The Complete A+ Guide to PC Repair

FIFTH EDITION UPDATE

The Complete A+ Guide to PC Repair

Cheryl A. Schmidt

FLORIDA STATE COLLEGE AT JACKSONVILLE

Boston   Columbus   Indianapolis   New York   San Francisco   Upper Saddle River
Amsterdam   Cape Town   Dubai   London   Madrid   Milan   Munich   Paris   Montreal   Toronto
Delhi   Mexico City   Sao Paulo   Sydney   Hong Kong   Seoul   Singapore   Taipei   Tokyo

Editorial Director: Marcia Horton
Editor-in-Chief: Michael Hirsch
Editorial Assistant: Stephanie Sellinger
Vice President, Marketing: Patrice Jones
Marketing Manager: Yezan Alayan
Senior Marketing Coordinator: Kathryn Ferranti
Vice President, Production: Vince O'Brien
Managing Editor: Jeff Holcomb
Senior Operations Supervisor: Alan Fischer
Manufacturing Buyer: Lisa McDowell
Art Director: Linda Knowles
Cover Designer: Joyce Cosentino Wells
Text Designer: Gillian Hall, The Aardvark Group
Manager, Visual Research & Permissions: Karen Sanatar
Photo Researcher: Tim Herzog and Lily Ferguson, Bill Smith Group
Cover Art: Shutterstock/Dino O.
Media Editor: Daniel Sandin
Media Project Manager: Wanda Rockwell
Full-Service Project Management: Andrea Stefanowicz, PreMediaGlobal
Composition: PreMediaGlobal
Art Production: Katherine Martin, LeeAnne Dollison, Donna McAfee Tucker, George Nicols, and KC Frick
Printer/Binder: Courier/Kendallville
Cover Printer: Lehigh-Phoenix Color/Hagerstown

Credits and acknowledgments borrowed from other sources and reproduced, with permission, in this text-book appear in the Credits section in the endmatter of this book.

Microsoft® and Windows® are registered trademarks of the Microsoft Corporation in the U.S.A. and other countries. Screen shots and icons reprinted with permission from the Microsoft Corporation. This book is not sponsored or endorsed by or affiliated with the Microsoft Corporation.

Many of the designations by manufacturers and sellers to distinguish their products are claimed as trade-marks. Where those designations appear in this book, and the publisher was aware of a trademark claim, the designations have been printed in initial caps or all caps.

Library of Congress Cataloging-in-Publication Data
Schmidt, Cheryl A.
  The complete A+ guide to PC repair update / Cheryl A. Schmidt. — 5th ed.
      p. cm.
  Includes bibliographical references and index.
  ISBN-13: 978-0-13-272759-4 (alk. paper)
  ISBN-10: 0-13-272759-5 (alk. paper)
  1. Microcomputers—Maintenance and repair—Examinations—Study guides. 2. Computer technicians—Certification—Study guides. 3. Computer networks—Examinations—Study guides.
4. Computing Technology Industry Association—Examinations—Study guides. I. Title.
  TK7887.S34 2012
  621.39'160288—dc22
                                                                        2010053317

10 9 8 7 6 5 4 3 2 1—CRK—15 14 13 12 11

Addison-Wesley
is an imprint of

www.pearsonhighered.com

ISBN 13: 978-0-13-272759-4
ISBN 10:   0-13-272759-5

Preface

The Complete A+ Guide to PC Repair, Fifth Edition Update, is intended for one or more courses geared toward A+ Certification and Computer Repair. It covers all the material needed for the following exams: CompTIA A+ Essentials 220-701® and CompTIA A+ Practical Application 220-702®. The book is written so that it is easy to read and understand because concepts are presented in building-block fashion. The book focuses on hardware, software, basic networking, and computer security.

Some of the best features of the book include the coverage of difficult subjects in a step-by-step manner, carefully developed graphics to illustrate concepts, photographs to demonstrate various technologies, reinforcement questions, critical thinking skills, soft skills that relate to chapter material, and hands-on exercises at the end of each chapter. Also, this book is written by a teacher who understands the value of a textbook in this field.

What's New in the Fifth Edition?

This update to the Fifth Edition has been revised to include coverage of Windows 7 in addition to Vista and XP. This edition differs from the Fourth in the following ways:

- Conformity with the latest CompTIA A+ Exam requirements, including CompTIA A+ Essentials 220-701 exam, as well as the CompTIA A+ Practical Application 220-702 exam.
- New sections in almost every chapter that relate to Windows Vista and 7.
- Emphasis on security and laptop components issues throughout all of the chapters.
- Added tools and exercises on topics such as subnetting, more wireless networking, striping and spanning of hard drive volumes, and use of dual monitors.
- Printers and video chapters integrated into a single peripheral devices chapter.
- Changed the serial devices chapter to Internet connectivity, removing older references and material related to serial devices except for analog modems. Focuses on Internet connectivity options and configuration.
- Windows Vista and 7 are integrated into the Windows XP Professional chapter. It includes all new Vista and 7 labs.
- Windows 2000 Professional chapter moved to the Companion Website.
- New look—including more technical tips and tables—makes detailed information easier to comprehend, with less wasted space in the exercise section of each chapter.
- Older technologies such as serial device configuration (except for analog modems) moved to the Companion Website.

Organization of the Text

The text is organized to allow thorough coverage of all topics, but also to be a flexible teaching tool; it is not necessary to cover all the chapters, nor do the chapters have to be covered in order.

- **Chapter 1** covers beginning terminology and computer part and port identification. Chapter 1 does not have a specific soft skills section as do the other chapters. Instead, it focuses on common technician qualities that are explored in greater detail in the soft skills sections of later chapters.

- **Chapter 2** details components, features, and concepts related to motherboards, including microprocessors, cache, expansion slots, and chipsets. Active listening skills are described in the soft skills section in this chapter.
- **Chapter 3** deals with configuration basics for the system and the different methods used to expand a system. System resources are also explained. Avoiding a "gun slinger" mentality is a focus area for soft skills in Chapter 3.
- **Chapter 4** steps the student through how to disassemble and reassemble a computer. Tools, ESD, EMI, and preventive maintenance are discussed for the first time. Subsequent chapters also include preventive maintenance topics. Basic electronics and computer power are also covered. Written communication tips are provided in this chapter for soft skills training.
- **Chapter 5** is a basic section covering troubleshooting skills and error codes. Good communication skills are stressed as a soft skill area.
- **Chapter 6** covers memory concepts, installation, preparation, and troubleshooting. The importance of teamwork is emphasized as a soft skill target area.
- **Chapter 7** deals with storage devices including floppy drive and IDE/SCSI hard drive installation, preparation, and troubleshooting. Phone communication skills is the target area for soft skills in this chapter.
- **Chapter 8** covers multimedia devices including CD and DVD technologies, as well as sound cards, scanners, and digital cameras. The chapter ends with a section on having a positive, proactive attitude.
- **Chapter 9** deals with peripheral devices including printers and video. The soft skills focus area is ethics.
- **Chapter 10** handles Internet connectivity including analog and digital methods. The focus area for soft skills is mentoring.
- **Chapter 11** details items that are common when working in a Windows environment, including common desktop icons, managing files and folders, the registry, and working from a command prompt including commands issued from Recovery Console. Chapter 11's soft skills area includes tips on how to stay current in a fast-paced field.
- **Chapter 12** is the Windows XP, Vista, and 7 chapter that details how to install and troubleshoot in the XP Professional/Vista/7 environment, including adding hardware, software, the management tools and remote management techniques. Avoiding burnout is the soft skill discussed in Chapter 12.
- **Chapter 13** is a chapter that introduces the students to networking. Basic concepts, terminology, and exercises make this chapter a favorite. An introduction to subnetting has been added. Being proactive instead of reactive is the focus of the soft skills section in this chapter.
- **Chapter 14** describes computer and network security issues including wireless network security. The exercises include file and folder security, event monitoring, and local policy creation. This chapter's soft skills area includes tips for dealing with irate customers—always a difficult situation for new technicians.

Features

- **Easy to Understand** Each section is written in a building-block fashion that begins at the most basic level and continues on to the more advanced. Students taught using this method understand new technologies better because of a solid foundation.
- **End-of-Chapter Review Questions** Each chapter contains numerous review questions in various formats, including true/false, multiple choice, matching, fill-in-the-blank, and open-ended.
- **Chapter Soft Skills Section** In each chapter a specific skill set related to soft skills is presented.
- **Tech Tips** Each chapter contains technical tips that are useful in the real-world of PC repair.
- **Hands-On Exercises** Computer repair cannot be learned by theory and lecture alone, but is reinforced through practice and experience. Exercises at the end of each chapter help with this task by allowing students to get their hands "dirty" to master the material they've studied.
- **Objectives** A list of objectives is provided at the beginning of each chapter.

- **Terminology** At the end of each chapter are the key terms that were defined and used throughout the chapter.
- **Soft Skills Exercises** The end of every chapter includes at least two soft skills activities that relate to the chapter.
- **Critical Thinking Skills** Every chapter includes at least two critical thinking activities that relate to the chapter material.

Supplemental Material

The following additional items are available to all readers of this book at its Companion Website (www.pearsonhighered.com/schmidt):

- Bonus chapters on Windows® 98, Windows NT Workstation, Floppy Drives, and Windows 2000 Professional
- Flashcards and crossword puzzles for review
- Web-based activities to reinforce concepts such as memory configuration, ports, and key concepts in the chapter
- Self-study quizzes

A complimentary access code for the book's Companion Website is available with a new copy of this book. Subscriptions may also be purchased online.

Instructor Support The following supplements are available to qualified instructors from the Pearson Education Instructor Resource Center (www.pearsonhighered.com/irc). Please visit the Instructor Resource Center, contact your Pearson Education/Addison-Wesley representative, or send an email to computing@pearson.com to register for access:

- Instructor's Manual
- PowerPoint® Presentation Slides
- Test Bank
- Computerized Test Bank

A Note to Instructors

Whenever people ask me what I do, my first response is "I fix computers." In my heart, I will always be a technician. Everything else is just a facet of that skill set, whether it is managing a computer and network support department, building a new lab and networking it, or teaching Voice over IP and quality of service. All of these boil down to knowing technical things. Sharing what I know is as natural as walking to me, but sitting still to write what I know is unnatural, so composing this text has been one of my greatest challenges. I managed to do it only because I needed a better textbook.

I taught computer repair classes long before I became a full-time faculty member. I was very frustrated with not having an appropriate book. Early on, I taught without a textbook and my students nicknamed me "the Handout Queen." I hope you are one of my colleagues who agrees that this book offers better support to both students and instructors. If there is any material you would like added or changed, please send a note to the author at cschmidt@fscj.edu.

A Note to Students

All the way through the book, I had to refrain from telling my stories, stay on track, and avoid using my mnemonics. Writing a textbook is really different from teaching class. My personality lies buried in this book. Only in a few places can you see or feel my teaching style, but I hope it comes through in subtle ways. My students are like my children except that I do not have to feed them and send them to college, so I am happy to claim any of you. I wish that I could be in each classroom as you start your computer career. How exciting!

Another thing that I tell my students is that I am not an expert and to watch out for those who say or think they are. Computer repair is an ever-changing field. I have been at it a long time, but there are always products and standards being developed that I do not know very much about. Humility is a wonderful trait to keep in computer repair because if you are not humble, the industry will prove you wrong sooner or later.

To my future technicians, I offer one important piece of advice:

Consistent, high-quality service boils down to two equally important things: caring and competence.

—Chip R. Bell and Ron Zemke

I can help you with the competence, but you are going to have to work on the caring part. Do not ever forget that there are people behind those machines that you love to repair. Taking care of people is as important as taking care of their computers.

Acknowledgments

Many people have helped me along my career and life paths. Thanks to the following people who have influenced my teaching: Ernie Friend, Amanda Bounds, Kevin Hampton, and Barbara Cansler (who happens to be my mother). Each of you has provided inspiration to me in my endeavors. Thanks also to Richard Jones of Scott/Jones Publishing for helping this book develop in its first three editions.

Thanks to the folks at my publisher, Addison-Wesley and Pearson. This book is something I am very proud of because of their efforts and professionalism working on the book and supporting me. Michael Hirsch is a wonderful manager. I also want to extend a special thank you to the other Addison-Wesley book team members, including Jeff Holcomb, Andrea Stefanowicz, Stephanie Sellinger, Tim Herzog, and Lily Ferguson.

No acknowledgments can be complete without mentioning the support and love of my family members—Karl, my husband, is the love of my life and completes me; Karalina and Raina, my daughters, are a constant joy to me and helped with some of the book sections; Sara and Josh Schmidt, Gavin, and Riley Redrick, whom I miss greatly; my mother, Barbara Cansler, and brother, Jeff Cansler, as well as my niece and nephew, Kirsten and Chance, bring a smile to my face when I talk to them during pre-press days.

Thanks to all my colleagues, adjuncts, and students at Florida State College at Jacksonville (formerly Florida Community College at Jacksonville), who have offered numerous valuable suggestions for improvement and have been testing some of the new material. Finally, the faculty members who reviewed individual chapters over the last four editions have my undying gratitude for their input.

Reviewers

Mike Beaver
University of Rio Grande

Mary Jane Beddow
Computing Energy, Inc.

Steven Blesse
The University of Southern Mississippi

Alan Block
Black Hawk Technical College

Sharon Brooks
Community College of Southern Nevada

Steve Cain
Tidewater Community College

Russell "Kelly" Campbell
Ozarks Technical Community College

Ron Carswell
San Antonio College

Don Casper
Eastern Idaho Technical College

Tracy Coady
Hillsborough Community College

David E. Cooke
Heart of Georgia Technical College

Sandra T. Daniels
New River Community College

Ross J. Decker
Brevard Community College

James Diehl
Delmar College

Terry R. Dummer
Midland Community College

Marvin L. Everest
Lake Washington Technical College

Russell Foszcz
McHenry County College

Bruce Gan
Palomar College

John Gazak
Herkimer County Community College

Richard Gohman
Yavapai Community College

Paula Greenwald
Niagara County Community College

Kevin Hampton
Florida State College at Jacksonville

John Haney
Snead State Community College

Richard Hernandez, Jr.
Arizona Western College

Kathy Himle
Salt Lake City Community College

Donald Hoffmann
Grayson County College

Glen Hovey
The University of Southern Mississippi

James Johnson
Pierce College

David V. Jones
Lenoir Community College

Richard Kalman
Atlantic Cape Community College

Martin Kanu
Canada College

Ronald E. Koci
Madison Area Technical College

Jee Laird
Nashville State Technical Community College

Michael Lehrfeld
Brevard Community College

Roger LeMarque
Florida Community College at Jacksonville

Jon Leong
Honolulu Community College

Doug Lundberg
Pierce College

Ron McDonald
Chattahoochee Technical College

KC Moore
Tidewater Community College

Jerry Moreau
Florida Community College at Jacksonville

Paul Nelson
Gateway Technical College

John O'Neal
Los Angeles Pierce College

Roger Peterson
Northland Community Technical College

Virginia Phillips
Youngstown State University

Lou Pierro
Ivy Tech State College

Scott Preedin
Florida Community College at Jacksonville

Phil Pursley
Amarillo College

Patricia Rausch
Lake-Sumter Community College

Phillip Regalbuto
Trident Technical College

Mark Risenhoover
Andrews High School

John S. Ruggirello
El Camino College

William Sawyer
Florida Community College at Jacksonville

Steven Sebili
Community College of Southern Nevada

Nancy Smith
Kirkwood Community College

Bob Starkey
Miami-Dade Community College

Greg Steffanelli
Carroll Community College

Zoltan Szabo
Richland College

Bruce Tate
Brevard Community College

Darla Tong
Northern Wisconsin Technical College

Cheryl Ucakar
Gateway Technical College

John Washington
Texas State Technical College

Robert Watts
Los Angeles Valley College

Doug Weaver
West Virginia University at Parkersburg

Belle Woodward
Temple Junior College

Brief Contents

Contents

Chapter 2 • On the Motherboard   27

Chapter 3 • System Configuration   67

Chapter 4 • Disassembly and Power 101

Chapter 5 • Logical Troubleshooting   151

Chapter 6 • Memory   163

Chapter 7 • Storage Devices   197

Chapter 8 • Multimedia Devices   263

Chapter 9 • Other Peripherals   305

Chapter 11 • Basic Windows and Windows Commands   391

Chapter 12 • Windows XP, Vista, and 7   473

Chapter 13 • Introduction to Networking   587

Chapter 14 • Computer and Network Security   663

List of Figures

Chapter 3 • System Configuration

Chapter 4 • Disassembly and Power

Chapter 5 • Logical Troubleshooting

Chapter 6 • Memory

Chapter 7 • Storage Devices

Chapter 8 • Multimedia Devices

Chapter 9 • Other Peripherals

Chapter 10 • Internet Connectivity

Chapter 11 • Basic Windows and Windows Commands

Chapter 14 • Computer and Network Security

List of Tables

Chapter 9 • Other Peripherals

Chapter 10 • Internet Connectivity

Chapter 11 • Basic Windows and Windows Commands

Chapter 12 • Windows XP, Vista, and 7

Chapter 13 • Introduction to Networking

Chapter 14 • Computer and Network Security

List of Tech Tips

Chapter 4 • Disassembly and Power

Chapter 5 • Logical Troubleshooting

Chapter 6 • Memory

Chapter 7 • Storage Devices

Chapter 8 • Multimedia Devices

Chapter 9 • Other Peripherals

Chapter 10 • Internet Connectivity

Chapter 11 • Basic Windows and Windows Commands

Chapter 12 • Windows XP, Vista, and 7

Chapter 13 • Introduction to Networking

Chapter 14 • Computer and Network Security

Introduction to Computer Repair

Objectives

After completing this chapter you will be able to

- Identify common technician qualities
- Understand basic computer terms
- Identify common computer parts
- Recognize and identify common computer ports

Overview

A computer technician must be a jack-of-all-trades: a software expert in various operating systems and applications; a hardware expert in everything ranging from processors to the latest laser printer; a communicator extraordinaire to handle the occasional irate, irrational, or computer-illiterate customer; a good listener to elicit computer symptoms from customers (and from the computer); an empathetic counselor to make customers feel good about their computers and confident in the technician's skills; and finally, a master juggler of time and priorities. These traits do not come overnight and not all of them can be taught—but a technician can constantly develop and fine-tune each of them.

This book covers computer support basics—the knowledge to get you started in the technology support industry. Standards relating to computer repair are important, and technicians must recognize old and current standards and stay abreast of emerging ones. Some computer standards allow a great deal of leeway for manufacturers and therefore cause more heartburn for computer technicians. However, if a technician understands the basics of computer repair, the problems from manufacturer design or hardware not covered in this book can still be resolved.

There is no substitute for experience, and no substitute for knowing the basics of how individual computer parts work. The basics help you understand other emerging technologies as well as proprietary devices. Once a technician has a job in the industry, past hands-on time will increase his or her depth of knowledge and experience. Use your classroom hands-on time wisely. The classroom is the place to learn the ropes—the basics.

Having a teacher to guide you through the basics, classmates with which to share information, and a book to supplement your instruction are important for getting you started. This book is a textbook, not a reference book. It serves as a supplement to your instructor of computer repair.

The best quality a technician can possess is logic. A good technician narrows a problem to a general area, subdivides the problem into possible culprits, and eliminates the possibilities one-by-one efficiently and logically. A technician is like a detective, constantly looking for clues, using common sense and deductive reasoning, gathering information from the computer and the computer user, and finally solving the mystery. As one computer teacher puts it, "a computer technician works smart, not hard." Detective work is integral to a technician's job; therefore, throughout this book **Tech Tips** provide important technical tips.

This book can help you achieve technical competence, but you should never forget the computer users. Many technicians like to work with things—computers, networks, printers, and so on—more than with people. This text cannot teach you to care about the people who use technology. You must remember that communication is as important as your technical skills.

An industry standard certification called A+ certification is important for new technicians. It does not guarantee you a job, but it helps you get an interview. The A+ certification consists of two exams: CompTIA A+ Essentials (220-701) and CompTIA Practical Application (220-702).

Repairing computers is rewarding, but it can be frustrating if you do not understand the basics. With good reasoning ability and a good foundation in computer repair, no problem goes unsolved. Remember that if every repair were simple, then no one would need technicians. Enjoy the class!

Safety Note

Safety is covered in each chapter, but especially in Chapter 4, but no book on computer repair can begin without stating that both the technician and the computer can be harmed by poor safety habits. To protect yourself and the computer, make sure the computer power is off when disassembling, installing, or removing hardware, or doing preventive maintenance (cleaning). Never take the monitor or power supply apart unless you have been specifically trained on these components. The power supply and monitor have capacitors (electronic parts that hold an electrical charge), which can hurt you even if the power has been removed. The type of equipment you need and things that you can do to prevent harm to the computer are covered more explicitly in Chapter 4 on power and disassembly.

Technician Qualities

Two of the most important qualities that a technician can have are active listening skills and attitude. Active listening means that you truly listen to what the person (who is having the problem) is saying. Having active listening skills involves good eye contact, nodding your head every now and then to show you are following the conversation, taking notes on important details, and avoiding distractions such as incoming cell phone calls or other activities. Clarify customer statements by asking pertinent questions and avoid interrupting the customer. Allow customers to complete their sentences. Many technicians jump into a problem the moment they hear the first symptom described by the user. Listen to the entire problem. Do not act superior because you know terms and things that they do not.

A positive attitude is probably the best quality a technician can possess. Many technicians treat customers abruptly, not taking the time to listen to their problem or to find the best solution. A good attitude is helpful when a user is upset because their computer or attached device is not working properly. Do not undermine the customer's problem; every problem is equally important to the computer user. A positive attitude is critical for being successful in the computer service industry.

A technician must be familiar with and thoroughly understand computer terminology to (1) speak intelligently to other technical support staff in clear, concise, and direct statements; (2) explain the problem to the user; and (3) be proficient in the field. The field changes so quickly that technicians must constantly update their skills.

Unfortunately, some computer technicians use the technical language of the trade when speaking with people who are not attuned to the lingo. Using too many technical terms around end users serves only to confuse and irritate them. A technician should avoid using slang, jargon, acronyms, and abbreviations. In addition to knowing and using the correct terminology, a technician must use it appropriately, and explain computer terms with simple, everyday language and examples. This book explains computer terminology in easy-to-understand terms and provides analogies that can be used when dealing with customers.

Basic Computer Parts

Computer systems include hardware, software, and firmware. **Hardware** is something you can touch and feel—the physical computer and the parts inside the computer are examples of hardware. The monitor, keyboard, and mouse are hardware components. **Software** interacts with the hardware. Windows, Linux, OS X, Microsoft Office, Solitaire, Google Chrome, Adobe Acrobat Reader, and WordPerfect are examples of software.

Without software that allows the hardware to accomplish something, a computer is nothing more than a doorstop. Every computer needs an important piece of software called an **operating system**, which coordinates the interaction between hardware and software applications. The operating system also handles the interaction between a user and the computer. Examples of operating systems include DOS, Windows XP, Windows Vista, Windows 7, OS X, and various types of Unix, such as Red Hat and Mandrake.

A **device driver** is a special piece of software designed to enable a hardware component. The device driver enables the operating system to recognize, control, and use the hardware component. Device drivers are hardware and operating system specific. For example, a printer requires a specific device driver when connected to a computer loaded with Windows 98. The same printer requires a different device driver when using Windows XP. Each piece of installed hardware requires a device driver for the operating system being used. Figure 1.1 shows how hardware and software must work together.

Software applications are normally loaded onto the hard drive. When a user selects an application, the operating system controls the loading of the application. The operating system also controls any hardware devices (such as the mouse, keyboard, monitor through the video adapter, and printer) that must be accessed by the application.

Firmware combines hardware and software into important chips inside the computer. It is called firmware because it is a chip, which is hardware, and it has software built into the chip. An example of firmware is the **BIOS** (basic input/output system) chip. BIOS chips always have

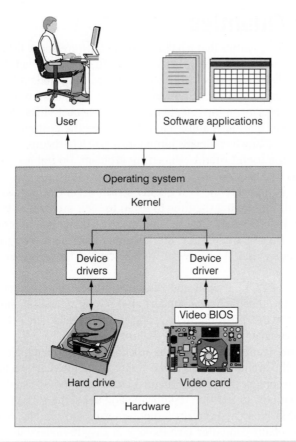

Figure 1.1   **Hardware and software**

software inside them. The BIOS has startup software that must be present for a computer to operate. This startup software locates and loads the operating system. The BIOS also contains software instructions for communication with input/output devices, as well as important hardware parameters that determine to some extent what hardware can be installed. For example, the system BIOS has the ability to allow other BIOS chips that are located on adapters (such as the video card) to load software that is loaded in the card's BIOS.

The simplest place to start to learn about computer repair is with the hardware components and their common names. A **computer**, sometimes called a microcomputer or a PC, is a unit that performs tasks using software applications. Computers come in three basic models: (1) a **desktop** model that normally sits on top of a desk; (2) a **tower** model that sits under a desk; and (3) a **laptop** model, which is portable. Laptops are sometimes called notebooks; smaller versions are called netbooks or nettops. A fourth type of computer is a handheld computer or palmtop computer. These replaced the **PDA** (personal digital assistant). The palmtype computer is normally incorporated into a cell phone. Figure 1.2 shows Apple's iPhone, which has the ability to send and receive phone calls and emails, view and listen to movies and songs, and take pictures.

A computer consists of a case (chassis), a **keyboard** that allows users to provide input into the computer, a **monitor** that displays information, and a **mouse** that allows data input or is used to select menus and options. Figure 1.3 shows a tower computer case, monitor, keyboard, and mouse.

Once the case is removed from the computer, the parts inside can be identified. The easiest part to identify is the **power supply**, which is the metal box normally located in a back corner of the case. A power cord goes from the power supply to a wall outlet or surge strip. One purpose of the power supply is to convert the AC voltage that comes out of the outlet to DC voltage the computer can use. The power supply also supplies DC voltage to the internal parts of the computer. A fan located inside the power supply keeps the computer cool, which avoids damage to the components.

Figure 1.2 Apple iPhones

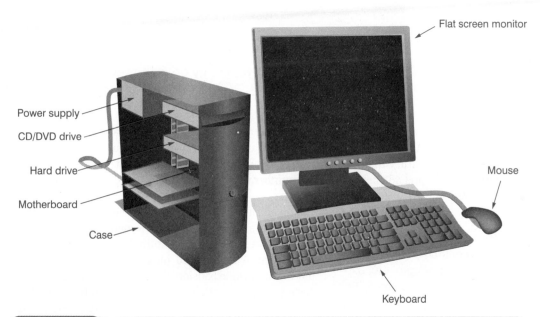

Flat screen monitor

Power supply

CD/DVD drive

Hard drive

Motherboard

Case

Mouse

Keyboard

Figure 1.3 Tower computer

A computer usually has a device to store software applications and files. Two examples of storage devices are the floppy drive and the hard drive. A slot in the front of the computer easily identifies the floppy drive. The **floppy drive** allows data storage to **floppy disks** (sometimes called diskettes or disks) that can be used in other computers. Floppy disks store less information than hard drives. The **hard drive**, sometimes called hard disk, is a rectangular box normally inside the computer's case that is sealed to keep out dust and dirt. In a desktop computer, the hard drive is normally mounted below or beside the floppy drive. A **CD drive** holds disks (CDs) that have data, music, or software applications on them. A popular alternative to a CD drive is a **DVD drive** (digital versatile disk drive), which supports CDs as well as music and video DVDs.

The **motherboard** is the main circuit board located inside a PC and contains the most electronics. It is normally located on the bottom of a desktop or laptop computer and mounted on the side of a tower computer. Other names for the motherboard include mainboard, planar, or systemboard. The motherboard is the largest electronic circuit board in the computer. The keyboard frequently connects directly to the back of the motherboard, although some computers have a keyboard connection in the front of the case. Figure 1.4 shows a different view of a tower computer with a hard drive, floppy drive, power supply, motherboard, and DVD drive. Notice that the floppy drive has a slot in the front of the computer, whereas the hard drive does not.

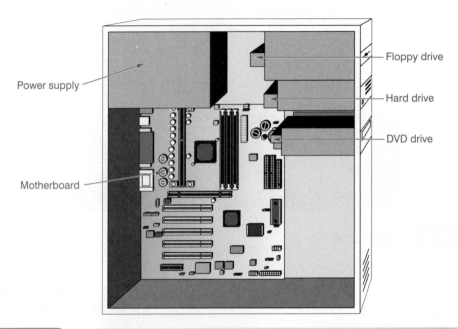

Power supply

Floppy drive

Hard drive

DVD drive

Motherboard

Figure 1.4   **Tower computer with hard drive, floppy drive, power supply, motherboard, and DVD drive**

Some devices have a cable that connects the device to the motherboard. Other devices require an adapter. **Adapters** are electronic circuit cards that normally plug into an **expansion slot** on the motherboard. Other names for an adapter are controller, card, controller card, circuit card, circuit board, and adapter board. The number of available expansion slots on the motherboard depends on the manufacturer.

Tech Tip

How to identify an adapter's function

Tracing the cable(s) attached to the adapter or looking at the device connected to the adapter can usually help with identifying an adapter's function. For example, typically a monitor has a cable going between it and a video adapter or motherboard.

An adapter may control multiple devices such as the DVD drive and speakers. An alternative to an adapter plugging directly into the motherboard is the use of a riser board. A **riser board** plugs into the motherboard and has its own expansion slots. Adapters can plug into these expansion slots instead of directly into the motherboard. Figure 1.5 is an illustration of a riser board and one adapter.

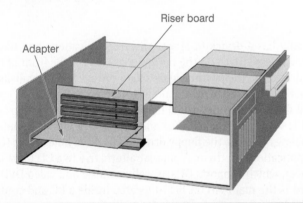

Riser board

Adapter

Figure 1.5   **Microcomputer with a riser board and one adapter**

A laptop has similar parts to a tower or desktop computer, but they are smaller. Portable computers (laptops) normally use a battery as their power source, but they can have an AC connection. Laptop batteries are normally modules that have one or two release latches that are used to remove the module. Figure 1.6 shows common laptop parts.

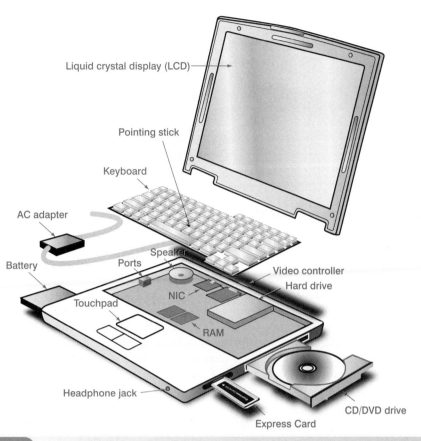

Liquid crystal display (LCD)

Pointing stick

Keyboard

AC adapter

Battery

Ports

Speaker

Video controller

Hard drive

Touchpad

NIC

RAM

Headphone jack

Express Card

CD/DVD drive

Figure 1.6 **Laptop battery**

When the laptop has the AC adapter attached, the battery is being recharged on most models. The laptop AC adapter converts the AC from the wall outlet to DC, which the laptop needs. Figure 1.7 shows the laptop port to which the AC adapter connects. The port sometimes has a DC voltage symbol below or beside it. This symbol is a solid line with a dashed line below it ($\overline{\overline{}}$).

Figure 1.7 **Laptop AC adapter and power port**

Laptops sometimes have one or more media bays to install removable drives such as a CD/DVD drive. A latch on the bottom of the laptop normally releases the drive. The bays allow hot swapping (device can be inserted with the power applied), but it is always safer to shut down the computer before installing a device unless you are sure it is hot swappable. Figure 1.8 shows the more commonly seen built-in CD/DVD drive.

Memory is an important part of any computer. Memory chips hold applications, part of the operating system, and user documents. Two basic types of memory are RAM and ROM. **RAM** (random access memory) is volatile memory meaning the data inside the chips is lost when power to the computer is shut off. When a user types a document in a word processing program, both the word processing application and the document are in RAM. If the user turns the computer off without saving the document to a disk or the hard drive, the document is lost because the information does not stay in RAM when power is shut off.

Figure 1.8   Laptop media bay

ROM (read-only memory) is nonvolatile memory because data stays inside the chip even when the computer is turned off. ROM chips are sometimes installed on adapters such as a network or video card.

RAM and ROM chips come in different styles: DIP (Dual In-line Package), DIMM (Dual In-line Memory Module), and RIMM (a memory module developed by Rambus). RAM chips can be any of the types, but they are usually DIMMs. Some ROM chips are DIP chips. They are usually distinguishable by a sticker that shows the manufacturer, version, and date produced. Memory chips are covered in great detail in Chapter 6 on memory. See Figure 1.9 for an illustration of a motherboard, various expansion slots, memory, and an adapter in an expansion slot.

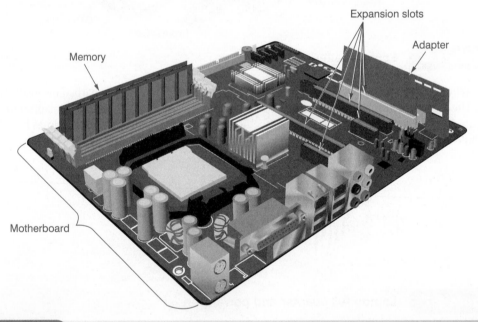

Figure 1.9   **Motherboard with expansion slots and adapter**

Part of the startup software the motherboard BIOS contains is **POST** (power on self test). POST performs a basic test of the individual hardware components such as the motherboard, RAM memory chips, keyboard, floppy drive, and hard drive. When a computer is turned on with the power switch, BIOS executes POST. Numbers appearing in the upper-left corner of the monitor indicate that POST is checking RAM. Turning the computer on with the power switch is known as a **cold boot**. Users perform a cold boot every time they power on their computers. A technician performs a cold boot when he or she is troubleshooting a computer and needs POST to execute.

You can restart a Windows XP computer with a warm boot by clicking the *Start* button, clicking *Shut Down*, selecting *Restart* from the drop-down menu, and clicking the *OK* button. It can also be performed by holding down the Ctrl key, the Alt key, and the Del key at the same time, selecting *Task Manager*, selecting the *Shut Down* option, selecting *Restart* from the drop-down menu, and clicking the *OK* button. Warm booting causes any changes that have been made to take effect without putting as much strain on the computer as a cold boot does. In Vista/7, click on the right arrow adjacent to the lock button and select *Restart* or press Ctrl+Alt+Del, select the up arrow in bottom right corner, and choose *Restart* from the menu.

External Connectivity

A **port** is a connector on the motherboard or on a separate adapter that allows a device to con-nect to the computer. Sometimes a motherboard has ports built directly into the motherboard. Motherboards that have ports built into them are called **integrated motherboards**. A technician must be able to identify these common ports readily to ensure that (1) the correct cable plugs into the port; and (2) the technician can troubleshoot problems in the right area.

Many port connections are referred to as male or female. **Male ports** have metal pins that protrude from the connector. A male port requires a cable with a female connector. **Female ports** have holes in the connector into which the male cable pins are inserted.

Many connectors on integrated motherboards are either D-shell connectors or DIN connec-tors. A **D-shell connector** has more pins or holes on top than on the bottom, so a cable connected to the D-shell connector can only be inserted in one direction and not accidentally flipped upside down. Parallel, serial, and video ports are examples of D-shell connectors. Many documents rep-resent a D-shell connector by using the letters DB, a hyphen, and the number of pins—for exam-ple, DB-9, DB-15, or DB-25.

A **DIN connector** is round with small holes and is normally keyed. When a connector is **keyed** it has an extra metal piece or notch that matches with an extra metal piece or notch on the cable, and the cable can only be inserted into the DIN connector one way. Older keyboard and mouse con-nectors are examples of DIN connectors. Today, keyboard and mouse connectors can also be USB connectors. These are covered later in the chapter. Figure 1.10 shows the back of a computer with an integrated motherboard. There are various DIN and D-shell connectors on the motherboard.

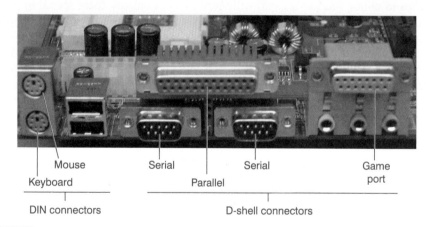

Mouse   Serial   Serial   Game
                                  port
Keyboard   Parallel

DIN connectors   D-shell connectors

Figure 1.10   **DIN and D-Shell connectors**

Video Port

A **video port** is used to connect a monitor. Today, there are two types normally seen and they both have three rows. The older one is a three-row, 15-pin female D-shell. The 15-pin female connec-tor is used to attach VGA, SVGA, XGA, SXGA, or UXGA monitors. These monitors have a CRT (cathode ray tube) and are heavier and bulkier than a flat panel monitor. Even though it can have different types of monitors attached, it is normally referred to as a **VGA port**. The newer port is called a **DVI port** (Digital Visual Interface) and it has three rows of square holes. This is the newer video port and is used to connect flat panel digital monitors. Flat panel monitors can also use the older VGA port. There are actually different types of DVI ports. They are covered in more detail in Chapter 9 on video. Some video adapters also allow you to connect a video device (such as a television) that has an S-Video port. Figure 1.11 shows a video adapter with all three ports. The top port is for S-Video, the center port is the DVI connector, and the bottom port is a VGA port.

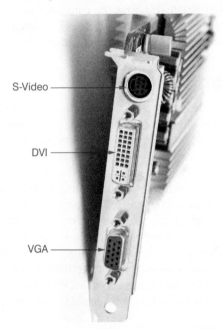

S-Video

DVI

VGA

Figure 1.11   **Video ports**

USB Port

USB stands for Universal Serial Bus. A **USB port** allows up to 127 devices to transmit at speeds up to 5Gbps (5 billion bits per second) with version 3.0. Compare these speeds to parallel port transfers of 1Mbps (1 million bits per second). Devices that can connect to the USB port include printers, scanners, mice, keyboards, joysticks, CD drives, DVD drives, tape drives, floppy drives, flight yokes, cameras, modems, speakers, telephones, video phones, data gloves, and digitizers. In order for the computer to use the USB port, it must have a Pentium or higher CPU; an operating system that supports USB, such as Windows 9x or higher, Apple OS X, or *nix (any flavor of Unix) and a chipset that acts as a host controller. Additional ports can sometimes be found on the front of computer cases. Figure 1.12 shows a close-up view of two USB ports. Figure 1.13 is a photograph of computer USB ports.

Figure 1.12   **USB ports**

Figure 1.13   **USB ports on the front of a computer**

USB ports and devices come in three versions—1.0, 2.0, and 3.0. Version 1.0 supported speeds of 1.5Mbps and 12Mbps. Version 2.0 increased the supported speed to 480Mbps; and Version 3.0 supports speeds up to 5Gbps. A symbol that looks like a trident is sometimes seen on the USB port or on the USB cable. A plus sign above one prong identifies a Version 2.0 port, but not all manufacturers use this symbol. Version 3.0 is sometimes referred to as SuperSpeed USB, and the logo has two S's on it. Figure 1.14 shows the USB symbols.

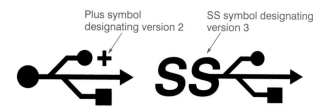

Figure 1.14   **USB symbols**

Converters are available to convert a USB port to a different type of connector (or vice versa), such as serial, parallel, PS/2 mouse/keyboard, or mini-DIN. Figure 1.15 shows a converter that inserts into a PS/2 mini-DIN connector and allows a USB mouse or keyboard to be connected.

Figure 1.15   **Mini-DIN to USB converter**

A smaller USB port used on small devices such as a USB hub, PDA, digital camera, and phones is known as a mini-USB port. There are three types of mini-USB ports: mini-A, mini-B, and mini-AB. The mini-AB port accepts either a mini-A or a mini-B cable end. The two leftmost connectors shown in Figure 1.16 are mini-B and standard A USB connectors. (The three connectors shown on the right are 6-, 4-, and 9-pin IEEE 1394 connectors, which are discussed later in this chapter.)

Figure 1.16   **Mini-B and a standard A USB connectors
(as well as IEEE 1394 connectors)**

Parallel Port

The **parallel port** is a 25-pin female D-shell connector used to connect a printer to the computer. Some motherboards have a small picture of a printer etched over the connector. Parallel ports transfer eight bits of data at a time to the printer or any other parallel device connected to the parallel port. Other parallel devices include tape drives, Iomega's Zip drive, scanners, and external hard drives. Parallel ports are becoming obsolete due to USB ports. Refer to Figure 1.10 for a photo of a parallel port.

Serial Port

A **serial port** (also known as a COM port, RS-232 port, or an asynchronous (async) port) can be a 9-pin male D-shell connector or a 25-pin male D-shell connector (on very old computers). Serial ports are used for a variety of devices including mice, external modems, digitizers, printers, PDAs, and digital cameras. Serial ports are becoming obsolete for the same reason that parallel ports are—USB ports. The most common reason to have a serial port would be for an external modem.

The serial port transmits one bit at a time and is much slower than the parallel port that transmits eight bits at a time. Serial ports sometimes have a small picture of two rows of square blocks (two digital square waves) tied together etched over the connector. The other type of picture sometimes shown above a serial port is a series of 1s and 0s. Figure 1.17 shows both types of markings. Figure 1.18 shows a USB to serial port converter if a serial port is needed and only USB ports are available. A converter may be purchased to convert a USB port to almost any other type of port.

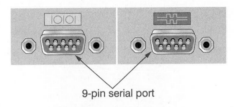

9-pin serial port

Figure 1.17   **Serial port markings**

Figure 1.18   **USB to serial port converter**

Serial and parallel ports are typically bidirectional, which means that data transfers to/from the port to the motherboard/adapter in both directions. Video, keyboard, and mouse ports are typically unidirectional. The mouse and keyboard are normally input-only devices, so data flows from the device to the computer. The monitor is normally an output device, and data flows from the computer to the monitor.

Mouse and Keyboard Ports

Mouse and **keyboard ports** have traditionally been 6-pin mini-DIN connectors, but some computer manufacturers are using USB ports to connect mice or keyboards. The mini-DIN port is sometimes called a PS/2 port. Refer to Figure 1.10 to see the mouse and keyboard ports. Most manufacturers color code the mouse and keyboard ports and/or put a small diagram of a keyboard and a mouse on the connectors.

Normal mouse use typically causes its internal parts to become dirty. Before explaining how to clean a mouse, understanding the basic internal mouse workings is important because the topics are interrelated. There are two basic types of mice—mechanical and optical. A **mechanical mouse** uses a rubber ball inserted into the bottom of the mouse. The rubber ball turns small metal, rubber, or plastic rollers mounted on the sides. The rollers relay the mouse movement to the computer. On the other hand, an **optical mouse** has optical sensors that detect the direction in which the mouse ball moves. It uses reflections from LEDs using a grid pattern mouse pad or almost any surface to detect mouse location.

A trackball is a replacement for the mouse. It sits in one location and does not move around on a mouse pad or desk. Instead, a person uses his or her palm to move the mouse pointer by means of a ball that rolls on bearings located inside the device.

Keyboards are input devices that connect to the keyboard port. There are two main types of keyboards: mechanical and capacitive. **Mechanical keyboards** are the cheapest and most common type. They use a switch that closes when a key is depressed. When the switch gets dirty, it sticks. Mechanical keyboards require more cleaning and are more error-prone than their capacitive counterparts. A **capacitive keyboard** is more reliable and more expensive than a mechanical keyboard because of the electronics involved in the design.

Tech Tip

Don't confuse the mouse and keyboard ports

On most motherboards, the mouse and keyboard ports are not interchangeable even though they are of the same pin configuration. The keyboard cable must plug into the keyboard port connector. The mouse cable must plug into the mouse port connector.

Wireless Input Devices

Many input devices have cordless connectivity. Two common devices are the keyboard and mouse. There are two types of technologies used with wireless input devices: infrared and radio. Whichever one is used, a transceiver is connected to a serial, PS/2 mouse/keyboard, or USB port. Infrared is used for shorter distances and is cheaper than the radio method. However, infrared devices must be kept within the line of sight of the transceiver (the device that picks up the wireless signal that attaches to the computer) and this can be cumbersome. Radio controlled wireless devices can have interference from other devices in the home or office such as microwave ovens, cordless phones, and other wireless devices (see Figure 1.19).

Figure 1.19   **Wireless devices**

If a wireless device is not operating properly, check to see if it has a battery and if the battery is losing its charge. Check for blocked line of sight if the device uses infrared. Move the device closer to the transceiver to see if performance is improved. Verify that the transceiver connects to the appropriate port. If the wireless device uses a radio frequency to communicate with the transceiver, ensure that no other device is causing interference by moving the wireless input device, hanging up the telephone, or shutting off other devices that could be causing the interference.

Mouse and Keyboard Preventive Maintenance

Mouse cleaning kits are available in computer stores, but normal household supplies also work. For an optical mouse, simply wipe the bottom of the mouse with a damp, lint-free cloth. For a mechanical mouse, the ball inside the mouse gets dirty and clogged with lint and dirt. Turn the mechanical mouse over and rotate the ball's retainer ring or access cover counterclockwise to remove it. Sometimes a mouse has screws that secure the ball's access cover. After removing the mouse cover, turn the mouse over while cupping your hand over the mouse ball. Catch the mouse ball as it falls into your hand. To clean the mouse ball, use a mild detergent, soapy water, contact cleaner, or alcohol. Rinse the mouse ball and dry completely with a lint-free cloth. With compressed air or your breath, blow out where the rubber ball sits in the mouse. A trackball's rollers are similar to a mouse ball's rollers and can be cleaned the same way.

The rollers inside a mechanical mouse also get dirty, which causes erratic mouse behavior. Use a cotton swab or lint-free cloth with alcohol to clean the rollers. If you are at a customer site with no supplies, use water to clean the mouse ball. Use a fingernail, small screwdriver, or unfolded paperclip to scrape the rollers. Occasionally, threads or hair get wrapped around the rollers. Unwrap the obstructions for better mouse performance. With an optical mouse, use a lint-free cloth or compressed air to clean the optical sensors. Any small piece of dirt or lint blocking the sensors causes poor mouse behavior and reaction.

Keyboards also need periodic cleaning, especially because most are mechanical. Keyboard cleaning kits and wipes are available at computer stores. Simply turn the keyboard upside down and shake it to remove the paper bits and paper clips. Compressed air also helps with keyboard cleaning. Obtain compressed air that has a plastic straw that attaches to the nozzle. If the keys are dirty from finger oils, turn the computer off before cleaning the keys. Then, using keyboard cleaning wipes or a cloth and all-purpose cleaner, wipe the keyboard keys. A cotton or lint-free swab can be used between the keys. The lint-free swab works best. Make sure the keyboard is completely dry before re-energizing.

Keyboard Troubleshooting

If a particular key is not working properly, remove the key cap. The chip removal tool included with PC tool kits is great for this. They are not great for removing chips, but they are good for removing key caps. A tweaker (small, flat-tipped) screwdriver also does a good job. After removing the key cap, use compressed air around the sticky or malfunctioning key.

If coffee or another liquid spills into the keyboard, all is not lost. Many people have cleaned their keyboard by soaking it in a bathtub, a flat pan of water, or the top rack of a dishwasher. If you use a dishwasher, run it through one rinse cycle only and do not use detergent. Distilled or boiled water cooled to room temperature works best. Afterward, the keyboard can be disassembled and/or scrubbed with lint-free swabs or cloths.

Keyboards and mice are normally considered throw-away technology. The customer's cost to pay a technician to keep cleaning a keyboard over and over again would pay for many new capacitive keyboards. Keep this in mind when troubleshooting the cheaper devices.

Other Input Devices

A variety of input devices are available. Most connect to the serial, PS/2, USB, or IEEE 1394 port. Installation and troubleshooting of these devices follows the same procedure as the common devices that attach to these ports. Table 1.1 lists a description of some of the common input devices. Figure 1.20 shows a digital tablet with a pen.

Sound Card Ports

A **sound card** converts digital computer signals to sound and sound to digital computer signals. A sound card is sometimes called an audio card and can be integrated into the motherboard or an adapter that contains several ports. The most common ports include a port for a microphone, one or more ports for speakers, and an input port for a joystick or MIDI (musical instrument digital interface) device. Examples of MIDI devices include electronic keyboards and external

Table 1.1	Common input devices
Device	**Description**
digital pen	Translates words written with the pen for input into the computer. The pen can also be used to control the cursor or mouse. The pen is frequently a wireless device and is sometimes used with a digital tablet.
digital tablet	Allows graphical or desktop publishing information to be input. The tablet can be wireless or connected to a USB or serial port. A tablet can come with an integrated mouse and/or digital pen. This is sometimes called a drawing tablet.
signature pad	Allows someone to sign and digitally store his or her name.
touch screen	Allows a finger or a pen-like device to control a special monitor. The screens are popular with bank ATMs and with kiosks such as those found in schools, hotels, and shopping malls.
track pad	Allows the pointer to be manipulated with fingertip movement by means of an integrated window or a place located on a laptop. Flat buttons that are similar to mouse control buttons are mounted above or below the track pad.
trackball	Allows a user to use the palm or fingertip to move the pointer on the screen. This is achieved by manipulating a device that has a ball mounted in the center.
TrackPoint (by IBM) or track stick	Controls pointer operations as an alternative to a mouse by means of a rubber nipple that is normally situated between keys in the center of the laptop keyboard.

Figure 1.20   **Digital tablet**

sound modules. The joystick port is sometimes known as a **game port**. Game ports are 15-pin female D-shell connectors, and are sometimes confused with older Ethernet connectors. Game ports are becoming extinct because of the popularity of USB ports. Another type of digital sound port that is gaining popularity is **S/PDIF** (Sony/Philips Digital Interface). There are two main types of S/PDIF connectors: an RCA jack used to connect a coaxial cable and a fiber-optic port for a TOSLINK cable connection. Sound cards, however, are still popular because people want better sound than what is available integrated into a motherboard. See Figure 1.21 for an illustration of a sound card. Figure 1.29 later in the chapter shows the S/PDIF ports.

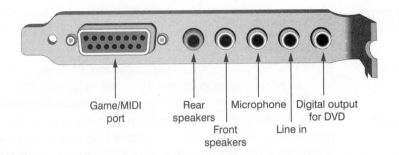

Game/MIDI port · Rear speakers · Front speakers · Microphone · Line in · Digital output for DVD

Figure 1.21   Sound card ports

IEEE 1394 Port

The IEEE 1394 standard is a serial technology developed by Apple Computer. Sometimes it is known as FireWire or i.Link, which is a Sony trademark. **IEEE 1394 ports** have been more predominant on Apple computers, but are now becoming a standard port on PCs. Windows and Apple operating systems support the IEEE 1394 standard. Many digital products now have an integrated IEEE 1394 port for connecting to a computer. IEEE 1394 devices include camcorders, cameras, printers, storage devices, DVD players, CD-R drives, CD-RW drives, tape drives, film readers, speakers, and scanners.

Speeds supported are 100, 200, 400, 800, 1200, 1600, and 3200Mbps. As many as 63 devices (using cable lengths up to 14 feet) can be connected with FireWire. The IEEE 1394 standard supports hot swapping (plugging and unplugging devices with the power on), plug and play, and powering low-power devices. The cable has six wires—four for data and two for power. Newer IEEE 1394 standards support the use of RJ-45 and fiber connectors. Figure 1.22 shows FireWire ports. Figure 1.23 shows three IEEE 1394 adapter ports.

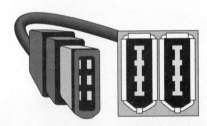

Figure 1.22   FireWire ports

Figure 1.23   IEEE 1394 adapter ports

Figure 1.24 shows an IEEE 1394 port on a laptop. This is similar to a port found on a camera or video device. Other common laptop ports are also shown.

Figure 1.24   **IEEE 1394 laptop port**

Network Ports

Network ports are used to connect a computer to other computers, including a network server. Two different network adapters, Ethernet and Token Ring, are available, but most networks use Ethernet ports. The ports on these adapters can be quite confusing because the connectors are sometimes the same. A network cable inserts into the network port.

Ethernet adapters are the most common type of **NIC** (network interface card/controller). They can have a BNC, an RJ-45, a 15-pin female D-shell connector, or a combination of these on the same adapter. The BNC connector attaches to thin coax cable. The 15-pin D-shell connector connects to thick coax cable. The RJ-45 connector connects to UTP (unshielded twisted-pair) cable and is the most common Ethernet port used. The 15-pin female D-shell connector is confusing because this connector is also used with game ports. The RJ-45 connector (the most common one) looks like a phone jack, but it uses eight wires instead of four. Figure 1.25 shows examples of different Ethernet adapter ports.

Figure 1.25   **Ethernet ports**

Today's Ethernet adapters have a single RJ-45 jack (port), as shown in Figure 1.26.

Figure 1.26   **RJ-45 Ethernet port**

Token Ring adapters are not as popular as Ethernet, and they can have two different connectors: RJ-45 and/or 9-pin female D-shell connectors. Some adapters have a little green sticker with the numbers 4/16 on it, which indicates the two speeds, 4Mbps and 16Mbps, at which Token Ring adapters can run. The 4/16 sticker is a helpful indicator that the port is a Token Ring port. Figure 1.27 shows examples of Token Ring ports.

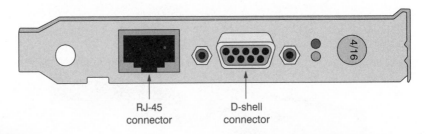

RJ-45   D-shell
connector   connector

Figure 1.27   **Token Ring ports**

Modem Ports

A **modem** connects a computer to a phone line. A modem can be internal or external. An internal modem is an adapter that has one or two RJ-11 connectors. An external modem is a separate device that sits outside the computer and connects to a 9-pin or 25-pin serial port. The external modem can also have one or two RJ-11 connectors. The RJ-11 connectors look like typical phone jacks. With two RJ-11 connectors, one can be used for a telephone and the other has a cable that connects to the wall jack. The RJ-11 connector labeled *Line* is for the connection to the wall jack. The RJ-11 connector labeled *Phone* is for the connection to the phone. An internal modem with only one RJ-11 connector connects to the wall jack. Figure 1.28 shows an internal modem with two ports.

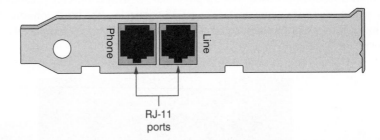

RJ-11
ports

Figure 1.28   **Internal modem with two ports**

Pros and Cons of Integrated Motherboards

An integrated motherboard provides expandability because ports are built in and do not require separate adapters. If the motherboard includes the serial, parallel, and video ports, there is more space available for other adapters such as network or sound cards. Some motherboards include the network connection and the ports normally found on sound cards. The number of available expansion slots in a system depends on the motherboard manufacturer. Figure 1.29 shows integrated motherboard ports.

Ports built into a motherboard are faster than those on an expansion board. All adapters in expansion slots run slower than the motherboard components. Computers with integrated motherboards are easier to set up because you do not have to install an adapter or configure the ports. Normally, systems with integrated motherboards are easier to troubleshoot because the components are on one board. The drawback is that when one port goes bad, you have to add an adapter that has the same type of port as the one that went bad.

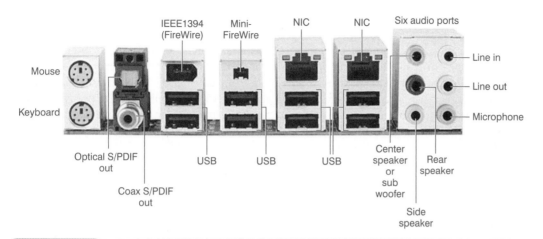

Figure 1.29   **Integrated motherboard ports**

Ports have different parameters set to keep one port from interfering with another. The ability to alter the configuration is important to a technician. Of course, having good documentation about the features and abilities of an integrated motherboard is crucial. Without documentation, you cannot disable a port or change a port's settings. In addition, proper documentation allows you to determine the features of the individual ports or of the other motherboard components. The Internet is a great resource for documentation when the original documentation is unavailable.

Docking Station and Port Replicator

Docking stations and port replicators add connectivity and expansion capability to laptop computers. A **docking station** allows a laptop computer to be more like a desktop system. A docking station can have connections for a full-size monitor, printer, keyboard, mouse, and printer. In addition, a docking station can have expansion slots or cards and storage bays.

To install a laptop into a docking station, close the laptop and slide the laptop into the docking station. Optionally (depending on the model), secure the laptop with locking tabs. Figure 1.30 shows a Hewlett-Packard laptop installed on a docking station.

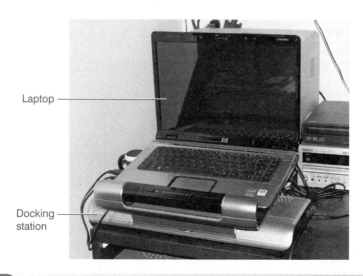

Figure 1.30   **HP laptop docking station**

The **port replicator** is similar to a docking station, but does not normally include an expansion slot or drive storage bays. The port replicator attaches to the laptop and allows more devices to be connected, such as an external monitor, keyboard, mouse, joystick, and printer. To use a port replicator, normally the external devices are connected first. Align the laptop connector with the port replication connector. Attach the port replicator to the laptop. Today, most laptops come with many integrated ports; therefore, docking stations and port replicators are not as popular. Also, port replicators and docking stations are normally proprietary, which means that if you have a particular brand of laptop, you must use the same brand docking station or port replicator.

Being able to identify ports quickly and accurately is a critical skill in computer repair. Table 1.2 lists the most common computer ports.

Table 1.2	Common computer ports		
Port	**Usage**	**Port color code**	**Common connector**
PS/2 mouse	Mouse	Green	6-pin mini-DIN
PS/2 keyboard	Keyboard	Purple	6-pin mini-DIN
IEEE 1394	Camcorder, video recorder, camera, printer, CD/DVD drive, scanner, speaker	Gray	6-pin IEEE 1394
USB	Printer, mouse, keyboard, digital camera, scanner, digitizer, plotter, external hard drive, CD/DVD drive	Black	USB Type A
Parallel	Printer, tape backup	Burgundy (dark pink)	25-pin female D-shell
Serial	External modem, digitizer, plotter	Teal or turquoise	9-pin male D-shell
Video	Analog monitor (VGA or higher)	Blue	3-row 15-pin female
Video	DVI digital or analog monitor	White	3-row DVI
S-Video	Composite video device	Yellow	7-pin mini-DIN
Audio	Analog audio input	Light pink	3.5mm jack
Audio	Analog line level audio input	Light blue	3.5mm jack
Audio	Analog line level audio output from main stereo signal	Light (lime) green	3.5mm jack
Audio	Analog line level audio for right to left speaker	Brown	3.5mm jack
S/PDIF	Digital audio output (sometimes used as an analog line output for a speaker instead)	Orange	3.5mm jack
Game port/MIDI	Joystick or MIDI device	Gold	15-pin female D-shell
Ethernet	UTP network	N/A	8-conductor RJ-45
Modem	Internal modem or phone	N/A	4-conductor RJ-11

Key Terms

adapter (p. 6)
BIOS (p. 3)
capacitive keyboard (p. 13)
CD drive (p. 5)
cold boot (p. 8)
computer (p. 4)
desktop (p. 4)
device driver (p. 3)
digital pen (p. 15)
digital tablet (p. 15)
DIN connector (p. 9)
docking station (p. 19)
D-shell connector (p. 9)
DVD drive (p. 5)
DVI port (p. 9)
Ethernet (p. 17)
expansion slot (p. 6)
female port (p. 9)
firmware (p. 3)
floppy disk (p. 5)
floppy drive (p. 5)
game port (p. 15)
hard drive (p. 5)

hardware (p. 3)
IEEE 1394 port (p. 16)
integrated motherboard
   (p. 9)
keyboard (p. 4)
keyboard port (p. 12)
keyed (p. 9)
laptop (p. 4)
male port (p. 9)
mechanical keyboard (p. 13)
mechanical mouse (p. 13)
memory (p. 7)
modem (p. 18)
monitor (p. 4)
motherboard (p. 5)
mouse (p. 4)
mouse port (p. 12)
network port (p. 17)
NIC (p. 17)
operating system (p. 3)
optical mouse (p. 13)
parallel port (p. 12)
PDA (p. 4)

port (p. 9)
port replicator (p. 20)
POST (p. 8)
power supply (p. 4)
RAM (p. 7)
riser board (p. 6)
ROM (p. 8)
S/PDIF (p. 15)
serial port (p. 12)
signature pad (p. 15)
software (p. 3)
sound card (p. 14)
Token Ring (p. 18)
touch screen (p. 15)
tower (p. 4)
track pad (p. 15)
track stick (p. 15)
trackball (p. 15)
USB port (p. 10)
VGA port (p. 9)
video port (p. 9)

Review Questions

1. List three qualities of a good computer technician.
2. Describe how a computer technician must be like a detective.
3. [T | F] Working inside a monitor can cause harm to an improperly trained technician.
4. List an example of an operating system.
5. Why is having a correct device driver so important?
6. List one purpose of a power supply.
7. List three common components found inside a computer.
8. Which holds more data, a hard drive or a CD?
9. What is an alternative to a CD drive?
10. Where is the motherboard located on a tower computer?
11. List three names for an adapter.
12. How can you determine an adapter's function?
13. What is the purpose of the laptop AC adapter?
14. What is the difference between RAM and ROM?
15. Which type of memory do you think the computer has more of, RAM or ROM?
16. List two types of RAM chips.
17. What is the difference between a cold boot and a warm boot?
18. What is another name for a connector on the motherboard or an adapter to which a cable normally attaches?
19. Why must technicians be able to identify common ports?
20. What is the difference between male and female ports?

21. What type of connector do keyboards and mice use?

22. Which video port is used to attach a flat panel monitor? [S-video | VGA | DVI]

23. What speeds are supported by USB?

24. How can you visually identify a Version 2.0 USB port?

25. List three devices that can connect to a USB port.

26. What is the difference in data transmission between the serial and parallel ports?

27. What is the one device that would most likely connect to a serial port today?

28. [T | F] Serial and parallel ports normally transmit in both directions.

29. How can you distinguish between a serial and a parallel port?

30. [T | F] The keyboard and mouse cables can always plug into either DIN port on the back of a computer.

31. How can one distinguish between an optical mouse and a mechanical mouse?

32. What is a drawback to using an infrared wireless mouse?

33. What can be used to clean mechanical mouse ball rollers?

34. Match the input device to its definition.

    _____ touch screen   a. A laptop input device that uses finger movement

    _____ track pad   b. A monitor that uses a pen or fingertip as an input device

    _____ digital tablet c. Used in computer-aided drawing and frequently comes with a mouse or pen

35. What type of card would have a MIDI port on it?

36. What is another name for the IEEE 1394 standard?

37. What speeds are supported by the IEEE 1394 standard?

38. What is the most common type of NIC?

39. What device converts analog signals to digital and vice versa as well as connects a computer to a phone line?

40. What type of connector is found on an internal modem?

41. [T | F] An internal modem with only one RJ-11 jack has a phone connected to the port.

42. Name at least two advantages of an integrated motherboard.

43. What is the difference between a docking station and a port replicator?

Fill-in-the-Blank

1. An operating system is an example of _____. The hard drive, keyboard, and monitor are examples of _____.

2. A small input device connected to the motherboard or an adapter is a/an _____.

3. The _____ provides DC voltage to various parts of a computer.

4. The most common device used to store data is a/an _____ that is sealed to keep out dust and dirt.

5. The largest electronic circuit board in the computer is the _____.

6. Adapters plug into a/an _____ on the motherboard.

7. A/An _____ plugs into the motherboard and holds adapters in some computer models.

8. Two basic types of memory found inside the microcomputer are _____ and _____.

9. The chip that contains software to start the computer is the _____.

10. _____ is a software program that performs a hardware check during a cold boot.

11. A/An _____ is a motherboard that has multiple ports built into it.

12. A connector with a notch or an extra metal piece that allows a cable to be inserted only one way is said to be _____.

13. A three-row, 15-pin female D-shell connector is commonly used to connect a _____.

14. A/An _____ monitor connects to three rows of square holes.

15. The 25-pin female D-shell connector is used to connect a/an _____.

16. The 9-pin or 25-pin male D-shell connector is a/an _____ port.

17. The keyboard or mouse connector can be a/an _____ or a/an _____ port.

18. A/An _____ port allows connection of up to 127 devices.

19. A/An _____ converts digital signals to audio.

20. The most common connector used on the Ethernet port is _____.

Hands-On Exercises

1. Identifying Tower Computer Parts

Objective: To identify various computer parts correctly

Procedure: Using Figure 1.31, identify each computer part.

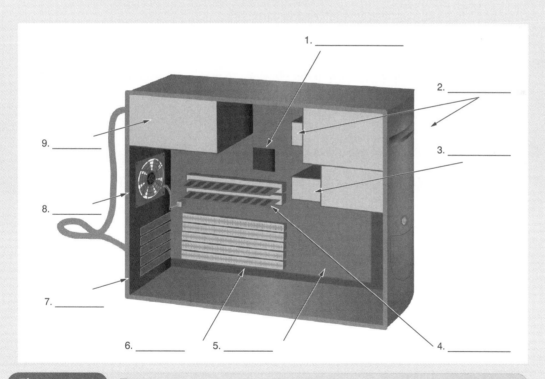

Figure 1.31   **Tower computer parts**

2. Identification of Computer Ports

Objective: To identify various computer ports correctly

Procedure: Using Figure 1.32, identify each computer port.

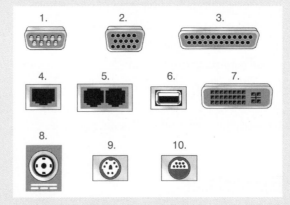

3. Port Identification

Objective: To identify various computer ports correctly

Parts: Computer ports, either built into a specific computer or as separate adapters

Procedure:

1. Contact your instructor for a computer on which to work or to obtain adapters.

2. Identify the computer port(s) given to you by the instructor. Using Table 1.3, fill in the connector type, number of pins, and port type.

Table 1.3   Connector identification

	Connector type (D-shell, DIN, etc.)	Number of pins	Port type (video, parallel, serial, etc.)
1.			
2.			
3.			
4.			
5.			
6.			
7.			
8.			
9.			
10.			

Internet Discovery

Objective: To obtain specific information on the Internet regarding a computer or its associated parts

Parts: Computer with Internet access

Procedure: Obtain the technical information on a computer. Answer the following questions based on the information. More documents may need to be obtained in order to answer the questions.

Questions:

1. What ports are available on the front of the computer?

2. What ports are available on the back of the computer?

3. How many drive bays are available to install devices such as hard drives, CD/DVD drives, tape drives, and so on?

4. Were the photos in the documentation clear enough to differentiate between the different ports? If not, explain what is wrong.

5. List three safety precautions or procedures the documentation offers.

Soft Skills

Objective: To enhance and fine tune a future technician's ability to listen, communicate in both written and oral form, and support people who use computers in a professional manner

Procedure:

1. In a team environment, list three qualities that would be found in a computer technician. Create scenarios that demonstrate these qualities. Share these findings in a clear and concise way with the class.

2. In a team environment, list three qualities that are not good practices for computer technicians. Create scenarios that demonstrate these qualities. Share these findings in a clear and concise way with the class.

Critical Thinking Skills

Objective: To analyze and evaluate information as well as apply learned information to new or different situations

Procedure:

1. Find an advertisement for a computer in a local computer flyer, newspaper, magazine, book, or on the Internet. List which components you know in one column and the components you do not know in the other column. Select one component you do not know and research that component. Write the new information and share with at least one other person.

2. Why do you think that computer components are considered "throw away" technology? List your reasoning. In groups of three or four, share your thoughts. Nominate a spokesperson who shares your group reaction in two sentences or less.

3. Provide five tips that might help someone identify the different computer ports. Each person in the class states a tip without duplicating someone else's tip if possible.

On the Motherboard

Objectives

After completing this chapter you will be able to

- Define the purpose of the major components on a motherboard including the BIOS, clock, front side bus, and expansion slots

- Explain the basic operation of a processor and what issues must be considered when upgrading it

- Recognize and identify the motherboard, CPU, and expansion slots

- Compare and contrast motherboard expansion slots

- Identify methods to add functionality to portable devices

- Explain different motherboard technologies such as HyperTransport, HyperThreading, and multi-core

- Learn the benefits of active listening

Processor Overview

At the heart of every computer is a special motherboard chip called the **processor** that determines, to a great extent, the power of the computer. The processor is also called the CPU (central processing unit) or microprocessor. The processor executes instructions, performs calculations, and coordinates input/output operations. Each motherboard has electronic chips that work with the CPU and are designed to exact specifications. Whether or not these other components can keep up with the processor depends on the individual component's specifications. The major processor manufacturers today are Intel, Motorola, VIA, and AMD (Advanced Micro Devices, Inc.). The processors designed by Motorola have been used in Apple computers for years.

Intel designed the processors IBM used in their first computers. IBM put microcomputers in the workplace and the home. Those early computers influenced much of what happened in the computer industry. The machines sold by companies who copied IBM's first computers were known as clones or IBM-compatibles. These two terms are still used in the computer industry. Another name for the computer is **PC** (personal computer). This book focuses on compatibles (non-Apple computers) because they are the majority used in businesses today. Intel and AMD processors are covered extensively because they are the most common in the computer industry.

Processor Basics

All processors use 1s and 0s. One 1 or one 0 is a **bit**. Eight bits grouped together are a **byte**. The letter A looks like 01000001 to the processor. Each character on a keyboard appears as one byte or eight bits to the processor. Approximately 1,000 bytes is a **kilobyte** (kB). (1,024 bytes to be exact, but the computer industry rounds off the number to the nearest thousand for ease of calculation.) Ten kilobytes is shown as 10K or 10kB. Approximately one million bytes is a **megabyte** (MB). 540 megabytes is shown as 540MB or 540M. A true megabyte is 1,048,576 bytes. Approximately one billion bytes (1,073,741,824 bytes) is a **gigabyte** and is shown as 1GB or 1G. Table 2.1 shows the different terms associated with computer storage and capacity.

Table 2.1	Byte table	
Term	**Abbreviation**	**Description**
Kilobyte	kB	~1 thousand bytes
Megabyte	MB	~1 million bytes
Gigabyte	GB	~1 billion bytes
Terabyte	TB	~1 trillion bytes
Petabyte	PB	~1,000 trillion bytes
Exabyte	EB	~1 quintillion bytes
Zetabyte	ZB	~1,000 exabytes
Yottabyte	YB	~1 million exabytes

When information needs to be expressed exactly, binary prefixes are used. For example, when describing a value of 2^{10} (1024), instead of saying that it is 1 kilobyte, which people tend to think of as approximately 1,000 bytes, the term **kibibyte** (KiB) is used. When describing a value of 2^{20} or 1,048,576, the term **mebibyte** (MiB) is used. Table 2.2 shows the terms used with binary prefixes or when exact measurements are needed.

Microprocessors come in a variety of speeds. The speed of processors is measured in **gigahertz** (GHz). Hertz is a measurement of cycles per second. One hertz equals one cycle per second. One gigahertz is one billion cycles per second or 1GHz. Older CPUs used megahertz (MHz) as the standard measurement. One megahertz is one million cycles per second or 1MHz.

Table 2.2	Binary prefixes	
Term	**Abbreviation**	**Description**
Kibibyte	KiB	2^{10} and closely associated with kilobyte
Mebibyte	MiB	2^{20} and closely associated with megabyte
Gibibyte	GiB	2^{30} and closely associated with gigabyte
Tebibyte	TiB	2^{40} and closely associated with terabyte
Pebibyte	PiB	2^{50} and closely associated with petabyte
Exbibyte	EiB	2^{60} and closely associated with exabyte
Zebibyte	ZiB	2^{70} and closely associated with zettabyte
Yobibyte	YiB	2^{80} and closely associated with yottabyte

The original PC CPU, the 8088 microprocessor, ran at 4.77MHz. Today's microprocessors run at speeds over 3GHz.

The number of bits processed at one time is the microprocessor's **register size (word size)**. Register size is in multiples of 8 bits (i.e., 8-, 16-, 32-, 64-, or 128-bit). Intel's 8086 processor's register size was 16 bits or two bytes. Today's CPUs have register sizes of 64 or 128 bits.

The 1s and 0s must travel from one place to another inside the processor as well as outside to other chips. To move the 1s and 0s around, electronic lines called a **bus** are used. The electronic lines inside the CPU are known as the **internal data bus** or system bus. In the 8086 the internal data bus comprises 16 separate lines with each line carrying one 1 or one 0. The word size and the number of lines for the internal data bus are equal. The 8086, for example, had a 16-bit word size, and 16 lines carried 16 bits on the internal data bus. In today's microprocessors, 64 or 128 internal data bus lines operate concurrently.

For the CPU to communicate with devices in the outside world, such as a printer, the 1s and 0s travel on the **external data bus**. The external data bus connects the processor to adapters, the keyboard, the mouse, the floppy drive, the hard drive, and other devices. The external data bus is also known as the external data path. One can see the external data lines by looking between the expansion slots on the motherboard. Some solder lines between the expansion slots are used to send data out along the external data bus to the expansion slots. The Intel 8088 had an 8-bit external data bus. Today's processors have 64- and 128-bit external data paths. Figure 2.1 shows the internal and external data buses.

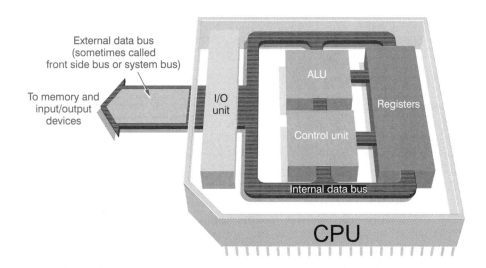

Figure 2.1   **Internal and external data buses**

Processors have a special component called the **ALU** (arithmetic logic unit), which does all the calculations and comparison logic needed by the computer. Refer to Figure 2.1 and see how the ALU connects to the registers, control unit, and internal bus. Today's processors actually have two ALUs, but Figure 2.1 simply shows how the buses connect. The control unit coordinates activities inside the processor. The I/O unit manages data entering and leaving the processor. The registers within the CPU are a very high speed storage area for 1s and 0s before the bits are processed.

To make sense of all of this, take a look at a letter typed on a computer that starts out: *Dear Mom*. To the computer, the letters of the alphabet are different combinations of eight 1s and 0s. For example, the letter *D* is 01000100; the letter *e* is 01000101. The 8086 microprocessor has a word size of 16-bits and an external data path of 16-bits. Therefore, the letters *D* and *e* travel together down the bus; the letters *a* and *r*, then the letters (space) and *M*, and finally the letters *o* and *m* travel as 1s and 0s. Each bit travels along a single data path line. Intel's 80386DX CPU has 32-bit internal and external data buses. In the same *Dear Mom* letter, the letters *D*, *e*, *a*, and *r* are processed at the same time, followed by (space), *M*, *o*, and *m*. An AMD 64-bit processor would allow the words *Dear Mom* to be sent all at one time. You can see that the size of the bus greatly increases performance on a computer.

Processors have multiple **pipelines** (separate internal buses) that operate simultaneously. To understand pipelining, take the example of a fast-food restaurant. In the restaurant, say there are five steps (and one employee per step) to making a burger and giving it to the customer: (1) take the order and input it into the computer system; (2) brown the buns and cook the burgers; (3) take the bun and burger and add the condiments; (4) wrap the burger, add fries, and insert it into the bag; (5) take the customer's money and give the bag to the customer. Keep in mind that the person taking the customer's order and inputting the order can serve another customer once he or she has completed this task for the first customer. The same is true for each person along the line. To make this burger process go faster, you could: (1) make your employees work faster; (2) break the tasks into smaller tasks (such as seven steps instead of five and have seven people); or (3) have more lines of people doing the exact same process tasks.

To relate this to processors, making the employees work faster is the same as increasing the CPU clock speed. Breaking the tasks into smaller tasks is the same as changing the structure of the CPU pipeline. Instead of the standard five tasks the CPU performs, 6, 7, 14, 20, or even more steps are created. This allows each step to be acted upon quicker, the task to be smaller, and production to be faster. Having more lines of people doing the same complete process is having multiple pipelines.

A 32- or 64-bit CPU can have separate paths, each of which handles 32 or 64 bits. For example, the Pentium has two pipelines. In the *Dear Mom* scenario, the letters *D*, *e*, *a*, and *r* can be in one pipeline, while (space), *M*, *o*, and *m* can be in the other pipeline.

AMD's Athlon has 9 execution pipelines and the Opteron has 12 pipelines for integers and 17 pipelines for floating point numbers (numbers that can have a decimal point in it). Intel Pentium 4 and Xeon CPUs have various models that contain anywhere from 20- to 31-stage pipelines. Debate continues about whether a longer pipeline improves performance.

Intel Processors

Traditionally, Intel has rated its processors by GHz and people have compared processors based on speed alone. Now, Intel arranges its products by family numbers. Within a family of microprocessors, you can compare things such as speed and the amount of cache memory and other technologies within the family. Table 2.3 shows Intel's processor families.

Intel also makes processors for more powerful computers such as network servers. The processors used by these computers include the Itaniums, Xeons, Pentium Ds, and Pentium 4s. The 64-bit Itanium Intel processors are based on the EPIC (Explicitly Parallel Instruction Computing) architecture that has been developed jointly by Hewlett-Packard and Intel. This type of technology is known as IA-64. The Itanium family of processors is best suited for network servers. With this architecture, up to 18EBs (exabytes) of memory can be accessed. This is 18,446,744,073,709,551,616 bytes. The 64-bit architecture is also backward compatible with 32-bit instructions. However, in Itanium 2 processors, the 32-bit instructions are done in an emulation mode, which could make them run slower. Figure 2.2 shows an Intel quad-core CPU.

Table 2.3	Intel processor families
Processor family*	**Comments**
Core i7	Multi-core (2 packages with 2 cores in each package) with 8MB L2 cache shared between cores Desktop processor for virtualization, graphic/multimedia design and creation, gaming On-board memory controller
Core2	Multi-core (single- and dual-core models in a single package; quad core has 2 processors in 2 packages for a total of 4 cores) with 6MB to 12MB L2 cache shared between cores Desktop/laptop processor for gaming and multimedia
Pentium	Single- or dual-core desktop/laptop processor for general computing
Celeron	Entry-level desktop processor for general computing
Centrino	Laptop processor for general computing that has extended battery life
Atom	Nettop/netbook/mobile Internet device** processor

*Intel is constantly upgrading processors. More information is available at www.intel.com.
**A nettop is smaller than a laptop used to extend Internet access at home. Mobile Internet devices are small enough to fit in a pocket. Netbooks are a portable version of your desktop used for Internet research, email, or streaming audio/video.

Figure 2.2	Intel quad-core processor

AMD Processors

AMD rivals Intel in processors. Anyone buying a processor should research all vendors, including Intel and AMD. Table 2.4 lists the characteristics of AMD processor families. The AMD Opteron processor is shown in Figure 2.3. The 64 indicates that it supports a 64-bit operating system and applications.

Table 2.4	AMD processor families
Processor family	**Comments**
Phenom	Multi-core (3 or 4 in a single package) high-end desktop for HD support, megamedia creation and editing, and virtualization Supports 32- and 64-bit computing, 3DNow!, SSE, SSE2, SSE3, SSE4a, HyperTransport, and DirectConnect technologies*
Athlon	Single- or dual-core desktop/notebook processor
Sempron	Lower-cost desktop/notebook processor for basic productivity, email, and web browsing
Turion	Dual-core notebook processor

*These technologies are covered later in the chapter.

2
On the
Motherboard

Figure 2.3   **AMD Opteron**

Speeding Up Processor Operations Overview

The processor speed can be determined by looking at the model number on the chip, but processors frequently have fans or heat sinks attached to them for cooling, which makes it difficult to see the writing on the chip. A processor commonly does not use its maximum speed in order to save power or cool down.

Tech Tip

Locating your processor speed

An easy way to tell processor speed with Windows XP is to open *Windows Explorer,* right-click the *My Computer* icon, and select the *Properties* option. The first tab (*General*) lists the processor speed toward the bottom of the window. In Vista/7, right-click the *Start* button and select *Explore*. Right-click the *Computer* option and select *Properties*.

We have already taken a look at how increasing the CPU pipeline to some extent can improve processor operations, but other technologies also exist. Some of the hardest concepts to understand about the motherboard revolve around understanding the computer's timing and interaction with the CPU with other components such as memory and expansion slots. We will start by defining some of the terms that relate to this area and associating those terms to concepts and the various technologies used. Table 2.5 list the terms related to speed.

Cache

An important concept related to CPU speed is keeping data flowing into the processor. Registers are a type of high speed memory storage inside the CPU and is an integral part of CPU processing. The data or instruction the CPU needs to operate on is usually found in one of three places: the cache, the motherboard memory (main memory), or the hard drive.

Cache memory is a very fast type of memory designed to increase the speed of CPU operations. When cache memory is integrated as part of the CPU, it is called **L1 cache**. Included in the processor packaging, but not part of the CPU is **L2 cache**, which some refer to as **on-die cache**. Finally, there is a third level of memory found when using higher end server processors called **L3 cache**, which can be located in the CPU housing or on the motherboard. CPU efficiency is increased when data continuously flows into the CPU. Cache gives the fastest access. If the information is not in cache, the microprocessor looks for it in the motherboard memory. If the information is not there, it is retrieved from the hard drive and placed into the motherboard memory or the cache. Hard drive access is the slowest of the three.

An analogy best explains this. Consider a glass of cold lemonade, a pitcher of lemonade, and a can of frozen lemonade concentrate. If you were thirsty, you would drink from the glass because it is the fastest and easily accessible. If the glass is empty, you would pour lemonade from the pitcher to refill the glass. If the pitcher is empty, you would go to the freezer to get the frozen concentrate to make more. The glass of lemonade is like cache memory. It is easily accessible. The pitcher of lemonade is like the motherboard memory. If the glass is empty, you have to get more lemonade from the pitcher. Likewise, if the 1s and 0s are not in cache,

Table 2.5	PC speed terms
Term	**Explanation**
clock or **clock speed**	The speed of the processor's internal clock, measured in gigahertz.
bus speed	The speed in which data is delivered when a particular bus on the motherboard is being used.
FSB (front side bus)	The speed between the CPU and some of the motherboard components. This is what most people would term the motherboard speed. Sometimes the speed is listed in megatransfers per second, or MT/s. With MT/s, not only is the speed of the FSB considered but how many processor transfers occur each clock cycle. A 266 MHz FSB that can do four transfers per second could list as 1064MT/s. The FSB is being upgraded with technologies such as AMD's HyperTransport and Intel's QPI (QuickPath Interconnect).
back side bus	The speed between the CPU and the L2 cache located outside the main CPU, but on the same chip.
PCI bus speed	The speed in which data is delivered when the PCI bus is being used. The PCI bus is the main bus used on the motherboard. Common speeds for the PCI bus are 33 and 66MHz allowing bandwidths up to 533MBps.
PCIe bus speed	The speed in which data is delivered when the PCIe bus is being used. This bus is used for PCI Express cards.
AGP bus speed	The speed in which data is delivered when the AGP bus is being used. The AGP bus is a 66MHz bus allowing 2.1GBps of bandwidth.
CPU speed	The speed at which the CPU operates. Some motherboards have a BIOS option to change the speed. Other motherboards either use motherboard jumpers or cannot be changed.
CPU throttling	Reducing the clock frequency in order to reduce power consumption and heat. This is especially useful in laptops.

they are retrieved from the motherboard memory chips. The pitcher holds more lemonade than the glass, just like motherboard memory holds more information than cache memory. The lemonade concentrate is like the hard drive—the lemonade concentrate takes longer to make and get to than the glass or the pitcher. In a computer, it takes roughly a million times longer to access information from the hard drive than it does from the memory on the motherboard or cache.

Usually the more cache memory a system has, the better that system performs, but this is not always true. System performance also depends on the efficiency of the cache controller (the chip that manages the cache memory), the system design, the amount of available hard drive space, and the speed of the microprocessor. When determining a computer's memory requirements, you must consider the operating system used, applications used, and hardware installed. The Windows 98 operating system takes a lot less memory than Windows 7. High-end games and desktop publishing take more RAM than word processing. Free hard drive space and video memory are often as important as RAM in improving a computer's performance. Memory is only one piece of the puzzle. All of the computer's parts must work together to provide good system performance. Figure 2.4 shows this hierarchy of data access for the CPU.

Clocking

The motherboard generates a clock signal that is used to control the transfer of 1s and 0s to the CPU. Processor clock timing signals go as fast as 100, 133, 166, 200, 266, or 333 MHz (millions of cycles per second). A clock signal can be illustrated as a sine wave. One clock cycle is from one point on the sine wave to the next point that is located on the same point on the sine wave later in time, as shown in Figure 2.5.

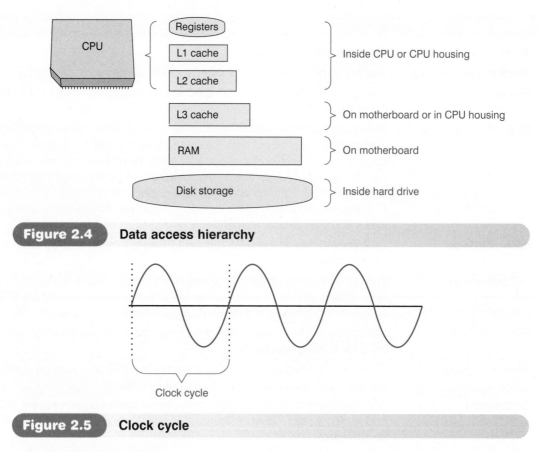

Figure 2.4   **Data access hierarchy**

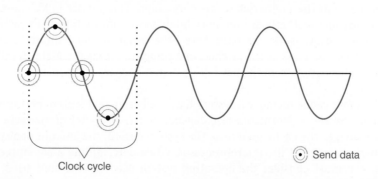

Figure 2.5   **Clock cycle**

In older computers, data was sent to the CPU only once during a clock cycle. Then, newer memory technologies evolved that allow data to be sent twice during every clock cycle. Today, data is sent four times during a single clock cycle, as shown in Figure 2.6.

Figure 2.6   **Clock cycle that clocks data four times per cycle**

We have considered various ways to speed up processor operations, including having more stages in the processor, increasing the speed of the clock, and sending more data in the same amount of time. Accessing L2 cache and motherboard components was a bottleneck in older systems because the CPU used the same bus to communicate with RAM and other motherboard components as it did with L2 and motherboard cache. Intel's Pentium Pro and AMD's Athlon/Duron CPUs take a different approach called DIB. With DIB (dual independent bus), two buses are used: a back side bus and a front side bus. The back side bus connects the CPU to the L2 cache. The FSB (front side bus) connects the CPU to the motherboard components. The FSB is considered the speed of the motherboard. Figure 2.7 illustrates the concept of a front side bus. Remember that the front side bus is more detailed than what is shown; the figure simply illustrates the difference between the back side bus and the front side bus.

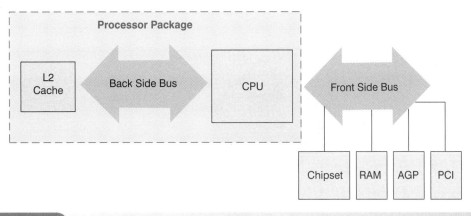

Figure 2.7   **Front side bus**

Many people think that the higher the CPU speed, the faster the computer. This is seldom true. Several factors contribute to computer speed. One factor is bus speed. Bus speed describes how fast the CPU can communicate with motherboard components, such as memory, chipset, or PCI bus. The first Pentium CPUs ran at the same speed as the bus—60Mhz; however CPUs got faster and buses stayed the same. Advances in technology have not reached the rest of the motherboard components (and it would cost too much to try to have them keep up).

Intel and AMD have new technologies to replace the front side bus in some parts. AMD's solution is DirectConnect. Intel has **QPI** (QuickPath Interconnect), a full-duplex (traffic can flow in both directions simultaneously) point-to-point connection between the processor and one or more motherboard components.

A multiplier is a number that, when multiplied by the bus speed, gives the CPU speed. Other names for the multiplier include CPU clock ratio, bus frequency multiple, and bus frequency ratio. The motherboard speed is increased to a faster rate for the CPU that can operate at the increased level of speed. For example, if the motherboard is using a 200Mhz clock speed and the CPU multiplier is set to 12, then the speed of the CPU is 2.4Ghz. Multipliers can be from 1.5 to 23 or higher. The available multiplier and the bus speed are determined by the motherboard manufacturer.

Settings for CPU installations

When upgrading a processor or installing a new one, sometimes there are two sets of motherboard jumpers or BIOS settings that can be important: CPU bus frequency and bus frequency multiple. The CPU bus frequency setting allows the motherboard to run at a specific speed, such as 200 or 266 MHz. This speed is the external rate data travels *outside* the processor. The bus frequency multiple enables the motherboard to recognize the *internal* processor speed.

Knowing the CPU's speed is no longer an issue unless you are upgrading the computer to a faster microprocessor or configuring the motherboard. Many motherboards accept processors with different speeds. The microprocessor settings can be configured through system BIOS or by **jumpers** (pins on the motherboard). The software in the BIOS requires a specific key to be pressed during startup to access the software. The processor settings are normally in the *Advanced Settings* section, which is covered in more detail in Chapter 3.

A motherboard manufacturer determines how the motherboard is configured and the number of jumpers (if any) on the motherboard. Jumpers are also found on devices and older adapters. Each jumper can have more than one setting. For example, consider a motherboard with a jumper block and three pins labeled 1, 2, and 3. The jumper can be placed over pins 1 and 2 for one setting or pins 2 and 3 for a different setting. For example, jumper pins 1 and 2 may need to be jumpered together to erase the password that has been forgotten. In that case, the jumper is placed over pins 1 and 2; pin 3 is left uncovered. Refer to Figure 2.8 for an illustration of JP1 pins 1 and 2 jumpered together.

Figure 2.8 shows an enlarged jumper; the jumper blocks and jumpers on a motherboard are much smaller. When a jumper is not in use, instead of putting it in a drawer somewhere, place the jumper over a single pin in the jumper block. This action does not enable anything and it keeps the jumper safe and convenient for when it is needed later.

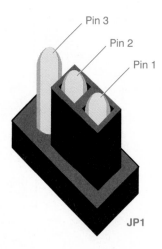

Pin 3
Pin 2
Pin 1

JP1

| Figure 2.8 | JP1 jumper block with pins 1 and 2 jumpered together |

Multi-Core Processors

Another way to speed up operations is to have two or more processors. Intel developed **HT** (hyperthreading technology), which is an alternative to using two processors. HT allows a single processor to handle two separate sets of instructions simultaneously. To the operating system, HT makes the system appear as if it has multiple processors. Even before HT, software was written so that instructions could be split and acted upon by multiple processors. In order to take advantage of Intel's technology the following requirements must be met:

- The CPU must support HT
- The chipset (covered later in the chapter) must support HT
- The BIOS must support HT
- The operating system must support HT

Intel claims that the system can have up to a 30 percent increase in performance, but studies have shown that this is application-dependent. In some instances it has actually slowed down performance. If the applications being used cannot take advantage of the multiple threading, then HT can be disabled in the BIOS.

In the past when two processors were installed, software had to be specifically written to support it. That is no longer true. A **dual-core CPU** combines two CPUs in a single unit. Both Intel and AMD offer dual-core processors. AMD offers a **tri-core CPU**, which has three processors in a single unit. Both Intel and AMD have **quad-core CPU** technologies, which is either two dual-core CPUs installed on the same motherboard (Intel's solution) or two dual-core CPUs installed in a single socket (AMD and Intel solution). Intel and AMD's dual and quad core technologies are different, especially in regard to how the CPU accesses L2 cache memory and motherboard RAM.

AMD core processors directly access RAM on the motherboard, and each core has its own L2 cache and, optionally, L3 cache. An advertisement that shows a 2x2MB cache means the computer has two sets of 2MB of cache memory, 2MB for each CPU. Intel processors share L2 cache and access RAM via an external memory controller or have an integrated memory controller within the CPU packaging. An Intel advertisement would just show the amount of shared L2 cache. Figures 2.9 and 2.10 show how the AMD and some of the Intel multi-processors can have integrated memory controllers.

In the past, dual processors were most beneficial in servers and gaming PCs where software could take advantage and was written for two-processor technology. Today, dual-core CPUs are useful to almost anyone who has multiple applications open at the same time. All applications can take advantage of the dual-core technology as well as the background processes that are associated with the operating system as well as the applications. This improves operations when multitasking or when running powerful applications that require many instructions to be executed, such as drawing applications and games.

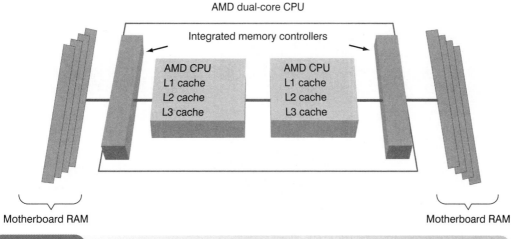

Figure 2.9   **AMD dual-core memory access**

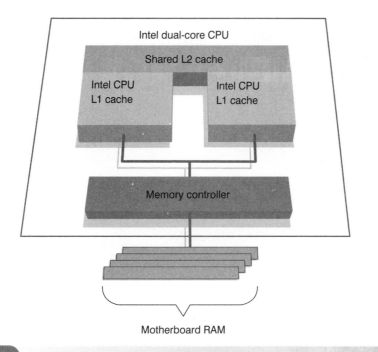

Figure 2.10   **Intel dual-core memory access**

Sockets and Slots

A processor inserts into a socket or slot depending on the model. Most processors today insert into a socket. There are different types of sockets: PGA (pin grid array), which has even rows of holes around the square socket; SPGA (staggered pin array), which has staggered holes so more pins can be inserted; PPGA (plastic pin grid array) used on Intel Celerons and Pentium 4s; µPGA (micro pin grid array) used by AMD; and LGA (land grid array) used with AMD and Intel processors. Figure 2.11 shows a LGA775 socket (also called a Socket T).

The processor sockets used today are called **ZIF sockets** (zero insertion force); even though people call all sockets with a lever a ZIF socket, they come in different sizes, depending on the processor installed. They have a small lever to the side of the socket that, when lifted, brings the processor slightly up out of the socket holes. When installing a processor, the CPU is aligned over the holes and the lever is depressed to bring the processor pins into the slot with equal force on all the pins. Refer to Figure 2.11 and notice the lever beside the socket.

Figure 2.11 LGA775 socket

Buy the right CPU

If you buy a motherboard and processor separately, it is important to ensure that the motherboard CPU socket is the correct type for the processor.

Table 2.6 lists the commonly used Intel CPU sockets and slots. Table 2.7 shows some of the AMD CPU sockets and slots that can be found.

Table 2.6 Intel desktop CPU sockets and slots

Socket or slot	Description
Slot 1	242-pin 2.8V and 3.3V connector for Pentium IIs, IIIs, and Celerons
Slot 2	330-pin 1.5V to 3.5V connector for Pentium II and III Xeons
Socket 423	423-pin 1.7V and 1.75V for Pentium 4s
Socket 478	478-pin 1.7V and 1.75V for Pentium 4s and Celerons
Socket 603	603-pin 1.5V and 1.7V for Pentium 4 Xeons, and Xeon MPs
Socket 604	604-pin for Pentium 4 Xeons
Socket 611	611-pin 3.3V for Itanium 2s
Socket 755	755-pin for Pentium 4s and Celerons
Socket 775	775-pin for Pentium 4s, Celerons, Core 2 Duo, Core 2 Extreme, and Core 2 Quads
Socket B or Socket 1366	1366-pin for Core i7s

Table 2.7 AMD desktop CPU sockets and slots

Socket or slot	Description
Socket A or Socket 462	462-pin 1.1V to 1.85V for Duron and Athlons
Socket AM2	940-pin for Athlon, Athlon X2, and Semprons
Socket AM2+	940-pin for Athlon X2, Phenom X3, and Phenom X4s
Socket AM3	940-pin for Phenom II X3 and Phenom II X4s
Socket 754	754-pin for Athlon and Semprons
Socket 939	939-pin for Athlon and Athlon X2s 1207-pin

Processor Cooling

In today's systems the fans and heat sinks are very large. A heat sink looks like metal bars protruding from the processor. The largest chip or cartridge on or inserted into the motherboard with a fan or a heat sink attached is easily recognized as the processor. Some systems have multiple fans to keep the CPU cool. Figure 2.12 shows a fan and a heat sink.

Additional motherboard components can also have heat sinks attached. These are normally the chipset and/or the I/O (Input/Output) controller chips. Figure 2.13 shows a motherboard with these cooling elements.

Heat sinks and fans attach to the processor using different methods. The most common methods are screws, thermal compound, or clips. Clips can use retaining screws, pressure release (press down on them and they release), or a retaining slot. Small screwdrivers can be used to release the clips that attach using the retaining slot. Clips for fans or heat sinks can be difficult to install.

Figure 2.12   **CPU fan and heat sink**

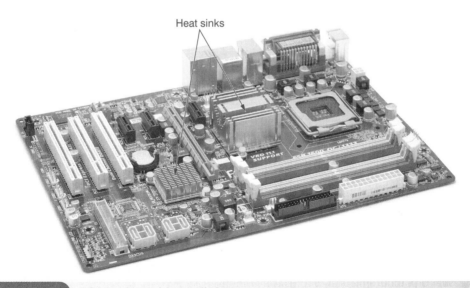

Heat sinks

Figure 2.13   **Motherboard heat sinks**

When installing a heat sink, a thermal pad or thermal compound may be used. A thermal pad provides uniform heat dispersion for the CPU. If thermal compound is used, only apply the prescribed amount. Spread the compound evenly in a fine layer over the portion of the CPU that comes in contact with the heat sink. Always follow the heat sink installation procedures.

Watch out for screwdrivers

Screwdrivers can cause damage to a motherboard. They can slip when trying to remove a retaining clip for a heat sink or fan and can gouge the motherboard. Be careful not to scratch the surface of the motherboard with a screwdriver.

Some heat sinks are known as active heat sinks. These have power provided by a motherboard connection or through one of the power supply drive connectors. Some motherboards come with sensors that monitor CPU temperatures, motherboard temperatures, and fan speed. The BIOS (covered further in Chapter 3) can be used to configure the CPU. Additional fans can be installed to provide additional cooling for the PC. Figure 2.14 shows extra cooling fans mounted in a case.

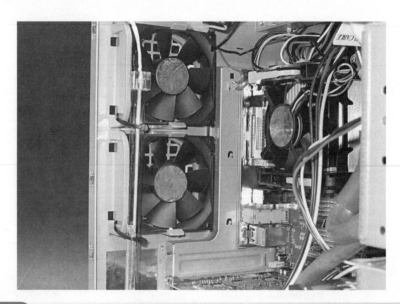

Figure 2.14   **Computer case auxiliary fans**

Because heat sinks generate a lot of heat, it is important to have the proper amount of airflow in the right direction. If you install an additional fan to help with cooling, there are two most likely places for fan placement: (1) near the power supply directly behind the CPU or (2) on the lower part of the front side of the case. Figure 2.15 shows two possible installation sites for an additional fan.

An alternative to a fan or heat sink for CPU cooling is a **liquid cooling system**. With a liquid cooling system, liquid is circulated through the system including through a heat sink that is mounted on the CPU. Heat from the processor is transferred to the cooler liquid. The now hot liquid is transported to the back of the system, converted to heat, and released outside the case.

Liquid cooling allows higher clock speeds and is quieter than using a fan. However, some liquid cooling systems are difficult to install and require space within the case. Some liquid systems require the liquid to be periodically refilled. The good part about a liquid cooling system is that the CPU temperature remains constant no matter how much usage the CPU is experiencing. This is not the case with heat sinks and fans. A similar, but expensive cooling technology is phase-change cooling (also known as vapor cooling).

Keep your computer cool

Air flow should be through the computer and over the motherboard to provide cooling for the motherboard components.

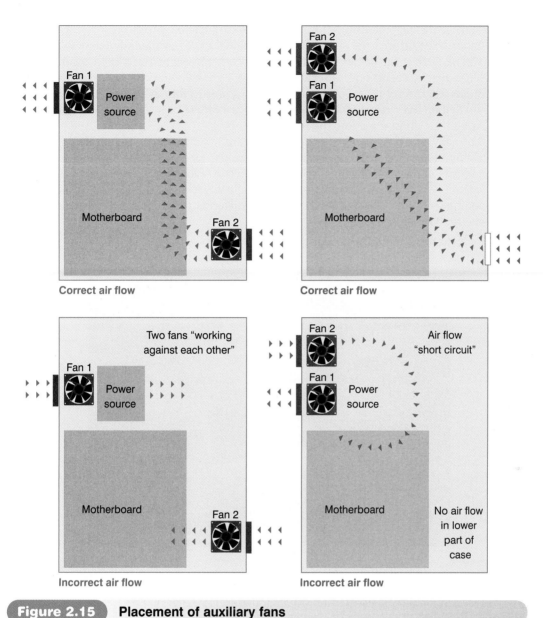

| Figure 2.15 | **Placement of auxiliary fans** |

Both Intel and AMD have technologies that reduce processor energy consumption (and heat) by turning off unused parts of the processor.

Installing Processors

Whenever a processor is purchased, it includes installation instructions. Also, motherboard manuals (documentation) include the steps to upgrade or install the CPU.

The following are the general steps for installing a processor:

> *Parts*: Proper processor for the motherboard
> (refer to motherboard documentation)
> Antistatic materials

1. Be sure power to the computer is *off* and the computer is unplugged.
2. Place the antistatic wrist strap around your wrist and attach the other end to a ground on the computer.

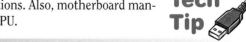

Handling the CPU

Always hold the CPU by the edges to avoid bending or touching the pins underneath. Do not lay the CPU down where the pins are on a flat surface because they can easily bend.

3. Remove the old processor by lifting the ZIF socket retaining lever.

4. Insert the CPU into the socket. When installing a CPU, it fits only one way into the socket. Look at the processor and the socket *before* inserting the chip to ensure proper alignment. A socket and CPU normally have a triangle marking or circular dot that shows where pin 1 goes. Processors insert only one way into the socket. If the socket has a retention lever, raising the socket lever allows a CPU to be inserted. Lowering the lever keeps the CPU inserted into the socket.

5. Normally, you must configure the motherboard by jumpers or through BIOS software configuration. Refer to the motherboard manual for exact steps. If needed, set any jumpers or switches on the motherboard necessary for proper operation or press the correct key to enter the setup program that allows you to set the CPU speed and proper multiplier. Some manuals refer to the multiplier as the stepping value. Refer to the motherboard documentation.

Figure 2.16 shows an AMD CPU being installed. Notice how the ZIF socket lever is raised.

Figure 2.16   **Installing an AMD CPU**

Tech Tip

Some motherboards have a retention mechanism used with processors equipped with mounted heat sinks.

Cooling the CPU

Do not apply power to the computer until the CPU and the heat sink, fan, and/or cooling unit are installed. Running the CPU without cooling it will overheat the CPU and destroy or weaken it.

Two common questions asked of technicians are "*Can* a computer be upgraded to a higher or faster processor?" and "*Should* a computer be upgraded to a higher or faster processor?" Whether or not a computer *can* be upgraded to a higher or faster processor depends on the capability of the motherboard. When a customer asks if a processor *should* be upgraded, the technician should ask, "What operating system and applications are you using?" The newer the operating system, the more advanced a processor should be.

When installing multiple processors, some motherboards require that the same processor model is used in each slot. This is not always true with the newer motherboards. Refer to the motherboard documentation. The motherboard's documentation is very important when considering a CPU upgrade. Read the documentation to determine if it can accept a faster processor.

When upgrading a CPU on an older or newer system, an important consideration is CPU voltage. Different CPUs require different voltage levels. Inserting a CPU into a socket that has a lower or higher voltage supplied to it will damage the new CPU. Now, a VRM (voltage regulator module) is integrated into the motherboard and can provide the appropriate voltage. Today's CPU can communicate to the VRM the voltage level desired and the VRM can provide it. Running a processor at lower speeds and lower voltages can save on power consumption, especially on a mobile platform.

Throttle management is the ability to control the CPU speed by slowing it when it is not being used heavily or is hot. Usually this feature is controlled by a system BIOS setting (which is covered in the next chapter) and the Power Options control panel. For an AMD CPU, this feature is called Cool'n'Quiet; Intel's version is SpeedStep. Some users may not want to use CPU throttling so that performance is at a maximum. Others, such as laptop users, may want to conserve power whenever possible to extend the time the laptop can be used on battery power.

Upgrading things other than the processor can also increase speed in a computer. Installing more memory, a faster hard drive, or a motherboard with a faster front side bus sometimes improves a computer's performance more than installing a new microprocessor. All devices and electronic components must work together transferring the 1s and 0s efficiently. The processor is only one piece of the puzzle. Many people do not realize that upgrading one computer component does not always make a computer faster or better.

Overclocking Processors

Overclocking is changing the front side bus speed and/or multiplier to boost CPU and system speed. Before describing the overclocking steps, we must discuss the issues.

- Because the CPU is normally covered with a heat sink and/or fan, you cannot easily tell the CPU speed. Be wary of vendors who sell a system advertised with a higher rated CPU speed than what is installed.
- CPU speed ratings are conservative.
- The CPU, motherboard, memory, and other components can be damaged by overclocking.
- Applications may crash, the operating system may not boot, and/or the system may hang when overclocking.
- The warranty is void on most CPUs if you overclock.
- When you increase the speed of the CPU, the processor's heat increases. Extra cooling by fans and larger heat sinks are essential.
- PCI and SCSI devices may not react well to overclocking.
- The hard drive PIO mode may need to be changed because of overclocking.
- The memory chips may need to be upgraded to be able to keep up with the faster CPU.
- Know how to reset the system BIOS in case the computer will not pass POST after making changes.

In order to overclock, you must have the motherboard documentation to determine whether the system board supports different CPU speeds and different multipliers. Many motherboard manufacturers do not allow changing the CPU, multiplier, and clock settings. The changes to the motherboard will be made through jumpers or through BIOS setup. Determine which method is used with your motherboard. Keep in mind that overclocking is a trial-and-error situation. The primary problem with overclocking is insufficient cooling. Make sure you purchase the larger heat sink and/or extra fans before starting the overclocking process. There are Web sites geared toward documenting specific motherboards and overclocked CPUs.

MMX, SSE, and 3DNow!

Today's applications require intense mathematical calculations because of the emphasis on video and audio integration. Inside the processor is a part called the FPU (floating-point unit), which is responsible for handling floating-point numbers. Floating-point numbers are those that use decimals such as 1024.7685 and −581.3724985 as compared to integers, which are numbers like 10, 561, and –86. Both video and audio applications use floating-point numbers. Today's FPUs use 128 bits.

Today's applications and games use 3-D graphics. A 3-D graphic is made up of small polygons. Each time the figure changes, the polygons have to be redrawn and each polygon corner has to be recalculated using floating-point numbers. One 3-D figure could be 1,500 polygons or more. Five things help speed up calculations with these types of intense applications: (1) a faster CPU (which also means a faster FPU); (2) more CPU pipelines; (3) multiple CPUs; (4) built-in 3-D instructions in the CPU that software applications can use; and (5) a good video adapter with a built-in processor and memory installed on the board. The 3D multimedia technologies supported by today's processors are summarized in Table 2.8.

Table 2.8	3D and multimedia
Term	**Description**
MMX	57 commands added to the processor for multimedia and communications software.
MMX2	Upgrades MMX with 70 new instructions.
3DNow!	AMD-sponsored with 21 instructions and support for SIMD (single instruction multiple data). SIMD allows one instruction to be executed by multiple data items. For example, a teacher could give instructions to class (SIMD) or as an alternative, tell each student the instructions individually. Upgrades include Enhanced 3DNow! and 3DNow! Professional.
SSE	(Streaming SIMD extensions) 50 new instructions that allow floating-point calculations to occur simultaneously. Uses 64-bit registers.
SSE2	Adds 144 new instructions. Used in Pentium III and 4 CPUs as well as AMDs 64-bit processors. Uses 128-bit registers.
SSE3	Adds 13 new instructions.
SSE4	Adds 54 instructions.
SSE4.1	A subset of SSE4 with only 47 instructions.
SSE4.2	A subset of SSE4 with the remaining instructions; used in Intel i7 Core processors.
SSE4a	An unofficial version used by AMD that contains a subset of 4 instructions from SSE4 as well as added two new instructions.

Expansion Slots

If the computer is going to be useful, the CPU must communicate with the outside world, including other motherboard components and adapters plugged into the motherboard. An expansion slot is used to add an adapter to the motherboard, and it has rules that control how many bits can be transferred at a time to the adapter, what signals are sent over the adapter's gold connectors, as well as how the adapter is configured. Figure 2.17 shows expansion slots on a motherboard.

Expansion slots used in PCs are usually some form of PCI (peripheral component interconnect) or AGP (accelerated graphics port). Other types of expansion slots that have been included with older PCs are **ISA** (industry standard architecture), EISA (extended industry standard architecture), MCA (micro channel architecture), and VL-bus (sometimes called VESA [video electronics standards association] bus). A technician must be able to distinguish among adapters and expansion slots and be able to identify the adapters/devices that use an expansion slot. The technician must also realize the abilities and limitations of each type of expansion slot when installing upgrades, replacing parts, or making recommendations.

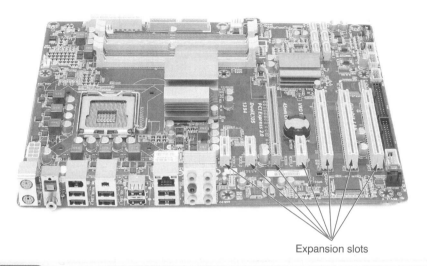

Expansion slots

Figure 2.17   Motherboard expansion slots

ISA (Industry Standard Architecture)

ISA is the oldest expansion slot. ISA allows 16-bit transfers to adapters installed in ISA slots. The number of expansion slots available depends on the motherboard manufacturer. ISA is also referred to as the AT bus. Because computer manufacturers want customers to be able to use their old adapters in an upgraded motherboard or a new computer, ISA is still available on the market.

ISA operates at 8MHz, although some vendors reliably achieve 10MHz throughput. Some vendors have achieved 12MHz, but the industry pronounced 10MHz the maximum speed for ISA. With today's microprocessor speeds, it's easy to see how the ISA architecture can be a detriment. Adapters that require high-speed transfers, such as network memory and video, are hampered by the slowness of the ISA standard.

ISA was designed to be backward compatible with IBM's first two computer models, the PC and the XT, which had an 8-bit external data bus. The only adapters that worked in the PC and the XT computers were 8-bit adapters. The ISA architecture allows an 8-bit adapter to fit and operate in the 16-bit ISA slot. Today, motherboards normally do not come with ISA slots.

PCI (Peripheral Component Interconnect)

A previously popular expansion slot is **PCI** (peripheral component interconnect) bus. PCI comes in four varieties: 32-bit 33MHz, 32-bit 66MHz, 64-bit 33MHz, and 64-bit 66MHz. Figure 2.18 shows the most common type of PCI expansion slot.

PCI expansion slots

Figure 2.18   PCI expansion slots

There are several different types of PCI slots, as shown in Figure 2.19. One type of PCI expansion slot used by some vendors is called a combo slot; it is a connector that combines ISA and PCI. The connector is one molded piece, but the piece contains both an ISA expansion slot and a PCI expansion slot for maximum flexibility.

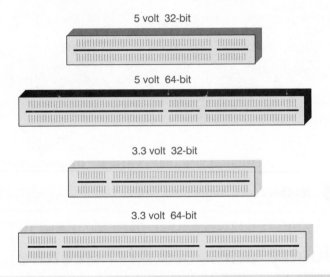

5 volt 32-bit

5 volt 64-bit

3.3 volt 32-bit

3.3 volt 64-bit

Figure 2.19   **3.3 volt and 5 volt PCI expansion slots**

An upgrade to the PCI bus is called **PCI-X**. PCI-X can operate at 66, 133, 266, 533, and 1066MHz. The PCI-X bus is backward compatible with the previous versions of the bus, but it allows faster speeds. A chip called the PCI bridge controls the PCI devices and PCI bus. With the PCI-X bus, a separate bridge controller chip is added. Figure 2.20 shows how the PCI-X bus integrates into the system board.

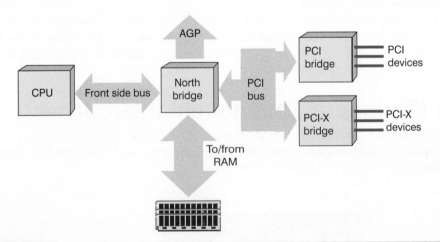

Figure 2.20   **PCI-X block diagram**

Tech Tip

PCI cards in PCI-X slots

Remember that older PCI cards can fit in a PCI-X expansion slot, but a PCI-X adapter *requires* a PCI-X expansion slot.

PCI-X adapters are more often found in network servers or high-end gaming workstations to control video, network adapters (such as gigabit Ethernet), and SCSI adapters (that control hard drives, tape drives, CD/DVD drives, scanners, and other internal and external peripherals). Today's motherboards have a limited number of PCI or PCI-X expansion slots because of a newer standard called PCI Express or PCIe, which is covered later in the chapter.

AGP (Accelerated Graphics Port)

AGP (accelerated graphics port) is a bus interface for graphics adapters developed from the PCI bus. Intel does the majority of the development for AGP and the specification was originally designed around the Pentium II processor. AGP speeds up 3-D graphics, 3-D acceleration, and full-motion playback.

With AGP, the processor on the video adapter can directly access RAM on the motherboard when needed. This helps with video-intensive applications. 3-D graphics, for example, are resource-intensive and use a lot of memory. Software developers can produce better and faster 3-D graphics using AGP technology. The best performance is achieved when applications use the RAM on the AGP adapter. However, because more memory than the amount on the adapter is needed, motherboard RAM is the next best option. Previous video adapters have been limited by the bottleneck caused by going through an adapter and a bus shared with other devices. With AGP, the video subsystem is isolated from the rest of the computer. The different versions of AGP are known as 1X, 2X, 4X, and 8X. All versions transfer 32-bits at a time. Table 2.9 summarizes the differences between the AGP versions.

Table 2.9	**AGP versions**			
AGP version	**1X**	**2X**	**4X**	**8X**
Bus Speed	66MHz	133MHz	266MHz	533MHz
Transfer Rate	266MBps	512MBps	>1GBps	>2GBps
Data Path	32 bits	32 bits	32 bits	32 bits
Connector Voltage	3.3V	3.3V	1.5V	1.5V

Figure 2.21 shows an illustration of an AGP slot compared with PCI and ISA expansion slots. All of the expansion slots previously covered are being replaced by PCIe (covered next). Figure 2.22 shows various expansion slots.

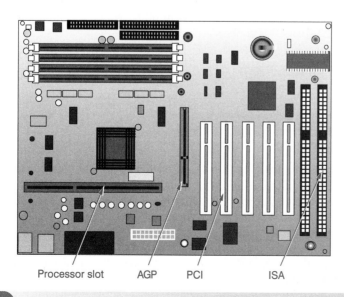

Processor slot   AGP   PCI   ISA

Figure 2.21   **AGP expansion slot**

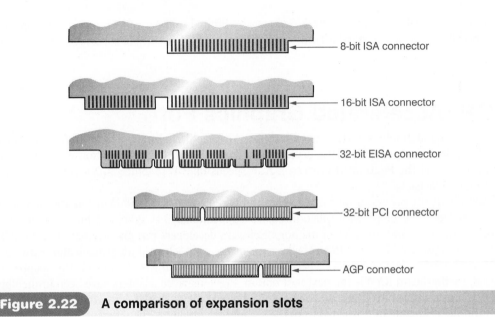

8-bit ISA connector

16-bit ISA connector

32-bit EISA connector

32-bit PCI connector

AGP connector

Figure 2.22   **A comparison of expansion slots**

PCIe (Peripheral Component Interconnect Express)

The PCI bus has almost reached its limit in terms of speed. PCI, PCI-X, and AGP are being replaced with **PCIe** (PCI Express), which is also seen as PCI-E. PCIe is better than the other types of PCI expansion slots. PCIe 3.0 allows transfers up to 1GBps per lane in one direction with a maximum of 32 lanes. PCIe 2.0 has a transfer rate from 2.5GT/s (gigatransfers per second) to 5.0 GT/s, and version 3.0 increases it to 8GT/s. This allows a 16-lane PCIe link to transfer data at a rate up to 32GBps. Competing technologies to PCIe include Rapid IO, HyperTransport, InfiniBand, and StarFabric. These are great types of technologies to research if you are interested in hardware development.

Tech Tip

PCI cards in PCIe slots

Older PCI, PCI-X, and AGP adapters will *not* work in any type of PCIe slots.

The older PCI standard is half-duplex bidirectional, which means that data is sent to and from the PCI or PCI-X card, but in only one direction at a time. PCIe sends data full-duplex bidirectionally; in other words, it can send and receive at the same time. Figure 2.23 shows this concept.

Tech Tip

Beware of the PCIe fine print

Some motherboard manufacturers offer a larger slot size (such as x8), but the slot runs at a slower speed (x1, for example). This keeps cost down. The manual would show such a slot as x8 (x1 mode) in the PCIe slot description.

The older PCI standard including PCI-X uses a parallel bus where data is sent with multiple 1s and 0s simultaneously. PCIe is a serial bus and data is sent one bit at a time. Another difference is that PCIe slots come in different versions depending on the maximum number of lanes that can be assigned to the card inserted into the slot. For example, an x1 slot can have only one transfer lane used by the x1 card inserted into the slot—x4, x8, and x16 slots are also available. An x16 slot accepts up to 16 lanes, but fewer lanes can be assigned. An x16 slot accepts x1, x4, x8, and x16 PCIe adapters. Figure 2.24 shows the concepts of PCIe lanes. Figure 2.25 (on page 50) shows some sample PCIe slots.

AMD has a different method of interfacing with PCI and PCIe interfaces than the traditional FSB. AMD uses a technology called **HyperTransport**, which is a high-speed bus used to connect

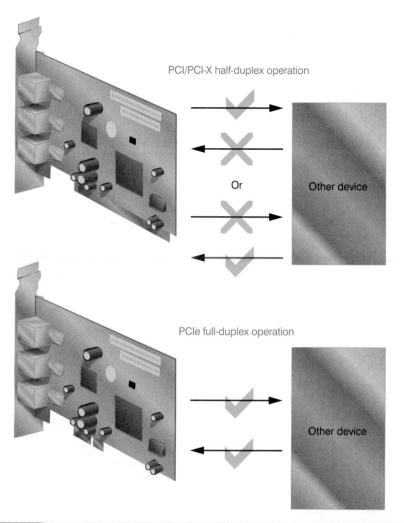

Figure 2.23   **A comparison of PCI/PCI-X and PCIe transfers**

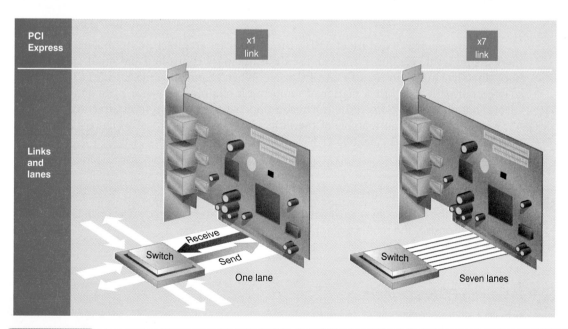

Figure 2.24   **PCIe lanes**

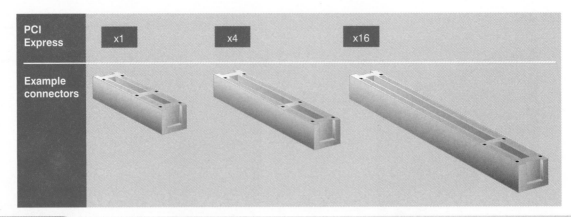

Figure 2.25   **PCIe expansion slots**

multiple CPUs, interface an AMD CPU with input/output devices, interface the CPU with PCI, PCI-X, and PCIe slots, and interface the CPU with RAM. Figure 2.26 shows how the HyperTransport bus connects various technologies.

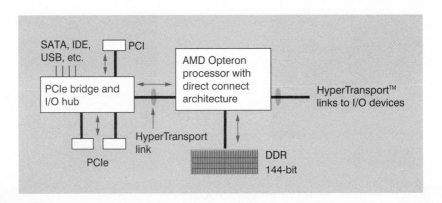

Figure 2.26   **HyperTransport used with AMD processors**

HyperTransport is a feature of AMD's Direct Connect architecture. With Direct Connect, there are no front side buses. Instead, the CPUs, memory controller, and input/output functions directly connect to the CPU at CPU speed. When removing an ISA, PCI, PCI-X, or AGP adapter, normally it is just a matter of removing a retaining screw or plate and lifting the adapter out of the slot. Some PCIe expansion slots have a retention lever attached.

Figure 2.27 shows an example of the PCIe adapter removal process. Figure 2.28 shows a motherboard with one x16 and two x1 PCIe slots. There are also four PCI slots.

Removing PCIe adapters

You must use the release lever to remove a PCIe adapter that has such a lever installed, or the board (and possibly the motherboard) could be damaged.

Installing PCIe adapters

A PCIe x1 slot accepts only x1 PCIe adapters. A PCIe x8 slot accepts x1, x4, and x8 adapters. A PCIe x16 slot accepts x1, x4, x8, and x16 adapters.

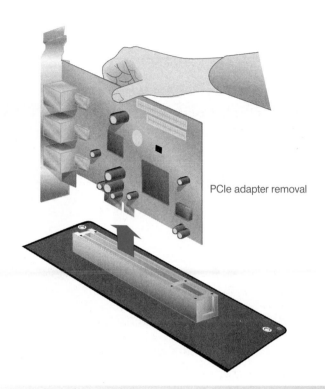

PCIe adapter removal

Figure 2.27   **PCIe adapter removal**

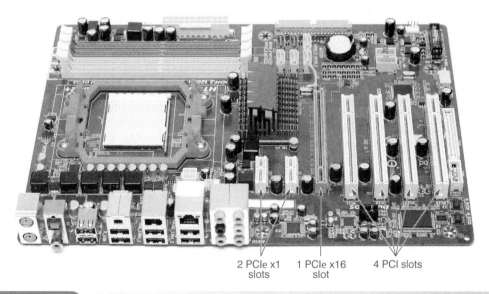

2 PCIe x1   1 PCIe x16   4 PCI slots
slots   slot

Figure 2.28   **Motherboard with PCIe slots**

Laptop Expansion

The **mini PCI** 32-bit 33MHz standard was developed to allow PCI upgrades and interface cards to be added to laptops, docking stations, and printers. Regular PCI cards are too large and require too much power for these technologies. Mini PCI cards allow SCSI, USB, IEEE 1394, wireless network, network, sound, modem, and other types of device or memory connectivity. Some mini PCI cards are combination cards that serve multiple functions such as a modem/network adapter.

Mini PCI cards have three form factors—Type I, II, and III. Type II cards have integrated connectors for RJ-11 or RJ-45 connections. Some laptops allow a choice of mini PCI card manufacturers and types. Manufacturers are now starting to use 52-pin mini PCIe cards. To install a mini PCI adapter, the laptop may have to be disassembled. Figure 2.29 shows a mini PCI adapter installed in a laptop. A screw in the back of the laptop had to be removed to access the slot.

Figure 2.29   **Mini PCI adapter installed in a laptop**

PC Cards are small credit card–size adapters that can be used to upgrade a laptop. PC Cards also come in three sizes: Type I, II, and III. They insert into a slot in the side of a laptop. PC Cards are being replaced by ExpressCards. **ExpressCard**® technology (http://www.expresscard.org/) is the latest high-performance, hardware expansion standard for mobile computers. ExpressCard modules give users the ability to add a wide variety of plug'n play applications to their computers, including memory, wired and wireless communications, multimedia, security, and networking.

Tech Tip

Universal slot is better

A laptop with a universal slot can accept either an ExpressCard/34 or an ExpressCard/54; however, an ExpressCard/34 slot accepts only ExpressCard/34 modules.

The ExpressCard Standard supports advanced technologies PCIe, e-SATA, IEEE 1394 (FireWire), or USB 3.0 connectivity through the ExpressCard slot. ExpressCard products are interoperable and hot swappable among computers. PC Cards do not fit in ExpressCard slots. ExpressCard products that pass a rigorous compliance program display the logo as shown in Figure 2.30.

ExpressCard™

Figure 2.30   **ExpressCard logo**

There are two types of ExpressCard: ExpressCard/34 and ExpressCard/54. The 34 means it is 34mm wide and the 54 means it is 54mm wide (in an L-type card). Figure 2.31 shows the two form factors.

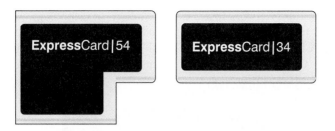

2
On the
Motherboard

Figure 2.31   **Types of ExpressCards**

PCI, PCI-X, AGP, and PCIe are important for connectivity in both workstation and portable computers. Traditional PCI connectivity will need to be supported for several more years in new machines for backward compatibility and in computers already in use. PCIe is the bus of the future for internal and external device connectivity. Figure 2.32 shows how AMD and Intel connect PCI and PCIe cards to other motherboard components.

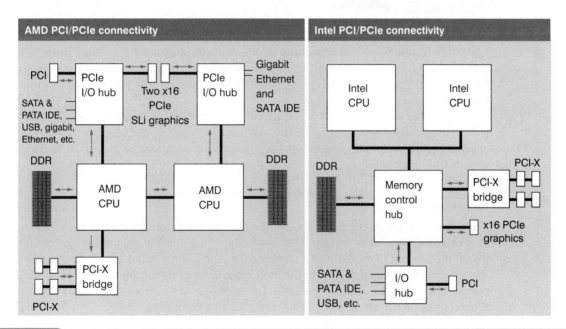

Figure 2.32   **How PCI and PCIe connect**

More Motherboard Connectors

Some connectors that are always a mystery to new technicians are AMR, CNR, and ACR. Intel developed AMR and CNR. **AMR** (audio/modem riser) is a connector on a motherboard that manufacturers use to offer a different version of the same motherboard. The motherboard manufacturer installs an adapter into the AMR slot, and the adapter can perform both sound card and modem duties and not take up one of the PCI slots. The cost is also lower to the manufacturer. The AMR connector is normally located beside or between the other motherboard expansion slots.

Know your chipset

A technician must keep informed about chipsets on the market; customers will always ask for recommendations about motherboard upgrades and new computer purchases. A technician should at least know where to find the information.

Tech
Tip

CNR (Communications Network Riser) is Intel's follow-on technology, which allows integration of network card functions with sound and modem. CNR is not backward compatible with AMR. CNR shares a PCI slot and it too is located beside or between the other motherboard expansion slots. AMR and CNR are usually found on motherboards that support Intel processors. Figure 2.33 shows a CNR expansion slot.

CNR slot

Figure 2.33   CNR slot

ACR (Advanced Communications Riser) was developed by a group of companies including AMD, VIA Technologies, Motorola, and 3Com. ACR not only supports audio, modem, and networking, but also supports DSL modems. ACR is an open specification and is found on motherboards that support AMD processors. The ACR connector is a 120-pin PCI connector that has been reversed (turned around).

Some older computers have an expansion slot built into the motherboard that is none of the common slots discussed. These expansion slots are proprietary: the adapters that fit in them are expensive and must be purchased from the motherboard or computer manufacturer (if that company is still in business).

Chipsets

The principle chips on the motherboard that work in conjunction with the processor are known as a **chipset**. These allow certain features on the computer. For example, chipsets control the maximum amount of motherboard memory, the type of RAM chips, the motherboard's capacity for two or more CPUs, and whether the motherboard supports the latest version of PCI. Common chipset manufacturers include Intel, Via Technologies, ATI technologies (now owned by AMD), Silicon Integrated Systems (SiS), AMD, and NVIDIA Corporation.

Usually a chipset goes with a particular processor and determines which memory chips a motherboard can have. Chipsets determine a lot about what a motherboard can allow or support. When buying a motherboard, pick a proper processor and a good chipset.

Let's take a look at one particular chipset to see the functionality it controls. Intel's 975X Express chipset supports Core 2, Core 2 Duo, Pentium Extreme, Pentium D, and Pentium 4 Intel processors; an 800- and 1066MHz bus; up to 8GB of DDR2 memory; 16 lanes of PCIe using two controllers to support either 2×8 or 1×16 operation; up to eight 2.0 USB ports; up to four serial ATA ports; and up to six traditional PCI slots. Figure 2.34 shows chipset interconnectivity.

Tech Tip

Finding your chipset

To locate the chipset, which may be one or two chips, look in the motherboard documentation for a diagram showing the location. If it's not shown, look in the documentation for the chipset manufacturer, then visually inspect the motherboard to locate the chip(s).

Notice in Figure 2.34 the **MCH** (memory controller hub). This important chip, sometimes called the north bridge, connects directly to an Intel CPU. On a motherboard that has an AMD CPU, the MCH would be incorporated into the CPU. Refer to Figure 2.32 to see the difference. Also notice the iCH7R chip. The **ICH** (I/O controller hub), also known as the south bridge, is a chip that controls what features, ports, and interfaces the motherboard supports.

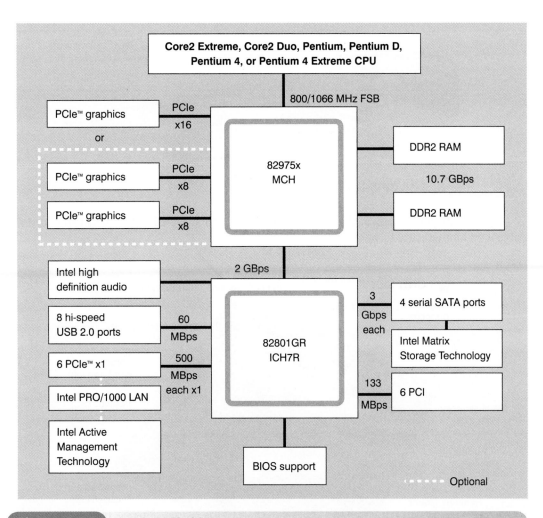

Figure 2.34   **Intel 975X chipset**

Types of Motherboards

Motherboards come in different sizes known as **form factors**. The most common motherboard is ATX. The different types of ATX are known as microATX (sometimes shown as µATX), miniATX, FlexATX, EATX, WATX, miniATX, nanoATX, picoATX, and mobileATX. Older form factors include AT, baby AT, NLX, LPX, and miniLPX. Some motherboards, such as the NLX and LPX form factors, had a riser board that attached to the smaller motherboard. Adapters go into the slots on the riser board instead of motherboard slots. Figure 2.35 shows this type of riser board. Refer to Figures 2.11, 2.13, and 2.28 for examples of ATX motherboards.

Motherboard form factor and case must match

The case used for the computer must match the motherboard form factor. Some cases can accommodate different form factors, but you should always check. When building a computer or replacing a motherboard, it is important to obtain the correct form factor.

The replacement for the ATX will probably be the BTX form factor. Within this family of form factors are the smaller versions called microBTX (sometimes shown as BTX), nanoBTX, and picoBTX. The WTX form factor is larger than ATX or BTX and is used with high-end workstations, such as those with multiple processors and more drives.

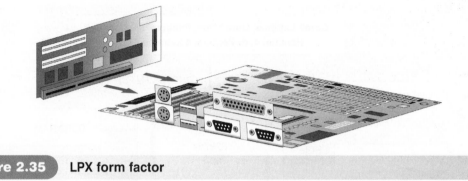

Figure 2.35 LPX form factor

Figure 2.36 shows many of the motherboard components labeled. A technician should stay current on motherboard technologies.

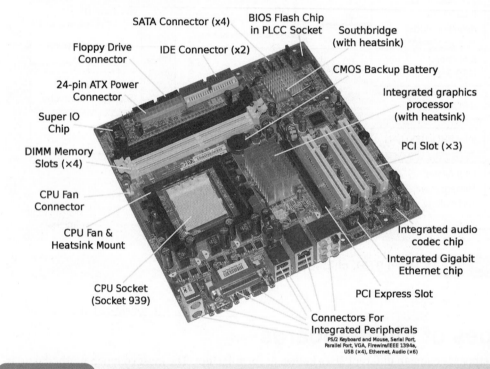

SATA Connector (x4)
BIOS Flash Chip in PLCC Socket
Southbridge (with heatsink)
Floppy Drive Connector
IDE Connector (x2)
CMOS Backup Battery
24-pin ATX Power Connector
Super IO Chip
Integrated graphics processor (with heatsink)
DIMM Memory Slots (×4)
PCI Slot (×3)
CPU Fan Connector
CPU Fan & Heatsink Mount
Integrated audio codec chip
Integrated Gigabit Ethernet chip
CPU Socket (Socket 939)
PCI Express Slot
Connectors For Integrated Peripherals
PS/2 Keyboard and Mouse, Serial Port, Parallel Port, VGA, Firewire/IEEE 1394a, USB (x4), Ethernet, Audio (x6)

Figure 2.36 Motherboard components

Tech Tip

Manufacturers can also design their case so that it requires a proprietary motherboard. With these designs, a replacement motherboard must be purchased from the original manufacturer and is usually more expensive.

Go green when buying a motherboard or CPU

When upgrading or replacing a motherboard and/or processor, consider going green. Select a board that uses 45nm silicon technology, one that is lead free, one that uses a lower amount of power (uses 22 watts instead of 65 or 90), one that uses a smaller form factor (such as microATX), one that has integrated video, or one that can do all of this.

Upgrading and Replacing Motherboards

When upgrading a motherboard or processor, several issues must be taken into account. The following list guides a technician through making the decision (or helping a customer make the decision) of whether to upgrade a motherboard.

- Why is the computer being upgraded? For example, does the computer need more memory? Are more expansion slots needed? Does the computer need a bigger/faster CPU to run certain operating systems or applications? Sometimes upgrading the motherboard does not help unless the other computer components are upgraded. The most expensive and fastest motherboard will not run applications well unless it has the proper amount of memory. Hard drives are another issue. If software access is slow, the solution might not be a new motherboard, but a faster and larger hard drive, more cache memory, or more RAM.

- Which type (ISA, PCI, AGP, or PCIe) and how many adapters are needed from the old motherboard? Does the new motherboard have the required expansion slots?
- Could any devices, such as the hard drive or CD or DVD drive that currently require an adapter, plug directly into the upgraded motherboard? If so, it would free up expansion slots as well as speed up the devices.
- What type of chipsets does the new motherboard support? What features, if any, would this bring to the new motherboard?
- Will the new motherboard fit in the current computer case or is a new one required?
- If upgrading the CPU, will the motherboard support the new type of CPU?
- Does the motherboard allow for future CPU upgrades?
- How much memory (RAM) does the motherboard allow? What memory chips are required on the new motherboard? Will the old memory chips work in the new motherboard or with the new CPU?

Before replacing a motherboard, keep the following list in mind:

- Remove adapters from expansion slots
- Remove memory chips from expansion slots
- Disconnect power connectors
- Disconnect ribbon cables
- Disconnect external devices such as mouse, keyboard, and monitor

Replacement motherboards do not normally come with RAM, so the old ones are removed from the bad motherboard. The motherboard may or may not come with a CPU. Make note of the CPU orientation before removing it from the motherboard. When installing the CPU into the replacement motherboard, refer to these notes. Some retailers sell kits that include the computer case, power supply, motherboard, and CPU so that the components match, function together correctly, and are physically compatible.

> **Tech Tip**
>
> **Use good antistatic measures when installing a motherboard**
> When replacing a motherboard or removing it from the case, place the motherboard on a nonconductive surface such as an antistatic mat or the antistatic bag that comes with the motherboard.

When upgrading any component or the entire computer, remember that the older part can be donated to a charity or educational institution. Something that is considered outdated by one person may be considered an upgrade to someone less fortunate. Educational institutions are always seeking components to use in the classroom.

Motherboards contain most of the circuitry for a microcomputer and are very important to its operation. Technicians must keep current with the options, features, microprocessors, and chipsets. Most technicians subscribe to computer magazines to help them fulfill this responsibility.

Motherboard Troubleshooting

Motherboards and power problems are probably the most difficult things to troubleshoot. Because various components are located on the motherboard, many things can cause an error. POST is one of the most beneficial aids for troubleshooting the motherboard. The meaning of any codes that appear on the screen should be researched. If multiple POST error codes appear, troubleshoot them in the order they are presented. The following list helps with motherboard troubleshooting:

- Is the motherboard receiving power? Check the power supply to see if the fan is turning. If the CPU or motherboard has a fan, see if it is turning. Check voltages going from the power supply to the motherboard.
- Check the BIOS settings for accuracy (covered more in Chapter 3).
- Check the motherboard jumper or BIOS settings to see if they have been changed or ask the user if they have changed anything in the BIOS.
- Check for overheating. Power down the computer and allow the computer to cool. Power on the computer with the cover off.

- Reseat the CPU and memory chips.
- Remove unnecessary adapters and boot.
- Plug the computer into a different power outlet and circuit if possible.
- Check if the motherboard is shorting out on the frame.
- Check the CMOS battery.
- Some motherboards have diagnostic LEDs. Check the output for any error code. Refer to the motherboard documentation or on-line documentation for the problem and possible solution.

Tech Tip

Concepts relate to Apple computers too

Even though this book focuses on PCs, concepts relating to CPU, motherboards, expansion slots, cache, and chipsets also apply to Apple computers. Apple computers and PCs have similar CPU and memory requirements.

Soft Skills—Active Listening

Active listening is participating in a conversation where you focus on what the customer is saying—in other words, listening more than talking. For a technician, active listening has the following benefits:

- Allows you to gather data and symptoms quickly
- Allows you to build customer rapport
- Improves your understanding of the problem
- Allows you to solve the problem quicker because you understand the problem better
- Provides mutual understanding between you and your customer
- Provides a means of having a positive, engaged conversation rather than having a negative, confrontational encounter
- Focuses on the customer rather than the technician
- Provides an environment where the customer might be more forthcoming with information related to the problem

Frequently, when a technician arrives onsite or contacts a customer who has a technical problem, the technician is: (1) rushed; (2) thinking of other things, including the problems that need to be solved; (3) assuming that they know exactly what the problem is even though the user has not finished explaining the problem; or (4) more interested in the technical problem than with the customer and the issues. Active listening changes the focus from the technician's problems to the customer's problems.

A common service call involves the technician doing most of the talking and questioning, filled with technical jargon and acronyms and presented in a flat or condescending tone. The customer, who feels vulnerable, experiences a heightened anxiety level. Active listening changes this scenario by helping you build a professional relationship with your customers. The following outlines how to implement active listening.

Have a positive, engaged professional attitude when talking and listening to customers

- Leave your prejudices behind
- Have a warm and caring attitude
- Do not fold your arms in front of your chest because it appears you are distancing yourself from the problem or the customer
- Do not blame others or talk badly about other technicians
- Do not act as if the problem is not your responsibility

Focus on what the customer is saying

- Turn off or ignore electronic devices
- Maintain eye contact; don't let your mind wander
- Allow the customer to finish explaining the problem; do not interrupt
- Stop all nonrelevant behaviors and activities
- Mentally review what the customer is saying

Participate in the conversation in a limited, but active manner

- Maintain a professional demeanor (suspend negative emotions)
- Acknowledge you are listening by occasionally nodding and making comments such as "I see"
- Use positive body language such as leaning slightly forward or taking notes
- Observe the customer's behavior to determine when it is appropriate to ask questions

Briefly talk with the customer

- Speak in a positive tone; use a tone that is empathetic and genuine, not condescending
- Restate or summarize points made by the customer
- Ask nonthreatening, probing questions related to the customer's statements or questions
- Do not jump between topics
- Do not use technical jargon
- Clarify the meaning of the customer's situation
- Identify clues to help solve the problem and reduce your troubleshooting time by listening carefully to what the customer says

Key Terms

3DNow! (p. 44)	ExpressCard (p. 52)	mebibyte (p. 28)
ACR (p. 54)	external data bus (p. 29)	megabyte (p. 28)
active listening (p. 58)	form factor (p. 55)	mini PCI (p. 51)
AGP (p. 47)	FSB (p. 33)	on-die cache (p. 32)
ALU (p. 30)	gigabyte (p. 28)	overclocking (p. 43)
AMR (p. 53)	gigahertz (p. 28)	PC (p. 28)
back side bus (p. 33)	HT (p. 36)	PCI (p. 45)
bit (p. 28)	HyperTransport (p. 48)	PCIe (p. 48)
bus (p. 29)	ICH (p. 54)	PCI-X (p. 46)
bus speed (p. 33)	internal data bus (p. 29)	pipeline (p. 30)
byte (p. 28)	ISA (p. 44)	processor (p. 28)
cache memory (p. 32)	jumper (p. 35)	QPI (p. 35)
chipset (p. 54)	kibibyte (p. 28)	quad-core CPU (p. 36)
clock (p. 33)	kilobyte (p. 28)	register size (p. 29)
clock speed (p. 33)	L1 cache (p. 32)	SSE (p. 44)
CNR (p. 54)	L2 cache (p. 32)	throttle management (p. 43)
CPU speed (p. 33)	L3 cache (p. 32)	tri-core CPU (p. 36)
CPU throttling (p. 33)	liquid cooling system (p. 40)	word size (p. 29)
dual-core CPU (p. 36)	MCH (p. 54)	ZIF socket (p. 37)

Review Questions

1. What is a processor?
2. List two processor manufacturers.
3. What is a PC?
4. Match the term on the left to the definition on the right.

    _____ bit   a. 8 bits

    _____ Kilobyte   b. a 1 or a 0

    _____ Megabyte   c. approximately 1,000 bytes

    _____ byte   d. approximately one million bytes

    _____ Gigabyte   e. approximately one billion bytes

5. What is a bus?

6. What is the difference between the internal data bus and external data bus?

7. [T | F] A computer's word size and external data path are always the same number of bits.

8. What are processor pipelines?

9. Which processors are designed by Intel? [Opteron | Pentium Dual Core | Celeron | Duron]

10. What does a "64" on an AMD processor mean?
    a. 64GHz speed
    b. 6.4GHz speed
    c. 64 bit operating systems supported
    d. 64 pipelines in the CPU
    e. 64 processes per second in the CPU

11. Which of the following microprocessor speeds is the fastest? [1GHz | 2GHz | 833MHz | 900MHz]

12. List two methods for determining processor speed.

13. Is the processor speed the same speed as the chips on the motherboard?

14. What is the name of the electronic component that provides timing signals to the motherboard?

15. Which type of cache memory is used first by the CPU? [L1 | L2 | L3]

16. [T | F] Cache memory is faster than RAM.

17. What is L3 cache?

18. [T | F] A PC normally has more RAM on the motherboard than hard disk storage.

19. List two common clocking speeds.

20. What is the difference between a front side bus and a back side bus?

21. A 2.6GHz processor is installed onto a motherboard that has a 266MHz bus. What multiplier is used?

22. A motherboard has no visible jumpers or switches. How would the multiplier be set on this type of system board?

23. Which of the following is not a requirement of HyperThreading?
    a. The operating system must support it.
    b. The CPU speed must be 900MHz or higher.
    c. The BIOS must support it.
    d. The proper chipset must be installed.

24. [T | F] Software must be specifically written in order to take advantage of dual-core CPUs' power.

25. Which multi-core processor manufacturer had a memory controller on the motherboard but now integrates it as part of the CPU packaging?

26. What is an advantage of having a SPGA over a PGA socket?

27. List an Intel socket used with iCore 7.

28. List an AMD socket used with Phenom II X4s.

29. What type of socket or slot is used for Intel's Core 2 Extreme?

30. [T | F] The processor must be inserted into the appropriate-sized socket.

31. What is the difference between a thermal pad and thermal compound?

32. Where are additional fans commonly placed?

33. [T | F] When installing a processor, the power supply should be off, but the power cord should stay attached.

34. [T | F] After installing a processor for the first time, apply power and ensure the computer boots before installing any heat sink or fan.

35. A customer wants to upgrade her processor. What questions are you going to ask before making a recommendation?

36. How can you tell if a motherboard accepts a faster or more powerful processor?

37. List three symptoms of problems seen when overclocking.

38. What is the most common problem with overclocking?

39. What is the difference between SSE4 and SSE4a?

40. What is an expansion slot?

41. Name three types of expansion slots.

42. Why must a technician be familiar with the different expansion slots?

43. What is ISA's biggest drawback?

44. [T | F] Computers today still use ISA.

45. List the four PCI versions.

46. [T | F] PCI-X is backward compatible with 32-bit 33MHz PCI.

47. [T | F] PCI-X adapters require a PCI-X slot.

48. What is a bus interface for graphic adapters developed to speed up 3-D applications?

49. Why is AGP a better solution for video than previous PCI versions?

50. What expansion slot replaced AGP?

51. PCI can send data in [super duplex | full CPU power | half duplex | super memory] mode.

52. List three competing PCIe technologies.

53. Older PCI cards [will | will not] work in a PCIe slot.

54. PCIe is a [serial | parallel] bus.

55. What type of PCI is used in laptops, docking stations, and printers?

56. What type of card allows PCIe connectivity in portable devices?

57. What open specification is a 120-pin reversed PCI connector?

58. Match the following definitions with the most correct term.

    _____ ISA   a. Primarily used in laptop computers

    _____ PC Card   b. The oldest expansion slot type

    _____ PCI   c. A 64-bit standard

    _____ PCIe   d. Has x1, x4, x8, and x16 slots

59. What is the motherboard form factor?

60. List at least three recommendations to remember when upgrading or replacing a motherboard.

61. What are two of the most difficult things to troubleshoot?

62. List two benefits of active listening.

63. List two things that frequently stop a technician from actively listening to a customer.

64. List two active listening techniques.

Fill-in-the-Blank

1. The main chip found on the motherboard that executes software instructions is the _____.

2. In computer technology, a 1 or a 0 is a/an _____.

3. A combination of eight 1s and 0s is a _____.

4. Approximately 1,000 (one thousand) bytes is a/an _____.

5. Approximately 1,000,000 (one million) bytes is a/an _____.

6. Approximately 1,000,000,000 (one billion) bytes is a/an _____.

7. Approximately 1,000,000,000,000 (one trillion) bytes is a/an _____.

8. The number of bits that the processor handles at one time is the processor's _____.

9. The term _____ is used to describe the data delivery rate for PCI adapters.

10. The rate of transfer between the processor and motherboard components is known as
_____.

11. The rate of transfer between cache on the processor die and the processor itself is known as
the _____ bus.

12. A processor speed is measured in _____.

13. A more technical term for what most call the motherboard speed is _____.

14. _____ is the type of memory that has always been found inside the processor.

15. The type of memory that was previously outside the processor on the motherboard, but now
is inside the processor packaging is _____.

16. When L1 and L2 cache are included with the CPU or in the processor packaging, any cache
installed on the motherboard is known as _____ cache.

17. Processor speed equals bus speed times the _____.

18. A plastic cover over two pins that enables a computer option is a _____.

19. A common use for a motherboard jumper is for _____.

20. _____ allows a CPU to process two sets of instructions at the same time.

21. Core 2 Duo is Intel's version of a _____-core CPU.

22. A/An _____ socket has a lever beside it to facilitate CPU insertion and removal.

23. The AMD Sempron inserts into a _____-pin socket or _____-pin socket.

24. Raising the ZIF lever is used when _____ a CPU because it lifts the CPU out of the
socket.

25. Besides the processor, two parts of the motherboard that frequently have heat sinks attached
are _____ and _____.

26. With a _____ fluid is pumped through the heat sink and throughout the computer to
cool it.

27. Increasing processor speed is commonly known as _____.

28. The _____ is the part of the processor that handles numbers with decimals, which is
important when dealing with complex graphics.

29. _____ microprocessors have 57 multimedia instructions built into them.

30. Intel tends to use _____ to provide support for 3-D technologies, whereas AMD would
use _____ that is different.

31. The oldest expansion slot is _____.

32. An upgrade to PCI that is backward compatible with older versions, but supports speeds up
to 1066MHz is _____.

33. A PCIe x4 slot can assign the card inserted into the slot up to _____ transfer lanes.

34. A PCIe x16 expansion slot accepts PCIe _____, _____, _____, and
_____ PCIe cards.

35. AMD's _____ is an alternative to FSB.

36. Some PCIe slots have a _____ that must be pushed to release the adapter to remove
it.

37. The two types of ExpressCard are _____ and _____.

38. The _____ connector allows a combination of sound card and modem to be attached.

39. The _____ works with the processor and determines whether or not the motherboard
supports PCIe.

40. Common _____ manufacturers include Intel, AMD, Via Technologies, and SiS.

41. _____ is focusing on someone else when they are talking.

42. When actively listening to a customer, you maintain good _____ contact when you are
not taking notes.

Hands-On Exercises

1. ATX Motherboard Parts Identification Exercise

Using Figure 2.37, label each of the ATX motherboard parts.

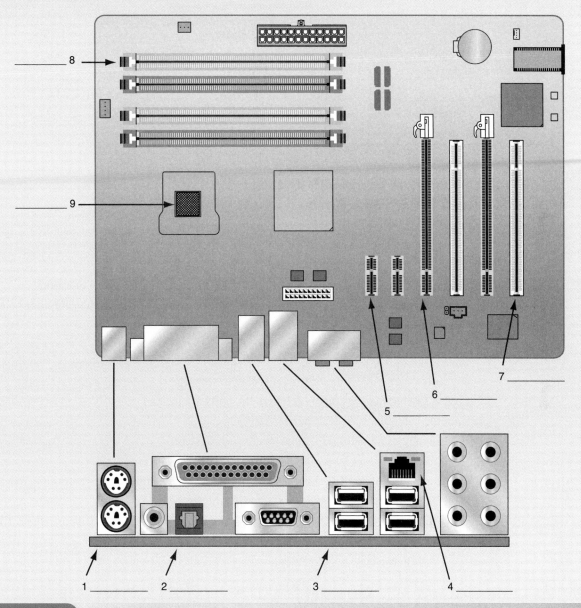

Figure 2.37   **Motherboard parts**

2. Determining CPU Frequency

The multiplier and bus speed are used to determine CPU frequency. Determine the CPU frequency, bus speed, or multiplier used when given two of the three parameters. Fill in the missing parameter using Table 2.10.

Table 2.10	CPU frequency parameters	
CPU Frequency	**Bus Speed**	**Multiplier**
_____	133MHz	22
1.8GHz	166MHz	_____
2.6GHz or 2660MHz	_____	20
_____	200MHz	13.5
3.6GHz	_____	11
2.5GHz	200MHz	_____
_____	266MHz	14
2.66GHz	266MHz	_____
3.5GHz	_____	15

3. Processor Speed, Processor Socket, USB Ports, and IEEE 1394 Ports

Objective: To identify various computer features such as the type of processor being used, processor socket, and additional expansion ports

Parts: Computer with Internet access

Procedure: Complete the following procedure and answer the accompanying questions.

1. Boot computer and determine the microprocessor speed by watching the computer boot.

   Write down the speed.

2. Power off the computer. Remove the cover.

   What type of processor socket or slot is on the motherboard? If unsure, use the Internet as a resource. Write down the processor socket or slot type.

3. Look at the back of the computer where the ports are located.

   Does the computer have USB ports?

   If the computer has USB ports, how many does it have?

   If the computer has at least one USB port, what type of connector is it?

4. Locate a picture of an IEEE 1394 port or connector on the Internet.

   Write down the URL for where you found this information.

5. Using the Internet, locate one vendor that makes a motherboard that supports IEEE 1394 or has an integrated IEEE 1394 port.

   Write down the vendor's name and the URL where you found the information.

Internet Discovery

Objective: To obtain specific information on the Internet regarding a computer or its associated parts

Parts: Computer with Internet access

Procedure: Locate documentation on the Internet for an Intel GIGABYTE GA-EX58-UD5P motherboard in order to answer Questions 1–12. Continue your Internet search in order to answer Questions 13 and 14.

Questions:

1. Does the motherboard support a multi-core processor?

2. What chipset is used?

3. How many PCI slots are on the motherboard?

4. What form factor does this motherboard use?

5. What processors can be used on this motherboard?

6. What is the speed of Intel's QPI?

7. What type of CPU socket does the motherboard have?

8. How many and of what type of PCIe slots are there?

9. What type of memory does this motherboard accept?

10. Does this motherboard have an integrated IEEE 1394 port?

11. How many USB ports does the motherboard have?

12. Write the URL where you found the motherboard information.

13. Find a vendor for a motherboard who accepts an AMD Phenom II X4 quad-core processor. Write the vendor's name and the URL where you found this information.

14. Find an Internet site that describes the difference between the Northbridge and the Southbridge, and write a brief description of each term.

Soft Skills

Objective: To enhance and fine tune a future technician's ability to listen, communicate in both written and oral form, and support people who use computers in a professional manner

Activities:

1. On a piece of paper or index card, list three ways you can practice active listening at school. Share this information with your group. Consolidate ideas and present five of the best ideas to the class.

2. Within a team environment, determine two situations in which team members have experienced a situation in which a support person (a PC support person, sales clerk, checkout clerk, a person being asked directions, and so on) could have provided better service if they had been actively listening. Share your findings with the class.

3. In teams of two, one person tells a story and the other person practices their active listening skills. The person telling the story critiques the listener. Exchange roles.

Critical Thinking Skills

Objective: To analyze and evaluate information as well as apply learned information to new or different situations

Activities:

1. Find an advertisement for a computer in a local computer flyer, newspaper, magazine, book, or on the Internet. Determine all the information about the motherboard and ports that you can from the ad. Write down any information you do not understand. Research this information and share with a classmate.

2. Why do you think that most motherboard settings are controlled through BIOS rather than the old way of setting jumpers and switches? What do you think is a drawback of configuring everything through BIOS?

3. Why do you think the motherboard has different buses that operate at different speeds?

2

On the
Motherboard

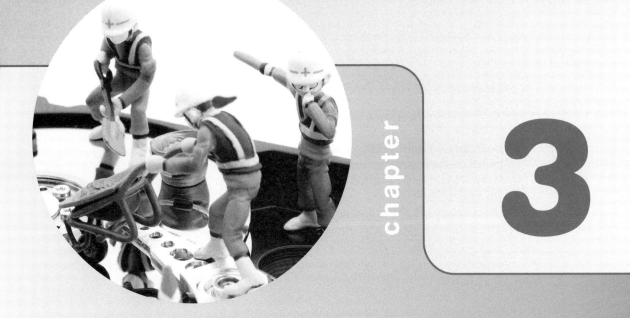

3

System Configuration

Objectives

After completing this chapter you will be able to

- Distinguish between the various methods used to configure a computer
- Describe how to replace a motherboard battery
- Identify system resources such as interrupts, DMA channels, memory addresses, and I/O addresses
- Differentiate between different PC buses and describe how to configure them
- Describe how to configure and install adapters/devices in a Windows environment
- Learn the benefits of a "one thing at a time" approach to problem solving

Configuration Overview

The BIOS (basic input/output system) is an important motherboard component. The BIOS has the following functions:

- Holds and executes POST (power on self test)—the program that identifies, tests, and initializes basic hardware components
- Holds a basic routine called a bootstrap program that locates an operating system and allows it to load
- Holds **Setup**, which is a program that allows device settings to be viewed and managed

When assembling, troubleshooting, or repairing a computer, a technician must go into a Setup program to configure the system. The Setup program is held in BIOS and through the Setup program you can see and possibly configure such things as how much RAM is in the computer, the type and number of drives installed, where the computer looks for its boot files, the current date and time, and so on. An error message is displayed if the information in the Setup program fails to match the hardware or if a specific device does not work properly.

There are two main ways to configure your system or an adapter—through the Setup program held in system BIOS or through the operating system. The Setup program is examined first.

Figure 3.1 shows an enlarged jumper; the jumper blocks and jumpers on a motherboard are much smaller. When a jumper is not in use, instead of putting it in a drawer, place the jumper over a single pin in the jumper block. This action does not enable anything and it keeps the jumper safe and convenient for when it is needed later.

Tech Tip

Use Setup to disable integrated ports and connectors

Motherboards also include connectors for hard drives, CD/DVD drives, floppy drives, and so on. If any of these connectors should fail, disable it through Setup and obtain a replacement adapter just like you would if an integrated port should fail.

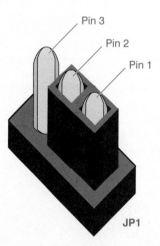

Pin 3
Pin 2
Pin 1
JP1

Figure 3.1   **JP1 jumper block with pins 1 and 2 jumpered together**

The Setup Program

Tech Tip

How to access setup

The key(s) to press to access Setup are normally displayed briefly during the boot process. Otherwise, look in the motherboard or computer documentation.

Most computers have Setup software built into the system BIOS chip on the motherboard and accessed by specific keystrokes determined by the BIOS manufacturer. During the boot process, most computers will display a message stating which keystrokes will launch the Setup program. The keystroke can be one key pressed during startup such as the [Esc], [Ins] (or [Insert]), [Del] (or [Delete]), [F1], [F2], or [F10] keys. Other BIOS manufacturers use a combination of keystrokes where two or more keys are held down simultaneously during the boot process: Ctrl+Alt+Enter, Ctrl+Alt+Esc, Ctrl+Alt+Ins, Ctrl+Alt+Shift, Ctrl+Alt+F1, Ctrl+Esc, or Ctrl+Alt+F11.

Flash BIOS

Flash BIOS is the most common type of BIOS that allows changing the BIOS without installing a new chip or chips. Common computer BIOS manufactures include AMI (American Megatrends, Inc.), Phoenix, and Insyde Software. Many computer companies produce their own BIOS chips or subcontract with AMI or Phoenix to customize the BIOS. The following procedure is one example of "flashing the BIOS":

1. Once the system BIOS upgrade is downloaded from the Internet, execute the update.
2. Follow the directions on the screen or from the manufacturer.
3. Reboot the computer.

There are various reasons why a computer may need a BIOS upgrade: to provide support for new or upgraded hardware, support for higher capacity hard drives, virus protection, password protection, or to solve problems with the current BIOS.

How to flash the BIOS

Updating the system BIOS involves downloading an updated file from the Internet and executing that file according to the instructions.

Some motherboards have a utility that allows recovery if a BIOS becomes corrupted or the BIOS update fails. Other motherboards come with a Flash recovery jumper or switch used for BIOS recovery. Another motherboard manufacturer option includes a backup BIOS in case a BIOS upgrade fails or stalls during the upgrade process. Also, an alternative is a portion of the BIOS that cannot be changed so that the computer can still boot even if a BIOS update fails. A computer without an operational BIOS cannot boot. See the motherboard manual or documentation for specific BIOS details and the method that is being used to protect the BIOS.

3 System Configuration

How to remove the BIOS write protection

Because the Flash BIOS is frequently write-protected, a motherboard jumper, switch, or BIOS setting may need to be changed to allow the update. Refer to the computer or motherboard documentation to find the exact procedure for removing the write-protection and updating the Flash BIOS.

Protect the Flash BIOS

Viruses can infect the Flash BIOS. Keep the BIOS write-protected until you need to update it.

CMOS Memory

Settings changed in system BIOS are recorded and stored in **CMOS** (complementary metal oxide semiconductor) found in the motherboard chipset (south bridge or I/O controller hub). CMOS is low-powered memory powered by a small coin-sized lithium battery when the system is powered off. The memory holds the settings configured through BIOS. Part of the BIOS software routine that runs after the computer is turned on checks CMOS for information about what components are supposed to be installed. These components are then tested.

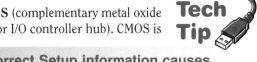

Incorrect Setup information causes POST errors

The wrong configuration information causes POST error codes or error messages that would normally indicate a hardware problem.

The information inside CMOS memory can be kept there for several years using a small coin-sized lithium battery. When the battery dies, all configuration information in CMOS is lost and must be re-entered.

Recall from Chapter 1 that POST (power on self test) runs whenever the computer cold boots and it performs a hardware check on installed components. POST knows what hardware is *supposed* to be in the computer by obtaining the settings from CMOS.

Keep a record of current Setup settings

Technicians should keep a record of the current settings for all the computers they service. If the wrong information is entered into the Setup program and saved in CMOS, a computer can operate improperly and may not boot.

When working on a computer with a POST error code, ensure that the user or another technician (1) has not changed the configuration through the Setup program or (2) removed or installed any hardware without changing the Setup program or updating the operating system. Correct Setup information is crucial for proper PC operation.

BIOS Configuration Settings

BIOS options vary according to manufacturer, but many options are similar. Table 3.1 shows some common BIOS settings and a brief explanation of each. Most Setup programs have help that can be accessed from within the Setup program to explain the purpose of each option.

Table 3.1   Common Setup options

Setup option	Description
System Information	Displays general information such as the processor, processor speed, amount of RAM, BIOS manufacturer, and BIOS date.
Boot Sequence or Boot Menu	Prioritizes from what device the computer looks for an operating system.
CPU Configuration or Advanced CPU Settings	Contains settings such as CPU TM function, which affects CPU throttle management (slows the CPU when overheated); Execute Disable Bit, which helps with virus protection; PECI, which affects how the thermal sensors report the core temperature of your CPU; Max CPUID, which is used to be compatible with older operating systems; CPU Ratio control, which sets the CPU multipliers; and Vanderpool Technology, which is used with Intel virtualization.
Video Options	Allows configuration such as DVMT (dynamic video memory technology) to control video memory, aperture size (the amount of system RAM dedicated for the AGP adapter use), and which video controller is primary or secondary.
Onboard Device Configuration	Allows modification of devices built into the motherboard such as any serial, network, USB, or video ports.
Power on Password, Password Options, Supervisor Password, or User Password	Allows configuration of a password to enter the Setup program, to allow the computer to boot, or to distinguish between someone who can make minor changes such as boot options or date and time (user password) and someone who can view and change all Setup options (supervisor password).
Virus Protection	A small virus scanning application located in BIOS. Some operating systems and software updates require disabling this option for the upgrade.
Numlock On/Off	Allows default setting (enabled or disabled) of the number lock key option after booting.
USB Configuration	Allows modification of parameters such as support for legacy devices, USB speed options, and the number of ports to enable.
HyperThreading	Allows enable/disable of HyperThreading technology.

Table 3.1   **Common Setup options (continued)**

Setup option	Description
Integrated Peripherals	Allows enabling/disabling and configuration of motherboard-controlled devices such as PATA/SATA drives, integrated ports including USB, audio, and network. Sets the amount of RAM dedicated for the AGP adapter's use. If the computer has an ample amount of RAM, increasing this setting can increase performance, especially in applications (such as games) that use high definition graphics.
HD Audio Controller	Enables/disables high definition audio controller.
Advanced BIOS Options	Allows configuration of options such as CPU and memory frequencies, CPU, front side bus, Northbridge, Southbridge, chipset, and memory voltage levels.
IDE Configuration	Allows manual configuration of IDE devices such as IDE, hard drives, and CD/DVD drives.
SATA Configuration	Allows viewing Serial ATA values assigned by BIOS and changing some of the related options.
PCI/PnP Configuration	Allows viewing and changing PCI slot configuration including IRQ and DMA assignments.
ACPI (advanced configuration and power interface)	Determines what happens if power is lost, power options if a call comes into a modem, power options when directed by a PCI or PCIe device or by mouse/keyboard action.
Hardware Monitor	Allows viewing CPU and motherboard temperature as well as the status of CPU, chassis, and power supply fans.

3
System
Configuration

For a new system, use default BIOS settings in the beginning
When installing a new system, use the default BIOS settings until all components are tested.

Some motherboards have pins that, when jumpered together, remove the power-on password. Look at the computer or motherboard documentation for the exact procedure to remove the power-on password. Some motherboards distinguish between supervisor and user passwords. Another security option of some BIOSs is whether a password is needed every time the computer boots or only when someone tries to enter the Setup program. The options available in Setup and Advanced Setup are machine dependent due to the different BIOS chips and the different chipsets installed on the motherboard. Always refer to the computer or motherboard documentation for the meaning of each option.

What to do for a forgotten BIOS password
When a power-on password is set and forgotten, some motherboards have pins that, when jumpered together, remove the power-on password. With other motherboards, the only way to remove the password is by jumpering pins together to clear all the CMOS settings. Refer to Figure 2.8 for a graphic of a jumper.

You must save your changes whenever you make configuration changes. Incorrectly saving the changes is a common mistake made by a new technician. The options available when exiting BIOS depend on the model of BIOS being used. Sample BIOS exit options are shown in Table 3.2.

Table 3.2	Sample configuration change options
Option	**Description**
Save & Exit Setup	A commonly used option that saves all changes and leaves the Setup program.
Exit without Saving	Used when changes have been made in error or more research is needed.
Load Fail-Safe Defaults	Sets the default settings programmed by the manufacturer. Used when getting unpredictable results after changing an option.
Load Optimized Defaults	An option programmed by the manufacturer. It has more aggressive settings than the *Load Fail-Safe Defaults* option.

Motherboard Batteries

The most common battery used today is a lithium battery about the size of a nickel. Figure 3.2 shows a photo of a lithium battery installed on a motherboard. If you cannot find the motherboard battery, refer to the motherboard or computer documentation for the exact location.

Battery

Figure 3.2	Computer motherboard battery

No battery lasts forever. Higher temperatures and powering devices that use batteries to power up and power down shorten a battery lifespan. Computer motherboard batteries last 3 to 8 years. Today, batteries last longer and people replace their computers more frequently; therefore, replacing batteries is not the issue it once was.

Tech Tip

Battery replacement hints

Before replacing a battery, write down or print the settings in Setup. Also, check the motherboard for any evidence of battery corrosion and verify that no battery acid has come in contact with the motherboard. If the motherboard is contaminated with battery acid, it will probably need to be replaced. A first indication that a battery is failing is the loss of the date or time on the computer. The battery should be replaced before more configuration information is lost.

When batteries fail, several options are available to the technician, depending on which type of battery is installed. Table 3.3 shows various battery options.

Table 3.3	Battery options
Option	**Replacement description**
Lithium	Replace with the same kind normally obtained at a local electronics or computer store or from the computer manufacturer. If on a motherboard, gently lift the clip that holds the battery in place and slide the battery out of the holder.
Battery pack	Note which way the battery wires connect to the motherboard. Replace with an approved part number. Some laptop batteries that are *not* from the original manufacturer may not have the Li-ion safety features in place or the "intelligence" used to monitor power levels.
AA or AAA	Replace the batteries the same as any electronic portable device by making note of polarity (positive and negative).

Refer to documentation for battery replacement procedures

Always refer to the motherboard documentation for the exact battery replacement procedure. Replace the battery with one of the proper voltage and check on any recharging procedures.

3
System Configuration

Plug and Play

Plug and play (PnP) allows automatic software configuration of an adapter. A PnP adapter plugs into an expansion slot without the technician having to configure the board or worry about the adapter conflicting with other adapters already installed in the system. The motherboard BIOS must be the type that supports plug and play. ISA, PCI, PCIe, and AGP adapters support plug and play. More information on configuring adapters that support plug and play is available later in the chapter and in the various hardware and operating system chapters.

Use a battery recycling program

Many states have environmental regulations regarding battery disposal. Many companies also have battery recycling programs. The earth911.com Web site has information regarding recycling and disposing of batteries and computer components by zip code or city/state.

Configuration through Switches

A **switch** (sometimes called a DIP switch) can be used to configure motherboard and adapter options. Switches can be found on older adapters and still can be found on motherboards and devices. There are two basic models of switches: slide and rocker. With the slide switch, a sliding tab sticks up from each switch in the switch bank. A switch bank is a group of switches. Each switch is normally numbered starting with 1. Each side of the switch bank is normally labeled with either On/Off, 1/0, or Closed/Open. On, 1, and Closed mean the same thing; Off, 0, and Open mean the same thing. The manufacturer determines how a switch bank is labeled.

To change a switch in the slide DIP switch bank, move the tab with an ink pen or small tweaker (flat-tipped) screwdriver to one of the two positions. For example, say that a switch needs positions 5 and 8 turned *on*. A technician turns the computer off, removes the computer cover, and moves the tabs in switch positions 5 and 8 to *on*. Figure 3.3 shows an example of a slide type DIP switch with the sliding tabs in positions 5 and 8 in the *on* position. Notice in Figure 3.3 that the switch bank has eight individual switch positions.

Use updated device drivers
Just because an adapter is PnP does not mean that an updated device driver does not have to be obtained and installed loaded. A device driver is a small piece of software designed to allow a specific operating system to detect, configure, and control a hardware device. A best practice is to let the operating system detect the device if possible and then obtain an updated driver. Even if an adapter is automatically recognized by the operating system, an updated driver may be available and should be used.

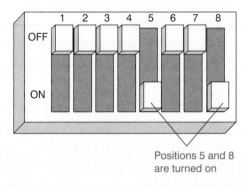

Positions 5 and 8 are turned on

Figure 3.3   Slide type switch

A rocker switch does not have sliding tabs. Instead, each switch position has a rocker switch that presses down to either the On or Off position. To change a rocker switch position, use an ink pen or small tweaker screwdriver to push *down* on one side of the rocker switch. One end of the switch will be pushed down into the switch bank and the other end will extend up from the switch bank. The side of the rocker switch that is pushed down determines whether the switch is On or Off, 1 or 0, or Open or Closed. For example, Figure 3.4 shows a rocker type switch with switch positions 1, 4, and 5 Closed (which also means On or 1). Positions 2, 3, and 6 are Open (which also means Off or 0).

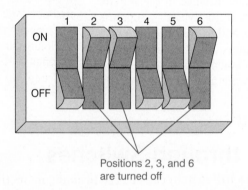

Positions 2, 3, and 6 are turned off

Figure 3.4   Rocker type switch

Use an ink pen or small tweaker screwdriver to change a switch
Never use a pencil to change a DIP switch because the pencil lead may break off into the switch. The lead is conductive. If it breaks off into the switch, the switch may be ruined. Instead, use an ink pen or small tweaker screwdriver to change the switch position.

Other Configuration Parameters

Other possible parameters contained and set via the Setup program or operating system are IRQs (interrupt requests), I/O (input/output) addresses, DMA (direct memory access) channels, and memory addresses. These parameters are assigned to individual adapters and ports, such as disk controllers, and the USB, serial, parallel, and mouse ports. Sometimes these ports must be disabled through Setup in order for other devices or adapter ports to work. No matter how the parameters are assigned, collectively they are known as **system resources**. These are not the same system resources that we refer to when we discuss Windows operating systems. Let's take a look at four important system resources: (1) IRQs; (2) I/O addresses; (3) DMA channels; and (4) memory addresses. Figure 3.5 shows how the operating system controls devices and is used to access them.

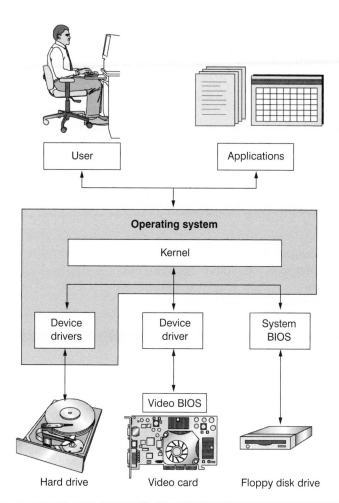

Figure 3.5 **How you, an application, an operating system, and hardware work together**

IRQ (Interrupt Request)

Imagine being in a room of 20 students when four students want the teacher's attention. If all four students talk at once, the teacher is overloaded and unable to respond to the four individuals' needs. Instead, the teacher needs an orderly process of acknowledging each request, prioritizing the request (which student is first), and then answering each question. The same thing happens when multiple devices want the attention of the CPU. For example, which device gets to go first if a key on the DIN-attached keyboard is pressed and the DIN-attached mouse is moved simultaneously? The answer lies in what interrupt request numbers are assigned to the keyboard and the mouse. Every device requests permission to do something by interrupting the processor (similar to a student raising his hand). The CPU has a priority system to handle such situations.

The processor prioritizes device requests through the use of IRQ. An **IRQ** (interrupt request) is a number assigned to expansion adapters or ports so orderly communication can occur between the device or port and the processor. For example, when a key is pressed and the mouse is moved simultaneously, the keyboard has the highest priority because of its IRQ number.

Older computers had 16 interrupts numbered 0 through 15. The chip that controls the interrupts is known as the interrupt controller chip. Today, computers have **APIC**s (advanced programmable interrupt controllers) that support more interrupt outputs (24, for example), which provides more flexibility than the traditional system, which did not normally support more than one device to an interrupt. APICs allow sharing interrupts between devices. There are two common types of APICs: **LAPIC** (local APIC) and **I/O APIC**. LAPIC is normally integrated into each CPU and has its own timer, whereas the I/O APIC is used throughout any of the peripheral buses and is integrated into the chipset. The chipsets used today have backwards compatibility with the traditional interrupts used.

Tech Tip

How IRQs are assigned to multiple-device ports

Ports such as USB, SCSI, IEEE 1394 (FireWire), and so on that support multiple devices, only require one interrupt per port. For example, a single USB can support up to 127 devices, but needs only one IRQ.

Interrupts for integrated ports and some devices can be set through the system's Setup program. Other adapter and device interrupts are set by using **Device Manager** in Windows or using various control panels. To access Device Manager in Windows XP Professional, perform the following: *Start → Settings → Control Panel → System → Hardware* tab → *Device Manager* button. Click the *View* menu option and select *Resources by Type*. Expand the *Interrupt request (IRQ)* option. In Windows Vista/7, click the *Start* button → *Control Panel → System and Maintenance* (Vista)/*System and Security* (7) → *Device Manager → View Hardware and Devices*. Select the *View* menu option and select *Resources by type*. Expand the *Interrupt request (IRQ)* option. Device Manager can also be accessed from a command prompt: `devmgmt.msc`. Figure 3.6 shows how IRQs appear in the Windows XP Device Manager window.

In Figure 3.6, notice that some interrupts have multiple entries. Multiple entries do not always indicate a resource conflict. They are allowed because PCI devices may share IRQs. The next section goes into more detail on this issue.

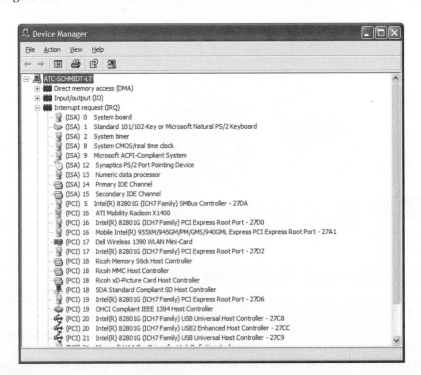

Figure 3.6   **IRQs in Device Manager**

The Computer Management console can also be used to access Device Manager: *Start → Control Panel → System and Maintenance* (Vista)/*System and Security* (7) *→ Administrative Tools → Computer Management*. The system resources for a particular device or part can be accessed through Device Manager. Expand the category within Device Manager, locate the device or port, right-click the device and select *Properties*. Click the *Resources* tab. Device Manager can also be accessed by right-clicking *My Computer* (XP)/*Computer* (Vista/7) through *Explorer*, selecting *Properties*, and selecting the *Hardware* tab. Figure 3.7 shows an integrated network card's properties that cannot be changed through Device Manager.

In Figure 3.7, notice how the *Change Setting* button is grayed out, meaning that the settings cannot be changed through Device Manager. However, they might be able to be modified through the system BIOS Setup program.

Verifying resources with Device Manager

When adapters or devices have resource conflicts or are disabled, Device Manager marks them with a yellow circle with an exclamation point inside or with a red X over the device icon. X means disabled, and ! usually is a resource conflict or missing driver. An i indicates that the Use Automatic setting feature is not being used for the device and resources were manually configured. You may have to click the plus sign beside each category type to see the indication.

Indications of a resource conflict (including IRQ, DMA, I/O address, and memory address conflicts) are as follows:

- The new device is installed and the new device or a device already installed does not work
- The computer locks up or restarts when performing a specific function; for example, when playing or recording audio
- The computer hangs during startup or shutdown
- A device does not work properly or fails to work at all

Use General tab for troubleshooting

On the *General* tab of any adapter or port properties, check the *Device status* section for any error codes including those for resource conflicts.

Figure 3.7   *Resources tab from Device Manager*

PCI Interrupts

When a PC first boots, the operating system discovers what AGP, PCI, and PCIe adapters and devices are present and what system resources each one needs. The operating system allocates resources such as an interrupt to the adapter/device. If the adapter or device has a ROM chip installed that contains software that initializes and/or controls the device, the software is allowed to execute during the boot process.

PCI devices use interrupts called INTA, INTB, INTC, INTD, and so on (depending on the number of PCI slots). Some motherboard documentation uses the numbers 1, 2, 3, and 4 to replace the letters A, B, C, and D. PCI devices are allowed to share interrupts if they need to. Table 3.4 shows common assignments. Each adapter and computer can be assigned differently.

Table 3.4	Common Windows APIC interrupt assignments
IRQ	Common assignment
0	Reserved internal timer
1	Reserved keyboard
2	Reserved to bridge IRQs 8-15
3	
4	COM1 (serial port)
5	
6	Floppy drive controller
7	LPT1 (first parallel printer port)
8	Reserved real-time clock
9	
10	
11	
12	On-board PS/2 mouse port
13	Reserved numeric data processor
14	Primary PATA/SATA (IDE)
15	Secondary PATA/SATA (IDE)
16	Available through PIRQA (programmable interrupt request A)
17	Available through PIRQB (programmable interrupt request B)
18	Available through PIRQC (programmable interrupt request C)
19	Available through PIRQD (programmable interrupt request D)
20	Available through PIRQE (programmable interrupt request E)
21	Available through PIRQF (programmable interrupt request F)
22	Available through PIRQG (programmable interrupt request G)
23	Available through PIRQH (programmable interrupt request H)

Tech Tip

When *not* to share a PCI IRQ

A technician should be able to verify the resources being used. If a device needs maximum performance, it should not share an IRQ with another PCI conventional device.

In Table 3.4, notice how IRQs 0, 1, 2, 8, and 13 are not available to adapters. Also notice that if a system did not use an APIC, only IRQs 0 through 15 would be seen and available. The chipset (specifically the I/O controller hub) can connect each PIRQ line internally to an available IRQ in the range of 3 through 15. PCI interrupts to USB, SATA devices, and PCIe devices are normally assigned dynamically as they are needed. Table 3.5 shows an example of how a motherboard might make PCI IRQ assignments.

PCI interrupts can also be mapped to one of the traditional interrupts, usually IRQ 9, 10, 11, and 12. With so few interrupts available and so many devices installed in today's computers, this presents a problem, which is solved with a technique called IRQ steering. IRQ steering allows multiple PCI adapters to be mapped to the same traditional IRQ. PCI steering (another name for IRQ steering) allows multiple devices to share the same interrupt.

| Table 3.5 | Sample PCI interrupt assignments |

	A	B	C	D	E	F	G	H
PCI slot 1						used		
PCI slot 2							shared	
PCI slot 3								shared
SATA		shared						
LAN		shared						
PCIe X16 1	shared							
PCIe X16 2	shared							
PCIe X1			shared					
USB controller 1							shared	
USB controller 2				shared				
USB controller 3			shared					
USB controller 4	shared							
USB controller 5		shared						
USB 2.0 controller 1							shared	
USB 2.0 controller 2		shared						
SATA controller 1		shared						
SATA controller 2				shared				

PCI cards should be able to share the same resources without conflicts. When IRQ steering is enabled and when a PCI/AGP adapter needs an interrupt, the operating system finds an available interrupt (which may be currently used by an ISA device that does not need it) and allows the PCI device to use it.

If you look at Device Manager, normally you see several PCI devices sharing IRQ9 because the PCI bus uses IRQ9 for IRQ steering. During the boot process, adapters are configured by the system BIOS. Windows examines the resources assigned by the BIOS and uses those resources when communicating with a piece of hardware.

What to do when a PCI conflict occurs

If you suspect a resource conflict with a PCI card, move the PCI card to another slot. PCI slot 1 in particular can cause resource conflicts with the AGP slot. Avoid using PCI slot 1 when an AGP video adapter is installed. If swapping PCI slots does not work, BIOS changes must be made.

Tech Tip

BIOS section titles differ, but a common one for PCI configurations is PCI/PnP configuration. The *Normal* setting is the common default and it automatically assigns resources to the PCI adapter. The *Manual* setting allows manual mapping of a permanent legacy IRQ to the PCI interrupt. Always refer to the motherboard documentation or BIOS help for more information about making BIOS changes.

I/O (Input/Output) Addresses

An **I/O address**, otherwise known as an input/output address or port address, allows the device and the processor to exchange data. The I/O address is like a mailbox number; it must be unique or the mailman gets confused. The device places data (mail) in the box for the CPU to pick up. The processor delivers the data to the appropriate device through the same I/O address

Tech Tip

When is an I/O address needed?

Remember that every device must have a separate I/O address. Otherwise, the CPU cannot distinguish between installed devices.

3 System Configuration

(mailbox number). I/O addresses are simply addresses for the microprocessor to distinguish among the devices with which it communicates. Remember that you cannot deliver mail without an address.

Most PCs have 65,535 different I/O addresses. I/O addresses are shown in hexadecimal format from 0000 to FFFF. Some outputs are shown with eight positions such as 00000000 to FFFFFFFF. Hexadecimal numbers are 0, 1, 2, 3, 4, 5, 6, 7, 8, and 9 just like the decimal numbers we use, but hexadecimal numbers also include the letters A, B, C, D, E, and F. Table 3.6 shows decimal numbers 0 through 15 and their hexadecimal and binary equivalents.

Table 3.6   Decimal, binary, and hexadecimal numbers

Decimal	Hexadecimal	Binary	Decimal	Hexadecimal	Binary
0	0	0000	8	8	1000
1	1	0001	9	9	1001
2	2	0010	10	A	1010
3	3	0011	11	B	1011
4	4	0100	12	C	1100
5	5	0101	13	D	1101
6	6	0110	14	E	1110
7	7	0111	15	F	1111

An example of an I/O address is 390h where the small "h" denotes hexadecimal. Table 3.7 uses this method and shows common I/O addresses used in computers.

Table 3.7   Common I/O addresses

I/O address	Device or port	I/O address	Device or port
000-00Fh	DMA controller (channels 0–3)	200-207h	Game port
020-021h	Interrupt controller 1	220-233h	Sound card
040-043h	System timers—clocks	278-27Fh	LPT2
060h	Keyboard	2E8-2EFh	COM4
070h or 071h	Real-time clock/CMOS/NMI mask	2FFh	COM2
081-083h and 087h	DMA page register (0–3)	330-331h	MIDI port
089-08Bh and 8Fh	DMA page register (4–7)	378-37Fh	LPT1
0A0-0A1h	Interrupt controller 2	388-38Bh	FM synthesizer
0C0-0DEh	DMA controller (channels 4–7)	3E8-3EFh	COM3
0F0-0FFh	Math coprocessor	3F0-3F7h	Floppy controller
170-177h	Secondary IDE controller	3F8-3FFh	COM1
1F0-1F7h	Primary IDE controller	FF80-FF9Fh	USB

The addresses in Table 3.7 are common assignments. Each adapter and computer can be assigned differently. Notice that the table's left column lists a range of I/O addresses. Normally, devices need more than one hexadecimal address location. The number of extra addresses depends on the individual device and what business it does with the processor. In manuals or documentation for a device or adapter, a technician might see that the adapter has an I/O address range instead of just one I/O address. Table 3.7 lists what I/O addresses *can* be used in computers. The manufacturer of the computer or an adapter can set the I/O address specifically or allow different I/O addresses to be set. I/O addresses are set for some devices and ports through the computer's Setup program, Device Manager in Windows or various control panels. Figure 3.8 illustrates a partial view of I/O addresses from the Windows XP Device Manager window.

What to do if only the starting hexadecimal number is shown

One problem for technicians is that some documentation and some Setup programs only give the starting hexadecimal I/O address and not the ending I/O address. The range of addresses the adapter uses can conflict with another adapter or device. Device Manager shows the full range.

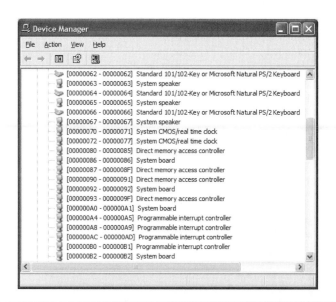

Figure 3.8   **Device Manager I/O addresses**

How to read I/O addresses

When reading the I/O addresses, notice that they are in numerical order with one or more leading zeros. In Figure 3.8, the output is shown with six leading zeros. For example, the System CMOS/real-time clock uses an address range of 72 to 77, which is shown as 00000072 – 00000077.

DMA Channels

A **DMA channel** (direct memory access channel) is a number assigned to an adapter. The DMA assignment allows the adapter to bypass the CPU and communicate directly with RAM. Transferring the data directly to memory speeds up transfers. Devices that frequently take advantage of DMA are drives, tape backup units, and multimedia adapters such as sound cards. A drawback to DMA transfers is that the processor may be put on hold until the DMA data transfer is complete. Well-written software allows the CPU to function periodically during the DMA operation.

Older computers have four DMA channels labeled 0, 1, 2, and 3. DMA channel 0 was normally reserved for refreshing the RAM chips. A single DMA controller chip controls four DMA channels. Later computers had two DMA controller chips, giving a total of eight DMA channels. DMA channel 4 is normally reserved for connecting the two DMA controller chips. Keep in mind that the DMA controller chips are integrated with the motherboard's chipset in today's computers.

A better capability than DMA is bus-mastering. A **bus-mastering** adapter takes control of the bus similarly to the microprocessor. Frequently, bus-mastering adapters have their own processor specific to the adapter's function.

DMA channels must be unique

No two devices or adapters should have the same DMA channel number.

Bus-mastering capabilities are much more efficient than DMA. Assign DMA channels through the system BIOS Setup program, Device Manager, or control panels.

Memory Addresses

The last important system resource is the memory address. A **memory address** is a unique address assigned to the BIOS, any other ROM chips installed on adapters, and RAM chips installed in the system. The memory address is used by the CPU when it accesses information inside the chip. Configuration problems can be caused by overlapping adapter ROM memory addresses.

Memory addresses are shown in hexadecimal. The memory address ranges used for all of the different ROM chips installed in the system are usually from A0000h to FFFFFh. This is the notation shown in books. However, some documentation drops the last digit and does not include the full memory range that the ROM chip takes. For example, a ROM chip on an adapter might be listed as C800h. In reality, this is C8000-C8FFFh. When you look at the memory address on the computer, the address may be shown with more hexadecimal places such as 000A0000-000AFFFFh.

Some ROM addresses are preset and cannot be changed. Others can be changed through jumpers, switches, Device Manager, or various Windows control panels. Some BIOS chips allow the contents of ROM chips to be copied into RAM. This is called ROM shadowing. Access from RAM is faster than from a ROM chip. Figure 3.9 shows memory addresses viewed from within Device Manager.

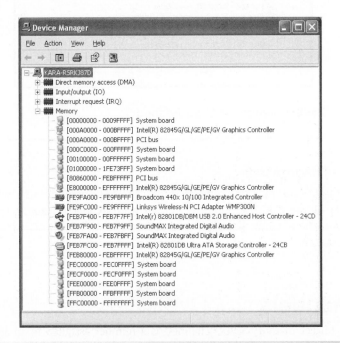

Figure 3.9 **Memory addresses within Device Manager**

ROM addresses must be unique

Every ROM chip must have a unique memory address or the CPU will be unable to access the information inside it. Memory address conflicts can prevent a device or adapter from functioning properly.

In Figure 3.9, notice how the video card (Intel® 82845G/GL/GE/PE/GV) is using the memory address ranges 000A0000–000BFFFFh, E8000000 to EFFFFFFF, and FEB80000 to FEBFFFFF. The ranges are for video RAM and the video ROM chip that is mounted on the adapter. Exercises at the end of the chapter help to identify IRQs, I/O addresses, DMA channels, and memory addresses for various devices and operating systems.

Configuration Overview

ISA, EISA, PCI, PCIe, and AGP adapters must be configured for the proper IRQ, I/O address, memory address, and DMA channel. The most common method used for changing resources for adapters is through the device properties accessed through Device Manager as follows: In the *Device Manager* window, locate the device → right-click it → *Properties* → *Resources* tab.

Adapter documentation is frequently available through the Internet. Technicians must become familiar with using the Internet to download documentation, updated device drivers, and support files related to adapters and devices.

Steps for installing adapters:

1. Use an antistatic wrist strap when handling adapters. ESD (electrostatic discharge) can damage electronic parts. (See Chapter 4 on Disassembly and Power for more details on ESD.)
2. Be sure the computer is powered off and unplugged.
3. Install the adapter in a free expansion slot. Remove any brackets from the case or plastic covers from the rear of the computer that may prevent adapter installation.
4. Attach any internal device cables that connect to the adapter as well as any cables that go to an external port on the adapter, if necessary.
5. Attach any external or internal devices to the opposite ends of the cable, if necessary.
6. Power on any external devices connected to the adapter, if applicable.
7. Reattach the computer power cord and power on the computer.
8. Load any application software or device drivers needed for the devices attached to the adapter.
9. Test the devices connected to the adapter.

The system BIOS plays an important role when the computer boots. Not only does it check hardware for errors as part of POST, but also as part of the startup routine the BIOS detects installed adapters and, together with the operating system, determines what resources to assign to the adapter. This information is stored in a part of CMOS known as the **ESCD** (extended system configuration data) area. Some system BIOS Setup routines allow resetting this information or manually configuring a resource such as an IRQ. Once configured the information stays in the ESCD area and does not have to be recomputed unless another device is added. After resources are allocated, the BIOS looks in the saved settings of CMOS to determine to what device it should look first for an operating system. This part of the BIOS routine is known as the bootstrap loader. If BIOS cannot locate an operating system in the first location specified in the saved settings, it tries the second device and continues on looking to each device specified in the saved settings for an operating system. Keep in mind that once an operating system is found, the operating system loads.

Configuration of PCI, AGP, and PCIe Adapters

PCI, AGP, and PCIe adapters are the easiest adapters to configure. Usually, they do not have problems with interrupt conflicts because the PCI standard allows interrupt sharing. A PCI device is configured through the BIOS and system Setup software as well as through software provided with the PCI adapter. PCI adapters have special registers that store the configuration information. When installing a PCI, AGP, or PCIe adapter, always refer to the documentation for installation instructions.

PCI adapters are configured with software and the standard supports bus-mastering. Bus-mastering allows an adapter to take over the external bus from the CPU and execute operations with another bus-mastering adapter without going through the processor. Not all PCI slots support bus-mastering. Always refer to the motherboard documentation to see the specifications on expansion slots.

When you install a PCI adapter in a Windows environment, the operating system detects installation and adds the adapter's configuration information to the registry. The **registry** is a central database in Windows that holds hardware information and other data. All software applications access the registry for configuration information instead of going to the adapter. In a plug and play operating system, the system prompts for either the operating system disks or CD, or for a software disk from the adapter manufacturer.

Windows works in conjunction with a PnP BIOS to configure adapters automatically. Windows attempts to make hardware installation easier and it keeps track of the computer's configuration. When Windows boots, it compares the saved configuration with what is detected during initialization. When adding hardware, the system automatically detects it or you can use Windows' Add New Hardware, Add/Remove Hardware, or Add Hardware wizards. This wizard lets the operating system search for the new piece of hardware or allows selection of the type of device or adapter.

One way to access the Add Hardware wizard is through the Windows Control Panel. The wizard asks if Windows should search for the new hardware. If *Yes* is chosen, then the operating system searches for new hardware. Directions for installation appear in the windows throughout the process. If *No* is chosen, a list of hardware types appears in a window. Click the hardware category, click *Next*, and follow the directions on the screen. Letting the operating system search for new hardware can be a time-consuming process. If you are familiar with installing hardware, select the *No* option and pick the hardware category to save time. Note that starting with Windows 7, the Add Hardware wizard cannot be accessed from a control panel. However, from a command prompt run as an administrator, the **hdwwiz.exe** command manually starts the Add Hardware wizard.

Windows XP, Vista, and 7 have a feature called **driver signing**, which means that a device driver for a particular piece of hardware has met certain criteria for WHQL (Windows hardware quality lab) tests. Some people call this having a signed driver. A signed driver is a device driver file that has not been altered and cannot be overwritten by another program's installation process. Conversely, an unsigned driver is simply one that has not gone through this process of becoming an "authorized" signed driver.

You can modify how your computer handles signed drivers by using the *System* control panel → *Hardware* tab → *Driver Signing* button. Figure 3.10 shows the three options available in XP.

Tech Tip

What to do if plug and play does not work

Plug and play (and sometimes a configuration utility supplied with the device) is used to configure system resources. Sometimes a reboot is required for the changes to take effect. If the device does not work after the reboot, reboot the computer again (and possibly a third time) to allow the operating system to sort out the system resources. Manual changes can be made if this does not work.

Tech Tip

Use the device driver provided by the adapter manufacturer

Whether or not Windows searches for the new hardware, use the specific operating system driver provided with the adapter for optimum performance. If the driver is missing, check the adapter manufacturer's Web site to see if a driver exists and if a new version is available.

Figure 3.10   **Windows XP driver signing options**

Microsoft Vista and 7 require driver signing as a security precaution. You can use the `verifier.exe` program from the command prompt to verify the drivers installed on the computer especially if you have unexplained computer problems due to faulty device drivers. Also, within Vista's Advanced Boot Options menu is the *Disable Driver Signature Enforcement* option. Use this if you suspect that Vista is not booting due to an unsigned driver. Note that Vista boots in normal mode (not Safe mode) when this option is active.

Configuration of PC Cards/ExpressCards

The **PC Card** architecture, previously known as PCMCIA (Personal Computer Memory Card International Association), expands laptops by allowing cards to be added that function as modems, hard drives, network adapters, and so on. The original standard was a 16-bit local bus standard later upgraded to **CardBus**, that allows 32-bit transfers at speeds up to 33MHz (133Mbps).

The number of PC Card slots available on a computer varies among manufacturers and computer models. A PC Card inserts into the PC Card slot. However, each PC Card can control more than one PC Card slot. The PC Card function can commonly be identified by the PC Card's thickness. A laptop computer with a Type II PC Card slot accepts Type II and Type I PC Cards, but only one at a time! The easiest way to think of this is that the thinner cards fit in the thicker slots; but a thick card cannot fit in the thinner slots.

Avoid upgrading laptop memory with a PC Card

Upgrading memory in a laptop with a 16- or 32-bit CardBus PC Card is not the best solution. A PC Card memory upgrade should be done only as a last resort.

Type III PC Cards are 10.5mm thick and are for rotating devices such as hard drives, CD/DVD drives, floppy drives, and so on. Type III PC Card slots also accept Type I and II PC Cards. Table 3.8 recaps the PC Card types, sizes, and uses.

Table 3.8	PC Cards	
PC Card type	**Size**	**Usage**
I	3.3mm	Memory and applications
II	5mm	Modems and network adapters
III	10.5mm	Storage devices such as floppy drive, hard drives, and CD-ROMs

PC Card slots are now being replaced with ExpressCards (although some manufacturers are including both slots or a combo slot due to these two technologies being incompatible with one another). PC Cards and ExpressCards now support power management in security tokens, GPS (global positioning system), wireless network adapters, sound cards, video capture/frame grabber cards, TV tuners, and video-conferencing cards. ExpressCard 2.0 complies with PCI Express 2.0 and SuperSpeed USB and is backward compatible with the original ExpressCard. Figure 3.11 shows the difference between the sizes.

Most PC Cards/ExpressCards support hot swapping. **Hot swapping** allows the cards to be inserted into the slot when the laptop is powered on. Each card takes up system resources, such as memory addresses and interrupts, just as other adapters do. Figure 3.12 shows a network PC Card being inserted into a Dell laptop while the laptop is powered.

When installing PC Cards/ExpressCards, some manufacturers recommend that you insert the installation CD or floppy, start the installation software, and then insert the adapter. Other manufacturers have you install the PC Card/ExpressCard with the power off and then boot the computer. Sometimes you may need the

Converter is available

An adapter is available to connect a PC Card to an ExpressCard/34 or /54 slot.

operating system CD to install a new device. Modems and network cards can be especially frustrating in their conflicts with other installed devices.

Figure 3.11   **PC Card and ExpressCard sizes**

Figure 3.12   **Hot swapping a PC Card**

Tech Tip

Use Device Manager to verify and troubleshoot PC Cards
If the PC Card/ExpressCard has two functions such as a LAN/Modem card, you should check that both devices are working by using Device Manager. Always use Device Manager first when an adapter is not working and to troubleshoot resource conflicts.

A message such as "This device is working properly." displays on the device's main *Properties* window. If a yellow exclamation mark shows in Device Manager, troubleshoot the resource conflict. If a red X appears over the device's icon, click the appropriate checkbox under *Properties* to enable the PC Card/ExpressCard device.

The following common problems can occur with PC Cards/ExpressCards:

- The card is not fully inserted into the slot.
- The computer's BIOS is not up-to-date.
- The system shows multiple installations of the same adapter.
- The appropriate cable is not connected properly or in the right connector.
- An old driver or a driver for the wrong operating system was used.
- If two devices will not work when installed simultaneously, but will work when only one or the other is installed, then reverse the order of installation. Install one device and test it, then install the second device. If this does not work, uninstall both devices and reverse the order.

Installing a USB Device

A USB device connects to a USB port or connects wirelessly. USB wired devices are hot-swappable; that is, they can be plugged into the computer or hub while the computer is powered, and they support plug and play. As mentioned in Chapter 1, there are three main versions of USB—1.0, 2.0, and 3.0. USB 1.0 operated at speeds of 1.5Mbps and 12Mbps; version 2.0 operates at speeds up to 480Mbps. Version 3.0 transmits data up to 5Gbps. USB 3.0 is backward compatible with the older versions, which means that the cables are the same and any 1.0 device works with a 2.0 port. Figure 3.13 shows the USB symbols found on devices.

For USB devices, always follow manufacturer's installation instructions

Even though USB devices are easy to install, always follow the USB device manufacturer's instructions.

Figure 3.13 **USB logos**

USB OTG (on-the-go) is a supplement to the USB 2.0 specification. Normally with USB a device that does not have too much intelligence built into it attaches to a host—specifically, a PC. USB on-the-go allows a USB device to have the capability of being the host device. This allows two USB devices to communicate without the use of a PC or a hub. The supplement allows a USB on-the-go device to still attach to a PC because USB on-the-go is backward compatible with the USB 2.0 standard.

Certified Wireless USB supports high-speed, secure wireless connectivity between a USB device and a PC at speeds comparable to Hi-Speed USB. Certified Wireless USB is not a networking technology; it is just another way that you can connect your favorite USB devices to a host. You just don't have to plug a cable into a USB port. Wireless USB supports speeds of 480Mbps at a range of three meters (~10 feet) or 110Mbps at 10 meters (~30 feet). Wireless USB uses UWB (ultra-wideband) low-power radio over a range of 3.1 to 10.5GHz.

To install a USB device, perform the following steps:

- Power on the computer.
- Optionally, install the USB device's software. Note that some manufacturers require that software and/or device drivers are installed before attaching the USB device.
- Optionally, power on the device. Not all USB devices have external power adapters or a power button because they receive power from the USB bus.
- Locate a USB port on the rear or front of the computer or on a USB hub. Plug the USB device

A USB port takes only one interrupt

Note that a USB port takes only one interrupt no matter how many devices connect to that port.

Safely remove USB devices

To remove a USB device, do not simply unplug it from the port. Instead, click on the *Safely Remove Hardware* icon from the systray. Select the USB device to remove. The operating system prompts when it is safe to unplug the device.

3
System Configuration

into a free port. The operating system normally detects the USB device and loads the device driver. The *Add New Hardware* window may appear and you may have to browse to the driver that is normally located on the disk shipped with the USB device. You should use the drivers that come with the device and download a newer device driver from the Internet once the driver loads properly.

Tech Tip

Do not use more than five USB hubs

When connecting multiple hubs, the rule is that no device's signal can pass through more than five hubs before reaching the computer. Each hub can have multiple hubs attached to it, but no more than five tiers of hubs.

A USB hub is quite popular for connecting more than one USB device to a USB port. A USB hub can connect to a computer's USB port and provide more ports for USB devices. A USB hub can also connect to another USB hub. The maximum distance between each hub is 16.4 feet (5 meters). Full-speed devices can connect to the hub or computer at a maximum of 16.4 feet, whereas low speed devices have a maximum of 9.8 feet (3 meters). A maximum of five hubs are allowed with a maximum range of 88.5 feet (27 meters). USB allows up to 127 devices to be connected using hubs.

To install a USB hub, optionally attach the AC adapter to the hub's power jack and AC wall outlet. Some USB hubs have power supplies that are purchased separately and are not included with the hub. Not all USB hubs are powered.

USB ports are known as upstream and downstream ports. The upstream port is used to connect to the computer or another hub. The downstream port is used to connect a USB device. These ports are commonly known as Type A and Type B. A standard USB cable has a Type A male connector on one end and a Type B male connector on the other end. The port on the computer is a Type A port. The Type A connector inserts into the Type A port. The Type B connector attaches to the Type B port on the USB device. Hubs normally have Type A ports on them. Figure 3.14 shows Type A and Type B connectors. There are also mini versions of the Type A and Type B connectors. Refer to Figure 1.16 in Chapter 1 for a photo of these two connectors.

Type A connector

Type B connector

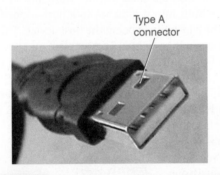
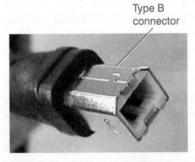

Figure 3.14   **USB Type A and Type B connectors**

Connect the USB-A connector to the available USB port or into another hub's downstream port. Connect the USB-B connector to the hub's upstream port. Attach USB devices as needed. Figure 3.15 shows how USB devices connect to a hub.

A USB device can be powered by the USB bus. Things commonly powered by the bus include flash drives, mice, and keyboards. Scanners, printers, and hard drives are types of devices that use an external power source.

Many hubs can operate in two power modes—self-powered and bus-powered—and the hub may have a switch control that must be set to the appropriate mode. Self-powered mode means the hub has an external power supply attached. Bus-powered means that no external power supply connects to the hub. Once all USB devices attached to the hub are tested, the hub's power supply can be removed and the devices retested. If all attached devices work properly, the hub power supply can be left disconnected.

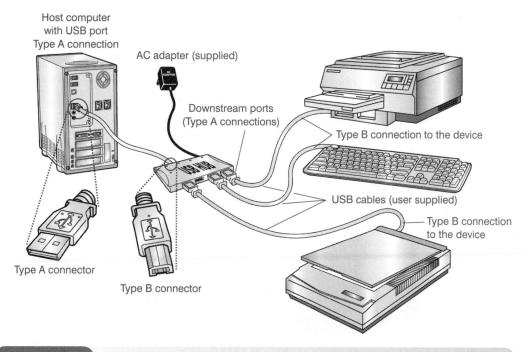

Host computer
with USB port
Type A connection

AC adapter (supplied)

Downstream ports
(Type A connections)

Type B connection to the device

USB cables (user supplied)

Type B connection
to the device

Type A connector

Type B connector

Figure 3.15   **USB hub connectivity**

USB Troubleshooting

To troubleshoot USB device problems, check the obvious first. Check the cabling and power. Verify if any USB device that plugs into a USB hub works. If none work, swap the hub. If some work and some do not, attach an external power source to the hub, change its configuration, if necessary, and retest the devices. Restart the computer and retest the USB device.

A USB device could be drawing more power than is allowed. If this is the case, the computer can disable the port. The only way to re-enable the port is to restart the computer. If a device is using less than 50 milliamps of power, the USB port never becomes active. Try plugging the USB device into a different USB port or verify it on another computer.

A USB device requires a driver that may be loaded automatically. The incorrect driver or outdated driver could be loaded and causing problems. The following list can also help when troubleshooting USB devices:

- Use Device Manager to ensure the hub is functioning properly.
- Ensure the BIOS firmware is up-to-date.
- Use Device Manager to ensure that no USB device has an IRQ assigned and shared with another non-USB device.
- USB devices sometimes do not work in safe mode and require hardware support configured through the BIOS.
- Sometimes USB devices stop working on hubs that have an external power source. Remove the hub's external power source and retest.
- Do not connect USB devices to a computer that is in standby mode. This may prevent the computer from coming out of standby mode.
- For intermittent USB device problems, disable power management to see if this is causing the problem.
- Test a device connected to a USB hub by connecting it directly into a USB port that has nothing else attached. The problem could be caused by other USB devices or a USB hub.
- Remove the USB device's driver and reinstall. Sometimes you must reboot the computer to give the new drivers priority over the general purpose drivers.

3
System
Configuration

- If a USB device is running slowly, try attaching it to a different port with fewer devices connected to the same port.
- Verify the USB port is enabled in BIOS if integrated into the motherboard or attached to the motherboard through an adapter cable. Always refer to the USB device manufacturer's Web site for specific troubleshooting details.

Installing an IEEE 1394 (FireWire) Device

The IEEE 1394 bus allows automatic installation and configuration of up to 63 devices such as a modem, keyboard, mouse, monitor, scanner, hard drive, CD or DVD drives, printer, hard disk audio recorders, video conferencing cameras, and an audio/video device. Each device can connect to up to 14.7 feet (4.5 meters) away, and up to 16 devices can be on a single chain. The maximum distance for all devices combined is approximately 236 feet (72 meters). IEEE 1394 (all versions) supports speeds up to 3200Mbps. IEEE 1394c and 1394d allow RJ-45 and fiber connectors/cabling to be used. IEEE 1394b (FireWire2) increases cable lengths to 328 feet (100 meters). Figure 3.16 shows an IEEE 1394 cable.

Figure 3.16   **IEEE 1394 cable**

IEEE 1394 has two data transfer modes—asynchronous and isochronous. The asynchronous mode focuses on ensuring the data is delivered reliably. Isochronous transfers allow guaranteed bandwidth (which is needed for audio/video transfers), but does not provide for error correction or retransmission.

IEEE 1394 supports plug and play like USB and the devices are hot swappable. IEEE 1394 devices (like USB devices) can receive power from the IEEE 1394 bus, or they can have an external power source, but FireWire is more expensive to implement than USB. When a device is attached or removed, all IEEE 1394 devices are reset. They reinitialize and all devices are assigned a unique number.

IEEE 1394 devices can connect to a port built into the motherboard, an IEEE 1394 port on an adapter, another IEEE 1394 device, and a hub. IEEE 1394 does not require a PC to operate; two IEEE 1394 devices can communicate via a cable. The IEEE 1394 bus is actually a peer-to-peer standard, meaning that a computer is not needed. Two IEEE 1394-compliant devices can be connected (such as a hard drive and a digital camera) and data transfer can occur across the bus. Many compare IEEE 1394 with USB or place them in competition with one another; but in the computer world, there are applications for each. IEEE 1394 was designed for high-speed audio and video devices, and the standard has much greater throughput for applications such as video conferencing. Figure 3.17 shows an IEEE 1394 device directly connected to a port.

The BIOS is used to disable/enable integrated ports on the motherboard. Most operating systems automatically detect that a FireWire adapter has been installed and no special software is needed. When connecting a FireWire device, always follow the manufacturer's instructions. Attach the device to an available port on the motherboard or an adapter, another IEEE 1394 device, or IEEE 1394 hub port.

Tech Tip

An IEEE 1394 port uses the same system resources to access any devices attached to the same port

If one or more FireWire devices connect to a FireWire port (integrated or on an adapter), the devices use the same system resources as assigned to the port.

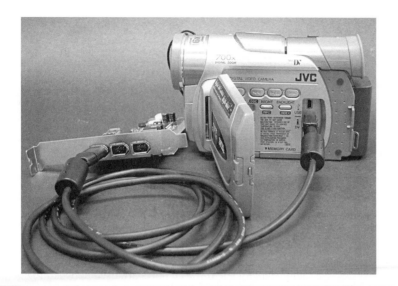

Figure 3.17   **IEEE 1394 cable connected to a port**

The following are generic steps for installing a FireWire adapter:

- Power off the computer and remove the AC power cord.
- Access the computer interior by removing the computer case.
- Locate an available expansion slot and optionally remove the slot cover and retaining screw. Not all computer cases have this now.
- Firmly insert the PCI FireWire adapter into the PCI expansion slot.
- Reinsert the retaining screw if necessary.
- Replace the computer cover and reattach the power cord.
- Power on the computer. The operating system normally detects the newly installed hardware. Insert the driver disk/CD that ships with the adapter and browse to the location of the driver file. Follow the prompts for installing the drivers. Windows normally detects the correct driver for the FireWire adapter, but the computer may have to be rebooted to recognize the adapter.

For an IEEE 1394 device or adapter, always follow manufacturer's installation instructions

Follow all FireWire adapter and device manufacturer directions.

IEEE 1394 Troubleshooting

Use Device Manager to verify the correct installation for an IEEE 1394 device or port. To verify installation in Windows open *Device Manager*, double-click the *1394 Bus Controller* option to verify that a IEEE 1394 host controller is present.

FireWire hubs can be self-powered or bus-powered like USB hubs. A slide switch may be used to select the appropriate power mode. Most FireWire hub manufacturers recommend powering the hub only during installation. Once installed, test the FireWire devices, remove the hub power, and retest the devices. If all devices operate properly, leave the FireWire hub power adapter disconnected. With a cable that has a 6-pin connector at both ends, connect the hub to the computer's FireWire port. Attach FireWire devices to the hub as needed.

What if IEEE 1394 is not working properly?

If a question mark appears by the IEEE 1394 host controller in Device Manager, remove or delete the driver and reinstall. You may need to download a newer driver from the adapter manufacturer's Web site. If this does not work, change the adapter to a different expansion slot. If a red or yellow symbol appears by the FireWire controller, the driver is corrupt, the driver is the wrong one, or there is a system resource conflict with another device.

3
System Configuration

What if I don't have the right IEEE 1394 cable?
FireWire devices can have three types of connectors—a 4-, 6-, and 9-pin. The 4-pin cable does not provide for voltage over the IEEE 1394 bus. Placing a 6-pin connection on a FireWire 800 cable reduces connection speeds to a maximum of 400Mbps. Converters can be purchased to convert 4- to 6-pin or 6- to 9-pin connectors.

Infrared Devices

Most laptop computers include an infrared port; some motherboards include a connector to add an infrared port. An **infrared port** is a small dark window that uses infrared light to perform wireless communication. Infrared transmissions are used in intrusion detection systems, home entertainment control devices, robotic toys and devices, and cordless microphones. Wireless communication can use either infrared light or radio frequencies. A few wireless input and output devices such as mice, keyboards, modems, or printers use infrared light to communicate, but most wireless devices use radio frequencies. Infrared ports are used between PDAs (personal digital assistants) to communicate or transfer data. See Chapter 13 on Networks (the wireless section) for information on using radio frequencies for wireless transmission.

Infrared is not as popular as radio frequency wireless transmission because it is limited in its distance range and it requires an unobstructed direct line of sight connection. However, infrared is cheaper to implement than a radio frequency-based wireless connection. In addition to external devices, infrared can be used to perform data transfers between two computers that have infrared ports installed.

Infrared communication requires an infrared transceiver. This transceiver can be integrated into the motherboard (which is common in laptop computers). You can also attach a transceiver to the computer's serial port or reconfigure the serial port as an infrared port if the system allows it. The last option is only allowed if the computer has an internal infrared device. Figure 3.18 shows a laptop's infrared port.

Infrared port

Figure 3.18   Infrared port

Once an infrared port is enabled in Windows XP, the only step necessary to establish communication with another infrared device is to aim the port at the other infrared port. Some ports work better if they are at least six inches apart. Ensure the ports are no more than three feet apart. A Windows taskbar icon can be used to set options for the infrared port. Once communication is established with another infrared port, an icon appears on the Windows taskbar. Figure 3.19 shows the two common infrared port Windows icons.

For any integrated infrared port, ensure the port is enabled through the BIOS. Common settings include Disable, Enable, and Auto. Older motherboards have the infrared port multiplexed with the second serial port. This means that to enable infrared communication, the serial port must be changed to the IrDA (infrared data association) mode. IrDA is an organization that creates international standards for wireless infrared communications.

Infrared taskbar icon

Infrared icon when
communicating

Figure 3.19   **Windows infrared port icons**

To verify an infrared device in Windows 2000 or XP, click the *Wireless Link* control panel, click the *Hardware* tab, select the infrared device, and select *Properties*. Device Manager can also be used to verify the infrared devices. Once Device Manager is open, look for a category called *Infrared Devices*. This option appears if the computer has an infrared transceiver. Double-click the *Infrared Devices* option. Right-click on the infrared device and select *Enable* to allow the device to work. If no devices are listed, check the BIOS settings to ensure the infrared port is enabled. Also, if it is an external infrared port, ensure the drivers have been loaded and that the device is listed as a *Virtual Infrared Port* under the *Ports (COM and LPT)* Device Manager heading. If the infrared device is listed but not enabled, perform troubleshooting.

Infrared ports are very easy to troubleshoot once the port is enabled and device driver is loaded. The following steps aid in infrared port troubleshooting:

- Ensure the distance between the infrared ports is at least six inches and no more than three feet.
- Ensure both devices that contain infrared ports are on a stable, level surface.
- Ensure no bright light such as sunlight is interfering with communication.
- Ensure there is no more than a 15 degree angle (some manufacturers allow up to 30 degrees) between the two devices.
- Ensure no obstructions are between the two infrared ports.

Soft Skills—A Good Technician Quality: One Thing at a Time

The least effective type of computer technician is a "gun slinger." The term gun slinger brings to mind images of wild west ruffians who had shooting matches with other gangsters in the town's main street. Gun slingers drew their guns frequently and with little provocation. They did not put much thought into their method or consider other possible resolutions. You must strive *not* to be this type of technician.

A gun slinger technician changes multiple things simultaneously. For example, if there is no display on the output, the technician will swap out the monitor, disable the on-board video port, add a new video adapter, power on the computer, and when output appears, call the problem "solved." If a computer problem is repaired using this technique, the technician never knows exactly what solved the problem.

A good technician, on the other hand, makes a list of symptoms (even if it is simply a mental list) followed by a list of things to try. Then the technician tries the possible solutions starting with the simplest one (the one that costs the least amount of time to the computer user). The technician documents each step. Each approach that is tried but does not fix the problem is put back to the original configuration before the next possible solution is attempted. This method keeps the technician focused on what has been tested and if another technician takes over, the steps do not have to be repeated. Best of all, when one of the possible solutions fixes the problem, the exact solution is known.

Gun slinger technicians do not learn as fast as other technicians because they do not determine the real cause of problems. Each time they are presented with a problem similar to one they have seen in the past, gun slinger technicians will go through the same haphazard troubleshooting method. These technicians are actually dangerous to an organization because they are not good at documenting what they have done and determining exactly what fixes a particular problem.

Key Terms

APIC (p. 76)
bus-mastering (p. 81)
CardBus (p. 85)
Certified Wireless USB (p. 87)
CMOS (p. 69)
Device Manager (p. 76)
DMA channel (p. 81)
driver signing (p. 84)
ESCD (p. 83)

Flash BIOS (p. 69)
hdwwiz.exe (p. 84)
hot swapping (p. 85)
I/O address (p. 79)
I/O APIC (p. 76)
infrared port (p. 92)
IRQ (p. 76)
LAPIC (p. 76)
memory address (p. 82)

PC Card (p. 85)
registry (p. 84)
Setup (p. 68)
switch (p. 73)
system resources (p. 75)
USB OTG (p. 87)
`verifier.exe` (p. 85)

Review Questions

1. What is the purpose of the Setup program?
2. What is the best source of information for finding out how to enter the Setup program?
3. What is the purpose of a Flash update?
4. A computer has a write-protected BIOS. What can you do to update the Flash BIOS?
5. [T | F] A virus can infect a Flash BIOS.
6. What is the difference between BIOS and CMOS?
7. How does the POST program know which hardware components to test?
8. [T | F] Entering the wrong Setup information can cause a POST error.
9. What component keeps the information in CMOS memory even when the computer is powered off?
10. What is the purpose of the Boot Sequence BIOS setting?
11. What is the difference between a user and a supervisor power on password?
12. What should you do if the password that is needed during power on (set from the BIOS Setup program) has been forgotten?
13. List two things to remember when replacing a battery inside a microcomputer.
14. What is one indication that a battery is beginning to fail?
15. Is it an acceptable practice to replace a computer battery with one that has a higher voltage (but not lower)?
16. How can you determine what battery recycling options are available in your city and state?
17. Using Figure 3.20, determine how the switches would be changed if positions 1, 2, and 6 are the only positions to be *enabled*.

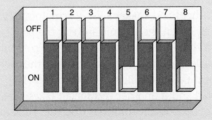

Figure 3.20

18. A switch block has the top labeled 1 and the bottom labeled 0, as shown in Figure 3.21. Which switches are off?

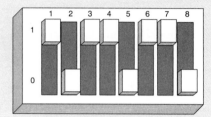

Figure 3.21

19. Using Figure 3.22, determine which side of each switch position is pressed if positions 1, 3, 4, and 6 are the only ones to be *disabled*?

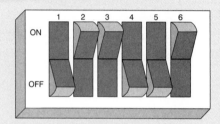

Figure 3.22

20. [T | F] A pencil should be used to change a DIP switch because the tip is thinner than an ink pen's tip.

21. What PC component supports more than 16 IRQs and is normally integrated into the chipset?

22. Describe two visual signs of a resource conflict detected by Device Manager.

23. What IRQs are normally unavailable for adapters?

24. What interrupt is normally assigned to the primary PATA IDE controller in a computer?

25. You suspect a conflict with PCI adapters. What is the first thing you should try?

26. [T | F] Every device must have a separate I/O address to communicate with the microprocessor.

27. What is the decimal number 14 in hexadecimal?

28. What is the common I/O address for the COM1 serial port?

29. List one disadvantage to using a DMA channel.

30. What type of address is unique for every ROM chip installed in the computer?

31. Which memory address is higher—C011111D or B2FFFE43?

32. [T | F] PCI adapters can be installed with power applied to the computer.

33. What Windows XP wizard allows the operating system to search for newly installed hardware?

34. What is driver signing?

35. What Vista boot option is used if a device driver is suspect?

36. What do you recommend if a company-issued network card is a PC Card and a computer user's newly purchased laptop takes only ExpressCards?

37. List two common PC Card/ExpressCard installation problems.

38. What is the maximum distance from a wireless USB device to the host PC if the user of this device needs maximum transfer rates?

39. A friend of yours bought a USB printer and asks you to install it. You look and there are no USB ports available on the motherboard or front of the computer. What will you recommend?

40. What is the maximum number of USB hubs allowed to connect to a single PC port?

41. Which type of USB connector normally connects to a printer? [Type A | Type B | Centronics | DB9 | DB15]

42. Can USB ports operate without an external power supply?

43. What is the maximum distance 16 IEEE 1394 devices can be from the IEEE 1394 port?

44. Are IEEE 1394 devices hot swappable?

45. [T | F] When an IEEE 1394 device is added to the bus, only the newly installed IEEE 1394 device is reset.

46. [T | F] Two IEEE 1394 devices can connect without using an integrated IEEE 1394 port or adapter.

47. What is the difference between the two IEEE 1394 cables?

48. Once Windows recognizes an infrared port, what must be done to establish communication with another infrared port or device?

49. Is being a gun slinger technician a good thing or a bad thing? Explain your answer.

50. List one thing you think a gun slinger technician might do if a port on a motherboard works only part of the time.

Fill-in-the-Blank

1. To set the configuration for today's computers, go into the _____ program.

2. The _____ holds the Setup program.

3. Two commonly used software programs to configure an adapter are _____ and _____.

4. A/An _____ connects two metal pins together on a motherboard, adapter, or device.

5. The type of BIOS used today is _____.

6. A special type of memory where configuration information is saved is _____.

7. The _____ keeps information in CMOS.

8. _____ batteries are the most common type used on motherboards.

9. On a rocker DIP switch, other settings for "on" are _____ or _____.

10. _____ is the name given when collectively referring to IRQs, I/O addresses, DMA channels, and memory addresses.

11. A/An _____ is a number assigned to an adapter so the microprocessor can recognize higher priority devices first.

12. The two types of APICs are _____ and _____.

13. _____ is used within Windows to view system resources such as IRQs.

14. The reason IRQ8 cannot be used for an adapter is because it is used for the _____.

15. A/An _____ allows communication between a microprocessor and an adapter.

16. An I/O address is normally shown using the _____ numbering system.

17. A/An _____ is a number assigned to an adapter that allows bypassing the microprocessor.

18. Memory addresses are shown as _____ numbers.

19. The _____ is a database for Windows that holds hardware configuration information.

20. _____ are also known as PCMCIA adapters.

21. Type _____ PC Cards are used for modems.

22. _____ allows laptop computers to be compatible with USB and PCIe interfaces.

23. Low-speed USB devices can be located a maximum of _____ from the USB port.

24. _____ and _____ are the two IEEE 1394 transfer modes.

25. A/An _____ port is sometimes found on a laptop and is used in wireless communication for a very limited distance.

Hands-On Exercises

1. Configuration Method Exercise and Review

Objective: To determine which configuration method a computer uses

Parts: A computer

Procedure: Open the computer and look at the motherboard. Determine whether the computer uses (1) jumpers; (2) a battery to maintain CMOS information; or (3) Flash BIOS.

Questions:

1. What is an advantage of having a battery that keeps CMOS information?

2. What jumper(s), if any, are on the motherboard?

3. How can you tell the purpose of the jumper(s)?

4. What is one of the first indications of a failing battery?

5. What determines the keystroke required to access the Setup program?

2. Interrupt, I/O Address, and DMA Channel Configuration through the Setup Program

Objective: To access a computer's resources through the Setup program

Parts: A computer that uses keystrokes to enter the Setup program

Procedure: Complete the following procedure and answer the accompanying questions.

1. Power on the computer.

2. Press the appropriate key(s) to enter the Setup program.

3. Go through the various menus or icons until you find an interrupt (IRQ) setting for a particular device or port. Write the device or port and the associated IRQ in the space below.

IRQ   **Device or Port**

_____   _____

Why do different devices generally not have the same interrupt?

4. Go through the various menus or icons until you find an I/O address setting for a particular device or port. Write the device or port in the space provided along with the associated I/O address.

I/O Address   **Device or Port**

_____   _____

Why must all devices and ports have a separate and unique I/O address?

Who assigns I/O addresses, interrupts, and DMA channels to different adapters?

What is the best source of information on how to set interrupts, I/O addresses, memory addresses, and DMA channels for technicians installing a new adapter into a system?

3
System
Configuration

5. Exit the Setup program.

6. Go into Device Manager and determine if the information collected in Steps 3 and 4 is the same.

Instructor initials: _____

3. Examining System Resources Using Windows XP or Vista

Objective: To be able to view and access system resources using Windows XP or Vista

Parts: A computer with Windows XP or Vista loaded

Procedure: Complete the following procedure and answer the accompanying questions.

1. Power on the computer and verify that Windows loads. Log on to the computer using the userid and password provided by the instructor or lab assistant.

2. Access the *Performance and Maintenance* control panel (XP) or the *System and Maintenance* control panel (Vista).

3. In XP click the *Hardware* tab. In either XP or Vista, access *Device Manager*.

4. Click the *View* menu option and select *Resources by type*.

   What are the four types of system resources shown?

5. Click the plus sign by *IRQ* (interrupt request).

   Are any interrupts in use by multiple PCI devices? If so, list one.

6. Click the help icon (a yellow question mark on top of a piece of paper or a question mark).

   What happened?

   Using the help function, determine how to start or stop a non-plug and play device. Document your findings.

7. Close the help window.

   What device, if any, is using IRQ4?

   Is this the standard IRQ for this device?

Instructor initials: _____

8. Click the plus sign by *Input/output (I/O)*.

   What is the first I/O address range listed for the first occurrence of DMA (direct memory access) controller?

9. Collapse the *Input/output* section. Click the plus sign by *DMA*.

   Are any DMA channels being used? If so, list them.

10. Click on any device listed in the IRQ section. Move your mouse slowly over the icons at the top until you locate the *Update Driver* icon. When the mouse is moved slowly enough, a description of the icon appears.

    What does the *Update Driver* icon look like?

11. Using previously learned steps, locate the *COM1 IRQ* and click it once to select it. If COM1 IRQ is not there, select the PATA or SATA (may be listed as ATA) IRQ.

12. Move your mouse slowly over the icons at the top until you locate the *Uninstall* and *Disable* icons. *Do not click these icons.* They can be used to troubleshoot problem devices.

13. Click the *Action* menu item and select *Properties*. The *Properties* window opens. Many devices have a *Troubleshooter* button located on the *General* tab.

14. Click the *Resources* tab. The resources tab shows what system resources a particular device is using.

    What resources are being used?

    What message displays in the *Conflicting Device List* section?

    Is the *Use automatic settings* checkbox enabled?

15. If the *Use automatic settings* checkbox is enabled, click inside the box to disable it. Click the *Setting based on* drop-down menu. Select each of the possible settings. Watch the resources change. Also look to see if any of the configuration settings cause a conflict.

    Did any of the selections cause a conflict?

16. In the *Resource settings* section under the *Resource type* column, click *IRQ*. Click the *Change Setting* button. The IRQ value is listed on the screen. To change the value, use the ⬆ and ⬇ keys. Change the value until a conflict appears.

    What IRQ value caused a conflict?

Instructor initials: _____

17. Click the *Cancel* button twice to return to Device Manager. Close Device Manager.

Internet Discovery

Objective: To obtain specific information on the Internet regarding a computer or its associated parts

Parts: Computer with Internet access

Procedure: Use the Internet to answer the following questions. Assume your customer owns a Gateway M1634u notebook computer in answering Questions 1–2.

Questions:

1. Determine the procedure for accessing the computer's Setup program. Write the key(s) to press, the page number, and the URL where you found this information.

2. How many (if any) PC Card/ExpressCard slots does this notebook have and what type of slot is it? Write the answer and the URL where you found the information.

3. Another customer owns a Tyan S7025 motherboard. How many and what type of PCIe slots does this motherboard have? Write the answer and the URL where you found the information.

4. On the same Tyan S7025 motherboard, what motherboard jumper is used to clear CMOS? Write the answer and the URL where you found the information.

5. On the same Tyan S7025 motherboard, what BIOS menu option is used to configure the I/O address and IRQ for the first serial port? Write the answer and the URL where you found the answer.

Soft Skills

Objective: To enhance and fine tune a future technician's ability to listen, communicate in both written and oral form, and support people who use computers in a professional manner

Activities:

1. In teams, come up with a troubleshooting scenario that involves a computer technician who uses gun slinging techniques and the same scenario involving a technician who is methodical. Explain what each technician type does and how they solve the problem. Also, detail how they treat the customer differently. Determine ways of how a gun slinger technician might be harmful to a computer repair business.

2. After exploring the BIOS options, turn to a fellow student, pretend they are a customer over the phone, and walk the other student through accessing Setup. Explain the purpose of at least five of the options. Reverse roles and cover five other options. Be sure to act like a typical computer user when playing that role.

3. Brainstorm a troubleshooting scenario in which you fix the problem that involves accessing the Setup program, and/or an adapter. Document the problem using a word processing application. Create an invoice using either a word processing or spreadsheet application. Share your documents with others in the class.

3
System
Configuration

Critical Thinking Skills

Objective: To analyze and evaluate information as well as apply learned information to new or different situations

Activities:

1. Why do you think so few computers today have ISA adapters or slots?

2. Compare and contrast a post office with IRQs, I/O addresses, and memory addresses shown in Device Manager. For example, how might something that happens in a post office relate to an IRQ in a PC (or I/O address or memory address)?

3. Your parents want to buy a new computer and they are doing research. They ask you to explain whether they should buy a PCIe or an AGP video adapter. Explain to them (either verbally or in writing) the differences between them and your recommendation.

Disassembly and Power

Objectives

After completing this chapter you will be able to

- Describe how static electricity can damage computer components
- Describe what type of equipment causes RFI and EMI and what to do when they occur
- List tools a technician needs
- Disassemble and reassemble a computer
- Define and apply basic electronic terms that relate to computer support
- Perform basic checks, such as voltage and continuity
- Describe the purposes of a power supply
- Install a power supply and connect the motherboard and devices to it
- Recognize the different power supply output voltages

- Recognize different power connectors
- Apply appropriate power saving techniques
- Research and upgrade or replace a power supply
- Solve power problems
- Define and describe the purpose of different power protection devices
- Describe what to do if an electrical fire occurs
- Detail what to do when a computer component fails and must be thrown away
- Detail alternatives for outdated computer parts, including recycling or appropriate disposal
- Describe good written communication techniques

Disassembly Overview

It is seldom necessary to completely disassemble a computer. However, when a technician is first learning about PCs, disassembly can be both informative and fun. Technicians might disassemble parts of a computer to perform preventive cleaning or to troubleshoot a problem. It may also be appropriate to disassemble a computer when it has a problem of undetermined cause. Sometimes, the only way to diagnose a problem is to disassemble the computer outside the case or remove components one by one. Disassembling the computer outside the case may help with grounding problems. A **grounding** problem occurs when the motherboard or adapter is not properly installed and a trace (metal line on the motherboard or adapter) touches the computer frame, causing the adapter and possibly other components to stop working.

Electrostatic Discharge (ESD)

Many precautions must be taken when disassembling a computer. The electronic circuits located on the motherboard and adapters are subject to ESD. **ESD** (electrostatic discharge) is a difference of potential between two items that causes static electricity. Static electricity can damage electronic equipment without the technician's knowledge. The average person requires a static discharge of 3,000 volts before he or she feels it. An electronic component can be damaged with as little as 30 volts. Some electronic components may not be damaged the first time static electricity occurs. However, the effects of static electricity can be cumulative, weakening or eventually destroying a component. An ESD event is not recoverable—nothing can be done about the damage it induces. Electronic chips and memory modules are most susceptible to ESD strikes.

Atmospheric conditions affect static electricity. When humidity is low, the potential for ESD is greater than at any other time. Keep humidity above 50 percent to reduce the threat of ESD.

A technician can prevent ESD by using a variety of methods. The most common tactic is to use an **antistatic wrist strap**. One end encircles the technician's wrist. At the other end, an alligator clip attaches to the computer. The clip attaches to a grounding post or a metal part such as the power supply. The electronic symbol for ground follows:

An antistatic wrist strap allows the technician and the computer to be at the same voltage potential. As long as the technician and the computer or electronic part are at the same potential, static electricity does not occur. An exercise at the end of the chapter demonstrates how to attach an antistatic wrist strap and how to perform maintenance on it. Technicians should use an ESD wrist strap whenever possible.

A resistor inside the wrist strap protects the technician in case something accidentally touches the ground to which the strap attaches while he or she is working inside a computer. This resistor cannot protect the technician against the possible voltages inside a monitor. Refer to Figure 4.1 for an illustration of an antistatic wrist strap.

When *not* to wear an antistatic wrist strap
Technicians should not wear an ESD wrist strap when working inside a CRT monitor because of the high voltages there.

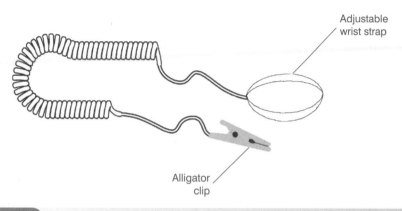

Adjustable wrist strap

Alligator clip

Figure 4.1   **Antistatic wrist strap**

Antistatic bags are good for storing spare adapters and motherboards when the parts are not in use. However, antistatic bags are not as effective after a few years. Antistatic mats are available to place underneath a computer being repaired; many of the mats have a snap for connecting the antistatic wrist strap. Antistatic heel straps are also available.

If an antistatic wrist strap is not available, you can still reduce the chance of ESD damage. After removing the computer case, if you are right-handed, place your bare left arm on the power supply. Remove the computer parts one by one, always keeping your left elbow (or some bare part of your arm) connected to the power supply. If you are left-handed, place your right arm on the power supply. By placing your elbow on the power supply, both hands are free to remove computer parts. This method is an effective way of keeping the technician and the computer at the same voltage potential, thus reducing the chance of ESD damage. It is not as safe as using an antistatic wrist strap. Also, removing the power cable from the back of the computer is a good idea. Power supplies provide a small amount of power to the motherboard even when the computer is powered off. Always unplug the computer and use an antistatic wrist strap when removing or replacing parts inside the computer!

EMI (Electromagnetic Interference)

EMI (electromagnetic interference, sometimes called EMR for electromagnetic radiation) is noise caused by electrical devices. Many devices can cause EMI, such as a computer, pencil sharpener, motor, vacuum cleaner, air conditioner, and fluorescent lighting. The electrical devices around the computer case, including the CRT-type monitor and speakers, cause more problems than the computer.

A specific type of electromagnetic interference that affects computers is **RFI** (radio frequency interference). RFI is simply those noises that occur in the radio frequency range. Anytime a computer has an intermittent problem, check the surrounding devices for the source of that problem. For example, if the computer only goes down when the pencil sharpener operates or when using the CD/DVD player, then EMI could be to blame. EMI problems are very hard to track to the source. Any electronic device including computers and printers can be a source of EMI/RFI. EMI/RFI can affect any electronic circuit. EMI can also come through power lines. Move the computer to a different wall outlet or to a totally different circuit to determine if the power outlet is the problem source. EMI can also affect files on a hard drive.

Tech Tip

Replace empty slot covers

To help with EMI and RFI problems, replace slot covers for expansion slots that are no longer being used. Slot covers also keep out dust and improve the airflow within the case.

Disassembly

Before a technician disassembles a computer, several steps should be performed or considered. The following list is helpful:

- Do not remove the motherboard battery or the configuration information in CMOS will be lost.
- Use proper grounding procedures to prevent ESD damage.
- Keep paper and pen nearby for note taking and diagramming. Even if you have taken computers apart for years, you might find something unique or different inside.
- Have ample workspace.
- When removing adapters, do not stack the adapters on top of one another.
- If possible, place removed adapters inside a special ESD protective bag.
- Handle each adapter or motherboard on the side edges. Avoid touching the gold contacts on the bottom of adapters. Sweat, oil, and dirt cause problems.
- Hard disk drives require careful handling. A very small jolt can cause damage to stored data.
- You can remove a power supply, but do not disassemble a CRT-style monitor or power supply without proper training and tools.

Tools

No chapter on disassembly and reassembly is complete without mentioning tools. Tools can be divided into two categories: (1) do not leave the office without and (2) nice to have in the office, home, or car.

Many technicians do not go on a repair call with a full tool case. Ninety-five percent of all repairs are completed with the following basic tools:

- Medium flat-tipped screwdriver
- Small flat-tipped tweaker screwdriver
- #1 Phillips screwdriver
- #2 Phillips screwdriver
- 1/4-inch nut driver
- 3/16-inch nut driver
- Pair of small diagonal cutters
- Pair of needlenose pliers

Screwdrivers take care of most disassemblies and reassemblies. Sometimes manufacturers place tie wraps on new parts, new cables, or the cables inside the computer case. The diagonal cutters are great for removing the tie wraps without cutting cables or damaging parts. Needlenose pliers are good for getting disks or disk parts out of disk drives, straightening bent pins on cables or connectors, and doing a million other things. Small tweaker screwdrivers and needlenose pliers are indispensable.

Many technicians start with a basic $15 microcomputer repair kit and build from there. A bargain table 6-in-1 or 4-in-1 combination screwdriver that has two sizes of flat blade and two sizes of Phillips is a common tool used by new technicians. A specialized Swiss army knife with screwdrivers is the favorite of some technicians. Other technicians prefer the all-in-one tool carried in a pouch that connects to their belt.

Do not use magnetized screwdrivers

Avoid using a magnetic screwdriver. It can cause permanent loss of data on hard or floppy disks. Magnetism can also induce currents into components and damage them. Sometimes, technicians are tempted to use a magnetic screwdriver when they drop a small part such as a screw into a hard-to-reach place or when something rolls under the motherboard. It is best to avoid using a magnetic screwdriver when working inside a computer.

Alternatives to the magnetic screwdriver include a screw pick-up tool and common sense. The screw pick-up tool is used in the hard-to-reach places and sometimes under the motherboard. If a screw rolls under the motherboard and cannot be reached, tilt the computer so that the screw rolls out. Sometimes the case must be tilted in different directions until the screw becomes dislodged.

There are tools that no one thinks of as tools, but which should be taken on a service call every time. They include: a pen or pencil with which to take notes and fill out the repair slip and a bootable disc containing the technician's favorite repair utilities. Usually a technician has several bootable disks or CDs for different operating systems and utilities. Often a flashlight comes in handy because some rooms and offices are dimly lit. Finally, do not forget to bring a smile and a sense of humor.

Tools that are nice to have, but not used daily, include the following:

- Multimeter
- Screw pick-up tool
- Screwdriver extension tool
- Soldering iron, solder, and flux
- Screw-starter tool
- Medium-size diagonal cutters
- Metric nut drivers
- Cable-making tools
- AC circuit tester
- Right-angled, flat-tipped, and Phillips screwdrivers
- Hemostats
- Pliers
- CD/DVD cleaning kit
- Network cable tester
- Nonstatic vacuum
- Disposable gloves

You could get some nice muscle tone from carrying all of these nice to have, but normally unnecessary tools. When starting out in computer repair, get the basics. As your career path and skill level grow, so will your toolkit. Nothing is worse than getting to a job site and not having the right tool. However, because there are no standards or limitations on what manufacturers can use in their product line, always having the right tool on hand is impossible. Always remember that no toolkit is complete without an antistatic wrist strap.

Reassembly

Reassembling a microcomputer is easy if the technician is careful and properly diagrams during the disassembly. Simple tasks such as inserting the CD/DVD drive in the correct drive bay become confusing after many parts have been removed. Writing down reminders takes less time than having to troubleshoot the computer because of poor reassembly. Reinsert all components into their proper place; be careful to replace all screws and parts. Install missing slot covers if possible.

Three major reassembly components are motherboards, cables, and connectors. Motherboards sometimes have plastic connectors called **standoffs** on the bottom. The standoffs slide into slots on the computer case. Do not remove the standoffs from the motherboard. Take the motherboard out of the case with the standoffs attached. The first step in removing a motherboard involves removing the screws that attach the motherboard to the case. Then, the motherboard (including the standoffs) slides to one side and lifts up. Some motherboards have retaining clips that must be lifted. Others have one or more retaining tabs that you must push while sliding the motherboard out of the case.

When reinstalling the motherboard, reverse the procedure used during disassembly. Ensure that the motherboard is securely seated into the case and that all retaining clips and/or screws are replaced. This procedure requires practice but eventually a technician will be able to tell when a motherboard is seated properly into the case. Visual inspection can also help. As a final step, ensure that the drives and cover are aligned properly when the case is reinstalled.

Cables and Connectors

When reassembling a computer, cables that connect a device to an adapter or motherboard can be tricky. Inserting a cable backward into a device or adapter can damage the device, motherboard, or adapter. Most cables are keyed so the cable only inserts into the connector one way. However, some cables or connectors are *not* keyed.

Each cable has a certain number of pins and all cables have a **pin 1**. Pin 1 on the cable connects to pin 1 on the connector.

Pin 1 is the cable edge that is colored

Pin 1 on a cable is easily identified by the colored stripe that runs down the edge of the cable.

In the unlikely event that the cable is *not* easily identified, both ends of the cable should be labeled with either a 1 or 2 on one side or a higher number, such as 24, 25, 49, 50, and so on, on the other end. Pins 1 and 2 are always on the same end of a cable. If you find a higher number, pin 1 is on the opposite end. Also, the cable connector usually has an arrow etched into its molding showing the pin 1 connection. Figure 4.2 shows pin 1 on a ribbon cable.

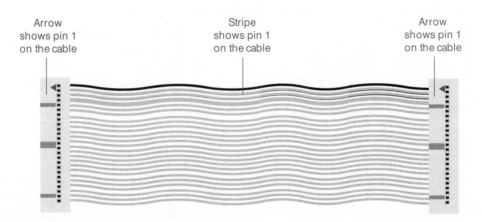

Arrow shows pin 1 on the cable   Stripe shows pin 1 on the cable   Arrow shows pin 1 on the cable

Figure 4.2   **Pin 1 on a ribbon cable**

Snug connections

When connecting cables to the motherboard or internal components, ensure that each cable is connected tightly, evenly, and securely.

Just as all cables have a pin 1, all connectors on devices, adapters, or motherboards have a pin 1. Pin 1 on the cable inserts into pin 1 on the connector. Cables are normally keyed so they only insert one way. Some manufacturers stencil a 1 or a 2 by the connector on the motherboard or adapter; however, on a black connector, it's difficult to see the small number. Numbers on adapters are easier to distinguish. When the number 2 is etched beside the adapter's connector, connect the cable's pin 1 to this side. Remember that pins 1 and 2 are always on the same side whether it is on a connector or on a cable. Some technicians use a permanent marker to label a cable's function. Figure 4.3 shows an example of a stenciled marking beside the adapter's connector. Even though Figure 4.3 illustrates the number 2 etched onto the adapter, other manufacturers do just the opposite; they stencil a higher number, such as 33, 34, 39, or 40, beside the opposite end of the connector.

Motherboard connectors are usually notched so that the cable only inserts one way; however, not all cables are notched. Some motherboards have pin 1 (or the opposite pin) labeled. Always refer to the motherboard documentation for proper cable orientation into a motherboard connector. Figure 4.4 shows three motherboard connectors.

Some manufacturers do not put any markings on the cable connector; even so, there is a way to determine which way to connect the cable. Remove the adapter, motherboard, or device from

Pin 1 of the cable
connects to
pin 1 on the
adapter connector

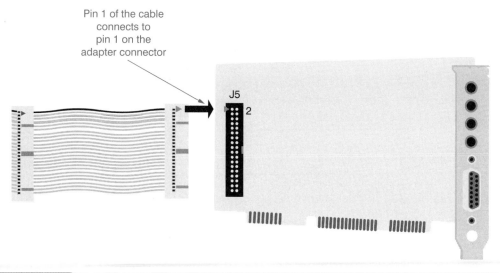

Figure 4.3   **Pin 1 on an adapter**

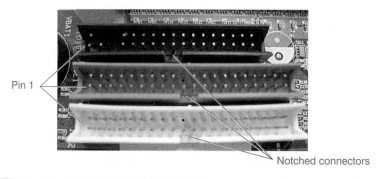

Pin 1

Notched connectors

Figure 4.4   **Three motherboard connectors**

the computer. Look where the connector solders or connects to the motherboard or adapter. Turn the adapter over. Notice the silver blobs, known as **solder joints**, on the back of the motherboard or adapter. Solder joints connect electronic components to the motherboard or adapter. The connector's solder joints are normally round, *except for the solder joint for pin 1*, which is square. Look for the square solder joint on the back of the connector. If the square solder joint is not apparent on the connector, look for other connectors or solder joints that are square. All chips and connectors mount onto a motherboard in the same direction—all pin 1 is normally oriented in the same direction. If one pin 1 is found, the other connectors orient in the same direction. Insert the cable so pin 1 matches the square solder joint of the connector. Figure 4.5 shows a square solder joint for a connector on the back of an adapter.

Tech Tip

Pin 1 is on the opposite end from the higher stenciled number

If a higher number is stenciled beside the connector, connect pin 1 of the cable *to the opposite end of that connector*.

Specific cables connect the motherboard to lights, ports, or buttons on the front panel. These include the power button, a reset button, USB ports, FireWire ports, a microphone port, a headphone port, speakers, fans, the hard drive usage light, and the power light, to name a few. Be very careful when removing and reinstalling these cables. Usually, each one of these has a connector that must attach to the appropriate motherboard pins. Be sure to check all ports and buttons once you have reconnected these cables. Refer to the motherboard documentation if your diagramming or notes (or lack of them) are inaccurate.

4
Disassembly and Power

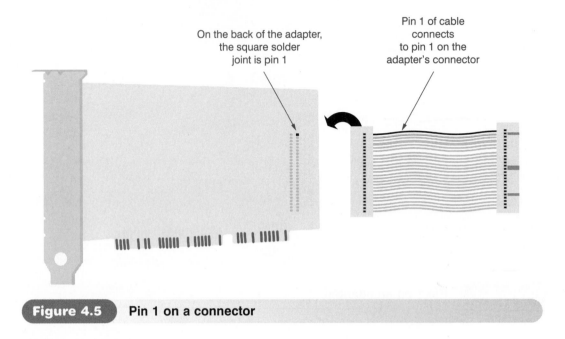

On the back of the adapter, the square solder joint is pin 1

Pin 1 of cable connects to pin 1 on the adapter's connector

Figure 4.5   **Pin 1 on a connector**

Hard Drives

Hard drives must be handled with care when disassembling a computer. Inside the hard drives are hard platters with tiny read/write heads located just millimeters above the platters. A small jolt can make the read/write heads drop down and touch the platter, causing damage to the platter and/or the read/write heads. The platter is used to store data and applications. With older hard drives, a head parking utility locks the heads in place away from the area where data is stored on the platter. Today's hard drives have self-parking heads that do not require software to make them pull away to a safe area. Instead, when the computer powers off, the heads pull away automatically. Always be careful neither to jolt nor to jar the hard drive when removing it from the computer. Even with self-parking heads, improper handling can cause damage to the hard drive. An exercise at the end of the chapter contains step-by-step directions for disassembling and reassembling a computer.

Preventive Maintenance

A computer should be cleaned at least once a year in a normal working environment. A computer runs longer and more efficiently if preventive maintenance is periodically undertaken. **Preventive maintenance** includes certain procedures performed to prolong the life of the computer. Some computer companies sell maintenance contracts that include a preventive maintenance program. Typical preventive measures include vacuuming the computer and cleaning the floppy drive heads, CD/DVD laser, keyboard keys, printers, and monitor screen. Preventive exercises for many individual devices are described in their respective chapters. For example, the steps detailing how to clean CD/DVDs are included in Chapter 8. This section gives an overview of a preventive maintenance program and some general tips about cleaning solvents.

Repair companies frequently provide a preventive maintenance kit for service calls. The kit normally includes a portable vacuum cleaner, special vacuum cleaner bags for laser printers, a can of compressed air, a floppy head cleaning kit, urethane swabs, monitor wipes, lint-free cloths, general purpose cloths, general purpose cleanser, denatured alcohol, mouse ball cleaning kit, an antistatic brush, gold contact cleaner, and a CD/DVD cleaning kit.

The vacuum is used to suck dirt from the inside of the computer. Ensure that you use non-metallic attachments. Some vacuum cleaners have the ability to blow air out. Vacuum first and then set the vacuum cleaner to blow. The blowing action is used to get dust out of hard-to-reach places. Compressed air can also be used in these situations. The floppy head cleaning kit is used to clean the read/write heads on the floppy drive. Monitor wipes are used on the front of the monitor screen. Monitor wipes with antistatic solution work best.

Urethane swabs are used to clean between the keys on a keyboard. If a laptop key is sticking, remove the laptop keyboard before spraying or using contact cleaner on it. Notebook touchpads normally require no maintenance except wiping them with a dampened lint-free cloth to remove residual finger oil.

Tech Tip

Be careful when cleaning LCD monitors and laptop displays

Use one of the following methods: (1) wipes specifically designed for LCDs; (2) a soft lint-free cloth dampened with either water or a mixture of isopropyl alcohol and water. Never put liquid directly on the display and ensure the display is dry before closing the laptop.

General-purpose cleanser is used to clean the outside of the case (after removing the case from the computer) and to clean the desktop areas under and around the computer. Never spray or pour liquid on any computer part. Liquid cleaners are used with soft lint-free cloths or lint-free swabs.

Denatured alcohol is used on rubber rollers, such as those found inside printers. An antistatic brush can be used to brush dirt away from hard-to-reach places. Gold contact cleaner is used to clean adapter contacts as well as contacts on laptop batteries and the contacts where the battery inserts. A useful CD/DVD cleaning kit can include a lens cleaner that removes dust and debris from an optical lens, a disk cleaner that removes dust, dirt, fingerprints, and oils from the disk, and a scratch repair kit used to resurface, clean, and polish CDs and DVDs.

When using cleaning solutions, many companies have **MSDS** (material safety data sheets) that contain information about a product, including its toxicity, storage, and disposal. Your state may also have specific disposal procedures for chemical solvents. Check with the company's safety coordinator for storage and disposal information.

When performing preventive maintenance, power on the computer to be certain it operates. Perform an audio and visual inspection of the computer as it boots. It is a terrible feeling to perform preventive maintenance on a computer, only to power it on and find it does not work. You will wonder if the cleaning you performed caused the problem or if the computer had a problem before the preventive maintenance. Once the computer powers up, go into Setup and copy the current settings in case the battery dies. Keep this documentation with the computer. Some technicians tape it to the inside of the case.

Tech Tip

Know your state aerosol can disposal laws

Some states have special requirements for aerosol can disposal especially if the can is clogged and still contains some product. Other states allow aerosol can disposal through normal waste disposal methods.

Power off the computer, remove the power cord, and vacuum it with a non-metallic attachment. Do *not* start with compressed air or by blowing dust out of the computer because the dirt and dust will simply go into the air and eventually fall back into the computer and surrounding equipment. After vacuuming as much as possible, use compressed air to blow the dust out of hard-to-reach places, such as inside the power supply and under the motherboard. If performing maintenance on a notebook computer, remove as many modules as possible, such as the CD/DVD drive, battery, and hard drive, before vacuuming or using the compressed air. Inform people in the immediate area that they might want to leave the area if they have allergies.

If you remove an adapter from an expansion slot, replace it into the same slot. If the computer battery is on a riser board, it is best to leave the riser board connected to the motherboard so the system does not lose its configuration information. The same steps covered in the disassembly section of this chapter hold true for performing preventive maintenance.

When you perform preventive maintenance, take inventory of what is installed in the computer, such as the hard drive size, amount of RAM, available hard drive space, and so on. During the maintenance procedure, communicate with the users. Ask if the computer has been giving them any trouble lately or if it has been performing adequately. Computer users like to know that you care about their computing needs. Also, users frequently ask common sense questions, such as whether sunlight or cold weather harms the computer. Always respond with answers the user can understand. Users appreciate it when you explain things in terms they comprehend and that make sense.

Tech Tip

Use the preventive maintenance call as a time for updates

A preventive maintenance call is a good time to check for BIOS, antivirus, and driver updates.

4

Disassembly and Power

The preventive maintenance call is the perfect opportunity to check computers for viruses. Normally, first you would clean the computer. Then, while the virus checker is running, you might clean external peripherals, such as printers. Preventive maintenance measures help limit computer problems as well as provide a chance to interact with customers and help with a difficulty that may seem minuscule, but could worsen. The preventive maintenance call is also a good time to take inventory of all hardware and software installed. In a preventive maintenance call, entry level technicians can see the different computer types and begin learning the computer components.

Basic Electronics Overview

A technician needs to know a few basic electronic terms and concepts when testing components. The best place to start is with electricity. There are two types of electricity: AC and DC. The electricity provided by a wall outlet is **AC** (alternating current) and the type of electricity used by computer components is **DC** (direct current). Devices such as radios, TVs, and toasters use AC power. Low voltage DC power is used for the computer's internal components or anything powered by batteries. The computer's power supply converts AC electricity from the wall outlet to DC for the internal components. Electricity is nothing more than electrons flowing through a conductor, just as water runs through a pipe. With AC, the electrons flow alternately in both directions. With DC, the electrons flow in one direction only.

Electronic Terms

Tech Tip

Voltage, current, power, and resistance are common electronic terms used in the computer industry. **Voltage**, which is a measure of the pressure pushing electrons through a circuit is measured in **volts**. A power supply's output is measured in volts. Power supplies typically put out +3.3 volts, +5 volts, –5 volts, +12 volts, and –12 volts. The term *volts* is also used to describe voltage from a wall outlet. The wall outlet voltage is normally 120VAC (120 volts AC). Exercises at the end of the chapter explain how to take voltage readings.

Polarity is only important when measuring DC voltage

When a technician measures the voltage coming out of a power supply, the black meter lead (which is negative) connects to the black wire from the power supply (which is ground). The red meter lead connects to either the +5 or +12 volt wires from the power supply.

Figure 4.6 shows a photograph of a DC voltage reading being taken on the power connectors coming from the computer's power supply. The meter leads are inserted correctly and the voltage level is of the correct polarity.

The reading on the meter could be the opposite of what it should be if the meter's leads are reversed. Since electrons flow from one area where there are many of them (negative polarity) to an area where there are few

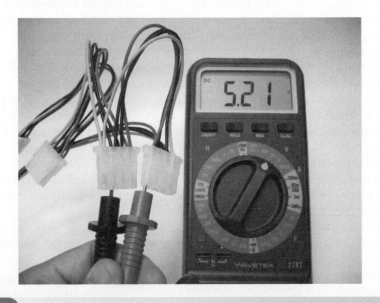

Figure 4.6   **DC voltage reading**

electrons (positive polarity), polarity shows which way an electric current will flow. Polarity is the condition of being positive or negative with respect to some reference point. Polarity is not important when measuring AC.

Monitors and power supplies can have dangerous voltage levels. Monitors can have up to 35,000 volts going to the back of the CRT (cathode ray tube). 120 volts AC is present inside the power supply. Power supplies and monitors have capacitors inside them. A **capacitor** is a component that holds a charge even after the computer is turned off. Capacitors inside monitors can hold a charge

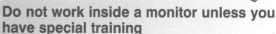

Do not work inside a monitor unless you have special training

Monitors require high voltage meters and special precautions.

for several hours after the monitor has been powered off. Capacitance is measured in farads. Note that a laptop display uses low DC voltage, not AC like that present in a desktop computer.

Another important consideration when taking voltage readings is to set the meter for the correct type of current. The AC voltage setting is for alternating current and the DC voltage setting is for direct current. Meters may have different symbols for AC and DC voltage, but the common symbols found on a meter for AC voltage are as follows:

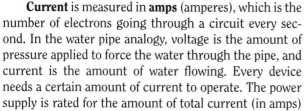

The common meter symbols for DC voltage are as follows:

$$— \quad \text{or} \quad \cdots \quad \text{or} \quad \overline{v}$$

Use the highest setting when measuring an unknown voltage

Some meters have multiple voltage range settings. When measuring an unknown voltage, set the meter to the highest setting before taking any readings. The meter may be damaged if it is set to a low range and the measured voltage is a much higher level.

Always refer to the meter's documentation if you are unsure of the symbols. Know whether you are measuring AC or DC voltage and set the meter to the appropriate setting. Also note that some meters have voltage ranges (such as 0–10V, 0–100V, etc.) that must be set *before* taking a measurement. Some meters automatically sense what type of voltage is being measured and do not have these settings.

Current is measured in **amps** (amperes), which is the number of electrons going through a circuit every second. In the water pipe analogy, voltage is the amount of pressure applied to force the water through the pipe, and current is the amount of water flowing. Every device needs a certain amount of current to operate. The power supply is rated for the amount of total current (in amps)

Current is what kills people when an electrical shock is received

Voltage determines how much current flows through the body. A high current and low voltage situation is the most dangerous.

it can supply at each voltage level. For example, a power supply could be rated at 20 amps for the 5-volt level and 8 amps for the 12-volt level.

Power is measured in **watts**, which is how much electrical work is being done. It is determined by multiplying volts by amps. Power supplies are described as providing a maximum number of watts. This is the sum of all outputs: For example, 5 volts × 20 amps (100 watts) plus 12V 8 amps (96 watts) equals 196 watts. An exercise at the end of the chapter explains how current and power relate to a technician's job.

All power supplies are not created equal

A technician needs to replace a power supply with one that provides an equal or greater amount of power. Search the Internet for power supply reviews. A general rule of thumb is that if two power supplies are equal in wattage, the heavier one is better because it uses a bigger transformer, bigger heat sinks, and more quality components.

Resistance is measured in **ohms**, which is the amount of opposition to current in an electronic circuit. The resistance range on a meter can be used to check continuity or check whether a fuse is good. A conductor in a cable or a good fuse will have very low resistance to electricity (close to zero ohms). A broken wire or a bad fuse will have very high resistance (millions of ohms, sometimes shown as infinite ohms). A **continuity** check is used to determine if a wire has a break in it. For example, a cable is normally made up of several wires that go from one connector to

4

Disassembly and Power

Tech Tip

Always unplug the computer before working inside it
The ATX power supply provides power to the motherboard, even if the computer is powered off. Leaving the power cord attached can cause damage when replacing components such as the CPU and RAM.

another. If you were to measure the continuity from one end of a wire to the other, it should show no resistance. If the wire has a break in it, the meter shows infinite resistance. Figure 4.7 shows an example of a good wire reading and a broken wire reading.

Good connection

Broken wire

Figure 4.7   Sample meter readings

Tech Tip

Dealing with small connections and a meter

Some connectors have small pin connections. Use a thin meter probe or insert a thin wire, such as a paper clip, into the hole and touch the meter to the wire to take your reading.

Tech Tip

Use the right fuse or lose

Never replace a fuse with one that has a higher amperage rating. You could destroy electronic circuits or cause a fire by allowing too much current to be passed by the fuse, defeating the fuse's purpose.

Digital meters have different ways of displaying infinity. Always refer to the meter manual for this reading. When checking continuity, the meter is placed on the ohms setting, as shown in Figure 4.7. The ohms setting is usually illustrated by an omega symbol (Ω).

Polarity is not important when performing a continuity check. Either meter lead (red or black) can be placed at either end of the wire. However, you do need a pin-out diagram (wiring list) for the cable before you can check continuity because pin 1 at one end could connect to a different pin number at the other end. An exercise at the end of the chapter steps through this process.

The same concept of continuity applies to fuses. A fuse has a tiny wire inside it that extends from end to end. The fuse is designed so that the wire melts (breaks) if too much current flows through it. The fuse keeps excessive current from damaging electronic circuits or starting a fire.

A fuse is rated for a particular amount of current. For example, a 5-amp fuse protects a circuit if the amount of current exceeds 5 amps.

Take the fuse out of the circuit before testing it. A good fuse has a meter reading of 0 ohms (or close to that amount). A blown fuse shows a meter reading of infinite ohms. Refer to the section on resistance and Figure 4.7. An exercise at the end of this chapter demonstrates how to check a fuse.

A technician needs to be familiar with basic electronic terms and checks. Table 4.1 consolidates this information.

Table 4.1	Basic electronics terms	
Term	**Value**	**Usage**
Voltage	Volts	Checking AC voltage on a wall outlet (typically 120VAC). Checking the DC output voltage from a power supply (typically +/– 12 and +/–5VDC).
Current	Amps (amperes)	Each device needs a certain amount of current to operate. The power supply is rated for total current in amps for each voltage level (such as 20 amps for 5-volt power and 8 amps for 12-volt power).
Resistance	Ohms	Resistance is the amount of opposition there is to electric current. Resistance is used to check continuity on cables and fuses. A cable that shows little or no resistance has no breaks in it. A good fuse shows no resistance. If a cable has a break in it or if a fuse is bad, the resistance is infinite.
Wattage	Watts	Watts is a measure of power and is derived by multiplying amps by volts. Power supply output is measured in watts. Also, UPS's are rated in Volt-Amps. The size of UPS purchased depends on how many devices plug in to it.

Power Supply Overview

The power supply is an essential component within the computer; no other internal computer device works without it. The power supply converts AC to DC, distributes lower voltage DC power to components throughout the computer, and provides cooling through the use of a fan located inside the power supply. The power supply is sometimes a source of unusual problems. The effects of the problems can range from those not noticed by the user to those that shut down the system.

There are two basic types of power supplies: switching and linear. A computer uses a switching power supply. It provides efficient power to all the computer's internal components (and possibly to some external ones, such as USB devices). It also generates minimum heat, comes in small sizes, and is cheaper than linear power supplies. A switching power supply requires a load (something attached to it) in order to operate properly. With today's power supplies, a motherboard is usually a sufficient load, but a technician should always check the power supply's specifications to be sure.

A good power supply has internal circuitry that shuts down the power supply if it is without a load—that is, it is connected to something. However, some cheap power supplies can be destroyed if powered on without a device or the motherboard connected. Exercises at the end of the chapter familiarize the technician with voltage checks on a computer. Use extreme caution when doing AC voltage checks; AC voltage is high enough to harm you! Also, be careful when checking DC voltages. Touching the meter to two different voltages simultaneously or to a DC voltage and another circuit can damage the computer.

Tech Tip

Powering on a power supply without anything attached could damage the power supply

Do not power on a power supply without connecting to the motherboard and possibly a device such as a floppy drive, CD/DVD drive, or hard drive. An ATX power supply usually requires a motherboard connection only.

4
Disassembly and Power

Power Supply Form Factors

Just as motherboards come in different shapes and sizes, so do power supplies. Today's power supply form factors are ATX, ATX12V v1.x, and ATX12V v2.x. Other form factors include LFX12V (low profile), SFX12V (small form factor), EPS12V (used with server motherboards and has an extra 8-pin connector), CFX12V (compact form factor), TFX12V (thin form factor), WTX12V (workstation form factor for high-end workstations and select servers), and FlexATX (smaller systems that have no more than three expansion slots). Both Intel and AMD certify specific power supplies that work with their processors. The same is true for video card manufacturers. A computer manufacturer can also have a proprietary power supply form factor that is not compatible with other vendors or even computer models. Laptop power supplies are commonly proprietary.

Tech Tip

The motherboard and power supply must be compatible

The motherboard form factor and the power supply form factor must fit in the case and work together. For optimum performance, research what connectors and form factors are supported by both components.

The ATX12V version 2 standard has a 24-pin motherboard connector that does away with the need for the extra 6-pin auxiliary connector and adds a SATA power connector. Some 24-pin motherboard connectors accept the 20-pin power supply connector. Table 4.2 lists the possible ATX power supply connectors.

Table 4.2	**ATX power supply connectors**	
Connector	**Notes**	**Voltage(s)**
24-pin	Main ATX power connector to the motherboard	+3.3, +5, +12, –12
20-pin	Main power connector to the motherboard	+3.3, +5, –5, +12, –12
15-pin	SATA connector	+3, +5, +12
8-pin	12V for CPU	+12V
6-pin	PCIe video; connects to PCI video adapter	+12V
6-pin	Sometimes labeled as AUX; connects to the motherboard if it has a connector	+3.3, +5
4-pin **Molex**	Connects to peripheral devices such as hard drives and CD/DVD drives	+5, +12
4-pin **Berg**	Connects to peripheral devices such as the floppy drive	+5, +12
4-pin	Sometimes labeled as AUX or 12V; connects to the motherboard for CPU	+12V
3-pin	Used to monitor fan speed	N/A

Tech Tip

Not all 24-pin motherboard connectors accept 20-pin power supply connectors

You can purchase a 24-pin to 20-pin power adapter. A Web site containing information regarding power supply form factors is http://www.formfactors.org.

Figure 4.8 shows a few ATX power supply connectors. Figure 4.9 shows the ATX power supply connectors. Figure 4.10 (on page 116) illustrates the compatibility between the two ATX motherboard connector standards. Notice in Figure 4.10 how the power cable is only one connector, notched so the cable inserts into it one way only. This is a much better design than older power supplies where two connectors were used that could be reversed. Also, notice that a **power good signal** (labeled PWR_OK in the figure) goes to the motherboard. When the computer is turned on, part of POST is to allow the power supply to run a test on each of the voltage levels. The voltage levels must be correct before any other devices are tested and allowed to initialize. If the power is OK, a power good signal is sent to the motherboard. If the power good signal is not sent from the power supply, a timer chip on the motherboard resets the CPU. Once a power good signal is sent, the CPU begins executing software from the BIOS. Figure 4.10 also shows the +5vsb connection to provide standby power for features such as Wake on LAN or Wake on Ring (covered later in the chapter).

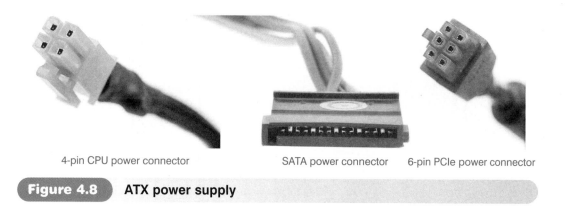

4-pin CPU power connector   SATA power connector   6-pin PCIe power connector

Figure 4.8   **ATX power supply**

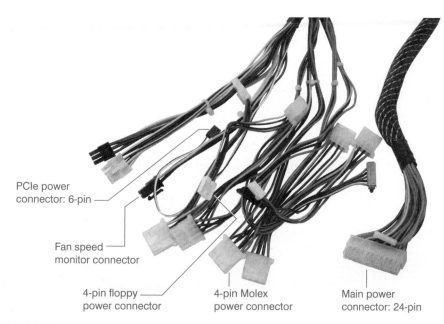

PCIe power
connector: 6-pin

Fan speed
monitor connector

4-pin floppy   4-pin Molex   Main power
power connector   power connector   connector: 24-pin

Figure 4.9   **ATX power supply connectors**

A high-quality power supply delays sending the power good signal until all of the power supply's voltages have a chance to stabilize. Some cheap power supplies do not delay the power good signal. Other cheap power supplies do not provide the power good circuitry at all, but instead tie five volts to the signal, sending a power good signal even when it is not there.

The number and quantity of connectors available on a power supply depends on the power supply manufacturer. If a device requires a Berg connector and the only one available is a Molex, a Molex-to-Berg connector converter can be purchased. If a SATA device needs a power connection, a Molex-to-SATA converter is available. Figure 4.11 shows a Molex-to-Berg converter and a Molex-to-SATA converter.

The power supply connectors can connect to any device; there is *not* a specific connector for the hard drive, the CD/DVD drive, and so on. If there are not enough connectors from the power supply for the number of devices installed in the computer, a Y power connector can be purchased at a computer or electronics store. The Y connector adapts a single Molex connector to two Molex connectors for two devices. Verify that the power supply can output enough power to handle the extra device being installed. Figure 4.12 shows a Y power connector.

Tech Tip

Power converters and Y connectors are good to have in your tool kit

When a service call involves adding a new device, having various power converters available as part of your tool kit is smart.

4

Disassembly and Power

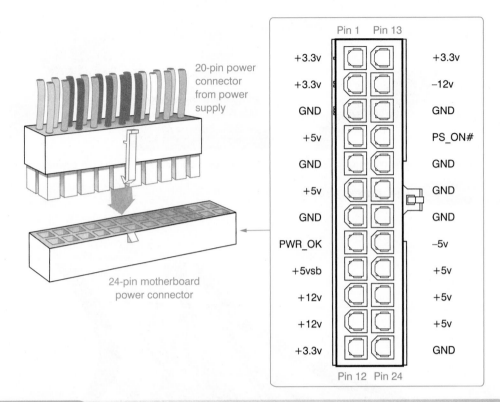

Figure 4.10   ATX 24- and 20-pin motherboard connectivity

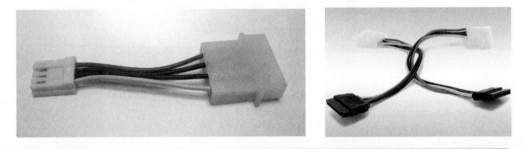

Figure 4.11   Molex-to-Berg and Molex-to-SATA converters

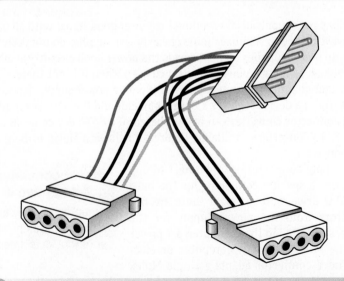

Figure 4.12   Y Molex connector

Purposes of a Power Supply

The power from a wall outlet is high voltage AC. The type of power computers need is low voltage DC. All computer parts (the electronic chips on the motherboard and adapters, the electronics on the drives, and the motors in the floppy drive, hard drive, and CD/DVD drive) need DC power to operate. Power supplies in general come in two types—linear and switching. Computers use switching power supplies. The main functions of the power supply include the following:

- Convert AC to DC
- Provide DC voltage to the motherboard, adapters, and peripheral devices
- Provide cooling and facilitate air flow through the case

One purpose of the power supply is to convert AC to DC so the computer has proper power to run its components. The ATX power supply does not connect to the front panel switch as the old AT-style power supplies did. With the ATX power supply, a connection from the front panel switch to the motherboard simply provides a 5-volt signal that allows the motherboard to tell the power supply to turn on. This 5-volt signal allows ATX power supplies to support ACPI, which is covered later in the chapter, and also lets the motherboard and operating system control the power supply. Figure 4.13 shows the front panel connections to the motherboard.

Tech Tip

On an ATX power supply that has an on/off switch, ensure it is set to the *on* position

If an ATX power supply switch is present and in the *off* position, the motherboard and operating system cannot turn the power supply on. Some ATX power supplies do not have external on/off switches and the operating system is the only way to power down the computer.

Figure 4.13 **Front panel connections to the motherboard**

Another purpose of the power supply is to distribute proper DC voltage to each component. Several cables with connectors come out of the power supply. With ATX motherboards, there is only a 20- or 24-pin connector used to connect power to the motherboard. The power connector inserts only one way into the motherboard connector. Figure 4.14 shows the ATX connector being inserted into the motherboard.

4
Disassembly and Power

Figure 4.14   **Installing the ATX power connector on the motherboard**

Tech Tip

Don't block air vents
Whether the computer is a desktop model, a tower model, or a desktop model mounted in a stand on the floor, ensure that nothing blocks the air vents in the computer case. For laptops, do not place the laptop on a blanket or pillow causing the vents to be blocked.

Tech Tip

Be careful when installing an auxiliary fan
Place the fan so the outflow of air moves in the same direction as the flow of air generated by the power supply. If an auxiliary fan is installed inside the case in the wrong location, the auxiliary airflow could work against the power supply airflow, reducing the cooling effect. Figure 2.15 in Chapter 2 details how air flow can be aided with an auxiliary fan.

Another purpose for the power supply is to provide cooling for the computer. The power supply's fan circulates air throughout the computer. Most computer cases have air vents on one side, both sides, or in the rear of the computer. The ATX-style power supply blows air inside the case instead of out the back. This is known as reverse flow cooling. The air blows over the processor and memory to keep them cool. This type of power supply keeps the inside of the computer cleaner than older styles. Refer to Figure 2.15 to refamiliarize yourself with airflow in an ATX computer.

Electronic components generate a great deal of heat, but are designed to withstand fairly high temperatures. Auxiliary fans can be purchased to help cool the internal components of a computer. Some cases have an extra mount and cutout for an auxiliary fan. Some auxiliary fans mount in adapter slots or drive bays.

Power Supply Voltages

Refer to Figure 4.10 and notice how +3.3, +5, –5, +12, and –12 volts are supplied to the motherboard. The motherboard and adapters use +3.3 and +5 volts. The –5 volts is seldom used. If the motherboard has integrated serial ports, they sometimes use +12 and –12 volt power. Hard drives and CD/DVD drives commonly use +5 and +12 volts. The +12 voltage is used to operate the device motors found in drives, the CPU, internal cooling fans, and the graphics card. Drives are now being made that use +5 volt motors. Chips use +5 volts and +3.3 volts. The +3.3 volts are also used for memory, AGP/PCI/PCIe adapters, and some laptop fans. The negative voltages are seldom used.

A technician must occasionally check voltages in a system. There are four basic checks for power supply situations: (1) wall outlet AC voltage, (2) DC voltages going to the motherboard, (3) DC voltages going to a device, and (4) ground or lack of voltage with an outlet tester. A **power supply tester** can be used to check DC power levels on the different power supply connectors.

Laptop Travel and Storage

When traveling with a laptop, remove all cards that insert into slots and store them in containers so that their contacts do not become dirty and cause intermittent problems. Remove all media discs such as CDs or DVDs. Check that drive doors and devices are securely latched. Ensure that the laptop is powered off or in hibernate mode (not in suspend or standby power mode, which is covered later in the chapter).

Carry the laptop in a padded case. If you have to place the laptop on an airport security conveyor belt, ensure that the laptop is not placed upside down, which could cause damage to the display. Never place objects on top of a laptop or pick up the laptop by the edges of the display when the laptop is opened. When shipping a laptop, place it in a properly padded box. The original shipping box is a safe container.

The United States has some regulations about lithium batteries on airplanes. If battery contacts come in contact with metal or other batteries, the battery could short-circuit and cause a fire. For this reason, any lithium batteries are to be kept in original packaging. If original packaging is not available, place electrical tape over the battery terminals or place each battery in an individual bag. Spare lithium batteries are not allowed in checked baggage but can be taken in carry-on bags. More tips for laptop and wireless network use when traveling follow.

- Most people do not need a spare Li-ion battery. If it is not being used constantly, it is best not to buy one. The longer the spare sits unused, the shorter the lifespan it will have.
- Buy the correct battery recommended by the laptop manufacturer.
- Do not use the DVD/CD player when running on battery power.
- Turn off the wireless adapter if a wireless network is not being used.
- In the power options, configure the laptop for hibernate rather than standby (covered later in the chapter).
- Save work only when necessary and turn off the autosave feature.
- Reduce the screen brightness.
- Keep the hard drive defragmented (before running on battery power).
- Avoid using external USB devices such as Flash drives or external hard drives.
- Add more RAM (to reduce swapping of information from the hard drive to RAM to CPU).
- Keep battery contacts clean (with a dab of rubbing alcohol on a lint free swab once a month).
- Avoid running multiple programs.
- Avoid temperature extremes.

Laptops have heating issues, as do any electronic devices. The following can help with laptop overheating:

- Locate air vents and keep them unblocked and clean. Do not place a laptop on your lap to work.
- In the BIOS settings, check the temperature settings for when fans turn on.
- Check laptop manufacturer Web site or documentation to see if any fan/temperature monitoring gauges are available.
- Place a laptop on something that elevates it from the desk, such as drink coasters. In addition, pads, trays, and mats can be purchased with fans that are AC powered or USB powered.

Laptop Power

A portable computer (laptop) uses either an AC connection or a battery as its power source. On most models, when the laptop connects to AC power, the battery normally recharges. Laptop batteries are usually modules with one or two release latches that are used to remove the module. Figure 4.15 shows a Dell laptop computer with its battery module removed. Battery technologies have improved in the past few years, probably due to the

Tech Tip

Check input voltage selector

Some power supplies and laptops have input voltage selectors; others have the ability to accept input from 100 to 240 volts for use in various countries. Ensure that the power supply accepts or is set to the proper input voltage.

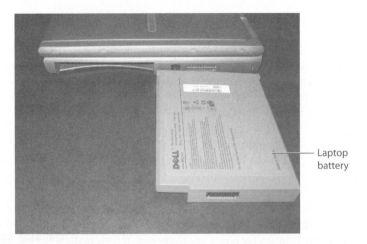

Laptop battery

Figure 4.15   Dell laptop battery

Tech Tip

Do not power on a laptop computer after a temperature change

Computers are designed to work within a range of temperatures. Any sudden change is not good for them. If a laptop computer is in a car all night and the temperature drops, then the laptop should be returned to room temperature before you power it on. It is bad for a computer to sit in direct sunlight, just as it is bad for a person to sit in the sun too long. Inside the computer case it is usually 40° hotter than outside. Direct sunlight will make a computer run hotter, which may cause a particular component to exceed its temperature rating.

Tech Tip

Do not fully discharge a Li-ion battery

Li-ion batteries do not suffer from the memory effect, as did some nickel-based batteries. Fully discharging a lithium battery, such as an Li-ion battery, is actually bad for it, but most lithium batteries have a circuit to prevent the battery from being totally discharged.

Tech Tip

Keep Li-ion batteries cool

Li-ion batteries last longer if they are kept cool (not frozen). If storing an Li-ion battery, the battery should only be 40 percent charged and placed in a refrigerator to prolong its life.

development of more devices that need battery power, such as digital cameras, portable CD and DVD players, and PDAs (personal digital assistants).

Until 1996 the NiCad (nickel cadmium) battery was the most popular type of portable computer battery. NiCad batteries were said to be subject to a memory effect, which means that the battery could not be fully recharged if it was not fully drained. In reality, the NiCad battery memory effect is rare.

NiCad batteries were replaced with lighter and more powerful **NiMH** (nickel-metal hydride) **batteries**. These batteries were replaced with **Li-ion** (lithium-ion) **batteries**, which are very light and can hold a charge longer than any other type. They are also more expensive. Besides laptops, mobile phones, portable media players, and digital cameras use Li-ion batteries. Li-ion batteries lose their charge over time even if they are not being used. Use your laptop with battery-provided power. Do not keep a laptop that has an Li-ion battery plugged into an AC outlet all the time. Calibrate a laptop battery according to manufacturer instructions so the battery meter displays correctly.

Li-ion polymer batteries are similar to Li-ion batteries, except they are packed in pouched cells. This design allows for smaller batteries and a more efficient use of space, which is important in the portable computer and mobile device industries. For environmentalists, the zinc-air battery is the one to watch. AER Energy Resources, Inc., has several patents on a battery that uses oxygen to generate electricity. Air is allowed to flow during battery discharge and is blocked when the battery is not in use. This battery holds a charge for extended periods of time. Another upcoming technology is fuel cells. Fuel cells used for a laptop can provide power for 5 to 10 hours.

ACPI (Advanced Configuration and Power Interface)

Today's computer user needs to leave the computer on for extended periods of time in order to receive faxes, run computer maintenance tasks, automatically answer phone calls, and download software upgrades and patches. Network managers want control of computers so they can push software upgrades out, perform backups, download software upgrades and patches, and perform tests. Laptop users have always been plagued by power management problems, such as short battery life, inconsistent handling of screen blanking, and screen blanking in the middle of presentations. These problems occurred because originally the BIOS controlled power. Power management has changed.

APM (Advanced Power Management) was originally developed by Microsoft, Toshiba, and Intel. APM allows the operating system to control devices such as the hard drive and monitor when the computer is not in use. APM further developed into a standard known as **ACPI** (Advanced Configuration and Power Interface), which combines the features of APM and plug and play to give the motherboard and operating system control over various devices' power and modes of operation. Common components that can be controlled through ACPI include the CPU, hard drive, CD/DVD drive, monitor, network adapter, and printer; and devices controlled through the computer, such as VCR, TV, phone, fax machine, and stereo. All ACPI user preferences are set through the operating system, although the computer must first have ACPI turned on through the system Setup program.

In Windows XP, the ACPI settings are controlled through the *Power Options* control panel. With Vista/7, the Power Options control panel can be accessed through *System and Maintenance* (Vista)/*Security* (7) and also the *Hardware and Sound* control panels. Vista/7 have three power plans (Balanced, Power Saver, and High Performance), and a customized plan can be created. Note that some devices, such as network card, can have a Power Management tab available through the *Properties* dialog box to control power for that particular device.

With ACPI, the user can control how the power switch operates and when power to specific devices, such as the hard drive and monitor, is lowered. For example, the *Instant On/Off* BIOS setting can control how long the power switch is held in before the power supply turns on or off. Case temperatures, CPU temperatures, and CPU fans can be monitored. The power supply can be adjusted for power requirements. The CPU clock can be throttled or slowed down to keep the temperature lower and prolong the life of the CPU and reduce power requirements especially in portable devices when activity is low or nonexistent. ACPI has six operating states that are shown in Table 4.3.

Two common BIOS and adapter features that take advantage of ACPI are Wake on LAN and Wake on Ring. The **Wake on LAN** feature allows a network administrator to control the power to a workstation remotely and directs the computer to come out of sleep mode. Software applications can also use the Wake on LAN feature to perform updates, upgrades, and maintenance tasks. The feature can also be used to bring up computers immediately before the business day starts. Wake on LAN can be used with Web or network cameras to start recording when motion is detected or to bring a network printer up so that it can be used when needed. The **Wake on Ring** allows a computer to come out of sleep mode when the telephone line has an incoming call. This lets the computer receive phone calls, faxes, and emails when the user is not present.

The Wake on LAN feature is enabled on adapters as well as through the motherboard for built-in network adapters. Wake on Ring is usually a pin connector on the motherboard that allows a cable connection between the motherboard and the device that uses Wake on Ring. Common BIOS settings related to ACPI are listed in Table 4.4.

Tech Tip

How to disable ACPI

When not all devices or applications support ACPI and generate system errors, when the computer randomly goes into standby mode, or when the computer freezes coming out of standby mode, you may need to disable ACPI. The best way to do this is through the computer's Setup program. Look for the key words ACPI or Power Management. If the system still has ACPI-related problems, disable ACPI through the operating system's *Power Options* or *Power Management* control panel.

4
Disassembly and Power

Table 4.3		ACPI operating states

Global System State	Sleep State	Description
G0 Working	(S0)	The computer is fully functional. Software, such as the AutoSave function used with Microsoft products, can be optimized for performance or lower battery usage.
G1 Sleeping		Requires less power than the G0 state and has multiple sleeping states.
	(S1)	CPU is still powered, and unused devices are powered down. RAM is still being refreshed. Hard disks are not running.
	(S2)	CPU is not powered. RAM is still being refreshed. System is restored instantly upon user intervention.
	(S3)	Power supply output is reduced. RAM is still being refreshed. Some info in RAM is restored to CPU and cache.
	(S4)	Lowest-power sleep mode and takes the longest to come up. Info in RAM is saved to hard disk. Some manufacturers call this the hibernate state.
G2	(S5)	Also called soft off. Power consumption is almost zero. Requires the operating system to reboot. No information is saved anywhere.
G3		Also called off, or mechanical off. This is the only state where the computer can be disassembled. You must power on the computer to use it again.

Table 4.4	Common BIOS power settings

Setting	Description
Delay Prior to Thermal	Defines the number of minutes the system waits to shut the system down once an overheating situation occurs.
CPU Warning Temperatures	Specifies the CPU temperature at which a warning message is displayed on the screen.
ACPI Function	Enables or disables ACPI. This is the preferred method for disabling ACPI in the event of a problem.
Soft-off	Specifies the length of time a user must press the power button to turn the computer off.
Wake Up by PCI Card	Allows the computer to wake when a PCI adapter contains the Wake on LAN feature.
Power on by Ring, Resume by Ring, or Wakeup	Allows the computer to wake when an adapter or an external device supports Wake on Ring.
Resume by Alarm	Allows a date and time to be set when the system is awakened from Suspend mode. Commonly used to update the system during non-peak periods.
Wake Up on LAN	Allows the computer to wake when a Wake on LAN signal is received across the network.
CPU THRM Throttling	Allows a reduction in CPU speed when the system reaches a specific temperature.
Power on Function	Specifies which key (or key combination) will activate the system's power.
Hot Key Power On	Defines the keystrokes that will reactivate system power.
Doze Mode	When the system is in a reduced activity state, the CPU clock is throttled (slowed down). All other devices operate at full speed.

Sometimes when a computer comes out of Sleep mode, not all devices respond and the computer's power or reset button has to be pressed to reboot the computer. The following situations can cause this to happen:

- A screen saver conflicts with ACPI
- All adapters/devices are not ACPI compliant
- An adapter/device has an outdated driver

Power values for energy-efficient monitors

Always keep the screen saver timeout value shorter than the power saver timeout value, especially with green (energy efficient) monitors!

To see if the screen saver causes the problem, use the *Display* control panel and set the screen saver option to *None*. Identifying a problem adapter, device, or driver will take Internet research. Check each adapter, device, and driver one by one. Use the *Power Options* control panel to change the power scheme. Also check all devices for a *Power Management* tab on the *Properties* dialog box. Changes can be made there.

The *Advanced* tab in Windows XP allows you to specify whether the power control icon appears in the taskbar, whether a password is required to bring the computer out of Standby mode, and how the computer's power (and possibly the sleep buttons) behave depending on the operating system. Figure 4.16 in Windows XP shows the *Advanced* tab settings.

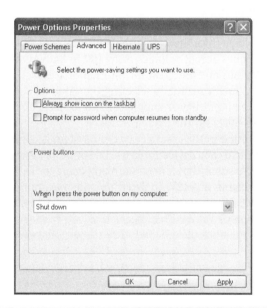

Figure 4.16   *Power Options Properties* window (*Advanced* tab)

In Vista and 7, use the Power Options control panel to edit the power settings. Select the *Change advanced power settings* link to configure passwords, standby power behavior, as well as other power-related settings. If the computer does not go into the Sleep mode, check the following:

- Determine if ACPI is enabled in BIOS
- Try disabling the antivirus program to see if it is causing the problem
- Set the screen saver to *None* to see if it is causing the problem
- Determine if all device drivers are ACPI-compliant
- Determine if power management is enabled through the operating system (use the *Power Options* control panel)
- USB devices can cause problems; disconnect them to see if this is the case

Replacing or Upgrading a Power Supply

Power supplies are rated in watts. Today's computers have power supplies with ratings ranging from 250 to 500 watts, although powerful computers, such as network servers, can have power supplies rated 600 watts or higher. Each device inside the computer uses a certain amount of power and the power supply must provide enough to run all the devices. The power each device or adapter requires is usually defined in the documentation for the device or adapter or on the manufacturer's Web site. The computer uses the wattage needed, not the total capacity of a power supply. The efficiency (more AC is converted to DC) is what changes the electricity bill.

Some power supplies list as being dual or triple (or tri) rail. A **dual rail power supply** has two +12V output lines, one of which is used for the CPU. Version 2 of the ATX standard requires that the CPU has a separate and independent power connection. A triple rail power supply simply has three +12V output lines for devices. Keep in mind that most manufacturers do not have two or more independent 12V sources; they all derive from the same 12V source but have independent output lines. The most important thing to remember about 12V output is that multi-core processors and video cards use 12V power in addition to devices that have motors (hard drives, CD/DVD drives, for example). Ensure that enough amperage is provided for all installed devices that use 12V power. Many power supplies have a sticker or stencil that shows the various voltage levels and the maximum current output in amps.

Tech Tip

Watch the wattage

Many manufacturers overstate the wattage. The wattage advertised is *not* the wattage available at higher temperatures, such as when mounted inside a computer. Research a model before purchasing.

Power supplies can be auto-switching or have a fixed input. An **auto-switching** power supply monitors the incoming voltage from the wall outlet and automatically switches itself accordingly. Auto-switching power supplies accept voltages from 100 to 240VAC at 50 to 60Hz. These power supplies are popular in laptops and are great for international travel. A power supply might also allow adjusting the input value by manually selecting the value through a voltage selector switch on the power supply. A fixed input power supply is rated for a specific voltage and frequency for a country, such as 120VAC 60Hz for the United States.

Some people are interested in the exact power their system is consuming. Every device in the computer consumes power and each device could use one or more different voltage levels (+5V, –5V, +12V, –12V, +3.3V). A power supply has a maximum amperage for each voltage level, for example 30 amps at +5 volts and 14 amps at +12V. To determine the maximum power in watts being used, multiply the amps and volts. If you add all of the maximum power levels, the amount would be greater than the power supply's rating. This means that you cannot use the maximum power at every single voltage level (but since the –5V and –12V are not used very often, normally this is not a problem).

In order to determine the power being consumed, every device must be researched to determine how much current it uses at a specific voltage level. Internet power calculators are available to help with this task. Table 4.5 lists sample computer components' power requirements.

Table 4.5	**Sample computer component power requirements**
Component	**Power consumption**
Motherboard (without processor)	5 to 50W
Processor	10 to 100W
Floppy drive	5W
IDE hard drive	3 to 15W
CD/DVD drive	10 to 25W
Non-video adapter	4 to 25W
Video adapter	20 to 300W

Table 4.6 shows a sample computer system and its +12V level usage.

Table 4.6	+12V power (total available 14 amps)
Component	**Current consumption**
Five expansion slots (.18 amp each)	.9 amp
Floppy motor	1 amp
Two hard drive motors (1 amp each)	2 amps
CD/DVD motor	1 amp
Total 12V power requirements	**4.9 amps**
Total 12V available power	**9.1 amps** (14 amps total minus 4.9 amps used)

Different physical sizes of power supplies are available. When replacing a power supply, purchasing a power supply for a new computer, or upgrading a power supply, verify that the power supply will fit in the computer case. Also, verify that the power supply produces enough power for the installed devices and for future upgrades. Do not forget to check that the on/off switch on the new power supply is in a location that matches the computer case.

When purchasing a new power brick for a laptop, ensure that it is approved by the manufacturer. Less expensive models might not provide the same quality as approved models. Ensure that the replacement has a power jack that does not wiggle once inserted into the laptop. Ensure that it has the appropriate DC voltage required by the laptop.

Power management on both laptops and desktops is important. Most computer components are available as energy-efficient items. ENERGY STAR is a joint effort by the U.S. EPA (Environmental Protection Agency) and Department of Energy to provide device standards and ratings that easily identify products (including computer components) that are energy efficient. Many computers today are on more than they are off, and settings such as power options, CPU throttling, and some advanced BIOS settings affect power settings. A technician must be aware of all these options and be willing to offer advice such as turn the computer off when finished working on it; set the power management option to one that allows work to be performed at an affordable cost; disable options not being used, such as wireless capabilities when wired networking is functioning; be aware of monitor costs (CRT-type monitors take the most energy, followed by plasma displays and then LCD or flat panel technology); and purchase energy-efficient parts and computers.

Power Supply Problems

When you suspect the power supply is the problem, swap the power supply, make the customer happy, and be on your way! Power problems are not usually difficult to detect or troubleshoot.

Do not overlook the most obvious power supply symptom. Start by checking the computer power light. If it is off, check the power supply's fan by placing your palm at the back of the computer. If the fan is turning, it means the wall outlet is providing power to the computer and you can assume that the wall outlet is functioning. Test the power outlet with another device. Ensure the power cord is inserted fully into the wall outlet and the computer. If you suspect the wall outlet, use an **AC circuit tester** to verify the wall outlet is wired properly.

On a laptop that is running on battery power, check the laptop battery charge icon through the operating system. Try using the laptop on AC power. If it works on AC power, try recharging the battery. If the battery does not recharge, replace it. Wiggle the AC power to see if the connection is loose. Remove the laptop battery for a moment and then re-insert it (and attach AC power if battery power does not work). See if the power brick has a power light on it and whether it is lit. Try a different AC adapter from the same manufacturer because AC adapters are proprietary between laptop vendors.

Tech Tip

Do not disassemble a power supply

Power supplies are not normally disassembled. Manufacturers often rivet them shut. Even when the power supply can be disassembled, you should not take it apart unless you have a background in electronics. Replace the entire power supply when it is faulty; power supplies are inexpensive.

4

Disassembly and Power

The following troubleshooting questions can help you determine the location of a power problem:

1. Did the power supply work before? If not, check the 115/230 switch on the power supply and verify that it is on the proper setting.
2. Is the power supply's fan turning? If yes, go to step 5. If not, check the wall outlet for proper AC voltages. If the wall outlet is OK, go to step 3.
3. Is a surge strip used? If so, check to see if the surge strip is powered on, then try a different outlet in the surge strip, or replace the surge strip.
4. Is the computer's power cord OK? Verify that the power cord plugs snugly into the outlet and into the back of the computer. Swap the power cord to verify it is functioning.
5. Are the voltages going to the motherboard at the proper level? Check the voltages to the motherboard. If they are low, something may be overloading the power supply. Disconnect the power cable to one device and re-check the voltages. Replace the power cable to the device. Remove the power cable from another device and re-check the motherboard voltages. Continue doing this until the power cord for each device has been disconnected and the motherboard voltages have been checked. A single device can short out the power supply and cause the system to malfunction. Replace any device that draws down the power supply's output voltage and draws too much current. If none of the devices is the cause of the problem, replace the power supply. If replacing the power supply does not solve the problem, replace the motherboard.

If a computer does not boot properly, but it does boot when you press Ctrl+Alt+Del, the power good signal is likely the problem. Some motherboards are more sensitive to the power good signal than others. An example is when a motherboard has been replaced and the system does not boot. At first glance, this may appear to be a bad replacement board, but the problem could be caused by a power supply failing to output a consistent power good signal.

Build the computer outside the computer case, on an antistatic mat if possible. Start with only the power supply, motherboard, and speaker connected. Even though it will normally

Tech Tip

Check the power good (sometimes called power OK) signal
Check the power supply documentation to see if the power supply outputs a power good signal (rather than the normal +5 volts). Turn on the computer. Check the power good signal going into the motherboard power connector. Do this before replacing the motherboard. A power supply with a power good signal below +3V needs to be replaced.

produce a POST audio error, verify that the power supply fan will turn. Most power supplies issue a click before the audio POST beeps. Next, verify the voltages from the power supply. If the fan turns and the voltages are correct, power down the machine and add a video adapter and monitor to the system. If the machine does not work, put the video adapter in a different expansion slot and try again. If placing the video adapter in a different expansion slot does not work, swap out the video adapter.

If the video adapter works, continue adding devices one by one and checking the voltages. Just as any one device can cause the system not to operate properly, so can any one adapter. If one particular adapter causes the system to malfunction, try a different expansion slot before trying a different adapter.

If the expansion slot proves to be a problem, check the slot for foreign objects. If none are found but the problem still occurs, place a note on the expansion slot so that no one will use it.

Symptoms of Power Supply Problems

The following list offers symptoms of a power supply problem:

- The computer power light is off
- The power supply fan does not turn when the computer is powered on

- The computer sounds a continuous beep (this could also be a bad motherboard or a stuck key on the keyboard)
- When the computer powers on, it does not beep at all (this could also be a bad motherboard)
- When the computer powers on, it sounds repeating short beeps (this could also be a bad motherboard)
- During POST, a 02X or parity POST error code appears (where X is any number); one of the POST checks is a power good signal from the power supply; a 021, 022, . . . error message indicates that the power supply did not pass the POST test
- The computer reboots without warning
- The power supply fan is noisy
- The power supply is too hot to touch
- The monitor has power light, but nothing appears on the monitor and no PC power light illuminates

Adverse Power Conditions

There are two adverse AC power conditions that can damage or adversely affect a computer: overvoltage and undervoltage. **Overvoltage** occurs when the output voltage from the wall outlet (the AC voltage) is over the rated amount. Normally, the output of a wall outlet is 110 to 130 volts AC. When the voltage rises above 130 volts, an overvoltage condition exists. The power supply takes the AC voltage and converts it to DC. An overvoltage condition is harmful to the components because too much DC voltage destroys electronic circuits. An overvoltage condition can be a surge or a spike.

When the voltage falls below 110 volts AC, an **undervoltage** condition exists. If the voltage is too low, a computer power supply cannot provide enough power to all the components. Under these conditions, the power supply draws too much current, causing it to overheat, weakening or damaging the components. An undervoltage condition is known as a brownout or sag. Table 4.7 explains these power terms.

Table 4.7	Adverse power conditions	
Major type	**Subtype**	**Explanation**
Overvoltage	**spike**	A spike lasts one to two nanoseconds. A nanosecond is a billionth of a second. A spike is harder to guard against than a surge because it has such short duration and high intensity.
	surge	A surge lasts longer (three or more nanoseconds) than a spike. Also called transient voltage. Causes of surges include lightning, poorly regulated electricity, faulty wiring, and devices that turn on periodically, such as elevators, air conditioners, and refrigerators.
Undervoltage	**brownout**	A brownout is when power circuits become overloaded. Occasionally, an electric company intentionally causes a brownout to reduce the power drawn by customers during peak periods.
	sag	A sag occurs when the voltage from the wall outlet drops momentarily.
	blackout	A total loss of power.

4

Disassembly and Power

Electric companies are offering surge protection for homes. Frequently, there are two choices. The basic package protects larger appliances, such as refrigerators, air conditioners, washers, and dryers. It allows no more than 800 volts to enter the electrical system. The premium package protects more sensitive devices (TVs, VCRs, stereos, and computers) and reduces the amount of voltage allowed to 323 volts or less. Some suppressors handle surges up to 20,000 volts. The exterior surge arrestor does not protect against voltage increases that originate inside the building, such as those caused by faulty wiring.

Adverse Power Protection

Power supplies have built-in protection against adverse power conditions. However, the best protection for a computer is to unplug it during a power outage or thunderstorm. Three devices are commonly used to protect against adverse power conditions: a surge protector, a line conditioner, or a UPS (uninterruptible power supply). Each device has a specific purpose and guards against certain conditions. A technician must be familiar with each device in order to make recommendations for customers.

Surge Protectors

A **surge protector**, also known as a surge strip or surge suppressor, is commonly a six-outlet strip with built-in protection against overvoltage. Figure 4.17 shows a picture of a surge protector.

Figure 4.17   Surge protector

Surge protectors do not protect against undervoltage; they protect against voltage increases.

Most surge protectors have an electronic component called an **MOV** (metal oxide varistor), which protects the computer or device that plugs into one of the outlets on the surge strip. The MOV is positioned between the AC coming in and the outlet into which devices are plugged. When a surge occurs, the MOV takes the extra voltage and prevents it from passing to the outlets. The MOV, however, has some drawbacks. If a large surge occurs, the MOV will take the hit and be destroyed, which is better than damaging the computer. However, with smaller overvoltages, each small surge weakens the MOV. A weakened MOV might not give the proper protection to the computer if there is a bigger surge. Also, there is no simple check for the MOV's condition. Some MOVs have indicator lamps attached, but these only indicate when the MOV has been destroyed, not when it is weakened. Still, having an indicator lamp is better than nothing at all. Some surge protectors also have replaceable fuses and/or indicator lamps for the fuse. A fuse only works once and then is destroyed during a surge in order to protect devices plugged into surge protector outlets.

Tech Tip

Do not create a trip hazard with a surge strip

When installing a surge protector, do not install it in such a manner that it causes a trip hazard because the cord lies in an area where people walk.

Several surge protector features deserve consideration. Table 4.8 outlines some of these features.

Table 4.8	Surge protector features
Feature	**Explanation**
Clamping voltage	The level at which the surge protector starts protecting the computer. The lower the value, the better the protection.
Clamping speed	How much time elapses before protection begins. The lower the value, the better the protection. Surge protectors cannot normally protect against power spikes (overvoltages of short duration) because of their rated clamping speed.
Joule dissipation capacity	The greater the number of joules that can be dissipated, the more effective and durable a surge protector is. This feature is sometimes called energy absorption. A surge protector rating of 630 joules is more effective than a rating of 210 joules.
TVS (Transient Voltage Suppressing) **rating**	This is also known as response time. The lower the rating the better. For example, a 330 TVS-rated surge protector is better than a 400 TVS-rated one.

Underwriters Laboratories developed the UL1449 standard to regulate surge suppressors—the 497A standard is for phone line protection, and the 1283 standard is for EMI/RFI.

The federal government designates surge suppressor grades—A, B, and C. Suppressors are evaluated on a basis of 1,000 surges at a specific number of volts and amps. A Class A rating is the best and indicates tolerance up to 6,000 volts and 3,000 amps.

Surge protectors are not the best protection for a computer system because most provide very little protection against other adverse power conditions. Even the good ones protect only against overvoltage conditions. Those with the UL1449 rating and an MOV status lamp are usually more expensive. Unfortunately, people tend to put their money into their computer parts, not the protection of those parts.

Which surge strip to buy?

When purchasing or recommending a surge protector, be sure it conforms to the UL1449 standard and has an MOV status lamp. Also, check to see if the vendor offers to repair or replace the surge-protected equipment in the event of damage during a surge.

Line Conditioners

An alternative for computer protection is the line conditioner. **Line conditioners**, sometimes known as power conditioners, are more expensive than surge protectors, but they protect the computer from overvoltages, undervoltages, and adverse noise conditions over electrical lines. The line conditioner monitors AC electricity. If the voltage is too low, a line conditioner boosts voltage to the proper range. If the voltage level is too high, a line conditioner clamps the voltage down and sends the proper amount to the computer. Figure 4.18 shows a line conditioner.

Be careful not to plug too many devices into a line conditioner

A line conditioner is rated for a certain amount of current. Laser printers, for example, can draw a great deal of current (up to 15 amps). Some line conditioners are not rated to handle these devices. Because laser printers draw so much current, if a computer and a laser printer are on the same electrical circuit, that circuit should be wired to a 20-amp circuit breaker. Most outlets in today's buildings are on 20-amp breakers.

4

Disassembly and Power

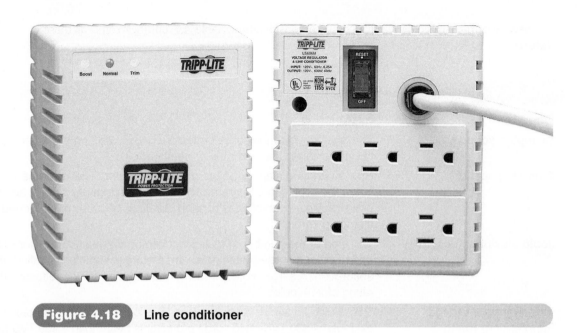

Figure 4.18   Line conditioner

Uninterruptible Power Supply (UPS)

A **UPS** (uninterruptible power supply), sometimes called online UPS or true UPS, provides power to a computer or device for a limited amount of time when there is a power outage. The UPS provides enough time to save work and bring the computer down safely. Some operating systems do not operate properly if power abruptly cuts off and the computer is not brought to a logical stopping place. A network server, the main computer for a network, is a great candidate for a UPS. Network operating systems are particularly susceptible to problems during a power outage. Some UPSs have a connection for a serial cable and special software that automatically maintains voltages to the computer, quits all applications, and powers off the computer. The UPS provides the necessary power and time to do this. Some newer UPSs will protect network cables. Figure 4.19 shows an APC UPS. Notice how the UPS has eight power outlets. Some UPS units have USB and/or network connections as well.

A UPS also provides power conditioning for the devices attached to it. The AC power is used to charge a battery inside the UPS. The battery inside the UPS supplies power to an inverter. The inverter makes AC for the computer. When AC power from the outlet fails, the battery inside the

Figure 4.19   Front and back of a UPS

UPS continues to supply power to the computer. The battery inside the UPS outputs DC power and the computer accepts (and expects) AC power. Therefore, the DC power from the battery must be converted to AC voltage. AC voltage looks like a sine wave when it is in its correct form, but cheaper UPSs produce a square wave that is not as effective. Some computer systems and peripherals do not work well on a 120VAC square wave. Figure 4.20 illustrates a sine wave and a square wave.

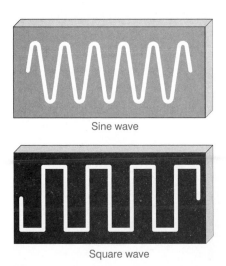

Sine wave

Square wave

Figure 4.20   Sine wave and square wave

Be sure the UPS produces a proper waveform for optimum operation. The UPS documentation should specify the waveform type. Keep in mind that the sine wave is the better form. The amount of time the UPS provides power to a computer or device and the number of devices that can attach to the UPS varies from model to model. Generally, the more time and the more devices a UPS can handle, the more expensive it is.

UPSs are the best protection against adverse power conditions because they protect against overvoltage *and* undervoltage conditions and they provide power so a system can be brought down and turned off properly. When purchasing a UPS, be sure that (1) the amount of battery time is sufficient to protect all devices; (2) the amount of current the UPS produces is sufficient to protect all devices; and (3) the output waveform is a sine wave.

Tech Tip

Do not plug a laser printer into a UPS unless it has a rating less than 1400VA

Most UPSs cannot handle the very high current requirements of a laser printer when it powers up.

To install a UPS, connect it to a wall outlet and power it on. When a UPS is first plugged in, the battery is not charged. See the UPS manufacturer's installation manual for the specific time it will take to charge. Power off the UPS. Attach device power cords, such as the PC, to the UPS. Ensure that the UPS is rated to supply power to the number and type of connected devices. Power on the UPS.

A UPS has a battery inside similar to a car battery (except that the UPS battery is sealed), which contains acid. Never drop a UPS or throw it in the trash. Research your state's requirements for recycling batteries. All batteries fail after some time and most UPSs have replaceable batteries. Again, do not throw the UPS battery in the trash. Recycle it!

UPS troubleshooting is not difficult. The following guidelines assist with this task. Keep in mind that you should always follow the manufacturer's recommendations for troubleshooting.

- If the UPS will not power on, check the on/off switch. Verify that the UPS is attached to an electrical outlet. Ensure the outlet has power and that the circuit breaker for the outlet has not been tripped. Ensure the battery is installed properly.
- Some UPS units have a self-test procedure and include a self-test button.

4

Disassembly and Power

- With some UPS units, a beep indicates a power interruption has occurred. This is a normal function.
- Some UPS units beep at a different rate when the battery is low. Others have a light indicator. Recharge or replace the battery.
- If a UPS is overloaded, that is, it has too many devices attached, the UPS may shut off, trip a circuit breaker, provide a beep, or have a light indication for this problem.

Figure 4.21 shows the front of an American Power Conversion UPS. Notice the diagnostic lights on it.

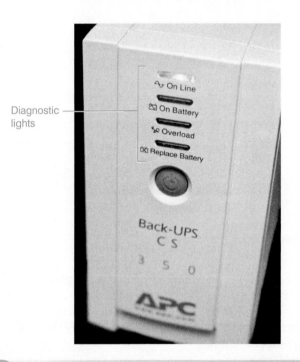

Diagnostic lights

Back-UPS C S 3 5 0

APC

Figure 4.21   **Front of an American Power Conversion UPS**

Standby Power Supply (SPS)

A device similar to the UPS is the **SPS** (standby power supply). An SPS contains a battery like the UPS, but the battery only provides power to the computer when it loses AC power. It does not provide constant power like the UPS. An SPS is not as effective as the UPS because an SPS provides no protection against noise or under/over voltages. The SPS must detect a power-out condition first, and then switch over to the battery to supply power to the computer. As a result, SPS switching time is important. Any time under five milliseconds is fine for most systems.

Phone Line Isolator

Just like AC power outlets, the phone outlet can experience power fluctuations. These enter the computer through a modem, a device used to connect a computer to a phone line. Not only can a modem be damaged by a power surge on the phone line, but also other electronics inside the computer, such as the motherboard, can be damaged. A **phone line isolator**, sometimes called a **modem isolator**, can be purchased at an electronics store. It provides protection against phone line surges. No computer connected to a phone line through a modem should be without one. Many surge protectors now come with a modem isolator built into the strip. Refer to Figure 4.17 in the surge protector section. Notice in the photograph how the surge strip has modem protection integrated into the unit.

Power supplies and associated protection equipment are not exciting topics, but they are very important to a technician. Power problems can catch you unaware. Always keep power in your mind as a potential suspect when troubleshooting a computer.

Electrical Fires

No discussion of power is complete without a brief warning about fire. Electrical fires are uncommon in computers, but if one occurs, a technician must know what to do. If a fire occurs inside a computer or peripheral, unplug the equipment if possible, but do not put yourself in harm's way attempting to do this. Use a **Type C** or a **Type A-B-C fire extinguisher** to put out the fire. Type C fire extinguishers are made specifically for Type C (electrical) fires. Type A-B-C fire extinguishers can be used for Class A, Class B, and Class C fires. Class A fires involve paper, wood, cloth, or other normal combustibles. Class B fires involve flammable liquids and gases. It is also a good idea to have a dry chemical 20lb ABC fire extinguisher in homes for the electronics (including computers) located there. Home computer equipment should be listed on the home insurance policy. Figure 4.22 shows a Type A-B-C fire extinguisher.

Figure 4.22   **Type A-B-C fire extinguisher**

When a fire occurs, pull out the fire extinguisher pin. Aim the fire extinguisher nozzle at the base (bottom) of the fire. Squeeze the fire extinguisher's handle and move the nozzle back and forth in a slow sweeping motion. With electrical fires, the smoke is a breathing hazard. Burning plastics produce lethal toxic fumes. Always evacuate the people in the building and call the fire department.

Computer Disposal/Recycling

Computers and electronic devices can contain materials such as lead, chromium, cadmium, mercury, beryllium, nickel, and zinc. These materials are increasing dramatically every year in the landfills and can pose a threat to our environment. Plastics that are part of computers are hard to isolate and recycle. CRTs (cathode ray tubes) are found in monitors and TVs and usually contain enough lead to be considered hazardous waste. However, the EPA has been successful in obtaining exclusions from the federal hazardous waste standards for unbroken CRTs so they can be recycled more effectively. Every state and many cities have specific guidelines as to how to dispose of electronics. These rules must be followed by technicians who replace broken computer equipment. For example, in Florida and New York, steps have been taken for more CRT recycling; however, other states regulate all CRTs as hazardous waste and they are banned from being sent to landfills. If you are unsure about how to get rid of any piece of broken electronics, contact your direct supervisor for instructions.

The following list provides alternatives and suggestions for being environmentally conscious about discarding electronics:

- Donate equipment that is operational to schools and charities so those that do not have access to technology can get some exposure. If the operating system is not transferred to another system, leave the operating system on it and provide proof of purchase along with documentation. Also, do not forget to erase all data stored on the computer before donating it.
- Recycle very outdated electronics. If the devices are so outdated that a school or charity does not want them, consider recycling them. Many companies accept old electronics and have determined ways to reuse some of their parts.
- Remove parts that do work and donate or recycle them.
- Buy electronics that are designed with saving resources in mind and are easy to upgrade, which extends their usefulness period; are energy efficient; contain fewer toxins; use recycled materials; and offer leasing or recycling programs.
- Check with the computer or component manufacturer to see if it has a recycling program. Most of them do.

Soft Skills—Written Communications Skills

When technicians are in school, they seldom think that the skills they should be learning involve writing. However, in the workplace, technicians use written communication skills when they document problems and use email. Advisory committees across the country state the same thing—in addition to technical knowledge, it is important that technicians are able to communicate effectively both written and orally, be comfortable working in a team environment, and possess critical thinking skills (be able to solve problems even though they have not been taught the specific problem).

Regardless of the size of a company, documentation is normally required. The documentation may only be the number of hours spent on a job and a basic description of what was done, but most companies require a bit more. Documentation should be written so others can read and understand it. Keep in mind that if another technician must handle another problem from the same customer, it saves time and money to have good documentation. The following list includes complaints from managers who hire technicians. Use the information to improve and avoid making the same mistakes:

- Avoids doing documentation in a timely manner
- Does not provide adequate or accurate information on what was performed or tried
- Uses poor grammar, capitalization, and punctuation skills
- Does not provide updates on the status of a problem

Email is a common means of communication for technicians. However, most technicians do not take the time to communicate effectively using email. The following list includes guidelines for effective email communication:

- Do not use email when a meeting or a phone call is more appropriate
- Include a short description of the email topic in the subject line
- Do not write or respond to an email when you are angry
- Send email only to the appropriate people
- Stick to the point; do not digress
- Use a spelling and grammar checker; if one is not included in the email client, write the email in a word processing application, check it, and then paste the document into the email
- Use proper grammar, punctuation, and capitalization; do not write in all uppercase or all lowercase letters
- Write each email as if you were putting the message on a billboard; you never know how the content might be used or who might see it

The number one complaint about technical support staff is not their lack of technical skills, but their lack of communication skills. Spend as much of your education practicing your communication skills as you do your technical skills.

Key Terms

AC (p. 110)	joule dissipation capacity (p. 129)	solder joint (p. 107)
AC circuit tester (p. 125)	Li-ion battery (p. 120)	spike (p. 127)
ACPI (p. 121)	line conditioner (p. 129)	SPS (p. 132)
amp (p. 111)	modem isolator (p. 132)	standoff (p. 105)
antistatic wrist strap (p. 102)	Molex (p. 114)	surge (p. 127)
auto-switching (p. 124)	MOV (p. 128)	surge protector (p. 128)
Berg (p. 114)	MSDS (p. 109)	TVS rating (p. 129)
blackout (p. 127)	NiMH battery (p. 120)	Type A-B-C fire extinguisher
brownout (p. 127)	ohm (p. 111)	(p. 133)
capacitor (p. 111)	overvoltage (p. 127)	Type C fire extinguisher (p. 133)
clamping speed (p. 129)	phone line isolator (p. 132)	undervoltage (p. 127)
clamping voltage (p. 129)	pin 1 (p. 106)	UPS (p. 130)
continuity (p. 111)	power (p. 111)	volt (p. 110)
current (p. 111)	power good signal (p. 114)	voltage (p. 110)
DC (p. 110)	power supply tester (p. 118)	Wake on LAN (p. 121)
dual rail power supply (p. 124)	preventive maintenance (p. 108)	Wake on Ring (p. 121)
EMI (p. 103)	resistance (p. 111)	watt (p. 111)
ESD (p. 102)	RFI (p. 103)	
grounding (p. 102)	sag (p. 127)	

Review Questions

1. How often does a technician normally disassemble a computer?
2. If someone says that a motherboard might be grounding out, what does that mean?
3. If you are out on a service call without an antistatic wrist strap, how can you reduce ESD?
4. How do you solve an RFI problem?
5. Why is it important to keep the battery attached to the motherboard?
6. Why should you not touch an adapter's gold contacts?
7. Which tools are usually necessary to disassemble a microcomputer?
8. Which tool is used to straighten bent pins on connectors, ports, or cables?
9. Which tool(s) should be avoided if a screw inadvertently rolls under the motherboard?
10. What can be done if a screw drops and rolls under the motherboard?
11. What does a cable being *keyed* mean?
12. How can you easily identify a ribbon cable's pin 1?
13. [T | F] On a cable, pin 2 is on the same end as pin 1.
14. [T | F] A square solder joint is on the opposite end from pin 1.
15. Is orienting cables a difficult task? Why or why not?
16. [T | F] Even with self-parking heads, improper handling can damage a hard drive.
17. List three common tasks performed during preventive maintenance.
18. What is the name of the test the computer performs to check hardware each time the computer powers on?
19. List three common things found in a preventive maintenance kit.

4

Disassembly and Power

20. [T | F] The first step in preventive maintenance is cleaning the computer with compressed air.

21. [T | F] Leaving the computer plugged in during disassembly is the best method for ensuring a good ground.

22. What is the most frustrating component of a computer to remove?

23. What is the most frustrating component to install when reassembling the computer?

24. How can the frustration referred to in Question 23 be avoided?

25. List two preventive maintenance tips for a notebook computer that do not really apply to a tower computer.

26. Describe the difference between AC and DC power.

27. What device provides DC power to the computer's internal components?

28. Describe how polarity is important when measuring DC voltage.

29. Name two devices with potentially dangerous voltage levels.

30. Of the two devices mentioned in Question 29, which one is the most dangerous?

31. Draw an AC voltage symbol found on a meter.

32. Draw a DC voltage symbol found on a meter.

33. If you do not know what the symbols on a meter mean, what would you do?

34. What meter setting is used when measuring an unknown voltage? [Infinite | Highest | Amps | Lowest]

35. What is current?

36. How is current related to computer repair?

37. How do watts relate to power?

38. What computer component's output is described in watts?

39. When replacing a power supply, how is wattage applicable?
    a. It must be lower than the total requirement of all components installed
    b. It is not applicable
    c. It relates to the amount of capacitance the power supply provides
    d. It must be equal to or greater than the total requirement of all components installed

40. When working inside an ATX computer, why should the computer be unplugged even if it is powered down?

41. What term describes the amount of opposition to current in a circuit? [Resistance | Wattage | Capacitance | Voltage]

42. What type of check is performed on a cable to determine if each wire is good?

43. [T | F] When checking continuity, polarity does not matter.

44. [T | F] When checking continuity on pin 2 on both ends of the cable, the meter will always show no resistance if the wire is good.

45. What type of check is performed on a fuse to determine whether it has blown?

46. What is different about an ATX12V v2.x power supply?

47. What is the purpose of the power good signal?

48. What can be done if a power supply does not have an available SATA connector and one is needed?

49. What can be done if a power supply does not have enough power connectors?

50. List three purposes of a power supply.

51. [T | F] An ATX power supply has 120VAC going to the front panel switch.

52. How do you power off a computer that has an ATX power supply?

53. What is reverse cooling, and what type of power supply uses it?

54. List one precaution to take when installing an additional cooling fan inside a computer.

55. What are the five output voltages of a power supply?
56. Of the five output voltages of a power supply, which are used for electronic chips?
57. Of the five output voltages of a power supply, which is used for most drive motors?
58. What type of batteries are most commonly used in laptops?
59. What is the difference between the soft off and hibernate ACPI modes?
60. What is the difference between Wake on LAN and Wake on Ring?
61. What factors should be taken into account when replacing a power supply?
62. [T | F] Power supplies are frequently disassembled for repair.
63. Describe how you can go about troubleshooting a power supply problem.
64. List three power supply problem symptoms.
65. What is the difference between a surge and a spike?
66. [T | F] Power supplies have their own internal protection against power problems.
67. What features should you look for in a surge protector?
68. Why is having an MOV status lamp in a surge protector important?
69. What is the optimum power protection for a computer during a storm?
70. [T | F] Powerful computers that are an important component in a network should always have a UPS attached for power protection.
71. What features are important in a UPS?
72. What is the difference between a UPS and an SPS?
73. [T | F] Power surges can occur over phone lines and damage internal components of a microcomputer.
74. What is the difference between a Class A and a Class C fire?
75. Describe how to use a fire extinguisher.
76. [T | F] Different states have different laws regarding how to dispose of a CRT.
77. List two tips for good technical documentation.
78. List the top three email tips that would help you communicate better.

Fill-in-the-Blank

1. _____ is static electricity that enters an electronic component causing damage to it.
2. _____ volts need to be present before an average person can feel static electricity.
3. As little as _____ volts of static electricity can damage an electronic component.
4. _____ and _____ are most susceptible to ESD strikes.
5. A/An _____ connects a technician to the computer and places both at the same potential.
6. An antistatic wrist strap should not be used when working inside a/an _____.
7. Random noise caused by a pencil sharpener that interferes with a computer speaker is an example of _____.
8. Use proper grounding procedures to prevent _____ damage.
9. _____ are good for straightening bent pins.
10. The plastic connectors on the bottom of a motherboard are _____.
11. Some motherboards have _____ or _____ that you must lift or push when removing the motherboard from the case.
12. Cable pin numbers _____ and _____ are always toward the cable stripe.
13. Hard drive _____ can be damaged by slightly banging the drive onto a flat surface.
14. Measures taken to prolong the life of computer components are collectively known as _____.

15. The _____ contains information about how to dispose of a particular chemical solvent.

16. A/An _____ can include a lens cleaner, scratch repair kit, and disc cleaner.

17. The type of power provided through a wall outlet is known as _____.

18. The type of power a computer uses is known as _____.

19. The measurement used to describe the power supply output is _____, which is also the term that describes how much pressure pushes electrons through a circuit.

20. Typical power supply output voltages are _____.

21. A wall outlet is typically _____ AC volts.

22. A/An _____ is an electronic component found in power supplies and monitors that stores a charge even after power is removed.

23. Capacitance is measured in _____.

24. Amps are a measurement of _____.

25. Power is measured in _____.

26. Ohms are a measure of _____.

27. When measuring a broken wire, the meter shows _____.

28. A good fuse shows _____ ohms on a meter.

29. There are two basic types of power supplies. Computers use a/an _____ type power supply.

30. Do not power on a power supply without a/an _____ because the power supply can be damaged.

31. The ATX _____ standard has a 24-pin motherboard connector.

32. The _____ determines how many and what type of power supply connectors are provided.

33. The _____ signal is sent to the motherboard when the power supply's voltages are at their proper levels.

34. The _____ ATX v2.x power connection provides power when a computer is in sleep mode.

35. If a Molex power connector is the only connector available and the device needs a Berg connector, use a/an _____.

36. A power supply converts _____ to _____.

37. When installing an auxiliary fan, the airflow must be in the _____ direction as/from the airflow generated by the power supply.

38. Li-ion batteries should not be _____ discharged.

39. U.S. flight regulations state that spare lithium batteries are not allowed in _____ baggage.

40. _____ combines APM and plug and play technologies to allow an operating system and BIOS to control various devices' power.

41. The _____ BIOS setting is used to enable/disable ACPI.

42. The best way to disable ACPI is through the _____.

43. The Windows XP _____ control panel is used to select a power scheme.

44. A laptop with a/an _____ power supply can be used in Europe and the United States without any switch being changed.

45. A/An _____ is used to test wall outlet connections.

46. A/An _____ condition is when the AC electrical force exceeds the rated amount.

47. Two overvoltage conditions are a/an _____ and a/an _____.

48. Two undervoltage conditions are a/an _____ and a/an _____.

49. A total loss of power is also known as a/an _____.

50. A/An _____ only protects against the overvoltage condition.

51. A common component in a surge protector is the _____.

52. The _____ guards against overvoltages and undervoltages, but not against a blackout.

53. The _____ provides power from a battery to the computer during a power outage and during normal power conditions.

54. A/An _____ provides power to the computer from a battery only during a power outage.

55. _____ provides protection for modems.

56. To extinguish a computer fire, use a Class _____ or _____ fire extinguisher.

57. An electrical fire is classified as a Class _____.

58. Never send an email when you are _____.

59. Write each email as if it were to be displayed on a/an _____.

Hands-On Exercises

1. Performing Maintenance on an Antistatic Wrist Strap

Objective: To understand how to care for and properly use an antistatic wrist strap

Parts: Antistatic wrist strap
Computer chassis
Multimeter

Note: Electrostatic discharge (ESD) has great potential to harm the electronic components inside a computer. Given this fact, it is vitally important that you practice proper ESD precautions when working inside a computer case. One tool you can use to prevent ESD is an antistatic wrist strap. This tool channels any static electricity from your body to the computer's chassis, where it is dissipated safely.

Procedure: Complete the following procedure and answer the accompanying questions.

1. Examine the wrist strap for any obvious defects such as worn or broken straps, loose grounding lead attachments, dirt or grease buildup, and so on.

2. If necessary, remove any dirt or grease buildup from the wrist strap, paying close attention to the electrical contact points such as the wrist contact point, the ground lead attachment point, and the computer chassis attachment clip. Use denatured alcohol to clean these contact points.

3. If possible, use a multimeter to check continuity between the wrist contact point and the computer chassis attachment clip. A reading of zero ohms of resistance indicates a good electrical pathway.

   How many volts of static electricity does it take to harm a computer's electrical components?

4. Adjust the wrist strap so it fits snugly yet comfortably around your wrist. Ensure that the wrist contact is in direct contact with your skin, with no clothing, hair, etc., being in the way.

5. Attach the ground lead to the wrist strap and ensure it snaps securely into place.

6. Attach the computer chassis attachment clip to a clean metal attachment point on the computer chassis.

7. Any static electricity generated or attracted by your body will now be channeled through the antistatic wrist strap to the computer chassis, where it will be safely dissipated.

   How many volts will an ESD be before you will feel it?

   Should you use an antistatic wrist strap when working inside a monitor?

Instructor initials: _____

2. Computer Disassembly/Reassembly

Objective: To disassemble and reassemble a microcomputer correctly

Parts: A computer to disassemble
             A toolkit
             An antistatic wrist strap (if possible)

Note: Observe proper ESD handling procedures when disassembling and reassembling a microcomputer.

Procedure: Complete the following procedure and answer the accompanying questions.

1. Gather the proper tools needed to disassemble the computer.

2. Clear as much workspace as possible around the computer.

3. Power on the computer.

   Why is it important to power on the computer before you begin?

External Cables

4. Turn the computer and all peripherals *off*. Remove the power cable from the wall outlet then remove the power cord from the computer.

5. Note where the monitor cable plugs into the back of the computer. Disconnect the monitor including the power cord and move it to a safe place. Take appropriate notes.

6. Remove all external cables from the back of the computer. Take notes on the location of each cable. Move the peripheral devices to a safe place.

   Did the mouse cable connect to a PS/2 or USB port?

Computer Case Removal

7. If possible, remove the computer case. This is usually the hardest step in disassembly if the computer is one that has not been seen before. Diagram the screw locations. Keep the cover screws separate from other screws. An egg carton or a container with small compartments makes an excellent screw holder. Label each compartment and reuse the container. Otherwise, open the case as directed by the manufacturer.

Adapter Placement

8. Make notes or draw the placement of each adapter in the expansion slots.

9. On your notes, draw the internal cable connections *before* removing any adapters or cables from the computer. Make notes regarding how and where the cable connects to the adapter. Do not forget to include cables that connect to the motherboard or to the computer case.

   List some ways to determine the location of pin 1 on an adapter or cable.

Internal Cable Removal

10. Remove all internal cables. **WARNING**: Do not pull on the cable; use the pull tab, if available, or use the cable connector to pull out the cable. Some cables have connectors with locking tabs. Release the locking tabs *before* you disconnect the cable. Make appropriate notes regarding the cable connections. Some students find that labeling cables and the associated connectors makes reassembly easier, but good notes usually suffice.

Adapter Removal

11. Start with the left side of the computer (facing the front of the computer) and locate the left-most adapter.

12. Write down any jumpers or switch settings for this adapter. This step may need to be performed after you remove the board from the computer if the settings are inaccessible.

13. If applicable, remove the screw or retaining bracket that holds the adapter to the case. Place the screw in a separate, secure location away from the other screws already removed. Make notes about where the screw goes or any other notes that will help you when reassembling the computer.

14. Remove the adapter from the computer.

    Why must you be careful not to touch the gold contacts at the bottom of each adapter?

15. Remove the remaining adapters in the system by repeating Steps 12–15. Take notes regarding screw locations, jumpers, switches, and so forth for each adapter.

Drives

16. Remove all power connections to drives, such as hard drives, floppy drives, CD/DVD drives, etc. Note the placement of each drive and each cable, and any reminders needed for reassembly.

17. Remove any screws holding the drives in place. Make notes where the screws go. Keep these screws separate from any previously removed screws.

18. Remove all drives.

    Why must you be careful when handling a hard drive?

Power Supply

19. Before doing this step, ensure that the power cord is removed from the wall outlet and the computer. Remove the connectors that connect the power supply to the motherboard.

20. Take very good notes here so you will be able to insert the connectors correctly when reassembling.

21. Remove the power supply.

    What is the purpose of the power supply?

Motherboard

22. Make note of any motherboard switches or jumpers and indicate if the switch position is on or off.

    What is the importance of documenting switches and jumpers on the motherboard?

23. Remove any remaining connectors except those that connect a battery to the motherboard. Take appropriate notes.

24. Remove any screws that hold the motherboard to the case. Place these screws in a different location from the other screws removed from the system. Write any notes pertaining to the motherboard screws. Look for retaining clips or tabs that hold the motherboard into the case.

25. Remove the motherboard. Make notes pertaining to the motherboard removal. The computer case should be empty after you complete this step.

Instructor initials: _____

Reassembly

26. Reassemble the computer by reversing the steps for disassembly. Pay particular attention to cable orientation when reinstalling cables. Before reconnecting a cable, ensure that the cable and the connectors are correctly oriented and aligned before pushing the cable firmly in place. Refer to your notes. The first step is to install the motherboard in the computer case and reconnect all motherboard connections and screws.

27. Install the power supply by attaching all screws that hold the power supply in the case. Re-attach the power connectors to the motherboard. Refer to your notes.

28. Install all drives by attaching screws, cables, and power connectors. Refer to your notes. Attach any cables that connect the drive to the motherboard.

29. Install all adapters. Attach all cables from the adapter to the connecting device. Replace any retaining clips or screws that hold adapters in place. Refer to your previous notes and diagrams.

30. Connect any external connectors to the computer. Refer to previously made notes when necessary.

31. Replace the computer cover. Ensure slot covers are replaced and that the drives and the front cover are aligned properly. Ensure all covers are installed properly.

32. Reinstall the computer power cable.

4
Disassembly and Power

33. Once the computer is reassembled, power on all external peripherals and the computer. A chassis intrusion error message may appear. This is just an indication that the cover was removed.

    Did the computer power on with POST error codes? If so, recheck all diagrams, switches, and cabling. Also, check a similar computer model that still works to see if you made a diagramming error. A chapter on logical troubleshooting comes next in the book. However, at this point in the course, the most likely problem is with a cable connection or with an adapter not seated properly in its socket.

Instructor initials: _____

3. Amps and Wattage

Objective: To determine the correct capacity and wattage of a power supply

Parts: Power supply

               Internet access (as needed)

Procedure: Complete the following procedure and answer the accompanying questions.

1. Locate the documentation stenciled on the power supply, if possible.

   Can you determine from the documentation how many amps of current the power supply is rated for at 5 volts? If not, proceed to Optional Step 2.

2. *Optional:* Use the Internet to find the power supply's documentation on the manufacturer's Web site. Use the information you find to answer the remaining questions.

   How many amps is the power supply rated for at 5 volts?

   How many amps is the power supply rated for at 12 volts?

   How many +12V rails does the power supply have?

   What is the maximum rated output power of the power supply in watts?

Instructor initials: _____

4. Continuity Check

Objective: To perform a continuity check on a cable and find any broken wires

Parts: Multimeter

               Cable and pin-out diagram

Procedure: Complete the following procedure and answer the accompanying questions.

1. Obtain a meter, cable, and pin-out diagram from your instructor.

2. Set the meter to ohms.

3. Power on the meter.

4. Lay the cable horizontally in front of you. The connector on the left is referred to as Connector A. The connector on the right is referred to as Connector B.

5. Determine the number of pins on the cable connector. On a separate sheet of paper, write numbers vertically down the left side of the paper, similar to the numbering used in Lab 5. There should be a number for each connector pin. At the top of the numbers write Connector A as the heading. Create a corresponding set of identical numbers vertically on the right side of the paper.

6. Check the continuity of each wire. Document your findings by placing a check mark beside each pin number with a good continuity check.

   What meter setting did you use to check continuity, and what meter symbol is used for this setting?

7. Power off the meter and return all supplies to the instructor.

Instructor initials: _____

5. Pin-Out Diagramming

Objective: To draw a pin-out diagram using a working cable

Parts: Multimeter

           Good cable

Procedure: Complete the following procedure and perform the accompanying activities.

1. Obtain a meter and a good cable from your instructor.
2. Set the meter to ohms.

Instructor initials: _____

3. Power on the meter.
4. Lay the cable horizontally in front of you. The connector on the left is referred to as Connector A. The connector on the right is referred to as Connector B.
5. Touch one meter lead to Connector A's pin 1. Touch the other meter lead to every Connector B pin. Notice when the meter shows zero resistance, indicating a connection. Using the table that follows, draw a line from Connector A's pin 1 to any Connector B pins that show zero resistance. Add more pin numbers as needed to the table or use a separate piece of paper. Remember that all pins do not have to be used in the connector.

Connector A	Connector B
☐ 1	☐ 1
☐ 2	☐ 2
☐ 3	☐ 3
☐ 4	☐ 4
☐ 5	☐ 5
☐ 6	☐ 6
☐ 7	☐ 7
☐ 8	☐ 8
☐ 9	☐ 9
☐ 10	☐ 10
☐ 11	☐ 11
☐ 12	☐ 12
☐ 13	☐ 13
☐ 14	☐ 14
☐ 15	☐ 15
☐ 16	☐ 16
☐ 17	☐ 17
☐ 18	☐ 18
☐ 19	☐ 19
☐ 20	☐ 20

6. Power off the meter.

Instructor initials: _____

7. Return all supplies to the instructor.

4

Disassembly and Power

6. Fuse Check

Objective: To determine if a fuse is good

Parts: Multimeter

             Fuse

Procedure: Complete the following procedure and answer the accompanying questions.

1. Obtain a meter and a fuse from your instructor.

2. Look at the fuse and determine its amp rating.

    What is the amperage rating of the fuse?

3. Set the meter to ohms.

Instructor initials: _____

4. Power on the meter.

5. Connect one meter lead to one end of the fuse. Connect the other meter lead to the opposite end.

6. Look at the resistance reading on the meter.

    What is the resistance reading?

    Is the fuse good?

7. Power off the meter.

Instructor initials: _____

8. Return all materials to the instructor.

7. Wall Outlet and Power Cord AC Voltage Check

Objective: To check the voltage from a wall outlet and through a power cord

Parts: Multimeter

             Computer power cord

Caution: Exercise extreme caution when working with AC voltages!

Procedure: Complete the following procedure and perform the accompanying activities.

1. Set the multimeter to AC VOLTAGE (refer to the meter's manual if you are unsure about this setting). **Important:** Using a current or resistance setting could destroy the meter.

2. Power on the multimeter. Locate an AC power outlet. Refer to Figure 4.23 for the power connections.

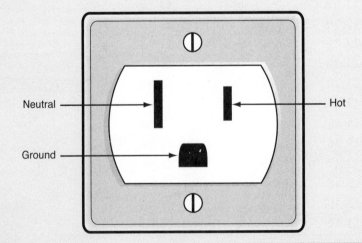

Figure 4.23   **AC outlet**

3. Insert the meter's **black** lead into the **round** (Ground) AC outlet plug.

4. Insert the meter's **red** lead into the **smaller flat** (Hot) AC outlet plug. The meter reading should be **aroun**d 120 volts. Use Table 4.9 to record the reading.

5. Move the meter's *red* lead into the *larger flat* (Neutral) AC outlet plug. The meter reading should be 0 volts. Use Table 4.9 to record the reading.

Table 4.9	Wall outlet AC checks	
Connections	**Expected voltage**	**Actual voltage**
GND to Hot	120VAC	
GND to Neutral	0VAC	
Hot to Neutral	120VAC	

6. Remove both leads from the wall outlet.

7. Insert the meter's *black* lead into the *smaller flat* (Hot) AC outlet plug.

8. Insert the meter's *red* lead into the *larger flat* (Neutral) AC outlet plug. The meter reading should be *around* 120 volts. Use Table 4.9 to record the reading.

9. Plug the computer power cord into the AC wall outlet that was checked using steps 3 through 8.

10. Verify the other end of the power cord is *not* plugged into the computer.

11. Perform the same checks you performed in Steps 3 through 8, except this time check the power cord end that plugs into the computer. Use Table 4.10 to record the reading.

Table 4.10	Power cord AC checks	
Connections	**Expected voltage**	**Actual voltage**
GND to Hot	120VAC	
GND to Neutral	0VAC	
Hot to Neutral	120VAC	

12. If the voltage through the power cord is correct, power off the meter. Notify the instructor of any incorrect voltages.

Instructor initials: _____

8. Device DC Voltage Check

Objective: To check the power supply voltages sent to various devices

Parts: Multimeter
            Computer

Procedure: Complete the following procedure and perform the accompanying activities.

1. Set the multimeter to DC VOLTAGE (refer to the meter's manual if unsure about the setting).

2. Power on the multimeter.

3. Power off the computer.

4. Remove the computer case.

5. Locate a Molex or Berg power connector. If one is not available, disconnect a power connector from a device.

6. Power on the computer.

7. Check the +5 volt DC output from the power supply by placing the meter's *black* lead in (if the connector is a Molex) or on (if the connector is a Berg) one of the grounds* (a black wire). Place the meter's *red* lead on th e +5 volt wire (normally a red wire) in or on the connector. Consult Figure 4.24 for the layout of the Molex and Berg power supply connections. Figure 4.24 also contains a table with the acceptable voltage levels.

*Use and check both ground connections (black wires going into the connector); do not check all the voltages using only one ground connection.

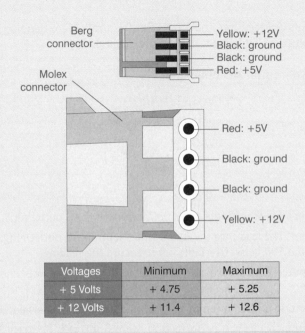

Voltages	Minimum	Maximum
+ 5 Volts	+ 4.75	+ 5.25
+ 12 Volts	+ 11.4	+ 12.6

Figure 4.24   **Molex and Berg power connectors**

Write the voltage level found for the +5 volt wire in Table 4.11.

Table 4.11   **+5 volt check**

Voltage being checked	Voltage found
+5 Volts	

8. Check the +12 volt DC output by placing the meter's *black* lead in (if the connector is a Molex) or on (if the connector is a Berg) one of the grounds. Place the meter's *red* lead on the +12 volt wire in or on the connector. See Figure 4.24 for the layout of the Molex and Berg power supply connections. The figure also contains a table with acceptable voltage levels. Write the voltage level found for the +12 volt wire in Table 4.12.

Table 4.12   **+12 volt check**

Voltage being checked	Voltage found
+12 Volts	

9. Notify the instructor of any voltages out of the acceptable range.
10. Power off the meter.

Instructor initials: _____
11. Power off the computer.

9. Windows XP Power Options

Objective: To be able to control power options via BIOS and Windows XP

Parts: Computer with Windows XP loaded

Procedure: Complete the following procedure and answer the accompanying questions.

1. Power on the computer and ensure it boots properly before the exercise begins.
2. Reboot the computer and access BIOS Setup.

   List the BIOS options related to power management.

   Can ACPI be disabled via BIOS?

3. Exit the BIOS setup program without saving any settings. Boot to Windows XP.

4. From the *Start* button, access *Control Panel*, Classic view, and the *Power Options* control panel.

On the *Power Schemes* tab, what is the current setting used?

Using the *Power Schemes* drop-down menu, list the power schemes available.

What is the current setting for the monitor power scheme?

What is the current setting for the hard drive power scheme?

What is the current setting for the system standby?

What is the maximum amount of time the monitor can be on and then be shut off by the operating system?

5. Select the *Advanced* tab.

Describe the power savings icon shown on this window.

What options are available for the power button?

6. Select the *Hibernate* tab.

How much disk space is required for hibernation?

7. Click *Cancel*.

10. Windows Vista Power Options

Objective: To be able to control power options via BIOS and Windows Vista

Parts: Computer with Windows Vista loaded

Procedure:

1. Power on the computer and ensure it boots properly before the exercise begins.

2. Reboot the computer and access BIOS Setup.

List the BIOS options related to power management.

Can ACPI be disabled via BIOS?

3. Exit the BIOS Setup program without saving any settings. Boot to Windows Vista.

4. Access the current power settings by using the *Start → Control Panel → System and Maintenance → Power Options*.

What power plan is currently configured?

5. Select the *Create a power plan* link on the left. Type a unique name in the *Plan name* textbox. Click *Next*.

6. Use the *Turn off the display* drop-down menu to select a time. Use the *Put the computer to sleep* drop-down menu to select a time for the computer to go into reduced power mode.

What global ACPI state do you think this would assign? Look back through the chapter to review.

7. Click the *Create* button. Notice that your new plan appears in the list of preferred plans. Also notice that the *Show additional plans reveal* arrow is in the center of the window on the right. Click on it, and other plans are revealed.

8. Click on the *Change plan settings* link under the plan you just created. Select the *Change advanced power settings* link.

List at least three devices for which you can have power controlled through this control panel.

9. Expand the *USB* settings, if possible, and the *USB selective suspend* setting.

What is the current setting?

10. Expand the *Processor power management* setting, if possible.

What is the minimum processor state?

What is the maximum processor state?

4
Disassembly and Power

11. Expand the *Multimedia* settings, if possible.

    What setting is configured with this option?

12. Click the *Cancel* button to return to the Change settings window. Click the *Cancel* button again. Show the instructor or lab assistant your settings.

Instructor initials: _____

13. To delete a power plan you created (the default ones cannot be deleted), select the radio button used when starting this lab. Refer to question 4, if necessary. Under the plan you created, select the *Change settings for the plan* link. Select the *Delete this plan* link and click *OK*. The plan should be removed from the power options list. Show the instructor or lab assistant that the plan has been deleted.

Instructor initials: _____

Internet Discovery

Objective: To obtain specific information on the Internet regarding a computer or its associated parts

Parts: Computer with Internet access

Procedure: Complete the following procedure and answer the accompanying questions.

1. Locate an Internet site that provides tips for doing computer preventive maintenance.

   Write 10 of the tips and the URL where you found the information.

2. Locate an Internet site that provides security devices for notebook computers.

   Make a list of three different devices and the URL where you found the information.

3. Locate a power company that provides surge protection service for homes.

   Write the cost(s) of the service if possible and the URL where you found the information.

4. A customer owns a Belkin 12-outlet surge protector with phone/Ethernet/Coaxial protection and an extended cord.

   What is the warranty amount for this surge protector and at what URL did you find this information?

5. A customer has a Sparkle Power, Inc. (SPI) ATX-450PA power supply.

   What is the power supply's maximum power output (in watts) and how many amps are provided for +3.3V, +5V, and +12V (combined amount for +12V)? Write the URL where you found this information as well.

6. A customer has an Enermax Liberty ELT500AWT power supply.

   Does this power supply comply with the ATXV12 Version 2.2 or higher specification?

   How many PCIe connectors are provided?

   Does the power supply have any SATA power connectors?

   At what Web site did you find this information?

7. What type of battery provides the longest amount of power for an HP dv2500t notebook computer and what URL provided this information?

8. Your company has a Tripp Lite Smart 700 UPS.

   What is the part number and cost for a replacement battery? At what Web site did you find this information?

9. Locate an A-B-C fire extinguisher.

   Give the model, cost, and URL where you found this information.

Soft Skills

Objective: To enhance and fine-tune a future technician's ability to listen, communicate in both written and oral form, and support people who use computers in a professional manner

Activities:

1. Using the information gathered in Critical Thinking Skills Activity 1 or research an appropriate replacement power supply for any computer, prepare a business proposal for the power supply as if you were offering it to a customer. Present your proposal to the class.

2. Work in teams to decide the best way to inform a customer about the differences between a line conditioner and a UPS. Present your description to the class as if you were talking to the customer. Each team member must contribute. Each classmate votes for the best team explanation.

Critical Thinking Skills

Objective: To analyze and evaluate information as well as apply learned information to new or different situations

Activities:

1. Locate a computer on the Internet that lists each device that is installed and the type of motherboard, integrated ports, and so on. Then, locate a power supply calculator. Find a replacement power supply based on the calculations performed. Write the details of what you looked for in the replacement power supply, the power supply, vendor, number and type of connectors, and cost.

2. For one of the computers in the classroom, locate an appropriate UPS that can provide power for 10 minutes. Write the details of your findings in a report.

4
Disassembly and Power

5

Logical Troubleshooting

Objectives

After completing this chapter you will be able to

- Perform basic procedures used when troubleshooting a PC
- Describe how the POST error codes help when troubleshooting a computer
- Describe the importance of good communication when dealing with the computer user

Troubleshooting Overview

When a computer does not work properly, technicians must exhibit one essential trait—the will to succeed. The main objective is to return the computer or peripheral to service as quickly and economically as possible. When a computer is down a business loses revenue and productivity. Therefore, a technician must have a good attitude and a large amount of perseverance and drive to resolve the problem at hand quickly and efficiently in a professional, helpful manner.

Technicians must also use all available resources. Resources can be documentation for a particular peripheral, motherboard, or computer; the Internet; another technician; corporate documentation; textbooks; experience with similar problems; training materials; previous service history on a particular customer/computer; or an online database provided by a company or partner. Technicians can be stubborn, but they must always remember that time is money and solving the problem quickly and with the least amount of downtime to the customer is a critical component of a computer support job.

Solving a computer problem is easier if a technician uses reasoning and takes logical steps. Logical troubleshooting can be broken down into the following six simple steps:

1. Identify the problem
2. Establish a theory
3. Divide and conquer: separate the problem into logical areas to isolate it
4. Repair the problem or go back to test another theory
5. Test the solution
6. Provide feedback to the user

Tech Tip

Back up data if possible

Before any changes are made to the system, ensure data is backed up if possible.

Identify the Problem

Computer problems come in all shapes and sizes. Many problems relate to the people who operate computers—the users. They may fail to choose the correct printer, push the wrong key for a specific function, or issue an incorrect command.

Have the user demonstrate or re-create the problem. Because the user is often the problem, you can save a great deal of time with this step. Do not assume anything! A user may complain that "my hard drive does not work" when in fact, there is no power to the computer. Often users repeat computer terms they have heard or read, but they do not use them correctly or in the right syntax. By asking a user to re-create a problem, a technician creates the chance to see the problem as the client sees it. Even during a phone consultation, the same rules apply:

- Do not assume anything; ask the user to re-create the problem step-by-step.
- Ask the user if anything has been changed, but do not be threatening. Otherwise, they will not be forthright and honest.
- Verify obvious things such as power to the monitor or speakers muted through the control panel.
- Do not assume that there is not a problem if it cannot be re-created by the user. Some problems are intermittent.
- Back up data, if possible, before making changes.

Establish a Theory

In order to establish a theory, you have to have heard or seen the problem as explained by the user. A lot of times, you establish a theory based on analyzing the problem and determining if the problem is hardware or software related (or both) by using your senses: sight, hearing, and smell can reveal a great deal. Smell for burning components. Watch the computer boot, look for lights, listen for beeps, and take notes. Frequently, a hardware problem is detected during POST (power on self-test) executed by the BIOS when the computer is first powered on. POST checks out the hardware in a sequential order and if it finds an error, the BIOS issues a beep and/or displays a numerical error code. Make note of any error codes or beeps. The number or duration of beeps and the numerical error codes that appear are different for different computers. The secret is knowing the BIOS chip manufacturer. Major manufacturers of motherboard BIOS chips include Award (now merged with Phoenix Technologies), AMI, IBM, and Phoenix. The computer or motherboard documentation sometimes contains a list of codes or beeps used for troubleshooting. A single beep is a common tone heard on a successful completion of POST because no hardware errors were detected. Table 5.1 lists the audio beeps heard on a computer with an AMI BIOS chip installed. Table 5.2 lists the POST error messages seen on a computer with an Award/Phoenix BIOS installed.

Table 5.1	AMI BIOS audio beeps
Beeps	**Description of problem**
1	OK if screen appears. If not, DRAM refresh (memory)
2	Parity circuit (memory)
3	1st 64KM of RAM or CMOS
4	System timer/memory
5	Microprocessor (memory/motherboard)
6	Keyboard controller or A20 line
7	Virtual mode exception error (CPU)
8	Video memory (read/write test)
9	BIOS
10	CMOS shutdown (read/write test)
11	Cache memory
1 long, 3 short	RAM
1 long, 8 short	Video

Table 5.2	Award (now Phoenix Technologies) BIOS POST error messages
Message	**Description**
BIOS ROM checksum error—System halted	The BIOS has a problem and needs to be replaced.
CMOS battery failed	Replace the motherboard battery.
CMOS checksum error—Defaults loaded	CMOS has detected a problem. Check the motherboard battery.
Floppy disk(s) failed	The system has been configured to have a floppy disk installed and the drive has not responded. Check the drive connectivity and power. If no drive is installed, change the setting in BIOS Setup.
Hard disk install failure	The BIOS could not find or initialize the hard drive. Check the hard drive connectivity and power.
Keyboard error or no keyboard present	The keyboard could not be found. Check the cabling.
Keyboard is locked out—Unlock the key	Ensure nothing rests on the keys during POST.
Memory test fail	A RAM error occurred. Swap the memory modules.
Override enabled—Defaults loaded	The current settings in CMOS could not be loaded and the BIOS defaults are used. Check the battery and CMOS settings.
Primary master hard disk fail	The PATA hard drive attached to the primary IDE connector and configured as master could not be detected. If a new installation, check the cabling, power, and master/slave/cable select settings. See Chapter 7 for more details.

5

Logical
Troubleshooting

Table 5.2	Award (now Phoenix Technologies) BIOS POST error messages (continued)
Message	**Description**
Primary slave hard disk fail	The PATA hard drive attached to the primary IDE connector and configured as slave could not be detected. If a new installation, check the cabling, power, and master/slave/cable select settings. See Chapter 7 for more details.
Secondary master hard disk fail	The PATA hard drive attached to the secondary IDE connector and configured as master could not be detected. If a new installation, check the cabling, power, and master/slave/cable select settings. See Chapter 7 for more details.
Secondary slave hard disk fail	The PATA hard drive attached to the secondary IDE connector and configured as slave could not be detected. If a new installation, check the cabling, power, and master/slave/cable select settings. See Chapter 7 for more details.

Phoenix BIOS is sold to various computer manufacturers, who are allowed to create their own error codes and messages. Other BIOS manufacturers do the same. Look in the motherboard/computer manual or on the manufacturer's Web site for a listing of exact error messages. Table 5.3 lists the audio beeps heard on a computer with a Phoenix BIOS chip installed.

Table 5.3	Phoenix audio beep codes
Beeps	**Description**
1-2-2-3	BIOS ROM (flash the BIOS/motherboard)
1-3-1-1	Memory refresh (RAM contacts/RAM)
1-3-1-3	8742 keyboard controller (keyboard/motherboard)
1-3-4-1	Memory address line error (RAM contacts/RAM/power supply/motherboard)
1-3-4-3	Memory error (RAM contacts/RAM/motherboard)
1-4-1-1	Memory error (RAM contacts/RAM/motherboard)
2-2-3-1	Unexpected interrupt (adapter/motherboard)
1-2	Adapter ROM error (video card memory/video adapter/adapter/motherboard)

In addition to hearing audio tones, a technician might see numerical error codes or a series of colored indicators displayed during POST. Some motherboards also have a numeric display that helps with hardware troubleshooting. The numeric codes can be found in the motherboard or computer manual. Like audio clues, the numerical error codes are BIOS dependent. Table 5.4 lists IBM POST codes. These codes are somewhat generic and similar to those found on other systems.

POST error codes direct a technician to the correct general area only. Sometimes multiple POST errors occur. If this is the case, start the troubleshooting process with the first error code detected.

Hardware errors might also occur. For example, the monitor might suddenly go black, the CD/DVD drive's access light might not go on when it attempts to access the CD disc, or the printer might repeatedly flash an error code. Hardware errors are usually obvious because of POST error codes or errors that occur when accessing a particular device. Also, some peripherals such as hard drives and printers include diagnostics as part of the software loaded when the device is installed. These diagnostics are frequently accessed through the device's Properties window or from the Windows All Programs software list.

Tech Tip

Motherboard manual or Web site lists latest error codes

Because manufacturers constantly produce BIOS upgrades, use the Internet to verify POST errors that occur and the recommended actions to take.

Software errors, on the other hand, occur when the computer user accesses a particular application or file, or when the system boots. Files that affect the booting process, such as files

Table 5.4	IBM POST error codes
Error	**Description**
01x	Undetermined problem
02x	Power supply
1xx	Motherboard error
2xx	RAM error
3xx	Keyboard error
6xx	Floppy drive error
9xx	Parallel port error
11xx	Serial COM1 error
12xx	Serial COM2, 3, or 4 error
104xx	IDE error
112xx	SCSI adapter error
113xx	Motherboard SCSI error
208xx	SCSI device error
209xx	SCSI removable disk error
210xx	SCSI hard drive error
215xx	SCSI CD drive error

in the Startup folder, are dependent on the operating system. If in doubt as to whether a problem is hardware or software related, use Windows Device Manager to test the hardware to eliminate that possibility. Every software program has problems (bugs). Software manufacturers offer a software **patch** or a **service release** that fixes known problems. Patches or service releases are usually available on the Internet from the software manufacturer. A **service pack** usually contains multiple patches and installs them at the same time rather than in multiple downloads.

Divide and Conquer

Divide the problem into logical areas and continue subdividing the problem until it is isolated. For example, if an error appears each time the computer user tries to write data to a CD, then the logical place to look is the CD/DVD drive system. The CD/DVD drive system includes the user's disc, the CD/DVD drive, electronics that tell the drive what to do, a cable that connects the drive to the controlling electronics, and the software program currently being used. Any of these may be the cause of the problem.

Ernie Friend, a technician of many years, advises students to divide a problem in half; then divide it in half again; then continue to divide until the problem is manageable. This way of thinking carries a technician a long way. Also, always keep in mind that you will beat the problem at hand! You are smarter than any problem!

Use Ernie's philosophy with the CD problem: divide the problem in half and determine if the problem is hardware or software related. To determine if the software application is causing the CD problem, try accessing the disc from another application. If the second application works, then the problem is in the first application. If both applications have problems, the problem is most likely in the disc or in the drive hardware system. The next easiest thing to eliminate as a suspect is the CD. Try a different disc. If a different disc works, then the first disc was the problem. If neither disc accepts data, the problem is the CD/DVD drive, cable, or electronics. Swap parts one at a time until you locate the problem. Always reinstall the original part if the symptoms did not change and continue troubleshooting.

If a hardware problem is evident once a POST error or peripheral access/usage error occurs, consider the problem a subunit of the entire computer. For example, if a POST error occurs for

5

Logical
Troubleshooting

Change or check the easy stuff first

When isolating the problem to a specific area, be practical; change or check the easy stuff first. Time is money—to the company or person whose computer is down and to the company that employs the technician.

the CD/DVD drive, the subunit is the CD/DVD drive subsystem. The subsystem consists of the drive, the cable, and the controlling circuits that may be on an adapter or the motherboard.

If the problem is software related, narrow it to a specific area. For example, determine if the problem is related to printing, saving, or retrieving a file. This may give you a clue as to what section of the application is having a problem or even lead you back to considering other hardware components as the cause of the problem.

When multiple things could cause the problem, make a list of possibilities and eliminate the potential problems one by one. If a monitor is down, swap the monitor with another before opening the computer and swapping the video adapter. Also, check with the computer user to see if anything about the computer has changed recently. For example, ask if anyone installed or removed something from the computer or if new software was loaded before or since the problem started. If the problem is hardware related, Device Manager and Windows troubleshooting wizards can narrow it down to a subunit. Isolating a problem frequently requires part swapping, but try not to replace good parts. If a replacement part does not solve the problem, put the old part back in.

Ethics are an important part of any job, including the job of being a technician. When a replacement part does not fix the job, do not leave it in the machine and charge the customer. Good technicians, like good automobile mechanics, take pride in doing an honest day's work. Start practicing these good habits in the classroom.

If you do not hear any unusual audio beeps or see any POST error codes and you suspect a software error, reboot the computer. In Windows, press the [F8] key to bring up a startup menu. Select a menu option, such as Step-by-Step Confirmation or Last Known Good Configuration.

Repair the Problem or Go Back to Test Another Theory

Swapping a part, checking hardware settings, and referring to documentation are necessary steps when troubleshooting. Noting error or beep codes is just one element in the diagnostic routine. Determining what the problem is usually takes longer than fixing it. Software problems frequently involve reloading software applications, software drivers, or getting software updates and patches from the appropriate vendor. The Internet is an excellent resource for these files and vendor recommendations. Hardware problem resolution simply involves swapping the damaged part. Sometimes it is necessary to remove or disable unnecessary components and peripherals. This is especially true with notebook computers.

If swapping a part or reloading the software does not solve the problem, go back to logical troubleshooting. Step 2 reminds you to divide the problem into hardware and software related issues. Go back to this step if necessary. Step 3 advises you to divide and conquer. This step is the most likely place to resume your troubleshooting. Eliminating what could be the problem is important. Take notes during these steps so that you know what you have tried. People who troubleshoot randomly—repairing parts or replacing files without a plan—are known as "gunslingers." Gunslingers are the most dangerous technicians to have on staff. Sometimes gunslingers get lucky and fix a problem faster than a logical technician would, but gunslingers frequently cause more problems than they solve. Consistent, logical troubleshooting is a better path to follow. If you are methodical there is no problem you cannot solve.

Test the Solution and Document

Never assume that the hardware component or the replaced software repairs the computer. The computer can have multiple problems, or the repair may not offer a complete solution. Test the computer yourself and have the user test the computer in normal conditions to prove that the problem is indeed solved. Document the solution.

Figure 5.1 shows a simple troubleshooting flowchart, but keep in mind that each chapter has one or more troubleshooting sections to help with problems. Also, the chapters toward the end of the book address problems related to the operating system.

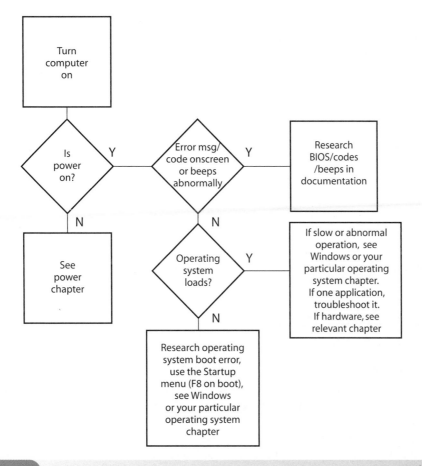

Figure 5.1 **Basic troubleshooting flowchart**

Soft Skills—Provide Feedback to the User

Unfortunately, one of the biggest problems with technicians is their inability to communicate effectively with users. The best computer technicians are the ones who users trust, and those who explain problems in a way customers can understand. A computer repair is never finished until the user is informed. Technical training on new equipment or a procedure/process may be necessary. Realize that computer users are intelligent, even if they are not proficient in technical terminology. The following list can be used as a reminder for good customer support skills:

- Use clear, concise direct statements when talking to customers. Be pleasant, patient, and professional.
- Listen to customers and allow them to complete their sentences. Do not interrupt.
- Ask questions when appropriate and when they are pertinent to the problem.
- Avoid using any technical slang, jargon, or acronyms.
- Respect the customer's privacy and property. Think about how you would want to be treated if someone was working in your office on your computer.
- Do not become defensive or judgmental. If the customer is unprofessional to a point that you cannot do your job, excuse yourself and contact your supervisor. Under no circumstance should you lose your own professional demeanor.
- Maintain a positive attitude and do the best job that you can.

A good recommendation is to follow up with the customer one week after the repair to make sure the customer is satisfied and that the problem is solved. If the customer is unhappy, jump

5

Logical
Troubleshooting

at the chance to make good on the repair. The best advertising is good referrals from satisfied customers. Keep in mind that the general rule of thumb is that if the customer is satisfied, he or she will tell one or two other people about the service. If the customer is dissatisfied, he or she will tell 10 other people about the problem.

Each computer repair is a different scenario because of the plethora of vendors, products, and standards in the marketplace. But that is what makes the job so interesting and challenging. Break down each problem into manageable tasks, isolate the specific issue, and use all available resources, including other technicians, documentation, and the Internet, to solve it. Never forget to give feedback.

The remaining chapters are dedicated to specific devices or areas of the computer. Each device or area covered includes troubleshooting techniques that can be used once a problem is narrowed down. For example, if you find you have a memory problem, read Chapter 6 on memory for details of operation and troubleshooting techniques.

Key Terms

patch (p. 155)
service pack (p. 155)
service release (p. 155)

Review Questions

1. Explain how users can be a computer problem.
2. How can a technician determine if a problem is hardware or software related?
3. [T | F] The manufacturer of the RAM chip determines what error codes are shown during POST.
4. If a computer beeps once during POST, what is the problem?
   a. There is no problem
   b. CPU register test
   c. DRAM refresh
   d. Video initialization error
5. If a computer beeps once then three times, then four times, then three more times during POST and the computer has a Phoenix BIOS, what is a possible suspect component?
   a. Keyboard
   b. BIOS
   c. Memory
   d. Video
6. What BIOS manufacturer uses multiple beeps with pauses in between; for example, two beeps, pause, four beeps, pause, and then three beeps? [AMI | Award | IBM | Phoenix]
7. Where can you find the latest information on POST error codes?
8. [T | F] Flash BIOS can be upgraded.
9. [T | F] After swapping a part in the computer and powering on, you can assume that the problem is solved.
10. What is the last and most important step in resolving a computer problem?

Fill-in-the-Blank

1. _____ checks out hardware sequentially.
2. The _____ chip executes POST.
3. An IBM POST error code _____ indicates a keyboard error.
4. To help determine if a problem is in the startup files, press the _____ key during the Windows boot process to bring up a menu that contains the Step-by-Step Confirmation option.

5. The _____ might contain a numeric display that contains an error code when a problem occurs.

6. If a problem is hardware related, _____ can be useful in getting the problem narrowed down to a subunit.

7. A computer problem is never solved until the user _____.

Hands-On Exercise

1. Logical Troubleshooting

Objective: To solve a computer problem with logic

Parts: Computer with a problem

Procedure: Complete the following procedure and answer the accompanying questions.

1. In teams of two, one person leaves the room while the other person installs a problem in the machine and powers it down.

2. The person who left the room powers on the computer with the problem and performs troubleshooting. Use the flowchart shown in Figure 5.2 and answer the questions that follow. Once the problem is solved, swap roles.

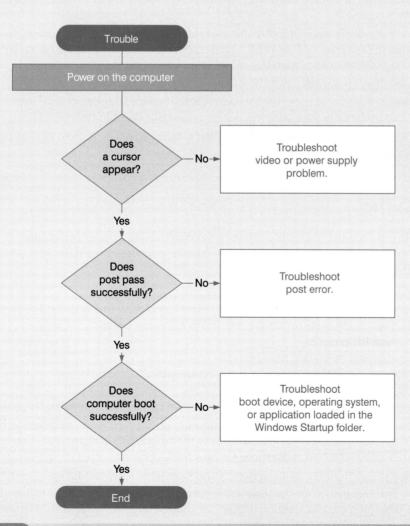

| **Figure 5.2** | **Troubleshooting flowchart** |

Do you hear any audio clues? If yes, list the symptoms.

Do any POST errors appear? If so, list them.

Are there any startup errors? If so, list them.

Are there any application-specific problems? If so, list them.

List any possible techniques to test. Test them one at a time. Document the solution.

Instructor initials: _____

Internet Discovery

Objective: To obtain specific information on the Internet regarding a computer or its associated parts

Parts: Computer with access to the Internet

Questions: Use the Internet to answer the following questions.

1. Locate a Web site that has a troubleshooting flowchart. Write three things the flowchart provides that you find helpful or confusing. Write the URL where the chart was found.

2. Locate one Web site that lists at least two BIOS vendor's error codes. Write the URL where this information was found.

3. What three fixes or updates does the Flash BIOS update for a Dell Precision 690 computer provide?

4. On an HP Pavillion dv2500t notebook computer, an error message appears that states, "Non-System Disk error or Disk Error." Find three recommended solutions from HP and list them along with the URL where this information was found.

5. A customer has an Acer Aspire L100 desktop computer and the Realtek HD audio control panel does not start and the error message "Illegal System DLL Relocation" appears. What caused this problem to start after the system previously worked fine?

6. A customer has a Gateway E6610D PC that has a damaged power switch. Find and note the URL that details how to replace the switch.

Soft Skills

Objective: To enhance and fine-tune a future technician's ability to listen, communicate in both written and oral form, and support people who use computers in a professional manner.

Activities:

1. Perform Critical Thinking Skills Activity 1 before completing this activity. The two technicians who solved the problem must perform the following tasks:
   - Document the problem.
   - List everything that *could* have been the problem.
   - List procedures that were tried in the order performed.
   - Document the final solution.

   The classmates who installed the problem must write a report detailing the following:
   - Positive comments and suggestions for how the technicians communicated verbally.
   - Positive comments and suggestions for how the technicians communicated nonverbally.
   - Positive comments and suggestions for how the technicians acted professionally.

2. Perform Critical Thinking Skills Activity 1 and Soft Skills Activity 1 before completing this activity. The four people on the team must present their written findings to the class and discuss their problem and solution. Other classmates evaluate the team on its presentation skills.

Critical Thinking Skills

Objective: To analyze and evaluate information as well as apply learned information to new or different situations.

Activities:

1. In teams of four, two people put a problem in the computer while the other two team members are out of the room. Once the two technicians return, one of the two students who installed the problem pretends to be a computer user with the problem. The two technicians act as a team to solve the problem. (See Soft Skills Activity 1 for the subsequent activity.)

2. Write a troubleshooting tip or procedure for any one computer item or step performed in class this term. Exchange your procedure with a classmate and critique each other's work by making comments and suggestions. Once your original paper is returned, rewrite it using suggestions you think are appropriate.

Memory

Objectives

After completing this chapter you will be able to

- Differentiate between different memory technologies
- Plan for a memory installation or upgrade
- Install and remove memory chips
- Describe how memory works with the operating system
- Optimize memory for Windows-based platforms
- Troubleshoot memory problems
- Understand the benefits of teamwork

Memory Overview

Computer systems need software to operate; the computer is an expensive doorstop without software. For the computer to operate, the software must reside in computer memory. Memory is simple to upgrade, but a technician must understand memory terminology, determine the optimum amount of memory for a system, install the memory, fine-tune it for the best performance, and finally, troubleshoot and solve any memory problems.

The two main types of memory are RAM (random access memory) and ROM (read only memory). RAM is found on the motherboard and stores the operating system, the software applications, and the data being used by all of the software. RAM is also found on adapters such as video cards. RAM is volatile memory; the information in RAM is lost when you power off the computer. ROM is nonvolatile memory; the information is in ROM even when the computer is powered off. ROM chips can also be found on adapters including SCSI, network, and video cards. The software contained inside the ROM chip is allowed to execute during the boot process and initialize the adapter and possibly detect devices attached to the adapter.

RAM is divided into two major types: **DRAM** (dynamic RAM) and **SRAM** (static RAM). DRAM is less expensive, but slower than SRAM. With DRAM, the 1s and 0s inside the chip must be refreshed. Over time, the charge, which represents information inside a DRAM chip, leaks out. The information, stored in 1s and 0s, is periodically rewritten to the memory chip through the **refreshing** process. The refreshing is accomplished inside the DRAM while other processing occurs. Refreshing is one reason DRAM chips are slower than SRAM.

Most memory on the motherboard is DRAM, but a small amount of SRAM can be found on a motherboard or, as is the norm for today's computers, inside the microprocessor. SRAM is also known as **cache memory**. The cache memory holds the most frequently used data so the CPU does not return to the slower DRAM chips to obtain the data. For example, on a motherboard with a bus speed of 100MHz, accessing DRAM could take as long as 180 nanoseconds. (A nanosecond (ns) is a billionth of a second.) Accessing the same information in cache could take as little as 45 nanoseconds.

The CPU fetches a software instruction from memory and then the processor sits idle. In a fast food restaurant, this is the same as not allowing waiting customers to be served until the first customer has his or her food. Most restaurants serve the next customer while the food is being prepared and open more registers when lots of customers are waiting. With pipelining, the processor is allowed to obtain more software instructions without waiting for the first instruction to be executed. Opening more registers is similar to how manufacturers use processor models with more pipelines. Using cache memory and using pipelining are popular technologies used today.

Tech Tip

The CPU should never have to wait to receive an instruction
Using pipelined burst cache speeds up processing for software applications.

The data or instruction that the microprocessor needs is usually found in one of three places: cache, DRAM, or the hard drive. Cache gives the fastest access. If the information is not in cache, the microprocessor looks for it in DRAM. If the information is not in DRAM, it is retrieved from the hard drive and placed into DRAM or the cache. Hard drive access is the slowest of the three. In a computer, it takes roughly a million times longer to access information from the hard drive than it does from DRAM or cache.

When determining a computer's memory requirements, you must take into consideration the operating system used, applications used, and hardware installed. The Windows 98 operating system takes a lot less memory than the Windows XP or 7. High-end games and desktop publishing take more RAM than word processing.

Free hard drive space and video memory are often as important as RAM in improving a computer's performance

RAM is only one piece of the puzzle. All of the computer's parts must work together to provide good system performance.

Memory Physical Packaging

A DIP (Dual In-line Package) chip has a row of legs running down each side. The oldest motherboards use DIP chips for the DRAM. SIMMs (Single In-line Memory Modules) came along next. Two types of SIMMs were used: 30-pin and 72-pin. The memory chip used today is a **DIMM** (Dual In-line Memory Module), which has 168, 184, or 240 pins. Figure 6.1 shows the progression of memory packaging.

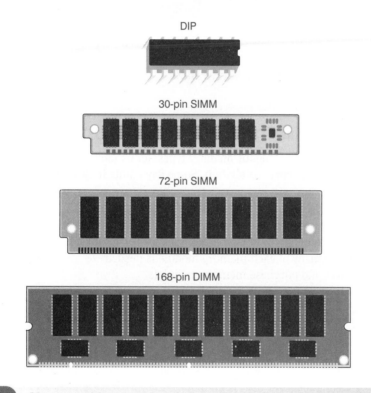

DIP

30-pin SIMM

72-pin SIMM

168-pin DIMM

Figure 6.1 **Memory chips**

Memory chips are also called memory sticks, or a technician might call one memory module a stick of memory or RAM. RIMMs are used in older Intel Pentium 4 computers. Figure 6.2 illustrates these types. Notice the single notch at the bottom of the 184-pin DDR DIMM. This distinguishes it from the other dual-notched DIMMs. The RIMM has two notches in the center.

Use tin or gold memory modules

Memory module contacts are either tin or gold (although most are gold). If the computer is designed to accept tin memory modules and you install gold ones, over time a chemical reaction between the metals can damage the connector. Memory errors also occur. Be certain to purchase the appropriate memory module for the computer by referring to the documentation or by examining other chips already installed.

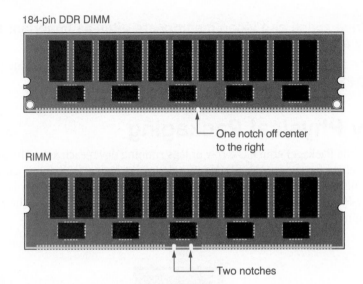

184-pin DDR DIMM

One notch off center to the right

RIMM

Two notches

Figure 6.2 **184-pin DDR DIMM and RIMM**

Planning the Memory Installation

Now that you know a little more about memory types, let us look at the practical side—how do you go about planning a memory installation. Some key points to discuss follow:

- Refer to the system or motherboard documentation to see what type of memory is supported
- Determine what features are supported
- Determine how much memory is needed
- Determine how many of each memory module is needed
- Research prices and purchase memory module(s)

Planning the Memory Installation— Memory Technologies

Technology has provided faster DRAM speeds without increasing the cost too greatly. These DRAM technologies include FPM (fast page mode) RAM, EDO (extended data out) RAM, BEDO (burst EDO) RAM, **SDRAM** (synchronous DRAM), DDR RAM, and **RDRAM** (Rambus DRAM). The motherboard must be designed to use one of these technologies or the faster memory *will not* speed up the computer. Table 6.1 explains some of the memory technologies.

Whether a motherboard supports faster memory chips is determined by the chipset, which performs most functions in conjunction with the microprocessor. A chipset is one to five electronic chips on the motherboard. The chipset contains the circuitry to control the local bus, memory, DMA, interrupts, and cache memory. The motherboard manufacturer determines which chipset to use.

Keep in mind that a DIMM could use EDO, be a DDR module, or be a DDR2 module. In other words, once you determine that you need a DIMM or a RIMM (or if it is really old, a SIMM), then you have to determine what type of DIMM you need.

Tech Tip

Use the type of memory chips recommended by the motherboard manufacturer

It is best to use the manufacturer-specified type of memory chips. The chipset and motherboard design are very specific as to what type, speed, and features the memory chips can have.

Table 6.1	Memory technologies
Technology	**Explanation**
FPM (fast page mode)	FPM, EDO, and Burst EDO speed up DRAM on sequential accesses to the memory chip. For example, if you have a 50ns DRAM and a 50ns FPM memory module, both types take 50 ns to access the chip the first time. On the second try, the FPM SIMM is accessed in 40ns. Used with SIMMs.
EDO (extended data out)	See explanation for FPM. A 50ns EDO memory module would take 50ns to access the chip, but on the second access, only 25ns are needed. Used with 72-pin SIMMs and 168-pin DIMMs.
BEDO (burst EDO)	See explanation for FPM. A 50ns BEDO memory module would take 50ns to access the chip, but on the second access, only 15ns are needed. Used with SIMMs.
SDRAM (synchronous DRAM)	Performs very fast burst memory access similar to BEDO. New memory addresses are placed on the address bus before the prior memory address retrieval and execution is complete. SDRAM synchronizes its operation with the CPU's clock signal to speed up memory access. Used with DIMMs.
PC100 SDRAM	Designed for the 100MHz front side bus.
PC133 SDRAM	Designed for the 133MHz front side bus, but will work with 100MHz motherboards (at 100MHz, not 133MHz). If you mix PC100 and PC133 DIMMs on the same motherboard, the memory and the bus will run at the lower speed (100MHz).
DDR (double data rate)	Sometimes called DDR SDRAM or DDR RAM and developed from SDRAM technology. With previous SDRAM, data was only sent on the rising clock signal. DDR RAM can send twice as much data as PC133 SDRAM because with DDR RAM, data is transmitted on both sides of the clock signal (rising and falling edges). A DDR DIMM uses 184 pins, and cannot be inserted into a DDR2 or DDR3 memory slot.
DDR2	An upgrade to the DDR SDRAM standard and sometimes is called DDR2 RAM. It includes the following modules DDR2-400, DDR2-533, DDR2-667, DDR2-800, and DDR2-1000. DDR2 uses 240-pin DIMMs and is not compatible with DDR; however, the higher end (faster) DDR2 modules are backwards compatible with the slower DDR2 modules.
DDR3	The latest in DDR SDRAM technology that is an upgrade from DDR2 for speeds up to 1600MHz. The technology better supports multi-core processor-based systems.
RDRAM (Rambus DRAM)	Developed by Rambus, Inc. and is packaged in 184-pin RIMMs (which is a trademark of Rambus, Inc.). Must be installed in pairs with dual and quad channel motherboards. The BIOS and chipset must both support the technology to use RDRAM. Examples of RIMMs include PC600, PC700, PC800, PC1066, PC1200, RIMM1600, RIMM3200, RIMM4200, RIMM6400, RIMM8500, and RIMM9600. When RIMMs are used, all memory slots must be filled even if the slot is not needed because the memory banks are tied together. Put a C-RIMM (Continuity RIMM), which is a blank module, in any empty (unfilled) slot.

Most people cannot tell the difference between a DDR, DDR2, or DDR3 memory module. Even though DDR uses 184 pins and DDR2 uses 240 pins, they are the same physical size. DDR3 modules also have 240 pins but will not fit in a DDR2 slot. Figure 6.3 shows DDR2 and DDR3 DIMMs and Table 6.2 lists many of the DIMM models.

Because a DIMM can be shown with either the PCx- or DDRx- designation, it can be confusing as to what you are buying. A brief explanation might help. DDR2-800 is a type of DDR2 memory that can run on a 400Hz front side bus (the number after DDR2 divided in half). Another way

DDR2 240-pin DIMM   DDR3 240-pin DIMM

Figure 6.3   **DDR2 and DDR3 DIMMs**

Table 6.2   **DIMMs**

Memory type	Other name	Clock speed	Data transfer rate (per second)
PC100	N/A	100MHz	100M
PC133	N/A	133MHz	133M
PC1600	DDR-200	100MHz	200M
PC2100	DDR-266	133MHz	266M
PC2700	DDR-333	166MHz	333M
PC3200	DDR-400	200MHz	400M
PC2-3200	DDR2-400	200MHz	400M
PC2-4200	DDR2-533	266MHz	533M
PC2-5300	DDR2-667	333MHz	667M
PC2-6400	DDR2-800	400MHz	800M
PC2-8000	DDR2-1000	500MHz	1G
PC2-8500	DDR2-1066	533MHz	1.07G
PC2-9200	DDR2-1150	575MHz	1.15G
PC2-9600	DDR2-1200	600MHz	1.2G
PC3-6400	DDR3-800	400MHz	800M
PC3-12800	DDR3-1600	800MHz	1.6G
PC3-16000	DDR3-2000	1000MHz	2G

of showing the same chip would be to use the designation PC2-6400, which is the theoretical bandwidth of the memory chip in MBps.

Planning the Memory Installation— Memory Features

In addition to having to determine what type of memory chips are going to be used, you must determine what features the memory chip might have. The computer system or motherboard

How parity works

If a system uses even parity and the data bits 10000001 go into memory, the ninth bit or parity bit is a 0 because an even number of bits (2) are 1s. The parity changes to a 1 only when the number of bits in the data is an odd number of 1s. If the system uses even parity and the data bits 10000011 go into memory, the parity bit is a 1. There are only three 1s in the data bits. The parity bit adjusts the 1s to an even number. When checking data for accuracy, the parity method detects if one bit is incorrect. However, if two bits are in error, parity does not catch the error.

documentation is going to delineate what features are supported. Table 6.3 helps characterize memory features.

Keep in mind that some motherboards may support both non-parity and ECC or may require a certain feature such as SPD. It is important that you research this *before* you look to purchase memory.

A memory module may use more than one of the categories listed in the two previous tables. For example, a DIMM could be a DDR2 module, be registered, and support ECC for error detection. Most registered memory also uses the ECC technology. DDR memory modules can support either ECC or non-ECC as well as be registered or unbuffered as the type of technology.

Memory technology is moving quite quickly today. Chipsets also change constantly. Technicians are continually challenged to keep up with the features and abilities of the technology so that they can make recommendations to their customers. Trade magazines and the Internet are excellent resources for updates. Never forget to check the motherboard's documentation when dealing with memory. Information is a technician's best friend.

Table 6.3	Memory features
Feature	**Explanation**
parity	A method for checking the accuracy of data going in or out of the memory chips.
non-parity	Non-parity memory chips are chips that do not use any error checking. Most memory modules today are non-parity because the memory controller circuitry provides error correction.
ECC (error correcting code)	An alternative to parity checking that uses a mathematical algorithm to verify data accuracy. ECC can detect up to four-bit memory errors and correct one-bit memory errors. ECC is used in higher-end computers such as network servers.
registered memory	Registered memory modules have extra chips (registers) near the bottom of the chip that, unlike unbuffered DDR or DDR2 modules, delay all data transfers by one clock tick to ensure accuracy. They are used in servers and high-end computers. If you install a registered memory module into a system that allows both registered and unbuffered memory, all installed memory must be registered modules.
unbuffered memory	The opposite of registered memory and is used in low- to medium-powered computers. Unbuffered memory is faster than registered or fully buffered memory.
fully buffered memory	A technology used in network servers and Apple computers. Requires a special memory controller. Fully buffered memory buffers the data pins from the channel and uses point-to-point serial signaling connections similar to PCIe. You sometimes see these chips advertised as FBDIMMs.
SPD (serial presence detect)	The memory modules have an extra EEPROM that holds information about the DIMM such as capacity, voltage, refresh rates, and so on. The BIOS can read and use this data to adjust motherboard timing for the best performance.

Planning for Memory— The Amount of Memory to Install

Memory is one of the easiest upgrades to do to a computer to improve performance. The amount of memory you need depends on what operating system you are using, what applications you are using, how many applications you want to have open at the same time, the type of computer you are using, and the maximum amount allowed by your motherboard. But first, we should look into memory capacities.

Think of a memory chip like a giant spreadsheet where each cell holds one bit. If you had 64 million cells, then the chip would hold 64 million bits. If each cell held eight bits, then the chip would hold 64 million bytes or 64MB. Common capacities for DIMMs are 256MB, 512MB, 1GB, 2GB, 4GB, and 8GB (and more before this book is revised). RIMMs come in 64MB, 128MB, 256MB, and 512MB capacities.

Memory chips are sometimes shown with varying numbers. For example, a chip may be shown as 32Mx64 and actually be a 256MB memory module. The 32Mx64 is describing the memory chip in more detail—there are 32 million locations with 64 bits in each location. 32 million times 64 is the chips capacity in mega*bits*. Divide by 8 and you get the chips capacity in *megabytes*. When parity is used with DIMMs, you see the second number as *72*; for example, 32Mx72 is still 256MB. Those extra 8 bits are used for error checking. Table 6.4 shows sample memory configurations.

Table 6.4	Memory capacities			
Module description	**Module locations (in millions)**	**Bits in each location**	**Capacity in megabits**	**Capacity in megabytes (divide by 8)**
8Mx64	8	64	512	64
8Mx72	8	64 (8 for parity)	512	64
16Mx64	16	64	1,024	128
16Mx72	16	64 (8 for parity)	1,024	128
32Mx64	32	64	2,048	256
64Mx64	64	64	4,096	512
128Mx64	128	64	8,192	1,024 (or 1GB)
256Mx72	256	64 (8 for parity)	16,384	2,048 (or 2GB)

The operating system you use determines to a great extent the starting point for the amount of memory to have. Generally, the older or less powerful your operating system is, the smaller amount of RAM you need. Table 6.5 is the *starting point* for calculating memory requirements. Remember that as you want to run more applications simultaneously and the higher the application function (such as gaming or photo/video/sound manipulation), the more memory you will need. Also note that the memory recommendations shown in Table 6.5 are not the minimum requirements listed by the operating system creators. Notice that an Apple computer (OS9 and OSX) have similar memory recommendations to PCs.

If upgrading memory, you need to know a couple of key pieces of information.

• How much memory you are starting with?
• How many motherboard RAM slots are currently being used and whether you have any slots free?
• What is the maximum amount of memory that your motherboard supports?

Table 6.5	General operating system memory recommendations
Operating system	**General amount of RAM to start calculations**
Windows 98	64 to 128MB
Windows XP Professional	512MB
Windows Vista/Windows 7	1GB
Mac OS9	384MB
MAC OSX	512MB (1+GB for multiple operating systems)
Linux	Depends on shell (some as little as 64MB)

Windows may have memory limitation

Even if your motherboard allows more memory, your operating system has the limitation. Upgrade your operating system if this is the case. Table 6.6 shows the Windows memory limits.

Table 6.6   **Windows XP/Vista/7 memory limits**

Operating system	32-bit version limit	64-bit version limit
XP Starter edition	512MB	N/A
XP (all other editions)	4GB	128GB
Vista/7 Starter edition	1GB (Vista)/2GB (7)	N/A (Vista)/2GB (7)
Vista/7 Home Basic	4GB	8GB
Vista/7 Home Premium	4GB	16GB
Vista/7 Business/Enterprise/Ultimate	4GB	128GB (Vista)/192GB (7)

To determine how much memory you have, access the *System Information* window (right click *My Computer* or *Computer → Properties*) or from the *Run* prompt, type MSINFO32 and press Enter. Scroll down to see the memory information. Figure 6.4 shows how a computer system currently has 1GB of RAM installed (1,024.00MB total physical memory).

To determine how many slots you are currently using and whether or not you have any free, you need to take the cover off of the computer and look on the motherboard. Some memory sites have a software program that determines the type of memory you are using and makes recommendations. However, since you want to be a technician, you can determine this for yourself.

Every motherboard has a maximum memory limitation

Your motherboard has a maximum amount of memory that it supports. You must check the computer or motherboard documentation to see how much this is. There is not a workaround for this limitation. If you want more than the motherboard allows, upgrade to a newer motherboard.

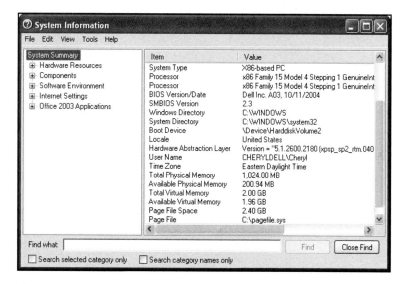

Figure 6.4   *System Information* **window**

Planning for Memory— How Many of Each Memory Type?

A motherboard has a certain number of memory slots determined by the motherboard manufacturer. What type of memory module inserts into the slot and the features that the memory module can have are all determined by the motherboard manufacturer. Two terms frequently seen in motherboard memory documentation are single-sided and double-sided. **Single-sided memory** refers to a memory module that the CPU accesses at one time. In other words, the memory module has one "bank" of memory and 64 bits are transferred out of the memory module to the CPU. A better term for single-sided memory is single-banked memory. Note that the memory module may or may not have all of its "chips" on one side. **Double-sided memory** means that a single memory module has been developed in such a way that it actually contains two memory modules in one container (two banks). If the motherboard slot has been designed to accept this type of memory module, data is still sent to the CPU 64 bits at a time. This is just a way for having more banks of memory on the motherboard without requiring more memory slots. Some people use the terms single-sided and double-sided to describe memory modules that have chips on one side (single-sided) or both sides (double-sided). Another name for single-sided memory is single-ranked and for double-sided memory is double-ranked memory.

Another related topic is dual-channel memory. **Dual-channel** means that the motherboard memory controller chip handles processing of memory requests more efficiently by handling two memory paths simultaneously. For example, say that a motherboard has four memory slots. Traditionally, the memory controller chip, commonly called the MCH or memory controller hub, had one channel through which all data from the four slots traveled. With dual-channeling, the four slots are divided into two channels with each channel having two slots each. Figure 6.5 shows this concept.

Dual-channeling increases a system performance. However, it only speeds things up if the memory modules match exactly—same memory type, same memory features, same speed, and same capacity. Note that on some motherboards the memory modules on Channel A or B do not have to be the same capacities, but the total capacity of the memory module in Channel A should match the total capacity of

Tech Tip

Dual-channel should use exact memory module pairs

Channel A and Channel B (sometimes labeled Channel 0 and Channel 1) should have matching memory modules. Buy a kit to ensure that the two modules are exact.

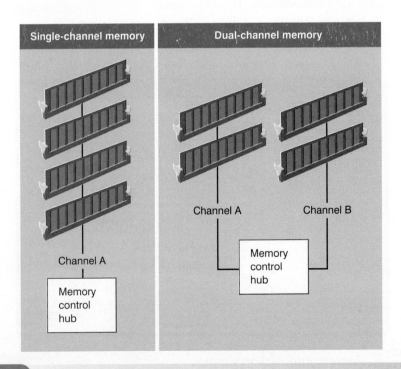

Figure 6.5   **Dual-channel memory**

the memory modules installed in Channel B. Some motherboards require this. Figure 6.6 illustrates this concept.

Notice in Figure 6.6 how in the first example two identical memory modules are inserted. One memory module is in Channel A and the other in Channel B. Frequently the motherboard manufacturer requires that the memory modules match in all respects: manufacturer, timing, and capacity in order to support dual-channeling.

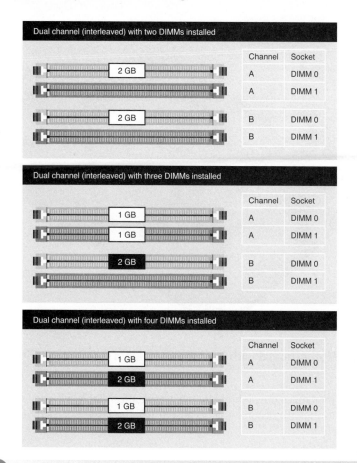

Figure 6.6 **The total capacity of the memory module installed in Channel A should match the total capacity in Channel B.**

In the next example, three DIMMs are used. Some manufacturers support dual-channeling with three DIMMS, but you should always check the motherboard or system documentation to ensure this is the case. Another example that is not shown in the figure is where an uneven amount of memory is installed in Channel A than in Channel B. For example, Channel A has 2GB and Channel B has a 1GB memory module. Some motherboards can dual-channel for the first 1GB. Only if the motherboard supports this can dual-channeling be achieved this way.

In the last example shown in Figure 6.6 all four DIMMs are installed. Notice how the Channel A total capacity matches the Channel B total capacity (3GB in both channels for a total of 6GB). When dual-channeling, buy memory modules in pairs from a single source. Memory vendors sell them this way.

To plan for the correct amount of memory, you must refer to the motherboard documentation and each motherboard is different. An example helps with this concept. Figure 6.7 shows a motherboard layout with four memory slots.

This motherboard allows 256MB, 512MB, 1GB, and 2GB unbuffered non-ECC DDR2-533 240-pin DIMMs for a maximum of 8GB. Pretend the customer wants 1GB of RAM. What could we do?

Beware of RAM over 4GB

Do not install over 4GB on a computer with a 32-bit operating system such as 32-bit Windows XP, Vista, or Windows 7. The operating system will not be able to see anything over 4GB. As a matter of fact, even when a system has 4GB installed, the 32-bit operating system shows the installed amount as slightly less than 4GB because some of that memory space is used for things attached to the PCI bus.

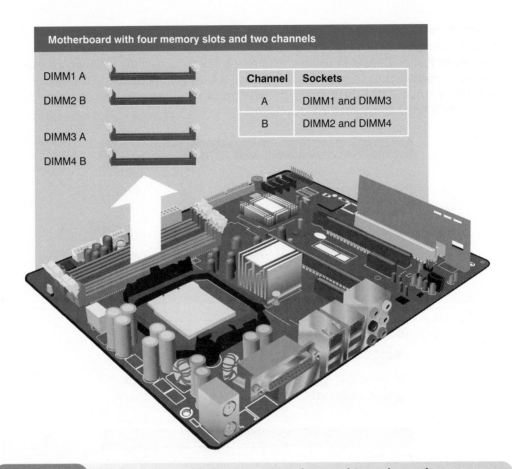

Motherboard with four memory slots and two channels

Channel	Sockets
A	DIMM1 and DIMM3
B	DIMM2 and DIMM4

DIMM1 A
DIMM2 B
DIMM3 A
DIMM4 B

Figure 6.7   **Motherboard with four memory slots and two channels**

How many memory modules do we buy and what capacities? Table 6.7 shows the possible solutions. The best solution is the second one because it has the largest capacity chips taking advantage of dual-channeling.

Table 6.7   **Possible solutions**

Solution	Number and size of memory module(s) needed
1	Four 256MB DIMMs installed in DIMM1, DIMM2, DIMM3, and DIMM4 slots (dual-channeling)
2	Two 512MB DIMMs installed in DIMM1 and DIMM2 slots (dual-channeling)
3	Two 512MB DIMMs installed in DIMM1 and DIMM3 slots
4	One 1GB DIMM installed in DIMM1

Planning for Memory—Research and Buy

The researching and buying step of planning for your memory installation/upgrade is most likely the step that can make your head spin. Different Web sites list memory differently. Some give you too much information, some too little. There are a few such as Kingston Technology (http://www.kingston.com) and Crucial (http://www.crucial.com) that specialize in memory and make it as painless as possible. Nevertheless, as a technician, you should be familiar with all aspects of memory and memory advertisements.

A confusing aspect of buying memory is memory speed. Memory speed can be represented as ns (nanoseconds), MHz, or the DDR PC rating. **Access time** describes how fast information goes into a memory chip or is removed from the chip and is measured in nanoseconds (ns). As for MHz or PC ratings, the higher the number is the faster the speed.

To understand memory, it is best to look at some examples. Table 6.8 shows sample memory advertisements.

Table 6.8	Sample memory advertisement
Memory module	**Advertisement**
2GB	DDR2 PC2-5300 • CL=5 • UNBUFFERED • NON-ECC • DDR2-667 • 1.8V • 256Meg x 64
2GB	DDR2 PC2-4200 • CL=4 • REGISTERED • ECC • DDR2-533 • 1.8V • 256Meg x 72
2GB kit (1GBx2)	DDR2 PC2-4200 • CL=4 • UNBUFFERED • ECC • DDR2-533 • 1.8V • 128Meg x 72
2GB	DDR2 PC2-5300 • CL=5 • FULLY BUFFERED • ECC • DDR2-667 • 1.8V • 256Meg x 72

Notice in Table 6.8 (as in most memory advertisements) that the memory capacity is shown first. The third advertisement down is a kit for a motherboard that had dual-channeling capabilities. It includes two 1GB memory modules for a total of a 2GB memory gain. Also pay attention to the type of memory module that is being advertised. Notice in Table 6.8 how the memory modules are DDR2 and show the PC2 rating. Later in the advertisement it also shows the front side bus speed of 533 or 667 (MHz).

Another listing in the memory advertisement shown in Table 6.8 is the **CL rating**. CL (column address strobe [CAS] latency), is the amount of time (clock cycles) that passes before the processor moves on to the next memory address. RAM is made up of cells where data is held. A cell is the intersection of a row and a column. Think of it as a spreadsheet application. The CAS signal picks which memory column to select, and a signal called RAS (row address strobe) picks which row to select. The intersection of the two is where the data is stored.

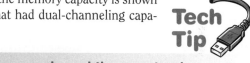

Nanoseconds and the race track

The lower the number of nanoseconds, the faster the access time of the memory chips. Think of access time like a track race—the person with the lowest time wins the race and is considered to be the fastest. Chips with lower access times (lower amount of nanoseconds) are faster than those with higher access times (larger numbers).

Buy the fastest type of memory the motherboard allows

Buying memory that is faster than the motherboard allows does no good. This is like taking a race car on a one lane unpaved road. The car has the ability to go faster, but it is not feasible with the type of road being used. Sometimes you must buy faster memory because the older memory is not sold. This is all right as long as it is the correct type such as DDR or DDR2.

Motherboard manufacturers sometimes list a minimum CL or CAS latency value for memory modules. Both motherboard documentation, memory magazine advertisements, and online memory retailers list the CL rating as a series of numbers such as 3-1-1-1. The first number is the CL rating or a CL3 in this example. The 3-1-1-1 is more detailed in that for a 32 bit transfer, it takes three clock cycles to send the first byte (eight bits), but the next three bytes are sent using one clock cycle each. In other words, it takes six clock cycles to transfer the 32 bits.

Also notice in Table 6.8 that the memory features are listed—fully buffered, unbuffered, and registered. Be sure that the type of memory for which you planned is the one you are researching to buy. The voltage level for the memory module is shown (these are standard values) as well as the capacity. With the capacity, if you see the number 64 at the end, the module does not use

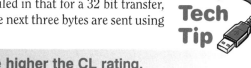

The higher the CL rating, the slower the memory

A rating of CL5 waits five clock cycles before moving to the next memory address. A rating of CL4 waits less time, or four clock cycles before moving to the next memory address.

parity. If you see 72, the memory module uses either parity or ECC. The majority of the time, it will be an ECC memory module.

Usually you can mix CL memory modules

Most systems allow mixing of CL modules; for example, a motherboard could have a memory module rated for CL2 and a different memory module rated for CL3. However, when mixing memory modules, the system will run at the slower memory speed (CL3), which has more clock cycles to wait.

Laptop Memory

Portable computers are a major part of today's business environment. The memory chips used with laptops are different from the ones used in desktop or tower computers. Portables that use DIMMs use special types such as a **SO-DIMM** (144-pin small outline DIMM) or a 172-pin **microDIMM**, and those that use RIMMs use SO-RIMM (small outline RIMM). Figure 6.8 shows a photo of a SO-DIMM.

Figure 6.8   SO-DIMM

Some laptop manufacturers require proprietary memory modules, but that is not as common as it once was. Many laptops only have one memory slot, so when you upgrade, you must replace the module that is installed. Always refer to the manufacturer's documentation when doing this. Always turn off the laptop and remove the battery pack before upgrading memory. You can also refer to the general memory installation instructions for each memory module type found later in this chapter. Laptops can also be upgraded with PC Cards, but this type of upgrade is not as fast as the memory installed on the motherboard.

Installing Memory Overview

The best method to determine which memory chips to install in each bank is described in the following steps:

1. Determine which chip capacities can be used for the system. Look in the documentation included with the motherboard or the computer for this information.
2. Determine how much memory is needed. Ask users which operating system is installed and which applications they are using. Refer to documentation for each application to determine the amount of RAM recommended. Plan for growth.
3. Determine what capacity chips go in each bank by drawing a diagram of the system, planning the memory population on paper, and referring to the documentation of the system or motherboard.

Depending on the type of motherboard, the number of banks available on the motherboard, whether the computer memory is being upgraded, or whether the memory is a new installation, some memory chips may need to be removed to put higher capacity chips into the bank. Look at what is already installed in the system, refer to the documentation, and remove any banks of memory necessary to upgrade the memory.

Memory safety reminder

Before installing a memory module, power off the computer, disconnect the power cord from the back of the computer, and use proper antistatic procedures. Memory modules are most susceptible to ESD. If ESD damages a memory module, a problem may not appear immediately and could be intermittent and hard to diagnose.

When installing memory into a portable computer, refer to the documentation to see if a retaining screw on the bottom of the unit must be removed or if the keyboard must be removed in order to access the memory slots. Be sure the laptop memory notch fits into the key in the memory slot. Laptop memory is normally installed at a 45 degree angle into the slot. Press down on the module until it locks into the side clips. The trick to memory is pushing firmly into the slot and then into the side clamps. Figure 6.9 shows accessing the memory module on a notebook computer.

Figure 6.9   **Accessing a laptop memory module**

Removing/Installing a DIMM/RIMM

When removing a DIMM or a RIMM and using proper ESD prevention techniques, push down on the DIMM retaining tabs that clasp over the DIMM. Be careful not to overextend the tabs when pushing on them. If a plastic tab breaks, the only solution is to replace the motherboard. The DIMM/RIMM lifts slightly out of the socket. Ensuring you are grounded to prevent ESD, lift the module out of the socket once it is released. Figure 6.10 shows how to remove a DIMM/RIMM.

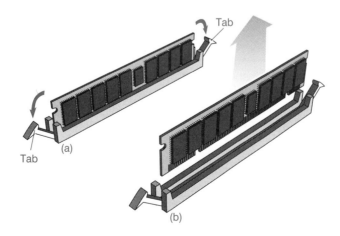

Figure 6.10   **DIMM/RIMM removal**

A DIMM/RIMM has one or more notches on the bottom where the gold or tin contacts are located. The DIMM inserts into the memory socket only one way. The DIMM memory socket has two tabs that align with the DIMM notches. Look at the DIMM and notice where the DIMM notches are located. Look at the DIMM socket and notice where the tabs in the socket are located. The DIMM will not insert into the memory socket unless it is oriented properly.

A DIMM/RIMM is inserted straight down into the socket, not at a tilt like the SIMM or a SO-DIMM. Make sure the side tabs are pulled out before you insert the DIMM, and close the tabs over the DIMM once it is firmly inserted into the socket. If the DIMM/RIMM does not go into the slot easily, do not force it and check the notch or notches for correct alignment. However, once the DIMM is aligned correctly into the slot, push the DIMM firmly into the slot and the tabs should naturally close over the DIMM or on the sides of the DIMM. Figure 6.11 illustrates how to insert a DIMM or a RIMM.

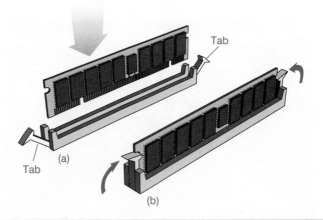

Figure 6.11   **DIMM/RIMM installation**

Today's motherboards automatically recognize new memory; however, some advanced BIOS options exist for tweaking memory performance. With some computers, the Setup program can be used to select parity, non-parity, or ECC options. Always refer to the motherboard or the computer system documentation.

Tech Tip

POST error codes are normal after a memory installation/upgrade

Some computers show a POST error message or automatically go into the Setup program. This is normal. The important thing to notice during POST is that the memory shown in BIOS should equal the amount of memory installed.

Adding More Cache/RAM

Most computers today have cache built into the processor. The motherboard manufacturer determines if any L3 cache can be installed. Check the documentation included with the motherboard or computer to determine the correct amount of cache (SRAM).

Adding more RAM can make a noticeable difference in computer performance (up to a point, of course). When a computer user is sitting in front of a computer waiting for a document to appear or waiting to go to a different location within a document, it might be time to install more RAM. If you have to have several opened applications on the taskbar, click one of them, and have to wait several seconds before it appears, it might be a good idea to upgrade your RAM.

Windows Disk Caching

Virtual memory is a method of using hard disk space as if it were RAM. Virtual memory allows the operating system to run larger applications and manage multiple applications that are loaded simultaneously. The amount of hard disk space used is dynamic—it increases or decreases as needed. If the system begins to page frequently and is constantly swapping data from RAM to the hard drive, the cache size automatically shrinks.

A **swap file** is a block of hard drive space used like RAM by applications. Other names for the swap file include page file or paging file. For optimum performance in any Windows operating system, set aside as much free hard disk space as possible to allow ample room for virtual memory and caching. Keep your hard drive cleaned of temporary files and outdated files/applications.

Hard drive swap file tips

If multiple hard drives are available, a technician might want to move the swap file to a different drive. Always put the swap file on the fastest hard drive unless that hard drive lacks space. It is best to keep the swap file on a hard drive that does not contain the operating system. You can configure the computer to place the swap file on multiple hard drives. The amount of virtual memory is dynamically created by the operating system and does not normally need to be set manually. If manually set, the minimum amount should be equal to the amount of RAM installed.

To adjust the virtual memory size in Windows XP, do the following:

1. Open the *System* control panel (select *Performance and Maintenance* if using Category view).
2. Click on the *Advanced* tab and locate the *Settings* button located in the Performance section.
3. Click on the *Advanced* tab and look for the *Change* button in the Virtual Memory section.
4. Change the size parameters and click on the *OK* button twice.

To adjust the virtual memory size in Windows Vista, do the following:

1. Open the *System* and *Maintenance* control panel.
2. Select *Performance Information* and *Tools* and select *Advanced* Tools from the Task panel on the left.
3. Select the *Adjust the appearance and performance of Windows* link. A UAC (User Account Control) dialog box appears. Select the *Continue* button.
4. Select the *Advanced* tab and click the *Change* button.

Windows 98 and higher use 32-bit demand-paged virtual memory, and each process gets 4GB of address space divided into two 2GB sections. One 2GB section is shared with the rest of the system while the other 2GB section is reserved for the one application. All the memory space is divided into 4KB blocks of memory called **pages**. The operating system allocates as much available RAM as possible to an application. Then the operating system swaps or pages the application to and from the temporary swap file as needed. The operating system determines the optimum setting for this swap file; however, the swap file size can be changed. Figure 6.12 illustrates how Windows 98 and higher operating systems use virtual memory.

In Figure 6.12, notice how each application has its own memory space. The Memory Pager maps the virtual memory addresses from the individual processes' address space to physical pages in the computer's memory chips.

Windows XP has a natural limitation of 4GB of physical memory. **PAE** (physical address extension) is provided by Intel for motherboards that support this feature and when 32-bit Windows operating systems are being used. PAE allows up to 64GB of physical memory to be used (if the motherboard supports it). You can view whether or not a system supports PAE by viewing the computer's properties through Windows Explorer. An exercise at the end of the chapter demonstrates this process.

Monitoring Memory Usage Under Windows

Windows has the **Performance utility** within Task Manager to monitor memory usage. To access this utility, press Ctrl+Alt+Esc → *Performance* tab. The Performance tab has graphs that visually demonstrate the CPU and memory usage. Figure 6.13 shows the Task Manager Performance tab and Table 6.9 lists the Task Manager Performance fields.

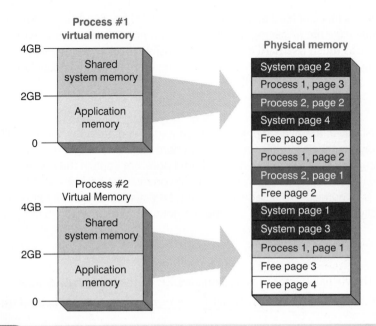

Figure 6.12   **Windows virtual memory usage**

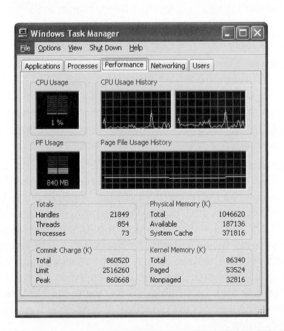

Figure 6.13   **Windows XP *Task Manager Performance* tab**

Old Applications Under Windows

Each 8- or 16-bit application runs in an NT/2000/XP process called NT Virtual DOS Machine (NTVDM). The NTVDM process simulates a 486 computer running DOS. Each older application runs in its own address space. However, 16-bit applications share address space in the NT environment. Many dated applications do not operate in the NT/2000/XP environment because these applications frequently make direct calls to hardware, which NT, 2000, and XP do not allow.

Microsoft states that some older software will not run in Windows Vista/7. One could configure virtual machines using virtualization software such as Microsoft's Virtual PC or VMware

Table 6.9	Task Manager Performance fields
Field	**Description**
Handles	The number of resources the operating system is currently dealing with
Threads	The number of objects contained within currently running processes that are executing program instructions
Processes	An executable program such as Notepad or a service that is currently running
Total Physical Memory	The amount of RAM installed
Available Physical Memory	The amount of physical memory not being used
System Cache	The amount of RAM used by the Input/Output subsystem to map recently used data from the disk
Total Commit Charge	The amount of RAM and virtual memory currently in use
Limit Commit Charge	The amount of virtual memory (page file) and RAM combined
Peak Commit Charge	The highest amount the total commit charge has reached since the computer last rebooted. If the peak amount is larger than your physical amount, then your computer is running low on memory and it is swapping back and forth between the hard drive and physical memory.
Total Kernel Memory	The memory used by the operating system kernel and device drivers
Page Kernel Memory	Memory that can be used by applications as needed that can be copied to the paging file (which frees up RAM)
Nonpaged Kernel Memory	This memory is only available to the operating system and stays in RAM

Workstation. A **virtual machine** allows you to reduce hardware costs by running multiple operating systems simultaneously on a single computer (without one interfering with the other).

Troubleshooting Memory Problems

You can get "out of memory" errors, system slowdowns, or application locking due to memory problems with any operating system. No matter which operating system is being used, check the amount of free space on the hard drive. Sometimes you must close all applications, reboot the computer, and open only the application that was running when the out of memory error occurred because some applications do not release the memory space they hold. The following tips and troubleshooting steps help with memory management:

- Add more RAM. To see the amount of physical memory (RAM) currently installed, right-click the *My Computer* or *Computer* Explorer option and click the *Properties* item.
- If you just installed new memory and an error appears, this is normal. Enter Setup because the BIOS knows something has changed.
- If you just installed new memory and the computer will not boot, check your installation by pushing harder on the memory module to ensure that it is fully seated into the slot. Check for loosened cables that you might have caused. Ensure that you are installing the right memory type. You might need to upgrade your BIOS so that your motherboard recognizes the increased amount of RAM.
- Delete files/applications that are no longer needed and close applications not being used. Empty the Recycle Bin.
- Adjust virtual memory size.
- Change the virtual memory settings so that it uses more hard drive space.
- Do not put the swap file on multiple partitions that reside on the same hard drive. Use multiple hard drives if necessary.
- Put the swap file on a hard disk partition that does not contain the operating system.
- Put the swap file on the fastest hard drive.
- Remove the desktop wallpaper scheme or use a plain one.

- Adjust your Temporary Internet Files setting. From Internet Explorer, click the *Tools* → *Internet Options* → *Settings* button. A slide bar allows you to adjust how much disk space is set aside for caching Web files. To increase the amount of disk space (faster access), move the sliding bar to the right. For those who do not have a lot of free hard disk space, move the sliding bar to the left.
- Defragment the hard drive. See Chapter 7 for steps.
- If you receive a message that the SPD device data missing or inconclusive, your motherboard is looking for SPD data that it cannot receive from the memory module. If this is a new module, ensure it supports SPD. If it is an older module, you need to replace one of your memory modules.

POST usually detects a problem with a memory chip, and most BIOS chips show an error code or message. If POST issues a memory error, turn off the computer, remove the cover, and press down on any memory modules and reboot. Another option is to clean the memory module slots with compressed air and reinstall the module.

The key to good memory chip troubleshooting is to divide and conquer. Narrow the problem to a suspected memory module, and then swap banks if possible. Keep in mind most memory problems are not in the hardware, but in the software applications and operating system.

Upgrading memory is one of the easiest ways to help with performance issues

Keep in mind that sometimes there is nothing to do but buy more RAM—but try the aforementioned tips first.

Adding more memory did not allow my application to load or run faster

Today's operating systems rely almost as much on hard drive space as they do RAM because of the multitasking (using multiple applications simultaneously). Lack of hard drive space is almost as bad as not having enough RAM. Also, not all applications can use available memory. Whether or not an application can use all the RAM in a system depends on the operating system/environment installed on the computer and the operating system for which the application is written.

Flash Memory

Flash memory is a type of non-volatile, solid state memory that holds data even when the computer power is off. PCs use flash memory as a replacement for the BIOS chip. Network devices use flash memory to store the operating system and instructions. Digital cameras use flash memory to store pictures; scanners use flash memory to store images; printers use flash memory to store fonts. Flash memory does not have to be refreshed like DRAM and it does not need constant power like SRAM. A drawback to flash memory is that it is erased in blocks rather than by bytes like RAM.

Various flash memory technologies that are used for storage applications have really advanced in the past few years. These technologies include CompactFlash, SmartMedia, and Flash drives. **CompactFlash** (CF) has two main standards, CompactFlash and CF+. CompactFlash is a small, 50-pin removable storage device that allows speeds up to 133MBps. The first CF device was introduced by the SanDisk Corporation. CF cards can store up to 137GB. The CF+ standard allows increased functionality with cards available for Ethernet, fax/modem/wireless, and barcode scanners.

The CF card can be inserted directly into many devices such as disk drives, cameras, PDAs, tablet PCs. The card uses flash memory, which does not require a battery to keep the data saved to it. CF cards can also be installed into computers with a Type II PC Card adapter

Make note of the CF card file system type

If Windows XP is used to format a CF card, it will place a FAT32 file system on the card. Some cameras can only use FAT16. Windows XP does have a setting for the FAT system that will allow the card to be used in the device that requires FAT16. See Chapter 7 for more information on FAT16 and FAT32.

or a CF card reader attached to a USB or IEEE 1394 FireWire port. The operating systems that support CF include Windows 9x and higher.

The CF technology is also used in solid state drives. Sometimes called microdrives, these devices fit in a Type II (5mm) CF card slot. The Type I (3.3mm) slot is a common one included in cameras. Solid state drives are covered in more detail in Chapter 7.

Another similar flash memory technology is SmartMedia, which is a trademark of Toshiba Corporation. SmartMedia flash cards are used in a variety of devices such as cameras, PDAs, musical instruments, printers, faxes, MP3 players, and scanners. A PC Card adapter can be used to install a SmartMedia card into a PC.

There are two versions of SmartMedia cards—3.3V and 5V. Some systems support both versions, but others support only one of the versions. It is important to purchase the appropriate version for the device being used. SmartMedia allows storage from 2MB to 256MB. Figure 6.14 shows from left to right a Sony Flash memory stick, an Olympus XD memory card, a SanDisk SD memory card, and a SanDisk CompactFlash memory card.

Figure 6.14   **Flash memory media**

USB flash drives (sometimes called thumb drives, memory bars, or memory sticks) allow storage up to 8GB with higher capacities expected. These drives connect to a USB port and are normally recognized by the Windows operating system. A driver may be required for an older operating system. After attaching the drive to a USB port, a drive letter is assigned and Windows Explorer can be used to copy files to the drive.

No. 1 cause of Flash drive failure is improper removal

When finished using the Flash drive, double-click the *Remove Hardware* icon located in the System Tray. The icon has a green arrow. You may have to click on the left arrow or up arrow to see this icon. Click *Safely Remove Hardware.* Select the appropriate Flash drive, then click *Stop* and *OK.* When a message appears that you can safely remove the drive, pull the Flash drive from the USB port.

Tech Tip

Various models are available including drives that fit on a neck chain, inside watches, and on a key ring. Security features that are available on the Flash drives include password protection to the drive and data encryption. Flash drives are a very good memory storage solution and they are inexpensive and easy to use. Figure 6.15 shows a flash drive.

Figure 6.15   **Flash memory thumb drive**

Memory is one of the most critical components of a computer and it is important for a technician to be well versed in the different memory technologies. Since memory is one of the most common upgrades, becoming proficient and knowledgeable about populating memory is important. Exercises follow that help prepare you for the workforce and installing/upgrading memory.

Soft Skills—Teamwork

Technicians, by their nature, do not like working in teams as much as they like working on their own. Much of a technician's job is done solely. However, normally a technician has one or more peers, a supervisor, and a network of partners involved with the job such as suppliers, subcontractors, and part-time help. It is easy to have tunnel vision in a technical support job and lose sight of the mission of the business. Many technical jobs have the main purpose of generating revenue—solving people's computer and network problems for the purpose of making money. Other technicians have more of a back-office support role—planning, installing, configuring, maintaining, and troubleshooting technologies the business uses to make money.

Technicians must focus on solving the customer's problems and ensuring that the customer feels his or her problem has been solved professionally and efficiently. However, you cannot lose sight of the business-first mentality—remember that you play a support role whether you generate revenue or not. You are a figure on someone's balance sheet and you need to keep your skills and attitudes finely tuned to be valuable to the company. No matter how good you are at your job, you are still better to a company if you are part of a team. Being the person who is late, takes off early, chats too much with customers, blames others, and so on, is not being a team member.

Technicians need to be good team players and have good sportsmanship when on the job. Teamwork is part of the skill set that employers seek as much as they want you to have technical skills. Think of ways that you can practice teamwork even as a student, and refine those skills when you join the workforce!

Key Terms

access time (p. 174)
cache memory (p. 164)
CL rating (p. 175)
CompactFlash (p. 182)
DDR (p. 167)
DDR2 (p. 167)
DDR3 (p. 167)
DIMM (p. 165)
double-sided memory (p. 172)
DRAM (p. 164)
dual-channel (p. 172)

ECC (p. 169)
flash memory (p. 182)
fully buffered memory (p. 169)
microDIMM (p. 176)
non-parity (p. 169)
PAE (p. 179)
pages (p. 179)
parity (p. 169)
Performance utility (p. 179)
RDRAM (p. 166)
refresh (process) (p. 164)

registered memory (p. 169)
SDRAM (p. 166)
single-sided memory (p. 172)
SO-DIMM (p. 176)
SPD (p. 169)
SRAM (p. 164)
swap file (p. 179)
unbuffered memory (p. 169)
USB flash drive (p. 183)
virtual machine (p. 181)
virtual memory (p. 178)

Review Questions

1. Describe the difference between RAM and ROM.

2. What is meant by "memory chip refreshing"?

3. Which types of memory chips require constant refreshing? (Pick all that apply.)
   [ROM | DRAM | SRAM | SDRAM | EDO | FPM | Burst EDO]

4. [T | F] Most memory on the motherboard is SRAM.

5. Describe how cache increases computer speed.

6. What physical packaging is most commonly used today for memory?

7. How is DDR SDRAM different from PC133 SDRAM?

8. What is another name for DDR RAM?

9. What is the difference between RDRAM and DDR2 RAM?

10. Which is faster DDR2 or DDR? Explain how they might be the same speed.

11. What is the difference between fully buffered and unbuffered SDRAM?

12. What is SPD and how is memory different with SPD?

13. Which type of memory is more likely to be used by people in a corporation? [registered | fully buffered | unbuffered]

14. Which type of memory is most likely to be used by college students on campus? [parity | non-parity]

15. [T | F] A motherboard could support SPD and ECC.

16. List three things that affect how much memory a computer needs.

17. A memory advertisement lists as 128Mx72. What is the total capacity for this module?

18. A memory module lists as 128Mx72. What feature does this module most likely use?

19. Describe how you can determine how much memory to install in a system.

20. What is another name for single-sided memory?

21. What is an advantage of having dual-channeling?

22. A customer has a motherboard that he wants you to install. He also wants you to recommend memory modules and install them. The manual states that the motherboard has two DIMM slots that support 64, 128, 256, 512MB, and 1GB 184-pin DDR single- and double-sided SDRAM modules. The maximum amount of RAM is 2GB. The customer wants 768MB of RAM. What memory modules will you recommend to the customer?

23. A customer has a motherboard that has two DIMM slots that support 64, 128, 256, 512MB, and 1GB 184-pin DDR single- and double-sided SDRAM modules. The customer wants 768MB of dual-channel RAM. What recommendations will you make?

24. Describe the three methods memory module speed might be represented.

25. [T | F] An 8ns memory chip is faster than a 10ns memory chip.

26. In the sample advertisements shown in Table 6.8, what front side bus is used with the PC2-5300 module?

27. [T | F] Installing faster memory chips always increases computer speed.

28. A DDR DIMM memory chip is advertised as 256MB CAS 2.5. What does CAS 2.5 mean?

29. Which is a better rating, CL2 or CL2.5?

30. How many clock cycles does it take to send 32 bits using a memory chip that has a rating of 4-2-1-1?

31. [T | F] Laptop memory is best upgraded with a PC Card.

32. List two common locations that the memory module is found on a laptop.

33. What could be a symptom of a computer that has had its memory weakened by static electricity during a memory upgrade?

34. How is a DIMM installation different from a SIMM installation?

35. [T | F] A POST error message is normal after upgrading memory on some computers.

36. [T | F] Processors today have cache built into them.

37. Explain how virtual memory works.

38. Which control panel is used in Windows XP to set virtual memory settings?

39. What is a swap file?

40. Which of the following is used in Windows XP/Vista to evaluate memory usage? [VCache tool | Task Manager | My Computer | System Monitor]

41. [T | F] All 16-bit applications operate in the Windows environment.

42. List four things to help with memory performance.
43. Which screen saver takes the least amount of memory?
44. [T | F] Flash memory contents are lost when power is removed.
45. List three ways a technician can demonstrate teamwork in a technical position.

Fill-in-the-Blank

1. The two main types of memory are _____ and _____.
2. An example of non-volatile memory is _____.
3. The major types of RAM are _____ and _____.
4. The SRAM chips contained in the CPU housing are known as _____.
5. DIMMs can have _____, _____, or _____ pins.
6. Memory modules have either _____ or _____ contact edges.
7. DDR is a type of _____ where twice as much data is sent as in PC133 modules.
8. Three DDR2 modules are _____, _____, _____.
9. DDR memory modules have _____ pins, whereas DDR2 modules use _____ pins.
10. Another name of DDR2-667 is PC2-_____.
11. All unused RIMM slots must contain a _____.
12. _____ transmits data on both sides of the clock signal and uses 184-pin DIMMs.
13. _____ is a method of memory error checking in which an extra bit is used to check a group of 8 bits going into the bank of memory.
14. _____ allows the BIOS to determine detailed information about a memory module.
15. DIMMs have capacities measured in _____ or _____.
16. The _____ applications you use simultaneously, the more RAM you need.
17. The My Computer or Computer _____ screen shows how much RAM is installed in the XP computer.
18. _____ has two memory modules in one package.
19. _____ is when the memory controller has two independent memory paths.
20. The _____ the PC number, the faster the memory module.
21. The _____ the MHz rating, the faster the memory module.
22. Three memory physical packaging types used in laptops are _____, _____, and _____.
23. The maximum amount of addressable RAM in a Windows XP 32-bit computer is _____.
24. Memory modules are susceptible to _____, which is where you induce current flow that weakens or destroys the module.
25. DIMM slots have _____ that keep the module firmly connected in the memory slot.
26. A/An _____ file is the use of some hard drive space by applications because there is not enough RAM.
27. _____ cards are commonly used in video equipment to store images.
28. A/An _____ is a common name for a Flash drive.
29. Use the _____ systray icon to remove a Flash drive.
30. The act of working toward a common business goal with other employees is _____.

Hands-On Exercises

1. Configuring Memory on Paper-1

Objective: To be able to determine the correct amount and type of memory to install on a motherboard

Parts: Internet access or access to magazines or ads that show memory prices

Procedure: Refer to Figure 6.16 and Table 6.10 to answer the questions. This motherboard supports 184-pin DDR SDRAM PC1600, PC2100, PC2700, and PC3200 modules. The capacities supported are 64MB through 1GB for a total of 3GB maximum.

Questions:

1. What memory modules are needed if the customer wants 1.25GB of RAM? (What capacities and how many of each capacity?)

2. What memory slots will be used to install the memory based on the information provided?

3. Using the Internet, a magazine, or a list of memory modules, determine the exact part numbers and quantities of memory modules that you would buy. List them with the location of where you obtained the information.

4. Based on your Internet research, did you change your mind about which memory modules you are buying if this was your own machine? Why or why not?

5. During your research of memory modules, did you come upon the words single-sided or double-sided? If so, in what context?

6. Can DDR2 memory modules be used with this motherboard? How can you tell?

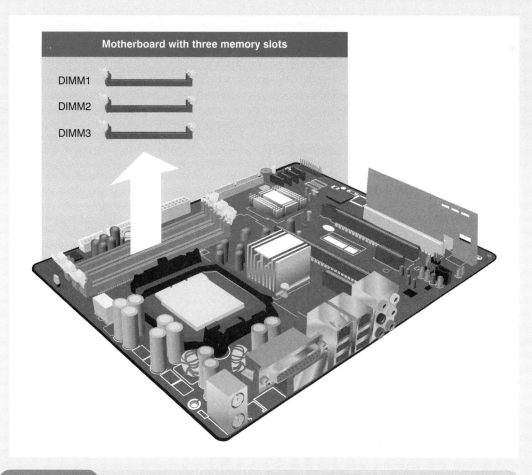

Figure 6.16   **Motherboard with three memory slots**

Table 6.10   **Motherboard memory combinations**

Number of DIMMs installed	DIMM1	DIMM2	DIMM3
1	x8 single-sided or x16		
1	x8 double-sided		
2	x8 single-sided or x16	x8 single-sided or x16	
2	x8 single-sided or x16	x8 double-sided	
2	x8 double-sided	x8 single-sided or x16	
2	x8 double-sided	x8 double-sided	
3	x8 single-sided or x16	x8 single-sided or x16	x8 single-sided or x16
3	x8 single-sided or x16	x8 single-sided or x16	x8 double-sided
3	x8 single-sided or x16	x8 double-sided	x8 single-sided or x16
3	x8 single-sided or x16	x8 double-sided	x8 double-sided
3	x8 double-sided	x8 single-sided or x16	x8 single-sided or x16
3	x8 double-sided	x8 single-sided or x16	x8 double-sided
3	x8 double-sided	x8 double-sided	x8 single-sided or x16
3	x8 double-sided	x8 double-sided	x8 double-sided

7. Is the parity, non-parity, or ECC feature used? How can you tell?

8. This motherboard already has 256MB of RAM installed in the DIMM1 slot. The customer would like to upgrade to 768MB of RAM. What memory modules are needed if the customer wants to go from 256MB to 768MB of RAM? (What capacities and how many of each capacity?)

9. What memory slots will be used to install the memory based on the information provided?

10. Using the Internet, a magazine, or a list of memory modules, determine the exact part numbers and quantities of memory modules that you would buy. List them with the location of where you obtained the information.

2. Configuring Memory on Paper-2

Objective: To be able to determine the correct amount and type of memory to install on a motherboard

Parts: Internet access or access to magazines or ads that show memory prices

Procedure: Refer to Figure 6.17 and Table 6.11 to answer the questions. This motherboard supports DDR 266, 333, and 400 memory modules. The capacities supported are 64MB through 1GB for a total of 4GB maximum. It is not recommended to use a three DIMM configuration with this board. Memory channel speed is determined by the slowest DIMM populated in the system.

Questions:

1. What memory modules are needed if the customer wants 1.5GB of dual-channel RAM? (What capacities and how many of each capacity?)

2. What memory slots will be used for each memory module type to install the memory based on the information provided?

3. Using the Internet, a magazine, or a list of memory modules, determine the exact part numbers and quantities of memory modules that you would buy. List them with the location of where you obtained the information.

4. This motherboard already has 256MB of RAM installed in the DIMM1 slot. The customer would like to upgrade to 2GB total memory, use the existing module if possible, and use dual-channel. What memory modules are needed? (What capacities and how many of each capacity?)

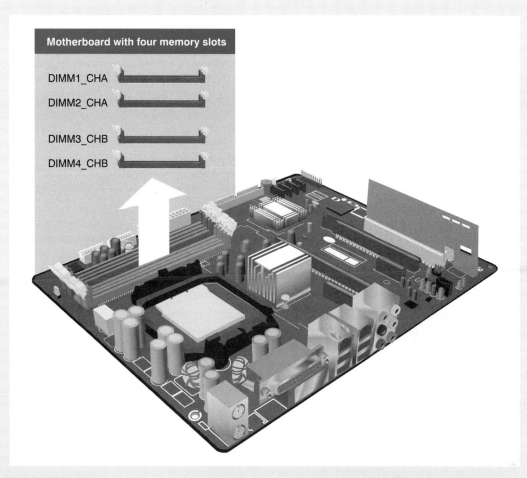

6
Memory

Figure 6.17   **Motherboard with four memory slots and two channels**

Table 6.11   **Motherboard single/dual-channel combinations**

		Sockets			
Mode	Scenario	DIMM1	DIMM2	DIMM3	DIMM4
Single	1	Populated			
	2		Populated		
	3			Populated	
	4				Populated
Dual-channel	1	Populated		Populated	
	2		Populated		Populated
	3	Populated	Populated	Populated	Populated

5. What memory slots will be used to install the memory based on the information provided?

6. What should you be concerned with regarding the already installed 256MB of RAM if you are going to use this module as part of the upgrade?

7. What does the documentation mean when referencing DDR 266/333/400 RAM?

8. How do you know which one of the 266, 333, or 400 type of module to use?

9. Using the Internet, a magazine, or a provided list of memory modules, determine the exact part numbers and quantities of memory modules that you would buy. List them with the location of where you obtained the information.

3. Configuring Memory on Paper-3

Objective: To be able to determine the correct amount and type of memory to install on a motherboard

Parts: Internet access or access to magazines or ads that show memory prices

Procedure: Refer to Figure 6.18 and Table 6.12 to answer the questions. This motherboard supports the following memory configurations:

- Up to 2GB utilizing 256Mb technology
- Up to 4GB utilizing 512Mb or 1Gb technology
- Up to 8GB utilizing 1Gb technology

The desktop board supports either single or dual-channel memory configurations. The board has four 240-pin Double Data Rate 2 (DDR2) SDRAM DIMM connectors with gold-plated contacts. It provides support for unbuffered, non-registered single or double-sided DIMMs, non-ECC DDR2 533/667/800MHz memory, and Serial Presence Detect (SPD) memory only.

Questions:

1. How can this motherboard support 8GB of RAM with only four slots?

2. What memory features, if any, are used? (Select all that apply) [parity | non-parity | ECC | registered | fully buffered | unbuffered | SPD]

3. What memory modules are needed if the customer wants 3GB of dual-channel RAM? (What capacities and how many of each capacity?)

4. What memory slots will be used to install the memory based on the information provided?

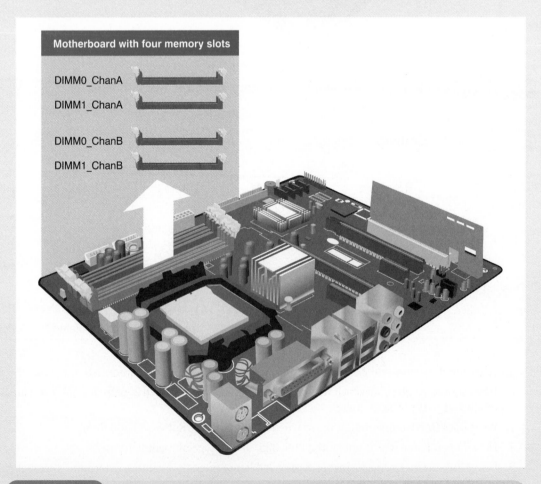

Figure 6.18 Motherboard with four memory slots and two channels

Table 6.12 **Motherboard single/dual-channel guidelines**

	Guidelines
2 DIMMs dual-channel	Install a matched pair of DIMMs equal in speed and size in DIMM0 of both Channel A and Channel B.
4 DIMMs dual-channel	Follow the directions for two DIMMs and add another matched pair of DIMMs in DIMM1 of both channels A and B.
3 DIMMs dual-channel	Install a matched pair of DIMMs equal in speed and size in DIMM0 and DIMM1 of Channel A. Install a DIMM equal in speed and total size of the DIMMs installed in Channel A in either DIMM0 or DIMM1 of Channel B.
Single channel	All other memory configurations result in single channel memory operation.

5. Using the Internet, a magazine, or a list of memory modules, determine the exact part numbers and quantities of memory modules that you would buy. List them with the location of where you obtained the information.

6. Will it matter if the motherboard has tin contacts in the memory slots? Why or why not?

7. Can DDR memory modules be used with this motherboard? How can you tell?

8. If this motherboard already has 1GB of RAM installed in the DIMM0_ChanA slot and the customer would like to upgrade to 2GB of dual-channel RAM, what memory modules are needed? (What capacities and how many of each capacity?)

9. What suggestions, if any, would you make to the customer before researching prices?

10. What memory slots will be used to install the memory based on the information provided?

11. Using the Internet, a magazine, or a list of memory modules, determine the exact part numbers and quantities of memory modules that you would buy. List them with the location of where you obtained the information.

4. Examining Memory Resources Using Windows XP

Objective: To be able to view memory resources currently being used by Windows XP

Parts: A computer with Windows XP installed

Procedure: Complete the following procedure and answer the accompanying questions.

1. Power on the computer and verify that XP loads. Log on to XP using the userid and password provided by the instructor or lab assistant.

2. Access the *Administrative Tools* control panel. (For the *Category* view, click *Performance and Maintenance*.)

3. Double-click the *Computer Management* icon. Click *Device Manager* in the left panel to select it. Click the *View* menu option and select *Resources by type*.

4. In the right window, click the memory option plus sign to expand the option. The first entry is normally the system board.

   What memory addresses are used by the system board?

5. Right-click the first system board memory address shown. Select *Properties*.

   What tabs are shown in the window?

6. Click the *Resources* tab. All memory resources used by the motherboard are shown.

   List the memory ranges used by the motherboard and shown on the *Resources* tab.

   Can the motherboard memory resources be changed on the *Resources* tab?

7. Click the *Cancel* button. Right-click any of the memory addresses that have adapters shown in the right panel. Access the *Resources* tab.

   Can any of the memory resources be changed?

8. Close the *Computer Management* window.

5. Using the System Information Tool in Windows XP to View Memory

Objective: To be able to view memory resources currently being used by Windows XP

Parts: A computer with Windows XP installed

Procedure: Complete the following procedure and answer the accompanying questions.

1. Open Windows Explorer.

2. Right-click *My Computer* and select *Properties*. (An alternate way to do this is to type **msinfo32** from the Run utility and press Enter.)

   On the *General* tab at the bottom of the screen, how much physical RAM is installed?

3. If the machine supports PAE, under the line that shows the amount of physical memory the words *Physical Address Extension* are shown.

   Does this computer have the PAE installed?

4. Click *Cancel* to close the *System Properties* window.

6. Using Windows XP Task Manager to View Memory

Objective: To be able to use the *Task Manager* tool to view memory resources currently being used by Windows XP

Parts: A computer with Windows XP installed

Procedure: Complete the following procedure and answer the accompanying questions.

1. Press Ctrl + Alt + Del keys.

2. Click on the *Performance* tab.

   What percentage of the CPU is being used?

   What is the significance of the number shown by *Threads*?

   Is the total amount of physical memory RAM, cache memory (virtual memory), or both?

   How much RAM is available?

   As a technician, what commit charge section is most important to you and why?

   How much memory is the operating system taking that no other applications can use?

   How can you tell how many applications and services are currently running?

3. Close the *Task Manager* window.

7. Examining Memory Resources Using Windows Vista

Objective: To be able to view memory resources currently being used by Windows Vista

Parts: A computer with Windows Vista installed and rights to use Device Manager

Procedure: Complete the following procedure and answer the accompanying questions.

1. Power on the computer and verify that Vista loads. Log on to Vista using the userid and password provided by the instructor or lab assistant.

2. Access the *System and Maintenance* control panel and select the *Device Manager* link. A UAC (User Account Control) dialog box appears. Select *Continue*.

3. Click the *View* menu option and select *Resources by type*. In the right window, click the memory option plus sign to expand the option. The first entry is normally the system board.

   What memory addresses are used by the system board?

4. Right-click the first system board memory address shown. Select *Properties*.

   What tabs are shown in the window?

5. Click the *Resources* tab. All memory resources used by the motherboard are shown.

   List the memory ranges used by the motherboard and shown on the *Resources* tab.

   Can the motherboard memory resources be changed on the *Resources* tab?

6. Click *Cancel*. Right-click any of the memory addresses that have adapters shown and access the *Resources* tab.

   Can any of the memory resources be changed?

7. Close the window.

8. Using the System Information Tool in Windows Vista to View Memory

Objective: To be able to view memory resources currently being used by Windows Vista

Parts: A computer with Windows Vista installed

Procedure: Complete the following procedure and answer the accompanying questions.

1. To access the System Information tool, click *Start* and select *Control Panel*. Select *System and Maintenance*. Click on the *Performance Information and Tools* link. Select *Advanced Tools* from the task panel on the left. Select the *View advanced system details in System Information* link. (An alternate way to do this is to run `msinfo32` from a command prompt as an administrator and press [Enter].)

   How much physical RAM is installed?

   How much physical RAM is available?

   How much total virtual memory does the machine have?

   How much available virtual memory does the machine have?

   What is the location and size of the page file?

2. Click the *Close Find* button to close the System Information window.

9. Using Windows Vista Task Manager to View Memory

Objective: To be able to use the *Task Manager* tool to view memory resources currently being used by Windows Vista

Parts: A computer with Windows Vista installed and a userid that is allowed to access Task Manager

Procedure: Complete the following procedure and answer the accompanying questions.

1. After logging on to a Windows Vista computer, press [Ctrl]+[Alt]+[Del] keys select *Task Manager* and access the *Performance* tab.

   What percentage of the CPU is being used?

   What is the significance of the number shown by *Threads*?

   Is the total amount of physical memory RAM, cache memory (virtual memory), or both?

   How much RAM is available?

2. Click the *Resource Monitor* button. A UAC (User Access Control) dialog appears. Click *Continue*.

   What is the percentage of used physical memory?

3. Expand the *Memory* section.

   List three executable (.exe) files running in memory.

4. Open an application such as the Calculator accessory. Locate the application in the memory list.

   How many kilobytes are shown for the application in the Commit column?

   How many kilobytes are shown for the application in the Working Set column?

   How many kilobytes are shown for the application in the Shareable column?

   How many kilobytes are shown for the application in the Private column?

5. In the Learn More area, click the *Resource View* Help link. Select *Identify Source Usage in Resource View*. Scroll down until you see the memory section.

   What is the purpose of the Working Set number?

   What is the purpose of the Shareable number?

   What is the purpose of the Private number?

   Looking back at your answers to Step 4, what do you think is the purpose of the Commit column? If possible, use the Internet to find the answer. If Internet access is unavailable, write your own opinion.

6. Close the *Help* window. Close the *Resource Monitor* window. Close the *Task Manager* window.

Internet Discovery

Objective: To become familiar with researching memory chips using the Internet

Parts: A computer with Internet access

Procedure: Use the Internet to complete the following procedure.

1. Power on the computer and start the Internet browser.

2. Using any search engine, locate three different vendors that sell memory chips.

3. Create a table like the one below and fill in your findings for each of the memory sites.

Internet site	Type of DIMM	Largest capacity DIMM	Pros of Web site	Cons of Web site

Of the three Internet sites you found, which one was your favorite and why?

Soft Skills

Objective: To enhance and fine tune a future technician's ability to listen, communicate in both written and oral form, and support people who use computers in a professional manner

Activities:

1. On your own, use the Internet to find a utility that tests soft skills or your personality. Compare your scores with others in the class. Make a list of how you might improve in specific weak areas. Present your findings to a group and share your group findings with another group.

2. Note that this activity requires two computers. In groups of two, have one person describe in great detail to the other person how to upgrade the computer's memory by removing memory from one computer and adding it to the other. The person doing the physical installation can do nothing unless the partner describes how to do it. Reverse roles for removing the memory and re-installing back in the original computer. At the end of the exercise, the two participants describe to the teacher what they experienced.

3. In small groups, find a video that describes how to do something on the computer. Critique the video for how the speaker might do a better job communicating to people who are not technicians. Share the video with the class along with your recommendations for doing it better. As an option, script a short presentation for how to do something. Tape it if possible and have the class critique each group's presentation.

Critical Thinking Skills

Objective: To analyze and evaluate information as well as apply learned information to new or different situations

Activities:

1. Refer to Figure 6.7 in the chapter. Compare and contrast solution 2 with solution 3 as it relates to dual-channeling. Write a list of your findings and share them with the class.

2. Using Figure 6.7 in the chapter again, list the repercussions of discovering that the motherboard supports both single-side and double-sided memory modules. What would the memory population look like for 8GB (the maximum) of RAM?

3. Download a motherboard manual from the Internet or use one provided in the classroom. Find the memory section and make a list of any terms or directions that are given that you do not understand. In groups of 4 or 5, share your lists and come up with as many solutions as possible. Share your group list with the class. Write any unsolved questions on the board and bring the answers to those questions back in a week.

Storage Devices

Objectives

After completing this chapter you will be able to

- Install or replace a floppy drive
- Define and explain fundamental hard drive terminology
- Compare and contrast IDE and SCSI technologies
- Install and configure storage devices
- Troubleshoot storage device problems
- Perform hard drive preventive maintenance
- Learn skills for effective communication on the phone

Floppy Drive Overview

The floppy drive subsystem consists of three main parts: (1) the electronic circuits or the controller, (2) the 34-pin ribbon cable, and (3) the floppy drive (sometimes called the "a" drive). The electronic circuits give the floppy drive instructions: "Floppy drive, go to this location and read some data! Floppy drive, go to this other location and write some data!" The electronic circuits can be on an adapter or built into the motherboard. For today's computers, the electronic circuits are normally built into the motherboard. The floppy cable connects the floppy drive to the electronic circuits. The floppy drive is the device that allows saving data to disk media.

Troubleshooting and installing floppy drives involves these three main areas and the media. Media refers to the disks inserted in the floppy drive. Note that today's floppy drives are 3.5-inch 1.44MB.

Floppy Media and Construction

Tech Tip

At the first sign of trouble on a floppy drive, clean the heads

Over time, the read/write heads become dirty. When a technician sees read/write errors occurring, the first step is to clean the read/write heads.

The media inserted in a floppy drive is a **disk** or floppy disk. On one side, a disk has a sliding write-protect window that allows the disk to be written to or protected from any writing or changing of data that is occurring. If you close the window, data can be written to the disk. If the window is open, the disk is write-protected and data cannot be written on the disk.

Floppy drives have two **read/write heads** responsible for placing the data, the 1s and 0s, onto the disk. The disk inserts between the two heads of the floppy drive. One read/write head mounts on the top, the other on the bottom.

Floppy Drive Installation or Replacement

Installation of floppy drives is simple after doing the following preliminary homework:

- An available drive bay
- An available power connection
- A motherboard floppy connector or install an additional adapter
- A floppy cable

Figure 7.1 shows a motherboard floppy connector.

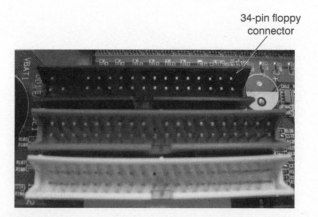

34-pin floppy connector

Figure 7.1   **Floppy connector on motherboard**

The floppy cable is unique to the computer because of the twist at the end of the cable that attaches to the floppy drive. Figure 7.2 shows a floppy drive cable that attaches from the motherboard to the floppy drive. Keep in mind the end with the twist is the one that connects to the drive.

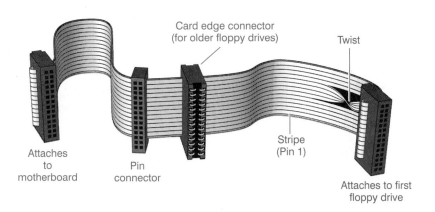

Card edge connector
(for older floppy drives)

Twist

Attaches
to
motherboard

Pin
connector

Stripe
(Pin 1)

Attaches to first
floppy drive

Figure 7.2   **Floppy drive cable**

Pin 1 on the cable needs to attach to pin 1 on the connector. Pin 1 on a cable is easy to find because of the colored stripe that is on one side of the cable. Pin 1 on an adapter or a motherboard is not always easy to locate. Some manufacturers put a small 1 or 2 by the end where the cable's pin 1 inserts. Other manufacturers put larger numbers at the opposite end. For example, if you see the number 33 or the number 34 on the motherboard where the floppy cable inserts, pin 1 and pin 2 are on the *opposite* end of the connector. Installation is nothing more than mounting the floppy drive to the computer case and connecting the cable between the drive and motherboard or adapter.

Attach cable correctly or destroy devices and components

Devices, adapters, controlling circuits, and so on, can be damaged if a cable plugs into the connector the wrong way. Some cables are keyed so they insert only one way into the connector. Most cables that connect to the floppy drive are keyed, but the other end of the cable that connects to the controlling circuits is sometimes not keyed.

Tech Tip

Hard Drive Overview

Hard drives are one of the most popular devices for storing data. They store more data than floppy drives and move data faster than tape drives. Today's hard drive capacities extend into the terabytes. Hard drives are frequently upgraded in a computer, so it is important for you to understand all the technical issues. These issues include knowing the parts of the hard drive subsystem, how the operating system and the BIOS work with a hard drive, how to configure a hard drive, and how to troubleshoot it. The hard drive subsystem can have up to three parts: (1) the hard drive; (2) a cable that attaches to an adapter or the motherboard; and (3) control circuits located on an adapter or the motherboard.

Hard Drive Geometry

Hard drives have multiple hard metal surfaces called **platters**. Each platter typically holds data on both sides and has two read/write heads, one for the top and one for the bottom. The read/write heads float on a cushion of air without touching the platter surface. If a read/write head touches the platter, a **head crash** occurs. This is sometimes called HDI (head to disk interference), and it can damage the platters or the read/write head, causing corrupt data. See Figure 7.3 for an illustration of a hard drive's arms, heads, and platters. Figure 7.4 shows the inside of a hard drive. You can see the top read/write head and the platters. Keep in mind that hard drives should not have their cover removed.

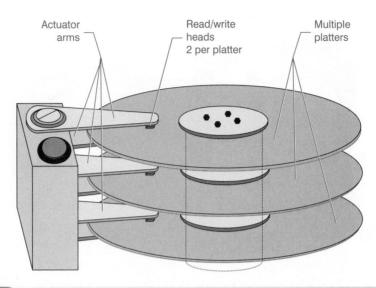

Actuator arms   Read/write heads 2 per platter   Multiple platters

Figure 7.3   **Hard drive geometry**

Figure 7.4   **Hard drive with cover removed**

Each hard drive surface is metallic and has concentric circles, each of which is called a **track**. Tracks are numbered starting with the outermost track, which is called track 0. One corresponding track on all surfaces of a hard drive is a **cylinder**. For example, cylinder 0 consists of all track 0s; all of the track 1s comprise cylinder 1, and so on. A track is a single circle on one platter. A cylinder is the same track on all platters. Figure 7.5 shows the difference between tracks and cylinders. Notice in Figure 7.5 how a concentric circle makes an individual track. A single track on all the surfaces makes an individual cylinder.

Each track is separated into **sectors** by dividing the circle into smaller pieces. 512 bytes are normally stored in each sector, as shown in Figure 7.6.

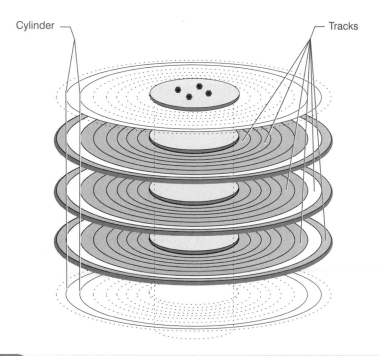

Figure 7.5   **Cylinders versus tracks**

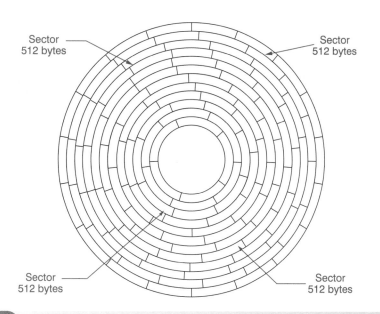

Figure 7.6   **Hard drive sectors**

Hard Drive Interfaces Overview

A hard drive system must have a set of rules to operate. These rules specify the number of heads on the drive, what commands the drive responds to, the cables used with the drive, the number of devices supported, the number of data bits transferred at one time, and so on. These rules make up a standard called an interface that governs communication with the hard drive. There are two major hard drive interfaces: **IDE** (integrated drive electronics), also known as the ATA (AT Attachment) standard, and **SCSI** (small computer system interface). IDE is the most common in home and office computers. SCSI is commonly found in network servers.

Both IDE and SCSI started out as parallel architectures. This means that multiple bits are sent over multiple paths. This architecture requires precise timing as transfer rates increase. Also with both types of devices, multiple devices can attach to the same bus. With parallel IDE, it was only two devices and with SCSI it was more, but the concept is the same. When multiple devices share the same bus, they have to wait their turn to access the bus and there are configuration issues with which to contend. Figure 7.7 shows the concept of parallel transfer.

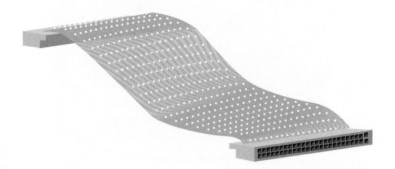

Figure 7.7   **Parallel transfer**

Today, there is a trend toward serial architectures. A serial architecture is a point-to-point bus where each device has a single connection back to the controller. Bits are sent one bit at a time over a single link. More devices can attach to this type of architecture because it scales easier and configuration is much easier. Figure 7.8 illustrates the concept of serial data transfer.

Figure 7.8   **Serial transfer**

IDE (Integrated Drive Electronics)

IDE (integrated drive electronics) is not only for hard drives, but for other internal devices such as tape, Zip, CD, and DVD drives. The original IDE standard was developed only for hard drives and is officially known as ATA (AT attachment). Later other devices were supported by the standard and the standard evolved to ATA/ATAPI (AT attachment packet interface). ATAPI increased support of devices such as CD/DVD and tape drives. There are two types of IDE—PATA (Parallel ATA) and SATA (Serial ATA).

PATA (parallel ATA) is the older IDE type, which uses a 40-pin cable that connects the IDE hard drive to an adapter or the motherboard and transfers 16 bits of data at a time. Each cable normally has either two or three connectors. Many motherboards have both SATA and PATA IDE connectors. Figure 7.9 shows the difference between a PATA and a SATA IDE motherboard connection.

A motherboard that has two IDE connectors can have up to four PATA devices, two per motherboard connection. Figure 7.10 shows a PATA IDE hard drive. Notice the 40-pin connector on the left and the power connector on the right.

SATA IDE
connectors   PATA IDE connector

Figure 7.9   **PATA and SATA motherboard connectors**

Figure 7.10   **PATA IDE hard drive**

If a PATA cable has two connectors and two devices are needed, buy another cable

One 40-pin motherboard PATA connector can support up to two PATA devices. However, some cables only have two connectors—one that connects to the motherboard and one that attaches to the PATA device. If a second device is added, a new cable must be purchased.

Tech
Tip

The original IDE interface supported up to two drives and is also known as the ATA-1 Standard (AT attachment standard). ATA-2 has faster transfer rates (8.3MBps, then later 16.6MBps) than the original ATA-1 standard of 3.3MBps. The ATA-2 standard also improves drive compatibility through an Identify Drive command that allows the BIOS to better determine the drive's properties. ATA-2 supports DMA transfers. **DMA mode** (direct memory access mode) allows data transfer between the hard drive and RAM without going through the CPU. The older method is known as PIO (programmed input/output) mode that was slower than DMA mode because data had to pass through the CPU. PIO is defined in different modes according to the transfer speed and will probably be removed in future ATA standards.

The latest type of DMA transfers is called **UDMA** (ultra DMA) or bus-master DMA. With UDMA the interface gains control of the PCI bus under the direction of the motherboard chipset. UDMA comes in different modes, which represent different transfer speeds. Table 7.1 shows the Ultra DMA modes for ATA hard drives.

Table 7.1	Ultra DMA modes for IDE hard drives
Ultra-DMA mode	Transfer rate (MBps)
UDMA0	16.7
UDMA1	25
UDMA2	33.3
UDMA3	44.4
UDMA4	66.6
UDMA5	100
UDMA6	133

ATA-3 includes power management and a technology called S.M.A.R.T (Self-Monitoring Analysis & Report Technology) that lets the drive send messages about possible data loss. The ATA-4 standard includes faster transfer modes (up to 33MBps) and is called Ultra ATA or Ultra DMA/33. It implements bus mastering and uses CRC for data integrity. **CRC** (cyclic redundancy checking) is a method of checking data for errors. The drive and controller (host) calculate a value based on an algorithm. If the value is different, the controller (host) drops to a slower transfer mode and requests a retransmission.

80-conductor PATA IDE cable is required with newer drives

The 80-conductor cable works with older IDE devices. UDMA modes 3 and higher require the 80-conductor (40-pin) cable.

The ATA-5 standard is also known as Ultra ATA/66 or simply ATA/66. A 40-pin cable is used with this standard as with the other standards, but the cable is different—it has 80 conductors. The 40 extra conductors are ground lines, which are situated between the existing 40 wires. These ground lines reduce crosstalk, improves the accuracy of data transfers, and allows faster speed. Crosstalk is when signals from one wire interfere with the signals on an adjacent wire. Figure 7.11 shows the older 40-pin cable and the newer 80-conductor cable. Table 7.2 shows the ATA standards.

The newer IDE standard is **SATA** (serial ATA). The original specification transfers data at 1.5Gbps (sometimes seen as 1.5Gb/s) with the latest release at 6Gbps. The SATA specification

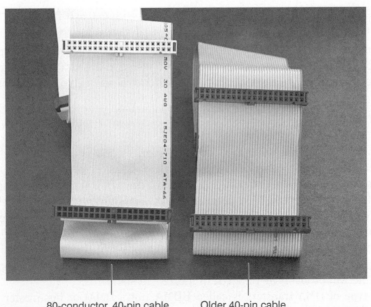

80-conductor, 40-pin cable   Older 40-pin cable

Figure 7.11	80- and 40-conductor cable

Table 7.2	IDE PATA standards		
ATA standard	**Speed (Mbps)**	**Cable**	**Notes**
ATA-1	3.3	40-pin	IDE hard drives
ATA-2	8.3 & 16.6	40-pin	Supports other devices besides hard drives; sometimes called EIDE
ATA-3	8.3 & 16.6	40-pin	Includes SMART
ATA-4	33	40-pin	Also called Ultra DMA/33 or Ultra ATA/33
ATA-5	66	40-pin (80 conductor)	Also called Ultra DMA/66 or Ultra ATA/66
ATA-6	100	40-pin	Also called Ultra DMA/100 or (80 conductor) Ultra ATA/100
ATA-7	133	40-pin (80 conductor)	Also called Ultra DMA/133 or Ultra ATA/133

was released as three different sections: SATA 1.5Gbps, SATA 1.5Gbps with extensions, and SATA 3.0Gbps. SATA 1.5Gbps uses the same commands as PATA and the same operating system drivers.

Serial ATA is a point-to-point interface, which means that (1) each device connects to the host through a dedicated link (unlike the traditional parallel IDE where two devices share the host link), and (2) each device has the entire interface bandwidth. Serial ATA uses a smaller cable that is more like a network cable than the traditional IDE ribbon cable. SATA supports both internal and external devices. Figure 7.12 shows a SATA drive. Figure 7.13 shows a SATA internal 7-pin device cable.

Figure 7.12   **SATA hard drive**

Figure 7.13   **SATA cable**

eSATA (external SATA) provides external device connectivity using the SATA standard. eSATA allows shielded cable lengths up to 2 meters (~6.56 feet), with faster connections than USB 2.0 or most IEEE 1394 types. However, the eSATA connection does not provide power to external devices. Furthermore, a single eSATA connector can attach to a **SATA-PM** (SATA port multiplier), which is similar to a USB hub. A SATA-PM can support up to 15 devices. Figure 7.14 shows an eSATA cable and eSATA port. An eSATA cable can be rated for 1.5Gbps or 3GBps. eSATA cables are limited to 1 meter (~3.3 feet) for 1.5Gbps devices and 2 meters (~6.6 feet) for 3.0Gbps transfers. The eSATA connector may be integrated (especially in a laptop) as a combination USB/eSATA port.

eSATA 3.0Gbps cable

eSATA port

Figure 7.14   **eSATA cable and port**

A SATA-PM requires that controllers support either command-based switching or FIS. With **command-based switching**, the host adapter/port can issue commands to only one drive at a time. This means that access is limited to one drive at a time. This technology is best suited for situations in which storage capacity is more important than performance. **FIS** (Frame Information Structure), in contrast, is a faster technology than command-based switching because the host to port multiplier link is used more efficiently, and multiple drives can be performing operations simultaneously.

SSD (Solid State Drive)

SSDs (solid state drives) are storage devices that use nonvolatile Flash memory technologies instead of hard drive technologies. SSDs eliminate the number-one cause of hard drive failure: moving parts. SSDs use Flash memory and can therefore be low heat producing, reliable, quiet, secure, long-lasting, and fast. SSDs are being installed in laptops and desktop models as internal and external units. They are being used to replace hard drives as a faster alternative and used in arenas where hard drive storage was not always possible or feasible. SSDs are used in the following industries:

- Medical—CRT/MRI image storage, monitoring equipment, portable devices
- IT—Video surveillance, wireless base stations, security appliances
- Industrial—Robotic systems, test equipment, manufacturing devices
- Automotive—Diagnostics, store safety information, store travel statistics

Another difference between hard drives and SSDs is how data is actually written. Write amplification and wear leveling are two terms used with SSDs that technicians should understand. To write data, an SSD may have to do an erase operation, move data to another location, and then write the information to memory. Still, overall performance is increased. **Write amplification** is the minimum amount of memory storage space affected by a write request. For example, if there is 4KB of information to be written and the SSD has a 128KB erase block, 128KB must be erased before the 4KB of information can be written. Writing takes longer than reading with SSDs.

Wear leveling is a technique used to erase and write data using all of the memory blocks instead of the same memory blocks repeatedly. SSD manufacturers are using various technologies: (1) software to track usage and direct write operations, (2) a certain amount of reserved memory blocks to use when a memory block does fail, and (3) a combination of the two techniques.

Two types of technologies used with SSDs are SLC and MLC. **SLCs** (single-level memory cells) store 1 bit in each memory cell and last longer than MLCs, but they are more expensive. **MLCs** (multi-level memory cells) store more than 1 bit in each memory cell and are cheaper to manufacturer, but they have slower transfer speeds.

The main drawback to SSDs is cost. SSDs are expensive compared to hard drives. As with Flash drives, each memory block of an SSD has a finite number of reads and writes. An SSD that writes data across the entire memory capacity will last longer. Some companies are including software with the drive that tracks or estimates end of life. Figure 7.15 shows the insides of an SSD.

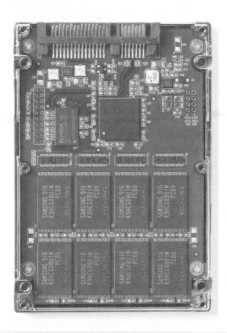

Figure 7.15   **Solid state drive**

SCSI (Small Computer System Interface)

SCSI (Small Computer System Interface) can control many different types of devices such as scanners, tape drives, hard drives, optical drives, printers, disk array subsystems, and CD/DVD drives. The SCSI standard allows connection of multiple internal and external devices to the same adapter. All devices that connect to the same SCSI controller share a common data bus called the SCSI bus (or SCSI chain). With features such as increased speed and multiple device support comes added cost. SCSI is more expensive than any other interface used with hard drives.

SCSI hard drives have the "intelligence" built into the drive, similar to IDE hard drives. The SCSI host adapter (usually a separate card, but it can be built into the motherboard) connects the SCSI device to the motherboard and coordinates the activities of the other devices connected. Three basic standards of SCSI are called SCSI-1, SCSI-2, and SCSI-3. The original SCSI standard is a parallel architecture. Figure 7.16 shows an SCSI hard drive.

The original SCSI standard is a parallel architecture. SCSI-1, left a lot of room for vendor specifications on the wide range of supported devices. Technicians had to cope with the fact that not all SCSI adapters handled all SCSI devices. SCSI-1 was primarily for hard drives; however, other device manufacturers such as those making tape drives, made do with SCSI-1 and adapted their devices as they saw fit. SCSI-1 supports up to eight devices (one host adapter and seven devices) on one SCSI 8-bit bus at a transfer rate of up to 5MBps. SCSI-2 supports 16 devices and speeds up to 20MBps. SCSI-2 hardware is compatible with SCSI-1 devices. SCSI-3 improves on data transfer rates and includes fiber optical cable standards. Figure 7.16 shows a SCSI hard drive.

Fast SCSI is a term associated with the SCSI-2 interface. It transfers data at 10MBps, eight bits at a time. 32-bit SCSI was defined in SCSI-2, but never adopted by the industry, so the 32-bit standard

Figure 7.16   **SCSI hard drive**

was dropped in SCSI-3, which is an improvement on the SCSI-2 interface. The various SCSI-3 standards all start with the word "Ultra." Ultra-Wide SCSI transfers 16 bits of data at 40MBps, Ultra2 SCSI transfers eight bits of data at 40MBps, and Ultra2-Wide SCSI transfers 16 bits of data at 80MBps.

SCSI-3 comprises different SPI (SCSI parallel interface) standards that include SPI, SPI-2, SPI-3, SPI-4, SPI-5, and SPI-6. SPI is commonly called Ultra SCSI; SPI-2 is called Ultra2 or Fast-40 SCSI; SPI-3 is called Ultra3, Ultra 160 SCSI, or Fast 80 DT; SPI-4 is known as Ultra4 or Fast-160DT SCSI; SPI-5 is known as Fast 320, transferring data at 640MBps; and SPI-6 is known as Fast 640. Table 7.3 shows a breakdown of the common parallel SCSI standards.

The latest SCSI devices that might be found in a PC are known as **SAS** (serial attached SCSI). SAS devices connect through a serial architecture which means they attach in a point-to-point bus. SAS devices are said to be more expensive than SATA IDE devices because they target the enterprise environment where high reliability and high MTBF (mean time between failures) is important.

Table 7.3   **SCSI standards**

SCSI standard	SCSI term	Speed (MBps)
SCSI-1	N/A	5
SCSI-2	N/A	5
	Fast	10
	Wide	20
	Fast-Wide	20
SCSI-3	Ultra	20
	Ultra	40
	Ultra-Wide	40
	Ultra2-Wide	80
	Ultra3	160
	Ultra160	160
	Ultra160+	160
	Ultra320	320
	Ultra640	640

SCSI storage devices are more frequently found in a network environment. Other types of SCSI used with networking include FC-AL (Fibre Channel Arbitration Loop), SSA (Serial Storage Architecture), and iSCSI.

Storage Device Configuration Overview

Drive configuration sometimes includes setting jumpers on the drive and sometimes on the associated adapter and proper termination. Termination is a method used to prevent signals from reflecting back up the cable. Each drive type has a normal configuration method. However, individual drive manufacturers may develop their own configuration steps. Always refer to the documentation included with the drive, adapter, or motherboard for configuration and installation information.

PATA Physical Installation

PATA IDE devices (including hard drives) are simpler to configure than parallel SCSI devices. The overall steps for installing a PATA device are as follows:

- Keep the drive in the protective antistatic container until you are ready to install
- Use proper antistatic handling procedures when installing the drive and handle the drive by the edges; avoid touching the drive electronics and connectors
- Turn off and remove the power cord when installing the drive
- Determine how many devices will attach to the same cable and configure their jumpers accordingly
- Physically mount and secure the device in the computer and attach the proper cable
- Configure the BIOS if necessary
- If a hard drive, prepare the drive for data as described later in the chapter

Actually, these steps apply to SATA and SCSI as well except for configuring jumpers and for SATA, determining how many devices attach to the same cable because SATA is a point-to-point architecture and only one device attaches to the connector.

Motherboards frequently have two PATA IDE connectors (although a few have three or four). The IDE connectors are known as the primary or primary IDE channel, secondary or secondary IDE channel, and if there are third or fourth connectors, they are known as the tertiary channel and quaternary channel respectively. Figure 7.17 shows a motherboard with four integrated IDE connectors.

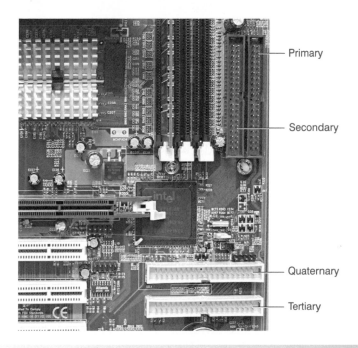

Figure 7.17   **PATA motherboard connectors**

7

Storage Devices

Each channel (connector) can have a master and a slave device. To distinguish between the devices, use the channel name followed by the words **master** or **slave**. The two settings are simply used to distinguish between the two devices because only one of the two devices (master or slave) can transmit data when connected to the same IDE channel (cable). For example, if two hard drives are installed on the primary channel, they are called primary master and primary slave. Table 7.4 shows the common IRQs and I/O addresses used by the IDE channels.

Table 7.4	PATA IDE system resources	
IDE channel	**IRQ(s)**	**I/O addresses**
Primary	14	1F0-1F7h and 3F6-3F7h
Secondary	15 or 10	170-177h and 376-377h
Tertiary	11 or 12	1E8-1EF and 3EE-3EF
Quaternary	10 or 11	168-16F and 36E-36F

PATA IDE devices are normally configured using jumpers. The four options commonly found are single, master, slave, and cable select. The **single** IDE setting is used when only one device connects to the cable. The master IDE setting is used in conjunction with the slave setting and both are used when two IDE devices connect to the same cable. One device is set to the master setting while the other device uses the slave setting. The **cable select** IDE option replaces the master/slave setting. The device automatically configures itself to either the master setting or the slave setting depending on the specific cable connector to which the device attaches. To use the cable select option, a special 80-conductor, 40-pin cable is needed. This cable has pin 28 disabled. Figure 7.18 shows the connections for the 80-conductor cable.

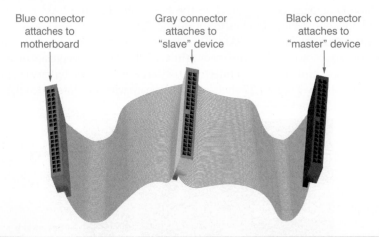

Blue connector attaches to motherboard   Gray connector attaches to "slave" device   Black connector attaches to "master" device

Figure 7.18	**80-conductor PATA IDE cable connections**

Tech Tip

Check your PATA IDE default setting

Most hard drives come preset to master or single whereas most other devices such as tape drives, CD/DVD drives, and Zip drives come preset to the slave setting. Devices that are set to slave and installed as the only device on the IDE cable still function properly. However, it is always best to check the settings of installed devices and of any new devices being installed.

All 80-conductor (40-pin) cables that meet the ATA specifications automatically support cable select, and the connectors, are color-coded according to the specifications. The 80-conductor (40-pin) cable must be used in Ultra DMA Mode 3 and higher, but can be used in lower modes as well.

Determining which cable select connector to use

When the cable select became a standard with ATA-5, the master connector (the black connector) is at the end of the cable. The slave connector (the gray one) is in the middle of the connector, and the blue connector attaches to the motherboard.

The following criteria must be met to use the cable select option:

1. A special IDE cable select cable or the 80-conductor (40-pin) cable must be used.
2. The host interface (controlling circuits) must support the cable select option.
3. The one or two attached devices must be set to the cable select option.

Do not use the 40-conductor 40-pin IDE cable with the cable select option

Do not set an IDE device to the cable select option unless the special cable is installed and the host interface supports this option. If two devices are set to the cable select option and a regular IDE cable is used, both devices are configured as master and will not work properly.

There are two methods of configuring PATA IDE devices: (1) configure one device as master and the other device as slave, or (2) configure both devices to the cable select option. By doing this, the device that connects to the black connector becomes the "master" and the device that connects to the gray connector becomes the "slave." Whichever method is used, the following are recommendations:

- When two IDE devices connect to the same cable, the faster or larger capacity device should be configured as master. Hard drives are normally the fastest IDE devices.
- When only one device (the master) connects to an older 40-conductor IDE cable, connect the device to the end connector (the one farthest from the motherboard) for best performance. Some devices show errors when there is only one IDE device and it connects to the center cable connector.
- If there are two IDE devices installed in the computer, a hard drive and a CD/DVD drive, install the hard drive on one IDE channel (primary) and the CD/DVD drive on the secondary IDE channel.
- Avoid putting a hard drive and an optical (CD or DVD) drive on the same channel. The optical device uses a more complicated command set than the hard drive and it can slow down the hard drive.
- If you have a CD-RW or DVD/RW drive and a CD-ROM or DVD drive and you transfer data frequently between the two, it is best to put them on separate channels. However, putting one of these devices with a hard drive is not a good idea either.
- For optimum performance, connect the hard drive that you boot from to the primary IDE motherboard connector and configure it as master.

Figure 7.19 illustrates how multiple PATA devices connect to the motherboard.

Watch out for PATA cable lengths

IDE devices connect to a 40-pin, 80-conductor ribbon cable. The maximum IDE cable length is 18 inches, which presents a problem with tower computers. Some companies sell 24- or 36- inch IDE cables. These do not meet specifications. If IDE problems or intermittent problems occur, replace the cable with one that meets specifications.

Almost all PATA IDE devices ship with cable select option selected. Figure 7.20 shows an illustration of two PATA IDE hard drives configured with the cable select option. Some drives can be limited to 2.1, 32, or 128GB. (The 128GB limitation is not supported on the drives shown.)

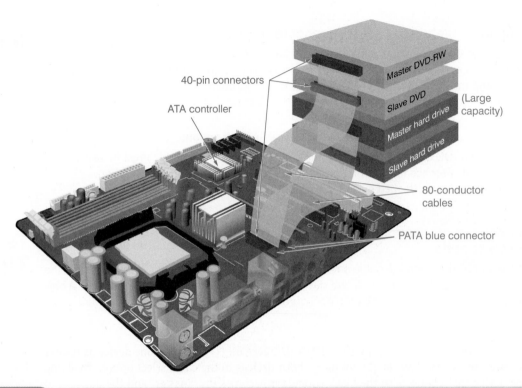

40-pin connectors

ATA controller

Master DVD-RW

Slave DVD

(Large capacity)

Master hard drive

Slave hard drive

80-conductor cables

PATA blue connector

Figure 7.19   **PATA device connectivity**

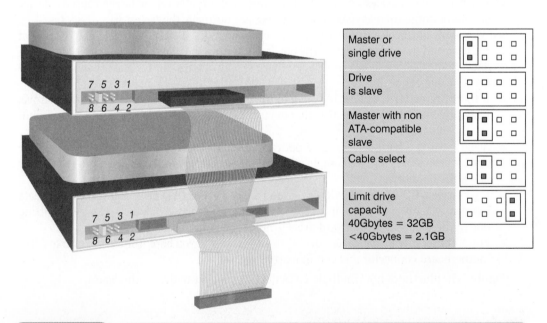

Master or single drive	▪ □ □ □ ▪ □ □ □
Drive is slave	□ □ □ □ □ □ □ □
Master with non ATA-compatible slave	▪ ▪ □ □ ▪ ▪ □ □
Cable select	□ ▪ □ □ □ ▪ □ □
Limit drive capacity 40Gbytes = 32GB <40Gbytes = 2.1GB	□ □ □ ▪ □ □ □ ▪

Figure 7.20   **Two PATA devices configured as cable select**

The table in Figure 7.20 shows several possible configurations. A similar table is found either on top of the hard drive or in the documentation included with the hard drive. The third alternative is to use the manufacturer's Internet site. If only one IDE hard drive is to be installed, the drive is to be configured as the master. Either leave the jumper set to cable select and simply attach to the black 80-conductor cable *or* move the jumper from pins 5 and 6 to pins 7 and 8 to configure the drive manually as master.

Closed means jumpered or enabled

Storage device documentation varies in how these are shown. When documentation shows an option as closed, jumpered, or enabled, this means to put a jumper over the two pins to configure the option.

Adjust to poorly written documentation

How a manufacturer uses the terms and configures a storage device is up to the manufacturer. The technician must learn to adjust to poorly written and sometimes confusing documentation. Jumpers other than the master/slave jumpers may be present, but you must refer to the hard drive's documentation for the proper settings. If documentation is unavailable, use the Internet; most manufacturers place their jumper setting documentation online and/or on top of the drive.

Figure 7.21 shows Western Digital's IDE hard drive with the documentation stenciled on top of the drive.

Figure 7.21   **Western Digital IDE hard drive**

If an IDE device has an SP setting, the setting is only used when installing two IDE devices on one cable where one device does not support the DASP signal. The SP setting, when set on the master device, tells it a slave device is present.

SATA Physical Installation

SATA drives are easy to install. Most internal drives require a special host adapter that supports one to four drives or an integrated motherboard connection. Each drive is seen as a point-to-point connection with the host controller.

SATA drives do not have any master/slave, cable select, or termination jumpers or settings. A serial 7-pin connector attaches from the SATA controller to the internal SATA drive. A longer cable connects power to the drive. The internal SATA power connector is not a Molex or Berg connector; it is a different type of connector. A cable converter can be obtained if a Molex connector is the only one available from the power supply. Figure 7.22 shows a Serial ATA hard drive with associated cabling. Notice the Molex-to-internal SATA cable converter in the photo.

There are also products available that allow a serial ATA hard drive to connect to a standard IDE controller. Figure 7.23 shows how two SATA drives attach to a motherboard that has two SATA connectors.

Tech Tip

Enable SATA port

Many manufacturers require that you enable the motherboard port through the system BIOS before any device connected to the port is recognized.

To install a SATA host adapter, power off the computer and remove the computer power cord. Remove the computer cover and locate an open expansion slot. Some adapters have jumpers for configurable options. Some common options include 16- and 32-bit PCI operations, adapter BIOS enabled/disabled, and Mode 0 enabled/ disabled. Some adapters may provide master/slave

Figure 7.22   **SATA hard drive and cables**

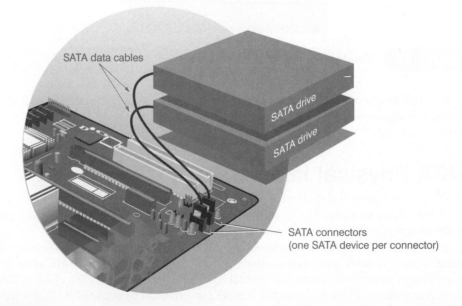

Figure 7.23   **SATA connectivity**

emulation options. Most adapters' default settings will work, but always refer to the adapter's documentation for details.

To install an internal SATA hard drive, power off the computer, and remove the computer's power cord. Physically mount the drive into a drive bay. Connect the SATA signal cable between the drive and the host controller. Connect the SATA power cord to the drive and an available Molex connector from the power supply. Figure 7.24 shows an installed SATA hard drive attached to a host adapter.

Figure 7.24   Installed SATA hard drive and adapter

An external (eSATA) drive normally has no jumpers, terminators, or switches to be configured. However, when installing a faster drive to a slower port—such as when installing a 3.0Gbps drive to a 1.5Gbps port—a jumper may need to be configured so the drive is compatible with the port. Always refer to the drive manufacturer's documentation when installing a drive. Attach the power cord to the drive, if applicable, and insert the other end of the power cord into a wall outlet. Attach one end of the eSATA cable to the drive. Plug the other end of the cable into an eSATA port on the computer. Note that some systems use the original SATA 1.5Gbps (sometimes called SATA I) port, and the drive may be a 3.0Gbps (sometimes called SATA II) drive. A cable converter may be necessary. Laptops sometimes have combination USB/SATA ports. eSATA ports are commonly disabled in BIOS and sometimes require BIOS changes, updates, and/or device drivers.

Before switching on eSATA drive power, ensure that the drive is positioned where it will stay during operation and that all data and power cords are attached securely. Switch on the drive power. The drive mounts. When a drive is mounted, a communications channel is opened between the drive and the operating system. Whenever the drive is to be disconnected, it is to be unmounted. Some drive manufacturers provide software for backing up data or configuring the drive in a RAID configuration. Use the Disk Management Windows tool to ensure that the drive is recognized.

Tech Tip

Unmounting an eSATA drive

To unmount an eSATA drive, click on the Safely Remove Hardware icon in the systray. Select the appropriate drive letter. Remove the drive when prompted by the operating system.

SSD Physical Installation

For a desktop computer, an SSD can be internally mounted and connected to a SATA/PATA motherboard or an adapter port. An SSD can also attach as an external device to a SATA, USB, or FireWire port. An SSD can be mounted as a replacement part for a laptop hard drive. SSDs do not normally require special drivers. Always refer to the SSD mounting directions provided by the manufacturer. The following steps are generic ones.

If installing an SSD internally into a desktop computer, power off the computer and locate an empty drive bay, a power connector of the appropriate type (or buy a converter), and an available SATA/PATA port or free PATA connector on a PATA cable. Attach mounting brackets to the SSD. Mounting brackets may have to be purchased separately, be provided with the drive, or be provided as spares that came with the computer. Slide the SSD into the drive bay and secure it, if necessary. Connect the data cable from the motherboard or adapter to the drive. Attach a power cable to the SSD. Reinstall the computer cover and power on the computer.

If installing an SSD internally into a laptop, power off the computer, disconnect the AC adapter, and remove the battery. Remove the drive bay access cover and install the SSD. Reattach the access cover, battery, and AC adapter, if necessary. Power on the laptop.

The BIOS should recognize an internally installed SSD. If it does not, go into the system BIOS setup and ensure that the connector to which the SSD attaches is enabled. Be especially careful with SATA ports and port numbering. Configure the system to automatically detect the new drive, save the settings, and reboot the system.

If installing an external SSD, attach the appropriate USB, SATA, or IEEE 1394 (FireWire) cable from the drive to the computer. Power on the SSD. The system should recognize the new drive.

Beware of static electricity

SSDs are Flash memory and are susceptible to static electricity. Use proper ESD handling procedures when installing an SSD.

Use only one technology

If an external drive supports more than one technology, such as eSATA, FireWire, and USB, attach only one type of cable from the drive to the computer.

Parallel SCSI Configuration

Configure a parallel SCSI device by doing the following:

1. Setting the proper SCSI ID
2. Terminating both ends of the SCSI chain
3. Connecting the proper cable(s)

The parallel SCSI chain consists of several SCSI devices cabled together. The SCSI chain includes SCSI devices and a single controller, sometimes called a host adapter. The SCSI controller is usually a separate adapter, but it may be built into the motherboard. The SCSI chain includes internal SCSI devices that connect to the SCSI host adapter and any external SCSI devices that connect to an adapter's external port. Multiple SCSI chains can exist in a system, and a computer can contain up to four SCSI host adapters. A SCSI-1 host adapter supports up to seven internal or external devices. SCSI-2 or higher adapters support up to 15 internal or external devices.

SCSI ID Configuration and Termination

Each device on a SCSI chain, including the SCSI host adapter, is assigned a **SCSI ID**. (Some SCSI hard drive manufacturers refer to this setting as the drive select ID.) The SCSI ID allows each device to share the same SCSI bus, and it assigns a priority for each device. The SCSI interface allows a SCSI device to communicate directly with another SCSI device connected on the same SCSI chain. The higher the SCSI number, the higher the priority of the device on the SCSI chain. SCSI IDs are normally set using switches, jumpers, SCSI BIOS software, or manufacturer-provided software.

Standard SCSI devices (8-bit devices) recognize SCSI IDs 0 through 7. Wide SCSI devices (16-bit devices) recognize SCSI IDs 0 through 15. The SCSI ID priority values are as follows from highest priority value to lowest. Figure 7.25 shows the SCSI priority numbers from highest to lowest.

Power on all external SCSI devices *before* turning on the computer
The host adapter detects all SCSI devices along the SCSI chain during the boot process. However, if a SCSI device is not used frequently the device can be powered off. The rest of the SCSI devices operate even if a SCSI device is powered off. If two devices have the same SCSI ID, a SCSI ID conflict occurs and the devices will not work properly. Setting an improper SCSI ID (priority) setting results in slower SCSI device performance.

Highest															Lowest
7	6	5	4	3	2	1	0	15	14	13	12	11	10	9	8

Figure 7.25   **SCSI ID priority levels**

The SCSI host adapter is normally preset to SCSI ID 7, the highest priority, and should not be changed. Slower devices such as scanners, CD/DVD drives, or video encoders should be assigned a higher SCSI ID such as 6 or 5 for a standard SCSI device and 15 or 14 for a Wide SCSI device, so they receive ample time to move data onto the SCSI bus. SCSI ID 0 is the default for most SCSI hard drives. A development that is helpful in setting SCSI IDs is SCAM (SCSI Configured AutoMatically).

Termination of SCSI devices is very important. Proper termination of SCSI devices keeps the signals from bouncing back up the cable and provides the proper electrical current level for the SCSI chain. The SCSI bus cannot operate properly without terminating both ends of the SCSI bus. Improper termination can make one, many, or all SCSI devices not work properly. Over time, improper termination can damage a SCSI adapter or a SCSI device. SCSI termination is performed in several ways: (1) by installing a SIPP; (2) by installing a jumper; (3) by setting a switch; (4) by installing a terminator plug; (5) by installing a pass through terminator; or (6) with software.

When setting or removing termination, refer to the documentation included with the adapter or device. If the terminator to an external SCSI device is not provided with the device, it must be purchased separately. Some internal SCSI cables do not have a terminator built into them.

Figure 7.26 shows a SCSI hard drive. The SCSI ID configuration is shown with the diagram on the bottom right side.

Figure 7.26   **SCSI hard drive**

There are several types of SCSI electrical signals and terminators. The three major categories are SE, HVD, and LVD. Table 7.5 explains these. The majority of terminators in use are either active or the FPT active terminator.

Table 7.5	SCSI electrical signals/terminator technologies
Technology/term	**Explanation**
SE (Single Ended) terminator	Terminators used by most SCSI devices. It can use passive and active terminators. It has a maximum bus length of 9 feet (2.7 meters).
Passive terminator	Terminators used on SCSI-1 devices. They are not good for long cable distances because they are susceptible to noise interference.
Active terminator	Terminators that can be used on SCSI-1, -2, and -3 devices. They allow for longer cable distances and provide the correct voltage for SCSI signals. This type must be used with Fast, Wide or Fast-Wide SCSI devices. A passive and an active terminator can be used on the same chain. SCSI-3 requires active termination.
FPT (Forced Perfect Termination)	A special type of active terminator that can be used with SE devices.
HVD (High Voltage Differential)	A technology that was used in a few SCSI-2 devices that allowed a longer SCSI bus length. HVD devices must use HVD terminators (sometimes called differential terminators).
LVD (Low Voltage Differential)	A technology that is backward compatible with SE and required on all devices that adhere to the Ultra SCSI standard. LVD bus length can be up to 39 feet (11.88 meters) depending on the number of devices. LVD devices use either LVD terminators or LVD/SE terminators.
Pass through terminator	A terminator used by most internal hard drives. It has an extra connector and allows a device that does not have terminators to be terminated through the connector that attaches to the cable.

Being able to distinguish among various SCSI devices is very difficult because there are many SCSI flavors. Special icons are placed on SCSI devices to differentiate them. Figure 7.27 shows these icons.

If only internal devices connect to the SCSI host adapter, terminate the adapter and the last internal device connected to the cable. Remove the termination from all other devices.

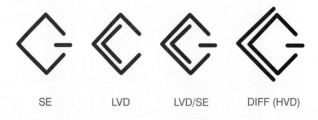

SE   LVD   LVD/SE   DIFF (HVD)

Figure 7.27	SCSI symbols

Tech Tip

Never connect an HVD device or terminator to SE, LVD, or LVD/SE bus

Never connect an HVD device/terminator to a SCSI bus/adapter that uses an SE, LVD, or LVD/SE bus. Equipment can be damaged!

When connecting only external devices to the SCSI host adapter or motherboard, terminate the adapter and the last external device. Remove the terminations from all other external devices.

Figure 7.28 shows SCSI IDs and termination for an internal and external device scenario. If both internal and external devices attach to the SCSI host adapter, the last internal device connected to the SCSI cable is terminated as well as the last external device. All other devices and the SCSI host adapter must have their terminators removed. The SCSI chain in Figure 7.28 consists of two internal SCSI devices (a CD drive and a hard drive) and two external SCSI devices (a tape drive and a scanner). The two ends of the SCSI chain that must be terminated are the CD drive and the scanner. All other devices are not terminated.

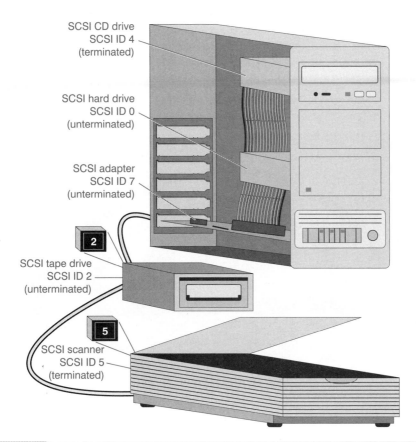

SCSI CD drive
SCSI ID 4
(terminated)

SCSI hard drive
SCSI ID 0
(unterminated)

SCSI adapter
SCSI ID 7
(unterminated)

2

SCSI tape drive
SCSI ID 2
(unterminated)

5

SCSI scanner
SCSI ID 5
(terminated)

Figure 7.28 **Internal and external SCSI devices—termination**

Use software that comes with the SCSI adapter for configuration

Newer SCSI cards have either a software utility that ships with the adapter or a software program built into the adapter's ROM chip that allows configuration through software instead of jumpers and switches. Refer to the adapter's documentation for configuration instructions.

Tech Tip

A smart technician plans the configuration of the drive before installing the drive in the system. A good plan of attack is the best strategy to avoid problems during installation. Draw the configuration on a piece of paper to help get the installation straight in your mind. To help new technicians with different configurations, the exercises at the end of the chapter contain sample practice configurations.

SCSI Cables

Parallel SCSI cabling allows multiple devices to be connected to one SCSI host adapter and share the same SCSI bus; this is called daisy chaining. Daisy chaining is like connecting multiple Christmas light sets together. If multiple internal SCSI devices attach to the SCSI adapter, then use an internal SCSI cable with multiple connectors. Most internal SCSI-1 and SCSI-2 cables are 50-pin ribbon cables. Internal SCSI-3 cables are 68-pin ribbon cables.

Tech Tip

Buy quality SCSI cables

Not all SCSI cables are created equal. Do not recommend or buy the cheaper, thinner SCSI cables available for external devices. These cheaper cables are susceptible to outside noise. The section on Configuration and Setup Procedures covers more cabling issues.

To connect external SCSI-1 devices, a 50-pin Centronics to 50-pin Centronics cable is used. The SCSI-1 cable is also known as an A Cable. The SCSI-2 standard has a different cable for connecting to the first external SCSI device. This cable has a 50-pin D-shell connector that connects to the SCSI host adapter, and a Centronics connector that connects to the external device. For 16-bit SCSI devices, a second 68-pin cable, called the B Cable, must be used in addition to the A Cable. This B Cable is not in the SCSI-3 specifications because industry did not fully support it. SCSI-3 has a 68-pin cable called the P Cable. Figure 7.29 illustrates some SCSI cables.

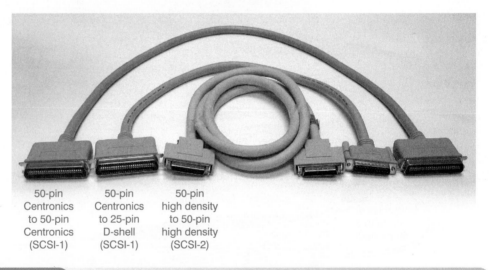

50-pin
Centronics
to 50-pin
Centronics
(SCSI-1)

50-pin
Centronics
to 25-pin
D-shell
(SCSI-1)

50-pin
high density
to 50-pin
high density
(SCSI-2)

Figure 7.29   **External SCSI cables**

Tech Tip

Install one SCSI device at a time and test

When installing multiple SCSI devices, install them one at a time and test each one before installing the next one.

Laptop Storage Devices

A laptop normally has a PATA or SATA hard drive installed but could have an SSD instead of or in addition to the hard drive. A mini PCI adapter can be used to connect the drive to the system, or the drive can be directly attached to the motherboard. Additional storage can be provided by devices that connect to USB, eSATA, or IEEE 1394 ports. PC Cards or ExpressBus hard drives can also be used to provide storage expansion.

Two methods are used with hard drives installed in portable computers: proprietary or removable. With the proprietary installation, the hard drive is installed in a location where it cannot be changed, configured, or moved very easily. Proprietary cables and connectors are used. With removable hard drives, the laptop has a hard drive bay that allows installation/removal through a 44-pin connector. This connector provides power as well as data signaling. The drive is usually mounted in a carrier that attaches to the 44-pin connector and is the primary master device. If a CD or DVD drive is installed, it is normally configured as the secondary master.

Many laptops use some type of hard drive casing or brackets to hold the drive. Upgrading a drive may include installing the new drive into the old drive's brackets or case and attaching it or sliding it into the laptop. Some vendors sell the drive with the drive casing, but it is usually more expensive than just buying the drive. Figure 7.30 shows a hard drive that is used in a portable computer.

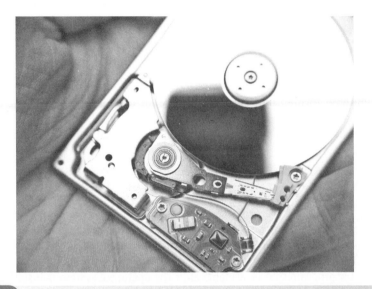

Figure 7.30   **Portable computer hard drive**

What to do if you want more storage space for a laptop

Laptops do not normally allow a second IDE hard drive. Instead, add an additional hard drive to the USB or eSATA port.

System BIOS Configuration for Hard Drives

The hard drive is configured through the system BIOS Setup program. As mentioned previously, Setup is accessed through keystrokes during the boot process. In the past, a drive type number was entered and the drive geometry information appeared to the right of the drive type number. In today's computers, the setting is Auto and the BIOS automatically detects the hard drive type. The drive type information is saved in CMOS.

IDE hard drives are normally configured using the Auto-Detect feature included with BIOS. The Auto-Detect feature automatically determines the drive type for the system. For SCSI hard drive installations, the most common CMOS setting for the hard drive type is type 0 or None. Once the system boots, the SCSI controller's BIOS initializes and the SCSI hard drive takes over and boots the system. Even though the drive type number is set to 0 or None, if this step is omitted, the hard drive will not operate.

Table 7.6 shows the most commonly used hard drive settings. Note that the BIOS is also where you select the drive that you want to boot the system.

Configure BIOS according to drive manufacturer's instructions

Drive manufacturers normally include documentation describing how to configure the drive in BIOS Setup. Also, they provide software for any system that does not recognize the drive.

Table 7.6	Common hard drive setup settings
Hard drive type	**Common setting**
IDE PATA/SATA	AUTO
SCSI	TYPE 0

Hard Drive Preparation Overview

Once a hard drive is installed and configured properly, and the hard drive type is entered into the Setup program, the drive must be prepared to accept data. The two steps of hard drive preparation are as follows:

1. Partition
2. High-level format

Partitioning the hard drive allows a drive letter to be assigned to one or more parts of the hard drive. **High-level formatting** prepares the drive for use for a particular operating system. This allows the drive to accept data from the operating system. For today's computers, a drive cannot be used until it has been partitioned and high-level formatted; thus technicians should be very familiar with these steps.

Partitioning

The first step in preparing a hard drive for use is partitioning. Partitioning a hard drive divides the drive so the computer system sees the hard drive as more than one drive. DOS and Windows 9x have a software program called FDISK that partitions hard drives. Windows NT and higher versions partitions can be set up during the operating system installation process, by using the **Disk Administrator** program that is available after the operating system is installed, or by using the **diskpart** utility from the command line. Disk Administrator is normally used to partition additional hard drives and to manage all of them. The first hard drive in the system is normally partitioned as part of the Windows installation process. Additional partitions can be created using Disk Administrator once the operating system is installed.

Partitioning provides advantages that include the following:

- Dividing a hard drive into separate subunits that are then assigned drive letters such as C: or D: by the operating system
- Organizing the hard drive to separate multiple operating systems, applications, and data
- Providing data security by placing data in a different partition to allow ease of backup as well as protection
- Using the hard drive to its fullest capacity

Tech Tip

How to determine what file system is being used

From the desktop, right-click the *My Computer* desktop icon and select the *Properties* option. The *General* tab shows the type of file system being used.

The original purpose of partitioning was to allow for loading multiple operating systems. This is still a good reason today because placing each operating system in its own partition eliminates the crashes and headaches caused by multiple operating systems and multiple applications co-existing in the same partition. The type of partition and how big the partition can be depends on the file system being used. A **file system** defines how data is stored on a drive. The most common file systems are FAT16, FAT32, and NTFS. The file system that can be used depends on what operating system is installed. Table 7.7 lists file systems and explains a little about each one.

When FDISK is used to partition the hard drive and you select the option to create a partition, a message appears that asks if you wish to enable large disk support. This option is what allows FAT32 to be installed. If you select *N* (No) when this question is asked, FAT32 will not be installed.

An even better reason for partitioning than loading multiple operating systems or separating the operating system from data is to partition the hard drive for more efficient use of space. The operating system sets aside one cluster as a minimum for every file. A **cluster** is the smallest

Table 7.7	File systems

File system type	Explanation
FAT12	Pre-DOS 3.x. Used on floppy disks smaller than 16MB.
FAT16	Also called FAT. Used with DOS 3.x+ and all versions of Windows including Vista and 7. 2GB partition limitation with DOS and Windows 9x. 4GB partition limitation with all versions of Windows higher than NT.
FAT32	Used with all versions of Windows 9x and higher. Supports drives up to 2TB. Can recognize volumes greater than 32GB, but cannot create them that big.
exFAT	Commonly called FAT64. A file system made for removable media (such as Flash drives and SD cards) that extends drive size support up to 64ZB in theory, but 512TB is the recommended max. Made for copying large files such as disk images and media files. Supported by Windows XP SP3, Vista, and 7. Use the format /? command to see if exFAT is available.
NTFS	Used with Windows NT, 2000, XP, Vista, and 7. Supports drives up to 16EB (16 exabytes that equals 16 billion gigabytes), but in practice is only 2TB (2 terabytes that equals 2 thousand gigabytes). Supports file compression and file security. NTFS allows faster file access and uses hard drive space more efficiently. Supports individual file compression and has the best file security.

How to convert partitions in NT, 2000, or XP

Use the **CONVERT.EXE** program in NT, to convert a FAT16 partition to NTFS, or in Windows to convert a FAT16/FAT32/exFAT partition to NTFS. Access a command prompt window. Type the following command:

CONVERT *x***: /FS:NTFS** (where *x* is the drive letter of the partition being converted to NTFS).

Press [Enter] and then press [Y] (Yes) and press [Enter]. Close the command prompt window and restart the computer. You can add a /v switch to the end of the command for a more verbose operation mode. Any type of partition conversion requires free hard drive space. The amount depends on the size of the partition.

amount of space reserved for one file and is made up of a specific number of sectors. Figure 7.31 illustrates the concept of a cluster. Keep in mind that the number of hard drive sectors per track varies. The outer tracks hold more information (have more sectors) than the inner tracks.

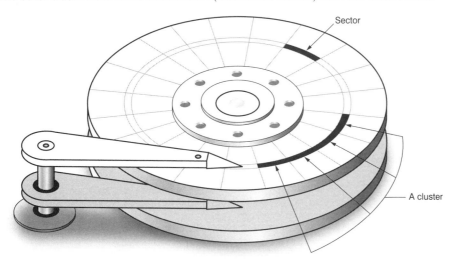

One cluster is the minimum amount of space for a file.

Figure 7.31	Clusters

Table 7.8 shows that partitioning large drives into one FAT partition wastes drive space. An efficiently partitioned hard drive allows more files to be saved because less of the hard drive is wasted.

Table 7.8	FAT16 partitions and cluster size	
Partition size	**Number of sectors**	**Cluster size**
0–15MB	8	4K
16MB–127MB	4	2K
128MB–255MB	8	4K
256MB–511MB	16	8K
512MB–1GB	32	16K
>1GB–2GB	64	32K
>2GB–4GB	128	64K

Tech Tip

Things to note about NTFS partitions

Windows 2000 and higher automatically convert older NTFS partitions to the newer type of NTFS.

Applications should be in a separate partition from data files. The following are some good reasons for partitioning the hard drive and separating data files from application files:

- Multiple partitions on the same hard drive divide the drive into smaller subunits, which makes it easier and faster to back up the data (which should be backed up more often than applications).
- The data is protected from operating system failures, unstable software applications, and any unusual software problems that occur between the application and the operating system.
- The data is in one location, which makes the files easier and faster to back up, organize, and locate.

Windows 9x, and higher systems can use FAT32 partitions. Flash drives are commonly formatted for FAT32 due to the NTFS "lazy write", which prolongs a write and might not release an external drive for some time. The FAT32 file system makes more efficient use of the hard drive than FAT16. Table 7.9 shows the cluster size for FAT32 partitions.

Table 7.9	FAT32 partitions and cluster size	
Partition size	**Number of sectors**	**Cluster size**
0–511MB	N/A	N/A
512MB–8GB	8	4K
>8GB–16GB	16	8K
>16GB–32GB	32	16K
>32GB	64	32K

The NTFS file system is a very efficient one. NTFS can use cluster sizes as small as 512 bytes per cluster. Table 7.10 lists the default cluster sizes for all versions of Windows since NT including Windows Vista and 7.

Table 7.10	NTFS partitions and cluster size	
Partition size	**Number of sectors**	**Cluster size**
0–16TB	8	4KB
16TB–32TB	16	8KB
>32TB–64TB	32	16KB
>64TB–128TB	64	32KB
>128TB–256TB	128	64KB

The Windows Setup installation program can be used to create a partition, and the Disk Management tool or `diskpart` utility can be used once the operating system is installed. Use the Disk Management tool to partition and manage any drive that is installed after the first hard drive. The first hard drive is partitioned initially through the Windows installation process. Figure 7.32 shows a screen capture from Windows XP.

Benefits of NTFS

NTFS supports disk quotas, which means that individual users can be limited on the amount of hard drive space. It can also automatically repair disk problems. For example, when a hard drive sector is going bad, the entire cluster is moved to another cluster.

Partitions are defined as primary and extended. If there is only one hard drive installed in a system and the entire hard drive is one partition, it is the **primary partition**. The primary partition on the first detected hard drive is assigned the drive letter `c:`.

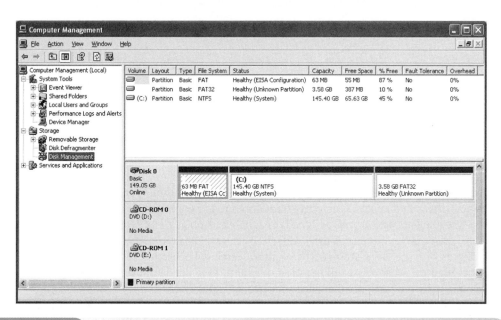

Figure 7.32   **Windows XP Disk Management tool**

eSATAs might already be partitioned
Some eSATA drives are already partitioned and formatted. Others have software that runs when the drive is connected for the first time. All of them should allow repartitioning and reformatting.

If the drive is divided so only part of the drive is the primary partition, the rest of the cylinders can be designated as the **extended partition**. An extended partition allows a drive to be further divided into **logical drives**. A logical drive is sometimes called a **volume**. A volume is assigned a drive letter and can include a logical drive as well as removable media such as a CD, diskette, DVD, or Flash drive. There can only be one extended partition per drive. A single hard drive can be divided into a maximum of four primary partitions. Remember that a partition is a contiguous section of storage space that functions as if it is a separate drive. See Figure 7.33 for an illustration of how one hard drive can be divided into partitions.

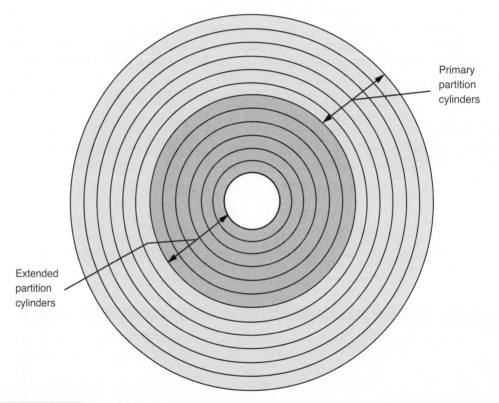

Primary partition cylinders

Extended partition cylinders

Figure 7.33   Hard drive partitioning

The first hard drive in a computer system must have a primary partition, but it does not require an extended partition. If the drive has an extended partition, it can be further subdivided into logical drives that appear as separate hard drives to the computer system. Logical drives created in the extended partition are assigned drive letters such as D:, E:, or others. The only limit for logical drives is the number of drive letters. An extended partition can have a maximum of 23 logical drives with the drive letters D: through Z:. A second operating system can reside in a logical drive. Figure 7.34 shows an illustration of a hard drive divided into a primary partition and an extended partition further subdivided into two logical drives.

If two hard drives are installed in a computer, the first hard drive *must* have a primary partition. The second hard drive is not required to have a primary partition and may simply have a single extended partition. If the second hard drive does have a primary partition, it can have an extended partition too.

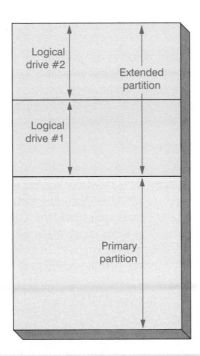

Figure 7.34   **Two logical drives**

When a hard drive is first installed and partitioned, the outermost track on the platter (cylinder 0, head 0, and physical sector 1) is reserved for the partition table. The partition table holds information about the types of partitions created and in what cylinders these partitions reside. The partition table is part of the **MBR** (master boot record) that contains a program that reads the partition table, looks for the primary partition marked as active, and goes to that partition to boot the system. Figure 7.35 shows the location of important parts of the hard drive that allows booting, partitions to be read, and files to be accessed.

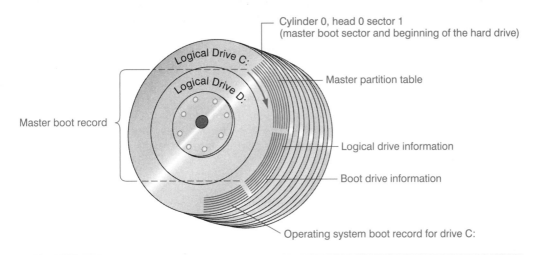

Figure 7.35   **Hard drive structure**

NTFS has two additional terms that you need to be aware of as a technician: system partition and boot partition. A Windows **system partition** is the partition on the hard drive that holds the hardware-specific files needed to load the operating system. A Windows **boot partition** is the partition on the hard drive that contains the operating system. The boot partition and the system partition can be on the same partition with Windows.

What happens when different types of partitions are deleted?

When a partition is deleted, all information in the partition is lost. A partition can be resized by deleting the partition and re-creating it, but the Disk Administrator program removes all information in the deleted partition. When logical drives in an extended partition are deleted, all data is lost. The other logical drives within the extended partition retain their information.

The ATA-4 standard included support for an HPA that has become quite popular with new computers. The **HPA** (Host Protected Area) is a hidden area of the hard drive used to hold a copy of the operating system; sometimes installed applications use the HPA when the operating system becomes so corrupted that a re-installation is necessary. Many manufacturers provide a BIOS setting or a keystroke that can be used when the system boots in order to access this area. The HPA is commonly found on the hard drive beyond the normal data storage locations; it reduces the amount of storage space available for data.

New partition type with Windows x64

A partition type known as GPT is available with Windows 64-bit operating systems. **GPT** (GUID, or globally unique identifier, partition table) allows up to 128 partitions and volumes up to 18EB. GPT partitioning is done through the Disk Management tool or the `diskpart` command-line utility. MBR-based partitions can be converted to GPT and vice versa, but data is not preserved.

How Drive Letters Are Assigned

Any operating system assigns drive letters to hard drives during the partitioning step. The order in which the partitions are assigned drive letters depends on three factors: (1) the number of hard drives; (2) the type of partitions on the hard drives (primary or extended); and (3) the operating system.

Note that if a new drive is installed, drive letters for these devices, volumes, partitions, or logical drives are added afterward. Drive letters can be changed through the Disk Management tool (right-click on the drive letter) or by using the `diskpart` command-line utility. Be careful, though, because some applications have pointers to specific files on a specific drive letter. Special products can be used that partition the hard drive and allow repartitioning without any data loss. Examples include Acronis Partition Manager, Power-Quest Corporation's Partition Magic, Avanquest's Partition Commander, and Symantec's Norton Partition Magic.

Determining what type of partition you have

To determine the type of partition on a computer, double-click the *My Computer* icon. Right-click a drive letter and select *Properties*. The *General* tab shows the type of file system used in the partition.

Windows Logical Disk Management

In the Windows environment, manage storage devices with a snap-in (an installable module) called Logical Disk Management. With Windows 2000 and higher, there are two types of storage: basic storage and dynamic storage. Table 7.11 explains these and other associated terms.

Table 7.11	Logical disk management terms
Term	**Description**
Basic storage	One of the two types of storage. This is what traditionally has been known as a partition. It is the default method because it is used by all operating systems.
Basic disk	Any drive that has been partitioned and setup for writing files. A basic disk has primary partitions, extended partitions, and logical drives contained within the extended partitions.
Dynamic storage	The second type of storage; contrast with basic storage. Allows you to create primary partitions, logical drives, and dynamic volumes on removable storage devices. More powerful than basic storage. Uses a dynamic disk (see this term for more information).
Dynamic disk	A disk made up of volumes. A volume can be the entire hard disk, parts of the hard disk combined into one unit, and other specific types of volumes, such as single, spanned, or striped volumes. Cannot be on a removable drive.
Simple volume	Disk space allocated from one hard drive. The space does not have to be contiguous.
Spanned volume	Disk space created from multiple hard drives. Windows writes data to a spanned volume in such a way that the first hard drive is used until the space is filled. Then, the second hard drive's space is used for writing. This continues until all hard drives in the spanned volume are utilized.
Striped volume	Data is written across 2 to 32 hard drives. It is different from a spanned volume in that each drive is used alternately. Another name for this is striping or RAID 0 (covered in the next section).
System volume	Holds the files needed to boot the operating system.
Boot volume	Holds the remaining operating system files. Can be the same volume as the system volume.
RAW volume	A volume that has never been high-level formatted and does not contain a file system.

Managing dynamic disks

Use the Disk Management tool (found in the Computer Management console) to work with dynamic disks or to convert a basic disk to a dynamic one. Once accomplished, the conversion process cannot be reversed.

Tech Tip

Figure 7.36 shows some of these concepts.

Fault Tolerance

RAID (redundant array of independent disks) allows reading from and writing to multiple hard drives for larger storage areas, better performance, and fault tolerance. **Fault tolerance** is the ability to continue functioning after a hardware or software failure. RAID can be implemented with hardware or software on IDE or SCSI hard drives. RAID comes in many different levels, but the ones implemented in the Windows environment are 0, 1, and 5. Some motherboards supported "nested"

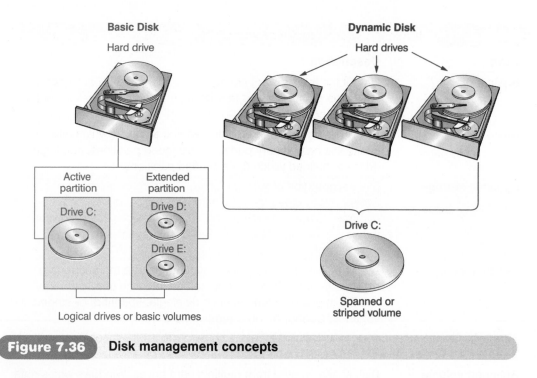

Figure 7.36 **Disk management concepts**

RAID which means RAID levels are combined. This method also increases the complexity of the hard drive setup. Table 7.12 explains these levels.

Table 7.12 **RAID**

RAID level	Description
0	Also called disk striping without parity. Data is alternately written on two or more hard drives, which increases system performance. These drives are seen by the system as one logical drive. **RAID 0** does not protect data when a hard drive fails.
1	Also called disk mirroring or disk duplexing. **RAID 1** protects against hard drive failure. **Disk mirroring** uses two or more hard drives and one disk controller. The same data is written to two drives. If one drive should fail, the system continues to function. With **disk duplexing**, a similar concept is used except that two disk controllers are used. Disk duplexing allows the system to continue functioning if one hard drive and one controller fail because of the redundancy.
0+1	A striped set and a mirrored set combined. Four hard drives minimum are required with an even number of disks. It creates a second striped set to mirror a primary striped set of disks. Also called RAID 01.
1+0	A mirrored set and a striped set combined with four hard drives as a minimum. Difference between 1+0 and 0+1 is that 1+0 has a striped set from a set of mirrored drives. Also called RAID 10.
5	Also called disk striping with parity. **RAID 5** writes data to three or more hard drives. Included with the data is parity information. If a drive fails, the data can be rebuilt from the other two drives' information.

Figure 7.37 shows the different types of RAID. With RAID 0, blocks of data (B1, B2, B3, etc.) are placed on alternating drives. With RAID 1, the same block of data is written to two drives. RAID 5 has one drive that contains parity information (P) for particular blocks of data such as B1 and B2.

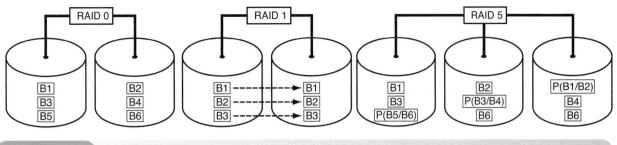

Figure 7.37 RAID concepts

High-Level Format

The last step in preparing a hard drive for use is high-level formatting. A high-level format must be performed on all primary partitions, logical drives located within extended partitions, and GPT partitions before data can be written to the hard drive. The high-level format sets up the file system so it can accept data.

NTFS allows support for multiple data streams and support for every character in the world. NTFS also automatically remaps bad clusters to other sections of the hard drive without any additional time or utility. Figure 7.38 shows the difference between how a FAT16 partition and an NTFS partition is set up when the high-level format step is completed.

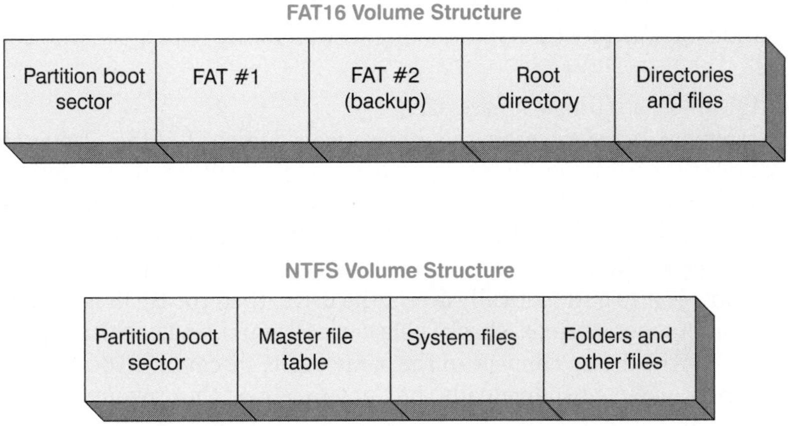

FAT16 Volume Structure

| Partition boot sector | FAT #1 | FAT #2 (backup) | Root directory | Directories and files |

NTFS Volume Structure

| Partition boot sector | Master file table | System files | Folders and other files |

Figure 7.38 FAT16 and NTFS volume structure

The high-level format creates two **FATs** (file allocation tables), one primary and one secondary. It also creates the root directory that renumbers the sectors. The FAT keeps track of the hard disk's file locations. It is similar to a table of contents in a book as it lists where the files are located in the partition. Table 7.13 shows the differences between the file systems.

Table 7.13 Comparing file systems

	FAT16	FAT32	NTFS
Maximum file size	4GB	4GB	~16TB
Maximum volume (partition) size	4GB (2GB if files are shared with DOS or Windows 95 computer)	32GB (max format) 2TB (max size can read)	2TB (or greater)*
Maximum files per volume	64KB	4MB	4GB

*Higher capacities are possible—up to 16EB (exabytes).

High-level formatting can be performed using the FORMAT command or by using Windows Disk Management tool. The area of the disk that contains information about the system files is the **DBR** (DOS boot record) and is located on the hard drive's cylinder 0, head 1, sector 1. The more common term for this today (since DOS is no longer a major operating system) is **boot sector** or volume boot record.

Additional drive partitions and drives installed after the first hard drive partition is created use the Windows Disk Management tool to high-level format the drive. The first hard drive partition is normally high-level formatted as part of the operating system installation process. The exercises at the end of the chapter explain how to partition and high-level format a hard drive.

How to change the cluster size

If you want to adjust the cluster size on a partition, you can do it during the high-level format step using the FORMAT command. The syntax for the command is **FORMAT *driveletter:* /FS:NTFS   /A:*clustersize*** where *driveletter* is the letter of the partition and *clustersize* is the size you want each cluster in the partition to be.

Troubleshooting Devices

Most problems with new drive installation stem from improper configuration of jumpers, SCSI ID settings, termination, or problems with cabling. The following steps assist with checking possible problems.

- Check the physical settings, if necessary.
- Check cabling. Pin 1 of the cable should be attached to pin 1 of the adapter connector.
- Check drive type setting in BIOS Setup. Refer to the documentation, contact the manufacturer of the drive for the correct setting, or use the Internet to obtain the setting.
- If after you have configured the drive, installed it, and powered it on, the BIOS shows the drive type as "None, Not installed," or displays all 0s in the drive parameters even though you set it to automatically detect the drive, then the BIOS is not able to detect it. Check all jumper settings, check cable connection(s), and check the power connection. If two PATA drives connect to the same cable, disconnect the slave drive. If the drives can be detected individually, but not together, they are incompatible on the same cable. In Setup, reduce any advanced features such as block mode, multi-sector transfer, PIO mode, 32-bit transfers, and so forth to their lowest values or disable them. Increase the amount of time the computer takes to initialize the hard drive by going into Setup and modifying such features as hard drive boot delay or set the boot speed to the lowest value. This gives the hard drive more time to spin up and reach its appropriate RPM before data is read from it. Make sure the motherboard port is enabled.
- Has the drive been partitioned and one partition marked as the active partition?
- Has the drive been high-level formatted?
- Verify that the mounting screw to hold the drive in the case is not too tight. Loosen the screw and power up the computer. Figure 7.39 shows the mounting screws for a hard drive installed in a tower case.

Stop 0x00000077 Kernel_Stack_Inpage error

If your computer has a boot sector virus or data cannot be read from the paging file, run antivirus software for the potential virus. If there is a paging file error, search for this error code on the Internet. Depending on the output shown, take the appropriate steps.

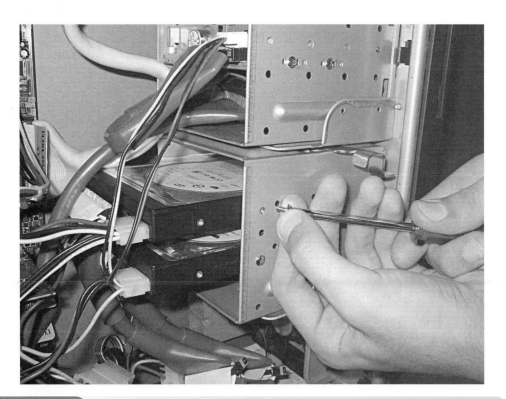

Figure 7.39 **Hard drive mounting screws**

- If during partitioning the "No fixed disks present" error appears, check the hard drive cabling, power connection, configuration jumpers (cable select, master/slave, SCSI ID), termination, and BIOS configuration.
- If the hard drive does not format to full capacity: (a) the drive parameters may be set incorrectly in Setup; (b) the BIOS does not support large hard drives; or (c) translation is not set up for the hard drive in the Setup program. Confirm the drive's parameters reported by the Disk Management tool with the drive's actual parameters and capacity.
- If the error message "Disk Boot failure" appears, check to see that the primary partition is marked active.
- If on initial boot after setting up a hard drive in BIOS Setup, you see the message "HDD Controller Failure, Press F1 to continue," then the system is not partitioned or high-level formatted. Press the necessary key and boot from a CD, then partition and high-level format the hard drive. If the message still continues, check the cabling and jumper configuration(s) on the hard drive.

Stop 0x0000007B Inaccessible_Boot_Device error
Your computer most likely has a boot sector virus. Run antivirus software.

Tech
Tip

- If during power-on the hard drive does not spin up or the hard drive spins down after a few seconds, check the power connector, the pin 1 orientation on the interface cable, the drive type in BIOS Setup, master/slave/cable select settings, energy management jumpers or settings in Setup, and any software that came with the drive that enables power management. Disable power management in BIOS Setup. Try installing the drive in another system.
- Run a virus checker on the system.

Stop 0x00000024 NTFS_File System error
The NTFS file system may be corrupt. Boot to Windows XP recovery console, back up data files, reinstall operating system.

- Try a warm boot (Ctrl+Alt+Del). If the drive is recognized after the warm boot, the Setup program may be running too fast for the drive to initialize. Refer to the hard drive documentation to see if the hard drive has a setting to help with this problem.
- Is the correct cable used?

The following are generic guidelines for hard drives that did work, but are now having problems.

- Run a virus-checking program after booting from a virus-free boot disk. Many viruses are specifically designed to attack the hard drive.
- Has there been a recent cleaning of the computer or has someone recently removed the top from the computer? If so, check all cables and verify that they correctly connect pin 1 to pin 1 of the adapter or motherboard. Check the power connection to the hard drive.
- If the hard drive flashes quickly on boot up, the controller is trying to read the partition table in the Master Boot Record. If this information is not found, various symptoms can be shown, such as the error messages "Invalid boot disk," "Inaccessible boot device," "Invalid partition table," "Error loading operating system," "Missing operating system," or "No operating system found." Use the DISKPART command from recovery console to see if the hard drive partition table is OK. Try running FDISK/MBR from Recovery Console or use a hard drive utility to repair the partition table.

Does your hard drive stick?
Place a hand on top of the drive as you turn on the computer. Does the drive spin at all? If not, the problem is probably a "sticky" drive or a bad drive. A hard drive must spin at a certain rpm before the heads move over the surface of the hard drive. To check if the drive is sticking, remove the drive and try spinning the spindle motor by hand. Otherwise, remove the drive, hold the drive in your hand, and give a quick jerk with your wrist. Another trick that works is to remove the hard drive from the case, place the drive in a plastic bag, and put in the freezer for a couple of hours. Then, remove the drive and allow it to warm up to room temperature. Reinstall the drive into the system and try it.

- Do you receive a message such as "Disk Boot Failure," "Non-System Disk," or "Disk Error"? These errors may indicate a boot record problem. The solution is to boot from a bootable disk or CD to see if drive C: is available. The operating system may have to be reloaded. Also, verify that the primary partition is marked as active.
- If you receive a message "Hard drive not found," "No boot device available," "Fixed disk error," or "Disk boot failure," the BIOS cannot find the hard drive. Check cabling.
- When Windows has startup problems, Recovery Console and the *Advanced Options* menu are used. Many times startup problems are due to a virus. Other utilities that help with MBR, boot sector, and system files are FIXBOOT, FIXMBR, System File Checker, and the *Advanced Options* menu. To use FIXBOOT, type FIXBOOT x: command where x: is the drive letter of the volume that has the problem. To use FIXMBR, type FIXMBR from a command prompt. FIXBOOT is used in XP Recovery Console to rewrite the boot sector. Vista and 7 use bootrec/FixMbr or bootrec/FixBoot.

Use System File Checker
The System File Checker program can be run from the *Run* dialog box by typing x:\Windows\System32\SFC.EXE /scannow where x: is the drive letter of the drive on which Windows is installed.

- Indications that there is a problem with the Master Boot Record or the system files are as follows: "Invalid partition table," "Error loading operating system," "Missing operating system," "A disk read error has occurred," "NTLDR is missing," or "NTLDR is corrupt."
- When Windows has startup problems due to incompatible hardware or software, or a corrupted installation process, the *Advanced Options* menu can help. This option can be selected by pressing the ⌷F8⌷ key during the boot process.
- If an insufficient disk space error appears, delete unnecessary files, including .tmp files, from the hard drive, empty the Recycle Bin, and save files to a CD/DVD, a Flash drive, or an external hard drive and remove the moved files from the hard drive. Use the Disk Cleanup and Defragmenter tool. Another option is to add another hard drive and move some (or all) data files to it.
- For eSATA drives, check the power cabling and data cabling. Ensure that the data cable is the correct type for the port and device being used. Partition and format the drive before data is written to it. Ensure that the port is enabled through BIOS. The BIOS may require an update, or a device driver may be required (especially if the drive is listed under "other devices" in Device Manager). BIOS incompatibilities are the most common issue with deployments. Note that some operating systems report SATA drives as SCSI drives.
- If the computer reports that the hard drive may have a defective area, use the hard drive error checking tool (right-click) on the hard drive volume, select *Properties*, select the *Tools* tab, and click the *Check now* button.
- A ticking sound is sometimes called by a failed or failing hard drive.

Table 7.14 shows some of the normal and problem drive status messages seen in the Windows Disk Management tool. These status messages can help with drive management, troubleshooting, and recovery.

Table 7.14   **Disk management status states**

Disk Management Status	Description
Active	The bootable partition, usually on the first hard drive, is ready for use.
Dynamic	An alternative to the basic disk the dynamic disk has volumes instead of partitions. Types of volumes include simple volumes, volumes that span more than one drive, and RAID volumes.
Failed	The basic disk or dynamic volume cannot be started; the disk or volume could be damaged; the file system could be corrupted; or there may be a problem with the underlying physical disk (turned on, cabled correctly) or with an associated RAID drive. Right-click the disk and select *Reactivate disk*. Right-click the dynamic volume and select *Reactivate volume*.
Foreign	A dynamic disk from another computer has just been installed. Right-click the disk and select *Import Foreign Disks*.
Healthy	The drive is ready to be used.
Not Initialized	A basic disk is not ready to be used. Right-click the disk and select *Initialize Disk*.
Invalid	Vista Home (any version) cannot access the dynamic disk. Convert the disk to a basic disk (right-click the disk number and select *Convert to basic disk*).
Offline	Ensure that the physical disk is turned on and cabled correctly. Right-click it and select *Reactivate Disk* or *Activate*.
Online (errors)	Use the hard drive error checking tool (in Explorer, right-click the hard drive partition and then select *Properties*, the *Tools* tab, and *Check now button*).
Unallocated	Space on a hard drive has not been partitioned or put into a volume.
Unknown	A new drive has not been initialized properly. Right-click it and select *Initialize disk*. The volume boot sector may be corrupted or infected by a virus.
Unreadable	The drive has not had time to spin up. Restart the computer and rescan the disk (use the *Action* menu item).

7

Storage Devices

Preventive Maintenance for Hard Drives

Keeping the computer system in a clean and cool operating environment extends the life of a hard drive. The most common hard drive failures are due to moving parts (heads and motors) and power fluctuations and/or failures. Performing preventive maintenance on the entire computer is good for all components found inside the computer, including the hard drive subsystem.

A program called **CHKDSK** can be executed from within the GUI or from Recovery Console and the program locates clusters disassociated from data files. These disk clusters occupy disk space. When CHKDSK executes and reports that there are **lost clusters**, it means that the FAT cannot determine to which file or directory these clusters belong.

In Windows you can perform this function by locating the drive partition in Explorer, right-click the drive letter and select *Properties → Tool* tab → *Check Now* button. Windows also has a program called **Disk Cleanup** that removes temporary files, removes offline Internet files, empties the Recycle Bin, compresses unused files, removes unused programs, and prompts you before doing any of this. To access Disk Cleanup use the following procedures:

Tech Tip

Running disk cleanup from a command prompt

An alternative method from the command prompt is CLEANMGR and then press Enter.

1. Click the *Start* button → *All Programs* → *Accessories* → *System Tools* → *Disk Cleanup*.
2. Select the drive letter, and click *OK*.
3. On the *Disk Cleanup* tab, click in the checkboxes for the options desired and click *OK*.

Data Security

Another preventive maintenance procedure for a hard drive is performing a backup of the data and operating system. Most people do not realize that the most important part of any computer is the data that resides within it. Data cannot be replaced like hardware can be. Traditionally, backups have been saved to magnetic tape (quarter-inch cartridge, LTO (linear tape-open) or DLT (digital linear tape) being the most common types), but CDs, DVDs, and external drives are viable alternatives today. Some people use CDs or DVDs to back up the data and periodically do a full backup to an external drive.

Tech Tip

A second hard drive makes an excellent backup device

Hard drives are inexpensive and easy to install. Install a second one to backup your data. Backups should be done routinely. Have a routine maintenance plan that you recommend to users. Important data should be backed up daily or frequently, but routine data is usually handled by a monthly backup. The sensitivity and importance of the data determines how frequent backups are performed.

Windows comes with a backup utility, but many of the external hard drives come with their own software that is easier to use, has more features, and allows easy and selective data backup scheduling. No matter what method of backup you use, test your backup for restoration. Install to a different drive if necessary.

Laptops sometimes have an additional password for their hard drive. That way if the laptop hard drive is stolen, it cannot be inserted into another device and used without knowing the hard

Tech Tip

For critical data, keep backups in a different location

Offsite storage for critical data is important even for home users in case of disaster such as flooding, fire, or theft. A safe deposit box can be used for important data records such as textbooks, income taxes, personal records (insurance policy numbers and financial data) and student tests (just kidding).

Don't use the same hard drive as a backup device
Backing up data to a different partition on the hard drive is *not* a good idea. Even though there is some chance that your data might be saved, it is more likely the drive will fail. The drive is a physical device with moving parts—motor, heads, and so on. Mechanical failure is always a possibility.

drive password. It is a password in addition to the power on password or Windows password. This option is configured through the BIOS if it is available.

Even though much data is stored locally for most users, many companies are favoring centralized storage even for individual users. One, this protects the company's interest and two it ensures backups are done on a regular and reliable basis. Some companies are moving toward a **thin-client** environment in which no hard drives are included with the system. Storage is provided across the network. This reduces hardware and software costs, PC maintenance staffing costs, and makes data security easier to manage.

When replacing a hard drive, destroy the drive so that data can never be retrieved. Open the drive and physically damage the platters. Scratch the platters with a screwdriver or other implement.

There are utilities that allow the entire drive to be rewritten with all ones or all zeros. Removing all partitions and re-partitioning and re-formatting the drive also helps.

Store data on remote servers
Many folks who travel frequently use data storage servers at their company or use the services of an Internet storage site. Part of their services includes backing up the data stored on their drives and having redundant hard drives in their servers.

Erase data from old drive
When upgrading (and removing) a hard drive, install the new drive, re-install data and/or applications, but ensure the data and remnants of data are no longer on the drive.

Removable Drive Storage

IDE and SCSI are the two most common types of hard drives, but these interfaces are also used for internal and external storage devices such as CD/DVD drives and tape drives. IDE PATA has traditionally only been internal devices, but now with SATA, external devices are available. SCSI has always supported internal and external devices. These external devices can also attach to the parallel port (not common today) or the USB port (a very popular option).

Tape drives can be attached using SCSI or IDE (SATA only) or attach to parallel, USB, eSATA, or IEEE 1394 ports if they are external devices. Tape drives are installed using similar methods of like devices that use these ports. When tapes are used, the most common types of tapes used for backups are DAT (digital audio tape) and Traven. The most common type of removable storage is optical (CD/DVD).

SSD defragmentation kills
Do not defragment an SSD as you would a magnetic hard drive. Defragmentation causes more reads and writes, which reduces the life span of the SSD.

Hard Drive Fragmentation

Over time, as files are added to a hard drive, the files become fragmented, which means that the clusters that make up the file are not adjacent to one another. Fragmentation slows down the hard drive in two ways: (1) the FAT has to keep track of scattered clusters, and (2) the hard drive read/write head assembly must move to different locations on the drive's surface to access a single file. Figure 7.40 illustrates fragmentation of

How to defragment in Windows
To access the defragmentation tool in Windows, open *Explorer*, locate a hard drive letter, right-click it, and select *Properties* → *Tools* tab → *Defragment Now* button.

7

Storage Devices

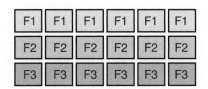

Three fragmented files · Three contiguous files

Figure 7.40 **Fragmented hard drive**

three files (F1, F2, and F3) and the results after defragmentation has been executed on the hard drive. **Defragmentation** is the process of placing files in contiguous sectors. Notice the results in Figure 7.40 of the defragmentation process.

Windows includes a program that defragments the hard drive. This program places the file clusters in adjacent sectors. Defragmenting the hard drive makes for faster hard disk access. These measures also extend the life of the hard drive because the drive's mechanical movements are reduced.

The DEFRAG command or the Defragment Windows tool come with some advanced options. Table 7.15 shows the XP defragmentation options.

Table 7.15 **Windows XP or DEFRAG command options**

Option	Description
Full Defragmentation	Takes the longest but is the best choice.
Defragment Files Only	Faster than Full Defragmentation but does not consolidate space on the hard drive.
Consolidate Free Space Only	Locates the largest amount of free space to place smaller clusters. Files could be more fragmented as a result.
Check Drive for Errors checkbox	Looks for and corrects lost clusters. Enabled by default.

Tech Tip

How often should you defragment a hard drive?

Periodically defragment files on a hard drive. Users who delete files often and have large files that are constantly revised should run these utilities more often. You can use the *Analyze* button in XP in Disk Defragmenter to check if a drive partition needs to be defragmented. Once the analysis is complete, click *View Report* to determine whether or not the drive partition needs to be defragmented.

Disk Caching/Virtual Memory

An easy way to speed up the hard drive is to create a **disk cache**. This puts data into RAM where it can be retrieved much faster than if the data is still on the hard drive. When data is read from the hard drive, the next requested data is frequently located in the adjacent clusters. Disk caching reads more data from the hard drive than requested. The data is placed in a reserved portion of RAM called the cache. Cache on a hard drive controller, sometimes called a data buffer, allows the read/write heads to read more than just one sector at a time. A hard drive can read up to an entire track of information and hold this data until needed without returning to the hard drive for each sector.

Both IDE and SCSI drives can contain 2MB to 16MB or more of RAM. Because drives are mechanical devices, they take time to reorder write data to the platters. With cache memory installed, information can be prefetched from the computer's system RAM and stored in the hard drive's cache memory. This frees up the system RAM for other tasks and improves the system and hard drive's performance.

A different way of using a hard drive is with virtual memory. Virtual memory is a method of using hard disk space as if it were RAM. The amount of RAM installed in a system is not normally enough to handle all of the operating system and the multiple applications that are opened and being used. Only the program and data of the application that is currently being used is what is in RAM. The rest of the opened applications and data are stored in what is called a swap file or a page file on the hard drive. When you click over to a different application that is held in the swap/page file, data is moved from RAM into the swap file and the data you need to look at is moved into RAM for faster access and data manipulation.

Windows uses **VMM** (Virtual Memory Manager). The disk cache is dynamic—it increases or decreases the cache size as needed. If the system begins to page (constantly swapping data from RAM to the hard drive), the cache size automatically shrinks. In Windows NT and higher, the virtual memory swap file (sometimes called the page file) is called `PAGEFILE.SYS`.

Where should you keep the swap file?

If multiple hard drives are available, a technician might want to move the swap file to a different drive. Always put the swap file on the fastest hard drive unless that hard drive lacks space. The swap file can reside on multiple hard drives. It is best to keep the swap file on a hard drive that does not contain the operating system.

How to adjust virtual memory in Windows 7

From the *Start* button or *Explorer,* right-click *Computer* → *Properties* → in left pane, select *Advanced system settings* → *Advanced* tab → in the *Virtual memory* section, click *Change*. Then to manually configure the settings, clear the *Automatically manage paging file size for all drives* and adjust the settings as needed.

32-bit Windows versions use 32-bit demand-paged virtual memory, and each process gets 4GB of address space divided into two 2GB sections. One 2GB section is shared with the rest of the system while the other 2GB section is reserved for the one application. All the memory space is divided into 4KB blocks of memory called "pages." The operating system allocates as much available RAM as possible to an application. Then, the operating system swaps or pages the application to and from the temporary swap file as needed. The operating system determines the optimum setting for this swap file; however, the swap file size can be changed.

Adding more physical RAM to the motherboard helps with caching

One of the most effective ways to speed up a computer is to reduce the amount of data that has to be swapped from the hard drive to RAM. This is done by increasing the amount of RAM on the motherboard. Accessing RAM is much faster than accessing a mechanical drive that rotates and has heads that have to move and find the data.

Soft Skills—Phone Skills

Technicians must frequently use the phone in the normal course of business. This includes speaking with customers who call in, those who you must call, and vendors and technical support staff. Many technicians' full-time job involves communication via the telephone.

Phone communication is different from in-person communication because on the phone you have only your words and voice intonation to convey concepts, professionalism, and technical assistance. When dealing with someone in person, you can use some of the following techniques that are not allowed during normal phone conversations:

- Gesture to emphasize points
- Draw a graphic to illustrate a concept
- Perform steps needed for troubleshooting faster because you can do them rather than step someone through them
- Show empathy easier with your body language, actions, and voice

When dealing with someone on the phone, the following pointers can help. Some of the tips apply to everyday technical support as well:

- Identify yourself clearly and pleasantly
- Avoid a condescending tone
- Be patient and speak slowly when giving directions
- Use active listening skills (covered in Chapter 2); avoid doing other tasks when on a call with someone
- Avoid using acronyms and technical jargon
- Avoid being accusatory or threatening
- If the customer is irate, try to calm him down and help him; however, if he continues to be belligerent, turn the call over to your supervisor
- Escalate the problem if it is beyond your skill level; do not waste the customer's time
- Do not leave people on hold for extended periods without checking back with them and updating them
- Speak clearly and loud enough to be heard easily
- Avoid having a headset microphone pulled away so it is hard to hear you; if you are asked to repeat something, speak louder or adjust the microphone or handset
- Avoid eating, drinking, or chewing gum when on the phone.

Good interpersonal skills are more important when on the phone than with face-to-face interactions. Before getting on the phone, take a deep breath and check your attitude. Every customer deserves your best game no matter what type of day you have had or what type of customer you have previously spoken to.

The rest of the chapter is devoted to questions and exercises to help with all hard drive concepts. Good luck with them!

Key Terms

basic disk (p. 229)
basic storage (p. 229)
boot partition (p. 227)
boot sector (p. 232)
boot volume (p. 229)
cable select (p. 210)
CHKDSK (p. 236)
cluster (p. 222)
command-based switching (p. 206)
CONVERT (p. 223)
CRC (p. 204)
cylinder (p. 200)
DBR (p. 232)
defragmentation (p. 238)
disk (p. 198)
Disk Administrator (p. 222)
disk cache (p. 238)
Disk Cleanup (p. 236)
disk duplexing (p. 230)
disk mirroring (p. 230)
diskpart (p. 222)
DMA mode (p. 203)
dynamic disk (p. 229)
dynamic storage (p. 229)
eSATA (p. 206)
exFAT (p. 223)

extended partition (p. 226)
FAT (p. 231)
FAT16 (p. 223)
FAT32 (p. 223)
fault tolerance (p. 229)
file system (p. 222)
FIS (p. 206)
GPT (p. 228)
head crash (p. 199)
high-level formatting (p. 222)
HPA (p. 228)
HVD (p. 218)
IDE (p. 201)
logical drive (p. 226)
lost cluster (p. 236)
master (p. 210)
MBR (p. 227)
MLC (p. 207)
NTFS (p. 223)
partitioning (p. 222)
PATA (p. 202)
platter (p. 199)
primary partition (p. 225)
RAID (p. 229)
RAID 0 (p. 230)
RAID 1 (p. 230)

RAID 5 (p. 230)
RAW volume (p. 229)
read/write head (p. 198)
SAS (p. 208)
SATA (p. 204)
SATA-PM (p. 206)
SCSI (p. 201)
SCSI ID (p. 216)
sector (p. 200)
simple volume (p. 229)
single (p. 210)
slave (p. 210)
SLC (p. 207)
spanned volume (p. 229)
SSD (p. 206)
striped volume (p. 229)
system partition (p. 227)
system volume (p. 229)
thin client (p. 237)
track (p. 200)
UDMA (p. 203)
VMM (p. 239)
volume (p. 226)
wear leveling (p. 206)
write amplification (p. 206)

7
Storage Devices

Review Questions

1. What drive letter is assigned to the first floppy drive detected in a system?

2. If a floppy cable has two connectors and only one drive is to be connected, to which connector do you attach the drive?

3. How do you know the proper orientation for connecting the cable onto the floppy controller?

4. List three considerations when installing a floppy drive.

5. What is the difference between a floppy drive and a hard drive?

6. How many surfaces are on a hard drive platter?

7. How many read/write heads are normally used with each hard drive platter?

8. What is the difference between a track and a cylinder?

9. List the two types of hard drives.

10. What is one difference between an architecture that transmits in parallel and one that transmits serially?

11. [T | F] Older IDE and SCSI standards are both serial architectures.

12. What are two types of IDE?

13. Which IDE type is the older technology?

14. How many pins are on a PATA IDE motherboard connector?

15. What is crosstalk?

16. How is the Ultra ATA/66 cable different from older IDE cables?

17. What is the minimum UDMA mode that requires the 80-conductor IDE cable?

18. [T | F] SATA supports internal and external devices.

19. What is the standards-based maximum length for an eSATA cable?

20. [T | F] An eSATA motherboard port can provide power to an external device, but an eSATA port on an adapter cannot.

21. A laptop has one eSATA port, but the customer wants to attach two external SATA drives. List two solutions.

22. What is the maximum number of devices that can be connected to a SATA-PM?

23. What is the difference between command-based switching and FIS?

24. What type of memory do SSDs use?

25. What is the primary cause of hard drive failures?

26. Which situation would *not* be appropriate for the use of SSDs?
    a. a manufacturing plant with heat-sensitive equipment
    b. a medical imaging office that needs high-capacity storage
    c. a research facility where noise must be kept to a minimum
    d. a military operation where fast access to data is critical

27. Describe how erasing is used for writing data onto an SSD.

28. What is an erase block as it relates to SSDs?

29. How can wear leveling extend the life of an SSD?

30. What is a drawback of SSDs? [cost] [speed] [reliability] [MTBF]

31. Which hard drive type has the ability to daisy chain over three devices using the same controller?

32. What SCSI standard has a maximum data transfer rate of 80MBps?

33. What SCSI standard is associated with the term *Ultra*?

34. List three steps used when installing a PATA drive.

35. [T | F] When two PATA IDE devices connect to the same IDE cable, only one device transmits at a time.

36. Describe the difference between primary master and secondary master.

37. [T | F] IDE hard drives are normally the fastest type of IDE device.

38. [T | F] When only one PATA device connects to an IDE cable, configure that device as master and attach the device to the center connector for optimum performance.

39. Describe how to configure two PATA IDE devices using cable select.

40. Explain what happens if two PATA devices are set to cable select and connected to a 40-conductor IDE cable.

41. [T | F] Two SATA devices can connect to a cable that has two device connectors and a motherboard connector.

42. [T | F] An eSATA drive requires setting or removing a termination jumper.

43. Through what utility would a technician verify whether an eSATA port is disabled or enabled? [Disk Management | BIOS | diskpart | System Tools]

44. What does it mean when a drive mounts?

45. [T | F] An SSD can attach to a SATA port.

46. Why would a technician remove a laptop battery before installing an SSD?

47. Why are SSDs more susceptible than hard drives to electrostatic discharge?

48. List three things to consider when adding a parallel SCSI hard drive.

49. What is a SCSI chain?

50. List at least two reasons why you should be careful in choosing the SCSI ID for a SCSI device.

51. What is the highest priority SCSI ID?

52. What SCSI ID is normally assigned to the SCSI adapter?

53. What SCSI ID is normally assigned to a bootable hard drive?

54. One SCSI device has ID 4 and another device on the same bus has SCSI ID 14. Which device has the highest priority?

55. List one reason why installing or removing terminators on a SCSI hard drive is important.

56. [T | F] A SCSI chain uses termination for proper operation.

57. List the three categories of SCSI terminators.

58. Which types of SCSI devices require active terminators?

59. [T | F] Passive and active terminators can be used on the same SCSI chain.

60. [T | F] An HVD device can use an LVD/HVD terminator otherwise known as a differential terminator.

61. Which type of terminator is backward compatible with SE signaling? [HVD | LVD | Differential | PSST]

62. What are the two types of terminators used with LVD devices?

63. Draw the SCSI symbol for SE.

64. If a SCSI adapter attaches to two internal hard drives, where do you install the terminators?

65. If a SCSI adapter attaches to an internal hard drive and an external tape drive, where do you install the terminators?

66. [T | F] IDE hard drives are the most common type used in laptops.

67. Explain how to add a second hard drive in a notebook computer.

68. What is the most common BIOS setting for IDE hard drives?

69. What does partitioning the hard drive mean?

70. [T | F] A newly installed hard drive can be partitioned as part of the operating system installation.

71. List three file systems.

72. [T | F] FAT32 supports disk compression.

73. Why should you partition a 2TB hard drive?

74. How many logical drives can an extended partition have?

75. Explain the difference between spanned and striped volumes.

76. What is the maximum partition size for NTFS?

77. What Windows tool is used to high-level format a hard drive?

78. List three things to check if a hard drive has recently been installed and it does not work properly.

79. When powering on a computer, you notice that the hard drive does not spin at all. What will you check?

80. Upon powering up a computer system, you receive a "Disk Boot Failure" error message. What should you do?

81. List three things to check when a working hard drive quits.

Use information in the following advertisement to answer Questions 82–84.

Computer for Sale:
Intel dual-core 2.8GHz processor
4GB DDR2-667MHz dual channel SDRAM
500GB SATA HDD
16x CD/DVD+/-R/RW
802.11b/g

82. If you were to buy another hard drive just like the one listed in the advertisement, which of the steps needed to allow data to be written to the hard drive would you have to do?

7

Storage Devices

83. Of the two major types of hard drive interfaces, which hard drive type does this computer use?

84. If you were to build a system like this and the two DVD drives are parallel IDE devices, how would you connect them to the system (which connectors and what settings on each device)?

85. What is CHKDSK?

86. How do you check a hard drive for lost clusters in a Windows XP-based computer?

87. What is the purpose of the Disk Cleanup Windows tool?

88. Does Windows XP come with a data backup application or must a third-party application be used?

89. Why is backing your data up to a different partition on the same hard drive a bad idea?

90. What is an advantage of using an Internet storage site?

91. List three interfaces that could be used with a removable data storage unit such as an external hard drive.

92. What is fragmentation as it relates to hard drives?

93. How do you defragment a hard drive installed in a Windows XP-based computer?

94. What is a swap drive as it relates to Windows XP?

95. Can you adjust the amount of hard drive space that is used as virtual memory? If so, how can this be done? If not, why is it not allowed?

96. [T | F] One of the most effective ways of increasing computer performance is to increase the size of virtual memory.

97. [T | F] One of the most effective ways of increasing computer performance is to add more RAM.

98. Why is it easier to deal with customers in person than on the phone?

99. List three tips for dealing with anyone when communicating over the phone.

100. Describe a phone conversation in which the person on the other end could have done something differently to make the communication process work. Describe what the person said. Describe your reaction. List at least one thing that could have been improved.

Fill-in-the-Blank

1. The _____ is a window on the left side of a 3.5-inch disk that, when closed, allows data to be written to the disk.

2. The _____ floppy drive attaches to the connector with the twist.

3. One hard disk metal plate is called a _____.

4. The _____ are the part of the hard drive that actually transmit or receive the 1s and 0s to or from the hard drive.

5. The _____ is a part of the hard drive that holds the read/write heads.

6. One particular track on each and every platter collectively is known as a/an _____.

7. A/An _____ is the smallest division on a hard drive surface. Tracks are divided into these.

8. A/An _____ hard drive is common in today's computers and cheaper than SCSI hard drives.

9. The ATA standard is associated with the _____ interface.

10. _____ is hard drive intelligence software used for error reporting.

11. The _____ IDE type is a point-to-point interface.

12. eSATA has a cable used for devices that transfer at _____ Gbps and a different cable for the higher speed of _____ Gbps.

13. 1.5Gbps eSATA devices can have a cable up to _____ in length; in contrast, 3Gbps eSATA devices can have a cable up to _____ in length.

14. A SATA-PM allows up to _____ devices to connect to one port.

15. _____ is a faster technology required for a system that has a SATA-PM attached.

16. A/An _____ hard drive is used in network servers and whenever expandability (adding devices that do not necessarily have to be hard drives) is an issue.

17. Another name for a SCSI bus is a _____.

18. _____ are SCSI devices that use a point-to-point bus.

19. PATA IDE drives are set up using _____.

20. The four most common PATA IDE jumper settings for hard drives are _____, _____, _____, and _____.

21. The primary PATA IDE motherboard connection normally uses I/O address _____ and IRQ _____.

22. The PATA IDE cable's maximum specified length is _____ inches.

23. The middle PATA cable select connector (slave setting) is the color _____ according to the specification.

24. An internal SATA drive only requires connecting a(n) _____ cable and a/an _____ cable.

25. If a power connector is available, but it is not a SATA power connector, a/an _____ must be obtained.

26. _____ drives can be used instead of hard drives, but these use memory technology instead of hard drive technology.

27. _____ is the minimum amount of memory space erased in order to write data on an SSD.

28. _____ technology uses memory cells evenly on SSDs.

29. SSD _____ technology stores 1 bit in each cell compared to _____, which stores more than 1 bit.

30. Another name for a SCSI controller is _____.

31. A number assigned to a SCSI device that determines the device's priority on the SCSI bus is the _____.

32. Standard SCSI devices can use SCSI IDs _____ through _____; 16-bit SCSI devices can use SCSI IDs _____ through _____.

33. The SCSI symbol ◇ designates a _____ device, terminator, or cable.

34. The step in preparing a hard drive that assigns drive letters to the hard drive is known as _____.

35. The step in preparing a hard drive that allows data to be written to the drive is _____.

36. The Windows _____ program can be used to partition a second hard drive or partitions other than the first partition on the first installed hard drive.

37. _____ is the command-line utility used to partition a drive for NTFS.

38. Windows XP and Vista support the _____, _____, and _____ file systems.

39. The _____ command changes a FAT partition to NTFS.

40. A/An _____ is the minimum amount of space a file occupies; the number of sectors for each one is determined by the size of the partition.

41. The first hard drive in a system is normally partitioned through the _____ installation process.

42. The first primary partition on the first hard drive receives the drive letter _____.

43. An extended partition holds _____ drives.

44. The _____ is where the hard drive's partition information is kept.

45. The first sector on a hard drive is called the _____.

46. The Windows partition that holds the majority of the operating system files is called the _____ partition.

47. The two types of storage defined by the Windows Logical Disk Management tool are _____ and _____.

48. A/An _____ volume writes data by alternating between two or more drives.

49. A/An _____ disk holds a spanned volume.

50. A/An _____ volume holds files used to boot the computer.

51. The _____ process sets up the file system.

52. RAID _____ does not provide data protection.

53. RAID _____ is disk mirroring.

54. RAID _____ requires three or more hard drives because one drive always contains parity data used to rebuild a failed drive.

55. The _____ is like the table of contents for a hard drive with at least two on every hard drive.

56. During the boot process, the hard drive light flashes briefly to indicate reading the _____ table.

57. A hard drive shows a status of foreign in Disk Management. This is common when a _____ disk has been moved to another computer.

58. The _____ Windows program removes temporary files, empties the Recycle Bin, as well as other storage space saving techniques.

59. A type of computer that does not include a hard drive is known as a(n) _____.

60. File _____ occurs when a file is located on non-consecutive clusters.

61. The _____ Windows program places files in contiguous (adjacent) sectors.

62. A disk _____ speeds up hard drive data access.

63. _____ memory is when hard drive space is used as RAM.

64. Phone communication is different from in-person communication because you only have _____ and _____ to convey your message.

65. When helping a customer on the phone, it is a good idea to avoid _____.

Hands-On Exercises

1. Configuring a PATA IDE Hard Drive on Paper

Objective: To be able to configure a PATA IDE hard drive

Procedure: Refer to the following figures and answer the accompanying questions.

Questions:

See Figure 7.41 to answer Question 1.

Jumper	Setting	Comments
J17	Cable Select	Open=disabled* Jumpered=enabled
J18	Master/Slave	Open=slave in a dual drive system Jumpered=master in a dual drive system Jumpered=master in a single drive system*
J19	Write Cache	Open=disabled Jumpered=enabled*
J20	Reserved	For factory use
J21	Spare	

*=Default setting

Figure 7.41

1. Using the following drawing, circle the jumpers to be enabled (set) to configure IDE Hard Drive #1 as if it is the only drive connected to an IDE port.

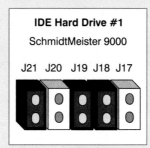

IDE Hard Drive #1

SchmidtMeister 9000

J21   J20   J19 J18 J17

See Figure 7.42 to answer Questions 2 and 3.

IDE Hard Drive #1

SchmidtMeister 9000

J21 J20 J19 J18 J17

Jumper	Setting	Comments
J17	Cable Select	Open=disabled*
		Jumpered=enabled
J18	Master/Slave	Open=slave in a dual drive system
		Jumpered=master in a dual drive system
		Jumpered=master in a single drive system*
J19	Write Cache	Open=disabled
		Jumpered=enabled*
J20	Reserved	For factory use
J21	Spare	

*=Default setting

IDE Hard Drive #2

SchmidtMeister 9000

J21   J20   J19 J18 J17

Figure 7.42

2. Using the following drawing, circle the jumpers to be enabled (set) to configure IDE Hard Drive #1 as the master drive connected to an IDE port. Keep in mind that IDE Hard Drive #2 shares the same cable with Hard Drive #1.

IDE Hard Drive #1

SchmidtMeister 9000

J21   J20   J19   J18   J17

3. Using the following drawing, circle the jumpers to be enabled (set) to configure IDE Hard Drive #2 as the slave drive. Keep in mind that IDE Hard Drive #2 shares the same cable with Hard Drive #1.

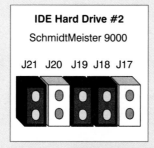

IDE Hard Drive #2

SchmidtMeister 9000

J21   J20   J19   J18   J17

See Figure 7.43 to answer Questions 4 and 5.

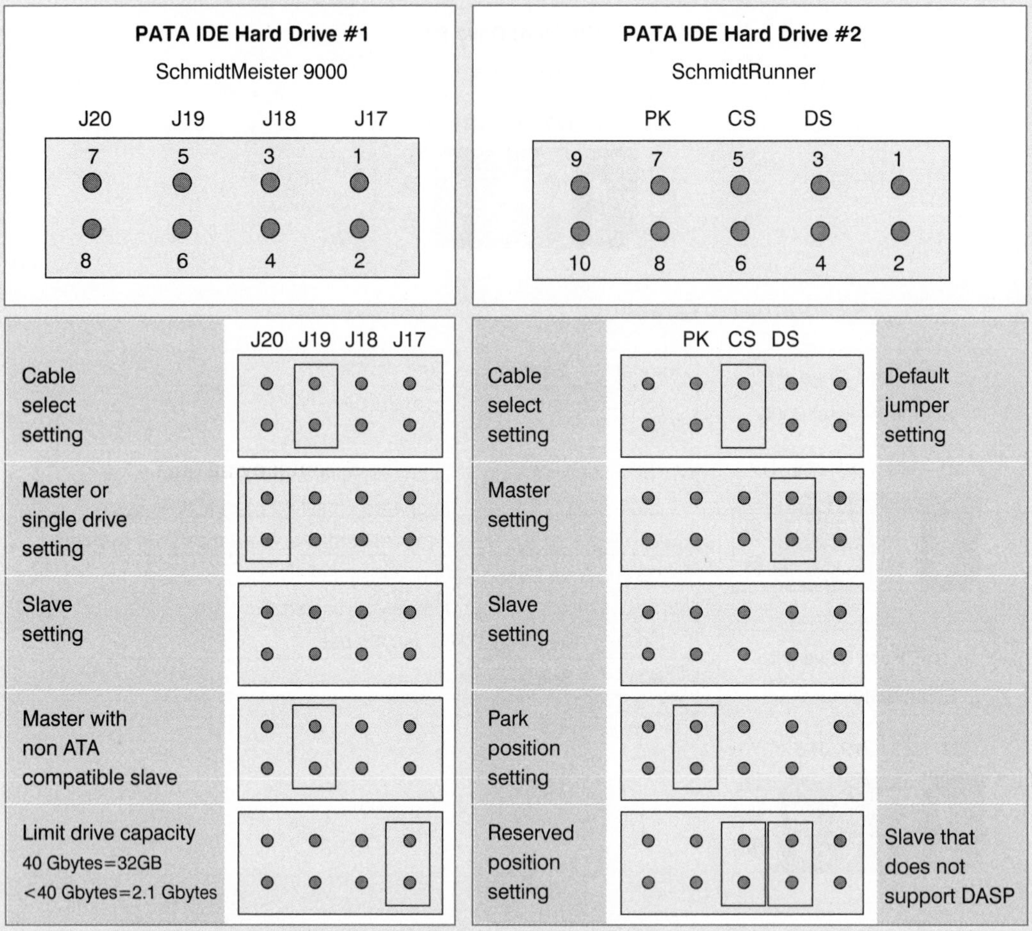

Figure 7.43

4. List the jumpers that will be enabled (set) to configure IDE Hard Drive #1 as the master drive connected to a PATA IDE port. Keep in mind that IDE Hard Drive #2 shares the same cable with Hard Drive #1.

5. List the jumpers that will be enabled (set) to configure IDE Hard Drive #2 as the slave drive. Keep in mind that IDE Hard Drive #2 shares the same cable with Hard Drive #1.

2. Configuring a PATA IDE Cable Select Configuration

Objective: To be able to configure a PATA IDE cable

Procedure: Refer to the following table and answer the accompanying question.

Question: The information in Table 7.16 relates to three PATA IDE devices being installed in a system.

1. All of the PATA IDE devices support cable select configuration. The system is supplied with two IDE motherboard connectors and two IDE 80-conductor 40-pin IDE cables. On a blank piece of paper, draw the motherboard connectors, IDE cables, and IDE cable connectors. Write the name of each device (Hard Drive #1, Hard Drive #2, and CD-RW Drive) by the PATA IDE cable connector to which it attaches. Designate the motherboard connections as Primary or Secondary. Designate the IDE devices as Primary master, Primary slave, Secondary master, or Secondary slave.

Table 7.16   **Three PATA IDE devices**

Device Name	Capacity	Cache
Hard Drive #1	750GB	8MB
Hard Drive #2	1TB	16MB
DVD/CD-RW Drive	N/A	2MB

3. Installing an IDE PATA/SATA Hard Drive with Windows XP Disk Management Tool, DISKPART, and CONVERT

Objective: To be able to configure and manage a hard drive using the Windows XP's Disk Management tool

Parts: Windows XP computer with an available PATA connection or SATA port
            IDE PATA/SATA hard drive

Procedure: Complete the following procedure and answer the accompanying questions.

Notes: Use proper antistatic and gentle handling procedures when dealing with hard drives. You must be a user who has administrator rights to configure hard drives. If two CD/DVD devices are installed, one can be replaced by the new hard drive to perform this lab.

1. Power on the computer and log in.

2. There are several ways to get to the window used to manage hard drives. Practice using both methods. Through Windows Explorer, right-click *My Computer* and select *Manage*.
   a. Click the *Start* button, click *Run*, and type **compmgmt.msc** and press (Enter).
   b. Click the *Start* button, click the *Control Panel* (ensure you are in Classic view), double-click the *Administrative Tools* control panel, and double-click the *Computer Management* icon.

3. In the console tree shown in the left window pane, select the *Disk Management* option. The disks and volumes already installed in the computer display in a graphical manner on the right.

4. Right-click the drive partition labeled C: and select *Properties*.

   What type of file system is being used? [FAT16 | FAT32 | NTFS]

   What is the total capacity of the drive?

   What is the amount of free space?

5. Shutdown the computer and remove the power cord.

6. Remove the computer cover. If PATA is being used, locate an available IDE PATA connector on the motherboard or an available PATA cable connector. If SATA is being used, locate a free SATA port on the motherboard and determine which port this is. Use the motherboard or system documentation, if necessary.

7. If a PATA is being installed, determine whether the other device on the same cable (if installed) uses cable select or master/slave jumpers by removing the drive and examining it. Handle the drive carefully.

   If a PATA drive is being installed, is there a second device on the same cable? If so does the device use the cable select, master, or slave jumper?

   If a SATA drive is being installed, what SATA port will be used for the new drive? Show the instructor.

8. If necessary, re-install the drive into the machine and reconnect the power and data cables. On the hard drive given to you by the instructor, if PATA is being used, configure the drive to the appropriate setting of cable select, master, or slave. If SATA is being used, power on the computer, enter Setup, and ensure that the SATA port is enabled. Enable the port, if necessary.

9. Mount the IDE hard drive (the one given to you by the instructor) into the case.

10. Attach the IDE data cable and attach a power cable.

11. Re-install the power cord and power on the computer. The *Found New Hardware* balloon appears.

12. Using previously described procedures, open the *Computer Management* tool. Click the *Disk Management* option in the left window pane. Notice that the drive appears as a new disk in the Disk Management window. If it does not appear as a new disk, right-click the disk number (not the area where you partition the drive) and select *Activate*. If this Activate option does not appear, power down the computer and check all cabling and settings. Note that the drive you were given may have been partitioned already and assigned a drive letter. If the drive was already partitioned and a drive letter assigned, right-click the drive and select *Delete Partition* and *Yes*.

    Was the drive already assigned a drive letter and partitioned?

13. Right-click the new drive you just installed and select *New Partition*. The *New Partition* wizard appears. If the SATA drive is detected in BIOS but not in the Disk Management tool, the drive will have to be initialized. The top half of the window shows devices that Windows knows how to access. Locate the new drive in the lower half of the screen. Because the disk does not contain a valid Windows signature, right-click the appropriate disk number (Disk 1, Disk 2, etc.) and select *Initialize Disk*. After installing a drive, Windows must prepare the drive before it is partitioned. When you first start the Disk Management tool, a wizard might appear. If you cancel the wizard before the disk signature is written, the drive status is not initialized and must be initialized before partitioning can begin.

    What is the difference between a primary partition and an extended partition?

    What is the maximum number of primary partitions as described on the screen?

14. Ensure the *Primary Partition* radio button is selected and click *Next*.

15. Enter a partition size that is 32GB or smaller.

    What partition size did you choose?

16. Click *Next*.

    How many drive letter devices are there?

17. Select the drive letter you want assigned (normally you would want the next drive letter available) and click *Next*. You are asked if you want to format the partition.

    What file systems does XP allow you to select for Disk Management when you use this tool?

    Are there any file systems supported by XP that are not shown? If so, what are they?

18. Select the *FAT32* option. Assign the volume label as a couple of letters from each of the lab partner's last names. Note that there is an 11 character maximum for FAT32 partitions and a 32 character maximum for NTFS partitions.

19. Select (enable) the *Perform a Quick Format* checkbox and click *Next*. Click the *Finish* button.

    How can you tell from the window whether a partition is FAT32 or NTFS?

20. Right-click in the unallocated drive space on the drive you just installed and select *New Partition*. The *New Partition* wizard appears. Click *Next*.

21. Select the *Extended Partition* radio button.

    According to the description information shown, what can an extended partition contain?

22. Click *Next*. The extended partition size needs to be the default amount shown (the rest of the drive). Click *Next*. Click *Finish*. The extended partition appears.

23. Right-click in the extended partition and select *New Logical Drive*. Click *Next*. The *Logical Drive* radio button is selected by default. Click *Next*.

24. The size for the logical drive needs to be one half the value currently shown on the screen.

    What amount of space did you choose for the logical drive size?

25. Click *Next*. Accept the drive letter default assignment and click *Next*.

26. Change the file system type to FAT32.

27. Make the volume label one of the partner's first name (up to 11 characters).

28. Select the *Perform a Quick Format* checkbox to enable. Click *Next* and click *Finish*.

29. Right-click the free space for the drive you installed. Using the same process, create an NTFS logical drive with the volume label as your first name and perform a quick format.

Instructor initials: _____ (Check: one FAT32 primary partition, one extended partition, two logical drives: one FAT32 and the other NTFS, two different volume labels for the logical drives)

30. You can change a FAT16 or FAT32 partition to the NTFS file system by using the convert command from a command prompt. Once it is changed, you cannot go back. Also, data is preserved (but should be backed up before the conversion just in case).

    Using the *Disk Management* window, what disk number is the drive you just installed? [0 | 1]

    Write the drive letter of the FAT32 primary partition on the drive you just installed. This drive letter will be used in the coming steps.

    Write the volume label used for this partition. This label is case sensitive, so write carefully.

31. Click the *Start* button. Select *Run*. Type **cmd** and press [Enter]. A command prompt window appears.

32. Type **convert /?** to see a list of options. These options tell you what to type after the convert command.

    What option is used to run convert in verbose mode?

    What option is used to convert a volume to NTFS?

33. Type **convert x:** (where *x*: is the drive letter you wrote down in Step 31) **/fs:ntfs**. For example, if the drive letter you wrote down is d: type convert d: /fs:ntfs. Notice the space between the drive letter and the /fs:ntfs.

    The /fs:ntfs is used to convert the existing file system (FAT16 or FAT32) to NTFS. You are prompted for the volume label for the drive. Enter the volume label you wrote down in Step 31 and press [Enter]. Don't forget that it is case sensitive. The partition is converted and can never be turned back into FAT32 unless the drive is reformatted.

34. Use the same process to convert the FAT32 logical drive to NTFS. Look up the volume label and the drive letter before starting.

Instructor initials: _____ (Look at the Computer Management screen and see that all the partitions and logical drives are NTFS—three drive letters)

35. From the *Computer Management–Disk Management* window, right-click the last logical drive on the hard drive you just installed.

36. Select the *Delete logical drive* option. Click *Yes*.

37. Partitions can be created from the Disk Management window, but they can also be created using the **DISKPART** command utility. Click the *Start* button, click *Run*, type **cmd** and press [Enter].

38. From the command prompt, type **DISKPART** and press [Enter].

    How does the prompt change?

39. Type **help** and press [Enter]. Use the help command to find out what commands are available.

    What command is used to make a new partition?

    What command can be used to give a drive partition a drive letter?

40. Type **create ?** and press [Enter].

    What two options can be used with create?

41. Type **create partition ?** and press [Enter].

    What type of partitions can be created?

7

Storage Devices

42. Press the ⬆ key once. The same command appears. Backspace and replace the **?** with **logical** so the command reads **create partition logical**. Press [Enter].

    What does the feedback say?

    What command do you think (based on help) would be used to select a drive?

43. Type **select disk** **x** (where **x** is the disk number you selected in the first question of Step 30). A prompt says the disk is selected.

44. Retype the **create partition logical** command or use your ⬆ and press it until that command appears and press [Enter].

45. Look back at your *Disk Management* window and see how the part of the drive previously marked as free space is now a logical drive.

46. At the command prompt, type **detail disk** to see the logical drive you just created. Notice how it does not have a file system or a drive letter assigned.

    Based on the command output, what drive letters are currently used?

47. At the command prompt, type **assign** and press [Enter].

    Look in the *Disk Management* window and see what drive letter was assigned. Write the drive letter.

48. At the command prompt, type **exit** to leave the **DISKPART** utility.

49. Type **help** at the command prompt to look for a command to help us high-level format the drive. The commands scroll by too fast, so type **help | more**. (The | keystroke is made by holding down the [Shift] key and pressing the key above the [Enter] key.) Press [Enter]. One page at a time is shown. Press the [Spacebar] once to see the next page of commands.

50. In the next command you are going to have to fill in some of the blanks to perform the step correctly. The parameters are as follows:

    x: is the drive letter documented in Step 47.

    /v:name where **name** is the second partner's first name (up to 32 characters).

    /fs:ntfs is telling the system to use the NTFS file system. Other options could be **/fs:fat** or **/fs:fat32**, but we are using NTFS this time.

    /q does a quick format.

    Type the command **format x: /fs:ntfs /v:name /q** and press [Enter]. When asked to proceed, press [Y] and press [Enter].

51. View the results in the Disk Management window. The last partition should be a logical drive that has a drive letter and is NTFS now.

52. Using whatever method you would like, copy one file to each of the three partitions you have created. Call the instructor over to show the three files and the *Disk Management* window. Do not proceed unless you have these parameters done.

    Instructor initials: _____ (three partitions that are all NTFS; three files, one in each of the partitions viewed through My Computer)

53. Starting with the partition on the far right in the *Disk Management* window for the drive you just installed, right-click each partition and delete each partition. Call the instructor over when the drive shows as one block (black) of unpartitioned hard drive space.

    Instructor initials: _____ (one space, no partitions, black colored)

54. Shut down the computer. Remove the power cord. Remove the IDE cable from the hard drive you just installed. Remove the power cord from the hard drive you just installed. Remove the hard drive. If necessary, re-install the CD/DVD drive, data cable, and power cord. Re-install the computer cover and the power cord.

55. Boot the computer. Open *My Computer* by clicking the *Start* button, and locating the *My Computer* icon. Ensure the CD/DVD drive is recognized. If it is not, redo Step 55.

56. Show the instructor the CD/DVD drive in the My Computer window and give the hard drive to the instructor.

    Instructor initials: _____ (ensure the CD/DVD drive is seen in My Computer)

4. Installing an IDE PATA/SATA Hard Drive with the Windows Vista Disk Management Tool, DISKPART, and CONVERT

Objective: To be able to configure and manage a hard drive using Windows Vista's Disk Management console

Parts: Windows Vista computer with an available PATA connection on the motherboard or an available PATA cable connection or motherboard SATA port

IDE PATA or SATA hard drive

Procedure: Complete the following procedure and answer the accompanying questions.

Notes: Use proper antistatic and gentle handling procedures when dealing with hard drives.

You must be a user who has administrator rights to configure hard drives.

If two CD/DVD devices are installed, one can be replaced by the new hard drive to perform this lab.

1. Power on the computer and log in.

2. There are several ways to get to the window used to manage hard drives. Practice using both methods.

   a. Click the *Start* button, click *Run*, type **compmgmt.msc**, and press Enter.

   b. In Windows Explorer, right-click *My Computer* and select *Manage*.

3. In the console tree shown in the left pane, select the *Disk Management* option. The disks and volumes already installed in the computer display in a graphical manner on the right.

4. Right-click the drive partition labeled **c:** and select *Properties*.

   What type of file system is being used? [FAT16 | FAT32 | NTFS]

   What is the total capacity of the drive?

   What is the amount of free space?

5. Shut down the computer and remove the power cord.

6. Remove the computer cover. If PATA is being used, locate an available IDE PATA port on the motherboard or an available PATA cable connector. If SATA is being used, locate a free SATA port on the motherboard and determine which port this is. Use the motherboard or system documentation, if necessary.

7. If PATA is being used, determine whether the other device on the same cable (if installed) uses cable select or master/slave jumpers by removing the drive and examining it. Handle the drive carefully.

   If a PATA drive is being installed, is there a second device on the same cable? If so, does the device use the cable select, master, or slave jumper? Show the instructor.

   If a SATA drive is being installed, what SATA port will be used for the new drive?

8. If necessary, re-install the PATA drive into the machine and reconnect the power and data cables. On the hard drive given to you by the instructor, if PATA is being used, configure the drive to the appropriate setting: cable select, master, or slave. If SATA is being used, power on the computer, enter Setup, and ensure that the SATA port is enabled. Enable the port if necessary.

9. Mount the IDE hard drive (that was given to you by the instructor) into the case.

10. Attach the IDE data cable and attach a power cable.

11. Re-install the power cord and power on the computer.

12. Using previously described procedures, open the *Computer Management* console. Click the *Disk Management* option in the left pane. Note that the drive you were given may have been partitioned already and assigned a drive letter. If the drive was already partitioned and a drive letter assigned, right-click the drive, select *Delete Partition*, and click *Yes*. If the drive shows the status of Invalid, right-click the drive and select the *Convert to basic disk option*.

    Was the drive already assigned a drive letter and partitioned?

13. Right-click the new drive you just installed and select *New Simple Volume*. The New Simple Volume Wizard appears. Click *Next*.

    What is the difference between a simple volume and a spanned volume?

    What is the minimum number of drives required to create a striped volume?

14. Enter a partition size that is less than 32GB. Click *Next*.

    What partition size did you choose?

    How many drive letter devices are there?

15. Select a drive letter (normally the next drive letter available) and click *Next*.

    What file systems are supported when you use this tool?

    Are there any file systems supported by Vista that are not shown? If so, what are they?

16. Select the *FAT32* option. Assign the volume label as a couple of letters from each of the lab partners' last names. Note that there is an 11-character maximum for FAT32 partitions and a 32-character maximum for NTFS partitions. Select (enable) the *Perform a quick format* check box and click *Next*. Click the *Finish* button.

    How can you tell from the window whether a partition is FAT32 or NTFS?

17. Right-click in the unallocated drive space on the drive you just installed and select *New Simple Volume*. The New Simple Volume Wizard appears. Click *Next*.

18. Click *Next*. Select a partition size less than 32GB. Click *Next*.

    What amount of space did you choose for the logical drive size?

19. Accept the drive letter default assignment and click *Next*.

20. Change the file system type to *FAT32*.

21. Make the volume label a unique name.

    Write the volume label chosen.

22. Select (enable) the *Perform a quick format* check box. Click *Next*, review the settings, and click *Finish*.

23. Right-click the free space for the drive you installed. Using the same process, create an NTFS simple volume, add a unique volume label, and perform a quick format.

Instructor initials: _____ (Check: two FAT32 primary partitions and one NTFS partition, with different volume labels on each)

24. You can change a FAT16 or FAT32 partition to the NTFS file system by using the **convert** command from a command prompt. Once a partition is changed, you cannot go back. Also, data is preserved (but should be backed up before the conversion, just in case).

    In the Disk Management console, what disk number is used for the newly installed drive?

    Write the drive letter of the first FAT32 primary partition on the newly installed drive. Note that this drive letter will be used in the coming steps.

    Write the volume label used for the first FAT32 partition. This label is case sensitive, so write it carefully.

25. Click the *Start* button. Locate the *Command Prompt* menu option. Normally, it is located in Accessories. Right-click the *Command Prompt* menu option and select *Run as administrator*. Click *Continue*.

26. Type **convert /?** to see a list of options. These options tell you what to type after the **convert** command.

    What option is used to run **convert** in verbose mode?

    What option is used to convert a volume to NTFS?

27. Type **convert x: /fs:ntfs** (where **x:** is the drive letter you wrote down in Step 24). For example, if the drive letter you wrote down is **d:** type **convert d: /fs:ntfs**. Notice the space between the drive letter and **/fs:ntfs**. **/fs:ntfs** is used to convert the existing file system (FAT16 or FAT32) to NTFS. You are prompted for the volume label for the

drive. Enter the volume label you wrote down in Step 24 and press Enter. Do not forget that the volume label is case sensitive. The partition is converted and can never be turned back into FAT32 unless the drive is reformatted.

28. Use the same process to convert the second FAT32 partition to NTFS. Look up the volume label and the drive letter before starting.

Instructor initials: _____ (Check: look at the Computer Management screen and see that all partitions are NTFS—three drive letters)

29. In the Computer Management—Disk Management window, right-click the last partition on the newly installed hard drive.

30. Select the *Shrink Volume* option. Reduce the amount of hard drive space and click *Shrink*.

    What was the result in the Disk Management console?

31. Right-click the second partition on the newly installed drive. Select *Extend Volume*. A wizard appears. Click *Next*. Use the space available on the same drive and click *Next* and then *Finish*.

    What message appeared?

    According to the information in the dialog box, do you think changing this volume to a dynamic disk will matter?

32. Click *Cancel* and return to the Disk Management console. Review the disks and determine the disk number and drive letter of the boot volume.

    Write the disk number of the boot volume.

    Write the drive letter of the partition that holds the boot volume.

33. Right-click on the second partition of the newly installed drive and select *Delete Volume*. Click *Yes*.

34. Partitions can be created from the Disk Management console, and they can also be created using the **DISKPART** command utility. Return to the command prompt.

35. At the command prompt, type **diskpart** and press Enter.

    How does the prompt change?

36. Type **help** and press Enter. Use the **help** command to find out what commands are available.

    What command is used to make a new volume?

    What command can be used to give a drive partition a drive letter?

37. Type **create ?** and press Enter.

    What two options can be used with **create?**

38. Type **create partition ?** and press Enter.

    What type of partitions can be created?

39. Press the up arrow ↑ key once. The same command appears. Backspace and replace the ↑ with **primary** so the command reads **create partition primary**. Press Enter.

    What does the feedback say?

    What command do you think (based on Help) would be used to select a drive?

40. Type **select disk x** (where **x** is the disk number you wrote for Step 24) and press Enter. A prompt says the disk is selected.

41. Retype the **create partition primary** command or press the up arrow ↑ key until that command appears and press Enter.

42. Look back at your Disk Management console and notice that the part of the drive previously marked as free space is now a partition.

    How is the drive partition different from the others?

43. At the command prompt, type **detail disk** and press Enter see the partition you just created. Notice that the partition has a RAW file system, but no drive letter is assigned.

    Based on the command output, what drive letters are currently used?

44. At the command prompt, type **assign** and press ⌨Enter⌨.

    Look in the Disk Management console and see what drive letter was assigned. Write the drive letter.

    What volume label, if any, was assigned?

45. At the command prompt, type **exit** and press ⌨Enter⌨ to leave the DISKPART utility.

46. Type **help** at the command prompt and press ⌨Enter⌨ to look for a command to help with the high-level formatting of the drive. The commands scroll by too quickly, so type **help | more** and press ⌨Enter⌨. (The | keystroke is made by holding down the ⌨Shift⌨ key and pressing the key above the ⌨Enter⌨ key.) One page at a time is shown. Press the space bar once to see the next page of commands.

47. The next command requires filling in some of the blanks to perform the step correctly. The parameters are as follows:

    x:, the drive letter documented in Step 44.

    /v:name, where **name** is a unique volume name with up to 32 characters.

    /fs:ntfs, which tells the system to use the NTFS file system. (Other options could be **/fs:fat** or **/fs:fat32**, but we are using NTFS.)

    /q, which does a quick format.

    Type the command **format x: /fs:ntfs /v:name /q** and press ⌨Enter⌨. Note that if you get a message that the arguments are not valid, you did not exit the **diskpart** utility and did not do Steps 45 and 46. Go back and do them. When asked to proceed, press ⌨Y⌨ and press ⌨Enter⌨.

48. View the results in the Disk Management console. The last partition should be a partition that has a drive letter and is NTFS.

49. Using whatever method you would like, copy one file to each of the three partitions you have created. Call the instructor over and show the instructor the three files and the Disk Management console. Do not proceed unless you have these parameters done.

Instructor initials: _____ (Check: three NTFS partitions; three files, one in each of the partitions viewed through Computer)

50. Starting with the partition on the far right in the Disk Management console for the newly installed drive, right-click each partition and delete each volume. Call the instructor over when the drive shows as one block (black) of unpartitioned hard drive space.

Instructor initials: _____ (Check: one space, no partitions, black colored)

51. Shut down the computer. Remove the power cord. Remove the data cable from the hard drive you just installed. Remove the power cord from the hard drive you just installed. Remove the hard drive. If necessary, re-install the CD/DVD drive, data cable, and power cord. Re-install the computer cover and the power cord.

52. Boot the computer. Open Windows Explorer and select *Computer*. Ensure that the CD/DVD drive is recognized. If it is not, redo Step 51.

53. Show the instructor the CD/DVD drive in *Computer* and give the hard drive and any cabling back to the instructor.

Instructor initials: _____ (Check: ensure that the CD/DVD drive is shown in Computer)

5. Striping and Spanning Using Windows Vista

Objective: To be able to configure and manage a striped volume or a spanned volume on a hard drive, using the Windows Vista Disk Management console

Parts: Windows Vista computer that boots
Motherboard or adapter that supports RAID 0/1
Two IDE PATA or SATA hard drives

Procedure: Complete the following procedure and answer the accompanying questions.

Notes: In the first part of the lab, you use the Windows Disk Management console to configure RAID. Use proper antistatic, gentle handling procedures when dealing with hard drives.

You must be a user who has administrator rights to configure hard drives.

This lab assumes that you can install and configure the two or more SATA or PATA hard drives and have them recognizable in the Disk Management console. The CD/DVD drive may have to be disconnected if PATA RAID is being used and only one PATA motherboard is available when a SATA drive boots the computer. If SATA RAID is being used, the motherboard SATA ports may need to be enabled through BIOS. Depending on the RAID controller, you may need to access the RAID menu or BIOS to designate which two drives are participating in the RAID.

1. Optionally install a RAID adapter. Cable the drives to SATA or PATA ports on the motherboard or on an adapter. Enable BIOS options as necessary.

2. Power on the computer and log in. Select the *Disk Management* option. The two newly installed hard drives should be visible in the Disk Management console. Initialize the drives, if necessary, by right-clicking them and selecting *Initialize Disk*.

   What disk numbers are assigned to the newly installed hard drives?

3. In the Disk Management console, right-click in the unallocated space of the newly installed drive with the lowest disk numbered. Select *New Spanned Volume*. A wizard appears. Click *Next*.

4. Select the second drive in the Available: pane and click *Add* to move to the Selected: pane. At least two drives should be listed in the Selected: pane. Click *Next*.

5. Select a drive letter to assign to the spanned volume. Click *Next*.

6. Select NTFS, using the drop-down menu and a volume label. Select (enable) the *Perform a quick format* checkbox. Click *Next*. Click *Finish*.

7. When a message appears to convert a basic disk to a dynamic disk, click *Yes*. Verify that the spanned volume appears.

   When using the Disk Management tool, how can you tell what two drives are a spanned volume?

8. Show the instructor the spanned volume.

Instructor initials: _____ (Check: two drives with purple-colored bars)

9. Use Windows Explorer to view the drive letters assigned and total capacity of each of the two drives.

   What drive letter was assigned to the spanned volume?

   What is the total capacity of the spanned volume?

   Which RAID level is spanning, if any?

10. In the Disk Management console, right-click in the created volume space and select *Shrink Volume*.

    How does the Disk Management tool change?

11. Show the instructor the shrunken volume.

Instructor initials: _____

12. In the Disk Management console, right-click in the spanned volume and select *Delete Volume*. When asked if you are sure, click *Yes*. Note that you may have to click *Yes* twice.

13. To create a striped volume from within the Disk Management console, right-click the lowest-numbered disk of the two newly installed drives. The New Striped Volume Wizard appears. Click *Next*.

14. In the Available: pane, select the second newly installed disk and click the *Add* button to move the drive to the Selected: pane. Click *Next*.

15. Select a drive letter or leave the default. Click *Next*.

7

Storage Devices

16. Leave the default file systemas NTFS and select (enable) the *Perform a quick format* check-box. Click *Next*. Click *Finish*. Click *Yes*.

    How do the disks appear differently than the spanned volumes in the Disk Management console?

17. Open Windows Explorer.

    How many drive letters are assigned to a RAID 1 configuration?

18. Copy a file to the RAID 1 drive. Show the instructor the file and the Disk Management console.

Instructor initials: _____ .

19. Right-click in the healthy volume space of either RAID 1 drive.

    Can a RAID 1 volume be shrunk?

20. Select the *Delete Volume* option. Click *Yes*. Note that you may need to click *Yes* a second time. Show the instructor the unallocated space.

Instructor initials: _____

21. Power down the computer, remove the power cord, and remove the two newly installed drives.

22. Power on the computer and, if necessary, return the BIOS settings to the original configuration. Ensure that the computer boots normally. Show the instructor that the computer boots normally.

Instructor initials: _____

6. Windows XP Backup Tool

Objective: To be able to backup data using Windows XP Backup tool

Parts: Windows XP computer

Procedure: Complete the following procedure and answer the accompanying questions.

Notes: You must be able to save data somewhere (floppy, USB drive, thumb Flash drive, hard drive, and so on) in order to perform this exercise.

1. Power on the computer and log in.

2. Click the *Start* button → *All Programs* → *Accessories* → *System Tools* → *Backup*. Another way of accessing it is to directly go to the partition that contains the information to be backed up (such as *c:*), right-click the drive letter in Windows Explorer, select *Properties*, select the *Tools* tab, and click the *Backup now* button.

3. Click *Next* to skip the opening page. Select *Backup files and settings* and click *Next*. The page where you must decide what to backup appears. For most users, the *My documents and settings* option backs up their data and that is all that is needed. For this exercise, select the *Let me choose what to back up* radio button. Select *Next*.

4. The Items to Back Up window appears. Expand any documents so that a couple of files show in the right window. Select two or three files to be backed up. Click *Next*.

5. Select a place to store the backup by using the *Browse* button. If unsure, contact your instructor or lab assistant. Click *Next*.

6. Click the *Advanced* button.

    What type of backups are allowed?

    When you select one of the backup types, a description is shown in the window. Based on the description shown, what is the difference between an incremental and a differential backup?

7. Ensure *Normal* is selected and click *Back*. Click *Finish*.

    How much time did Windows take to back up the files?

8. Click the *Report* button when done.

    How many bytes were backed up?

9. Close the log window.

Instructor initials: _____

10. Click the *Close* button.

7. Windows XP/Vista Hard Disk Tools

Objective: To be able to use the tools provided with Windows XP to manage the hard disk drive

Parts: A computer with Windows XP/Vista loaded and administrator rights/password

Procedure: Complete the following procedure and answer the accompanying questions.

Note: The defragmentation and *Check Now* (CHKDSK) process can take more than 60 minutes on larger hard drives.

1. Power on the computer and log on using a userid and password provided by the instructor or lab assistant that has administrator rights.

2. Click the *Start* button, select *All Programs*, select *Accessories*, select *System Tools*, and click *Disk Cleanup*.

3. If on Vista, select the *My files only* link. The drive selection window appears. Using the ⬇, select a drive letter and click the *OK* button.

4. The *Disk Cleanup* window appears. Ensure that *only* the following checkboxes are checked (enabled) for lab purposes:

    Temporary Internet files

    Recycle Bin

    Web client/Publisher Temporary Files (XP)

    Temporary Files

    Compress Old Files (XP)

    Click the *OK* button.

5. When prompted, if you are sure, click the *Yes* (XP) or *Delete Files* (Vista) button. Enter the administrator password, if necessary.

    List at least two related topics that are available from the Help and Support Center when getting help on the topic of disk cleanup.

    Instructor initials: _____

6. Click the *Start* button, select *All Programs*, select *Accessories*, select *System Tools*, and click *Disk Defragmenter*.

7. In XP, select a drive volume in the top portion of the window. In Vista, click on *Select volumes*. Select a particular drive to use. Vista users proceed to step 10 after answering the question for this step.

    What percentage of free space is shown for the drive?

    In Vista, select the *How does Disk Defragmenter help*? link. What does Vista help say about using the computer during defragmentation?

8. In XP, click the *Help* button (the button that looks like a piece of paper with a question mark on it). Click the *Best practices* hyperlink.

    Based on the XP help information shown, should hard drive volumes be analyzed before defragmenting them?

9. Close the XP *Help* window and click the *Analyze* button on XP computers. When finished answering the question for this step, click the *Close* button.

    Is defragmentation recommended?

10. In XP, click the *Defragment* button. In Vista, click the *Defragment now* button and the *OK* button.

    What would be the determining factor for you in recommending how often a particular computer user should make use of this tool?

    List one more recommendation that you would make to a user regarding this tool.

11. In XP, click the *View Report* button. In Vista, skip this step and the questions related to this step.

Instructor initials: _____

How many files are fragmented?

List one file that did not defragment.

What is the average file size?

12. Click on the *Close* button and close the *Disk Defragmenter* window.

13. Open Windows Explorer. Locate and right-click the hard drive (C:) and select *Properties*. Select the *Tools* tab and the *Check now* button. In Vista, if the User Account Control window appears, click *Continue*.

14. In the window that appears, select the *Scan for and attempt recovery of bad sectors* check box and ensure that the *automatically fix file system errors* check box is not checked (not enabled). Click *Start*.

For Vista users, click on the *View details* link to answer these questions:

How many files were processed?

What happens during stage 2?

How much space does the system take?

15. Call the instructor over when the utility is finished (before you click *OK*). Click *OK* again and close the utility window.

Instructor initials: _____

Internet Discovery

Objective: To obtain specific information on the Internet regarding a computer or its associated parts

Parts: Computer with Internet access

Questions: Use the Internet to answer the following questions. Write the answers and the URL of the site where you found the information. Assume you have just purchased a Maxtor Basics 1TB SATA II/300 hard drive kit in answering Questions 1–3.

1. What type of cable is needed for this drive? Does it come with the drive? Write the answer and the URL where you found this information.

2. How much cache does this drive have?

3. If the computer does not have an available Molex connector or SATA connector, what one recommendation could you make?

4. A customer has purchased a Western Digital 100Mb/s PATA WD3200AAKB Caviar Blue PATA hard drive. What is the default jumper setting for this drive? Write the answer and the URL where you found this information. [Single | Dual (Master) | Dual (Slave) | Cable Select]

5. Based on the same drive as in Question 4 and information you learned in this chapter, if a customer had a drive already configured to cable select and wanted you to install the Western Digital drive, what setting must be set on the new drive? [Single | Dual (Master) | Dual (Slave) | Cable Select]

6. Find an eSATA and an internal SATA hard drive that are equal or close to equal in capacity. What is the price difference between the two? Write the answer and the URL where you found this information.

Soft Skills

Objective: To enhance and fine tune a future technician's ability to listen, communicate in both written and oral form, and support people who use computers in a professional manner

Activities:

1. In groups of two pretend one of you has a hard drive problem. The other student pretends to help you on the phone. Share your phone conversation with two other groups. Select the best group and scenario.

2. With two other classmates, come up with 10 additional tips for good phone support that were not listed in the chapter. Share your ideas with the class.

3. As a team, plan the installation of three IDE devices. Two of these devices are PATA and the other one is SATA. In addition there are two SCSI devices to attach to the same controller. In your plan, detail what things you will check for, how you obtain the documentation, and what obstacles could appear as part of the installation process. Share your plan with others.

Critical Thinking Skills

Objective: To analyze and evaluate information as well as apply learned information to new or different situations

Activities:

1. List three things that could cause a computer to lock up periodically. What could you do to fix, check, or verify these three things?

2. A customer wants to either upgrade or replace his hard drive. Go through the steps you would take from start to finish to accomplish this task.

3. You have a department of 20 workstations. Develop a backup plan for the department. Use the Internet to research other backup plans.

Multimedia Devices

Objectives

After completing this chapter you will be able to

- Differentiate between various CD and DVD technologies
- Determine a CD or DVD X factor from an advertisement or specification sheet
- Explain the basics of how a CD/DVD drive works
- State the various interfaces and ports used to connect CD/DVD drives
- Recommend, install, configure, and troubleshoot CD/DVD drives
- Explain the basic operation of a sound card
- Install, configure, and troubleshoot a sound card
- Use Windows to verify CD/DVD drive and sound card installation
- Explain the basic principles of how a scanner works
- Install, configure, and test a scanner
- Define digital camera connectivity and options
- Provide support with a positive, proactive attitude

Multimedia Overview

The term *multimedia* has different meanings for people because there are many types of multimedia devices. This chapter focuses on the most popular areas—CD and DVD technologies, sound cards, cameras, and speakers. A CD/DVD drive can be internally mounted and attached to a PATA or SATA interface, or it can be an external unit like some of the other multimedia devices that attach to USB, IEEE 1394 (FireWire), or eSATA ports. Internal CD/DVD drives usually cost less than external ones. The chapter is not intended to be a buyer's guide or an electronics "how it works" book; instead, it is a guide for technicians with an emphasis on installation and troubleshooting. Multimedia devices can be a lot of fun once they are installed. However, they can also cause headaches during installation.

CD Drive Overview

A CD drive (compact disc) is sometimes called a CD-ROM (CD read-only memory) and it uses discs that store large amounts of information (628MB and higher). The disc for the CD drive is known as a **CD**, CD-ROM disc, or simply disc. Figure 8.1 shows a BenQ U.S.A. Corp.'s CD drive and its various front panel controls.

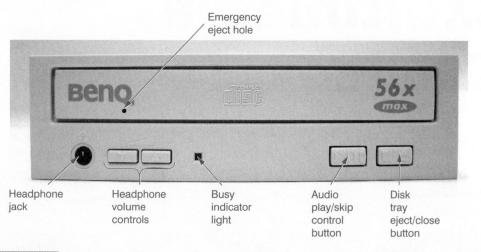

Figure 8.1   **BenQ CD drive front panel controls**

A CD has pits or indentations along the track. Flats, sometimes called lands, separate the pits. Reading information from a CD involves using a laser diode or similar device. The laser beam shines through the protective coating to an aluminum alloy layer, where data is stored. The laser beam reflects back through the optics to a photo diode detector that converts the reflected beam of light into 1s and 0s. The transitions between the pits and lands create the variation of light intensity. Figure 8.2 shows an inside view of a CD drive.

CD Drive Speeds

CD drives come in a variety of types classified by the X factor: 1X (single speed), 2X (double speed), 32X, 48X, 52X, and higher. Table 8.1 shows the transfer rates for several drive types. There are drives being advertised as 100X that use hard drive space to cache the CD contents and provide faster speeds (1.5MBps). See the next section, *CD Drive Buffers/Cache*, for information on how this works.

Take, for example, a 48X CD drive installed in two different computers. One computer has a 2GHz computer, 512MB of RAM, and an AGP video adapter with 64MB of video memory. Another 2GHz computer has 1GB of RAM and a PCIe video adapter with 128MB of video memory. The CD drive in the second example can put graphics on the screen or play audio files much faster than the first drive. The increased amount of system RAM, increased amount of video adapter RAM, and the

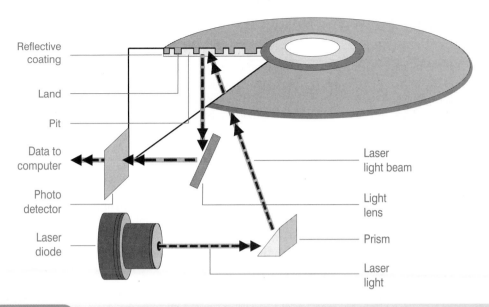

Figure 8.2   Inside a CD drive

Table 8.1   CD drive transfer speeds

Type of CD-ROM drive	Typical transfer rate (in kilobytes per second)
1X	150
2X	300
16X	2,400
24X	3,600
32X	4,800
36X	5,400
40X	6,000
48X	7,200
52X	7,800

use of a video card that is PCIe or AGP, not ISA, all contribute to the performance increase. Buying a faster CD drive does not necessarily mean the drive performs to expectations. As with all computer devices, components in the computer must work together to provide the fastest data transfer. Many people do not realize buying the latest and greatest X factor CD drive does not provide faster access. The drawback to CD drives is that they operate much slower than hard drives.

What affects CD drive performance?

The particular CD drive performance depends on several factors—the microprocessor installed, how much RAM is in the system, what video card is used (PCIe, PCI, AGP, ISA), and how much video memory is on the video card. Note that DVD drives have the same dependency factors and also use X factors.

Two confusing specifications of these drives are average seek time and average access time. The **average seek time** is the amount of time the drive requires to move randomly around the disc. The **average access time** is the amount of time the drive requires to find the appropriate place on the disc and retrieve information. Another comparison point is **MTBF** (mean time between failures), which is the average number of hours before a device is likely to fail. Keep in mind that the lower the access time number, the better the performance.

CD drive access times are much slower than hard drives and CD drive manufacturers usually quote access times using only optimum test conditions. When buying or recommending a CD drive to a computer user or customer, check magazines or online data for the latest test performance results.

CD Drive Buffers/Cache

One way to reduce CD data transfer time is through buffer memory located on the CD drive. When requesting data, the drive looks ahead on the CD for more data than requested and places the data in the buffers. The buffer memory ensures data is constantly sent to the microprocessor instead of the microprocessor waiting for the drive's slow access time. Buffer sizes typically range from 64KB to 2MB and higher. A drive should not be installed or purchased unless it has a minimum of 500KB buffer.

CD-R and CD-RW

Being able to create CDs is important in today's home and business environments. Two CD technologies, CD-R (compact disc recordable) and CD-RW (CD rewritable) allow this to become a reality. The two technologies have many similarities and CD-RW is the most popular. Technicians should understand the differences between the two. Table 8.2 lists the different CD technologies.

Table 8.2	CD technologies
Technology	**Description**
CD-ROM	Drive that can play pre-recorded discs
CD-R	Drive that can play pre-recorded discs and record on media during one session
CD-RW	Drive that can play pre-recorded discs and record, erase, and re-record on media during one session or multiple sessions
MultiRead	The OSTA (Optical Storage Technology Association)–defined term that describes drives that can read audio CD, CD-ROM, CD-R, and CD-RW discs

How to read the CD-RW numbers

CD-RW drives are frequently shown with three consecutive numbers such as 52×32×52. The first number is the CD-R write speed, the second number the CD-RW speed, and the last number is the read speed used when reading a pre-recorded disc.

Most CD-R blank discs hold 650MB (sometimes labeled as 74min). However, some manufacturers distribute 700MB discs. Not all CD-Rs can write or read CDs of this capacity. There are software packages that allow writing to 700MB discs such as Roxio, Inc.'s Easy CD Creator.

Some CD-RW drives are backward compatible

MultiRead or MultiRead2 is an OSTA (optical storage technology association) specification that states the CD-RW drive is backward compatible with CD-ROM and CD-R discs.

Another type of disc used in CD-Rs is the mini-disc. Many CD drives can accept both the common 5-inch and the mini 3-inch CDs. Look at the drive tray to see if there is a 3-inch diameter depression in the center of the tray. If so, the depression is for the 3-inch CDs. Place the mini CD in the depression, close the tray, and most CD drives will be able to read the disc. Figure 8.3 shows a mini CD disc.

Keep the data coming to the writable CD

One problem with CD-R drives occurs when data is written to the CD-R disc. If the CD-R drive does not receive data in a steady stream, a buffer underrun error occurs and the CD-R disc is ruined. To avoid this problem, do not perform other tasks while creating a disc.

Some older CD drives cannot read the discs created by a CD-R drive

On the problem CD drives, the laser is not calibrated to read recordable discs that have a surface different from that on regular CDs. An indication of this problem is if a disc created by a CD-R drive is readable by some CD drives, but not others. There is no solution to this problem except to replace the drive.

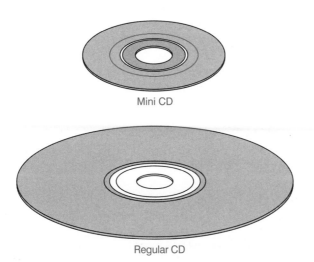

Mini CD

Regular CD

Figure 8.3 **A mini CD compared to a regular CD**

When creating a CD, the computer must transmit a steady stream of data that is written in a continuous format on the CD. The memory buffers included with the CD-R drive help with this task, but a computer that does not have enough free hard drive space or RAM can still slow down or abort the recording process.

Creating a CD takes time

You should not perform other tasks such as playing games or working in another application when recording a CD. This takes away from CPU time, available RAM, and available hard drive space.

Most CD creation software packages allow you to select the hard drive partition where the data is cached before it is written to the CD. Make sure you select a partition that has twice the amount of free space as the data being written. For example, if 100MB of data is going onto a CD, make sure 200MB of hard drive space is available. If the computer continuously displays errors when writing a CD, most CD recording software allows you to reduce the recording speed. This will take longer, but increases chances of success. Turn off power management and screen savers when creating a CD (or DVD).

Some people like creating an emergency boot CD that allows the computer to start in case of hard drive failure. Many computer manufacturers supply a CD for restoring a system back to factory defaults. However, all applications and operating system environment settings are lost. There are software programs that help create a bootable CD such as Roxio, Inc.'s Easy CD Creator; there are freeware programs available too. The software used to create the bootable CD is loaded and the CD is created. Always test a bootable CD *before* a hard drive failure occurs.

Consider the specifications for a CD-RW drive found in Table 8.3. The cache size is how much buffer memory the drive has installed. The speeds that follow in the left column are what is normally seen in the first line of the advertisement—CD-RW 52×24×52 USB/FireWire Drive. The load type is a tray that comes out when the eject button is pushed. The top item in the right column tells us this drive has both USB and IEEE 1394 ports. What it does not mention anywhere is whether or not cables are shipped with the drive. The specifications tell us that the drive is external and can read and write to CD-R and CD-RW discs.

The writing modes shown in Table 8.3 are Disk-at-Once, Multisession, and Track-at-Once. A **multisession** drive has the ability to store data on a disc and, later, add more data to the disc. **Disc-at-Once** (sometimes called DAO) means that the disc is created in one pass rather than the alternative of **Track-at-Once** (sometimes called TAO) which the laser stops writing normal data after a track is finished. Track-at-Once supports the disc having both audio and data. A writing mode that is not shown in Table 8.3, **Session-at-Once**, allows multiple sessions to be recorded on a single disc. These discs can normally be read by computer-based CD drives, but not audio CD drives such as ones found in a vehicle. The supported formats section are the standards supported by this drive.

Also mentioned in the specification are the supported formats. Commonly called CD Book standards, they are associated with a specific color. For example, CD-DA is the Red Book standard for digital audio, and CD-i/FMV is the Green Book standard for full motion video.

Table 8.3	CD-RW sample advertisement specifications
Specification	**Specification**
Cache Size: 2MB	Interface Types: USB 2.0 and IEEE 1394
CD Write Speed: 52×	Enclosure Type: External
CD Rewrite Speed: 24×	Compatible Writable Media: CD-R and CD-RW
CD Read Speed: 52×	Writing Modes: Disc-at-Once, Multisession, and Track-at-Once
Load Type: Tray	Supported Formats: CD-DA, CD-i/FMV, CD-ROM XA, CD-RW, and Enhanced CD

Magneto-Optical Drives

A similar technology used for reading and writing compact discs is magneto-optical (MO). Magneto-optical discs cannot be used in regular CD drives; they require a magneto-optical drive. Magneto-optical drives are great for data backups and archiving. They use a laser beam to heat the surface of the disc, and then a magnet applies a charge to the surface. They can be erased by reheating the disc and using the magnet to erase the data. Magneto-optical discs are read using the laser similar to CD drive technology.

DVD Drives

The DVD drive has made the CD drive obsolete. DVD-ROM originally stood for digital video disc, then digital versatile disc. Some people confuse DVD-Video with DVD-ROM. DVD-Video holds a video DVD and the DVD-Video player connects to a TV. DVD drives can be both internal and external devices connected to PATA IDE (internal), SATA IDE, SCSI, IEEE 1394 or USB. There are other DVD technologies covered later in the chapter.

DVD discs provide more storage capacity than a CD disc, but can still play CDs. The discs used with DVD drives are the same diameter and thickness as traditional CDs and like CDs, the DVD discs tolerate dust, dirt, and fingerprints. The data on the DVD disc has pits that are smaller and more closely spaced than CD discs. Because of this, DVDs cannot be read by CD drives. DVD discs provide high video resolution and high quality sound unmatched in the computer industry.

Tech Tip

Transfer rate is different between CD and DVD drives

When you see a DVD × factor, do not use the same numbers as used with CD drives. A 1× DVD has a 1.32MBps transfer rate compared to a 150KBps transfer rate for a CD drive.

The DVD-ROM drives currently come in two different configurations, 4.7GB and 8.5GB. The 4.7GB format (sometimes known as DVD-5) has a single layer of data on one side of the disc. The 8.5GB capacity (known as DVD-9) uses two layers on the same side to increase storage capacity.

Two other capacities are 9.4GB and 17.1GB. The 9.4GB disc (also referred to as DVD-10) uses a single layer on both sides of the disc. The 17.1GB disc (also known as DVD-18) has two layers on both sides of the disc. This capacity disc is difficult to manufacture.

A software development that helps with DVD technology is Microsoft's **DirectX**. DirectX allows people who write software such as games and Web design not to have to write code to access specific hardware directly. DirectX translates generic hardware commands into special commands for the hardware, which speeds up development time for hardware manufacturers and software developers. DirectX is available in Windows.

Decoders

MPEG (Moving Picture Experts Group) created a compression technique called MPEG2, which is used by DVDs. The computer must decompress the video and audio from the DVD. This is called decoding. There are two methods for decoding: hardware and software. A hardware decoder requires a PCI adapter and less work is put on the computer's CPU because the adapter does the decoding. The adapter decodes both video and audio. This solution is good for slower computers. Figure 8.4 shows how a hardware decoder connects to a DVD drive.

A **software decoder** does not need a PCI adapter, but CPU power is needed. A 400MHz processor is the minimum to use. Software decoders provide varying playback quality. The installed video adapter must support DirectX's overlay mixers in order to do software decoding. Most video cards now include this feature but not all do.

Tech Tip

Verifying DVD decoder in Windows

When you insert a DVD disc into the drive, a window appears asking you what you want Windows to do with the disc. If you click *Play DVD*, you should see the contents of the DVD and you have an encoder installed. If you get a message saying that a DVD decoder is not installed, contact the PC manufacturer (if the DVD shipped with the PC) or contact the DVD drive manufacturer (if the DVD drive was purchased separately).

8 Multimedia Devices

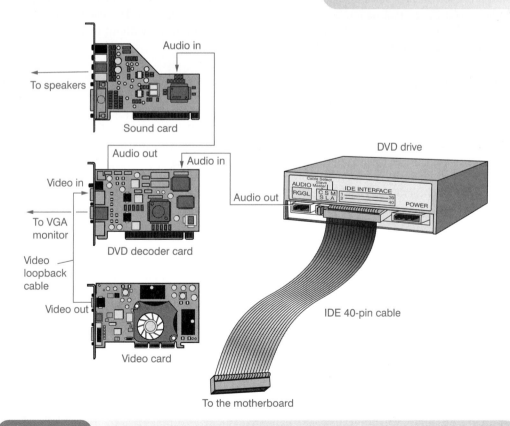

Figure 8.4   **DVD data flow**

Some software decoders require an AGP or PCIe video card, or their performance is weak. Software decoding also requires a PCI/PCIe or integrated sound card that supports 48KHz decoding for DVDs.

DVD Region Codes

To protect DVD software, movies, and audio, a DVD drive has a **region code**. The world is divided into six regions and the DVD drive must be set for the correct region code or else the DVDs made for that area do not work. When a DVD is inserted, the decoder checks what region it is configured for (or in the case of software decoding, what region the drive is configured for) and then checks the DVD region code. If the two match, then the movie plays. Table 8.4 shows the region codes.

Table 8.4	DVD region codes
DVD region code	**Geographic area**
1	United States and Canada
2	Europe, Near East, Japan, and South Africa
3	Southeast Asia
4	Australia, Middle America, and South America
5	Africa, Asia, and Eastern Europe
6	China

Some DVD drives do not require this setting (it is region free). The current standards allow five region changes before the drive is locked. If you have a hardware decoder, make sure that you configure it for the appropriate region. If you are using software decoding, the program must be configured for the correct region and it too normally allows five changes. There are freeware programs on the Internet to check the drive for its region requirements without incrementing the number of times the region code has been changed.

Other DVD Technologies

In addition to DVD-ROM, there are other types of DVD technologies currently in the marketplace: DVD-RAM, DVD-R, DVD+R, DVD-RW, DVD+RW, DVD±RW, DVD-R DL, and DVD+R DL. DVD-ROM is the most common, but that is changing. Compatibility with the various CDs and DVDs are issues to be aware of today. Table 8.5 shows these technologies.

Several technologies have been developed to write on the disk to label it without having to apply a paper label. LightScribe by Hewlett-Packard, DiscT@2 by Yamaha, and LabelFlash (introduced by NEC using DiscT@2 improvements) are three such technologies.

DVD Book Types

At the beginning of every DVD is a field where four bits define the type of DVD format the disc will use. A DVD drive reads this field to determine whether or not the drive can read the disc. The book type field values are as follows: DVD-ROM 0000, DVD-RAM 0001, DVD-R and DVD-R DL 0010, DVD-RW 0011, DVD+RW 1001, DVD+R 1010, DVD+RW DL 1101, and DVD+R DL 1110.

Blu-ray Drives

Blu-ray is a development in optical disc technology that uses blue-violet laser technology rather than the red laser technology currently used by CD/DVD drives. Blue-violet laser technology has a shorter wavelength, which means that smaller data pit sizes can be used to create higher disk capacities. This laser technology is also more expensive than red laser.

Table 8.5	DVD technologies*
Technology	**Explanation**
DVD-RAM	These discs are incompatible with older DVD-ROM drives, but look for the MultiRead2 capability. Discs include the following: 2.6 and 4.7GB (one side) and 5.2 and 9.4GB (two sides). Can usually write to a DVD-RW disc and can read them.
DVD-R	Uses WORM technology. Can record one time and uses one or two sided discs. Has capacities of 3.95, 4.7, and 9.4GB. Sometimes two different types are shown: DVD-R(A) and DVD-R(G). The DVD-R(A) targets the authoring business for professional development of DVDs. The DVD-R(G) is more for home users and lay people.
DVD+R	Can record (one time per disc) up to 4.7 or 9.4GB on single-sided DVD+R discs.
DVD-RW **(DVD-Rewritable)**	Similar to DVD-R except you can erase and rewrite data. Uses 4.7 or 9.4GB discs and most DVD-ROM drives and DVD-Video players support this format. Sometimes known as DVD-R/W or DVD-ER.
DVD+RW	Backward compatible with DVD-ROM drives and DVD video players. Discs hold 4.7 or 9.4GB per side. Reads most CD, DVD, DVD-R, DVD-RW, and DVD+R DL discs. Writes to CD-R, CD-RW, DVD+R, and DVD+RW discs.
DVD±RW	Reads most CD, DVD, and DVD+R DL discs. Writes to CD-R, CD-RW, DVD+R, DVD-R, DVD-RW, and DVD+RW discs.
DVD-R DL (dual layer)	Similar to DVD-R except it uses double-layered discs to store up to 8.5GB.
DVD+R DL	Similar to DVD+R except it uses double-layered discs to store up to 8.5GB.

*The formats shown with a + (plus sign) are supported by the DVD+RW Alliance. The formats shown with a − (minus sign) are supported by the DVD Forum.

Blu-ray has a higher data transfer rate (36Mbps) compared to DVD (10Mbps) and stores 25GB on a single-sided disc and 50GB on a dual-side disc. Blu-ray drives frequently have the Blu-ray symbol on them, as shown in Figure 8.5.

Figure 8.5	Blu-ray logo

Blu-ray was developed by industry leaders—Apple, Dell, Hitachi, HP, JVC, LG, Mitsubishi, Panasonic, Pioneer, Philips, Samsung, Sharp, Sony, TDK, and Thomson. The target market is for high-definition video and data storage. Blu-ray discs that can be written to once are known as BD-Rs and discs that are rewritable are known as BD-REs. Both have a 25GB capacity for single-layer discs and 50GB for dual-layer discs. Blu-ray discs have region codes. The A/1 code is used for North and South America, but most Blu-ray discs are region-free. Figure 8.6 shows a Blu-ray drive.

CD/DVD drives cannot read Blu-ray discs

Currently installed CD/DVD drives cannot read Blu-ray discs because CD/DVD drives use a red laser and Blu-ray drives use a blue-violet laser. Drives that have both lasers installed are available.

Tech Tip

8
Multimedia Devices

Figure 8.6 Blu-ray drive

CD/DVD Drive Interfaces and Connections

CD and DVD drives can use PATA IDE, SATA IDE, eSATA, USB, and IEEE 1384. In both desktop and portable computers, the IDE interface is the most common for internal devices and USB for external devices. The differences between these are great. Review Chapters 1, 2, 3, and 7 for more information on each of these technologies and review the installation techniques. The particular interface the technician recommends to the customer depends on several factors. The following questions will help customers decide what interface to use:

- Is the drive going to be an external device? If so, SATA, USB, and IEEE 1394 are the choices, and USB is one of the most popular.
- Is the drive going to be an internal device? If so, is price an issue? Internal drives can be PATA IDE, SATA IDE, or SCSI. Either of the IDE options is cheaper than SCSI.
- Does the customer plan to add more devices such as a scanner or tape backup unit in the near future? If so, SCSI, USB, eSATA, and IEEE 1394 have more expandability than IDE.

Tech Tip

PATA IDE connectivity

When connecting a drive to a PATA IDE connector with a hard drive connected, verify that the CD/DVD device is configured as the slave or connected to the gray (middle) slave connector and cable select is configured. For the best performance, connect the CD/DVD drive as secondary master by putting it on a separate PATA interface from any installed hard drive(s) or use SATA.

CD/DVD Drive Upgrades

If the customer wants to upgrade a drive, find out why. Many times, slow access is due to other components in the computer, not the drive. Use the same questions listed previously for a new drive. If it is a slow CD drive, such as a 1x, 2x, 4x, or 8x drive, upgrade the drive but be sure the other parts of the computer complement the CD/DVD drive's performance. The following questions help when upgrading drives:

- Does the customer want sound (speakers)? If so, a CD/DVD kit that includes speakers might be the best solution. If the customer is an audiophile, then special speakers may be needed.
- Is there an available slot in the computer for a sound card? Also, check if there are sound connections built into the motherboard. If so, a sound card may not be needed. The sound card should use PCI or PCIe and support 48KHz decoding if software decoding is being used.

- Is the customer going to be using discs that are video intensive? If so, what type of interface is the video adapter? AGP and PCIe provide the best throughput and performance for video. How much memory is on the video adapter? If DVDs are being used, 8MB of memory should be the minimum amount installed on the video card. DVDs require that the video adapter support DirectX's overlay mixers if software decoding is being used.
- Does the customer have enough RAM on the motherboard for the type of disc used?
- Are movies to be played? In order to achieve the best DVD effects, connect a sound system that accepts digital audio input and supports Dolby Digital surround sound.

Preventive Maintenance for CD/DVD Drives and Discs

When LP records were used, handling of the records was quite a problem. Fingerprints, dust, and dirt negatively affected the performance of the record. CDs and DVDs are less prone to these problems because they have a protective coating over the aluminum alloy-based data layer.

When reading information, the laser beam ignores the protective coating and shines through to the data layer. Even if the disc has dirt on the protective coating, the laser beam can still operate because the beam is directed at the data layer rather than the disc surface. An exception to this is surface material with reflective properties. The reflection could reflect and distort the laser beam, thus causing distortion or data corruption. Another exception is if the dust or dirt completely blocks the laser beam. A heavy accumulation of dust and dirt can reduce the quality of the data retrieved from the disc. Special cleaning discs, cloths, and kits are available for cleaning CD/DVD disks.

Handling CDs and DVDs

Always handle a disc by the edges and keep the disc in a sleeve or case. Proper handling of the disc aids in good performance. As with audio CDs, handle the disc on the outside edge of the disc. Never touch the surface of the disc, and store the disc in a cool location.

If a disc is scratched, mild abrasives or special disc repair kits are available. Examples of mild abrasives include plastic, furniture, or brass polish. When applying the abrasive, do not rub in circles. Instead, use the same technique as cleaning: start from the innermost portion of the disc and rub outward. The abrasive can remove the scratch if it is not too deep. A wax such as furniture or car wax can be used to fill the scratch if it is not removed by the abrasive.

Cleaning CDs and DVDs

When using the cleaning cloth, wipe the disc from the inside (near the center hole) to the outside of the disc (*not* in a circular motion) on the side of the disc that has data. (If you cannot tell, wipe both sides.)

A special component of the CD/DVD drive, the **laser lens** (also known as the objective lens), is responsible for reading information from the disc. If the laser lens gets dust, dirt, or moisture on it, the drive may report data or read errors. Some drives have the lens encased in an airtight enclosure and others have a self-cleaning laser lens. If the drive does not have this feature, laser lens cleaning kits are available at computer and music stores. Also, the laser lens can be cleaned with an air blower like ones used on a camera lens. Cleaning the laser lens should be a preventive maintenance routine. Some drive manufacturers include a special plate to keep dust away from the internal components. In any case, keep the disc compartment closed to prevent dust and dirt from accumulating on the laser lens and other drive parts.

CD/DVD Drive Installation

The following steps for installing an internal drive are similar to installing any drive:

1. Install any necessary mounting brackets onto the drive.
2. Check what interface (PATA IDE, SATA IDE, or SCSI) the drive uses. Set the appropriate master/slave, SCSI ID, or termination according to the drive interface type, if necessary. Refer to the documentation included with the drive for the proper configuration of these settings.

Some PATA IDE drives are pre-configured as the slave device
Always check the drive's master/slave/cable select setting and refer to the drive documentation for configuration issues.

3. Turn off computer power and optionally install the appropriate adapter or expansion hub if necessary.
4. Install the drive into the computer.
5. Attach the power cable from the power supply and interface cable from the drive to an adapter or motherboard.
6. (Optional) Attach the audio cable from the drive to the motherboard or sound card.

The drive is now installed, but is not operational until software drivers are installed properly and the drive is tested by reading from it or writing to it. Refer to the manufacturer's installation instructions.

External drives can be USB, IEEE 1394, eSATA, or a combination of any or all of these three technologies. For external USB or eSATA CD/DVD drives, attach the drive to external power if necessary. Some USB devices require external power; others take two USB ports. Attach the USB cable from the drive to the USB port or hub. Many manufacturers also include software tools that can be installed once the drive is operational. Some manufacturers may require you to install provided software before attaching the drive. Once installed, use Device Manager to ensure the drive is recognized by the operating system. Test the drive.

For external FireWire connectivity, attach external power to the drive if necessary. Install the manufacturer provided software, which frequently includes the driver. Attach the FireWire cable between the FireWire port and CD/DVD drive. Once installed, use Device Manager to ensure the drive is recognized by the operating system. The drive may appear under the IEEE 1394 Devices section. Test the drive.

Always test the installation
As with any hardware installation, test the installation by using the device. Ensure the customer tries the device and is comfortable with the changes caused by the installation.

Laptop CD/DVD Drive

Many laptop computers have drive bays that allow storage devices to be exchanged. PATA or SATA IDE interfaces are commonly used for internally mounted drives including CD/DVD drives. Usually these drive bays have a lock on them that prevents the drive from sliding out. Slide the lever to one side and the drive can be removed. Different laptop models use different part numbers and models for removable CD/DVD drives. Laptops sometimes have removable CD/DVD internal drives, and some of them are hot swappable. Always refer to the laptop manufacturer's documentation before removing the drive with power applied. Laptops sometimes have slot-loaded CD/DVD drives. Such a drive does not have a tray that holds the disc. Instead, the disc inserts into a slot, similar to that in an automobile CD player. Figure 8.7 shows a laptop with a slot-loaded drive.

To access an internally mounted drive, the keyboard is frequently removed to access the drive. Always refer to the laptop manual for instructions on replacing a drive.

For external notebook connectivity, use a USB or IEEE 1394 connection. USB is the most common. The external device can be attached with power applied and can be used with other portable computers.

Minimum requirements to play video on a laptop
In order to play video DVDs on a laptop, your computer must be faster than 400MHz and have at least an MPEG-2 decoder. This can be integrated into your computer as hardware or software that comes with your DVD player application.

Figure 8.7 Laptop slot-loaded CD/DVD drive

Troubleshooting CD/DVD Drive Problems

Windows has troubleshooting tools in the Help and Support Center:

1. Click *Start* and select *Help and Support*.
2. Select the *Fixing a problem* Help topic (XP)/*CDs and DVDs* (Vista)/or type `troubleshooting` in the search textbox (7).
3. Select the *Games, Sound, and Video Problems* link (XP)/an appropriate topic (Vista)/or *Open the Hardware and Devices troubleshooter (7)*.
4. In the right panel, use the *Games and Multimedia Troubleshooter* link (XP).

Check the easy stuff first

Verify a CD/DVD disc is inserted in the drive. Ensure the disc is inserted correctly (label-side up). Test the disk in another drive. Verify that the drive has a drive letter assigned by using the *My Computer* desktop or *Explorer* icon. If no drive letter is present for the device, check power and cabling and configuration settings. If a drive letter is available, use Device Manager to see if any resource conflicts exist. Update the driver if a new service pack has been installed.

The following is a list of problems with possible solutions or troubleshooting recommendations:

- If a drive tray cannot be opened, make sure there is power attached to the drive. Some drives have an emergency eject button or a hole that you can insert a paper clip to eject the disc.
- If a CD or DVD drive is not recognized by the operating system, check cables, power cords, and configuration (master/slave, cable select, port enabled in BIOS).
- If a CD or DVD drive busy indicator light flashes slower than normal, the disc or the laser lens may be dirty. Refer to the manufacturer's Web site for their recommendations on cleaning the laser lens. See the Preventive Maintenance section for details on how to clean a disc.
- If a CD/DVD drive cannot read a disc, refer to the drive manual to see what discs are supported. Not all disc formats are supported by all drives. Ensure the disc label is facing up. You may need to install a software application for the particular disc being used. Ensure the disc is clean and without scratches.
- If a CD-R or CD-RW drive is not recognized as a recordable device (if you view the properties and you don't have a *Recording* tab), a registry edit is required. Locate the Microsoft resolution.

- If a DVD sound track works, but the video is missing or distorted, check the cabling between the video adapter and DVD decoder. Verify the video drivers and that the video adapter supports DVD playback. Set the display resolution to a lower resolution and number of colors using the *Display* control panel.

If a CD or DVD doesn't work properly

Try the disc in another machine or try a different disc.

- If a movie stops playing, the DVD may be double-sided and needs to be flipped. Ensure that you have not paused the movie and check the video resolution.

8
Multimedia
Devices

- If you receive an illegal DVD region error or region code error, change the region.
- If a DVD drive only reads CDs, then the most likely problem is with bus mastering or the DVD drivers. Go to the manufacturer Web site for the latest drivers.
- Many DVD problems are solved by (1) reinstalling DirectX or obtaining the latest version of DirectX, (2) installing the latest drivers for the DVD drive, video adapter, and sound card, or (3) changing the screen resolution if it's too high. A computer should have approximately 80 percent free system resources when playing DVDs. For optimum performance, do not multitask (have other applications loaded).
- If you add DVD to a system, be careful that the video adapter can handle DVD playback. Sometimes a DVD player error occurs stating that you have low video memory. Make sure the latest video card drivers are loaded. If playback is still a problem, adjust the video card refresh rate to a lower value.
- When troubleshooting Windows XP multimedia applications and devices, two tools are handy—Sounds & Multimedia or Sounds and *Audio Devices* control panel and the DirectX Diagnostic tool. The *Hardware* tab contains a *Properties* button and a *Troubleshoot* button. Under the device section, click (right or double) on the device you want to check. The *Properties* button shows the version of driver being used. Windows XP allows the driver to be rolled back to a previous version with this option. The *Troubleshoot* button helps when diagnosing a specific multimedia device.
- A misapplied label on the disc can cause problems with the disc being read. Peeling labels can also cause insertion/ejection problems.
- If you cannot hear sound when playing a DVD, but you can when playing a CD, and your computer meets hardware and software requirements for DVD playback, obtain the latest DVD driver from your PC manufacturer (if the drive shipped with the computer) or from the DVD drive manufacturer.
- If your computer meets hardware and software requirements for DVD playback, your video driver may need updating. Also, if your video disappears or turns a different color, turn off video overlays. In Windows Media Player, select *Options* from the *Tools* menu. Select *Performance* tab, *Advanced* button, and in the Video Acceleration area, uncheck the *Use overlays* checkbox.

Tech Tip

You can see video, but you can't hear sound or vice versa

Verify that your computer has the hardware and software requirements for DVD playback.

The DirectX Diagnostic Tool is used in troubleshooting multimedia devices and DirectX drivers. You can view the driver, view system information, and test multimedia devices with this tool. Access the DirectX Diagnostic tool by clicking *Start*, accessing *Run*, typing *dxdiag* and pressing Enter in XP. In Vista/7, select *Start*, select *Help and Support*, type dxdiag, and press Enter. Select the *DirectX Diagnostic Tool* link.

Sound

CD and DVD technology emphasizes video and sound; therefore, no chapter on multimedia is complete without talking about sound. CD and DVD drives have the capability of producing sound, usually through a front headphone jack and through a connection to sound through the motherboard or an installed sound adapter. Audio CDs can be played on these drives, but the CDs do not sound as good through headphone jacks as they do through a stereo system or speakers. A cable optionally connects from the back of the CD or DVD drive to the sound card.

Many sound cards have a **MIDI** (musical instrument digital interface) built into the adapter, and a jack for microphone input. MIDI is used to create synthesized music. A 15-pin female connector on the back of the sound adapter connects a joystick or a MIDI device such as a MIDI keyboard. Figure 8.8 shows a typical sound board and ports. Ports for speakers and headphones are typically 1/8" connectors that accept TRS (tip ring sleeve) cables.

Notice in the figure the connection for S/PDIF. **S/PDIF** (Sony/Phillips digital interface format) defines how audio signals are carried between audio devices and stereo components. It can also be used to connect the output of a DVD player in a PC to a home theater or some other external device.

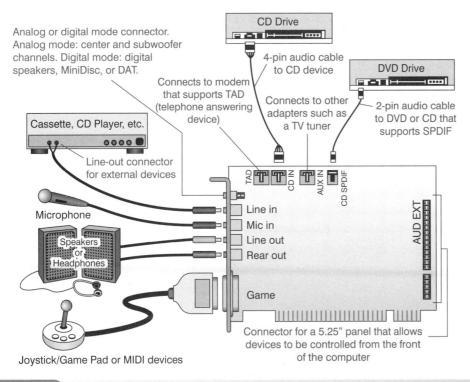

Analog or digital mode connector. Analog mode: center and subwoofer channels. Digital mode: digital speakers, MiniDisc, or DAT.

CD Drive

4-pin audio cable to CD device

DVD Drive

Connects to modem that supports TAD (telephone answering device)

Connects to other adapters such as a TV tuner

2-pin audio cable to DVD or CD that supports SPDIF

Cassette, CD Player, etc.

Line-out connector for external devices

Microphone

Speakers or Headphones

TAD   CD IN   AUX IN   CD SPDIF

Line in
Mic in
Line out
Rear out

AUD EXT

Game

Joystick/Game Pad or MIDI devices

Connector for a 5.25" panel that allows devices to be controlled from the front of the computer

Figure 8.8   **Multimedia Sound Blaster sound card ports**

A cable does not have to attach from the CD/DVD drive to the sound card

With Windows XP, enable CCDA (compact disc digital audio) and you do not have to attach a cable from the CD/DVD drive to the sound card or motherboard. Sound is output via the CD/DVD drive interface cable that connects to the motherboard. Access *Device Manager*; locate and right-click the CD/DVD drive and select *Properties* tab; enable the *Enable digital CD audio* checkbox. This option is not available in Vista.

Tech Tip

8
Multimedia
Devices

S/PDIF connectors can be used with coaxial cable (RCA jack) or fiber-optic cable (TOSLINK connector). Motherboards sometimes come with S/PDIF connectors. Figure 8.9 shows the two types of S/PDIF connectors.

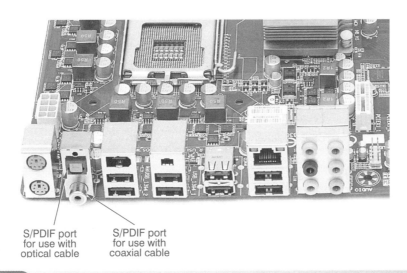

S/PDIF port for use with optical cable

S/PDIF port for use with coaxial cable

Figure 8.9   **S/PDIF connectors**

An initiative between Microsoft and Intel resulted in the PC Design Guides, which are available at http://www.pcdesguide.org. Connector colors and connector icons (labeling) are defined. With sound cards having so many connectors on the card, understanding the common labeling is imperative. The documentation may not always be handy or easy to get. Figure 8.10 illustrates the recommended port icons relating to sound cards. Table 8.6 shows common coloring used for sound ports.

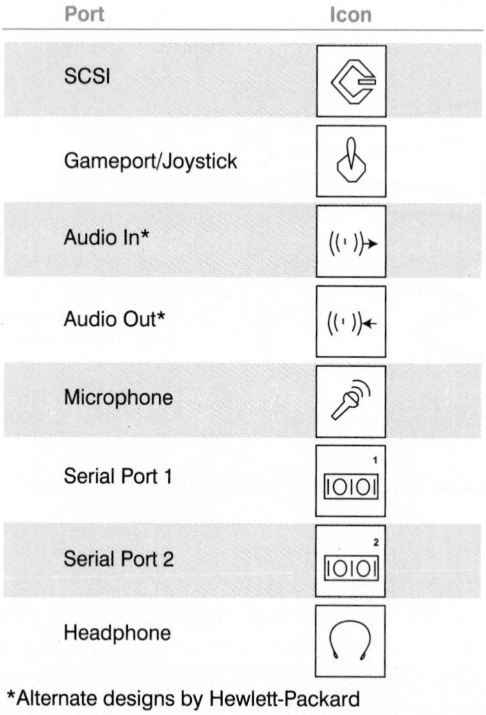

Port	Icon
SCSI	
Gameport/Joystick	
Audio In*	
Audio Out*	
Microphone	
Serial Port 1	
Serial Port 2	
Headphone	

*Alternate designs by Hewlett-Packard

Figure 8.10 PC design symbols

Table 8.6 Sound ports

Color	Purpose
Orange	Center speaker or subwoofer
Black	Rear speaker
Light blue	Line In
Lime	Line out
Pink	Microphone
Gray	Side speaker

Tech Tip

Sound card IDE ports do not have to be used

Even if a sound card has an interface connection for the drive, the CD/DVD drive does not have to connect to the sound card. Instead, the drive can connect to an IDE PATA or SATA motherboard connector or to another IDE adapter installed in the system.

The audio subsystem needs to make the digital audio stream available to the operating system kernel. This allows USB and IEEE 1394 devices to accept the audio digital signal and convert it in the external device. This keeps noise inside the computer from interfering with this digital signal.

Two major types of sound files are MIDI (.MID) and Wave (.WAV). Most multimedia discs use Wave files for sound, but most game CDs use MIDI files. Getting a sound adapter that can process both files is important. An alternative format is **MP3** (MPEG-1 Audio Layer-3) that compresses a file into about one-twelfth its original size. Windows has a player built into the operating system and others are available on the Internet. MP3 files have a file extension of *mp3*. MP3 is slowly being replaced by **AAC** (advanced audio compression), which does better coding and is found in Apple, PlayStation, Sony, and Nintendo products as well as others.

Sound Card Theory of Operation

Sound cards have a variety of options that can include an input from a microphone, an output to a speaker, a MIDI interface, and the ability to generate music. Take the example of bringing sound into the computer through a microphone connected to a sound card. Sound waves are shown as an analog waveform, as shown in Figure 8.11.

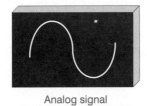

Analog signal

Figure 8.11   **Sound wave**

Computers work with digital signals (1s and 0s), so the sound card must take the analog signal and convert it to a digital format to send the sound into the computer. Sound cards can also take the digital data from a CD and output the sound to the speakers. To convert an analog waveform to 1s and 0s, samples of the data are taken. The more samples taken, the truer the reproduction of the original signal.

The first sound cards made for the computer sampled the data using eight bits. Eight 1s and 0s can give a total of 256 ($2^8 = 256$) different values. The analog waveform goes above and below a center value of 0. Because one of the eight bits denotes negative or positive value, only seven bits can represent sampled values. $2^7 = 128$. The values can be 0 through +127 or 0 through –127 (total value range is between –127 and +127). Figure 8.12 shows an example of sampling.

The more samples taken by the sound card, the closer the reproduction is to the original sound signal. The sound card's **frequency response** is dependent on the sample rate. This can also be known as the sample rate or sample frequency. For a good reproduction of sound, the sound wave is sampled at twice the range desired. For example, a person's hearing is in the 20Hz to 20KHz range. Twice that range is approximately 40,000 samples per second. The frequency response for a musical CD is 44,100 samples per second, a good quality sound reproduction for human ears. The first sound cards for computers used eight bits to sample the sound wave and had a frequency response of approximately 22,000 samples per second (22KHz). The sound produced from the original sound cards was better than the beeps and chirps previously heard from the computer. The sound was still grainy, better than an AM radio station but not as good as an FM radio station or a musical CD.

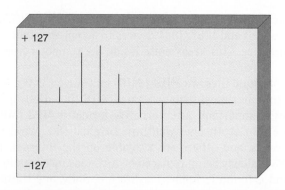

Figure 8.12 8-bit sampling

Next, 16-bit sound cards arrived for computers. The number of possible levels sampled with 16 bits is 65,536 (2^{16} = 65,536). When positive and negative levels are sampled, the range is –37,768 to +37,768. The frequency response with 16-bit sound cards is 44KHz, the same resolution as stereo audio CDs. 24-bit sampling results in a 96kHz sample rate that is sometimes called the audio resolution. The increase in the number of sampling levels and the frequency response allows sound cards to produce quality sound equal to audio CDs/DVDs. See Figure 8.13 for an example of 16-bit sampling. Keep in mind that when more samples are taken, the sound card provides a better frequency response.

DVDs require a 48KHz sampling rate for audio output. Therefore, sound card sampling rates should be a minimum of 48KHz for DVDs and 44.1KHz for CDs.

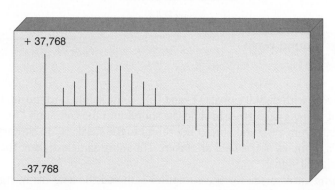

Figure 8.13 16-bit sampling

Tech Tip

What to look for in a sound card

Be sure it is a PCI/PCIe adapter that uses a minimum of 16 bits for sampling. For DVDs, make sure the sound card supports 48KHz, especially when using DVD software decoding.

Installing Sound Cards

The steps to installing a sound card are similar to any other adapter. Always refer to the manufacturer's instructions when installing devices and adapters. Power off the computer, remove the computer case, and locate an empty expansion slot (make sure it is the appropriate type of slot).

Attach appropriate cables such as the audio cable from the CD or DVD to the adapter. Attach external devices such as speakers. Power on the computer. Windows should detect that new hardware has been installed (if Windows does not, use the *Add Hardware* control panel). Load the appropriate device drivers for the sound card. Once a sound card is installed, there are normally other programs and utilities from the sound card manufacturer that you can install as you would any other application.

Disable motherboard sound when installing an adapter

If you install a sound card into a computer that has sound built into the motherboard, you must disable the onboard sound before installing the new adapter.

Sound Cards Using Windows XP/Vista/7

With Windows XP, the *Sounds and Audio Devices* control panel, or in Vista/7, the *Hardware and Sound* control panel link is used to change sound and adjust multimedia settings. All Windows operating systems allow controlling volume through a taskbar volume icon located in the lower-right portion of the screen. This icon, can be used to mute or adjust sound.

If sound is not coming from the computer

Check the *Mute* checkbox or icon located in the volume control in the systray.

Audio drivers are vastly improved in Windows XP. Microsoft has WDM (Windows Driver Model), which accommodates multiple streams of real-time audio and allows a kernel-mode process to handle audio management. This means that the operating system can control all aspects and improve audio performance. Digital audio can be redirected to any available output including USB and IEEE 1394 (FireWire).

Windows also includes a set of APIs (Application Programming Interface), which are commands that developers use to communicate with the sound card. DirectX has specific APIs that have commands relating to audio. In DirectX, Microsoft adds such things as DirectSound3D that has more 3-D audio effect commands, supports hardware acceleration, and allows simulation of audio sounds in certain environments, such as a tunnel or underwater. It allows software and game developers to create realistic audio environments such as muffling effects and audio directional effects (i.e., the direction a sound comes from).

You can tell whether or not a device has integrated sound or a sound adapter installed by inspecting the Sound, video and game controller category in Device Manager. The left side of Figure 8.14 shows a screen capture of Device Manager from a computer that has integrated sound on the motherboard. The Device Manager screen capture on the right is from a computer that has a sound card installed. Note that integrated sound may be located in the *System devices* category.

Portable Sound

Portable computers are more limited in what sound options they can have, but some laptops have upgraded sound integrated into the motherboard. Another option for laptops and desktop computers is adding an USB sound card. USB sound devices work with both analog and digital signals. Insert the sound card into a USB port and have instant quality sound.

Wireless sound connectivity is also an option. A PC or a laptop that has wireless network connectivity can have music stored on it. A wireless receiver allows music to be played anywhere within wireless network range.

Speakers

Most people connect speakers to a sound card or integrated sound ports. The quality of sound is personal—sounds acceptable to one person are not always acceptable to someone else. Table 8.7 shows some features to look for in speakers.

Figure 8.14   **Integrated sound and a sound card in Device Manager**

Table 8.7   **Speaker features**

Feature	Explanation
Amplification	Increase the strength of the sound. Sound cards usually have built-in amplification to drive speakers. Amplification output is measured in watts and most sound cards provide up to four watts of amplification (which is not enough for a full-bodied sound). Many speakers have built-in amplifiers to boost the audio signal for a much fuller sound.
Power rating	How loud the volume can go without distorting the sound. This is expressed in watts-per-channel. Look for the RMS (root-mean-square) power rating. 10 to 15 watts-per-channel is an adequate rating for most computer users.
Frequency response range	The range of frequency (sounds) that the speaker can reproduce. Humans can hear from 20Hz to 20KHz and the range varies for each person. Therefore, whether or not a computer speaker is appropriate, depends on the person listening to the speaker because speaker quality is subjective. Room acoustics and speaker placement also affect sound quality.
Shielding	Cancels out magnetic interference and keeps magnetic interference away from other devices. Speakers usually have a magnet inside them that can cause distortion to a device such as a monitor. These magnets can also cause damage to disks and other storage media. The best CD/DVD drive and sound card combination can be downgraded by using inexpensive, poorly shielded speakers.

Tech Tip

When choosing speakers

Listen to them without headphones using an audio (non-software) CD.

Most computers come with speakers. Sometimes these speakers are very inexpensive; often they are powered by batteries only. Speakers with an external power source are best. One speaker commonly connects to the sound card port and the other speaker is daisy-chained to the first speaker. Some speakers have an external volume control. Be careful of this. It is just another thing to check for when sound does not occur. Figure 8.15 shows computer speakers that are powered with an AC adapter.

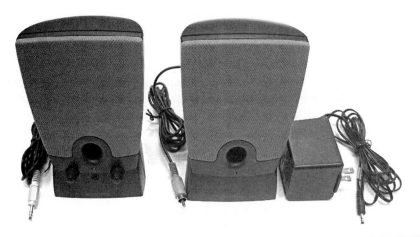

Figure 8.15   **Front view of powered speakers**

USB, IEEE 1394 (FireWire), and wireless can also be used to provide connectivity for speakers. This is a good solution because digital audio is sent over the bus and the external speaker converts the signal into sound. When audio is converted inside the computer, interference from internal electronic components and external sources (especially if an expansion slot does not have an adapter installed and the case has an opening) can cause audio interference. The drawback to USB is that it puts more work on the CPU. However, with today's multi-processor environment, this may not be an issue. The following is a list of extras to look for in speakers:

- An external volume control
- Headphone jacks
- Headphone and microphone pass-through connectors (so you do not have to dislodge the computer to reach the jacks)
- AC adapter
- Connectors for the speakers to connect to the sound card (if the connectors are wrong, Radio Shack or music stores carry converters)
- If the sound card is capable of 3D sound, a four or six speaker system is an enhancement

Two speakers are normally joined by a cable that may or may not be removable. Figure 8.16 shows how a cable that plugs into the right speaker would have the other end connected to the left speaker.

When speakers power on, there may be a popping sound emitted from them. This is normal, but if the sound continues after the speakers are powered on, the speaker is probably picking up interference from the computer or another device. Try moving the speakers farther away from the computer.

Figure 8.16   **Speaker connections**

Troubleshooting Sound Problems

The following is a list of common problems and solutions:

- If the speaker is emitting unwanted sounds, make sure there are no empty adapter slots in the computer. Next, check the speaker wires for cuts, move the sound card to another expansion slot, and move the speakers farther away from the computer. Finally, move the computer away from the offending device or the offending device away from the computer. If the speakers produce a humming noise and are AC powered, move the speaker power cord to a different wall outlet. Plugging the speakers into the same circuit as the computer is best.

Tech Tip

Check the easy stuff first

1. Are speakers plugged into the correct port on the sound card?
2. Is the volume control muted? If so, take it off mute.
3. Is the volume control on the speakers turned up?
4. If from within Windows, the device appears to be playing the disc, but no sound can be heard, then the problem is definitely in the sound system.
5. Do the speakers have power?

- If sound is a problem or if any solution directs you to update your sound driver, access *Device Manager* and expand the *Sound, Video, and Game Controllers* or *System Devices* option. Locate and right-click the integrated sound or the sound card and select *Properties*. Select the *Driver* tab and the *Update driver* button.
- If the sound card is not working, check Device Manager to see if the sound card is listed twice. If there are two entries for the same sound card, remove both of them by clicking each entry and clicking the *Remove* button. Restart Windows and the operating system should detect the adapter and either install a device driver or prompt for one. For best results, use the latest device driver from the sound card manufacturer or computer manufacturer, in the case of integrated ports.
- If you do not see a sound icon in the bottom-right corner of the screen, use the *Sounds and Audio Devices* (Windows XP) control panel to ensure the sound card is listed. On the *Volume* tab, ensure the *Place volume icon in the taskbar* checkbox is enabled. In Vista/7, open the *Appearance and Personalization* link. In the Taskbar and Start Menu section, select *Customize icons on the toolbar*. Select the *Notification area* tab and locate the System icons section. The *Clock* checkbox can be enabled to display the icon or disabled to remove it from the systray.
- If audio is low no matter what disc or system sound is played, the speakers may not be amplified speakers or they may not be connected to the correct sound card port. Also, do not forget to check the computer sound settings through the icon on the taskbar or the *Sounds and Audio Devices* (XP) or *Hardware and Sound* (Vista) control panel.
- If one disc does not output sound, but other discs work fine, the disc may use a later version of DirectX than the one installed. Check the recommended DirectX version for the disc. Also, the disc may have a problem.
- If building a computer, install the sound card after installing the video card, hard drive, and CD/DVD drive, but before anything else. Some sound cards are inflexible about system resource changes.

If sound does not come out of the CD/DVD drive after the drivers and software load, the following troubleshooting tips will help.

- Be sure an audio CD or a CD containing audio files is inserted into the CD/DVD drive.
- If sound no longer comes out of the speakers, check the speaker cables.
- Check the proper installation of the audio cable.
- Check that the speakers or headphones connect to the CD/DVD drive or to the sound card or integrated sound port.
- If using speakers, check the insertion of the cable jack on the back of the sound card. Verify the speakers have batteries installed or an AC adapter connected.

- If using headphones, verify that the headphones work on another device before using them to test the drive.
- Get updated drivers from the sound card manufacturer's Web site.
- If the monitor's image quality decreases after installing a sound card with speakers, move the speakers farther away from the monitor.

For more in-depth, product-specific troubleshooting, refer to the documentation or the Web site of the sound card or CD/DVD drive manufacturer.

Scanners

A **scanner** is a popular input device that allows documents including text and pictures to be brought into the computer and displayed, printed, emailed, pressed to CD/DVD, and so on. The most common types of scanners are listed in Table 8.8.

Table 8.8	Types of scanners
Scanner type	**Comments**
Flatbed (sometimes called desktop scanner)	Most popular; can scan books, paper, photographs, and so on; takes up a great deal of desk space
Sheetfed	Document is fed through an automatic document feeder similar to a fax machine; good for scanning many documents simultaneously
Handheld	Portable unit that slowly moves across the document; user must have patience and a steady hand
Film	Used to scan picture film instead of picture prints
Barcode reader	Handheld scanner used to read barcodes in checkout lanes and in retail establishments

Figure 8.17 shows a handheld scanner.

Figure 8.17   **Handheld scanner**

Scanners normally attach to the computer using one of the following methods:

- Parallel
- USB
- IEEE 1394 (FireWire)

Some scanners support multiple methods such as parallel and USB connectivity. Parallel port scanners are the traditional physical connection. However, since most computers have only one parallel port, scanners frequently have a second port with which to connect the printer.

The scanner connects to the computer's parallel port and the printer attaches to the second port on the scanner. Some scanners must be left powered on in order for the printer to work. USB is the most common connectivity option.

USB devices are very easy to install and USB hubs allow the system-integrated USB ports to be turned into multiple USB ports. To install a USB scanner, always follow the manufacturer's directions. The steps that follow are generic ones: (1) Install software and drivers. (2) Unpackage and unlock or remove special packaging. (3) Connect the data or network cable as well as the power cable. (4) Power on the scanner. Some scanners have a calibration program that needs to be performed. (5) Configure options and default settings. (6) Scan a document to test. (7) Ensure the customer is trained and has all scanner documentation. Figure 8.18 shows a Mustek flatbed scanner that uses a USB connection.

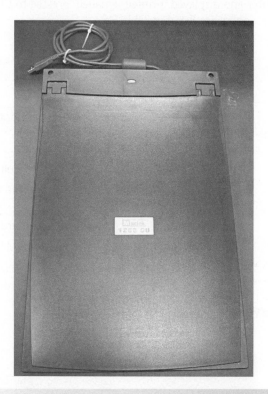

Figure 8.18   **Flatbed USB scanner**

The following list outlines how a flatbed scanner works:

1. A document is placed on the scanner's glass plate. There is a lamp under the glass.
2. The lamp (fluorescent, CCFL [cold cathode fluorescent lamp], or Xenon) turns on. Light reflects from the document.
3. The scan head is used to capture the reflected light. It moves slowly down the document by way of a belt that attaches to a stepper motor. The light reflects through a series of mirrors to the CCD (charge-coupled device) array.
4. The CCD array holds light sensitive diodes. The diodes convert light into varying voltage levels. The voltage levels are sent to an ADC (analog to digital converter).
5. The ADC converts the voltage levels to pixels. A pixel is a dot and is the smallest unit in a picture or document.
6. The pixels are sent through the scanner interface to the computer where the image is displayed.

A scanned image can be saved in several formats. When scanning a document or graphic for Web pages, select JPEG or GIF format. The most common graphic file formats are listed in Table 8.9. There are many terms associated with scanning and Table 8.10 lists the most common.

Table 8.9 Scanner file formats

File format	Comments
JPEG (Joint Photographic Experts Group)	Small file size; good for Web pictures; not good for master copies; always compresses the file; file extension is .jpg
GIF (Graphic Interchange Format)	Limited to 256 colors; small in size; good for Web pictures; file extension is .gif
TIFF (Tag Image File Format)	Good for master copies; large size; file extension is .tif
PNG (Portable Network Graphics)	Newest type; not supported by all applications or older applications; supports 24- and 48-bit color; file extension is .png

Table 8.10 Scanner terms

Scanner term	Comments
Resolution	Measured in dpi (dots per inch); determined by the number of sensors in the CCD array and by the precision of the stepper motor; common resolutions include 300, 600, 1200, 2400, 3200, 4800, and 9600
Bit depth	The number of bits used for color; the more bits, the more colors and color depth; common configurations are 24-, 30-, 36-, and 48-bits
Interpolation	Software used by the scanner to achieve a greater resolution by filling in the pixels around the scanned pixels
OCR (Optical Character Recognition)	Software that processes printed or written text characters; not all scanners ship with OCR software
TWAIN	A driver that is used so that applications can access and acquire images directly from the scanner

8 Multimedia Devices

Resolution is a difficult concept in scanning because the same term is used with printers and monitors. When scanning a document, always think about whether the output is intended for the printer or the monitor. Setting the scanner's resolution to the maximum amount for every scan is not a good idea. Table 8.11 shows some sample resolutions for scanning.

Table 8.11 Scanner resolutions

Type of document	Use	Scanner color setting	Recommended resolution (dpi)
Any	Displaying on a monitor	Color, grayscale, or black and white	150
Text	Copying or emailing	Color, grayscale, or black and white	150
Black-and-white photo	Saving, using in a Web site or email	Grayscale	75–300
Color photo	Copying, printing, or creating a document such as a photo or postcard	Color	300
	Using in a Web site or email	Color	75–150
	Saving	Color	75–300

Tech Tip

Cleaning your scanner

Never spray or pour any type of cleaning solution directly onto the scanner's glass. Always put the cleaning solvent on the cloth first and then wipe the glass. Do not use rough paper towels on the glass surface.

The scanner's plate glass needs to be cleaned periodically. The best method is to use optical-surface cleaning fluid with an antistatic cleaning cloth.

A commercial glass cleaner and denatured alcohol can also be used. Be careful to use a soft cloth and remove all cleaner residuals from the glass. To test the cleaning, scan a full page without a document loaded onto the scanner. See if the results yield any smudges or streaks.

Digital Cameras

A **digital camera** stores photographs in digital form and these photographs can be transferred to a computer or printer. Once the photographs are in the computer they can be displayed, changed, printed, emailed, pressed to CD/DVD, and so on. Digital cameras sometimes connect to the computer through a USB port to transfer the photographic images. However, FireWire and older serial/parallel digital cameras are also available.

A digital photograph can be saved in several formats. JPEG and TIFF are the most common. Refer to the scanner section for more information about these file formats. Some earlier digital camera manufacturers saved the photographs in a proprietary format, which meant that only the computer that had that manufacturer's software on it could be used to open the photographs. Some cameras that have advanced options can save files in WAV and AVI format for sound and motion.

Digital cameras usually run on AC and DC. For AC, the camera is plugged into an electrical outlet. This is especially useful for transferring photographs from the camera to the computer. For DC, batteries are used. Table 8.12 lists the most common digital camera battery types.

Table 8.12	Digital camera batteries
Battery type	**Comments**
AA	Easy to find; does not last long; inappropriate for cameras with movie-making features
NiCad (Nickel Cadmium)	Rechargeable; more expensive than AA but less expensive than the other types; loses approximately 1 percent of its power daily; must be fully discharged before recharging
NiMH (Nickel Metal Hydride)	More expensive than NiCads but last longer; must be recharged about once a month
Li-Ion (Lithium Ion)	Most expensive; best longevity; usually requires a special charger

A digital camera resolution is measured in pixels. The resolution is the number of horizontal and vertical pixels the camera can use to capture or display an image. Today, digital camera resolution technology has evolved into megapixels. If a camera has a 1 megapixel resolution, it means that the camera can process an image with approximately one million pixels. The camera's photosensors (usually CCD, like scanners or CMOS) determine how many pixels can be used. Common resolutions for today's digital cameras are 4–10 (and higher) megapixels.

Tech Tip

Caring for your digital camera

Remove disposable (alkaline) batteries from your digital camera when it's not being used for an extended period so they do not leak battery fluids into the camera.

Digital cameras traditionally have connected to the computer through a traditional interface such as serial, parallel, USB, SCSI, and FireWire. However, removable storage media has also become popular. Table 8.13 lists the more common digital camera storage media.

Table 8.13	Digital camera data storage
Storage type	**Comments**
Compact Flash (CF)	Introduced by SanDisk; uses flash memory; does not require a battery to store photos once power is removed; includes CF-I and CF-II
SmartMedia	Developed by Toshiba; smaller and lighter than CF; can purchase an adapter card with PC Card ATA adapter for data transfers
Memory Stick	Created by Sony; small in size; can read/write with a standard floppy disk drive with the purchase of a Memory Stick floppy disk adapter; includes MS (memory stick), MSD (memory stick duo), M2 (memory stick micro)
Secure Digital	Size of a postage stamp; does not require power to retain data; uses flash memory technology; has the ability for cryptographic security; different types include SD, miniSD, microSD, and SDHC
PC Card drives	One type is IBM MicroDrive; consumes more power than memory technology
MMC (multimedia card)	A type of flash memory used in many portable devices including cameras; works in many devices that support SD cards and is less expensive; types include MMC, RS-MMC (reduced size MMC), MMCmicro, DV-MMC (dual voltage), MMCplus (faster), MMCmoblile, and MiCard (has two detachable parts—one side for USB and the other side for use with a card reader)

The number of photographs stored on media is directly related to the amount of storage available and the type of file of each photograph saved. Digital cameras usually have one or more of the following file formats shown in Table 8.14.

Table 8.14	Digital camera file formats
File type	**Description**
RAW	Outputs raw, unprocessed data; does something with the photos after being removed from the camera
JPEG	Most common type; saves more photos due to compression
TIFF	Larger file size (fewer photos) due to retaining image quality

A reader is a popular device that many people attach to their PC or have integrated into a computer. A reader has multiple slots that allow different memory media to be read. This device is called many names, but common ones include 15-in-1 reader, 8-in-1 reader, or 5-in-1 reader (depending on how many different slots or types of memory modules it accepts). The reader instantly recognizes inserted memory cards, which can be copied into the computer and manipulated. The media card slots are assigned drive letters that are accessible through Windows Explorer. Figure 8.19 shows one of these readers.

Digital cameras normally have a button or a menu setting that allows photograph deletion. Sometimes a photograph is accidentally deleted. For cameras with flash memory technology, there are software programs that can undelete a photograph. Note that some cameras clear the image once the photograph is deleted and it cannot be recovered. Most software developers of this type of product have a compatibility chart or program to run to see if the application works with the camera.

Another popular type of digital camera is a **Web cam**, which is short for Web camera and sometimes seen as Webcam (one word)—a digital camera that attaches to a PC for use in

Tech Tip

No drive letter

If the media does not appear in Windows Explorer, the reader may have been temporarily uninstalled. Use the Safely Remove Hardware tool in the systray, unplug the cable from the port, and reinsert the cable to ensure the operating system recognizes the reader. If the card reader or ports are still not available or if they are integrated into the computer, restart the computer.

8

Multimedia Devices

Figure 8.19   **Memory card reader**

transmitting live video across the Internet. Web cameras can also be found that attach to VoIP phones and activate when a phone session occurs for instant Web conferencing. Most Web cams have a small visor that can be flipped over the lens to prevent video when desired. Figure 8.20 illustrates a Web cam. Web cams can also connect wirelessly to a PC or a laptop.

Figure 8.20   **Web cam**

Regardless of what multimedia device connects to a computer, all devices attach and install similarly. When installing a new device for a customer, don't forget to allow the customer to test the device while you are still there. Also, remember to leave all documentation related to the installation with the customer. They paid for the device and are entitled to the documentation.

Soft Skills—Attitude

A technician's attitude is one of his or her greatest assets. Some consider having a good attitude as simply being positive at work, but this is not the entire picture. A technician with a good attitude has the following traits:

- **Is proactive, not reactive.** A good technician actively looks for a solution rather than waiting for someone to instruct him or her.
- **Seeks solutions instead of providing excuses.** A positive technician does not continually apologize or talk in a subservient tone. For example, a positive technician explains issues such as late deliveries in a professional, positive manner.
- **Accepts responsibility for actions taken.** If a technician forgets something or takes a misstep, then the technician should apologize and explain to the customer what happened.

Truth goes a long way with customers. A positive technician does not constantly shift blame to other departments or technicians. Even if the other department or technician is responsible, the technician with a positive attitude handles the customer and then talks to the other department or technician about the problem.

- **Deals with priority changes professionally.** In the IT field, computer and network problems arise that cause us to reprioritize tasks weekly, daily, and even hourly. These are normal occurrences and a technician with a positive attitude understands this.
- **Cooperates and enjoys working with others.** A positive attitude is contagious and others like being around it.
- **Maintains professionalism even when working with a coworker who is unethical, unprofessional, or uncooperative.** A technician with a good attitude does not let someone else's poor attitude be a negative influence.
- **Embraces problems as challenges to learn and develop skills.**

You should exhibit all of these traits consistently to establish a positive mental attitude and make it part of your daily habits.

A common complaint of people who hire technicians is how the technicians talk to customers. For example, a computer repair teacher enters a computer retail store and is looking for a USB to 9-pin male serial port converter for her new laptop. A sales representative approaches her and asks if he can help. The teacher says "Yes" and explains what she wants. The salesperson tells her in a condescending tone that there is no such adapter and wants to know why the teacher wants such a converter. The teacher explains that she knows for a fact there is such a thing and it is used to attach a serial cable from the laptop to a router. The salesperson tells her that she does not need a male port for that, but a female one. The teacher explains that she will look for it on her own or purchase it online. The salesperson retorts "You are not going to find that on the Internet because there is no such thing" and walks away.

There are a couple of things to be learned from this scenario: (1) The salesperson appears to be a know-it-all—this is a common attitude among technicians who know a little. No one knows everything about technology and as a technician you must be humble. (2) Do not use a condescending tone with a customer. Usually when you tell a technician that they are using acronyms, "techie talk," or "geek speak," the technician reacts by using a tone as if they were speaking to a child—a condescending tone. The technician acts as if they are slowing down their intelligence to speak to a lower species and customers pick up on it. Do not use acronyms or technical lingo to impress or simply to do your job; furthermore, keep your tone professional at all times, especially if the customer is angry.

8
Multimedia
Devices

Key Terms

AAC (p. 279)
amplification (p. 282)
average access time (p. 265)
average seek time (p. 265)
Blu-ray (p. 270)
CD (p. 264)
CD-R (p. 266)
CD-RW (p. 266)
digital camera (p. 288)
DirectX (p. 269)
Disc-at-Once (p. 268)
DVD-R (p. 271)

DVD+R (p. 271)
DVD-R DL (p. 271)
DVD+R DL (p. 271)
DVD-RAM (p. 271)
DVD-RW (p. 271)
DVD+RW (p. 271)
DVD±RW (p. 271)
frequency response (p. 279)
frequency response range
  (p. 282)
laser lens (p. 273)
MIDI (p. 276)

MP3 (p. 279)
MTBF (p. 265)
multisession (p. 268)
power rating (p. 282)
region code (p. 270)
S/PDIF (p. 276)
scanner (p. 285)
Session-at-Once (p. 268)
shielding (p. 282)
software decoder (p. 269)
Track-at-Once (p. 268)
Web cam (p. 289)

Review Questions

1. What are some other names for discs that operate in CD drives?
2. [T | F] CD drives can be external devices.
3. Describe how a CD drive reads data.
4. What is a CD drive's X-factor?
5. [T | F] A CD drive that has a 400ms access speed is faster than one with a 250ms access speed.
6. [T | F] CD drives are slower than hard drives.
7. For what are CD buffers used?
8. A CD-R is listed as a 32×48. What does this mean?
9. What is a buffer underrun?
10. What is a mini-disc?
11. List three factors that influence CD creation.
12. [T | F] Session-at-Once drives can normally be used by a car CD player.
13. What is the difference between DVD-Video and DVD-ROM?
14. What is DVD-9?
15. A DVD has a listed DVD+R write capability of 22x. What is the approximate transfer rate this drive uses?
16. How can you determine if Windows XP has a software decoder installed?
17. What is the DVD region code for the U.S.?
18. [T | F] DVD+R drives can use both sides of the disc.
19. What type of DVD is endorsed by the DVD Forum and can read, write, and erase discs?
20. What DVD Book Type field defines DVD-RW?
21. What is the difference between writing discs with a DVD±RW drive and writing discs with a Blu-ray drive?
22. [T | F] A drive can write to both Blu-ray discs and DVD-RW discs.
23. What type of interface is most common for external CD/DVD drives?
24. What interfaces are available for CD and DVD drives?
25. What are some considerations when choosing a CD or DVD drive interface?
26. A customer has a Pentium 4 computer with 512MB of RAM running Windows XP. The video adapter is an AGP adapter with 64MB of video memory on the adapter. The user has a SATA IDE hard drive installed in the computer that plugs directly into the motherboard. The customer wants to upgrade the computer by adding a CD/DVD drive and sound card. What interface and drive setting would you recommend?
27. What are some considerations when upgrading a CD drive?
28. How can a disc be read even if a spot of dust is on the surface?
29. In what direction should a CD or DVD be cleaned? [clockwise in a circular pattern | counterclockwise in a circular pattern | inner-most circle to outermost circle using circular motions | innermost to outermost part of the disc in a linear motion]
30. What is another name for an objective lens?
31. [T | F] All CD drives have a self-cleaning laser lens.
32. List three things to do when installing an internal CD/DVD drive.
33. List three things to do when installing an external CD/DVD drive.
34. [T | F] Commonly, removable internal CD/DVD drives are interchangeable between laptop manufacturers.
35. What is the minimum decoder required to play video DVDs on a laptop?
36. List two easy things to check if having problems with a CD/DVD drive.

37. [T | F] A drive's headphone jack plays CDs as well as a stereo.

38. How do you verify if CCDA is enabled in Windows XP?

39. [T | F] A CD connected to a PATA IDE motherboard connector can play sound through a sound card.

40. What would normally connect to the Line Out sound card port?

41. Draw the PC Design symbol for a game port.

42. What is the PC Design recommended port color for Line In?

43. What normally connects to a speaker port that is orange?

44. What is MP3 and what software is replacing it?

45. Why is 40,000 samples per second a good sampling rate for a sound card?

46. What does having a 16-bit sound card mean?

47. If 24 bits are used for sampling, what is the audio resolution?

48. What sampling rate is required for DVD?

49. [T | F] Sound cards require a device driver.

50. A motherboard has integrated sound ports. You install a sound card, but the drivers will not load. What should you do?

51. What are APIs as they relate to sound?

52. List two options for upgrading sound on a notebook computer.

53. What is shielding as it relates to speakers?

54. What is a drawback to using USB speakers?

55. Sound does not emit from the speakers. What is the first thing to check?

56. A sound icon does not appear on the desktop. What should you check?

57. What is a possible problem if one disk outputs sound and another disc does not?

58. What are three common interfaces used with scanners?

59. Which scanner file format is good for pictures posted on the Internet, is small in size but is *not* limited to 256 colors?

60. How is scanner resolution different from printer resolution?

61. What is the best method for cleaning a scanner's glass plate?

62. List three interfaces that could be used with digital cameras.

63. What are the two most common digital camera file formats?

64. What advantage does a Secure Digital flash card have over the other digital camera storage methods?

65. Why do you think someone would buy a MiCard?

66. List ten technical terms or acronyms used in this chapter that should not be used with non-technical people.

Fill-in-the-Blank

1. If a CD drive uses the _____ interface, the drive must be an internal unit.

2. A 52x CD drive transfers data at _____ kBps.

3. On a CD, a/an _____ is an indentation along the spiral track.

4. On a CD, the area that separates the pits is a/an _____.

5. The CD drive _____ reads data from the CD.

6. The CD drive _____ specification is the time it takes to find specific data.

7. The amount of time before a device is likely to have a problem is the _____.

8. A/An _____ CD drive can write data to a disc and then add more data at a later date.

9. The _____ CD writing mode creates a disc in one pass.

10. The _____ is an alternative to DAO and supports writing both audio and data.

11. A CD drive listing that shows it supports CDi/FMV means the drive supports interactive and _____ discs.

12. A/An _____ drive uses a laser beam to read the CD and then writes data to the disc.

13. _____ drives combine audio and video entertainment with backward compatibility with CDs.

14. Microsoft's _____ contains multimedia software to speed up development of video and audio applications.

15. The _____ decoder requires a PCI adapter.

16. A DVD technology that can read, write, and erase discs but is not endorsed by the DVD Forum is _____.

17. DVD+R DL discs are different from DVD+R discs in that they are _____.

18. _____ is a technology developed by Hewlett-Packard that allows a disc label to be created on a CD or DVD.

19. The Book Type field code of 1001 is for _____ discs.

20. _____ drives use blue lasers instead of red.

21. The most common internal CD/DVD interface is _____.

22. Always handle a CD/DVD disk by its _____.

23. When cleaning a CD/DVD, do not wipe in circle; instead, wipe from _____ to _____.

24. Internal notebook CD/DVD drives usually attach to the _____ or _____ interface.

25. Some CD/DVD drives have an emergency eject _____ used when a disc is stuck.

26. Type _____ in Windows XP to run the DirectX Diagnostic tool.

27. The _____ interface is used to create synthesized music.

28. _____ is an audio interface that can have a coaxial or fiber-optic cable attached.

29. The _____-colored sound port is used for a rear speaker in a surround sound system.

30. Multimedia discs normally use sound files with the _____ file extension.

31. Most game CDs use sound files that have the _____ file extension.

32. Frequency response for a sound card is determined by the card's _____.

33. When installing a sound card into a system that has integrated sound ports, the integrated ports should be disabled through _____.

34. A rating for how loud the volume can be without distorting sound is a speaker's _____.

35. The _____ is the range of sounds a speaker or sound card can reproduce.

36. The Windows XP _____ control panel allows you to see whether an internal sound card is installed.

37. In XP, _____ is selected from the *System* control panel to update sound drivers.

38. A/An _____ scanner is used with picture film; a _____ scanner, on the other hand, is normally used for photographs or slides.

39. The _____ interface is the most common for scanner connectivity.

40. The _____ scanner file extension is good for compressed scanned pictures to be used on a Web page.

41. The _____ file extension is commonly used for 48-bit scanned color images.

42. The number of _____ determines a digital camera's resolution capabilities.

43. A digital camera storage media that has the ability to encrypt stored files is _____.

44. A/An _____ accepts many types of memory storage media.

45. A/An _____ is a multimedia device designed for video transmission on the Internet.

Hands-On Exercises

1. Sound and CD/DVD Drives in Windows XP

Objective: To be able to use the tools provided with Windows XP to manage sound devices and CD drives

Parts: A computer with Windows XP loaded

Procedure: Complete the following procedure and answer the accompanying questions.

Note: Parts of this lab may be different due to the hardware installed and the version of XP installed.

1. Power on the computer and log on using the userid and password provided by the instructor or lab assistant.

2. Click the *Start* button and click *Control Panel*. If in Category view, click *Sounds, Speech, and Audio Device*. Open the *Sounds and Audio Devices* control panel.

   What are the five tabs shown in the *Properties* window?

   Is the *Place volume icon in the taskbar* checkbox enabled or disabled?

3. The *Volume* tab is used to control the default sound device. In the Device volume section, a slide bar controls sound volume. The *Mute* checkbox turns sound off completely. If the *Place volume icon in the taskbar* checkbox is unchecked, click in the checkbox and click the *Apply* button. A volume control icon appears in the task-bar. Click the *OK* button.

4. Double-click the volume control icon in the task bar. The *Playback Control* window opens. This window is where sound might be muted if sound is not emitting from speakers. Close this window.

5. Right-click the volume control icon in the taskbar and select *Adjust Audio Properties*. The *Sound and Audio Devices Properties* window opens.

6. Return the *Place volume icon in the taskbar* checkbox to its original setting. Refer to Question 2. Click the *Apply* button.

7. Click the *Advanced* button in the Device volume section. The *Playback Control* window opens. This window is used to adjust sound volume for individual sound devices. Close the *Playback Control* window.

8. Click the *Speaker Volume* button. A checkbox at the bottom allows you to keep the left and right speaker controls the same as they are changed. Click the *Cancel* button.

9. Click the Speaker settings section's *Advanced* button. The *Advanced Audio Properties* window appears. This screen allows you to select the speaker type or to disable external speakers.

10. Click the *Performance* tab. Click the *Help* button (the button with a question mark) and point to the Hardware acceleration slide bar.

    Based on the information found in the Help screen, what is the purpose of the hardware acceleration slide bar?

11. The four settings for hardware acceleration are listed in Table 8.15.

Table 8.15	Hardware acceleration settings
Performance setting	**Purpose**
None	No acceleration; the computer operates in emulation mode
Basic	Only the required acceleration features are enabled
Standard	DirectSound is enabled
Full	DirectMusic and DirectShow are enabled

8 Multimedia Devices

12. Click somewhere in the *Advanced Audio Properties* window to remove the *Help* window. Use *Help* to determine the purpose of the *Sample rate conversion quality* slide bar.

Based on the information found in the *Help* screen, what is the purpose of the *Sample rate conversion quality* slide bar?

13. Close the *Help* screen, click the *Cancel* button, and click the *Sounds* tab.

What is the current setting, if any, for the *Sound scheme*?

14. Click the *Sound scheme* down arrow and select *Windows Default*. In the Program events section, click the *Asterisk* option. Click the *Play* button (the right arrow button located beside the *Browse* button).

15. Set the *Sound scheme* back to the original setting and click the *Apply* button. Refer to Step 13 if necessary.

16. Click the *Audio* tab, which allows you to specify audio devices such as the default playback device, recording device, and MIDI playback device used for different tasks.

17. Click the *Voice* tab, which has a similar purpose except it is for voice playback and recording devices.

18. Click the *Hardware* tab. This is an important tab for technicians. Devices are listed in the window. Select a CD or DVD drive and click the *Properties* button. Ensure the *Properties* window contains a *Driver* tab.

What device was selected?

19. Click the *Driver* tab. The driver tab can be used to upgrade a driver, list the current driver version, roll back to an older driver version, and uninstall the driver.

What driver version is currently installed?

20. Click the *Cancel* button and click the *Troubleshoot* button. The *Help and Support Center* window appears.

List one problem shown in the *Help and Support Center* window.

Instructor initials: _____

21. Close the *Help and Support Center* window. Click the *Cancel* button. Double-click the *My Computer* desktop icon.

What device letters are listed in the *Devices with Removable Storage* section?

22. Right-click the CD or DVD drive icon.

Tech Tip

What to do if a CD is stuck

The *Eject* option can be used when a CD is stuck in a CD drive.

23. Click *Properties* and select the *AutoPlay* tab. Press the ⬇.

List two devices shown in the drop-down menu.

24. Click the *Help* button and click somewhere in the *AutoPlay* window.

Based on the information found in the *Help* window, what is the purpose of the *AutoPlay* tab?

What actions can be performed on a Music CD?

25. Click the *Sharing* tab, which allows others access to the CD over a network. Click the *Share this folder* radio button.

26. Click the *Permissions* button, which assigns specific network users and specific permission to the drive. This is particularly important for CD-RW drives. Click the *Cancel* button.

27. Click the *Caching* button.

    What are the three caching settings?

Instructor initials: _____

28. Click the *Cancel* button. In the *Properties* window, click the *Cancel* button.

2. Sound and CD/DVD Drives in Windows Vista

Objective: To be able to use the tools provided with Windows Vista to manage sound devices and CD/DVD drives

Parts: A computer with Windows Vista loaded and that has Internet access

Procedure: Complete the following procedure and answer the accompanying questions.

Note: Parts of this lab may be different due to the hardware installed and the version of Vista installed.

1. Power on the computer and log on using the userid and password provided by the instructor or lab assistant.

2. Click the *Start* button and access the *Sound* control panel.

    What tabs are shown in the window?

    What is the default playback device?

3. With the default playback device selected, click the *Configure* button.

    What audio channels are available?

4. Select the *Test* button. As directed, click on the speaker.

    What was the result?

5. Click the *Cancel* button and ensure the *Playback* tab is selected. Click *Properties*. The Speakers Properties window opens.

    What jack information displays?

6. Click *Properties*.

    What is the device status?

7. Select the *Driver* tab.

    What is the driver version?

    What is the purpose of the Roll Back Driver button?

    Can the audio be disabled from this window?

8. Click the *Cancel* button. Select the *Levels* tab.

    What audio options are available?

9. Click the *Advanced* tab.

    How many bits are used for sampling?

    What is the frequency response?

10. Click *Cancel*. Select the *Recording* tab.

    Are any devices attached to the Line In port?

11. Select the *Sounds* tab. In the Program window, select any task that has a speaker icon to the left of it. Click *Test*.

    What was the test result?

12. Select the *Sound Scheme* drop-down menu.

    What options are available?

    For what is the checkbox in this section used?

8

Multimedia
Devices

13. Click *Cancel*. Close the control panel window.

14. Open Windows *Explorer*. Right-click the CD/DVD drive. Notice the Eject option, which can be used to eject a stuck disc.

15. Select the *Share* option. The Sharing tab opens. This option allows you to share a disc with others.

16. Select the *Hardware* tab. In the All disk drives window, select the CD/DVD drive.

    What is the device status?

17. Select the *Properties* button. Select the *DVD region* tab if a DVD drive is installed.

    What is the DVD region code? Write *Not applicable* as your answer if a CD drive is installed.

18. Select the *Driver* tab.

    What version of the driver is installed?

    What is the date of the driver?

19. Use the Internet to determine whether a new device driver is available. Show this driver to the instructor or lab assistant.

Instructor initials: _____

20. From the window, click *Cancel*.

21. From the CD/DVD drive properties window, select the *Customize* tab.

    What type of things can you customize from this tab?

22. Click the *Cancel* button. Close the Windows Explorer window.

23. Click the *Start* button and open *Help and Support*.

    Using the Help and Support link, list three suggestions about what to do if disc burning will not begin.

    Using the Help and Support link, list two more suggestions about what to do if disc burning stops before completion.

24. Close the *Help and Support* window.

3. CD/DVD Drive Installation Lab

Objective: To install, configure, and test a CD/DVD drive

Parts: A computer with Windows XP loaded.

   A CD, DVD, or CD/DVD drive with accompanying cable and mounting equipment if necessary

Procedure: Complete the following procedure and answer the accompanying questions.

1. Obtain a CD/DVD drive designated by the instructor or student assistant.

    What type of drive is this?

    [CD-ROM I CD-R I CD-RW I DVD-R I DVD+R I DVD+RW I DVD-RW I DVD±RW I DVD-R DL I DVD+R DL I BD-R I BD-RE]

    List the drive manufacturer and model number.

    If possible, determine if a driver is available for Windows XP and list the Web site on which you located this information.

    What is the latest driver revision number or date of the latest revision?

    What type of interface does the CD/DVD drive use? [PATA IDE I SATA I SCSI I Parallel I USB I FireWire]

2. Power off the computer, remove the power cord, open the computer if necessary, and determine if a cable and interface are available to install the drive. If not, obtain them.

3. Configure the drive as necessary for the type of interface being used.

    What drive settings did you select?

4. If appropriate, install the drive into the computer and attach power.

5. If an external device is being installed, a device driver may need to be installed at this point. Always refer to the device installation instructions. Whether the drive is internal or external, attach the correct interface cable to the drive.

6. Power on the computer, load a device driver if necessary and ensure the operating system recognizes the drive. Troubleshoot as necessary until the drive works.

   What tests did you perform to ensure the drive works?

7. Tell the instructor when the drive is successfully installed.

Instructor initials: _____

8. Remove the drive and re-install the computer cover.

Instructor initials: _____

4. DirectX Diagnostics in Windows XP

Objective: To be able to use the DirectX tool provided with Windows XP

Parts: A computer with Windows XP loaded and administrator rights

Procedure: Complete the following procedure and answer the accompanying questions.

1. Power on the computer and log on using the userid and password provided by the instructor or lab assistant.

2. Click *Start*, *Run*, type **dxdiag**, and press Enter. The DirectX tool may ask you to agree to allow an Internet connection for an update.

   Once the tool is shown and the *System* tab is displayed, what DirectX version is running?

3. Click the *Next Page* button. The DirectX Files tab information displays.

   What notes, if any, display?

4. Click the *Display* tab.

   How much RAM is on the video adapter? Are any DirectX features enabled? If so, which ones?

5. If available, test Direct3D by clicking the *Test DirectDraw* button. Click *Yes*, *OK* and answer the questions that follow.

6. If available, test Direct3D by clicking the *Test Direct3D* button. Click *Yes, OK* and answer the questions that follow.

7. Click the *Next Page* button.

   What acceleration setting, if any, is set?

8. If the *Test DirectSound* button is available, click it after attaching speakers and turning the volume up slightly.

   Could you tell the difference between the sounds?

9. Click the *Music* tab.

   What ports are available on this page?

10. Click the *Next Page* button.

    What input-related devices are there?

11. Click the *Network* tab. Select the *DirectPlay Voice Options* button. Click the *Run wizard* button. Follow the directions on the screen. When finished, click *Exit*.

5. DirectX Diagnostics in Windows Vista

Objective: To be able to use the DirectX tool provided with Windows Vista

Parts: A computer with Windows Vista loaded and with administrator rights and Internet access

Procedure: Complete the following procedure and answer the accompanying questions.

Note: This lab may vary due to the equipment installed and the Vista version and service pack.

8
Multimedia
Devices

1. Power on the computer and log on using the userid and password provided by the instructor or lab assistant.

2. Click the Windows *Start* button, select *Help and Support*, type **dxdiag**, and press ⌇Enter⌇. Select the *DirectX Diagnostic Tool* link. The DirectX tool may ask you to agree to allow an Internet connection for an update.

   Once the tool is shown and the System tab is displayed, what DirectX version is running?

   How much RAM is installed in the computer?

   What is the size of the paging file?

   How much of the paging file is currently used?

3. Click the *Next Page* button. The next tab displays.

   What notes, if any, appear on the tab?

4. Ensure you are on the *Display* tab.

   How much RAM is on the video adapter?

   Are any DirectX features enabled? If so, which ones? Research the words RAM, video adapter, and DirectX on the Internet and give a brief description of the features.

5. Ensure the *Sound 1* tab is being used.

   What is the device type being used?

   What is WDM? If you do not know, review the chapter.

   What system file is being used?

   What does WHQL Logo'd mean? If you do not know, look it up on the Internet.

6. Click the *Input* tab.

   List any direct input devices displayed.

7. Expand any USB devices in the Input Related Devices section.

   List any USB devices that are considered to be input devices.

8. Expand any PS/2 devices in the Input Related Devices section.

   List any PS/2 devices that are considered to be input devices.

9. Click *Exit*. Close the Help and Support window.

6. Installing a Sound Card and Speakers

Objective: To install and configure a sound card

Parts: A computer with Windows XP loaded, integrated sound, and an available expansion slot

                Sound card

                Speakers

                Optional audio CD

Procedure: Complete the following procedure and answer the accompanying questions.

Note: The available expansion slot and sound card should be the same type.

1. Power on the computer and log on using the userid and password provided by the instructor or lab assistant.

2. Examine the sound port(s) available on the computer.

   How many ports that could be found on a sound card are integrated into the motherboard? For what is each port used?

3. Connect power to the speakers if necessary and attach speakers to the computer.

4. Access the *Sounds and Audio Devices* control panel. On the *Volume* tab, notice that there is a checkbox for Mute. This checkbox is a common cause for sound not coming out of speakers. Also notice that there is a *Place volume icon in the taskbar* checkbox. Enable this checkbox and click the *Apply* button. The sound icon appears in the System Tray portion of the taskbar.

5. Select the *Speaker volume* button.

   Can you adjust the left and right volume separately from this window?

6. Click the *Advanced* button located in the Speaker Settings section.

   What does the *Speakers* tab allow you to configure?

   On the *Performance* tab, what is the default setting for Hardware acceleration?

   On the *Performance* tab, what is the default setting for the Sample rate conversion quality?

7. Click the *Cancel* button. Select the *Sounds* tab. Locate and click the *Exit Windows sound* in the *Program events* window. Any sound that has the sound icon to the left of it can be played as a test of the speakers. Click the *Play* button ▸, which is located beside the *Browse* button.

   Can you hear the sound even though a CD is playing? If not, troubleshoot as necessary. Do not proceed until you hear sound.

8. Click the *Audio* tab.

   What is the default sound playback device?

9. Click the *Hardware* tab. Locate and select the I*ntel 82802BA/BAM AC'97 Audio Controller* or whatever audio controller is installed. Click the *Troubleshoot* button. The sound troubleshooter opens.

   What is the first statement listed in the possible problems?

10. Close the *Sound Troubleshooter* window. Click the *Cancel* button in the *Sounds and Audio Devices Properties* window.

11. Access Device Manager. Expand the Sound, video and game controllers section. Right-click the Intel 82802BA/BAM AC'97 Audio Controller or whatever integrated audio controller is installed. Select *Properties* and click the *Resources* tab.

    What I/O address ranges are used by the integrated sound card?

    What interrupt is used?

12. Click the *Cancel* button to leave this window.

13. Reboot the computer and access the BIOS Setup program. Locate and disable the integrated sound ports. Save the settings.

    What key did you press to enter the Setup program?

14. Power off the computer and remove the power cord.

15. Access the computer expansion slots and remove any slot covers on retention bars if necessary.

16. Install the sound adapter and ensure it fits snugly into the expansion slot. Re-install any retention bar as necessary.

17. Re-install the power cord to the computer and power on the computer. The *Found New Hardware* balloon should appear. You may be prompted for a device driver and to restart the computer in order to use the new PCI adapter.

18. Attach the speakers to the newly installed sound card.

19. Using the process previously described, play a Windows sound or an audio CD using the newly installed adapter.

20. Access Device Manager. Expand the Sound, video and game controllers section. Right-click the newly installed sound card option and select *Properties*. Click the *Resources* tab.

    What I/O address does the adapter use?

    What interrupt does the PCI Sound Card use?

21. Click the *General* tab.

    What location is the card located in according to the information displayed?

    What is the device status according to the information displayed?

22. Power down the computer and remove the power cord.

23. Remove the sound adapter and reattach any slot covers.

24. Re-install any covers necessary to access the expansion slots and the power cord. Power on the computer and enter the Setup program.

8
Multimedia
Devices

25. Through BIOS Setup, re-enable the integrated sound ports. Save the settings.

26. Reattach the speakers to the integrated sound and test them. Troubleshoot as necessary.

Instructor initials: _____

7. Installing a USB Scanner

Objective: To be able to install a USB scanner and driver on a Windows-based computer

Parts: USB scanner, USB cable, scanner driver, scanner software/utilities, computer with Windows loaded

Procedure: The procedures outlined below are guidelines. Refer to the scanner's installation instructions for exact procedures.

Installing the Scanner Driver

1. Insert the scanner driver into the drive. The system normally recognizes CDs, but if necessary, use the *Add/Remove Software* (or similar name) control panel to install the USB driver. Sometimes you must also select what type of interface connection is going to be used. If this is the case, select *USB*. The software installer sometimes includes additional software programs that can be used to control the scanner and to manipulate scanned images. Many drivers require the computer to be restarted once the installation process is complete.

Connecting the Scanner

2. Some scanners ship with a carriage safety lock. If this is the case, remove the safety lock.

3. With the computer powered on, connect one end of the USB cable to the scanner's USB port and attach the other end to a USB computer port or a USB hub port.

4. If necessary, attach the power cable to the scanner. Attach the other power cable end to an electrical outlet.

5. Power on the scanner.

6. Optionally, if the scanner has a calibrate routine, execute the calibration.

Using the Scanner

7. If the scanner software program(s) did not install during driver installation, install the scanner software programs now.

8. Insert a document to be scanned.

9. Access the scanner software program through the *Start* button and scan the document.

Instructor initials: _____

8. Changing the Drive Letter of a CD/DVD Drive Using the DISKPART Utility

Objective: To reassign the CD/DVD drive letter

Parts: Windows computer with administrator rights

Procedure: Complete the following procedure and answer the accompanying questions.

1. Using Windows Explorer, determine the current CD/DVD drive letter.

   What drive letter is being used by the CD/DVD drive?

2. At a command prompt, type **diskpart** and press [Enter]. Type **list volume** and press [Enter]. Look down the Type column for a CD or DVD drive. Locate the drive to be changed. Ensure that the drive letter in the Ltr column is the same drive letter as written down in Step 1.

   Write the volume number that is listed in the same row as the CD/DVD drive.

3. At a command prompt, type **select volume *x*** (where *x* is the number you wrote in Step 2). A message appears, stating that the volume is selected. If the message does not appear, recheck your steps, starting from the beginning of the lab.

4. Type **assign letter=x** (where *x* is a drive letter to which you would like to move the CD/DVD drive). A message appears, stating that the drive letter assignment was successful. If this message does not appear, redo the exercise.

5. Use Explorer and refresh the screen, if necessary, to verify the reassignment. Show the instructor or lab assistant your reassigned drive letter.

Instructor initials: _____

6. In the **diskpart** utility, return the drive to the original drive letter by typing **assign letter x** (where *x* is the original drive letter). Refer to the answer to the question in Step 1 if you do not remember the drive letter. Use Windows Explorer to show the instructor or lab assistant that the drive letter has been reassigned.

Instructor initials: _____

Internet Discovery

Objective: To obtain specific information on the Internet regarding a computer or its associated parts

Parts: Computer with access to the Internet

Questions: Use the Internet to answer the following questions.

1. Find an Internet site that sells DVD drives.
   List the cost of the drives and the Web site URL.

2. What is the cost of a disc that works in a DVD+RW drive?
   List the cost and Web site URL.

3. Find an Internet site that tells you whether or not a DVD+RW drive is backward compatible with CD-R and CD-RW drives.
   List the URL for the site.

4. An HP G4050 Scanjet scanner attaches to a Windows Vista computer. When the scanning software is accessed, the error "The computer cannot communicate with the scanning device" appears.
   List the six recommended steps.

5. The President of the company has just bought a Canon SX20 IS digital camera.
   What type of memory media does this camera accept? Write the answer and URL where the answer was found.

6. A customer has a Plextor PX880SA DVD+/-RW drive.
   How much buffer memory does the drive contain and what interface(s) does it support? Write the answers and URL.

Soft Skills

Objective: To enhance and fine tune a future technician's ability to listen, communicate in both written and oral form, and support people who use computers in a professional manner

Activities:

1. List some tips on how to determine if a computer has a CD or DVD installed as if you were stepping through it over the phone with a customer who is not a technician. Practice with a fellow classmate using your instructions.

2. The class is divided into groups of five. Each group makes a list of three "categories" they would like that relate to multimedia devices. The five groups share their lists and determine which group works on which category. In 30 minutes, each team comes up with five answers with the corresponding questions for their category. The answers are rated from 100 to 500 with 100 being the easiest question. The teams play *Jeopardy* with the rule that no team may pick its own category.

8 Multimedia Devices

Critical Thinking Skills

Objective: To analyze and evaluate information, and apply information to new or different situations

Activities:

1. For this activity, you need an advertisement of a CD, DVD, or Blu-ray drive, including the technical specifications. Make a list of all terms related to the drive that you do not know. Using books, the Internet, or other resources, research these terms and define them.

2. For this activity, form groups of two. Several multimedia devices are needed. The devices are numbered. Each team selects a number and installs, configures, and tests the associated device. Each team documents its installation and shares its experience (including lessons learned) with the rest of the class.

9

Other Peripherals

Objectives

After completing this chapter you will be able to

- Describe the components of the video subsystem
- Differentiate among monitor types including laptop displays
- Define basic monitor theory and terminology
- Describe issues regarding video memory
- Install a video adapter and associated software
- Perform basic video troubleshooting techniques
- Explain basic printing concepts
- Describe how each type of printer operates
- Perform a printer installation, including print driver
- Perform preventive printer maintenance
- Control printers from Windows and make appropriate printer adjustments
- Solve common printer problems
- Demonstrate ethical and professional behavior when solving computer problems

Chapter Overview

Even though the book has covered many peripherals so far, such as hard drives, CD and DVD drives, mice, keyboards, and other USB/IEEE 1384 devices, other peripherals that have unique characteristics and technologies are still to be explored. Two of these technologies are video and printing. Each has associated terminology, concepts, and installation/troubleshooting tips. Let's explore video first.

Video Overview

Video quality is very important to computer users. The monitor, which displays the data, is one of the most expensive computer components. Users usually derive the most gratification from their monitor, although sound quality is now becoming as important. Technicians must look at video as a subsystem that consists of the monitor, the electronic circuits that send the monitor instructions, and the cable that connects them. The electronic video circuits are on a separate video adapter or built into the motherboard. Figure 9.1 illustrates a computer's video subsystem.

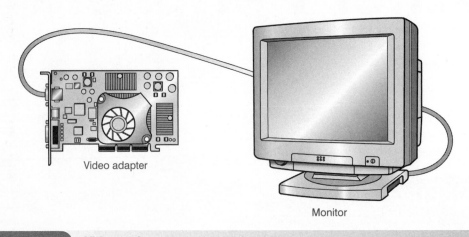

Video adapter

Monitor

Figure 9.1   **Video subsystem**

Types of Video Output Devices

Video output devices such as monitors and projectors are commonly used with desktop and laptop computers. Monitors can be classified several ways—color or non-color, analog or digital signals used to produce colors, and the type of video adapter used. The easiest way to classify video output is by the way in which the output is created—the technology. Table 9.1 lists some of the most popular display output technologies.

Other technologies used in video output include LCoS, SED, FED, OLED, and plasma. LCoS (liquid crystal on silicon) is similar to DLP except that it uses liquid crystals instead of mirrors for higher resolutions. SED (surface-conduction electron-emitter display) and FED (field emission display) technologies are similar: both use electron emitters to energize color phosphor dots to produce an image. The electron emitter used is what makes them different. An OLED (organic light-emitting diode) display does not require a backlight, like LCDs. An OLED has a film of organic compounds placed in rows and columns that can emit light.

Tech Tip

Recycle CRTs

CRTs contain toxic substances that can cause health risks to humans if CRTs are disposed of improperly. Consider donating a CRT or using a Web site such as www.crtusedmonitors.com instead of throwing it away.

Table 9.1	Video output technology
Technology	**Description**
CRT	CRT (cathode ray tube) monitors are the traditional-looking monitors. They are bulky and resemble TVs. A CRT monitor has three color beams (red, green, and blue) directed at a phosphorous dot on the back of the monitor tube. The phosphorous dot is a **dot triad** (three colored dots grouped together). The result is a single image on the screen called a **pixel**, or picture element. Figure 9.2 shows how that dot triad makes a pixel. Dot pitch is the distance between like-colored phosphorous dots on adjacent dot triads. **Dot pitch** is measured in millimeters. The lower a monitor's dot pitch, the smaller the distance between the dot triads and the sharper the image. CRTs have been replaced with flat panel monitors or LCDs.
LCD	LCD (liquid crystal display) technology is used in laptops, flat panel monitors, TVs, and projectors. Two glass substrates have a thin layer of liquid crystal between them. One glass substrate is the color filter, with three main colors—red, green, and blue—that allow more than 16 million colors to be displayed on a screen. The other glass substrate is the **TFT** (thin film transistor) array, which has the technology to direct the liquid crystal to block the light. A **backlight** (that used to be a fluorescent lamp but now can be **LED** technology) extends behind the combined glass assembly, and the light is always on. This is why an LCD monitor appears to sometimes glow even when it's off and why crystals are needed to block some of the light to create the intensities of light. Liquid crystals are sensitive to temperature changes. Laptop displays may appear distorted in cold or hot temperatures due to the liquid crystals. Figure 9.3 shows the inside parts of an LCD monitor.
DLP	DLP (Digital Light Processing) is a technology used in projectors and rear projection televisions. It is also a trademark owned by Texas Instruments. DLP has an array of mounted miniature mirrors, one of which is smaller than the width of a human hair and represents one or more pixels. The mirrors are used to create a light or dark pixel on a projection surface by being repositioned to different angles to reflect light. A color wheel or LEDs are used for the primary colors red, green, and blue. Figure 9.4 illustrates the concepts of DLP technology.

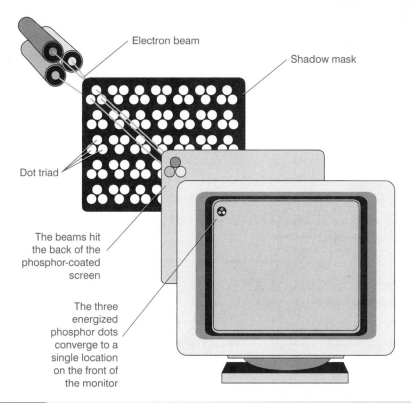

Figure 9.2 **Video theory of operation**

9

Other Peripherals

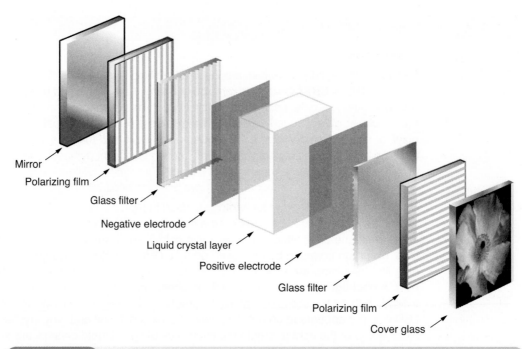

Figure 9.3   LCD technology

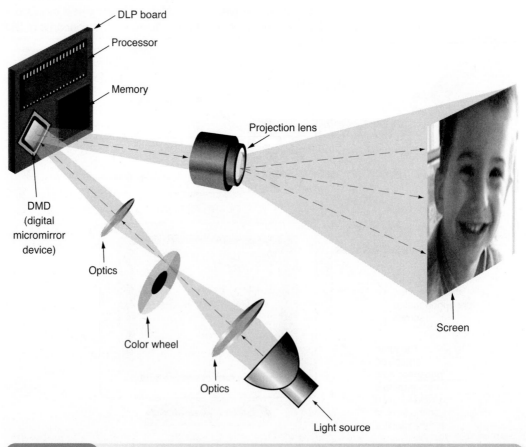

Figure 9.4   DLP technology

Plasma displays work very similarly to LCDs, except that they have plasma gas in little chambers. When electricity is applied inside the chambers, excited electrons hit red, green, and blue phosphorous dots that glow. Many believe that plasma displays require less energy than CRTs. This is not necessarily true. However, LCDs do take less energy than CRTs. Figure 9.5 shows the size difference when using CRT and LCD technologies.

Touch screen monitors connect to PCs and respond to contact on the screen rather than keyboard or mouse input. They are both an input and output device and are used in situations where information is to be controlled and in public areas such as kiosks in airports, malls, and entrance areas of schools or businesses. Touch screen monitors normally attach to a USB, IEEE 1394, VGA port, DVI port, a combination of these ports, or wirelessly. Special drivers and software are used to control the monitor.

Tech Tip

The video adapter must match the monitor
One of the most important things to remember about video is that the video adapter must match the type of monitor. Video adapters that allow two or more video output devices to be connected can be purchased.

Figure 9.5 **Flat panel versus regular-sized monitor**

There are several technologies used to manufacture a touch screen monitor. The two most common ones are resistive and capacitive. Resistive touch screen monitors have a flexible membrane stretched over the face of the monitor. The membrane contains a special metal oxide coating and has spacers that are used to locate the touched spot on the screen. Resistive touch screen monitors are good in manufacturing or medical areas where the personnel wear gloves. A stylus pen can also be used with these types of monitors.

Capacitive touch screen monitors are more durable than resistive monitors. They respond to a touch on the screen and easily detect contact. Most touch screen monitors are the capacitive type. There are also some companies that make a touch screen that attaches to a regular monitor.

To install a touch screen monitor, attach the cable(s) to the appropriate port(s), install the software driver, and install the software that comes with the monitor. Always follow the manufacturer's instructions and, if possible, test the monitor using a variety of applications.

Video Terminology and Theory

Video has unique terminology associated with it. It is important for a technician to be familiar with video terminology. Let's start with an important term—resolution. A monitor's **resolution** is the maximum number of pixels on the monitor. Two numbers separated by an x (meaning *by*) describe a monitor's resolution, such as 640×480 (640 "by" 480). The first number, 640, is the

9 Other Peripherals

number of pixels that fit horizontally across the screen. The second number, 480, describes the number of pixels that fit vertically on the screen. The possible monitor resolutions depend on the monitor and the video adapter. Table 9.2 shows terms used with resolution and the different modes that can be chosen for the display output. Table 9.3 lists important video features with which technicians need to be familiar.

Determining the number of pixels

To determine the number of pixels a display has, look at the resolution such as 1920×1200. Multiply the horizontal pixel number (the first number or 1920 in the example), by the vertical number of pixels, (the second number shown or 1200 in the example). The result is the total number of pixels or 2,304,000 (approximately 2.3 million pixels).

The monitor refresh rate is for a specific resolution. If the electron beam has to handle more pixels, it will naturally take longer. Video card capabilities are the main factor in determining what refresh rate the monitor uses, provided the monitor can perform it.

To set the refresh rate for the monitor on an XP computer, use the *Display* control panel. Select the *Settings* tab and click the *Advanced* button. Select the *Adapter* tab and click the *Refresh rate* down arrow. A listing of possible settings is displayed. The Optimal setting is the default. If you select another setting, click the *Apply* button and a warning message normally appears. Click the *OK* button and the monitor changes. A dialog box asks if you want to keep this setting. Selecting *No* will reset back to the default. If the mouse does not work or the mouse pointer does not appear on this screen, just press [Enter] and the *No* selection will be accepted.

Table 9.2   Video adapters/monitor types*

Video adapter	Description
VGA (Video Graphics Array)	Connects to a 15-pin, three-row, female D-shell connector. Resolutions are up to 640×480. (Resolution is how many dots go across the screen and how many rows of dots there are. This is explained in greater technical detail later in the chapter.)
SVGA (Super VGA)	Not really a standard, but some monitor manufacturers advertise that they provide higher resolution than VGA. VESA (Video Electronics Standards Association) came up with a standard for this that covers resolutions up to 1280×1024.
UVGA (Ultra VGA)	Not really a standard, but usually refers to the 1024×768 resolution.
XGA (eXtended Graphics Array)	Developed by IBM to describe resolutions of 1024×768 and up to 64K of colors.
SXGA (Super XGA)	Describes resolutions up to 1280×1024 and over 16 million colors.
SXGA+	An improvement over SXGA to support resolutions up to 1400×1050.
UXGA (Ultra XGA)	Describes resolutions up to 1600×1200 and over 16 million colors. Sometimes used on powerful laptops and using applications that more of the screen needs to be seen (such as with a spreadsheet).
WXGA (Wide XGA)	Describes resolutions up to 1366×768 and over 16 million colors. There are variations called WSXGA or WUXGA. This is for those who like viewing wide screen DVDs on a computer monitor.
WUXGA (Wide UXGA)	Describes resolutions up to 1920×1200.
QXGA (quad XGA)	Describes resolutions up to 2048×1536.
QSXGA	Describes resolutions up to 2560×2048.
WQSXGA	Describes resolutions up to 3200×2048.
WQUXGA (wide quad ultra XGA)	Describes resolutions up to 3840×2400.
HXGA (hex XGA)	Describes resolutions up to 4096×3072.
HUXGA (hex ultra XGA)	Describes resolutions up to 6400×4800.
WHUXGA (wide hex ultra XGA)	Describes resolutions up to 7680×4800.

*Note that resolutions are always improving over time.

Table 9.3	Video features
Feature	**Explanation**
Refresh rate	In CRTs, the maximum times a screen is scanned or redrawn in one second. Measured in Hertz (Hz). An electron beam continuously sweeps left to right, scanning every row of pixels.
Horizontal scanning frequency	The speed that the beam traverses the screen to refresh the pixels. The rate for one line to be drawn. Determined by the video adapter and ranges from 35 to 90kHz.
Vertical scan rate	The number of times the electron beam draws from the top-left corner to the bottom-right corner and back again to the top left. A slow rate can cause a monitor to appear to flicker.
Multi-scan monitor	A monitor that can lock onto different vertical and horizontal scanning frequencies. Also called multi-synch or multiple-frequency.
Interlacing	A monitor that scans only the odd-numbered pixel rows. Then the electron beam returns and scans the even-numbered pixel rows. Causes a flickering on the screen.
Degauss	In CRT monitors, removal of a magnetic field that can build up around the monitor, causing distortion on the display. The method used to degauss depends on the manufacturer, but common methods include (1) power cycling the monitor; (2) using a degauss button located on the front of the monitor; and (3) accessing the monitor menu, using a front panel button, and locating the degauss option (which may be an omega symbol [Ω]).

To set the resolution in Vista/7, access the *Personalization* control panel and click the *Display settings* link. Use the *Resolution* and the *Colors* options to customize the display. To adjust the refresh rate, click the *Advanced Settings* button in this window. Select the *Monitor* tab and use the *Screen refresh rate* drop-down menu to customize.

Monitors frequently have a button that allows a menu to be accessed or have several buttons used to adjust the image quality. Common buttons include the following:

- Power—Powers the monitor on or off
- Input—Available when both analog and digital (VGA and DVI) input connectors are on the monitor and used to select between the two
- Auto adjust—Automatically refines the monitor settings, based on the incoming video signal
- Brightness—Controls the intensity of the image or the luminance of the backlight on an LCD
- Contrast—Adjusts the degree of difference between light and dark
- Position—Moves or adjusts the viewing area by using horizontal and vertical controls
- Reset—Resets the monitor to default settings

Tech Tip

The higher the resolution, the smaller the pixel appears on the screen

Selecting a higher resolution will make the icons in Windows appear smaller. Many users do not know or understand this concept and set their resolution too high relative to their monitor size.

Tech Tip

Use a 75Hz or greater refresh rate

An improperly configured refresh rate can cause monitor flicker, which can lead to headaches or eye strain. Usually, a 75Hz or greater refresh rate produces less flicker.

9 Other Peripherals

LCD (Liquid Crystal Display)

LCD is a video technology used with laptops and flat screen monitors that are powered by a low-voltage DC power source. They are more reliable and have a longer life span than CRT monitors. There are two basic types of LCD: passive matrix and active matrix. The difference between the two lies in how the screen image is created. A video on the LCD creation process can be found at http://www.auo.com/auoDEV/content/technology/technology_tftprocess_popup_en.htm.

The cheaper of the two, passive matrix, is made up of rows and columns of conductors. Each pixel is located at the intersection of a row and a column. (This is a similar concept to a cell in a spreadsheet.) Current on the grid determines whether a pixel is turned on or off. Each pixel has three cells in a color monitor: one for red, one for green, and one for blue. Another name for passive matrix is STN (SuperTwist Nematic), which is a technology that twists light rays to improve the display's contrast. Passive matrix displays are not as bright as active matrix displays.

Active matrix displays have a transistor for each pixel. The number of transistors depends on the maximum resolution. A 1280×800 resolution requires 1,024,000 transistors (1280 times 800 and more are added for color). This technology provides a brighter display (more luminance). Active matrix monitors take more power than passive matrix, but both of them require less power than CRT-based displays. Another name for active matrix monitors is TFT (Thin Film Transistor). TFT displays use three transistors per pixel (one for each color). Table 9.4 lists some common LCD terms and explanations.

Table 9.4	LCD characteristics
LCD characteristic	**Explanation**
Viewable size	The diagonal length of the LCD screen surface. Sometimes called VIS (Viewable Image Size).
Native resolution	The optimum setting for an LCD, shown as the number of pixels that go across the screen followed by the number of pixels that go down the screen. Examples include 1024×768 and 1280×800.
Response time or synchronization rate	The time it takes to draw one screen (lower is faster and better).
Pixel response rate	How fast a pixel can change colors in milliseconds (lower number is faster).
Viewing angle	At certain angles, the LCD becomes hard to read. The viewing angle is the maximum angle that you can view the LCD and still see the image properly. Some displays have different viewing angles for horizontal and vertical perspectives.
Aspect ratio	A ratio of monitor width to height. Common monitor aspect ratios are 4:3 or 5:4, but new widescreen formats such as 16:9 or 16:10 are available.
Contrast ratio	The difference in light intensity between the brightest white and darkest black, but measured in different ways by manufacturers. A higher contrast ratio such as 800:1 is better than 500:1.
Portrait/landscape mode	Some monitors can be physically turned so that the edge of the monitor that is on the left is turned to be the top or bottom of the monitor.
Luminance or brightness	How much light the monitor can produce expressed in cd/m² (candelas per square meter) or nits. An example of a computer display is 50 to 500 nits (200 to 250 is acceptable for most users, but 500 is better if video clips or movies are used).
Dead pixel	The number of pixels that do not light up on an LCD due to defective transistors. LCD panels with dead pixels can still be used and are common. Dead pixels can be (and usually are) present on LCDs—even new ones. Research the LCD manufacturing standard from a particular vendor for dead pixels before purchasing an LCD.

LCDs do not have multiple frequency settings like CRTs do, nor do they flicker (no beam tracing across and down the screen). The number of pixels on a screen is a fixed amount. Manufacturers use image scalers to change LCD resolution. Pixelation is the effect caused by sending a different resolution out to the LCD than the monitor was designed for. The LCD

Set the LCD resolution to the native resolution

You can change the resolution for an LCD monitor through the *Display* (XP) or *Personalization* (Vista/7) control panel, but it is best if left to the resolution for which it was designed. Otherwise, the output will not be as sharp as it can be.

monitor must rely on interpolation or scaling of the output rather than having things displayed in the LCD native resolution (the optimum choice).

LCDs are found in the desktop and laptop computer markets. The desktop monitors that use this technology are called flat panel displays. With flat panel displays, the viewing area is the same as the LCD measurements (so no trick advertisements). Popular sizes include 14-, 15-, 17-, 18-, and 21-inch.

Laptops use LCDs and have a video cable that connects the LCD to the motherboard. A backlight bulb is used on many models so images on the screen can be seen. The bulb connects to an inverter. The inverter converts low DC voltage to high AC voltage for the backlight bulb. Figure 9.6 demonstrates this concept.

Liquid crystals are poisonous

Be careful with cracked LCDs. If liquid crystals (which are not liquid) get on you, wash with soap and water and seek medical attention.

Is it worth fixing a laptop display?

Most laptop LCDs are expensive to repair, but if it is the inverter that is faulty, it might be cheaper to repair than replace.

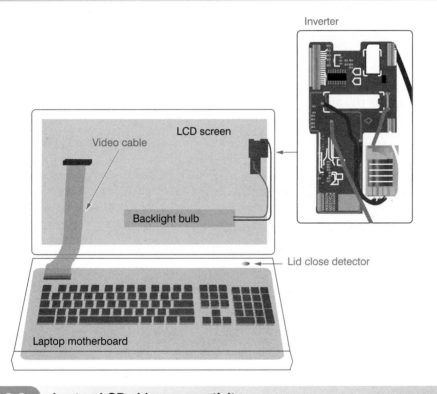

Figure 9.6   **Laptop LCD video connectivity**

The lid close detector can be a physical switch or magnetic switch located close to the back edge of the keyboard portion of a laptop. The laptop can be configured through power management configuration to go into hibernation or standby mode when the laptop is closed.

Video Ports

Flat panel monitors are digital, but some can work off an analog adapter (like the one most likely installed in your computer now). These digital monitors are more expensive, but offer better quality. The issue of colors with the old digital monitors is no longer relevant since the monitors use transistors to control colors. With the better flat panel monitors, you need an AGP or PCIe adapter that has a **DVI** (Digital Video/Visual Interface). Figure 9.7 shows an adapter with VGA, DVI, and TV out ports. The DVI port is a 24-pin connector.

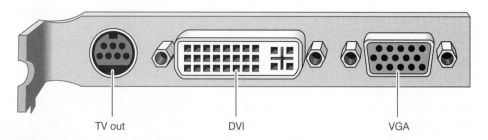

TV out   DVI   VGA

Figure 9.7   Video adapter with S-video (TV out), DVI, and VGA ports

Tech Tip

Use a digital adapter for a flat panel monitor

Using an analog adapter is not recommended for connecting a flat panel display unless the flat panel accepts analog input. The computer uses digital signals. The digital signals get converted to analog at the video adapter, it is sent to the monitor as analog, and then the monitor has to convert it back to digital for the display output.

There are several types of DVI connectors and the one used depends on the type of monitor being connected. Two terms used with the connectors are dual link and single link. A **single link** connection allows video resolutions up to 1920×1080. With a **dual link** connection, more pins are available to send more signals, thus allowing higher resolutions for a monitor designed for it. The two major types of DVI are DVI-D and DVI-I. **DVI-D** is used for digital connectivity only. **DVI-I** is used for both digital and analog monitors and is the most common. A less common type is DVI-A, which is used for only analog output. Figure 9.8 shows the different DVI pinouts.

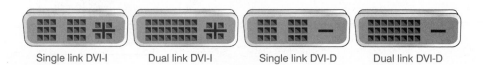

Single link DVI-I   Dual link DVI-I   Single link DVI-D   Dual link DVI-D

Figure 9.8   DVI connectors

Tech Tip

Video adapter DVI connection must match the monitor DVI connection type

Be careful when installing a video subsystem. Ensure that the video card installed matches the DVI connection type for the monitor. Converters can be purchased to adapt to VGA.

Tech Tip

Maximum DVI cable length is 5 meters

The specification for DVI states that the maximum cable length for DVI is 5 meters (approximately 16 feet) although there are longer ones available.

An upgrade to DVI is HDMI (High-Definition Multimedia Interface), which is a digital interface that can carry audio and video over the same cable. HDMI is already found on cable TV boxes and televisions, but is now appearing on video cards. Figure 9.9 shows a video adapter from XFX that has an S-video connector on the far left, an RCA jack, the HDMI connector, and a dual link DVI-I connector.

S-video

RCA

HDMI

DVI-I

Figure 9.9   **Video ports including an HDMI connector**

The S-video connector shown in Figure 9.9 is called HDTV by the vendor for a connection to a TV, possibly a high-definition TV. The RCA jack is used for RGB connections (analog three color—red, green, blue) such as to a scanner or camera. Another type of connection you may see on a video card that is not very common is **component/RGB video**—three RCA jacks labeled YPrPb (Y is for the luminescence or brightness, Pr and Pb are for the color difference signals). This type of connection is of higher quality than the single RGB connection and is more commonly found on TVs, DVD players, and projectors.

Converting DVI to HDMI

A DVI to HDMI cable can be used to connect a PC with a DVI port to a device such as a home theater system or flat screen TV that has an HDMI port.

To have two monitors connected to a single computer, you have several options.

- Use the two video ports on the motherboard (not common).
- Use the integrated motherboard port and buy a video card with one video port. (This is the cheapest solution, but the motherboard might disable the integrated video port automatically, and that setting has to be changed through BIOS.)
- Buy a video card that has two video ports (best option).
- Buy two video cards. (Usually the motherboard has one expansion slot for a video card, and that means using an older and slower technology expansion slot for the second video card.)

Once Windows recognizes the second monitor (two monitors appear in Device Manager), right-click the Windows desktop → *Properties* (XP)/*Personalize and Display settings* link (Vista)/ *Personalize, Display, Change display settings* (7) → *Settings* tab (XP). Two displays are shown, with the numbers 1 and 2. An exercise at the end of the chapter demonstrates this.

Another variation that some people or businesses want is the ability to use the same monitor (and sometimes mouse and keyboard) for two different computers. This is best done through

9

Other Peripherals

Dual monitor modes of operation

You can have the same information shown in both monitors, extend your desktop across two monitors, or use dual view, where you can choose what items are on each desktop.

a **KVM** (keyboard, video, mouse) **switch**, which allows at least one mouse, one keyboard, and one video output to be used by two or more computers. Many people would rather use software to do this function and remotely access the desktop of another computer. Windows calls this feature Remote Desktop.

A specialized use of video is with TV tuner cards and video capture cards. A **TV tuner card** allows TV signals to be brought into the computer and output to the monitor. Some TV tuner cards have the ability to record video. Figure 9.10 shows a photo of a TV tuner card.

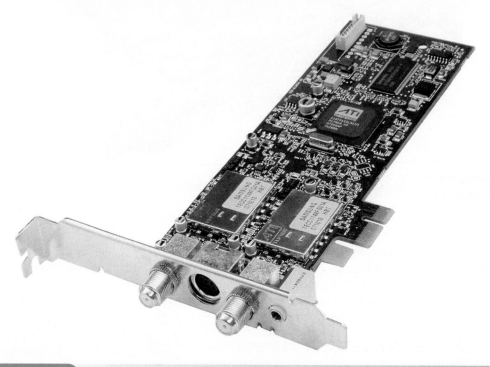

Figure 9.10   **TV tuner adapter**

A **video capture card** usually has specialized software that allows video to be captured from a camera, tape, DVD, recorder, or live audio and video and manipulated into a presentation, an archived file, or a saved document or streamed onto the Internet. Not all video capture cards support audio. Video surveillance systems sometimes use video capture cards.

Another specialized use of video is SLI (scalable link interface) from Nvidia. SLI links two or more PCIe video cards to share processing on graphics-intensive operations.

Projectors

Tech Tip

Monitors, cameras, TVs, and scanners are not the only peripherals that connect to computer video ports. Projectors are becoming a common device with which technicians must be familiar. A projector allows what is being displayed on the computer to be projected onto a larger screen.

Using an external monitor or projector with a laptop

For most laptops, you can hold down the Fn key and press a specific function key to (1) use only the LCD display; (2) use only the external monitor or projector that attaches to the external video port; or (3) use both the LCD and the external video device.

A projector has similar connections as those described for video cards. Cables that convert between the different formats are available. Figure 9.11 shows some of the connectors available on a projector including the previously discussed component video.

Notice in Figure 9.11 the three RCA jacks to the left of the VGA ports. These are used for RGB/component video. To connect a projector to a PC and a monitor you need a video distribution (sharing) device or two video

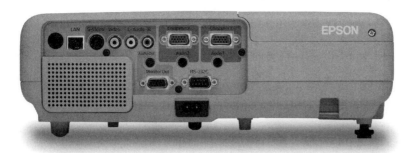

Figure 9.11 Video projector ports

ports with which many video adapters ship. A laptop frequently has a video port available for connecting an external monitor or a projector. Do not immediately unplug the power to a projector after a presentation so the projector can cool down.

The specific numbered function key depends on the laptop manufacturer. Most vendors put a small graphic that looks like a monitor on the function key or the words CRT/LCD. Table 9.5 shows some commonly used configurations. Figure 9.12 shows the common laptop keys used with the [Fn] key when connecting a laptop to a projector and using the external video port.

Table 9.5 Laptop external monitor/projector keystrokes

Vendor	Keystrokes used
Acer	[Fn] + [F5]
Compaq	[Fn] + [F4]
Dell	[Fn] + [F8]
HP	[Fn] + [F4] or [F5]
IBM	[Fn] + [F7]
Sony	[Fn] + [F7]
Toshiba	[Fn] + [F5]

Figure 9.12 Laptop external monitor keys

Monitor Preventive Maintenance

It is simple to perform preventive maintenance on a monitor. Static builds up on the face of the monitor and the screen attracts dust and dirt like a television. Antistatic cleaning wipes are available at computer and office supply stores. Some monitors also have a button on the front that, when pushed, removes static electricity from the front of the monitor.

A CRT monitor can also be cleaned with a soft dampened cloth and mild household detergent, glass cleaner, or isopropyl alcohol. Do not allow any liquid to get near the edge of the CRT. The liquid can seep inside the monitor case and cause damage. If using a CRT cleaning spray or glass cleaner, spray the cleaner on the cloth, not on the monitor. If the monitor has a non-glare screen or any type of special coating, see the manufacturer's instructions for cleaning it.

Unless specifically trained for monitor repair, never remove the monitor case

A CRT monitor holds 20,000 or more volts (depending on the monitor size and components). Voltage can still be present after turning off the power. Most technicians who work on monitors have special training in working on high-voltage equipment.

LCDs can be cleaned with wipes specifically designed for LCDs. Also, a soft cloth dampened with water or a mixture of isopropyl alcohol and water can be used to wipe an LCD. Never apply liquid directly to a monitor of any type. On a laptop, ensure that the display is dry before closing the laptop lid.

Monitor Energy Efficiency

A monitor's life span is normally 20,000 to 60,000 hours. The heat generated inside a monitor can reduce the life span of the monitor's components. Some monitors called green monitors have energy conservation capabilities. These monitors have software that reduces the power, leaving only enough to allow the monitor to be reactivated to a usable state quickly. The Environmental Protection Agency produced Energy Star guidelines (www.energystar.gov) to which many monitor manufacturers adhere. Many BIOS chips now support and have settings for energy-efficient monitors.

Microsoft and Intel developed the APM (Advanced Power Management) standard that allows the BIOS to control hardware power modes. With Windows 98 and higher, Microsoft presented **ACPI** (Advanced Configuration and Power Interface) that expanded the old APM standard to also control power modes for CD/DVD drives, network cards, printers, and other attached devices. Chapter 4 has more information on ACPI.

The following are some best practices for monitor energy efficiency:

- Turn off the monitor with the power switch when you are through for the day.
- Use Windows Power Options to enable Sleep mode for the monitor after a period of inactivity.
- On a laptop, adjust the contrast or brightness level to a lower one to prolong the life of the backlight.
- If buying a new laptop, consider one that uses an LED backlight instead of CCFL. In addition to the power savings, this technology can have better color accuracy.

To modify the power saving feature, use the *Display* (XP)/*Power Options* (Vista/7) control panel. In XP, click the *Screen Saver* tab and click the *Settings* button to display the *Power Management Properties* window. In Vista/7, select the *Change plan settings* link.

Energy efficiency monitor settings

Use energy efficiency BIOS settings, energy efficiency software, or Windows energy efficiency settings only if the monitor supports them. A non-green monitor can be damaged if you enable these settings. Check the monitor documentation to determine if it supports energy efficiency modes.

Screen Savers

In the past when monitors did not have fast refresh rates, screen savers were very important. A screen saver changes the image on the monitor constantly to keep any particular image from burning into the screen. With old monitors, if an image stayed on the screen for an extended period of time, an imprint of the image was left on the screen permanently. Today's monitors have high enough refresh rates so that screen savers are not necessary, but now they are an entertainment art form. LCDs use a different technology than CRTs and have never needed screen savers.

Screen savers can provide password protection that may be important to some users. With the password screen saver enabled, a user can leave his or her work area and no one can access the computer without the screen saver password.

In Windows XP, to enable the screen saver, use the *Display* control panel. In Vista/7, use the *Personalization* control panel along with the *Display settings* link. Click the *Screen Saver* tab and click the *Screen Saver* down arrow to display an options list. The *Blank Screen* option takes the least amount of memory and does not use CPU time. Another resource saver is to remove the display's wallpaper option (also found through the *Display* control panel).

Video Adapters

Using millions of colors, motion, sound, and video combined, the computer's video subsystem has made dramatic technological advances. The video adapter controls most of the monitor's output. Video adapters use the PCI, AGP, or PCIe interface. The bus connects the video card to the processor. The processor accepts data in 16-, 32-, or 64-bit chunks depending on the processor and the bus interface. One of the challenges of interfacing video is finding a good video adapter that uses a high-performance system architecture such as PCIe.

On the motherboard, the processor and the chipset are responsible for how quickly data travels to and from the video adapter. Such things as upgrading the chipset, the processor, or the video adapter to a faster interface speed up video transfer to the monitor. However, special features on the video adapter can also speed up video transfer.

Some video adapters have their own processor. The **video processor** (sometimes known as a video coprocessor or video accelerator) assists in video communication between the video adapter and the system processor. Figure 9.13 shows a video adapter with a video processor. The processor has a fan installed on top of it.

Figure 9.13   **Video processor**

Some video processors are 64- or 128-bit processors. Many users (and technicians) have a hard time understanding how a 128-bit video processor works in a 32-bit or 64-bit expansion slot. The 64 or 128 bits refers to the number of bits the video adapter's accelerator chip accepts at one time. The 64-bit (or higher) video processor controls many video functions on the video adapter otherwise handled by the microprocessor. Anytime information is processed on the adapter rather than the microprocessor, performance is faster. When signals pass to the microprocessor through an expansion slot, performance slows. Most video cards today contain a video processor because video is one of the biggest bottlenecks in a computer system.

Video Memory

One of the most important functions of the video processor is to transfer data to and from the video adapter's memory. Memory chips on the video adapter can be regular DRAM chips (including DDR2 and DDR3). Table 9.6 lists some video memory technologies.

Table 9.6	Video memory types
Memory type	**Description**
VRAM (video RAM)	A type of dual-ported memory, which means that it has separate read and write data paths and can be written to and read from simultaneously. This is in contrast to DRAM, which is single-ported memory (that can have a single data path in and out of the chip).
RDRAM (Rambus DRAM)	Proprietary technology developed by Rambus. A type of single-ported memory that is sometimes called Direct Rambus DRAM.
SGRAM (synchronous graphics RAM)	A form of SDRAM for graphics cards. Allows the video data to clock up to four times quicker than traditional DRAM technologies. It is single-ported memory.
GDDR3 SDRAM (graphics double data rate SDRAM)	Designed by ATI Technologies and is similar to DDR2. Has data rates up to 2Gbps.
GDDR4 SDRAM	A power-efficient video memory with speeds as high as 3.2GHz.
GDDR5	A type of SGRAM that has two parallel sets of data lines with data rates up to 4Gbps or higher.
XDR2 DRAM (extreme data rate 2 DRAM)	Designed by Rambus and based on RDRAM technologies and used in video cards and networking equipment.

The objective is to get data in and out of the video card memory chips as fast as possible for a reasonable cost. The adapter must handle a large amount of data due to the increasing number of pixels and colors displayed. Ample, fast memory on the video card allows higher resolutions and more colors to appear on the screen without the screen appearing to flicker. **Dual-ported memory** allows for faster data flow in and out of the memory chips.

All parts of the video subsystem must work together to get a clear picture on the screen. A very expensive video adapter with 16 trillion megabytes of memory connected to a monitor with a poor dot pitch will display a distorted picture on the screen. An expensive monitor connected to a PCI video adapter with only 256KB of memory will not provide the fastest refresh rates. The monitor appears to flicker as a result. The video adapter needs to be an AGP or PCIe card. Furthermore, the adapter needs to contain enough memory to sustain the number of colors at the specific resolution at which the user must work. A technician cannot perform magic on poorly matched video components. The only solution is to upgrade the weak link.

Memory on the video card stores screen information as a snapshot of what appears on the screen. Common memory chip capacities include 128MB, 256MB, 512MB, 768MB, 1GB, and 2GB. The video adapter manufacturer determines the maximum amount of video memory. Some manufacturers make video adapters that are not upgradable. Check the adapter's documentation before making a purchase or recommendation. The ability to upgrade video card memory is important to computer users.

To determine the amount of video memory an adapter needs, multiply the total number of pixels (the resolution) by the number of bits needed to produce a specific number of colors. Different combinations of 16 1s and 0s create 65,536 (64K) possible combinations as $2^{16} = 65,536$. For example, take a system that needs 65,536 colors at the resolution of 1024×768. To determine the minimum video memory necessary, multiply 16 (number of bits needed for 64K of colors) times 1024 times 768 (the resolution). The result, 12,582,912, is the number of bits needed to handle the combination of 65K colors at 1024×768. Divide the bits by 8 for the number of *bytes* needed. This is the minimum amount of memory needed on the video card: 12,582,912 divided by 8 = 1,572,864 or 1.5MB. The user needs more video memory if more colors, a higher resolution, or video motion is desired.

What if a user wants 256K colors at an 800×600 resolution? What is the minimum amount of video memory needed for the system? Different combinations of 18 1s and 0s produce 256K colors (2^{18} = 262,144). Eighteen times 800 times 600 equals 8,640,000 bits. 8,640,000 divided by 8 equals 1,080,000 bytes. The user would need at least 1MB of video RAM. Table 9.7 lists the number of bits required for different color options.

Tech Tip

How much video memory?

The amount of video adapter memory will determine the number of colors available at a specific resolution.

Table 9.7	Bits required for colors
Number of bits	**Number of colors**
4	16
8	256
16	65,536 (65K)
24	16,777, 216 (16M)

There are also video cards that offer 32-bit color. The extra bits are used for color control and special effects such as animation and game effects. If determining the amount of video memory seems confusing, an exercise at the end of the chapter provides practice for configuring different scenarios. Table 9.8 contains a chart that helps with the minimum amount of video memory needed for specific configurations.

If 2-D or 3-D graphics are being used, the calculations shown in Table 9.8 can be used, but more memory is needed. For 2-D graphics, multiply the answer by 16 more bits. For 3-D graphics, multiply the final number by 48 bits. (One byte is used to process the front dimension, one byte to process the back dimension, and one byte for the third dimension.) Then divide by 8 to find out how many bytes.

Video RAM is RAM that is used for video exclusively. When this RAM is not enough, motherboard RAM is used. When motherboard RAM is being used in addition to video card RAM, the amount of motherboard RAM being used is known as **shared system memory** or shared video memory. This is seen when you examine the video display properties. Some systems allow customization through system BIOS or a special control panel provided by the video adapter manufacturer. Common system BIOS options to control shared system memory include AGP Aperture Size and Onboard Video Memory Size.

Table 9.8	Minimum video memory requirement examples	
Amount of memory	**Color depth**	**Resolution**
1MB	16-bit (65,536 colors)	640×480
2MB	24-bit (16 million colors)	800×600
2MB	16-bit (65,536 colors)	1024×768
4MB	24-bit (16 million colors)	1024×768
6MB	32-bit (true color)	1400×1050
6MB	24-bit (16 million colors)	1600×1200
8MB	32-bit (true color)	1600×1200

9

Other Peripherals

Checking how much video memory you have

Use the Windows XP *Display* control panel → *Properties* → *Settings* tab → *Advanced* button → *Adapter* tab. For Vista/7, use the *Personalization* control panel → *Display settings* link → *Advanced* button → *Adapter* tab. Total available RAM is the RAM on the motherboard plus the video RAM. Dedicated video memory is RAM on the video card. Shared system memory is how much motherboard RAM is being used.

Installing a Video Adapter

Installing a new video adapter

When you install a new video adapter, if it does not work, disable the onboard video port by accessing system BIOS setup.

The first step in installing a video adapter is to do your homework: (1) Make sure that you have the correct interface type and an available motherboard slot. PCI and AGP are the most common, but keep in mind that monitors can attach to a USB or IEEE 1394 (FireWire) port. (2) Gather tools, if needed. The most common tool needed is a screwdriver to remove the slot-retaining bracket and to re-insert the screw that holds the adapter. (3) Download the latest drivers for the video adapter including any video BIOS updates. (4) Make sure the adapter has a driver for the operating system you are using.

Before installing the adapter, power the computer off and unplug it. For best results and to prevent component damage, use an antistatic wrist strap. Access the motherboard by removing a side panel or removing the computer's cover. Remove any previously installed video adapters (if performing an upgrade) by removing the screw. Use both hands and lift the board upward; you may need to rock the board slightly from side to side to remove it. If no video adapters are installed, remove the slot-retaining screw and remove the expansion slot cover. Place the retaining screw to the side.

Sometimes with tower computers, it is best to lay the computer on its side to insert the video adapter properly. Line the video adapter's metal connectors up with the interface slot. Push the adapter into the expansion slot. Make sure the adapter is flush with the expansion slot. Figure 9.14 shows a video adapter being installed in a tower. Notice how the technician is observing proper ESD procedures.

Make sure sections of the adapter's gold connectors are not showing because the card is skewed. Re-install the retaining screw, if necessary. Connect the monitor to the external video connector. Power on the monitor and computer.

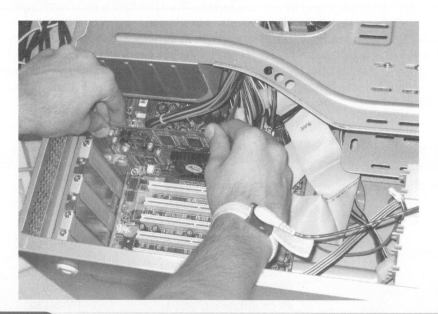

Figure 9.14   **Video adapter installation**

A video adapter usually has a set of drivers or software to enable the adapter to work to its full potential. Individual software drivers from the manufacturer provide system compatibility and performance boosts. The Internet provides a wonderful way for technicians to obtain current video drivers from adapter manufacturers. Be sure to use the proper video driver for the operating system. Always follow the adapter manufacturer's instructions for installing their drivers. The next paragraph lists generic steps.

On Windows the system usually prompts with the *Found New Hardware* dialog box. Click the *Next* button. Continue through the next two screens until the point where you can select where the driver is located. This is so you can install the drivers downloaded from the Internet. Use the *Browse* button to select the driver location and follow the prompts on the screen until finished.

Troubleshooting Video

When troubleshooting a video problem, check simple solutions first. Do not assume anything! Verify that the monitor's power light is on. If not, check the power cable connectors and the wall outlet. Verify that the brightness and contrast settings have not been changed. Double-check the monitor cable connected to the video port. Ask the user if any new software or hardware has been recently installed or upgraded.

In the video subsystem, if a piece of hardware is defective, then it is the monitor, adapter, or cable. If replacement is necessary, always do the easiest solution first. Replace the monitor with one that is working. If monitor replacement is not practical, then check for a conflict with non-energy-efficient monitors. Disconnect the monitor from the adapter, then power on the monitor and turn the brightness control to its highest position. Is there a raster? A **raster** is the monitor's brightness pattern—a bright white screen. If the raster appears, the problem is likely the video adapter. When disconnecting energy-efficient monitors from the video adapter, the monitors go into their low power mode. This check does not work on monitors in the low power mode.

Most video problems are *not* hardware related; most are software related. There are many symptoms of a software driver problem. Anything wrong on the display can be a result of a bad driver, an incompatible driver, or an incorrect driver. The best way to be sure is to download the exact driver for the monitor or the display adapter from the Internet, or obtain it from the manufacturer and load it. Some troubleshooting tips relating to video follow. Remember, these are only suggestions. Research and contact, if necessary, the monitor manufacturer or video adapter manufacturer for specific instructions on troubleshooting their equipment.

- If the monitor screen is completely black, check the monitor power light. If it is off, check the power connection at the monitor, wall outlet, and surge protector. Try a different outlet or surge protector. Verify that the wall outlet has power. If the monitor power light is on, check the brightness and contrast settings. Try disconnecting the monitor from the adapter to determine if there is a raster. If a blank screen saver is enabled, press a key or move the mouse. If pranksters are around, look for black letters on a black background setting. Boot to Safe Mode and change the settings.
- Carefully examine the monitor's cable ends. The pins can easily bend and not fit properly into the connector, yet the cable appears to plug correctly into the connector. If you find one or more bent pins, carefully use needlenose pliers to gently straighten the pins.
- If the CRT goes bad, it is probably more cost effective to replace the entire monitor. One monitor component that frequently goes bad is the **flyback transformer** that boosts the voltage to the high levels the CRT requires. The cost of flyback transformers varies from model to model. Get a price quote before replacing.

Laptop LCD troubleshooting

To troubleshoot a laptop LCD, connect an external monitor to the video port. Use the Fn and appropriate keystroke to enable the external monitor port. If the external monitor works, the video circuits are fine.

Tech Tip

9 Other Peripherals

- If you suspect a video driver problem, change the video driver to a standard (generic) driver to see if the problem is resolved and to prove that it is a software driver problem. If the screen appears distorted around the edges of the monitor or the color appears distorted, check for any other equipment such as other monitors, speakers, magnets, and fluorescent lighting that might cause interference with the monitor. Move the monitor from its current location to see if the situation improves or move the computer to another location to see if the problem goes away.

- Another possible problem with color distortion is CRT magnetization from an outside source. Degaussing circuits neutralize a magnetic field. Some monitors have degaussing controls built into them, so try letting the monitor's internal degaussing circuits fix the problem. Turn on the monitor and computer for one minute. Then, turn off the monitor. Leave the monitor off for 30 minutes. Then, turn the monitor on again for one minute followed by turning it off and leaving it off for 30 minutes. Continue to do this for several cycles. Do not use a degausser on an LCD monitor. On LCD monitors, use the vendor-provided software to make adjustments for distortion.

- If the screen has intermittent problems, check the video adapter documentation to see how to lower the refresh rate. The monitor and the adapter's refresh rates must match. Check the monitor's documentation for its refresh settings. Set a laptop to the native resolution (the resolution for which the LCD was made).

- If a cursor appears momentarily before the computer boots then nothing is displayed or a distorted display appears, check for a video driver problem.

What to do if a laptop LCD goes black, red, dim, or pink

Most likely this is because the backlight bulb is faulty. Otherwise, it is the inverter. Connect an external monitor to the laptop external video port. If the external monitor works, most likely the backlight bulb is the culprit.

- A laptop may start normally, but its screen may not display the Windows startup screen. Sometimes a faint image seems to be evident. The inverter most likely needs to be replaced. This is the most commonly replaced component in an LCD.

- If a laptop sometimes flickers or the display appears and then disappears if you move the laptop lid, this is usually a result of a bad or poorly connected video cable. Horizontal or vertical stripes on the screen are also signs of this problem.

- If you change the resolution or number of colors and the output is distorted, change the settings back to the original settings if possible, reboot to Safe Mode, or use the Last Known Good Configuration boot option, and reduce the resolution or number of colors.

Laptop LCD is black and there is no power indication

Check the laptop LCD close switch that is located in the main part of the laptop close to the back nearby to where the LCD attaches to the laptop. Check power management settings in that they can be configured to go into hibernate or standby if the laptop is closed. Also check the video cable from the motherboard to the display.

- Monitor flickering is normally caused by an incorrect refresh rate setting. It can also be caused by proximity to other video devices, speakers, refrigerators, and fluorescent lighting. Move the monitor or offending device. Buying a monitor with better shielding is also an option.

Monitor disposal rules

Note that if a monitor is replaced, the state may have specific disposal procedures that must be followed.

- Windows is not supposed to hang during the boot process because of video driver incompatibility. Instead, the operating system loads a default video driver. If video is a problem while working in Windows, boot to Safe Mode or use the Last Known Good Configuration boot option and then load the correct driver. You could also use the driver rollback option if a new driver has just been installed.
- Always check the monitor settings to verify that the monitor detection is accurate. In Windows XP, use the *Display* control panel's *Settings* tab. In Vista/7, use the *Personalization* control panel with the *Display settings* link. Then access the *Settings* tab.
- To check for resource conflicts, use the Device Manager.
- If nothing outputs once you have installed an adapter, check the following: card inserted fully into the slot, connectors not properly attached, adapter not supported by the motherboard, adapter does not have auxiliary power attached, insufficient power from the power supply, and improper driver installed.
- Any monitor that won't come out of power saver mode might need one of the following steps: (1) update the video driver, (2) flash the system BIOS, (3) check the BIOS power settings to ensure ACPI is enabled so Windows settings can be used, or (4) determine whether the problem is being caused by the monitor or the port. Connect a different monitor. If the video port is built into the motherboard, disable it through BIOS and insert a video card; otherwise, replace the video adapter to see if the port/adapter is causing the problem. Most likely it is a driver/Windows/BIOS ACPI setting problem.
- If video performance appears to be slow, adjust the monitor to a lower resolution or a lower number of colors (or both). See the exercise at the end of this chapter for step-by-step instructions. Check the video adapter driver to determine if it matches the installed adapter or if it is generic. Obtain the specific adapter's latest driver from the Internet.

Printers Overview

Printers are a difficult subject to cover because many different models exist (of course, that can be said about any peripheral); but the principles are the same for different categories of printers. The best way to begin is to look at what printers have in common. All printers have three subsystems: (1) the **paper transport** subsystem; (2) the **marking** subsystem; and (3) the **print engine** subsystem. Table 9.9 explains each of these subsystems.

Table 9.9	Printer subsystems
Subsystem	**Explanation**
Paper transport	Subsystem that pulls, pushes, or rolls paper through the printer. This can be done using a belt, tractor fee, or rollers. Some printers can even have a duplexer, which is an attachment option that allows printing on both sides of the paper.
Marking	Parts responsible for placing the image on the paper (also called the marking engine). This includes ribbons, ink (print) cartridges, toner cartridges, any moving part that is inside one of these, and anything else needed to print the image.
Print engine	The brains of the operation. It accepts data and commands from the computer and translates these commands into motion. It also redirects feedback to the computer.

Keep the three printer subsystems in mind when setting up a printer and troubleshooting it. Knowing how a specific type of printer places an image on the paper also helps when troubleshooting the printer.

9

Other Peripherals

Printer Ports

Printers connect to the parallel (IEEE 1284), serial, infrared, IEEE 1394 (FireWire), or USB ports. They can also connect through a wireless network. Most printers attach to a PC using the USB port. With USB printers, the USB host controller (built into the motherboard or on an adapter) powers up and queries all USB devices as to what type of data transfer they want to perform. Printers use bulk transfer on the USB, which means that data is sent in 64-byte sections. The USB host controller also assigns each USB a device so that the host controller can track them. Even though USB can provide power to smaller devices, a USB printer normally has its own power source.

USB is a good solution for printers because it is fast, and there are usually several ports available, or a hub can be added to provide more ports. USB uses only one interrupt for the devices connected to the bus.

Networked Printers

Many home users and almost all businesses use networked printers (printers that can be used by more than one computer). Printers can be networked using the following methods:

- A printer that is connected to a computer can be shared or made available to other computers through the Windows operating system. The other computers must be networked in some way.
- A printer can have a network card integrated into it or installed that allows it to participate as a network device. This includes wireless networks.
- A printer can attach to a device called an external **print server** (similar to attaching a printer to a computer) and the print server attaches to the network.

A networked printer can reduce costs. Laser printers can be expensive—especially ones that produce high speed, high volume, high quality, color output. Buying one printer and allowing users to access it from their individual desktops can be cost effective. It also reduces the amount of office or home space needed. Network printing is a viable alternative to using a computer's parallel or USB port.

Print servers are becoming quite common, even in homes. A print server connects to the network and allows any computer that is also connected to a network to print to it if the networks are the same or connected to one another. There are some print servers available that handle both wired and wireless connections. The print server attaches to a network switch and a network wireless router or wireless access point attaches to the same switch. Any PCs (wired or wireless) can print to the printer that attaches to the print server. Figure 9.15 illustrates this concept.

Wireless Printers

A PC can connect wirelessly to a printer using different methods: (1) the print server to which the printer connects can have wireless capabilities and wireless PCs can connect to the printer through the print server (as previously described and illustrated); (2) the printer can have a wireless NIC (network interface card) installed, attached via a USB port, or integrated and other devices on the wireless network can print to the printer; (3) the printer can have integrated Bluetooth capabilities or a Bluetooth adapter attached via a USB port. Printers with wireless capabilities are common, but the wireless adapter may have to be purchased separately. Refer to the Networking and Security chapters for more information on wireless networking theory and issues related to installing wireless devices.

Categories of Printers

Printers can be categorized according to how they put an image on paper. Printer categories are dot matrix, ink jet, and laser. There are more types, but these make up the majority of printers used in the workplace and home. Computer users normally choose a printer based on the type of printing they require. Table 9.10 describes the three major printer categories.

Each of the three basic printer types is discussed in greater detail in the next sections. The theory of operation for each printer type mainly concerns the marking subsystem.

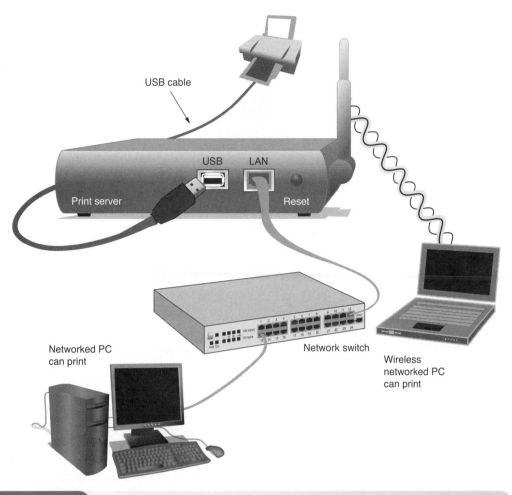

Figure 9.15   **Wireless and wired print server connectivity**

Table 9.10   **Printer categories**

Type of printer	Description
Dot matrix	Good for text printing with multiple copies and can produce limited graphics. Uses ribbons, which keeps costs down. The only printer that can do multiple-part forms and supports the 132-column-wide paper needed by some industries.
Ink jet	Much quieter, weighs less, and produces higher-quality graphics than dot matrix. Uses a **print cartridge**, sometimes called an ink cartridge, that holds the ink used to produce the text and graphics; these cost $10 to $60 and last 100 to 200 pages, depending on manufacturer and print quality settings. Color can be done by dot matrix, but ink jet is best for color printing.
Laser	Produces the highest quality output at the fastest rate. Cartridges can cost $20 to $350. Common in the corporate network environment where users share peripherals. Used for graphic design and computer-generated art where high quality printing is a necessity. Some can produce color output, but at a much higher cost. Some even have stapling capabilities like copy machines.

Dot Matrix Printers

Dot matrix printers are called impact printers because of the way they create an image on the paper. They have a **printhead** that holds tiny wires called **printwires**. Figure 9.16 shows an Oki Data Americas, Inc. printhead. The printwires are shown on the front of the printhead. The printwires can get out of alignment and produce misformed characters.

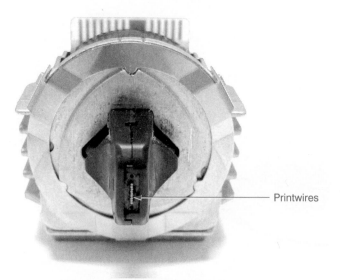

Printwires

Figure 9.16   **Dot matrix printhead**

The wires individually strike a ribbon hard enough to create a dot on the paper. The dots collectively form letters or images. The speed that the printhead can place characters on the page is its **cps** (characters per second) rating. The number of printwires in the printhead determines the quality of print; the more printwires, the better the print quality. The most common printwires are 9, 18, and 24. The 24-pin printers can print NLQ (near letter quality) output.

Each printwire connects to a solenoid coil. When current flows to the printwire, a magnetic field causes the wire to move away from the printhead and out a tiny hole. The print wire impacts a ribbon to create a dot on the paper. Figure 9.17 shows a dot matrix printhead. To show the individual printwires, the casing that covers the printwires has been removed from the illustration.

Each wire connects to a spring that pulls the printwire back inside the printhead. The images created are nothing more than a series of dots on the page. Dot matrix printers are impact printers because the printwire springs out of the printhead. The act of the printwire coming out of the printhead is called pin firing. The impact of the printer physically striking the ribbon, which in turn touches the paper, causes dot matrix printers to be noisy.

Because the printwire impacts the ribbon, one of the most common points of failure with dot matrix printers is the printhead. It can be expensive to replace printheads frequently in a high-usage situation; however, refurbished printheads work fine and they are available at a reduced price. The companies who refurbish them usually replace the faulty wires and test the printhead thoroughly.

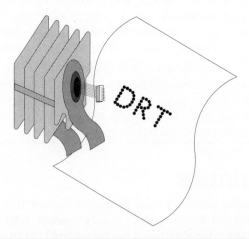

Figure 9.17   **Dot matrix printhead operations**

Dot matrix printers are the workhorses of printers. One advantage to a dot matrix printer is that it will print multiple-part forms such as invoices, purchase orders, shipping documents, and wide forms. Multiple-part forms print easily on a dot matrix printer because the printer impacts the paper so very hard. The maximum number of multiple copies each dot matrix printer handles depends on the printer model. Laser and ink jet printers cannot produce multiple-part forms. They can only make multiple copies of the same document.

Tech Tip

One direction is not a problem

Most dot matrix printers print bidirectionally. When the printhead gets too hot, the printer prints only in the left-to-right direction. This is normal.

Do not stack things on top of any printer, especially a dot matrix printer. The printhead gets hot and you should not add to the heat by stacking things on top of the printer. Keep the printer in a cool environment to avoid overheating. If the printer is used continuously, thus keeping the printhead hot, consider purchasing a second printer to handle the workload.

Ink Jet Printers

Ink jet printers are much quieter than dot matrix printers. They also have a printhead, but the ink jet's printhead does not have metal pins that fire out from the printhead. Instead, the ink jet's printhead has many tiny nozzles that squirt ink onto the paper. Each nozzle is smaller than a strand of human hair. Figure 9.18 shows a photo of a Hewlett Packard print cartridge.

Figure 9.18 **Hewlett-Packard ink cartridge**

One great thing about ink jet printers is that the printhead includes the nozzles and the reservoir for ink. When the ink runs out, you replace the entire printhead. The ink jet printer's printhead is known as the print cartridge. An ink cartridge has up to 6,000 nozzles instead of the 9-, 18-, or 24-metal pin configuration the dot matrix has. This is one reason why the ink jet quality is preferable to a dot matrix printer. Furthermore, with some manufacturers, the print cartridge is the printer printhead. Replacing the printhead, one of the most frequently used parts, keeps repair costs low but consumable costs are high. Two alternatives are for the manufacturers to use (1) a combination of a disposable printhead that is replaced as needed and a disposable ink tank, or (2) a replaceable printhead similar to the dot matrix printer. Figure 9.19 shows an expanded view of the front of the ink cartridge.

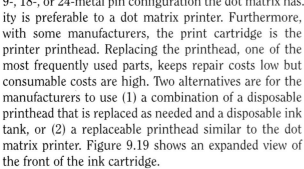

Tech Tip

Run the calibration test when you install a new ink cartridge or as needed

Many ink jet printers have a calibration routine that automatically executes when a new cartridge is installed. Other manufacturers provide it as an option through the printer software or through the printer *Properties* window. If you find that the print output is not as clean and sharp as it should be, use this routine to adjust the print cartridge output.

Ink jet printers, also called bubble jet or thermal printers, use thermal (heat) technology to place the ink onto the paper. Each print nozzle attaches to a small ink chamber that attaches to a larger ink reservoir. A small amount of ink inside the chamber heats to a boiling temperature. Once the ink boils, a vapor bubble forms. As the bubble gets hotter, it expands and goes out through the print cartridge's nozzle onto the paper. The size of the ink droplet is approximately two ten-thousandths (.0002) of an inch, smaller than a human hair. As the small ink chamber cools down, suction occurs. The suction pulls more ink into the ink chamber for the production of the next ink droplet.

9

Other Peripherals

Figure 9.19   Ink jet cartridge nozzles

Tech Tip

Be aware of optimized dpi

Many ink jet printers now show their dpi as optimized dpi. Optimized dpi is not describing how many drops of liquid are in an inch, but in a specific grid.

An alternative for producing the ink dots is to use piezo-electric technology, which uses pressure, not heat, to eject the ink onto the paper. Some companies use this technology to obtain 5760×1440 dpi and higher resolutions. **DPI** is the number of dots per inch a printer outputs. The higher the dpi, the better the quality of ink jet or laser printer output.

Most ink jet printers have different modes of printing. The draft mode uses the least amount of ink and the NLQ (near letter quality) mode uses the most ink. The quality produced by the ink jet printer is close to a laser printer, but in most high-end ink jet printers, the output is actually a higher dpi.

Color ink jet printers usually have a black cartridge for normal printing and a separate color cartridge for the colored ink or separate cartridges for each color. Buying an ink jet printer that uses a single cartridge for colors is cheaper on the initial printer purchase but more expensive in the long run. The black ink usually runs out much quicker than the colored ink. Users should buy an ink jet model with separate cartridges for black ink and colored ink.

There are some variations on the ink jet technology. Table 9.11 outlines three of them.

Table 9.11   Other printer technologies

Type of printer	Description
Solid ink	Sometimes called phase change or hot melt printers; uses colored wax sticks to create vivid color output. The wax stick is melted and sprayed through tiny nozzles onto the paper. The wax is smoothed and pressed as the paper is sent through rollers. The sticks can be installed one at a time as needed. The wax does not melt or bleed onto hands, clothing, or internal printer parts. It can print more colors, is faster, has fewer mechanical parts, and is cheaper than color laser printers, but is more expensive than normal ink jet printers.
Dye sublimation	Also known as dye diffusion thermal transfer printers; uses four film ribbons that contain color dyes. The ribbons are heated and applied to the paper. The quality is high, but the printers are expensive.
Thermal wax transfer	Uses wax-based inks like the solid ink printer, but prints in lower resolutions.
Large format ink jet	A wide printer to print large-scale media such as CAD drawings, posters, and artwork.

Inkjet printers are perfect for small businesses, home computer users, and individual computer office work. Some models of ink jet printers include faxing, scanning, copying, and printing capabilities. For higher output, the laser printer is more appropriate. A drawback to using ink is that sometimes the ink smears. Ink manufacturers vary greatly in how they respond to this problem. If the paper gets wet, some ink jet output becomes messy. The ink also smears if you touch the printed page before the ink dries. The ink can also soak into the paper and bleed down the paper. Using good quality paper and ink in the ink cartridge helps with this particular problem. Some manufacturers have a printer operation mode that slows down the printing to give the ink time to dry or a heating process to prevent smudges. See this chapter's section on printer supplies for more information on choosing the correct paper for different printers.

Laser Printers

The term *laser* stands for light amplification by stimulated emission of radiation. A laser printer operates similar to a copy machine's electrophotographic process. Before describing how a laser printer works, identifying the major parts inside the printer helps to understand how it works. Figure 9.20 shows a side view of a laser printer with a toner cartridge installed.

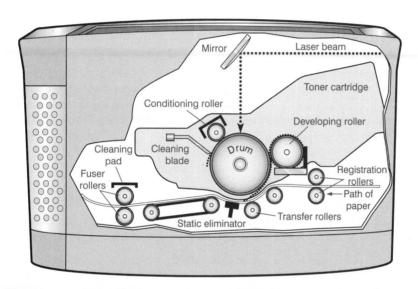

Figure 9.20   **Laser printer parts**

The computer sends 1s and 0s out the port and down the cable to the printer. Data transmits either through an array of LEDs or through a laser beam. The light beam strikes the photosensitive drum located inside the toner cartridge. Laser toner particles are attracted to the drum. The paper feeds through and the toner transfers to the paper. The toner is then fused or melted onto the paper.

Hewlett-Packard developed steps for the laser printing process. The six steps describe what happens when a laser printer prints a page. A computer technician must be familiar with the laser printing process to be certified and to troubleshoot laser printers. Table 9.12 lists the steps and explains them.

Do not get burned when working inside a laser printer

Remember to allow a laser printer to cool down completely before working in the fusing roller area.

A **fuser cleaning pad** located above the top **fusing roller** lightly coats the roller with silicon oil to prevent the paper from sticking to the roller, which is often coated with Teflon. The cleaning pad also removes any residual toner from the roller. The cleaning pad is usually replaced when the toner cartridge is replaced. Figure 9.21 shows a fuser cleaning pad being removed.

Laser printers *do* make weird noises

A laser printer frequently makes an unusual noise. The noise heard is the fusing rollers turning when the printer is not in use. Otherwise, the fusing rollers would have an indentation on one side. Users not familiar with laser printers sometimes complain about this noise but it is a normal function of the laser printer.

Table 9.12	Laser printing process steps
Step	**Description**
Conditioning	Get the drum ready for use. Before any information goes onto the drum, the entire drum must have the same voltage level. The **primary corona** (main corona) is a thin wire located inside the toner cartridge. It has up to –6000vdc applied to it. A primary control grid is located behind the corona and it controls the amount of voltage applied to the drum's surface (approximately –600 to –1000 volts). Some manufacturers use a conditioning roller instead of a primary corona. No matter what method is used, the drum gets a uniform electrical charge.
Writing	Put 1s and 0s on the drum surface. Whether the printer uses a laser beam or an LED array, the light reflects to the drum surface in the form of 1s and 0s. Every place the beam touches, the drum's surface voltage reduces to approximately –100 volts (from the very high negative voltage level). The image on the drum is nothing more than dots of electrical charges and is invisible at this point.
Developing	Get toner on the drum (develop the image). A **developing cylinder** (or developing roller) is inside the toner cartridge (right next to the drum) and contains a magnet that runs the length of the cylinder. When the cylinder rotates, toner is attracted to the cylinder because the toner has iron particles in it. The toner receives a negative electrostatic charge. The magnetic charge is a voltage level between –200 and –500 volts. The magnetized toner particles are attracted to the places on the drum where the light beam strikes. A **density control blade** controls the amount of toner allowed through to the drum. The image is no longer transparent on the drum. The image is black on the drum surface.
Transferring	Transfer the image to the paper. A **transfer corona** (roller or pad) is located at the bottom of the printer. It places a positive charge on the back of the paper. The positive charge is strong enough to attract the negatively charged toner particles from the drum. The particles leave the drum and go onto the paper. At this point, the image is on the paper, but the particles are held only by their magnetic charge.
Fusing	Melt the toner onto the paper. Heat and pressure make the image permanent on the paper. The paper, with the toner particles clinging to it, immediately passes through fusing rollers or a belt that apply pressure to the toner. The top roller applies intense heat (350°F) to the toner and paper that literally squeezes and melts the toner into the paper fibers.
Cleaning	Wipe off any toner left on the drum. Some books list this as the first step, but the order does not matter because the process is a continuous cycle. During the cleaning stage a wiper blade or brush clears the photosensitive drum of any excess toner. Then an **erase lamp** neutralizes any charges left on the drum so the next printed page begins with a clean drum.

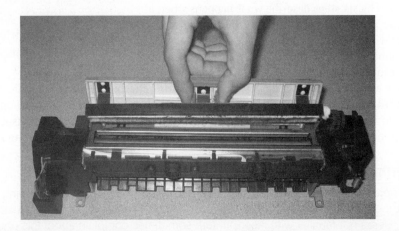

Figure 9.21   Fuser cleaning pad

Some books, manuals, and reference materials use the six phases of the electrophotographic process instead of Hewlett-Packard's (HP) terms. The six phases are listed in Table 9.13 with the equivalent HP terms. Keep in mind the same thing happens in each phase, only the terms differ.

Table 9.13 **Laser printer process terms**

Electrophotographic phase and term	Electrophotographic process	HP term
Phase 1 Charge	Charge the photoconductive drum	Conditioning
Phase 2 Expose	Expose the photoconductor	Writing
Phase 3 Develop	Develop the image	Developing
Phase 4 Transfer	Transfer the image onto the paper	Transferring
Phase 5 Fuse	Fuse the image to the paper	Fusing
Phase 6 Clean	Clean the photoconductor	Cleaning

Every laser printer that uses the six-phase process is known as a write-black laser printer. These laser printers produce a black dot every place the beam touches the drum. Most laser printers use the write-black technology. Write-white laser printers reverse the process and the toner attracts everywhere the light beam does *not* touch the drum surface. Write-black printers print finer details, but write-white laser printers can produce darker shades of black areas.

To help with the inundation of data, Table 9.14 lists the major parts of a printer with a short description of the purpose of each part.

Table 9.14 **Laser printer parts**

Part	Purpose
AC power supply	The main power supply for the printer
Cleaning blade	Wipes away excess toner from the drum before printing the next page
Cleaning pad	Applies oil to the fusing roller to prevent sticking; also removes excess toner during the fusing stage
Conditioning roller	Used instead of a primary corona wire to apply a uniform negative charge to the drum's surface
Control panel assembly	The user interface on the printer
Density control blade	Controls the amount of toner allowed on the drum (usually user adjustable)
Developing cylinder	Rotates to magnetize the toner particles before they go on the drum (also called the developing roller)
Drum (photo-sensitive)	Accepts light beams (data) from LEDs or a laser; can be permanently damaged if exposed to light; humidity can adversely affect it
ECP (electronic control package)	The main board for the printer that usually holds most of the electronic circuitry, the CPU, and RAM
Erase lamp	Neutralizes any residual charges on the drum before printing the next page
Fusing assembly	Holds the fusing roller, conditioning pad, pressure roller, and heating unit
Fusing rollers	Applies pressure and heat to fuse the toner into the paper
High voltage power supply	Provides a charge to the primary corona or conditioning roller, which in turn puts a charge on the drum
Main motor	Provides the power to drive several smaller motors that drive the gears, rollers, and drum *(continued)*

Table 9.14	Laser printer parts (*continued*)
Part	**Purpose**
Primary corona (main corona)	Applies a uniform negative charge to the drum's surface
Separation pad	A bar or pad in a laser printer that can have a rubber or cork surface that rubs against the paper as it is picked up
Scanner unit	Includes a laser or an LED array that is used to write the 1s and 0s onto the drum surface
Toner	Powder made of plastic resin particles and organic compounds bonded to iron oxide
Toner cartridge (EP cartridge)	Holds the conditioning roller, cleaning blade, drum, developing cylinder, and toner; always remove before shipping a laser printer
Transfer corona wire (transfer roller)	Applies a positive charge on the back of the paper to pull the toner from the drum onto the paper

Figure 9.22 shows a laser printer toner cartridge.

Figure 9.22	Laser toner cartridge

Be careful working inside laser printers

Be very careful when working inside a laser printer. There are high voltages in various parts as well as high temperatures in the fusing area. Turn off the printer and let it cool down before servicing. Always remove power from the printer when possible.

A word about spilled toner

Toner melts when warmed; small toner spills outside the printer can be wiped using a cold, damp cloth. Toner spills in the printer require a special type of vacuum with special bags. Toner on clothing can normally be removed by washing in cold water. Do not put the clothing in a dryer if the toner is not yet removed.

Paper

The type of paper used in a printer can affect its performance and cause problems. Dot matrix printers are the most forgiving because a mechanism physically impacts the paper. On the other hand, ink jet printers spray ink onto the paper, so the quality of paper determines how well the ink adheres. If the paper absorbs too much of the ink, the printout appears faded. For the laser printer, how well the paper heats and absorbs the toner also affects the printed output. Paper is a big factor in the quality of how long color lasts and the quality of print produced.

Erasable bond paper also does not work well in laser printers because the paper does not allow the toner to fuse properly. Every type of paper imaginable is available for ink jet and laser printers: transparency paper for overhead projectors, high gloss, water resistant ink jet paper, fabric paper, greeting cards, labels, recycled paper, and so on. Recycled paper may cause printer jams and produce lower print quality.

The highest quality paper available does not work well if the surrounding area has too much humidity. Humidity is paper's worst enemy. It causes the paper to stick together and it reduces the paper's strength, which causes feed problems. Paper affected by humidity is sometimes noticeable because of the lumpy look it gives the paper. If you detect damaged paper, discard and recycle it immediately. For best printing results, keep paper stored in a non-humid storage area.

Another simple and useful approach is to fan the paper before you insert it into the printer's bin. For best results, fill a printer's paper bin three-quarters full only. Do not overfill the bin.

Paper options also relate to printers. Some dot matrix printers allow you to remove the normal paper feeder and attach a paper option that allows continuous paper to be fed through the printer. Both dot matrix and ink jet printers have special feeders or you move a slide bar to feed envelopes or unusual sized paper through. Laser printers sometimes ship with additional trays and must be configured for this option. Laser printers normally allow manual feeding and have a front cover that allows paper, labels, transparencies, and other unusual sizes and types of paper to be used.

How to control printer trays and manual feed options

The *Paper* tab on the printer *Properties* tab is commonly used to configure where you want the printer to look for paper to be used. Most printers also allow the default order in which the printer looks for paper to be configured through either the manufacturer-provider software, the printer *Properties* window.

Refilling Cartridges, Reinking Ribbons, and Recycling Cartridges

Much controversy exists when it comes to reinking dot matrix printer ribbons, refilling ink jet cartridges, or buying remanufactured laser cartridges. Many people who are concerned about the environment recycle their cartridges. Even if a company or an individual user decides not to purchase remanufactured products, some send their old empty cartridges to companies that do the remanufacturing. Refilling ink cartridges significantly lowers the printing costs.

If you refill the ink cartridges, add new ink before the old cartridge runs completely dry. If refilling ink cartridges, be sure the refill ink emulates the manufacturer's ink. Some ink refill companies use inferior ink that, over time, has a corrosive effect on the cartridge housing. A leaky cartridge or one that bursts causing ink to get into the printer is nothing but trouble.

Beware of toner cartridges
Toner powder is harmful if inhaled. Wear gloves when replacing the toner cartridge.

Some ink refill companies have an exchange system. The old ink cartridges are placed into a sealed plastic bag and returned to the company where they are remanufactured. In return, the company ships a remanufactured cartridge filled with ink. If the empty ink cartridge sent to the company does not fit its standards criteria, the cartridge is thrown away. Some states have disposal requirements for ink jet cartridges.

When it comes to laser cartridge remanufacturing, the most important components are the drum and the wiper blade that cleans the drum. Many laser cartridge remanufacturers use the same parts over and over again. A quality refill company will disassemble the cartridge and inspect each part. When the drum and wiper blade are worn, they are replaced with new parts. Some states have disposal requirements for laser printer cartridges.

Reinking a dot matrix printer ribbon is not a good idea. It can cause a mess and the ink is sometimes an inferior quality that causes deterioration of the printhead over time. Because dot matrix printer ribbons are so inexpensive, you should just replace them.

Print Drivers

How an application outputs to a printer is determined by the operating system used. A **print driver** is a small piece of software specifically written for a particular printer. The print driver enables the printer's specific features and allows an application to communicate with the printer. Windows applications use a single print driver—one written for the specific printer.

Printers must accept as much data as possible from the computer, process that data, output it, communicate to the computer the need for more data, accept more data, and repeat the process. With Windows, a print spooler is used. A **print spooler**, or print manager, is a software program that intercepts the printer's request to print. Instead of going directly to the printer, the data goes to the hard drive. The spooler then controls the data from the hard drive going to the printer. Some printers come with their own print manager that replaces the one included with Windows.

Use the latest driver from the printer manufacturer

Windows ships with various print drivers, all of which allow basic communication and access to the printer. For best results and performance, use the driver provided by the manufacturer or better yet, one downloaded from the Internet. Use the driver designed for the operating system installed.

The print spooler transmission retry option is the number of seconds the print manager waits before giving up on trying to send the printer more data. If the document contains multiple fonts, font sizes, or graphics, the transmission retry settings may need to be changed. For Windows, use the *Printers* control panel, right-click the specific printer, and select *Properties*. Note that the tab used to select options for transmission retry may vary between printer manufacturers.

Fonts

A font is a group of printable characters from a particular style such as Times New Roman, Script, Arial, and Courier. The font style refers to the appearance of the type such as bold or italic. The font size is in points such as 10pt or 12pt. The larger the point size, the larger the type appears on the paper. Point size is different from cpi (characters per inch). The larger the cpi, the smaller the font size. Table 9.15 explains the basic types of fonts.

Table 9.15	Font types
Font type	**Description**
Raster	The most basic type and is nothing more than dots creating an image; dot matrix printers use raster fonts.
Vector	These are created from a mathematical formula. All characters are simply a series of lines between two points. Also known as outline fonts. The outline of each character is used to produce the printed output. The outline defines the shape of the character, but not the size. These are scalable, which means that the character can be created at any size.
TrueType	The most advanced type of outline (vector) font. Characters can be scaled (enlarged or shrunk) and rotated.

Watch out for PostScript drivers

If a document is created in a computer that has a PostScript printer driver loaded, and the document is taken to another computer without a PostScript printer driver, there is a good chance the document will not print properly.

Each printer has its own **PDL** (Page Description Language) that is a translator between the computer and the printer. The page description language handles the overall page look and has commands that treat the entire document as a single graphic. The two most popular page description languages are Adobe Systems Inc.'s **PostScript** and Hewlett-Packard's **PCL** (printer command language).

GDI (graphics device interface) is the part of Windows that handles representing and transmitting graphical objects to output devices such as printers, monitors, and overhead projectors. In Windows XP, GDI+ is the improved model. It handles graphical images better as well as supports file formats such as JPEG and PNG. Windows Vista/7 further upgrades GDI with **XPS** (XML paper specification) and documents sent to printers that support XPS will not have to be converted to a printer-specific language. XPS not only affects printing, but also document viewing. XPS is the replacement for **EMF** (enhanced metafile format), a graphics language for print drivers.

Printer Installation

A printer is one of the easiest devices to install. Always refer to the printer documentation for exact installation and configuration specifics. The following steps explain how to install a printer that attaches to a USB port:

1. Take the printer out of its box and remove the shipping materials. The number one cause of new printers not working properly is that all the shipping safeguards are not removed properly.
2. Connect the power cord from the printer to the wall outlet, surge protector, or UPS outlet. Note that most UPS units are not rated high enough for a laser printer to be connected to it.
3. Load paper and ribbon/ink/cartridge into the printer according to manufacturer's instructions. Most ink jet printers have a calibration routine that should be utilized as part of the installation routine.
4. Turn on the printer and verify that the power light is on.
5. Install the print driver by following the manufacturer's instructions for the particular operating system being used.
6. Attach the USB cable from the printer to the computer. Note that this cable might not be provided with the printer.
7. Configure options and default settings.
8. Perform a test print to verify communication between the computer and printer. Most ink jet printers have a calibration process that must be performed before normal printing. This calibration procedure is also performed when an ink cartridge is replaced.
9. Train the user on printer operation and leave all printer documentation with the customer.

Tech Tip

Educate the user on printer functionality and print cartridges

As part of the installation process, ask the user to print something and show them any features with which they may not be familiar. Inform them that the cartridge that comes with the printer does not last long and that they should order a new one as soon as possible.

Tech Tip

For a successful printer installation

The key to a successful printer installation is to read the printer documentation, use a good cable, load the latest printer drivers (from the manufacturer), and test. Many hours of frustration for the computer user and the technician can be avoided by doing the research before the install, not after a problem occurs.

Upgrading Printers

Printers can be upgraded in many ways, and the options available are vendor- and printer-dependent. The most common upgrades include memory and tray/paper feed options. The most commonly upgraded printers are ink jet and laser printers.

The most common upgrade for laser printers is memory. The amount of memory storage available for printers (especially those shared by multiple users) is very important because printing errors can occur with too little memory. It is also important to have some means of storage so that the documents can be sent and stored away from the computer that requested the print job. This frees up the computer's memory and hard drive space to do other tasks.

9

Other Peripherals

Printer memory upgrades

Many memory technologies are available for printers, but the common ones are RAM modules, flash memory, and PC Cards. These technologies are installed in the same manner they are installed into a computer. Always follow the manufacturer's installation instructions. Hard drives can also be attached to printers for additional storage.

The paper storage trays and feeders are another common upgrade. Laser printers frequently come with various paper storage tray options. When multiple people share a printer, a small capacity paper tray can be a nuisance. Ink jet printers often have different paper feed options relating to photograph printing. Paper designed for printing photographs is available in various sizes. Special paper feed options can be purchased that are mounted onto the printer for these rolls or different sizes of paper. With the increased popularity of digital photography, these printer options are quite popular.

Printer Preventive Maintenance

People sometimes forget to plug their printer into an uninterruptible surge protector (UPS). The printer can be damaged by electrical storms and power fluctuations just as a computer can. The laser printer AC power module and fuser assembly are especially susceptible to power problems. Protect any printer as well as the computer, but always make sure that the UPS has the ability to handle the higher power laser printer.

Dot matrix printers usually require cleaning more often than any other type of printer because they are frequently used for continuous fed paper or multiform paper and are often installed in industrial environments. Paper chafe, dust, and dirt cause an insulating layer of heat to the printer components, which causes them to fail faster. Vacuum dot matrix printers more often than other printers.

Ink jet printers require little preventive maintenance. Keep the interior and exterior clean of dust and particles. Use a soft brush or non-metallic vacuum nozzle to remove dust. Do not use any type of lubricants on the print cartridge bar. Use the printer's software or maintenance procedure for aligning the print cartridge each time it is replaced. Some printers have a "clean" maintenance procedure that can be done through the software that ships with the printer. Some of these processes do not clean the printhead well even when using this procedure and the printheads tend to clog during usage. Remove the printhead and clean with a lint-free cloth or with a dampened cotton swab. Allow the cartridge to dry thoroughly and reinstall.

Laser printers, on the other hand, do require some periodic maintenance. Be careful using compressed air to clean a laser printer that has loose toner in it. The compressed air could push the toner in to hard-to-reach places or to parts that heat up and cause the part to fail. Vacuum the laser toner before using compressed air.

Laser preventive maintenance is important

If any toner appears inside the printer, do *not* use a normal vacuum cleaner. The toner particles seep through the vacuum cleaner bag into the vacuum's motor (where the particles melt). Also, the toner can become electrically charged and ignite a fire. Special HEPA (high-efficiency particulate air) vacuum bags are available for some vacuum cleaners.

If the laser printer has a transfer corona instead of a transfer roller, clean it when you replace the toner cartridge. Some laser printers include a small cleaning brush to clean the corona wire. Some toner cartridges come with a cotton swab for cleaning the transfer corona. The transfer corona wire is normally in the bottom of the printer protected by monofilament wires. Be extremely careful not to break the wires or the transfer corona.

Ozone is a gas produced by larger business-type laser printers. The printer's ozone filter removes the gas as well as any toner and paper dust particles. The ozone filter needs replacing after a specific number of usage hours. Check the printer documentation for the filter replacement schedule. Simply vacuuming the ozone filter will not clean it. The ozone molecules are trapped and absorbed by the ozone filter. If you forget to replace the ozone filter, people in the immediate vicinity may develop headaches, nausea, irritability, and depression. Most home and small office laser printers do not have an ozone filter. When using these printers, the surrounding area must be well ventilated.

The fuser cleaning pad (sometimes known as the fuser wand) sits above the top fusing roller and is normally replaced at the same time as the toner cartridge. However, the cleaning pad sometimes becomes dirty before it is time to replace the cartridge. If so, remove the cleaning pad. Hold the pad over a trash can. Take a small flat-tipped screwdriver and use the shaft to rub along the felt pad. Replace the cleaning pad and wipe the screwdriver with a cloth.

The fusing roller sometimes has particles that cling to it. Once the assembly cools, *gently* scrape the particles from the roller. A small amount of alcohol on a soft, lint-free cloth can help with stubborn spots.

If the laser printer uses a laser beam to write data to the photosensitive drum, the laser beam does not directly touch the drum. Instead, at least one mirror is used to redirect the laser beam onto the drum's surface. The mirror(s) need to be cleaned periodically with a lint-free cloth.

For some printers, preventive maintenance kits are available for purchase. Quality printer replacement parts and preventive maintenance kits are important to the technician. If a printer must be sent out for repair, warranty work, and so on, make sure to remove the toner cartridge, platen knobs, and power cords before packing the printer in a box. Check with the receiving company to see if you should send the toner cartridge separately.

Tech Tip

What if you just performed maintenance on a printer and now the print looks bad?

After performing preventive maintenance on a printer, the pages may appear smudged or slightly dirty. Run a couple of print jobs through the printer to allow the dust to settle (so to speak). Never do any kind of maintenance on any computer part or peripheral without testing the results of the maintenance or the repair.

Printers in the Windows Environment

The operating system plays a big part in controlling the printer. When working in a Windows environment, there are three essential areas for a technician to know (besides knowing how to print): (1) configuration utilities; (2) resource allocation and viewing; and (3) printer settings. Sometimes these areas overlap.

To print in Windows, use one of the following methods:

- Open the file in the appropriate application. Click the *File* menu item and click the *Print* option.
- Drag the file to print to the printer's icon in the *Printers* folder.
- Create a shortcut icon on the desktop for a specific printer and drag the file to this icon.
- Right-click the filename and select the *Print* option.
- From within the application, press the Ctrl+P keys and the *Print* window appears.
- From within an application, click the printer icon located under the menu bar.

Tech Tip

Using the printer icon in the system tray

When a print job occurs, Windows normally shows an icon of a printer in the system tray (right side of the task bar). When the print job is still accessible, you can double-click the printer icon, click the document, and pause or cancel the print job through the *Documents* menu option.

If multiple print jobs are in the printer queue, they can be reordered by right-clicking on the document and selecting *Properties*. On the General tab, change the priority. A lower number is a lower priority than a higher number.

The *Printers and Faxes* control panel is used frequently to add a printer, remove a printer, temporarily halt a print job (pause the printer), and define or change printer settings such as resolution, paper type, and paper orientation. The Windows Add Printer wizard steps you through the installation process. This utility starts automatically when Windows detects a newly installed printer. Once the wizard starts you must select whether the printer is a local printer (used by only one computer) or a network printer. If the local printer option is selected, you will have to install a print driver. For best performance, use the latest printer manufacturer's driver for the operating system installed. You must also select the port to which the printer attaches (e.g., COM, LPT, or USB). The wizard also asks if this printer is to be the default printer.

Tech Tip

Setting a printer as the default printer

To configure a printer as a default printer, access the *Printers* control panel → right-click the appropriate printer → *Set As Default*. The default printer has a check mark above the printer icon in the *Printers* control panel window.

A **default printer** is the one that applications use without any configuration changes. Even if you reply *No* to this prompt, a printer can be changed to the default printer at a later date. Right-clicking a *printer* icon also gives you access to the *Properties* option. Through this selection, several tabs are available (depending on the printer model). Common tabs include *General*, *Sharing*, *Ports*, and *Advanced*. Figure 9.23 shows a printer's *Properties* window.

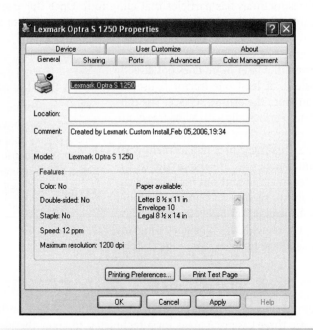

Figure 9.23   **Printer *Properties* window**

Use Windows Device Manager and System Information tools to examine system resources and check for problems.

- To access Device Manager in XP, open the *System* control panel → *Hardware* tab → *Device Manager* button. In Vista/7, access the *System* control panel → *Device Manager*.
- To access the System Information tool in XP, click the *Start* button → *All Programs* → *Accessories* → *System Tools* → *System Information* → expand *Hardware Resources* → click *Conflicts/Sharing*. In Vista/7, access the *Performance Information and Tools* control panel → *Advanced Tools* from the *Tasks* list → View *advanced systems details in System Information* link → expand the *Hardware Resources* category → *Conflicts/Sharing*.

A printer's *Properties* option contains useful tools and settings. Table 9.16 lists the common printer *Properties* window tabs and their general purpose.

Table 9.16   **Printer *Properties* tabs overview**

Tab	Comments
General	Displays the printer name and has a button for printing a test page
Sharing	Shares the printer over a network
Ports	Sets the LPT port number
Advanced	Allows setting resolution, graphics intensity (darkness), graphics mode, spooling (transmission delay), and defaults
Paper	Selects different paper trays, paper size, and two- sided printing on some models
Fonts	Displays and installs printer fonts
Device Options	Adjusts print density and quality, displays amount of RAM installed in the printer, and adjusts printer memory tracking

The *General* tab's *Print Test Page* button is important for a technician to determine if the operating system can perform basic communication with the printer. On one of the printer *Properties* tabs or from one of the configuration buttons, the *Spool Settings* option details how the print spool operates. Figure 9.24 shows an example of these settings.

In Windows, this option is frequently on the *Advanced* tab and it is called *Spool the document* (for enabling spooling) or *Print directly to a printer* (for no print spooling). If spooling is turned on (enabled), then data is sent to the hard drive temporarily. Whenever the printer is ready to accept data, it is retrieved from the hard drive. This frees up the application while your printer is doing other tasks.

Tech Tip

Printer *Properties General* tab has print test button

The *General* tab is normally where you find a button that allows communication between the PC and the printer to be tested with a test page.

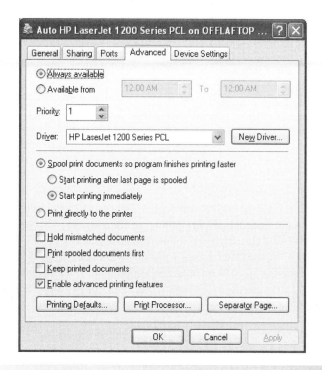

Figure 9.24   **Spool settings**

The SPOOL32.EXE program controls the spooling function. Also, when troubleshooting printer problems, the spooler can be disabled to eliminate it as the problem source.

Once spooling is enabled, there are two more choices: *Start printing after the last page is spooled* or *Start printing after the first page is spooled*. These two selections determine when data is sent from the spooler (hard drive) to the printer: after the entire document has been written to the hard drive or as soon as the first page has been written to the drive.

The next section is also important—Spool data format. This setting determines how the data is stored on the hard drive. The EMF (enhanced metafile) is the default setting and it is a 32-bit non-printer dependent format that performs faster than RAW. If you are having printing problems, and the documentation or your research directs you to change the spooling data format, this is the setting referenced. The RAW data format is printer-specific and it requires extra time to convert the printing data before it is saved to the hard drive.

Tech Tip

When to use spooling

Spooling should be disabled if the computer does not have at least 300MB of free hard drive space. Note that if a printer is shared (other computers can print to the printer through a network), spooling must be enabled and free hard drive space made available as much as possible. Some people use older computers to connect printers to a network. These computers are not used for anything but print spooling. They are designated as print servers.

Windows Printer Troubleshooting

The most common printing test is a test page from an application or from the specific printer's *Properties General* tab. Remember that Windows uses a single print driver for all applications. Check the status lights on the front of the printer for any abnormal indications. Windows has a Troubleshooter tool. Access Windows XP's Troubleshooter tool by clicking *Start → Help and Support → Troubleshooter* in the *Search* window. You may have to click the *Full-text search* matches to see the *List of troubleshooters* option. Scroll down in the right pane to see and click *Printing*. For Vista/7, click the *Start* button → *Control Panel* → type troubleshooting in the search box → *Troubleshooting* → locate *Hardware and Sound* → *Use a printer*.

Try printing from Notepad, a simple Windows-based application

If the self-test worked, try printing from Notepad. Restart the computer and click the *Start* button. Point to *Programs* and then point to *Accessories.* Click the *Notepad* option. Type a few characters in the blank window. Click the *File* menu option and click *Print.* If the file prints, then your problem may involve printing from only one application.

If the Troubleshooter tool does not help, run a self-test on your printer. If the self-test works, the printer is usually fine and the problem lies in the cable, port, software driver, or printer settings.

Free hard drive space is important for print spooling. Insufficient free space can cause print jobs to have problems. Even if there appears to be enough hard drive space to spool the printing job, the printer may still need more RAM installed to print a large or complex document.

If the printer works, then the printer, port, and printer cable are all operational and the problem is in the operating system. To see if the printer driver is the problem, use the *Add Printer* wizard to install the Generic/Text Only printer driver. See Hands-On Exercise 1 at the end of this chapter for more information.

If you reload the printer driver, the old printer driver must be removed first. Some manufacturers have very specific instructions for removing their driver. Always follow their directions. Most of them do something similar to the following: click the *Start* button and select the *Settings* option followed by the *Printers and Faxes* option. Right-click the specific printer icon and click the *Delete* option. Click the *Yes* button when prompted if all the associated printer files are to be deleted. To re-install the printer, use the Add Printer wizard. Refer to the Hands-On Exercise 1 at the end of the chapter if necessary.

General Printer Troubleshooting

The printing hardware subsystem consists of the printer, cable, and communications port. If something is wrong with the hardware, it is normally one of these three areas. Always check the connections and the power between each area. The printer has the highest failure rate of the three because it is a mechanical device with motors, plastic gears, and moving parts. Printers normally have a self-test routine. Refer to the printer's documentation to determine how to run the test. If a printer's self-test operates properly, the printer is operational. If the printer checks out, the problem is the port, cable, or software.

Another problem could be that the printer is not configured for the correct port. Check that the printer is configured for the proper port. Refer to the printer's documentation for specifics on how to configure the printer for a specific port.

Some printers have upgradable firmware. Just like the computer's Flash BIOS can be upgraded, printers may need a firmware upgrade to correct specific problems. Printer firmware

The paper gets stuck

If the printer is having trouble feeding paper, the first clue is to see how far the paper has gone along the paper path before it jammed or could not go any farther. Many paper feeding problems are due to poor paper quality or the inefficiency of the rubber rollers that move the paper along the paper path. Rubber rollers are normally found in the paper transport system on all printer types and over time, the rollers become slick from use and they do not work properly.

What to do with slick printer rollers

Special cleaners such as Rubber Rejuvenator are available for rubber printer rollers that have a hard time picking up the paper and sending it through the printer. Some printers have a special cleaning page for cleaning the rollers. Refer to the printer's manual for exact procedures. If a cleaner is unavailable, scrub the rollers with a wire brush or sandpaper to roughen them up a bit, which will enable them to pick up the paper better. If you do not have a wire brush or sandpaper, use the sharp edge of a paper clip to roughen up the rubber part of the roller so it can grip the paper.

updates can normally be obtained from the printer manufacturer's Web site. Always follow the manufacturer's instructions when installing firmware upgrades.

Connect a working printer to the port, install the proper print driver and verify the port works. If the printer uses the USB, the following is a checklist for troubleshooting.

- If the computer stops responding and the USB device is suspect, power the computer off and then back on again.
- The BIOS settings may have to be enabled for USB devices. Different BIOS manufacturers list the USB settings differently. The USB settings may be located in a heading *Enabling on-board USB* or within the PCI section. If you install a USB host adapter and the motherboard also supports USB ports, you may have to disable the motherboard ports through BIOS.
- Use Device Manager to check and see if USB is listed. Look at the Universal Serial Bus controllers section. If it is not, check the BIOS settings or update BIOS. If the USB device is listed, ensure that there are no resource conflicts.
- If there is a USB hub connected to the USB port, disconnect the hub and connect the USB printer directly into the USB port to see if the problem is the hub.
- With the computer's power on, disconnect the USB printer and reconnect it. Go into Device Manager and ensure that there is only one listing for the USB printer.
- Some USB devices have device drivers. Check the Internet for updated drivers.
- Disconnect the USB printer while the computer is powered on. Power down the computer. Then power on the computer. Insert the USB printer cable into the USB port. The system should automatically detect and install the printer.
- Verify the USB device works by plugging it into another USB port or another computer's USB port.
- Check that the proper USB cable is being used.

The last part to check is the printer cable. Remember: Cables are not normally faulty. A USB cable can be rated as high-speed or low-speed. The high-speed cables have more shielding and can support the higher speeds. If a high-speed USB device attaches to a low-speed cable, data loss can occur. Make sure you have the proper USB cable for a printer that attaches to a USB port.

On the software side, troubleshooting involves narrowing down the problem to the print driver. Because Windows uses one print driver for all applications, check the printing from within several software packages. Use a simple text program such as Notepad to see if simple text will print. Printers need memory to print multiple pages of complex graphics. If the printer prints a couple of pages and then stops, or prints half a page, ejects the paper, and then prints the other half of the page and ejects the paper, then the printer's memory needs upgrading. If printing does not occur in all of the software packages tested, the problem is most likely the software driver. See the earlier section for specific Windows printer troubleshooting tips.

The paper could be the culprit

If the printer has trouble feeding the paper, always be sure you are using the correct type of paper and that printing occurs on the correct side. Refer to this chapter's section on paper. One vendor quotes that 80 percent of all paper jams are due to inferior paper quality, poor paper condition such as damage due to humidity, or an operator-related problem such as the wrong paper size selected in the software program.

9

Other Peripherals

Dot Matrix Printer Troubleshooting

When technicians state that a printhead is not firing, one or more of the printwires are not coming out of the printhead to impact the ribbon. A printhead that is not firing is evidenced by one or more white lines that appear where the printed dots should be. On a printed page, the white line appears horizontally in the middle of a line. The most likely problem is the printhead. However, be aware that the problem could be a bad driver transistor on the main circuit board or a loose cable that attaches to the printhead. But, because the printhead is a mechanical part, it is the most suspect.

If the print is light, then dark, the printer ribbon may not be advancing properly. One of the shafts that insert into each end of the ribbon may not be turning or the set of gears under the shaft may not mesh properly. Also, there is a motor that handles ribbon movement; the motor may need replacement. A faulty ribbon can also cause the carriage to seize up. Remove the ribbon and power up the printer. If the carriage moves when the ribbon is removed, but it will not move when the ribbon is installed, replace the ribbon. Some printers have belts that move the printhead across the page. A worn, loose, or slipping belt can cause erratic printing.

Tech Tip

Dot matrix light printing can be caused by several things

Adjust the printhead gap to place the printhead closer to the ribbon or replace the ribbon. Also, the platen could be misaligned with the bottom paper feed rollers.

If the printer prints continuously on the same line, be sure the setting for tractor-fed paper or friction-fed paper is correct. Or, the motor that controls paper movement may need replacement. If the printer moves the paper up a small bit after printing, the model may have the Auto Tear Off feature enabled. The Auto Tear Off feature is used with perforated forms needed in many businesses. See the printer's documentation to disable this feature.

Ink Jet Printer Troubleshooting

Ink jet printers frequently have a built-in printhead cleaning routine. Access the routine through the printer's buttons or through software. Most manufacturers recommend cleaning the ink jet cartridge only when there is a problem such as lines or dots missing from the printed output. Otherwise, cleaning the ink jet cartridge with this method wastes ink and shortens the print cartridge's life span.

Usually, ink jet manufacturers include an alignment program to align the dots more precisely. Use the alignment program when vertical lines or characters do not align properly. Always refer to the printer's documentation for troubleshooting programs such as the printhead cleaning and alignment routines.

Laser Printer Troubleshooting

Lasers have more mechanical and electronic circuitry than the other printer types, which means that there are more things that can go wrong. The following list contains some common symptoms and possible solutions:

- Black streaks appear on the paper or the print is not sharp—check the fuser cleaning pad for toner particles and use a small screwdriver to scrape off the excess particles before re-installing.
- Output appears darker in some spots than others—remove the toner cartridge. Gently rock the toner cartridge back and forth to redistribute the toner. If this does not fix the problem, turn down the toner density by using the *Printers* control panel or software provided by the printer manufacturer. Also, the paper could be too smooth.
- Print appears light—adjust the darkness setting on the printer or through the printer's operating system settings. The toner cartridge could be low. Damp paper could also cause this symptom. Use fresh paper of the proper weight and finish. If the print appears consistently dark, adjust the darkness setting.
- A horizontal line appears periodically throughout the printout—the problem is one of the rollers. Check all rollers to see if one is dirty or gouged and needs replacing. The rollers

in the laser printer are not all the same size; the distance between the lines is the circumference of the roller. This is an easy way to tell which rollers are definitely not the problem or which ones are likely candidates.

- White vertical line(s) appear—the corona wires may have paper bits or something else stuck on them. This can also be caused by something being caught in the developer unit (located in the cartridge). Replace the cartridge to see if this is the problem.
- Opposite side of printed page has smudges or appears dirty—the fuser could be faulty, the wrong type of paper could be being used, or the toner may be leaking.
- Creases in paper—check the paper path for labels or debris.

Many laser problems involve the toner cartridge, which is a good thing because the cartridge is a part people normally have on hand. Various symptoms can occur because of the toner cartridge: smearing, horizontal streaking, vertical streaking, faded print, one vertical black line, one horizontal black line, a white streak on one side, wavy image, and so on. One of the easiest things to do is to remove the toner cartridge, hold the cartridge in front of you with both hands, and rock the cartridge away from you and then back toward you. Re-insert the cartridge back into the printer and test.

Sometimes, the primary corona wire or the conditioning roller inside the toner cartridge needs to be cleaned. Clean the corona wires with the provided brush or with a cotton swab. Dampen the cotton swab with alcohol, if necessary. Clean the conditioning roller with a lint-free cloth. Dampen the cloth with alcohol, if necessary.

To prove if a problem is in the toner cartridge or elsewhere in the printer, send any output to the printer. When the printer is through with the writing stage and before the toner fuses to the paper, open the laser printer cover and remove the paper. (Determining exactly when to open the cover may take several attempts.) If the paper is error-free, the problem is most likely in the transfer corona (or transfer roller) or fusing assembly.

Another common problem occurs when the laser printer does not have enough memory. One symptom is that when printing, the printer blinks as if it is accepting data. Then, the printer quits blinking and nothing appears or the printer prints only half the page. This could also be caused by insufficient hard drive space when spooling is enabled. Some printers give an error code if there is not enough memory. For example, in a Hewlett-Packard laser printer, the error code 20 indicates insufficient memory.

Experience is the best teacher when it comes to printers. Work on a couple of dot matrix models, a couple of ink jet printers, and a couple of laser printer models, and you will see the majority of problems. Each type of printer has very few circuit boards to replace. Normally the problems are in the moving parts or are software related.

Tech Tip

What if the printer needs more memory?

Of course, the obvious answer is to upgrade it, but an alternative is to send the print job fewer pages at a time, reduce the printer resolution (e.g., from 1200 dpi to 600 dpi), reduce the size of the graphics, or standardize the fonts. Font standardization can be accomplished by not using as many font types, styles, or font sizes. When print spooling is enabled, make sure there is ample free hard drive space. Delete old files/applications and run the disk management tool to make more available space.

9

Other Peripherals

Soft Skills—Work Ethics

Ethics are a set of morals by which you live or work. Employers want employees who possess a high standard of ethics. This means they want people who are honest, trustworthy, and dependable. IT technicians are exposed to many personal things—passwords, private data, visited Internet sites, just to name a few. Employers do not want to worry about their technicians taking things that belong to others, looking at data that does not relate to the computer problem at hand, and taking or giving away things from the office.

The best ruling factor in ethics is to always be professional. Therefore, if you are in a situation where someone asks you to give them another person's password, ask yourself if divulging the information is professional or not. When opening a customer's documents and reading them, ask yourself, am I being professional? If the answer is no, stop reading. If you are in a customer's office and accidentally see their password taped to a CD case, let them know that you have seen it, suggest that they do not write down their passwords in a conspicuous place, and recommend that they change passwords. One of the biggest assets an IT professional can have is his or her reputation. Being ethical at work goes a long way in establishing a good reputation.

Lastly, every IT person can probably remember at least one instance when he or she was asked to do something unethical—charge for more time than was actually spent on the job, provide access to a room or area where access is normally restricted, or grant privileges that others at the same level do not have. When put in this situation, there are a few options: (1) be polite and refuse; (2) adamantly refuse; (3) report the person to their supervisor. Recommending what to do is difficult, but for most offenses, being polite and refusing is the best course of action and is the most professional. If the request is against corporate policy or could hurt others in the company, you need to report this to a company manager or security. Your own boss may be the best person to inform.

Key Terms

ACPI (p. 318)
active matrix (p. 312)
aspect ratio (p. 312)
backlight (p. 307)
cleaning (p. 332)
component/RGB video (p. 315)
conditioning (p. 332)
conditioning roller (p. 333)
contrast ratio (p. 312)
cps (p. 328)
CRT (p. 307)
default printer (p. 340)
degauss (p. 311)
density control blade (p. 332)
developing (p. 332)
developing cylinder (p. 332)
DLP (p. 307)
dot matrix printer (p. 327)
dot pitch (p. 307)
dot triad (p. 307)
dpi (p. 330)
dual link (p. 314)
dual-ported memory (p. 320)
DVI (p. 313)
DVI-D (p. 314)

DVI-I (p. 314)
EMF (p. 337)
erase lamp (p. 332)
flyback transformer (p. 323)
fuser cleaning pad (p. 331)
fusing (p. 332)
fusing roller (p. 331)
GDDR4 SDRAM (p. 320)
GDI (p. 336)
ink jet printer (p. 327)
KVM switch (p. 316)
laser printer (p. 327)
LCD (p. 307)
marking (p. 325)
native resolution (p. 312)
paper transport (p. 325)
PCL (p. 336)
PDL (p. 336)
pixel (p. 307)
PostScript (p. 336)
primary corona (p. 332)
print cartridge (p. 327)
print driver (p. 336)
print engine (p. 325)
print server (p. 326)

print spooler (p. 336)
printhead (p. 327)
printwire (p. 327)
raster (p. 323)
refresh rate (p. 311)
resolution (p. 309)
SGRAM (p. 320)
shared system memory (p. 321)
single link (p. 314)
SXGA+ (p. 310)
TFT (p. 307)
transfer corona (p. 332)
transferring (p. 332)
TV tuner card (p. 316)
UXGA (p. 310)
video capture card (p. 316)
video processor (p. 319)
viewable size (p. 312)
writing (p. 332)
WUXGA (p. 310)
XGA (p. 310)
XPS (p. 337)

Review Questions

1. What components make up a computer's video subsystem?

2. What are two common output devices?

3. What video output technology more closely resembles a traditional TV than the others?

4. What is a dot triad?

5. What component directs the CRT electron beam to the proper location on the front of the monitor screen?

6. What video technology is commonly found in laptops? [CRT | LCD | DLP]

7. What two technologies are used for LCD backlights?

8. What effect do liquid crystals have on laptop displays?

9. What is the purpose of the miniature mirrors used with units that use DLP?

10. How are colors produced when DLP is being used?

11. What is DMD, and what do you think is the purpose of this component?

12. How are plasma displays different from LCDs?

13. [T | F] Plasma displays take less power than CRTs.

14. What can be done with a CRT that is being replaced by an LCD?

15. What video technology would be used with kiosks?

16. How many pixels does a monitor have if the monitor resolution is 1400×1050?

17. What is the maximum video resolution provided by WUXGA?

18. What determines the monitor refresh rate?
    a. The monitor specifications
    b. The video adapter specifications
    c. The video adapter and the monitor specifications
    d. The motherboard
    e. The motherboard BIOS
    f. The system processor

19. Why is the vertical scan rate important?

20. What is a good refresh rate for a monitor?

21. [T | F] Today's monitors normally support only one refresh rate.

22. What term best describes when a monitor electron beam scans the odd pixel rows and then scans the even pixel rows? [refreshing | interlacing | beaming | video skipping]

23. What does the word *degauss* mean in relation to a CRT?

24. What Windows XP tab is used to view the monitor refresh rate?

25. What is the purpose of the *Input* monitor button?

26. What type of video technology is used with laptop displays?

27. Describe the difference between active and passive matrix displays.

28. If an active matrix display uses TFT technology, how many transistors are required for an 800×600 resolution?

29. What is aspect ratio as it relates to monitors?

30. What are nits in relation to computer video?

31. [T | F] Having one or two dead pixels is common in a new LCD.

32. When would a technician change the resolution on an LCD monitor? Explain your answer.

33. What is pixelation as it relates to LCDs?

34. How would a technician determine the native resolution for an LCD on a laptop on which the technician was working?

35. Draw a basic diagram of the video subsystem in a laptop.

36. What two methods are used on a laptop lid close detector?

37. Explain why having an analog adapter is not the preferred method for connecting a flat screen monitor.

38. Describe the difference between single and dual link video connections.

39. What DVI connector is most common?

40. What do component video ports look like?

41. How can you connect an HDMI cable to a DVI port?

42. List two methods used to connect two monitors to a single computer.

43. Even though there are several ways to upgrade a computer so that two monitors can be used, what is the preferred method?

44. Describe the difference between a TV tuner and a video capture card.

9

Other Peripherals

45. What is another name for the three RCA jacks found on a projector?

46. Draw the two symbols commonly found on a laptop key and is used in conjunction with the Fn key to send video output through an external laptop port.

47. How do you keep a monitor static free?

48. [T | F] Monitors are frequently disassembled by technicians because the parts are so inexpensive.

49. Should a monitor be left on 24 hours a day? Explain your answer.

50. What is a green monitor?

51. What Vista control panel is used to enable a monitor's energy-saving features?

52. [T | F] A non-green monitor can be damaged if energy-efficiency software is enabled.

53. What is the most energy-efficient method for a laptop LCD backlight?

54. [T | F] Today's analog monitors require a screen saver, or an image could permanently burn into the display.

55. A computer user has a flat screen monitor. What do you recommend in regard to a screen saver?

56. What adapter interface would you recommend for video? [ISA | EISA | MCA | VL-bus | PCI | AGP | PCIe] Explain your answer.

57. What is a video accelerator?

58. List three ways to increase video performance on a computer.

59. Why is having memory on the video adapter so important?

60. What is the minimum amount of video memory needed for true color (32-bit) at 1024×768? [1MB | 2MB | 4MB | 512KB | 8MB | 16MB]

61. How many colors can a 24-bit video adapter display? [16 | 256 | 64K | 256K | 1M | 16M]

62. What steps should be performed *before* installing a video adapter?

63. [T | F] Monitors can use USB and IEEE1394 to attach to a system.

64. When troubleshooting a non-green monitor, you disconnect the monitor cable and the monitor has a raster. Is the problem most likely in the monitor or with the video adapter?

65. Why are software problems more prevalent than hardware problems in the video subsystem?

66. How do you prove that the video driver is causing the problem?

67. A monitor has had its resolution and number of colors set too high and now the output looks horrible. List two things a technician can do to solve this problem.

68. What subsystems do all printers have in common?

69. What major printer subsystem handles dot matrix printer ribbon movement?

70. What major printer subsystem handles moving the paper from the fuser rollers to a laser printer's output bin?

71. What major printer subsystem tells the printer how to print a particular font size?

72. What major printer subsystem sends an error message that the ink jet printer is out of paper?

73. [T | F] Most printers connect to the parallel or serial port.

74. If a customer asks for a printer recommendation, which type of printer would you recommend and why?

75. List two ways to share a printer with another computer.

76. Explain how a printer can participate in a wireless network.

77. What type of printer is best for multiple-part forms?

78. What are some common dot matrix printhead pin configurations?

79. What does a dot matrix printhead *not firing* mean?

80. A dot matrix printer that normally prints bidirectionally starts printing only left to right. Why does this occur?

81. Why are some ink jet cartridges better than a dot matrix printhead?

82. What is the major difference between ink jet printers and dot matrix printers?

83. [T | F] Most ink jet printers use heat to make the ink squirt onto the paper.

84. What can a user do if ink is smearing on an ink jet printer's output?

85. What stage of the laser printing process prepares the photosensitive drum for use?

86. Explain how data is written to the laser printer drum.

87. [T | F] The laser printer's conditioning phase precedes the writing phase.

88. How does the toner inside a laser printer's toner cartridge get magnetically charged?

89. [T | F] The amount of toner allowed onto the laser printer's drum is normally adjustable.

90. Explain how the toner permanently adheres to the paper from a laser printer.

91. A customer calls to explain that her new laser printer makes a funny sound as if it is printing something every 30 minutes, but nothing comes out of the printer. What is the solution to this problem?

92. [T | F] In the laser printing process, another name for the Conditioning phase is the Expose stage.

93. Match the laser part on the left with a description on the right.

   _____Cleaning pad   a. is an alternative to a primary corona wire
   _____Conditioning roller   b. neutralizes charges on the drum
   _____Density control blade   c. applies oil to the fusing roller
   _____Drum   d. allows a particular amount of toner onto the drum
   _____Erase lamp   e. accepts data from LEDs and should not be exposed to light

94. How do you clean toner from clothing?

95. Do reinked dot matrix printer ribbons produce the same output as new ribbons? Explain your answer.

96. Do refilled ink jet cartridges produce the same output as a new ink jet cartridge? Explain your answer.

97. Explain criteria to expect when purchasing remanufactured laser toner cartridges.

98. A Windows XP computer has Microsoft Visio and Office, Adobe Illustrator, and Paint Shop Pro applications loaded. How many print drivers are needed for this computer?

99. Explain what a hard drive has to do with a print spooler.

100. [T | F] PostScript is a page description language every laser printer supports.

101. What printer check proves that the printer is operational (not checking for communication between the operating system and the printer)?

102. [T | F] Educating the user is part of the printer installation process.

103. List one piece of advice to give a customer who has just had a new printer installed.

104. What is the best preventive maintenance routine for a dot matrix printer?

105. Why should you *not* use compressed air to remove toner from a laser printer?

106. Why should you *not* use a regular vacuum cleaner to remove toner from a laser printer?

107. List two ways to print from Windows.

108. What Windows utility steps through the printer installation process?

109. What is the difference between a network printer and a local printer?

110. List an instance when a printer *would not* be chosen as a default printer during the installation process.

111. What printer *Properties* tab contains the *Print test page* button?

112. What is the purpose of print spooling?

113. What is the default spool data format?

114. [T | F] Windows Office and Adobe Acrobat could conceivably use a different print driver for the same printer if Windows XP is being used.

115. If a test page does not print, what should you check on the printer?

9

Other Peripherals

116. Describe the steps to access the printer troubleshooting tool in Windows XP.

117. If the troubleshooting tool does not solve a printing problem, what is your next step?

118. List two USB troubleshooting tips.

119. If a white line appears across one row of dot matrix print, what are the possible suspect components?

120. What is the most likely laser printer suspect component if a horizontal white line appears periodically throughout a printed page?

121. List one symptom of insufficient memory on a laser printer.

122. List two things you can do if an ordered memory upgrade has not arrived, but the laser printer is demonstrating out of memory errors.

123. List one instance of someone being unethical in a work environment. How would you recommend that he or she act more professionally?

124. List three tips for demonstrating good work ethics. Give an example with each tip.

Fill-in-the-Blank

1. The smallest image on a display is a/an _____.

2. The measurement that describes the distance between red dots on a screen is _____.

3. Dot pitch is measured in _____.

4. The part of the LCD that blocks the light is the _____.

5. An LCD is technically always on except for the part of the light that is being blocked. This "always on" trait is provided by the _____ LCD part.

6. Video technology used by projectors is _____.

7. One port used to connect a touchscreen monitor is a/an _____ port.

8. A SXGA+ video adapter could provide a video resolution up to _____.

9. The total number of pixels on a monitor is the monitor's _____.

10. The speed at which the horizontal beam crosses the monitor is the _____.

11. The vertical scan rate is more commonly called a monitor's _____.

12. A monitor that has the ability to use various vertical and horizontal scan rates is a/an _____.

13. The Vista _____ control panel is used to view the refresh rate on a monitor.

14. A symbol sometimes seen on a monitor button used to remove unwanted magnetism from a monitor is the _____ symbol.

15. The _____ monitor button is used to adjust the viewing angle on some monitors.

16. The _____ type of passive matrix LCD improves brightness by twisting light rays.

17. An active matrix display with a resolution of 1024×768 has _____ transistors.

18. _____ is another term for response time or how long it takes to draw a screen on an LCD monitor.

19. How fast a pixel changes colors is the LCD monitor _____ rate.

20. The _____ is where you can still see the image of the LCD monitor even though you are not directly in front of it.

21. Candelas per square meter are used in measuring an LCD monitor's _____.

22. _____ displays are LCDs used on tower computers.

23. A/An _____ provides AC voltage to the backlight bulb on an LCD monitor.

24. A 24-pin port on a video adapter is commonly called a/an _____.

25. The maximum DVI cable length, according to the standards, is _____ feet.

26. An upgrade to the DVI port is _____, which can carry both audio and video.

27. A _____ allows one set of input devices to control multiple computers.

28. A _____ card allows video signals normally seen on a TV to be viewed on a computer.

29. A _____ card is sometimes used to accept video from a surveillance camera.

30. A/An _____ displays PC output on a large screen.

31. On a Dell laptop, control the display output by using the [Fn]+ _____ keys.

32. A/An _____ offers password protection and entertainment for today's computer users, but on an older computer, it is used to prevent an image from burning into the screen.

33. The _____ does processing on the video adapter that is normally performed by the motherboard processor.

34. Memory chips with separate read and write data paths are said to be _____.

35. _____ video memory is a type of SDRAM for video cards.

36. _____ video memory is designed by Rambus and is a competitor or GDDR SDRAM.

37. The monitor's brightness pattern is its _____.

38. A laptop display flickers when the cover is moved because the _____ is most likely loose or bad.

39. A monitor that will not come out of power saver mode might need a/an _____ or _____ update.

40. The _____ printer system has rollers that pull and push paper through the printer.

41. The _____ printer subsystem includes the laser printer toner cartridge.

42. The _____ printer subsystem allows a user to print a test page from the Windows environment.

43. The _____ port is the most popular for connecting a printer to a computer.

44. USB printers accept data in _____-byte chunks because it uses USB bulk transfers.

45. The USB controller assigns a USB printer a/an _____ used in tracking the printer.

46. A/An _____ connects a printer to the network and allows multiple computers to print to this printer.

47. A/An _____ printer produces color output at a moderate price.

48. The _____ printer produces the highest quality output at the fastest rate.

49. The _____ printer is also called an impact printer.

50. The dot matrix _____ houses the printwires that strike the ribbon to produce a dot on the paper.

51. A dot matrix printer speed is measured in _____.

52. The _____ on a dot matrix printer needs replacing at times because the pins strike a ribbon.

53. _____ printers have tiny nozzles from which ink squirts onto the paper.

54. The _____ holds an ink jet printer's ink and functions as the printhead.

55. Ink jet and laser printer output is commonly measured in _____. The higher this number, the better the quality of the output.

56. _____ printers operate on the same principle as a copy machine.

57. The way in which 1 s and 0s write to the laser printer's surface is by using a/an _____ or a/an _____.

58. The _____ or the _____ applies a uniform negative voltage to the laser drum.

59. _____ is powder made of plastic resin particles and organic compounds bound to iron oxide.

60. The _____ controls the amount of toner allowed onto the drum.

61. The _____ or the _____ applies a positive voltage on the back of the paper in a laser printer.

62. The _____ sits on top of the fusing roller and lubricates it.

63. A/An _____ is a piece of software needed for printer operation.

64. Storing data on the hard drive until the printer needs it is called _____.

65. _____ fonts are the most basic type.

66. _____ fonts are created from a mathematical model.

67. _____ fonts can be rotated.

68. _____ and _____ are the two most common page description languages for laser printers.

69. _____ is the Windows Vista upgrade to GDI.

70. Special vacuum _____ are needed when cleaning laser printers.

71. When a document has been sent to the printer a printer icon appears in the _____ indicating you can still cancel the print job.

72. The Windows XP _____ control panel is used to add a printer.

73. The default Windows printer has a/an _____ above the printer icon in the *Printers* window.

74. An alternative to the EMF spool data format is _____.

75. Windows has a/an _____ tool to help with printing problems.

76. Ink jet printers frequently have a built-in _____ cleaning routine to clean the ink jet cartridge.

77. Clean a laser conditioning roller with a/an _____.

78. A set of morals used at work is known as _____.

Hands-On Exercises

1. Exploring Video in Windows XP

Objective: To explore video properties using Windows XP

Parts: A computer with Windows XP installed

Procedure: Complete the following procedure and answer the accompanying questions.

1. Power on the computer and log on using the userid and password provided by the instructor or lab assistant.

2. Click the *Start* button and click *Control Panel*.

3. If in Category View, click *Performance and Maintenance*. In both views, open *Administrative Tools* and double-click the *Computer Management* icon.

4. In the left window, click *Device Manager*. In the right window, expand the *Display Adapters* option.

   Assuming that the monitor flickers and redraws the screen incorrectly when a window is moved or resized, what three things are recommended?

5. Right-click a specific video adapter and select *Properties*.

   What bus does the video adapter use?

   Can the display adapter be disabled through the *General* tab?

6. Click the *Driver* tab and click the *Driver Details* button.

   What video driver version is being used?

   List the driver files being used including the path.

7. Click the *OK* button.

   What three other things can be done through the *Driver* tab?

8. Click the *Resources* tab.

   List the memory addresses used by the video adapter.

   What IRQ does the video adapter use?

9. Click the *Cancel* button to return to Computer Management. Expand the *Monitors* option. Right-click a specific monitor and select *Properties*.

What tabs are available in the monitor's *Properties* window?

Can the monitor's refresh rate be changed with the *Properties* window? If so, what tab is used? If not, what method is used to change the refresh rate?

Instructor initials: _____

10. Click the *Cancel* button. Close the *Computer Management* window.

2. Exploring Video in Windows Vista

Objective: To explore video properties using Windows Vista

Parts: A computer with Windows Vista installed

Procedure: Complete the following procedure and answer the accompanying questions.

1. Power on the computer and log on using the userid and password provided by the instructor or lab assistant.

2. Click the *Start* button and select *Control Panel*.

3. Open the *System* control panel.

4. In the left window, click *Device Manager*. Expand the *Display Adapters* category and select a video adapter.

Assuming that the monitor flickers and redraws the screen incorrectly when a window is moved or resized, what three things are recommended?

5. Right-click on a specific video adapter and select *Properties*.

What bus does the video adapter use?

Can the display adapter be disabled through the *General* tab?

6. Click the *Driver* tab.

What video driver version is being used?

Can the display adapter be disabled through the *Driver* tab?

7. Click the *Driver Details* button.

List at least two driver files being used including the path.

8. Click the *OK* button.

What three other things can be done through the *Driver* tab?

9. Click the *Resources* tab.

List at least three memory address ranges used by the video adapter.

What IRQ does the video adapter use?

10. Click the *Cancel* button to return to Device Manager. Expand the *Monitors* category. Right-click on a specific monitor and select *Properties*.

What tabs are available in the monitor's *Properties* window?

Can the monitor's refresh rate be changed with the *Properties* window? If so, what tab is used? If not, what method is used to change the refresh rate?

Instructor initials: _____

11. Click the *Cancel* button. Close the *Device Manager* window. Close the *System* control panel window.

9

Other Peripherals

3. Configuring a Second Monitor Attached to the Same PC

Objective: To connect two monitors and configure XP/Vista

Parts: A computer with Windows XP/Vista loaded

Two video adapters with monitors attached *or* one video adapter that has two video ports with monitors attached

Note: One monitor should be installed, configured, and working *before* beginning this exercise.

Procedure: Complete the following procedure and answer the accompanying questions.

1. Power on the computer and log on using the userid and password provided by the instructor or lab assistant.

2. Enter *BIOS Setup* and verify if an option exists to select the order video adapters initialize. Ensure the adapter that is currently installed initializes first. Save the settings.

3. Power off the computer, remove the power cord, and install the second video adapter if necessary. Attach the second monitor to the video port on either the newly installed video adapter or the second video port on the original video adapter.

4. Power on the computer. If a new video adapter has been installed, Windows will prompt you for the appropriate driver. If this does not occur, manually add the adapter using the *Add Hardware* control panel.

5. Right-click an empty space on the desktop and select *Properties* (XP) or *Personalization* → *Display settings* link (Vista). Click the *Settings* tab. Two blue numbered boxes appear in the top section. If you arrange the boxes to be side by side, the monitor output will be spread across the two monitors from left to right. If you vertically arrange the boxes, the desktop will be shown on both screens from top to bottom. Windows XP supports up to 10 monitors in a single system.

6. Select the *Display* drop-down menu to select the individual monitor. Once selected, the resolution and quality can be adjusted. Ensure the *Extend my Windows desktop onto this monitor* checkbox is enabled. Click *Apply*. For some monitors, Windows may have to be started.

4. Determining the Amount of Video Memory

Objective: To determine how much memory should be installed on a video adapter based on customer requirements

Parts: None

Questions: Answer the questions using the situation given.

1. What is the minimum memory (512KB, 1MB, 2MB, 4MB, or 8MB) a video adapter needs if a user wants a 1024×768 resolution with 16 million colors available?

2. What is the minimum memory (512KB, 1MB, 2MB, 4MB, or 8MB) a video adapter needs if a user wants an 800×600 resolution with 65,536 colors available?

3. A video card has 512MB of memory and is a 32-bit color adapter. The user wants to display 16 million colors at a resolution of 1024×768 and plays games that have 3D graphics. Is the amount of installed memory on the video adapter adequate? Justify your answer.

4. A video card has 256MB of memory. The user complains that when watching video clips, the sound and video are sometimes choppy. Upon investigation, the technician determines that the total graphics memory is 1535MB, dedicated memory is 256MB, and shared system memory is 1279MB. What does this mean, and what would you recommend to this customer if you were the technician?

5. What is the minimum recommended memory for a video card purchased for a brand new system? Explain your answer.

5. Determining the Minimum Video Memory Installed

Objective: To understand how to calculate the amount of video memory based on the number of color bits and resolution settings

Parts: Windows XP/Vista computer

Procedure: Complete the following procedure and answer the accompanying questions.

1. Turn on the computer and verify that the operating system loads. Log in using the userid and password provided by the instructor or lab assistant.

2. Right-click an empty Desktop space and select *Properties* → *Settings* tab (XP) or *Personalize* → *Display settings* link (Vista). The *Display Properties* window opens.

3. Answer the questions that follow. When finished, close any open windows.

4. Click the *Settings* tab.

Questions:

1. In the Colors section, what is the number of bits used for color?

2. How many colors can be displayed using the number found in Question 1?

3. What is the current resolution setting? (This number is listed as *x* by *x* pixels.)

4. Calculate the amount of memory required by multiplying the two numbers that make up the resolution. These numbers are your answer to Question 2. (For example, if the resolution is listed as 800×600, the calculation would be 800 times 600 equals 480,000.)

$$\underline{\hspace{3cm}} \times \underline{\hspace{3cm}} = \underline{\hspace{3cm}}$$
horizontal bits   vertical bits   TOTAL 1

5. Take the result of Question 3 (TOTAL 1) and multiply by the number of color bits (the answer to Question 1). The result is the minimum amount of video memory installed *in bits*.

$$\underline{\hspace{3cm}} \times \underline{\hspace{3cm}} = \underline{\hspace{3cm}}$$
TOTAL 1   color bits   TOTAL 2

6. Take the result of Question 4 (TOTAL 2) and divide by eight to determine the minimum amount of video memory installed *in bytes*.

$$\underline{\hspace{3cm}} \div \underline{\hspace{3cm}} = \underline{\hspace{3cm}}$$
TOTAL 2   8   video memory in bytes

6. Installing a Generic/Text Only Print Driver on a Windows XP Computer

Objective: To install a generic print driver on a Windows XP computer and examine printer properties

Parts: A computer with Windows XP installed

Notes: (1) A printer is not required to be attached to the computer for this lab to be executed; (2) in order to install a printer, you must log on as Administrator (or use a userid that belongs to the Administrator's group) or a userid that belongs to the Power Users' group (that has the specific permission to load/unload a device driver).

Procedure: Complete the following procedure and answer the accompanying questions.

1. Power on the computer and log on using the userid and password provided by the instructor or lab assistant.

   Is a printer attached to the PC? If so, does it attach using the parallel port or the USB port?

2. Click the *Start* button → *Printers and Faxes* and the *Add a Printer* wizard appears → *Next* → disable (uncheck) the *Automatically detect and install my Plug and Play printer* radio button → *Next* → ensure the LPT1 port is chosen (no matter if a printer attaches to the PC already—you will not be printing from this print driver) → in the *Manufacturer* column, select *Generic* → in the *Printers* column, select *Generic/Text Only* → *Next* → in the *Printer name* textbox, type **Class Printer** → select *No* when asked if you want to use this printer

Other Peripherals 9

as the default printer (unless there is no printer attached and the system forces you to select *Yes*) → *Next* → *Next* → *No* when you are asked *Do you want to print a test page* → *Finish*.

3. From the *Printers and Faxes* control panel, locate the *Class Printer*, right-click it, and select *Properties*.

   What tabs are available with the generic print driver? On the *General* tab, what button do you think would be useful to a technician when troubleshooting a printing problem?

4. Click the *Printing Preferences* button. Click the *Landscape* radio button.

   For what do you think this feature is used?

5. Select the *Paper/Quality* tab. Click the *Paper Source* drop-down menu.

   What options are available even with a generic print driver?

6. Select the *Advanced* button.

   List three paper size options.

7. Click *Cancel*; click *Cancel* again. Click the *Sharing* tab.

   What do you think is the purpose of the *Sharing* tab?

8. Click the *Ports* tab. Notice how LPT1 is checked. If you made a mistake during installation and selected the wrong port, you could change it here. Click the *USB* option and *Apply*.

9. Click the *Question Mark* button in the upper right corner of the *Properties* window. Hold the mouse pointer over the *Enable printer spooling* option at the bottom of the *Ports* tab and click. A help window appears.

   What is the purpose of the Enable printer spooling based on the information shown in the help window?

10. Select the *Advanced* tab. Notice the spooling options in the middle of the window.

    What is the default print spooling option?

11. Select the *Printing Defaults* button. Through this option you can select the default quality and orientation the printer uses to print. Users must change the settings if they want something other than this. Click *Cancel*. Click the *Separator Page* button.

    What is the purpose of a separator page?

12. Click *Cancel*. Click *OK*.

13. To rename the Class Printer driver, ensure *Class Printer* is selected in the *Printers and Faxes* control panel. Select the *Rename this printer* link in the left panel. The *Class Printer* name highlights and is able to be renamed. Type **IT Group Printer**. Click in any blank space in the window.

14. To delete the IT Group Printer, ensure IT Group Printer is selected in the *Printers and Faxes* control panel. Select the *Delete this printer* link in the left panel → *Yes*.

7. Installing a Local Printer on a Windows XP Computer

Objective: To install a local printer on a Windows XP computer

Parts: A computer with Windows XP installed and a printer physically attached to an LPT, COM, or USB port

            Appropriate printer driver for XP

Notes: (1) Always refer to the printer installation guide for installing a new printer. Some printers have their own CD and installation wizard that installs the driver and software; (2) in order to install a printer, you must log on as an Administrator (or use a userid that belongs to Administrators group) or a userid that belongs to the Power Users group (that has the specific permission to load/unload a device driver); (3) printers can be plug and play or non-plug and play. Refer to the appropriate section for installation instructions. If unsure, try the plug and play directions first.

Procedure: Complete the following procedure and answer the accompanying questions.

Plug and Play Instructions

1. Power on the computer and log on using the userid and password provided by the instructor or lab assistant.

2. Attach the printer cable to the correct computer port. Attach the power cord to the printer if necessary and insert the other end into a wall outlet. Power on the printer.

3. Windows normally detects a plug and play printer and may complete all the installation steps automatically.

   Did Windows XP automatically detect and install the printer?

4. If the Found New Hardware wizard appears, select the *Install the software automatically (recommended)* option and click *Next*. Follow the installation instructions on the screen. Print a test document to ensure the printer works correctly.

   Did the printer print correctly? If not, follow the non-plug and play instructions.

Instructor initials: _____

Non-Plug and Play Instructions

5. Power on the computer and log on using the userid and password provided by the instructor or lab assistant.

6. Attach the printer cable to the correct computer port. Attach the power cord to the printer if necessary and insert the other end into a wall outlet. Power on the printer.

7. Click the *Start* button and select *Printers and Faxes*. Double-click the *Add Printer* icon. Click the *Next* button.

8. Select the *Local printer attached to this computer* radio button and click the *Next* button. Windows automatically searches for a printer and if it finds one, the printer driver automatically installs.

   Did Windows automatically find the printer?

9. If a printer is not found, a printer port must be chosen. Using the drop-down port menu, select the appropriate printer port and click *Next*. Select the appropriate printer manufacturer and model and click *Next* or insert printer driver disk or CD and click *Have Disk*. Type a printer name or accept the default name. Optionally, select the printer as the default printer and click *Next*. In this exercise, you will not be sharing the printer across a network. Click *Next* and click *Finish*. Print a test document to verify printer operation.

   Did the printer print correctly? If not, perform appropriate troubleshooting.

Instructor initials: _____

8. Exploring a Windows Vista Printer

Objective: To explore printer options available through Windows Vista

Parts: A computer with Windows Vista installed and a printer available through the computer

Procedure: Complete the following procedure and answer the accompanying questions.

1. Power on the computer and log on using the userid and password provided by the instructor or lab assistant.

2. Select *Start* button → *Control Panel* → *Printer* link. Right-click the installed printer and select *Printing Preferences*.

   What is the default quality mode for this printer?

   Is this the most cost-efficient mode available? If not, what is?

3. Click the *Cancel* button. Right-click the installed printer.

   List one instance in which a technician might use the *Pause Printing* option. If you do not know, research the answer on the Internet.

9

Other Peripherals

4. Select the *Sharing* option.

   List the steps necessary to share this printer with other computers.

5. Right-click the installed printer.

   When would a technician use the *Use Printer Offline* option? If you do not know, research the answer on the Internet.

6. Select *Properties*.

   List information that might be important for business documentation purposes.

   What button would a technician commonly use in troubleshooting a printer problem?

7. Click the *Ports* tab.

   To what port does the printer attach?

8. Click the *Cancel* button.

Internet Discovery

Objective: To obtain specific information on the Internet regarding a computer or its associated parts

Parts: Computer with access to the Internet

Questions: Use the Internet to answer the following questions.

1. A customer states that while playing Spore Galactic Adventures produced by Electronic Arts, the following message comes on the screen: "Could not start the renderer. Please ensure your display is set to 32 bits. [1001]." Write the solution and the URL where you found the answer.

2. The following statement is found on the Internet, "When a monitor goes bad you are usually stuck with replacing it." List the URL where you found this quote. Expand on this idea in stating with whether you agree with it or not and why.

3. What does the term *pincushion distortion* mean as it relates to monitors? Find a Web site that puts it in plain English and make a note of the URL.

4. Locate a Web site that has a video of how to upgrade laptop memory. Write the URL and a few sentences describing the helpfulness of the video and whether you would recommend this video to a student new to laptop upgrades. Use correct capitalization, punctuation, and grammar.

5. Using the Internet, determine what type of ports an Epson Stylus C88+ printer supports. Write the ports and the URL where you found this information.

6. Could this printer be connected to a wireless network based on information learned in the chapter? If so, how? If not, why not?

7. A customer has a Lexmark E460 laser printer connected to a computer that has just been upgraded to Windows Vista. Does Lexmark provide a Vista-capable printer driver for this printer? Which level of reset is a full factory reset? Write the answer and the URL where you found the solution.

8. How do you reset the HP LaserJet P2035 to factory default settings? Write the answer and list the URL where you found the answer.

Soft Skills

Objective: To enhance and fine-tune a future technician's ability to listen, communicate in both written and oral form, and support people who use computers in a professional manner

Activities:

1. Access a monitor setup menu. Make a list of some of the settings that would be helpful to a computer user. Include in your list a description of the function. Document this in such a way that it could be given to users as a how-to guide.

2. Write a paragraph describing someone with a negative attitude including explanations of how the person exhibited the negative traits. Then write a paragraph that details how the person with the negative attitude could have done things in a more positive way. Share your findings with an assigned group.

3. The class is divided into six groups. Each group is assigned a laser printing process. The group has 20 minutes to research the process. At the end of 20 minutes each team explains the process to the rest of the class.

4. Pretend you have a job as a computer technician. You just solved a printer problem. Using good written communication skills, document the problem as well as the solution in a professional format. Exchange your problem/solution with a classmate and critique each other's writings. Based on their suggestions and your own background, refine your documentation. Share your documentation with the rest of the class.

Critical Thinking Skills

Objective: To analyze and evaluate information as well as apply learned information to new or different situations

Activities:

1. A person wants to build a computer and needs help with the video system. Using materials or magazines provided by the instructor or Internet research, recommend the PC video system keeping in mind that the customer has a motherboard with PCIe slots, uses Word processing, spreadsheets, and Web browsing, and has a budget of $500 for these components.

2. A person wants to build a computer and needs help with the video system. Using materials or magazines provided by the instructor or Internet research, recommend the PC video system keeping in mind that the customer has a motherboard with multiple AGP slots, plays a lot of computer-based games, and does not have a particular budget for these components.

3. Two networked PCs and a printer are needed for this activity. Connect a printer to a PC. Install the printer, configure the default settings to something different from the current settings, share the printer, and print from another PC that connects to the same network.

4. Interview a technician regarding a printing problem. List the steps they took and make notes as to how they might have done the steps differently based on what you have learned. Share the experience with the class.

9

Other Peripherals

Internet Connectivity

Objectives

After completing this chapter you will be able to

- Describe the difference between serial and parallel data transfers
- Configure a serial port and an external modem and all associated system resources and individual settings; configure an internal modem with all associated settings
- Define basic handshaking between a DTE device and a DCE device
- Use Windows tools to determine which system resources can be assigned to serial devices and determine if they are working properly
- Explain basic modem concepts and analog modem limitations
- Compare and contrast different modems such as analog, cable, digital, fax, satellite, and wireless modems
- Perform basic modem troubleshooting
- Explain the benefits of mentoring in the IT field

Internet Connectivity Overview

Connecting to the Internet can be done in a variety of ways: via analog modem, ISDN, cable modem, DSL modem, satellite modem, wirelessly, powerline, or cellular network. Each of these technologies has its own installation method and configuration, but they all have in common the ability to connect a computer to an outside network. Each of these technologies is a viable option for connectivity in a specific situation. By examining the technologies and understanding them, you can offer customers connectivity options. More information about troubleshooting network connectivity is provided in Chapter 13. Let's start with the oldest method—analog modems.

Modems Overview

Tech Tip

One of the few serial devices left is a modem. Traditionally, there were other serial devices including mice, trackballs, printers, digitizers, plotters, and scanners to name a few. Serial printers might still be found today if a printer needs to be located 50 feet or less from the computer.

A modem (modulator/demodulator) connects the computer with the outside world through a phone line. Modems can be internal or external peripheral devices. An internal modem is an adapter installed in an expansion slot. An external modem attaches to a serial port. A modem converts a signal transmitted over the phone line to digital 1s and 0s to be read by the computer. It also converts the digital 1s and 0s from the computer and modulates them onto the carrier signal and sending out to the phone line. Modems normally connect to a remote modem through the phone line. Figure 10.1 shows two modems connecting two computers.

When connecting a modem to a phone line, be careful with the cabling

Some modems have two jacks on the back. The labeling varies, but one jack is usually labeled PHONE and the other labeled LINE. The LINE jack is for the cable that goes from the modem to the phone wall jack. The modem's PHONE jack is an optional jack to connect a telephone to the modem. Figure 10.2 shows the ports on an internal modem.

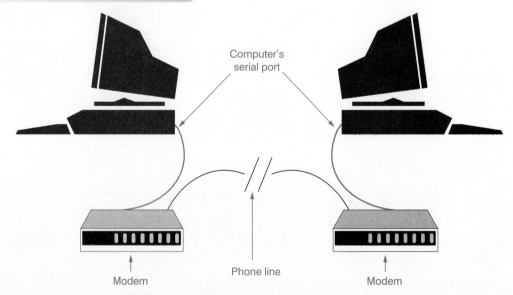

Figure 10.1   **Sample modem connection**

Figure 10.2   **Internal modem ports**

Serial Communication Overview

Serial devices such as modems transmit or receive information one bit at a time. In contrast, parallel devices transmit data eight bits at a time. Serial transmissions are much slower than parallel transmissions because one bit is sent at a time instead of eight. Figure 10.3 compares serial and parallel transmissions.

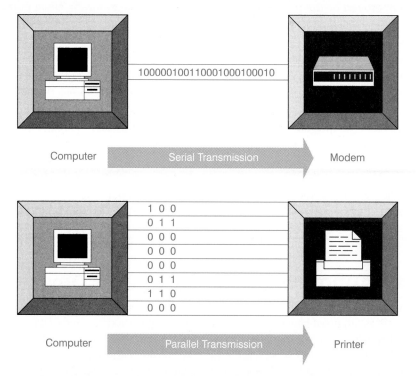

Figure 10.3   **Serial versus parallel transmissions**

Even though serial transmissions are slower than parallel, they travel longer distances more accurately than parallel transmissions. Serial cables should be no more than 50 feet long. The possibility for data loss is more likely in distances greater than 50 feet. Parallel cables should be no longer than 15 feet.

Serial devices are frequently external and connect to a serial port. A device such as an internal modem may be on an adapter. Serial ports are also known as asynchronous ports, COM ports, or RS232 ports. **Asynchronous** transmissions add extra bits to the data to track when each byte starts and ends. Synchronous transmissions rely on an external clock to time the data reception or transmission. Basic terminology associated with asynchronous transmissions is found in Table 10.1. Figure 10.4 illustrates a 9-pin serial port found on a motherboard.

Tech Tip

Configuring transmission speeds

When configuring the serial port or using an application such as HyperTerminal, the configured speed is the rate at which the serial port transmits. This is *not* the speed for an external serial device that connects to the port (such as a modem).

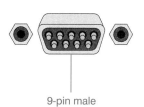

9-pin male

Figure 10.4   **9-pin serial port**

10

Internet
Connectivity

Table 10.1	Serial asynchronous transmission terminology
Term	**Description**
start bit	Used in asynchronous transmissions to signal the start of the data.
stop bit	Used in asynchronous transmissions to signal the end of the data.
RS232C	Standard approved by the EIA (Electronics Industries Alliance) for the serial port used on a computer. Because serial devices use the 9- or 25-pin connector defined by this standard, they are commonly called RS232 serial devices.
bps (bits per second)	A measurement used to describe the transmission speed of serial devices and ports. Settings include 110, 300, 1200, 2400, 4800, 9600, 19200, 38400, 57600, and 115200. The application software must match the serial device or serial port's bits per second rate.
baud	The number of times an analog signal changes in one second. Some used to use this term to speak of the modem speed. With today's modulation techniques, modems can send several bits in one cycle, so it is more accurate to specify modem speed in bits per second, or bps.
UART (Universal Asynchronous Receiver/ Transmitter)	A chip on the motherboard for an integrated serial port or on the adapter of an internal modem. It converts a data byte into a serial data stream of single 1s and 0s for transmission. It also receives the bit stream and stores data in its own buffers until the processor can accept the data.

How to Configure Serial Ports and Devices

Serial ports and devices such as internal modems have three important configuration parameters (and others as well, as discussed later): interrupt, I/O (input/output) address, and COM port number. An internal modem has all these parameters; an external modem uses these same parameters, but they are assigned to the serial port to which the external modem connects. Serial devices are normally assigned IRQ3 or IRQ4. An IRQ allows each device to request the attention of the processor.

Each serial port or device *must* be assigned a different I/O address. An I/O address is comparable to a device's mailbox number so that the processor can differentiate between devices. No single I/O address may be shared by two devices. The assigned I/O address determines the serial port's COM port number.

Every serial device or port must also have a different COM port number. External serial devices inherit the COM port name assigned to the motherboard or adapter serial port to which the serial device connects. The operating system assigns the serial port a COM port number such as COM1, COM2, COM3, or COM4.

On boot up, the BIOS looks for serial devices at I/O addresses 3F8, 2F8, 3E8, and then 2E8 *in that exact order*. The serial device or port at I/O address 3F8 is assigned the COM port number COM1. If BIOS finds a serial device or port at I/O address 2F8, that port or device is assigned COM2. Then, for I/O addresses 3E8 followed by 2E8, the attached serial devices or ports are assigned the COM port numbers COM3 and COM4, respectively. Table 10.2 lists the common IRQs, I/O addresses, and COM port assignments for serial devices and serial ports.

Table 10.2	Serial port assignments	
I/O address	**COM port name**	**IRQ**
3F8	COM1	4
2F8	COM2	3

The system BIOS setup program can be used to configure integrated serial ports. Common BIOS settings include IRQ, I/O address, COM port name, and disable. Use the setup program rather than Windows to configure integrated ports initially.

Application settings and hardware settings must match

Applications that communicate or control serial devices must have the application settings match the hardware settings or communication will not occur.

Most software applications used with serial devices require configuration. For example, if using a communication software package with a modem, the communications software must be configured for the specific interrupt, I/O address, and COM port that the modem uses.

Exercises at the end of the chapter show how to view serial device resources. No matter which operating system is being used, a technician must be aware of the hardware resources used and the resources available for serial devices.

More Serial Port Settings

A good understanding of how serial devices operate is essential to a technician's knowledge base. Before installing a serial device and configuring its associated software, a technician must be familiar with the terminology associated with serial device installation. Table 10.3 lists the various serial port settings.

The two common methods for flow control are XON/XOFF (software method) and RTS/CTS (hardware method). The **XON/XOFF** handshaking sends special control characters when a serial device needs more time to process data or is ready to receive more data. If one modem needs the remote modem to wait, it will send a certain character (usually [Ctrl]+[S]). Then, when the modem is ready to accept more data, a different control character (usually [Ctrl]+[Q]) is sent.

How does parity work?

Most think of parity as even parity or odd parity. Take the example of a computer that uses even parity. If the data sent is 10101010, a total of four 1s is sent, plus a 0 for the parity bit. Four is an even number; therefore, the parity bit is set to a 0 because the total number of 1s must be an even number when even parity is used. If the data sent is 10101011, a total of five 1s is sent, plus an extra 1 for the parity bit. Because five is an odd number and the system uses even parity, then the extra parity bit is set to a 1 to make the total number of 1s an even number.

Table 10.3	Serial port settings
Setting	**Explanation**
Data bits	Determines how many bits make up a data word. It is usually 8 bits per data word, but can be 7 or lower.
Parity	A simple method of checking data accuracy. When parity is used, both computers must be set to the same setting. The choices for parity include none, odd, even, space, and mark. With a space parity setting, both computers always set the parity bit to 0. With the mark parity setting, both computers always set the parity bit to 1. The most common setting is none for modems.
Stop bits	The number of bits sent to indicate the end of the data word. The number of stop bits can be 1, 1.5, or 2. One stop bit is the common choice.
FIFO setting	Used to enable or disable the UART chip's FIFO buffer. This setting gives the processor time to handle other tasks without the serial device losing data. If data is lost, it will have to be retransmitted later when the microprocessor turns its attention back to the serial device.
Flow control	Determines how two serial devices communicate. Can be set using software or physical pins on the serial port (hardware). Also called handshaking, which allows a serial device to tell the sending serial device, "Wait, I need a second before you send any more data."
Handshaking	The order in which things happen to allow two serial devices to communicate. Knowing this order helps with troubleshooting.

10

Internet
Connectivity

RTS/CTS (hardware handshaking) uses specific wires on the serial connector to send a signal to the other device to stop or start sending data. The **CTS** (clear to send) and the **RTS** (request to send) signals indicate when it is OK to send data. Modem communication normally uses hardware flow control (RTS/CTS) instead of software flow control. Table 10.4 delineates the hardware flow control.

Table 10.4	Hardware handshaking	
Order of execution	**Explanation**
Both devices (the DTE and the DCE) power on and are functional.	
The DTE sends a signal over the DTR (data terminal ready) line.	The DTE says, "I'm ready."
The DCE sends a signal over the DSR (data set ready) line.	The DCE says, "I'm ready, too."
The DTE sends a signal over the RTS (request to send) connector pin.	The DTE (such as the computer) says, "I would like some data."
The DCE sends a signal on the CTS (clear to send) connector pin.	The DCE (such as the modem) says, "OK, here comes some data."
Data transmits one bit at a time over a single line.	

The RS232 serial communication standard was developed during a time when mainframes were the norm. A mainframe terminal known as a DTE connected to a modem known as a DCE. In today's world, **DTE** (data terminal equipment) includes computers and printers. On a DTE serial connector, certain pins initiate communication with a DCE device, such as a modem. Table 10.5 shows the common signal names as well as the common abbreviations for the signals used with DTE devices.

Table 10.5	DTE signal connections	
Signal abbreviations	**Signal name**
TD	Transmit Data
DTR	Data Terminal Ready
RTS	Request to Send

DCE (data circuit-terminating equipment) includes devices such as modems, mice, and digitizers. On the DCE side, the signal names relate more to receiving data. Table 10.6 lists the common signal names used with DCE devices.

Table 10.6	DCE signal connections	
Signal abbreviation	**Signal name**
RD	Receive Data
DSR	Data Set Ready
CTS	Clear to Send
CD	Carrier Detect
RI	Ring Indicator

Serial Device Installation

Installing serial devices can be very frustrating. To avoid problems, install the internal modem or attach the serial device, and determine what the COM port, IRQ, and I/O settings have been assigned to the device. Check Device Manager to ensure no conflicts have occurred. Install and configure any software application that controls the device to match these settings. If the application or device has any self-test feature, use it.

Serial Device Troubleshooting

Most serial device problems are IRQ, I/O address, or COM port related. The serial device may not be working properly due to the following reasons: (1) a configuration setting conflicting with another device; (2) BIOS reassigning the COM port setting; or (3) a software's configuration setting not matching the serial device setting. Symptoms for this problem include the following: (1) the serial device does not work; (2) a different device quits working; (3) the serial device works and then locks: or (4) the computer locks during boot up. To solve this problem, go back to the discovery stage. Find out what is already installed in the computer. Try disabling serial ports not being used. Verify every setting through documentation and Device Manager.

Other problems with serial devices are provided in the following list:

- Always check the simplest solution first. Check the cable attachment. Check for bent connector and cable pins. This is more common than you would think.
- If the device is external, check to see if it needs an external power source and, if so, that the external power source is working. Be sure you plugged the external device into the correct COM port and that the cable fits securely to the connector. The PC Design recommends that teal be used to color-code serial ports. The PC Design port markings are as follows:

First serial port

Second serial port

- Using the wrong serial cable can cause many problems. The serial device may work intermittently or not at all. If possible, swap with a known good cable. Make sure you have not used a null modem cable by mistake. External modems need a **straight-through serial cable** to connect the modem to the computer. A **null modem cable** is used to connect two computers without the use of a modem.
- Check the system BIOS settings and verify the COM port used by an external serial device is not disabled in Setup, or does not conflict with an internal serial device.

Pros and Cons of Internal and External Modems

The pros and cons of external modems are numerous. Internal modems require less space than an external modem, but they do require an expansion slot, generate more heat, and place a larger load on the computer's power supply. External modems connect to an existing serial port. Internal modems are cheaper than external modems. External modems can easily connect to a different computer without taking the computer apart. External modems have lights on the outside, which are great for troubleshooting. However, many shareware programs exist, as well as software included with the internal modems, which allow a simulation of the external modem lights that can be used when troubleshooting.

Choosing between an internal modem and an external modem narrows down to the following questions:

- Is there an existing expansion slot for an internal modem?
- Is there an existing serial port available for an external modem? If not, use an internal modem (as long as you have an available slot).
- Is money an issue? If so, get an internal modem.
- Is desk space an issue? If so, get an internal modem.

When installing an internal modem, follow all guidelines for any adapter installation. When installing an external modem, connect it to an existing serial port and configure the port accordingly.

Modem Speeds and Standards

Modems transmit and receive at different speeds. A faster modem means less time on the phone line and less time for microprocessor interaction. However, because modems connect to other modems, the slowest modem determines the fastest connection speed. A slow modem can only operate at the speed for which it was designed. Connecting to a faster modem will not make the slower modem operate any faster. Fortunately, speedy modems can transmit at lower speeds.

Communication mode standards developed by CCITT (Comité Consultantif Internationale de Téléphonie et de Télégraphie) help with modem compatibility. For two modems to communicate with one another, they must adhere to the same protocol or set of rules. The CCITT V standards regulate modem speeds and compatibility. CCITT standards are now listed in articles or textbooks as ITU (International Telecommunications Union) standards. For all communication standards, check the TIA (Telecommunications Industry Association) and ITU Web sites. ITU V.10 through V.34 are standards for interfaces and voiceband modems. ITU V.35 through V.37 standards deal with wideband modems. ITU standards V.40 through V.42 deal with error control.

Modem **error correction** ensures the data is correct at the modem level rather than have the computer's CPU handle or oversee it. A modem with error correction capabilities provides for overall faster computer performance. Microcom, Inc. has its own standards for error correction as well as CCITT. The **MNP** (Microcom Network Protocol) Levels 1 through 4 determine standards for error correction. Some of the CCITT standards include the MNP data compression standard levels as well.

Like error correction, data compression is also a part of some of the modem standards. **Data compression** converts data into smaller sizes before transmitting it. Compressing the data allows faster transmissions (less data to be transmitted). A drawback to modems using some types of data compression occurs with files such as ZIP, GIF, or JPG. These files have already been compressed. The modem tries to uncompress the files, and then re-compress them for transmission. This process may actually slow down the computer's overall performance. Some of the ITU standards concern data compression. MNP Level 5 is the data compression standard from Microcom. Table 10.7 lists some of the modem standards and their features.

Analog modems are the slowest type of Internet connectivity. As a general rule of thumb, the modem's speed setting should be set to its maximum throughput. If the modem supports data compression, higher speeds are possible. Table 10.8 lists the maximum modem speeds based on the type of modem and the type of data compression used. Check the modem's documentation for the maximum speed setting.

56Kbps Modems

The phone line limit was once thought to be 28.8Kbps, then 33.6Kbps. Now modem manufacturers push even that limit. The 56Kbps data transfer rate is only possible if the transmitted (analog) signal converts to digital one time during the data transmission. Digital phone lines are

Table 10.7	Communications standards
Standard	**Comments**
V.17	14.4Kbps and lower fax ITU standard
V.22	1200bps modem ITU standard
V.22bis	2400bps modem ITU standard
V.29	9600bps and lower fax ITU standard
V.32	9600bps and lower modem ITU standard
V.32bis	14.4Kbps and lower modem ITU standard
V.32turbo	Non-CCITT (ITU) standard for 12Kbps data transfer
V.FAST	Non-CCITT (ITU) standard for 28.8Kbps data transfer. The working name for the V.34 standard until the standard became a reality.
V.FC	(Also known as V.Fast Class) Rockwell 28.8Kbps standard with data compression and error correction. Does not support speeds less than 14.4Kbps.
V.34	28.8 Kbps modem ITU standard. In October 1996, the standard changed to allow 33.6Kbps transfers. Automatically adjusts to lower speeds if line problems occur.
V.34bis	ITU data compression standard
V.42	ITU error correction standard. Covers Microcom's Levels 1 through 4 for error correction. Also known as LAPM (Link Access Procedure for Modems).
MNP-4	Microcom error correction standard
V.42bis	ITU data compression standard
V.44	ITU data compression standard
MNP-5	Microcom data compression standard
V.59	A standard for performing diagnostics
V.90	56K modem ITU standard. In February 1998, the standard resolved the battle between the two 56Kbps standards: X.2 and K56flex.
MNP-10	Microcom standard for monitoring line conditions. Can adjust modem speed up or down depending on the state of the line.
V.92	Increases data rates and supports Quick Connect as well as Modem on Hold. Quick Connect allows faster initial modem connections (handshaking). Modem on Hold allows modem connectivity even when a phone conversation is occurring on the same line.

Table 10.8	General guidelines for maximum modem speeds	
Modem type	**Type of data compression**	**Speed setting (in bps)**
V.22bis	MNP-5	4800
V.22bis	V.42bis	9600
V.32	MNP-5	19200
V.32	V.42bis	38400
V.32bis	V.42bis	38400 or 57600

10
Internet
Connectivity

quieter than their analog counterparts, have less noise on the line, and allow faster data transmissions. For example, consider the scenario of a person dialing into an office network from home, as shown in Figure 10.5.

Notice in Figure 10.5 how the signal converts twice. The first time is when the analog signal enters the phone company's central office. Between central offices, the signal stays digital.

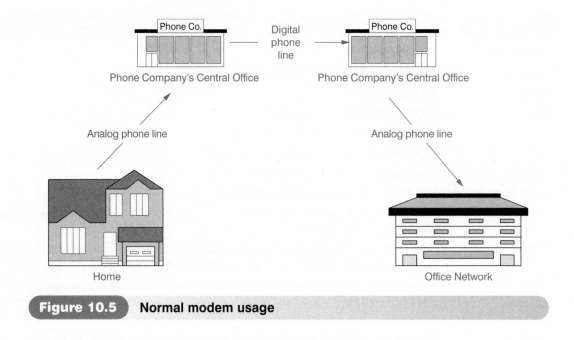

Figure 10.5 **Normal modem usage**

Then, when the signal leaves the central office to travel to the work building, the signal converts from a digital signal to an analog signal. 56Kbps transmission speeds do not support two conversions.

If the workplace has a digital line from the phone company or if a person dials into an Internet provider that has a digital phone connection, 56Kbps throughput on a 56Kbps modem is achievable. Figure 10.6 shows the difference.

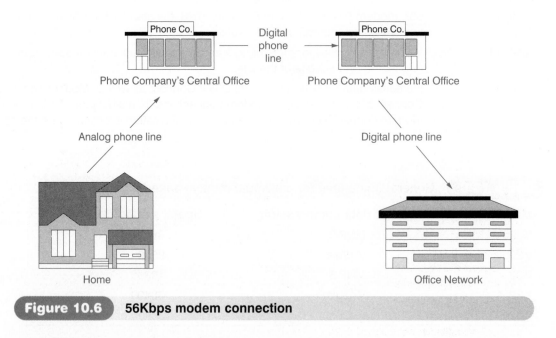

Figure 10.6 **56Kbps modem connection**

In Figure 10.6, only one analog to digital conversion exists—the one between the home and the first central office. 56Kbps speeds, in theory, can exist when only one conversion exists. However, if the modem cannot run at 56Kbps, the modem supports lower speeds such as 33.6Kbps and 28.8Kbps. Studies estimate that 56Kbps will run at 56Kbps 10 to 20 percent of the time, about the same estimated percentage of time 33.6Kbps and 28.8Kbps modems run at their top speed.

Fax Modems

A **fax modem** allows a modem to use the computer and printer as a fax machine. The modem portion brings the data to the computer. The facsimile (fax) software allows viewing, printing, replying to, or sending a fax. A regular modem sends data differently from how a fax machine sends data, so a modem can send faxes only if it is a fax modem. Not all computer-based fax machines can handle modem data transfers, but a fax modem can do both modem and fax transfers.

Fax standards handled by CCITT (ITU now) are in groups. Group I through Group IV concern fax machines. Group I and Group II are slow. A Group III bis fax modem transfers data up to 14,400bps. Group IV fax modems transmit over a digital ISDN line at speeds up to 64Kbps. ISDN technology is discussed later in the chapter.

The Internet has changed fax capabilities. Fax machines can now be used to send a fax that is received in an email account at the final destination. The fax machine can connect to a phone line that connects to a fax gateway. The fax gateway connects to a network and sends the message in email format to the final destination. A fax machine that adheres to the ITU T.37 iFax standard allows a fax machine to be connected to the data network. The fax machine formats the fax into email format for distribution to a person's email account or to the destination fax machine that has its own email address account and connects to a network.

VoIP (Voice over IP), which allows traditional voice traffic to be transmitted over the Internet or data networks rather than the traditional phone network, has affected fax capabilities. A fax machine can have a VoIP adapter installed and connect to a VoIP gateway. The VoIP gateway connects to a phone line that has a destination fax machine attached. One must realize that once something is converted into 1s and 0s, if that device can be networked, then it is just data to the network and can be transmitted.

Modem Installation

Windows has an Install New Modem wizard that automates the modem installation process. Often conflicts arise and other devices stop working or the modem does not work after using this wizard. Many technicians avoid using the wizard to detect the modem automatically. Instead, they manually select from a list of manufacturers and models or use the disk from the modem manufacturer. If the wizard selects the modem type, it might pick a compatible model. This frequently causes conflict, and the modem does not work or does not have all of its capabilities. Some plug and play modems require specific settings on power up. The settings can be manually input through the Device Manager.

Analog Modem Troubleshooting

In Windows, if the modem is not dialing at all, check the port setting by using the *Phone and Modem Options* control panel. On the *General* tab, select the correct modem. Click the *Properties* button to see the port listing and check the port settings by using the *Modem* tab. Windows has a Modem Diagnostic Tool available through the *Diagnostic* tab. Many modems have an *Advanced Port Settings* button that allows you to modify and view buffer settings. Device Manager can be used to disable error control change the flow control setting. In Device Manager, locate the modem and click the *plus* symbol. Double-click the modem, click the *Properties* tab, *Connection* tab. And select the *Advanced* button. Adjust the error control and flow control by clicking in the checkboxes beside each option.

Sometimes Windows disables a modem. To verify that the modem is enabled, use Device Manager. Verify the Device Usage checkbox next to the modem configuration. Click the *Resources* tab to determine if Windows detects a resource conflict with any other installed device. Resolve resource conflicts the same way you would resolve any other I/O address, IRQ, or memory address conflict. Refer to Chapter 3 for more resource conflict information.

If the modem keeps losing connection, use the prior troubleshooting tips and try placing the modem at a lower speed. Use the *Modem* control panel to set the lower speed. If the modem works using the Windows HyperTerminal program, but will not work with a different 32-bit communication application, try reinstalling the communication program.

All the previously mentioned troubleshooting tips for serial ports also apply to modems. However, the following additional tips specifically apply to modems:

- If the modem is an external unit, turn the modem's power off and back on, then try the modem again. If the modem is internal, reboot the computer and try the steps again.
- If the modem does not dial the number or does not output a dial tone, or if a message appears stating that the modem is not responding, check that the phone cord connects to the correct jack on the modem and to the wall phone jack. Also, be sure the correct serial cable is used, the cable secures properly to the modem and the computer, and the COM port setting is correct. Check the flow control setting or check to see if the phone line requires a special number such as a 9 to dial an outside line. Remove the cable from the phone outlet to the modem and plug it into a phone. The phone outlet should have a dial tone and work correctly.

Tech Tip

Modem hangs up or "No dial tone" appears

If the modem starts to dial but then hangs up, check to see if the phone cable from the wall jack to the modem inserts into the correct modem jack. This symptom also occurs if the "No dial tone" message appears.

- If the modem hangs up after some time, other equipment (such as fax machines, answering machines, and portable phones) can be the cause of the problem. Also, other people picking up the phone line and disconnecting the modem's connection is a common occurrence. To verify that other equipment is causing the problem, disconnect the other devices on the phone line and see if the problem is resolved. Another problem can be the call waiting feature. Is call waiting enabled on the same phone line the modem uses? If so, disable call waiting or place a *70 (or whatever number disables call waiting for your phone) before the phone number to be dialed. Check with the modem at the other end to see if it is having problems. Lower the speed of the modem and try to connect. Turn off data compression or error checking to see if one of these settings is causing the problem.
- Phone line problems can cause a modem to transmit at a lower speed. Some modems try to correct or compensate for phone line noise. This is a very common occurrence. Have the phone company check the line. Special modem lines provide a cleaner line and are available for home users. Check with the local phone company for details.
- If garbage (random characters) appears on the screen, check the handshaking, parity, stop bit, and baud rate settings. Most dial-up services require some type of emulation settings, such as VT-100 or ANSI. Check with the system provider or operator for the proper settings (or try each setting until one works).
- Verify that the modem works by using the Windows HyperTerminal program. After setting the modem's parameters, type ATE1M1V1 (using all caps—some modems are case-sensitive when using modem commands). Press Enter. The modem should reply with an *OK* on the screen. If not, the modem may not be a Hayes-compatible modem. The ATE1M1V1 is from the U.S. Robotics and Hayes modem command set. AT in ATE1M1V1 means Attention and must precede all other commands. E1 tells the modem to echo whatever is sent out. M1 turns on the modem's speaker. V1 places the modem in verbal mode. Check the modem's documentation to be sure it understands the ATE1M1V1 command. If that is not the problem, the modem may be set up on the wrong COM port in the Terminal settings. Go back and reconfigure the settings for a different COM port. The Hayes modem command ATZ resets the modem. Each modem normally comes with a manual that lists each command it understands. Table 10.9 lists common modem commands.

Table 10.9	**Common modem commands**
Command	**Purpose**
AT	Precedes modem commands
ATDT	Dials a number using touch-tone; put a space after this command and follow it with the phone number
AT&F	Resets to factory default settings
ATZ	Resets to power on settings
*70	Disables call waiting

- Another HyperTerminal check is as follows: after setting the modem's parameters, type ATDT and press [Enter]. The DT in this command tells the modem to use touch-tone dialing. A dial tone should emit from the modem speaker. If not, the modem may not be a Hayes-compatible modem and it may not understand the command ATDT. Check the modem documentation to be sure it understands the command. Then, check the modem's connection to the wall jack and the modem's speaker volume level. Refer to the modem manual. If the phone line requires a special number to connect to an outside phone line, place that number immediately after the ATDT command.
- Type AT&F to restore the factory settings and often solve obscure problems.
- If a modem is having trouble connecting, disable the error control feature. Check with the other modem site to determine if the other modem and modem settings are operational.
- If a letter appears twice on the screen for every letter typed, check the **echo mode setting** in the communications software package. The echo mode setting is sometimes called the local echo setting and, when enabled, it sends typed commands through the modem to the screen. The setting needs to have the local echo turned off. If nothing appears on the screen when you type, turn the local echo setting on. Some software settings refer to turning the local echo off as the full-duplex mode and turning the local echo on as the half-duplex mode. **Full-duplex** means that two devices can send each other data simultaneously. **Half-duplex** means that two devices can send each other data, but only one device can transmit at a time.
- If the modem dials, but the high-pitched, screeching noise that indicates connection to another modem or fax does not sound, check the phone number. The phone number dialed may be incorrect or the prefix such as a 1 for long distance may be inadvertently omitted. Another possibility is that the modem is dialing too fast for the phone line. Consult the modem's manual for slowing down the dialing.
- Use an external modem's lights to troubleshoot the problem. Manufacturers label the external lights differently, but the concept is the same. Most modems use hardware handshaking, so watching the lights and listening for the dial tone and the high-pitched noises are good troubleshooting hints. Refer to Table 10.4 for the order in which handshaking occurs. An internal modem frequently has software to show a pictorial status of it as if the modem was external. Table 10.10 shows the common external modem status lights.

Table 10.10	Common external modem lights
Abbreviation	**Purpose**
CD	Carrier detect
MR	Modem ready
RD	Receive data
SD	Send data
TR	Terminal ready

Digital Modems and ISDN

Digital modems connect the computer directly to a digital phone line rather than to a traditional analog phone line. One type of digital phone line available from the phone company is an ISDN line. An **ISDN** (Integrated Services Digital Network) line has three separate channels: two B channels and a D channel. The B channels handle data at 64Kbps transmission speeds. The D channel is for network routing information and transmits at a lower 16Kbps. The two B channels can combine into a single channel for video conferencing, thus allowing speeds up to 128Kbps. They are available in large metropolitan areas for reasonable rates, making it an affordable option for home office use, but due to recent technologies, such as cable modems and xDSL modems (covered in the next two sections), ISDN is not a popular option today.

Cable Modems

One of the most popular items in the modem industry is the **cable modem**, which connects a computer to a cable TV network. Cable modems can be internal or external devices. If the cable modem is external, two methods commonly exist for connectivity to a PC—a NIC (network interface card) is installed in the computer and a cable attaches between the NIC and the cable modem or the cable modem connects to a USB port. Figures 10.7 and 10.8 show these two types of connections.

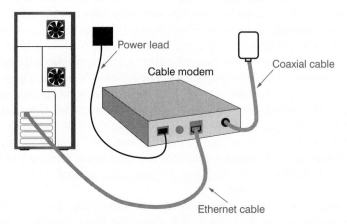

| **Figure 10.7** | **Cable modem and NIC connectivity** |

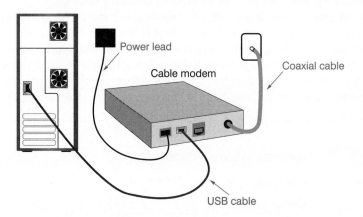

| **Figure 10.8** | **Cable modem and USB connectivity** |

The cable modem operation is not hard to understand. Internet data comes in through the cable TV coax cable. The coax cable plugs into the cable modem. The cable modem then sends the information out its built-in Ethernet port. A network cable connects from the cable modem's Ethernet port into an Ethernet port on the computer. To send data to the Internet, the reverse happens. The computer sends the data out its Ethernet port into the cable modem. The cable modem sends the data out the coax cable onto the cable TV company's network.

Two terms that are often associated with cable modems are upstream and downstream. **Upstream** refers to data that are sent from your home to the Internet. **Downstream** refers to the data pulled from the Internet into your computer, as when you download a file or view a Web page. With cable modems, downstream transfer rates are faster than upstream transfers. Downstream speeds can be as high as 35Mbps, but are normally in the 1.5–3Mbps range for consumers and higher speeds for businesses. Upstream speeds vary; with an external cable modem they tend to be between 384Kbps and 10Mbps. Even though upstream speeds are slower, cable modems are a huge improvement over analog modems.

The speed of a cable modem connection depends on two things: (1) your cable company, and (2) how many people in your neighborhood share the same cable TV provider. Each cable channel uses 6MHz of the cable's bandwidth. **Bandwidth** is the capacity of the communications channel. Bandwidth is also known as throughput or line speed. The cable company designates one of the 6MHz channels as Internet access. Several homes can use the same channel, which reduces the amount of bandwidth each house has available. If you have three neighbors who all use the same cable vendor and they all are Internet warriors, you will have slower access than if you were the only person in the neighborhood connected.

> **Tech Tip**
>
> **Cable TV and cable modem**
>
> Some cable modem Internet providers will not provide Internet access through their network unless you have the cable TV service as well.

The minimum amount of hardware needed to have a cable modem depends on the cable company's specifications. Whether or not you need an internal modem, Ethernet card, and so on, depends on the company from which you receive the cable modem. Some companies include them as part of their rate. Some cable companies install the cable modem and associated software and hardware as part of their package. If required to install the modem, always follow the manufacturer's installation instructions. The modem installs similar to any other adapter. Chapter 13 has tips on configuring network adapters.

xDSL (Digital Subscriber Line) Modems

xDSL is another modem technology that is growing in popularity. The x in the term xDSL refers to the various types of DSL that are on the market. The most common one is ADSL (Asymmetrical DSL), but there are many others. ADSL uses faster downstream speeds than upstream. This performance is fine for most home Internet users. Figure 10.9 shows a Cisco Systems, Inc.'s 675 DSL modem.

Figure 10.9   **A Cisco Systems, Inc. DSL modem**

With DSL modems, bandwidth is not shared between people in the same geographical area. The bandwidth paid for is exclusive to the user. DSL is not available in all areas. The DSL Reports Web site (http://www.dslreports.com) has a listing of major DSL vendors and geographical areas plus a rating on the service. Table 10.11 shows the most common DSL types.

With DSL, an internal or external DSL modem can be used and connected to the regular phone line. The phone line can be used for calls, faxes, and so on, at the same time as the modem. If external, the modem can connect to a USB port or an Ethernet network card. Figure 10.10 shows the DSL modem ports including the Ethernet connector, which is labeled ENET. Note that this modem does not have a USB connectivity option.

If the DSL implementation uses an internal modem, it occupies an expansion slot (usually PCI) and configures the same way an internal modem does. Always follow the manufacturer's installation instructions. Some vendors install the DSL modem and configure the computer as

Table 10.11	DSL technologies
DSL type	**Comments**
ADSL	Asymmetrical DSL—most common, faster downloads than uploads; upstream speeds from .5 to 3.5Mbps; downstream speeds from 5 to 150Mbps; uses a different frequency level for upstream and downstream communications
G.SHDSL	Symmetric High-speed DSL—upgrade to SDSL that supports symmetric data rates up to 4.6Mbps
HDSL	High bit-rate DSL—symmetrical transmission (equal speed for downloads/uploads); speeds up to 1.5Mbps
PDSL	Powerline DSL modulates data speeds from 256K to 2.7Mbps onto electrical lines and sometimes called Broadband over Powerline, or BPL
RADSL	Rate-Adaptive DSL—Developed by Westell and allows modem to adapt to phone line conditions; speeds up to 2.2Mbps
SDSL	Symmetric DSL—same speeds (up to 1.5Mbps) in both directions
UDSL	Also known as Uni-DSL or Ultra high speed DSL with speeds up to 200Mbps and backward compatible with ADSL, ADSL2+, VDSL, and VDSL2
VDSL2	Upgrade of VDSL that supports voice, video, data, and HDTV with speeds from 1 to 150Mbps downstream

Figure 10.10   DSL modem ports

part of their package. Also note that the DSL connection is viewed by the PC as a network connection.

A drawback to DSL is that the DSL signal needs to be separated from the normal phone traffic. DSL providers normally ship phone filters that must connect to each phone outlet and a phone, fax machine, or voice recorder attaches to the filter. The connection from the DSL modem to the phone outlet does not have a filter on it.

This chapter does not go into firewalls and network security; they are discussed in later chapters. It is very important when installing cable modems and DSL modems to look at information on proxy servers, firewalls, disabling file sharing, and so on. When using these technologies, the computer is more prone to attacks, viruses, taking/looking at the computer files, or taking over the computer. Figure 10.11 shows three different ways to connect a cable or DSL modem. The example on the left is the least secure. File sharing should not be enabled on the computers if connected in this manner.

Troubleshooting Cable and DSL Modems

Since most cable and DSL modems are external, the best tool for troubleshooting connectivity problems are the lights on the front of the modem. The lights will vary between vendors, but common ones include those shown in Table 10.12

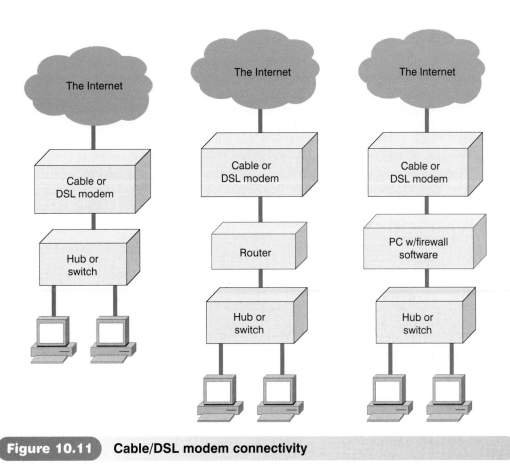

Figure 10.11   **Cable/DSL modem connectivity**

Table 10.12   **Cable/DSL modem lights and troubleshooting***

Light	Explanation
Power	Indicates power to the modem
ENET, E, or Ethernet	Usually indicates connectivity between the PC and the modem; if unlit, ensure you are using Ethernet (if using USB this will be unlit), check cabling, and check PC network card settings
USB or U	Usually indicates connectivity between the PC and the modem; if unlit, ensure you are using USB (if using a NIC, this light will be unlit), check cabling, and check Device Manager to see if the modem is recognized
Internet, Ready, or Rdy	Stays lit when the modem has established an Internet connection
PC	Used instead of Ethernet or USB lights to show the status of the connection between the modem and the PC
Cable, data, or D/S	Usually blinks to indicate connectivity with Internet provider
Link status	Usually flashes when acquiring a connection with a provider and is on steady when a link is established

*Note that you should always refer to the modem documentation for the exact status of the lights.

Once you have checked lights and possibly checked cables, if you still feel you have a problem, power off the modem, power it back on, and reboot your computer. Give the modem a couple of minutes to initialize. Most modems have a reset button that can also be used, but powering off and powering back on works. Lastly, if the modem is still not working, contact the modem service provider.

10
Internet
Connectivity

Satellite Modems

An option available to areas that do not have cable or DSL service is satellite connectivity. The satellite relays communication back to receivers on Earth. Satellite connectivity requires a satellite dish and a **satellite modem** as a minimum. It may also require an analog modem and other equipment depending on the satellite provider. If connected via satellite, the data would go from the computer to the satellite dish mounted outside your home, to another satellite dish (and maybe more), up to the satellite orbiting Earth, down to the ISP, from the ISP to the Web site requested, and the Web page returns back the same path it took. Satellite connectivity is not as fast as cable or DSL connectivity, but it can be five to seven times faster than dial-up. The downstream speeds can be from 9Kbps to 24Mbps but typically are around 500Kbps. Some providers provide the same upstream speeds.

With a satellite modem, TV programs accessed via the satellite can be watched at the same time Web pages are downloaded from the Internet. However, drawbacks to satellite modems are important to mention.

- Initial costs of installing a satellite modem can be high.
- If other people in your area subscribe to the same satellite service, speed is decreased during peak periods.
- Initial connections have a lag time associated with them, so multiplayer games are not very practical.
- VPNs (virtual private networks) are normally not supported.
- Weather elements such as high winds, rain, and snow affect performance and connectivity.

Laptop Modems

Portable computers sometimes have a modem PC Card or ExpressCard installed in them. Modem PC Cards are Type II cards that fit into a Type II or a Type III slot. Some modem cards are combo cards—they are both a modem and a NIC. Modem PC Cards have a special connector called a dongle that attaches to them and allows an RJ-11 cable to be plugged into the card. Dongles can also be used with laptop network PC Cards. Some vendors' dongles are proprietary. A spare dongle is recommended in the laptop case. Figure 10.12 shows a NIC modem PC Card with a dongle attached.

An increasingly popular feature with laptops is connectivity called **wireless broadband**, with download speeds up to 45Mbps. This technology is sometimes referred to as wireless or cellular WAN. Cell phone companies and Internet providers are offering PC Cards, ExpressCards, USB modems, mobile data cards,

Tech Tip

Laptop wireless WAN connectivity

Laptops that ship with integrated wireless WAN capabilities do not need an additional adapter or antenna. However, the BIOS must have the option enabled. Some laptops might have a key combination or switch to enable the connection. The wireless application software is available through the Start button.

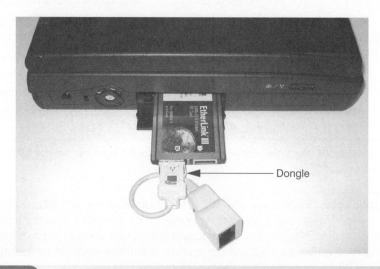

Figure 10.12 **3Com NIC/modem combo PC Card with a dongle**

or integrated laptop connectivity to have the ability to receive, create, and communicate Internet information within a coverage area. For people who travel a lot, this option gives them connectivity in places where data connectivity has not previously been feasible.

Modem Preventive Maintenance

The old adage "an ounce of prevention is worth a pound of cure" is never truer than in the case of modems. A power surge can come across a phone line just as it can travel through an electrical outlet. Most people think and worry about the computer problems that could be a result of power surges, but they do not stop to think about surges through the phone line. To provide protection for the modem and the computer, purchase a special protection device called a phone line isolator or a modem isolator at any computer or phone store. A power surge through the phone line can take out many components inside the computer, including the motherboard.

Some surge protectors also have modem protection. A phone cable from the computer plugs into the surge protector. A separate phone cable connects to another jack on the surge protector and the other end plugs into the phone wall jack. The surge protector must, of course, be plugged into a grounded outlet.

Soft Skills—Mentoring

Every great technician can tell you that they had at least one mentor along the way. When you hear the word mentor, it conjures up other words in your head—coach, guidance, teacher, adviser, positive influence, leadership, setting an example, and so on. No technician can attain his or her ultimate level without being mentored and mentoring someone else along their career path. Also, no technician can learn everything from a book or from experience. It takes others helping us along the way to learn faster and more efficiently.

When you enter your first (second, third, or fourth) job in the IT field, you should take a few days to look around the company. Find someone who appears to be very professional and knowledgeable—someone who you would like to emulate. Talk to this person and explain your goals. Ask if he or she would mentor you and detail what you would like, whether it is helping you with problems you cannot solve or advising you about office politics.

Mentoring is an important part of life. Not only should you consider being mentored, but also, along your career path, you should consider mentoring others. Many technicians tend to hoard information from other technicians and computer users. There are many who consider knowledge power (and it is to some extent), but by sharing information with others and helping them along the way, you cement and expand your own knowledge.

Key Terms

10 Internet Connectivity

Review Questions

1. List two serial devices that might be found attached to a computer today.

2. If a modem has only one RJ-11 port, what plugs into the port?
   a. A cable that connects to another modem
   b. A cable that plugs into a phone
   c. A cable that plugs into a phone outlet
   d. A cable that connects to another computer

3. Which device transmissions travel farther, serial or parallel?

4. Which device transmissions travel faster, serial or parallel?

5. [T | F] Serial devices transmit seven bits at a time.

6. Explain the difference between serial and parallel transmissions.

7. A serial port on a PC normally transmits [asynchronously | synchronously].

8. Which of the following are names for a computer's serial port? (Pick all that apply.)
   [COM port | Asynchronous port | Synchronous port | LPT port | RS232 port]

9. List five common modem speed settings.

10. Describe the most common type of serial port found on a computer.

11. Which of the following controls the computer's serial port? [UART | BIOS | CMOS | CPU]

12. Where can a UART chip be located? (Pick all that apply.)
    a. On the motherboard
    b. On a serial adapter
    c. In an external modem
    d. On an internal modem

13. What is the purpose of UART buffers?

14. List three parameters that must be configured for serial ports.

15. Which of the following is the correct order for I/O addresses that BIOS assigns COM port numbers?
    a. 2E8, 2F8, 3E8, 3F8
    b. 2E8, 3E8, 2F8, 3F8
    c. 3F8, 2F8, 3E8, 2E8
    d. 3F8, 3E8, 2F8, 2E8

16. [T | F] Serial ports always receive COM port numbers in I/O address order.

17. Which COM port is normally assigned to IRQ4? [COM1 | COM2 | COM3 | COM4]

18. What setting determines how two serial devices establish communication?
    [Data bits | Stop bits | Parity | Flow control]

19. What are two common flow control methods?

20. Define handshaking.

21. What does CTS stand for?

22. What does RTS stand for?

23. Explain what happens when hardware handshaking is used.

24. Explain the difference between a DCE and a DTE.

25. List three recommendations to remember when installing a serial device.

26. List three troubleshooting tips for serial ports.

27. Describe two advantages of external modems.

28. Describe two advantages of internal modems.

29. What ITU standards deal with modem data compression?

30. What ITU standards deal with fax modems?

31. What modem feature does the V.44 standard target?

32. What is a drawback to modem data compression?

33. [T | F] A modem should be set to its maximum speed.

34. What is the biggest limitation to a 56Kbps modem transmitting at 56Kbps?

35. What ITU standard allows a fax machine to connect to a data network?

36. Describe how a networked fax machine might interact with email.

37. [T | F] A fax machine can have a VoIP adapter installed.

38. List five troubleshooting tips for modems.

39. What happens if call waiting is enabled on a phone line that has a modem attached?

40. List at least two things that can cause a modem to transmit at a speed lower than the maximum speed.

41. If a modem does not sound a dial tone, what is the most likely conflict if the modem worked before?

42. What does a TR modem light indicate? [Terminal Ready | Transmit/Receive | Transmit Ready | Transmit Reset]

43. [T | F] A cable modem is a good investment for a home modem. Explain your answer.

44. Explain when a NIC would be used with a cable modem.

45. List one drawback to a cable modem.

46. What does *asymmetrical* mean in relation to an ADSL modem?

47. Can a phone be used at the same time as a DSL modem?

48. What interface does a DSL internal modem use?

49. What is the first thing you should check if your Internet connectivity is down and you have a DSL modem installed?

50. What is wireless broadband?

51. A new laptop has an integrated wireless WAN. The customer thinks there is a missing wireless antenna. What should you advise the customer?

52. A customer has a new laptop with wireless WAN capabilities; however, the software does not connect to the Internet. What would you suggest to the customer?

53. What is a phone line isolator?

54. List two ways mentoring can help in the IT field.

Fill-in-the-Blank

1. A device that allows a computer to connect to a phone line is a/an _____.

2. A/An _____ takes a signal from the phone line and converts it to digital format for input into the computer.

3. _____ transmissions require a clock to send or receive data.

4. The _____ bit is used with asynchronous transmissions and signals the beginning of transmission.

5. The _____ bit is used with asynchronous transmissions and signals the end of transmission.

6. A serial device transmission speed is measured in _____.

7. A/An _____ converts a data byte into single transmission bits.

8. Serial devices are normally assigned the interrupts _____ or _____.

9. The normal parity setting for a modem is _____.

10. The _____ modem setting enables the UART buffers.

11. The _____ flow control method uses specific wires to signal data transmission.

12. The _____ flow control method uses control characters to signal data transmission.

13. Modems use a/an _____ cable.

14. A modem that has _____ keeps the processor from having to verify the accuracy of the data.

15. A modem that has _____ must transmit less data than one that does not have this ability.

16. Two features in the V.92 standard are _____ and _____.

17. An analog modem can transmit at a maximum of _____ if only one analog-to-digital conversion occurs; otherwise, data transmits at a lower rate.

18. _____ allows voice traffic to be sent over a traditional data network.

19. The Windows XP _____ wizard handles a modem installation.

20. The Windows XP Modem _____ tab allows you to troubleshoot the modem by running procedures on the modem.

21. _____ is used in XP to determine whether a modem is enabled.

22. The Hayes modem command _____ causes a Hayes-compatible modem to perform as if picking up a phone—it issues a dial tone.

23. The Hayes modem command _____ resets a Hayes-compatible modem.

24. A type of digital phone line that has three channels is _____.

25. An ISDN line consists of two _____ channels and one _____ channel.

26. The ISDN B channel transfers data at _____ bps.

27. The ISDN D channel transfers data at _____ bps.

28. A/An _____ modem connects a computer to a TV network using coaxial cable.

29. When using a cable modem, the term _____ refers to data pulled from the Internet.

30. _____ is a type of DSL that allows speeds up to 150Mbps.

31. _____ allows a DSL transfer of voice and HDTV transmissions in addition to data.

32. A/An _____ modem allows connectivity in remote places, using devices in orbit around Earth.

33. A/An _____ is used with a laptop to connect a modem to a phone line.

34. Another name for wireless broadband is _____.

Hands-On Exercises

1. Exploring Serial Devices in Windows XP

Objective: To explore serial devices and their properties using Windows XP

Parts: A computer with Windows XP installed and, optionally, a modem

Procedure: Complete the following procedure and answer the accompanying questions.

1. Power on the computer and logon using the userid and password provided by the instructor or lab assistant.

2. Click the *Start* button and click *Control Panel*.

3. If in Category View, click *Performance and Maintenance*. In both views, open *Administrative Tools* and double-click the *Computer Management* icon.

4. In the left window, click *Device Manager*. In the right window, expand the *Ports* option.

5. Right-click *Communications Port (Com1)* and select *Properties*.

    What options are available under the Device Usage drop-down menu?

    What is the status of the serial port?

6. Click the *Troubleshoot* button. Once the generic hardware device troubleshooter opens, click the *Next* button.

7. Click the *Yes, my hardware is on the HCL* or *I have already contacted the manufacturer and installed updated drivers, but I still have a problem* radio button and click *Next*.

   What is the next question the troubleshooter poses?

   If a new driver was just installed, what new Windows XP feature can be used?

8. Close the *Help and Support Center* window and click the *Port Settings* tab.

   What is the default serial port speed setting?

9. Click the *Driver* tab and click the *Driver Details* button.

   List any drivers including the complete path associated with the serial port.

10. Click the *OK* button.

    What is the purpose of the roll back driver button?

11. Click the *Resources* tab.

    What IRQ and I/O addresses are assigned?

Instructor initials: _____

12. Click the *OK* button.

Modems

Note: *Skip this section if a modem is not installed. If unsure, perform the tasks to see if the steps work.*

13. Expand the *Modems* Device Manager category. Right-click a specific modem and select *Properties*. Click the *Modem* tab.

    What COM port does the modem use?

    What is the maximum port speed?

    Is 115,200bps the speed at which the modem transmits over the phone line? Explain your answer.

14. Click the *Diagnostics* tab and click the *Query Modem* button.

    What was the first AT command sent to the modem?

15. Click the *View log* button.

    Scroll to the bottom of the log. What communications standard(s) does the modem use?

16. Close the Notepad log. Click the *Resources* tab.

    What IRQ and I/O addresses does the modem use?

Instructor initials: _____

17. Close the *Modem Properties* window. Close the *Computer Management* window.

2. Exploring Serial Devices in Windows Vista

Objective: To explore serial devices and their properties using Windows Vista

Parts: A computer with Windows Vista installed and either a serial port with an external modem attached, an internal modem, or both

Procedure: Complete the following procedure and answer the accompanying questions.

1. Power on the computer and log on using the userid and password provided by the instructor or lab assistant.

2. Click the *Start* button and click *Control Panel*.

3. Double-click the *System and Maintenance* or *System* control panel.

4. Click *Device Manager*. Note that you may have to scroll down to see this option.

5. Expand the *Ports* option.

6. If *Communications Port (Com1)* is available, right-click and select *Properties*.

   What tabs are available?

   What is the status of the serial port?

7. Click the *Port Settings* tab.

   What is the maximum number of bits per second?

8. Click the *Advanced* button.

   What UART is being used?

   What COM port is assigned?

9. Click *Cancel*.

10. Click the *Driver* tab and click the *Driver Details* button.

    List any drivers, including the complete path associated with the serial port.

11. Click the *OK* button.

    What is the purpose of the Roll Back Driver button?

12. Click the *Resources* tab.

    What IRQ and I/O addresses are assigned?

Instructor initials: _____

13. Click the *OK* button.

Modems

Note: Skip this section if an internal modem is not installed. If unsure, perform the tasks to see if the steps work.

14. Expand the *Modems* Device Manager category. Right-click a specific modem and select *Properties*. Click the *Modem* tab.

    What COM port does the modem use?

    What is the maximum port speed?

    Is the setting for the maximum bits per second on a serial port the speed at which the external modem transmits over the phone line? Explain your answer.

    Why would you want the speaker volume enabled when first installing a modem?

15. Click the *Diagnostics* tab and click the *Query Modem* button.

    What was the first AT command sent to the modem?

16. Click the *View log* button. Scroll to the bottom of the log.

    What communications standard(s) does the modem use?

17. Close the Notepad log. Click the *Resources* tab.

    What IRQ and I/O addresses does the modem use?

Instructor initials: _____

18. Close the *Modem Properties* window. Close the *Device Manager* window.

19. Close the *Control Panel* window.

3. Windows XP Direct Cable Connection

Objective: To connect two computers using either a serial or parallel null cable so that one computer can access files or resources on the other computer

Parts: Two Windows XP computers

  A null serial or parallel cable Windows XP installation CD

Note: Networking must previously be installed or installed during the Direct Cable Connection installation. The steps of this process are beyond the scope of this chapter.

Procedure: Complete the following procedure and answer the accompanying questions.

1. Connect the null serial or parallel cable between the two computers.

2. Power on the computer and logon as an administrator or with a userid that has administrator permissions. See the instructor or lab assistant for more details.

3. Before installing Windows XP's Direct Cable Connection, check to see if a null serial cable is being used. Look to see if the cable attaches to the serial or parallel port. If it is a serial connection, the cable must first be installed as a modem. If a null serial cable is being used, go to the Serial Connection Pre-installation section. If a serial connection is not being used, skip this section.

Serial Connection Pre-installation

4. Access the *Phone and Modem Options* control panel and select the *Modems* tab. Click the *Add* button.

5. Enable the *Don't detect my modem, I will select it from a list* checkbox and click *Next*.

6. Locate the *Standard Modem Types Manufacturer* option and click it. In the right pane, select *Communications cable between two computers* and click *Next*.

7. Select the port that has the null serial cable attached. Click *Finish* and click *OK*.

Direct Cable Connection Installation

8. Click the *Start* button and click *Control Panel*. Double-click *Network Connections*.

9. Under Network Tasks, click the *Create a new connection icon*, and click *Next*. Under Network Connection Type, select *Set up an advanced connection* and click *Next*. If configuring the first computer (the host), select *Accept incoming connections* in the *Type of Connection You Want* window and click *Next*. If configuring the second computer (the guest), select *Connect directly to another computer* and click *Next*. The host computer is the one sharing resources. The guest computer is the one that is accessing the shared resources. Click the *Next* button.

10. Select the type of cable being used checkbox and click *Next*.

11. Select the *Do not allow virtual private connections* radio button and click *Next*.

12. Select the users who will be allowed to connect and click *Next*.

13. In the *Networking software* window, ensure that a networking protocol such as TCP/IP and File and Printer Sharing are enabled. Note that the *Properties* button can be used if necessary to configure the networking protocol parameters. See Chapter 13 for more details on TCP/IP addressing. Click *Next* and click the *Finish* button.

14. Go to the second computer and perform the exact procedure except select *Connect directly to another computer* in Step 2.

Instructor initials: _____

4. Internal and External Modem Installation

Objective: To be able to install an internal and an external modem and establish communication between two computers

Parts: Internal modem

External modem with serial cable

Two Windows XP computers

Windows XP HyperTerminal communication software

Two RJ-11 phone cables

Two analog phone ports or a simulator such as one from Adtran

Note: Two internal or two external modems could also be used to perform this lab with very few adjustments.

Procedure: Complete the following procedure and answer the accompanying questions.

1. Power on the computer and ensure it boots properly before the exercise begins.

2. Shut down the computer properly and remove the power cord from the back of the computer.

Internal Modem Installation

3. Install the internal modem into an available slot.

4. Re-install the computer cover, re-install the computer power cord, and power on the computer. The *Found New Hardware* wizard appears if this is the first time the computer has had this adapter installed.

5. Install the correct modem driver either using the one from Microsoft or the one provided with the modem.

6. Access the Device Manager through the *System* control panel (or *Performance and Maintenance* category and then the *System* control panel). Click the *Hardware* tab and click *Device Manager*. Expand the *Modems* category. Right-click the internal modem that was just installed and select *Properties*.

   Under the *General* tab, what is the device status? It should be that the modem is working properly. If it is not, perform appropriate troubleshooting until it does display that message.

7. Click the *Diagnostics* tab. Click the *Query modem* button.

   List at least two AT commands and the response that is shown in the information window.

8. Click the *View log* button.

   What do you think a technician could do with this information?

9. Close the *Notepad log* window.

10. Click the *Resources* tab.

    What memory range is used by the adapter?

    What IRQ is the adapter using?

11. Click the *Advanced* tab.

    When do you think you would use the Extra initialization commands textbox?

12. Click the *Advanced Port Settings* button.

    What COM port is used with this adapter?

    Are FIF0 buffers used by default?

13. Click the *Cancel* button on the next two screens to exit the *Properties* window.

14. Connect an RJ-11 phone cable from the internal modem port (the one that is **not** labeled phone) to the analog phone line or to a port on the simulator.

External Modem Installation

15. On the second computer, attach the power cord to the external modem and attach the other end to power outlet. Connect the serial modem cable between the modem and the PC.

    What COM port are you attaching the modem? If you do not know, research this until you do. Do not proceed until you determine the COM number assigned to the serial port being used.

16. Turn on the external modem. A *Found New Hardware* balloon normally appears. If Windows detects it, after a short period a message appears that the hardware is ready to use.

17. Access the *Phone and Modem Options* control panel. Click the *Modems* tab.

    Does the modem appear in the list? If not troubleshoot until it does.

    What COM port lists in the "Attached to" column of the display?

18. Ensure the correct modem is selected and click the *Properties* button.

    On the *General* tab, what is the device status?

19. Click the *Modem* tab. The modem tab is where you can control the speaker volume, maximum port speed, and the dial control option. Click the *Diagnostics* tab and click the *Query Modem* button. Watch the lights on top of the modem as the PC communicates with the external modem. This ability to watch the connectivity is an advantage of having an external modem.

    List the first command and response listed in the dialog window as a result of the modem query.

    Click the *Advanced* tab. What is allowed to be done from this option?

20. Click the *Driver* tab.

    What is the purpose of the *Roll Back Driver* option?

21. Click the *Cancel* button on the next two screens to exit the *Properties* window.

22. Notice the documented markings for the external modem's phone ports. The port that has the symbol for an RJ-11 connection is used to connect to a phone outlet. The port that has the symbol for a phone is where you can optionally attach an analog phone to the modem. Connect an RJ-11 phone cable from the external modem port to another phone outlet or to a phone network simulator.

    What phone number is assigned to the wall outlet or port used for the internal modem?

    What phone number is assigned to the wall outlet or port used for the external modem?

Communication Between the Two Modems

23. The HyperTerminal program is a communications program that ships with Windows products since the first version of Windows. On the computer that has the external modem attached, access the HyperTerminal application (normally available through the *Accessories* option). The *New Connection* window appears. Figure 10.13 shows this window.

Figure 10.13   **HyperTerminal window**

24. Click the *Cancel* button. From the *File* menu option, select *Properties*. In the *Connect using* drop-down list, select the modem. Figure 10.14 shows how the modem appears in the drop-down list.

25. Click the *Configure* button.

    What is the default flow control used by this external modem?

    Is error compression enabled or disabled by default?

26. Click the *Advanced* tab.

    What is the default setting for the number of data bits, whether parity is used or not, the number of stop bits, and the type of modulation used?

27. Click the *Cancel* button. From the *Properties* window, click the *OK* button. From the HyperTerminal window, type **AT** and press Enter. The modem responds with the message *OK* when the modem is working properly. The AT command tells the modem that you want its "ATtention."

Figure 10.14   **HyperTerminal modem selection**

28. On the computer that has the internal modem, access HyperTerminal. In the Name textbox, type your name and click *OK*. Enter the area code in the area code textbox and ensure the *Connect using drop-down* option is selected to the internal modem. Click *OK* and *Cancel*.

29. From the HyperTerminal window for the external modem, type **ATE1** so that your commands that you type will show in the window. From the HyperTerminal window, type **ATDT XXXXXXX** (where the Xs are replaced with the phone number of the other modem). ATDT gets the modem's attention and tells it to dial using the "tone" method. The number that follows is the phone number to dial. If the external modem volume is turned up, you will hear a phone ringing.

30. From the HyperTerminal window for the internal modem, click the *Call* menu option and select *Wait for call*.

    What message appears in the HyperTerminal window that is used to control the external modem?

31. From the HyperTerminal window that is used to control the external modem, type **Hello to you**. Look at the HyperTerminal window for the internal modem.

    What indication, if any, is seen in the HyperTerminal window?

32. Show the HyperTerminal message to the teacher.

33. From the HyperTerminal window that controls the external modem, select the *Call* menu option, and select *Disconnect*.

    What indication do you have in the HyperTerminal window that controls the internal modem that the modem connection is no longer active?

34. Power off the external modem. Disconnect the phone cable. Remove the power connector. Remove the serial modem cable from the back of the PC and the back of the external modem. Replace all parts to their storage location.

35. Disconnect the analog phone cable from the internal modem.

36. On the computer that has the internal modem, power off the computer, remove the power cord, and remove the internal modem. Place the modem inside the antistatic bag. Return the modem, phone cable, and software to the proper storage location.

Internet Discovery

Objective: To obtain specific information regarding a computer or its associated parts on the Internet

Parts: Computer with Internet access

Questions: Use the Internet to answer the following questions.

1. Locate a cable modem Web site that explains how to increase speed on a cable modem. Write the URL where you found the answer as well as the recommendation.

2. Determine if cable or DSL modems are supported in your area. If so, determine as many vendors as you can for these products.

3. Find one vendor of VDSL in the United States and write the vendor and the URL where you found the answer.

4. Find an Internet site that describes how modem chat scripts are done and provides examples of one. Write the URL and your own explanation of chat scripts.

5. You have a customer who has a USRobotics 3CP5610 external PCI 56K data modem. What should the switches be set to for this modem? Write the answer, the page number in the PDF chapter where you found this answer, and the web address where you found this solution.

6. Find a vendor in your state that sells wireless broadband for a laptop. What type of technology does it use (USB, PC Card, CardBus, integrated, etc.)? Write the URL, the vendor and model number, as well as the cost.

Soft Skills

Objective: To enhance and fine-tune a future technician's ability to listen, communicate in both written and oral form, and support people who use computers in a professional manner

Activities:

1. The class is divided into three groups—two groups who will be debating against one another and a third group who will be the judges. The judges have 45 minutes to determine the rules and consequences of how the debate is to be conducted. During the same 45 minutes, the two debating groups will be researching material and planning a strategy for either cable modems or DSL modems. At the end of 45 minutes, the debate will start with the judges mediating with the rules they establish and presenting to the two teams before the debate begins. The judges, along with the instructor, determine which group proved their point the best.

2. Using whatever resources are available, research one of the following that has been assigned to you. Share the results individually with the class.
   * What is the largest number of IRQs supported by an analog modem that you could find?
   * What is the fastest DSL, cable, or analog connection in a 60 mile radius from your school?
   * What is the most common type of Internet connectivity from home users in your area?
   * What is the most common type of Internet connectivity businesses use in your area?
   * What is the type and speed of Internet connectivity from your school?
   * What is the type and speed of Internet connectivity from a college in your state?
   * Which types of DSL services are available in your state?
   * Which types of cable modem services are available in your state?

10
Internet
Connectivity

Critical Thinking Skills

Objective: To analyze and evaluate information as well as apply learned information to new or different situations

Activities:

1. In groups of three, write a chat script to automate a modem that connects to another modem.

2. In groups of two, write two analog/cable/DSL modem problems on two separate 3×5 cards. Give one problem to another class group and the other problem to a different class group. Your group will receive two 3×5 cards from two different groups as well. Solve the problems given to you using any resource available. Share your group findings with the class.

11

Basic Windows and Windows Commands

Objectives

After completing this chapter you will be able to

- Identify, explain, and use common desktop icons
- Manage files and folders including attributes, compression, and encryption
- Modify the Start button appearance
- Describe the purpose of the registry and how it is organized into subtrees
- Work from a command prompt and perform basic functions using commands (to access the file structure, create a file, view a file, copy and delete files, and set attributes on files and directories)
- Describe methods used to stay current in technology areas

Basic Operating Systems Overview

Computers require software to operate. An **operating system** is software that coordinates the interaction between hardware and any software applications, as well as the interaction between a user and the computer. An operating system contains commands and functions that both the user and the computer understand. For example, when you select a file from Windows Explorer and select *Copy* the computer understands that you want to make a copy of the file you just selected. **Windows Explorer** (sometimes called Explorer) is the most common application used to create, copy, or move files or folders; however, the My Computer (XP) or Computer (Vista/7) window can also be used in a similar fashion. A **file** is an electronic container that holds computer code or data. Other ways of looking at it is thinking of a file as a box of bits or an electronic piece of paper with information on it. A **folder** holds files and can also contain other folders.

Explorer is a **GUI** (graphical user interface) application. From a command prompt, you can type commands that are specific to the operating system. For example, say that you type the word `hop` from a command prompt. The word `hop` is not a command that the computer understands (has been programmed to understand). If you type the word `hop`, the computer does not know what to do. However, if you type the letters `DIR` from a command prompt, the computer recognizes the command and displays a directory or a listing of files. Operating systems also handle file and disk management. Examples of operating systems include Apple's Mac OS X, Sun Solaris, Windows XP, Vista, and 7, and the different types of UNIX (besides Solaris) such as Red Hat and SuSE. Mac OS X and Windows Vista/7 have similar memory and hardware requirements, whereas the UNIX and Linux requirements vary depending on version and type of operating system being used. One advantage of open source operating systems such as Linux is that all the code that makes up the operating system is open to view and improve upon or change. This sometimes allows for more community-driven features that are not as easily changed in closed source or proprietary software such as Windows or OSX.

Which Edit functions to use

When you are copying a file or folder, use the *Copy/Paste* function from the *Edit* menu option. When you are moving a file or folder, use the *Cut/Paste* functions.

Basic Windows Usage Overview

When a Windows-based operating system first boots, there may be a logon screen. A userid and password is created when the operating system is loaded. Once in the Windows environment, the desktop appears. The **desktop** is the area on the screen where all work is performed. The desktop is part of a GUI environment. It is the interface between the computer user and computer files, applications, operating system, and installed hardware. The desktop contains **icons**, which are pictures that provide access to various devices, files, and applications on the computer. The desktop can be customized so that the most commonly accessed applications or files are easily accessible. Figure 11.1 shows the major components of the desktop.

By default, Windows XP/Vista/7's desktop displays the Recycle Bin icon only. However, most people like to have the normal Windows icons displayed. Common desktop icons are listed in Table 11.1.

The Google Chrome icon shown in Figure 11.1 is a desktop icon called a shortcut. A **shortcut** represents a **path** (a location on a drive) to a file, folder, or program. It is a link (pointer) to where the file or application resides on a disk. When a shortcut icon is double-clicked, Windows knows where to find the specific file

Accessing the local Administrator account

Note that Windows XP's welcome screen does not contain the local Administrator account (the master account that is allowed to change everything on the local machine) icon on the welcome screen. Press [Ctrl]+[Alt]+[Del] twice and log in with the Administrator account userid and password.

Quickly spotting a shortcut

A shortcut is an icon that has a bent arrow in the lower-left corner.

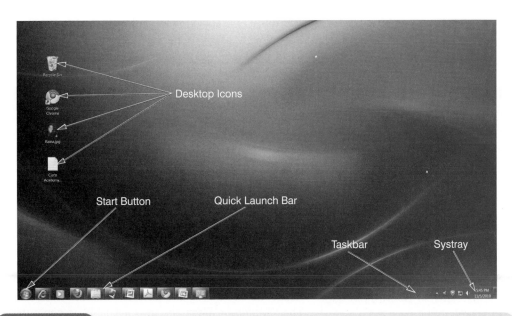

Figure 11.1   **Windows desktop**

Table 11.1   **Common Windows desktop icons**

Icon	Purpose
My Documents/Documents	Used to access a folder located on the hard drive that is the default storage location for files
My Computer/Computer	Used to access hardware, software, and files
My Network Places/Network	Used to access network resources such as computers, printers, scanners, fax machines, and files
Recycle Bin	Holds files and folders that have been deleted
Internet Explorer	Starts the Internet Explorer application; used to access the Internet

the icon represents by the associated path. Users and technicians frequently place shortcuts on the desktop and it is important to know how to create or troubleshoot one.

To discover the path to the original file used to create the shortcut, right-click the shortcut icon and select *Properties*. Click the *Shortcut* tab and look in the *Target* textbox for the path to the original file. The *Find Target* (XP) or *Open File Location* (Vista/7) button can be used to locate the original file.

An important desktop icon is the Recycle Bin, which is used to hold files and folders that the user deletes. When a file or folder is deleted, it is not really gone. Instead, it goes into the Recycle Bin, which is actually just a folder on the hard drive. The deleted file or folder can be removed from the Recycle Bin just as a piece of trash can be removed from a real trash can. Deleted files and folders in the Recycle Bin use hard drive space.

One way to modify the desktop is by changing the wallpaper scheme. A wallpaper scheme is a background picture, pattern, or color. Other changes to the desktop include altering the color scheme that is used in displaying folders and enabling a screen saver, which is the picture, color, or pattern that displays when the computer is inactive. Hands-On Exercises 1 and 2 at the end of the chapter explain how to change these settings.

Keeping the desktop organized

Sometimes the desktop is cluttered with icons the user puts on it. To organize the desktop nicely, right-click an empty desktop space, point to the *Arrange icons* (XP) or *View → Auto arrange icons* (Vista/7) option.

How to delete a file permanently

If you hold down the [Shift] key when deleting a file, it is permanently deleted and does not go into the Recycle Bin.

Need hard drive space? Empty the Recycle Bin

A technician must remember that some users cannot (or do not) empty the Recycle Bin. Empty the Recycle Bin to free up space on the hard drive.

Whenever anything is double-clicked in Windows, a window appears. Windows are a normal part of the desktop as are the taskbar, Start button, and Quick Launch bar. The **taskbar** is the bar that commonly runs across the bottom of the screen. The taskbar holds buttons that represent applications or files currently loaded into the computer's memory. The taskbar also holds icons that allow access to system utilities such as a clock for the date and time and a speaker symbol for access to volume control. Refer to Figure 11.1 to see the taskbar.

The **Start button** is located in the desktop's lower-left corner and is used to launch applications and utilities, search for files and other computers, obtain help, and add/remove hardware and software.

The *Shut Down, Turn Off Computer,* or *Restart,* Start button option is used to shut the computer off, restart the computer, and put the computer in standby. The *Standby* or *Sleep* option is available on computers that support power saving features.

What to do if the Start button is not on the desktop

If the Start button does not appear on the desktop, hold down the [Ctrl] key and press the [Esc] key. Another way to bring up the Start menu is by pressing the [⊞] key on the keyboard, which is the key with the Windows graphic on it. Figure 11.2 shows the Windows XP *Start* button.

Figure 11.2   Windows XP *Start* button menu

In Vista and 7, the *Switch User, Lock, Sleep, Shut Down, Restart,* and *Log Off* options are available from a right arrow on the Start button, as shown in Figure 11.3.

Figure 11.3   **Vista restart options**

The **Control Panel** Start button option allows computer configuration such as add software, remove software, add hardware, remove hardware, adjust the monitor settings, configure a screen saver, and configure the mouse for a left-handed person. Control Panel is one of the most commonly used Start menu options used by technicians.

The **Quick Launch bar** is a set of icons to the right of the Start button that allow applications to be launched with one click of an icon. Refer to Figure 11.1 to see the Quick Launch bar. An important icon on the Quick Launch bar is the Show Desktop icon (the one closest to the *Start* button). Single-click the Show Desktop icon to reduce all windows on the screen and display the desktop. Click the icon a second time and the original document (that was on the screen when the Show Desktop icon was first clicked) reappears. Another Quick Launch icon is *Internet Explorer,* which is used to access the Internet quickly.

The *Show Desktop* option is also available by simply right-clicking an empty space on the taskbar. Figure 11.4 shows the Vista Start button and three of the common Quick Launch icons; from left to right, they are Show Desktop, Switch between Windows, and Internet Explorer. Hands-On Exercises 1 through 4 at the end of the chapter demonstrate how to use and control the Windows desktop environment.

Technicians frequently interact with the Windows operating system through a **dialog box**. A dialog box is used by the operating system and with Windows applications to allow configuration

Figure 11.4   **Vista Start button and Quick Launch area**

and operating system preferences. The most common features found in a dialog box are a **checkbox**, a textbox, tabs, a drop-down menu, a Help button, a Close button, an **OK button**, and a **Cancel button**. Figure 11.5 shows a sample dialog box.

How to modify the buttons shown on the Quick Launch bar

In XP, the Quick Launch bar shows three icons. The three that are shown on the taskbar can be modified in XP by clicking on the Quick Launch bar double arrows, followed by selecting and dragging the application name and icon to the taskbar. In all Windows versions, drag an application icon to the Quick Launch area.

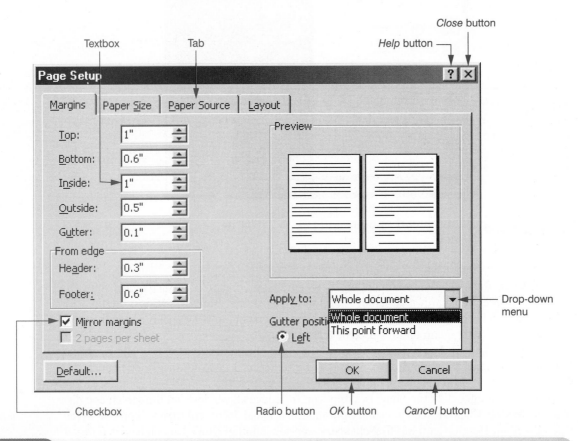

Figure 11.5   **Windows dialog box components**

A **textbox** is an area where you can type a specific parameter. When the inside of a textbox is checked, a vertical line appears. This is the insertion point. Any typed text is placed to the right of the insertion point. In Figure 11.5, options such as Top, Bottom, Inside, and Outside are textboxes. Textboxes sometimes have up and down arrows that can be used to select an option or the parameter can just be typed inside the textbox.

Tabs frequently appear across the top of a dialog box. Each tab holds a group of related options. Click once on the tab to bring that particular major section to the window's forefront. The tabs shown in Figure 11.5 are Margins, Paper Size, Paper Source, and Layout.

The **Help button**, which is indicated by a question mark and located in the upper-right corner of the dialog box, is used to provide context sensitive assistance. Once the Help button is clicked, the cursor turns into an arrow with a question mark attached. Click any item for which you would like basic information and a pop-up window appears on the screen. Close the pop-up window by clicking anywhere on the screen. The **Close button**, which is indicated by an X, is used to close the dialog box window. When the *Close* button is used, changes made inside the dialog box are not applied.

When checked, a checkbox option is enabled (turned on). Clicking inside a checkbox option places a check mark inside the checkbox, such as the one for Mirror margins, shown in Figure 11.5. A similar dialog box option is a radio button. A **radio button** is a circle that when enabled has a solid dot inside it. If a radio button that already has a dot in it is clicked, the dot disappears and the option is disabled. The *Left* radio button is enabled in Figure 11.5.

Drop-down menus are presented when you click a down arrow. Figure 11.5 shows the drop-down options of *Whole document* and *This point forward*. Once the drop-down menu option is selected, the option appears in the drop-down menu. The OK button and Cancel button are standard in a dialog box. When the OK button is clicked, all options selected or changed within the dialog box are applied. When the Cancel button is clicked, anything changed within the dialog box is not applied—the options are left in their original state. Another common dialog box option that is not shown in Figure 11.5 is the Apply button. The **Apply button** is used to make changes immediately (before clicking the OK button).

Click *OK* or *Apply* to make it work

When they want to apply a change, inexperienced technicians often make the mistake of clicking the *Close* button (the button with an X on it) instead of the OK or Apply button. When a dialog box is closed with the Close button, changes in the dialog box are not saved or applied.

Tech
Tip

Managing Files and Folders

Technicians are always creating, deleting, and moving files and folders. You need to be able to do these tasks quickly and without error. It is important to remember to think about what file and folder you want to work with, where the files and folders are located now, and where you want the files or folders to be eventually.

A drive letter followed by a colon represents every drive in a computer. For example, the floppy drive is represented by A: and the first hard drive partition is represented by C:. The CD, DVD, and Flash drives are all represented by a drive letter followed by a colon. Disks or drives hold files. A file is kept on some type of media such as a floppy disk, flash drive, hard drive, tape, or CD. Each file is given a name called a filename. An example of a filename is WIN7CHAP.DOCX.

Files are usually kept in folders to organize them. In older operating systems, a folder was called a directory. Every file and folder is given a name and an extension. An **extension** is added to the filename, and the extension can be three or more characters in length. The filename and the extension are separated by a period. An example of a filename with an extension is BOOK.DOCX where BOOK is the name of the file and DOCX is the extension.

It is easier to understand file and folder names if filename rules in an older operating system such as DOS are examined. In DOS, the maximum number of characters in the filename is eight. For this reason, older filenames are called **short filenames** or 8.3 filenames. Filenames in Windows can be up to 255 characters long. These extended filenames are commonly called **long filenames**. An example of a long filename is WINDOWS 7 CHAPTER.DOCX.

Normally with Windows, the application automatically adds an extension to the end of the filename. In most views, Windows does not automatically show the extensions. To view the extensions in XP Windows Explorer, perform the following steps: *Tools → Folder Options → View* tab → *Hide file extensions for known file types* checkbox (to disable the option and remove the check from the checkbox) → *OK*. In Vista/7, click on the Start button and select *Control Panel → Appearance and Personalization* link → *Folder Options → View* tab → *Advanced Settings* section → uncheck the *Hide extensions for known file types* checkbox.

Tech Tip

Characters you cannot use in file and folder names

Folders and filenames can have all characters, numbers, letters, and spaces *except* the following: / (forward slash), " (quotation marks), \ (backslash), | (vertical bar), ? (question mark), : (colon), and * (asterisk).

When Windows recognizes an extension, the operating system associates the extension with a particular application. Filename extensions can tell you a lot about a file, such as what application created the file or what its purpose is. Table 11.2 lists the most common file extensions and their purpose or what application creates the extension.

Table 11.2	Common file extensions
Extension	**Purpose or application**
AI	Adobe Illustrator
BAT	Used to execute commands from one file and is commonly known as a batch file
BMP	Bitmap file
CAB	Cabinet file—a compressed file that holds operating system or application files
COM	Command file—an executable file that opens an application or tool
DLL	Dynamic Link Library file—contains executable code that can be used by more than one application and is called upon from other code already running
DOC or DOCX	Microsoft Word
DRV	Device driver—a piece of software that enables an operating system to recognize a hardware device
EPS	Encapsulated postscript file
EXE	Executable file—a file that opens an application
GIF	Graphics interchange file
HLP	Windows-based help file
INF	Information or setup file
INI	Initialization file—Used in older Windows environments to be backwards compatible with Windows 3.x.
JPG or JPEG	Joint Photographic Experts Group file format—graphics file
MPG or MPEG	Movie clip file
NLS	National language support file
ONE	Microsoft OneNote file
PCX	Microsoft Paintbrush
PDF	Adobe Acrobat—portable document format
PPT or PPTX	Microsoft PowerPoint
RTF	Rich text format
TIF or TIFF	Tag image file format
TXT	Text file
VXD	Virtual device driver
WKS	Lotus worksheet
WPS	Microsoft Works text file format
WRI	Microsoft WordPad
XLS or XLSX	Microsoft Excel
ZIP	Compressed file

When saving a file in a Windows application, the application automatically saves the file to a specific folder. This is known as the default folder. With Windows, this folder is the *My Documents* (XP) or *Documents* (Vista/7) folder. In documentation, installation instructions, and when writing the exact location of a file, the full path is used. A file's path is like a road map to the file and includes the drive letter plus all folders and subfolders as well as the filename and extension. For example, if the CHAP1.DOCX file is in the *Documents* folder on the first hard drive partition, the full path is C:\DOCUMENTS\CHAP1.DOCX. The first part is the drive letter where the document is stored. The C: represents the first hard drive partition. The name of the document is always at the very end of the path. In the example given, CHAP1.DOCX is the name of the file. Everything in between the drive letter and the filename is the name of one or more folders where the CHAP1.DOCX file is located. The folder in this example is the *DOCUMENTS* folder.

If the CHAP1.DOCX file is located in a subfolder called *COMPUTER BOOK* that is located in the folder called *DOCUMENTS* (sometimes called the parent folder), then the full path is C:\DOCUMENTS\COMPUTER BOOK\CHAP1.DOCX. Notice how the backslashes are always used to separate the folder names as well as the drive letter from the first folder name. Figure 11.6 shows how the WINDOWS XP TABLES.VSD long filename looks in graphical form using Windows Explorer.

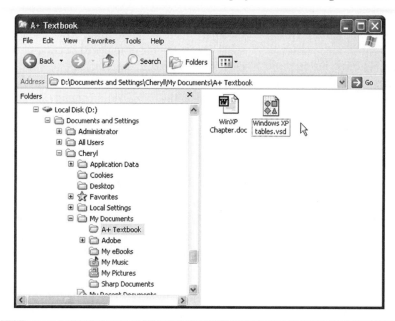

Figure 11.6   **Long filename in Windows Explorer**

Floppy/Zip disk or thumb (Flash) drive files are permanently deleted

When deleting a file or folder from a floppy disk, Zip disk, CD/DVD, memory card, MP3 player, digital camera, remote computer, or Flash drive, the file or folder is permanently deleted. It does not go into the Recycle Bin as the case when a file is deleted from a hard drive.

The contents of the Recycle Bin take up hard drive space. To change how much space is reserved for the Recycle Bin or the drive on which the deleted files in the Recycle Bin are stored, right-click on the Recycle Bin and select *Properties*. Hands-On Exercises at the end of the chapter illustrate how to copy, move, and delete files and folders (Hands-On Exercises 4 and 11) and empty the Recycle Bin (Hands-On Exercises 1 and 2).

Attributes, Compression, and Encryption

My Computer (XP), Computer (Vista/7), and Explorer can be used for setting attributes for a file or folder. The file and folder attributes are read-only, hidden, archive, and system. The **read-only attribute** marks a file or folder so that it cannot be changed. The **hidden attribute** marks a file or folder so that it is not visible through My Computer, Computer, or Explorer unless someone changes the default view for the window. Some applications use the **archive attribute** to control which files or folders are backed up. The **system attribute** is placed on certain files used to boot Windows.

How to change a file or folder's attributes

To change a file or folder's attributes, locate the file or folder using My Computer, Computer, or Explorer and right-click the filename or folder name. Select *Properties* and click one or more attribute checkboxes to enable (if checked) or disable an attribute. If the file is not a system file, the system attribute is unavailable. Click the *Apply* button.

If the hard drive is partitioned for the NTFS file system, files and folders can be compressed or encrypted with Windows NT and higher. **Compression** is compaction of a file or folder to take up less disk space. All Windows-based applications can read and write compressed files. The operating system decompresses the file, the file is available to the application, and the operating system decompresses the file when it is saved.

You can enable file compression by using Windows Explorer or My Computer/Computer using the following steps: Locate the file or folder to be compressed, and right-click it → *Properties* → *Advanced* → *Compress contents to save disk space* or *Compress* checkbox → *OK*. If this applies to a folder, the *Confirm Attribute Changes* dialog box appears. You must select whether the compression applies to only this folder or to this folder and all subfolders.

Compression causes your computer to slow down

When compression is enabled, the computer's performance can degrade. This is because when a compressed file is opened, the file must be decompressed, copied, and then recompressed in order to open. Degradation can also occur if a compressed file is transferred across a network because the file must be uncompressed before it is transferred.

What happens when a compressed file is moved or copied?

Moving or copying a compressed file or folder can alter the compression. When moving a compressed file or folder, the file or folder remains compressed. When copying a compressed file or folder, it is only compressed if the destination folder (where you are moving it to) is already compressed. When adding a file to an encrypted folder, the file is automatically encrypted.

Encryption is a method of securing data from unauthorized users. Windows 2000 and higher use an encryption feature called **EFS** (encrypting file system). Note that Vista and 7 Starter, Home Basic, and Home Premium versions do not fully support encryption. In these versions, the cipher command can be used from the command prompt to decrypt files, modify an encrypted file and copy an encrypted file to the computer. The EFS algorithm originally used DES (Data Encryption Standard), which uses 56- or 128-bit encryption but now uses AES (Advanced Encryption Standard), SHA (Secure Hash Algorithm), smart-card-based encryption, and, in Windows 7, ECC (Elliptical Curve Cryptography).

When a file or folder is encrypted with EFS, only authorized users can view or change the file. Administrators designated as recovery agents have the ability to recover encrypted files if necessary. EFS is not compatible with any Windows versions prior to Windows 2000.

Compressed files, system files, and read-only files cannot be encrypted. Windows Explorer is used to encrypt a file or folder. The hard drive volume must be partitioned as NTFS to enable encryption. The following steps outline how to encrypt a file or folder. Right-click the file or folder to be encrypted, select *Properties* → *General* tab → *Advanced* button → *Encrypt contents to secure data* checkbox → *OK* button → *Apply* button → *OK* button. If a folder is marked as encrypted, the Confirm Attribute Changes dialog box appears and asks if only the folder is to be encrypted or if subfolders are to be encrypted as well. Hands-On Exercises 6 and 12 at the end of the chapter demonstrate how to manipulate file attributes, compression, and encryption.

What happens when an encrypted file is moved or copied?

Encrypted files and folders that are moved or copied on NTFS volumes remain encrypted. If a file or folder is moved or copied to a FAT(16) or FAT32 volume, the file or folder is decrypted and the user making the move must have encryption authorization.

Determining the Windows Version

The version of an operating system is very important to a technician. With any Windows version, upgrades or patches to the operating system are provided by service packs. A **service pack** has multiple fixes to the operating system. A technician must determine what operating system version is on the computer so that he or she can research whether or not a service pack is needed. Several ways to determine what version of Windows is loaded on a computer follow:

- Right-click the *Start* button → *Explore* → *Help* → *About Windows*
- *Start* button → *Run* → type winver and press Enter
- *Start* button → *All Programs* → *Accessories* → *System Tools* → *System Information*
- Right-click the *Start* button → *Explore* → locate *Computer* → right-click on *Computer* → *Properties*
- In the *Start Search* textbox, type winver and press Enter
- *Start* button → *All Programs* → *Accessories* → *System Tools* → *System Information*
- *Start* button → *Control Panel* → *System and Maintenance* (Vista)/*System and Security* (7) → *System*

Windows Registry

Every software and hardware configuration is stored in a database called the **registry**. The registry contains such things as folder and file property settings, port configuration, application preferences, and user profiles. A **user profile** contains specific configuration settings such as what applications the user has access to, desktop settings, and the user's network configuration for each person who has an account on the computer. The registry loads into RAM (memory) during the boot process. Once in memory, the registry is updated continuously by changes made to software, hardware, and user preferences.

The registry is divided into five subtrees. Subtrees are also sometimes called branches or hives. The five standard subtrees are as follows: HKEY_LOCAL_MACHINE, HKEY_USERS, HKEY_CURRENT_USER, HKEY_CURRENT_CONFIG, and HKEY_CLASSES_ROOT. Each of these subtrees has keys and subkeys that contain values related to hardware and software settings. Table 11.3 lists the five subtrees and their functions. The registry can contain other subtrees that are user defined or system defined, depending on what hardware or software is installed on the computer.

Table 11.3   Windows registry subtrees

Registry subtree	Subtree function
HKEY_LOCAL_MACHINE	Holds global hardware configuration. Included in the branch is a list of hardware components installed in the computer, the software drivers that handle each component, and the settings for each device. This information is not user-specific.
HKEY_USERS	Keeps track of individual users and their preferences.
HKEY_CURRENT_USER	Holds a specific user's configuration such as software settings, how the desktop appears, and what folders the user has created.
HKEY_CURRENT_CONFIG	Holds information about the hardware profile that is used when the computer first boots.
HKEY_CLASSES_ROOT	Holds file associations and file links. The information held here is what allows the correct application to start when you double-click a filename in Explorer or My Computer (provided the file extension is registered).

Editing the Windows Registry

Most changes to Windows are done through the various control panels, but sometimes the only way to make a change is to edit the registry directly. Hands-On Exercise 7 at the end of the chapter illustrates this procedure.

Depending on the Windows operating system being used, one or two 32-bit registry editors are available. They are called **REGEDIT** and **REGEDT32**. Both registry editors can be used to change the registry; however, there are some differences between the two. The big difference is how information is displayed. With REGEDIT, the five major subtrees are in one window. With REGEDT32, the subtrees are in individual windows. In 32-bit Windows XP and Vista, even though both commands are available, they display the same. Figure 11.7 shows Windows XP's REGEDIT utility.

Make a backup of the registry before you change it

Before making changes to the registry, you should make a backup of it. That way, if the registry changes do not work properly or affect the computer in a negative way, the changes can be reversed easily.

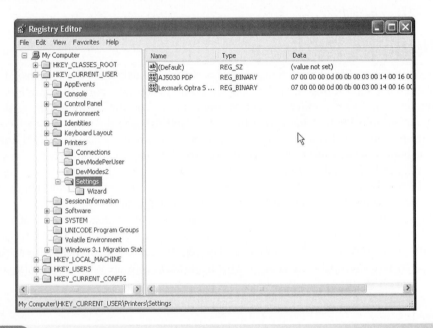

Figure 11.7   REGEDIT **in Windows**

Notice in Figure 11.7 how subtrees, such as HKEY_CLASSES_ROOT and HKEY_CURRENT_USER, list in the left window. By clicking the + (plus) symbol beside each subtree, more subkeys appear. After several layers, when you click a folder in the left window, values appear in the right window. These values are the ones you must sometimes change to fix a problem. Hands-On Exercises 1, 2, and 7 at the end of the chapter demonstrate how to modify the registry.

For 64-bit versions of Windows XP and Vista, the registry is divided into 32- and 64-bit keys. The 32-bit keys are kept in a subfolder called WOW6432Node, located within the HKEY_LOCAL_MACHINE key (Software folder). On some machines, the vendor may have a subfolder under Software; it is this vendor subfolder that contains the WOW6432Node folder. Just do a search for WOW6432Node to find it.

Accessing the 64-bit registry editor

To access the 64-bit registry editor, you must know where the operating system is stored. The common location is C:\Windows. If this is the case, then the command to open the 64-bit registry from the Start Search textbox is C:\Windows\syswow64\regedit (then press Enter). Otherwise, replace C:\Windows with the drive letter and folder where the operating system files are located.

Recovering the Operating System

When a computer starts performing badly and the operating system tools do not seem to help, it is common to replace the operating system. A virus could also cause extensive damage, resulting in needing an operating system recovery. How this process is done depends on what measures have been taken (or not been taken, in some cases) and the type of environment where the computer is located (home or work). The list that follows describes some of the common methods used to recover an operating system:

- Recovery CD/DVD provided by the computer manufacturer
- Recovery partition or section of the hard drive (sometimes called the HPA, or host protected area) created by the computer manufacturer and commonly accessed through Advanced Boot Options (which you access by pressing F8 while booting) or through a keystroke defined by the computer manufacturer
- Imaging software—Companies frequently have a standard image stored on a server used to replace failing operating systems or new computers
- Backup/restore software provided by an external hard drive manufacturer
- Booting to Recovery Console from Advanced Boot Options and selecting the recovery tool. The Recovery Console is covered in greater detail in the next section.
- Original operating system disks—This method is a risky one because the original disks do not contain updated service packs. Download service packs and copy the service pack to a CD/DVD *before* reinstalling the operating system. Research the service pack requirements before installing. Ensure the computer is disconnected from any network before reinstalling the operating system and service packs! Do not connect to the network until the service packs have been installed, or virus infection may result.
- Booting to safe mode or Recovery Console from Advanced Boot Options (F8 while booting) and using the System Restore tool to restore the operating system back to a time when it worked.

Recovery Console

Recovery Console is used when Windows 2000 or XP do not boot and other startup options do not solve a problem. Recovery Console allows access to hard drive volumes without starting the GUI (graphical user interface). In other words, Recovery Console allows you access to a command prompt from which you use commands to start and stop services, repair and access hard drive volumes, replace corrupt files, and perform a manual recovery.

Recovery console is not loaded onto the system by default, but it can be installed from the XP CD and then loaded through the boot menu or executed from the XP CD. Normally technicians run Recovery Console from the CD because it is needed when there is a problem.

To run Recovery Console from the XP CD, use the XP CD to start XP. If the CD is unavailable or the computer does not support booting from a CD, use XP setup boot disks (obtained from Microsoft). Press R at the Welcome to Setup screen to select the repair the installation option and the Recovery Console window appears. Press the number that corresponds to the partition where XP is loaded. An administrator password prompt appears. Type the Administrator password and press Enter. A command prompt appears. Technicians must sometimes work from the command prompt when the system is not working properly.

Recovery Console requires the Administrator password

You must have the Administrator password to access the full potential of Recovery Console. Without it, many options are not available and the system will not be able to be repaired.

Vista/7 Recovery Console missing

The Recovery Console has been removed from Vista and Windows 7. Tools are available through a special recovery partition accessed through Advanced Boot Options (F8 while booting) or from the original Vista installation discs. Boot from the Vista installation disc, select *Repair your computer*, and use the *System Recovery Options*. This is known as WinRE (Recovery Environment).

Administrator password not required in Recovery Console if the registry is corrupt

If the registry is corrupt or has been deleted, you are not prompted for an Administrator password. Instead, the system boots to a prompt where you can use basic commands like CHKDSK, FIXBOOT, and FIXMBR to repair the system. However, you cannot access any folders on the hard drive.

The drive letters available at the Recovery Console command prompt might not be the same ones you used in the GUI environment. Use the MAP command to see the drive letters (and the volumes that do not have drive letters).

If partition is FAT16, you must re-install Recovery Console

If using FAT(16) and you install the Recovery Console and you convert the partition to NTFS, the Recovery Console must be re-installed.

Some of the commands most frequently used from the Recovery Console command prompt are outlined in this chapter. Some commands have different options when used within Recovery Console. To get help from a command prompt running within Windows XP or from within Recovery Console, type help to see a list of commands; type help command_name (where command_name is the command itself); or type command_name /?

The copy command can be used through Recovery Console to restore the two important files, system and software hives. These are used to build two important registry keys, hkey_local_machine\system and hkey_local_machine\software. Frequently when one of these two hives have problems you will get an error that Windows could not start because the following file is missing or corrupt: \Windows\System32\Config\System (or Software). If the unresolved problem relates to hardware, replace the "system" file first. If the problem relates to software, replace the "software" file first. Do not replace both files at the same time because the system or software hive files may not be current, which means that drivers or service packs may have to be re-installed after replacement.

Backup the system and software files before problems occur

It is a good idea to make a backup of the system and software hive files *before* Windows XP crashes or before replacing them. To make a copy using Recovery Console, type cd system32\config at the prompt. To copy the system file, type copy system *path* (where *path* is the drive letter and path to where the backup is to be stored). To copy the software file, type copy software *path* (where *path* is the drive letter and path to where the backup is to be stored).

To replace the system or software hive file, type copy ..\ ..\ repair \ system or copy ..\ ..\ repair \ software or put the path where the latest backup copy of the system and software files are located. To update the software and system hive files kept in the Repair folder, use the Backup utility and save the System State. When the *System State backup* option is enabled, the Repair folder is updated.

Recovery Console has four default limitations of which a technician should be aware:

- No text editor is available in Recovery Console by default
- Files cannot be copied to removable media such as floppy disks or Flash drives while in Recovery Console; write access is disabled
- The Administrator password cannot be changed from Recovery Console
- Some folders, such as Program Files and Documents and Settings, are inaccessible from the Recovery Console prompt

Working from a Command Prompt Overview

Quite a few computer problems are software-related and many hardware installations have software programs that allow the hardware to work. Running diagnostic software is something a technician also performs from time to time. Even with the advent of newer and more powerful operating systems, a technician still must enter basic commands into the computer while troubleshooting. Being able to function from a command prompt is a skill that a technician still must use sometimes. When an operating system does not work, the technician must be able to input commands from a prompt.

An operating system has two types of commands—internal and external. **Internal commands** are not visible when viewing files on a disk, flash drive, or hard drive, but after you enter the commands, they will execute. Internal commands are built into the operating system and execute much faster than external commands. Two examples of internal commands are DIR and COPY. Use the DIR command to view a listing of files and directories. Use the COPY command to make a duplicate file or folder.

External commands can be seen when viewing files on a disk or a hard drive. External commands execute slower than internal commands because the external commands must retrieve data from a disk or hard drive. For example, you can do a search through Windows Explorer (using the *Search* option from the Start button

Tech Tip

Run Device Manager from a prompt

From a command prompt or from the *Search text* textbox in Vista, type `mmc devmgmt.msc` to start Device Manager.

or *Search text* textbox in Vista) and find the ATTRIB.EXE command, but you cannot find the COPY command. Both commands work from a command prompt, but ATTRIB.EXE is an external command and COPY is an internal command. The ATTRIB command is used to set an attribute such as read-only or hidden on a file or folder manually.

There are several ways to access a command prompt when the computer is functional. These methods follow:

- *Start → Run* (XP) or *Start Search* textbox in Vista/7 → type cmd and press [Enter]
- *Start → Run* (XP) or *Start Search* textbox in Vista/7 → type command and press [Enter]; note that when this option is used, the keyboard arrow keys do not bring up previously used commands as the CMD command does
- *Start → All Programs → Accessories → Command Prompt* (XP, Vista, and Windows 7)

Working from a Command Prompt Basics

Drive letters are assigned to hardware devices when a computer boots. For example, the first floppy drive gets the drive letter A:. The colon is part of the device drive letter. The first hard drive in a system gets the drive letter C:. The devices detected by the operating system can use drive letters A: through Z:.

All communication using typed commands begins at the **command prompt**, or simply a prompt. A command prompt might look like A:\> or C:\> or C:\WINDOWS>. Commands are typed using a keyboard. Capitalization does not matter when using a command prompt, but commands *must* be typed in a specific format and in a specific order. Practicing commands from a command prompt is the best way to become proficient at using them.

Files can be organized like chapters in a book; however, on a computer, these file groupings are called a folder (GUI environment) or a **directory** (command prompt environment). The starting point for all directories is the **root directory**. From the root directory, other directories can be made. The root directory is limited as to how many files it can hold.

When looking at a file structure from within Windows Explorer, you can see some of these concepts. Figure 11.8 shows that the root directory of the C: drive contains folders such as *Binaries*, *Config.Msi*, *Dell*, and *Documents and Settings*.

Tech Tip

Maximum number of files in the root directory

A FAT (FAT16) formatted partition or Flash drive can hold a maximum of 512 files or directories. A drive will send an "out of space" error message if there are more than 512 files in the root directory. The drive may have gigabytes of available space and still give the error just because the root directory is filled. Creating directories is a good way to organize files and keep the root directory uncluttered.

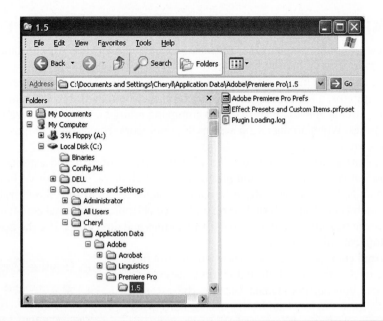

Sample file structure

When the + sign beside the *Documents and Settings* folder is clicked, the folders within the folder, such as the folder for *Administrator*, *All Users*, and *Cheryl*, are displayed. Within the *Cheryl* folder, there is a folder within called *Application Data*. When you expand the *Application Data* folder, one folder that exists is called *Adobe*. When the *Adobe* folder is expanded, three folders are shown: *Acrobat*, *Linguistics*, and *Premier Pro*. Within the *Premier Pro* folder is another folder called *1.5*. When you click the *1.5* folder, the contents of the folder displays on the right—*Adobe Premiere Pro Prefs*, *Effect Presets and Custom Items.prfpset*, and *Plugin Loading.log*. The path to the *Plugin Loading.log* file is shown at the top of the *Windows Explorer* window. You would have to add the name of the file to the end of the path that is shown for the complete path:

```
C:\Documents and Settings\Cheryl\Application Data\Adobe\
     Premiere Pro\1.5\Plugin Loading.log
```

Every folder along the path is shown starting with the root directory of C: (C:\). The path tells you exactly how to reach the file.

Notice in Figure 11.8 how each folder (directory) has a unique name. An infinite number of files can exist under each directory. Each filename within a directory must be unique, but other directories can contain the same file. For example, let us assume that the *CHERYL.TXT* file exists in the *WINDOWS* directory. A different *CHERYL.TXT* file (or the same one) can exist in the *LOTUS* or *UTILITY* directory (or all three directories for that matter). It could also be the exact same file called *CHERYL.TXT* that exists in all three folders. However, a second *CHERYL.TXT* file cannot exist in the same folder (directory).

Files are kept in directories (folders) or in the root directory. A **subdirectory** can be created beneath another directory. For example, if a directory (folder) has the name *BOOK*, below the directory can be subdirectories titled *CHAP1*, *CHAP2*, *CHAP3*, and so on. In Figure 11.8, the three folders under the *Adobe* folder would be considered subdirectories.

Moving Around from a Command Prompt

The most frequently used command for moving around in the cumbersome tree structure is **CD** (change directory). Take, for example, a disk with a *TEST1* directory that has subdirectories called *SUB1*, *SUB2*, and *SUB3*, as shown in Figure 11.9.

Assume the prompt is at A:\>. To move to the *SUB2* subdirectory (subfolder), type the command CD TEST1\SUB2. The prompt changes to A:\TEST1\SUB2>. Another command that works is CD A:\TEST1\SUB2.

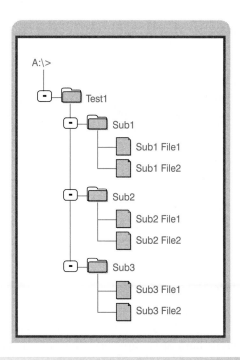

Figure 11.9   **Sample tree structure**

To move to a subdirectory that is on the same level as the *SUB2* directory (such as *SUB1* or *SUB3*), several commands are possible. One way is to type CD.. to move back one level and then type CD SUB1. Notice there is not a backslash (\) between the CD and the SUB1. Omit the backslash only when moving one level down the tree structure shown in the figure. From the A:\Test1> prompt, you can type CD SUB1, CD\TEST1\SUB1, or CD A:\TEST1\SUB1 to get to the *SUB1* subfolder. However, if the prompt shows you are at the root directory (A:\>), either A:\TEST1\SUB1 or CD TEST1\ SUB1 must be used. The other commands given do not operate properly because of the current location within the tree structure. Practice is the only way to master moving around from a prompt. Hands-On Exercises 10, 11, and 12 at the end of the chapter help with this concept.

The TYPE Command

Another useful command is the **TYPE** command, which is used to display text (.TXT) or batch (.BAT) files on the screen. Many times *README.TXT* or *READ.ME* files are included with software applications and utilities. The TYPE command allows viewing these files; however, most of the time, these files occupy more than one screen. So, using the | more parameter after the TYPE command permits viewing the file one screen at a time. After viewing each screen, the (Spacebar) is pressed. For example,

```
TYPE README.TXT | MORE
```

allows viewing the text file one page at a time.

Copying Files

The **COPY** command is used to make a duplicate of a file. The COPY command is an internal command meaning it cannot be found as an executable file on the hard drive or Windows CD/DVD. The operating system can always find an internal command no matter where in the directory structure the command is located. The command allows you to copy a file to a different disk, copy a file from one directory to another, copy a group of files using wildcards, or rename a file as it is being copied. A **wildcard** replaces one or more characters. ? and * are examples of wildcards, where ? represents a single character and * represents any number of characters.

The `COPY` command has three parts with each part separated by a space:

1. The command itself (`COPY` or `XCOPY`)
2. The source (the file being copied)
3. The destination (where the file is being copied to)

The destination is optional if the file copies into the current directory. For example, if working from the `A:\>` command prompt and copying a file called *DOCUMENT.TXT* from the hard drive's root directory, then the command could be `COPY C:\DOCUMENT.TXT`. The destination is omitted because the file automatically copies to the current drive and directory (which is `A:\`). The same function can be accomplished by typing `COPY C:\DOCUMENT.TXT A:\`, which has all three parts—the `COPY` command, the source (a file called *document.txt* located on the hard drive or `C:\DOCUMENT.TXT`), and the destination (the root directory of A or `A:\`).

The command requires all three parts if the destination is *not* the current drive and directory. For example, take the situation of being at the `C:\>` command prompt. To copy the `FORMAT.COM` command from the hard drive to a disk located in the `A:` drive, type the following command:

```
COPY C:\WINDOWS\SYSTEM32\FORMAT.COM A:\
```

Note that the `COPY` command is first. Then the source, the location, and name of the file being copied—`C:\WINDOWS\SYSTEM32\FORMAT.COM`—is next. Last is the destination, `A:\` or the root directory of the floppy disk where the file is to be placed. If the current directory is the `C:\WINDOWS\SYSTEM32` hard drive directory, then the source path does not have to be typed. Instead, the command would look like the following:

```
C:\WINDOWS\SYSTEM32> COPY FORMAT.COM A:\
```

The backslash (`\`) after the `A:` is not necessary if the floppy drive does not have directories (folders). The `COPY` command does not need the entire path in front of the command because `COPY` is an internal command.

Tech Tip

Use the complete path if you are unsure about what command to use
New technicians commonly make mistakes in specifying a command's correct path. If you are a beginner, the safest way is to type the complete path of the command, source, and destination locations.

Before using any command, consider the following questions:

- What command do you want to issue?
- Where is the command located in the directory structure?
- Where in the directory structure are you currently working?
- If you are copying a file or moving a file, in what directory does the file need to be placed?

The `ATTRIB` Command

The **`ATTRIB`** command sets, removes, or shows the attribute of a file or a directory. Attributes change how a file or directory is displayed on the screen or what can be done with the file or directory. Possible attributes include read-only, archive, system, and hidden.

- The read-only attribute protects files so they cannot be accidentally changed or deleted
- The archive attribute marks files that have changed since they were last backed up by a backup program
- The system attribute designates a file as a system file; files with this attribute do not show in directory listings
- The hidden attribute allows file hiding and even directory hiding

Set each attribute using the +*x* switch where *x* is `R` for read-only, `H` for hidden, or `S` for system. Remove each attribute using the −R, −S, −H, or −A switch with the `ATTRIB` command. One command can set more than one attribute on files or directories. For example, to make the *CHERYL.TXT* file hidden and read-only, type `ATTRIB +R +H CHERYL.TXT`.

Windows Command Format

When Windows does not boot, a technician must work from a command prompt. Some of the most frequently used commands are outlined on the following pages. Items enclosed by

How to get help when working from a prompt

To get help from a command prompt running within Windows, type `Help` to see a list of commands; type `Help command_name` (where `command_name` is the command itself); or type `command_name /?`.

brackets are optional. Items in italics are command specific values that you must enter. When the items are separated by a | (bar), one of the items must be typed. Note that not all options shown may be available when using Recovery Console. Some commands have different options when used within Recovery Console. The items with an asterisk (*) before them are available from both a command prompt and from within Recovery Console (although not all options are available).

*ATTRIB

This command is used to control the attribute for a file or folder.

Syntax: `attrib [+|-h] [+|-r] [+|-a] [+|-s][drive:][path]filename`
               `[/S][/D]`

Explanation: + adds an attribute.

          – takes an attribute away.

          h is the hidden attribute.

          r is the read-only attribute.

          a is the archive file attribute.

          s is the system attribute.

          `[drive:]` is the drive where the file is located.

          `[path]` is the directory/subdirectory where the file is located.

          `filename` is the name of the file.

          `[/S]` includes subfolders.

          `[/D]` includes folders

Example: `attrib +h c:\cheryl.bat` sets the hidden attribute for a file called *CHERYL.BAT* located on the hard drive.

Notes: The `DIR` command (typed without any switches) is used to see what attributes are currently set. You may set more than one attribute at a time.

BCDEDIT

The `bcdedit` command is used from the command prompt or System Recovery environment in Windows Vista and Windows 7 to modify and control settings contained in the BCD (boot configuration data) store, which controls how the operating system boots. The BCD store is similar to the *BOOT.INI* file in previous editions of Windows.

Syntax: `bcdedit [/createstore] [/export] [/import] [/store]`
               `[/copy] [/create] [/delete] [/deletevalue] [/set] [/enum]`
               `[/v] [/bootsequence] [/default] [/displayorder] [/timeout]`
               `[/toolsdisplayorder] [/bootems] [/ems] [/emssettings]`
               `[/bootdebug] [/dbgsettings] [/debug]`

Explanation: `[/createstore]` creates a new empty BCD store that is not a system store.

[/export] exports the BCD system store to a remote destination file that can be used to restore the BCD system store.

[/import] uses a previous backed-up copy of the BCD system store to replace the existing BCD system store.

[/store] is used in conjunction with other commands to specify a specific BCD store to use.

[/copy] is used to make a copy of a specific boot entry contained in the BCD store.

[/create] is used to create a new entry in the BCD store.

[/delete] is used to delete an element from a specific entry in the BCD store.

[/deletevalue] is used to delete a specific element from a boot entry.

[/set] is used to set a specific entry's option value.

[/enum] is used to list entries in a store.

[/v] is used to set BCDEDIT to verbose mode.

[/bootsequence] is used to specify a display order that is used one time only. The next time the computer boots, the original display order is shown.

[/default] selects the entry used by the boot manager when the timeout expires.

[/displayorder] is used to specify a display order that is used each time the computer boots.

[/timeout] is used to specify, in seconds, the amount of time before the boot manager boots using the default entry.

[/toolsdisplayorder] specifies the display order for the Tools menu.

[/bootems] enables or disables EMS (Emergency Management Services) for the specific entry.

[/ems] enables or disables EMS for the specified operating system boot entry.

[/emssettings] sets global EMS settings.

[/bootdebug] enables or disables the boot debugger for a specified boot entry.

[/dbgsettings] specifies the global debugger settings.

[/debug] enables or disables the kernel debugger for a specified boot entry.

Example: `bcdedit / set Default debug on`

This command troubleshoots a new operating system installation for the operating system that is the default option that appears in the Boot Manager menu.

Notes: Use the `bcdedit /? TYPES` command to see a list of data types. Use the `bcd /? FORMATS` command to see a list of valid data formats. To get detailed information on any of the options, type `bcdedit /?` followed by the option. For example, to see information on how to export the BCD, type `bcd/ ?/ export`.

*BOOTCFG

This command is used to change, delete, configure, or query entries set in the *BOOT.INI* file for Windows XP and earlier.

Syntax: When used from a command prompt within the operating system:

`bootcfg [/copy|/delete|/query|/raw|/timeout|/default|/ems|`
`/debug|/addsw|/rmsw|/dbg1394][arguments]`

Syntax when used from Recovery Console:

```
bootcfg [/add|/rebuild|/scan|/list|/disableredirect|
/redirect [port_number baud_rate]| useBiosSettings]|
/redirect|/default]
```

Explanation: `[/copy]` creates a copy of the current boot entry [operating systems] section of *BOOT.INI* and this can be used to add options.

  `[/delete]` is used to delete the existing boot entry [operating systems] section of *BOOT.INI*. An argument must be used to specify which boot entry is to be deleted.

  `[/query]` displays the current boot entries.

  `[/raw]` allows the user to specify switch options for a specific boot entry in the *BOOT.INI* file.

  `[/timeout]` is used to change the timeout value for the *BOOT.INI* file.

  `[/default]` is used to change the default operating system defined in the *BOOT.INI* file.

  `[/ems]` allows the /redirect switch to be configured.

  `[/debug]` is used to configure the port and speed for debugging a boot entry found in the *BOOT.INI* file.

  `[/addsw]` allows a user to add predefined switches for a specific boot entry.

  `[/rmsw]` allows a user to remove a predefined switch for a specific boot entry.

  `[/dbg1394]` allows a user to configure the FireWire port to debug a specific boot entry.

  `[arguments]` are options normally available with a specific command. To see what arguments are available for a specific parameter type `bootcfg`, then a forward slash (`/`), then the specific parameter such as `copy` or `delete`, press the `Spacebar` once, and type `/?`. An example is `bootcfg /copy /?`.

  `[/add]` adds a windows installation to the boot list.

  `[/rebuild]` iterates through all Windows installations and allows the user to choose which installation to add to the boot list. `[/scan]` checks all disks for Windows installations.

  `[/list]` lists entries contained in the current boot list.

  `[/disableredirect]` disables redirection of the boot loader.

  `[/redirect [port_number baud_rate | useBiosSettings]` enables redirection in the boot loader. An example is `bootcfg /redirect com1 115200`.

Example: `bootcfg /delete /id 1` deletes the second boot entry from the *BOOT.INI* file.

BOOTREC

The `bootrec` command is used from Recovery Console (XP) or the System Recovery environment (Vista/Windows 7) to repair and recover from hard drive problems.

Syntax: `bootrec [/FixMbr] [/FixBoot] [/ScanOs] [/RebuildBcd]`

Explanation: `[/FixMbr]` repairs the hard drive MBR (master boot record) by copying a new MBR to the system partition. The existing partition table is not altered.

  `[FixBoot]` repairs the hard drive boot sector if it has been corrupted and replaces it with a non-Windows Vista/Windows 7 boot sector or, if an earlier version of Windows has been installed, *after* Windows Vista or Windows 7.

  `[/ScanOs]` looks for compatible operating system installations that do not currently appear on the Boot Manager list.

  `[/RebuildBcd]` scans all disks for operating systems compatible with Windows Vista or Windows 7 and optionally rebuilds the BCD (boot configuration data). The

Example: BCD store provides structured storage for boot settings that is especially helpful in multiple operating system environments. Discovered operating systems can be added to the BCD store.

Example: `bootrec /fixmbr`

This command could be used if a virus has destroyed the master boot record.

Notes: If you receive an "Element not Found" error when using the `bootrec` command, the hard drive partition might not be active. Use the Vista/Windows 7 recovery environment command prompt and the `diskpart` command to select the drive disk number (if you only have one and it has one partition, it will be the command *select disk 0*, as an example), and then type the command *active*. Exit the *diskpart* utility and reboot the computer. Re-access the System Recovery environment and rerun the `bootrec` command.

If the system needs a new BCD and rebuilding it did not help, you can export the existing BCD and then delete the current BCD. To export the BCD, type `bcdedit /export x:\`*folder* (where `x:\`*folder* is the location to where you want the BCD store exported). Then type `c:`, `cd boot`, `attrib bcd -s -h -r`, `ren c:\boot\bcd bcd.old`, `bootrec/RebuildBcd` to create a backup copy of the BCD store, make it so it is not hidden and can be deleted, and then rebuilds it.

*CD

This command is used to navigate through the directory structure.

Syntax: `cd [`*drive:*`][`*path*`][..]`

Explanation: `[`*drive:*`]` specifies the drive (if a different one than the current drive) to which you want to change.

`[`*path*`]` is the directory/subdirectory to reach the folder.

`[..]` is used to change to the parent directory (moves you back one directory in the tree structure).

Example: `C:\WINDOWS>cd..`

`C:\>`

This command moves you from the *WINDOWS* directory (folder) to the parent directory, which is the root directory (`c:\`).

`C:\>cd \WINDOWS`

This command moves you from the root directory to the *WINDOWS* directory on the `c:` drive.

*CHKDSK

This command checks a disk for physical problems, lost clusters, cross-linked files, and directory errors. If necessary, the `chkdsk` command repairs the disk, marks bad sectors, recovers information, and displays the status of the disk.

Syntax: `chkdsk [`*drive:*`][/r][/c][/f][/i][/l:`*size*`][/v][/x][/b]`

Explanation: `[`*drive:*`]` specifies the drive to check.

`[/r]` locates bad sectors and attempts recovery of the sector's information.

`[/c]` skips cycle checking of NTFS volume folders.

`[/f]` fixes drive errors.

`[/i]` checks only index entries on NTFS volumes.

`[/l:`*size*`]` the /l: must be part of the command followed by the size (in kilobytes) of the log file for NTFS volumes.

[/v] With a FAT volume, the /v switch shows the full path for every file. With an NTFS volume, cleanup messages are displayed.

[/x] With NTFS, the switch forces the volume to dismount before checking the volume.

[/b] With NTFS, the switch re-evaluates bad clusters.

Example: chkdsk d: This command checks the disk structure on the D: drive.

Notes: This command can be used without switches. In order for this command to work, the *AUTOCHK.EXE* must be loaded in the *SYSTEM32* folder or used with the correct path and run from the Windows CD.

*CIPHER

The cipher command displays or alters file or folder encryption.

Syntax: cipher [/e|/d] [/s:*dir*] [/a] [/i] [/f] [/q] [/h] [/k] [/u[/n]] [*path*|[/r:*PathNameWithoutExtension*]|[/w:*PathName*]

Explanation: [/e] encrypts the specified folder, including files that are added in the future.

[/d] decrypts the specified folder.

[/s:*dir*] performs an operation defined by another switch in the specified folder and includes subfolders.

[/a] performs an operation defined by another switch for files and directories.

[/i] ignores any errors encountered.

[/f] forces encryption or decryption because, by default, files that have already been encrypted or decrypted are skipped.

[/q] reports essential information about the encryption or decryption.

[/h] shows files that have the hidden or system attribute set.

[/k] creates a new file encryption key.

[/u] updates the encryption key to the current one for all encrypted files if the keys have been changed. /u works only with the /n option.

[/n] finds all encrypted files. It prevents keys from being updated. It is used only with /u.

[*path*] a pattern, file, or folder.

[/r:*PathNameWithoutExtension*] creates a new recovery agent certificate and private key and writes them to files with the filename specified in *PathNameWithoutExtension*.

[/w:*PathName*] removes data on unused portions of a volume, as specified by *PathName*.

[/?] shows help.

Example: cipher /e Book\Chap1

This command encrypts a subfolder called Chap1 that is located in a folder called Book.

cipher /e /s:Book

This command encrypts all subfolders in the folder called Book.

cipher Book

This command displays whether the Book folder is encrypted.

```
cipher Book\Chap 1\*
```
This command display whether any files in the Chap1 subfolder of the Book folder are encrypted.

Notes: Multiple parameters are separated with spaces. Read-only files and folders cannot be encrypted.

*CLS

The `cls` command clears the screen of any previously typed commands.

Example: C:\WINDOWS>cls

CMD

The `cmd` command is executed from the *RUN* dialog box. (Click *Start* button → *Run* → type CMD.EXE → press Enter.) A command prompt window appears. Type EXIT to close the window.

Syntax: cmd [/c *string*]

Explanation: [/c *string*] specifies that the command interpreter is to perform the command specified by the *string* option and then stop.

Example: cmd /c chkdsk d: This command runs the `chkdsk` program on the D: hard drive volume using the command line.

Notes: This command is not available in Recovery Console.

*COPY

The `copy` command is used to copy a single file to the destination that you specify from Recovery console. Multiple files can be copied from within the Windows command prompt environment.

Syntax: copy [/a] [/v] [/y] [/-y] *source* [*target*]

Explanation: [/a] indicates an ASCII text file.

[/v] verifies that files are written correctly.

[/y] suppresses the prompt to overwrite an existing file.

[/-y] prompts to overwrite an existing file.

source is the file that you want to copy and it includes the drive letter and the path if it is different from your current location.

[*target*] is the location you want to put the file and it includes the drive letter and path if it is different from your current location.

Example: copy c:\cheryl.bat a:\

This command takes a file called *CHERYL.BAT* that is located in the root directory of the hard drive and copies it to the floppy drive.

Notes: You cannot use wildcard characters such as * and ? with this command in the Recovery Console. You do not have to put a target if the file is going to the current location specified by the command prompt. If a file already exists, you will be prompted whether or not to overwrite the file. Compressed files that are copied from the Windows CD are automatically uncompressed to the hard drive as they are copied.

DEFRAG

The `defrag` command is used to locate and reorder files so they are contiguous (not fragmented) and improve system performance.

Syntax: defrag [*drive:*] [/a] [/c] [/e] [/h] [/m] [/t] [/u] [/v] [/x]

Explanation: [*drive:*] is the drive letter where the files are located.

[/a] is used to analyze the drive volume specified.

[/c] includes all volumes.

[/e] excludes certain volumes (and the rest are used).

[/h] executes at the default priority of low.

[/m] executes on each volume in parallel as a background task.

[/t] tracks a currently running operation on a specific volume.

[/u] prints the operation progress on the screen.

[/v] prints the verbose output.

[/x] consolidates free space on the specified volume.

Example: `defrag c: d: /a`

This command defragments the C: and D: drives and analyzes them.

Notes: Multiple switches can be used as long as spaces appear between them. Multiple drive letters (volumes) can be used with a single command.

*DEL

The del command is used to delete a file.

Syntax: `del name [/p][/f][/s][/q][/a]`

Explanation: name is the file or directory (folder) that you want to delete and it includes the drive letter and the path if it is different from your current location.

[/p] is used to prompt for confirmation before deleting.

[/f] is used to force read-only files to be deleted.

[/s] is used to delete files from all subdirectories.

[/q] means quiet mode, which does not prompt for confirmation.

[/a] is used to select files based on their attribute where the attributes are R, H, S, and A. A + (plus sign) before the attribute means "select it" and a − (minus sign) before the attribute means "do not select it."

Example: `C:\WINDOWS>del c:\cheryl.bat`

This command deletes a file called *CHERYL.BAT* that is located in the *WINDOWS* directory on the hard drive.

Notes: You cannot use wildcard characters such as * and ? with this command while in the Recovery Console.

*DIR

The dir command is used to list files and folders and their attributes.

Syntax: `dir [drive:][path][filename][/a][/b][/c][/d][/l][/n][/o] [/p][/q][/s][/t][/w][/x][/4]`

Explanation: [drive:] is the drive letter where the files are located.

[path] is the directory/subdirectory to reach the folder.

[filename] is the name of a specific file.

[/a:attribute] is used to display files that have specific attributes where the attributes are D, R, H, A, and S. D is for directories; R is for read-only; H is for hidden; A is for archive; and S is for system files.

[/b] is for barebones format (it does not show heading or summary information).

[/c] shows the file sizes with the thousands separator.

[/d] displays the file listing in a wide format sorted by column.

[/l] displays the listing in lowercase.

[/n] displays the listing in long list format.

[/o] displays the listing in sorted order. Options you can use after the "o" are E, D, G, N, and S. E is by alphabetic file extension; D is by date and time with the oldest listing shown first; G shows the directories listed first; N displays by alphabetic name; and S displays by size from smallest to largest.

[/p] displays the information one page at a time.

[/q] displays the owner of the file(s).

[/s] includes subdirectories in the listing.

[/t] controls which specific time field is shown where the types of time fields are A, C, and W. A is for the last access date/time with the earliest shown first; C is for the creation date/time; and W is for the last written date/time.

[/w] shows the listing in wide format.

[/x] shows the 8.3 filename listing for long filenames.

[/4] displays four digit years instead of two digit years.

Example: dir c:\windows

This command shows all of the files and folders (and their associated attributes) for the *WINDOWS* folder that is located on the c: drive.

Notes: You can use wildcard characters such as * and ? with this command in the Recovery Console. The attributes you can see are (1) *a* for archive, (2) *c* for compressed, (3) *d* for directory, (4) *e* for encrypted, (5) *h* for hidden, (6) *p* for reparse point, (7) *r* for read-only, and (8) *s* for system file.

DISABLE

From Windows XP Recovery Console, the disable command is used to disable a system service or hardware driver.

Syntax: disable *name*

Explanation: *name* is the name of the service or driver that you want to disable.

Notes: You can use the listsvc command to show all services and drivers that are available for you to disable. Make sure that you write down the previous *START_TYPE* before you disable the service in case you need to restart the service.

*DISKPART

The diskpart command is used to manage and manipulate the hard drive partitions.

Syntax: diskpart [/add|/delete][*devicename*]
              [*drivename*|*partitionname*][*size*]

Explanation: [/add|/delete] is used to create a new partition or delete an existing partition.

[*devicename*] is the name given to the device when creating a new partition such as \Device\HardDisk0.

[*drivename*] is the drive letter used when deleting an existing partition such as E:. [*partitionname*] is the name used when deleting an existing partition and can be used instead of the *drivename* option. An example of a *partitionname* is Device\HardDisk0\Partition2.

[*size*] is used when creating a new partition and is the size of the partition in megabytes.

Notes: You can just type the diskpart command without any options and a user interface appears that helps when managing hard drive partitions.

DXDIAG

This command is used to perform DirectX diagnostics.

Syntax: dxdiag [/dontskip] [whql:on|/whql:off] [/64bit *target*]
[/x *filename*] [/t *filename*]

Explanation: [/dontskip] causes all diagnostics to be performed even if a previous crash in dxdiag has occurred.

[/whql:on] checks for WHQL digital signatures.

[/whql:off] prevents checking for WHQL digital signatures.

[/64bit *target*] uses 64-bit DirectX diagnostics.

[/x *filename*] saves XML information to the specified *filename* and quits.

[/t *filename*] saves TXT information to the specified *filename* and quits.

Notes: When DirectX diagnostics checks for WHQL digital signatures, the Internet may be used.

ENABLE

From Windows XP Recovery Console, this command is used to enable a system service or hardware driver.

Syntax: enable *name* [*start-type*]

Explanation: *name* is the name of the service or driver that you want to disable.

[*start-type*] is when you want the service or driver scheduled to begin. Valid options are as follows:

SERVICE_BOOT_START

SERVICE_SYSTEM_START

SERVICE_AUTO_START

SERVICE_DEMAND_START

Example: enable DHCP client service_auto_start

Notes: You can use the listsvc command to show all services and drivers that are available for you to enable. Make sure that you write down the previous value before you enable the service in case you need to restart the old service or driver.

*EXIT

This command closes Recovery Console and restarts the computer. When an operating system is loaded and an command prompt window is open, the exit command closes the command prompt
window.

Example: C:\WINDOWS>exit

*EXPAND

The expand command is used to uncompress a file from the Windows CD or a CAB file. A CAB file is a shortened name for a cabinet file. A **CAB file** holds multiple files or drivers that are compressed into a single file. Cabinet files are normally located in the i386 folder on the Windows CD. Technicians frequently copy the CAB files onto the local hard drive, so that when hardware and/or software is installed, removed, or re-installed, the Windows CD does not have to be inserted.

Syntax: expand [-r] [-d] [-i] *source* [/f:*filespec*][*destination*]
[/y][/d]

Explanation: [-r] renames expanded files.

[-d] displays files in *source*.

[-i] renames files but ignores the directory structure.

source is the name of the file, including the path that you want to uncompress.

[/f:*filespec*] is the parameter used if a source contains more than one file.

[*destination*] is the path to where you want to place the uncompressed file.

[/y] is the parameter used if no overwrite prompt is desired.

[/d] is the parameter used when the folder that is contained in the source parameter is not to be expanded.

Example: expand   d:\i386\access.cp_   c:\windows\system32\access.cpl
expands (uncompresses) the compressed file *ACCESS.CP_* and puts it into the *C:\WINDOWS\SYSTEM32* folder with the name *ACCESS.CPL*.

Notes: You may not use wildcard characters with the source parameter. You may use wildcard characters with the /f:*filespec* parameter.

FIXBOOT

From Windows XP Recovery Console, this command is used to rewrite the hard drive's boot sector.

Syntax: fixboot [*driveletter*:]

Explanation: [*driveletter*:] is the drive letter (and a colon) of the hard drive volume that you want to place in a new boot sector.

Example: fixboot c:

Notes: If you do not specify the *driveletter*: parameter, the boot sector that is repaired is the system boot volume's boot sector.

FIXMBR

From Windows XP Recovery Console, this command rewrites the startup partition's Master Boot Record.

Syntax: fixmbr [*name*]

Explanation: [*name*] is the name of the device that you want to repair its Master Boot Record.

Example: fixmbr \Device\HardDisk0

Notes: If you do not type the *name* parameter, Disk 0 is the default. Use the map command to see valid device names. Run an anti-virus scan before using this command.

*FORMAT

The format command is used to format a disk and can be used to format it for a particular file system.

Syntax: format   [*driveletter*:][/q][/fs:*filesystem*][/a:*size*][/c]
[/f:*size*][/n:*sectors*][/t:*tracks*][/v:*label*][/x]

Explanation: [*driveletter*:] is the drive letter for the disk or hard drive volume that you want to format.

[/q] is the parameter used if you want to perform a quick format.

[/fs:*filesystem*] is the parameter used if you want to specify a file system. Valid values are as follows: FAT, FAT32, exFAT, and NTFS.

[/a:*size*] The a: must be part of the command followed by the default allocation unit size. The different units supported by the three file systems follow:

NTFS: 512, 1024, 2048, 4096, 8192, 16K, 32K, and 64K

FAT: 512, 1024, 2048, 4096, 8192, 16K, 32K, 64K, and (128K, 256K for sector size that is larger than 512 bytes)

FAT32: 512, 1024, 2048, 4096, 8192, 16K, 32K, 64K, and (128K, 256K for sector size that is larger than 512 bytes)

[/c] is used to compress the files on the volume by default.

[/f:*size*] The /f: must be part of the command followed by the size for floppy disk to format. The different sizes supported are as follows: 160, 180, 320, 360, 640, 720, 1.2, 1.44, 2.88, or 20.8.

[/n:*sectors*] The /n: must be part of the command followed by the number of sectors per track.

[/t:*tracks*] The /t: must be part of the command followed by the number of tracks per disk side.

[/v:*label*] The /v: must be part of the command followed by the name of the volume assigned.

[/x] is used to dismount the volume first, if necessary.

Example: format c: /fs:ntfs

Notes: If no /fs:*filesystem* parameter is specified, the NTFS file system is used. FAT is FAT16. FAT16 hard drive volumes cannot be more than 4GB in size, but should be formatted to 2GB to be compatible with DOS, Windows 3.x, and Windows 9x.

*HELP

This command displays information about specific Recovery Console and command prompt commands.

Syntax: help [*command*]

Explanation: [*command*] is the name of the command for which you want help.

Example: help expand

Notes: If you do not specify the *command* parameter when using the Help command, all commands are listed.

*IPCONFIG

This command is used to view and control information related to the network adapter.

Syntax: ipconfig [/allcompartments] [/all|/renew [*adapter*] |
/release [*adapter*]|/renew6 [*adapter*]|/release6
[*adapter*]|/flushdns|displaydns|registerdns|/showclassid
[*adapter*]|/setclassid *adapter* [*classid*]|/showclassid6
[*adapter*]|/setclassid6 *adapter* [*classid*]]

Explanation: [/allcompartments] displays information regarding all compartments and, when used with the /all option, shows detailed information about all compartments.

[/all] displays all configuration information, including IP and MAC addresses.

[/renew] renews the IPv4 address optionally for a specific adapter.

[/release] releases the IPv4 address optionally for a specific adapter.

[/renew6] renews the IPv6 address optionally for a specific adapter.

[/release6] releases the IPv6 address optionally for a specific adapter.

[/flushdns] removes all entries from the DNS resolver cache.

[/displaydns] shows the contents of the DNS resolver cache.

[/registerdns] refreshes DHCP leases and re-registers recently used DNS names.

[/show *classid*] displays all configured IPv4 DHCP class IDs allowed optionally for a specific adapter.

[/setclassid *adapter*] configures an adapter for a specific IPv4 DHCP class ID. A class ID is used to have two or more user classes that are configured as different DHCP scopes on a server. One class could be for laptops, while a different class could be for desktop computers in an organization.

[/showclassid6 *adapter*] displays all configured IPv6 DHCP class IDs allowed optionally for a specific adapter.

[/setclassid6 *adapter*] configures an adapter for a specific IPv6 DHCP class ID.

Examples: ipconfig /all

ipconfig /release

ipconfig /renew

Notes: The three commands above are essential to a technician. ipconfig /all verifies whether an IP address has been configured or received from a DHCP server. ipconfig /release releases a DHCP-sent IP address. ipconfig /renew starts the DHCP request process.

Operation requires elevation

If a message ever appears from within the command prompt window that the requested operation requires elevation, close the command prompt window. Re-locate the *Command Prompt* Windows Accessory and right-click on the option. Select *Run as administrator* and re-execute the command from the prompt.

LISTSVC

In Windows XP Recovery Console, this command lists all of the services, hardware drivers, and their start-types available. The listsvc command is useful to use before using the disable or enable command.

Syntax: listsvc

Example: C:\WINDOWS>listsvc

LOGON

In Windows XP Recovery Console, the logon command is used to list all Windows 2000, NT, and XP installations and prompts for the local administrator password.

MAP

In Windows XP Recovery Console, the map command is used to list the computer's drive letters, types of file systems, volume sizes, and physical device mappings.

Syntax: map [*arc*]

Explanation: [*arc*] is the Advanced RISC Computing path instead of the Windows device paths. This parameter is used when you are repairing or recreating the *BOOT.INI* file.

*MD

This command is used to create a directory (folder).

Syntax: md [*driveletter:*][*dirname*]

Explanation: [*driveletter*:] is the drive letter for the disk or volume on which you want to create a directory (folder). It can also include the path.

[*dirname*] is the parameter used to name the directory (folder).

Example: md c:\TEST

Notes: You may not use wildcard characters with this command. The mkdir command can also be used to create a directory.

*MORE

The more command is used to display a text file.

Syntax: more *filename* [/c][/e][/p][/s][/t#]

Explanation: *filename* is the path and name of the text file you want to display on the screen.

[/c] clears the screen before displaying a page of information.

[/e] enables extended features.

[/p] expands form feed characters.

[/s] takes multiple blank lines and condenses them into one blank line.

[/t#] The /t must be part of the command followed by the number of spaces used to expand tabs. The normal setting is eight spaces.

Example: more c:\boot.ini

Notes: The [Spacebar] allows you to view the next page of a text file. The [Enter] key allows you to scroll through the text file one line at a time. The [Esc] key allows you to quit viewing the text file.

MSCONFIG

The msconfig command is used to start the System Configuration utility from a command prompt instead of a control panel. The System Configuration utility is commonly used to troubleshoot boot issues specifically related to software and services. The Startup tab lists software loaded when the computer boots, and a checkbox allows you to disable and enable the particular application. The same concept is used with the Services tab, which contains checkboxes beside services started when the computer boots.

Syntax: msconfig

MSINFO32

The msinfo32 command is used to bring up the System information window from a command prompt. The System information window contains details about hardware and hardware configurations as well as software and software drivers.

Syntax: msinfo32 [/pch] [/nfo *path*] [/report *path*] [/computer *computer_name*] [/showcategories] [/category *id*]

Explanation: [/pch] shows the history view.

[/nfo *path*] saves the exported file with an .nfo extension.

[/report *path*] saves the exported file in .txt format.

[/computer *computer_name*] starts the System Information utility for a remote computer.

[/showcategories] starts the System Information utility with category IDs instead of the normal names.

[/category *id*] starts System Information with a specific category selected.

Examples: msinfo

msinfo /computer Cheryl_Dell

*NET USE

The `net use` command is used to attach to a remote network device.

Syntax: `net use [drive_letter] [\\server_name\share_name /user:domain_name\user_name [password] [/smartcard] [/savecred] [[/delete] [/persistent:{yes | no}]]`

Explanation: `drive_letter` is the letter (followed by a colon) that NET USE assigns to the network device connection.

`\\server_name` is the name of the network device to which to connect.

`share_name` is the name of the share.

`domain_name` is the domain used to validate the user.

`user_name` is the user to be validated.

`[password]` is an optional entry so the system does not prompt for a password. If this option is not entered, a password prompt appears and the system automatically assigns a drive letter once a connection is made.

`[/smartcard]` uses credentials found on a smart card.

`[/savecred]` keeps the provided credentials and reuses them.

`[/delete]` the specified network connection is removed. An asterisk (*) removes all network connections.

`[/persistent]` saves all network connections by default and uses them on the next logon. Use the *no* option to prevent saving the network connection.

Example: `net use \\ATC227-01\cisco /user:cisco\student`

Notes: Not all NET commands can be used from Recovery Console.

NSLOOKUP

The `nslookup` command is used for troubleshooting DNS issues.

Syntax: `nslookup [-option] [hostname] [server]`

Explanation: `[-option]` is a variety of options that can be used, such as `exit`, `finger`, `help`, `ls`, `lserver`, `root`, `server`, and `set`. See Microsoft TechNet for a complete listing.

`[hostname]` is a name of a host, such as the computer name for a specific computer in the organization.

`[server]` is the URL of a specific server, such as www.pearsoned.com.

Examples: `nslookup www.pearsoned.com`

`nslookup -querytype=hinfo -timeout=10`

Notes: The second example changes the default query type to a host and the timeout to 10 seconds. You must have at least one DNS server IP address configured on a network adapter (which you can view with the `ipconfig /all` command) in order to use the `nslookup` command. There are two modes of operation: non-interactive and interactive. The non-interactive has more commands than shown in the examples given. The interactive mode is started by simply typing `nslookup` and pressing Enter.

*NTBACKUP

The `ntbackup` command is used in Windows XP and lower to perform backup operations.

Syntax: `ntbackup backup [systemstate] "@bks_file_name" /j {"job_name"} [/p {"pool_name"}] [/g {"guid_name"}] [/t {"tape_name"}] [/n {"media_name"}] [/f {"file_name"}] [/a] [/v:{yes|no}] [/r:{yes|no}] [/l:{f|s|n}] [/m {backup_type}] [/hc:{on|off}] [/snap:{on|off}]`

Explanation: [systemstate] sets the backup type to normal (or copy) because the System State data is backed up.

"*@bks_file_name*" specifies the name of the backup selection file (.bks file) to be used for the backup. The @ symbol must precede the name of the file.

/j {"*job_name*"} is the name of the job to be used in the log file.

[/p {"*pool_name*"}] is the media pool from which you want to use media. This option cannot be used with the /a, /g, /f, or /t options.

[/g {"*guid_name*"}] overwrites or appends to a tape. This option cannot be used with the /p option.

[/t {"*tape_name*"}] overwrites or appends to a tape. This option cannot be used with the /p option.

[/n {"*media_name*"}] gives the tape a name. This option cannot be used with the /a option.

[/f {"*file_name*"}] defines the logical path and filename to be used with this backup. This option cannot be used with the /p, /g, or /t options.

[/d {"*set_desc*"}] configures a descriptive label for each backup set.

[/a] appends data to a backup. The /g or /t options must be used with this option, but the /p option cannot be used with it.

[/v:{yes|no}] determines whether or not data is verified.

[/r:{yes|no}] restricts backup access to the owner or a member of the Administrators group.

[/l:{f|s|n}] determines the type of log file used, where f is full, s is summary, and n is no log file created.

[/m {*backup_type*}] determines the type of backup done (normal, copy, differential, incremental, or daily).

[/hc:{on|off}] determines whether or not hardware compression is used, if available, on the backup media.

[/snap:{on|off}] determines whether or not the backup is a volume shadow copy.

Example: ntbackup backup \\cheryl-Dell\c$ /j "CSchmidt Backup 1" /f "d:\backup1.bkf"

*PING

The ping command is used to test connectivity to a remote network device.

Syntax: ping [-t] [-a] [-n *count*] [-l *size*] [-f] [-i *ttl*]
[-v *tos*] [-r *count*] [-s *count*] [[-j *host_list*] |
[-k *host_list*]] [-w *timeout*] [-R] [-S *source_addr*] [-4]
[-6] *target*

Explanation: [-t] pings the destination until stopped with [Ctrl] +C keystrokes. To see the statistics and continue, use the [Ctrl]+Break keys.

[-a] resolves IP addresses to host names.

[-n *count*] defines how many pings (echo requests) are sent to the destination.

[-l *size*] defines the buffer size (length of packet).

[-f] sets the do not fragment flag in an IPv4 packet.

[-i *ttl*] defines a time to live value from 0 through 255.

[-v *tos*] defines a type of IPv4 service.

[-r *count*] records the route for a specified number of IPv4 hop counts.

[-s *count*] defines a timestamp for a specific number of IPv4 hop counts.

[[-j *host_list*] is used for a loose source route along a specified *host_list* in an IPv4 environment.

[-k *host_list*] is an alternative to the -j option for a strict source route along a specified host_list in an IPv4 environment.

[-w *timeout*] defines the time, in milliseconds, to wait for each echo reply.

[-R] is used in IPv6 to use a routing header to test the reverse route as well as the forward route.

[-S *source_addr*] defines the source IP address to use.

[-4] forces the use of IPv4.

[-6] forces the use of IPv6.

target is the destination IP address.

Examples: ping -t www.pearsoned.com

ping -n 2 -l 1450 165.193.130.107

Notes: The first example pings the Pearson Technology Education Web site indefinitely until the Ctrl+C keys are used. The second example sends two echo requests (pings) that are 1450 bytes to the Pearson Technology Education Web site.

*RD

This command is used to remove a directory (folder).

Syntax: rd [*driveletter:*][*path*]

Explanation: [*driveletter:*] is the drive letter for the disk or hard drive volume from which you want to remove a directory (folder).

[*path*] is the optional path and name of the directory (folder) you want to remove.

Example: rd c:\TEST\JUNKDATA removes a directory (folder) called *JUNKDATA* that is a subdirectory under a directory (folder) called *TEST*. This directory is located on the hard drive (c:).

Notes: You do not have to use the *driveletter:* parameter if the default drive letter is the same as the one that contains the directory to be deleted.

*REN

The ren command is used to rename a file or directory (folder).

Syntax: ren [*driveletter:*][*path*] *name1 name2*

Explanation: [*driveletter:*] is the drive letter for the disk or hard drive volume in which you want to rename a file or a directory (folder).

[*path*] is the optional path telling the operating system where to find the file or directory (folder) you want to rename.

name1 is the old name of the file or directory (folder) that you want to rename.

name2 is the new name of the file or directory (folder).

Example: ren c:\cheryl.bat c:\newcheryl.bat

Notes: The renamed file cannot be placed in a new location with this command. Move or copy the file after you rename it if that is what you want to do. The * and ? wildcard characters are not supported.

*SET

The set command is used to display and view different Recovery Console variables.

Syntax: set [*variable = value*]

Explanation: *variable* is one of the following:

AllowWildCards, which is the variable used to enable wildcard support for the commands that normally do not support wildcards.

`AllowAllPaths`, which is the variable that allows access to all of the computer's files and folders.

`AllowRemovableMedia`, which is the variable that allows files to be copied to removable media (floppy disk).

`NoCopyPrompt`, which is the variable that disables prompting when overwriting a file.

`value` is the setting associated with the specific variable.

Example: `set allowallpaths = true` allows access to all files and folders on all drives.

`set allowremovablemedia = true` allows you to use a Flash (thumb) drive or floppy.

`set allowwildcards = true` allows you to use wildcards from the command prompt.

Notes: To see all of the current settings, type `set` without a variable and the current settings display. The `set` command can be used only if it is enabled using the Group Policy snap-in.

SFC

This command is used to start the System File Checker utility from a command prompt. The System File Checker verifies operating system files.

Syntax: `sfc [/scannow] [/verifyonly] [/scanfile=file_name]`
`[/verifyfile=file_name] [/offwindir=windows_directory]`
`[/offbootdir=boot_directory]`

Explanation: `[/scannow]` is used to scan all protected system files and repair those that are damaged, if possible.

`[/verifyonly]` scans all protected system files but does not repair any detected problems.

`[/scanfile=file_name]` scans the specified file and repairs it if necessary. `file_name` should contain the full path.

`[/verifyfile=file_name]` verifies the specified file but does not repair it. `file_name` should contain the full path.

`[/offwindir=windows_directory]` is used in Vista for offline repairs for the specified Windows directory.

`[/offbootdir=boot_directory]` is used in Vista for offline repairs for the specified boot directory.

Examples: `sfc /scannow`

`sfc /release`

`sfc /scannow /offwindir=c:\windows`

SYSTEMROOT

The `systemroot` command sets the current directory as the system root.

Syntax: `systemroot`

Notes: The `systemroot` command is only available through Recovery Console.

TELNET

This command is used in Windows XP and earlier operating systems to access a remote network device. A better tool to use would be SSH.

Syntax: `telnet [destination]`

Explanation: `[destination]` is the name or IP address of the remote network device.

TRACERT

This command is used to verify the path taken by a packet from source device to destination.

Syntax: tracert [-d] [-h max_hops] [-j host_list]
          [-w msec_timeout] [destination]

Explanation: [-d] does not attempt to resolve intermediate router IP addresses to names and speeds up the tracert process.

[-h max_hops] specifies the maximum number of hops to search for the destination. The default is 30.

[-j host_list] where host_list is a list of IP addresses listed in dotted-decimal notation and separated by spaces. The echo request message IP header uses the loose source route option with the set of intermediate destinations specified by host_list.

[-w msec_timeout] specifies the time to wait for an ICMP time exceeded or echo reply message to be received. This time is specified in milliseconds, with the default being 4000, which is 4 seconds.

[destination] is the targeted end device, listed by IP address or name.

Example: tracert -d www.pearsoned.com

*TYPE

The type command is used to display a text file.

Syntax: type filename

Explanation: filename is the path and name of the text file you want to display on the screen.

Example: type c:\boot.ini

Notes: The [Spacebar] allows you to view the next page of a text file. The [Enter] key allows you to scroll through the text file one line at a time. The [Esc] key allows you to quit viewing the text file.

WSCRIPT

The wscript.exe is the command used to bring up a Windows-based script property sheet. This property sheet is used to set script properties. The command line version is CSCRIPT.EXE.

XCOPY

The xcopy command is used to copy and backup files and directories.

Syntax: xcopy source [destination] [/a] [/m] [/d[:date]] [/p] [/s]
          [/e] [/v] [/w] [/c] [/i] [/q][/f] [/l] [/g] [/h] [/r]
          [/t] [/u] [/k] [/n] [/o] [/x] [/y] [/-y] [/z] [/b] [/j]
          [/exclude:file1 [+file2]...]

Explanation: source is the full path from where the file(s) are copied.

[destination] is the optional destination path. If the destination is not given, the current directory is used.

[/a] copies files with the archive attribute set but does not change the archive attribute.

[/m] copies files with the archive attribute set and turns off the archive attribute.

[/d:date] copies files changed on or after the specified date.

[/p] causes a prompt to appear to verify the copying of each file.

[/s] copies all directories and subdirectories except for those that do not contain files.

[/e] copies all directories and subdirectories including empty ones.

[/v] verifies the size of the copied file.

[`/w`] prompts to press a key before the copying begins.

[`/c`] continues copying even if errors occur.

[`/i`] directs the operating system that the destination is a directory if the destination does not exist and more than one file is being copied.

[`/q`] suppresses displaying of filenames while copying.

[`/f`] displays full source and destination filenames while copying.

[`/l`] displays files that would be copied.

[`/g`] copies encrypted files to a destination that does not support encryption.

[`/h`] copies hidden and system files.

[`/r`] overwrites files in the destination that have the read-only attribute set.

[`/t`] creates a directory structure but does not copy files. It does not include empty directories or subdirectories unless it is used with the `/e` option.

[`/u`] copies only files that already exist in the destination location.

[`/k`] copies original attributes of the source file.

[`/n`] copies using the generated shortened filenames.

[`/o`] copies the file ownership and ACL information.

[`/x`] copies the file audit settings, file ownership, and ACL information.

[`/y`] suppresses the prompt that asks if you want to overwrite an existing destination file.

[`/-y`] displays a prompt asking if you want to overwrite an existing destination file.

[`/z`] copies networked files in restartable mode.

[`/b`] copies the symbolic link itself rather than the target of the link.

[`/j`] copies using unbuffered I/O; this is recommended when transferring large files.

[`/exclude:file1 [+file2]...`] removes particular files from the list of files to be copied.

Example: `xcopy c:\users\cheryl\my documents\chap1\chap1.docx`
`e:\book\chap1`

This command copies a file called `chap1.docx` from the `chap1` subfolder (which is located in folder called `chap1` that is a subfolder of the My Documents folder) to the E: drive and places it in the `chap1` subfolder that is contained in the book folder.

Notes: The `xcopy` command normally resets read-only attributes when copying.

Soft Skills—Staying Current

Technicians must stay current in the rapidly changing field of computers. Benefits of staying current include (1) being able to understand and troubleshoot the latest technologies; (2) being able to recommend upgrades or solutions to customers; (3) saving time troubleshooting (and time is money); and (4) being someone considered for promotion. A variety of methods are used by technicians to stay current, including the following:

- Subscribe to a magazine or an online magazine
- Subscribe to a newslist that gives you an update in your email
- Join or attend association meetings or seminars
- Take a class
- Read books
- Talk to your department peers and supervisor

Staying current in technology in the past ten years has been a challenge for all, but the rapidly changing environment is what draws many of us to the field.

Key Terms

Apply button (p. 397)
archive attribute (p. 400)
ATTRIB (p. 408)
CAB file (p. 417)
Cancel button (p. 396)
CD (p. 406)
checkbox (p. 396)
Close button (p. 397)
CMD (p. 414)
command prompt (p. 405)
command switch (p. 461)
compression (p. 400)
Control Panel (p. 395)
COPY (p. 407)
DEL (p. 415)
desktop (p. 392)
dialog box (p. 395)
DIR (p. 415)
directory (p. 405)
drop-down menu (p. 397)
EFS (p. 400)
encryption (p. 400)
extension (p. 397)

external command (p. 405)
file (p. 392)
folder (p. 392)
GUI (p. 392)
Help button (p. 396)
hidden attribute (p. 399)
icon (p. 392)
internal command (p. 405)
Internet Explorer (p. 393)
long filename (p. 397)
MD (p. 420)
My Computer/Computer
  (p. 393)
My Documents/Documents
  (p. 393)
My Network Places/Network
  (p. 393)
OK button (p. 396)
operating system (p. 392)
path (p. 392)
Quick Launch bar (p. 395)
radio button (p. 397)
RD (p. 424)

read-only attribute (p. 399)
Recovery Console
  (p. 403)
Recycle Bin (p. 393)
REGEDIT (p. 402)
REGEDT32 (p. 402)
registry (p. 401)
root directory (p. 405)
service pack (p. 401)
short filename (p. 397)
shortcut (p. 392)
sidebar (p. 445)
Start button (p. 394)
subdirectory (p. 406)
system attribute (p. 400)
taskbar (p. 394)
textbox (p. 396)
TYPE (p. 407)
UAC (p. 443)
user profile (p. 401)
wildcard (p. 407)
Windows Aero (p. 445)
Windows Explorer (p. 392)

Review Questions

1. List two operating systems.

2. What is the name of a graphical representation of a file, application, or folder?

3. What Windows XP desktop icon is used to access files located on various drives?
   [My Computer | Internet Explorer | Network Neighborhood | Recycle Bin]

4. Describe an easy way to tell if an icon is a shortcut.

5. What Windows XP desktop icon is used to access files that have been deleted?

6. What happens when you double-click a shortcut icon for a document?

7. Explain what a shortcut icon represents.

8. [T | F] Deleted files can be recovered from the Recycle Bin.

9. Describe why items placed in the Recycle Bin take up hard drive space.

10. What keystroke(s) bring up the *Start* menu?

11. Where is the Vista *Start* button located?

12. What *Start* menu option is used to access various icons that can be used to configure the computer?

13. List three items commonly found in a dialog box.

14. What is the insertion point as it relates to a textbox found in a dialog box?

15. What dialog box is represented by an X? [Help | Close | Performance | Lock out]

16. What happens when a dialog box is closed using the *Close* button instead of clicking *Apply*?

17. How can you tell when a radio button option is disabled?

18. What button is used to apply changes to a dialog box? [OK | Enable | Set | Change]

19. Describe the most common mistake made when working with dialog boxes.

20. What drive letter is assigned to the first floppy drive?

21. [T | F] A disk drive is always represented by a drive letter and a colon.

22. What is another name for a folder?

23. What is the normal number of characters used in a file extension?

24. With the filename *VISTA QUIZ 4.DOCX*, what characters represent the extension?

25. List three characters that cannot be used in Windows-based long filenames.

26. List three characters that can be used in Windows-based filenames.

27. Give an example of a long filename.

28. [T | F] By default, Windows Explorer displays file extensions.

29. Describe the process to set Windows Explorer so that file extensions are shown.

30. What extension is used for an encapsulated postscript file?

31. What file extension do compressed files normally use? [COM | ZIP | WKS | INF]

32. A user is working in Microsoft Word. He saves the document called *LTR1.DOC* to a folder called *WORDDOCS*. The *WORDDOCS* folder is a subfolder of the *MY DOCUMENTS* folder located on the D: hard drive volume. Write the complete path for the *LTR1.DOC* file.

33. What device contains the file A:\REVIEW1.XLS?

34. What is the parent folder for the path C:\MY DOCUMENTS\GAME1.PPT?

35. A file called *QUIZ1.DOC* is located in the *TEST* folder, which is a subfolder of *WINDOWS CLASS*. The *WINDOWS CLASS* folder is located in the *MY DOCUMENTS* folder on the first hard drive partition. Write the complete path for the *QUIZ1.DOC* file.

36. List three file attributes and the purpose of each attribute.

37. Describe the steps to set or remove a file attribute.

38. [T | F] Folders can have attributes configured.

39. [T | F] Compression is not supported on an NTFS partition.

40. [T | F] File and folder compression can degrade a computer's performance.

41. What Windows Vista versions do not support encrypting a file with software provided in the operating system?

42. List three algorithms used to encrypt files on Windows.

43. Describe what is contained in a user profile.

44. During the boot process, the registry loads into what type of memory? [ROM | EEPROM | RAM | FLASH]

45. Which registry key holds user profiles?

46. What are the five basic registry branches?

47. What registry hive has a list of hardware components and software drivers?

48. What registry branch holds the currently installed hardware profile?

49. You double-click a document called *TEST GRAPHICS.VSD* and the Visio application opens with the *TEST GRAPHICS.VSD* file active in a window. What registry hive tracked the file extension and associated it with the Visio application?

50. [T | F] The registry can only contain five subtrees.

51. What should you create before making changes to the registry? [boot disk | backup tape | boot CD | registry backup]

52. [T | F] 64-bit Windows Vista has both 32-bit and 64-bit registry keys.

53. What subfolder holds the Windows Vista 64-bit registry editor by default?

54. List one reason why a system might need to have the operating system recovered.

55. List three methods used to recover an operating system.

56. Which operating system recovery method do you think a home user with a Windows Vista-based computer is most likely to use and why?

57. [T | F] Recovery Console is a GUI environment.

58. [T | F] Recovery Console is loaded as a standard Windows XP boot option.

59. What type of user account is required to have access to Recovery Console? [Guest | Standard | Advanced | Administrator | Power User | Power Administrator]

60. List two limitations of using Recovery Console.

61. DIR is an example of an [Internal | External | Recoverable | Recovery Console Only] command.

62. List one method of accessing a command prompt when Windows XP is operational.

63. If a CD/DVD drive has the drive letter of D:, what would a command prompt look like if that drive was being accessed?

64. [T | F] The FAT16 root directory has a maximum number of files or directories that it can hold.

65. Why should directories be created on a hard disk instead of placing every file in the root directory?

66. What is the difference between a directory and subdirectory?

67. Consider the following directory structure from the C: drive root directory.

    2011_Term (directory)
        COMPREPAIR (subdirectory)
        OPSYS (subdirectory)
        CISCO8 (subdirectory)
        VOIP (subdirectory)

    If the prompt is C:\2011_TERM> and you wanted to move into the *VOIP* subdirectory, what command would you type?
    a. CD VOIP
    b. CD..
    c. CD C:\
    d. CD C:\VOIP

68. Which of the following commands is for viewing the contents of text files on the screen? [VIEW | SCREEN | OUTPUT | TYPE | EDIT]

69. Consider the following directory structure from the C: drive root directory:

    COMPUTER_REPAIR (directory)
        Quiz 1.doc (file)
        Quiz 2.doc (file)
        Midterm.doc (file)

    If the command prompt is C:\COMPUTER_REPAIR>, what command would you type to copy the *Quiz1.doc* to the root directory of C:?
    a. copy C:\Quiz1.doc C:\
    b. copy C:\COMPUTER_REPAIR C:\
    c. copy Quiz1.doc C:\
    d. copy Quiz1.doc C:\COMPUTER_REPAIR

70. Consider the following command:

    Copy G:\TESTS\CET2186\Quiz1.docx C:\My Documents

    To where does the *Quiz1.docx* file get copied? [TESTS | CET2186 | My Documents | Root directory of C: | Root directory of G:]

71. What are some mistakes that technicians commonly make when they are using the COPY or XCOPY commands?

72. [T | F] The ATTRIB command cannot hide directories.

73. List two file attributes.

74. What command is used from a Vista command prompt to decrypt and encrypt a file?

75. What command could be used from a prompt to reorder files on a hard drive volume so they are contiguous?

76. From a command prompt, what switch is used with the DEL command so that no confirmation prompt appears?

77. What Recovery Console command is used to show all services and drivers eligible to be disabled?

78. What command is used to change the name of a file?

79. List one method of staying current in technology that is *not* listed in the textbook.

Fill-in-the-Blank

1. Windows _____ is the most common Windows application used to move a file or folder.

2. Commands that can be executed from a prompt are specific to the _____.

3. _____ is the area where all work is done in the Windows environment.

4. The _____ Windows XP desktop icon is used to access a networked printer.

5. The _____ Windows XP desktop icon is frequently used to access the Web.

6. David Brown, a local network user, has shared a folder on his computer so others can access the documents. Lance Wallace wants to access David's folder. Therefore, he would use the _____ Windows XP desktop icon.

7. A/An _____ is a special icon used for quick file or application access and is shown with a bent arrow on the icon.

8. Shortcuts are normally placed on the _____.

9. The _____ Windows XP desktop option is used to keep desktop icons from being moved.

10. Deleted files from the hard drive volume go into the _____.

11. A/An _____ is a picture, pattern, or color used for the desktop background.

12. A/An _____ is the picture, color, or pattern that appears when the computer is idle.

13. The _____ holds buttons that represent open applications.

14. The _____ button is the place to begin in the Windows environment to access programs, get help, and find specific files.

15. The _____ or _____ Shut Down/Turn Off Computer option is used for saving power.

16. The _____ Windows XP *Quick Launch* option has an icon that looks like a desk with a pencil touching a piece of paper.

17. A/An _____ is the part of a dialog box that allows typed entries.

18. Click a dialog box's _____ to access a screen of related options.

19. In a dialog box, the _____ button is represented by a question mark.

20. When you click an empty checkbox, a/an _____ appears in the checkbox to show the option is enabled.

21. With a _____ dialog box button, the circle is darkened when enabled.

22. The drive letter _____ represents the first hard drive partition/volume.

23. A/An _____ holds data.

24. A/An _____ holds files.

25. *.DOCX* is an example of a/an _____.

26. *NTTEST1.DOC* is an example of a/an _____.

27. *HOMEWORK ASSIGNMENT.XLSX* is an example of a/an _____ filename.

28. The _____ application uses the .PDF extension.

29. The _____ and _____ file extensions are used with executable files.

30. The _____ file extension has executable code used by multiple applications.

31. Consider the following name: `C:\My Documents\Windows Class\Homework Assignment 1.docx`. In this name, `C:\My Documents\Windows Class\` is an example of a/an _____.

32. When working with a path, folders and filenames are always separated by the _____ character.

33. Both _____ and _____ can be used to set file attributes.

34. _____ folders take less space than folders that do not have this feature enabled.

35. The Windows database that stores hardware and software configuration information is called the _____.

36. The _____ registry hive holds file links.

37. The _____ registry branch holds Lance Wallace's desktop settings such as his custom motorcycle wallpaper scheme.

38. A computer just booted. The registry hive that has the current hardware profile is _____.

39. The two registry editors for Windows XP are _____ and _____.

40. The _____ folder holds Vista's 64-bit registry editor.

41. Performing operating system recovery from a partition/volume on the hard drive is normally accessed through _____ Boot Options or a/an _____ defined by the computer manufacturer.

42. _____ is used when Windows XP does not boot and other recovery options do not help.

43. The Recovery Console tools are accessed from a Windows Vista installation disc, specifically through the _____ option.

44. The drive letter _____ represents the first hard drive partition.

45. When working from a command prompt, another name for a folder is _____.

46. A/An _____ is a folder within a folder.

47. The _____ command is used to move around in the directory structure.

48. You are in the G:\TESTS directory on a Flash drive. You want to move into a subdirectory called *CET2186*. To do this you would type _____ *CET2186*.

49. In the path of *G:\TESTS\CET2186\Quiz1.docx*, *Quiz1.docx* is a/an _____.

50. In the path *G:\TESTS\CET2186\Quiz1.docx*, *TESTS* is a/an _____.

51. The _____ command can be used to remove the hidden attribute from a file.

52. The _____ command checks drives for errors.

53. The _____ switch is used with CHKDSK to speed up the process by checking only NTFS index entries.

54. The _____ XP Recovery Console command is used to rewrite the master boot record.

Hands-On Exercises

1. XP Basic Usage

Objective: To be able to work effectively with the Windows XP desktop including working with the *Start* button, managing the display through the *Control Panel*, changing *Start* button properties, obtaining help, performing file, folder, and computer searches, and accessing programs

Parts: Computer with Windows XP and Notepad installed

Procedure: Complete the following procedure and answer the accompanying questions.

1. Power on the computer and log on to Windows XP if necessary.

Working with the *Start* Menu

2. Click the *Start* button located in the bottom-left corner. The top of the *Start* menu shows who is currently logged on to the computer. Users are created so that the system can be individualized when multiple people use the same computer.

   Is your computer loaded with the classic *Start* button menu or the simple *Start* menu? Note that the classic *Start* button looks like previous Windows versions (a single column of words).

3. To see a dialog box and make changes to the *Start* button menu, right-click the *Start* button → *Properties* → *Start Menu* tab → *Customize* button.

   The *General* tab has three sections: *Icon size*, *Programs*, and *Show on Start* menu. The *Icon size* section controls the size of *Start* menu program icons. The *Programs* section has an option for setting the number of frequently used software shown on the left side of the *Start* menu. The *Clear List* button is used to clear the most frequently used software list being tracked by the operating system. It does not clear the software listed under the

Programs Start button option. The *Show* on *Start* section allows you to select the software used to access the Internet and email software.

4. Click the *Advanced* tab. The *Advanced* tab contains three sections: *Start menu settings*, *Start menu items*, and *Recent documents*. The *Start menu items* section controls which items display on the *Start* menu.

   Using the scroll bar in the *Start menu items* section, determine if the *Network Connections* option displays by default on the *Start* menu. Document your findings.

5. The *Clear List* button in the *Recent documents* section is used to clear the current list of recently accessed documents. Click the *Cancel* button.

6. Click the *Cancel* button and then click the *Start* button. Shortcuts for this step include pressing Ctrl+Esc or pressing the Windows key (if available).

   What are the top four options in the *right* column of the *Start* menu?

7. The *My Documents* option represents a folder that is the default storage location for saved files. *My Pictures*, *My Videos*, and *My Music* are subfolders (a folder within a folder) of the *My Documents* folder. A file is document. A folder is a storage unit for files. Click the *My Computer* Start button option. The *My Computer* option contains access to drives installed or connected to the computer. Floppy drives, hard drives, CD-ROM drives, DVD drives, Zip drives, tape drives, and so on are given drive letters such as A: or C:.

   What drives are available through the *My Computer* option?

Working with Control Panels

8. Close the *My Computer* window by clicking the *Close* button (the red X button) in the upper-right corner. Click *Start → Control Panel*. The *Control Panel* option allows access to control panel icons that are used to configure the computer. There are two ways to view control panels: *Classic control panel* and *Category control panel*. The default XP view is by category. If the words "Pick a category" *do not* appear at the top of the screen, click the *Switch to the Category View* option located in the left pane.

   List two control panel categories shown on the screen.

9. Click the *Switch to the Classic View* option located in the left window.

   List three control panel categories shown on the screen.
   Table 11.4 shows common XP control panels and functions of each one.

   Fill in the following table with the correct control panel. Use a computer that has XP installed to discover the correct control panel.

Control panel	Task
	Used to configure the mouse buttons for a left-handed person
	Used to mute the computer speaker sound
	Used to configure the date to be April 15, 2011
	Used to define how fast a character repeats when a specific key is held down
	Used to define what page (home page) appears every time Internet Explorer starts
	Used to configure the computer's network (IP) address
	Used to install a printer
	Used to access Device Manager

Working with the *Display* Control Panel

10. Double-click the *Display* control panel.

    What five tabs are listed across the top of the window?

11. Click the *Screen Saver* tab. Click the *Screen Saver* down arrow to see a list of pre-installed screen savers and click one of the options. Click the *Preview* button. The screen saver appears. Move the mouse to regain control.

Table 11.4   **Common Windows XP control panels**

Control panel	Function
Accessibility Options	Used to change the way the keyboard, sounds, display, and mouse function within Windows; used for people with disabilities
Add/Remove Hardware	Used to install and remove hardware devices
Add/Remove Programs	Used to install and remove software applications
Administrative Tools	Used to monitor and configure Windows
Date/Time	Used to change the date and time
Display	Used to control monitor functions such as desktop appearance, screen saver, and size of objects
Folder Options	Used to change file associations and how folder contents are displayed
Fonts	Used to add or remove system fonts
Internet Options	Used to change settings related to an Internet connection
Keyboard	Used to change the keyboard driver, repeat rate, and cursor blink rate
Mouse	Used to change the mouse driver, click speed, and pointer shape
Network and Dial-up	Used to add, remove, and configure network connections
Phone and Modem Options	Used to install a modem and control modem and dialing properties
Power Options	Used to reduce electrical power use in devices such as a monitor or hard drive
Printers	Used to add, remove, or change the properties of a printer
Regional Options	Used to set the time zone and to set the format for numbers and currency
Scheduled Tasks	Used to schedule things such as backups and disk defragmentation utilities
Sounds and Multimedia	Used to add/remove multimedia device drivers, set system event sounds, and change audio/video settings for multimedia devices
System	Used to view system configuration information, configure the computer for multiple hardware configurations, and change system settings
User and Passwords	Used to add/remove user accounts, set passwords, and set/view various security settings

12. Click the *Power* button. The *Power Options Properties* window appears. Table 11.5 shows the various power options available in Windows XP.

    What power option would your teacher use if he or she was using the computer to teach class and document why you think this?

Table 11.5   **Windows XP power schemes**

Power option	Purpose
Home/Office Desk	Monitor turns off after 15 minutes of inactivity, hard drive(s) turns off after 30 minutes, and the computer turns off after 20 minutes
Portable/Laptop	Same times as *Home/Office Desk* settings
Presentation	Standby options for hard drive, monitor, and computer system are disabled
Always On	Monitor turns off after 30 minutes of inactivity, hard drive(s) turn off after 1 hour, and the computer system never goes into standby
Minimal Power Management	Monitor turns off after 15 minutes of inactivity
Max Battery	Same as *Minimal Power Management* standby options

13. Click the *Cancel* button. You return to the *Display Properties* window. Click the *Cancel* button.

14. In the *Control Panel* window, click *Switch to Category View* to return to the default view. Close all control panel windows. Click the *Start* button.

Obtaining Help

15. Click *Help and Support*. The *Help and Support* window contains links to online and locally stored help topics.

16. The most commonly used help topics are listed on the left. On the right are the custom manufacturer options and a *Did you know?* category. Across the top are *Index*, *Favorites*, *History*, *Support*, and *Options*. Click the *Index* icon.

    What is the first item listed on the left.

17. Locate the *Performance and Maintenance* link. Select the *Advanced Performance* and *Maintenance Tools* option on the left.

    What is the first problem listed?

18. Note that instead of scrolling through topics, you can type a subject in the *Search* textbox and topics appear for you to select. To see a list of Windows XP troubleshooting topics, type **troubleshooting** in the *Type in the keyword to find*: textbox. A list of troubleshooting topics immediately displays.

    Is sound listed as one of the troubleshooting topics?

19. Close the *Help and Support Center* window.

Searching for Files, Folders, and Computers

20. Click the *Start* button and select *Search*. The *Search* option is used to hunt for files, other computers on the network, people listed in your address book, and information located on the Internet.

21. Click the *All files and folders* option. In the *All or part of the file name* box, type ***.hlp**. The ***** means the entire first part of any filename. The **.** (period) separates the filename from the file extension. The extension is automatically added by software applications. Windows help files all have the *.hlp* extension. So, the search criteria specified is for all Windows help files. Click the *Search* button.

    How many help files did the system find?

22. Locate and click the *Show Desktop* taskbar button. The button looks like a desk blotter with a pencil in the center and is normally located to the immediate right of the *Start* button.

23. Right-click the *My Computer* icon and select *Properties*. Click the *Computer Name* tab.

    Write the computer name.

    Find another computer or ask a classmate for the name of a different computer. Write the other computer name.

What to do if *My Computer* is not on the desktop

If the *My Computer* icon does not show on the desktop, click the *Start* button and point to the *Control Panel* option. If the *Control Panel* window shows the classic control panels, click the *Switch to Category View* option in the left panel. Select the *Appearance and Themes* control panel category. Click the *Change the computer's theme task*, click the *Desktop* tab, click the *Customize Desktop* button, and in the *Desktop icons* section, select the desktop icons to be added. Click the *OK* button twice and close the *Control Panel* window.

Tech
Tip

---

24. Click the *Cancel* button and then click the *Search Results* taskbar button, which brings you back to the same search window used before. Click the *Start a new search* option in the left window.

25. Click the *Computers or people search* option. At the *What are you looking for?* window, click *A computer on the network*. At the *Computer Name*: prompt, type the name of

your classmate's computer and Click *Search*. The computer should appear in the right window pane.

26. Close the search results window.

Starting Applications

27. Software applications are accessed through the *Start* button. Click the *Start* button. The left column contains the most recently used applications. If a program is not listed there, you can access it through the *All Programs* option. Point to *All Programs*. Point to *Accessories* and click *Notepad*. The Notepad application opens.

28. Type **This is a test**. Click the *File* menu bar option, Save, then type **text** in the *File name* textbox, and click the *Save* button. Click the *Close* button in the upper-right corner. Reaccess the *Start* button menu.

    Does the Notepad application now appear in the left column of the *Start* menu?

29. Click the *Start* button and click *Run*. Run is used to type a command or search for a particular executable file. An executable file is one that has *.exe*, *.com*, or *.bat* as a file extension. In the *Open* textbox, type **notepad** and click *OK*. The Notepad application opens. Close the Notepad application using the *Close* button.

Using the *Run* Option

30. Click *Start* and click *Run* again. Click the *Browse* button. The *Browse* option allows you to search for a particular executable file. Most people keep their documents in the *My Documents* folder. Click the *My Documents* icon in the *Browse* window's left panel. Click the *Cancel* button and return to the *Run* window. Click the *Cancel* button.

Recycle Bin

31. Use the *Search* option previously covered to locate the test file created in Notepad. Click once on the file icon and press the ⌈Del⌋ key. A *Confirm file delete* window appears. Click *Yes*. The file is sent to the *Recycle Bin*, which is a desktop icon that represents a folder on the hard drive.

    The Recycle Bin holds deleted files and folders. When a file or folder is deleted, it is not immediately discarded; instead, it goes into the *Recycle Bin* folder. Once a file or folder is in the Recycle Bin, it can be removed. This is similar to a piece of trash being retrieved from an office trash can. A technician must remember that the files and folders in the Recycle Bin take up hard drive space and that users frequently forget to empty the files and folders. Click the *Show Desktop* taskbar icon.

32. Double-click the *Recycle Bin* desktop icon. The document should be listed in the window.

    Does the *text.txt* file appear in the *Recycle Bin* window? If not, redo the steps to create and delete the file.

33. Click the *File* menu option and click *Empty Recycle Bin*. A *Confirm file delete* window appears. Click *Yes*. The name disappears from the *Recycle Bin* window (as well as any other files that were located in the Recycle Bin). Close the *Recycle Bin* window.

Creating a Shortcut

34. Click *Start* → *All Programs* → *Accessories* → *Windows Explorer* → *Search* icon. The search icon is used the same way the search *Start* menu option works. Click the *All files and folders* option. In the *All or part of the filename* textbox, type **notepad.exe**. Click the *Look in* down arrow and select *Local hard drives*. Click the *Search* button.

35. More than one Notepad file may exist. Pick one and right-click the file icon. Click the *Create shortcut* option. A window appears stating that a shortcut cannot be created here and prompts if the shortcut is to be created on the desktop. Click *Yes*. Close the *Search* window.

36. Access the desktop and verify that the Notepad shortcut is on the desktop.

Instructor initials: _____

37. Delete the shortcut and empty the Recycle Bin using the previous steps.

Instructor initials: _____

38. When finished working on the computer for the day, the computer needs to be turned off or shut down properly. All applications and windows should be closed and then special steps need to be taken for shutting down. Click *Start* and select *Turn off computer*. The *Turn off computer* dialog box appears, as shown in Figure 11.10.

Figure 11.10   Windows XP *Turn off computer* dialog box

If the computer has ACPI (Advanced Configuration and Power Interface) enabled, the computer shows a *Stand By* option. If ACPI is not enabled, the computer shows a *Hibernate* button instead of a *Stand By* button on the left side of the window. The *Cancel* button can be used to return to the Windows work environment. The four turn off options that can be shown in the dialog box and their purpose are listed in Table 11.6.

Table 11.6   Windows XP *Turn off computer* options

Option	Purpose
Hibernate	Saves the current work to disk and powers the computer down. When power is restored, the programs currently being used are available. *Power Options* control panel must be enabled.
StandBy	Keeps the current work, but puts the computer in low power mode. *Power Options* control panel must be enabled.
Turn Off	Used to shut the computer off
Restart	Used when new software or hardware has been installed or when the computer locks

39. Click the *Turn off* option to turn off the computer properly.

2. Vista/7 Basic Usage

Objective: To be able to work effectively with the Windows Vista/7 desktop, including working with the Start button; managing the display through the Control Panel; changing Start button properties; obtaining help; performing file, folder, and computer searches; and accessing programs

Parts: Computer with Windows Vista or 7 and the Windows Notepad application installed

Procedure: Complete the following procedure and answer the accompanying questions.

1. Power on the computer and log on to Windows if necessary.

Working with the *Start* Menu

2. Click the *Start* button. The top right of the Start menu on some systems shows who is currently logged on to the computer. Users are created so that the system can be individualized when multiple people use the same computer.

What do you think is the difference between the applications listed on the top left and those listed below the line on the left Start button column?

3. You can make changes to the Start button menu by right-clicking the *Start* button →
   Properties → *Start Menu* tab → *Customize* button.

   What is the current setting for the Control Panel option?
   [Display as a link | Display as a menu | Don't display this item]

   What is the current setting for Games?
   [Display as a link | Display as a menu | Don't display this item]

   How many recent programs are currently set to display?

4. Click *Cancel*. Select the *Taskbar* tab.

   List three options that can be customized through this tab.

5. Select the *How do I customize the taskbar* link. Using the information available, answer the
   questions that follow.

   How can you tell if the taskbar is locked or unlocked without moving it?

   What toolbars can be added to the taskbar?

   How can a taskbar that is hidden be reactivated?

6. Close the Windows Help and Support window.

7. Click on the *Notification Area* tab (Vista) or the *Customize* button in the Notification area (7).

   List three system icons.

8. Click the *Toolbars* tab.

   List any enabled toolbars.

9. Click *Cancel*. Press the Ctrl+Esc or press the *Windows* key to re-access the
   Start button.

   What are the top four options in the right column of the *Start* menu?

10. The *Documents* option represents a folder that is the default storage location for saved files.
    Pictures, *Music*, and *Games* also represent folders. A folder can contain another folder, and
    this folder is commonly called a subfolder. A file is a document created by an application.
    Files are stored and organized in folders. Click the *Computer* Start button option. The
    Computer option contains access to drives installed or connected to the computer. Floppy
    drives, hard drives, CD-ROM drives, DVD drives, Zip drives, tape drives, and so on are given
    drive letters such as A: or C:.

    What drives are available through the *Computer* option?

Working with Control Panels

11. Select the *Control Panel* Start button option. *Control Panel* allows access to control panel
    icons or links used to configure the computer. There are two ways to view control panels:
    Classic and *Category*. The default view is by category. In Vista, if the words "System and
    Maintenance" *do not* appear in the right pane, select the *Control Panel Home* link in the
    left pane. In Windows 7, select *Category* in the View by: drop menu.

    List two control panel categories shown on the screen.

12. In Vista, click the *Classic View* option located in the left window. In Windows 7, select
    Large icons or *Small icons* in the View by: drop menu. The classic view/large or small
    icons is the older method for accessing any particular control panel. Return to the
    Category control panel view.

    Table 11.7 shows common Vista/7 control panel categories and types of functions performed
    within each one. Some systems have special control panels due to the hardware installed or
    type of computer such as a nettop or tablet. Notice how some of the options are found in
    multiple categories.

    Fill in Table 11.8 with the correct control panel category and subcategory.

Table 11.7	Common Windows Vista or 7 control panel categories*	
Control panel category	**Subcategory**	**Function**
System and Maintenance (Vista) System and Security (7)	Welcome Center (Vista)	Used to access basic computer information, information on how to use Windows Vista, and Vista help videos
	Backup and Restore	Used to save or restore files and folders to or from a different location
	System	Used to view basic computer properties, such as RAM, processor type, and computer name
	Windows Update	Used to customize how Vista/7 updates are received and installed
	Power Options	Used to configure power saving modes
	Indexing Options*	Used to configure how Vista searches for files and folders more efficiently
	Problem Reports and Solutions (Vista)	Used to receive help with or view a history of computer problems
	Performance Information and Tools (Vista)	Used to obtain information about the computer speed and possible solutions related to speed
	Device Manager (Vista)	Used to view and update hardware settings
	Administrative Tools	Used for such tasks as freeing up hard disk space, managing hard drive partitions, scheduling tasks, and viewing event logs
	Action Center (7)	Used to view personal information, view a history of computer problems, view performance information, configure backup, troubleshoot problems, and restore the computer to a previous time
Security (Vista)	Security Center (Vista)	Used to view and modify computer firewall and update settings
	Windows Firewall	Used to enable and customize security firewall features
	Windows Update	Used to customize how updates are received and installed
	Windows Defender*	Used to scan the computer for unwanted software
	Internet Options (Vista)	Used to customize Internet Explorer
	Parental Controls (Vista)	Used for changing, enabling, and disabling settings related to family member access
	BitLocker Drive Encryption (7)	Change or use encryption options
Network and Internet	Network and Sharing Center	Used to check the status and modify network-related settings as well as share files, folders, and devices on the network
	Internet Options	Used to customize Internet Explorer
	People Near Me*	Used to configure the computer for software such as Windows Meeting Place
	Sync Center*	Used to synchronize mobile devices or network shares
	HomeGroup (7)	Used to view and change sharing and password options

*Note that in Windows 7, particular options can be found by typing in the subcategory in the *Search Control Panel* textbox.

(continued)

11

Basic Windows

Table 11.7   Common Windows Vista/7 control panel categories (continued)*

Control panel category	Subcategory	Function
Hardware and Sound	Printers (Vista)	Used to add, delete, or customize printer settings
	Devices and Printers (7)	Used to add/remove a device, scanner, camera, printer, and mouse as well as access Device Manager
	AutoPlay	Used to change how media is automatically handled when a disc or type of file is added or inserted
	Sound	Used to manage audio devices and change sound schemes
	Mouse (Vista)	Used to customize mouse and mouse button settings
	Power Options	Same as found in the System and Maintenance/System and Security category
	Personalization (Vista)	Used to customize the desktop, adjust monitor settings, select a theme, or change the mouse pointer
	Scanners and Cameras (Vista)	Used to add, delete, or customize settings related to scanners or cameras
	Keyboard*	Used to customize keyboard settings
	Device Manager (Vista)	Same as found in the System and Maintenance category
	Phone and Modem Options*	Used to install a modem and control modem and phone dialing properties
	Game Controllers*	Used to add, remove, and customize USB joysticks, gamepads, and other gaming devices
	Windows SlideShow (Vista)	Used to customize SlideShow settings
	Pen and Input Devices	Used to configure pen options for a tablet PC
	Color Management*	Used for advanced color settings on disc plays, scanners, and printers
	Tablet PC Settings	Used to configure tablet and screen settings on a tablet PC
	Display (7)	Used to adjust resolution, configure an external display, or make text larger/smaller
Programs	Programs and Features	Used to uninstall and change programs as well as enable/disable Windows features such as games, telnet server, telnet client, TFTP client, and print services
	Windows Defender*	Same as found in the Security category
	Default Programs	Used to remove a startup program, associate a file extension with a particular application, or select the program used with a particular type of file
	Windows SideShow (Vista)	Same as found in the Hardware and Sound category
	Windows Sidebar Properties (Vista)	Used to add gadgets to the sidebar as well as customize the gadgets displayed on the desktop

*Note that in Windows 7, particular options can be found by typing in the subcategory in the *Search Control Panel* textbox.

Table 11.7	Common Windows Vista/7 control panel categories (continued)*	
Control panel category	**Subcategory**	**Function**
	Desktop Gadgets (7)	Used to add/remove/restore desktop interactive objects
Mobile PC	Windows Mobility Center	Used on laptops to adjust screen brightness, audio volume, wireless enabling and strength status, presentation settings, and external display control
	Power Options	Used on laptops and has the same function as found in the System and Maintenance category
	Personalization	Used on laptops and has the same function as found in the Hardware and Sound category
	Tablet PC Settings	Used on laptops and has the same function as found in the Programs category
	Pen and Input Devices	Used on laptops and has the same function as found in the Hardware and Sound category
	Sync Center	Used on laptops and has the same function as found in the Network and Internet category
User Accounts and Family Safety	User Accounts	Used to add, remove or modify accounts allowed access to the computer
	Parental Controls	Same as found in the Security (Vista)/System and Security (7) category
	Windows CardSpace	Used to manage relationships and information such as a userid and password for Web sites and online services. The personal card information is kept encrypted on the local hard drive.
	Credential Manager (7)	Used to store username/password in a vault for easy logon to sites and/or computers
Appearance and Personalization	Personalization	Same as found in the Hardware and Sound category
	Taskbar and Start menu	Used to customize the Start menu and taskbar by adding or removing icons
	Fonts	Used to customize available fonts
	Folder Options	Used to configure how folders are viewed and acted upon including what files are seen
Clock, Language, and Region	Date and Time	Used to configure time, date, time zone, and clocks for different time zones
	Region and Language Options	Used to configure the format for date, time, currency, etc. that are region specific. Also used to customize keyboard settings
Additional Options		Holds special control panels that are system specific, such as a NVIDIA video display or Java control panel

*Note that in Windows 7, particular options can be found by typing in the subcategory in the *Search Control Panel* textbox.

11

Basic Windows

Table 11.8 Determine the correct control panel

Control panel category	Control panel subcategory	Task
		Used to configure the mouse buttons for a left-handed person
		Used to mute the computer speaker sound
		Used to configure the date to be in the format April 15, 201X
		Use to define how fast a character repeats when a specific key is held down
		Use to define what page (home page) appears every time Internet Explorer starts
		Used to configure an IP address on a wireless network adapter
		Used to set a printer as the default printer
		Used to see if Windows recognizes a particular piece of hardware

Working with the display

13. Select the *Hardware and Sound* control panel category. In Vista, select the *Personalization* link; select *Display Settings* (Vista). In Windows 7, select *Display*. Note that you may be required to search throughout this area to answer the questions.

    What is the current resolution?

    How many bits are used for color?

14. Continuing with the Display link locate and select the *Advanced Settings* button or link.

    What adapter is being used?

    How much video memory does the adapter have?

    How much total video memory is available?

15. Click the *Monitor* tab.

    What refresh rate is used?

16. Click *Cancel* on this window and the next. In Vista, click the *Screen Saver* link. In Windows 7, select the *Personalization* link in the bottom left; select the *Screen Saver* link in the bottom right. Use the *Screen Saver* down arrow to see a list of pre-installed screen savers and click one of the options. Click the *Preview* button. The screen saver appears. Move the mouse to regain control.

17. Click the *Change power settings* . . . link. The Power Options Properties window appears. Table 11.9 shows the various power options available in Windows Vista and 7.

Table 11.9 Windows Vista/7 default power schemes*

Power scheme	Purpose
Balanced (Vista/7)	Default mode; processor adapts to activity being performed; performance provided when the computer is in use; power savings when the computer is inactive. Display powers down after 15 minutes; hard drive powers down after 20 minutes and goes to sleep after 20 minutes.
Power saver (Vista/7)	Provides maximum battery life for laptops. Display and hard drive power down after 20 minutes, and the system goes to sleep after one hour.
High performance (Vista)	Maximum system performance and responsiveness. Display and hard drive power down after 20 minutes, but the system never sleeps.
Customized (Vista/7)	A scheme created by the user that has different settings than the default three schemes

*Note that a computer manufacturer may provide additional power schemes.

What power option would a teacher use when using a laptop to teach a four-hour class?

18. Close all control panel windows.

Obtaining Help

19. Click *Help and Support* from the Start button menu. The Help and Support window contains links to online and locally stored help documents.

20. In Vista the standard help links are *Windows Basics, Table of Contents, Security and Maintenance, Troubleshooting, Windows Online Help*, and *What's New*. In Windows 7 the standard three links are *How to get started with your computer, Learn about Windows Basics,* and *Browse Help topics*. In both Vista and 7 the *Search Help* textbox is used by typing a word or series of words on a specific topic. Note that the Help and Support window may vary depending on the computer manufacturer.

    What is the first link listed in the help window?

21. In either Vista or 7, type **monitor quality** and press Enter.

    List three settings used to improve display quality.

22. To see a list of troubleshooting topics, type **troubleshooting** in the *Search help* textbox. A list of troubleshooting topics immediately displays. Select the *Offline Help* menu arrow.

    What menu options appear?

23. Select *Settings*. Notice how you can customize the type of help you receive by enabling or disabling the online help checkbox.

24. Close the *Windows Help and Support Center* window.

Searching for Files, Folders, and Computers

25. Click the *Start* button and find the *Start Search* (Vista)/*Search programs and files* (7) textbox, located directly above the Start button. This option is used to hunt for files, other computers on the network, people listed in your address book, and information located on the Internet.

26. In the textbox, type **system configuration**, but do not press Enter. Notice how the program shows in the panel. Always keep in mind that applications are simply a type of file that brings up the specific software. Also, any files that contain the words "System Configuration" appear under the files list. Select the *System Configuration* program from the list. Close the window once the question has been answered.

    List five tabs found in the System Configuration window.

27. Bring up the search list for system configuration (but don't press Enter) again. In Vista, click the *Search the Internet* option at the bottom of the list. In Windows 7, click on the *See more results* link and scroll to the bottom of the list; locate and select the *Internet* icon.

    List one URL that the system found.

28. Locate the name of the computer, using a control panel previously explored. Exchange computer names with a classmate.

    Your computer name _____

    Classmate's computer name _____

29. Return to the computer *Start Search* (Vista)/*Search programs and files* (7) textbox and type in your classmate's computer name and press Enter. In the resulting window in the Folders panel on the left, select the *Network* option.

    Does the remote computer name appear?

    Instructor initials: _____

30. Close the window.

Tech Tip

UAC (User Access Control)

Windows Vista/7 has a **UAC** dialog box that frequently appears, asking for permission to do something. The UAC settings can be disabled through the System configuration utility (**msconfig** from a command prompt). Use the *Tools* tab in the System Configuration window to locate the *Disable UAC* (Vista)/*Change UAC Settings* (7) option. Select the option and click the *Launch* button. Select the desired level.

Starting Applications

31. Software applications are accessed through the Start button. Click the *Start* button. The left column contains the most recently used applications. If a program is not listed there and the application is installed, you can access it through the All Programs option. Point to *All Programs*; locate and click the *Accessories* option. Locate and click *Notepad*. The Notepad application opens.

32. Type **Whatever you are be a good one. —Abraham Lincoln.** Click the *File* menu option, *Save*, then type **quote** in the *File name* textbox. Notice the path for where the document is saved located at the top of the window. The folder and subfolders are separated by arrows.

    Write the path for where the document will be saved.

33. Click the *Save* button. Click the *Close* button (the button with the X) in the right corner. Reaccess the *Start* button menu.

    Does the Notepad application now appear in the left column of the Start menu?

34. In the *Start Search* (Vista)/*Search programs and files* (7) textbox, type **notepad**, but do not press the ⌈Enter⌋ key. The Notepad application is listed under the Programs section. In the *Start Search* (Vista)/*Search programs and files* (7) textbox, delete the word *notepad* and type **quote**, but do not press ⌈Enter⌋. Your file (and any others that have the word "quote" in the filename or document) will appear under the Files section of the list. Notice the icon beside the file name. Click on the *Quote* document. The document opens. Close the document and application.

Recycle Bin

35. Right-click the *Start* button and select the *Explore* (Vista)/*Open Windows Explorer* (7) option. Using the information you wrote down for Step 32, click on the first folder you wrote down. It should be located under the Folders (Vista), Desktop (7), or Documents section of the left panel. Double-click on the second (and any subsequent) folder you wrote down. Locate the file called *quote*. Do not open the file, just browse until the file name appears in the major window.

Tech Tip

Files deleted from Recycle Bin cannot be retrieved.

Once the Recycle Bin has been emptied the file cannot be recovered without the use of special software.

36. Right-click on the *quote* file name. Notice that there is a Delete option. Do not click on this option. Click away from the file name on an empty part of the window and then click once on the *quote* file name to select it. The name is highlighted when it is selected. Press the *Delete* key. The *Are you sure you want to move this file to the Recycle Bin?* dialog box appears. Click *Yes*. The file is sent to the Recycle Bin, which is just a folder on the hard drive.

    The Recycle Bin holds deleted files and folders. When a file or folder is deleted, it is not immediately discarded; instead, it goes into the Recycle Bin folder. Once a file or folder is in the Recycle Bin, it can be removed. This is similar to a piece of trash being retrieved from an office trash can. A technician must remember that the files and folders in the Recycle Bin take up hard drive space and that users frequently forget to empty these deleted files and folders.

37. From the window where you located the now-deleted *quote* document, locate the *Recycle Bin* icon in the Folders panel (Vista); for Windows 7, the Recycle Bin icon is commonly located on the desktop—select *Desktop* from the Favorites section. Double-click on this icon.

    Does the *quote* text document appear in the Recycle Bin window? If not, redo the steps in this section to create and delete the file.

    Instructor initials: _____

38. Select the *Empty the Recycle Bin* option from the top menu. A confirmation window appears, asking if you are sure you want to permanently delete the file. Click *Yes*. The name disappears from the Recycle Bin window (as do those of any other files that were located in the Recycle Bin). Close the window.

Pinning an Application to the Start Menu

39. Click *Start → All Programs → Accessories* and locate the *Notepad* application. Right-click the *Notepad* application and select the *Pin to Start Menu* option.

40. Click the *Start* button. Notice how the Notepad application appears at the top of the Start menu. Once the application is pinned, it always appears in that top list.

    Instructor initials: _____

41. Right-click the *Notepad* Start button option and select *Unpin from Start Menu*. The application is removed immediately but still resides in All Programs.

Other Windows Vista/7 Differences

42. One of the things that is different in Windows Vista and 7 from Windows XP is the sidebar. The **sidebar** is a collection of gadgets that stay on the desktop. By default they load to the left, but you can customize them to be on top of or below windows. You can also customize which gadgets appear. Microsoft calls this new look and feel **Windows Aero**, and it is available in all Vista/7 versions except for Home Basic.

    What gadgets are currently on the desktop?

Windows Vista/7 Shutdown Options

43. When finished working on the computer for the day, the computer needs to be turned off or shut down properly. All applications and windows should be closed, and then special steps need to be taken for shutting down. Click *Start* and locate the *Start Search* (Vista)/*Search programs and files* (7) textbox you have been using. Immediately to the right of that textbox are two symbols and a right arrow in Windows Vista or a Shut down button in Windows 7. See Figure 11.11.

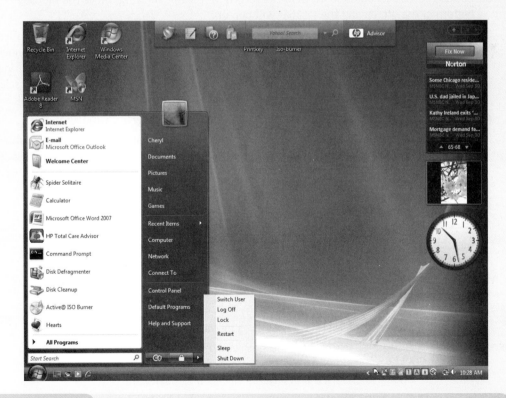

Figure 11.11   **Windows Vista log off and power options**

The shutdown options that commonly appear are listed in Table 11.10, along with the purpose of each one.

Table 11.10	Windows Vista/7 shutdown options
Option	**Purpose**
Switch User	Allows another user to switch to his or her own environment (desktop, files, etc.).
Log Off	Keeps the computer powered on but logs off the current user.
Lock	Locks the computer, such as when someone goes to lunch. All settings and current applications are left untouched.
Restart	Used when new software or hardware has been installed or when the computer locks
Sleep	Reduces power consumption but keeps the applications and settings that are currently on the screen.
Shut Down	Powers off the computer.

44. Select the Shut Down option unless directed otherwise by the instructor or lab assistant.

3. Windows XP/Vista/7 Taskbar Options

Objective: To be able to interact with and customize the Windows Taskbar

Parts: Computer with Windows XP/Vista/7 installed

Procedure: Complete the following procedure and answer the accompanying questions.

1. Turn on the computer and verify that the operating system loads. Log on if necessary.

Taskbar Options

2. Locate the taskbar on the bottom of the screen. If it is not showing, move the mouse to the bottom of the screen and the taskbar will pop up.

3. To modify or view the Taskbar settings, right-click a blank area of the taskbar. A menu appears. *Note*: In XP, you can also use the *Start → Control Panel →* if categories are shown, select *Appearance and Themes → Taskbar and Start Menu*. If the *Control Panel* classic view is used, the *Taskbar and Start Menu* control panel is used. In Vista or 7 control panels, select the *Appearance and Personalization* link followed by the *Taskbar* and *Start Menu* link.

4. Click the *Properties* option. The *Taskbar and Start Menu Properties* window appears.

5. Click the *Taskbar* tab. The options available on this screen relate to how things are shown on the taskbar. The items with a check in the checkbox to the left are active. To remove a check mark, click in the checkbox that already contains a check in it. To put a check mark in a box, click once in an empty box. Table 11.11 shows the functions of the options.

   Which of the five options are currently enabled, if any?

   What is the current taskbar location? [bottom | right | left | top]

Table 11.11	Windows taskbar appearance options
Option	**Function**
Lock the taskbar	Prevents the taskbar from being moved
Auto hide the taskbar	Hides the taskbar until the pointer is moved to the taskbar area; use the *Keep the taskbar on top of other windows* option in conjunction with this option to ensure the taskbar is visible when selected
Keep the taskbar on top of other windows (XP/Vista)	Ensures the taskbar is visible even when a maximized window displays of other windows
Group similar taskbar buttons (XP/Vista)	Collapses multiple windows used by the same application buttons into one button
Show Quick Launch (XP/Vista)	Displays the Quick Launch bar on the taskbar

Table 11.11	Windows taskbar appearance options (continued)
Option	**Function**
Show window properties (thumbnail) (Vista)	Available on Vista Home Premium and higher; shows a miniature version of open windows
Taskbar location on screen (7)	Sets whether the taskbar appears at the bottom (default), or to the left, right, or top.
Taskbar buttons (7)	Optionally combines similar labels

6. Ensure the *Auto-hide the taskbar* option is enabled and all other taskbar options are disabled. Click the *Apply* button and click *OK*. The taskbar disappears from view.

7. Point to the screen where the taskbar is normally located. The taskbar appears. Click *Start → All Programs → Accessories → WordPad*. Maximize the screen by clicking the maximize button, which is the center button at the top right side of the window.

   What happened to the taskbar?

8. Move the pointer to the screen area where the taskbar is normally located.

   Did the taskbar appear?

9. Close the *WordPad* window. Bring the taskbar options back up and reset them to their original configuration. Refer to the answer to Question 5 for enabled options.

Instructor initials: _____

10. Right-click an empty taskbar space and select *Properties*. At the bottom of the *Taskbar* tab is the *Notification area* section (XP) or click on the *Notification Area* tab (Vista). The notification area is also called the Systray. A sign (<, <<, or ▲) marks the beginning of the area. Two common options are *Show the clock* and *Hide inactive icons*. The *Show the clock* option displays the time in the notification area. The *Hide inactive icons* option hides taskbar icons that are not currently in use. On the taskbar, click the notification area sign to view hidden inactive icons. The *Customize* button is used to change the settings in Windows 7.

    Did the computer have any inactive icons that displayed once the < was clicked?

11. Back in the Taskbar and Start Menu properties window, click the *Start Menu* tab. The two XP or Vista options shown are *Start menu* and *Classic Start menu*. These are used to determine how the *Start* menu displays. The *Classic Start* menu option displays the *Start* menu like older Windows versions. Windows 7 has a privacy section that determines whether recently opened programs or items display.

    Which *Start* menu option is currently selected on this machine?

12. Click the *Customize* button.

    List three things that can be changed through this option.

    In XP, the General tab controls the *Start* menu icon size, number of programs shown in the Start menu's left pane, and what options (if any) are displayed for Internet and email applications. The Clear List button is used to clear the most frequently accessed programs displayed in the left pane.

    In Vista/7, the options can be customized using radio buttons and checkboxes. Scroll through the options to see the selections. Even the size of the Start menu icons can be set in this window. In Vista, stay in this window to answer the next question.

    Using the information shown, how many applications currently can display in the *Start* menu's left pane?

13. In XP, click the *Advanced* tab. The Advanced tab contains Start menu settings and controls how items appear as well as the Recent Documents setting. In Vista/7, use the scroll bar to determine how documents appear on the Start menu.

    Using the vertical scroll bar, determine whether Help or Help and Support is enabled, meaning that it displays as a Start menu item. Is Help enabled?

14. Click the *Cancel* button (twice in Vista or 7).

Customizing the Quick Launch Toolbar (XP/Vista) or Taskbar (7)

15. Quick Launch is the taskbar area located to the immediate right of the Start button in XP or Vista. In 7, buttons are simply attached to the taskbar. There are several ways to add an item to the Quick Launch bar. The easiest way is demonstrated here. Use the *Start* menu → *Search* (XP), *Start Search* textbox (Vista), or *Search programs and files* (7) → *All files and folders link* (XP only). In XP, Vista, or 7, type **wordpad** in the textbox and in XP press [Enter]. In Vista/7 do not press [Enter].

16. In the Search results window, right-click the *WORDPAD.EXE* filename and drag the file to the Quick Launch or taskbar area. Release the right mouse button and *Copy Here*, *Move Here*, *Create Shortcuts Here*, and *Cancel* options (XP), *Move to Quick Launch* (Vista), or *Pin to taskbar* (7) display.

17. Select the *Copy Here* option (XP), *Move to Quick Launch* (Vista), or *Pin to taskbar* (7). To access the *WordPad* Quick Launch icon, click the double arrows in the *Quick Launch* window or just click on the WordPad icon. Any items that have been added to the Quick Launch or taskbar area appear and can be selected. If the *WordPad* option is not available, redo Steps 15 and 16.

18. Click the *WordPad Quick Launch* option. The WordPad application displays. Close WordPad. Close the *Search results* window (XP).

Instructor initials: _____

19. To remove the *WordPad* icon from the Quick Launch toolbar or taskbar, right-click the Quick Launch area or taskbar *WordPad* option. Select the *Delete* (XP/Vista) or *Unpin this program from taskbar* (7) option. A warning message appears that states that the WordPad option will not be available if it is deleted. Click *Yes* and the WORDPAD.EXE file used in the Quick Launch bar is sent to the Recycle Bin. Note that as long as the *Copy Here* option (XP) was selected, the WordPad application is still available.

20. Use the *Accessories* Start menu option to access the WordPad application.

Is the WordPad application still available? If so, show the window to the instructor or lab assistant. If WordPad does not start, you did not select the *Copy Here* option in Step 17. If this is the case, the WordPad application must be removed from the Recycle Bin and placed in its proper folder. The default folder is Program Files\Windows NT\Accessories.

Instructor initials: _____

21. Power off the computer properly.

Tech Tip

What to do if Quick Launch toolbar is missing

If the Quick Launch toolbar is missing from the taskbar, right-click an empty taskbar space, select *Toolbars* and click the *Quick Launch* option. The Quick Launch toolbar then displays on the taskbar.

4. Windows XP/Vista/7 File and Folder Management

Objective: To be able to create folders, move files, and copy files to new locations

Parts: Computer with Windows XP/Vista/7 installed

   Formatted 3.5-inch disk, ZIP disk, or Flash drive

Procedure: Complete the following procedure and answer the accompanying questions.

Note: There are multiple ways to do some of the steps in this exercise. The steps that have an alternate method have the letters ALT: before the step. For these steps, you may use either method.

1. Click *Start → All Programs → Accessories → Notepad*. Type the following:

   ```
   Develop a passion for learning. If you do, you will never cease
   to grow.
   —Anthony J. D'Angelo
   ```

2. Click the *File* menu option and click *Save*.

3. Insert a formatted disk into the floppy (**A:**) drive, Zip drive, or attach a Flash drive. Click the down arrow in the *Save in* textbox (XP) or the down arrow next to the left of the user name in the top pane (Vista), or down arrow (7) as shown in Figure 11.12. Select *Computer*, then the appropriate drive option for the media you are using. In the *File name* textbox, type **Quote 1** and select the *Save* button.

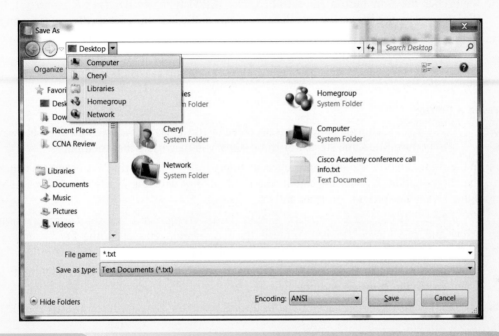

Figure 11.12   **Windows 7 path selection arrow**

4. In Notepad, click the *File* menu option and select *New*. Type the following:

   ```
   The man who graduates today and stops learning tomorrow is
   uneducated the day after.
   —Newton D. Baker
   ```

5. Click *File → Save* from the menu options. The *Save in textbox* (XP) or top line (Vista/7) should show the drive option you selected previously. If it does not, select the appropriate drive media. In the *File name* textbox, type **Quote 2** and select *Save*.

6. Click *File → New*. Type the following:

   ```
   Don't just learn the tricks of the trade. Learn the trade.
   —James Bennis
   ```

7. Click *File → Save*. The *Save in* textbox (XP) or top line (Vista/7) should show the drive option selected previously. If it does not, select the appropriate drive media. In the *File name* textbox, type **Quote 3** and select *Save*.

8. Click *File → New*. Type the following:

   ```
   Nine-tenths of education is encouragement.
   —Anatole France
   ```

9. Click *File → Save*. The *Save in* textbox (XP) or top line (Vista/7) should show the drive option selected previously. If it does not, select the appropriate drive media. In the *File name* textbox, type **Quote 4** and select *Save*.

10. Click *File → New*. Type the following:

    ```
    Technology is dominated by two types of people—Those who
    understand what they do not manage, and those who manage what
    they do not understand.
    —Source Unknown
    ```

11. Click *File → Save*. The *Save in* textbox (XP) or top line (Vista/7) should show the drive option selected previously. If it does not, select the appropriate drive media. In the *File name* textbox, type **Quote 5** and select *Save*.

12. Close the Notepad application by clicking the *Close* button (which is the button in the upper-right corner with an X).

13. Right-click the *Start* button and select *Explore* (XP/Vista)/*Open Windows Explorer* (7). In the left window, use the vertical scroll bar to locate and select the drive media you are using.

14. In the right window, locate the five files you just created called *Quote 1*, *Quote 2*, *Quote 3*, *Quote 4*, and *Quote 5*. If the files are not there, redo the steps used to create them.

Instructor initials: _____

Create a Folder

Note: The method shown below that is preceded by the label *Alternative* is an alternate way to perform the same steps. For these steps, you may use either method.

15. In the right *Explorer* window, right-click an empty space. Point to the *New* option and click the *Folder* option. A folder appears in the right window with the words *New Folder* highlighted. Type **Learning Quotes** and press ⏎Enter.

    XP Alternative: Click the *File* menu option. *Vista Alternative*: Click the *Organize* down arrow and select *New Folder*. Point to the *New* option and click the *Folder* option. *7 Alternative*: Click the *New folder* option from the top line.

    In all versions, a folder appears in the right window with the words *New Folder* highlighted. Type **Learning Quotes** and press ⏎Enter.

16. Create another new folder called *General Quotes* using the steps outlined in Step 15.

Instructor initials: _____

Copy a File

17. In the right *Explorer* window, right-click the file named *Quote 1*. A submenu appears. Select the *Copy* option.

    Alternative: In the right *Explorer* window, click the file named *Quote 1*. Click the *Edit* menu option. In Vista/7, click the *Organize* down arrow.

    Then in all operating system versions, click the *Copy* option from the drop-down menu.

18. In the right window, double-click the *Learning Quotes* folder. Notice in XP how the *Windows Explorer Address* textbox changes to `X:\Learning Quotes` (where *X:* is the drive letter you are using). In Vista/7, the path appears across the top of the window. The right window is empty because the folder does not have any files or subfolders in it yet.

19. In the right window, right-click and a submenu appears. Click *Paste* and the Quote 1 file appears in the right window.

    XP Alternative: Click the *Edit* menu option. *Vista/7 Alternative:* Click the *Organize* down arrow.

    In both XP and Vista, select *Paste*. The Quote 1 file appears in the right window.

20. In the left window, click the drive option for the media you are using. Notice in XP how the *Window Explorer Address* textbox changes to a different drive letter. In Vista/7, the path across the top of the window changes.

21. Copy the files named *Quote 2* and *Quote 3* into the *Learning Quotes* folder using the methods outlined in previous steps.

Copy Multiple Files

22. In the left window, click the drive option for the media you are using.

23. Locate the files called *Quote 4* and *Quote 5* in the right window.

24. In the right window, click once on the *Quote 4* filename. The name is highlighted.

25. Hold the (Shift) key down and click once on the *Quote 5* filename. Both the *Quote 4* and *Quote 5* filenames are highlighted. *Note*: The (Shift) key is used to select files that are consecutive in a list (one right after the other). If you wanted to select files that are not consecutive, use the (Ctrl) key to select the files.

26. Right-click the files named *Quote 4* and *Quote 5*. A submenu appears. Click the *Copy* option.

    XP Alternative: Click the *Edit* menu option and select *Copy*. *Vista/7 Alternative:* Click the *Organize* down arrow and select *Copy*.

27. Double-click the *General Quotes* folder. In XP, notice how the *Windows Explorer Address* textbox and in Vista/7, the path across the top changes to `X:\General Quotes` (where `X:` is the drive media you are using) and the right window is empty because the folder does not have any files or subfolders in it yet.

28. In the right window, right-click an empty space and a submenu appears. Select *Paste*. The *Quote 4* and *Quote 5* files appear in the right window.

    XP Alternative: Select the *Edit* menu option. *Vista/7 Alternative:* Click the *Organize* down arrow and select *Paste*.

    The *Quote 4* and *Quote 5* files appear in the right window.

    How many folders are located in the root directory? _____

    How many files are located in the root directory? _____

    How many files are located in the *Learning Quotes* folder? _____

    How many files are located in the *General Quotes* folder? _____

Instructor initials: _____

Copying a File from One Folder to Another

29. In the left window, click the drive option for the media you are using.

30. Open the *Learning Quotes* folder located under the drive option that you are using. The files *Quote 1*, *Quote 2*, and *Quote 3* appear in the right window.

31. In the right window, right-click the *Quote 3* file. From the submenu that appears, select *Copy*.

    XP Alternative: In the right window, click the *Quote 3* file. Click *Edit* from the menu and select *Copy*. *Vista/7 Alternative:* In the right window, click the *Quote 3* filename. Click *Organize* from the menu and select *Copy*.

32. Open the *General Quotes* folder located under the drive media option you are using. The *Quote 4* and *Quote 5* files appear in the right window and the Address textbox shows General Quotes.

33. In the right window, right-click an empty space and a submenu appears. Select *Paste* and the *Quote 3*, *Quote 4*, and *Quote 5* files appear.

    XP Alternative: Click the *Edit* menu option. Select *Paste* and the *Quote 3*, *Quote 4*, and *Quote 5* files appear. *Vista/7 Alternative:* Click the *Organize* down arrow and select *Paste*. The Quote 3, Quote 4, and Quote 5 files appear.

34. Using the same procedures previously described, copy the *Quote 1* and *Quote 2* files from the *Learning Quotes* folder into the *General Quotes* folder. At the end of this step you should have three files (*Quote 1*, *Quote 2*, and *Quote 3*) in the *Learning Quotes* folder and five files (*Quote 1*, *Quote 2*, *Quote 3*, *Quote 4*, and *Quote 5*) in the *General Quotes* folder.

Moving a File

35. Create a folder on the disk you are using called *My Stuff*. Refer to the steps earlier in the exercise if you need assistance.

36. Open the folder called *General Quotes*. In the right window, all five files appear.

37. In the right window, click once on the *Quote 1* file to highlight it. Hold down the (Ctrl) key and click the *Quote 3* file. Both the *Quote 1* and *Quote 3* filenames are highlighted. *Note:*

The Ctrl key is used to select nonconsecutive files, whereas the Shift key is used to select files that are listed consecutively (one right after another).

38. Right-click either the *Quote 1* or *Quote 3* filename. Select the *Cut* option.

    XP Alternative: Select the *Edit* menu option. Click *Cut*. The *Cut* option is used to move a file from one folder to another. *Vista/7 Alternative:* Click the *Organize* down arrow and select *Cut*. The *Cut* option is used to move a file from one folder to another.

39. Open the *My Stuff* folder. The right window is empty because no files have been copied or moved into the *My Stuff* folder yet. In the right window, right-click and select *Paste*. The *Quote 1* and *Quote 3* files appear in the right window.

    XP Alternative: Select the *Edit* menu option and click *Paste*. The *Quote 1* and *Quote 3* files appear in the right window. *Vista/7 Alternative:* Click the *Organize* down arrow and select *Paste*. The Quote 1 and Quote 3 files appear in the right window.

The purpose of Cut and Paste

The *Cut* and *Paste* options are used to move a file from one folder to another.

40. Using the procedures just learned, move the *Quote 1* file from the *Learning Quotes* folder into the *General Quotes* folder.

    How many files are located in the *Learning Quotes* folder? _____

    How many files are located in the *General Quotes* folder? _____

    How many files are located in the *My Stuff* folder? _____

Instructor initials: _____

Deleting Files and Folders

41. Open the *My Stuff* folder. The *Quote 1* and *Quote 3* files appear in the right window.

42. In the right window, select the *Quote 1* and the *Quote 3* files. Both the *Quote 1* and *Quote 3* filenames are highlighted.

43. Press the Del key on the keyboard. A message appears on the screen asking, *Are you sure you want to delete these 2 items?* Click *Yes*.

    XP Alternative: Select the *File* menu option and choose *Delete*. A *Confirm Multiple File Delete* message appears on the screen asking, "Are you sure you want to delete these 2 items?" Select *Yes*. *Vista/7 Alternative:* Click on the *Organize* down arrow and select *Delete*. A confirmation message appears. Select *Yes*.

Deleted files on external media are not put in Recycle Bin

When deleting files from a floppy disk, Zip disk, thumb drive, or other external media, the files are not placed in the Recycle Bin. They are deleted. When deleting files from a hard drive, the files get placed in the Recycle Bin when you press the Del key or select the *Delete* option from the *File* menu option.

44. Select the *My Stuff* folder. The *My Stuff* folder is highlighted. Press the Del key on the keyboard. A *Confirm Folder Delete* message appears on the screen asking, "Are you sure you want to remove the folder "My Stuff" and all its contents?" Click the *Yes* button.

    XP Alternative: Select the *File* menu option and choose *Delete*. A *Confirm Multiple File Delete* message appears on the screen asking, "Are you sure you want to remove the folder "My Stuff" and all its contents?" Click the *Yes* button. *Vista/7 Alternative:* Click the *Organize* down arrow and select *Delete*. A confirmation message appears. Select *Yes*.

Skipping the Recycle Bin for deleted hard drive files

If you want to permanently delete a file from a hard drive (the file will not get placed in the Recycle Bin), hold the Shift key down while pressing the Del key.

> **Retrieving a deleted file**
>
> To restore a file that has been accidentally placed in the Recycle Bin, open the Recycle Bin, right-click the file, and click the *Restore* option or click *Restore this item*.
>
> **Tech Tip**

Instructor initials: _____

45. Using the previously demonstrated procedures, delete the *Learning Quotes* folder and the *General Quotes* folders and all files contained within each folder as well as the original *Quote* files.

46. Close the *Windows Explorer* window.

Challenge

47. Using Notepad, create three text files and save them to the external media in a folder called *My Files*.

48. On the hard drive or on external media, create a folder called *Computer Text*.

49. Copy the two of the three text files from the *My Files* folder into the folder called *Computer Text*.

50. Move the third text file from the *My Files* folder into the folder called *Computer Text*.

Instructor initials: _____

51. Permanently delete the folder called *Computer Text* and all files within this folder.

Instructor initials: _____

52. Delete the folder called *My Files* and all files within this folder.

Instructor initials: _____

5. Windows XP/Vista/7 File Extension

Objective: To be able to associate a file extension with a file type

Parts: Computer with Windows XP/Vista/7 installed

Formatted 3.5-inch disk, ZIP disk, or Flash drive

Procedure: Complete the following procedure and answer the accompanying questions.

1. Select *Start → All Programs → Accessories* option and click the *Notepad* menu selection. Type the following:

   ```
   I hear and I forget. I see and I remember. I do and I
   understand.
   —Confucius
   ```

2. Select the *File* menu option and choose *Save*.

3. Insert a formatted disk into the floppy (A:) drive, Zip drive, or attach a Flash drive. Select the appropriate drive option for the media you are using. In the *File name* textbox, type **Junk**. Click the *Save* button.

4. Close the Notepad application.

5. Right-click the *Start* button and select *Explore* (XP/Vista)/*Open Windows Explorer* (7).

6. In XP, select the *Tools* menu option and choose *Folder Options*. In Vista/7, select the *Organize* menu option and select *Folder and Search Options*. Click the *View* tab. If the *Hide (file) extensions for known file Types* checkbox contains a check mark, click inside the checkbox to remove the check mark. If the checkbox is empty, ignore this step. Click *OK*.

7. In the left *Explorer* window, use the vertical scroll bar to locate and select the disk media you used to save the file. Locate the *Junk.txt* file in the right window and double-click the icon.

   What happened? Did the Notepad application open with the *Junk* file open?

8. Close the Notepad application.

9. In the Explorer window, right-click the file called *Junk*. Click the *Rename* option. Ensure the entire file name, *Junk.txt*, is highlighted. Type **junk.abc** and press Enter. *Junk.txt* is renamed to *junk.abc*. A Rename warning box appears stating that, "If you change a file name extension, the file may become unusable." It also asks, "Are you sure you want to change it?" Click *Yes*.

   What does the *junk.abc* file icon look like now?

10. Double-click the *junk.abc* file icon.

    What happened when you double-clicked on the *junk.abc* file icon?

11. Click the *Select the program from a list of installed programs* radio button and click *OK*. Scroll until you reach the *Notepad* icon. Click the *Notepad* icon and then click *OK*.

    What happened when you clicked the *OK* button?

12. In the Notepad application, select the *File* menu option and choose *New*.

13. Type the following:

    The only real mistake is the one from which we learn nothing.
    —John Powell

14. Select the *File* menu option and click *Save as*. Ensure the disk media option that you are using is the destination. In the *File name* textbox, type **Junk2** and click *Save*.

15. Close the Notepad application.

16. Using Explorer, rename the *Junk2.txt* file to **Junk2.abc**. A Rename warning box appears stating that, "If you change a file name extension, the file may become unusable." It also asks, "Are you sure you want to change it?" Select *Yes*. Notice the file icon after the change.

    How is the icon different from before?

17. Double-click the *Junk2.abc* icon.

    What happened when you double-clicked the *Junk2.abc* icon?

Instructor initials: _____

6. Windows XP/Vista/7 Attributes, Compression, and Encryption

Objective: To be able to identify and set file and folder attributes, compression, and encryption

Parts: Computer with Windows XP/Vista/7 installed

               Formatted 3.5-inch disk, ZIP disk, or Flash drive

Procedure: Complete the following procedure and answer the accompanying questions.

Note: The compression and encryption portions of this exercise require an NTFS partition.

Managing File Attributes

1. Click *Start → All Programs → Accessories → Notepad*. Type the following:

   Aim for success, not perfection.
   —Dr. David M. Burns

2. Select the *File* menu option and choose *Save*. Insert a formatted disk into the floppy (**A:**) drive, Zip drive, or attach a Flash drive. Select the appropriate drive option for the media you are using. In the *File name* textbox, type **ATTRIBUTE FILE** and click *Save*.

3. Close the Notepad application.

4. Right-click the *Start* button and select the *Explore* (XP/Vista)/*Open Windows Explorer* (7) option.

5. In the left pane, click the option for the disk media you are using. The *ATTRIBUTE FILE* file should be listed in the right panel. If not, redo the previous steps to create the file.

6. Select the *ATTRIBUTE FILE* file in the right pane. In XP, select the *File* menu option and select *Properties*. In Vista/7, select the *Organize* menu option and select *Properties*. The

same results can be obtained by right-clicking the file and selecting *Properties*. The file attributes are listed at the bottom.

What three file attributes are listed for the *ATTRIBUTE FILE* file?

What file attribute is enabled by default?

7. The Archive attribute is enabled so that the file is selected for backup by default. Backup applications use this attribute when backing up data. Click the *Read-only attribute* check-box and click *OK*.

8. Double-click the *ATTRIBUTE FILE* filename. The application opens with the typed text shown. Add the following to the quote:

   Never give up your right to be wrong, because then you will lose the ability to learn new things and move forward with your life.

9. Click the *File* menu option and select *Save*. Click the *Save* button.

   What happens when the Save option is chosen?

10. Click the *OK* button and then click *Cancel*.

11. Click the *Close* button in the Notepad window. When asked if you want to save the changes, click *No* (XP) or *Don't Save* (Vista/7). The read-only attribute prevented the file from being changed.

12. In the *Windows Explorer* window, right-click the *ATTRIBUTE FILE* file and select *Properties*. Select the *Hidden* file attribute checkbox and click *OK*.

13. In the XP *Windows Explorer* window, select the *View* menu option and click *Refresh*. This step is not needed in Vista/7.

    What happened to the *ATTRIBUTE FILE filename*?

14. In the *Windows Explorer* window, select the *Tools* (XP)/*Organize* (Vista/7) → *Folder Options* (XP) or *Folder and Search Options* (Vista/7) → *View* tab → *Hidden files and folders* folder → *Show hidden files and folder* (XP/Vista)/*Show hidden files, folders, and drives* (7) radio button. This option is used to see files or folders that have the hidden attribute set or enabled. To make this change applicable to all folders, click the *Apply to all folders* (XP) or *Apply to Folders* (Vista/7) button. A *Folder views* dialog box appears stating that the change will occur the next time the folder is opened. Click *Yes* and then click *OK*.

    Does the *ATTRIBUTE FILE* file appear in the Windows Explorer right pane? If not, press the F5 key to refresh the window or select the *Refresh* option from the *View* menu (XP).

    How does the file icon differ from before?

15. Click the *Windows Explorer View* (XP)/*Views* (Vista) menu option and select *Thumbnails* (XP)/*Small Icons* (Vista). In Windows Explorer for Windows 7, click the *Change your view* icon that contains a down arrow on the right side of the menu bar; select *Small icons*.

    How do the icon(s) now appear in the Windows Explorer right pane?

16. Under the *View* (XP)/*Views* (Vista)/*Change your view* (7) menu option, select the *List* option.

    How does the *ATTRIBUTE FILE* filename now appear in the right pane?

17. From the Windows Explorer menu, select *View* (XP)/*Views* (Vista)/*Change your view* (7) and then select *Details*.

    Why do you think that a technician would prefer the Details view option over any other option?

18. Delete the *ATTRIBUTE FILE* file from the external media.

    Did either the hidden or read-only attribute stop the ATTRIBUTE FILE file from being deleted? [Yes | No]

19. To reset all folder options back to the default attributes, select the *Tools* (XP)/*Organize* (Vista/7) option from the Windows Explorer menu → *Folder Options (XP) Folder and Search Options* (Vista/7) → *View* tab → *Restore defaults* → *Apply to all folders* (XP) or *Apply to folders* button (Vista/7). A folder views dialog box appears. Click *Yes* followed by *OK*.

Instructor initials: _____

Using Compression

Note: The disk volume must have an NTFS file system on it in order to do this section. To check the file system, open *My Computer* (XP)/*Computer* (Vista/7). Right-click the hard drive volume that contains Windows and select *Properties*. In the Properties window near the top, the type of file system is listed.

20. Create a file called *COMPRESSION FILE* using Notepad and save it in the *My Documents* (XP)/*Documents* (Vista/7) folder on the hard drive. If necessary, refer to a previous exercise for steps. The text to be placed in the file follows. Copy this text repeatedly in the document until you have four pages of text.

    The most successful career must show a waste of strength that might have removed mountains, and the most unsuccessful is not that of the man who is taken unprepared, but of him who has pre-pared and is never taken. On a tragedy of that kind, our national morality is duly silent. —Edward M. Forster

21. Close the *Notepad* application window. Using Windows Explorer, locate *COMPRESSION FILE*.

    What is the current *COMPRESSION FILE* file size?

22. Right-click the filename and select *Properties*. Click the *Advanced* button. In the Advanced Attributes dialog box, locate the *Compress or Encrypt attributes* section. Click the *Compress contents to save disk space* checkbox. This option is used to compress a file or folder. Click the *OK* button. Again, click the *OK* button to finish the process. Keep in mind that in order to save disk space efficiently, the file needs to be at least 4K of disk space.

    Using Windows Explorer, locate the file called *COMPRESSION FILE* and determine the file size. Document the file size.

    Instructor initials: _____

23. Permanently delete the *COMPRESSION FILE*.

    Have a classmate verify the file deletion by printing his/her name. Is the file *completely* deleted?

Enabling Encryption

Note: The disk volume must have an NTFS file system on it in order to do this section.

24. Create a file called *ENCRYPTION FILE* using Notepad and save it to *My Documents* (XP)/*Documents* (Vista/7). If necessary, refer to a previous exercise for steps. The text to be placed in the file follows:

    I do not fear computers. I fear the lack of them.
    —Isaac Asimov

25. Close the *Notepad* application window. Using Windows Explorer, locate the file named *ENCRYPTION FILE*.

    What is the current *ENCRYPTION FILE* file size?

26. Right-click the filename and select *Properties*. Click the *Advanced* button. In the Advanced Attributes dialog box, locate the *Compress or Encrypt attributes* section. Click the *Encrypt contents to secure data* checkbox, the option used to encrypt a file or folder. Note that the checkbox may not be available on some Vista/7 versions. See the Tech Tip. Click the *OK* button twice. A dialog box appears asking if you want to encrypt the file and the parent file or encrypt only the file. Click the *Encrypt the file only* radio button and click *OK*.

    What is the current *ENCRYPTION FILE* file size after encryption?

Tech Tip

Limited encryption support on Vista/7 Home

Vista/7 Starter, Home Basic, and Home Premium versions do not fully support encrypting files. In these versions, the **cipher** command can be used from the command prompt to decrypt files, an encrypted file can be modified, and an encrypted file can be copied to the computer.

Instructor initials: _____

27. Permanently delete the *ENCRYPTION FILE*.

    Have a classmate verify the file deletion by printing his or her name. Is the file *completely* deleted?

28. Properly power off the computer.

7. Using REGEDIT in Windows XP/Vista/7

Objective: To become familiar with the REGEDIT registry editing utility

Parts: Computer with Windows XP/Vista/7 installed and administrator rights

    Formatted 3.5-inch disk, ZIP disk, or Flash drive

Procedure: Complete the following procedure and answer the accompanying questions.

Notes: REGEDIT is a utility used for editing the Windows registry. With REGEDIT, you can view existing registry settings, modify registry settings values, or create new registry entries to change or enhance the way Windows operates. In this lab, you will use REGEDIT to view the System BIOS and Video BIOS information on your computer.

Caution: Editing the registry can cause your computer to run erratically, or not run at all! When performing any registry editing, follow *all* directions carefully, including spelling, syntax use, and so on. Failure to do so may cause your computer to fail!

Viewing Registry Information

1. In XP, from the *Start* menu → *Run* → type **REGEDIT** → *OK*. In Vista/7, from the *Start Search* (Vista)/*Search programs and files* (7) textbox, type **REGEDIT** → in the *Programs* section, click on *Regedit* → *Continue* (Vista)/*Yes* (7) button, if necessary. The REGEDIT utility opens.

2. In the left window, expand *HKEY_LOCAL_MACHINE*, *HARDWARE*, and *DESCRIPTION* by clicking the + (plus) symbol (XP) or arrow (Vista/7) located to the left of the name. Click the *System* option located under *DESCRIPTION*. In the right window, the system BIOS and video BIOS information display.

    What is the system BIOS date?

    Who is the manufacturer of the system BIOS?

    When was the video BIOS manufactured?

Instructor initials: _____

Exporting and Importing a Registry Section

3. REGEDIT can be used to backup and restore part or all of the registry. To illustrate this point, a portion of the registry will be exported to disk and then imported into the registry. Ensure the following option is still selected in the Registry Editor window:

    HKEY_LOCAL_MACHINE\Hardware\Description\System

4. Select the *File* menu option and choose *Export*. The Export Registry File window opens.

5. Insert a formatted disk into the floppy (**A:**) drive, Zip drive, or attach a Flash drive. Click the down arrow in the *Save in* textbox and select the appropriate drive option for the media you are using. In the *File name* textbox, type **Registry System Section** and click the *Save* button. The specific registry key is saved to disk.

6. To restore the registry (or a portion of it as in this exercise), click the *File* menu option and select *Import*. The screen should list the file located on the external disk media, but if it does not, select the appropriate drive letter option for the disk media you are using.

7. Click the *Registry System Section* filename and click the *Open* button. A message appears when the section is successfully inserted into the registry. Show this message to the instructor or lab assistant.

8. Close the REGEDIT utility.

Instructor initials: _____

8. Modifying the Windows XP Start Button

Objective: To be able to modify the *Start* button menu

Parts: A computer with a Windows XP operating system loaded

Procedure: Complete the following procedure and answer the accompanying questions.

Start Menu Icon Size

1. Once Windows boots, right-click the *Start* button → *Properties* → *Customize* button. The *General* tab contains two radio buttons that control the size of the icons found on the start menu.

    What start menu icon size radio button is currently selected?

2. Select the opposite radio button. Click *OK* → *Apply* → *OK*.

3. Select the *Start* button to test the icon size change.

4. Return the icon size to the original setting.

Customizing the Number of *Start* Menu Programs Shown

5. Right-click the *Start* button → *Properties* → *Customize* button. Locate the *Programs* section. The number of programs shown on the left side (bottom portion) of the *Start* button menu can be modified in this section.

    How many programs are currently set to appear on the *Start* button?

6. Click the *Cancel* button and when returned to the previous menu, click *Cancel* again. Click the *Start* button and verify that the number of programs shown is correct. Windows automatically adds the most often utilized programs to the list, but the maximum is set through the *General* tab from which you just returned.

7. Right-click the *Start* button → *Properties* → *Customize* button.

    What is the maximum number of programs that you can have on the *Start* button?

8. Increase the number of programs shown on the *Start* button menu. When finished click *OK* → *Apply* → *OK*.

9. Click the *Start* button. The number of programs shown on the bottom of the Start menu should be the number specified on the *General* tab. If not, access an application not listed on the menu, close the application, and click the *Start* button again.

10. Return the number of *Start* button menu programs to the original setting.

Modifying Default Icon Settings

11. By default, Windows XP displays Web browser and email client icons in the upper section, left column of the *Start* menu. To change this behavior, right-click *Start* button → *Properties* → *Customize* button. Locate the *Show on Start menu* section.

    Is Internet enabled (checked)?

    Is Email enabled (checked)?

12. Change the two settings in the *Shown on Start menu* section to something different. Click *OK* → *Apply* → *OK*.

13. Select the *Start* button.

    Have the changes been implemented?

14. Return the *Show on Start menu* section to the original settings. Verify by selecting the *Start* button.

Customizing the Start Menu Programs

15. By default, the Windows XP *Start* menu has links to My Computer, My Documents, My Pictures, My Music, Help and Support, Run, and so on in the right column. Click the *Start* button.

    Write three items found in the *Start* button menu right column.

16. Right-click the *Start* button → *Properties* → *Customize* button → *Advanced* tab. Locate the *Start menu items* section. Some of the options located there have three possible selections: (1) *Display as a link*; (2) *Display as a menu*; and (3) *Don't display this item*.

    Display as a link means that when the menu option is selected, it opens in a new window. With *Display as a menu*, the option will have an arrow to the side allowing you to access all options that windows would normally contain.

    What is the current setting for *Control Panel*?

17. Click the *Cancel* button and when returned to the previous menu, click *Cancel* again. Click the *Start* button and observe the current *Control Panel* option on the menu.

    Does the *Control Panel* option appear as described?

18. Right-click the *Start* button → *Properties* → *Customize* button → *Advanced* tab. Locate the *Start menu items* section. Change the *Control Panel* menu option to one of the other menu settings. Click *OK* → *Apply* → *OK*.

19. Select the *Start* button and select the *Control Panel* menu option.

    How is the *Control Panel* option different?

20. Return the *Control Panel Start* menu item to its original setting.

Adding a Program to the Start Menu

21. Click *Start* button → *Search* → *All Files and Folders* link → type **charmap** in the *All or part of the file name* textbox → *Search* button. *charmap* is the file used to execute the Character Map program. It is commonly found in the *C:\Windows\System32* folder if you do not want to wait on the Search program. *Note:* If the *charmap* file is not installed, any program file can be used for this part of the exercise.

22. Right-click the *charmap* file. Select the *Pin to Start Menu* option. Click the *Start* button.

    Where on the *Start* button menu is the Character Map application added?

23. To remove a customized application, click the *Start* button, right-click the unwanted item (*charmap* in this case), and select *Unpin from Start Menu*.

Instructor initials: _____

9. Modifying the Windows Vista/7 Start Button

Objective: To be able to modify the *Start* button menu

Parts: A computer with the Windows Vista or 7 operating system loaded

Procedure: Complete the following procedure and answer the accompanying questions.

Start Menu Icon Size

1. Once Windows boots, right-click the *Start* button → *Properties* → *Customize* button. The radio buttons and checkboxes are used to configure the look of the Start menu. Icon size is controlled by a checkbox at the end of the list.

   What Start menu icon size radio button is currently selected? [Normal | Large]

2. Set the setting to the opposite (that is, if the box is already checked, uncheck it, and if the box is unchecked, then check it). Click *OK* → *Apply* → *OK*.

3. Click the *Start* button to test the icon size change.

4. Return the icon size to the original setting.

Customizing the Number of *Start* Menu Programs Shown

5. Right-click the *Start* button → *Properties* → *Customize* button. Locate the *Number of recent programs to display* selectable number option. The number of programs shown on the left side (bottom portion) of the *Start* button menu can be modified using the up and down arrows that control the number.

   How many programs are currently set to appear on the *Start* button?

6. Click the *Cancel* button and, when returned to the previous menu, click *Cancel* again. Click the *Start* button and verify that the number of programs shown is correct. Windows

automatically adds the most often utilized programs to the list, but the maximum is set through the window from which you just returned.

7. Right-click the *Start* button → *Properties* → *Customize* button.

What is the maximum number of programs that you can have on the *Start* button?

8. Increase the number of programs shown on the *Start* button menu. When finished, click *OK* → *Apply* → *OK*.

9. Click the *Start* button. The number of programs shown on the bottom left of the Start menu should be the number specified. If it is not, access an application not listed on the menu, close the application, and click the *Start* button again.

10. Return the number of *Start* button menu programs to the original setting.

Modifying Default Icon Settings

If Windows 7 is installed, proceed to Step 15.

11. By default, Windows Vista displays Web browser and email client icons in the upper section of the left column of the *Start* menu. To change this behavior, right-click *Start* button → *Properties* → *Customize* button. Locate the *Show on Start menu* section.

Is the Internet link enabled (checked)?

Is the E-mail link enabled (checked)?

12. In Vista, change the two settings in the *Shown on Start menu* section to something different. Click *OK* → *Apply* → *OK*.

13. Select the *Start* button.

Have the changes been implemented?

14. Return the Start menu to the original settings. Verify by selecting the *Start* button.

Customizing the Start Menu Programs

15. By default, the Start menu has links to Documents, Pictures, Music, Help and Support, and so on in the right column. Click the *Start* button.

What are three items found in the Start button menu right column?

16. Right-click the *Start* button → *Properties* → *Customize* button. Locate the *Computer* section. Some of the options located in this window have three possible selections, similar to the Computer section: (1) Display as a link, (2) Display as a menu, and (3) Don't display this item.

Display as a link means that when the menu option is selected, it opens in a new window. With *Display as a menu*, the option will have an arrow to the side allowing you to access all options that windows would normally contain.

What is the current setting for Control Panel?

17. Click the *Cancel* button and, when returned to the previous menu, click *Cancel* again. Click the *Start* button and observe the current *Control Panel* option on the menu.

Does the Control Panel option appear or not appear as configured?

18. Right-click the *Start* button → *Properties* → *Customize* button. Locate the *Control Panel* section. Change the *Control Panel* menu option to one of the other menu settings. Click *OK* → *Apply* → *OK*.

19. Select the *Start* button and select the *Control Panel* menu option.

How is the Control Panel option different?

20. Return the *Control Panel* item to its original setting.

Adding a Program to the Start Menu

21. Click *Start* button → type **charmap** in the *Start Search* (Vista)/*Search programs and files* (7) textbox. CHARMAP is the file used to execute the Character Map program. It is commonly found in the C:\Windows\System32 folder. *Note:* If the CHARMAP file is not installed, any program file can be used for this part of the exercise.

22. Locate *charmap* in the resulting *Programs* list. Right-click the *charmap* file and select the *Pin to Start Menu* option. Click the *Start* button.

    Where on the Start button menu is the Character Map application added?

23. To remove a customized application, click the *Start* button, right-click the unwanted item (*charmap* in this case), and select *Unpin from Start Menu*.

Instructor initials: _____

10. Basic Commands from a Command Prompt

Objective: To execute basic commands from a command prompt

Parts: A Windows-based computer with command prompt access

    The ability to save a file to the hard drive *or* access to a floppy drive/Zip/Flash drive

Procedure: Complete the following procedure and answer the accompanying questions.

Note: For each step requiring a typed command the [Enter] key must be pressed to execute the command. This instruction will *not* be given with each step.

1. Power on the computer and log on if necessary. When Windows loads, exit to a command prompt.

    Windows XP: (1) *Start → Run →* type **CMD** *→ OK*; (2) *Start→All Programs → Accessories → Command Prompt*. Windows Vista/7: (1) *Start Search* (Vista)/*Search programs and files* (7) textbox → type **CMD** → press [Enter].

    Does a prompt display? If not and you followed every step correctly, contact your instructor.

    What prompt displays on the screen? This is the folder (directory) from which you are starting.

2. From the command prompt, type the following: **CD**

    The prompt changes to c:\>. If a message appears stating invalid command or invalid directory, you made a typing error. If you suspect an error, verify the backslash is after CD and that there are no extra spaces. The backslash starts from the left side and goes to the right (\ ). Other commands use a forward slash, which would be in the opposite direction /.

    CD is the command for Change Directory, which tells the operating system to go to a different directory in the tree structure. The \ after the CD command tells the operating system to go to the root directory. An alternative way of typing this command is CD \. Notice the space between the CD command and the backslash. There are usually different ways to do every command from a prompt. Note that the CD\ command allows you to return to the root directory at any time.

3. At the command prompt, type **DIR**

    A list of files and directories appears. Files are the items that show an extension to the right of the filename, file size, and file creation date. File extensions frequently give clues as to which application created the file. Directories have a <DIR> entry to the right of the name.

    List one file including its extension and one directory shown on the screen. Using the table provided in the chapter, try to determine what application created the file and write that application (if found) beside the filename.

4. When the number of files shown exceeds what can be displayed on the screen, the files quickly scroll off the screen until all files finish displaying. The DIR command has a switch that controls this scrolling. A **command switch** begins with a forward slash and enhances or changes the way a command performs. At the command prompt, type **DIR /P**.

    After looking at the data on the screen, press [Enter] again. Continue pressing [Enter] until the prompt reappears. The DIR command's /P switch tells the operating system to display the files one page at a time.

5. At the prompt, type **DIR /W**

    What is the function of the /W switch?

6. Multiple switches can be used with a DOS command. At the prompt, type **DIR /W/P**.

  Using the DIR command /W and /P switches cause files to display in a wide format, one page at a time.

7. Different versions of Windows have documentation with online help. To find out the operating system version loaded on the computer, type **VER**.

  Who is the operating system manufacturer and what version is being used on the computer?

8. At the prompt, type **DIR /? | more**. To create the vertical bar used in the command, hold down the [Shift] key and, while keeping it held down, press the key directly above the [Enter] key. It is the same key as a backslash. A short explanation of the command appears followed by the command's syntax (instructions or rules for how the command is to be typed). A technician needs to be able to understand command syntax to determine what commands to type when unfamiliar with a command. The | symbol is called the pipe symbol. The | more command tells the operating system to display the output one page at a time. Perform the following activities and then press any key to continue until you return to a prompt.

  Write the DIR syntax.

  Write one switch that can be used with the DIR command along with a short explanation of its purpose.

9. Type **CD*XXXXX*** where the *XXXXX* is replaced by the name of the directory you wrote as the answer to Question 3. For example in Question 3, if I wrote the directory name *CASINO*, I would type CD\CASINO at the prompt. The prompt changes to the name of the directory (folder) that I just typed.

10. Type the following command: **DIR A*.***

  The A*.* is not a switch. This command is directing the operating system to list all files or subdirectories that start with the letter A. The *.* part means all files. The directory you chose may not have any files or subdirectories that start with the letter A. If this occurs, the operating system displays the message "File not found." The * is known as a wildcard. A wildcard substitutes for one or more characters. The first asterisk (*) is the wildcard for any name of a file. The second asterisk is the wildcard for any extension.

  Does the operating system list any files or subdirectories that start with the letter A? If so, write one of them in the following space. If not, did the operating system let you know this? If so, write the message displayed.

11. Type the following command: **CD..**

  The .. tells the operating system to move back (or up if you think about the structure in Windows Explorer) one directory in the directory structure. Since you are one level down (because of typing the CD*XXXXX* command), this command returns you to the root directory.

  If you wanted to display a list of all files in the root directory that start with the letter C, what command would you type? Try this command on the computer to see if it works.

  Do any commands start with the letter C? If so, write at least one of them down.

  Does the *COMMAND.COM* file appear in the list of commands that start with the letter C?

On Your Own

a. Change to the directory that contains Windows. The directory's name is normally *WINDOWS* or *WINNT*. If you cannot determine what directory contains Windows, use the **dir** command again or contact your instructor or lab assistant.

  Write the command you used to do this.

  List two Windows files that begin with the letter D.

b. Return to the root directory.

  Write the command you used.

12. *Note*: If you are not allowed to create and save a file on the hard drive, you can do this part from the root directory of another drive such as the floppy drive or a Flash drive.

  From the root directory (*X*:\), you are going to create a file using the COPY CON: command that will later be read using a different command. The name of the file will be

LADYVOLS.TXT. You are going to type the commands below exactly as they appear and at the end of each line press ⏎Enter. Note that no message appears.

```
COPY CON: X:\LADYVOLS.TXT
This is a fine mess you've gotten me into Ollie.
This computer is about to EXPLODE if you press Enter one more time.
Go get that Earth creature and bring back the Uranium Pew36 Space Modulator.
Can you sing Rocky Top?
```

Press ⌷F6. A caret Z (^z) appears on the screen. Press ⏎Enter. A message appears stating that one file copied. If this did not occur, repeat this step.

13. From the root directory, use the `Type` command to view the text file you just created by using the following command: **TYPE LADYVOLS.TXT**

    What is the result of using the `Type` command? Can you edit and change the file using this command? Have a classmate verify your file displays and sign his or her name beside your answer.

14. The `DEL` command is used to delete files. From the root directory, delete the file you just created using the following command: **DEL LADYVOLS.TXT**

    Why do you think you did not have to type DEL `X:\LADYVOLS.TXT` (the full path) in the last step?

11.   COPY, MD, DEL, and RD Command

Objective: To correctly use the COPY, MD, DEL, and RD command

Parts: A Windows computer with command prompt access

               The ability to save a file to the hard drive *or* access to a floppy drive/Zip/Flash drive

Procedure: Complete the following procedure and answer the accompanying questions.

Note: For each step requiring a typed command, the ⏎Enter key must be pressed to execute the command. This instruction will *not* be given with each step.

1. Power on the computer and log on if necessary. When Windows loads, access a command prompt. There are multiple methods that can be used. Use a previous lab for instructions.
   Note: This next section requires the ability to create folders and files. If this is not permitted on the hard drive, do this section from a floppy disk, Zip disk, or Flash drive.

2. At the command prompt type the command to go to the drive you will be using. For example, if you are using the floppy drive, type **A:** and press ⏎Enter. If you are using a Flash drive that uses the drive letter G, you would type **G:** and press ⏎Enter. The command is as follows: **X:** (where *X* is the drive letter where you are allowed to create files). The prompt changes to the appropriate drive. From the command prompt, type the following command: **CD**

   What is the purpose of the CD command?

   What is the purpose of the CD\ command?

3. Create a directory (folder) called *CLASS*: **MD CLASS**

4. Use the DIR command to verify the directory creation. If it is not created, redo Step 3.

5. When the directory is created, move into the *CLASS* directory using the CD command:
   CD CLASS

   If you use the DIR command at this point, what two entries are automatically created in a directory?

6. Within the *CLASS* directory, create a subdirectory (subfolder) called *SUBFOLDER1*:
   MD SUBFOLDER1

7. Move from the *CLASS* folder into the subfolder just created: **CD SUBFOLDER1**

   In Step 7, would the CD `X:\CLASS\SUBFOLDER1` (or whatever media you are using) command have worked as well? Why or why not?

8. From the *SUBFOLDER1* directory, move back one directory: **CD..**

   What does the prompt look like at this point?

9. Make another subdirectory called *SUBFOLDER2*.

   Have a fellow student verify that both subdirectories have been created by using the DIR command. Have them sign their name on your answer sheet if the *CLASS* directory has two subdirectories that have the correct title.

10. Return to the root directory.

On Your Own

a. Using the COPY CON: command as described in a previous lab, create two text files within the *SUBFOLDER1* directory. Name the files with your first initial and last name and a 1-1 and a 1-2. The file extension will be *txt*. For example, the filenames of *cschmidt1-1.txt* and *cschmidt1-2.txt* would be in *SUBFOLDER1*.

b. Within *SUBFOLDER2*, create two files. Name the files with your first initial and last name and a 2-1 and a 2-2. The file extension will be *.txt*. For example, the filenames of *cschmidt2-1.txt* and *cschmidt2-2.txt* would be located in *SUBFOLDER2*.

c. Use the DIR command to verify the two files exist in the two subdirectories.

   Have a fellow student verify that two files are created in the two subdirectories. Ensure that the two names are correct and are readable. Have him/her sign his/her name and write the command he/she used to verify what you typed inside each file.

d. Return to the root directory of the *X:* drive (the media where you are allowed to create files).

   Draw an image of your directory structure that you have created.

   Since you are sitting at the root directory of the drive, what do you think would be the results of the following command? COPY C:\WINDOWS\SYSTEM32\ATTRIB.EXE

11. *Note*: This step assumes that Windows has been loaded in a directory (folder) called *WINDOWS*. If it is loaded in a different directory, substitute the name of that directory for *WINDOWS* in the commands. You have to substitute *X:*\CLASS with a drive letter different from *X:* for the drive letter you are using to create these files.

    From the root directory, type the following command:

    COPY *C:*\WINDOWS\SYSTEM32\ATTRIB.EXE *X:*\CLASS

    To what location do you think the file was copied?

12. From the root directory verify that the command has been copied by typing the following command: **DIR \CLASS**

    What is the size of the *ATTRIB.EXE* file?

13. To copy the ATTRIB.EXE command from the *CLASS* folder into *SUBFOLDER2* (from the root directory), use the following command:

    COPY \CLASS\ATTRIB.EXE \CLASS\SUBFOLDER2

14. Verify that the file copied correctly using the following command:

    DIR \CLASS\SUBFOLDER2

    The *ATTRIB.EXE* file should be listed. If it is not, redo Step 13.

    What is the size of the *ATTRIB.EXE* file in the *SUBFOLDER2*?

15. Copy your first text file from your second subdirectory into your first subdirectory using the following command. *FLAST2-1.TXT* is your first initial and last name followed by *2-1.txt*.

    COPY \CLASS\SUBFOLDER2*FLAST*2-1.TXT \CLASS\SUBFOLDER1

16. Verify that the file copied: **DIR \CLASS\SUBFOLDER1**

    Write the exact command you would use to copy the first text file from *SUBFOLDER1* into *SUBFOLDER2* from the root directory. Have the instructor or lab assistant verify your command. •

17. Execute the command to copy the first text file from *SUBFOLDER1* into *SUBFOLDER2* from the root directory command prompt. Verify the copy.

    What command was used to verify the copy in Step 16?

    Write the exact command to copy the first text file from *SUBFOLDER2* into the *CLASS* directory.

18. A directory can be created within a subdirectory from the root directory. To create a subdirectory called *FUN* within the *SUBFOLDER2* directory, use the following command from the root directory. Notice how you must insert the backslashes when you have multiple directories to go through to create the subdirectory. We just used a space before.

    MD \CLASS\SUBFOLDER2\FUN

19. Verify the subdirectory creation: **DIR \CLASS\SUBFOLDER2**
    A directory called *FUN* should be listed in the output.

    What is the total amount of space the three files located within *SUBFOLDER2* occupy?

20. To copy all the files located in *SUBFOLDER2* into the newly created *FUN* subdirectory, the following command is used:

    COPY \CLASS\SUBFOLDER2 \CLASS\SUBFOLDER2\FUN

21. Use the **DIR** command as follows to verify the copy:

    DIR \CLASS\SUBFOLDER2\FUN

22. Wildcards can be used with the **COPY** command. To copy all the files that start with the letter A from the *FUN* subdirectory into the *SUBFOLDER1* subdirectory, the following command is used:

    COPY \CLASS\SUBFOLDER2\FUN\A*.* \CLASS\SUBFOLDER1

    How many files were copied?

Instructor initials: _____

23. The **DEL** command is used to delete files. Wildcards can also be used with this command. Delete all the files located in the *FUN* subdirectory using the following command. The *.* is the wildcard representing all files with any extension.

    DEL \CLASS\SUBFOLDER2\FUN*.*

    When prompted if you are sure, type **Y** and press Enter. Verify the files are deleted with the **DIR** command:

    DIR \CLASS\SUBFOLDER2\FUN

24. The **RD** command is used to remove directories and subdirectories. Remove the *FUN* subdirectory:

    RD \CLASS\SUBFOLDER2\FUN

25. Type the command used to remove the *SUBFOLDER2* subdirectory:

    RD \CLASS\SUBFOLDER2

    What was the operating system response and what do you think has to be done as a result?

26. Delete the files in the *SUBFOLDER2* subdirectory:

    DEL \CLASS\SUBFOLDER2*.*

    When prompted if you are sure, type **Y** and press Enter. Verify the files are deleted with the **DIR** command:

    DIR \CLASS\SUBFOLDER2

27. Remove the *SUBFOLDER2* subdirectory:

    RD \CLASS\SUBFOLDER2

    Verify the results:

    DIR \CLASS

On Your Own

a. Using the DEL, RD, and DIR commands, delete all files, subdirectories, and directories that you have created and verify the deletions.

Write each command you are going to use *before* attempting this part.

Write each command used to delete the files, subdirectories, and directories that have been created as part of this exercise.

Have another student verify your work. Have them sign as well as print their name verifying that all of the files created during this lab have been deleted.

12. ATTRIB **Command and Moving Around in the Directory Structure**

Objective: To use the ATTRIB command and to work correctly from a prompt when dealing with directories and subdirectories

Parts: A computer with a Windows operating system loaded

Access to modify files on the hard drive or a disk such as a floppy disk, ZIP disk, or Flash drive

Procedure: Complete the following procedure and answer the accompanying questions.

Note: For each step requiring a typed command the [Enter] key must be pressed to execute the command. This instruction will *not* be given with each step.

1. Power on the computer and log on if necessary. Access a command prompt.

2. From the root directory of a disk that can have files and directories created, type the following command to create a directory called *Junk*: **MD JUNK**

3. Under the *JUNK* directory, make subdirectories called *SUB1*, *SUB2*, and *SUB3*. Use the following commands.

   CD JUNK
   MD SUB1
   MD SUB2
   MD SUB3

4. Return to the root directory. Verify by looking at the command prompt after returning to the root directory.

   What command makes the root directory the current directory?

   Write the command prompt as it appears on your screen.

5. Make a new directory called *TRASH* from the root directory. Within the *TRASH* directory, make subdirectories called *SUB1*, *SUB2*, and *SUB3*. Use the following commands:

   MD TRASH
   CD TRASH
   MD SUB1
   MD SUB2
   MD SUB3

6. Return to the root directory.

On Your Own

a. Make a new directory called *GARBAGE* from the root directory. Within the *GARBAGE* directory, make subdirectories called *SUB1*, *SUB2*, and *SUB3*. Verify the directory and subdirectories were created.

Write the commands to create a directory called *GARBAGE* and the three subdirectories.

b. Using previously described commands and exercises, create three files called *SPECIAL1.TXT*, *SPECIAL2.TXT*, and *TICKLE.TXT*. Place them in the *GARBAGE\SUB1* subdirectory.

Write the commands to create the files for the SUB1 subdirectory.

c. From the root directory, copy all files that begin with the letter *S* from the *GARBAGE\SUB1* subdirectory and place them in the *TRASH\SUB3* subdirectory.

Write the commands to copy *S* files from the GARBAGE SUB1 subdirectory to the TRASH SUB3 subdirectory.

How many files copied?

d. Copy any file that begins with *T* from the *GARBAGE\SUB1* subdirectory and place them in the *SUB2* subdirectory of the *JUNK* directory.

Write the commands to copy T files from one subdirectory to another subdirectory.

How many files copied?

Draw a diagram of how your directory structure that you have created in this exercise including all directories, subdirectories, and files.

7. To make all files in the *SUB3* subdirectory of the *TRASH* directory read-only, use the `ATTRIB` command with the +R switch. From the root directory, type the following command.

   `ATTRIB +R \TRASH\SUB3\*.*`

8. To verify the read-only attribute is set, type the following command.

   `ATTRIB \TRASH\SUB3\*.*`

   The *SUB3* subdirectory should list two files. Both have an R beside them indicating that the read-only attribute is set. If the two files do *not* have the read-only attribute set, perform the previous step again.

9. The best way to prove that the files are read-only is to try to delete them. Type the following command.

   `DEL \TRASH\SUB3\*.*`

   When asked if you are sure, type **Y** and press (Enter). A message appears on the screen stating, "Access is denied." Then, the command prompt appears. If the access denied message does not appear, the files were deleted which means the read-only attribute was not set. If this is the case, redo this exercise starting with *On Your Own* Step c above.

10. Hide the *JUNK\SUB2* subdirectory using the following command:

    `ATTRIB +H \JUNK\SUB2`

    No message appears on the screen. The command prompt appears again.

11. To verify that the directory is hidden, type the following command:

    `DIR \JUNK`

    The *SUB2* subdirectory should not appear in the list.

12. Use the `ATTRIB` command to verify that the directory is hidden by typing the following command: `ATTRIB \JUNK\SUB2`

    The directory listing appears with an H beside the name.

13. Some operating system files are automatically marked as system files when the operating system is installed. From the root directory of the `c:` drive, type the following command to see what files are marked already as system files.

    `ATTRIB`

    List any files that have the system attribute.

On Your Own

a. Hide the *SPECIAL1.TXT* file located in the *SUB1* subdirectory of the *GARBAGE* directory.

   Write the command you used for the previous step.

b. Verify that the *SPECIAL1.TXT* file is hidden by using the `DIR` and `ATTRIB` commands.

   Write the command you used for the previous step.

   Have a classmate print his/her name and his/her signature as well as a statement describing how the person verified that you were in the correct directory.

Instructor initials: _____

   c. Remove the hidden attribute from the *SPECIAL1.TXT* file in the *SUB1* subdirectory of the *GARBAGE* directory. If necessary, use `Help` to find the switch to remove an attribute.

     Write the command used in the previous step.

   d. Have a classmate verify that the *SPECIAL1.TXT* file is no longer hidden.

     Have the classmate write the command he/she used, his/her printed name, and his/her signature.

14. Ensure you are at the root directory.

15. Moving around within subdirectories can be a challenge when you are first learning commands. Move to the *SUB3* subdirectory of the *TRASH* directory.

    What command did you use to perform Step 15?

16. To move to the SUB1 subdirectory from within the *SUB3* subdirectory, type `CD..`; then type `CD SUB1` to move into the correct subdirectory.

    What does the command prompt look like now?

17. A shortcut to move up one directory is to type `CD..` from within the *SUB1* subdirectory. The prompt immediately changes to one level up (the *TRASH* directory). Type `CD..`
       The command prompt changes to *X:*`\TRASH>`.

18. Using the `CD..` command again returns one level back in the directory structure to the root directory. Type `CD..` and the command prompt changes appropriately.

On Your Own

   a. From the root directory change to the *SUB2* subdirectory of the *GARBAGE* directory.

     Write the command used in the previous step.

     How can one verify that the current directory is *GARBAGE\SUB2*?

   b. From the `GARBAGE\SUB2` subdirectory, change the current directory to the *SUB3* subdirectory of the *TRASH* directory.

     Write the command you used in the previous step.

     Have a classmate print his/her name and his/her signature as well as a statement describing how the person verified that you were in the correct directory.

19. Using the `CD..` command, move from *TRASH\SUB3* to *TRASH*.

20. Using the `CD..` command, move from *TRASH* to the root directory.

On Your Own

   a. Using the `ATTRIB`, `DEL`, and `RD` commands, delete the *TRASH* and *GARBAGE* directories including all subdirectories underneath them. Write all commands before you attempt this step.

     Write all commands used in the previous step.

   b. Using the `ATTRIB`, `DEL`, and `RD` commands, delete the *JUNK* directory and all subdirectories. Write all commands before attempting this step.

     Write all commands used in the previous step.

Instructor initials: _____

13. Creating a Boot Floppy Disk within Windows XP

Objective: To create a bootable floppy disk in the Windows XP environment

Parts: A Windows XP-based computer that has a floppy drive installed
         1 blank formatted disk

Procedure: Complete the following procedure and answer the accompanying questions.

1. Boot the computer and log on if necessary.

2. Insert the floppy disk into the drive.

3. Open Explorer. Right-click the *3 1/2 Floppy (A:)* option. Select *Format . . .*

4. Select the *Create an MS-DOS startup disk* checkbox to enable it.

5. Click the *Start* button followed by *OK*. When the format is finished, click *OK*.

6. Ensure the computer BIOS is set to boot from floppy disk and the disk is inserted into the drive. Reboot the computer to a command prompt using the disk.

Instructor initials: _____

Can you use any of the commands you have learned? If so, which ones?

7. Remove the disk and reboot the computer normally.

14. Installing and Exploring Windows XP Recovery Console

Objective: To install Recovery Console onto a computer hard drive and have it available as a boot option

Parts: Windows XP computer with permissions to install software

Windows XP installation CD, XP service pack CD, or access to the folder where the service pack is installed

Procedure: Complete the following procedure and answer the accompanying questions.

Note: In order to access Recovery Console, the administrator password is required.

1. Insert the Windows XP installation CD into the CD drive. If the welcome screen appears, close it.

2. Click the *Start* button → *Run* → type `X:\I386\WINNT32  /CMDCOMS` (where *X*: is the drive letter for the CD drive) → `Enter`. This starts the Recovery Console installation process.

   Note that if you receive an error message stating that you have a service pack installed that is higher than the CD version, you have two choices: (1) use a Windows XP service pack CD or (2) install Recovery Console using the XP service pack installation file. If you choose the latter, you must know or locate the folder that holds the service pack. This is commonly in the root directory of `C:` and called I386.

3. When asked if you want to install Recovery Console, click *Yes*, and follow the prompts on the screen.

4. Once Recovery Console is installed, restart the computer. When the computer restarts, a menu appears with both Windows XP or Recovery Console listed. Select the *Recovery Console* option.

5. After the Recovery Console loads a list of numbered partitions that contains Windows lists. A prompt asks which Windows installation you would like to log onto. Most machines only have 1. Type `1` and press `Enter`.

6. When prompted for the Administrator password, type it and press `Enter`.

7. Type `dir`. A listing of the files in the *Windows* folder appears one page at a time. Press the `Spacebar` to see another page. Press `Esc` to exit the listing. The letters to the side designate attributes for the files.

a=archive	h=hidden
d=directory	r=read-only
e=encrypted	s=system

   From the output shown, list three entries that are directories and three entries that are system files.

8. Type `map`. Drive letters that are available through Recovery Console display.

   What drive letters do you have available?

   Are you allowed access to a CD/DVD drive through Recovery Console?

9. Type `help`. Commands that are available in this mode list on the screen.

   Based on the output displayed, determine whether a command is available or not through Recovery Console.

Command	Available	Not Available
Attrib		
Cipher		
Copy		
Disable		
Enable		
Expand		
Fdisk		
Fixboot		
Prompt		
Rd		
Set		
Tree		

10. Type `listsvc` to see a listing of services that are available. The `enable` and `disable` commands are used to start and stop a service that might be causing problems.

    List three services that are automatically started in Recovery Console mode.

11. From the prompt, type **CD**.

    What happened? Why do you think this behaves this way?

12. Type `exit` to leave Recovery Console and boot normally.

Internet Discovery

Objective: Access the Internet to obtain specific information regarding a computer or its associated parts

Parts: Access to the Internet

Procedure: Complete the following procedure and answer the accompanying questions.

1. Locate an Internet site that has a tutorial for basic Windows usage.

   Write the URL and the name of the tutorial.

   What is the latest service pack for Windows XP Professional? Write the service pack number and the URL of the location where you found this information.

   What is the URL for the Windows XP Professional resource kit?

2. Find a Web-based article on the differences between Windows XP Home and Professional editions.

   Write the name of the article and the URL.

3. The Windows registry can be edited to allow users to automatically be logged into the Windows environment. Locate a Web site that demonstrates how to edit the Windows registry for any version of the Windows Vista operating system.

   Write the URL and one tip you discovered.

4. Locate a Web site that describes three things to do if Vista (any version) will not boot.

   Write the URL.

Soft Skills

Objective: To enhance and fine-tune a future technician's ability to listen, communicate in both written and oral form, and support people who use computers in a professional manner

Activities:

1. On a piece of paper or index card, list two topics you would like to hear about if you were to attend a local association PC Users group meeting. Share this information with your group. Consolidate ideas and present five of the best ideas to the class.

2. In a team environment, select one of the five ideas in the class to research. Every team member presents something about a latest technology to the rest of the class. The class votes on the best presented topic and the most interesting topic.

3. On a 3×5 card, document a question that several students have asked the teacher about how to do a particular task. Exchange cards with one classmate. Correct each other's grammar, punctuation, and capitalization. When you have your original card, exchange your card with a different classmate and perform the same task. Rewrite your 3×5 card based on the recommendations of your classmates. Keep in mind that all their suggestions are just that, suggestions. You do not have to accept their suggestions. A complaint of industry is that technicians do not write well. Practice helps with this issue.

Critical Thinking Skills

Objective: To analyze and evaluate information as well as apply learned information to new or different situations

Activities:

1. Windows Vista will not boot. What will be the first thing, second thing, and third thing you try? Explain your reasoning.

2. In a paragraph, explain why or why you would not use Recovery Console as a first attempt in a Windows boot failure.

3. Explain a situation of when you would use a Windows boot CD or find one on the Internet. Detail the drawbacks to using it.

4. Find a specific problem on the Internet and what the person did to repair the problem using Recovery Console. Share your findings with the class.

12

Windows XP, Vista, and 7

Objectives

After completing this chapter you will be able to

- Distinguish between Windows XP, Vista, 7, and other operating systems
- Back up and restore the System State
- Configure and use the System Restore utility
- Install, configure, and troubleshoot Windows XP, Vista, and 7
- Use the proper Windows control panel to control hardware and software
- Install hardware and software on a Windows computer
- Use the driver roll back feature
- Use Windows administrative tools including Microsoft Management console
- Explain the boot process and troubleshoot boot problems using various boot options
- Define when to access and how to use Computer Management console, Task Manager, and Event Viewer

Before beginning this chapter or any of the exercises, review Chapter 11 on basic Windows to become familiar with working in the Windows environment.

Windows XP Professional Overview

Windows XP is a 32- and 64-bit operating system. Microsoft created several different types of Windows XP: Home, Professional, Professional x64, Tablet PC, and Media Center. Table 12.1 summarizes the differences among the versions.

Table 12.1 Windows XP editions

XP version	Description
Windows XP Professional	The most common version used by businesses; many home users use as well. Supports encryption, network domains, widest range of support tools, remote access, and security.
Windows XP Professional x64	The 64-bit operating system that can run 64-bit applications as well as the older 32-bit applications designed for XP Professional. Virtual memory is expanded to 16 terabytes. Requires a 64-bit processor, 256MB of RAM, and 1.5GB of hard disk space as a minimum.
Windows XP Home	Similar to XP Professional, but not as robust; does not allow connecting to a network domain or support encryption.
Windows XP Tablet PC	Specifically designed for notebook and laptop computers. Has more pen and speech capabilities, such as converting handwriting to text or using the input panel designed for people on the go.
Windows XP Media Center	Designed for home multimedia (video, music, pictures) computers as well as tools for online entertainment; has higher hardware requirements than the other 32-bit XP versions because of the entertainment focus: 1.6GHz or higher CPU and 256MB RAM.

Windows XP Home and Windows XP Professional are the two most popular versions available. Table 12.2 lists features of both versions.

Table 12.2 Windows XP Home and Professional features

Supports disk quotas to limit users on storage space
Supports NTFS, FAT32, and FAT16 file systems
Supports CDFS and UDF for CD/DVD media
Has core reliability and stability like Windows 2000
Has enhanced support for movies, pictures, and music
Contains Windows Messenger, which is a collaboration tool for instant messaging, voice and video conferencing, and application sharing
Contains an Internet connection firewall, which can help with Internet attacks
Offers improved boot and power resume performance
Configures automatically for 802.11x wireless networks
Supports DualView, which allows different outputs to multiple monitors simultaneously
Can make CDs by using drag-and-drop or CD Writing wizard
Allows communication between software applications and image-capturing devices with WIA (Windows Image Acquisition); the Scanner and Camera wizard is used to retrieve images from any WIA-enabled devices
Supports ClearType, which is a new text display technology that provides better output for LCD (Liquid Crystal Display) monitors
Can switch between users without rebooting

There are quite a few differences between Windows XP Professional and Windows XP Home. Table 12.3 lists some of these differences.

Table 12.3   Windows XP Home and Professional differences

Professional	Home
Two CPUs	One CPU
Roaming profiles	Not applicable
Remote Desktop and Remote Assistant	Remote Assistant only
Computer Management and Performance monitor	Not applicable
Can join to a Windows-based server domain	Workgroups only
Can simplify user and group administration with the Group Policy tool	No Group Policy tool
EFS (Encrypting File System)	No encryption
Dynamic disk support	No dynamic disks
IPSec, which is a group of security protocols and services used to safeguard TCP/IP data	No IPSec
Upgradable from 98, ME, NT 4, or 2000 Professional	Upgradable from 98 or ME
IIS Web server software	No Web server software installed
File-level access control	Folder level access control only

Windows XP Professional supports 32-bit Windows applications, 16-bit applications, and some DOS applications (only those that do not access hardware directly); every 32-bit application runs in its own 2GB memory space; all 16-bit Windows applications run in a single virtual machine; a virtual machine simulates a single computer with its own memory, hardware devices, and software configuration.

DOS and 16-bit Windows applications run in a single 2GB memory space. The Windows XP VMM (virtual memory manager) handles allocating memory to applications. A single block called a page is 4KB. A **page** is used to store files and may also retrieve a file located on a disk. This file is called a paging file.

Windows XP supports **WFP** (Windows file protection). WFP protects system files (files critical to the operating system) and some TrueType fonts. WFP runs in the background. When WFP detects that a file has been altered or deleted, it copies a replacement file from the WINDOWS\SYSTEM32\ DLLCACHE folder, the Windows XP CD, or a network share (a shared folder that contains a copy of the XP CD).

Windows Vista/7 Overview

Like Windows XP, Vista and 7 come in 32- and 64-bit versions: Starter, Home Basic, Home Premium, Business (Vista), Professional (7), and Ultimate. Depending on the version, enhanced features include improved security; a graphical environment called **Windows Aero** that is a Windows sidebar containing gadgets such as a clock, live thumbnails (hold your mouse over an application icon and all documents are shown in a separate thumbnail), transparent icons (icons that you can see through), animations, and themes; quick access to tools and files; the Narrator text-to-speech program that reads the screen; an on-screen keyboard; the **UAC** (User Account Control) to notify you of potential security issues before anything is added to or removed from the system; disk partitions that can be resized without loss of data; the Startup Repair Tool instead of Recovery Console; and full support of IP version 6 (IPv6). Figure 12.1 shows an example of the thumbnails and a Windows Aero desktop.

In order to use Windows Aero, the following minimum requirements must be met:

- Vista/7 Home Premium or higher
- 1GHz 32-bit processor or higher
- 1GB of RAM or higher
- 128MB graphics memory
- Graphics card set to 32-bit color or higher
- Monitor refresh rate 10Hz or higher
- Windows theme set to Windows Vista or 7
- Display color scheme set to Windows Aero
- *Appearance and Personalization* control panel → *Personalization* link → *Windows color* option → *Enable transparency* option enabled (checked)

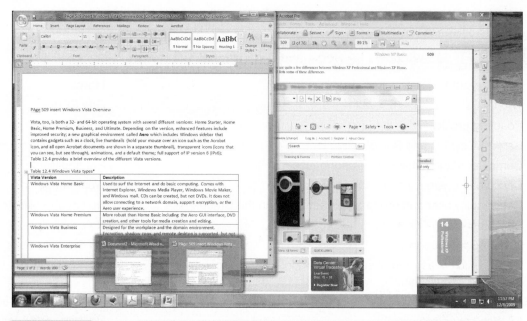

Figure 12.1   **Windows Aero desktop with thumbnails**

Table 12.4 provides a brief overview of the different Vista versions.

Table 12.4   **Windows Vista versions***

Vista version	Description
Windows Vista Starter	Sold with lower-cost computers in countries other than the U.S., Japan, Australia, or Europe for beginning computer users.
Windows Vista Home Basic	Used to surf the Internet and do basic computing. Comes with Internet Explorer, Windows Media Player, Windows Movie Maker, and Windows Mail. CDs can be created, but not DVDs. It does not allow connecting to a network domain, support encryption, or provide the Aero user experience.
Windows Vista Home Premium	More robust than Home Basic, includes the Aero GUI interface, DVD creation, and other tools for media creation and editing.
Windows Vista Business	Designed for computers in the workplace and the domain environment. Aero, encryption, shadow copy, and remote desktop are supported, but not all the multimedia capabilities.
Windows Vista Enterprise	Designed for the corporate environments where multimedia editing and creation are used; supports BitLocker drive encryption (covered in Chapter 13) multi-lingual support. Not sold through retail centers but to corporate and educational institutions using bulk licensing.
Windows Vista Ultimate	Contains all the Vista Business features including support for multiple processors, but includes some extras that are downloadable from Microsoft. These include fun utilities and work-related tools such as the Windows BitLocker Drive Preparation Tool (which does not come with Vista Business).

*Each comes in a 32- and 64-bit version

Besides having to choose a Windows version, deciding on a 32-bit or 64-bit version is also required. This decision is based on the type of processor that is installed. Through Windows Explorer, right-click on the computer and select *Properties* to see the current version. 64-bit processors have been available for some time, but a 64-bit operating system is a big step. It took over 12 years for a 32-bit operating system to become the norm in business and home computing environments. Even though Windows XP had a 64-bit version, many consumers have not considered using a 64-bit operating system until Windows Vista and 7. Many books and advertisements refer to a 32-bit processor as an x86 chip. 64-bit processors are frequently shown as x64. Table 12.5 lists the differences between 32-bit and 64-bit Windows.

Table 12.5	32-bit and 64-bit Windows
32-bit Windows	**64-bit Windows**
32-bit or 64-bit processor	64-bit processor
4GB RAM limitation	1 to 128+GB RAM supported (Home Basic 8GB; Home Premium 16GB; Business, Enterprise, and Ultimate 128GB+ maximum)
32 bits are processed at a time	64 bits are processed at a time.
32-bit drivers required	64-bit device drivers required, and they must be digitally signed.
32-bit applications and some support of older 16-bit applications	32- or 64-bit application support. 16-bit application support using the **Program Compatibility wizard** or download and use Windows XP mode (covered later in the chapter).
	Protection for the operating system kernel (the core of the operating system)
	Better support for multiple processors
DEP (Data Execution Prevention) prevents a specific type of security attack by using both hardware and software technology	"Always on" DEP support for 64-bit processes

12
Windows XP, Vista, and 7

Windows Vista and 7 improve upon WFP with **WRP** (Windows Resource Protection) that protects operating system files, folders, and important registry keys using ACLs (access control lists). Changes made to a monitored file or folder cannot be changed even by an administrator unless he or she takes ownership and adds the appropriate ACEs (access control entities). Any file that cannot be repaired by `SFC.EXE` (System File Checker), can be identified with the following administrator command:

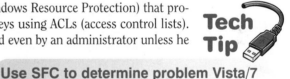

>   findstr /C:"[SR] Cannot repair member file"
> `%windir%\logs\cbs\cbs.log>sfcdetails.txt`

Use Notepad or the `EDIT` command to open the file (normally located in C:\Windows\System32 folder). From an elevated command prompt, the following commands are used to grant administrators access to the protected files, so they can be replaced.

>   takeown /f *filename_including_path* (where *filename_including_path* is the full path and file name to the problem file)
>   icacls *filename_including_path*/GRANT ADMINISTRATORS:F

Then use the COPY command to replace the file with a known good one.

>   copy *source_filename destination_filename* (where the source and destination are the full path and file)

Tech Tip

Use SFC to determine problem Vista/7 system file

Use the `SFC /scannow` command as an administrator to replace any protected system files that have problems.

Logging on to Windows

With Windows the first screen to appear when you boot the computer is the welcome screen, which allows users to log in. A user can log in to the local computer, a workgroup (peer-to-peer network), or a domain (a network with a server). See Chapter 13 on networking for more information on network types. To log in, click a user account icon and enter a password (if necessary) or press [Ctrl]+[Alt]+[Del] to go to the Log On to Windows box.

Logging on with local Administrator

Note that the local Administrator account (the master account that is allowed to change everything on the local machine) is not a user icon. You must press Ctrl+Alt+Del twice in Windows XP and enter the correct userid and password to use the Administrator account.

WINLOGON.EXE controls the user login process on a Windows computer and this file is located in the \Windows\System32 folder. This file also controls how the desktop looks for individual users through the HKEY_CURRENT_USER registry key. Starting with Vista and continuing on with 7, the WINLOGON process can work with credential providers such as a password or smartcard that can be user selected or event driven.

Pre-Installation of Windows

Windows XP, Vista, or 7 can be installed from a central location or locally. The pre-installation of any operating system is more important than the installation process. Technicians who grab a disc and load a new operating system without going through a logical process are asking for trouble. There are two major portions of any new operating system installation—hardware and software. The hardware and possibly software already installed in the system must be compatible with the operating system and researched before any installation steps are taken. The steps to take before installing Windows follow:

1. Decide whether the installation will be an upgrade or clean install and which version of the operating system is to be loaded.
2. Determine the file system(s) to be used. Also plan the partition/volume size.
3. Decide whether the computer will have more than one operating system installed.
4. Scan for viruses, and then disable the virus protection during the installation.
5. Determine if the hardware is compatible.
6. Obtain any drivers, upgrades, or hardware replacements.
7. Decide if the software applications are compatible.
8. Obtain any patches, upgrades, or software replacements.
9. Delete any unwanted files and uninstall any unwanted applications.
10. Back up any data files necessary or plan for data migration, as needed.
11. Remove any power management or disk management tools.

Antivirus software interferes with operating system installation

Whether doing a clean install or upgrade, disable the antivirus protection until after the installation.

The first decision to make when planning to install an operating system is whether to upgrade from another operating system or to perform a clean install. An **upgrade** or in-place upgrade is when a computer already has an older operating system on it and a newer operating system is being installed. A **clean install** puts an operating system on a computer that does not have one, or removes the computer's existing operating system and replaces it. There are three reasons to perform a clean install:

1. The computer does not have an operating system already installed.
2. The current operating system is not upgradable to the desired Windows version.
3. The current operating system is upgradable to a specific Windows version, but the existing files and applications are going to be reloaded.

When you decide to upgrade, you must take into account what operating system is already installed, what hardware (RAM, CPU, and hard disk space are important) is on the computer, what applications are being used, and whether they are compatible and whether they are compatible with the new operating system.

If the decision is made to upgrade, then you need to determine what operating system is already installed. Windows XP Professional supports upgrading from Windows 98, Windows Me, NT Workstation 4, 2000 Professional, and XP Home edition. Windows XP Home edition only supports upgrades from Windows 98 and Windows ME. When Windows is installed as an upgrade, the user's applications and data are preserved if the operating system is installed in the same folder (directory) as the original operating system. If Windows is installed in a different folder, then all applications must be reloaded.

Microsoft describes an in-place installation as one that requires no movement of files. Upgrading from a version of Windows XP to Vista and keeping operating system settings and files is not always possible for an in-place upgrade. Even when Microsoft states that it *can* be done, there is no guarantee that all applications and settings will work in Vista after the upgrade. Only certain versions of Windows XP can be upgraded to Vista (not 7); however the Easy Transfer program or the USMT tool discussed at the end of this section could be used when replacing XP with Windows 7. Table 12.6 shows the Windows XP versions and corresponding Vista versions that can be used for an in-place upgrade.

Table 12.6	Windows Vista in-place upgrade scenarios			
	Vista Home Basic	Vista Home Premium	Vista Business	Vista Ultimate
XP Professional	No	No	Yes	Yes
XP Professional x64	No	No	No	No
XP Home	Yes	Yes	Yes	Yes
XP Media Center	No	Yes	No	Yes
XP Tablet PC	No	No	Yes	Yes

A Windows 2000 Professional computer can have Vista or 7 installed, but it must be installed to a separate hard drive partition; it cannot be "upgraded" or have an in-place upgrade just like taking XP to Windows 7. All of the "in-place" upgrade scenarios in Table 12.6 that have "No" as an in-place option can have a clean installation performed on a separate hard drive partition. The **Upgrade Advisor** application should always be used before upgrading Windows. Upgrade Advisor is a software tool that you can download to see if a Windows XP or Vista computer can function well with a higher version of Windows Vista or 7. It might seem unusual to think you would run it on a Vista- or 7-based computer,

Plug in everything

Be advised that any devices normally used with a computer, especially USB-based ones, should be connected to the computer before starting Upgrade Advisor.

but with the different versions of Vista and 7, the Upgrade Advisor is commonly used to see if a more powerful version is an option.

Another decision you must make if upgrading is whether or not to convert the hard drive partition to NTFS. Once a partition is converted to NTFS, the partition cannot be changed. If you are unsure whether or not to convert the partition, leave it unchanged and later use the convert.exe command to upgrade. NTFS is the better file system for the following reasons:

- Security (individual files can be protected with NTFS)
- More efficient use of cluster space (the cluster size can be defined based on the user's needs when using NTFS)
- NTFS supports file compression
- NTFS supports larger hard drive partition sizes
- NTFS includes journaling, which helps to rebuild the file system after a crash or power failure. FAT is non-journaling—it does not track changes made to the file system.

Using the CONVERT command

The CONVERT command can be used to change a FAT(16) or FAT32 partition to NTFS. The format of the command is CONVERT *x:* /fs:ntfs (where *x:* is the drive to be converted to NTFS).

What is the difference between a patch and a service pack?

A **patch** is an update to an operating system. Microsoft releases service packs when they are needed for emergency fixes to vulnerabilities and routinely about once a month. A **service pack** consists of a group of patches, which makes it easier to install one update rather that a large number of separate patches.

In order to take advantage of Windows reliability, enhancements, and security features, sometimes a clean installation is the best choice. Because a clean installation involves formatting the hard drive, the user's data must be backed up and all applications re-installed once the Windows installation is complete. Also, all user-defined settings are lost. Note that OEM (original equipment manufacturer) Windows or a version of Windows that is sold as part of a computer sale is not transferable to another computer. In contrast, retail versions of Windows (where the Windows version is purchased separately) can be uninstalled on one computer and put on a different computer. The retail version of one copy of Windows cannot be installed on two computers at once. Another important point to remember is that not all Windows 9x applications are compatible with Windows XP or higher. You should contact the company that developed the application to see if it is compatible. You can also try using the Program Compatibility wizard or download and use Windows XP Mode (covered later in the chapter).

The third decision that must be made is whether to install more than one operating system. This situation is often called a **dual-boot** or multi-boot scenario. If Windows XP, Vista, or 7 is to coexist with one or more other operating systems, a separate hard disk partition should be created and used for each operating system. When doing a dual-boot or multi-boot configuration, make sure that the newest operating system is installed *after* the other operating systems. For example, if the goal is to have a Windows XP machine dual-boot with Windows 7, install XP first and then Windows 7 in a separate partition.

What does dual-boot mean?

Dual-boot means that the computer can boot from two operating systems. Multi-boot means that the computer can boot from two or more operating systems.

The fourth step in planning for a Windows installation is to scan the system for viruses. Viruses can cause havoc on a new upgrade. The next section provides more information about the most common types of viruses.

The fifth step when installing Windows is to determine what computer hardware is installed. Table 12.7 lists the minimum and preferred hardware requirements for installing Windows XP Professional. Table 12.8 lists the Microsoft minimum and recommended hardware standards for Vista Home Basic. Table 12.9 lists the requirements for the remaining Vista versions. One of the things that might influence your choice of Windows version is the amount of memory supported by the different flavors. Table 12.10 lists those maximums, and Table 12.11 shows the requirements to install Windows 7.

Ensure the BIOS update is the right one

Do *not* download a BIOS update unless you are sure it is compatible with your computer. Installing an invalid update can damage your computer system and cause it not to operate.

Once hardware has been verified, you may have to obtain Windows XP, Vista, or 7 device drivers from the hardware manufacturer's Web site. The hardware device may have to be upgraded or replaced.

Table 12.7	Windows XP Professional hardware requirements	
Component	**Minimum requirements**	**Recommended requirements**
CPU	Intel Pentium or AMD K6/Athlon/Duron 233MHz	300MHz or higher
RAM	64MB	128MB or higher
Hard disk space	1.5GB	>1.5GB
Video	VGA or higher	SVGA with plug and play monitor
CD/DVD	CD or DVD drive	CD or DVD drive (12x or higher)
Input device	Keyboard and mouse or pointing device	Keyboard and mouse or pointing device

Table 12.8 **Vista Home Basic hardware requirements**

Component	Minimum	Recommended
Processor	800MHz 32-bit or 64-bit multiple core	1GHz 32-bit or 64-bit multiple core
RAM	512MB	512MB
Hard drive space	20GB drive with a minimum of 15GB of space	20GB drive with a minimum of 15GB of space
Graphics	SVGA	32MB of video memory and support for DirectX9 or higher
CD/DVD	CD-ROM	DVD-ROM
Sound		Audio output
Network		Internet connectivity

Table 12.9 **Vista Home Premium, Business, and Ultimate recommended hardware requirements***

Component	Minimum	Recommended
Processor	800MHz 32-bit or 64-bit multiple core	1GHz 32-bit or 64-bit multiple core and dual processors
RAM	512MB	1GB
Hard drive space	20GB drive with a minimum of 15GB of space	40GB drive with a minimum of 15GB of space
Graphics	SVGA	128MB of video memory and support for DirectX9 or higher with WDDM driver, Pixel Shader 2.0 in hardware, 32-bit color
DVD	CD-ROM	DVD-ROM
Sound		Audio output
Network		Internet connectivity

*Note that a tablet PC or touch screen monitor is required to use Windows Tablet and Touch Technology that is available in these versions. Windows BitLocker encryption tool requires a USB 2.0 Flash drive or a TPM version 1.2 or higher motherboard chip.

Table 12.10 **Windows Vista memory maximum**

Windows Vista version	32-bit maximum memory	64-bit maximum memory
Starter	1GB	N/A
Home Basic	4GB	8GB
Home Premium	4GB	16GB
Business, Enterprise, and Ultimate	4GB	128GB*

*as of press time

Table 12.11 **Windows 7 hardware requirements**

Component	Minimum
Processor	1GHz
RAM	1GB for 32-bit or 2GB for 64-bit
Graphics	Support for DirectX9 or higher with WDDM driver
Hard drive space	16GB for 32-bit or 32GB for 64-bit

12

Windows XP, Vista, and 7

Sometimes older operating system drivers do work, but many times the older drivers do not function at all or properly. This is the cost of going to a more powerful operating system. The customer may also decide at this point not to upgrade, but to buy a computer with the desired version of Windows already installed instead.

The seventh determination you must make before upgrading Windows is whether or not any existing software applications are compatible. Use the Upgrade Advisor or contact the developer of each software application to determine if it is compatible. The information may be posted on the software developer Web site. Also, Microsoft has a list of compatible software on their Web site. Not all 16-bit applications can be used in 64-bit Windows versions, but try the Program Compatibility wizard once Windows is installed: *Start* button → *Control Panel* → *Programs* → *Programs and Features* → *Use an older program with this version of Windows*.

If the Program Compatibility wizard does not work, the Windows XP mode is an option. **Windows XP mode** is an optional program that can be downloaded and used in Windows Vista and 7 Professional, Ultimate, and Enterprise versions. Once it is downloaded and installed, access it by clicking on the *Start* button → *All Programs* → *Windows Virtual PC* → *Virtual Windows XP*. Hardware including CD/DVD and USB drives are normally accessible through Windows XP mode, but not all hardware may work in this environment. Also, Windows XP mode is not suited for graphic-intensive games or applications.

Windows XP mode can be customized for a specific Windows version. Right-click on the Windows XP mode *Start* button option and select *Properties* → *Compatibility* tab. A drop-down compatibility mode menu allows the choice of Windows versions starting with Windows 95. Note that an application installed in Windows XP mode appears in both the Windows XP mode application list (within the Windows Virtual PC folder) and in the Windows 7 application list.

Tech Tip

Use Windows Help and Support for software compatibility verification

Windows has a help function that can check for software compatibility. To access this tool, *Start* → *Help and Support* (XP)/*Search programs and files* (7) → type `Program Compatibility wizard`.

Once you have determined whether the software is compatible with Windows, you may have to obtain software patches, upgrades, or buy a new version. This is best done before installing Windows. Be proactive, not reactive—solve any problems you can *before* upgrading or installing any operating system. Such preparation is usually more work than the actual installation process, but any omitted steps will cost you more time.

In any upgrade, hardware change, or software change, backing up data is an essential step. Whether you do a clean install or an upgrade, if the user has data on the computer, it must be backed up before starting the installation process. Also, before backing up data, remove any unwanted files and/or applications that are no longer needed in order to free up hard drive space.

A "clean install" is when you install Windows on a hard drive partition (called *volumes* in Vista/7) that has no other operating system installed. With a clean install, you often need to migrate data from an old computer or another volume. Microsoft has a product that can be downloaded called Windows Easy Transfer. Windows Easy Transfer (`migwiz.exe`) copies files and operating system settings to another drive, to removable media, over a network, or to another storage location; the operating system is installed; and then the files and settings are re-applied to the upgraded computer. This tool can also be used when a computer is being replaced and a data migration is required, such as when Windows 7 is replacing XP.

Microsoft also has the **USMT** (User State Migration Tool), which IT staff use to perform large deployments of Windows. This tool is used from a command line for more control and customized settings including registry changes. The `scanstate.exe` and `loadstate.exe` commands are used to transfer file and user settings.

The last step in the pre-installation checklist is to remove any power or disk management tools that are loaded. They can interfere with the new tools provided with Windows and can prevent an operating system from installing.

Viruses

Before installing a new operating system on a computer that already has an operating system loaded, you should run a virus scan with the latest virus scanning software version. A **virus** is a computer program that is designed to do something to your computer that changes the way the computer originally operated. Examples include infecting the computer so it does not boot, infecting a particular application so it does not operate or performs differently, and erasing files. Some viruses are not written to cause harm but simply to cause mischief, such as a program that puts a picture on the screen.

Viruses can cause many unusual and frustrating problems during an operating system installation. Some technicians think that by high-level formatting the hard drive no virus can exist. This is a mistake. Do not take that chance. Take a few moments to scan the hard drive for viruses. Table 12.12 shows common virus types and their descriptions.

Table 12.12 **Virus types**

Virus	Description
BIOS virus	Designed to attach computers with Flash BIOS. Rewrites the BIOS code so the computer does not boot.
Boot sector (MBR) virus	Replaces or alters information in boot sectors or in the Master Boot Record. These viruses spread whenever you boot off a disk. Examples include Michelangelo, Junkie, and Ohio.
File virus	Replaces or attaches itself to a file that has a COM or EXE extension (an executable file). By attaching itself to this type of file, a virus can prevent the program from starting or operating properly. It can also be triggered for a particular event such as a date as well as load into RAM and affect other COM or EXE files. Examples include Friday the 13th, Enigma, Loki, and Nemesis.
Macro virus	Written in a specific language and attaches itself to a document created in a specific application such as Excel or Word. Once the document (along with the virus) is opened and loaded into memory, the virus can attach itself to other documents.
Trojan (horse) program	Does not replicate as a virus does, but does destroy data. Frequently hides a virus problem because it appears a legitimate program to a virus checker. When the virus executes, the computer does something the user does not expect such as put a message or picture on the screen. The virus does not replicate (copy itself somewhere else), but it can be used to gather information such as userids and passwords that can later be used to hack into the computer. Examples include Aids Information, Twelve Tricks A and B, and Darth Vader.
Stealth virus	Written to avoid antivirus software detection. When the antivirus program executes, the stealth virus provided the antivirus software with a fake image.
Polymorphic virus	Constantly changes in order to avoid detection by an antivirus program.
Worm virus	Makes a copy of itself from one drive to another and can use a network to replicate itself. The most common types of worm viruses today are in the form of email messages.
Phage virus	Re-writes an executable file with its own code, then destroys other programs and files.

Common symptoms of a virus are as follows:

- Computer does not boot
- Computer hard drive space is reduced
- Applications will not load
- An application takes longer to load or function than necessary
- Hard drive activity increases (especially when nothing is being done on the computer)
- An antivirus software message appears
- The number of hard drive sectors marked as bad steadily increases
- Unusual graphics or messages appear on the screen
- Files are missing (deleted)
- A message appears that the hard drive cannot be detected or recognized
- Strange sounds come from the computer

Tech Tip

Be responsible

A technician is responsible for ensuring that any computer deployed has an antivirus application installed and that the application is configured to receive virus signature updates. Educate users about viruses and what to do if a computer gets one.

If a virus is detected or even suspected, run an antivirus program. Note that the computer may have to be booted into Safe Mode, Recovery Console (XP), or System Recovery Options (Vista/7). Antivirus applications can be configured to run in manual mode (on demand) or as scheduled scans. Also quarantine the infected computer(s). This means you should disconnect the computer from the network until the computer is virus-free. Some antivirus programs can quarantine a computer automatically if the computer has a virus. Many antivirus software programs have the ability to quarantine files—files that appear to the antivirus program as possible virus-infected or suspicious files that might be dangerous. A message normally appears with a list of files that have been quarantined, and each one must be identified as a valid file or to be left in the quarantine (unusable) until a new version of the antivirus signature files has been updated and can identify the file.

The time to get an antivirus program is *before* a virus infects the computer because the damage may be irreversible, especially if backups are not performed. Always backup data files before upgrading to a new operating system. Backups are an important part of any computer support plan.

Some antivirus software can be set to load into memory when the computer boots and runs continuously. The antivirus software can prevent the upgrade or patch (service pack) from installing. Make sure you disable this feature when installing an operating system patch (service pack) or upgrade. Other types of software that can prevent an operating system from being upgraded are power management and disk management software/tools. Disable these utilities and applications before attempting an operating system installation or upgrade.

DEP (Data Execution Prevention)

DEP is a security measure implemented in both hardware and software to prevent malicious software from running on a Windows-based computer. DEP is always on and enabled for 64-bit versions of Windows, but the policy can be managed. With DEP that is hardware-based, the CPU supports enforcing no execute (AMD processors) or execute disable (Intel processors). The processor marks memory with an attribute indicating that data inside that memory location should not be executable (it should just be another type of data or code). Different processors have different capabilities, but at a minimum, the processor can display a message if code tries to execute from those memory locations marked as no execute or execute disable. Even if your CPU does not support this, you can have some protection through software-based DEP.

With software-enforced DEP, if a program tries to run from a memory location that should not have executable code, the application is closed and a message appears. Software-enforced DEP is available in Windows XP Service Pack 2 and higher and all versions of Vista and 7. To see this feature in Vista or 7, *System* (Vista) or *System and Security* (7) control panel link → *Security* (7) → *Advanced System Settings* link → in the *Performance* area, *Settings* button → *Data Execution Prevention* tab. Figure 12.2 shows the two options.

Notice in Figure 12.2 that you can turn off DEP for an individual program that you trust. You select the *Turn on DEP for all programs and services except those I select* radio button, select a program from the list displayed, and click *Add* or browse for a specific executable

Figure 12.2 **DEP on Vista and 7**

program and add it manually. The Data Execution Prevention window also shows at the bottom of the window whether the processor is capable of DEP.

Installation/Upgrade of Windows

After all the pre-installation steps are completed, you are ready to install Windows. The installation process is easy if you performed the pre-installation steps. Hands-on exercises follow that guides you through a clean installation (one where no other operating system is on the machine), an upgrade of XP, an installation of Vista, and an installation of Windows 7. The number one piece of advice to heed is to do your homework first. The number of possible problems will be greatly reduced.

During the Windows XP installation process, the computer must be restarted three times. This has been improved upon by the Windows Vista and 7 installation process. In the XP first phase, a selection must be made whether to upgrade or perform a clean installation, the product key must be entered, and a basic hardware check including available disk space must be accomplished. The computer restarts. After the restart, the second phase begins and setup runs in text mode. During this process, a partition to install Windows can be chosen and setup files are copied to the partition. The computer restarts and the third phase begins. During this portion, devices are installed, administrator password is entered, and the operating system is created. The system restarts a final time and the logon screen is presented. Windows Vista and 7 have a similar process in that you can partition the drive, select a preconfigured partition, and select a password.

Tech Tip

Windows XP/Vista/7 mandatory activation

Microsoft requires activation of Windows within 30 days. You can activate over the phone or the Internet. No name or personal information is required, but activation must occur.

Corporate Windows Deployment

Corporate computer installations are much more involved than any other type of deployment when adding new computers or upgrading old operating systems. Companies need automated installation tools to help with this process. Tools that can help with this are Windows XP's Sysprep tool, Symantec Corporation's Ghost program, Microsoft's Setup Manager, Windows SIM (System Image Manager), and MDT (Microsoft Deployment Toolkit).

The Sysprep tool is found on the XP CD in the Support\Tools folder. On Windows Vista and 7 it is now installed by default and located in the Windows\System32 folder. The purpose of Sysprep is to remove all unique identifiers (SIDs) from a machine before the computer is cloned (an exact copy of it is made). A **SID** (security identifier) is a unique number assigned by a network domain controller to every Microsoft-based computer.

Sysprep is used on a computer once it has Windows installed on it an all applications have been loaded. After the computer has been configured properly with updated drivers and each application has been tested, the cloning or disk imaging software is executed. An example of this type of software is Symantec Corporation's Ghost.

The disk imaging software makes an exact copy (a binary copy) of the files loaded on the hard drive. The copy is then pressed to a CD or put on a network drive to be copied onto other computers. Every computer must have the same basic hardware components as the original image. A program must be used after each computer is cloned to assign the unique identifiers. The third-party utility (such as Ghost Walker from Symantec) can be used to do this or Microsoft's Sysprep program can be used.

Microsoft's Setup Manager creates a text file that contains all the answers to questions asked during the installation process. The Setup Manager tool prompts for the installation process questions so an answer file called `UNATTEND.TXT` is created. This file is then used across the network to answer the questions without end user intervention.

Windows **SIM** (System Image Manager) is used in Windows Vista and 7 to create and configure answer files, install applications, apply service packs and updates to an image, and to add device drivers. Windows Vista/7 use the `UNATTEND.XML` file as an answer file.

To install Windows XP across a network, you must have a network card installed; the computer cabled to the network; and, the appropriate network protocol such as TCP/IP installed and configured. After logging onto the network, the technician installs XP using the `winnt` or `winnt32` command. Normally the company has an answer file so that once the process is started, the installation requires no interaction from the person doing the installation. One drawback when using this method is that network bandwidth is used to copy the installation files. Of course, this only installs the operating system and does not put any applications onto the computer that may be needed. Microsoft provided RIS (Remote Installation Services) and has since updated to WDS (Windows Deployment Services) to help when deploying Windows Vista and 7 across a network without using an optical disc.

When deploying Windows Vista or 7, licensing is handled a bit differently. Larger businesses buy a VLK (volume license key). When deploying Vista or 7, technical support staff have two choices—MAK or KMS. With **MAK** (Multiple Activation Key), the Internet or a phone call must be used to register one or more computers. This method has a limited number of activations, but more licenses can be purchased. The **KMS** (Key Management Service) method is used in companies with 25 or more computers to deploy. Technical support staff can also use a deployment tool that allows automating product key entry and customizing disc installation images so the computer users are not prompted for a key the first time they use a software package. KMS is a software application installed on a computer. All newly installed Vista- or 7-based computers register with the computer that has KMS installed. Every 180 days, the computers are re-activated for the Windows license. Each KMS key can be used on two computers up to 10 times.

WDT (Windows Deployment Toolkit) is a GUI shell that makes managing Windows deployment in a corporate environment easier. Tools such as USMT, mentioned earlier, ACT (Application Compatibility Toolkit), **MAP** (Microsoft Assessment and Planning Toolkit), and the volume licensing application are inside the MDT shell. From there, Windows can be deployed in LTI (Lite Touch Installation) mode, which deploys Windows without any other system management tool or in ZTI (Zero Touch Installation) mode. In ZTI mode, the MDT is used in conjunction with Microsoft's Configuration Manager.

An alternative method is to use a third-party utility to make an image of a manually configured hard drive. An example of this type of utility is Symantec's Ghost. A drawback to this method and any method that deploys across a network is that network bandwidth can be affected. An advantage of this method is that the operating system as well as applications can be loaded at one time.

Any existing data can be backed up to another hard drive, a network drive, or pressed to one or more optical discs. Remember to restore the data once the upgrade has been completed or the new computer installed.

Tech Tip

Back up data before upgrading

If upgrading an operating system, the user's data should be backed up before the upgrade process.

Verifying the Installation

In any upgrade or installation, verification that the upgrade is successful is critical in both the home and the business environment. If an upgrade has been done, verify that all applications still function. If a new installation has just been completed, ensure that all installed hardware is detected by Device Manager.

Reinitialize antivirus software

If the antivirus software was disabled through BIOS and/or through an application, re-enable it after the operating system installation is complete. Verify that all settings are in accordance with the user requirements and/or departmental/organizational standards.

12

Windows XP, Vista, and 7

Troubleshooting the Windows Installation

Installation problems can be caused by a number of factors. The following list shows the most common causes of problems and their solutions:

- Incompatible BIOS—Obtain compatible BIOS, replace the motherboard with one that has compatible BIOS, or do not upgrade/install Windows XP/Vista.
- BIOS needs to be upgraded—Upgrade (flash) the BIOS.
- Incompatible hardware drivers—Obtain the appropriate Windows version drivers from the hardware manufacturer (not Microsoft).
- Incompatible applications—Obtain upgrades from the software manufacturer, do not use the software, or do not upgrade the operating system.
- Minimum hardware requirements have not been met—Upgrade the hardware. The most likely things to check are the CPU and RAM.
- A virus is present—Run an antivirus program and remove the virus.
- Antivirus software is installed and active. It is halting the installation/upgrade—Disable through BIOS and/or through the application. Restart the Windows installation and re-enable once the operating system installation is complete.
- Pre-installation steps have not been completed—Go back through the list.
- The installation disc is corrupted (not as likely as the other causes)—Try the disc in another machine and see if you can see the contents. Check if a scratch or dirt is on the disc surface. Clean the disc as necessary.
- Incorrect registration key—Type in the correct key to complete the installation. The key is located on the disc or disc case.
- If the Windows XP installation cannot find a hard drive, it is most likely due to a SATA drive being used and a driver is not available for the controller. Download the driver, put on a floppy/Flash drive or use a software program such as nLite to create a custom XP installation CD that includes the downloaded driver.
- A STOP message occurs when installing a dual-boot system—Boot from the Windows XP, Vista, or 7 installation disc rather than the other operating system.

Installation halts

Try removing any nonessential hardware, such as network cards, modems, and USB devices, and start the installation again. Re-install the hardware once Windows is properly installed.

- The computer locks up during setup and shows a blue screen (commonly called the blue screen of death)—Check the BIOS and hardware compatibility. Also, if an error message appears, research the error on the Internet.
- A message appears during setup that a device driver was unable to load—Obtain the latest device drivers that are compatible and restart the setup program.
- After upgrading to Windows 7, the computer freezes. Boot to Safe Mode and check Device Manager for errors. If none seen, disable the following devices if present: video adapter, sound card, network card, USB devices and controller (unless keyboard/mouse is USB), CD/DVD, modem, unused ports. Enable each disabled device one at a time until the blue screen appears. Once the problem device is known, obtain the appropriate replacement driver.

- After the file copying has been completed, setup displays the message that it cannot set the required XP configuration information—A hardware conflict is normally the cause.
- A STOP 0x0000001E (0x800000003, 0xBFC0304, 0X0000000, 0x0000001) error occurs—There is either not enough disk space to load Windows, an incompatible or outdated driver installed, or the motherboard BIOS needs updating.
- A STOP 0x00000ED (0x, 0x, 0x, 0x) UNMOUNTABLE_BOOT_VOLUME error appears (the hexadecimal numbers may vary)—The problem is either the UDMA cable or settings or the file system is damaged. Check to see if a UDMA PATA IDE hard drive is installed and verify that the correct 80-wire, 40-pin cable is being used. If the cable is fine, go into the computer BIOS and use the *Fail-Safe* options for the IDE hard drive. If this is not the problem, use the CHKDSK /R command to repair file system damage.
- The Windows 7 0xC004F061 activation error is caused by a product key being used for an upgrade Windows 7 version and a previous Windows version was not on the computer when the installation was performed. If the drive was formatted *before* starting the installation, the upgrade product key cannot be used. Install 7 with the current Windows running or if you want to format the hard drive and an upgrade version is being used, do so through the Windows 7 installation process: boot with upgrade DVD, click *Custom (advanced)*, and select *Drive options (advanced)*.
- In Vista, the "upgrade" option has been disabled—To upgrade, start the installation from Windows" message appears—This might occur if you double-click the SETUP.EXE file from the installation DVD. If the computer has no operating system, boot from the Vista disc and select *Custom (advanced)*. Click to ensure the current operating system is upgradable to the Vista version being selected. If a 32-bit version of Windows is being upgraded, exit setup, remove the Vista installation disc, restart the computer with the 32-bit operating system, and restart the installation. If a 64-bit version of Windows is already installed, a Vista upgrade is not possible—only a clean install of Vista can be done.
- The following message appears: "The legacy OS does not meet the software update requirements: Service Pack 2 for Windows XP"—Exit the installation process, remove the installation media, reboot the computer to the original operating system, upgrade XP to the latest service pack, and start the Vista installation upgrade again.
- When booting from the Vista installation DVD, the Upgrade option does not display—Ensure the current operating system is upgradable to Vista. Then restart the computer and boot to the original operating system. Insert the Vista DVD. If it does not automatically start, use Windows Explorer to locate and double-click on the STARTUP.EXE file. Select the *Upgrade* option.

Two text files located in the folder in which Windows XP was loaded can be helpful in determining the installation problem—SETUPLOG.TXT and SETUPAPI.LOG. These files can be opened with any word processor including Notepad. Vista has two similar files called SETUPAPI.DEV.LOG and SETUPAPI.APP.LOG. Table 12.13 lists important log files that are created during Windows 7 setup.

Table 12.13   **Windows 7 Setup log files**

Log file location	Description
X:\Windows\setupapi.log	Device and driver changes, service pack and hotfix installations
X:\$Windows.~BT\Sources\Panther\setupact.log	Setup actions performed during the install
X:\$Windows.~BT\Sources\Panther\setuperr.log	Setup installation errors
X:\$Windows.~BT\Sources\Panther\PreGatherPnPList.log	Initial capture of devices information
X:\$Windows.~BT\Sources\Panther\miglog.xml	User directory structure and SID information
X:\WINDOWS\INF\setupapi.dev.log	Plug and play devices and driver information
X:\Windows\INF\setupapi.app.log	Application installation information
X:\Windows\Panther\PostGatherPnPList.log	Device information after the online configuration

Dual-Booting Windows

Sometimes users like to try a new operating system while keeping the old operating system loaded. A computer that has two operating .systems loaded is known as a dual-boot computer. If Windows is installed on an NTFS partition, only a Windows version that supports NTFS (NT and higher) can access files in the partition, if required.

When dual-booting, do the oldest operating system first

Any time a dual-boot or multi-boot situation is desired, the oldest operating system should be installed first. The operating systems need to be in separate hard disk partitions.

Once installed, the Windows Boot Manager window appears, showing the older version of Windows as "Earlier Version of Windows" and the newly added "Microsoft Windows Vista", "Windows 7" or both. From this screen you can choose the older operating system with the "Earlier Version of Windows" option or accept the default option. In Windows XP, these settings can be changed using the following process:

1. Open *Windows Explorer* and right-click on *Computer*. Select *Properties*.
2. Select the *Advanced system settings* link from the left pane.
3. From the Startup and Recovery section, select the *Settings* button. The default operating system can be selected from the drop-down menu in the System startup section. The time to display the options in the Windows Boot menu is selectable in seconds as well as via an enable/disable checkbox.

In Windows Vista or 7, the boot settings are changed using the `bcdedit` command.

1. Click *Start* button, click *All Programs*, and select *Accessories*.
2. Right-click on the *Command Prompt* option and select *Run as administrator*.
3. Type `bcdedit /?` to see a list of switches.

Tips for working with the BCDEDIT command follow in Table 12.14.

Table 12.14 **BCDEDIT tips**

BCDEDIT command	Description
`bcdedit /export` *filename*	Used to export the current BCD registry in case of mistake
`bcdedit /import` *filename*	Used to restore the BCD from a backup file
`bcdedit /enum`	Used to view the existing boot menu entries
`bcdedit /default` *id*	Used to configure the default entry. *id* is the identifier for the specific Windows version; for example, if the older version of Windows XP is shown as {*ntldr*}, then the command would be `bcdedit /default {ntldr}`.
`bcdedit /timeout` *seconds*	Used to change the time the menu displays

Reloading Windows

Sometimes it's necessary to do a re-installation (sometimes called an in-place upgrade or a repair installation) of Windows XP, Vista, or 7, such as when Windows will not start normally, in Safe Mode, or has a registry corruption that cannot be solved with System Restore. Before you reload Windows, back up any existing data. The installation process should not disturb the data, but there is always that chance.

There are two ways to reload Windows XP from the XP CD: (1) from within a booted XP environment or (2) by booting from the XP CD. If you boot XP and insert the

All existing system restore points are removed when Windows is re-installed

Once Windows has been installed, no preexisting restore points are kept. You should ensure that the System Restore utility is enabled and backup your data once Windows is installed. You should also apply any service packs and patches once the re-installation is complete.

CD, select the *Install Windows XP option* → *Upgrade (Recommended)* in the *Installation Type* menu → *Next* → accept the license → *Next* → enter the product key → *Next* → select *I accept this agreement* → *Next* → follow the instructions on the screen. If you boot from the CD, press Enter to setup Windows XP now → press F8 on the license agreement → select your current Windows XP installation → press R to repair XP → follow the directions on the screen.

This is less common with Vista and 7. Also, Windows Vista and 7 have tools that help with startup problems, a corrupt registry, and missing or corrupt boot configuration files. These tools are covered later in the chapter.

Updating Windows

Almost daily new vulnerabilities are found in every operating system. Windows has a method called Windows Update or Automatic Updates for upgrading the operating system. To configure Windows XP for automatic updates, click the *Start* button → *Control Panel* → *Classic* view → *System* control panel → *Automatic Updates* tab. Figure 12.3 shows this screen and Table 12.15 details the options.

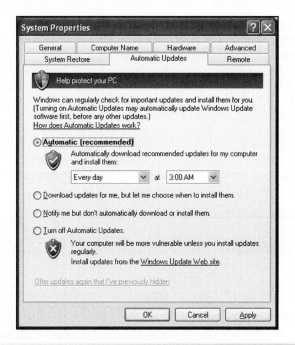

Figure 12.3   **Windows XP Automatic Updates window**

Table 12.15   **Windows XP Automatic Updates options**

Automatic Update Option	Description
Automatic (recommended)	The computer automatically downloads an update from Microsoft across the Internet and installs the update(s). You can do it daily or weekly and choose the time. The computer must be on.
Download updates for me, but let me choose when to install them	Once the updates are downloaded an icon appears in the notification area. You can point to the icon to get a message about the status. You can double-click the icon to install the updates.
Notify me but don't automatically download or install them	Windows recognizes when you connect to the Internet and searches for updates, but does not download them. A message appears telling you when an update is available and asks if you want to download or install it.
Turn off automatic updates	Automatic updates are disabled. Sometimes this option is required when installing some software, but it is not an option that you would normally choose.

Some Windows updates require a computer restart

After some updates have been downloaded and installed on the computer, a restart is necessary. However, if you are working on something important, you have the option of restarting later.

One way to access Windows Update settings in Vista or 7 from the *Start* button → *All Programs* → *Windows Update* → *Change Settings*. From this window in Vista, only two options are available: (1) Use recommended settings and (2) Install important updates only. The recommended settings option automatically updates and installs updates classified as "Important" and "Recommended." The second setting automatically downloads and installs only updates that are classified as "Important" by Microsoft. For better fine tuning, technicians should always use the *Windows Update* control panel link in Vista and 7.

Windows XP/Vista notification update icon

In the taskbar notification area, an icon appears when an update has been downloaded and is ready to be installed in XP and if a member of the Administrator group in Vista. The icon that appears in XP is shown on the left.

The Windows Vista and 7, *Windows Update* link is available from the *System and Maintenance* (Vista)/*System and Security* (7) control panel link → *Windows Update* (Vista/7) → *Change Settings*. The Important Updates section has the following options:

- Install updates automatically (recommended)
- Download updates but let me choose whether to install them
- Check for updates but let me choose whether to download and install them
- Never check for updates (not recommended)

See Table 12.15 for the descriptions since Windows Vista and 7 options are worded similarly.

There are also some options such as how to handle recommended options, whether or not all users on the computer can install updates, and whether or not to receive updates for other Microsoft products such as Internet Explorer at the same time as receiving operating system updates. If a newly installed service pack causes problems and must be removed, use the `SPUNINST.EXE` command.

Updates must be installed

Depending on which option is chosen from the System control panel, updates may be downloaded, but you may have to manually install them. The system is not protected unless the updates are installed.

To customize how the notifications appear in Vista, right-click on the *Start* button and select *Properties*. Select the *Notification Area* tab and click on the *Customize* button. In Windows 7, right-click the *Start* button → *Properties* → *Taskbar* tab → locate the *Notification area* section → *Customize* button → locate *Windows Update* option under *Icons* column → select the appropriate behavior.

You must be an administrator to change Automatic Update settings

You must be logged in as the computer administrator (Windows XP Home Edition) or as administrator or a user that is a member of the Administrators group (Windows XP Professional Edition, Vista, or 7) in order to modify Automatic Updates settings.

Backing Up/Restoring the Windows Registry

The **registry** is a database that contains information about the Windows environment including installed hardware, installed software, and users. The registry should be backed up whenever the computer is fully functional and when any software or hardware changes are made.

Back up the registry

The registry should be backed up and restored on a working computer *before* disaster hits. The time to learn how to restore the registry is not when the computer is down.

The registry can be backed up and restored several different ways. The three most common methods are the REGEDIT program, the Backup utility, and the System Restore tool (covered later in the chapter). The REGEDIT program allows you to export the registry to a file that has an extension of .REG. The file can be imported back into the computer if the computer fails. The REGEDIT program and the Backup utility both back up the entire registry.

The Backup utility in XP is accessed through *Start* button → *All Programs* → *Accessories* → *System Tools* → *Backup*. In Vista from the *Start* menu → *System and Maintenance* control panel → *Backup and Restore Center* link. The Backup utility is the preferred method for backing up the Windows registry, but in Vista/7 the full version of the Backup tool (the part that can back up the registry) is only available in Windows Vista/7 Business, Professional, Enterprise, or Ultimate versions. The backup option to look for specifically in Windows XP is the System State, which is discussed in the next section.

Backing Up and Restoring the Windows System State

One option available in the Windows XP Backup utility is the System State. The **System State** is a group of important Windows XP files including the registry, the system files, the boot files, and the COM+ Class Registration database. With the Backup utility, you cannot backup or restore these items individually. They are all needed because they depend on one another to operate properly. The Backup utility is accessed through *Start* button → *All Programs* → *Accessories* → *System Tools* → *Backup*. The Windows XP System State Backup exercise demonstrates this process. The registry files are located in a folder normally labeled *%systemroot%*\Repair\ Regbackup (which is normally C:\WINNT\REPAIR\BACKUP or C:\WINDOWS\REPAIR\ BACKUP, depending on the type of installation). The registry can be restored without having to restore the other System State files.

Who can use the *Backup* program?

In order to use the *Backup* program, you must be an Administrator (XP, Vista, or 7) or in XP, a member of the Backup Operators group.

In order to correct a problem with the system files, registry, or Windows XP boot failure, you must restore the registry. You may also have to restore the System State files (which includes the registry) to make the system operational again. To start the restoration process, install Windows XP to the same folder that it was installed in originally. When you are prompted to format the hard drive volume or leave it, select the *Leave the current file system intact* option. Use the Backup utility to restore the System State and/or the registry (*All Programs* → *Accessories* → *System Tools* → *Backup*). Click the *Restore* tab and select the device that holds the backed-up files.

The Windows Vista and 7 Backup and Restore link can also be used to backup the system state (even though that option is not shown like it is in XP). This link can also be used to backup files and an entire disk image. To access this link, click on the *Start* button → *Control Panel* → *System and Maintenance* (Vista)/*System and Security* (7) → *Backup and Restore* → *Create a system repair disc*.

Configuring Windows Overview

One of the most common windows used by technicians is the *Control Panel* window. A control panel is a method for configuring various components. Each Control Panel icon represents a Windows utility that allows you to customize a particular part of the Windows environment. The number of control panels displayed depends on the type of computer and the components contained within the computer. Windows has two control panel views—*Classic* and *Category*. Figure 12.4 shows the Windows 7 control panel using Category view.

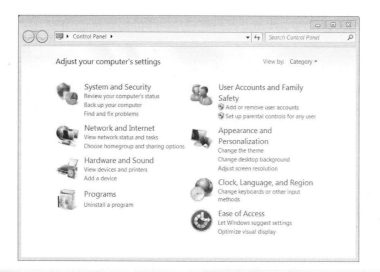

Figure 12.4   **Windows 7 control panel categories**

Technicians must know which control panel category to use for changing a computer's configuration. Table 12.16 shows the common Windows XP control panel categories and the function of each. Table 12.17 shows the control panels for Windows Vista and 7. Hands-on exercises at the end of the chapter help familiarize you with several control panel categories.

Table 12.16   **Windows XP control panel categories**

Control panel	Function
Appearance and Themes	Used to change the computer's theme, background color, screen saver, and resolution. Also used to access the traditional Display, Folder options, and Taskbar and Start Menu control panels.
Network and Internet Connections	Used to configure or change an Internet connection, connect to a business' network, and configure/change a home network. Also used to access the traditional Internet options and Network Connections control panels.
Add or Remove Programs	Used to add, change, or delete software.
Sounds, Speech, and Audio Devices	Used to adjust system volume, change sound scheme, and change speaker settings. Also used to access the traditional Sounds and Audio Devices and Speech control panels.
Performance and Maintenance	Used to view basic computer information, adjust visual effects, make more hard disk space available, perform a backup, perform hard disk maintenance. Also used to access the traditional Administrative Tools, Power Options, Schedule Tasks, and System control panels.
Printers and Other Hardware	Used to access printers or fax printers and add a new printer. Also used to access the traditional Game Controllers, Keyboard, Mouse, Phone and Modem Options, Printers and Faxes, and Scanner and Cameras control panels.
User Accounts	Used to create or change an account, change the way a user logs on or off, and view each user account.
Date, Time, Language, and Regional Options	Used to set date and time, change the format of numbers, and add a language. Also used to access the traditional Date and Time and Regional and Language Options control panels.
Accessibility Options	Used to configure screen contrasts and configure vision, hearing, and mobility features. Also used to access the traditional Accessibility Options control panel.

Table 12.17	Windows Vista/7 control panel categories*
Control panel category	**Function**
System and Maintenance (Vista)/System and Security (7)	Used to access the Backup and Restore utility, System, Windows Update, Power Options, Device Manager, and Administrative Tools. The Windows Firewall and Action Center are available in Windows 7.
Security (Vista)	Used to access the Security Center, Windows Firewall settings, Windows Update, Windows Defender, Internet Options, and Parental Controls
Network and Internet	Used to access the Network and Sharing Sharing Internet Options, People Near Me, Change your home page, and Sync Center
Hardware and Sound	Used to access the Printers, AutoPlay, Sound, Mouse, Power Options, Personalization, Scanners and Cameras, Keyboard, Device Manager, Phone and Modem Options, Game, Windows SlideShow, Pen and Input Devices, Color Management, and Tablet PC Settings
Programs	Used to access the Programs and Features, Windows Defender, Default Programs, Windows SlideShow, and Windows Sidebar Properties
Mobile PC	Used on laptops to access the Windows Mobility Center, Power Options, Personalization, Tablet PC Settings, Pen and Input Devices, and Sync Center
User Accounts and Family Safety	Used to access the User Accounts, Parental Controls, and Windows CardSpace
Appearance and Personalization	Used to access the Personalization as well as the Taskbar and Start menu links
Clock, Language, and Region	Used to access the Date and Time as well as the Region and Language Options links
Additional Options	Holds special control panels that are system-specific such as a NVidia video disc play or Java control panel.

*Some Vista/7 versions or computers will not have all of the selections within a category or even a specific category.

Configuring Windows

Technicians must frequently add new hardware and software using the operating system. Windows has specific tools for these functions. Using the correct procedure is essential for success. The following sections highlight many of the tasks a technician must perform:

- Adding devices
- Removing hardware components
- Adding a printer
- Installing/removing software

Hardware devices are physical components that connect to the computer. A **device driver** is a piece of software that allows hardware to work with a specific operating system. Some device drivers are automatically included with Windows and are updated continuously through Windows updates. A technician must be aware of what hardware is installed into a system so that the latest compatible drivers can be downloaded and installed.

Adding Devices

Plug and play devices are hardware and software designed to automatically be recognized by the operating system. These devices include USB devices; IEEE 1394 devices; SCSI devices; PC Card and CardBus devices; PCI/PCIe devices; and printers. USB, IEEE 1394, PC Card devices, and CardBus devices can be added or removed with power applied. Adapters are installed and removed with the computer powered off and the power cord removed.

The key to a successful device installation includes the following:

- Possessing the most up-to-date device driver for the specific installed operating system
- Following the directions provided by the device manufacturer

Once a device is installed, power on the computer. The Windows *Found New Hardware* wizard appears. Windows XP attempts to find a driver for the new device. Plug and play devices make use of a special `.CAB` (cabinet) file called `DRIVER.CAB` located in *%winroot%*\Driver *Cache\i386* folder (where *%winroot%* is normally `C:\WINNT` or `C:\WINDOWS`). This file contains over 2,500 compressed files. If Windows XP detects new hardware, it will automatically search `DRIVER.CAB` for a driver. If a driver cannot be found, a dialog box appears. The best policy with any operating system is to use the latest driver even if the operating system detects the device. Hands-On Exercise 16 outlines how to install a new hardware driver.

Windows Vista and 7 do not use the `DRIVER.CAB` system. Instead, it uses driver packages that are stored in an indexed database. The drivers are stored in the Windows\System32\DriverStore\FileRepository folder. All driver files that are not part of the operating system must be imported into this folder before the driver package can be installed. Drivers created for earlier Windows versions may require updating.

Installing a device driver requires Administrator rights

Remember that if the operating system cannot configure a device and prompts for a device driver, you must have Administrator rights to install the driver.

Tech Tip

Some Windows device drivers use **digital signatures**, which is sometimes called driver signing. The digital signature confirms that the hardware or updated driver being installed is compatible with Windows and has not been changed. The digital signature indicates that the driver was tested with Windows and is compatible with the operating system. Digital signatures are required for 64-bit kernel mode drivers in Windows Vista and 7.

In Windows XP, there are three file signature verification options—*Ignore*, *Warn*, and *Block*. Table 12.18 shows what these three options do.

Table 12.18	Windows XP file signature verification options
Option	**Purpose**
Ignore	Allows all device drivers to be installed regardless if a digital signature is present or not
Warn	Displays a warning message whenever a driver that does not have a digital signature is attempted
Block	Prevents any device drivers that do not have a digital signature from being installed

To modify how drivers are handled in Windows Vista, access the *System and Maintenance* control panel → *System* → *Advanced system settings* link → *Continue* button → *Hardware* tab → *Windows Update Driver Settings* button. The three options available are as follows.

- Check for drivers automatically (recommended)
- Ask me each time I connect a new device before checking for drivers
- Never check for drivers when I connect a device

For Windows 7, use the *System and Security* control panel → *System* → *Advanced system settings* link → *Hardware* tab → *Device Installation Settings* button. The options available in Windows 7 are as follows.

- Yes, do this automatically (recommended)
- No, let me choose what to do
  - ❏ Always install the best driver software from Windows Update
  - ❏ Install driver software from Windows Update if it is not found on my computer
  - ❏ Never install driver software from Windows Update

Windows XP has a control panel called *Add Hardware* or if using control panel categories, the *Printers and Other Hardware* category → *Add Hardware*. The *Add Hardware* wizard allows hardware configuration and is used for hardware that is not automatically recognized by Windows XP. It is also used for plug and play devices that don't install properly with Windows XP's automatic detection. You must have Administrator privileges in order to load device drivers for new hardware.

In Vista and 7, most hardware is automatically detected. In Vista, there is no Add Hardware control panel, but in Windows 7 there is an *Add a device* link in the Hardware and Sound control panel group. Hands-On Exercise 18 explains how to do this.

Driver roll back requires Administrator rights

You must have Administrator rights to access or use the *Driver roll back* option.

Device Manager is used to view installed hardware devices, enable or disable devices, troubleshoot a device, view and/or change system resources such as IRQs and I/O addresses, update drivers, and access the *Driver roll back* option. The **Driver roll back** option is a new feature in Windows XP and is available in Windows Vista and 7. It allows an older driver to be re-installed when the new driver causes problems.

If the device driver has not been updated, driver roll back will not be possible and a message screen displays stating this fact. The troubleshooting tool should be used instead to troubleshoot the device. Hands-On Exercise 16 details how to use the driver roll back feature.

Sometimes Windows can install the wrong driver for an older device or adapter. From Device Manager, right-click the device and you can uninstall the device driver or disable it. Sometimes the computer must reboot and Windows will re-install the wrong driver (again). The solution to this is to disable the device and then manually install it. Hands-On Exercise 17 illustrates how to disable a device. To manually install new hardware in Windows XP, use the following steps:

Put oldest adapters closest to the power supply

Place older adapters closest to the power supply because Windows checks expansion slots in order starting with the closest to the power supply. By putting the older adapters in these slots, Windows will allocate system resources to the older adapters first and there is less chance of system resource conflicts.

1. Click the *Start* button and select the *Control Panel* option.
2. If in *Category* view → *Printers and Other Hardware* → *Add Hardware* from the left pane. If in *Classic* view → double-click the *Add Hardware* icon. The *Add Hardware* wizard starts.
3. Make sure the new hardware is physically connected. Select *Yes, I have already connected the hardware* → *Next*.
4. Use the Installed hardware scroll bar to find and select the *Add a new hardware device* checkbox → *Next*.
5. Select the manual option and select the type of hardware being installed. Scroll through the manufacturer list or have an XP-compatible driver ready and click the *Have Disk* button to install the appropriate driver. Click the *Next* button to finish the device driver installation.

Too many tray icons

Many programs and some drivers place icons in the system tray (the area to the right of the taskbar). Vista and 7 do a better job of consolidating them, but if they are not used, remove them. Right-click on *Start* button → *Properties* → *Notification Area* tab → *Customize* button.

To manually install a driver in Windows Vista or 7, follow these steps:

1. Open the *Device Manager* link by using the *System and Maintenance* (Vista)/*System and Security* (7) control panel.
2. Expand categories as needed to locate the device for which the driver is to be installed. Note that to display hidden devices in Device Manager, select the *Show hidden devices* from the *View* menu option.
3. Right-click on the device name and select *Update Driver Software*.
4. Select *Browse my computer for driver software*, click *Let me pick from a list of device drivers on my computer*, and select *Have Disk*. Click the *Browse* button to locate the extracted files. Click on the *.inf* file designed to work with Vista.
5. Follow the dialogs that continue to update the driver. If you are prompted with a warning about driver compatibility, you can click *No* and continue installing the driver. You can always remove it or roll back the driver if it does not install correctly or work.

If an `.INF` file cannot be found in a folder from your driver download, look in subfolders or other folders that might hold the file. You could always download the driver again and pay attention to the folder name in which the driver is stored. If there are multiple `.INF` files in the folder, you may have to try them one at a time until you find the one that works with your hardware. Always reboot Windows after a driver installation, even if the system does not prompt for a reboot.

In Vista or 7, if you cannot install a device driver by its installation program, you can try running the installation program in compatibility mode, try using administrative credentials, or try manually installing it using Device Manager. To run the driver installation program in compatibility mode, locate and right-click on the executable file for the driver installation program. Select *Properties* → *Compatibility* tab → enable the *Run this program in compatibility mode for* checkbox → select a version of Windows XP → click *OK*. Double-click the executable file to start the installation process.

To use administrative credentials in Windows Vista or 7, locate the executable file used to start the driver installation process. Right-click on the filename and select *Run as administrator*. Provide the administrator password if required. Click *Continue*. Follow the installation instructions as normal.

System Restore

If an unsigned device driver installing/uninstalling incompatible software, installing incompatible device drivers that will not uninstall, or downloading content causes a problem, you might be able to use the System Restore utility. The **System Restore** utility is a program that makes a snapshot image of the registry and backs up certain dynamic system files. The program does not affect your email or personal data files. This program is similar to the Last Known Good Configuration Advanced Boot Options menu item (but more powerful). Each snapshot is called a **restore point**, and multiple restore points are created on the computer and you can select which one to use. Restore points are usually created once a day, but you can do one at any time especially before doing an important upgrade. System Restore is your number one tool for solving problems within the operating system and registry.

System Restore can also be used if you suspect that the registry is corrupt. For example, if an application that worked fine yesterday, but today displays a message that the application cannot be found, you may have a virus, a corrupt application executable file, or a corrupt registry. Run an antivirus check first with updated virus definitions. If free of viruses, use the System Restore utility to roll back the system to yesterday or the day before this problem occurred. Sometimes System Restore works best if executed from Safe Mode (covered later in the chapter). If System Restore does not fix the problem, re-install the application.

> **If low on disk space, disable System Restore**
>
> If disk space is an issue, you can disable the *System Restore* utility until you add a second hard drive or upgrade the one you have. Open *Windows Explorer*, right-click *My Computer* (XP)/*Computer* (Vista/7) → select *Properties* → *System Restore* tab (XP)/*Advanced system settings* then *System Protection* tab (7) → *Turn off System Restore* checkbox.

System Restore requires NTFS and can be executed from Windows Vista/7 by typing `system restore` or `rstrui` in the *Start Search* (Vista)/*Search programs and files* (7) textbox from the *Start* menu. Windows Vista and 7 use a different type of System Restore technology than Windows XP used; Vista and 7 use **Shadow Copy**, which uses a block-level image instead of monitoring certain files for file changes. Backup media can be CDs, DVDs, Flash devices, other hard drives, and server storage, but not tape.

Tech Tip

You can run System Restore from a command prompt

If Windows XP does not load properly, you can execute it from a command prompt with the command `%systemroot%\system32\restore\rstrui.exe`. In Windows Vista/7 the path is `%systemroot%\system32\rstrui.exe`.

Adding a Printer

Printers can be connected to a computer through the printer's parallel port, USB port, or a local area network (wired or wireless). Only USB printers will be covered in this chapter. Networked printers will be discussed in Chapter 13 on networks.

Windows can automatically detect printers. If Windows detects a printer, the operating system has the potential to automatically install drivers, update the registry, and allocate system resources to the printer. Automatically detected printers are normally USB, FireWire, or infrared printers.

To install a USB printer, always follow the manufacturer's directions. Normally, there is an installation disk that may have to be executed before connecting the printer. Connect the printer to the appropriate computer port with a cable. Power on the printer. A wizard normally detects and leads you through the installation process. Update the driver once the installation process has finished.

In Windows Vista and 7, some drivers are available from the operating system and some are available through Windows Update. In other cases, you need to install the drivers using a disc or downloaded file provided by the printer manufacturer. To install or update printer drivers using Vista/7, follow these steps:

1. Open the *Hardware and Sound* control panel and select the *Printers* (Vista)/*Devices and Printers* (7) link.
2. Right-click on the printer for which you need a new driver and select *Run as administrator*. Right-click on the printer again and select *Properties*. (Note that some printers have their own control panel and have their driver accessed through the *Printer Properties* link rather than the *Properties* link.) Provide an Administrator password if required.
3. Select the *Advanced* tab.
4. Select *New Driver* and follow the directions on the screen provided by the Add Printer Driver wizard.

The most effective method is to download the driver from the printer manufacturer's Web site. To determine what version of Windows you are using, use the *Start* menu to select *All Programs*. Select *Accessories* and *System Tools*. Ensure *System Summary* is selected on the left. The *OS Name* and *Version* are on the right.

If a printer connected to a Windows XP computer has a TCP/IP connection, manually install the printer using the preceding steps, except instead of selecting the *Local printer* option, select *Standard TCP/IP Port* → *Next* twice → enter the printer name or IP address, the port name → *Next*. The *Install Printer Software* window appears and the same steps are used as a local printer.

Tech Tip

Identifying the default printer

In the Printers folder, the default printer has a check mark next to the icon.

In Vista or 7, to install a network printer, always use the information that comes with the printer. Windows Vista has a wizard that helps with this. From the *Printers* section accessed from the *Hardware and Sound* control panel, select the *Add a printer* link. From the

Add Printer Wizard, select *Add a network, wireless or Bluetooth printer*. To configure a printer as a default printer (the printer that applications normally use), locate and right-click on the printer. Click on *Set as Default Printer*.

Removing Hardware Devices

Windows normally detects when hardware has been removed and the operating system automatically removes the device's driver(s). If Windows does not automatically detect the device removal, you must manually remove the drivers. Hands-On Exercise 17 describes how to remove the driver.

If you are removing a printer from a Windows XP system, use the *Printers* control panel: *Start* button → *Settings* → *Printers* → right-click the printer you want to delete → *Delete*. In Vista or 7, use the *Hardware and Sound* control panel link, *Printers* (Vista)/*Devices and Printers* (7), right-click on the printer, and select *Delete*.

Installing/Removing Software

No computer is fully functional without software. One thing you should know about the newer Windows versions is that they may not support some of the older 16-bit software. Use the Program Compatibility wizard or download and use the Windows XP mode virtual environment for older applications loaded in Windows Vista and 7. Most software today is 32-bit, comes on CD or DVD and includes an autorun feature. If the disc has the autorun feature, an installation wizard steps you through installing the software when the disc is inserted into the drive. If there is not an autorun feature on the disc, then the Add or Remove Programs control panel is used to install or remove the software.

To access the Add or Remove Programs control panel in Windows XP, click the *Start* button → *Control Panel* → *Add or Remove Programs* → *Add New Programs* → *CD or Floppy* button and ensure the software disc is inserted in the appropriate drive. If a SETUP.EXE file cannot be found on the designated disk, the system prompts with a dialog box. Use the *Browse* button to locate the installation file. Click the *Finish* button to complete the process.

To remove a software application in Windows XP, use the same Add or Remove Programs control panel; instead of clicking Add New Programs, click the *Change or Remove Programs* icon in the left panel. A list of installed applications appears. Locate the software to be removed and click its name → *Remove* → when asked if you are sure you want to remove this software, click the *OK* button and close the *Control Panel* window. Some applications have their own uninstall program. Refer to the application's *Help* file or look in the application's folder for an uninstall icon. The *Add or Remove Programs* control panel can also be used to update operating system components. Hands-On Exercises 20 and 21 illustrate these concepts.

In Windows Vista and 7, the *Programs* control panel is used to add and remove applications. This link is also used to configure which programs are the default programs such as for email or a Web browser. Desktop gadgets in the Aero environment can be customized from here as well.

Once an application is installed in Windows XP, Vista, or 7, launch the application by clicking the *Start* button → *All Programs* → locate the application name and click it. If the application does not appear on the list, do not panic. The most frequently used program names appear in the left Start button panel.

Microsoft Management Console

The **Microsoft Management console**, more often called **Computer Management console**, holds snap-ins or tools used to maintain the computer. To access the console, click the *Start* button → *Control Panel*. In XP, select the *Performance and Maintenance* category → *Administrative Tools* → *Computer Management*. In Vista, select the *System and Maintenance* control panel; in Windows 7, select the *System and Security* control panel link → *Administrative Tools* → double-click on *Computer Management*.

12

Windows XP, Vista, and 7

Tech Tip

Adding Administrative Tools to the *Start* button

To add the administrative tools to the *Start* button's *All Programs* option, right-click an empty space on the *Taskbar → Properties → Start Menu* tab → *Customize*. In XP, select the *Advanced* tab → use the *Start* menu items section's vertical scroll bars to locate the *System Administrative Tools* section → *Display on the All Programs menu* radio button → *OK* button twice. In Vista/7, scroll to the *System Administrative Tools* section and select a radio button to put the tools either on All Programs or on the Start menu.

Figure 12.5 shows the Microsoft Computer Management console screen.

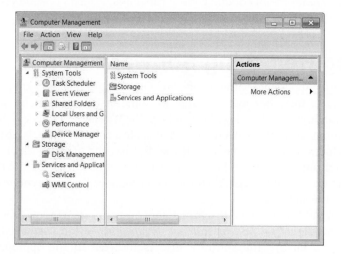

Figure 12.5   **Microsoft Computer Management console**

The Computer Management console allows a technician to manage shared folders and drives, start and stop services, look at performance logs and system alerts, and access Device Manager to troubleshoot hardware problems.

The three major tool categories found in the Computer Management console are *System Tools*, *Storage*, and *Services and Applications*. The System Tools include Event Viewer and Performance Logs and Alerts (XP), Shared Folders, Local Users and Groups, Task Scheduler (Vista/7), Reliability and Performance (Vista), Performance (7), and Device Manager.

The Shared Folders tool is used to view shares, sessions, and open files. Shares can be folders that have been shared on the computer, printers, or a network resource such as a scanner. Sessions list network users who are currently connected to the computer as well as the network users' computer names, the network connection type (Windows, NetWare, or Macintosh), how many resources have been opened by the network user, how long the user has been connected, and whether or not this user is connected using the Guest user account. Open files are files that are currently opened by network users. In order to use the Shared Folders tool, you must be a member of the Administrators or Power Users group (XP only).

In the left Computer Management window's pane, expand the *Shared Folders* option and click the *Shares* option. The computer's network shares appear in the right pane. Double-click any of the shares to view the Properties window. From this window, using the *Share Permissions* or *Security* tabs, permissions can be set for shared resources. Permissions are covered later in the chapter. Figure 12.6 shows the Properties window for a shared folder called *Sharp*.

The Local Users and Groups tool is used to create and manage accounts for those who use the computer or computer resources from a remote network computer. These accounts are considered local users or local groups and are managed from the computer being

Figure 12.6   Computer Management console—*Shares* window

worked on. In contrast, domain or global users and groups are administered by a network administrator on a network server. Permissions are granted or denied to files, folders, and network resources such as a shared printer or scanner. Rights can also be assigned. Rights are computer actions such as performing a backup or shutting down the computer. Open the *Local Users and Groups* option by expanding the *Local Users and Groups* selection in the *Computer Management* window. Double-click the *Users* option and a list of current users displays in the right pane. Figure 12.7 shows an example of local users that have been created for a Windows 7 computer.

Notice in Figure 12.7 how the Guest account has a small down arrow in the lower-right corner of its icon. (In Windows XP, it is a red X.) This means that the account has been disabled. In Vista or 7, double-click the *Guest* icon. Look at the *Account is disabled* checkbox to see if the account is disabled. The box is checked by default, meaning that the Guest account is not available for use. In XP, Vista, and 7, to create a new user click the *Action* menu option and select *New User*.

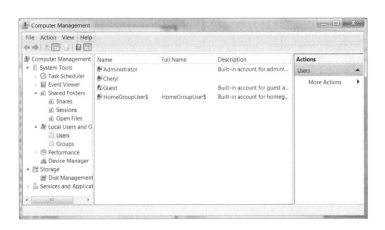

Figure 12.7   Computer Management console Local Users and Groups—*Users* window

Windows Vista and 7 have two types of user accounts: Standard User and Administrator. The Administrator account has full control over the system, as it always has in Windows. By default, the Standard User cannot install most applications or change system settings. All users on the computer should have a standard user account that is used for everyday use. Any account designated as an Administrator account should be used only to log onto the system to make system changes and install new software. These two accounts are affected by a new feature in Windows Vista/7 called UAC (User Access Control). UAC works in conjunction with Internet Explorer 7 and higher, Windows Defender, and Parental Controls to provide a heightened awareness to security issues. A UAC message appears anytime something occurs that normally would require an administrator-level decision to make changes to the system. An application that has a security shield icon overlay is going to display a UAC prompt when executed. If a standard user is logged in, a message appears stating that the task is prohibited or that Administrator credentials must be provided (and the Administrator password entered to proceed). This is to protect users from themselves as well as software that is trying to change the system. Even if a person is logged in with an Administrator account, the UAC prompt appears to confirm the action that is about to be performed.

The following configurations help with UAC:

- To configure a specific application to run in an elevated mode—meaning it has the administrator access token given to it or permission given to it to run—right-click on the application and select *Properties → Compatibility* tab → under the Privilege level select *Run this program as administrator → OK*.
- If a user demands that the UAC be disabled, use the System Configuration window (`msconfig`) *Tools* tab. Select the *Disable UAC* option (Vista) or *Change UAC Settings* (7). Also, an individual account can be changed through the *Change security settings* (Vista)/*Change User Account Control settings* (7) link from within the User Accounts control panel.
- To disable the administrator approval mode in Vista Business, Enterprise, and Ultimate, and Windows 7 Professional and Ultimate, type `secpol.msc` in the *Start Search* (Vista)/*Search programs and files* (7) textbox and press ⏎Enter. In the Local Security Settings section, double-click *Local Policies* → double-click *Security Options* → scroll down, locate, and double-click on *User Account Control: Run all administrators in Admin Approval Mode* → select *Disabled → OK*.
- To disable UAC from prompting for credentials to install applications in Vista Business, Enterprise, or Ultimate or Windows 7 Professional or Ultimate, type `secpol.msc` in the *Start Search* (Vista)/*Search programs and files* (7) textbox and press ⏎Enter. From the *Local Security Settings* section, double-click *Local Policies* → double-click *Security Options* → scroll down, locate, and double-click on *User Account Control: Detect application installations and prompt for elevation* → select *Disabled → OK*.

Device Manager is used after installing a new hardware device and seeing if Windows recognizes the device. It is also used to change or view hardware configuration settings, view and install device drivers, return (roll back) to a previous device driver version, disable/enable/uninstall devices, and print a summary of all hardware installed. Expand a section. Double click any device and the Properties window appears. The General tab can contain a *Troubleshoot* button that can help diagnose hardware problems. Click the *Device Manager* option in the Computer Management window's left pane and the Device Manager hardware categories appear in the right pane. Expand any category to view the individual hardware devices. Double-click any hardware device to open the device's Properties window. Figure 12.8 shows the Device Manager window.

The Storage Computer Management category includes Removable Storage, Disk Defragmenter, and Disk Management tools in Windows XP and just the Disk Management tool in Windows Vista/7. The Removable Storage XP tool allows creation and management of media libraries that track where data is stored on removable disks such as Zip disks, CDs, disk changers, and jukeboxes.

The Windows Disk Defragmenter tool analyzes hard drive volumes and consolidates files and folders into contiguous (one right after another) space. Files and folders become fragmented due to file creation and

Tech Tip

Defragmentation requires Administrator rights

Note that only a member of the Administrators group can defragment a hard drive.

Figure 12.8   **Computer Management console—*Device Manager* window**

deletion over a period of time. A defragmented volume has better performance than a volume that has files and folders located throughout the drive. In Vista/7, this tool is accessed by right-clicking on a drive letter from Windows Explorer and selecting *Properties → Tools* tab → *Defragment Now*.

The Disk Management tool is used to manage hard drives including volumes or partitions. Drives can be initialized; volumes created; volumes formatted for FAT, FAT32, and NTFS; RAID configured; and remote drives managed.

The Services and Applications section can contain a multitude of options depending on the computer and what is loaded on it. Common options include Telephony, WMI Control, Services, and Indexing Service. A frequently used option is Services. A service is an application that can be started using this window or configured so it starts when the computer boots. By clicking the *Services* option, a list of services installed on the computer is displayed in the right window. Double-click any service and the service's Properties window appears. From this window on the *General* tab, a service can be started, stopped, paused, resumed, or disabled on the local computer and on remote computers, but you must be logged on as a member of the Administrators group to change a service. Figure 12.9 shows the Management Console Services window and some examples of installed services.

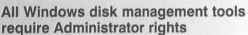

All Windows disk management tools require Administrator rights

You must be a member of the Administrators group to perform any disk management tasks.

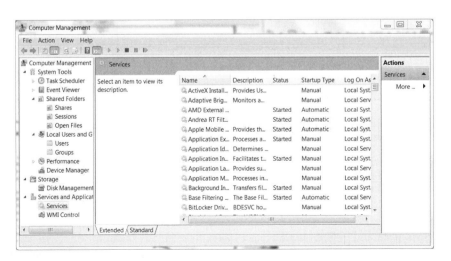

Figure 12.9   **Computer Management console—*Services* window**

If you double-click on a service, the Recovery tab is a nice tool for technicians. It allows a technician to determine what happened when a service fails the first time, the second time, and even a third time. For example, if the print service fails the first time, a restart occurs. Once the print service fails a second time, the print server can be restarted automatically. The third time the print service fails, a file that pages a technician can be executed.

Permissions

Monitoring the users and groups and things they have access to is important. Permissions are a way to control what can or cannot be done to files, folders, and devices from a remote connection. Permissions that users assign can cause havoc. Network administrators and end users can set permissions on folders, and these permissions can affect another user's access to files and folders. Technicians need to be familiar with permissions.

There are two types of permissions that can be assigned in Windows: Shared folder permissions and NTFS file/folder permissions. Shared folder permissions provide access to data across a network. Shared folder permissions are the only way to secure network resources on FAT16 or FAT32 drives. NTFS file/folder permissions provide tighter control than shared folder permissions. NTFS permissions can only be used on NTFS drives.

In XP, to share a folder using shared folder permissions, locate the folder using *Explorer* → right-click the folder → *Sharing and Security* → *Sharing* tab → *Share this folder*. Permissions are set by clicking the *Permissions* button. Besides sharing this folder and allowing access to another user across the network, you can limit the number of users who can access this folder. Figure 12.10 shows this window.

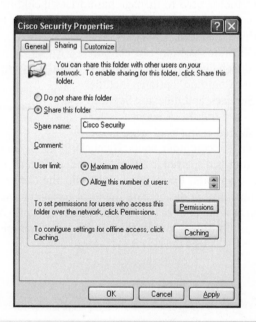

Figure 12.10   **Folder permissions—*Sharing* tab**

Tech Tip

Vista/7 password protection

You can enable or disable password protection through the Network and Sharing Center on a workgroup computer. If password protection is enabled, the person with whom the folder is being shared must have a user account and password on the computer with the share.

Windows Vista and 7 support sharing a folder in a similar fashion as XP, but another way is through a new folder called the Public folder. The default path for the Public folder is C:\Users\Public. You can copy or move any files to the Public folder. The Public folder makes it easier to share files with someone, but files that are copied into it take twice as much hard drive space because they are in two folders.

If sharing is enabled for the Public folder, anyone with a user account and password on the computer that contains the data, in addition to any user on the network, can see all files and folders in the Public folder. You can set permissions so that the Public folder is inaccessible or restrict anyone from changing files or creating new files. However, you cannot pick and choose what files can be seen by individuals.

In Vista/7, to share a folder other than the Public folder, use *Windows Explorer* → right-click the folder → *Share* (Vista)/*Share with* (7). You can do one of the following at this point:

- Type the name of the person with whom you want to share the folder and click *Add*.
- If the computer is attached to a network domain, click the arrow to the right of the textbox, click *Find*, type the name of the person with whom you want to share the folder, click *Check Names*, and click *OK*.
- If the computer is on a workgroup, click the arrow to the right of the textbox, click the appropriate name, and click *Add*. If the name does not appear, click the arrow to the right of the textbox and click *Create a new user* to create the user account.

In Windows 7, libraries are used. A **library** is similar to a folder, but a library contains files that are automatically indexed for faster searching, viewing, and access. For example, a teacher might store training video clips in a library and share them from a library. This library could contain files from different folders, an external drive, or even a network share.

Windows 7 is configured to have four default libraries: Documents, Printers, Music, and Videos. Explorer automatically shows the Documents library instead of the traditional My Documents (XP and below) or Documents (Vista/7). If you right-click on the Documents library and select Properties, you can see that both a particular user's Documents folder is shown as well as a public Documents folder. Notice the *Include a folder* button in this window as shown in Figure 12.11. This button allows more folders to be included in the Documents library. No matter the source of the files, they are all controlled through a single library as if the contents were stored in a single location. Each default library has two locations configured as shown in Figure 12.11. The public location is used by any user logged onto the computer. Only one location can be configured as the default save location for files that are moved, copied, or saved to the library.

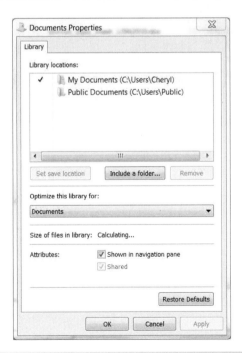

Figure 12.11   **Windows 7 libraries**

Some people find Windows Vista/7 folder sharing more difficult than sharing in Windows XP. The Windows XP method can be used in Vista/7 by right-clicking on a folder and selecting *Properties* → *Sharing* tab → *Advanced Sharing* button → enable the *Share this folder* checkbox → *Permissions* button.

12

Windows XP,
Vista, and 7

To share files on a home network, create a homegroup. In Windows 7 Home Basic and Starter, you can only join a homegroup, not create one. Right-click on a folder, and use the *Share with* menu option.

You can also share files and folders using the public folder. In Windows Explorer, expand any of the libraries and notice the Public folder as shown in Figure 12.12. Drop a file or folder into one of these public folders and others have access. Note that "Public" file sharing is turned off by default and you cannot restrict individual files within any of the Public folders.

Once you share a folder, the permissions are set by clicking the *Permissions* button. To test a shared folder permission, go to another computer and use My Network Places (XP) or Network (Vista/7) to locate the computer and share what was just created. The permissions that can be set are Full control, Change, and Read, as shown in Figure 12.13. Table 12.19 shows the effects of setting one of these permissions.

On an NTFS partition, additional security protection is available through Windows. To share a folder using NTFS permissions, locate the folder using Windows Explorer. Right-click the folder and select *Sharing and Security* (XP), *Sharing* (Vista), or *Properties* (7), and click the *Security* tab.

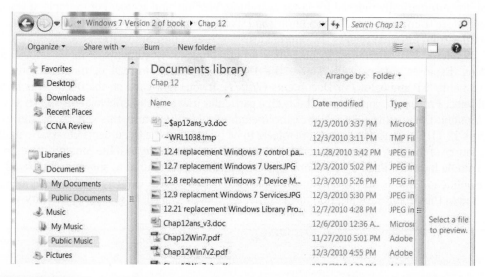

Figure 12.12   **Windows 7 Public Documents folder**

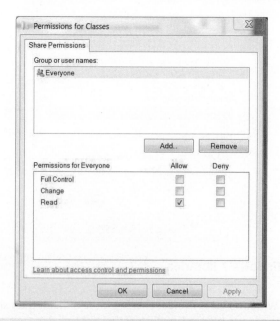

Figure 12.13   **Folder permissions—share permissions**

Table 12.19	Share permissions
Permission	**Description**
Full Control	Users can do everything, such as change the file permissions, take ownership of files, and perform everything that can be done with the *Change* permission.
Change	Users can add a new folder, add files to a folder, change the data in file, add data to files, change the file attributes, delete folders and files, and do all the tasks that you can do with the *Read* permission.
Read	Users can look at file and folder names and attributes. Also, files and scripts can be executed.

Figure 12.14 shows this window. Notice how there are more permissions that can be administered on an NTFS partition using NTFS permissions rather than share permissions. Table 12.20 defines these permissions.

Figure 12.14 Windows 7 NTFS permissions—*Security* tab

Table 12.20	NTFS permissions
Permission	**Description**
Full Control	Users can do anything in the files and folder including delete, add, modify, and create.
Modify	Users can list items in a folder, read data, write data, but cannot delete subfolders and files and cannot take ownership.
Read & Execute	Users can list items in a folder, read a file, but they cannot change or delete the file or create new files. Users can execute applications contained within the folder.
List Folder Contents	Users can only look inside a folder.
Read	Users can display folder and subfolder attributes and permissions as well as look at a particular file.
Write	Users can add files or folders, change attributes for the folder and add or append to data in a file.

Tech Tip

Effective permissions are the final permissions granted to a person for a particular resource. Effective permissions are important when you combine shared folder permissions given to an individual, shared folder permissions given to a group, and individual permissions. The list that follows outlines some helpful tips when sharing folders and files across a network:

Shares are only available from a remote computer

Notice that shared folder permissions are only applicable across a network. This type of share does not prevent someone sitting at the computer from accessing files and folders. For the best protection across a network and at the computer, use NTFS file and folder permissions.

- Folder permissions are cumulative—when you grant folder permissions to a group and then grant an individual permissions to that same folder, the effective permissions for that person is the combination of what the group gets and what the person gets. For example, if the group gets the Write permission and the person gets only the Read permission (and the person is a member of the group that has the Write permission), the person can both read and write files to the folder.

- Deny overrides any allowed permission set for a user or a group. For example, if a group is denied access to a folder, but a person is specifically allowed access to the folder, the person is not allowed to access the folder.

- When NTFS and shared folder permissions are both used, the most restrictive of the two is the effective permissions.

Windows Vista and 7 have help in determining effective permissions. In Vista, right-click on the shared folder and select *Properties* → *Sharing* tab → *Advanced* button → *Effective Permissions* tab → *Select* → click on a specific user or group → *OK*. In Windows 7, right click on a file or folder → *Properties* → *Security* tab → *Advanced* button → *Effective Permissions* tab. Permissions are a common problem and a computer technician must be familiar with the effects of misconfiguring them.

Overview of the Boot Process

With Windows there are two types of partitions that are important during the boot process—the system partition/volume and the boot partition/volume. The **system partition** (XP and lower) or **system volume** (Vista and higher) is the active drive partition that has the files needed to load the operating system. The system partition is normally the c: drive (the active partition). The **boot partition** (XP and lower) or **boot volume** (Vista and higher) is the partition or logical drive where the operating system files are located. One thing that people sometimes forget is that the system partition and the boot partition can be on the same partition. These partitions are where certain boot files are located.

Every operating system needs specific files that allow the computer to boot. These files are known as **system files** or startup files. The system files and their specific location on the hard drive are listed in Table 12.21.

Reading about Windows files can be confusing because the file locations frequently have the entries *%systemroot%* and *%systemdrive%*. This is because computers can be partitioned differently. If you install Windows onto a drive letter (a partition or logical drive) other than the active partition (normally c:), the startup files can be on two different drive letters. Also, you do not have to take the default folder name of WINNT or WINDOWS (depending on the type of installation) to install Windows. To account for these different scenarios, Microsoft uses the *%systemroot%* to represent the boot partition, the partition and folder that contains the majority of the Windows files. *%systemdrive%* represents the root directory. On a computer with a single operating system, this would be c:\.

Tech Tip

Example of *%systemdrive%* and *%systemroot%*

If Windows XP is installed onto the c: drive and the c: drive is the active partition, then the BOOT.INI, BOOTSECT.DOS, HYBERFIL.SYS, NTBOOTDD.SYS, NTDETECT.COM, and NTLDR files would all be in the root directory of c:. The HAL.DLL and NTOSKRNL.EXE files would be located in the SYSTEM32 folder (located in either the WINNT or WINDOWS folder) on the c: drive.

Table 12.21   **Windows XP and higher system files**

Startup filename	File location
BOOT.INI (XP and lower)	Root directory of system partition
BOOTMGR.EXE (Vista and higher)	Root directory of system partition
BOOTSECT.DOS (needed with XP and lower if the computer is a dual- or multi-boot system)	Root directory of system partition
HAL.DLL	%systemroot%\System32*
NTBOOTDD.SYS (used on XP and lower with SCSI drives that have the SCSI BIOS disabled)	Root directory of system partition
NTDETECT.COM	Root directory of system partition
NTLDR (Windows XP and lower)	Root directory of system partition
NTOSKRNL.EXE	%systemroot%\System32*
WINLOAD.EXE	%systemroot%\System32*
WINRESUME.EXE	Root directory of system partition
BCD	%systemroot%\Boot
SYSTEM (registry file)	%systemroot%\System32\Config\System
WINLOGON.EXE	%systemroot%\System32

*%*systemroot*% is the boot partition and the name of the folder under the folder where Windows is installed (normally C:\WINNT *or* C:\WINDOWS)

Another example would be if you installed Windows XP onto the D: drive, but the C: drive is the active partition. The BOOT.INI, BOOTSECT.DOS, HYBERFIL.SYS, NTBOOTDD.SYS, NTDETECT.COM, and NTLDR files would all be in the root directory of C:. The HAL.DLL and NTOSKRNL.EXE files would be located in the SYSTEM32 folder (that is located under the WINNT or WINDOWS folder) on the D: drive.

The boot process for any Windows version is actually quite involved, but the major steps for Windows XP are as follows:

1. Power on the computer.
2. POST executes.
3. BIOS searches BIOS saved configuration for the boot device order and checks for a boot sector. If the boot device is a hard drive, BIOS reads the Master Boot Record, and locates and loads the information into sector 0 of the system partition. The contents of sector 0 define the type of file system and the location of the bootstrap loader file, and start the bootstrap loader. With Windows XP, this file is NTLDR.
4. NTLDR starts in real mode so that 8- and 16-bit software can be loaded. Then XP is switched to 32-bit mode and the file system begins to load.
5. NTLDR reads the BOOT.INI file and displays the various operating system choices contained within the BOOT.INI file. If something other than Windows XP is chosen, the BOOTSECT.DOS file takes over. If Windows XP is chosen, the NTDETECT.COM file executes.
6. NTDETECT.COM detects the computer's hardware and ACPI tables are read so that XP can detect power management features.
7. NTLDR passes the hardware information to the NTOSKRNL.EXE file.
8. The operating system kernel, NTOSKRNL.EXE, executes and the HAL.DLL file loads. **HAL** (hardware abstraction layer) is a layer between the operating system and the hardware devices. The HAL allows Windows XP to run with different hardware configurations and components without affecting (or crashing) the operating system.
9. The registry key Hkey_Local_Machine\System loads. This registry key is located in the %*systemroot*%\System32\Config\System file. This key has information found during the hardware detection process and is used to determine which device drivers to load.

10. The operating system kernel initializes and NTLDR passes control to it. The Starting Up process bar displays. During this time, a hardware key is created, device drivers load, and services start.

11. The WINLOGON.EXE file executes and the logon screen appears. While the logon process is occurring, XP detects plug and play devices.

The Windows Vista boot process has changed dramatically from the Windows XP process:

1. Power on the computer.

2. POST executes.

Tech Tip

Installing Vista/7 with older operating systems

Be careful installing Vista or 7 with an older operating system. Windows Vista or 7 overwrites the MBR, boot sector, and boot files. That is why very few Windows versions are upgradable to Vista or 7.

3. BIOS searches the BIOS saved configuration for the boot device order and checks for a boot sector. If the boot device is a hard drive, BIOS reads the MBR and locates and loads the information into sector 0 of the system partition. The contents of sector 0 define the type of file system and the location of the bootstrap loader file and start the bootstrap loader. With Windows Vista, this file is BOOTMGR.EXE.

4. The Windows Boot Manager (BOOTMGR.EXE) reads boot configuration data from the BCD (Boot Configuration Data) database file. Boot Manager replaces the older BOOT.INI file, can be edited with bcdedit.exe, and allows better support for non-Windows operating systems to coexist with Vista/7. On multi-boot systems, a menu appears. Note that Boot Manager can be accessed by pressing the space bar during startup.

5. If Vista/7 is chosen or the only choice, WINLOAD.EXE takes control as the operating system boot loader. This file takes the place of NTLDR and is responsible for loading the operating system kernel (NTOSKRNL.EXE) and device drivers.

Speeding up the Boot Process

The following tips can help reduce the time Windows takes to become operational.

- Configure BIOS boot options so that the drive used to boot Windows listed as the first option.
- Configure BIOS for the fast boot option or disable hardware checks.
- If multiple operating systems are installed, use the msconfig utility *Boot* tab to reduce the boot menu timeout value.
- Remove unnecessary startup applications using the msconfig utility.
- Have available hard disk space and keep the drive defragmented. Note that Vista and 7 are automatically configured to defragment the hard drive at 1:00 a.m. on Wednesday. If the computer is powered off, defragmentation occurs when the computer next boots.
- Disable unused or unnecessary hardware using Device Manager.
- Use Windows ReadyBoost to cache some startup files to a 256MB+ flash drive, SD card, or CF card. Right-click the device to access the *Properties* option and select the *ReadyBoost* tab. Note that ReadyBoost does not increase performance on a system that boots from a SSD, so Windows 7 (not Vista) disables ReadyBoost as an option when an SSD is in use.
- Use *Control Panel* → *Administrative Tools* → *Services* to change services that are not needed the moment Windows boots to use the *Automatic (Delayed Start)* option instead of Automatic.

Troubleshooting the Boot Process

Quite a few things can cause Windows to not boot properly. For example, a non-bootable disk inserted into the floppy drive can cause Windows not to boot. If none of the hard drives contain an active partition or if the hard drive's boot sector information is missing or corrupt (see Chapter 7), any of the following messages could appear:

- Invalid partition table
- Error loading operating system
- Missing operating system
- Boot: Couldn't find NTLDR (XP or lower)

- NTLDR is missing (Windows XP and lower)
- Windows has blocked some startup programs
- The Windows boot configuration data file is missing required information (Windows Vista and higher)
- Windows could not start because the following file is missing or corrupt

Also, if you receive a message that you have an invalid boot disk, a disk read error, or an inaccessible boot drive, troubleshoot your hard drive and/or BIOS settings.

Windows has a wealth of tools and start modes that can be used to troubleshoot the system. If Windows boots, but still has a problem, try to solve the problem without booting into one of these special modes. For example, if one piece of hardware is not working properly and the system boots properly, use Device Manager and the troubleshooting wizards to troubleshoot the problem. Another problem can be caused by an application that loads during startup.

How to stop programs that automatically load at startup from running

To disable startup programs, hold down the [Shift] key during the logon process and keep it held down until the desktop icons appear.

For a permanent change to an application starting automatically, move or delete the startup shortcuts from the one of the following places:

- *%systemdrive%*\Documents and Settings\Username\Start Menu\Programs\Startup
- *%systemdrive%*\Documents and Settings\All Users\Start Menu\Programs\Startup
- *%systemdrive%*\Users\All Users\Microsoft\Windows\Start Menu\Programs\Startup
- *%windir%*\Profiles\Username\Start Menu\Programs\Startup
- *%windir%*\Profiles\All Users\Start Menu\Programs\Startup
- *%windrive%*\Profiles\All Users\Microsoft\Windows\Start Menu\Programs\Startup

If a startup problem appears to occur before the "Starting Windows" logo appears, the causes are typically missing startup files, corrupt files, or hardware problems. The Windows Vista and 7 BOOTSECT /NT60 ALL (or a drive letter instead of ALL if multiple operating systems are installed) can be used to manually repair the boot sector. The BOOTSECT.EXE file is available from the BOOT folder of the Windows Vista/7 DVD and can be executed from within Windows Recovery Environment (WinRE) covered later in the chapter or from within Windows. If the Windows logo appears, but there is a problem before the logon prompt appears, the problem is usually with misconfigured drivers and/or services. If problems occur after the logon window appears, then look to startup applications (hold the [Shift] key down during startup).

Advanced Boot Options Menu

When Windows does not boot properly, the Windows Advanced Boot Options menu can be used. Tools that can be used to troubleshoot Windows boot problems include Last Known Good Configuration, Safe Mode, Recovery Console (XP) or Windows Recovery Environment (Vista or higher), and Automated System Restore wizard (XP) or Startup Repair Tool (Vista or 7). Table 12.22 gives a brief description of these options.

What loads when booting into Safe Mode?

When the computer boots in Safe Mode, the mouse, keyboard, CD/DVD, and 640 x 480 default video device drivers are the only items loaded.

When to use the *Last Known Good Configuration* boot option

Whenever the **Last Known Good Configuration** option is used, all configuration changes made since the last successful boot are lost. However, since the changes are the most likely cause of Windows not booting correctly, Last Known Good Configuration is a useful tool when installing new devices and drivers that do not work properly.

Table 12.22	Windows Advanced Boot Options window
Boot Option	**Description**
Safe Mode	Uses a minimum set of drivers and services to start Windows. A commonly used option.
Safe Mode with Networking	Same as Safe Mode, but includes an NIC driver.
Safe Mode with Command Prompt	Same as Safe Mode except Windows Explorer (GUI mode) is not used, but a command prompt appears instead. This option is not used very often.
Enable VGA Mode (XP only)	Used when Safe mode does not work and you suspect the default video driver is not working.
Enable low resolution video (640x480) (Vista or 7)	Used when Safe mode does not work and you suspect the default video driver is not working.
Last Known Good Configuration	A very popular option used when a change that was just implemented caused the system to not boot properly.
Debugging Mode	Debugging information can be sent through the serial port to another computer running a debugger program. This option is not used very often.
Enable Boot Logging	Enables logging for startup options except for the *Last Known Good Configuration* option. The logging file is called ntbtlog.txt.
Disable automatic restart on system failure (Vista or 7)	Prevents Windows from automatically rebooting after a system crash.
Disable Driver Signature Enforcement (Vista or 7)	Allows drivers that are not properly signed to load during startup.
Start Windows Normally	Restarts Windows and attempts to boot normally.
Repair Your Computer (Vista or 7)	Used if system recovery tools are installed on the hard disk. Otherwise, these tools are available when booting from the Windows installation DVD.
Reboot	Restarts Windows.

If Last Known Good Configuration does not work properly, boot the computer into Safe Mode, which is covered in the next section. If Windows works, but a hardware device does not work and a new driver has been recently loaded, use the *driver roll back* option for the device.

Safe Mode is used when the computer stalls, slows down, or does not work right, or problems are caused by improper video, intermittent errors, or new hardware/software installation. Safe Mode is used to start Windows with minimum device drivers and services. Software that automatically loads during startup is disabled in Safe Mode and user profiles are not loaded.

Safe Mode allows you to access configuration files and make necessary changes, troubleshoot installed software and hardware, disable software and services, and adjust hardware and software settings that may be causing Windows to not start correctly. The bottom line is that Safe Mode puts the computer in a "bare bones" mode so you can troubleshoot problems.

Tech Tip

Press F8 during startup

When Windows is booting, press the F8 key to access the Windows Advanced Boot Options menu.

Windows XP Recovery Console

Recovery Console is used when Safe Mode and other startup options do not solve a Windows XP or earlier version-based problem. Recovery Console allows access to hard drive volumes without starting the GUI (Graphical User Interface). In other words, the Recovery Console allows you access to a command prompt from which you use commands to start and stop services, repair and access hard drive volumes, replace corrupt files, and perform a manual recovery.

Administrator rights are needed for all of the Recovery Console tasks
You must have the Administrator password to access the full potential of Recovery Console.

Recovery Console is not loaded onto the system by default, but it can be installed from the XP CD and then loaded through the boot menu or executed from the XP CD. Normally technicians run Recovery Console from the CD because it is needed when there is a problem. Once Recovery Console is installed, restart the computer. Recovery Console appears as a boot option. Use the arrow keys to select the *Recovery Console* option and press [Enter]. A command prompt appears.

How to install Recovery Console
To install Recovery Console, insert the XP CD into the CD drive. If the welcome screen appears, close it. Click the *Start* button, click the *Run* option, and type in the appropriate path to access the i386 folder and the `WINNT32 /CMDCOMS` command. An example is `F:\I386\WINNT32 /CMDCOMS`. This starts the Recovery Console installation process. When asked if you want to install Recovery Console, click the *Yes* button and follow the prompts on the screen.

12
Windows XP,
Vista, and 7

Technicians must sometimes work from the command prompt when the system is not working properly. That is what the Recovery Console tool is all about. You may want to review Chapter 11 on basic Windows to understand the process and procedures needed when working from a command prompt.

How to get to a command prompt
There are several ways to access a command prompt when the computer is functional. The methods are listed as follows:
- Click the *Start* button, click the *Run* option, and type `cmd` in the dialog box.
- Click the *Start* button, click the *Run* option, and type `command` in the dialog box. Note that when this option is used, the keyboard arrow keys do not bring up previously used commands as the `cmd` command does.
- Click the *Start* button, point to the *All Programs* option, point to the *Accessories* option, and click the *Command Prompt* option.

Reload Recovery Console if you just converted a FAT16 partition to NTFS
If using FAT16 and you install the Recovery Console and you convert the partition to NTFS, the Recovery Console must be re-installed.

The `copy` command can be used through Recovery Console to restore the two important files, system and software, that are used to build two important registry keys, Hkey_Local_Machine\System and Hkey_Local_Machine\Software. If the unresolved problem relates to hardware, try replacing the system file first. If the problem relates to software, replace the software file first. Do not replace both files at the same time because the system or software files may not be current, which means that drivers or service packs may have to be re-installed after replacement.

How to make a copy of the system and software Windows XP files
It is a good idea to make a backup of the system and software files *before* Windows XP crashes or before replacing them. To make a copy of them using Recovery Console, type `cd system32\config` at the prompt. To copy the system file, type `copy system path` (where `path` is the drive letter and path to where the backup is to be stored). To copy the software file, type `copy software path` (where `path` is the drive letter and path to where the backup is to be stored).

To replace the system or software files, type `copy ..\ ..\ repair \ system` or `copy ..\ ..\ repair \ software` or put the prompt where the latest backup copy of the system and software files are located. To update the system and software files kept in the *Repair* folder, use the Backup utility and save the System State. When the *System State backup* option is enabled, the Repair folder is updated.

Recovery Console has four default limitations of which a technician should be aware.

1. No text editor is available in Recovery Console by default.
2. Files cannot be copied to removable media such as floppy disks while in Recovery Console. Write access is disabled.
3. The Administrator password cannot be changed from Recovery Console.
4. Some folders, such as Program Files and Documents and Settings, are inaccessible from the Recovery Console prompt.

Windows XP ASR (Automated System Recovery)

ASR (Automated System Recovery) replaces the Emergency Repair Disk used by NT and 2000 Professional and it uses the Backup tool to backup important system files used to start Windows XP. Automated System Recovery does not backup data files (although the Backup program can be used to backup data too).

To create an Automated System Recovery disk, you will need a 1.44MB floppy disk and media such as a CD (if the machine has a CD-RW drive) or tape (for a tape drive). The floppy is used to boot the system and then you can restore the files if the hard drive crashes or the operating system is inoperable.

To access the Backup tool, click *Start* → *All Programs* → *Accessories* → *System Tools* → *Backup*. The Backup wizard begins. On the initial screen, click the words *Advanced Mode*. The words are underlined in the window. Click the *Tools* menu option and select *ASR Wizard*. The Automated System Recovery wizard starts.

To use the disk and media created with Automated System Recovery, you will need the floppy disk created when the system was backed up, the backup media written to when the system was backed up, and the original Windows XP CD. Start the computer using the Windows XP CD. During the Setup process, press the `F2` key. A prompt appears to insert the Automated System Recovery floppy disk into the floppy drive. Insert the disk and follow the screen directions to restore the system.

Windows Recovery Environment

In Windows Vista and 7, Microsoft replaced the Recovery Console and ASR with the **WinRE** (Windows Recovery Environment), which is accessed by booting from a Windows Vista or 7 installation DVD → select the language parameters → click *Repair your computer* → select an operating system → click *Next*. Some computers have a recovery partition that would contain these tools or it is available through the Advanced Boot Options `F8` menu. See the computer documentation for details. The tools are shown in Figure 12.15 and explained in Table 12.23.

Windows Vista and 7 have a great command-line utility to use when the Startup Repair option does not work after multiple attempts—`bootrec.exe`:

- `bootrec /FixMbr`—Used to resolve MBR issues; writes a Windows Vista or 7 compatible MBR to the system partition.
- `bootrec /FixBoot`—Used if the boot sector has been replaced with a non-Windows Vista or 7 boot sector, if the boot sector has become corrupt, or if an earlier Windows version has been installed *after* Windows Vista or 7 was installed and the computer was started with the NTLDR instead of `BOOTMGR.EXE`.
- `bootrec /ScanOs`—Used when any Windows Vista or 7 operating system has been installed and is not listed on the Boot Manager menu; scans all disks for any and all versions of Windows Vista or 7.

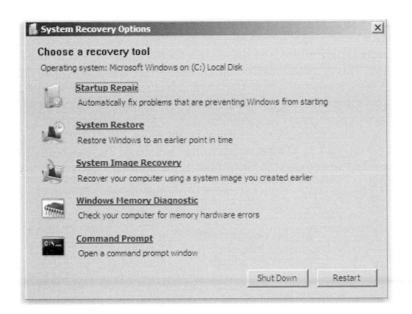

Figure 12.15 Windows 7 WinRE menu

Table 12.23 WinRE tools

Tool	Description
Startup Repair	Analyzes a computer and tries to fix any missing or damaged system files or BCD (Boot Configuration Data) files. This tool can be run multiple times. After a single repair and system reboot, try the tool again (and again). The system could have multiple problems.
System Restore	Works like the System Restore utility in Windows but is used to return the system to an earlier time, such as before a service pack was installed and the system stopped booting.
Complete PC Restore (Vista)/System Image Recovery (7)	Available in Vista Business, Enterprise, and Ultimate and all versions of Windows 7 to restore the contents of the hard drive from some type of backup media, such as another hard drive or DVDs.
Windows Memory Diagnostic Tool	Used to heavily test RAM modules to see if they are causing the system to not boot. The tool runs tests repeatedly until it is manually stopped. Microsoft states that it is unlikely that repeating the test will result in a newly detected error. An extended test is available from the diagnostic menu.
Command Prompt	Unlike the Windows XP Recovery Console, which has a limited number of executable commands, the Command Prompt option allows execution of any command-line program.

- `bootrec /RebuildBcd`—Used when the BCD file needs to be rebuilt; gives the option to select the installation to add to the BCD store. If rebuilding the BCD file does not fix the startup issue, the current BCD can be exported, deleted, and then rebuilt. The following commands can be used:

```
bcd edit /export x:\BCD_BACKUP
c:
cd boot
attrib bcd -s -h -r
ren c:\boot\bcd bcd.old
bootrec /RebuildBcd
```

System Configuration Utility

The **System Configuration utility** is used to disable startup programs and services one at a time or several at once. This graphical utility reduces the chances of making typing errors, deleting files, and other misfortunes that occur when technicians work from a command prompt. Only an Administrator or a member of the Administrators group can use the System Configuration utility.

To start the System Configuration utility in Windows XP, click *Start → Run →* type `msconfig` and press Enter. In Windows Vista's *Start Search* or 7's *Search programs and files* textbox, type `msconfig` and press Enter. Figure 12.16 shows the System Configuration utility's General tab.

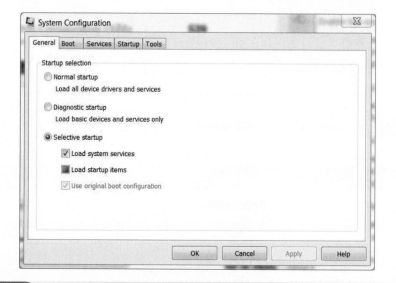

Figure 12.16   **Windows 7 System Configuration utility—*General* tab**

In Windows Vista and 7, the SYSTEM.INI, WIN.INI, and BOOT.INI tabs are not available like they are in XP. Instead, the first tab is *Boot*, which allows you to control and modify the Windows boot environment similarly to the BOOT.INI tab in XP. The Boot tab functions include selecting the default operating system and the time allotted to wait for the default operating system to load if no other operating system is chosen from the boot menu in a multiple operating system situation. Advanced options on this tab include defining the number of processors and maximum memory as well as whether PCI Lock and Detect HAL are enabled.

The General tab has three radio buttons: Normal startup, Diagnostic startup, and Selective startup. Normal startup is the default option and all device drivers and services load normally when this radio button is selected. The Diagnostic startup radio button is selected when you want to create a clean environment for troubleshooting. When *Diagnostic startup* is chosen and Windows is restarted, the system boots to Safe Mode and only the most basic device drivers and services are active.

The Selective startup radio button is the most common troubleshooting tab on the General tab. When *Selective startup* is chosen, you can pick which startup options load. Using the divide-and-conquer method of troubleshooting, find the startup file that is causing boot problems. Start with the first checkbox, *Load system services*, and deselect the checkbox. Click *OK* and restart the computer. Once you determine which file is causing the problem (the problem reappears), click the System Configuration tab that corresponds to the problem file and deselect files until the exact problem file is located.

The Services and Startup tabs in the System Configuration window are also quite useful when troubleshooting boot problems. Certain applications, such as an antivirus program, run as services. Many services are started during the boot process. The *Services* tab can be used to disable and enable these boot services. Enabling the *Hide all Microsoft Services* option allows you to view and manipulate third-party (non-Microsoft) services. The *Startup* tab allows you to enable and disable Windows-based startup programs. Figure 12.17 shows a sample Startup tab screen.

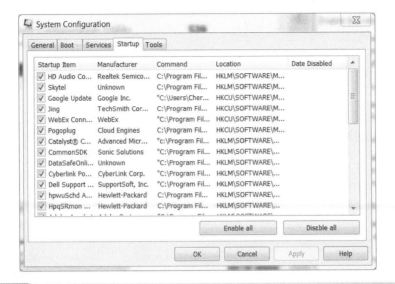

Figure 12.17 **System Configuration utility—*Startup* tab**

Another tab available in Vista/7 System Configuration that was not in XP is Tools. The *Tools* tab allows launching such options as Task Manager, Performance Monitor, and Internet Options from Internet Explorer—items that might need to be changed as a result of a startup issue.

Windows XP and Vista do not have an Emergency Repair Disk

Windows XP and Vista do not support creating an Emergency Repair Disk in the same way that NT Workstation and Windows 2000 Professional do. A set of installation disks can be obtained from Microsoft and would be needed only if the computer does not support booting from CD.

Windows Defender

Windows Defender is available in all versions of Windows Vista and higher and is available for download for computers that have Windows XP SP2 and higher. Windows Defender works in the background looking for spyware. Windows Defender can be customized in terms of when updates are downloaded and how often it scans the computer, and it shows detailed information about software that is installed on the computer. Hands-on Exercise 27 explores some of the Windows Defender options.

Task Manager and Event Viewer

Task Manager is a Windows-based utility that displays applications currently loaded into memory, processes that are currently running, processor usage, and memory details. To activate Task Manager, press Ctrl+Alt+Del. Another way of accessing Task Manager is to right-click the taskbar and select *Task Manager* (XP/Vista) or *Start Task Manager* (7).

Microsoft created the **Dr. Watson** Windows XP utility to create a text log that could be used to help Microsoft and a technician in discovering the cause of a system crash. The Dr. Watson utility is not available in any version of Windows Vista or 7. In Windows Vista, Microsoft has the Problem Reports and Solutions window that helps check for solutions to problems. These solutions can be saved and viewed later. In Windows 7, the troubleshooting tool can be used. From the Start menu, type `troubleshooting` in the *Search programs and files* textbox. The troubleshooting tool lists first in the output list. These control panel links can also be accessed through `msconfig` *Tools* tab, as demonstrated in Lab 28.

Event Viewer is a Windows tool used to monitor various events in your computer such as when a driver or service does not start properly. The Event Log (XP) or Windows Event Log (Vista/7) service starts automatically every time a computer boots to Windows. This service is what allows the events to be logged and then Event Viewer is used to see the log.

Tech Tip

What to do if the system is not responding

One of the common uses of Task Manager is to exit from an application that is "hung up" or not responding. Once inside the Task Manager window, click the *Applications* tab. Locate the name of the troublesome application and click on the name. Click on the *End Task* button. Normally, if an application is causing a problem, the status shows the application as "not responding." Figure 12.18 shows the Task Manager Applications tab.

Access Event Viewer in Windows XP by clicking the *Start* button → *Control Panel* → if in *Category* view, *Performance and Maintenance* → *Administrative Tools* → *Event Viewer*. In Vista, select the *System and Maintenance* control panel or in Windows 7, select the *System and Security* control panel → *Administrative Tools* → *Event Viewer*. The left window contains the Event Viewer logs. In Windows XP, these include the application log, the security log, and the system log. The application log displays events associated with a specific program. The programmers who design software decide which events to display in the Event Viewer's application log. The security log displays events such as when different users log in to the com-puter (both valid and invalid logins). A technician can pick which events are displayed in the security log. All users can view the system log and the application log, but only a member of Administrators can enable security log information.

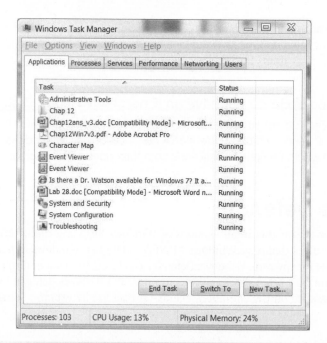

Figure 12.18   **Task Manager—*Applications* tab**

The most commonly used log is the system log. The system log displays events that deal with various system components such as a driver or service that loads during startup. The type of system log events cannot be changed or deleted. Click the system log option in the left panel. The system log events displays in the right window. Figure 12.19 shows an example of Windows XP Event Viewer system log.

Windows Vista and 7 improve on Event Viewer by no longer having a 300MB limit as in prior versions, forwarding Event Viewer information, and collecting copies of events from multiple remote computers. Windows Vista/7 Event Viewer has two types of logs: Windows logs and Applications and Services logs, as shown in Figure 12.20.

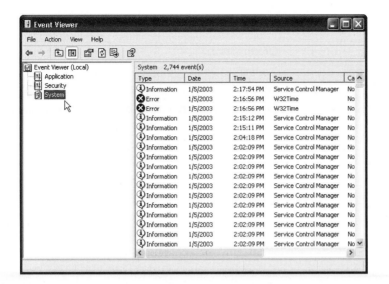

Figure 12.19   **Windows XP Event Viewer—System log**

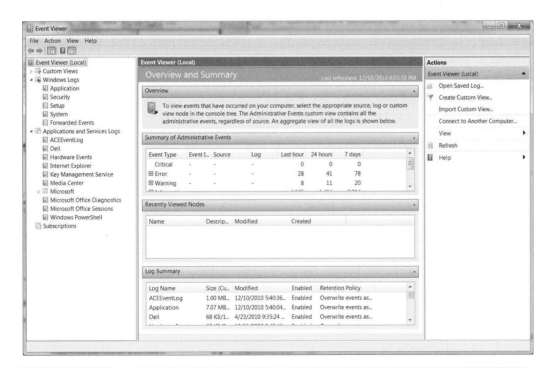

Figure 12.20   **Windows 7 Event Viewer**

Within the Windows Logs section, there are the traditional application, security, and system logs, along with two new ones: setup and forwarded events. Also, there is a new Applications and Services Logs section. Table 12.24 summarizes the types of things you might see in these logs. Event Viewer can display five different types of events. The events are shown in Table 12.25.

Double-click an Event Viewer event to see more information about it. Figure 12.21 shows a System log warning event window. Event viewer logs can be saved as files and viewed later. This is especially useful with intermittent problems. Use the *Action* menu item (XP) or *Actions* section (Vista/7) to save and retrieve saved event viewer log files.

Table 12.24 Windows Vista/7 Event Viewer logs

Major Log Category	Log	Description
Windows Logs	Application	Contains events logged by software applications. The company who writes the software applications decide what to log.
	Security	Contains events specified by administrators such as valid and invalid logon attempts, and network share usage.
	Setup	Contains setup events logged by software applications.
	System	Contains Windows system events such as when a driver or service fails to load or start.
	Forwarded Events	Contains events from remote computers.
Applications and Services Logs	Vendor-specific	Contains logs from a specific application or Windows component. The logs can be one of four types: admin, operational, analytic, and debug. The admin log is for normal users and technical support staff. The operational event is used by technical staff to analyze a problem. The analytic and debug events would more likely be used by the application developer. Both create a large amount of entries and should be used for a short period of time only.

Table 12.25 Event Viewer symbols

Symbol	Type of Event	Explanation
Lowercase "i"	Information	Normal system operations such as the system being initialized or shut down.
Exclamation mark	Warning	An event that is not critical, but one that you might want to take a look at. The system can still function, but some feature(s) may not be available.
X	Error	A specific event failed such as a service or device that failed to initialize properly.
Yellow key	Success Audit	You can audit a specific event. If successful, this symbol appears and the exercise of a user right succeeded.
Yellow lock	Failure Audit	When you specify a specific event to audit and the event fails, the yellow lock appears. An example is when you are auditing a system login and someone tries to log in that does not have a valid username or password, then the system creates a Failure Audit event.

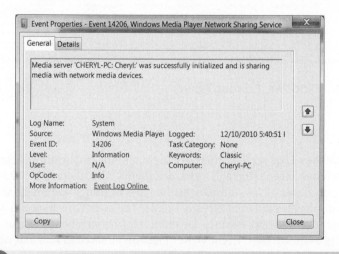

Figure 12.21 Event Viewer—System log event

What to do if the XP Event Viewer log is full

If an error message appears stating that the Event Viewer log is full, start Event Viewer. Click the *Action* menu option → *Properties* → *General* tab → *Clear log* button. The *Log Size* option may need to be changed to one of the following: *Overwrite events older than 0 days, Maximum log size,* or *Overwrite events as needed*. Note that you must be an Administrator or a member of the Administrators group to perform this procedure.

Troubleshooting a Service that Does Not Start

Some Windows services start automatically each time the computer boots. If one of these services has a problem, there is normally an error message that appears during the boot sequence. You can use the System Configuration utility (`msconfig`) previously discussed to enable and disable startup services. You can also use Event Viewer to see if the service loaded properly. Another program that you can use is the Services snap-in used from the Computer Management tool. Or, from a command prompt type `services.msc`, and press [Enter]. The *Services* tool allows you to view what services have been started and stopped and, if desired, allows you to stop a service. Open the Services snap-in and double-click any service. The Service window opens and on the General tab are the *Stop* and *Start* buttons that can be used to control the service. Figure 12.22 shows the iPod service. The service loads every time the computer starts. Notice in Figure 12.22 that because the iPod service is already started, the only action that can be performed is to stop the service by clicking the *Stop* button.

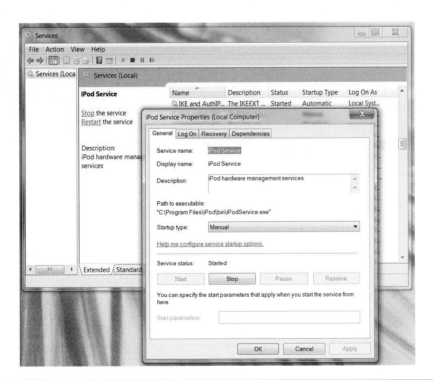

Figure 12.22　**Services snap-in—*General* tab window**

Shut Down Problems

Windows should be shut down properly when all work is finished. Before Windows can shut down, the operating system sends a message to all devices, services, and applications. Each device or system service that is running sends a message back saying it is OK to shut down now. Any active application saves data that has not been previously saved and sends a message back to the operating system that it is OK to shut down.

If the system has trouble shutting down, it is due to devices, services, or applications. The most common problem is an application that does not respond. When this happens, press Ctrl+Alt+Del to access Task Manager. Manually stop any applications that show a status of not responding. You can also click any other applications and stop them to see if they are causing the problem. Sometimes a program will not show a status of not responding until you try to manually stop the application from within Task Manager. If a single application continually prevents Windows from shutting down, contact the software manufacturer to see if there is a fix or check online.

For services problems, boot the computer into Safe Mode and then shut down the computer. Notice whether or not the computer had any problems shutting down. If the process works, use the System Configuration window *General* tab *Selective startup* radio button in conjunction with the *Services* tab to selectively disable services. Because there are so many services loaded, you might try the divide and conquer method—disable half of the services to narrow the list.

A device does not cause a shut down problem frequently, so eliminate services and applications first. Then, while working on the computer, notice what devices you are using. Common devices are video, hard drive, CD/DVD drive, keyboard, and mouse. Boot to the Advanced Options menu by pressing F8 during booting. Select *Enable Boot Logging*. Once the system boots, locate the NTBTLOG.TXT file in the *Windows* folder. You may have to set folder options within Windows Explorer to list the file and access it. Verify that all of your devices have the most up-to-date driver loaded and that the driver is compatible with the installed version of Windows.

Tech Tip

Try the restart option instead of the shut down option

If you cannot stop the problem application or determine if the problem is a service or hardware, try restarting the computer instead of shutting down. Once the computer restarts, try shutting down again. As a last resort, use the computer power button to power the computer off.

Sometimes USB or IEEE1394 FireWire ports can stop a computer from shutting down or powering off. Check event logs to see if any device did not enter a suspend state. A feature called USB selective suspend allows the Windows hub driver to suspend a particular USB port and not affect the other USB ports. This is particularly important to laptops and nettops because of power consumption. Suspending USB devices when the device is not in use conserves power. If this is causing the problem, this default behavior can be modified using the *Power options* control panel link and accessing the *Advanced power settings*.

Monitoring System Performance

It is important for a technician to understand how a computer is performing and to be able to analyze why a computer might be running slow. In order to do that, a technician must know what applications are being run on the computer and their effects on the computer resources. A technician must also be able to monitor the computer's resource usage when problems occur, change the configuration as needed, and observe the results of the configuration change.

Utilities commonly used to monitor system performance include Task Manager, Windows XP's System Monitor and Performance Logs and Alerts, and Windows Vista/7's Reliability Monitor and Performance Monitor. Task Manager is used to monitor your current system's performance. **System Monitor** is used to monitor real-time data about specific computer components. **Performance Logs and Alerts** allows creating logs about the computer performance and creating alerts that notify you when a specific instance being monitored reaches a defined threshold. It includes a summary graph of processor and memory usage. **Performance Monitor** is a visual graph in real time or from a saved log file providing data on specific computer components. **Reliability Monitor** provides a visual graph of system stability and details on events that might have affected the computer's reliability.

Although Task Manager has been discussed in a previous section, how to use it to monitor computer performance was not discussed. Access Task Manager and click the *Performance* tab. Task Manager immediately starts gathering CPU and memory usage statistics and displays them in graph form in the window as shown in Figure 12.23.

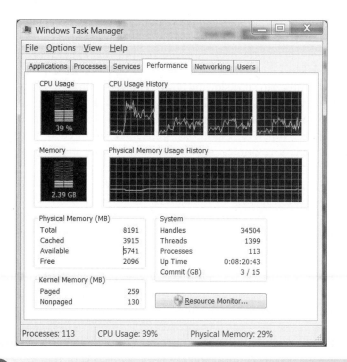

Figure 12.23 Task Manager—*Performance* tab

The first window on the left, CPU Usage, shows the processor usage percentage, or what percentage of time the processor is working. Actually, the percentage of time the processor is running a thread is a more accurate statement. A thread is a type of Windows object that runs application instructions. The window on the right, CPU Usage History, is a graph of how busy the processor is over a period of time.

The second window on the left for Windows XP is PF Usage, and it shows the amount of virtual memory (the paging file) being used. If the display shows that the paging file is near the maximum, you can adjust the page file size with the following steps:

- Click the *Start* button and select *Control Panel*.
- If in *Category* view, select *Performance and Maintenance* followed by the *System* control panel icon. If in *Classic* view, double-click the *System* control panel icon.
- Click the *Advanced* tab, locate the *Performance* section, and click the *Settings* button.
- Click the *Advanced* tab, locate the *Virtual Memory* section, and click the *Change* button.

In Vista or 7, the second window on the left displays memory usage for the current moment. The graphic on the right is memory usage over time. To see how much memory an individual process is using, use the *Processes* tab and locate the program executable file. The CPU and memory usage show in separate columns on the *Processes* tab.

Memory is a frequent bottleneck for computer performance issues. Task Manager can also be used to see the total amount of RAM installed and how much RAM is available. Look in the *Physical Memory* information section of the Task Manager *Performance* tab to see this information.

What to do if you think memory is the problem

If you determine that memory is a problem, there are several things you can do, such as increase the amount of RAM installed in the system; create multiple paging files when multiple hard drives are installed in the system; manually set the paging file size; run applications that require a lot of memory with all other applications closed; close any unnecessary windows; avoid having too many applications open; upgrade the hard drive or add another hard drive; and run the disk defragmenter program provided with Windows.

Tech Tip

Task Manager also has the *Networking* tab that is useful to technicians. The *Networking* tab shows a graph of network performance. The information shown can also be changed by selecting the *View* menu option, clicking the *Select Columns* option, clicking in the available checkboxes, and clicking the *OK* button.

Sometimes a computer can start slowing down. The most common cause of slowdown is that the computer's resources are insufficient or an application is monopolizing a particular resource such as memory. Other causes of slowdowns include a resource that is not functioning properly or is outdated, such as a hard drive; a resource that is not configured for maximum performance and needs to be adjusted; or resources, such as hard drive space and memory, that are not sharing workloads properly and need to be adjusted.

Tech Tip

When do I need to do a baseline?

A baseline report is needed before a computer slowdown occurs.

Viewing system performance when a problem occurs is good, but it is easier if the normal performance is known. A baseline can help with this. A **baseline** is a snapshot of computer performance during normal operations (before it has problems).

Task Manager can be used to get an idea of what normal performance is, but the Windows XP System Monitor and Performance Logs and Alerts tools and the Windows Vista/7 Performance Monitor and Reliability Monitor tools are better suited to capturing and analyzing specific computer resource data.

To access the Windows XP Performance tool (which contains System Monitor and Performance Logs and Alerts), perform the following steps: From the *Start* menu → *Control Panel* → in *Category view* select *Performance and Maintenance* → *Administrative Tools* → double-click *Performance*. In Windows Vista, from the *Start* menu → *Control Panel* → *System and Maintenance* → *Performance information and Tools* → *Advanced Tools* → *Reliability and Performance Monitor* link. In Windows 7 from the *Start* menu → *Control Panel* → *System and Security* → *Administrative Tools* → double-click on *Performance Monitor*.

The Performance tool can also be accessed from a command prompt by typing `perfmon.msc`, and pressing Enter. In Windows XP, click the *System Monitor* option and the tool starts collecting and displaying real-time data about the local computer or, if configured, from remote computers. A previously captured log file can also be loaded. Data can be displayed in Graph, Histogram, and Report views.

In Windows Vista and 7, select the *Performance Monitor* option from the left pane in the *Reliability and Performance* tool. In Windows 7, use the *System and Security* control panel → *Administrative Tools* → double-click on *Performance Monitor*. Inside Performance Monitor, counters are used. A **counter** is a specific measurement for an object. Common objects include cache, memory, paging file, physical disk, processor, network interface, system, and thread. Select the + (plus sign) in Performance Monitor to select various counters. At the bottom of the window is a legend for interpreting the graph including what color is used for each of the performance measures and what counter is being used. Table 12.26 shows common counters used while within Performance Monitor. Figure 12.24 shows an example of the Performance Monitor within Windows 7. The counters chosen are the ones shown in Table 12.26.

The Windows 7 **Resource Monitor** (previously found on the main page of Windows Vista's *Performance Monitor* option) is a nice graphical tool that requires little work, but shows the main components of a system. Access the tool by selecting the *Open Resource Monitor* link from

Table 12.26   **System Monitor counters**

Computer component	Object name	Counters
Memory	Memory	Available Bytes and Cache Bytes
Hard Disk	Physical Disk	Disk Reads/sec and Disk Writes/sec
Hard Disk	Logical Disk	% Free Space
Processor	Processor	% Processor Time (All instances)

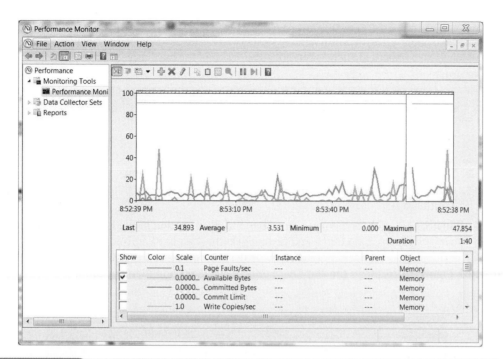

Figure 12.24　**Windows 7 Performance Monitor**

within the Performance Monitor window or access the *System and Security* control panel →
System → *Performance Information and Tools* link at the bottom of the left panel → *Advanced
tools* → *Open Resource Monitor*. Figure 12.25 shows the Resource Monitor in Windows 7.

The Windows Vista/7 *Performance Information and Tools* control panel link shows a rating
for major installed components. The scale is from 1.0 to 7.9. The higher the number the better

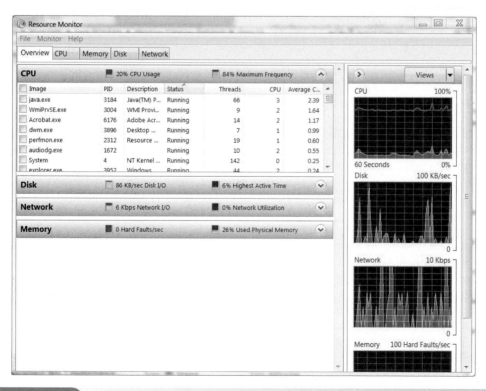

Figure 12.25　**Windows 7 Resource Monitor**

the score. This rating is measuring the capability of your hardware and software configuration to give you an overall rating for your Windows experience. The base score is actually the lowest rate of an individual component such as memory, the desktop, the hard drive transfer rate, and graphics performance.

Running any performance monitor tool affects the computer performance, especially when using the Graph view and sampling large amounts of data. The following steps help when running any performance monitoring tool:

1. Turn off any screen saver.
2. Use *Report* view instead of Graph view to save on resources.
3. Keep the number of counters being monitored to a minimum.
4. Sample at longer intervals such as 10 to 15 minutes rather than just a few seconds or minutes apart.

In Windows XP, click the *Performance Logs and Alerts* option in the Performance window to be able to create graphs, bar charts, and text reports that can be saved and viewed at a later time, as well as set parameters that generate a system alert when a certain counter's threshold has been reached. Figure 12.26 shows the standard Performance Logs and Alerts window.

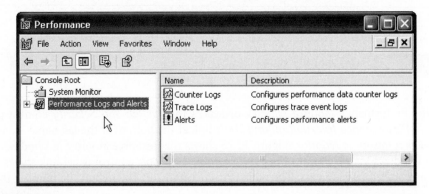

Figure 12.26 Performance tool—Performance logs and alerts window

As seen in Figure 12.26, there are three types of logs or alerts. The Counter Logs option is used to create a log file using objects and counters that you select. Trace Logs is used to trigger data recording once a certain threshold has been reached. Alerts is used to select objects and counters and set when the tracking is to begin, how often the system is monitored, and how alerts are to be handled. Alerts by default are sent to Event Viewer in the application event log. For example, an alert was created to trigger any time the memory available bytes counter goes above a value of 1. (This is not a practical example but one used to illustrate how alerts are handled.) The alert is configured so that Event Viewer's application event log is updated whenever memory goes above this threshold. Figure 12.27 shows the information alert in Event Viewer.

Another tool that is available (but only in XP) is Dr. Watson. Dr. Watson is a utility that automatically loads when an application starts. Dr. Watson can detect and display troubleshooting information as well as create a text log file (DRWTSN32.LOG) when a system or application error occurs. A technician might need this information when communicating with Microsoft or the application developer's technical support. Make notes of any messages that appear on the screen when any type of problem occurs.

To start Dr. Watson in Windows XP, click the *Start* button, click the *Run* option, and type drwtsn32 and press Enter. Click the application error and click the *View* button. The default location for the log file is C:\Documents and Settings\All Users\ Application Data\Microsoft\DrWatson. When an error occurs, Dr. Watson appends information to the end of this log file.

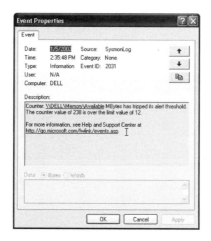

Figure 12.27 Event Viewer—application event log alert

Blue screen of death

Sometimes when Windows XP crashes, a blue screen with an error code and numbers appears on the screen. Try to reboot with the power button, but it may require you to remove the computer's power cord, reinsert the power cord, and re-power on the computer. Once restarted, you can research the error message and problem on the Internet.

Windows XP is the first version of a Windows operating system that has Windows Error Reporting tool that is based on the Dr. Watson technology. Through this feature, the application code that is stored in memory is provided to Microsoft via the Internet. Sometimes, possible solutions are sent back including links to updated files that solve particular application problems. Microsoft states that many of the fixes for Windows XP came from problems reported using this tool.

Microsoft Vista does not include the Dr. Watson tool but has the Problem Reports and Solutions window instead. The settings allow Windows Vista/7 to automatically report problems and check for solutions, to check for solutions only when a problem occurs, or to report problems and check for solutions at any time. In Vista, access the *System and Maintenance* control panel and select the *Problem Reports and Solutions* link. In Windows 7, access the *System and Security → Action Center → Maintenance* section.

Windows Vista and 7 handle the logs and reports differently than Windows XP. A **data collector set**, which organizes data to be viewed, logged, and reviewed later, can contain performance counters, event trace data and system information such as registry key values. To create a data collector set, use the Performance Monitor tool to create counters to monitor. From the *Action* menu item, select *New → Data Collector Set*. Type a name for the set and click *Next*. The default directory for the saved set is the *%systemdrive%*/PerfLogs/Admin/ folder. Click *Finish*.

Expand the *Data Collector Sets* item in the left pane and expand the *User Defined* section. Right-click on the saved performance monitor and select *Start*. The data gathering starts. Right-click on the data collector set name again and select *Stop*. Expand the *Reports* section and the *User Defined* area. Expand the named data collector set and double-click on the saved file.

The Vista/7 Reliability Monitor is also new, and it is used to give a visual and detailed report on the reliability of the computer by category. The details are to help technicians troubleshoot the cause of something that causes the system to become unreliable. In Vista, the Reliability Monitor is found as an option within the Reliability and Performance Monitor. In Windows 7 it is a separate tool found by typing `reliability monitor` in the *Search programs and files* textbox from the *Start* menu. Figure 12.28 shows this tool.

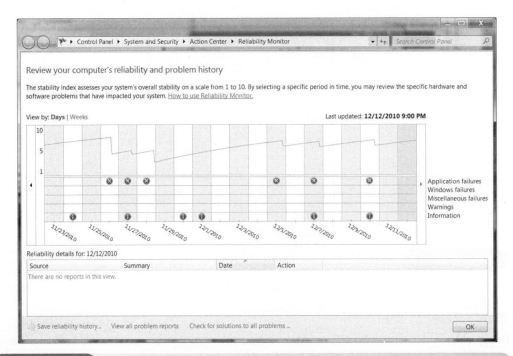

Figure 12.28   **Windows 7 Reliability Monitor**

Supporting Windows Computers Remotely

Windows XP and Vista/7 Professional and higher support accessing a PC remotely using two Microsoft products—Remote Desktop and Remote Assistance. Both products allow a computer to be accessed remotely. The difference is that Remote Assistance displays a prompt at the remote computer asking permission to allow the computer to be viewed remotely and Remote Desktop does not display this prompt.

Using Remote Desktop (`mstsc` command) requires the following elements:

- The remote desktop must have some type of network connectivity
- The computer used to access the remote desktop must be Windows XP Professional, Windows Vista/7 Professional or higher, Windows Server, or have some type of terminal services running
- Any firewalls between the two computers must allow ports 3389 and 80 to be open
- The remote PC must have the Remote Desktop application installed
- You need to know the computer name of the remote PC
- You need to have a user account with a password on the remote PC

Tech Tip

What type of network connectivity does Remote Desktop require?

If you are connecting to the remote PC from another computer on the same network, then of course, both computers must have network connectivity. If you are connecting to the remote PC from an entirely different network in a different location such as a different city or state, then of course the PCs must have Internet connectivity.

Both Remote Desktop and Remote Assistance are useful for those working a help desk and for technicians who must support computers located in other locations. With Remote Assistance, one computer user (the Expert) views another computer user's (the Novice) desktop.

Tech Tip

Remote Assistance using Windows XP Home version

If Windows XP Home is installed, the computer user functioning in the "Novice" role must be logged in and using an "Owner" type of account.

Remote Assistance (`msra` command) can be initiated using any of the following methods:

- Windows Messenger service
- Email an invitation
- Send an invitation as an email attachment

Of the three methods available, Windows Messenger is the only method that works in real time.

How to get started with Windows XP Remote Assistance

If you have never configured Windows Messenger service, the Remote Assistance wizard steps you through the process. *Start* button → *Help and Support* → *Invite a friend to connect to your computer with Remote Assistance* link → *Invite someone to help you* link. Through this link you can configure and use Windows Messenger, email, or save the invitation as a file.

Tech Tip

12 Windows XP, Vista, and 7

Remote Desktop is disabled by default in Windows Vista or 7. Open *Windows Explorer* and right-click on *Computer* → *Properties* → *Remote Settings* link from left panel. In the Windows Vista and 7 environment, Remote Assistance now supports computers that use NAT (network address translation); however, you may have to go into the Windows Firewall application and in the left panel select *Allow a program through Windows Firewall*. Select the *Exceptions* tab and locate *Remote Assistance*. You must also set up a password for the guest user and manually send the password to the person being invited to take over the computer.

Preventive Maintenance for Your Operating System

Your operating system is a key component of a working system. No application or hardware can work without an operating system. It is important that you keep your operating system healthy. The following suggestions can help:

- Always have an antivirus software program that has up to date virus definitions.
- Make frequent data backups.
- Have a backup of your operating system. Many external hard drives include backup software. Remember that Windows XP Home and Vista Home Basic/Premium do not include a backup utility.
- Ensure that the System Restore utility is enabled.
- Update the operating system with service packs and patches.

Soft Skills—Avoiding Burnout

Many technicians get tired of the fast pace of technology. As a person matures, it seems to takes more effort to stay current in the skills required for business. One of the attractions to technology for many students is how technology is always changing; however, it is this speed of change that provides such a challenge even to seasoned veterans. Sometimes, a technician is in the same job for more than three years, and burnout is evident. Burnout—commonly caused by too much work and stress—is a mental state that can also affect emotional and physical capabilities. Technicians should monitor their own attitude and mental state constantly and watch for warning signs associated with burnout:

- Overreaction to common situations
- Constant tiredness
- Reduced productivity
- Poor attitude
- Lack of patience with customers or peers
- Feeling of a loss of control
- Use of food, drink, or drugs as coping mechanisms

Burnout can be prevented and dealt with if it is recognized. Working too much, having too many responsibilities, and expecting too much of yourself also lead to burnout. The following list can help you recognize and cope with burnout:

- Take vacations during which you do not stay in contact with work
- Set reachable goals, even on a daily basis
- Take a couple of breaks during the day and do something nontechnical
- Learn something new that is not related to technology
- Have good eating, sleeping, and exercising routines
- Subscribe to a positive saying or joke of the day
- Smile more

Key Terms

ASR (p. 514)
baseline (p. 524)
boot partition (p. 508)
boot volume (p. 508)
clean install (p. 478)
Computer Management console (p. 499)
counter (p. 524)
data collector set (p. 527)
DEP (p. 477)
device driver (p. 494)
digital signature (p. 495)
Dr. Watson (p. 517)
driver roll back (p. 496)
dual-boot (p. 480)
effective permissions (p. 508)
Event Viewer (p. 518)
HAL (p. 509)
KMS (p. 486)
Last Known Good Configuration (p. 511)

library (p. 505)
MAK (p. 486)
MAP (p. 486)
Microsoft Management console (p. 499)
page (p. 475)
patch (p. 480)
Performance Logs and Alerts (p. 522)
Performance Monitor (p. 522)
Program Compatibility wizard (p. 477)
Recovery Console (p. 512)
registry (p. 491)
Reliability Monitor (p. 522)
Resource Monitor (p. 524)
restore point (p. 497)
Safe Mode (p. 512)
service pack (p. 480)
Shadow Copy (p. 498)
SID (p. 486)

SIM (p. 486)
System Configuration utility (p. 516)
system file (p. 508)
System Monitor (p. 522)
system partition (p. 508)
System Restore (p. 497)
System State (p. 492)
system volume (p. 508)
Task Manager (p. 517)
UAC (p. 475)
upgrade (p. 478)
Upgrade Advisor (p. 479)
USMT (p. 482)
virus (p. 483)
WDT (p. 486)
WFP (p. 475)
Windows Aero (p. 475)
Windows Defender (p. 517)
Windows XP mode (p. 482)
WinRE (p. 514)
WRP (p. 477)

Review Questions

1. Match the Windows XP version on the left with the environment on the right.
   _____ Home   a. corporate environment
   _____ Media Center   b. low end student computer
   _____ Professional   c. computer for scrapbook and photo album creation

2. List three features of Window XP.

3. What is the difference between Windows XP Home and Professional versions?

4. Explain how WFP works.

5. Windows Vista and 7 are a [16 | 32 | 64 |128 | 256]-bit operating system. (Select all that apply.)

6. Aero is a/an [system tool | screen saver | startup repair tool | graphical environment].

7. Describe the purpose of the Windows UAC.

8. How much video RAM is needed to run Aero?

9. List all Vista versions available for home users in the U.S.

10. [T | F] 32-bit Windows 7 can be installed on a computer with a 64-bit processor.

11. What is the maximum amount of RAM that can be recognized by any version of 32-bit Windows 7?

12. What is the maximum amount of RAM supported by Windows 7 Home Basic?

13. A customer has an older 16-bit game as well as some newer 32-bit games. The customer is considering upgrading to 64-bit Windows 7. Will there be any issues with this? If so, what are they and how might they be resolved?

14. What SFC switch is used to replace a corrupt system file in Windows 7?

15. What type of files does WRP protect?

16. List three steps to be taken *before* installing Windows XP, Vista, or 7.

17. [Yes | No] Can Windows XP be upgraded directly to Windows 7? Explain your answer.

18. What Windows XP versions can be upgraded to Vista Business?

19. Can Windows 2000 Professional be upgraded to Vista? [Yes | No]

20. [Yes | No] Is the Upgrade Advisor tool available from the Windows Vista or 7 installation disc?

21. List two reasons to use the NTFS file system.

22. What is journaling, and what file system supports it?

23. What Microsoft tool checks software applications after Windows XP or Vista is loaded?

24. List two symptoms of a virus.

25. Who is responsible for ensuring that a newly deployed computer has an antivirus application installed and configured as well as educating the customer about what to do if the computer contracts a virus? [the user | the customer's boss | the corporate helpdesk | the technician | the computer manufacturer]

26. What is hardware-based DEP?

27. What are the two software-based DEP options available in Windows 7?

28. [T | F] Microsoft requires Windows 7 activation within 10 days of installation.

29. A large college would most likely use [MAK | KMS] for activating Vista licenses.

30. How many times can a KMS key be used?

31. How is network bandwidth affected when computer cloning is being performed?

32. List three possible errors that could occur during installation.

33. What is the best solution for dual-booting Windows 7 with another operating system? [Put the operating systems on separate hard drive volumes | Put Windows 7 on an external USB hard drive | Put Windows 7 on an eSATA drive | Run Windows 7 from a DVD]

34. List a reason why you might have to reload Windows.

35. Describe the steps technicians use to customize Windows Vista or 7 updates.

36. [T | F] Existing restore points are deleted if Windows is re-installed.

37. What utility is used to modify the Windows Vista/7 registry?

38. What utility is used to create an emergency copy of the System State?

39. Match the following tasks with the appropriate Windows XP control panel category:

    _____ Printers and Other Hardware
    _____ Performance and Maintenance
    _____ Network and Internet Connections
    _____ Appearance and Themes
    _____ Sounds, Speech, and Audio Devices

    a. Used to access options when connecting to the Web
    b. Used to select speaker settings
    c. Used to set the *Start* menu to the traditional setting
    d. Used to access keyboard settings
    e. Used to select a power option

40. Match the following tasks with the appropriate Windows 7 control panel category. Note that each category has only one definition when the other definitions are taken into account, even though some definitions can be accessed through multiple control panel links.
    _____ Programs
    _____ Action Center
    _____ Network and Internet
    _____ User Accounts (and Family Safety)
    _____ System and Security
    a. Used to access Internet Options
    b. Used to access the troubleshooting wizards
    c. Used to change the desktop gadgets
    d. Used to access the System properties
    e. Used to reset a user password

41. [T | F] Device drivers are specific for a particular Windows operating system version.

42. A device driver is best described as [firmware | hardware | software].

43. In what way does a Windows update affect device drivers?

44. What are the two most important steps for a successful device installation?

45. What does Windows 7 use instead of the .CAB system for drivers?

46. How does a digital signature help a technician?

47. What user group is allowed to perform the driver rollback?

48. If a device has to be manually installed in Vista, what utility is used and what file extension is required for the driver?

49. What is the purpose of the System Restore utility?

50. How is System Restore on a Windows Vista/7 computer different from the same utility on a Windows XP system?

51. How can you tell which printer is the default on a Windows computer?

52. List two suggestions to help with a problem getting an older application to function in the Windows 7 environment.

53. What Windows XP control panel is used to remove applications?

54. What Windows Vista/7 control panel is used to customize desktop gadgets?

55. List the three major components of the Microsoft Management Console.

56. How can you tell if a user account has been disabled in Windows 7?

57. What Windows tool is used to analyze a hard drive and consolidate files and folders?

58. What Service Properties tab contains a *Start*, *Stop*, *Pause*, or *Resume* button used to control a particular service?

59. What Service Properties tab allows you to see what happens when a service fails multiple instances?

60. What NTFS permissions are not available with share permissions?

61. Alice has a Windows 7 computer participating in a workgroup network and has password protection enabled. She wants to share files with Joe. What does Alice have to do once she shares the folder to ensure that Joe can access the files in the shared folder?

62. What are effective permissions?

63. Daniel has granted Jennifer the NTFS permission to look at the contents of a shared folder. Jennifer belongs to a group called *Writers* that is allowed through NTFS permissions to read and execute applications contained in the shared folder. What are Jennifer's effective permissions?

64. What type of Windows partition holds the majority of the operating system files?

65. [T | F] On Windows XP, the boot partition and the system partition can be the same partition.

66. Where is the NTLDR file located on the hard drive when Windows XP is loaded?

67. What does the Microsoft term *%systemroot%* mean?

68. What Windows 7 file causes multiple operating system choices to appear as a boot menu?

69. What Windows Vista/7 file replaced the Windows XP NTLDR file?

70. You just installed a new sound card and loaded the driver, but when Windows boots, the computer locks. What boot option should you use to help with this problem?

71. [T | F] Whenever the *Last Known Good Configuration* boot option is used, all configuration changes since the last successful boot are lost.

72. List three suggestions to reduce the amount of time a Windows 7 computer takes before being usable.

73. What log file is created when Enable Boot logging is used?

74. [T | F] *Recovery Console* is a boot option by default with Windows XP.

75. [T | F] The Windows XP Administrator password can be changed from Recovery Console.

76. [T | F] While in Recovery Console, files can be copied to Zip disks but not floppy disks.

77. What is used instead of the Emergency Repair Disk with Windows XP?

78. What Windows Recovery Environment tool is used to take the Windows Vista or 7 system files back to an earlier time?

79. What Vista versions are required to do a complete restore of the operating system from an external hard drive backup?

80. [T | F] The WinRE command prompt has fewer commands available to be executed than Windows XP Recovery Console.

81. What command is used if the Startup Repair WinRE option cannot fix an MBR problem?

82. What three tabs were available through the Windows XP System Configuration utility, but are not available in Windows Vista and 7?

83. What is the purpose of the Boot tab in Windows Vista/7 System Configuration window?

84. When would a technician use the Windows Vista/7 System Configuration Tools tab?

85. What keystrokes bring up Task Manager in Windows?

86. When would a technician use Event Viewer?

87. When you see an Event Viewer event that has an exclamation mark beside it, what do you do?

88. What type of Windows Vista/7 Event Viewer log would list events from a different computer?

89. What do you do if you see an error message that states that the Event Viewer log is full on a Windows XP computer?

90. What two tools would be best to use if a service does not start?

91. List two tools used to monitor computer performance on a Windows 7 computer?

92. Detail specifically how Task Manager can be used to monitor computer performance?

93. For what is the Task Manager CPU Usage performance factor used?

94. [T | F] When System Monitor is actively capturing computer data, the system performance can be degraded.

95. List three things a student can do to avoid burnout in school.

Fill-in-the-Blank

1. Windows handles memory blocks in 4K chunks known as a/an _____.

2. Press _____+_____+_____ twice to access the Windows XP Administrator account login screen.

3. A/An _____ is done when an older operating system is already loaded and XP is installed to replace it.

4. The Windows Vista/7 _____ feature notifies the user of potential security risks when an application is trying to modify important files on the system.

5. _____ protects certain Windows Vista/7 registry keys using ACLs.

6. A _____ is the type of installation that must be used when a customer wants Windows 7 on a computer that currently has Windows XP installed.

7. The _____ Microsoft tool is used to check for hardware and software compatibility problems *before* Windows is installed.

8. A/An _____ changes the way the operating system, applications, and/or files behave.

9. Hardware-based _____ is known as no execute on an AMD CPU-based motherboard and as execute disable on an Intel CPU-based motherboard.

10. A computer has Windows 7 installed. Another computer has been built and the Windows 7 for the first computer _____ [can | cannot] be used on the second computer.

11. A/An _____ is a number assigned by a Windows domain controller to every computer on the network.

12. The two user groups authorized to use the Backup utility by default in Windows XP are _____ and _____.

13. The *Change your home page* control panel link is found in the _____ Windows 7 control panel.

14. A/An _____ enables a piece of hardware to work with Windows.

15. Use the _____ Windows tool to install hardware devices that are not automatically detected by the operating system.

16. The _____ folder holds device drivers known to Windows Vista/7.

17. You must be a member of the _____ group to install a new hardware driver.

18. A/An _____, otherwise known as driver signing, is used by a device driver known to be compatible with Windows.

19. A/An _____ is one snapshot of the operating system taken by the System Restore utility.

20. Management tools are contained in Windows _____.

21. In order to use the *Shared Folders* Computer Management Console tool in XP, you must be a member of the _____ or _____ group.

22. _____ contains a Windows XP troubleshooting tool for hardware devices.

23. The _____ tool is used to create hard disk partitions.

24. The Windows 7 _____ Computer Management section holds the WMI Control tool.

25. The _____ Device Manager tab contains a *Troubleshoot* button that is used when a device is not working properly.

26. The _____ and _____ share permissions cannot take ownership of files.

27. The _____ Windows partition contains files that are needed to boot Windows.

28. The BOOT.INI Windows XP file is located in the _____.

29. The term *%systemdrive%* is a Microsoft term that represents the _____ directory.

30. _____ is the acronym for the layer between hardware devices and Windows.

31. _____ is the most common boot mode option used when the computer slows down or does not work properly.

32. _____ is the same as Safe Mode except that it loads network drivers and services.

33. _____ is used only when other Windows XP boot options do not solve the computer problem. This mode starts the computer in command prompt mode and only typed commands can be used.

34. The _____ is the Windows Vista/7 menu that contains *Startup Repair* which can be used to fix the computer when Windows does not boot properly.

35. The _____ utility is used to disable startup programs selectively.

36. _____ is used to stop currently loaded programs that have halted unexpectedly.

37. _____ is used to monitor computer events.

38. The Windows 7 _____ Event Viewer log is used to monitor system components that load during startup.

39. The _____ Event Viewer symbol is used to signify that a specific event has failed.

40. The _____ system performance tool can be used to quickly see processor utilization.

41. The Windows _____ Task Manager tab is used to show the amount of virtual memory being used.

42. A _____ is a report that is done before the computer has problems and it shows how the computer normally performs.

Hands-On Exercises

1. Windows XP Clean Installation

Objective: To be able to install Windows XP on a hard drive that does not have an operating system installed or any partitions

Parts: Computer with a hard drive that does not have partitions or an operating system installed and that has a CD drive installed

Windows XP CD

Note: If partitions currently exist on the hard drive, see Chapter 7 on hard drives for removing partitions.

Procedure: Complete the following procedure and answer the accompanying questions.

1. Insert the Windows XP CD into the CD-ROM drive and turn on the computer. Some computers require you to press a key or require special BIOS settings to boot from the CD. Perform the appropriate steps to allow the computer to boot from the CD. The setup screen displays. If the CD is an evaluation copy of XP, press Enter to display the licensing agreement.

2. Press F8 to accept the licensing agreement. The hard drive partitioning screen appears.

3. Check with the instructor on how much space is desired for the partition. The partition must be a minimum of 2GB.

   What size partition did you choose for the Windows XP installation?

4. Select a hard drive area that is unpartitioned and press C to create a partition. A prompt appears asking for the partition size. Use the answer obtained in Step 3 and enter this information. Note that Enter can be pressed to use all available space for the partition. Press Enter to install Windows XP on the partition just created.

5. A screen appears prompting you to format the newly created partition. Select *NTFS* as the type of file system used. The drive is formatted and setup files are copied to the drive.

6. When prompted to restart the computer, remove the CD from the drive and press Enter.

7. When prompted to insert the CD into the drive, re-insert the Windows XP CD into the drive and click the *OK* button.

8. Accept the default path for the Windows XP installation by clicking the *OK* button. After copying more files, you are prompted for regional settings. Set the appropriate language and click *Next*.

9. The Personalize Your Software page appears. This is what applications use for product registration and document identification. Leave this information blank and click the *Next* button. The Product Key page appears.

10. Enter the product key located on the back of the Windows XP case, written on the CD, or provided by the student assistant or instructor. Click the *Next* button.

    Check with the lab assistant or instructor for the name that will be given to the computer as well as the Administrator password. Document this information.

    Computer name: _____

    Administrator password: _____

11. The setup program prompts for the computer name and Administrator password. Type the computer name and Administrator password. Click the *Next* button.

12. If a modem is installed, the modem dialing information is displayed. The correct country, area code, number to access an outside line, and so on, are required. Contact the lab assistant or instructor for this information, enter it, and click the *Next* button. If a modem is not installed (or after this information is entered), the date and time page appears. Set the date and time as appropriate and click the *Next* button.

13. If a network card is installed in the computer, the network settings page displays. Enter the appropriate networking information provided by the instructor and click *Next*. The setup process continues copying files and installing the operating system and then restarts the computer. After the restart, the Welcome to Microsoft Windows screen appears.

    Does the welcome screen appear? Show this screen to the instructor.

Instructor initials: _____

14. Click the *Next* button and the Internet Connection screen appears. Select *skip this step*.

15. When asked if you want to activate Windows, select the *wait until later* option.

16. When prompted, do not select to set up user accounts. This process is covered in another lab.

17. Click the *Finish* button.

    Does Windows boot properly after the installation process?

Instructor initials: _____

2. Windows XP Upgrade Installation

Objective: To be able to install Windows XP on a hard drive that already has an operating system installed

Parts: Computer with a hard drive that has Windows 98, Windows Me, NT Workstation 4.0, or Windows 2000 installed and that has a CD drive installed

               Windows XP CD

Procedure: Complete the following procedure and answer the accompanying questions.

1. Power on the computer and log on as necessary. Contact the instructor or lab assistant for the userid and password if necessary. Insert the Windows XP CD into the CD-ROM drive. The Welcome to Microsoft Windows XP screen should appear. Click *Install Windows XP*. The setup process collects information about the computer to ensure it is upgradable.

2. When asked what type of installation to use, select *Upgrade* and click the *Next* button.

3. Click the radio button to accept the licensing agreement and click the *Next* button.

4. Enter the product key located on the back of the CD case, written on the CD, or provided by the instructor or lab assistant and click the *Next* button.

5. The Dynamic Update is optional and can only be used if an Internet connection is available. The Dynamic Update updates installation files. Contact the instructor or lab assistant to determine if the Dynamic Update is necessary.

   Was the Dynamic Update performed?

6. The setup process copies installation files and restarts. When prompted to choose a Windows installation, *do not select anything*. Windows automatically selects the correct version. The XP logo appears, more files are copied, and the computer reboots again.

7. You may be asked to enter a computer name if the old computer name is not appropriate. If necessary, type an appropriate computer name and click the *Next* button. The Tour Windows screen appears.

8. When asked to activate the product, select the option to bypass this step. Click the *Finish* button.

9. When asked to setup user accounts, contact the instructor or lab assistant to verify if any should be created.

   Were any user accounts created? If so, list them.

10. Click the *Next* button and the XP desktop appears.

3. Windows Vista Installation

Objective: To be able to install Windows Vista on a hard drive that does not have an operating system installed or any partitions

Parts: Computer with a hard drive that does not have partitions or an operating system installed and that has a CD/DVD drive installed

Windows Vista DVD

Note: The screens may appear a little differently with different service packs and Vista versions.

Procedure: Complete the following procedure and answer the accompanying questions.

1. Insert the Windows Vista installation disc into the CD/DVD drive and turn on the computer. Some computers require you to press a key or require specific BIOS settings to boot from the CD/DVD drive.

   Perform the appropriate steps to allow the computer to boot from the CD/DVD drive.

2. The Install Windows screen appears. Ensure the language, time and currency format, and keyboard are set to the correct values and click *Next*.

3. Notice on the next screen the option to discover what to do and know before installing Windows. These are the types of things you should have read in the chapter in the pre-installation section. Also notice the *Repair your computer* option. The R is underlined because if you press the R key, this option is chosen. The Repair your computer option is the replacement for the Recovery Console utility found in Windows XP. Because there is not a boot problem, click the *Install now* button.

4. Type the product key provided by your instructor or lab assistant or found on the DVD case and click *Next*.

   Note that if you leave the product key textbox empty and click *Next*, a message appears asking if you want to enter the product key now. If you select *No* to this question, Setup asks you what Vista version you purchased. You can select any Vista version and experiment with it for 30 days. To extend that time period for another 30 days, access a command prompt as Administrator (right-click on the Command Prompt Accessory and select *Run as administrator*) and type **slmgr-rearm**. This process can be used to extend the trial period to a maximum of 120 days.

5. Read and confirm the license by selecting the *I accept the license terms* checkbox and click *Next*. A prompt appears asking what type of installation you want.

6. Select *Custom (advanced)* unless directed otherwise by your instructor or lab assistant.

7. The Where do you want to install Windows? prompt appears. Select the hard drive partition on which Vista will be installed and click *Next*. The Installing Windows window appears, and this step may take approximately 40 to 45 minutes.

8. Click the *Restart now* button, or the system will automatically restart itself after a period of time. When the message appears to press a key to boot from the CD or DVD, *do not* press any key so the system will boot from the hard drive partition.

9. The installation process may cause the computer to reboot during the next portion of the setup process. This is normal. Eventually, the system will prompt to enter a user name and

picture. In the *Type a user name (for example, John)* textbox, type a name provided by the instructor or lab assistant.

10. Type a password provided by the instructor or lab assistant in the *Type a password (recommended)* textbox as well as the *Retype your password* textbox. Note that passwords are case sensitive. Also type a password hint, as directed by the instructor or lab assistant.

    Print the exact password used, using appropriate uppercase and lowercase letters.

    _____

11. Click *Next*. Type a computer name in the *Type a computer name (for example Office-PC)* textbox and select a desktop background. Click *Next*.

12. When the Help protect Windows automatically window appears, check with the instructor or lab assistant for the option to select. If the instructor or assistant is not available, click on the *Use recommended settings* option.

13. Select the appropriate time zone and date and click *Next*.

14. Select the appropriate computer location, as recommended by your instructor or lab assistant. If the instructor or assistant is not available, select the *Work* option.

15. Click the *Start* button. The login window appears. Enter the password selected in Step 10. Click the *right arrow* button.

16. The Windows Vista welcome screen appears.

Instructor initials: _____

4. Windows 7 Installation

Objective: To be able to install Windows 7 on a hard drive that does not have an existing operating system

Parts: Computer with the minimum hardware requirements for Windows 7 and a DVD drive
Windows 7 DVD or virtual image of the installation disc

Note: The screens may appear a little differently with different service packs and Windows 7 versions.

Procedure: Complete the following procedure and answer the accompanying questions.

1. Configure the BIOS to boot from the CD/DVD drive.

2. Insert the Windows 7 installation DVD into a DVD drive and turn on the computer. The Windows 7 Setup program starts automatically if the BIOS was configured correctly.

3. Select the appropriate regional options and click *Next*.

4. Select *Install Now* to start the Windows 7 installation.

5. Read the EULA (end user licensing agreement). Select the *I accept the License Terms* option and click *Next*.

6. The two options that appear for Windows 7 is to upgrade or to perform a custom installation. To install Windows 7 as a clean install, click the *Custom (Advanced)* option.

7. When prompted for where to install Windows 7, select the *Drive options (advanced)* option.

8. Delete a partition, create a partition, and format a partition as needed. When finished selecting the partition, click *Next*. If a RAID or SCSI driver is needed, install it at this point.

9. The computer restarts and Windows 7 loads and completes the installation. A username and a computer name are required. The computer name must be unique. Contact the instructor or lab assistant for a unique name if necessary.

10. Contact the instructor for a password for the user account.

    Print the exact password to be used using appropriate upper and lowercase letters.

    _____

11. Enter the password, hint, and click *Next*.

12. Enter the product key provided. Check with the instructor or lab assistant if you do not have one. Note that you can leave this blank to experiment with the different versions of Windows 7. They all come on the same DVD. You must eventually install a version for which you have a license. Do not experiment with different Windows 7 versions if upgrading from a prior version of Windows as this is not allowed once the old version is upgraded.

13. In the Help Protect Your Computer and Improve Windows Automatically dialog box, select the *Use Recommended Settings* option.

14. In the Review Your Time and Date Settings dialog box, select the appropriate time zone and date options. Click *Finish*.

15. Contact your instructor or lab assistant for the appropriate computer location. If the instructor or assistant is not available, select the *Work* option.

16. Click *Start* and the Windows logon appears.

Instructor Initials _____

5. Using REGEDIT in Windows XP/Vista/7

Objective: To become familiar with the REGEDIT registry editing utility

Parts: Computer with Windows XP, Vista, or 7 installed

          Formatted 3.5-inch disk or Flash drive

Note: REGEDIT is a utility used for editing the Windows registry. With REGEDIT, you can view existing registry settings, modify registry setting values, or create new registry entries to change or enhance the way Windows operates. In this lab, you will use REGEDIT to view the system BIOS and video BIOS information on your computer.

Caution: Editing the registry can cause your computer to run erratically or not run at all! When performing any registry editing, follow *all* directions carefully including spelling, syntax use, and so forth. Failure to do so may cause your computer to fail!

Procedure: Complete the following procedure and answer the accompanying questions.

Viewing Registry Information

1. From the *Start* menu in Windows XP, choose *Run*, type **REGEDIT**, and click *OK*. In Vista/7 from the *Start* menu, type **regedit** in the *Start Search* (Vista)/*Search programs and files* (7) textbox and press Enter. Click *Continue* (Vista)/*OK* (7) if necessary. The REGEDIT utility opens.

2. In the left window, expand both the *HKEY_LOCAL_MACHINE*, *HARDWARE*, and *DESCRIPTION* sections by clicking the + (plus) symbol in XP or the ▷ in Vista/7 (located to the left of the name). Click the *System* option located under *DESCRIPTION*. The system BIOS and video BIOS information display in the right window.

What is the system BIOS date?

Who is the manufacturer of the system BIOS?

When was the video BIOS manufactured?

Instructor initials: _____

Exporting and Importing a Registry Section

3. REGEDIT can be used to backup and restore part or all of the registry. To illustrate this, a portion of the registry will be exported to disk and then imported into the registry. Ensure the following option is still selected in the Registry window:

HEKY_LOCAL_MACHINE\Hardware\Description\System

4. Click the *File* menu option and select *Export*. The Export Registry File window opens.

5. Insert a blank formatted disk into the A: drive or insure the Flash drive is attached and recognized by the operating system. Click the *Save in* down arrow (at the top of the window) and select the appropriate drive letter.

6. In the *File name* textbox, type **Registry System Section** and click the *Save* button. The specific registry key is saved to disk.

7. To restore the registry (or a portion of it as in this exercise), click the *File* menu option and select *Import*. The screen should list the file located on the drive to which it was saved, but if it does not, select the correct drive option from the *Look in* drop-down menu (XP), or browse using the Favorite Links section (Vista) or the left portion (7) of the window.

8. Click the *Registry System Section* file name and click the *Open* button. A message appears when the section is successfully inserted into the registry. Show this message to the instructor or lab assistant.

Instructor initials: _____

9. Close the REGEDIT utility.

6. Windows XP/Vista/7 Registry Modification

Objective: To be able to modify the Windows XP, Vista, or 7 registry when given directions to do so

Parts: Computer with Windows XP, Vista, or 7 loaded

Notes: You must be an Administrator or a member of the Administrators group to change registry settings. Sometimes you are given directions by Microsoft to edit the registry in order to fix a problem. It is very important that you follow the directions exactly as shown.

Procedure: Complete the following procedure and answer the accompanying questions.

1. Power on the computer and verify that Windows loads. Log on to the computer using the userid and password provided by the instructor or lab assistant.

2. Open Windows Explorer and right-click any folder.

   Which editing options are available for a folder? Select all that apply. [*Cut* | *Copy* | *Paste* | *Copy To Folder* | *Move To Folder* | *Delete* | *Rename* | *Send To*]

3. In XP, select the *Start* button → *Run* → type **regedit** and press ⏎. In Vista/7, locate the *Start* button *Search* (Vista)/*Search programs and files* (7) textbox, type **regedit**, and press ⏎.

4. Expand the *HKEY_CLASSES_ROOT* option by clicking the + (plus sign) in XP or the ▷ in Vista/7.

5. Scroll down to locate and expand *AllFileSystemObjects*. Note that items beginning with character such as . (period), are before the alphabetized list of other objects.

6. Expand the *shellex* object and locate *ContextMenuHandlers*. Shellex is a shell extension key that lets you customize the Windows interface.

7. Right-click *ContextMenuHandlers* → *New* → *Key*. When the new folder (key) appears, type **Copy To** because this registry modification adds a new option to the right-click menu called *Copy To*.

8. The Copy To object should still be selected in the left window. Double-click the *(Default)* name in the right panel. The Edit String window appears.

9. In the *Value data* textbox, type the following value exactly as shown (the 0s are zeroes):
   {C2FBB630-2971-11D1-A18C-00C04FD75D13}
   Click *OK*.

10. Verify the change has occurred. Open *Windows Explorer* and right-click any folder.

    Does the *Copy To Folder* option appear as an option? If not, redo the lab.

Instructor initials: _____

11. Using the same process, create another new key under *ContextMenuHandlers* and name the key *Move To*. The value data for the Move To key is as follows:

    {C2FBB631-2971-11D1-A18C-00C04FD75D13}

12. Use Windows Explorer to create two new folders. Copy a couple of files into each folder. Use the new *Copy To* and *Move To* options you just created.

13. Delete any folders that you have created.

14. To delete keys in Registry Editor, select the *Copy To* key in the left panel. From the *Edit* menu option, select *Delete* and select *Yes* when asked to verify. Delete the *Move To* key using the same process.

Instructor initials: _____

15. Close the *Registry Editor* window.

    Using the Internet or magazines, locate a registry edit that you think would improve Windows. Write the URL or magazine title and date as well as a brief description of the edit.

7. Windows XP System State Backup

Objective: To be able to backup the Windows XP system state using the Backup utility

Parts: Computer with Windows XP installed

Note: In order to do this exercise, the student must have local Administrator privileges. The System State can be quite large (a common size is 400MB), so adequate hard drive or Flash drive space must be available.

Procedure: Complete the following procedure and answer the accompanying questions.

1. Turn on the computer and verify that the operating system loads.

2. Log on to Windows XP using the userid and password provided by the instructor or lab assistant.

3. Click the *Start* button and point to the *All Programs* selection. Point to the *Accessories* option, point to *System Tools*, and click the *Backup* menu selection. The *Backup* wizard starts.

4. Click the *Advanced Mode* option (which is an underlined option in the words appearing in the window).

5. Click the *Backup* tab and select the *System State* checkbox to enable it.

6. Select where the backup is to be stored by clicking the *Browse* button.

    What drive and folder is being used to store the System State backup?

7. Click the *Start Backup* button. The *Backup Job information* dialog box appears. Click the *Start* button located in the window to start the backup.

8. When the backup finishes, the *Backup Progress* window shows that the backup is complete. Show this to your instructor.

Instructor initials: _____

9. Click the *Close* button. Close the *Backup Utility* window.

10. Use Windows Explorer to locate the BACKUP.BKF file and permanently delete it.

    Have a classmate verify the BACKUP.BKF file is *permanently* deleted.

Classmate's printed name: _____

8. Windows Vista Backup

Objective: To be able to backup Windows Vista using the Backup utility

Parts: Computer with Windows Vista Business, Enterprise, or Ultimate installed

Note: In order to do this exercise, the student must have local Administrator privileges. The backup can be quite large, so adequate hard drive or R/W DVDs (2–14) must be available.

Procedure: Complete the following procedure and answer the accompanying questions.

1. Turn on the computer and verify that the operating system loads.

2. Log on to Windows using the userid and password provided by the instructor or lab assistant.

3. Access the *System and Maintenance* control panel to access the *Administrative Tools* link. Double-click on *Services*. Place a checkmark by any service that has a status of *Started* in Table 12.27. Add any not listed to the bottom of the table.

4. Unplug this computer from any network by removing the network cable from the NIC.

Table 12.27 Started services

Service	Checkmark (if enabled)	Service	Checkmark (if enabled)
Application Experience		Secondary Logon	
Application Information		Secure Socket Tunneling Protocol Service	
Background Intelligent Transfer Service		Security Accounts Manager	
Base Filtering Engine		Security Center	
COM+ Event System		Server	
Cryptographic Services		Shell Hardware Detection	
DCOM Server Process Launcher		Software Licensing	
Desktop Window Manager Session Manager		SSDP Discovery	
DHCP Client		Superfetch	
Diagnostic Policy Service		System Event Notification Service	
Diagnostic System Host		Tablet PC Input Service	
Distributed Link Tracking Client		Task Scheduler	
DNS Client		TCP/IP NetBIOS Helper	
Function Discovery Resource Publication		Telephony	
Group Policy Client		Terminal Services	
Human Interface Device Access		Themes	
IKE and AuthIP IPsec Keying Modules		UPnP Device Host	
IP Helper		User Profile Service	
IPsec Policy Agent		Web Client	
KtmRm for Distributed Transaction Coordinator		Windows Audio	
Multimedia Class Scheduler		Windows Audio Endpoint Builder	
Network Connections		Windows Defender	
Network List Service		Windows Driver Foundation— User-mode Driver Framework	
Network Location Awareness		Windows Error Reporting Service	
Network Store Interface Service		Windows Event Log	
Offline Files		Windows Firewall	
Plug and Play		Windows Image Acquisition (WIA)	
Portable Device Enumerator Service		Windows Management Instrumentation	
Print Spooler		Windows Search	
Program Compatibility Assistant Service		Windows Time	
ReadyBoost		Windows Update	
Remote Access Connection Manager		WinHTTP Web Proxy Auto-Discovery service	
Remote Procedure Call (RPC)		Workstation	

5. Disable (do not uninstall) virus protection software and disk scanning software.

   List the programs that have been disabled.

6. Starting at the top of the Services list, click on the name of the first one that has a status of *Started*. A description of the service and a link to stop or restart the service is provided. For example, the first service might be Application Experience. Click once on it, and the description appears to the left. To stop the service, either click on the *Stop* link or right-click on the service name and select *Stop*. The status column changes to empty (no words) once a service stops.

   For each service, do the following:
   (a) Determine the purpose of the service.
   (b) Determine if you would consider the service one that puts a lock on files or one that is noncritical. Examples of services that put a lock on files include antivirus, disk scanning, and indexing services.
   (c) If the service fits one of these categories, stop the service and place an X beside the checkmark in Table 12.27 to identify it as one you have stopped.

7. Open the Registry Editor.

8. Expand the following keys: HKEY_LOCAL_MACHINE → SYSTEM → CurrentControl Set → Services → TCPIP. Double-click on the *Start* subkey in the right pane.

   What is the current value of the Start subkey?

9. Set the value to *1* and click *OK*.

10. From the *System and Maintenance* control panel, access the *Backup and Restore Center* link. Select the *Back up files* button.

11. Select *On a hard disk, CD, or DVD,* select a location, and click *Next* or select *On a network* and select a networked computer, select the shared folder location, and enter a username and password for that networked computer and click *Next*.

    List at least three types of file types available.

    According to the note at the bottom of the screen, what type of disks can be backed up with the Backup utility?

    Can the file backup utility be used to backup system files, executable files, and temporary files?

12. Click *Cancel*. Select the *Back up computer* button.

13. Select *One or more DVDs* and click *Next*. Click Start *backup*. Insert DVDs as directed.

14. Once the backup has finished and the *Backup completed successfully* window appears, click *Close*.

Instructor initials: _____

Note that to restore a system from a DVD backup, you start a computer from a Vista installation DVD and select the *Repair your computer* option. Select *Complete PC Restore*. Select the operating system to repair if any are listed. If it is a blank hard drive, none will be listed. Remove the installation DVD and insert the first backup DVD. Select *Windows Complete PC Restore* and follow the directions.

If a computer is participating in a computer domain, the security channel can be tested with the following commands.

nltest /sc_query:*domain_name*—If a failure condition is reported, then the security channel needs to be reset.

nltest /sc_reset:d*omain_name*—Resets a security channel.

Another command you can use to put the computer back on the domain if you are a domain administrator is netdom. You use **netdom query trust/verify** to test the security channel:

netdom reset computer_name/domain:domain_name/usero:administrator/ passwordo:password

15. Use the Internet to locate the Microsoft TechNet bulletin on the `netdom` command.

    Document another `netdom` command that you think would be useful to a technician. Include the syntax and description.

16. Return to the Services menu and put all services back to the original configuration. See Step 3, Table 12.27, for the original settings and which ones to modify.

Instructor initials: _____

9. Windows 7 Backup

Objective: To be able to backup files including the operating system if necessary using the Backup and Restore utility

Parts: Computer with Windows 7 installed and administrator rights

Procedure: Complete the following procedure and answer the accompanying questions.

Note: Even though only three files are backed up using this process, the same process can be used to backup the computer.

1. Create a new folder called *Stuff* under *Documents*.

2. Create three text files of any name and place them in the new *Stuff* folder.

3. Access the *System and Security* control panel link → *Backup and Restore* → *Set up backup* link (Note that if the Backup and Restore link has already been accessed, then the *Change settings* link can be used to complete the lab.) → select a backup destination designated by the instructor or lab assistant → *Next* → select the *Let me choose* radio button.

Note: The *Let Windows choose* radio button could be used to back up the entire operating system and files.

4. Deselect all enabled checkboxes → expand *OS (C:)* by clicking on the arrow beside it → expand *Users* → expand the user name used to log into the computer → expand *Documents* → select the *Stuff* folder *to* enable it for backup → *Next* → *Save settings and run backup* button.

5. The backup executes. Show the instructor the completed backup.

Instructor Initials _____

6. Delete the *Stuff* folder and the three files contained within it.

10. Windows Automatic Update Utility

Objective: To be able to configure a computer for automatic updates to the Windows XP operating system.

Parts: Computer with Windows XP, Vista, or 7 loaded

   Internet access

Note: You must be an Administrator or a member of the Administrators group to change Automatic Updates settings.

Procedure: Complete the following procedure and answer the accompanying questions.

1. Power on the computer and verify that Windows loads. Log on to the computer using the userid and password provided by the instructor or lab assistant.

2. In XP, select the *Start* button → *Control Panel* → *Classic* view → *System* → *Automatic Updates* tab. In Vista, select the *System and Maintenance* control panel → *Windows Update* link. Click on the *Change settings* link. In Windows 7, click the *Start* button → *Control Panel* → *System and Security* link → *Windows Update* link.

    What option is currently selected?

    Which option do you think most large corporations would want as standard and why do you think this?

3. Close the Windows Update window.

4. Click the *Cancel* button to close the Automatic Updates window.

11. Windows XP Mouse, Keyboard, Accessibility, and Sound Options

Objective: To be able to use the appropriate control panels to configure a mouse and keyboard, and enable disabilities options

Parts: Computer with Windows XP installed

Procedure: Complete the following procedure and answer the accompanying questions.

1. Turn on the computer and verify that the operating system loads.

2. Log on to Windows XP using the userid and password provided by the instructor or lab assistant.

3. Click the *Start* button and select the *Control Panel* option. Pick a Category should display in the right window. If it does not, click the *Switch to Category View* option in the left pane.

Keyboard Configuration

4. Click the *Printers and Other Hardware* control panel category. Click the *Keyboard* icon. The Keyboard Properties window appears.

5. Click the *Speed* tab. The *Keyboard Properties* window contains two tabs—*Speed* and *Hardware*. The *Speed* tab has three settings: repeat delay, repeat rate, and cursor blink rate.

   List the current keyboard settings for each of the three options.

6. The *repeat delay* option configures the duration of wait time before a key starts repeating. This is especially important for people who do not type well or who have to use a device such as a pencil to press keys. The *repeat rate* is an adjustment for how fast characters repeat across the screen. The *cursor blink rate* controls how many times the cursor blinks per second. Adjust each of these settings and test them using the *Click here and hold down a key to test repeat rate* area.

7. Configure the keyboard settings back to their original configuration. Refer to the settings determined after Step 5.

8. Click the *Hardware* tab. The Hardware tab is used to access the keyboard troubleshooting wizard and the keyboard driver. Click the *Properties* button.

   What is the current device status as shown in the window?

Instructor initials: _____

9. Click the *Driver* tab. The Update driver button is used to load a new keyboard driver. Click the *Cancel* button twice and return to the *Printers and Other Hardware* control category window.

Mouse Configuration

10. Click the *Mouse* icon. The Mouse Properties window appears. Some of the settings are standard, but others depend on the mouse manufacturer.

    List the tabs that are available in the Mouse Properties window.

11. On the Buttons tab, there are three standard options—*Button configuration*, *Doubleclick speed*, and *ClickLock*. The *Button configuration* section is where the mouse buttons can be reversed for left-handed people.

    Is the *Switch primary and secondary buttons* option enabled for left-handed people?

    What is the current setting for the Double-click speed?

12. Adjust the Double-click speed and test it using the test folder located in the right window of this section.

13. Reset the Double-click speed setting to its original configuration. Refer to the answer determined after Step 11.

14. The ClickLock setting is so you can select an option and drag the mouse without holding down the left mouse button. Once a click is made for more than a second, the button locks and the icon can be dragged. When a second click is made, the mouse unlocks.

    Is the *Turn on ClickLock* option enabled or disabled?

15. The mouse troubleshooter and driver is accessed through the Hardware tab. Click the *Hardware* tab. Click the *Troubleshoot* button. The Mouse Troubleshooter window appears. Close the *Mouse Troubleshooter*.

16. Reaccess the Mouse control panel's *Hardware* tab. Click the *Properties* button.

    In the Mouse Properties window, what is the mouse's device status?

Instructor initials: _____

17. Click the *Driver* tab. Just like with the keyboard, the Update Driver button is used to load a new mouse driver.

18. Click the *Cancel* button twice to return to the Printers and Other Hardware control panel category. Click the *Back* button to return to the control panel categories.

Accessibility Options

19. Accessibility options are not just for people with disabilities. The settings can be adjusted by any computer user to make his or her computer environment more comfortable. Click the *Accessibility Options* category. Click the first task, *Adjust the contrast for text and colors on your screen*. The Accessibility Options window opens with the Display tab active.

20. The two configuration sections are High Contrast and Cursor Options. Click the *Use High Contrast* checkbox to enable it and click the *Apply* button. A "Please wait" message appears and then the screen changes.

Instructor initials: _____

    What is different about the display when the high contrast option is enabled?

21. Click the *Use High Contrast* checkbox to disable it and click *Apply*. The screen returns to normal. Click the *Cancel* button and the Accessibility Options control panel category window reappears.

22. Click the second task, *Configure Windows to work for your hearing, vision, and mobility needs*. The Accessibility wizard appears. This wizard steps through visual, auditory, and motor skills settings. Click the *Next* button. The Text Size window appears.

    What is the default text size setting?

23. Click the *Next* button and the Display Settings window appears.

    What options are currently enabled?

24. Click the *Next* button and the Set Wizard Options window appears.

    What four options are available?

25. The option that is probably the most vague is the Administrative option. This option is used to turn certain accessibility features off if the computer sits idle and make the accessibility features available to one user or all users. Click the *Cancel* button. A Save Changes message box appears. Click the *No* button so that the configuration changes are not kept.

Instructor initials: _____

    Table 12.28 lists available XP accessibility features and their functions.

Controlling Sound

26. Access the *Sounds, Speech, and Audio Devices* control panel category. Select the *Adjust the system volume* task.

    What are the five tabs in the *Sounds and Audio Devices Properties* window?

27. The Volume tab is used to control the volume for the entire computer system and speaker configuration. The Mute checkbox is used to mute all of the computer's sound. The Place volume icon in the taskbar is used to add a volume control icon in the taskbar in the

Table 12.28	**Windows XP accessibility options**
Option	**Function**
StickyKeys	Used for one finger or mouth stick typing and permits one keystroke at a time; used with key combinations such as Ctrl + A.
FilterKeys	Adjusts the keyboard so inadvertent adjacent keystrokes are ignored
ToggleKeys	Emits a beep when Num Lock, Caps Lock, or Scroll Lock keys are pressed (on)
Microsoft Magnifier	Enlarges a small portion of the screen
The Narrator	Reads information displayed on the screen
MouseKeys	Allows pointer manipulation with one finger, mouth stick, or the numeric keypad
ShowsSound	Applications that have closed-caption ability can provide visual feedback
SoundSentry	Sends a visual cue when a computer sound is generated
NetMeeting	Allows Internet conferencing for hearing impaired users

12
Windows XP,
Vista, and 7

notification area. The Device Volume slide bar sets the computer's value settings. Click the *Advanced* button located in the Device Volume section. The Play Control window opens.

What is the current status of the mute buttons displayed in the Play Control window? Use the following table to document the findings.

Play control setting	**Enabled or disabled**
Play Control Mute all	
Wave Mute	
MIDI Mute	
CD Audio Mute	
Line-In Mute	

28. Click the *Play Control Mute all* checkbox to enable it. If it is already enabled, leave the setting turned on (enabled). Close the *Play Control* window. Return to the *Sounds and Audio Devices Properties* window. You will have to reaccess the control panel category.

What is the current status of the Mute checkbox located in the Device Volume section? [Enabled | Disabled]

29. Return all Play Control settings back to their original settings and return to the *Sounds and Audio Devices Properties* window.

Instructor initials: _____

30. Click the *Speaker volume* button. The Speaker volume screen has a left and right speaker volume. This setting does not affect speakers that simply plug into the Line out connection on the sound adapter or built into the motherboard. Click the *Cancel* button.

31. The *Advanced* button in the Speakers settings section is used to configure speakers for such things as headphone usage and surround sound. Click the *Advanced* button in the Speakers settings section and click the *Speakers* tab. The Speakers setup list is used to specify external speakers. Computers such as ones in a business environment or a lab can be configured for no speakers.

What speaker, if any, lists in the *Speakers setup* drop-down list?

32. To disable speakers, click the *Speakers setup* down arrow and select the *No Speakers* option. Click the *Cancel* button twice and close the Control Panel window.

33. Power off the computer properly.

12. Configuring Windows 7 Ease of Access

Objective: To be able to configure Windows 7 for customers who need customized environment for visual, auditory, and physical reasons

Parts: Computer with Windows 7 installed

Procedure: Complete the following procedure and answer the accompanying questions.

1. To access the Ease of Access Center, click on the *Start* button → *Control Panel* → *Ease of Access* link.

2. Select the *Let Windows suggest settings* link.

    What recommendations does Microsoft make available to someone at the workplace who has trouble seeing images on the screen because of the office lighting? Note that you have to make selections to obtain this information.

3. You should be at the *Recommended settings* window after answering the last question. If not, redo Steps 1 and 2 and read the accompanying note. Ensure the computer has speakers attached and, on the recommendation screen, select the *Turn on Narrator* checkbox and leave the automatically enabled recommendations enabled. Click *Apply*.

4. In the Microsoft Narrator window, ensure the *Echo User's Keystrokes* and *Announce System Messages* options are enabled. They are normally enabled by default.

5. Enable the *Announce Scroll Notifications* checkbox and select the *Voice Settings* button.

    What are the default voice, speed, volume, and pitch settings?

6. Click the *Cancel* button; select the *Exit* button. Click *Yes*. From the Recommend settings window, click *OK*.

7. Select the *Start Narrator* link from the Ease of Access Center.

    How do you think this setting would be beneficial in a work environment?

    List at least one disadvantage of this setting.

8. Click *Exit* from within the Microsoft Narrator window. Click *Yes*.

9. Select the *Get recommendations to make your computer easier to use* link. Disable the *Lighting conditions make it difficult to see images on my monitor checkbox.*

10. Select the *Images and text on TV are difficult to see (even when I'm wearing glasses)* checkbox. Click *Next* four times and then click *Done* to view Microsoft's recommendations.

    What three options are recommended (checked) by Microsoft for this situation?

11. In the *Change the color and size of mouse pointers* section, select the *Large Inverting* radio button. Select *Apply*.

12. Move the mouse and open *Windows Explorer*.

    Describe your experience.

    Do you think office workers who do not have a visual impairment would enjoy this feature?

13. Change the mouse pointer back to *Regular white*. Disable the *Turn on Narrator* checkbox. Ensure that the *High contrast color scheme* is selected, with all associated checkboxes enabled. Select *Apply*.

14. Hold down the left [Alt] key and while keeping the key held down, press and hold the left [Shift] key. While holding down both of these keys, press the [Print Screen] key (ALT+left Shift+PrtScn). Release all three keys.

    What audio signal do you hear?

    From information in the message, document how to disable the keyboard shortcut if these specific keys are used for another application.

15. Click *Yes*.

    Describe the difference in screen appearance.

    Do you like the high contrast?

16. Use the same keys again to disable the high-contrast setting. Click *Cancel* in the Recommended settings window.

17. Re-select the *Get recommendations to make your computer easier to use link*. Remove the enabled option checkbox from the *Eyesight* window and click *Next*.

18. In the *Dexterity* window, select the *Pens and pencils are difficult to use* checkbox. Click *Next* or *Done* until you reach Microsoft's recommendations.

    What option(s) are recommended by Microsoft?

    What are Toggle Keys?

19. Open *Notepad*. Notice the blinking cursor in the top left corner.

20. Back in the *Recommended settings* window, notice the setting for *Set the thickness of the blinking cursor*. Change the thickness of the blinking cursor to *5*. Click *Apply*.

21. Return to Notepad and notice the difference in the blinking cursor.

22. Return to the *Recommended Settings* window and return the thickness to the default setting of *1*. Close *Notepad*.

23. Return to the *Recommended Settings* window.

    What are Sticky Keys?

    Who might benefit from Sticky Keys?

24. Click on the *Set up Filter Keys* link.

    What are Filter Keys?

    What is the default amount of time the Shift key has to stay depressed to toggle on Filter Keys?

    By default, do you see a warning message, do you hear a tone, or do you get both a message and a tone when Filter Keys is active? [warning message | tone | both]

    What are Bounce Keys?

    What is the default time between keystrokes if the Bounce Keys feature is enabled?

    Is this setting adjustable? [Yes | No]

25. Click in the *Type text here to test settings* textbox. Type **hello**.

    What happened?

26. Click the *Set up Repeat Keys and Slow Keys* link.

27. Click in the *Type text here to test settings* textbox. Click and hold the **h** key down until it appears in the textbox. Finish typing the word **hello** as a message.

    What indication did you get, besides seeing it appear in the textbox, that the letter "took"?

Instructor initials: _____

28. Click *Cancel* to return to the *Set up Filter Keys* screen.

    What are the other settings this window offers?

29. Click *Cancel* to return to the *Ease of Access Center*.

30. Re-access the *Get recommendations to make your computer easier to use* link. Return to the *Dexterity* window and clear the checkbox for *Pens and pencils are difficult to use*. Click *Next*.

31. On the *Hearing* window, select the *Conversations can be difficult to hear (even with a hearing aid)* checkbox. Click *Next* or *Done* until you reach the Microsoft recommendations.

    What options are available?

32. Enable the *Turn on visual notifications for sounds (Sound Sentry)*. Select the visual warning of *Flash active window*. Click *Apply*. Leave that window open and access the *Hardware and Sound* control panel. In the *Sound* section, select the *Change system sounds* link. On the *Sounds* tab, select a Windows notification that has a speaker beside it. Click the *Test* button.

    Even if your computer does not have speakers, what visual clue do you get that a sound is being made?

33. Click *Cancel* and return to the *Recommended Settings* window. Remove the check from the *Turn on visual notifications for sounds (Sound Sentry)*. Click *Apply*. Click *Cancel* to return to the Ease of Access Center.

34. Re-access the *Get recommendations to make your computer easier to use* link. Return to the *Hearing* window and disable the *Conversations can be difficult to hear (even with a hearing aid)* option. Click *Next* to advance to the *Speech* options screen. Enable the *Other people have difficulty understanding me in a conversation (but not due to an accent)* option. Click *Next* or *Done* until you reach Microsoft's recommendations.

    What is Microsoft's recommendation?

35. Click the *Completing the questionnaire again* link. Return to the *Speech* page and enable the *I have a speech impairment* checkbox.

    Did this change Microsoft's recommendations? If so, what is the recommendation(s)?

36. Return to the questionnaire and disable all options from the *Speech* page and click *Next* to advance to the Reasoning window. Select the *I have a learning disability, such as dyslexia* option. Click Done.

    What does Microsoft recommend for this type of person?

Instructor initials: _____

37. Click *Cancel*. Close the *Ease of Access Center* window.

13. Windows XP System Restore Utility

Objective: To be able to configure and use the System Restore utility

Parts: Computer with Windows XP loaded

Notes: You must be an Administrator or a member of the Administrators group to perform System Restore. If the system has System Restore disabled, this lab may need to be done in two different class periods.

Procedure: Complete the following procedure and answer the accompanying questions.

1. Power on the computer and verify that XP loads. Log on to XP using the userid and password provided by the instructor or lab assistant.

2. Select the *Start* button → *All Programs* → *Accessories* → *System Tools* → *System Restore* → *System Restore Settings* link.

3. If System Restore is turned off, uncheck the *Turn off System Restore* checkbox and complete this lab later.

    On the System Restore tab, is System Restore turned on or off?

    How much disk space is being used for System Restore?

4. Click the *Apply* button if changes have been made and click *OK* to close the System Restore window.

5. Back on the Welcome to System Restore window, ensure that the *Restore my computer to an earlier time* radio button is enabled and click *Next*.

6. A calendar appears where you can select a day when System Restore has created a restore point. Only the bolded days are valid. Select a valid system restore point and click *Next*. Click *Next* again. The system restarts.

7. A status bar appears showing the System Restore progress. The computer restarts and a message appears that the system has successfully been restored. Show the instructor this screen.

Instructor initials: _____

8. Click *OK*.

14. Windows Vista System Restore Utility

Objective: To be able to configure and use the System Restore utility

Parts: Computer with Windows Vista loaded

Notes: You must be an Administrator or a member of the Administrators group to perform System Restore. If System Restore has been disabled, this lab may have to be done over two class periods. One class period would be used to enable it and schedule a restore point and the next class period to perform the system restore. Also note that an antivirus update or a Windows update might have to be re-installed as a result of the system restore.

Procedure: Complete the following procedure and answer the accompanying questions.

1. Power on the computer and verify that Vista loads. Log on to Windows using the userid and password provided by your instructor or lab assistant.

2. Select the *System and Maintenance* control panel to access the *Back and Restore Center* link.

3. Select the *Use System Restore to fix problems and undo changes to Windows* link available at the bottom of the window.

4. Select the *Choose a different restore point* radio button. Click *Next*.

   List the last three restore points.

   What triggered the latest restore point?

   How can you view restore points that are older?

5. Select the latest restore point and click *Next*.

6. Click *Finish*. Click *Yes* to the dialog message. The system restarts.

Instructor initials: _____

7. Click the *Close* button.

8. Once the system has been restored to an earlier time, install any antivirus or Windows updates that have been affected by this system restore. See the answer to the second question in Step 4.

Instructor initials: _____

15. Windows 7 System Restore Utility

Objective: To be able to configure and use the System Restore utility

Parts: Computer with Windows 7 installed and administrator rights

Notes: You must be an administrator to perform System Restore. If System Restore has been disabled, this lab may have to be done over two class periods. One class period would be used to enable it and schedule a restore point and the next class period to perform the system restore. Also note that an antivirus update or a Windows update might have to be re-installed as a result of the system restore.

Procedure: Complete the following procedure and answer the accompanying questions.

1. Power on the computer and verify that Windows 7 loads. Log on to Windows using the userid and password provided by the instructor or lab assistant.

2. Select the *System and Security* control panel link. Select the *Backup and Restore* control panel link.

3. Select the *Recover system settings on your computer* link at the bottom of the window.

4. Select the *Open System Restore* button.

   What are two reasons that system restore might be used?

   [T | F] System restore does not affect personal data documents.

   [Yes | No] Can a recently installed application be affected by using the System Restore utility?

   [Yes | No] Is the System Restore process reversible?

5. Click the *Next* button.

Are any restore points available? If so, list the latest one.

6. Select the *Show more restore points* checkbox.

What is the oldest restore point available?

7. Select the newest (one at the top of the list) restore point and click *Next*.

What does Windows recommend creating if you have recently changed your Windows password?

8. Click *Finish* to confirm rolling back your system to an earlier time.

Under what conditions can the System Restore changes *not* be undone?

9. Click *Yes* to the dialog message. The system restarts as part of the System Restore process.

Instructor Initials _____

10. Log into Windows 7 and ensure the system works.

11. Once the system has been restored to an earlier time, install any antivirus or Windows updates that have been affected by this system restore. See the answer to the question in Step 5.

16. Upgrading a Hardware Driver and Using Driver Roll Back Using Windows XP/Vista/7

Objective: To install an updated driver under the Windows XP, Vista, or 7 operating system

Parts: Computer with Windows XP, Vista, or 7 installed

Internet access

Note: In this lab a new driver is loaded, but then the old driver is re-installed with the driver roll back feature. The student must be logged in as a user with local Administrator rights to perform this lab.

Procedure: Complete the following procedure and answer the accompanying questions.

1. Turn on the computer and verify that the operating system loads. Log in to Windows using the userid and password provided by the instructor or lab assistant.

2. Pick an installed hardware device and locate an updated driver using the Internet. Download the driver to the hard drive. Note that some drivers may come in a compressed file and must be uncompressed before continuing the procedure.

What device did you select to upgrade?

What location (folder, desktop, etc.) was used to download the driver?

Instructor initials: _____

Installing the Driver

3. Open *Device Manager*.

4. Click the + (plus sign) beside the hardware category that contains the device being upgraded.

5. Right-click the device name and click the *Properties* selection.

6. Click the *Driver* tab.

7. In Windows XP, click the *Update Driver* button. The *Update Hardware* wizard screen appears. Select the *Install from a list or specific location (Advanced)* radio button and click *Next*. Click the *Don't search. I will select the driver to install* radio button and click *Next*. Click the *Have Disk* button, use the *Browse* button to locate the downloaded file, and click *OK*. A list of models might appear. If so, select the correct model and click *Next*. Finish the driver update.

In Windows Vista/7, click the *Update Driver* and select *Search automatically for updated driver software* to not only look on the computer for an updated driver but also search the

Internet. Note that if a driver has been downloaded, use the *Browse my computer for driver software* link to locate the downloaded driver.

Instructor initials: _____

Using Driver Roll Back

8. Use *Device Manager*, right-click the device name again, and select *Properties*.

9. Click the *Driver* tab and click the *Roll Back Driver* button. Click the *Yes* button to roll back the driver. If the device driver has not been updated, driver roll back will not be possible and a message screen will display this fact.

Instructor initials: _____

10. Close all windows and power off the computer properly.

17. Disabling a Hardware Driver Using Windows XP, Vista, or 7

Objective: To disable a driver under the Windows XP, Vista, or 7 operating system

Parts: Computer with Windows XP, Vista, or 7 and a network adapter installed

Note: The student must be logged in as a user with local Administrator rights to perform this lab. In this lab, a driver is disabled and then re-enabled. Sometimes Windows can install the wrong driver, in which case the driver must be disabled and then manually re-installed.

Procedure: Complete the following procedure and answer the accompanying questions.

1. Turn on the computer and verify that the operating system loads. Log in to Windows using the userid and password provided by the instructor or lab assistant.

2. Using *Device Manager*, expand the *Network adapters* category.

   What network adapter is installed in the computer?

Instructor initials: _____

3. Right-click a network adapter and click the *Disable* selection.

   What message displays on the screen?

4. Click the *Yes* button.

   In Device Manager, how is a device that has its driver disabled displayed differently from any other device?

Instructor initials: _____

5. In *Device Manager*, right-click the same network adapter and click the *Enable* option. The device is re-enabled and appears normally in the window.

Instructor initials: _____

6. Close the *Device Manager* window and all other windows.

18. Installing Hardware Using Windows XP/Vista/7

Objective: To install a new hardware component under the Windows XP, Vista, or 7 operating system

Parts: Computer with Windows XP, Vista, or 7 installed

   New device to install

   Access to the Internet

Note: The student must be logged in as a user with local Administrator rights to perform this lab. In this lab, the Internet is used to obtain the device's installation instructions and latest device driver, and then the new hardware device is installed.

Procedure: Complete the following procedure and answer the accompanying questions.

1. Log in using the userid and password provided by your instructor or lab assistant.

2. Using the Internet, locate the manufacturer's instructions for installing the device.

   Who is the device manufacturer?

3. Using the Internet, locate the latest device driver that is compatible with the version of Windows being used.

   Does the device have an appropriate driver for the version of Windows being used?

   What is the device driver version being downloaded?

4. Connect the device to the computer using the proper installation procedures.

5. Boot the computer. Usually Windows automatically detects the new hardware and begins the Found New Hardware wizard. If it does not present this wizard, look to see if the hardware device vendor supplied an installation program. If so, use this program to install the device. If no vendor-supplied installation program is available, use the *Add Hardware* control panel (XP), *Device Manager* (Vista), or *Devices and Printers/Add a device* link (7) as described in the chapter, to install the device. Install the device driver based on the device type and manufacturer's instructions.

   Did the Found New Hardware wizard begin?

6. Test the device installation.

Instructor initials: _____

19. Installing Administrative Tools in Windows XP

Objective: To be able to install Administrative Tools in Windows XP

Parts: Computer with Windows XP installed Userid that has Administrator rights Windows XP CD

Note: In this lab, if Administrative Tools is already loaded, it will be removed and re-installed.

Procedure: Complete the following procedure and answer the accompanying questions.

1. Turn on the computer and verify that the operating system loads. Log in to Windows XP using the userid and password provided by the instructor or lab assistant. Ensure the userid is one that has Administrator rights.

Verifying if Administrative Tools Is Already Loaded

2. Click the *Start* button, point to *All Programs,* and look for an *Administrative Tools* item.

   Does the Administrative Tools item appear in the All Programs list?

Removing Administrative Tools from the Start Menu

Note: The steps in this section are performed because the Administrative Tools item is already installed in the system. If Administrative Tools is not already installed, skip to the *Installing Administrative Tools* section.

3. Right-click the *Start* button and select the *Properties* option. Click the *Start Menu* tab.

4. Click the *Customize* button. The Customize Start Menu window opens. In the Start Menu items section, locate the System Administrative tools section and click the *Don't display this item* radio button. Click the *OK* button. Click the *OK* button again. Verify that the Administrative Tools no longer displays in the All Programs list.

Instructor initials: _____

Installing Administrative Tools to the Start Menu

5. Right-click the *Start* button and select the *Properties* option. Click the *Start Menu* tab.

6. Click the *Customize* button. The Customize Start Menu window opens. In the Start Menu items section, click the *Advanced* tab, locate the *System Administrative tools* section and click in the *Display on the All Programs menu* radio button. Click the *OK* button. Click the *OK* button again. Verify that the Administrative Tools displays in the All Programs list.

Note: An alternate way of accessing Administrator Tools is *Start → Control Panel → Classic* view *→ Administrative Tools*.

Instructor initials: _____

Does the All Programs menu contain Administrative Tools? If not, redo the Installing Administrative Tools section.

List two administrative tools provided with XP.

20. Installing and Removing Windows XP Components

Objective: To be able to install and remove Windows XP components

Parts: Computer with Windows XP installed

Userid that has Administrator rights

Approximately 18MB of free hard disk space

Note: In this lab if Windows XP's Accessories and Utilities component is already installed, it is removed and re-installed. If the Accessories and Utilities component is not already installed, it will be installed, removed, and re-installed. The Accessories and Utilities component requires about 17.5MB of hard disk space. The final objective of this lab is to have Accessories and Utilities installed.

Procedure: Complete the following procedure and answer the accompanying questions.

1. Turn on the computer and verify that the operating system loads. Log in to Windows XP using the userid and password provided by the instructor or lab assistant. Ensure the userid is one that has Administrator rights.

Verifying if Accessories and Utilities Are Already Loaded

2. Click the *Start* button and click the *Control Panel* option. Access the Add or Remove Programs control panel by clicking the *Category* view or double-clicking the *Classic view* control panel icon.

3. Click the *Add/Remove Windows Components* icon located on the left portion of the Add or Remove Programs window. The Windows Components window opens.

Is the Accessories and Utilities option enabled (checked)?

If so, proceed to the *Removing Accessories and Utilities* section below. Remove the components and then proceed to the *Installing Accessories and Utilities* section to re-install the components. If the Accessories and Utilities option is not installed (unchecked), proceed to the *Installing Accessories and Utilities* section, install the components, then go to the *Removing Accessories and Utilities* section and uninstall the components, then, finally, re-install the components. When this lab is complete, the Accessories and Utilities component should be installed.

4. You can double-click any component to view the subcomponents. Try this procedure on your own. Close all windows and proceed to the appropriate section based on the answer to the question in Step 3.

Removing Accessories and Utilities

5. Click the *Start* button and click the *Control Panel* option. Access the Add or Remove Programs control panel by clicking the *Category* view or double-clicking the *Classic* view control panel icon.

6. Click the *Add/Remove Windows Components* icon located on the left portion of the Add or Remove Programs window. The Windows Components window opens.

7. Click the *Accessories and Utilities* checkbox to deselect (uncheck) it and click the *Next* button. The files are deleted.

8. Click the *Finish* button and verify that accessories and utilities are uninstalled using the previously described procedures.

Has the Accessories and Utilities component been removed? Have a classmate verify.

Classmate's printed name: _____

Classmate's signature: _____

Installing Accessories and Utilities

9. Click the *Start* button and click the *Control Panel* option. Access the Add or Remove Programs control panel by clicking the *Category* view or double-clicking the *Classic view* control panel icon.

10. Click the *Add/Remove Windows Components* icon located on the left portion of the Add or Remove Programs window. The Windows Components window opens.

11. Click the *Accessories and Utilities* checkbox to select (enable) it. If the box is already checked, go to the *Removing Accessories and Utilities* section. Click the *Next* button. A prompt appears to insert the Windows XP CD. Insert the CD and the files copy.

12. Click the *Finish* button, close all Add/Remove Components control panel windows, and verify that Accessories and Utilities are installed using the previously described procedures.

    Is the Accessories and Utilities Windows XP component installed? Show this component to your instructor.

Instructor initials: _____

21. Installing and Removing Windows Vista/7 Components

Objective: To be able to install and remove Windows Vista/7 components

Parts: Computer with Windows Vista/7 installed and administrator rights

Procedure: Complete the following procedure and answer the accompanying questions.

1. Turn on the computer and verify that the operating system loads. Log in to Windows using the userid and password provided by your instructor or lab assistant. Ensure that the userid is one that has Administrator rights.

Verifying and Installing Windows Features

2. Open *Windows Explorer*, right-click *Computer*, and select *Properties*. Select the *System Protection* link.

3. Create a system restore point by clicking the *Create* button. In the description textbox type **class** followed by the current date. Click *Create*. A dialog box appears when the restore point has been successfully created. Click *OK*.

    According to the chapter text, what makes Windows Vista's System Restore utility different from the one used in Windows XP?

4. Click *OK* in the System Properties window.

5. Access the *Programs* control panel to select the *Turn Windows features on or off* link from the Programs and features section.

    List three enabled Windows features.

    List three Windows features that are turned off.

6. Notice how the Games option is controlled through this section. Expand the *Games* option.

    List three available games.

7. Check with your instructor or lab assistant for a specific feature to turn on. One option would be to turn on the TFTP client if it is not enabled.

    List the program to be enabled.

8. Select the checkbox for the feature to be enabled and click *OK*. Note that enabling the feature might take a few minutes.

9. Re-access the *Turn Windows features on or off* link to verify that the feature now shows as enabled.

Instructor initials: _____

10. Remove the check from the feature you just enabled and verify that the feature is removed successfully.

11. Select the *Default Programs* link (from the *Programs and Features* (Vista)/*Programs* (7) control panel link). Select the *Set your default programs* link.

   List the options available from this window.

12. Select *Internet Explorer* from the Programs list. Select the *Choose defaults for this program* link.

   List the extensions that are automatically opened by Internet Explorer.

   List protocols that are automatically recognized from the address line in Internet Explorer.

13. Click *Cancel* and *OK* to return to the Default Programs window.

14. Select the *Associate a file type or protocol with a program* link.

   List one program that does not have an extension or protocol associated with it.

15. Leave this window open and create a Notepad document with a message in it called **Superdog.txt**.

   Document the location where this document is saved.

16. Open *Windows Explorer* and locate the `Superdog.txt` file. In Vista, select the *Views* menu option. In Windows 7, select the *Views* drop-down arrow as shown in this graphic: ▦▾

   What is the current view?

17. Select the *List* view. Select the *Organize* menu option and select *Folder and Search Options*. Select the *View* tab.

   What is the current setting for *Hide extensions for known file types*? [Enabled | Disabled]

18. Ensure that the *Hide extensions for known file types* option is disabled (unchecked). Click *OK*.

19. Return to Windows Explorer and ensure that the `.txt` extension is visible on the `Superdog.txt` filename. Right-click on the `Superdog.txt` file and select *Rename*. Rename the `.txt` extension to `.cas` (or your own initials, if they are not a common file extension). When the message window appears, click *Yes*.

   How did the appearance of the file change?

20. Right-click on the `Superdog` file and select *Properties*.

   What application does Windows assign to open the document?

21. Click the *Change* button. Notice that the *Always use the selected program to open this kind of file* checkbox at the bottom of the window is enabled. Select *Notepad* and *OK*. Click *Apply* and *OK*.

22. Locate the `Superdog` file in Windows Explorer and double-click the icon.

   Does the file open? If so, in what application?

23. Close the `Superdog` file. Return to the *Set Associations* window. Scroll down until you see the extension you used when you renamed the *Superdog* filename. Show your instructor or lab assistant the file extension.

Instructor initials: _____

24. Select the file extension in the list and click on the *Change program* button. Use the *Browse* button to find the WordPad application. Use the Search feature inside Browse, if necessary. Once you find WordPad, select it and click *Open*. Click *OK*.

25. Close the *Set Associations* window. Return to *Windows Explorer*. Locate the `Superdog` file and double-click the icon.

   Does the file open? If so, in what application?

26. Close the file. Permanently delete the file by holding down the *Shift* key while pressing *Delete*. Click *Yes* to permanently delete the file.

27. On your own, create another file that ends in the same file extension. Try to open it.

   What happens?

28. Close the file and permanently delete the file.

29. Re-open the *System Restore* utility.

12

Windows XP, Vista, and 7

30. Select the *Choose a different restore point* radio button and click *Next*.

31. Select the *class+date* restore point and click *Next*. Click *Finish*. Read the message that appears and click *Yes*. The system restores the system to the time before this lab was started. The system reboots, and a dialog box appears, telling you whether the restore point was successful. Click *Close*.

32. Re-open the *Programs* control panel and select the *Make a file type always open in a specific program* link.

33. Scroll through the list.

    Is the unique file extension used in this lab located in the list?

34. Show the instructor or lab assistant the file extension (or lack of one).

Instructor initials: _____

35. Close the *Set Associations* window.

22. Windows XP Microsoft Management Console

Objective: To be able to access Microsoft Management Console, see what folders are being shared, view and add a user, access Device Manager, access disk management tools, and view current services

Parts: Computer with Windows XP and Administrative Tools installed

Note: If Administrative Tools is not already installed, use Hands-On Exercise 19, *Installing Administrative Tools in Windows XP*, to install it.

Procedure: Complete the following procedure and answer the accompanying questions.

1. Turn on the computer and verify that the operating system loads. Log in to Windows XP using the userid and password provided by the instructor or lab assistant. Ensure the userid is one that has Administrator rights.

2. To access Microsoft Management Console, click the *Start* button, point to the *Control Panel* option, point to *Administrative Tools*, and click the *Computer Management* option.

    Using the Help menu item, determine what each of the three major Computer Management sections are used for and complete the following table. Write the description found in Help.

Computer Management section	Purpose
System Tools	
Storage	
Services and Applications	

3. Return to the Computer Management window and, if necessary, click the plus sign beside System Tools to expand it. If necessary, click the + (plus sign) beside Shared Folders to expand it and click the *Shares* folder. Shares are used when the computer is in a network environment. Other users on different computers can access resources on this computer. When networking is enabled, default administrative shares are created for each hard drive partition. Administrative shares can be easily identified by the $ (dollar sign) after the share name.

    List two default shares located on this machine. If none are available, document this fact.

4. If necessary, click the + (plus sign) by *Local Users and Groups* to expand it and click the *Users* folder.

    List two users shown in the *Computer Management* window.

5. To add a new user who will have access to this computer, click the *Action* menu option and select *New User*. The New User window opens. Click the *Question mark* icon located in the upper-right corner of the window. An arrow with an attached question mark appears as the pointer. Move the pointer to inside the *User name* textbox and click. A *Help* box appears.

Based on the information in the help balloon, what is the maximum number of characters the user name can contain?

Can spaces be used within the user name?

6. In the *User name* textbox, type **Jeff Cansler**. In the *Full name* textbox, type **Jeffrey Wayne Cansler**. In the *Description* textbox, type **Brother**. In the *Password* and the *Confirm password* textboxes, type **test**. Click in the *User must change password at next logon* checkbox to disable it. Click in the *User cannot change password* textbox to enable this option. Click the *Create* button. Click the *Close* button. The Jeff Cansler user icon appears in the Computer Management console window.

Have a classmate verify the Jeff Cansler user icon. Have him/her double-click the icon to verify your settings. Are the settings correct? If not, redo the previous step.

Classmate's printed name: _____

Classmate's signature: _____

7. Log off the computer and log back on using the Jeff Cansler user name with a password of test.

Did the logon work correctly? If not, log back on using the userid and password given to you in the beginning of the lab by the lab assistant or instructor and redo Step 6.

8. Log off the computer and log back on using the userid and password given to you by the lab assistant or instructor. Access the *Computer Management* window and double-click the *Jeff Cansler* user icon. Click the *Member of* tab.

To what group does the *Jeff Cansler* user automatically belong?

9. Click the *Add* button. The Select Groups window opens. In the *Enter the object names to select* textbox, type **Administrators** and click the *Check Names* button. Click the *OK* button. The display changes to Jeff Cansler belonging to both the Users and Administrator groups. Click the *Apply* button and then the *OK* button.

Instructor initials: _____

10. Return to the Jeff Cansler user window and click the *Profile* tab. The Profile tab is used to specify a home directory for the user, run a logon script that sets specific parameters for the user, input a path that specifies where the user stores files by default, or input a shared network directory where the user's data is placed. The *Profile path* textbox is where you type the location of the profile using a UNC. An example is `\\ocsic\profiles\jcansler`. The Logon script textbox is where you type the name of the logon script file, for example, `startup.bat`. The *Home folder Local path* textbox is where you type the full path for where the user's data is stored by default. An example is `d:\users\jcansler`. The *Connect* radio button is used to assign a network drive letter and specify the location of a network directory where the user's data is stored. An example is `\\ocsic\users\jcandata`. Click the *Cancel* button to return to the Computer Management window. Notice that users that are disabled have a red *X* on their icon.

Are any users disabled? If so, list them.

11. In the Computer Management window, click the *Groups* folder.

List two default groups.

12. Double-click the *Administrators* group icon. The Administrators group has total control of the local machine.

Are any users listed as part of the Administrators group? If so, list them.

Fill in the following table with the purpose of each user group type. Use the *Help* menu item for more information than what is shown in the window.

Group	Purpose
Administrators	
Backup Operators	
Guests	
Users	

12

Windows XP, Vista, and 7

13. Click the *Cancel* button and then click the *Users* folder located in the Computer Management window. Click the *Jeff Cansler* user icon. Click the red *X* button or click the *Action* menu item and select *Delete*. A message appears asking if you are sure that you want to delete this user. Click the *Yes* button.

14. Go into the Administrators group and verify that Jeff Cansler no longer appears there.

    Have a classmate verify that the Jeff Cansler user icon is deleted. Is the Jeff Cansler user icon deleted? If not, redo the previous step.

Classmate's printed name: _____

Classmate's signature: _____

15. Click the *Device Manager* option located in the Computer Management window. Device Manager is used to access and manage hardware devices installed in the computer. It is also used to load new drivers and roll back to old drivers.

16. Click the + (plus sign) by the computer's name if the list is not already expanded. Click the + (plus sign) by the *Computer* category.

    Does the computer have ACPI enabled? This would be evidenced by a computer subcategory.

17. If the computer has ACPI enabled, double-click the *ACPI* option. The window that opens is similar to all individual device windows although the tabs may vary depending on the device.

Tech Tip

Don't always believe the message that the device is working properly

Just because Windows states that a device is working does not make it so. There is also a *Troubleshooter* button on the General tab that can be used to troubleshoot the individual device.

The *General* tab has a device status window where you can see whether Windows believes the device is working properly.

The *Driver* tab contains information about the driver version, a button to update the driver, and a button to roll the driver back to a previous version.

18. Click the *Cancel* button and, if necessary, click the + (plus sign) beside the *Storage* category to expand it. Click the *Disk Management* subcategory. The right Computer Management window displays information about each type of hard disk partition created on the drive.

    The top window shows information about each disk partition including total capacity, file system, free space percentage, and so forth. The bottom windows show the partitions in graphical form.

19. Right-click the first disk partition (Disk 0) graph in the lower window and select the *Properties* option. An alternate method for getting to this screen is to click the *Action* menu item and select *Properties*. The Disk Properties window opens.

20. On an NTFS partition, the General tab contains a Disk Cleanup button that can be used to clean up temporary files and delete applications not used, Windows components not used, log files, and old system restores. Click the *Tools* tab.

    What tools are listed on the *Tools* tab?

    Match the following tool to its associated task.
    Backup   a. Scans the disk for damage
    Error-checking   b. Used to restore system files that have been saved
    Defragmentation   c. Locates file clusters that are not consecutive (contiguous) and
                           places the files in order

21. The Disk Management tool can be used to create disk partitions, delete partitions, convert partitions to NTFS, create logical drives, and convert basic disks to dynamic disks. Click the *Cancel* button.

22. If necessary, click the + (plus sign) by the *Services and Applications Computer Management* category to expand it. Click the *Services* subcategory. A service is an application that runs in the background (you do not see it on the taskbar). The Services window is used to start, stop, pause, resume, or disable a service. You must be a member of the Administrators group to use this tool.

    List two services that start automatically when the computer starts and two services that require manual starting.

23. Double-click the *Computer Browser* service. The *General* tab is used to start, stop, pause, or resume a service (depending on its current state). The buttons in the *Service status* section are used to control these actions. The *General* tab is also used to set whether or not the service starts when the computer boots. Click the *Startup type* down arrow to see a menu of startup options.

24. Close the *Service* window without making any changes to the service and close the *Computer Management* window.

Instructor initials: _____

23. Windows 7 Microsoft Management Console

Objective: To be able to access and use the major utilities found in the Microsoft Management Console

Parts: Computer with Windows 7 installed and administrator rights

Notes: You must be an administrator to utilize the Microsoft Management Console utilities.

Procedure: Complete the following procedure and answer the accompanying questions.

1. Power on the computer and verify that Windows 7 loads. Log on to Windows using the userid and password provided by the instructor or lab assistant.

2. To access Microsoft Management Console, click the *Start* button → *Control Panel* → *System and Security* link → *Administrative Tools* → double-click the *Computer Management* option.

    Determine the subcategories for each of the major Computer Management sections. Write the subcategories.

Computer Management section	Subcategories
System Tools	
Storage	
Services and Applications	

3. Return to the Computer Management window and, if necessary, click the arrow beside *System Tools* to expand the section. If necessary, click the arrow beside *Shared Folders* to expand that section. Click the *Shares* folder. Shares are used when the computer is in a network environment. Other users on different computers can access resources on this computer. When networking is enabled, default administrative shares are created for each hard drive partition. Administrative shares can be easily identified by the $ (dollar sign) after the share name.

    List two default shares located on this machine. If none are available, document the fact.

4. If necessary, expand *Local Users* and *Groups* and click the *Users* folder.

    List the users shown in the Computer Management window.

5. To add a new user who will have access to this computer, click the *Action* menu option and select *New User.* The New User window opens. Click the *Question mark* icon located in the upper-right corner of the window. An arrow with an attached question mark appears as a pointer. Move the pointer to inside the *User name* textbox and click. A Help box appears.

    Based on the information in the help balloon, what is the maximum number of characters the user name can contain?

    Can a plus sign (+) be used within the user name?

6. In the *User name* textbox, type **Jeff Cansler**. In the *Full name* textbox, type **Jeffrey Wayne Cansler**. In the *Description* textbox, type **Brother**. In the *Password* and the *Confirm password* textboxes, type **test**. Ensure the *User must change password at next logon* checkbox is disabled (not checked). Click in the *User cannot change password* checkbox to enable this option. Click the *Create* button. Click the *Close* button. The Jeff Cansler user icon appears in the Computer Management window.

Have a classmate verify the Jeff Cansler user icon. Have the classmate double-click the icon to verify your settings. Are the settings correct? If not, redo the previous step.

Classmate's printed name: _____

Classmate's signature: _____

7. Log off the computer and log back on using the Jeff Cansler username with a password of *test*.

Did the log on process work correctly? If not, log back on using the userid and password given to you by the lab assistant or instructor for the beginning of the lab and redo Step 6.

8. Log off the computer and log back on using the userid and password given to you by the lab assistant or instructor (the original userid and password). Access the *Computer Management* window and double-click the *Jeff Cansler* user icon. Click the *Member of* tab.

To what group does the Jeff Cansler user automatically belong?

9. Click the *Add* button. The Select Groups window opens. In the *Enter the object names to select* textbox, type **Administrators** and click the *Check Names* button. Click the *OK* button. The information shown changes to the user, Jeff Cansler, belonging to both the Users and Administrator groups. Click the *Apply* button and then the *OK* button.

Instructor initials: _____

10. Re-open the Jeff Cansler user window and click the *Profile* tab. The *Profile* tab is used to specify a home directory for the user, run a logon script that sets specific parameters for the user, input a path that specifies where the user stores files by default, or input a shared network directory where the user's data is placed. The *Profile path* textbox is where you type the location of the profile using a UNC. An example is `\\ocsic\profiles\jcansler`. The *Logon script* textbox is where you type the name of the logon script file, for example `startup.bat`. The *Home folder Local path* textbox is where you type the full path for where the user's data is stored by default. An example is `D:\users\jcansler`. The *Connect* radio button is used to assign a network drive letter and specify the location of a network directory where the user's data is stored. An example is `\\ocsic\users\jcandata`. Click the *Cancel* button to return to the Computer Management window. Notice that users that are disabled have a small down arrow on their icon.

Are any users disabled?

11. In the Computer Management window, click the *Groups* folder.

List two default groups.

12. Double-click the *Administrators* group icon. The Administrators group has total control of the local machine.

Are any users listed as part of the Administrators group? If so, list them.

Fill in the following table with the purpose of each group type. Use the *Help* menu item for more information than what is shown in the window.

Group	Purpose
Administrators	
Backup Operators	
Guests	
Users	

13. Click the *Cancel* button and then click the *Users* folder located in the Computer Management window. Click the *Jeff Cansler* user icon. Click the red *X* button or click the *Action* menu item and select *Delete*. A message appears asking if you are sure that you want to delete this user. Click the *Yes* button.

14. Go into the *Administrators* group and verify that Jeff Cansler no longer appears there.

    Have a classmate verify that the Jeff Cansler user icon is deleted. Is the Jeff Cansler user icon deleted? If not, redo the previous step.

    Classmate's printed name: _____

    Classmate's signature: _____

15. Click the *Device Manager* option located in the Computer Management window. This utility can also be accessed by typing `devmgmt.msc`. Device Manager is used to access and manage hardware devices installed in the computer. It is also used to load new drivers and roll back to an older driver.

16. Click the arrow by the computer's name if the list is not already expanded. Expand the *Computer* category.

    Does the computer have ACPI enabled? This would be evidenced by a computer subcategory.

17. If the computer has ACPI enabled, double-click the *ACPI* option. The window that opens is similar to all individual device windows although the tabs may vary depending on the device. The *General* tab has a device status window where you can see whether Windows believes the device is working.

Don't always believe Windows when it says the device is working properly
Just because Device Manager states a device is working properly does not make it so. Some devices have a *Troubleshooter* button on the *General* tab that can be used to troubleshoot a problem with the device.

Tech Tip

The *Driver* tab contains information about the driver version, a button to update the driver, and a button to roll the driver back to a previous version. The *Details* tab shows additional information about the specific device.

18. Click the *Cancel* button and, if necessary, expand the *Storage* category. Click the *Disk Management* subcategory. The right Computer Management window displays information about each type of hard disk partition created on the drive. The top window shows information about each disk partition including total capacity, file system, free space percentage, and so forth. The bottom windows show the drives and partitions in graphical form.

19. Right-click the first disk partition (Disk 0) graph in the lower window and select the *Properties* option. An alternate method is to click the *Action* menu item and select *Properties*. The Disk Properties window opens.

20. On an NTFS partition, the General tab contains a *Disk Cleanup* button that can be used to clean up temporary files and delete applications not used, Windows components not used, log files, and old system restores. Click the *Tools* tab.

    What tools are listed on the Tools tab?

    Match the following tool to its associated task.
    Backup   a. Scans the disk for damage
    Error-checking   b. Used to restore system files that have been saved
    Defragmentation   c. Locates file clusters that are not consecutive (contiguous) and
                           places the files in order

21. The Disk Management tool can be used to create disk partitions, delete partitions, convert partitions to NTFS, create logical drives, and convert basic disks to dynamic disks. Click the *Cancel* button.

22. If necessary, expand the *Services and Applications* Computer Management category. Click the *Services* subcategory. A service is an application that runs in the background (you do

not see it on the taskbar). The Services window is used to start, stop, pause, resume, or disable a service. You must be a member of the Administrators group to use this tool.

List two services that start automatically and two services that require manual starting.

23. Double-click the *Computer Browser* service. The General tab is used to start, stop, pause, or resume a service (depending on its current state). The buttons in the *Service status* section are used to control these actions. The General tab is also used to set whether or not the service starts when the computer boots. Click the *Startup type* down arrow to see a menu of startup options.

24. Close the *Service* window without making any changes to the service and close the *Computer Management* window.

Instructor initials: _____

24. Exploring Windows XP Boot Options

Objective: To explore Windows XP boot options that are used to troubleshoot startup problems

Parts: Computer with Windows XP installed that has the ability to boot from a CD

               Userid that has Administrator rights

               Windows XP CD

Note: In this lab, you will boot without startup programs loaded, boot to Safe Mode, boot to Safe Mode with Command Prompt, boot to Enable Boot Logging and examine the NTBTLOG.TXT file, and boot to Recovery Console and examine commands using the command prompt.

Procedure: Complete the following procedure and answer the accompanying questions.

1. Turn on the computer and verify that the operating system loads. Log in to Windows XP using the userid and password provided by the instructor or lab assistant. Ensure the userid is one that has Administrator rights.

Verifying *Startup* Folder Contents

2. Right-click the *Start* button and click the *Explore* option.

3. Locate the *Documents and Settings* folder and expand it if necessary. Locate the *All Users* folder (located under *Documents and Settings*) and expand it if necessary. Locate the *Start Menu* subfolder (located under *All Users*) and expand it if necessary. Locate the *Programs* subfolder (located under the *Start Menu* folder) and expand it if necessary. Click the *Startup* folder located under the *Programs* folder.

Are there any program shortcuts listed in the Startup folder? If so, list at least one of the programs.

Classmate's printed name: _____

Classmate's signature: _____

If there is no program shortcut, create a shortcut to the Notepad application and place it in the *Startup* folder.

4. Restart the computer and verify that the program listed in the Startup folder starts automatically when the computer boots. If it does not, redo the lab.

Instructor initials: _____

Preventing Startup Programs from Loading

5. Restart the computer and while the computer boots and the login process occurs, hold down the ⇧Shift key until the desktop icons appear. Holding down the ⇧Shift key stops startup programs from loading automatically. This technique works when any program that starts automatically is causing problems. If this does not work for you, shut down the computer properly, power off, power back on, log in, and hold down the ⇧Shift key during the login process.

What indication do you have that holding down the [Shift] key while booting stopped the application from loading?

6. Using Windows Explorer, delete the shortcut located in the *Startup* folder.

   Have a classmate verify that you only deleted the shortcut and not the application. Has the shortcut been deleted?

Classmate's printed name: _____

Classmate's signature: _____

Using Boot Options

7. Restart the computer and press the [F8] key as the computer boots. The Windows Advanced Options menu appears. If it does not, repeat this procedure until it does. Select the *Safe Mode* option and press [Enter].

   What is different about the Windows XP login screen?

   Why do you think the *Administrator* user icon appears in Safe Mode and not during the regular boot sequence?

8. Log in as Administrator.

   How do you know that the computer is running in Safe Mode?

9. Click the *Yes* button.

   Did your program in the *Startup* folder automatically start?

   Are Administrative Tools available through the *Start* button's *All Programs* list?

   To what *Control Panel* view does the system default?

10. Double-click the *Administrative Tools* control panel. Double-click the *Computer Management* icon. Access the *Services* folder.

    List two automatic services that have a status of *started*?

11. Notice how there are quite a few services that are automatic services that did not start in Safe Mode. Close the *Computer Management* screen and the *Administrative Tools* window.

12. Restart the computer and press the [F8] key to see the Windows Advanced Options menu.

    List the boot options available.

    Match the following definitions to the appropriate boot option:

    ____ Safe Mode
    ____ Safe Mode with Command Prompt
    ____ Enable Boot Logging
    ____ Last Known Good Configuration

    a. Starts the system with minimum files and drivers and only typed commands can be used
    b. Records the boot process into a text file that can later be viewed and used for troubleshooting
    c. Starts the system with minimum file and drivers including VGA video drivers
    d. Used when a newly installed piece of hardware or software causes the system not to boot properly

13. Select the *Safe Mode with Command Prompt* option and log in as Administrator.

    What is different about the desktop appearance?

14. Click the *minimize* button, which is the left-most button in the upper-right corner of the `cmd.exe` window.

    What does the screen look like now?

15. The *Safe Mode with Command Prompt* option is used to start the system with minimum files and drivers and a command prompt where you must type commands instead of working through a graphical interface. Type **exit** at the command prompt.

    What happened to the screen?

Instructor initials: _____

12

Windows XP,
Vista, and 7

16. Press ⌜Ctrl⌝+⌜Alt⌝+⌜Del⌝ and the Task Manager window appears. Click the *Shut Down* menu option and select *Restart*. Restart the computer, press the ⌜F8⌝ key to see the Windows *Advanced Options* menu. Select the *Enable Boot Logging* option.

    Does the Administrator userid appear as a login choice?

17. Log in to Windows XP.

    How does the desktop appear when using the *Enable Boot Logging* option?

18. Using Windows Explorer, locate the file **NTBTLOG.TXT** and double-click the file icon to open the file.

    List two drivers that loaded properly.

    List two drivers that did not load.

Instructor initials: _____

19. Close the **NTBTLOG.TXT** window and close all Windows Explorer windows.

Recovery Console

20. Shut the computer down and power off. Insert the Windows XP CD into the drive and power on the computer. The Welcome to Setup screen appears. If the computer does not boot from the Windows XP CD, the BIOS settings probably need to be adjusted. Press ⌜R⌝ at the Welcome to Setup screen. The Recovery screen appears.

21. Press the number that corresponds to the partition that contains XP.

22. Type the Administrator password. Contact a lab assistant or the instructor if the password is unknown. The Recovery Console loads.

    Write down what the prompt looks like.

23. The Recovery Console is used as a last resort—when other boot options do not solve the problem. At the prompt, type **copy** and press ⌜Enter⌝. An error message appears. Command prompt usage must be very precise and exact commands with proper switches must be used.

24. Type **help copy** and press ⌜Enter⌝. Help information on the copy command appears.

25. Type **copy /?** and press ⌜Enter⌝. Again, help information appears.

26. Type **help** and press ⌜Enter⌝. A list of Recovery Console commands appears. Press the ⌜Spacebar⌝ to see the rest of the command list.

Instructor initials: _____

27. Remove the XP CD and type **exit.** The system boots normally.

25. Exploring Windows 7 Boot Options

Objective: To explore Windows 7 boot options that are used to troubleshoot startup problems

Parts: Computer with Windows 7 installed that has the ability to boot from a CD/DVD

    Userid that has Administrator rights

    Windows 7 DVD or virtual image of the DVD

Note: In this lab, you will boot without startup programs loaded, boot to Safe Mode, boot to Safe Mode with Command Prompt, boot to Enable Boot Logging and examine the **NTBTLOG.TXT** file, and boot to Recovery Console and examine commands using the command prompt. If the Windows 7 DVD or image of the installation disc is not available, then that one section could be skipped.

Procedure: Complete the following procedure and answer the accompanying questions.

1. Turn on the computer and verify that the operating system loads. Log in to Windows using the userid and password provided by your instructor or lab assistant.

Using Boot Options

2. Restart the computer and press the ⟨F8⟩ key as the computer boots. If the *Advanced Boot Options* window does not appear, shut down the computer and restart. Press ⟨F8⟩ as the computer boots. The *Advanced Boot Options* menu appears. Select the *Safe Mode* option and press ⟨Enter⟩. Log in as Administrator, as necessary.

When would a technician use the Safe Mode option as opposed to the Safe Mode with Command Prompt option?

How does the look of the screen in Safe Mode differ from the look of the normal Windows desktop?

What Windows Help and Support topic automatically displays?

According to the information presented, how can you easily tell you are running in Safe Mode?

According to the information displayed, if Windows successfully boots into Safe Mode, what suspect problems are eliminated?

What information is displayed as a suggestions for what to try next if the Safe Mode boot process is successful?

3. Access the *Administrative Tools* control panel link. Open *Computer Management*. Expand the *Services and Applications* category. Access the *Services* option.

4. Notice that there are quite a few services that are automatic services that did not start in Safe Mode.

List two services that did not automatically start because Safe Mode with Networking was used.

5. Close the *Computer Management* and any control panel windows.

6. Restart the computer and press the ⟨F8⟩ key to access the Advanced Boot Options menu.

List the boot options available.

Match each of the following definitions to the appropriate boot option:

_____ Safe Mode

_____ Safe Mode with Command Prompt

_____ Enable Boot Logging

_____ Last Known Good Configuration (advanced)

a. Starts the system with minimum files and drivers, and only typed commands can be used

b. Records the boot process into a text file that can later be viewed and used for troubleshooting

c. Starts the system with minimum files and drivers, including the default video drivers

d. Used when a newly installed piece of hardware or software causes the system not to boot properly

7. Select the *Safe Mode with Command Prompt* option. Log in using the same user name and password.

What is different about the desktop appearance compared to the desktop before the reboot?

8. Click the *minimize* button, which is the left-most button in the upper-right corner of the `cmd.exe` window.

What does the screen look like now?

9. The *Safe Mode with Command Prompt* option is used to start the system with minimum files and drivers and a command prompt where you must type commands instead of working through a graphical interface. Re-access the `cmd.exe` window. Type **dir** at the command prompt.

How many files are available?

How many directories are available?

Instructor initials: _____

10. Type **dir r*.*** at the command prompt.

    List three files that are executables that start with the letter R.

11. Type **rstrui** at the command prompt.

    What happened as a result of typing this command?

12. Close the window that appeared.

13. From the command prompt window, type **exit**.

    What happened as a result of typing this command?

14. Press `Ctrl`+`Alt`+`Del` Select the *red power button* menu in the lower-right corner and select *Restart*. Restart the computer and press the `F8` key to see the Advanced Boot Options menu. Select the *Enable Boot Logging* option.

    How does the desktop appear when using the *Enable Boot Logging* option?

15. Using the Start button *Search programs and files* textbox, locate and access the NTBTLOG.TXT file.

    List two drivers that loaded properly.

    List two drivers that did not load.

Instructor initials: _____

16. Close all windows.

Recovery Environment

17. Shut the computer down and power off. Insert the Windows 7 installation disc into the drive and power on the computer. If prompted, press a key to start Windows from the disc. A menu appears with a default option selected. Press `Enter`. If the computer does not boot from the Windows disc, the BIOS settings probably need to be adjusted.

18. Choose the appropriate language settings and click *Next*.

19. Select *Repair your computer*. In the System Recovery Options window, select the *Use recovery tools that can help fix problems starting Windows*. Enable the *Select an operating system to repair* radio button.

20. Ensure that the operating system is selected and click *Next*.

    List the recovery tool options

    Which option would be used to repair a system file?

    Which option would be used to check RAM?

    Which option would be for advanced technicians?

    Which option configures the system to an earlier time such as before a Windows update?

Instructor initials: _____

21. Select the *Memory Diagnostic* link. Select the *Restart now and check for problems (recommended)* link. Do not press a key when the system reboots and asks "Press a key to boot from CD or DVD."

    List one status message.

22. Once the test executes and the computer reboots, again, do not press any key even when the message prompts to press a key to boot from CD or DVD. Once Windows reboots, log in again. Open Event Viewer by accessing the following control panel links: *System and Security → Administrative tools*. Double-click *Event Viewer* to open the tool.

22. Expand *Windows Logs*. Right-click on *System* and select *Find*.

23. In the *Find what* textbox, type the following:

    MemoryDiagnostics-Results

    Be very careful that you type exactly as shown and click *Find Next*. The corresponding line highlights.

24. Close the *Find* window. Double-click on the highlighted line to see the results of the memory diagnostic check. Select the *Details* tab.

    What are the results shown in the friendly view?

    What Event ID did Windows assign?

25. Close all windows. Remove the Windows disc and return to the instructor or lab assistant.

26. Windows XP System Configuration Utility

Objective: To be able to use the System Configuration utility to troubleshoot boot problems

Parts: Computer with Windows XP installed

Userid that has Administrator rights

Note: In this lab, create a shortcut to an application and then use the System Configuration utility to prevent it from loading. Explore various options that can be used within the System Configuration utility.

Procedure: Complete the following procedure and answer the accompanying questions.

1. Turn on the computer and verify that the operating system loads. Log in to Windows XP using the userid and password provided by the instructor or lab assistant. Ensure the userid is one that has Administrator rights.

Creating an Application Shortcut in the *Startup* Folder

2. Right-click the *Start* button and click the *Explore* option.

3. Locate the *Documents and Settings* folder and expand it if necessary. Locate the *All Users* folder (located under Documents and Settings) and expand it if necessary. Locate the *Start Menu* subfolder (located under *All Users*) and expand it if necessary. Locate the *Programs* subfolder (located under the *Start Menu* folder) and expand it if necessary. Click the *Startup* folder located under the *Programs* folder.

4. Use the *Search* Start button option to locate the original Notepad application (`notepad.exe`). Create a shortcut to the Notepad application and place it in the *Startup* folder located under the *Programs* folder (see Step 3). Hands-On Exercise 1 in Chapter 11 explains how to create a shortcut.

    Have a classmate verify your shortcut (especially that it is a shortcut and not a copy of the application or the application itself). Is the icon in the Startup folder a shortcut icon?

Classmate's printed name: _____

Classmate's signature: _____

5. Restart the computer and verify that the Notepad program starts automatically when the computer boots. If it does not, redo.

Instructor initials: _____

System Configuration Utility

6. Click the *Start* button, click the *Run* option, type **msconfig** and press ⟨Enter⟩. The System Configuration utility window opens.

    What is the purpose of the System Configuration utility?

    What five tabs are available through the System Configuration utility?

7. Click the *Diagnostic Startup—load basic devices and services only* radio button. Click the *Apply* button and then click the *Close* button. A System Configuration message box appears. Click the *Restart* button. When the computer restarts, log in with the same userid used previously.

    What is different about the way Windows XP loads?

    Did the Notepad application automatically start?

8. Click the *OK* button. Click the *Selective Startup* radio button found on the *General* tab. Checkboxes are now available so that you can select the startup files that are to be loaded

the next time the computer boots. Click the *Load Startup Items* checkbox. Click the *Apply* button and then click *Close*. Click the *Restart* button and the system restarts. Log in using the same userid and password.

Did the Notepad application automatically start? Why or why not?

9. Click the *OK* button. Click the *Normal Startup—load all device drivers and services* option located on the *General* tab.

10. Click the *Startup* tab. Click the *Shortcut to notepad* checkbox to disable it.

Instructor initials: _____

11. Click the *Apply* button and then click *Close*. Click the *Restart* button. When the computer restarts, log in using the same userid and click *OK*.

Did the Notepad application automatically start? Why or why not?

What is different about the System Configuration utility's General tab?

Match the correct System Configuration utility tab to its characteristic.

_____ General	_____ BOOT.INI
_____ SYSTEM.INI	_____ Services
_____ WIN.INI	_____ Startup

a. Contains the [386enh] section

b. Contains applications that begin every time the computer boots

c. Contains a section called [boot loader] that details operating system boot options

d. Has an option to choose which boot files are processed

e. Contains an option called Application Management

f. Used with old Windows 3.x applications and contains a section called [fonts]

12. Click the *General* tab and select the *Normal Startup* radio button. Click the *Apply* button and then click *Close*. Click the *Restart* button. Log in using the same userid.

13. Once the computer reboots, remove the shortcut to the Notepad application from the *Startup* folder.

Is the Notepad shortcut (and not the original application) deleted?

Instructor initials: _____

27. Vista System Configuration and Windows Defender

Objective: To be able to use System Configuration and Windows Defender to troubleshoot boot and spyware problems

Parts: Computer with Windows Vista installed

          User logon that has administrator rights

Note: In this lab, you will explore various options that can be used within the System Configuration and Windows Defender windows.

Procedure: Complete the following procedure and answer the accompanying questions.

1. Turn on the computer and verify that the operating system loads. Log in to Windows Vista using the userid and password provided by your instructor or lab assistant.

2. Open *Windows Explorer*. From the *Organize* menu option → *Folder and Search Options* → *View* tab.

What is the current setting for the Hidden files and folders section?
[Do not show hidden files and folders enabled | Show hidden files and folders enabled]

What is the current setting for the Hide extensions for known file types option? [Enabled | Disabled]

What is the current setting for the Hide protected operating system files (Recommended) option? [Enabled | Disabled]

3. Configure the following settings:
   - *Show hidden files and folder radio button*—enabled
   - *Hide extensions for known file types*—enabled
   - *Hide protected operating system files (Recommended)*—enabled

   Click *Yes* (if prompted) → *Apply* → *OK*. Close *Windows Explorer*.

4. Re-open *Windows Explorer* and locate the *Start* folder using the path that follows:

   C:\Users\All Users\Microsoft\Windows\Start Menu\Programs\Startup

   Leave the Windows Explorer window open after you find this folder. Put a shortcut to the WordPad application in the Startup folder.

5. Restart the computer and ensure that WordPad opens. Do not immediately suspect that something is wrong if WordPad does not open right away. Windows services and drivers load first. If WordPad does not open eventually, redo the lab. Close WordPad.

6. Open the *Start* menu and select *All Programs* → *Windows Defender*. Select the *Tools* menu option → *Options*.

   What actions are defined from this window?

7. Select the *Tools* menu option → *Quarantined items*.

   List any software that Windows Defender has prevented from executing.

8. Select the *Tools* menu option → *Allowed items*.

   List any software that has been selected to not be monitored by Windows Defender.

   What happens if an item is removed from the list?

9. Select the *Tools* menu option → *Software Explorer* to view or manage software currently running on the computer.

   What categories are available to be controlled through Software Explorer?

10. From the *Categories* drop-down menu, select *Currently Running Programs*.

    List two applications that are currently running.

11. Select the *Microsoft Desktop Window Manager*.

    Where is the executable file located for this application?

    Is this application classified as Auto Start by Microsoft?

    When was this file installed?

    Is this application eligible for SpyNet voting?

12. Notice that you can end an application with the *End Process* button (but do not do so). Select the *Startup Programs* category.

13. Select the *Show for all users* button.

14. Locate the *Microsoft Windows WordPad* application. If it is not there, redo the steps required to put WordPad in the Startup folder. Close the *Windows Defender* window.

15. Click the *Start* button. In the *Start* Search textbox type **msconfig** and press [Enter]. The System Configuration window opens.

    What is the purpose of the System Configuration utility?

    What five tabs are available through the System Configuration utility?

16. On the General tab, select *Selective Startup*. Ensure that the *Load startup items* checkbox is disabled (unchecked). This setting is used when a problem occurs and you suspect a startup application. Leaving system services enabled allows services configured through the Administrative Tools/Services control panel link to load (even though these services may be the problem). By doing this, you can divide the problem in half by proving that one of the startup applications is the problem or that none of the startup applications are causing the problem. If the computer starts and the problem does not appear, one of the services may be the problem. Click the *Startup* tab.

    What options, if any, are automatically checked now?

17. Click the *Enable all* button. Scroll through the list to locate the *Microsoft Windows Operating System* item. It is frequently the last item. Expand the *Startup Item* column temporarily to see the full words by holding the mouse over the line that separates the Startup Item column from the *Manufacturer* column until the mouse cursor turns into a crosshairs symbol. Click on the separating line and drag it to the right slowly to increase the Startup Item column width. When finished, return the column to the original size.

18. Select the *Microsoft Windows Operating System* item and expand the *Command* column to ensure that the path is correct for the *wordpad.exe* file. If it is not, select another item with the words *Microsoft Windows Operating System* and the path for the *wordpad.exe* file. Disable (click to remove the checkmark) this item. This prevents the WordPad application from opening, but all other services and startup files execute.

19. Click *Apply*. Click *OK*. A System Configuration Manager application message box appears. Select the *Restart* button.

    What is different about how the system boots now?

20. Re-access the System Configuration window.

    How does the Load startup items checkbox appear and, what do you think this means?

21. The Selective startup radio button and the Startup tab are probably the best diagnostics you can use for a startup problem. Normally you would disable them all and then re-enable until you find the problem. Also, the reverse can be tried—enable all of them and disable them one by one until you find the problem.

    Click the *Diagnostic Startup—load basic devices and services only* radio button. Click the *Apply* button and then click *OK*. Select the *Restart* button. When the computer restarts, log in using the same userid and password.

    What is different about the way Windows Vista loads now?

    Did the WordPad application automatically start?

22. Re-access the System Configuration window. Select the *Allow* link. Click the *Normal Startup—load all device drivers and services* option located on the General tab.

23. Select the *Boot* tab.

    List three boot options that can be customized.

    What is the default timeout for the default boot menu option?

24. Select the *Services* tab.

    What services are enabled currently?

25. Select the *Tools* tab that is new to Windows Vista. Select *Registry Editor* and click *Launch*. The Registry Editor opens.

26. Close the *Registry Editor* window.

27. Click *Apply*. Click *OK*. Select the *Restart* button.

28. Once the computer restarts, log in using the same userid and password.

    Does the WordPad application start?

    Show the instructor or lab assistant the startup.

Instructor initials: _____

29. Re-access the *Startup* folder and remove the *WordPad shortcut*.

30. Re-access *Windows Explorer* and configure the settings to the original configuration. See the answers to Step 2.

    Show the instructor or lab assistant the correct Windows Explorer settings.

Instructor initials: _____   **(See Step 2 answers for Windows Explorer settings.)**

28. Windows 7 Startup Configuration

Objective: To be able to use the System Configuration tool to troubleshoot startup problems

Parts: Access to Windows 7 with a user ID that has administrator rights

Procedure: Complete the following procedure and answer the accompanying questions.

1. Turn on the computer and verify that the operating system loads. Log in to Windows 7 using the userid and password that has full administrator rights and that is provided by your instructor or lab assistant.

2. Open *Windows Explorer* → locate and select the *Organize* menu option → *Folder and Search Options* → *View* tab.

   What is the current setting for the *Hidden files* and *folders* option?
   [Don't show hidden files, folders, or drivers | Show hidden files, folders, and dirvers]

   What is the current setting for the *Hide extensions for known file types*? [Enabled | Disabled]

   What is the current setting for *Hide protected operating system files (Recommended)*?
   [Enabled | Disabled]

3. Configure the following settings:
   - *Show hidden files, folders, and drives*—enabled
   - *Hide extensions for known file types*—enabled
   - *Hide protected operating system files (Recommended)*—enabled

   Click *Yes* (if prompted) → *Apply* → *OK*. Close *Windows Explorer*.

4. Re-open *Windows Explorer* and locate the *Start* folder using the path that follows:

   x:\ProgramData\Microsoft\Windows\Start Menu\Programs\Startup (where *x*: is the drive where Windows is installed, such as C:)

   Leave the Windows Explorer window open once the Startup folder has been found. Place a shortcut to the *WordPad* application in the Startup folder. Refer to a previous lab if you cannot do this task. Click *Continue* if prompted.

5. Restart the computer and ensure the WordPad application automatically opens. Do not immediately suspect something is amiss if WordPad does not open quickly. Windows services and drivers load first. If WordPad does not open eventually, redo the lab until the WordPad application opens automatically as part of the startup process.

Instructor initials: _____

6. From the *Start* menu, type `msconfig` in the *Search programs and files* textbox and press [Enter]. The System Configuration window opens.

   What is the purpose of the System Configuration utility?

   What five tabs are available in the System Configuration utility window?

7. On the *General* tab, select *Selective Startup*. Ensure that the *Load startup items* checkbox is disabled (unchecked). This setting is used when a problem occurs and you suspect a startup application is the culprit. Leaving system services enabled allows services configured through the Administrative Tools/Services control panel link to load (even though these services may be the problem). By doing this, you can divide the problem in half by proving that one of the startup applications is the problem or that none of the startup applications are causing the problem. If the computer starts and the problem does not appear, one of the services may be the problem. Click the *Startup* tab.

   What options, if any, are automatically checked now?

8. Click the *Enable all* button. Scroll through the list to locate the *Microsoft Windows Operating System* item. (Note that it is frequently the last item. You can expand the *Startup Item* column temporarily to see the full words by holding the mouse over the line that separates the *Startup Item* column from the *Manufacturer* column until the mouse cursor turns into a double arrow symbol. Click on the separating line and drag it slowly to the right to increase the *Startup Item* column width. When finished return the column to the original size.)

9. Select the *Microsoft Windows Operating System* option to deselect it. Expand the *Command* column temporarily to ensure that the path is correct for the `wordpad.exe` file. If this is not the correct option, select another option with the words *Microsoft Windows Operating System* that has the path for the `wordpad.exe` file. Ensure the

checkmark is removed from this item. This prevents the WordPad application from opening as part of the boot process, but all other services and startup files/applications execute.

10. Click *Apply* → *OK*. A System Configuration Manager application message box appears. Select the *Restart* button. When the computer restarts, log in using the same userid and password.

    What is different about how the system boots now?

11. Open the *System Configuration* utility again.

    How does the Load startup items checkbox appear and what do you think this means based on what you have done?

12. The *Selective startup* (and associated options) as well as the *Startup* tab are some of the best tools you can use for a startup problem. Normally you would disable all applications and then re-enable an application one application at a time until you find the problem. Also, the reverse can be tried—enable all applications and then disable them one by one until you find the problem.

    Click the *Diagnostic Startup—Load basic devices and services only* radio button. Click the *Apply* button → *OK* → *Restart*.

    What is different about the way Windows loads now?

    Did the WordPad application automatically start?

13. Open the *System Configuration* utility again. Click the *Normal Startup—Load all device drivers and services* option located on the *General* tab.

14. Select the *Boot* tab.

    List three boot options that can be customized.

    What is the default timeout value for the boot menu?

15. Click *Apply* → *OK* → *Restart*.

16. Once the system restarts, reopen the *System Configuration* utility. Select the *Services* tab.

    List three services currently enabled.

17. Select the *Tools* tab that is new to Windows Vista and 7.

    List all utilities that can be started from the *Tools* tab.

18. Select the *Registry Editor* option and click *Launch*. The Registry Editor opens.

19. Close the Registry Editor window. Close the System configuration utility window.

20. Re-access the *Startup* folder and delete the *WordPad* shortcut.

21. Reopen *Windows Explorer* and configure the *View* tab as it was originally set in Step 2.

    Show the instructor or lab assistant the correct Windows Explorer settings.

Instructor initials: _____ **(See Step 2 answers for Windows Explorer settings.)**

29. Halting an Application Using Task Manager in Windows XP/Vista/7

Objective: To use Task Manager to halt an application

Parts: Computer with Windows XP, Vista, or 7 installed

Note: At times, it may become necessary to halt an application that is hung or stalled. Windows provides a method to accomplish this through the Task Manager utility.

Procedure: Complete the following procedure and answer the accompanying questions.

1. Turn on the computer and verify that the operating system loads. Log in to Windows using the userid and password provided by the instructor or lab assistant. Ensure the userid is one that has Administrator rights.

2. From the *Start* menu, choose *All Programs*, *Accessories*, and then select *Notepad*. The Notepad utility opens.

3. To access Task Manager, simultaneously press [Ctrl], [Alt], and [Del]. In Vista/7, select the *Start Task Manager* link. The *Task Manager* window opens.

   What type of things can you view from Task Manager?

4. Select the *Applications* tab.

   What applications, if any, are listed as open?

5. Click the *Untitled—Notepad* option and click the *End Task* button. Notepad closes.

   Were you able to close the Notepad application from within Task Manager?

6. Close the *Task Manager* window.

Instructor initials: _____

30. Using Windows XP Event Viewer

Objective: To be able to use the *Event Viewer* program to troubleshoot problems

Parts: Computer with Windows XP installed and a userid that has Administrator rights

Note: In this lab, evaluate a computer event to see how to gather information using Event Viewer.

Procedure: Complete the following procedure and answer the accompanying questions.

1. Turn on the computer and verify that the operating system loads. Log in to Windows XP using the userid and password provided by the instructor or lab assistant. Ensure the userid is one that has Administrator rights.

2. Event Viewer is used to monitor various events such as when drivers and services load (or fail to load and have problems). Click the *Start* button and click the *Control Panel* option. If in control panel *Category* view, click the *Performance and Maintenance* category and click *Administrative Tools*. If in *Classic* view, double-click the *Administrative Tools* control panel icon and then double-click the *Event Viewer* icon. The *Event Viewer* window opens.

3. Click the *Application* log located in the left pane. Application events are listed in the right pane.

   Are there any warning events listed? If so, list one of them.

   Are there any information events listed? If so, list one of them.

4. Double-click any application event.

   Do you have any way of copying the event's information to the clipboard where it can later be copied into a text file? If so, list the details of how to do this in the space below.

5. Close the *Event Properties* window. Click the *System* log located in the left pane. System events are listed in the right pane.

   What is the most common type of system event?

6. Double-click any of the individual events. Click the button that looks like two pieces of paper directly under the *Up* and *Down* arrow buttons.

7. Click the *Start* button. Click the *Run* option. Type `clipbrd` and press [Enter]. The event is copied to the Clipboard and the `clipbrd` command opens the Clipboard Viewer.

8. Open Notepad by clicking the *Start* button, pointing to *All Programs*, pointing to *Accessories*, and clicking the *Notepad* option.

9. Click the *Edit* menu option and select *Paste*.

   What appeared in Notepad?

Instructor initials: _____

10. The event information can be saved as a text file and referenced later especially when there is a problem. Close *Notepad* without saving the document. Close *Event Viewer*.

31. Using Windows Vista/7 Event Viewer

Objective: To be able to use the Event Viewer program to troubleshoot problems

Parts: Computer with Windows Vista or 7 installed and a userid that has Administrator rights

Note: In this lab, evaluate a computer event to see how to gather information using Event Viewer.

Procedure: Complete the following procedure and answer the accompanying questions.

1. Turn on the computer and verify that the operating system loads. Log in to Windows using the userid and password provided by your instructor or lab assistant. Ensure that the userid is one that has Administrator rights.

2. Event Viewer is used to monitor various events such as when drivers and services load (or fail to load and have problems). From the *Start* menu → *Control Panel* → *System and Maintenance* (Vista)/*System and Security* (7) → *Administrative Tools* → double-click *Event Viewer*. The Event Viewer window opens to the Overview and Summary window.

   How many total warning administrative events occurred on this computer?

3. Scroll down in *Summary of Administrative Events* and expand the *Audit Success* category. Select and double-click on the line with the highest audit success event ID.

   From the General tab, what was the account name?

4. In the right panel, select the *Attach Task to This Event*. Type your first initial and last name as the name of the basic task, for example cschmidt. Click *Next* on the following two windows.

   What three actions can be taken from this screen?

5. Click *Cancel*.

6. Expand the *Windows Logs* category in the left panel. Select the *Application* subcategory.

   List the application that caused the first event.

7. Select the *Security* subcategory from the left panel. Double-click on the first *Audit Success* event.

   What account name was used?

8. Close the *Event Properties* window. Select the *System* subcategory from the left panel. Double-click on the first event listed.

   List the source of the first event.

9. Select the *Copy* button.

10. From the *Start* menu → *All Programs* → *Notepad* → *Edit* menu item → *Paste*.

    What appeared in Notepad?

Instructor initials: _____

11. The event information can be saved as a text file and referenced later, especially when there is a problem. Close Notepad without saving the document. Close the *Event Properties* window.

12. In Event Viewer, expand *Applications and Services Logs*. Expand the *Microsoft* folder and the *Windows* folder. Expand the *TaskScheduler* to locate and click on the *Operational* event log.

    What is the first informational TaskScheduler *event logged?*

13. Close *Event Viewer*.

32. Using Task Manager to View Performance

Objective: To be able to use the Task Manager program to evaluate basic computer performance

Parts: Computer with Windows XP, Vista, or 7 installed

              Userid that has Administrator rights

Note: In this lab, evaluate a computer event to see how to gather information using Event Viewer.

Procedure: Complete the following procedure and answer the accompanying questions.

1. Turn on the computer and verify that the operating system loads. Log in to Windows using the userid and password provided by the instructor or lab assistant. Ensure the userid is one that has Administrator rights.

2. Press the Ctrl+Alt+Del keys to bring up Task Manager. In Vista/7, select *Start Task Manager*. Click the *Performance* tab. The Performance tab is used to view CPU and page file usage (Vista)/memory usage (7).

3. Open *Notepad*, access the Internet if possible, open a game if possible, and start other applications.

   What happens to the CPU usage as displayed in Task Manager?

   What is the page file usage (PF Usage) in XP or the Memory usage in Vista/7?

   What is the total physical memory?

   How much memory is available?

Instructor initials: _____

4. Task Manager is a great way to see a snapshot of the status of two of the most important pieces of hardware, the CPU and RAM (even though the Task Manager application increases both the CPU and memory usage). Close all windows.

33. Using the System Monitor Utility in Windows XP

Objective: To use the System Monitor utility to track individual computer components

Parts: Computer with Windows XP installed and Administrative Tools loaded

Procedure: Complete the following procedure and answer the accompanying questions.

1. Turn on the computer and verify that the operating system loads. Log in to Windows XP using the userid and password provided by the instructor or lab assistant. Ensure the userid is one that has Administrator rights.

2. Click the *Start* button and click the *Control Panel* option. If in Category view, click the *Performance and Maintenance* category and click *Administrative Tools*. If in Classic view, double-click the *Administrative Tools* control panel icon and then double-click the *Performance* icon. The Performance window opens. The Performance utility allows you to track individual computer component's performance. This is done through individual counters.

3. In the left window, click the *System Monitor* item.

4. Click the *Add* button (the button that has a plus sign on it) or right-click in the right window and click the *Add Counters* option. The Add Counters dialog box opens.

5. Click the *Performance object* down arrow. A list of system components appears such as processor, physical disk, paging file memory, etc. Select the *Memory performance* object.

6. Once a system component has been selected, individual counters for that component can be selected and monitored. In the Select counters from list window, click the *Available Bytes* counter. Click the *Add* button.

7. Click the *Performance* object down arrow. Select the *Paging File performance* object.

8. In the Select counters from list window, click the *%Usage* counter. Click the *Add* button.

   Using the Explain button, find out for what the *%Usage* counter is used. Document the purpose of the %Usage counter.

9. Close the *Explain text* message box. Using the method outlined in Steps 5 through 8, select two more counters to be monitored.

   What two counters did you add?

10. Click the *Close* button. The right window in the Performance window displays a graph of the various counters. You may need to start some applications, do some cutting and pasting, or surf the Internet to see some of the counter activity. When finished, close the *Performance* window.

Instructor initials: _____

34. Using the Performance Monitor Utility in Windows XP

Objective: To use the System Monitor utility to track individual computer components

Parts: Computer with Windows XP installed and Administrative Tools loaded

Procedure: Complete the following procedure and answer the accompanying questions.

1. Turn on the computer and verify that the operating system loads. Log in to Windows XP using the userid and password provided by the instructor or lab assistant. Ensure the userid is one that has Administrator rights.

2. Click the *Start* button and click the *Control Panel* option. If in control panel Category view, click the *Performance and Maintenance* category and then click *Administrative Tools*. If in Classic view, double-click the *Administrative Tools* control panel icon and then double-click the *Performance* icon. The Performance window opens. The Performance utility allows you to track individual computer component's performance. This is done through individual counters.

3. Click the *Performance Logs and Alerts* option in the left panel. Click the + (plus sign) if necessary to expand the *Performance Logs and Alerts* category.

   What are the three types of logs tracked by this utility?

4. Counter logs are used to create a log file using objects and counters you select. Click the *Counter logs* option in the left panel.

5. Click the *Action* menu item and select *New Log Settings*.

6. In the *Name* textbox, type **Memory Usage** and click the *OK* button.

7. Click the *Add Counters* button. Click the *Performance* object down arrow and select Memory. In the *Select counters from list* window, click the *Available bytes* counter, and click the *Add* button. In the *Select counters from list* window, click the *Cache bytes* counter, and click the *Add* button. Click the *Close* button. The counters appear in the Counters window.

8. Click the *Log Files* tab. The Log Files tab is used to select what type of file is created. The default type of file is a binary file, but a text file can be selected. Click the *Log file type* down arrow and select the *Text File (Comma delimited)* option.

9. The Configure button is used to specify the location of the log file. Click the *Configure* button.

   What is the default location (folder) for the log file?

10. Click the *Cancel* button. Click the *Schedule* tab. The Schedule tab is used to define the start and stop time for the log file. The default is to start the log and keep going until it is manually stopped. In the Stop log section, click the *At* radio button. Change the time to two minutes after the current time. Make sure the date is today's date. (The default is one day later.) In other words, you will only be logging for two minutes. Click the *Apply* button and click the *OK* button. The Memory Usage log file appears in the right panel.

11. After two minutes, access the WordPad accessory. Click the *File* menu option and select *Open*. Click the *Files of type* down arrow and select *All Documents*. Use the *Look in* drop-down box or the icons on the left to locate the Memory Usage file. Reference your answer following Step 9 for the name of the folder and drive letter. Click the file name and click the *Open* button. The Memory Usage log file appears. The first set of numbers is the date followed by the time. The next two numbers are the counters that were requested: Available bytes and Cache bytes.

    On the first logged event line, what is the number of available bytes and cache bytes?

Instructor initials: _____

12. Return to the Performance window and click the *Memory Usage* counter log that you created earlier. Click the red *X* (delete) icon. An alternative method for doing the same thing is to click the *Action* menu item and click the *Delete* option.

13. Click the *Alerts* log in the left panel. Click the *Action* menu item and select *New Alert Settings*. In the *Name* textbox, type `Memory Alert` and click the *OK* button. The *Alerts* option is used to set a counter that triggers an alert event to be sent to Event Viewer.

14. Click the *Add* button. In the *Performance* object drop-down menu, select *Memory*. In the *Select counters from list* window, use the scroll bars to locate the *Available Bytes* counter. Click the *Explain* button.

    What does the Available Bytes counter log do?

15. Close the *Explain Text* window. Click the *Add* button. Click the *Close* button. On the *General* tab, type **1** in the *Limit* textbox. (Note that this is not a value you would normally pick, but is used for illustration purposes.) Click the *Action* tab. The Action tab is used to specify what happens when an alert is generated. The default is to send an alert into the application event log.

16. Click the *Schedule* tab. The Schedule tab is used to define the start and stop time for the log file. The default is to start the log and keep going until it is manually stopped. In the *Stop log* section, click the *At* radio button. Change the time to two minutes after the current time. Make sure the date is today's date. In other words, you will only be logging for two minutes. Click the *Apply* button and click the *OK* button. The Memory Alert log file appears in the right panel.

17. Open Event Viewer and open the Application event log by clicking *Application* in the left panel. Look in the right panel. The first few application events should have event code 2031. Double-click one of these events.

Instructor initials: _____

    Write down the event description.

18. Close Event Viewer and return to the Performance window. Click the *Alerts Performance Logs and Alerts* category. Click the *Memory Alert* log. Click the red *X* (delete) icon. An alternative method for doing the same thing is to click the *Action* menu item and click the *Delete* option.

    Have a classmate verify that the counter log and alert log you created in this exercise are deleted.

Classmate's printed name: _____

Classmate's signature: _____

19. Close the Performance window.

35. Performance and Reliability in Windows Vista

Objective: To be able to use the Reliability and Performance tool to troubleshoot problems

Parts: Computer with Windows Vista installed and a userid that has Administrator rights

Note: In this lab, evaluate a computer's performance and reliability to see how to gather information when a problem occurs.

Procedure: Complete the following procedure and answer the accompanying questions.

1. Turn on the computer and verify that the operating system loads. Log in to Windows using the userid and password provided by your instructor or lab assistant. Ensure that the userid is one that has Administrator rights.

2. From the *Start* menu → *Control Panel* → *System and Maintenance* → *Administrative Tools* → double-click *Reliability and Performance Monitor*. The Resource Overview window opens. Let the system run at least two minutes before answering the questions. During this time, access the Internet, open a game, and open a word processing document, photo, or graphic. In other words, do things on the computer.

What is the CPU usage?

Describe the Disk graph.

Did the Network graph show activity that reflected your activity? [Yes | No]

What percentage of the memory is Used Physical memory?

3. Expand the *Monitoring Tools* object in the left pane. Select the *Performance Monitor* tool.

What is the default counter shown?

4. Select the plus symbol (+) from the graphical menu at the top of the chart. Scroll through the counters list until you locate and click on the down arrow (∨) for the *PhysicalDisk* counter. Click once on the *Disk Reads/sec* counter. In the *Instance of selected object* window, select the number that corresponds to your primary hard drive partition. Click *Add*. Continue by adding the following counters:

- PhysicalDisk   Disk Writes/sec
- LogicalDisk   % Free Space
- Memory   Available Bytes
- Memory   Cache Bytes
- Processor   % Processor Time (All instances)

Click *OK*. If a message appears saying that one of the counters is already enabled, click *OK*.

5. Allow the system to run for at least two minutes. Do things on the computer during this time. Afterward, click the *Freeze Display* menu icon that looks like a Pause button on a CD/DVD player or press Ctrl + F.

6. Select the *Change Graph Type* drop-down menu to *Histogram bar*. This is the third icon from the left on the graphic menu at the top of the graph. Select the *Available bytes* counter.

What is the average number of available bytes of memory?

7. Click on the *Cache Bytes* counter row.

What is the maximum number of bytes in cache memory?

Look at the bar graph. Which is higher: the number of disk reads per second or disk writes per second?

Instructor initials: _____

8. Change the graph type to the *Report* view.

Which one of these views do you think will be most used by a technician?

9. From the left pane, select *Reliability Monitor*. If any events appear in the System Stability chart, double-click on it to see more information in the report section.

Describe any event that the system considered important enough to potentially affect the computer's reliability.

10. Close all windows.

36. Performance and Reliability in Windows 7

Objective: To be able to use Windows 7 tools to verify performance, measure reliability, and troubleshoot startup problems

Parts: Access to Windows 7 with a user ID that has administrator rights

Procedure: Complete the following procedure and answer the accompanying questions.

1. Turn on the computer and verify that the operating system loads. Log in to Windows 7 using the userid and password that has full administrator rights and that is provided by your instructor or lab assistant.

2. From the *Start* menu → *Control Panel* → *System and Security* → *Administrative Tools* → double-click *Performance Monitor* → select the *Open Resource Monitor* link. The information shown on the overview tab is known as the key table. It always contains a complete list

of running (active) processes for the system. You can filter the data and look at the information more granularly by using the specific tabs.

3. Select the *CPU* tab. Notice the individual processes in the Processes section. Select a particular process by clicking in the checkbox by the process name. The top graph shows that particular process in relation to the total CPU usage.

   How many CPU threads are used by the Performance Monitor application?

4. Deselect the individual process(es) you selected in the Processes section. Expand the *Services* section. Notice the last column—Average CPU. This column shows the average percentage of CPU consumption by a particular service.

   What service is taking the most CPU power?

5. Select the *Memory* tab. Notice the Commit (KB) column. This column shows the amount of virtual memory reserved by Windows for a particular process.

   List two processes and the amount of virtual memory being used by the system for each process.

6. The Working Set column shows the amount of physical memory used by a particular process.

   Which process is using the most motherboard RAM?

7. Select the *Disk* tab. Open any file and save it to a different location on the hard drive if possible. Return to the *Disk* tab and notice the disk activity.

8. Select the *Network* tab. Connect to the Internet and return to this tab.

   How many TCP connections are active?

9. Close the *Resource Monitor* window and return to the *Performance Monitor* window.

10. Ensure the top object, *Performance,* is selected in the left panel. Notice the *System Summary* section in the center of the right panel.

    What is the available memory in megabytes?

    Scroll down to see the *PhysicalDisk* component. What is the percentage of idle time?

    Locate the *Processor Information* section. What is the total percent of processor time?

11. Expand the *Monitoring Tools* object in the left panel. Select the *Performance Monitor* tool.

    What is the default counter shown?

12. Select the plus symbol (+) from the graphical menu at the top of the chart. Scroll through the counters list until you locate and click on the *PhysicalDisk* counter down arrow (▼). Click once on the *Disk Reads/sec* counter. In the *Instances of selected object* window, select the number that corresponds to your primary hard drive partition. Click *Add*. Continue by using the same process to add the following counters.

    - PhysicalDisk   Disk Writes/sec
    - LogicalDisk   % Free Space
    - Memory   Available Bytes
    - Memory   Cache Bytes
    - Processor   % Processor Time (All instances)

13. Click *OK*. If a message appears saying that one of the counters is already enabled, click *OK*.

14. Allow the system to run at least two minutes. Do things on the computer during this time. Afterward, click the *Freeze Display* menu icon that looks like a pause button on a CD/DVD player or use the (Ctrl)+(F) keystrokes.

15. Select the *Change Graph Type* drop-down menu item to *Histogram bar*. Note that this is the third icon from the left on the graphic menu at the top of the graph. Select the *Available bytes* counter.

    What is the average number of available bytes of memory?

16. Click on the *Cache Bytes* counter row.

    What is the maximum number of bytes in cache memory?

    Look at the bar graph. Which is higher, the number of disk reads per second or the disk writes per second?

Instructor initials: _____

17. Change the graph type to the *Report* view.

   Which one of these views do you think will be most used by a technician?

18. Click the *Start* button. Type **reliability monitor** in the *Search programs and files* textbox. Select the *View reliability history* link from the resulting list.

   Describe any event that the system considered important enough to potentially affect the computer reliability.

19. Close all windows.

20. Click the *Start* button → *Control Panel* → *System and Security* → locate (but don't click on) the *System* section → locate and click on the *Check the Windows Experience Index* link.

   What is the base score?

   What component(s) rate the highest subscore?

21. Close all windows.

37. Installing and Using Remote Desktop in Windows XP

Objective: To be able to configure a computer for remote accessing using the Remote Desktop tool as well as access and administer the computer remotely

Parts: Two computers with Windows XP loaded

   Windows XP CD

Note: You must have the ability to create users on the remote computer or have a user ID already created that has a password assigned.

Procedure: Complete the following procedure and answer the accompanying questions.

Remote Computer

1. On the computer that is to be accessed remotely, power it on and verify that XP loads. Log on to XP using the userid and password provided by the instructor or lab assistant.

2. If the computer has a user ID that has a password, this step can be skipped. Otherwise, access the *User* control panel by selecting the *Start* button → *Control Panel* → *Classic* view → *User Accounts* → *Create a new account* → type **tester** in the *Name* textbox → select *Next* → *Limited radio* button → *Create Account* button. Add a password by clicking the *Change an account link* → *tester* → *Create a password link* → in the *Type a new password* textbox, type **tester** → in the *Type the password again to confirm* textbox, type **tester** → *Create password*. Close the User Accounts window.

3. Install the Remote Desktop application by clicking the *Start* button → *Control Panel* → *Add or Remove Programs* → *Add/Remove Windows Components* → *Internet Information Services* → *Details* button → *World Wide Web Service* → *Details* button → *Remote Desktop Web Connection* checkbox → *OK* → *OK* → *Next* → you may be prompted to insert the XP CD → *Finish* button. Close the Add or Remove Programs window. Close the Control Panel window.

4. Ensure the computer has all the latest security updates by temporarily disabling the World Wide Web publishing service and obtaining/installing the updates. Click the *Start* button → *Run* → type **net stop w3svc** and press Enter. A message appears stating the World Wide Web publishing service has been stopped. Install Microsoft Windows updates by clicking the *Start* button → *All Programs* → *Windows Update* and follow the directions on the screen. Once updated, re-enable the World Wide Web publishing service by clicking the *Start* button → *Run* → type **net start w3svc** and press Enter. The **net** command is used by networking and PC support staff. Table 12.29 lists some of the more common commands used.

5. Start the Remote Desktop configuration by obtaining the computer name—click the *Start* button → *Control Panel* → *Classic* view → *System* → *Remote* tab.

   Write the name of the computer exactly as it is shown.

Table 12.29	**NET commands**
Command	Description
`net start`	Can start services within Windows when enclosed within quotation marks. Examples include alert, browser, DHCP client, event log, plug and play, server, workstation, schedule, and spooler. It can also be sued to start non-Windows services.
`net stop`	Can stop services. See `net start` explanation.
`net use`	Used to connect or disconnect a computer from a network resource as well as view information about network connections.
`net view`	Lists computers in a workgroup or a specific computer's shared network resources.

6. Configure Remote Desktop for the particular user by ensuring the *Allow users to connect remotely to this computer* checkbox is enabled → *Apply* button → *Remote Users* button → *Add* button → in the *Enter object names to select* textbox, type **tester** → *OK*.

7. Click *OK* and close the System Properties window.

Firewall Configuration

8. Ensure that any firewalls enabled between the remote system and the PC used to connect to the remote allow Remote Desktop to be used. If using Windows Firewall on the PC being accessed remotely, click the *Start* button → *Control Panel* → *Classic* view → *Security Center* → *Windows Firewall* link → *Exceptions* tab → enable the *Remote Desktop* checkbox (and ensure a group policy does not override this setting). If using a third party firewall software application, ensure ports 3389 and 80 are open.

Second Computer Configuration

9. On the computer used to access the first computer, access the Remote Desktop application by clicking the *Start* button → *All Programs* → *Accessories* → *Communications* → *Remote Desktop Connection*. In the *Computer* textbox, type in the computer name previously recorded (the computer name of the remote desktop) and click *Connect*.

10. In the *User name* textbox, type **tester** → in the *Password* textbox, type **tester** → *OK*. Add a shortcut desktop icon to any application not already shown. Show the new shortcut icon to the instructor.

Instructor initials: _____

11. Experiment with the controls at the top of the *Remote Desktop* window. Notice how you can minimize the window and be back on your own desktop. Notice the push pin icon on the far left. This keeps the Control Panel window active at the top of a full screen. If you click the push pin to turn the icon sideways, the Control Panel window recedes. To get the window to reappear, move your mouse pointer to the top of the window for a moment. Click the push pin again to make the Control Panel stay.

12. Close the Remote Desktop connection by clicking the *Close* button at the top of the screen.

Removing the User and Shortcut

13. On the original computer, remove the shortcut that was just created.

14. On the original computer, remove the *tester* user using the User Accounts control panel. Show the changes to the instructor.

Instructor initials: _____

38. Windows 7 Remote Desktop

Objective: To be able to configure a computer for remote access using the Remote Desktop tool

Parts: Two computers with Windows 7 loaded

Notes: The Remote Desktop tool is disabled by default and is only available in Windows 7 Professional, Business, and Ultimate.

You must have the ability to create users on the remote computer or have a userid already created that has a password assigned.

Procedure: Complete the following procedure and answer the accompanying questions.

1. On the computer that is to be accessed remotely, power it on and verify that Windows 7 loads. Log in using the userid and password provided by the instructor or lab assistant.

2. If both computers have a userid with full administrator rights and a password, this step can be skipped. Otherwise, access the *Start* button → *Control Panel* → *User Accounts and Family Safety* → *User Accounts* → *Manage another account* → *Create a new account* link → type **tester** in the *New account name* textbox → select the *Administrator* radio button → select the *Create Account* button. Add a password by clicking the *tester* icon → *create* a *password* link → in the *New password* textbox, type **tester** → in the *Confirm new password* textbox, type **tester** → click on the *Create password* button. Close the User Accounts window. Login using the "tester" account on both computers.

3. On both computers, open *Windows Explorer*. Locate and right-click on the *Computer* item. Select *Properties*.

   Document the full computer name for both computers.

   Computer 1 _____

   Computer 2 _____

4. On both computers, select the *Remote settings* link. The *Remote* tab should be active.

   What is the current setting? [Don't allow connections to this computer | Allow connections from computers running any version of Remote Desktop (less secure) | Allow connections only from computers running Remote Desktop with Network Level Authentication (more secure)]

5. In the *Remote Desktop* section, select the *Allow connections from computers running any version of Remote Desktop (less secure)* radio button.

   What warning appears, if any?

6. If necessary, click *OK* on the message. Click *OK*.

7. On computer 1, select the *Start* button → *All Programs* → *Accessories* → *Remote Desktop Connection*.

8. In the Remote Desktop Connection window, type the other computer's full computer name in the *Computer* textbox. Click *Connect*.

9. Enter a password. Click *Yes* on the request for a certification or if a certificate warning appears.

   What happened to the remote computer?

10. On the computer that is doing the controlling, add a new shortcut to the desktop of the remote computer. When finished, click on the close button in the blue control panel located in the top center of the screen. Click *OK*.

11. On the remote computer, login. Notice the new desktop shortcut.

Instructor Initials: _____ (check for new desktop shortcut)

12. Delete the newly installed desktop shortcut on the remote computer.

13. Return all settings back to the original configuration. See Step 4 answer.

14. Remove the *tester* user account from any computer if it was created.

Internet Discovery

Objective: To access the Internet to obtain specific information regarding a computer or its associated parts

Parts: Access to the Internet

Procedure: Use the Internet to answer the following questions.

1. Find a Web site that offers Windows 7 freeware tools. Write the name of the Web site and the URL where this information was found.

2. What is the latest service pack available from Microsoft for Windows 7? Write the answer and the URL where you found the answer.

3. Find a Web site that details how to set up DualView. Write the Web address as well as the questions to configure DualView.

4. Microsoft always has minimum requirements for any of its operating systems. Find a Web site that tells you what your system should have to run Windows 7 Ultimate efficiently. Write the name of the company that posts the recommendation, the minimum requirements cited, as well as the URL.

5. You get the error code 0x80072F8F on a Windows Vista computer when trying to get a Windows update. Find a Web site that describes this error and write the cause and URL.

6. Find a certification related to a Microsoft operating system. List the certification and the average salary associated with the certification. List any and all URLs used to find this information.

Soft Skills

Objective: To enhance and fine tune a future technician's ability to listen, communicate in both written and oral form, and support people who use computers in a professional manner

Activities:

1. In groups of two or three students, one student puts a problem related to Windows XP, Vista, or 7 on the computer. The other two students use the Remote Desktop utility to solve the problem. Document each problem along with the solution provided. Exchange roles so that each student practices the repair and documentation.

2. Divide into five groups. The following are five questions about operating systems: (1) What should you do *before* installing an operating system, (2) What are alternatives to XP, Vista, or 7 as an operating system and what are pros/cons of these alternatives? (3) What is the difference between an active partition, system partition, and boot partition in regards to XP, Vista, or 7? (4) What operating systems can be upgraded to Windows XP, Vista, or 7? What is the difference between a clean install and an upgrade and what determines which one you do? (5) What differences can be seen for a Windows hard drive that has a FAT32 partition and one that has an NTFS partition? Each group is assigned one of these five areas or another set of five questions related to Windows XP, Vista, and/or 7. Each group is allowed 20 minutes (and some white board space or poster-sized paper) to write their ideas. Each group member helps to present his/her ideas to the class.

3. Find a magazine article related to a Windows solution or feature. Share your findings with the class.

Critical Thinking Skills

Objective: To analyze and evaluate information as well as apply learned information to new or different situations

Activities:

1. Based on the information given in the chapter about Remote Assistance, along with any directions found on the Internet or through Windows help, configure two computers for Remote Assistance and allow a person to take over a computer remotely. Write the steps needed to do this process. Share the steps with other groups and refine the steps until non-technical people could use the steps provided as a class to configure a computer for Remote Assistance.

2. Find a Windows registry hack online, in a book, or from a magazine. Analyze the hack for whether or not it is beneficial to normal users, whether it is beneficial to technicians, whether or not you would recommend it to a fellow student, and whether or not you would recommend it to your parents. Write a brief description of your findings including the implications of installing the registry modification.

3. Using any research method and resource, determine the pros and cons of upgrading to Windows Vista from Windows XP Professional. Make a list of things to check before upgrading.

13

Introduction to Networking

Objectives

After completing this chapter you will be able to

- Differentiate between peer-to-peer/workgroup and server-based/domain networks
- Identify commonly used network topologies
- Compare and contrast types of network cabling
- Explain the differences between various network access methods
- Explain how Ethernet works
- Identify OSI and TCP/IP model layers and the network devices that work at each layer
- Articulate commonly used network protocols
- Identify and define the purpose of a MAC address and an IPv4 and IPv6 address
- Apply IP addressing concepts

587

- Define the purpose of DHCP and DNS
- Configure a computer for network connectivity
- Use common network troubleshooting tools
- Access a network printer
- Define common networking terms
- Identify and define the function of the basic parts of a wireless network
- Distinguish between ad hoc and infrastructure wireless networks
- List the different types of wireless NICs
- Explain the purpose of an SSID and channel ID
- List the three non-overlapping channel IDs used in wireless networks
- Contrast dBd with dBi
- Define and explain how to perform a basic wireless site survey
- Compare and contrast the 802.11a, 802.11b, 802.11g, and 802.11n wireless standards
- Explain the basic protocols used with email
- Describe how to be a proactive technician

Networking Overview

Many networks are found all around us. Some of them follow:

- The network of roads and interstate highways
- The telephone network
- The electrical network that provides electricity to our homes
- The cellular network that allows cell phones to connect to one another as well as connectivity between cell phones and the wired telephone network and the Internet
- Air traffic control network
- Our network of friends and family

A **network** as it relates to computers is two or more devices that have the ability to communicate with one another and share resources. A network allows computer users to share files; communicate via email; browse the Internet; share a printer, modem, or scanner; and access applications and files. Networks can be divided into four major categories based on the size of the network—PAN, LAN, MAN, and WAN. Table 13.1 describes these different networks.

Today, networks are vital to businesses. They can also be found in many homes. A technician must have a basic understanding of the devices that make up networks and learn how to connect them into an existing network.

Types of Local Area Networks

There are two basic types of LANs, a server-based network and a peer-to-peer network. With a server-based network, computer users log in to a main computer called a server where they are authenticated (authorized to use the network). The server is a more powerful computer than a normal workstation. The server contains information about who is allowed to connect to the

Table 13.1	Types of networks
Network type	**Description**
PAN (Personal Area Network)	Personal devices such as PDAs, cell phones, laptop computers, and pocket video games that can communicate in close proximity through a wired network or wirelessly. Playing a game between two laptop computers wirelessly is an example of a PAN.
LAN (Local Area Network)	A group of devices that can share resources in a single area such as a room, home, or building. The most common type of LAN is Ethernet. A LAN can be wired or wireless. The computers in a networked classroom is an example of a LAN.
MAN (Metropolitan Area Network)	Connectivity between sites within the same city. A MAN connects multiple LANs. MANs can be wireless or use fiber optic cabling. Multiple college campuses connected together is an example of a MAN.
WAN (Wide Area Network)	Communication between LANs on a larger geographic scale. The Internet is an example of a WAN just as two networks located in two cities is a WAN.

network, and to what network resources (files, printer, and applications) the network user is allowed access. Another name for a server-based network is **client/server network**. Windows computers in a server-based network are commonly called a **domain** that has dedicated servers known as domain controllers. One or more dedicated domain controllers log and track users and resources. Domains are commonly found in the business environment.

A peer-to-peer network does not have a centralized server. Instead, each computer is its own server and resources are shared between the workstation computers. The computer user sets up passwords to allow others access to the resources on or directly connected to that computer. A person uses the network to access remote files, printers, applications, and so forth from his/her own workstation. Server-based networks are more common in businesses, whereas peer-to-peer networks are more common in homes and very small businesses. A server-based network can consist of 10 or more computers; in contrast, a peer-to-peer network usually has fewer (2 to 9 computers).

Windows computers in a peer-to-peer network are known as a **workgroup**. Two or more computers configured with the same workgroup name can share devices such as printers as well as files and folders. No central server or domain controller is used. Many homes and small businesses use a workgroup environment.

A server-based network is more secure than a peer-to-peer network. This is because the server is normally in a locked network room or wiring closet. Also, the network users and what they are allowed to do (their network rights and permissions) are configured and stored on the network server. Servers have a special operating system loaded on them called a NOS (network operating system). Examples of network operating systems are Novell OES (Open Enterprise Server), Microsoft 2008 Server, Red Hat Enterprise Linux, and Sun Solaris. A network operating system has utilities that allow computer user management (who is allowed onto the network), resource management (what network applications, files, printers, and so on a user can use), and security management (what a user is allowed to do with a resource such as read, write, and read and write). One userid and password is all a remote user needs to access many network resources located throughout the business organization. A network user can sit down at any computer in the organization, log on to the server, and start working with the network resources.

Figure 13.1 shows how a server-based network can be configured. The network has one server in the center, four workstations, and two laser printers. The server has a database of users, CSchmidt, RDevoid, and MElkins, and their associated passwords. The server also has three applications loaded—Microsoft Excel, Microsoft Project, and Microsoft Word. These applications and associated documents are stored on the server. Whether or not the users can access

13
Introduction to Networking

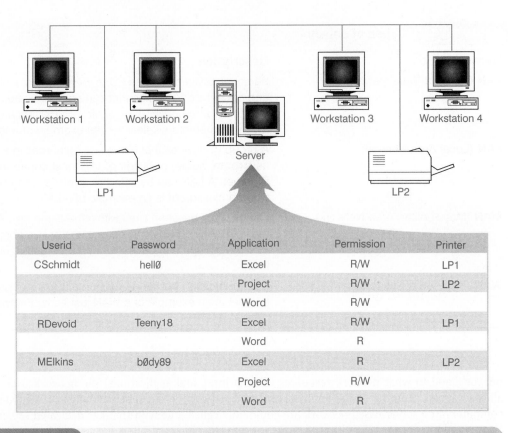

Userid	Password	Application	Permission	Printer
CSchmidt	hellØ	Excel	R/W	LP1
		Project	R/W	LP2
		Word	R/W	
RDevoid	Teeny18	Excel	R/W	LP1
		Word	R	
MElkins	bØdy89	Excel	R	LP2
		Project	R/W	
		Word	R	

Figure 13.1 **Server-based network**

these applications and documents and what they can do within each document is also stored on the server. In the Permission column of the table located in Figure 13.1 is either R for Read or R/W for Read/Write. This is an indication of what the user can do in a particular application. For example, user CSchmidt has read and write access to Excel, Project, and Word. This means that she can open, look at, and modify documents in any of these three applications. MElkins can only read Excel and Word documents, but she can read and write Microsoft Project documents. CSchmidt can print to either of the laser printers, but RDevoid prints only to the LP1 laser printer.

Another benefit of server-based networks is that a user can sit down at any workstation, log in to the server with his or her userid and password, and have access to all of the network resources. For example, in Figure 13.1, RDevoid can sit down at any workstation and have access to her Excel and Word documents and print to laser printer LP1.

A peer-to-peer network is not as expensive, or as secure as a server-based network. A server is more expensive than a regular workstation plus it requires a network operating system. Since peer-to-peer networks do not use a dedicated server, costs are reduced. Instead of a network operating system, each workstation uses an operating system such as Windows XP, Windows Vista, or Windows 7. A peer-to-peer network is not as secure as a server-based network because each computer must be configured with individual userids and passwords. Figure 13.2 shows how a peer-to-peer network is configured.

In Figure 13.2 there are three workstations labeled Workstation 1, 2, and 3. Workstation 2 has a shared printer. A shared printer is a printer connected to the computer that has been configured so that other network users can print to it. There are three people in this company, Raina Devoid, Cheryl Schmidt, and Melodie Elkins. RDevoid normally works at Workstation 1 and she has shared a folder on the hard drive called *WORDDOCS* that has a password of Stealth2. CSchmidt and MElkins can access the documents located in

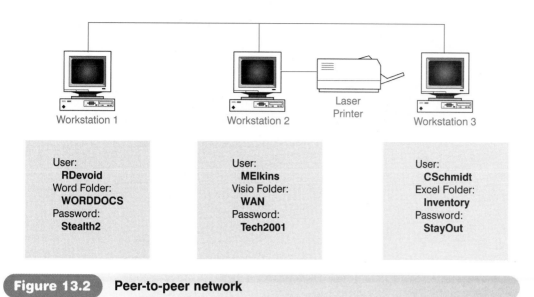

Figure 13.2 **Peer-to-peer network**

WORDDOCS from their own workstations as long as they know the password is Stealth2. If RDevoid (who is sitting at Workstation 1) wants to access MElkins' *WAN* folder, RDevoid must know and remember that the password is Tech2001. If MElkins' changes the password on the *WAN* folder, MElkins must remember to tell the new password to anyone who needs access. The password is only used when accessing the *WAN* folder documents.

A peer-to-peer network password is only effective across the network. The password is not effective if someone sits down at the workstation. For example, if a summer intern, Ken Tinker, sits down at Workstation 3, Ken has full access to the *Inventory* folder and documents. Even though the folder is password protected for the peer-to-peer network, Ken is not using the network

> **Peer-to-peer networks are for small networks**
>
> You can see that the more resources that are shared on a peer-to-peer network, the more passwords and more cumbersome password management will be. That is the reason peer-to-peer networks are used in very small network environments.

to access the folder so the password is useless. Ken could be prevented from accessing the folder if userids and passwords are implemented for individual machines. The problem of having access to a workstation and all its resources simply by sitting down at a computer is not as much of a threat today because of the newer operating systems' features.

Management of network resources is much harder to control on a peer-to-peer network than on a server-based network. Each user is required to manage the network resources on one computer and password management can become a nightmare. Remember with peer-to-peer networks that anyone who knows the password can access the folder across the network. Server-based networks are normally more secure because (1) passwords are managed centrally at the server and (2) the server is normally locked in a wiring closet.

In order to have a network, the following are required: network adapters (NICs), network media (cabling or air), and an operating system with network options enabled. The following sections explore these concepts.

Network Topologies

The physical network topology is how the network is wired. Figure 13.3 shows the physical topologies used in networking. Keep in mind that a large business may have combinations of these topologies. A topology that combines multiple topologies is known as a hybrid topology.

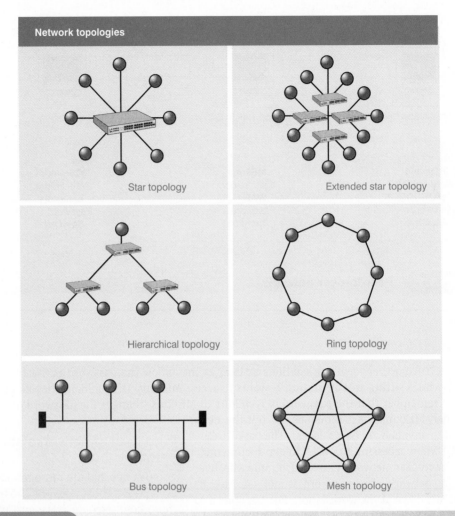

Figure 13.3   **Network topologies**

Tech Tip

Ethernet networks are physically wired in a star

The most common network topology used today is the **star topology** because it is used with Ethernet networks.

Ethernet networks are the most common type of network. Each network device connects to a central device, normally a hub or a switch. Both the **hub** and the **switch** contain two or more RJ-45 network jacks. The hub is not as intelligent as a switch. The switch takes a look at each data frame as it comes through the switch. The hub is not able to do this. Figure 13.4 illustrates a hub or switch.

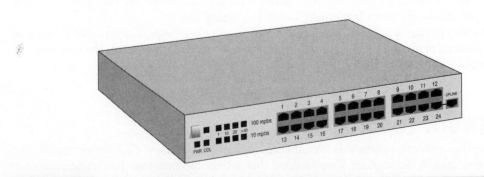

Figure 13.4   **Hub (switch)**

In a star topology, each network device has a cable that connects between the device and the hub or switch. If one computer or cable fails, all other devices continue to function. However, if the hub or switch fails, the network goes down. The hub or switch is normally located in a central location, such as a network wiring closet. Figure 13.5 shows how a star topology is cabled. By looking at how each device connects to a central location, you can easily see why it is called a star.

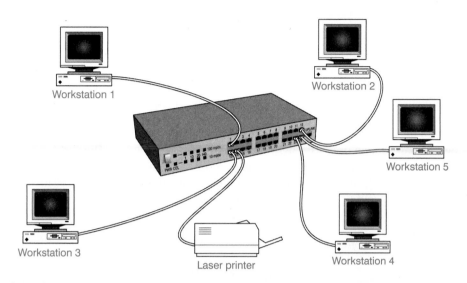

Figure 13.5   **Star topology**

More cable is used in wiring a star topology than with the old bus topology, but the type of cable used is comparatively cheap. Star topologies are easy to troubleshoot. If one network device goes down, the problem is in the device, cable, or port on the hub/switch. If a group of network devices goes down, the problem is most likely in the device that connects them together (hub or switch). Refer to Figure 13.5. If workstations 1, 2, 3, 4, and 5 cannot communicate with one another, the problem is the switch in the middle. If only Workstation 3 cannot communicate with the other network devices, the problem is in Workstation 3, the cable that connects Workstation 3, or in port 13 on the switch. Table 13.2 summarizes information about different network topologies.

Tech Tip

Network two PCs without a switch or hub

If you have two PCs with Ethernet NICs installed, you can connect them with a crossover cable attached to the RJ-45 jack on each NIC. If the two PCs do not have NICs installed, but have IEEE 1394 FireWire ports, you can connect a normal FireWire cable between the two PCs and have a network.

Table 13.2   **Network topologies**

Topology	Description
Bus	Not common anymore. Takes less cable (cheaper), but with a break in the bus, the network is down.
Mesh	With a break in the cable, the network still works (very fault tolerant), but it takes a lot of cabling. It is expensive and complex (hard to reconfigure). More likely to be used in a WAN than a LAN.
Ring	Each network device connects to two adjacent network devices. Is easy to install, but requires expensive parts. **FDDI** (Fiber Distributed Data Interface) networks use a ring topology.
Star	Is the easiest to install, is the most common, and a break in a workstation cable does not affect the rest of the network.

13

Introduction to Networking

Network Media Overview

Networks require some type of medium to transmit data. This medium is normally some type of cable or air. The most common types of cable are twisted-pair copper and fiber-optic, although some very old networks used coax cable and video networks use coax. Air is used in wireless networking where data is sent over radio frequencies.

Copper Media

The most common type of copper media used with computer networking is UTP (Unshielded Twisted-Pair) cabling. Most people are familiar with **twisted-pair cable** because this type of cable is used in homes for telephone wiring. Twisted-pair cable actually comes in two types—shielded and unshielded. The acronyms used with this type of cable are **STP** (shielded twisted-pair) and **UTP** (unshielded twisted-pair). STP cable has extra foil shielding that provides more shielding. Shielded twisted-pair cable is used in industrial settings, such as a factory, where extra shielding is needed to prevent outside interference from interfering with the data on the cable.

Twisted-pair cabling used with networking has eight copper wires. The wires are grouped in colored pairs. Each pair is twisted together to prevent crosstalk. **Crosstalk** occurs when a signal on one wire interferes with the signal on an adjacent wire. The wires are wrapped in a vinyl insulator. Figure 13.6 shows unshielded twisted-pair cable.

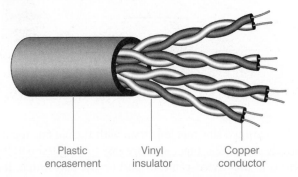

Plastic encasement   Vinyl insulator   Copper conductor

Figure 13.6   **UTP cable**

UTP cabling is measured in gauges. The most common sizes of UTP cabling are 22-, 23-, 24-, or 26-gauge unshielded twisted-pair cables. UTP cables come in different specifications called categories. The most common are categories 5e (which is an enhanced version of 5) and 6. People usually shorten the name Category 5 to CAT 5 or CAT 5e or CAT 5E. The categories determine, in part, how fast the network can run. Table 13.3 shows some of the categories of UTP cabling.

Table 13.3   **UTP cable categories**

Category	Description
3	Mainly installed for telephone systems in many office buildings. Commonly called voice grade cable, but has the ability to run up to 10Mbps Ethernet or 16Mbps Token Ring topologies.
5	No longer recognized standard as it was replaced by CAT 5e.
5e	Known as CAT 5 enhanced. Can be used with 10BaseT, 100BaseT, and 1000BaseT (Gigabit) Ethernet networks. Cables are rated to a max of 100 meters (~328 feet), but this is usually done by a maximum of 90 meters (~295 feet) and a 5 meter (~16 feet) patch cable from the wall to the network device. Supports frequencies up to 100MHz per pair.
6	Supports Gigabit Ethernet better, but uses larger gauge (thicker) cable. Supports frequencies up to 250MHz per pair. Higher specifications to prevent crosstalk (signals from one wiring going over into another wire).
6a	Supports 10GbaseT Ethernet and frequencies up to 500MHz.

A special type of UTP or STP cable is plenum cable. Plenum is a building's air circulation space for heating and air conditioning systems. **Plenum cable** is treated with Teflon or alternative fire retardant materials so it is less of a fire risk. Plenum cable is less smoke producing and less toxic when burning than regular networking cable.

The alternative to plenum cable is **PVC** (polyvinyl chloride) cable that has a plastic cable insulation or jacket. PVC is cheaper than plenum cable, but it can have flame-retardant added to make it flame-retardant if necessary to become compliant with building codes. PVC is usually easier to install than plenum.

In order to avoid extra troubleshooting time, most businesses install their network cabling according to the ANSI/TIA/EIA-568-A or 568-B standard. This standard specifies how far the cable can extend, how to label it, what type of jack to use, and so forth. Figure 13.7 illustrates the common RJ-45 cabling standards used in industry.

Tech Tip

Push the cable firmly into the jack

When installing network cabling, it is important to insert the UTP cable fully into the RJ-45 jack and to insert the colored wires in the standardized order. One of the most common mistakes that new technicians make when putting an RJ-45 connector on UTP cable is putting on the RJ-45 connector upside down.

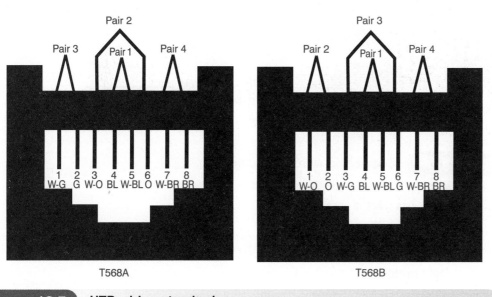

Figure 13.7 **UTP wiring standards**

Figure 13.8 shows the location of pin 1 on an RJ-45 connector.

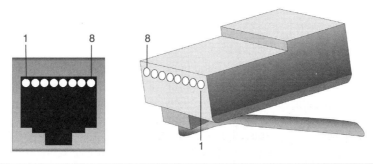

Figure 13.8 **RJ-45 pin 1 assignments**

Another common mistake is not pushing the wires to the end of the RJ-45 connector. Before crimping (securing using a tool called a crimper) the wires into the connector, look at the end of the RJ-45 connector. You should see each wire jammed against the end of the RJ-45 connector. With twisted-pair cable, all network devices connect to one central location such as a patch panel, hub, or switch.

Another type of copper cabling is **coaxial cable** (usually shortened to coax). Coax cable is used in older Ethernet 10Base2 and 10Base5 networks, mainframe and minicomputer connections, as well as video networks such as those that connect TVs in a school.

Most people have seen coax cable in their homes. The cable used for cable TV is coax cable, but is a different type than network cabling. Coax cable has a center copper conductor surrounded by insulation. Outside the insulation is a shield of copper braid, a metallic foil, or both, that protects the center conductor from EMI. Figure 13.9 shows a coax cable. Coax is used in star and bus topologies.

Tech Tip

Label both cable ends

When installing any type of network cabling, you should label both ends with a unique identifier that normally includes the building and/or room number.

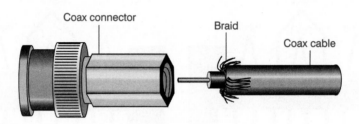

Figure 13.9   **Coax cable with connector**

Table 13.4 lists types of coax cables.

Table 13.4   **Coax cable types**

Coax cable type	Description
RG*-58 A/U	Used in 10Base2 (Thinnet) networks and it allows distances up to 185 meters.
RG-8	Used in 10Base5 (Thicknet) networks and allows distances up to 500 meters; it is also known as the yellow garden hose.
RG-6	This is the least likely type of cable to be used in a network. It is suitable for distributing signals for cable TV, satellite dish, or rooftop antenna. It has better shielding than RG-59.
RG-59	This type of cable is not used in LANs. It is used in video installations.

*RG stands for Radio Grade

Fiber Media

Fiber-optic cable is made of glass or a type of plastic fiber and is used to carry light pulses. Fiber-optic cable can be used to connect a workstation to another device, but in industry, the most common use of fiber-optic cable is to connect networks together forming the network **backbone**. Copper cable is used to connect workstations together. Then fiber cable is used to interconnect the networks, especially when the network is located on multiple floors or multiple buildings.

There are many different types of fiber connectors and many of them are proprietary. Three of the most common types of connectors used with fiber-optic cable are MT-RJ, ST, SC, and LC. Figure 13.10 shows these connectors.

ST type

SC type

LC type

Figure 13.10   **Fiber-optic connector types**

Fiber-optic cabling has many advantages including security, long distance transmission, and bandwidth. Fiber-optic cabling is used by many government agencies because of the high security it offers. Light signals that travel down fiber are impossible to detect remotely, unlike signals from other cable media. Also, because light is used instead of electrical signals, fiber-optic cable is not susceptible to interference from EMI- or RFI producing devices. Fiber-optic cable is the most expensive cable type, but it also handles the most data with the least amount of data loss. Figure 13.11 shows fiber-optic cable.

Tech Tip

Two cables are normal with fiber

Each fiber-optic cable can carry signals in one direction, so an installation normally has two strands of fiber-optic cable in separate jackets. Fiber is used in the ring and star topologies.

The two major classifications of fiber are single-mode and multi-mode. **Single-mode** fiber-optic cable has only one light beam sent down the cable. **Multi-mode** fiber-optic cable allows multiple light signals to be sent along the same cable.

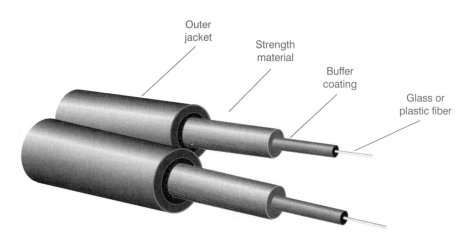

Outer jacket

Strength material

Buffer coating

Glass or plastic fiber

Figure 13.11   **Fiber-optic cable**

13
Introduction to Networking

Tech Tip

Which fiber should I use?

Multi-mode fiber is cheaper and more commonly used than single-mode fiber and is good for shorter distance applications; but single-mode fiber can transmit a signal farther than multi-mode and supports the highest bandwidth.

Single-mode cable is classified by the size of the fiber core and the classing. Common sizes include 8/125 to 10/125 microns. The first number represents the size of the core; the second number is the size of the cladding. Single mode cable allows for distances up to 80,000 meters (which is more than 50 miles). Multi-mode cable (50/125 and 62.5/125 microns) on the other hand, can support distances up to 2,000 meters or over a mile.

Protecting Your Network and Cable Investment

Quite a bit of money is applied to network cabling. Professional cable management systems can help keep cabling organized. Network devices should be locked in a secure room or cabinet when possible. Figure 13.12 shows a lockable network cabinet that can have network devices as well as cabling installed inside it.

Network cabling can be pulled through walls and over ceilings, but should be installed in conduit or raceways if possible. Ensure that network cabling is not a tripping or other safety hazard in any location. Of course this really increases the cost of the network installation, but it protects the network cabling. Figure 13.13 shows a typical network wall outlet.

Figure 13.12   **Network lockable cabinet**

Figure 13.13   **Network wall outlet**

Ladder racks are also a popular network cable accessory installed to hold multiple cables going across a room or from one side of the room to a network rack that is located away from the wall. Figure 13.14 shows a network cable ladder rack that has tubes through which fiber cable is pulled.

Figure 13.14   **Network cable ladder rack**

Ethernet Issues and Concepts

Ethernet is the most common type of LAN, and more time must be spent on understanding it because technicians constantly add and remove devices from an Ethernet network. Some issues related to Ethernet include full-duplex and half-duplex transmissions, network slowdowns, and increasing bandwidth.

Ethernet networks were originally designed to support either half-duplex or full-duplex data transmissions. **Half-duplex** transmission is data transmitted in both directions on a cable, but not at the same time. Only one network device can transmit at a time. One example of half-duplex transmission is using a walkie-talkie. **Full-duplex** transmission is data transmitted in both directions on a cable simultaneously.

Ethernet networks were originally designed for half-duplex transmission on a 10Mbps bus topology. The more workstations on the same network, the more collisions occur and the

13

Introduction to Networking

more the network slows down. In addition, with half-duplex Ethernet, less than 50 percent of the 10Mbps available bandwidth could be used because of collisions and the time it takes for a network frame to transmit across the wire.

What does CSMA/CD mean to a network?

In the acronym **CSMA/CD**, the CS stands for "Carrier Sense," which means that it checks the network cable for other traffic. "Multiple Access" means that multiple computers can access the network cable simultaneously. "Collision Detect" provides rules for what happens when two computers access the network at the same time. CSMA/CD is the access method used with Ethernet networks.

Today's Ethernet networks support speeds of 10Mbps, 100Mbps, 1,000Mbps (1Gbps), and 10,000Mbps (10Gbps). Most Ethernet NIC cards are 10/100/1000, which means they can run at either 10, 100, or 1000Mbps. Table 13.5 lists the different types of Ethernet networks.

When considering the term 100BaseT, the 100 means that the network runs at 100Mbps. The T at the end of 100BaseT means that the computer uses twisted-pair cable. The 1000 in 1000BaseT means that 1000Mbps is supported. Base means that the network uses baseband technology. Baseband describes data that is sent over a single channel on a single wire. In contrast, broadband is used in cable TV systems and it allows multiple channels using different frequencies to be covered over a single wire.

Why full-duplex is better than half-duplex

Collisions are not a problem because full-duplex takes advantage of the two cable pairs (one for receiving and one for transmitting). Full-duplex Ethernet creates a direct connection between the transmitting station at one end and the receiving circuits at the other end and allows 100 percent of the available bandwidth to be used in each direction.

Full-duplex more than doubles the amount of throughput on a network because of the lack of collisions and transmitting both directions simultaneously. Full-duplex is used when a switch is used to connect network devices together. Full-duplex connectivity uses four wires (two pairs). Two of the wires are used for sending data and the other two wires are used for receiving data. This creates a collision-free environment. Using a switch instead of a hub as a central connectivity device speeds up Ethernet transactions because a switch has more intelligence than a hub and creates a collision-free full-duplex environment. Switches are very common devices in today's business network environment.

Table 13.5 Ethernet standards

Ethernet type	Description
10BaseT	10Mbps over CAT 3 or 5 UTP cable
100BaseT	100Mbps over CAT 5 or higher UTP cable
1000BaseT	Also known as Gigabit Ethernet. 1000Mbps or 1Gbps over CAT 5 or higher UTP cable
1000BaseSX	1Gbps using multi-mode fiber
1000BaseLX	1Gbps using single-mode fiber
10GBaseSR	10Gbps over multi-mode fiber
10GBaseLX4	10Gbps over multi-mode and single-mode fiber
10GBaseLR	10Gbps up to 10 km using single-mode fiber
10GBaseER	10Gbps up to 40 km using single-mode fiber
10GBaseT	10Gbps over UTP (CAT 5e or higher) or STP cable

Why a switch is better than a hub

When a workstation sends data to a hub, the hub broadcasts the data out all ports except for the port the data came in on. A switch, on the other hand, keeps a table of addresses. When a switch receives data, the switch looks up the destination MAC address in the switch table and forwards the data out the port for which it is destined. A switch looks very similar to a hub and it is sometimes hard to distinguish between the two.

Network Standards

IEEE (Institute for Electrical and Electronics Engineers) committees create network standards called the 802 standards. Each standard is given an 802.x number and represents an area of networking. Standardization is good for the network industry because different manufacturers' network components work with other manufacturers' devices. Table 13.6 lists the various 802 standards.

Table 13.6	IEEE 802 standards
802 standard	**Purpose**
802.1	Bridging and Management
802.2	Logical Link Control
802.3	CSMA/CD Access Method
802.4	Token-Passing Bus Access Method
802.5	Token Ring Access Method
802.6	DQDB (Distributed Queue Dual Bus) Access Method
802.7	Broadband LAN
802.8	Fiber-Optic
802.9	Isochronous LANs
802.10	Security
802.11	Wireless
802.12	Demand Priority Access
802.15	WPANs (Wireless Personal Area Networks)
802.16	Broadband Wireless Access
802.17	Resilient Packet Ring

13 Introduction to Networking

For more information about the 802 standards, access the IEEE Web site at the following address: http://standards.ieee.org/about/get/802/802.html.

OSI Model

The International Standards Organization (ISO) has developed a model for network communications known as the OSI (Open Systems Interconnect) model. The **OSI model** is a standard for information transfer across the network. The model sets several guidelines including (1) how the different transmission media are arranged and interconnected; (2) how network devices that use different languages communicate with one another; (3) how a network device goes about contacting another network device; (4) how and when data gets transmitted across the network; (5) how data is sent to the correct device; and (6) how it is known if the network data was received properly. All of these tasks must be handled by a set of rules and the OSI model provides a structure into which these rules fit.

Can you imagine a generic model for building a car? This model would state that you need some means of steering, a type of fuel to power the car, a place for the driver to sit, safety standards, and so forth. The model would not say what type of steering wheel to put in the car or what type of fuel the car must use, but is just a blueprint for making the car. In networking, the OSI model is such a model.

The OSI model divides networking into different layers so that it is easier to understand (and teach). Dividing the network into distinct layers also helps manufacturers. If a particular manufacturer wants to make a network device that works on layer three, the manufacturer only has to be concerned with layer three. This division makes networking technologies emerge much faster. Having a layered model also helps to teach network concepts. Each layer can be taught as a separate network function.

The layers of the OSI model (starting from the top and working down) are application, presentation, session, transport, network, data link, and physical. Figure 13.15 shows this concept.

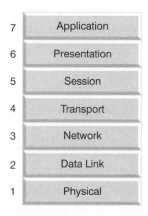

7	Application
6	Presentation
5	Session
4	Transport
3	Network
2	Data Link
1	Physical

Figure 13.15   **OSI model layers**

Tech Tip

OSI mnemonic

A mnemonic to help remember the OSI layers is: A Person Seldom Takes Naps During Parties. For example, *A* in the phrase is to remind you of the application layer. *P* in Person is to remind you of the presentation layer, and so on.

Each layer of the OSI model uses the layer below it (except for the physical layer which is on the bottom). Each layer provides some function to the layer above it. For example, the data link layer cannot be accessed without first going through the physical layer. If communication needs to be performed at the third layer (the network layer), then the physical and data link layers must be used first.

Certification exams contain questions about the OSI model and knowing the levels is a good place to start preparing for the exams. Each first letter of the mnemonic phrase is supposed to remind you of the first letter of the OSI model layers.

Each layer of the OSI model from the top down (except for the physical layer) adds information to the data being sent across the network. Sometimes this information is called a header. Figure 13.16 shows how a header is added as the packet travels down the OSI model. When the receiving computer receives the data, each layer removes the header information. Information at the physical layer is normally called bits. When referring to information at the data link layer, use the term **frame**. When referring to information at the network layer, use the term **packet**.

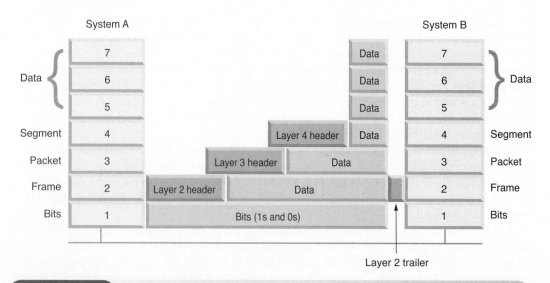

Figure 13.16   **OSI peer communication**

Each of the seven OSI layers performs a unique function and interacts with the layers surrounding it. The bottom three layers handle the physical delivery of data across the network. The **physical layer** (sometimes called layer one) defines how bits are transferred and received across the network media without being concerned about the structure of the bits. The physical layer is where connectors, cable, and voltage levels are defined. The **data link layer** (sometimes called layer two) provides the means for accurately transferring the bits across the network, and it groups (encapsulates) the bits into usable sections called frames. The **network layer** (sometimes called layer three) coordinates data movement between two devices. This layer provides path selection between two networks. Most companies and even some homes have a router that they use to connect to the Internet through their **ISP** (Internet service provider). An ISP is a vendor that provides Internet access.

The top four layers handle the ins and outs of providing accurate data delivery between computers and their individual processes, especially in a multitasking operating system environment. The **transport layer** (sometimes called layer four) provides a service to the upper layers so they do not have to worry about the details of how data is sent. The transport layer provides such services as whether the data should be sent "reliably" or not. This is similar to getting a return receipt for a package at the post office.

The **session layer** manages the communication and synchronization between two network devices. The **presentation layer** provides a means of translating the data from the sender into data the receiver understands. This allows all types of computers to communicate with one another even though one computer may be using one language (such as EBCDIC) while another computer uses a different language (such as ASCII). The **application layer** provides network services to any software applications running on the network. The application layer provides network services to a computer. This allows the computer to participate or enter the OSI model (the network). Some of the services the application layer provides include negotiating **authentication** (what type of authentication will be used in the communication), negotiating who has responsibility for error recovery, and negotiating quality of service across the network.

The OSI model is very confusing when you are first learning about networking, but it is very important. Understanding the model helps when troubleshooting a network. Knowing where the problem is occurring narrows the field of what the solution may be. For example, if a computer has problems communicating with a computer on the same network, then the problem is most likely a layer one or a layer two problem because layer three takes care of communication between two networks. Check the cabling and NIC settings. Table 13.7 summarizes the OSI model for you.

Tech Tip

What device works at what OSI layer?

Cables, connectors, repeaters, hubs, and patch panels all reside at layer 1 of the OSI model, the physical layer. Part of the network card resides at layer one (the connector or antenna), and part of the network card resides at layer two. Most books state that the network card resides at layer two because it has a layer two MAC address embedded into it. A switch also resides at layer two, the data link layer. A **router**, a network device that determines the best path to send a packet, works at layer three, the network layer.

13 Introduction to Networking

Table 13.7	OSI model

OSI model layer	Purpose
Application	Provides network services (file, print, and messaging services) to any software application running on the network.
Presentation	Translates data from one character set to another.
Session	Manages the communication and synchronization between network devices.
Transport	Provides the mechanisms for how data is sent, such as reliability and error correction.
Network	Provides path selection between two networks. Routers reside at the network layer. Encapsulated data at this layer is called a packet.
Data Link	Encapsulates bits into frames. Can provide error control. MAC address is at this layer. Switches reside at data link layer.
Physical	Defines how bits are transferred and received. Defines the network media, connectors, and voltage levels. Data at this level is called bits.

The TCP/IP Model

A network protocol is a data communication language. A protocol suite is a group of protocols that are designed to work together. **TCP/IP** (Transmission Control Protocol/Internet Protocol) is the protocol suite used in networks today. It is the most common network protocol and is required when accessing the Internet. Most companies (and homes) use TCP/IP as their standard protocol. The TCP/IP protocol suite consists of many protocols, including TCP (Transmission Control Protocol), IP (Internet Protocol), DHCP (Dynamic Host Configuration Protocol), FTP (File Transfer Protocol), and HTTP (Hypertext Transfer Protocol), to name a few. The TCP/IP model describes how information flows through the computer when TCP/IP-based protocols are being used. The TCP/IP model has only four layers, in contrast to the seven layers in the theoretical OSI model. Because there are fewer layers and because the TCP/IP model is made up of protocols that are in production, it makes it easier to study and understand networking from a TCP/IP model prospective. Figure 13.17 shows the TCP/IP model, and Table 13.8 describes the layers.

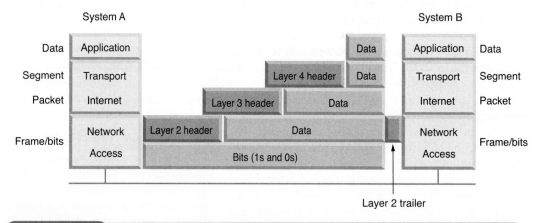

Figure 13.17 TCP/IP message formatting

Table 13.8 TCP/IP model layers

TCP/IP model layer	Description
Application	TCP/IP-based application-layer protocols format data specific for the purpose. Is equivalent to the application, presentation, and session layers of the OSI model. Protocols include HTTP, Telnet, DNS, HTTPS, FTP, TFTP, TLS, SSL, POP, SNMP, IMAP, NNTP, and SMTP.
Transport	Transport-layer protocols add port numbers in the header so the computer can identify which application is sending the data. When data returns, this port number allows the computer to determine into which window on the screen to place the data. Protocols include TCP and UDP.
Internet	Sometimes called the internetwork layer. IP is the most common Internet layer protocol. IP adds a source and destination IP address to uniquely identify the source and destination network devices. An **IP address** is a unique 32-bit number assigned to a NIC.
Network access	Called link layer in the original RFC. Defines how to format the data for the type of network being used. For example, if Ethernet is being used, an Ethernet header, including unique source and destination MAC addresses, will be added here. A **MAC address** is a unique 48-bit hexadecimal number burned into a chip on the NIC. The network access layer would define the type of connector used and put the data onto the network, whether it be voltage levels for 1s and 0s on the copper cable or pulses of light for fiber.

To see the TCP/IP model in action, imagine opening a Web browser with two separate windows: www.pearsoned.com and www.google.com. Two separate packages of data would be formed. For example, since HTTP data is being sent, HTTP will specify how the data is to be formatted at the application layer. So, web page 1 gets HTTP data at the application layer and moves down to the transport layer (inside the computer). At the transport layer, TCP is used for HTTP traffic, and TCP adds a source port number of 51116 and a destination port number of 80 as part of building the transport-layer header. All of this HTTP and TCP information moves down to the Internet layer, where IP adds a source and destination IP address. Because Pearson Education's Web server has the IP address 74.125.47.99, that is the destination IP address. The packet continues moving down the model to the network access layer where, and because the LAN is an Ethernet LAN, a source MAC address and destination MAC address are added. The data and all the headers are placed onto the Ethernet cable and sent on their way. The same thing happens with the second web page, except that at the transport layer, TCP adds port number 51117 and destination port number 80.

Use `netstat` to view current connections

To see current connections and associated port numbers, bring up a command prompt and type `netstat`.

When the Pearson Education Web server delivers the Web page to the computer, the data of course is from the Web server, but the TCP port numbers are reversed. The Web server places port number 80 as the source port number and port number 51116 as the destination port number. The source and destination IP addresses and MAC addresses are reversed as well. When the original computer gets the message, it knows which browser window generated port number 51116, and it places the Pearson Education book information from the Web server into the correct browser window. The same is true when the Google request comes back from the Google Web server. TCP/IP-based protocols are required to send and receive data through the Internet.

Network Addressing

Network adapters normally have two types of addresses assigned to them—a MAC address and an IP address. The MAC address is a 48-bit unique number that is burned into a ROM chip located on the NIC and is represented in hexadecimal. A MAC address is unique for every computer on the network. However, the MAC address has no scheme to it except that the first 24 bits represent the manufacturer. The MAC address is known as a layer two address or a physical address. A MAC address is normally shown in one of the following formats shown in Table 13.9.

Table 13.9	MAC address formats
Format style	**Description**
00-11-11-71-41-10	Every group of two hexadecimal digits is separated by a hyphen.
01:11:11:71:41:10	Every group of two hexadecimal digits is separated by a colon.
0111.1171.4110	Every group of four hexadecimal digits is separated by a period.

The IP address is a much more organized way of addressing a computer and it is sometimes known as a layer three address, in reference to the OSI network layer. There are two types of IP addresses: IPv4 (IP version 4) and IPv6 (IP version 6). **IPv4** is the most common IP address used on LANs. The IPv4 address is a 32-bit number that is entered into a NIC's configuration parameters. This address is used when multiple networks are connected and when accessing the Internet. The IPv4 address is shown using dotted decimal notation, such as 192.168.10.4.

What is in an IPv4 address?

An IPv4 address is separated into four sections called octets. Each number is separated by periods and represents eight bits. The numbers that can be represented by eight bits are 0 to 255.

IPv6 addresses are 128 bits in length and shown in hexadecimal format. An example of an IPv6 address is fe80::13e:4586:5807:95f7. Each set of four digits represents 16 bits. Anywhere there are just three digits, such as 13e, there is a zero in front that has been left off (013e). Anywhere there are double colons (::), a string of zeros has been omitted. Only one set of double colons is allowed in an IPv6 address. Many network cards are assigned IPv6 addresses, even though IPv6 is not being used.

IPv4 addresses are grouped into five classes called Class A, B, C, D, and E. Class A, B, and C addresses are used by network devices. Class D is used for multicasting (sending traffic to a group of devices such as in a distributed video or a web conference session) and Class E is used for experimentation. It is easy to tell which type of IP address is being used by a device. All you have to look at is the first number shown in the dotted decimal notation. Table 13.10 shows the classes of addresses used by devices connected by the Internet.

Table 13.10	Classes of IPv4 addresses
Class	**First octet (number) of the IP address**
Class A	0 to 127
Class B	128 to 191
Class C	192 through 223

If a computer has an IP address of 12.150.172.39, the IP address is a Class A address because the first number is 12. If a computer has an IP address of 176.10.100.2, it is a Class B IP address because the first number is 176. A computer with an IP address of 200.1.1.1 uses a Class C address.

IP Addressing

An IP address is broken into two major parts—the network number and the host number. The **network number** is the portion of the IP address that represents which network the computer is on. All computers on the same network have the same network number. The **host** portion of the IP address represents the specific computer on the network. All computers on the same network have unique host numbers or they will not be able to communicate.

The number of bits that are used to represent the network number and the host number depends on which class of IP address is being used. With Class A IP addresses, the first eight bits (the first number) represent the network portion and the remaining 24 bits (the last three numbers) represent the host number. With Class B IP addresses, the first 16 bits (the first two numbers) represent the network portion and the remaining 16 bits (the last two numbers) represent the host number. With Class C IP addresses, the first 24 bits (the first three numbers) represent the network portion, and the remaining eight bits (the last number) represent the host number. Figure 13.18 illustrates this point.

In order to see how IP addressing works, it is best to use an example. A business has two networks connected with a router. On each network, there are computers and printers. Each of the

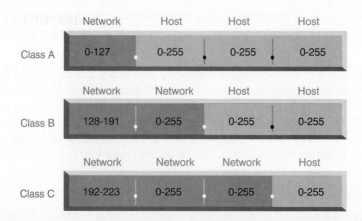

Figure 13.18   IP addressing (network and host portions)

two networks must have a unique network number. For this example, one network has the network number of 193.14.150.0, and the other network has the network number of 193.14.151.0. Notice how these numbers represent a Class C IP address because the first number is 193.

With a Class C IP address, the first three numbers represent the network number. The first network uses the numbers of 193.14.150 to represent the network part of the IP address. The second network uses the 193.14.151 numbers in the network part of the address. Remember that each network has to have a different network part of the IP address than any other network in the organization. The last part of the IP address (the host portion) will be used to assign to each network device. On the first network, each device will have a number that starts with 193.14.150 because that is the network part of the number and it stays the same for all devices on that network. Each device will then have a different number in the last portion of the IP address, for example, 193.14.150.3, 193.14.150.4, 193.14.150.5.

On the second network, each device will have a number that starts with 193.14.151 because that is the network part of the IP address. The last number in the IP address changes for each network device, for example, 193.14.151.3, 193.14.151.4, 193.14.151.5, and so on. No device can have a host number of 0 because that number represents the network and no device can have a host number of 255 because that represents something called the broadcast address. A **broadcast address** is the IP address used to communicate with all devices on a particular network.

In the example given, no network device can be assigned the IP addresses 193.14.150.0 or 193.14.151.0 because these numbers represent the two networks. Furthermore, no network device can be assigned the IP addresses 193.14.150.255 or 193.14.151.255 because these numbers represent the broadcast address used with each network. An example of a Class B broadcast is 150.10.255.255. An example of a Class A broadcast is 11.255.255.255. Figure 13.19 shows this configuration.

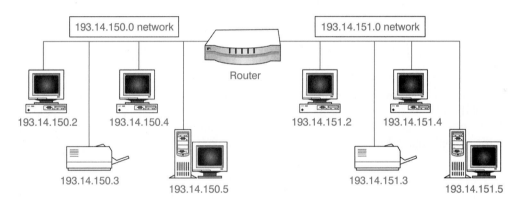

Figure 13.19 IP addressing (two network example)

Notice in Figure 13.19 how each device to the left of the router has an IP address that starts with 193.14.150 (the network number) and each device has a unique last number. The same is true for the devices to the right of the router except they are on the 193.14.151.0 network.

In addition to assigning a computer an IP address, you must also assign a subnet mask. The **subnet mask** is a number that the computer uses to determine which part of the IP address represents the network and which portion represents the host. The subnet mask for a Class A IP address is 255.0.0.0; the subnet mask for a Class B IP address is 255.255.0.0; the subnet mask for a Class C IP address is 255.255.255.0. Table 13.11 recaps this important information.

Table 13.11 IP address information

Class	First number	Network/host number	Subnet mask
A	0–127	N.H.H.H*	255.0.0.0
B	128–191	N.N.H.H*	255.255.0.0
C	192–223	N.N.N.H*	255.255.255.0

*N = Network number and H = Host number

Subnetting Basics

In business, the subnet mask used does not usually correspond to the class of IP address being used. For example, at a college, the IP address 10.104.10.88 and subnet mask 255.255.255.0 are assigned to a computer. The 10 in the first octet shows that this is a class A IP address with a default mask of 255.0.0.0. The 255 in the subnet mask is made up of eight 1s in binary in the first octet (11111111) followed by all 0s in the remaining octets (00000000.00000000.00000000).

The purpose of the subnet mask is to tell you (and the network devices) what portion of the IP address is the network part. The rest of the address is the host portion of the address. The network part of any IP address is the same 1s and 0s for all computers on the network. The rest of the 1s and 0s can change and be unique addresses for the network devices on the same network.

Important rules that relate to subnetting follow:

- The network number *cannot* be assigned to any device on the network.
- The network number contains all 0s in the host portion of the address. Note that this does not mean that the number will be 0 in decimal. This is explained next.
- The broadcast address (the number used to send a message to all devices on the network) *cannot* be assigned to any device on the network.
- The broadcast address contains all 1s in the host portion of the address. Note that this does not mean that the number will be 255 in decimal. This is explained next.

Consider the IP address and mask used as an example before—10.104.10.88 255.255.255.0. Put these numbers in binary, one number on top of the other, to see the effects of the subnet mask.

```
      10             104           10             88
  0 0 0 0 1 0 1 0 . 0 1 1 0 1 0 0 0 . 0 0 0 0 1 0 1 0 . 0 1 0 1 1 0 0 0

  1 1 1 1 1 1 1 1 . 1 1 1 1 1 1 1 1 . 1 1 1 1 1 1 1 1 . 0 0 0 0 0 0 0 0
```

The 1s in the subnet mask show which bits in the top row are the network part of the address. The subnet mask is always a row of consecutive 1s. Where the 1s stop is where the network portion of the address stops. Keep in mind that this does not have to be where an octet stops, as in this example. A good technique is to draw a line where the 1s in the subnet mask stop, as shown in the example that follows:

```
      10             104           10        |    88
  0 0 0 0 1 0 1 0 . 0 1 1 0 1 0 0 0 . 0 0 0 0 1 0 1 0 | 0 1 0 1 1 0 0 0

  1 1 1 1 1 1 1 1 . 1 1 1 1 1 1 1 1 . 1 1 1 1 1 1 1 1 | 0 0 0 0 0 0 0 0
```

Tech Tip

Subnet mask in prefix notation

Subnet masks in network documentation are commonly shown in **prefix notation**, using a slash with the number of consecutive 1s found in the subnet mask. For example, 10.104.10.88 255.255.255.0 is shown as 10.104.10.88/24, and 192.168.10.213/27 is the same as a 255.255.255.224 subnet mask.

At this point, there is no other purpose for the subnet mask. You can get rid of it, as shown in the example that follows:

```
      10             104           10        |    88
  0 0 0 0 1 0 1 0 . 0 1 1 0 1 0 0 0 . 0 0 0 0 1 0 1 0 | 0 1 0 1 1 0 0 0
```

All 1s and 0s to the left of the drawn line are the network portion of the IP address. All devices on the same network will have this same combination of 1s and 0s up to the line. All 1s and 0s to the right of the drawn line are in the host portion of the IP address:

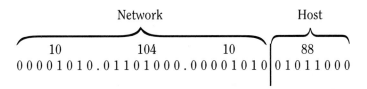

The network number, the IP address used to represent an entire single network, is found by setting all host bits to 0. The resulting number is the network number:

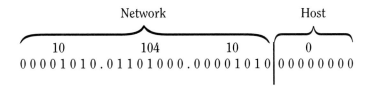

The network number for the network device that has the IP address 10.104.10.88 is 10.104.10.0. To find the broadcast address, the IP address used to send a message to all devices on the 10.104.10.0 network, set all the host bits to 1:

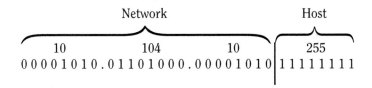

The broadcast IP address is 10.104.10.255 for the 10.104.10.0 network. This means that hosts can be assigned any addresses between the network number 10.104.10.0 and the broadcast address 10.104.10.255. Another way of stating this is that IP addresses 10.104.10.1 through 10.104.10.254 are usable IP addresses on the 10.104.10.0 network.

Consider the IP address 192.168.10.213 and the subnet mask 255.255.255.224 assigned to a computer in a college. What would be the network number and broadcast address for this computer? To find the answer, write 192.168.10.213 in binary octets. Write the subnet mask in binary under the IP address:

```
        192              168             10             213
  1 1 0 0 0 0 0 0 . 1 0 1 0 1 0 0 0 . 0 0 0 0 1 0 1 0 . 1 1 0 1 0 1 0 1
  1 1 1 1 1 1 1 1 . 1 1 1 1 1 1 1 1 . 1 1 1 1 1 1 1 1 . 1 1 1 0 0 0 0 0
```

Now draw a line where the 1s in the subnet mask stop:

```
        192              168             10            213
  1 1 0 0 0 0 0 0 . 1 0 1 0 1 0 0 0 . 0 0 0 0 1 0 1 0 . 1 1 0|1 0 1 0 1
  1 1 1 1 1 1 1 1 . 1 1 1 1 1 1 1 1 . 1 1 1 1 1 1 1 1 . 1 1 1|0 0 0 0 0
```

Remove the subnet mask because it is not needed anymore:

```
        192              168             10            213
  1 1 0 0 0 0 0 0 . 1 0 1 0 1 0 0 0 . 0 0 0 0 1 0 1 0 . 1 1 0|1 0 1 0 1
```

Set all host bits to 0 to find the network number:

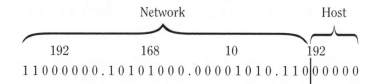

The network number for the network device that has IP address 192.168.10.213 is 192.168.10.192. To find the broadcast address, set all host bits to 1.

Set all host bits to 1 to find the broadcast address:

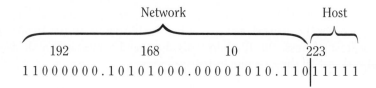

The broadcast address for the network device that has the IP address 192.168.10.213 is 192.168.10.223. Notice how all eight bits are used to calculate the number 223 in the last octet. Valid IP addresses are any numbers between the network number 192.168.10.192 and the broadcast IP address 192.168.10.223. In other words, the range of usable IP addresses is from 192.168.10.193 (one number larger than the network address) through 192.168.10.222 (one number less than the broadcast address). Practice problems in an exercise at the end of the chapter help you explore this concept.

DUN (Dial-Up Networking)

DUN is used when a remote computer that dials into the Internet or into a company network device uses a modem. The type of connection, protocol, and settings that you configure on the remote computer depends on the company to which you are connecting. A connection protocol used with dial-up networking is PPP. PPP (Point-to-Point Protocol) is a connection-oriented, layer two protocol that encapsulates data for transmission over various connection types.

One type of connection used by a PC is a phone line. In Windows XP use the *Network and Internet Connections* control panel category to select *Network Connections* and *Create a new connection*. In Vista, use the *Network and Sharing Center* control panel link to access the *Connect to a network* option.

Before creating a remote connection, you should always determine what parameters are to be entered *before* starting the configuration. Contact the network administrator for exact details on how to configure the remote connection. If the connection is to the Internet via an ISP, detailed instructions are available on the ISP's Web site and/or with the materials that come with the Internet package from the ISP.

There are many types of network connections. Dial-up networking normally uses POTS (Plain Old Telephone Service) or ISDN. Businesses use various types of network connections leased from the local phone company or a provider. Table 13.12 shows the types of network connections and bandwidth.

Wireless Networks Overview

Wireless networks are networks that transmit data over air using either infrared or radio frequencies. Most wireless networks in home and businesses use radio frequencies. Wireless networks operate at layers one and two of the OSI model.

Table 13.12	Network connections
Connection type	**Speed**
POTS (Plain Old Telephone Service)	2400bps to 115Kbps analog phone line
ISDN (Integrated Services Digital Network)	64Kbps to 1.544Mbps digital line
Frame Relay	56K to 1.544Mbps
56K point to point	56K guaranteed bandwidth between two points
T1	1.544Mbps guaranteed bandwidth between two points
T3	44Mbps guaranteed bandwidth between two points
DSL (Digital Subscriber Line)	256Kbps and higher; shares data line with voice line
Broadband cable or satellite	56Kbps (broadband satellite) to 30Mbps and higher
ATM (Asynchronous Transfer Mode)	Up to 2Gbps

Wireless networks are very popular in home and business computer environments and are great in places that are not conducive to having cabling, such as outdoor centers, convention centers, bookstores, coffee shops, and hotels, as well as between buildings and in between non-wired rooms in homes or businesses. Wireless networks can be installed indoors or outdoors.

Laptops and portable devices are frequently used to connect to a wireless network and have wireless capabilities integrated into them. Laptops also normally have a wired network connection. A technician must be familiar with installation, configuration, and troubleshooting of both wired and wireless technologies.

What if I want wireless connectivity for my desktop computer?

Desktop workstations sometimes have integrated RJ-45 Ethernet connections, but if wireless networking is desired, then a wireless NIC usually has to be added.

13 Introduction to Networking

Bluetooth

Bluetooth is a wireless technology for PANs (personal area networks). Bluetooth devices include PDAs (personal digital assistants), audio/visual products, automotive accessories, keyboards, mice, phones, printer adapters, cameras, wireless cell phone headset, sunglasses with a radio and wireless speakers, and other small wireless devices. Bluetooth works in the 2.4GHz range similar to business wireless networks, has three classes of devices (1, 2, and 3) that have a range of approximately 6 meters (19.6 feet), 22 meters (72.1 feet), and 100 meters (328 feet), respectively, and a maximum transfer rate of 24Mbps. Bluetooth supports both data and voice transmissions. Up to eight Bluetooth devices can be connected in a piconet (a small network). Bluetooth has always had security features integrated including 128-bit encryption (scrambling of data that is discussed later in the chapter) that uses a modified form of SAFER+ (Secure and Fast Encryption Routine). Bluetooth is a very viable network solution for short-range wireless solutions. Figure 13.20 shows a Bluetooth cell phone headset.

Windows Vista and 7 support Bluetooth better than Windows XP. With Windows XP, when you connect a Bluetooth adapter to the computer, it should work if Windows XP Service Pack 2 or higher has been installed. If the Bluetooth adapter is one that Windows XP does not recognize, Windows XP may provide generic software support. You should always use drivers and installation instructions from the Bluetooth device manufacturer.

The *Hardware and Sound* Windows XP/Vista/7 control panel link provides access to the *Bluetooth Devices* control panel. The *Devices* tab shows all Bluetooth devices configured on the computer, has the *Add* button used to add a device, and is used to view the properties of a specific Bluetooth device. Through the properties, the name can be changed and you can see whether a passkey is needed when pairing with the device. The *Options* tab

Missing Bluetooth control panel

If the Bluetooth Devices control panel does not display or if the Bluetooth icon is not in the notification area (systray) on the taskbar, type `bthprops.cpl` at a command prompt.

Figure 13.20 Bluetooth cell phone headset

has the checkbox *Turn discovery* on, which is used to allow Bluetooth devices to discover the computer and make a connection. Another important option on this page is the *Allow Bluetooth devices to connect to this computer* checkbox. If it is disabled (not checked), no Bluetooth devices can connect to the computer. For Bluetooth printers, use the *Add a printer* link from the *Hardware and Sound* control panel link.

A Bluetooth PAN (personal area network) provides computer-to-computer connectivity between Bluetooth devices. Each computer must support a PAN to join the network. Once a Bluetooth device is added, you can use the Bluetooth systray option to select *Join a Personal Area Network*. A dialog box will appear, showing devices to which the computer can connect. Select a device and click *Connect*.

The list that follows provides troubleshooting tips for dealing with Bluetooth devices:

- If the Bluetooth device has batteries, ensure that they are installed correctly and are functioning.
- Change the location of the Bluetooth device—try moving it closer to and further from the computer.
- Ensure that no other devices that could interfere in the 2.4GHz range (in which Bluetooth operates) are in the area. These include wireless networks, X10 automatic lighting and remote controls, microwave ovens, and cordless phones.
- Remove all other Bluetooth devices to aid in troubleshooting the problematic device.
- Remove any unused USB devices.
- If a Bluetooth transceiver is used, move the transceiver to another USB port.
- Use the *Administrative Tools* control panel to access the *Computer Management* tool. Select *Services and Applications* in the list on the left. Click *Services* in the right panel. Locate and double-click *Bluetooth Support Service*. Ensure that the service is set to automatic and is started.

Wireless Network Types

There are two main types of wireless networks: ad hoc and infrastructure. An ad hoc mode wireless network is also known as a peer-to-peer or IBSS (independent basic service set) mode. An ad hoc wireless network is when at least two devices such as two computers have wireless NICs (network interface cards) installed. The two devices transmit and receive data.

Major types of wireless NICs include: PC Card, USB, PCI, and PCIe. Figure 13.21 shows a wireless NIC that could be installed in a laptop computer.

Figure 13.21   Wireless NIC

PCI wireless NICs allow desktop or tower computers to access a wireless network. Figure 13.22 shows D-Link Systems Inc.'s PCI wireless NIC.

Figure 13.22   PCI wireless NIC

The third type of wireless NIC attaches to the USB port and is often found in home networks. Figure 13.23 shows a LinkSys USB wireless NIC.

Figure 13.23   LinkSys USB wireless NIC

An ad hoc mode wireless network is used when two people want to play a network-based game, two or more computers need to transfer data, or one computer connects to the Internet and the other computer(s) are not wired into the same network. Figure 13.24 shows an ad hoc mode wireless network that consists of two laptops communicating over airwaves.

The **infrastructure mode** wireless network connects multiple wireless network devices through an access point. An **access point** is a device that receives and transmits data from multiple computers that have wireless NICs installed. Figure 13.25 shows a D-Link access point. The access point has two connectors on the side—an Ethernet connector and a power connector.

13
Introduction to Networking

Laptop   Laptop

Figure 13.24 **Ad hoc wireless network**

Figure 13.25 **A D-Link access point**

The easiest way to describe an access point is to think of it as a network hub—it connects the wireless network. Figure 13.26 shows an infrastructure mode wireless network with an access point and multiple wireless devices.

The access point can also be wired to another wireless network or a wired network. The access point can then relay the transmission from a wireless device to another network or to the

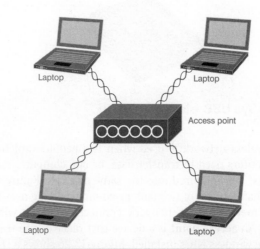

Figure 13.26 **Infrastructure mode wireless network**

Figure 13.27 **D-Link access point connected to NETGEAR switch**

Internet through the wired network. Figure 13.27 shows a D-Link access point connected to a NETGEAR switch. This switch could also be further connected to other network infrastructure devices such as another switch or a router.

When multiple devices connect to an access point (whether that access point is wired to a LAN or not), the configuration is known as a BSS (basic service set). Home networks frequently use an integrated services router that allows wireless and wired connectivity. Figure 13.28 shows

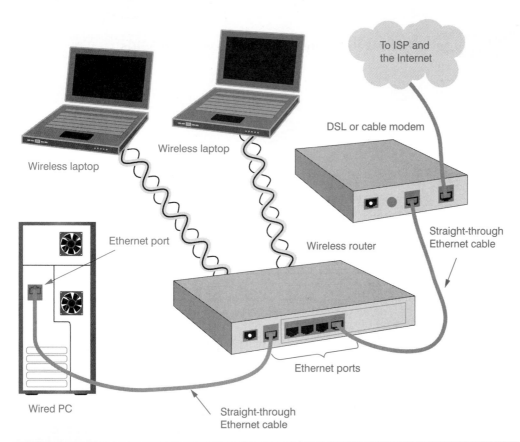

Figure 13.28 **Wireless and wired network connectivity**

how a wireless access point connects in this type of environment. Notice how the access point connects to a wired network and gives the wireless devices access to the Internet. When multiple access points connect to the same main network (known to some as the distribution system), the network design is known as an ESS (extended service set).

Each access point can handle 60 to 200 network devices depending on vendor, wireless network environment, amount of usage, and the type of data being sent. Each access point is assigned an **SSID** (Service Set Identifier). An SSID is a set of 32 alphanumeric characters used to differentiate between different wireless networks. Wireless NICs can automatically detect an access point or can be configured manually with the access point's SSID.

If two access points are used and they connect two different wireless networks, two different SSIDs would be used. Figure 13.29 shows this concept. If two access points connect to the same wireless network, the same SSID is used. Figure 13.30 shows this concept.

In addition to SSIDs, an access point can be configured with a password and a channel ID. When an access point is purchased, a default password is assigned. Because default passwords are

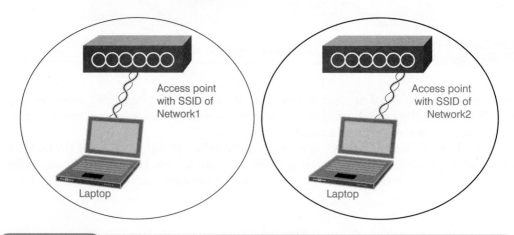

Figure 13.29   **Two separate wireless networks with two SSIDs**

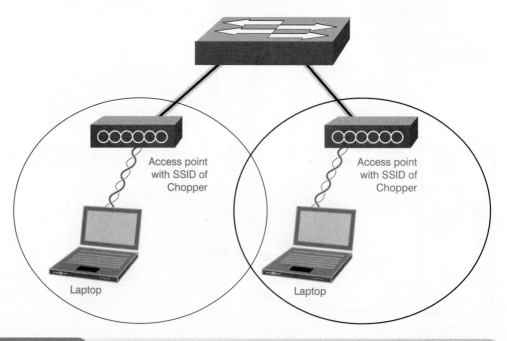

Figure 13.30   **One extended wireless network with the same SSID on both access points**

available through the Internet, the password needs to be changed immediately so that unauthorized access is not permitted. The **channel ID** defines at what frequency the access point operates. With the 802.11b standard, up to 14 channels are available depending on what part of the world the wireless network is being deployed. In the United States, only 11 channels are used and they are listed in Table 13.13.

Table 13.13	802.11b/g/n frequency channels
Channel ID number	**Frequency (in GHz)**
1	2.412
2	2.417
3	2.422
4	2.427
5	2.432
6	2.437
7	2.442
8	2.447
9	2.452
10	2.457
11	2.462

The frequencies shown in Table 13.13 are center frequencies. The center frequencies are spaced 5MHz apart. Each channel is actually a range of frequencies. For example, Channel 1's range is 2.401 to 2.423 with the center frequency being 2.412. Channel 2's range is 2.406 to 2.428 with the center frequency being 2.417.

What is really important about channel IDs is that each access point must have a different frequency or nonoverlapping channel ID. Channel IDs should be selected at least five channel numbers apart so they do not interfere with one another. The wireless devices that connect to an access point have the same frequency setting as the access point. For most devices, this is an automatic detection feature.

The three commonly used nonoverlapping channel IDs are 1, 6, and 11. By using these three channel IDs, the three access points would not interfere with one another. This is because each center frequency overlaps with the adjacent frequency channels. Figure 13.31 shows this concept.

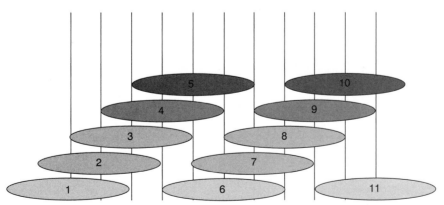

802.11b, g, and n
Center Frequencies
(in GHz)

2.412 2.417 2.422 2.427 2.432 2.437 2.442 2.447 2.452 2.457 2.462

Figure 13.31	802.11b/g/n 2.4GHz nonoverlapping channels

13
Introduction to Networking

Notice in Figure 13.31 how each center frequency is 5MHz from the next center frequency. Also notice how each channel is actually a range of frequencies shown by the shaded ovals. Channels 1, 6, and 11 clearly do not overlap and do not interfere with each other. Other nonoverlapping channel combinations could be channels 2 and 7, channels 3 and 8, channels 4 and 9, as well as channels 5 and 10. The combination of channels 1, 6, and 11 is preferred because it gives you three channels with which to work. Figure 13.32 shows a different way of looking at how channels 1, 6, and 11 do not overlap.

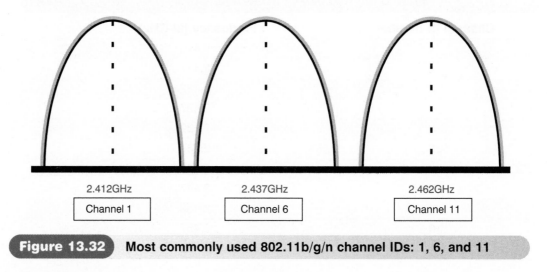

| 2.412GHz | 2.437GHz | 2.462GHz |
| Channel 1 | Channel 6 | Channel 11 |

Figure 13.32 Most commonly used 802.11b/g/n channel IDs: 1, 6, and 11

Figure 13.33 shows how the three nonoverlapping channels can be used to have extended coverage even with multiple access points.

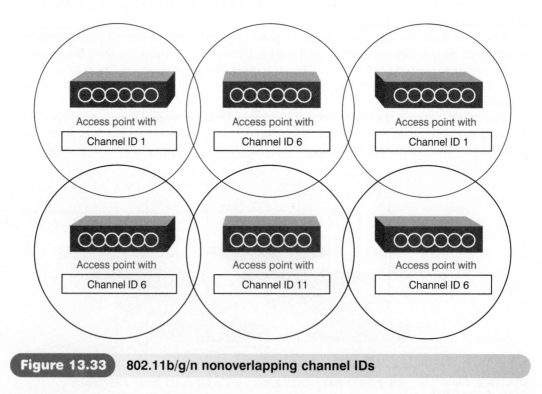

Access point with Channel ID 1

Access point with Channel ID 6

Access point with Channel ID 1

Access point with Channel ID 6

Access point with Channel ID 11

Access point with Channel ID 6

Figure 13.33 802.11b/g/n nonoverlapping channel IDs

With 802.11a, twelve 20MHz channels are available in the 5GHz range. Out of these twelve channels, eight can be nonoverlapping. The 802.11a standard breaks the 5GHz range into three subranges called UNII1 (UNII stands for Unlicensed National Information Infrastructure), UNII2, and UNII3. UNII1 is for indoor use only, UNII2 is for both indoor and outdoor use, and UNII3 is for outdoor use only. In the United States, most chipsets support only UNII1 and UNII2, so four channels can be chosen from the UNII1 range and four channels from the UNII2 range.

Some access points can be configured as a repeater to extend the coverage area of the wireless network. In this instance, the access point cannot normally be connected to the wired LAN. Instead, the repeater access point attaches to a "root" access point. The repeater access point allows wireless devices to communicate with it and relays the data to the other access point. Both access points will have the same SSID. Figure 13.34 shows this concept.

Channel ID must match

The channel ID (frequency) must be the same between the access point and wireless NIC for communication to occur between any wireless devices on the same network.

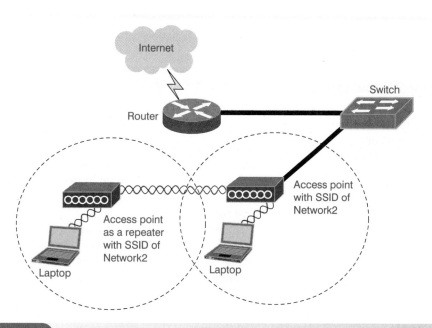

Figure 13.34   **Access point as a repeater**

Antenna Basics

Wireless cards and access points can have either external antennas or antennas built into them. An **antenna** is used to radiate or receive radio waves. Some access points also have integrated antennas. Wireless NICs and access points can also have detachable antennas depending on the make and model. With external antennas, you can simply move the antenna to a different angle to obtain a better connection. With some laptops, you must turn the laptop to a different angle to attach to an access point. External antenna placement is important in a wireless network.

There are two major categories of antennas: omnidirectional and directional. An **omnidirectional antenna** radiates energy in all directions. A **directional antenna** radiates energy in a specific direction. Each antenna has a specific radiation pattern. A radiation pattern (sometimes called a propagation pattern) is the direction(s) the radio frequency is sent or received. It is the coverage area for the antenna that is normally shown in a graphical representation in the antenna manufacturer's

Where is the wireless antenna on a laptop?

For laptops that have integrated wireless NICs, the wireless antenna is usually built into the laptop display for best connectivity. This is because the display is the tallest point of the laptop and therefore closest to the wireless receiving antenna. The quality of these integrated antennas is diverse.

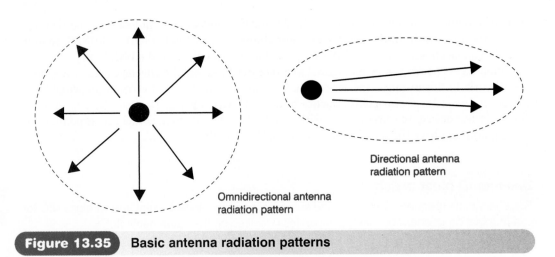

Omnidirectional antenna
radiation pattern

Directional antenna
radiation pattern

Figure 13.35 **Basic antenna radiation patterns**

Tech Tip

specifications. Figure 13.35 shows the difference in radiation patterns with omnidirectional and directional antennas.

The higher the wireless decibel rating, the better the signal

As a wireless device is moved farther away from the access point or other wireless device, the more attenuation occurs. Walls, trees, obstacles, or other radio waves can cause attenuation. The type of radio antenna and length of antenna cable can also be a factor in attenuation.

Tech Tip

What is gain?

Antenna gain is the antenna's output power in a particular direction compared to the output power produced in any direction by an isotropic or dipole antenna.

Tech Tip

Understanding gain

A 3dB gain is twice the output power. 10dB is 10 times the power, 13dB is about 20 times the power, and 20dB is 100 times the power. Gain that is shown with a negative value means there is a power loss. For example, a –3dB gain means the power is halved.

As a wireless network installer, you must be familiar with the antenna's radiation pattern so that the appropriate type of antenna can be chosen for the installation. As a signal is radiated from an antenna, some of the signal is lost. **Attenuation** is the amount of signal loss of a radio wave as it travels (is propagated) through air. Attenuation is sometimes called path loss.

Attenuation is measured in decibels. The decibel is a value that represents a measure of the ratio between two signal levels.

Things that affect an antenna's path loss are the distance between the transmitting antenna and the receiving antenna, what obstructions are between the two antennas, and how high the antenna is mounted. Another factor that affects wireless transmission is interference, including radio frequencies being transmitted using the same frequency range and external noises. Other wireless devices, wireless networks, cordless phones, and microwave ovens are common sources of interference.

An important concept in relationship to antennas is gain and in order to understand gain, an isotropic antenna must be discussed. An isotropic antenna is not real; it is an imaginary antenna that is perfect in that it theoretically transmits an equal amount of power in all directions. The omnidirectional radiation pattern shown in Figure 13.35 would be one of an isotropic antenna.

Antenna gain is measured in **dBi**, which is a measurement of decibels in relationship to an isotropic antenna. (The "i" is for isotropic.) Some antennas are shown with a measurement of **dBd** instead of dBi. This measurement is referenced to a dipole antenna. (The "d" at the end is for dipole.) 0 dBd equals 2.14 dBi. More gain means more coverage in a particular direction. Gain is actually logarithmic in nature.

Imagine a round balloon that is blown up. The balloon represents an isotropic radiation pattern—it extends in all directions. Push down on the top of the balloon and the balloon extends out more horizontally than it does vertically. Push on the side of the balloon and the balloon extends more in one horizontal directional than the side being pushed. Now think of the balloon's shape as an antenna's radiation pattern. Antenna designers can change the radiation pattern of an antenna, by changing the antenna's length and shape similar to how a balloon's looks can be changed by pushing on it in different directions. In this way, different antennas can be created to serve different purposes.

A **site survey** is an examination of an area to determine the best wireless hardware placement. Temporarily mount the access point. With a laptop that has a wireless NIC and site survey software, walk around the wireless network area to see the coverage range. Most vendors provide site survey software with their wireless NICs.

The site survey can also be conducted by double-clicking the network icon on the task bar. The signal strength is shown in the window that appears. Move the access point as necessary to avoid attenuation and obtain the largest area coverage. Radio waves are affected by obstructions such as walls, trees, rain, snow, fog, and buildings, so for a larger project the site survey may need to be done over a period of time.

There are many different types of antennas, but four common ones are parabolic, Yagi, patch, and dipole. Parabolic antennas can come in either grid or dish type models and they are usually used in outdoor environments. Parabolic dishes are used to provide the greatest distances in a wireless network. Parabolic dish antennas may not come with mounting hardware, so you should research if additional hardware is needed before purchasing. Figure 13.36 shows a parabolic dish antenna.

Figure 13.36   **Parabolic dish antenna**

A Yagi antenna can be used indoors or outdoors depending on the manufacturer. It is used for long distance communication and normally is not very large or hard to mount. The Yagi may or may not have mounting hardware. Figure 13.37 shows a Yagi antenna.

Figure 13.37   **Yagi antenna**

A patch antenna can also be used indoors and outdoors. Patch antennas can be mounted to a variety of surfaces including room columns or walls. Figure 13.38 shows a patch antenna.

13

Introduction to Networking

Figure 13.38   Patch antenna

The last type of antenna covered in this section is a dipole antenna. A dipole antenna is frequently referred to as a rubber ducky. A dipole antenna attaches to wireless NICs and access points and is used in indoor applications. Of all the previously mentioned antenna types, the dipole has the lowest range. Figure 13.39 shows a dipole antenna attached to an access point from D-Link Systems, Inc.

Figure 13.39   Dipole antenna from D-Link Systems

Wireless Network Standards

The IEEE 802.11 committees define standards for wireless networks and these can be quite confusing. Table 13.14 shows the different standards as well as proposed standards.

Table 13.14	IEEE 802.11 standards
Standard	**Purpose**
802.11a	Came after 802.11b standard. Has speeds up to 54 Mbps, but is incompatible with 802.11b. Operates in the 5GHz range.
802.11b	Operates in the 2.4000 and 2.4835GHz radio frequency range with speeds up to 11Mbps.
802.11g	Operates in the 2.4 GHz range with speeds up to 54Mbps and is backwards compatible with 802.11b.
802.11i	Relates to wireless network security and includes AES (Advanced Encryption Standard) for protecting data.
802.11n	Operates in the 2.4 and 5Ghz ranges and is backward compatible with 802.11a, b, and g equipment. Speeds up to 600Mbps using MIMO (multiple input/multiple output) antennas.

802.11-based wireless networks use CSMA/CA (Carrier Sense Multiple Access/Collision Avoidance) as an access method. Network devices listen on the cable for conflicting traffic, as with CSMA/CD; however, with CSMA/CA, a workstation that wants to transmit data sends a jam signal onto the cable. The workstation then waits a small amount of time for all other workstations to hear the jam signal, and then the workstation begins transmission. If a collision occurs, the workstation does the same thing as CSMA/CD: The workstation stops transmitting, waits a designated amount of time, and then retransmits.

Data transfer speed between the wireless NIC and an access point or another wireless device is automatically negotiated for the fastest transfer possible. The farther away from an access point a wireless device is located, the lower the speed. Figure 13.40 shows this concept.

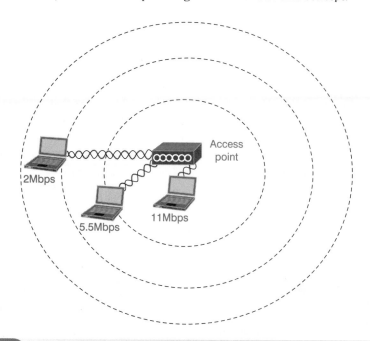

Figure 13.40 **Access point speed ranges**

Wired or Wireless NIC Installation

When you install an NIC card in a computer, there are four things that must be configured before connecting to the network.

1. Determine that an appropriate slot, port, or integrated wireless NIC is available. For example, an NIC can be integrated into the motherboard, require a PCI/PCIe slot, connect to a USB port, or insert into a laptop slot (CardBus or CF NIC—a CompactFlash card that has an RJ-45 NIC port).
2. Obtain and install the appropriate NIC driver.
3. Give the computer a unique name and either a workgroup name or a domain name.
4. Configure TCP/IP.

There are always other things that could be required depending on the network environment. For example, if the system is a peer-to-peer network, then file and print sharing must be enabled. If TCP/IP is configured, some other configuration parameters may be necessary. Hands-On Exercises 1, 2, and 8 at the end of the chapter demonstrate these concepts.

When configuring TCP/IP, an IP address and subnet mask must be assigned to the network device. The IP address is what makes the network device unique and what allows it to be reached by other network devices. There are two ways to get an IP address: (1) statically define the IP address and mask or (2) use DHCP.

When an IP address is statically defined, someone manually enters an IP address and mask into the computer through the *Network Connections* (XP) or *Network and*

Tech Tip

How to name a computer

Name a computer using the *Network Connections* (XP) or *System* (Vista/7) control panel. Each device on the same network must be given a unique name.

Sharing Center (Vista/7) control panel. Most support staff do not statically define IP addresses unless the device is an important network device such as a Web server, database server, network server, router, or switch. Instead, DHCP is used.

What happens if you assign the same IP address?

Entering an IP address that is a duplicate of another network device renders the new network device inoperable on the network.

DHCP (Dynamic Host Configuration Protocol) is a method of automatically assigning IP addresses to network devices. A DHCP server (software configured on a network server or router) contains a pool of IP addresses. When a network device has been configured for DHCP and it boots, the device sends out a request for an IP address. A DHCP server responds to this request and issues an IP address to the network device. DHCP makes IP addressing easier and keeps network devices from being assigned duplicate IP addresses.

Another important concept that relates to IP addressing is a default gateway (sometimes called gateway of last resort). A **default gateway** is an IP address assigned to a network device that tells the device where to send a packet that is going to a remote network. Default gateway addresses are important for network devices to communicate with network devices on other networks. The default gateway address is the IP address of the router that is directly connected to that immediate network. Keep in mind that the primary job of a router is to find the best path to another network. Consider Figure 13.41.

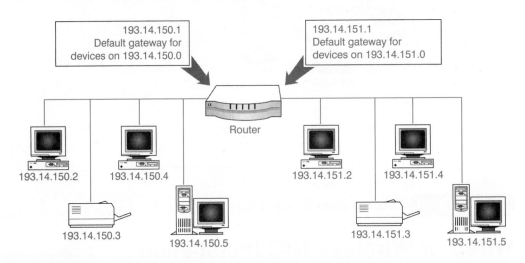

Figure 13.41   **Default gateway**

What happened if I have my computer configured for DHCP, but I get a crazy IP address like 169.254.0.5?

Windows computers support **APIPA** (Automatic Private IP Addressing), which assigns an IP address and mask to the computer when a DHCP server is not available. The addresses assigned are 169.254.0.1 to 169.254.255.254. No two computers get the same IP address. APIPA will continue to request an IP address from the DHCP server at five minute intervals. To see if APIPA is configured, open a command prompt window and type `ipconfig /all`. If you see the words *Autoconfiguration Enabled Yes*, APIPA is turned on. If the last word is *No*, APIPA is disabled.

How do I assign a default gateway?

If you are statically assigning an IP address, the default gateway address is configured using the *Network Connections* (XP) or *Network and Sharing Center* (Vista/7) control panel. Your computer can automatically receive a default gateway through DHCP just like receiving an IP address and mask.

Network devices on the 193.14.150.0 network use the router IP address of 193.14.150.1 as a default gateway address. When a network device on the 193.14.150.0 network wants to send a packet to the 193.14.151.0 network, it sends the packet to the default gateway, the router. The router, in turn, looks up the destination address in its routing table and sends the packet out the other router interface (193.14.151.1) to the device on the 193.14.151.0 network.

The default gateway address for all network devices on the 193.14.151.0 network is 193.14.151.1, the router's IP address on the same network. Any network device on 193.14.151.0 sending information to another network sends the packet to the default gateway address. For network devices on the 193.14.151.0 network, the gateway address is 193.14.151.1.

My computer does not have the same IP address

The IP address can change each time the computer boots because with DHCP, you can configure the DHCP server to issue an IP address for a specific amount of time.

Other elements of TCP/IP information that may need to be configured or provided through DHCP include DNS server IP addresses. A **DNS** (Domain Name System) **server** is an application that runs on a network server that provides translation of Internet names into IP addresses. DNS is used on the Internet, so you do not have to remember the IP address of each site to which you connect. For example, DNS would be used to connect to Addison/Wesley Publishing by translating the **URL** (uniform resource locator) of www.aw.com into the IP address 165.193.123.218. A computer can receive the DNS server's IP address from DHCP if the DHCP server has been configured for this. A technician can also manually configure the system for one or more DNS server IP addresses through the *Network* (XP) or *Network and Sharing Center* (Vista/7) control panel.

One DHCP server can provide addresses to multiple networks

DHCP server can give out IP addresses to network devices on remote networks as well as the network to which the DHCP server is directly connected.

13
Introduction to
Networking

If a DNS server does not know a domain name (it does not have the name in its database), the DNS server can contact another DNS server to get the translation information. Common three letter codes used with DNS (three letters used at the end of a domain name) are com (commercial sites), edu (educational sites), gov (government sites), net (network-related sites), and org (miscellaneous sites).

A WINS (Windows Internet Naming Service) server keeps track of computer NetBIOS names. When connecting to another computer, a user types a computer's name and not the computer's IP address. The WINS server translates the name to an IP address.

WINS is not normally needed on a Windows machine

WINS is not normally needed by Windows computers unless the computer has an application that needs NetBIOS name resolution.

Newer DNS servers provide name resolution

If a Windows computer is on an Active Directory domain, Active Directory automatically uses DNS to locate other hosts and services using assigned domain names.

Windows 7 makes it easier to create a network at home with the **HomeGroup** option. Be aware, though, that Windows 7 Starter and Home Basic versions can join, but not create a HomeGroup. To access the HomeGroup wizard to create or join a network, click the *Start* button → *Control Panel* → *Network and Internet* link → *HomeGroup*. Part of the process is to create a password that is used to add other computers to the HomeGroup. Another part of the configuration process is to determine what to share such as pictures, music, videos, documents, and printers. These particular libraries are then made available to other computers on the same network.

If Windows XP or Vista computers are to be used on a HomeGroup network, then use the *User* control panel link on the Windows 7 computer to create a new *Standard user* account. Then, from a Vista computer, use Windows Explorer to access the *Network* option in the left panel. Double-click on the Windows 7 computer that has the shared documents. Enter the user name and password that was created on the Windows 7 computer. Double-click on the *Users* share that appears in the window and all file and folders shared with the HomeGroup option on the Windows 7 computer are accessible.

On a Windows XP computer, access a HomeGroup by selecting *My Network Places* from Windows Explorer or the Start button menu. Select the *View Workgroup Computers* link from the left upper panel. If the Windows XP computer and the Windows 7 computer are members of the same workgroups, double-click on the name of the Windows 7 computer. Otherwise, select the *Other Places* panel and locate the appropriate HomeGroup. In both cases, once the computer is found, open the *Users* share to access the shared folders and/or printers.

Wired and wireless adapters require IP addresses, default gateways, and DNS configuration, but before any wireless adapters are installed or configured, the basic configuration parameters should be determined. The following list helps with these decisions:

- Will the wireless adapter be used in an ad hoc environment or infrastructure mode?
- What is the SSID?
- Is WEP, WPA, WPA-PSK, WPA2-PSK, TKIP, AES, or any other security option enabled?*
- What security key lengths, security keys, or passphrases are used?*
- What is the most current driver for the operating system being used?

    *Note that these options are discussed in Chapter 14.

Wireless network adapters can be USB, PCI, PCIe, ISA, IEEE 1394, PC Card, or ExpressCard. Each of these adapters install like any other adapter of the same type. Not all computers in the wireless network have to have the same type of wireless NIC. For example, a desktop computer could have a PCIe wireless NIC installed, a laptop computer in a cubicle office could have an integrated wireless NIC, and another laptop in another cubicle could have a PC Card wireless NIC. All three can access the same wireless network and access point.

With most wireless NICs, the manufacturer's software is normally installed before the NIC is installed or attached to the computer. With all wireless NICs, the latest driver for the particular version of Windows should be downloaded from the manufacturer's Web site before the card is installed. Once the adapter is inserted or attached and the computer is powered on, Windows recognizes that a new adapter has been installed and prompts for the driver. You must browse to the location of the new downloaded driver. Another method is to install the driver that comes with the adapter and then upgrade it once installed.

Once the wireless adapter is installed, SSID and security options can be installed. These parameters are normally configured through a utility provided by the wireless NIC manufacturer or through Windows network control if Windows XP is installed. Figure 13.42 shows the wireless NIC properties screen that is accessible through the Windows XP *Network Connections* control panel.

To access the configuration for the wireless network, click the *Wireless Networks* tab in Windows XP as shown in Figure 13.43.

Disable Windows control of the wireless NIC if other utilities are used

If a vendor provides a method of controlling the wireless NIC with utilities associated with the NIC, use those and *not* Windows. Windows and the vendor utility cannot both be used. To use the vendor-supplied utility, go into Windows first and uncheck the *Use Windows to configure my wireless network settings* checkbox.

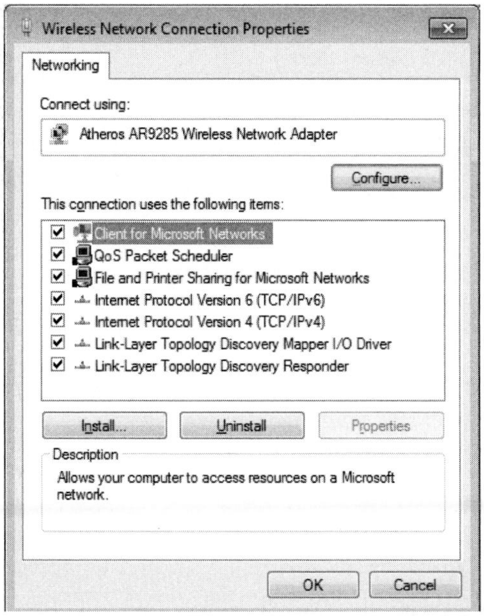

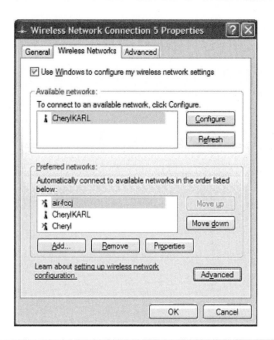

Figure 13.42 *General* **tab of the wireless NIC properties window**

Figure 13.43 *Wireless Networks* **tab**

To configure the wireless network adapter for ad hoc mode or infrastructure mode, click the *Advanced* button at the bottom of the window. In Windows XP, to select a wireless network, use the *Wireless Networks* tab, select the *Add* button to configure the wireless NIC for a wireless network. On this screen, the SSID can be input, WEP can be enabled, and the shared key can be input. Figure 13.44 shows this window.

In Windows Vista and 7, use the *Network and Sharing Center* control panel link to configure the wireless NIC for a specific wireless network. Figure 13.45 shows this window. Use the *Set up a new connection or network* link to access the *Manually connected to a wireless network* option. Figure 13.46 shows the wireless configuration options in Windows Vista or 7.

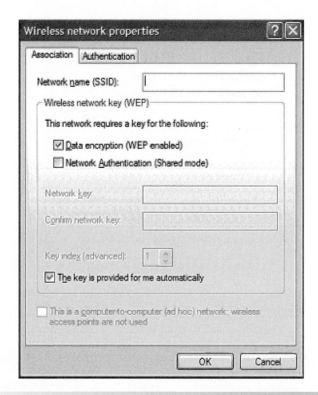

Figure 13.44 Windows XP wireless NIC configuration screen

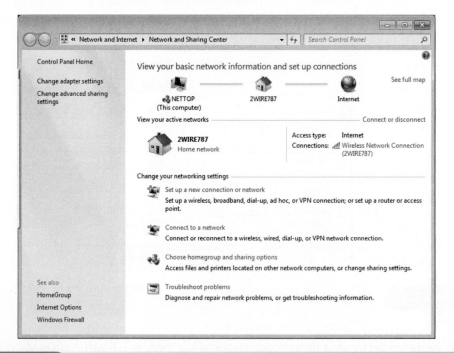

Figure 13.45 Windows 7 Network and Sharing Center

Wireless NICs are very easy to install. The utilities that are provided with the NICs are quite sophisticated and easy to use. Always follow the manufacturer's instructions. All of the screens and configuration utilities have the same type of information. Understanding what the configuration parameters means is important. The hardest part about configuring wireless NICs is obtaining the correct parameters before installation begins. Incorrectly inputting any one of the parameters

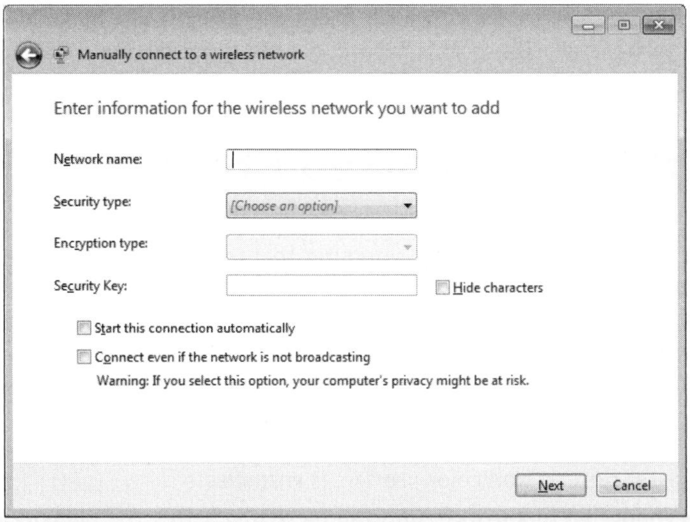

Figure 13.46   **Windows 7 wireless network configuration window**

will cause the wireless NIC not to associate with the access point or remote wireless device and not transmit. Planning is critical for these types of cards.

Access Point/Router Installation

Many wireless access points have the ability to route. The router connects the wired network and the wireless network together. A router is also good to have so that DHCP can be provided for both the wired and the wireless networks and to provide a firewall for network security. Firewalls are covered in Chapter 14.

Many of the parameters needed for wireless NIC configuration are also needed for access point installation. However, an access point is more involved because it is the central device of the wireless network. The following list helps with access point installation. The questions should be answered *before* the access point is installed. Some of these security options are discussed in Chapter 14.

- What is the SSID to be used?
- Is WEP, WPA, WPA-PSK, WPA2-PSK, TKIP, AES, or any other security option enabled?*
- What security key lengths, security keys, or passphrases are used?*
- Is MAC address filtering enabled?*
- Is there power available for the access point? Note that some access points can receive power through an in-line switch.
- How will the access point be mounted? Is mounting hardware provided with the access point or does extra equipment have to be purchased?
- Where should the access point be mounted for best coverage of the wireless network area? Perform a site survey to see best performance. Temporarily mount the access point. With a laptop that has a wireless NIC and site survey software, walk around the wireless network area to see the coverage range. The site survey can also be conducted by double clicking the network icon on the task bar; the signal strength is shown in the window that appears. Move the access point as necessary to avoid attenuation and obtain the largest area coverage.
- What channel ID will be used?
- Will the access point connect to the wired network and, if so, is there connectivity available where the access point will be mounted?

*Note that these options are discussed in Chapter 14.

Wireless networking is an important and popular technology. Technicians today must be familiar with this technology as corporations and home users install these types of products.

Because the technology is reasonably priced, many new technicians install their own wireless network for the experience. Enjoy this technology because more wireless technologies are evolving.

Configuring a Networked Printer

There are three ways to network a printer.

1. Connect a printer to a port on a computer that is connected to the network and share the printer.
2. Setup a computer or device that is designated as a print server. Connect the print server to the network.
3. Connect a printer with a network connector installed directly on the network. Printers can also be password protected on the network. A networked printer is very common in today's home and business computing environment. Networking expensive printers such as laser printers and color printers is cost effective.

A printer that is connected to a workstation can be shared across the network by enabling File and Print Sharing. An exercise at the end of the chapter explains how to do this.

Do your configuration homework

Whether installing a wired or wireless network printer, obtain IP address, subnet mask, default gateway, SSID, and security information before starting the installation.

With Microsoft operating systems, networked printers are much easier to configure than they used to be. To connect and use a networked printer, use the *Add Printer* wizard. A prompt is available that asks whether the printer is local or networked. A local printer is one that is directly attached to the computer and a networked printer is one attached to another workstation, a print server, or directly connected to the network.

The steps for installing a wireless printer are similar to installing a wired network printer once the printer is attached to the wireless network. Before installing a wireless printer, you need to ensure a functional wireless network is in the area. You need to know the SSID and any security settings configured on the wireless network. Normally, wireless printers are configured with one of the following methods:

- Install software that comes with the printer *before* connecting the printer. Then use the software to enter the wireless network SSID and optional security parameters.
- Use front panel printer controls to configure the wireless settings.
- Use a USB connection to the printer until the wireless network configuration options are entered.

Gathering the wireless configuration information is mandatory before configuring any device, including printers for a wireless network.

Network Troubleshooting

One way to troubleshoot a network is to determine how many devices are affected. For example, if only one computer cannot communicate across a network, it will be handled differently than if several (or all) computers on a network cannot communicate. The easiest way to determine how many devices are having trouble is by using a simple test. Since most computers use TCP/IP, one tool that can be used for testing is the ping command.

For what is `ping` used?

The **ping** command can be used to determine if the network path is available, if there are delays along the path, and whether the remote network device is reachable. Ping sends a packet to an IP destination (that you determine) and a reply is sent back from the destination device (when everything is working fine).

The `ping` command can be used to check connectivity all around the network. Figure 13.47 shows a sample network that is used to explain how ping is used to check various network points.

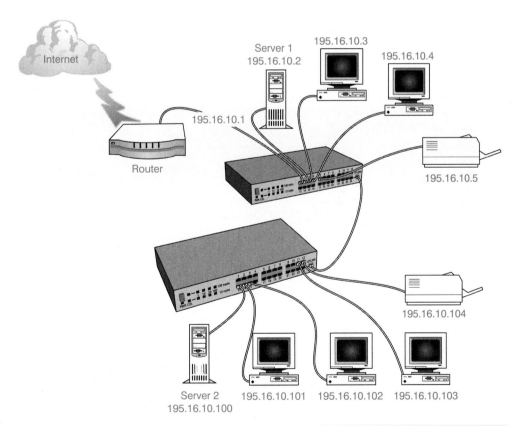

Figure 13.47   **Sample network troubleshooting scenario**

The network consists of various network devices including two servers and two laser printers. The devices connect to one of two switches that are connected using the uplink port. This port allows two similar devices to be connected with a standard Ethernet cable or fiber cable. A router connects to the top switch and the router connects to the Internet.

The 195.16.10.3 workstation cannot access a file on Server2 (195.16.10.100). The first step in troubleshooting is to ping Server2. If this is successful, the problem is in Server2 or the file located on the server.

If the ping is unsuccessful, there is a problem somewhere between the workstation and the server or on the server. Ping another device that connects to the same switch—from workstation 195.16.10.3, ping Server1 (195.16.10.2). A successful ping tells you the connection between the 195.16.10.3 workstation and the switch is good, the switch is working, the cable connecting to Server1 is fine, and Server1 is functioning.

Now ping workstation 195.16.10.101 (a device other than the server on the remote switch). If the ping is successful, (1) the uplink cable is operational; (2) the second switch is operational; (3) the cable that connects workstation 195.16.10.101 to the switch is good; and (4) the 195.16.10.101 workstation has been successfully configured for TCP/IP. If the ping is unsuccessful, one of these four items is faulty. If the ping is successful, the problems could be (1) Server2's cable; (2) the switch port to which the server connects; (3) server NIC; (4) server configuration; or (5) the file on Server2.

To see the current IP configuration, use the `ipconfig` command from a command prompt. The `ipconfig /all` command can be used to see both wired and wireless NICs if both are installed as shown in Figure 13.48. Click the *Start* button → *All Programs* → *Accessories* → *Command Prompt*. Hands-On Exercises 1, 4, 5, and 8 at the end of the chapter guide you through the processes of configuring an NIC, TCP/IP, and sharing network resources.

Use the `ping` command followed by the name of the device being tested, for example, `ping www.pearsoned.com`. A DNS server translates the name to an IP address. If the site can be reached by pinging the IP address, but not the name, there is a problem with the DNS server.

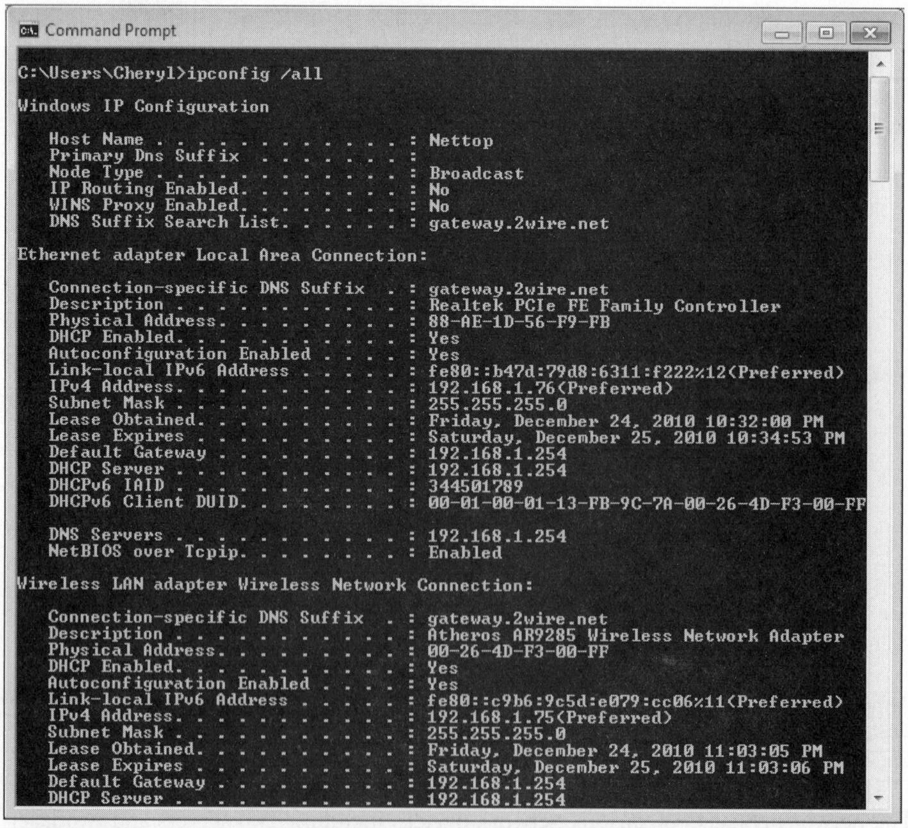

Figure 13.48 IPCONFIG and IPCONFIG /ALL

Nslookup is a program tool that helps with DNS server troubleshooting. `Nslookup` allows you to see domain names and their associated IP addresses. When an Internet site (server) cannot be contacted by its name, but can be contacted using its IP address, there is a DNS problem. `Nslookup` can make troubleshooting these types of problems easier. To see this tool in action, bring up a command prompt and type `nslookup http://www.pearsonhighered.com` and press Enter. The IP address of the Pearson Web server appears. Type `quit` to return to the command prompt.

The **tracert** command is also a commonly used tool. The `tracert` command is used to display the path a packet takes through the network. The benefit of using the `tracert` command is that you can see where a fault is occurring in a larger network. You can also see the network latency. Network **latency** is the delay measured from source to destination.

The following list contains methods that can help with NIC troubleshooting:

- From a command prompt window, `ping 127.0.0.1` to test the NIC.
- Ping another device on the same network.
- Ping the default gateway.
- Ping a device on a remote network.
- Use the `tracert` command to see if the fault is inside or outside the company.
- Check the status light on the NIC to see if the physical connection is good. Different NICs have different colored lights, but the two most common colors used with status lights to indicate a good connection are green and orange. Some status lights indicate the speed at which the NIC is operating (10Mbps, 100Mbps, or 1Gbps).
- Check the status light on the hub or switch that is used to connect the workstation NIC to the network. Green is a common color for a good connection on these devices.
- Check cabling. Even though the status lights may indicate that the connection is good, the cabling can still be faulty.
- Update the device driver by obtaining a newer one from the NIC manufacturer Web site.
- Check the IP addressing used. Use the `ipconfig` command from a prompt to ensure the NIC has an IP address assigned.
- If on laptop, ensure that the wireless NIC is enabled. Look for a button or a keystroke combination that re-enables the wireless antenna, as well as ensuring the NIC is not disabled in the *Network Connections* (XP)/*Network and Sharing Center* control panel link → *Change adapter settings* link (Vista/7).

Network Printer Troubleshooting

To begin troubleshooting a networked printer, do all the things that are normally done when troubleshooting a local printer. Check the obvious things first. Does the printer have power? Is the printer online? Does the printer have paper? Are the printer's connector(s) secured tightly? Is the correct printer driver loaded? If all of these normal troubleshooting steps check out correctly, the following list can help with networked printers:

- Print a test page and see if the printer's IP address outputs or see if the printer is labeled with its IP address. If so, ping the printer's IP address to see if there is network connectivity between the computer and the printer. Use the `tracert` command to see if there is a complete network path to the printer.
- Check the printer's *Properties* page to see if the printer has been paused.
- Cancel any print jobs in the print queue and resubmit the print job.
- Reset the printer by powering it off and back on. If it connects to a print server device, reset it too.
- If the printer has never worked, try a different version of the print driver.

Network Terminology

In the networking field, there are a great many acronyms and terms with which you must be familiar. Table 13.15 shows a few of the most common terms.

13

Introduction to Networking

Table 13.15	Common network terms

Term	Explanation
Backbone	The part of the network that connects multiple buildings, floors, networks, and so on together.
Bandwidth	The width of a communications channel that defines its capacity for data. Examples include up to 56Kbps for analog modems, 64 to 128Kbps for ISDN and up to 10Gbps for an Ethernet network.
Baseband	The entire cable bandwidth is used to transmit a digital signal. Because LANs use baseband, there must be an access method used to determine when a network device is allowed to transmit (token passing or CSMA/CD).
Broadband	Cable bandwidth is divided into multiple channels. On these channels, simultaneous voice, video, and data can be sent.
CDMA (Code Division Multiple Access)	A protocol used in cellular networks as an alternative to GSM.
FastEthernet	An extension of the original Ethernet standard that permits data transmission of 100Mbps. FastEthernet uses CSMA/CD just like the original Ethernet standard.
FDDI (Fiber Distributed Data Interface)	A high-speed fiber network that uses the ring topology and the token passing method of access.
FTP (File Transfer Protocol)	A protocol used when transferring files from one computer to another across a network. Later exercises demonstrate this protocol.
GSM (Global System Mobile)	The most widely used digital technology for cellular networks.
HTML (Hypertext Markup Language)	The programming language used on the Internet for creating Web pages.
HTTP (Hypertext Transfer Protocol)	A protocol used when communicating across the Internet.
HTTPS (Hypertext Transfer Protocol over Secure Socket Layer or HTTP over SSL)	Encrypted HTTP communication through an SSL session. Web pages are encrypted and decrypted for better security.
Infrared	A few laptop computers have infrared ports that allow them to communicate with other devices (such as another computer or printer) across a wireless network. The common term used with this is IrDA (Infrared Serial Data Link).
LPR (Line Printer Remote)	A protocol used to send print jobs to non-Windows clients.
NAT/PAT (Network Address Translation/Port Address Translation)	A method of conserving IP addresses. NAT uses private IP addresses that become translated to public IP addresses. PAT does the same thing except uses fewer public IP addresses by "overloading" one or more public IP addresses by tracking port numbers.
POP (Point of Presence)	A POP is an Internet access point.
POP (Post Office Protocol)	POP is used to retrieve email from a network server. Commonly known as POP2 or POP3, but a newer version called POP4 is due to be released. POP2 requires SMTP, but with POP3, SMTP is optional.
SNMP (Simple Network Management Protocol)	A protocol that supports network monitoring and management.
SSH (Secure Shell)	A protocol used to exchange data securely between two network devices. Commonly used to remotely access a network device.
SSL (Secure Sockets Layer)	A protocol used to transmit Internet messages securely. This protocol is used with HTTPS and online shopping Web sites to secure credit card information.

(continued)

Table 13.15	Common network terms *(continued)*
Term	**Explanation**
TCP (Transmission Control Protocol)	A layer 4 connection-oriented protocol that ensures reliable communication between two devices.
Telnet	An unsecure application that allows connection to a remote network device. Use SSH instead.
UDP (User Datagram Protocol)	A layer four connectionless protocol that applications use to communicate with a remote device.
VoIP (Voice over IP)	Sending a phone conversation over traditional network data connectivity instead of traditional telephone circuits and wiring. This can include connectivity through the Internet. VoIP can be implemented by installing software on your computer and using speakers or headphones and an integrated or external microphone. Another method can use special network-enabled phones that connect to an RJ-45 jack on your DSL or cable modem the same way your computer connects. In businesses, VoIP phones connect to an RJ-45 data jack that is wired to a network switch. Figure 13.49 shows a Cisco IP Phone.

Figure 13.49 Cisco IP phone

Sharing

When you double-click *My Network Places* desktop icon, you can view other network devices by their assigned names. They can also be viewed by typing nbtstat -n from a command prompt. Knowing a network device name is important when accessing a network share across the network. A **network share** is a folder or device that has been shared and is accessible from a remote computer.

The command prompt can also be used to access network shares by typing the computer name and the share name using the **UNC** (Universal Naming Convention). For example, a computer called *CSchmidt* has a network share called *TESTS*. By typing \\CSchmidt\TESTS at the command prompt, you can access the network share.

How to share a folder

To share a folder, use *My Computer* (XP), *Computer* (Vista/7), or *Explorer.* Locate the folder to be shared and right-click it → *Sharing and Security* → *Sharing* tab → *Share this folder on the network* checkbox. In the *Share Name* text box, type a name for the network share. This name appears in other computers' My Network Places (XP) or *Network* (Vista/7) when accessed across the network. Click *OK* and test the share from a remote computer. Figure 13.50 shows the *Sharing* tab.

Tech Tip

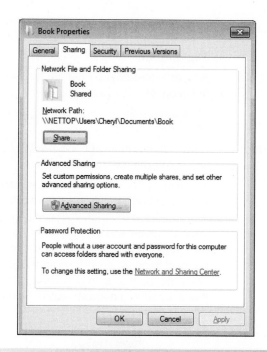

Figure 13.50   Windows XP *Sharing* tab

Tech Tip

Mapping from a prompt

A drive can be mapped from a command prompt. Use the `net /?` command for more help. For example, a computer with the name *TECH01* has a share called *Cheryl*. The following command can be used to attach to it using the drive letter `M:`. `net use m: /persistent:yes \\TECH01\Cheryl`

In a network, it is common to map a drive letter to a frequently used network share. To map a drive letter to a network share, click the *Start* button → *Computer* (Vista/7) → *Map Network Drive* → select a drive letter in the *Drive* box → in the *Folder* text box, type the UNC for the network share or use the *Browse* button to select the network share. The *Reconnect at Logon* check box allows you to connect to the mapped drive every time you log on. Figure 13.51 shows the windows to map drive letter `z:` to the shared folder called *Book*.

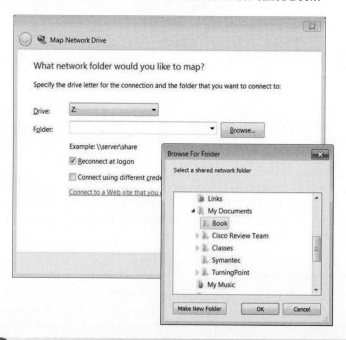

Figure 13.51   Windows 7 *Map Network Drive* window

Computer users commonly have network shares mapped to a drive letter for frequently used network shares. It is faster accessing a network share by drive letter than searching around for the share through My Network Places (XP) or Network (Vista/7).

Email

Another common Internet software application is an email (electronic mail) package to send messages across the Internet. Microsoft operating systems come with Windows Messaging (Inbox). Another popular freeware email software program is Eudora Light. Many Internet providers also have their own email package.

When you send an email to someone, your email client software formats the message and sends it to an email server. The email server has the following functions:

- Has a database of email accounts
- Stores messages (email) sent and received
- Communicates with other email servers
- Uses the DNS protocol to locate the other servers

As a reminder, a DNS server keeps a database of locations and can contact a higher level DNS server if a location is unknown.

SMTP (Simple Mail Transport Protocol) is used to transmit (send) email across the Internet. To receive email into a particular person's account, either **POP3** (Post Office Protocol and soon to be POP4) or **IMAP** (Internet Mail Access Protocol) is used. POP3 downloads the received message to the user's computer, whereas with IMAP, the message stays on the server. **MAPI** (Messaging Application Programming Interface) is a Microsoft-proprietary alternative protocol for use with email.

A technician must be familiar with troubleshooting browser and email applications. A good place to start is with the userid and password, POP3, and SMTP settings. In Internet Explorer, a technician needs to be familiar with the settings that can be configured under the *Internet Options* section from the *Tools* menu item. The *Connections* tab is a great place to start.

Forwarding email

To configure a particular application such as Google Gmail to be forwarded to another application such as Outlook, key information must be gathered: (1) a list of protocols used to send and receive email such as IMAP, SMTP, POP, and SSL, and (2) associated protocol port numbers. The technician must then go into the email application and configure an incoming mail server and an outgoing mail server settings, based on the gathered information.

Soft Skills—Being Proactive

A good technician is proactive, which means that the technician thinks of ways to improve a situation or anticipates problems and fixes them before being told to. A proactive technician follows up after a service call to ensure that a repair fixed the problem rather than waits for another help desk ticket that states that the problem is unresolved. When something like a theft or a problem with a customer occurs, a proactive technician provides a list of recommended solutions or procedural changes to the supervisor rather than waits for the supervisor to delineate what changes must occur.

For example, consider a college technician. The technician is responsible for any problems logged by computer users through the help desk. The technician is also responsible for maintaining the computer classrooms used by various departments. Each term, the technician reloads the computers with software updates and changes requested by the teachers. A proactive technician checks each machine and ensures that the computer boots properly and that the load is successful. The technician does not wait for the first day of the term or for a teacher to report a problem to the help desk.

Another example involves checking new software. When the computers are reloaded each term, a faculty member is asked to check the load. A proactive technician has a list of "standard" software loaded on the computer such as the operating system, service pack level, and

13
Introduction to Networking

any applications that are standard throughout the college. A separate list would include the changes that were applied to the computer. Then the faculty member can simply look at the list and verify the load. Being proactive actually saves the technician and the faculty member time each term.

The opposite of being proactive is being reactive. A reactive technician responds to situations only when there is a problem. The technician is not looking for ways to avoid problems. For example, a proactive technician ensures a computer is configured for automatic updates of virus scanning software. A reactive technician waits until a help desk ticket is created for a computer that exhibits unusual behavior (it has a virus).

As a student, practice being proactive with your life. Start an assignment a day before you would normally start it. Talk to your teacher about your grade in advance (before the day preceding the final). Bring a pencil and paper to school (don't wait until you arrive at school before realizing that you don't have them and have to borrow from someone).

Key Terms

access point (p. 613)
antenna (p. 619)
antenna gain (p. 620)
APIPA (p. 624)
application layer (p. 603)
attenuation (p. 620)
authentication (p. 603)
backbone (p. 596)
bandwidth (p. 634)
Bluetooth (p. 611)
broadcast address (p. 607)
channel ID (p. 617)
client/server network (p. 589)
coaxial cable (p. 596)
crosstalk (p. 594)
CSMA/CD (p. 600)
data link layer (p. 603)
dBd (p. 620)
dBi (p. 620)
default gateway (p. 624)
DHCP (p. 624)
directional antenna (p. 619)
DNS server (p. 625)
domain (p. 589)
DUN (p. 610)
Ethernet (p. 592)
FDDI (p. 593)
fiber-optic cable (p. 596)
frame (p. 602)
FTP (p. 634)
full-duplex (p. 599)
half-duplex (p. 599)

HomeGroup (p. 625)
host (p. 606)
HTML (p. 634)
HTTP (p. 634)
HTTPS (p. 634)
hub (p. 592)
IMAP (p. 637)
infrared (p. 634)
infrastructure mode (p. 613)
IP address (p. 604)
`ipconfig` (p. 632)
IPv4 (p. 605)
IPv6 (p. 606)
ISP (p. 603)
LAN (p. 589)
latency (p. 633)
MAC address (p. 604)
MAN (p. 589)
MAPI (p. 637)
multi-mode (p. 597)
NAT/PAT (p. 634)
network (p. 588)
network layer (p. 603)
network number (p. 606)
network share (p. 635)
`nslookup` (p. 633)
omnidirectional antenna (p. 619)
OSI model (p. 601)
packet (p. 602)
PAN (p. 589)
physical layer (p. 603)
`ping` (p. 630)

plenum cable (p. 595)
POP (p. 634)
POP3 (p. 637)
prefix notation (p. 608)
presentation layer (p. 603)
PVC (p. 595)
router (p. 603)
session layer (p. 603)
single-mode (p. 597)
site survey (p. 621)
SMTP (p. 637)
SNMP (p. 634)
SSID (p. 616)
star topology (p. 592)
STP (p. 594)
subnet mask (p. 607)
switch (p. 592)
TCP (p. 635)
TCP/IP (p. 604)
`tracert` (p. 633)
transport layer (p. 603)
twisted-pair cable (p. 594)
UDP (p. 635)
UNC (p. 635)
URL (p. 625)
UTP (p. 594)
VoIP (p. 635)
WAN (p. 589)
wireless network (p. 610)
workgroup (p. 589)

Review Questions

1. List three types of networks you saw on the way to school today.
2. What type of network is a large business most likely to have?

3. Match the network type on the left with the scenario on the right.

    _____ MAN   a. Home network of four PCs

    _____ LAN   b. City of Schmidtville networks

    _____ PAN   c. Hewlett-Packard corporate networks

    _____ WAN   d. Bluetooth network of two devices

4. Which type of network is least secure—peer-to-peer or server-based? Why?

5. List three things needed for networking.

6. What device is normally at the center of a star topology?

7. Which type of network topology takes the most cable and why?

8. Which type of topology does an Ethernet network use?

9. Which type of physical network topology is used with fiber connections?

10. List three types of network media.

11. Match the following:

    a. CAT 3 UTP   Common type of LAN cable

    b. CAT 5e UTP   Delivers TV stations inside a home

    c. Coax   Voice-grade phone network cable

    d. Fiber   Backbone cable

12. Describe the difference between plenum and PVC cable.

13. What cabling standard is the most common for UTP cable?

14. When installing UTP, what is the most common mistake technicians make?

15. What is the most expensive type of cable? [Coax | Fiber | UTP | STP]

16. What are the two types of fiber-optic cable and what is the difference between the two?

17. List two ways to protect your network cabling investment.

18. What type of access method do Ethernet networks use?

19. What type of access method is used when network devices "listen" to the cable before transmitting?

20. What does the *CD* mean in the term CSMA/CD and how does this affect Ethernet networks?

21. Explain the difference between half-duplex and full-duplex transmissions.

22. [T | F] Ethernet networks support half- and full-duplex transmissions.

23. List the speeds at which Ethernet networks can operate.

24. What type of Ethernet handles speeds up to 10Gbps for 20 miles?

25. What does the *100* mean in the term 100BaseT?

26. What does the T mean in the term 1000BaseT?

27. What does the *Base* mean in 100BaseT?

28. Explain how full-duplex transmission helps with Ethernet collisions.

29. Which network device works at layer one and sends received data out all its ports?

30. Match the networking standard on the left with the situation on the right. Note that not all standards will be used.

    _____ Network security   a. 802.8

    _____ Wireless networks   b. 802.3

    _____ Wireless PANs   c. 802.11

    _____ Access method used by Ethernet   d. 802.10

                                                           e. 802.15

                                                           f. 802.1

31. List three guidelines provided by the OSI model.

32. Describe a benefit of using a layered model approach to networking.

33. Write down your own mnemonic phrase that describes the OSI model from bottom to top (layer one to layer seven).

34. What layer of the OSI model encapsulates data into frames?

13

Introduction to Networking

35. What is an ISP?

36. The analogy of a post office return receipt is used to describe what OSI model layer? [Session | Network | Data link | Transport]

37. Sometimes, when logging on to a network, you must provide a userid and password or authenticate yourself. What OSI layer handles authentication? [Session | Presentation | Application | Transport]

38. At what OSI model layer does a hub reside?

39. At what OSI model layer does a router reside?

40. What is the most common network protocol suite?

41. At what TCP/IP model layer does HTTP operate?

42. At what TCP/IP model layer does UDP operate?

43. At what TCP/IP model layer does an IP address reside?

44. At what TCP/IP model layer does a NIC operate?

45. Which type of address is 48 bits long?

46. In a MAC address, how many bytes are used to represent the NIC manufacturer?

47. Which type of address is called a layer three address?

48. How many bits does each number (one octet) represent in an IP address?

49. Write Class A, B, or C as the class of IP address for each IP address shown.
    _____ 156.122.10.59
    _____ 122.6.158.2
    _____ 172.10.148.253
    _____ 201.56.199.45
    _____ 194.194.194.194
    _____ 58.22.12.10

50. Draw a vertical line between the network number and the host number for each of the following IP addresses (assuming the default subnet mask):

    141.2.195.177
    193.162.183.5
    100.50.70.80

51. Explain why no network device can have the last octet number of 255 as its host number.

52. What is the network number for 172.16.117.88/26?

53. What is the broadcast address for 10.155.97.185/27?

54. What is the network number for 192.168.10.205/28?

55. What does DUN stand for and what does this term mean?

56. Match the network connection method on the left with the description on the right.
    _____T1   Uses traditional home phone network
    _____DSL   1.54Mbps
    _____POTS   High speed home or business connection that shares voice line with data

57. List three characteristics of wireless networks.

58. What is a popular wireless technology used with PANs?

59. What is the maximum transfer rate and range for Bluetooth?

60. Describe the difference between an ad hoc wireless network and an infrastructure wireless network.

61. Complete the following chart with the appropriate type of wireless NIC.

Features	Wireless NIC type
Used in laptops	
Attaches to a computer port	
Installs into a motherboard expansion slot	

62. List one reason to configure a wireless ad hoc network.

63. [T | F] An access point must connect to a wired network.

64. [T | F] An access point can connect to another access point.

65. Two access points connect two *different* wireless networks. List the SSIDs for each access point in the following chart.

Access Point	SSID
Access Point 1	
Access Point 2	

66. Two access points connect and extend *the same* wireless network. List the SSIDs for each access point in the following chart:

Access Point	SSID
Access Point 1	
Access Point 2	

67. How many channels are available in the United States 2.4GHz range for 802.11-based wireless networks?

68. Two 802.11g access points (AP1 and AP2) have overlapping coverage areas. List the two channel IDs to assign to each access point by filling in the following chart:

Access Point	Channel ID
AP1	
AP2	

69. For what is the UNII2 band used? [Indoor only | Outdoor only | Both indoor and outdoor | Bridge mode only]

70. [T | F] When communicating with an access point, a wireless NIC and access point must be configured to the same frequency.

71. What are the two major types of antenna classifications and how do they differ?

72. List three things that can cause attenuation.

73. Describe how an isotropic antenna is important to understanding any other type of antenna.

74. What is dBi and how is this measurement important for antennas?

75. What is a site survey and how does it relate to antennas?

76. [T | F] Most vendors provide site survey software with their wireless NIC.

77. Compare and contrast a parabolic antenna with a Yagi antenna.

78. Match the following definitions. Note that not all options on the right are used.

    _____ 802.11a   a. Operates in the 2.4GHz range with speeds up to 54Mbps

    _____ 802.11b   b. Operates in the 2.4GHz range with speeds up to 2Mbps

    _____ 802.11g   c. Operates in the 2.4GHz range with speeds up to 11Mbps

    _____ 802.11i   d. Security specification

    _____ 802.11n   e. Operates in the 5GHz range with speeds up to 54Mbps

                                        f. Specifies interoperability between access points

                                        g. Standard for quality of service

                                        h. Standard for wireless interference

                                        i. Backward compatible with 802.11a, b, and g

79. List four configuration tasks used to connect a PC to a network.

80. List two methods of assigning an IP address to a network device.

81. [T | F] Workstation IP addresses are normally statically defined.

82. Reference Figure 13.52. What IP address is the default gateway for host 150.10.5.2?

83. [T | F] DHCP can provide IP addresses of the DNS and WINS servers to a host.

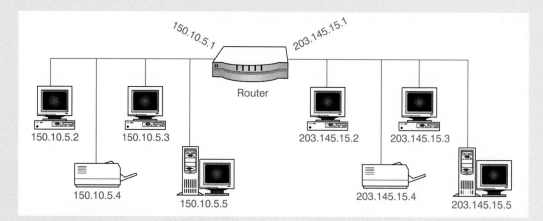

Figure 13.52 **Network scenario**

84. List three things that should be decided *before* installing a wireless NIC.

85. [T | F] Both Windows and a utility provided by the wireless NIC manufacturer can be used to control the wireless NIC so that any access point and SSID can be detected and provide a backup for each other.

86. What Windows XP wireless NIC *Properties* tab allows configuration of infrastructure or ad hoc mode? [General | Wireless Networks | Security | Advanced]

87. List three things to determine *before* installing a wireless AP.

88. List three ways to network a printer.

89. What command is used to determine if another network device is reachable?

90. What IP address is known as the NIC loopback address?

91. What is the Windows command used to view the current IP configuration including DNS information?

92. What Windows command is used to troubleshoot DNS problems?

93. What tool is used to determine the path a packet takes through a network?

94. List two troubleshooting steps when a print job does not print to a networked printer.

95. What is the term given for the part of the network that connects multiple buildings or floors?

96. What is a better protocol to use than Telnet for remotely accessing and configuring a network device?

97. What is the name of the transport layer protocol that is connectionless?

98. List one way to view network device names.

99. A folder called CHAP1 is located in a subfolder called Book, which is found in the My Documents folder. The CHAP1 folder has been shared, and the share is called CHAPTER1 on a computer that has been named CHERYLOFFICE. What is the UNC for this share?

100. List two examples of how a technician can be proactive that were not given in the chapter.

Fill-in-the-Blank

1. A/An _____ is a group of devices connected together for the purpose of sharing resources.

2. The two basic types of networks are _____ and _____.

3. Another name for server-based networks is _____ networks.

4. A home user has two computers connected together. Both computers have folders that are shared and accessible by the other computer. One computer has a printer attached that the other computer can also use. This is an example of a/an _____ network.

5. Of the two basic types of networks, the _____ network is more secure.

6. A/An _____ network should consist of no more than 10 computers.

7. The term used to describe how a network is wired is _____.

8. The _____ network topology is the most common, used with Ethernet networks, and has a direct connection between a network device and a centrally located hub or switch.

9. Data from one cable interferes with another cable. This is known as _____.

10. _____ cable carries light pulses.

11. With a fiber-optic cable installation, _____ strands are normally used, one for each direction.

12. The type of fiber used for the longest distances is _____.

13. A network accessory used in wiring closets to take multiple cables from the wall to a network cabinet is a/an _____.

14. _____ is the access method or set of rules for how workstations transmit on an Ethernet network.

15. _____ transmission is when data is transmitted in both directions simultaneously.

16. A phone conversation is an example of _____ transmission.

17. The _____ in 100BaseT means that twisted-pair cable is used.

18. A/An _____ is better than a hub in Ethernet networks because this device is a layer two device and keeps a table of addresses for the network devices attached.

19. Fiber-optic networks are defined in the IEEE _____ standard.

20. The term given for encapsulated layer two data is _____.

21. A UTP cable resides at the _____ layer of the OSI model.

22. The _____ OSI model layer provides best path selection through the network and the Internet.

23. The _____ OSI model layer provides reliable connectivity.

24. A mainframe terminal has data in one data format and a workstation has data in another format. Both devices are able to communicate across a network with the help of the _____ OSI model layer because this layer translates from one language to another.

25. A switch resides at the _____ layer of the OSI model.

26. Data found at layer three of the OSI model is called a/an _____.

27. A switch works at the _____ TCP/IP model layer.

28. Data at the network access layer of the TCP/IP model is called both a/an _____ and a/an _____.

29. The MAC address is considered an OSI model layer _____ address.

30. MAC addresses are represented in _____ format.

31. Each position in an IP address can be a number from _____ to _____.

32. 153.12.250.14 is a Class _____ IP address.

33. The term associated with sending a packet to all devices on a single network is _____.

34. The _____ is used to determine which part of an IP address is the network number.

35. The standard mask used with a Class C IP address is _____.

36. A technician configures a workstation to automatically receive an IP address. The IP address comes from a/an _____ server.

37. A/An _____ is used when a network device wants to communicate with another network device located on a remote network. This address is the router IP address.

38. A subnet mask shown as /27 instead of 255.255.255.224 is in _____ format.

39. The broadcast address for 172.16.120.200 255.255.192.0 is _____.

40. _____ is a layer two protocol used with dial-up networking.

41. Wireless networks operate at OSI model layers _____ and _____.

42. A Bluetooth network consisting of up to eight devices is called a/an _____.

43. _____ is a wireless network type that has a minimum of two wireless devices (and neither of the devices is an access point).

44. A wireless network device connected in _____ mode is the most commonly used type of network in homes and businesses.

45. A/An _____ is used in infrastructure mode and it connects multiple wireless devices together.

46. The _____ uniquely identifies a wireless network.

47. Three commonly used channel IDs with 802.11g access points are _____, _____, and _____.

48. _____ channel IDs are specified in the 802.11b standard, but only _____ are used in the United States.

49. The part of the wireless network that is responsible for sending and receiving radio waves is the _____.

50. Another name for a propagation pattern is _____.

51. _____ can be defined as the amount of radio wave signal loss.

52. The comparison measurement between an antenna's radiation pattern and an isotropic antenna's radiation pattern is _____.

53. The _____ measurement is to show an antenna's gain as compared to a dipole antenna.

54. _____ dBi equals _____ dBd.

55. Four common types of antennas are _____, _____, _____, and _____.

56. An appropriate type of antenna to be used in a room that has a column in it or in a long hallway would be a _____.

57. Another name for a rubber ducky antenna is _____.

58. _____ provides translation between a URL and an IP address.

59. _____ servers provide computer name to IP address translation.

60. To configure an SSID on a wireless NIC, the manufacturer's _____ is used or Windows XP's _____ control panel is used.

61. The _____ wireless NIC properties tab in Windows XP allows you to view automatically detected SSIDs.

62. Where an access point should be mounted is determined by doing a _____.

63. The command used to test the TCP/IP protocol suite on an NIC is _____.

64. The _____ command is used to troubleshoot a remote network fault and to see the path a packet takes through several networks.

65. A layer 4 connection-oriented protocol is _____.

66. \\BlackDell\AppsShare is an example of the _____ convention.

67. To start the process of sharing a folder use My Computer (XP), Computer (Vista), or the _____ application.

68. When you _____ a drive letter, you give a single drive letter such as t: to a network share.

69. Three protocols with email are _____, _____, and _____.

70. A better quality for a technician is to be _____ rather than being the opposite and being _____.

Hands-On Exercises

1. Installing and Configuring an NIC Using Windows XP

Objective: To be able to configure an NIC using Windows XP

Parts: Computer with Windows XP installed

NIC adapter

Optional NIC driver disk or CD

Note: The method used to install an NIC in Windows XP is vendor-specific. Always follow the NIC manufacturer's instructions when installing an NIC. The directions given below are generic for most adapters. Also, you must have rights to install hardware on the computer. Check with the lab assistant or instructor if the computer will not allow hardware to be installed.

Procedure: Complete the following procedure and answer the accompanying questions.

Who is the NIC manufacturer?

Installing an NIC

1. If possible, download the latest driver for the NIC to be installed later in the exercise.

2. Power off the computer and remove the computer's power cord.

3. Remove the computer cover and install the NIC into an available expansion slot. Use proper ESD precautions when installing an adapter.

4. Re-install the computer's power cord and power on the computer. If necessary, log on to Windows XP using the appropriate userid and password.

5. Windows XP recognizes that new hardware has been installed and the *Found New Hardware* wizard starts.

6. Insert any CD or disk that came with the NIC, if available. Follow the prompts on the screen. Windows XP may have a driver for the NIC if one is not available. If not, use the downloaded driver. An NIC cannot operate without a driver. Once the wizard completes, click the *Finish* button. The computer may have to be reloaded.

Checking the Installation

7. Click the *Start* button and select *Control Panel*.

8. If in *Category* view, select *Network and Internet Connections*, and select *Network Selections*. If in *Classic* view, double-click the *Network Connections* icon.

9. Right-click the icon that represents the NIC that was just installed and select *Properties*.

10. Click the *Configure* button.

    Does the *Device Status* window show that the device is working properly? If not, reboot the computer and check again. If it still shows a problem, perform appropriate troubleshooting.

11. Click the *Advanced* tab.

    What value is assigned to the Media Type?

12. Click the *Driver* tab.

    What is the driver version?

    Can the driver be updated from this tab?

    What is the purpose of the *Roll Back Driver* button?

13. Click the *Resources* tab.

    What IRQ is the adapter using?

Instructor initials: _____

14. Click the *Cancel* button.

13 Introduction to Networking

2. Creating a Straight-Through CAT 5, 5e, or 6 Network Patch Cable

Objective: To create a functional CAT 5, 5e, or 6 UTP network cable

Parts: UTP cable

         RJ-45 connectors

         CAT 5 stripper/crimper tool

         UTP cable tester

Note: Standard Ethernet networks are cabled with either UTP cable or RG-58 coaxial cable. In this exercise, you create a standard cable for use with Ethernet networks connected through a central hub or switch.

Procedure: Complete the following procedure and answer the accompanying questions.

1. Category 5 UTP cable consists of four twisted pairs of wires, color coded for easy identification. The color-coded wires are colored as follows:
   Pair 1: White/Orange and Orange
   Pair 2: White/Blue and Blue
   Pair 3: White/Green and Green
   Pair 4: White/Brown and Brown

2. Using the stripper/crimper tool, strip approximately 1/2 inch of the protective outer sheath to expose the four twisted pairs of wires. Most strippers have a strip gauge to ensure stripping the proper length. See Figure 13.53.
   Note: In order to make it easier to sort the wire pairs, the sheathing can be stripped farther than 1/2 inch, then the wires can be sorted properly and trimmed to the proper length.

3. Untwist the exposed wire pairs. Be careful that you do not remove more twist than necessary. Sort the wires according to the following:
   Wire 1: White/Orange
   Wire 2: Orange
   Wire 3: White/Green
   Wire 4: Blue
   Wire 5: White/Blue
   Wire 6: Green
   Wire 7: White/Brown
   Wire 8: Brown

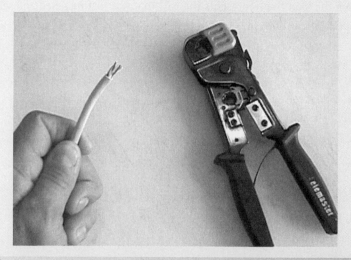

Figure 13.53   Strip the cable sheathing

Ethernet cabling utilizes wires 1, 2, 3, and 6. Using the above wiring scheme means that the cable will use the White/Orange-Orange and White/Green-Green wire pairs.

Will both ends of the cable need to follow the same wiring schematic?

4. Insert the sorted and trimmed cable into an RJ-45 connector. The RJ-45 connector key (tang) should face downward with the open end toward you while you insert the wires. Verify that all eight wires fully insert into the RJ-45 connector and that they are inserted in the proper order. See Figure 13.54.

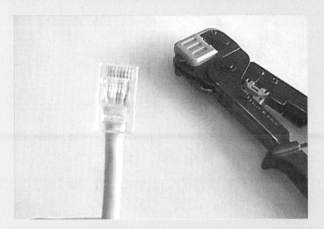

Figure 13.54   **Push wires firmly into the RJ-45 connector in the correct order**

5. Insert the cable-connector assembly into the stripper/crimper tool and crimp the connector firmly. See Figure 13.55.

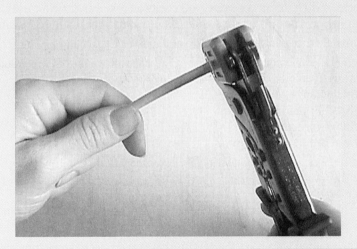

Figure 13.55   **Crimp the RJ-45 connector firmly**

6. Remove the cable/connector assembly from the stripper/crimper tool and verify that the wires fully insert into the connector and that they are in the proper order.

7. Repeat Steps 2 through 6 for the other end of the CAT 5 UTP cable.

Can the cable be used at this point?

8. Before using the cable, it should be tested with a cable tester. This verifies that you have end-to-end continuity on individual wires and proper continuity between wire pairs. Insert the RJ-45 connector into the proper cable tester receptacle and verify that the cable is functional. See Figure 13.56.

Instructor initials: _____

13

Introduction to
Networking

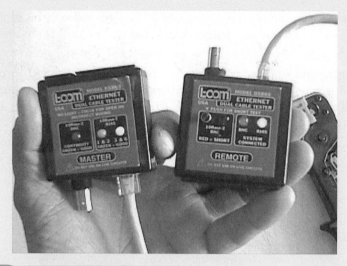

Figure 13.56 Network cable testers

3. Creating a CAT 5, 5e, or 6 Crossover Network Cable

Objective: To create a functional UTP crossover cable

Parts: UTP cable

RJ-45 connectors

Stripper/crimper tool

UTP cable tester

Note: In normal situations, straight-through UTP cabling is used to connect to a central hub or switch. In this exercise, you create a crossover cable for use when connecting two network devices (computers *without* using a central hub or switch).

Procedure: Complete the following procedure and answer the accompanying questions.

1. Category 5 UTP cable consists of four twisted pairs of wires that are color coded for easy identification. The color-coded wires are as follows:
Pair 1: White/Orange and Orange
Pair 2: White/Blue and Blue
Pair 3: White/Green and Green
Pair 4: White/Brown and Brown

2. Using the stripper/crimper tool, strip approximately 1/2 inch of the protective outer sheath to expose the four twisted pairs of wires. Most tools have a strip gauge to ensure stripping the proper length.
   Note: In order to make it easier to sort the wire pairs, the sheathing can be stripped farther than 1/2 inch. The wires can then be sorted properly and trimmed to the proper length.

3. Untwist the exposed wire pairs. Be careful that you do not remove more twist than necessary. Sort the wires as follows:
Wire 1: White/Orange
Wire 2: Orange
Wire 3: White/Green
Wire 4: Blue
Wire 5: White/Blue
Wire 6: Green
Wire 7: White/Brown
Wire 8: Brown
   Ethernet networks utilize wires 1, 2, 3, and 6. Using the above wiring scheme means the cable will use the White/Orange-Orange and White/Green-Green wire pairs.

When making a crossover cable, will both ends of the cable need to follow the same wiring schematic?

4. Insert the sorted and trimmed cable into an RJ-45 connector. The RJ-45 connector key (tang) should face downward with the open end toward you while you insert the wires. Verify that all eight wires fully insert into the RJ-45 connector, and that they are inserted in the proper order.

5. Insert the cable-connector assembly into the stripper/crimper tool and crimp the connector firmly.

6. Remove the cable/connector assembly from the stripper/crimper tool and verify that the wires are fully inserted into the connector and that they are in the proper order.

7. To create the crossover cable, the wire pairs must be put in a different order. To accomplish this, repeat Steps 2 through 6 on the *opposite* end of the cable, but when sorting the wire pairs, use the following color codes.

Wire 1: White/Green   Wire 5: White/Blue
Wire 2: Green   Wire 6: Orange
Wire 3: White/Orange   Wire 7: White/Brown
Wire 4: Blue   Wire 8: Brown

8. Verify both ends of the cables ensuring the tang is downward and the colored wires are in the correct order. You can also check the very ends of the connectors to see if you see the tip of the copper wire pushed against the end. See Figure 13.57.

Can the crossover cable be used at this point?

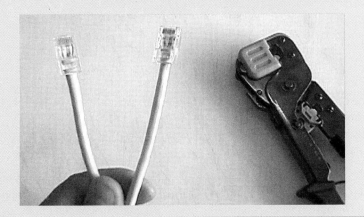

Figure 13.57   **Verify the color codes on both connectors**

9. Before using the crossover cable, it should be tested with a cable tester. This verifies that you have end-to-end continuity on individual wires and proper continuity between wire pairs. Insert the RJ-45 connector into the proper cable tester receptacle and verify that the cable is functional.

Note: Your cable tester must have the capability to test crossover cables.

Instructor initials: _____

4. Networking with Vista/7

Objective: To be able to put two Windows Vista/7 computers into a network workgroup

Parts: Two computers with Windows Vista or 7 installed

One crossover cable OR two straight-through cables and a hub or switch

Procedure: Complete the following procedure and answer the accompanying questions.

1. Power on the first computer and log on to Windows Vista/7 if necessary. Do one of the following: (1) connect a crossover between the two computers NICs or (2) connect a straight-through cable from each computer to the hub or switch and power on the switch.

2. Right-click the *Start* button and select *Explore* (Vista)/*Open Windows Explorer* (7). Right-click *Computer* in the left pane and select *Properties*. Locate the *Computer name, domain, and workgroup settings* section.

13
Introduction to
Networking

Document the current settings:

Original Computer 1 name: _____

Original Full computer 1 name: _____

Original Computer 1 description, if entered:_____

Is Computer 1 on a workgroup or domain? [Workgroup | Domain]

Original workgroup/domain name for Computer 1: _____

3. Select the *Change settings* link to the right of the computer name section. Click *Continue*, if necessary.

4. Select the *Computer Name* tab. Click the *Change* button. Select the *Workgroup* radio button. Name the Workgroup something unique.

Changed workgroup/domain name: _____

5. Click the *OK* button, and a Computer Name/Domain Changes window appears. Click *OK*. Click the *OK* button when prompted, click *Close*, and click *Restart now*.

6. Power on the second computer and log on to Windows Vista/7, if necessary.

7. Right-click the *Start* button and select *Explore*. Right-click *Computer* in the left pane and select *Properties*. Locate the *Computer name, domain, and workgroup settings* section.

Document the current settings:

Original Computer 2 name: _____

Original Full computer 2 name: _____

Original Computer 2 description if entered: _____

Is Computer 2 on a workgroup or domain? [Workgroup | Domain]

Original workgroup/domain name for Computer 2: _____

8. Select the *Change settings* link to the right of the computer name section. Click *Continue*, if necessary.

9. Select the *Computer Name* tab. Click the *Change* button. Select the *Workgroup* radio button. Name the Workgroup something unique.

Changed workgroup/domain name : _____

10. Click the *OK* button, and a Computer Name/Domain Changes window appears. Click *OK*. Click the *OK* button when prompted, click *Close*, and click *Restart now*.

11. When both computers have rebooted, the IP addresses need to be configured manually. On both computers, click on the *Start* button → *All Programs* → *Accessories* → *Command prompt*. In the new window type `ipconfig /all`.

On Computer 1, what is the IPv4 address on the Ethernet adapter?

On Computer 1, what is the IPv6 address on the Ethernet adapter?

On Computer 1, what is the subnet mask?

On Computer 1, what is the default gateway?

On Computer 1, what is the MAC address?

On Computer 2, what is the IPv4 address on the Ethernet adapter?

On Computer 2, what is the IPv6 address on the Ethernet adapter?

On Computer 2, what is the subnet mask?

On Computer 2, what is the default gateway?

On Computer 2, what is the MAC address?

Who is the network adapter manufacturer for Computer 2?

How many hexadecimal characters are shown in the Computer 1 IPv6 address?

How many bits does this represent?

12. Complete this step on both computers. Close the Command Prompt window. Select the *Start* button → *Control Panel* → *Network and Internet* link (Vista)/*Homegroup and Sharing options* (7) → *Network and Sharing Center* link.

Document the current Sharing and Discovery settings for both computers:

	Computer 1	Computer 2
Network discovery	_____	_____
File sharing	_____	_____
Public folder sharing	_____	_____
Printer sharing	_____	_____
Password protected sharing	_____	_____
Media sharing/streaming	_____	_____

13. On both computers from the Network and Sharing Center, select the *Manage network connections* (Vista)/*Change adapter settings* (7) link from the left menu. Right-click the *Local Area Connection* adapter and select *Properties*. Click *Continue*, if prompted. Locate and select the *Internet Protocol Version 4 (TCP/IPv4)* option. Click *Properties*.

Document the settings for Computer 1 and Computer 2:

Computer 1 IP address, mask and default gateway OR obtains an IP address automatically?

Computer 1 Preferred and alternate DNS server(s) IP addresses OR obtains DNS server address automatically?

Computer 2 IP address, mask and default gateway OR obtains an IP address automatically?

Computer 2 Preferred and alternate DNS server(s) IP addresses OR obtains DNS server address automatically?

14. On Computer 1, select the *Use the following IP address* radio button and type in the following information:

IP address: **192.168.1.1**

Subnet mask: **255.255.255.0**

Default gateway: **192.168.1.254**

Click the *OK* button on the next two screens to apply the changes.

15. On Computer 2, select the *Use the following IP address* radio button and type in the following information:

IP address: **192.168.1.2**

Subnet mask: **255.255.255.0**

Default gateway: **192.168.1.254**

Click the *OK* button. Click the *Close* button at the bottom of the *Local Area Connection Properties* screen.

16. On both computers, using previously described procedures, open a command prompt and verify that the IPv4 address has been applied.

From a Computer 1 command prompt, type `ping 192.168.1.2`.

What was the response?

17. Access the *Network and Sharing Center* control panel link. Turn *on* the following settings by clicking on the double arrows, selecting the appropriate radio button, clicking the *Apply* button, clicking *Continue*, if necessary, and selecting the appropriate option in any dialog window that appears.
   - Network discovery
   - File sharing
   - Public folder sharing—anyone with network access with open files

18. On Computer 1, using Windows Explorer locate the *Public* folder. Create a text file in the folder called *Surprise.txt* with the following message typed in it:

13
Introduction to
Networking

> **Technology makes it possible for people to gain control over everything, except over technology. —John Tudor**

19. On Computer 2, use Windows Explorer to access the *Network* option from the left pane. In the right pane, double-click the Computer 1 name. Note that if no passwords are assigned to the existing user account, a password will have to be applied to the account on both machines.

20. Double-click the *Public* folder. Double-click the *Public Documents* folder. Open the *Surprise.txt* document. Try modifying the text inside and saving it on Computer 1.

    Were you successful? [Yes | No]

21. Close the *Surprise.txt* document on both computers. From Computer 1, try pinging Computer 2 now.

    Was the **ping** successful? [Yes | No]

    Which Network and Sharing Center option that was enabled do you think allowed the ping through?

    What is a disadvantage to sharing files through the Public folder?

Instructor initials: _____

22. On both computers, access the *System and Maintenance* (Vista)/*System and Security* (7) control panel → *Administrative Tools* → *Windows Firewall with Advanced Security* in the right pane. Click *Continue*, if necessary. Select the *Inbound rules* option from the left pane. Expand the *Name* column section by placing the cursor over the dividing line between the *Name* column and the *Group* column. When the cursor turns to a crosshairs symbol, click and drag the line to the right to widen the *Name* column.

    Is the domain profile for *Connect to a Network Projector (TCP-in)* inbound rule enabled? [Yes | No]

    Is *Core Networking—Destination Unreachable (ICMPv6-In)* enabled for any profile? [Yes | No]

    What do the green and gray checkmarks on the left indicate?

    How many types of network discovery rules are available for selection? [Fewer than 10 | Between 10 and 20 | More than 20]

    Is *Remote Assistance* allowed on this computer? If so, for what profile?

    Is *Remote Desktop* allowed on this computer? If so, for what profile?

    Locate the name of the rule that affects the echo request and echo reply ICMP messages for IPv4. Document the name of the rule.

23. Close all windows.

24. Place both computers back in the original workgroup/domain. Refer to Step 7 for the original settings.

25. Configure both computers to the original Sharing and Discovery settings. Refer to Step 12 for the original settings.

26. Place both computers to the original IPv4 IP address, mask, default gateway, and DNS settings. Refer to Step 13 for the original settings. Have a classmate verify the original workgroup/domain settings from Step 7, the Sharing and Discovery settings from Step 12, and the original IPv4 IP address, mask, default gateway, and DNS settings from Step 13.

    Classmate printed name _____

    Classmate signature _____

27. Remove the cable and put the computers back to the original cabling configuration. Ensure that the computer works and has the same access as it had before you began this lab.

Instructor initials: _____

5. Connecting to a Windows XP/Vista/7 Shared or Networked Printer

Objective: To be able to properly share a printer and use a shared or networked printer using Windows XP/Vista/7

Parts: Two networked computers with a printer attached to one and either Windows XP or Vista installed

Procedure: Complete the following procedure and answer the accompanying questions.

1. Power on the computer that has the printer attached. If necessary, log on to Windows using the appropriate userid and password.

2. Click the *Start* button and select *Control Panel*.

3. In Windows XP, if in *Category* view, select the *Printers and Other Hardware* option and then select *Printers and Faxes*. If in XP *Classic* view, double-click the *Printers and Faxes* option.

   In Windows Vista/7, access the *Network and Sharing Center* control panel. Ensure that *Printer sharing* is enabled. Lab 4 detailed how to do this. Then in Vista/7, access the *Printers* control panel.

4. Right-click the printer to be shared and select the *Properties* option.

5. Click the *Sharing* tab and select the *Share this printer* radio button/checkbox. If the option is grayed out, select the *Change sharing options* button (Vista)/*Network and Sharing Center* link (7). Make changes as necessary. Back in the original printer properties window, ensure the *Share this printer* and *Render print jobs on client computers* checkboxes are enabled. Click *OK* if necessary.

6. In the *Share* name textbox, type in a unique printer name and limit it to eight characters if possible. It is very important that this name is unique.

   What name was assigned to the printer? _____

7. Click the *OK* button.

Printing to a Shared or Networked Printer

8. On the second computer, open the *Printers and Faxes* (XP)/*Devices and Printers* (7)/ *Printers* (Vista/7) control panel using the previously described steps.

9. On Windows XP, in the *Printer Tasks* window on the left side, click the *Add a printer* option.

   In Vista/7, click the *Add a Printer* menu option. The *Add Printer* wizard opens. Click the *Next* button.

10. In XP, click the *A network printer*, or *A printer attached to another computer* radio button.

    In Vista/7, click the *Add a network, wireless, or Bluetooth printer* option.

11. In Windows XP, there are two methods to finding a shared or networked printer and they follow:
    - Select the *Find a printer in the directory* radio button, click *Next*, click the *Browse* button, select the printer location, and click the *OK* button. Click the *Find Now* button, select the printer, and click the *OK* button.
    - Select the *Connect to this printer* (or to browse for a printer, select this option and click *Next*) radio button. Either type the name of the printer using the following format: \\computer_name\printer_share_name, or browse the network for the printer name, click the *Next* button, select the printer in the *Shared printers* window, and click the *Next* button.

    In Vista/7, the printer link should list in the window. Click *Next* if the printer is there, then select the *Install driver* button. If the printer is missing, click *The printer that I want isn't listed*. Three methods can be used to find a shared or networked printer:
    - Click the *Browse for a printer* radio button and click *Next*. Double-click the computer icon that has the printer attached. Select the printer and click the *Select* button and click *Next*.
    - Select the *Shared printer by name* radio button. Either type the name of the printer using the following format: \\computer_name\printer_share_name or browse the network for the printer name, click the *Next* button, select the printer, and click *Next*.

- Select the *Add a printer using a TCP/IP address or hostname* radio button and click *Next*. Type the hostname or IP address. Click *Next*.

12. For all versions of Windows, select one of these options and locate the shared printer. Print a test page to the shared printer.

    Does the test page print properly? If not perform appropriate printer troubleshooting.

Instructor initials: _____

6. Installing a Dial-Up Connection Using Windows XP

Objective: To understand how to create a dial-up connection when using Windows XP

Parts: Windows XP computer with a modem and Dial-up Network installed correctly

        Phone number of a dial-up server

        Optionally a username and password to the access server

Note: The Windows Dial-up Network (DUN) utility allows you to create and configure dial-up connections that allow connectivity to access servers. In this exercise, you create a dial-up connection using Windows XP.

Procedure: Complete the following procedure and answer the accompanying questions.

1. Power on the computer. If necessary, log on to Windows XP using the appropriate userid and password.

2. Click the *Start* button and select the *Control Panel* option.

3. If in *Category* view, select the *Network and Internet Connections* option and select *Network Connections*. If in *Classic* view, double-click the *Network Connections* icon.

4. In the *Network Tasks* window on the left, select the *Create a new connection* option. The *New Connection* wizard opens. Click the *Next* button.

5. Select the *Connect to the Internet* radio button and click *Next*.

6. Select the *Set up my connection manually* radio button and click *Next*.

7. Select the *Connect using a dial-up modem* radio button and click *Next*.

8. In the ISP Name, type a name that refers to the dial-up connection you are creating.

   What name was chosen for the dial-up connection?

9. Click the *Next* button. In the *Phone number* textbox, type in the phone number given to you by your instructor or lab assistant. This is the phone number to the dial-in access server. Once typed, click the *Next* button.

10. Some servers require a username and password to access the server. Type the username, password, and retype the password in the *Confirm password* textbox. Click the *Next* button. Click the *Finish* button.

11. Return to the *Network Connections* window and an icon with the dial-up connection name chosen in Step 8 lists in the window. Double-click the icon and test the connection.

    Did the dial-up connection work? If not, perform appropriate troubleshooting.

Instructor initials: _____

7. Identifying Basic Wireless Network Parts

Objective: To be able to identify basic parts of a wireless network and determine the type of wireless network being used

        Using Figure 13.58, identify the major parts of a wireless network. For the number 5 blank, write the type of wireless network being illustrated.

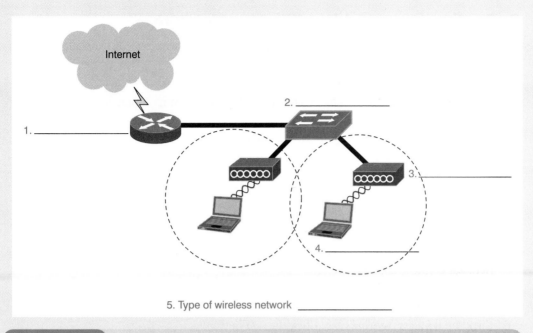

Figure 13.58 **Wireless network components**

8. Installing a Wireless NIC

Objective: To install a wireless NIC into a computer and have it attach to an access point

Parts: A computer with access to the Internet and permission to download files

A wireless NIC

An access point that has already been configured by the instructor or lab assistant

Note: In order to verify that a wireless NIC works once installed, it must have another wireless device such as another computer with a wireless NIC installed or an access point. This lab assumes that an access point is available and allows attachment of wireless devices. The students will need any security information such as WEP key before they begin. Each student will download the installation instructions and driver for the wireless NIC. Frequently these files may be in zipped or PDF format. The computer they are using may need to have Adobe's Acrobat Reader and/or a decompression software package loaded.

Procedure: Complete the following procedure and answer the accompanying questions.

1. Determine what type of wireless NIC is being installed.

   What type of wireless NIC is being installed? [PCI | USB | PC Card]

   Who is the manufacturer of the wireless NIC?

   What operating system is being used on the computer in which the wireless NIC will be installed?

2. Using the Internet, determine the latest version of wireless NIC driver for the operating system being used and download the driver.

   What is the latest driver version?

3. Using the Internet, download the installation instructions for the wireless NIC being used.

   What is the name of the installation document?

4. Open the document that details how to install the wireless NIC.

5. Follow the directions and install the wireless NIC.

   Does the wireless NIC automatically detect a wireless network? If not, contact the lab assistant or instructor for any settings that must be configured on the wireless NIC.

   List any specifications given to you by the instructor/lab assistant.

13

Introduction to Networking

9. Configuring an Ad Hoc Wireless Network

Objective: To configure two Windows XP computers that have wireless NICs installed as an ad hoc wireless network

Parts: Two Windows XP-based computers that have wireless NICs installed

Note: Students must have rights to change the hardware configuration on the computer for this lab.

Procedure: Complete the following procedure and answer the accompanying questions.

1. Power on the computer and gain access to the desktop.

2. Click the *Start* button and select *Control Panel*.

3. If in *Category* view, select *Network and Internet Connections* and then *Network Connections*.

4. If in *Classic* view, double-click the *Network Connections* icon.

5. Right-click the *Wireless Network Connection* icon and select *Properties*. If the *Wireless Network Connections* icon is unavailable, install a wireless NIC or perform troubleshooting as appropriate.

   What type of wireless NIC is installed?

6. Click the *Wireless Networks* tab. Click the *Add* button.

7. In the SSID box, type **happy**. If available, click *This is a computer-to-computer (ad hoc) network; wireless access points are not used* checkbox. Click the *OK* button.

8. Click the *Advanced* button.

   Which of the three options is currently selected: (1) Any available network (access point preferred); (2) Access point (infrastructure) networks only; or (3) Computer-to-computer (ad hoc) network; wireless access points are not used?

9. Select the *Computer-to-computer (ad hoc) networks only* radio button and click the *Close* button. Click the *OK* button.

10. Go to the second computer and do the same procedure. Once associated to each other, both computers should show a network icon on the bottom that looks like two computers stacked on top of one another. A red X should not be over the icon.

    Do both computers have the wireless network icon available? If not, perform appropriate troubleshooting. The computers may have to have their antennas adjusted or, if a laptop, the laptop may have to be turned at a different angle to perform association.

11. Point to the wireless network icon on the task bar. Do not click or double-click this icon. A balloon should appear.

    What words appear in the wireless network icon balloon?

12. Using the wireless network connection *Properties* screen, reconfigure the wireless network card to the original mode type. Refer to the answer given in Step 7 if unknown.

    Is the wireless connection still available?

Instructor initials: _____

10. Configuring a Wireless Network

Objective: To be able to configure a wireless AP (access point) or router and attach a wireless client

Parts: One wireless access point or router

A computer with an integrated wireless NIC or a wireless NIC installed as well as an Ethernet NIC

One straight-through cable

Procedure: Complete the following procedure and answer the accompanying questions.

1. Obtain the documentation for the wireless AP or router from the instructor or the Internet.

2. Reset the wireless AP or router as directed by the wireless device manufacturer.

   Document the current Ethernet NIC IPv4 settings. [DHCP | Static IP address]

   If a static IP address is assigned, document the IP address, subnet mask, default gateway, and DNS configuration settings.

3. Attach a straight-through cable from the computer's Ethernet NIC to the wireless AP or router.

4. Power on the computer and log on, if necessary.

5. Configure the computer with a static IP address or DHCP as directed by the wireless device manufacturer.

6. Open a Web browser and configure the wireless AP or router with the following parameters:
   - Change the default SSID
   - Leave SSID broadcasting enabled for this lab
   - Do not configure wireless security at this time
   - Change the default password used to access the wireless AP/router

   Document the current settings:

   SSID: _____

   Password for wireless device access: _____

7. Save the wireless AP or router configuration.

8. Disconnect the Ethernet cable.

9. Enable the wireless NIC and configure it for the appropriate SSID.

10. Configure the wireless NIC for a static IP address or DHCP as directed by the wireless AP or router manufacturer.

11. Open a Web browser and access the wireless AP or router. If access cannot be obtained, troubleshoot as necessary or reset the wireless AP or router to default configurations and restart the lab.

    What frequency (channel) is being used by the wireless AP or router and the wireless NIC for connectivity?

12. Show the instructor the connectivity.

Instructor initials: _____

13. Reset the wireless AP or router to the default configuration settings.

14. Reset the computer(s) to the original configuration settings.

Instructor initials: _____

11. Wireless Network Case Study

Objective: To design and price a wireless network based on parameters given

Parts: Computer with Internet access

Note: The instructor or lab assistant can speak on behalf of the faculty members if any design questions arise.

Scenario: A building has just been renovated to include faculty offices and two new classrooms, as shown if Figure 13.59. The only wired networks are in the computer classroom (not shown) and the administrator's office (not shown). The wired network allows access to the Internet. The wired network connections are in the wiring closet shown in the diagram at the intersection of the two hallways. Five faculty members are being issued laptop computers. The laptops do not include wireless NICs. The faculty members want to be able to use their laptops in their classrooms and offices. There are also comfortable chairs in the hallways and faculty would like to be able to use their laptops in the hallways as well. The faculty would like (1) access to the Internet and (2) access to a printer. Currently there are no printers in the classrooms or the faculty area that they can use.

13
Introduction to
Networking

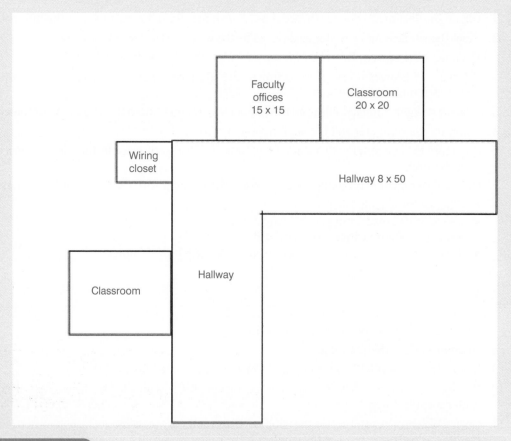

Figure 13.59

Tasks:

- Design a wireless network to allow faculty to use their laptops and gain access to the Internet. Provide this drawing in electronic form to the instructor. This can be done in Word, Visio, or some other drawing package.

- Provide a detailed list of wireless network parts, part numbers, price, and a Web link where the prices were obtained. This will include antenna type, a printout of the wireless antenna radiation pattern, and antenna coverage range.

- Provide the instructor with a typewritten list of policies and configuration settings for the wireless network. You are the designer and implementer and what you decide goes.

12. FTP Server and Client

Objective: To transfer files from one network device to another using FTP server and client software

Parts: An application or freeware application that provides the FTP server service

         An application or freeware application that provides the FTP client service

Procedure: Complete the following procedure and answer the accompanying questions.

FTP Server

1. Download, install, and open an FTP server freeware application. This lab has directions specifically for Home FTP Server, but the steps are similar.

2. Start the FTP server. You may need to start the FTP server or the FTP server service. In the Home FTP Server application, click the *FTP Server* tab → *Start Server*.

3. Some FTP server applications allow anonymous users or anyone who connects to the server to download files. Also, some applications allow you to specify what the anonymous user can do such as download, upload, and delete files and directories. To enable anonymous logins within Home FTP Server, click the *FTP Server* tab → enable *Allow anonymous users (allow all active)* checkbox. This same tab can be used to enable specific permissions for creation and deletion of files and directories.

   Make a note as to where the default anonymous directory is located.

4. FTP server applications frequently allow Web connectivity. To enable the Web interface within Home FTP Server, select the *Web interface* tab → enable the *Web interface enabled* checkbox.

   What is the default port number used for FTP server?

   What is the IP address of the FTP server?

5. Copy some files into the default anonymous directory on the FTP server.

FTP Client

6. Download, install, and open an FTP client freeware application. This lab has directions specifically for SmartFTP client, but the steps are similar.

7. Usually a client requires the following configuration:
   - (a) address of FTP server
   - (b) user login ID and password OR anonymous login selected.

   In SmartFTP client, type in the FTP server IP address in the *address* textbox → click the *Anonymous* button (option) → click the green arrow to connect. The FTP client displays the files that were copied into the anonymous directory.

Instructor initials: _____

Tightening Security

8. Create a user on the FTP server. In Home FTP Server, click the *New Member* button → *General* tab → type a name in the *User Name* textbox → type **class999** in the *Password* textbox. Make a note of the home directory and permissions for this user. Click *Apply*.

9. Test the user account from the FTP client application by creating a new entry with the appropriate userid and password. In SmartFTP, click the *File* menu option → select *disconnect* to disconnect the previous login session. Click the *File* menu option → *New Remote Browser* → in the *Host* textbox, type the FTP server IP address → in the *User name* textbox, type the *exact* user name as was typed in the FTP server application → In the *Password* textbox, type **class999** → in the *Name* textbox, type **FTP with login** → *OK*. The client connects to the FTP server.

Instructor initials: _____

10. Within the client application, close the FTP session. For Smart FTP client, use the *Close* button in the upper-right corner of the *FTP with login* tab. Close all tabs and sessions.

11. Delete FTP client entries. From within SmartFTP client, click the *Favorites* menu option → *Edit Favorites Quick Connect* option in the left pane → click once on the FTP server IP address in the right pane → *Edit* menu option → *Delete* → *Yes*. Delete the FTP with login option using the same technique.

Instructor initials: _____

13. Subnet Practice Lab

Objective: To be able to determine the subnet number, broadcast address, and IP addresses that can be assigned to network devices

Parts: None needed

Procedure: Complete the following procedure and answer the accompanying questions.

1. Determine the subnet number for the following IP address and subnet mask combinations.
   210.141.254.122 255.255.255.192
   206.240.195.38 255.255.255.224
   104.130.188.213 255.255.192.0
   69.89.5.224 255.240.0.0
   10.113.71.66 255.128.0.0

2. Determine the broadcast address for the following IP address and subnet mask combinations.
   166.215.207.182 255.255.255.240
   198.94.140.121 255.255.255.224
   97.57.210.192 255.255.224.0
   133.98.227.36 255.255.192.0
   14.89.203.133 255.128.0.0

3. Determine the valid IP addresses on the networks that contain the following IP address and subnet mask combinations.
   131.107.200.34 255.255.248.0
   146.197.221.238 255.255.255.192
   52.15.111.33 255.255.248.0
   192.168.10.245/30
   209.218.235.117 255.255.255.128

Internet Discovery

Objective: To access the Internet to obtain specific information regarding a computer or its associated parts

Parts: Access to the Internet

Procedure: Complete the following procedure and answer the accompanying questions.

1. On an HP Pavilion dm3z laptop, you cannot get the wireless NIC to attach to the wireless network. What are some steps you can take as recommended by HP to help in this situation? Write at least three solutions as well as the URL where you found the solution.

2. What does the term *Wake on Wireless* mean and at what URL did you locate the answer?

3. A computer with a LinkSys LNE 100TX 10/100 Ethernet NIC on a Windows Vista computer cannot access the Internet. What are four things LinkSys recommends you do? Write the answers and the URL where you found the answer.

4. Find an Internet forum that discusses Bluetooth and Windows Vista on Lenovo laptops. Write the URL where you found the information.

5. Find an Internet site that explains the differences between CAT 5e and CAT 6 UTP cable. Write one difference between the two standards, the name of the article or site, and the URL where you found the information.

Soft Skills

Objective: To enhance and fine-tune a future technician's ability to listen, communicate in both written and oral form, and support people who use computers in a professional manner

Activities:

1. Using the Internet, find and access a utility that tests your soft skills. Compare your scores with others in the class and determine how you might improve in specific weak areas.

2. In groups of two, one person puts a network problem in the computer while the other person is out of the room. When the other person comes back, they troubleshoot the problem

by asking questions of the user (as if they were on the phone helping them). The person performing the troubleshooting cannot touch the computer.

3. In groups of two or three, brainstorm three examples of a technician being reactive rather than proactive. List ways the technician could have been more proactive for each example. Share your findings with other teams.

Critical Thinking Skills

Objective: To analyze and evaluate information as well as apply learned information to new or different situations

Activities:

1. A home user connects to the Internet. The ISP provides hard drive space for the user's Web page. Is this a network? Why or why not? Write your answer in a well-written paragraph using good grammar, capitalization, and punctuation.

2. Use the Internet, magazines, newspapers, or books to find a network installation case study. Make a table of terms they use that were introduced in this chapter. On the left side list the term and on the right side define or describe how the term relates to the network installation. Analyze the installation and discuss with a team. Make a checklist of approved processes and of recommended changes to implemented processes. Share your team findings with the class.

3. In a team environment, design a wired and wireless network for a small business with 10 computers. Name the business, provide a design and implementation plan, provide a list of items for which you should do more research. Share your plan with the class.

13

Introduction to
Networking

14

Computer and Network Security

Objectives

After completing this chapter you will be able to

- Detail common components contained in a security policy
- Describe techniques and devices used in computers and networks
- Recommend laptop security methods and devices
- Detail and perform operating system and data protection
- Optimize a Windows-based system for security
- Define common wireless security terms
- Plan, configure, implement, and troubleshoot a basic wireless network with security implemented
- Explain common techniques used when dealing with irate customers

Security Overview

Computer and network security relates to the protection of PC hardware, software, and data and techniques used when communicating across a wired or wireless network. Books with multiple editions are devoted to the topic of computer and network security. This chapter focuses on issues related to a PC technician job and the processes and terminology with which the technician should be familiar. Security needs to be a concern of everyone from the person who greets customers, sales clerks, administrative support staff, supervisors, to of course, the people who repair and support PCs—the technicians. A technician must be able to implement and explain security concepts.

Security Policy

A **security policy** is one or more documents that provide rules and guidelines related to computer and network security. Every company, no matter what size or how many employees, should have a security policy. Small businesses tend to have general operating procedures that are passed verbally from one employee to another, but it is best to have these processes documented in detail. Common elements of a security policy are shown in Table 14.1.

Table 14.1	Security policy elements
Security policy component	**Description**
Physical access	Describes who is allowed into a building and to what part of the building they have access. Defines who has keys to the wiring closets and server rooms as well as who is allowed in such places. Delineates what type of security log is kept when a person is allowed access to a space.
Antivirus	States whether antivirus software is required on every system, possibly what product is used, how updates are obtained, and steps taken when a machine is not compliant or if a person refuses to be compliant.
Acceptable usage	Defines who has access to and what level of usage is appropriate for the company-provided information resources such as email and Internet. Sometimes it defines what data can be taken from the company and data storage limitations such as no personal data is to be stored on a server or workstation PC. This section normally includes statements about gaming and Web surfing during work hours as well as consequences for violations. The details might include defining what Web browser and hardware platforms are supported. It might include the process for assigning folder and file rights and what to do if an account has been disabled.
Password	Guidelines for protecting passwords such as not writing them down, a timeline for changing passwords, the number and type of characters required, and processes for forgotten passwords such as whether or not the new password can be given by phone or by email only.
Email usage	Defines who owns the email because it resides on a company server, how long email is stored, proper usage of email, and when it is backed up. Lawsuits related to this area continue to find for the company regarding email rights since the data is stored on company-owned and provided servers.
Remote access	Contains statements relevant to who is allowed, type(s) of remote access permitted, company resources that can be accessed remotely, the process to obtain desired rights and access, and what type of security level is required.
Emergency procedures	Details what to do when something is missing. And the steps to take if a natural disaster such as a hurricane occurs. Stipulates who overrides a security policy and authorizes access to someone.

Even though not all companies have a security policy, specific points relating to the security policy are referenced through the rest of the chapter. Whether written or just accepted company guidelines, many implementations are based upon the particular company's rules for computer and network security.

Physical Security

Typical physical security includes door locks, cipher locks, keys, guards, and fences, but physical security regarding computers can mean much more. For several years companies have been using **electronic key cards** for physical access to rooms instead of keys. Electronic key cards are part of an access control system which includes the key cards, door readers, and software to control and monitor the system. Electronic key cards have many benefits, including the following:

- They are easy to program and issue/revoke than the time it takes to issue a key or to get back a key from a dismissed employee or one who quits.
- Data is stored on a database instead of a checkout form.
- Access to information, such as who entered a room and at what time, can be logged and monitored more easily than with a checkout sheet.
- More layers of control can be exercised with key cards. With metal keys, the usual process is to give a key for each room, issue a submaster key for an entire wing, or issue a master key for the entire building.
- When keys are issued and one is lost, the lock must be rekeyed and new keys issued. When an electronic key card is lost, the old card is deactivated, and a new one is issued.

Other electronic devices and technologies also provide access to computers and rooms. Table 14.2 lists and describes security devices that help with the physical security of computers.

Table 14.2	Computer physical security devices
Device/technology	**Description**
Smart card	A small ID-sized card that can store data, be encrypted (scrambled so it cannot be read), require authorization for changing, and interact wirelessly with a card reader or the card is swiped through a card reader. Used in government IDs and contains service member's medical/dental records. It is also used in mobile phones as a subscriber identification module, driver's licenses, and employee badges.
Key fob	Used for keyless entry to cars and buildings and interior doors such as a fitness room in an apartment complex.
RFID (radio frequency ID)	A technology that allows automatic identification of people, objects, or animals. Uses an RFID tag that is read by wirelessly by an RFID reader. Used in libraries, inventory systems, as a security device for computers and hospital equipment, and in locating lost pets.
Security token	Also known as a hardware token, DES card, authentication* token or card. May be in a form of a smart token, key fob, small calculator-sized, or USB-attached device. To use the device, a PIN is frequently required, and a security token (think of it like a password) is generated. The user types this security token at the appropriate screen to be allowed access to a network.
TPM (Trusted Platform Module)	A microcontroller chip on a motherboard that is used for hardware and software authentication. The chip stores information such as security certificates, passwords, and encryption keys. It can authenticate hardware devices. Applications can use the TPM for file and folder encryption, local passwords, email, VPN/PKI authentication, and wireless authentication.

*Authentication is a term used when describing the process of proving who you are before being allowed onto the computer, to remotely access into a corporate network, or to be allowed access to a network resource such as a printer or shared document.

Smart cards or security tokens are often described as using two-factor authentication. This type of authentication is familiar to some—you need something you have such as your ATM card or your security token device and something you know such as a PIN number. This is more secure than a password which is only one factor. Figure 14.1 shows a smart card; Figure 14.2 illustrates a key fob; Figure 14.3 shows a photo of a security token.

Figure 14.1 Smart card

Figure 14.2 Electronic key fob

Figure 14.3 Security token

An expanding field related to this is **biometrics**, which is authenticating (proving who someone is) based on one or more physical traits such as a fingerprint, eyeball (retina), or hand. Behavioral traits can also be used such as voice and signature. Voice can actually be both physical and behavioral. A less complex system could just compare voice with a stored voice print. The more complex systems compare tone and inflection too, which is more in the behavioral realm.

Multifactor authentication is when two or more methods are required to gain access to a computer, network room, or other shared media. Using a bank ATM requires multifactor authentication: (1) the ATM card and (2) a PIN code. With computers, one of the two things could be something the users know such as a password or PIN and the second security measure could be a token, smart card, USB security key device, or a biometric device such as a fingerprint reader or face recognition through a webcam. Biometrics add one more security layer to authentication.

Biometrics are more secure because it is difficult to bypass such as is the case when someone uses your userid and password. The trait is less likely to be lost like a password. Also, biometrics requires that the person being authenticated is present when gaining access. Biometrics is more expensive to implement than a userid/password scheme. Examples of biometric devices used to allow someone to gain access to a room, locker, or device are listed in Table 14.3.

Table 14.3	**Biometric devices**
Device	**Description**
Fingerprint reader	Requires a finger to be placed against a reader and compared against a stored image. Used in the notebook market with some vendors having these devices already installed. Can be attached to an existing computer easily via a PC Card, CardExpress, or USB.
Face recognition system	Takes a photo and compares it with an image database (resource intensive).
Hand scanner	Requires a palm of the hand to be placed against a reader and is more secure than a fingerprint reader. Higher-end systems can analyze veins in the palm.
Retinal scanner	Sometimes called an eye scanner or an iris scanner. According to LG Electronics, the human iris is the most distinguishable characteristic.
Voice recognition	A person speaks into a microphone before gaining access to a computer or physical space. Also called speech recognition, but not the same as the software used to input data instead of typing.

Applications for biometric devices are not limited to computer/network security. Disney World uses biometrics to ensure the same person uses a multiday pass. Airports use biometrics for employee-only area access. Police departments use biometrics to gain access to evidence and gun lockers. These devices will need to be installed and maintained by the computer and network support staff. Figures 14.4 and 14.5 show a fingerprint scanner and a retinal scanner.

Most computers have BIOS options that prevent others from altering the settings. Two common levels exist—supervisor and user. The supervisor password has unrestricted access to all BIOS settings. The user password allows a limited number of configuration changes such as time and boot sequence. Some computers also have a BIOS option for a boot or power-on password. This password is required before the BIOS looks for an operating system to load.

Use the *Lock Computer* option

When away from your desk, use the *Lock Computer* option for Windows computers connected to a domain. Press [Ctrl]+[Alt]+[Del] and select *Lock Computer*.

Figure 14.4   **Fingerprint scanner**

Figure 14.5   **Iris scanner**

Laptop computers have special security needs and locking and tracking devices are available for them. Use a nondescript bag to carry the laptop to have less chance of it being stolen and carry PC Cards/ExpressCards in a separate bag. Have an engraved permanent asset tag attached. Most laptops have a USS (universal security slot) that allows a cable lock or laptop alarm to be attached. Special software packages exist that have the laptop automatically contact a tracking center in case of theft. Figure 14.6 shows a USS on a notebook computer.

Figure 14.6   **Universal security slot**

Protecting the Operating System and Data

Several chapters have contained important security-related tips, steps, and information related to protecting the operating system and data. Some of the more important ones follow:

- Use the NTFS file system.
- Back up data often and keep the backups in a different location in case of natural disaster or fire. There are different types of backups which are done using a file's archive bit status. A full backup backs up all selected files and sets the archive bit to off. An incremental backup backs up all files that have changed since the last backup. The files selected are the ones that have the archive bit set to on. The backup software resets those bits to off. A differential backup backs up files that have changed since the last full backup (files that have the archive bit set to on), but the backup software does not reset the archive bit like the incremental backup does.
- Back up the System State.
- Ensure operating system and application service packs and updates are applied regularly.

- Install antivirus software with the latest virus definitions.
- Encrypt data that needs to be protected.
- Use BitLocker and TPM (Trusted Platform Module). **BitLocker** encrypts an entire disk volume, including the operating system, user files, swap files, and hibernation files. It is available on Vista/7 Enterprise and Ultimate and requires two NTFS disk partitions.
- Optionally place operating system files and data files on separate hard drive partitions.
- Set share permissions appropriately.
- If donating an older computer or replacing a hard drive, the data needs to be removed, and if feasible, the hard drive partition(s) deleted and recreated; some hard drive manufacturers have a utility that rewrites the hard drive with all 1s or all 0s to prevent data remnants from being recovered. Use the `format x: /p:n` (where `x:` is the drive letter and *n* is the number of passes) to format a disk volume with a zero in every sector. Then use the `cipher /w x:`, where `x:` is the letter of the hard drive volume from which you want to remove data by overwriting all unused sectors on the disk with zeros, then ones, and then a random number. Because this command does this on unused sectors, it is important to remember to use the `format` command first. Hard drives not donated can also be recycled. A company that has extremely sensitive data stored on a hard drive should destroy the hard drive according to the security policy and should shred CD/DVD discs.

If you suspect that your system has a virus, run the antivirus program after first checking for any updated virus signatures from the antivirus software vendor. If the system still performs unusually, try booting into Safe Mode and running the virus checker from there. If you purchased an antivirus disc, run the software from the CD. If all else fails, most vendors have instructions on their Web site for booting to a command prompt and executing the virus scan from the prompt.

Besides backing it up, the following are several things you can do to protect your locally stored data.

Manually delete files if necessary

If the antivirus software or other preventive software applications state that a particular file cannot be deleted, make a note of the file and its location. Try deleting the file from Windows Explorer. You may have to set Explorer to allow you to view hidden or system files. Once viewed, the hidden or system attribute may need to be removed before deletion can occur.

- If the computer you are using does not need to share files or a printer with others on the network, disable *File and Print Sharing* from the *Network* (XP) or *Network and Sharing Center* (Vista/7) control panel.
- To create a shared folder that is not seen by any others across the network, add a $ (dollar sign) to end of the share name. An example of a hidden shared folder is Book$.
- In XP, make any folder in your user profile private such as *My Documents*, *Desktop*, *Start Menu*, *Cookies*, and *Favorites* (or any subfolder of these). Note that Vista/7 does not support private folders. Hands-On Exercise 2 at the end of the chapter demonstrates these techniques.
- Encrypt (scramble so they cannot be read) files or folders.

All subfolders are shared when a folder is shared

When you share a folder, all subfolders are automatically shared unless you make the subfolders private.

NTFS volumes can have files, folders, and subfolders encrypted using **EFS** (encrypting file system). When a folder or subfolder is encrypted, all newly created files within the folder or subfolder are automatically encrypted. If any files are copied or moved into an encrypted folder or subfolder, those files are automatically encrypted. System files cannot be encrypted. EFS can use a CA (certificate authority) such as one issued from a server or use a self-signed certificate as demonstrated in Hands-On Exercise 1 at the end of the chapter.

Can you encrypt someone else's files?

The answer is yes if you have the write attribute, create files/write data and list folder/read data permissions for the file.

Prevent a computer from being seen through the network

In XP, *Start → Control Panel → Classic* view and *Administrative Tools;* in Vista/7 *System* control panel *→ Administrative Tools →* in XP, Vista, and 7, *Services →* double-click *Computer Browser → Startup type* drop-down menu, select *Disabled → Apply → OK →* restart the computer.

Ten concurrent users

A maximum of 10 users can simultaneously use the same shared folder.

When a new computer is purchased, data and applications may need to be migrated to the new machine. Several options are possible. If only data (no applications) needs to be transferred, the data can be copied to CD/DVDs, a Flash drive, or an external hard drive. Otherwise, a special cable can be used between the two computers' serial, parallel, USB, FireWire, or network ports and data copied from one machine to the other. If data and applications need to be transferred, special software can help with this process. Keep in mind that if an external NTFS-formatted hard or Flash drive is used, Windows uses what is known as a "lazy write" to the drive. This means that the system doesn't always write quickly to the external drive exactly when you clicked "Copy." The result of this is that external drives sometimes do not "eject" from a USB port when requested. Consider using a FAT32 or exFAT-based drive to avoid this issue.

All versions of Windows Vista/7 have the Windows Easy Transfer Wizard that transfers user accounts, files and folders, program data files and settings, photos, music, videos, Windows settings, and Internet settings. Note that applications are *not* transferred, and an Easy Transfer cable (from a computer store), a wired or wireless network, a removable hard drive, or a CD/DVD can be used in conjunction with this program.

Beware of migration software applications that do not allow you to select the software

Some migration utilities do not allow you to specify which applications are transferred to the new machine. This is fine if every application needs to be moved, but this is not always the case.

Protecting Access to Local and Network Resources

Several techniques exist to protect computer access and some of them have been considered as part of the physical access section. Authentication is used to determine what network resources can be used. **Authorization** is the part of the operating system or network controls in place to determine what resources such as files, folders, printers, video conferencing equipment, fax machines, scanners, and so on, can be accessed and used.

A great analogy for authentication is the clubhouse that many of us made as children. A secret tap at the door or a special password was the only way to gain access to the private domain. Most people are familiar with the userid and password method of authentication. Other means could be used including the previously discussed biometric devices, such as the fingerprint scanner, retinal scanner, or palm scanner. All of these provide an additional layer of security beyond the userid and password method. Windows and other operating systems and applications use the Kerberos protocol to provide authentication. Kerberos uses a KDC (key distribution center) to authenticate users, applications, and services. Password protection is a common method used though, and some password guidelines are listed in Table 14.4.

Windows allows several userid and password options, including the following:

- Local userid and password created and maintained on the local PC
- Computer that is part of the workgroup where the userid and password are created, stored, and maintained on the local computer (similar to the local PC)
- Computer that is part of a domain and the userid and password are created, stored, and maintained on a centralized network server

A workgroup environment is a LAN where each computer maintains its own networked resources such as whether a file or printer is shared with others. Workgroup networks are more

Table 14.4	Computer/network password guidelines
Device/technology	**Description**
Reminders	Do not write down your password. Most computer users write down their password and keep it close to the computer. Do not put your password in a document stored on the same computer.
Number of characters	Use eight or more characters with uppercase and lowercase letters interspersed with numerals and characters.
Format	Do not use consecutive letters or numbers on the keyboard such as *asd* or *123* because it is easy for someone who is watching the password being typed to guess the password. Do not use passwords that are words such as *children* or *happiness* because there are password dictionaries that are used to hack passwords. These dictionaries contain the same words as normal dictionaries, including foreign words and names.
Social	People's eyes tend to stray toward movement. If someone is standing near you when you are logging in, ensure their eyes are averted or wait until they move to type your password into the system.

common in home and small business environments and are sometimes called peer-to-peer networks. A domain environment is more common in the business world where network servers are used to authenticate logins, provide for file storage, and provide services such as email and Web access. Another name for a domain environment is server-based network. Figure 14.7 illustrates a workgroup environment; Figure 14.8 shows how a domain environment is different.

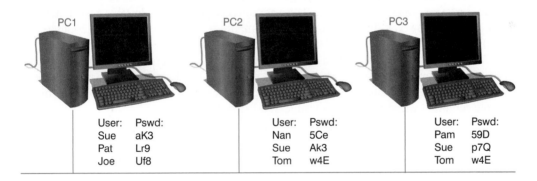

Figure 14.7   **Windows workgroup model**

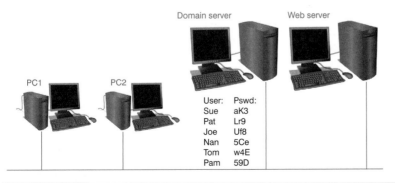

Figure 14.8   **Windows domain model**

14

Computer and
Network Security

Another method of controlling login passwords is through a local- or domain-based account policy. Policies can define the desktop, what applications are available to users, what options are available through the *Start* menu, whether or not users are allowed to save files to external media, and so on. A domain or group policy can be created and applied to every computer on the domain.

A local policy is created on a computer, and it could be used to disable auto-playing of CD/DVDs, turn off personalized menus, or keep someone from changing the Internet Explorer home page. A local policy might be implemented in a workgroup setting. A group policy is more common in a corporate environment, and a group policy can overwrite a local policy. The local policy is accessed by typing `gpedit.msc` from a command prompt or in the *Search* textbox in Windows Vista or 7.

Through the defined policy, criteria for auditing can also be set. **Auditing**, sometimes called event logging or just logging, is the process of tracking events that occur on the network such as someone logging into the network. In the business environment, a server with special auditing software is sometimes devoted to this task because it is so important to security. Hands-On Exercise 6 at the end of the chapter details how to configure a local security policy, log events, and view those audited items.

File and folder security protection is also a concern. A subfolder and any files created within that subfolder all inherit security permissions from the parent folder or the folder that contains the subfolder. This feature can be disabled when necessary. Exercise 3 at the end of the chapter demonstrates this concept.

Files and folders can be shared in either a network workgroup or domain. A **local share** is something—a printer, folder, or media device—shared on a specific computer. **Administrative shares** are shares created by Microsoft for drive volumes and the folder that contains the majority of Window files. An example of an administrative share is a drive volume letter (such as C) followed by the dollar sign ($) symbol (C$). The admin$ administrative share is used to access to the folder that contains the Windows operating system files.

Windows automatically creates these administrative shares, but by default Windows Vista and 7 prevent local accounts from accessing administrative shares through the network. If this feature is desired in Windows Vista or 7, a registry edit must be made. In Windows XP and lower versions, the `net share` *share_name*`$ /delete` command can be used to disable a particular administrative share. However, this is reset when the computer is restarted. A batch file could be created and put in the startup folder to make this a more permanent solution.

Any local share can be made a **hidden share**, which is a share that is not seen by default through the network. To make a share a hidden share, add the dollar sign ($) symbol to the share name. This might be beneficial to a computer user who wants to access something from his or her remote computer without making it visible to other network users.

Internet Security

Tech Tip

Why keep your Windows and Web browser current?

Internet hackers frequently target browsers and constant updates are provided that help with these attacks.

Before upgrading an Internet browser, you must determine the current Web browser version. With any Windows-based application, the version is determined by starting the application, clicking the *Help* menu option, and selecting the *About x* (where *x* is the name of the application) in Windows XP or selecting the question mark menu item in Vista or Windows 7. With Internet Explorer, the first two numbers listed are the software version numbers. There is another value called cipher strength that is a bit value for encryption; **encryption** is a protection method used to change data so it cannot be recognized.

Some companies use a **proxy server** to protect the company's network. This server acts as an agent (a go-between) between an application like a Web browser and a real server. A proxy server can also cache frequently accessed Web pages and provide them when requested from a client instead of accessing the real Web server. To configure any device or application for a proxy server, obtain the following information:

- IP address of the proxy server
- Port number of the proxy server
- Optionally a username and password, but some organizations use server-based authentication

To configure Internet Explorer to use a proxy server, use the *Internet Options* from the *Tools* menu bar option → *Connections* tab → *LAN Settings* button → select the *Use a proxy server for your LAN* checkbox → in the *Address* textbox, type the proxy server IP address → type the proxy server port number in the *Port* textbox. This information can be obtained from the company's network administrator or through **WPAD** (Web Proxy AutoDiscovery) protocol. Click on the *Advanced* button to set individual IP addresses and port numbers for different protocols. Note that if you don't want the proxy server to be used when accessing resources in the local domain (and speed up this type of access), select the *Bypass proxy server for local addresses* checkbox.

Computer security is a huge concern. If the computer connects to the Internet it should be connected behind a firewall. A **firewall** protects one or more computers from outside attacks. A firewall can be a software application or hardware and should be implemented for any computer that connects to another network, especially a computer that connects to the Internet. A firewall keeps hackers from accessing a computer that connects to the Internet. A software firewall is a good solution for individual computers. A hardware firewall is a good solution for home and business networks. Both can be used concurrently. Microsoft Windows XP, Vista, and 7 have a software firewall installed that examines packets travelling to and from the computer and filters them (denies or allows them) based on a configured ACL (access control list). Options chosen through the Windows Security Center affect this ACL. **Port forwarding** is a term used when a packet is allowed through the firewall based on a particular port number/protocol. Port triggering is a similar concept. **Port triggering** allows data into a computer temporarily based on a configured situation.

Tech Tip

Antivirus and antispyware applications are still needed even when a firewall is installed

A computer protected by a firewall still needs antivirus and antispyware applications for protection. Having a firewall on each computer on a network as well as on a router or modem that connects to the Internet (or a device dedicated to providing firewall services) is common in both the home and business environment.

The concept of a firewall is similar to building a moat with a drawbridge around a castle. The castle is the inside network, the moat with the drawbridge is the firewall, and everything outside the castle is "outsiders." The drawbridge can control who or what has access to the castle and who or what leaves the castle.

To verify if Windows XP has the Windows firewall enabled, click the *Start* button → *Control Panel* → *Classic* view → *Security Center*. In Vista/7, *Start* button → *Control Panel* → *Security* → *Windows Firewall*. Use the `wf.msc` command to access the Vista/7 Advanced Windows configuration page. To see open firewall ports, use the `netsh firewall show state` command.

Figure 14.9 shows the Windows 7 Firewall control window. In XP, the *Don't Allow Exceptions* checkbox is used to block all incoming traffic when a computer is used in a restaurant or public place. In Vista/7, the *Block all incoming connections* checkbox provides the same security option.

Tech Tip

Allowing a program Internet access through Windows Firewall

Locate and right-click the program you want to allow Internet connectivity. Select *Properties* → *Shortcut* tab → right-click in the *Target* textbox (the path highlights) → *Copy* → *Cancel* button. In both Vista and XP, open the Security Center and Windows Firewall. Select the *Exceptions* tab → *Add Program* button → *Browse* button → right-click in the *File name* textbox and select *Paste* → *OK* → *OK*. Windows Firewall will now allow that application to have Internet connectivity.

When Windows Firewall is installed and enabled on a Windows computer and another computer or application tries to connect, Windows Firewall blocks the connection and prompts with a security alert to allow a choice of *unblock*, *keep blocking*, or *ask me later*. Table 14.5 describes these options.

When people connect to the Internet, they normally do so through a Web browser. Any Web browser can usually be configured for various security options. Since Microsoft operating systems ship with Internet Explorer, it is covered here. But, similar options are available in most browsers.

Windows Vista/7 have up to three possible network location settings (depending on the Windows version) that configures the firewall differently. The *Private (Home or Work)* network location setting turns file sharing and network discovery on through the firewall so communication will easier at work or in a private home network. The *Public* setting configures these settings

Figure 14.9   **Windows 7 firewall**

Table 14.5   **Windows firewall security alerts**

Alert	Description
Unblock this program	The program is allowed to execute and the program is automatically added to the Windows Firewall exceptions list.
Keep blocking this program	The program is not allowed to execute or listen. Use whenever you do not know the source of the alert.
Keep blocking this program, but ask me again later	Does not allow the program to execute or listen, but the next time you access the site, the security alert will prompt you again.

to be off through the firewall to help protect your computer when you are on a public network such as when you are in an airport. The *Domain* setting is when the computer participates in a Windows Active Directory domain environment.

To access the security options (as well as other ones), open Internet Explorer, click the *Tools* menu option, and select *Internet Options*. Figure 14.10 shows this window.

There are five major sections to the Internet Options *General* tab: *Home page*, *Browsing history*, *Search*, *Tabs*, and *Appearance*. Table 14.6 shows the function of each section.

Most Web browsers allow some method of deleting cookies. A **cookie** is a special program written to collect information and store it on the hard drive. A cookie could be used for a variety of things, but some examples include your preferences when you visit a Web site, rotating banner ads at the top of a Web site so you do not see the same ones repeatedly, and tracking what Internet sites you visit. Internet Explorer stores cookies as a separate file. Netscape stores cookies in a single file called *cookies.txt*.

You can configure the Web browser to accept all cookies, block all cookies, or notify you every time a cookie is offered by a Web server. In Internet Explorer 7 or 8, access the *Tools* menu option → *Internet Options* → *Browsing History* section. The *Delete* button gets rid of cookies, passwords, form data, history, and temporary Internet files.

Cookies can also be controlled through the Internet Zone Settings located on the *Security* tab in Internet Explorer. The zones are the four categories shown with icons at the top of the page in Figure 14.11.

Click the *Internet zone* (the world icon) to adjust the settings. The Internet zone is the default zone that all Web sites fall into unless a Web site is specifically added to another zone such

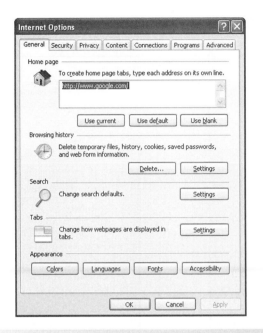

Figure 14.10   *Internet Options* window

Table 14.6   Internet Options *General* tab sections

Section	Purpose
Home Page	Defines the default URL that opens automatically when Internet Explorer is accessed. The address textbox is used to type in a new URL and click the *Use Current* button.
Browsing history	Keeps track of URLs that have been visited in the past. You can define the number of days to keep these. Use the *Delete* button to clear the list of recently visited Web sites, cookies, passwords, form data, and temporary Internet files.
Search	Allows customization of which service providers list in the search box.
Tabs	Allows multiple Web sites to be opened within the same main browser window. Each Web site is on a particular tab.
Appearance	Allows customization of how Web sites are displayed in terms of colors, fonts, and languages.

as the Trusted sites zone. Use the slide bar to adjust the security levels. These settings help against rogue spyware installations and advertisement pop-ups.

Active scripting is an important security setting in a Web browser. Active scripts are programs written for the Internet and are used on news sites, online shopping sites, and Web-based email sites to make a Web page more dynamic and one that constantly changes. However, some active scripting can be harmful because it can be used as a mechanism to transmit a worm virus into the computer. For this reason, a technician should define what Internet sites are often used that might be programmed with scripting. If active scripting is used on a site not listed, a message appears on the screen and you can either view the page or refuse it.

To configure Internet Explorer to handle active scripting this way, open Internet Explorer, select the *Tools* menu option *Internet Options Security* tab *Trusted Sites*. Click the *Sites* button. In the *Add this Web site to the zone* textbox, type the Web address for a site you visit often that might use active scripting. Click the *Add* button. Continue adding as many sites as you need. Click the *OK* button when finished adding sites.

From the *Security* tab, select the *Internet* icon. Click the *Custom Level* button. Figure 14.12 shows this window. Each of the security settings can be manually configured and Table 14.7

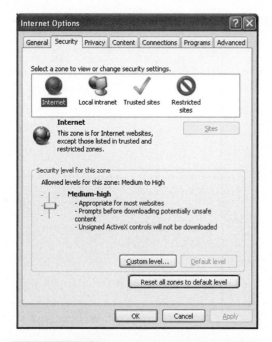

Figure 14.11   **Internet Explorer—**
Security tab

Figure 14.12   **Custom level security settings**

explains the options. Table 14.8 shows Windows firewall issues and solutions to help with troubleshooting.

Many Internet sites send unwanted code to the computer via the Web browser. This unwanted code can be offered as a special utility to speed up Internet access or is included as part of a downloaded song or application. Table 14.9 lists some of these malicious types.

There are freeware programs available as well as full security suites such as ones from McAfee or Symantec that include software firewalls and components to prevent these types of malicious software applications from executing. Microsoft Vista and 7 come with Windows Defender, which works with Internet Explorer 7 and higher to warn for spyware. The MBSA (Microsoft Security Baseline Analyzer) can be used to identify security misconfigurations on computers.

Spam is another problem. **Spam** comes in unsolicited email from a company or person previously unknown. People who send this type of email are known as spammers. Most email applications have filters for spam, but they cannot catch all of them. Most email applications also allow you to create a rule to block messages from a particular source or subject line.

Other issues related to email include how email messages are sent in clear text. If the email is intercepted, the message is easy to read. PGP (pretty good privacy) and S/MIME (secure multipurpose Internet mail extension) are frequently used to provide encryption and authentication for email messages.

All technicians (and employees) should be aware of social engineering. **Social engineering** is a technique used to trick people into divulging information including their own personal information or corporate knowledge. Social engineering does not just relate to computers, but can be done over the phone, through an online survey, or through a mail survey. No auditing or network security applications and devices can help with such deviousness.

Table 14.7   **Custom settings options**

Option	Description
Disable	Skips prompting and automatically refuses the action or download.
Enable	Automatically proceeds with the option.
Prompt	Prompts for approval before proceeding with the option. Note that not all options have a Prompt choice.

Table 14.8   **Windows firewall troubleshooting**

Windows firewall issue	Resolutions
The firewall is blocking all connections	Access Windows Firewall and disable the *Don't allow exceptions* (XP) or *Block all incoming connections* (Vista/7) checkbox.
The firewall is blocking a specific application	If a dialog box appears, select the *Unblock* option to allow it through. If the dialog box does not appear, access Windows Firewall and use the *Exceptions* tab to create a rule that will allow the application through the firewall.
No one can ping my Vista/7 computer	Ensure *File and Print Sharing* is enabled through the *Network and Sharing Center* control panel. Access the *Administrative Tools* link and select *Windows Firewall with Advanced Security*. Select *Inbound rules* in the left pane. Select *New Rule* in the *Actions* column. Select the *Custom* radio button and *Next*. Select the *All programs radio* button and *Next*. Select *ICMPv4* from the *Protocol Type* drop-down box. Select the IP addresses to which this rule will apply and name the rule.
Windows Firewall is turned off every time the computer restarts	Another security firewall is installed.
No one can access local files and/or a shared printer	File and print sharing has not been enabled.

Table 14.9   **Unsolicited Internet message types**

Type	Description
spyware	Collects personal information without consent through logging keystrokes, accessing saved documents, and recording Internet browsing. Results in unsolicited pop-ups and identify theft.
adware	A program that automatically displays marketing advertisements as an integrated part of a Web site or as a pop-up.
malware	Also known as badware and includes software code that is designed to damage a computer system.
grayware	A generic term for applications or files that are not viruses, but that affect computer performance and/or cause unexpected and unsolicited events to occur. Can come from downloading shareware or freeware, infected emails, selecting an advertisement shown in a pop-up window, or through a Trojan virus. Spyware, adware, and malware are all types of grayware.

A related concept is phishing. **Phishing** (pronounced fishing) is a type of social engineering that attempts to get personal information, and it comes through email from a company that appears legitimate. Phishing emails target ATM/debit or credit card numbers and PINs, Social Security numbers, bank account numbers, Internet banking login IDs and passwords, email addresses, security information such as a mother's maiden name, full name, home address, or phone number. Internet Explorer 7 and higher includes a phishing filter, which proactively warns the computer user when he or she goes to a site that is a known phishing site or when a site contains characteristics common to phishing sites.

Attacks can come from outside or from within a corporate network. Table 14.10 lists various types of network attacks.

A popular business solution for security is VPN. **VPN** (virtual private networking) is a special type of secure network created over the Internet from one network device to another. One example is a home PC that connects to a corporate server and has access to company resources that cannot be accessed any other way except by being on a computer on the inside network. The VPN connection makes it appear as if the home computer is on the inside corporate network. Another example

Table 14.10   **Types of network attacks**

Type of attack	Description
Access	Frequently uses multiple dictionaries including foreign ones to gain access to accounts, databases, servers, and/or network devices. Types of attacks include man-in-the-middle, port redirection, buffer overflow, and password.
ARP spoofing	Sending of an Ethernet frame with a fake source MAC address to trick other devices to sending traffic to a rogue device.
Backdoor	Also known as trapdoor. A planted program executes to bypass security and/or authentication.
Brute force	Repeated attempts to check all possible key combinations to gain access to a network device or stored material.
DoS (denial of service)	A string of data/messages sent to overload a particular firewall, router, switch, server, access point, computer, etc. in an attempt to deny service to other network devices.
DDoS (distributed denial of service)	A group of infected computers attack a single network device by flooding the network with traffic.
Reconnaissance	Attempts to gather information about the network before launching another type of attack. Tools used include port scanners, pings, and packet-sniffing programs.
Replay	A valid network message or certificate is re-sent, usually in an attempt to gain logon procedures.
Smurf	Uses the ICMP protocol to ping a large amount of network traffic at a specific device to deny that device network access, ping a nonexistent device to generate a lot of network traffic, or ping all network devices to generate a lot of traffic in ICMP replies.
TCP/IP hijacking	A stolen IP address is used to gain access and/or authorization information from the network.
Vulnerability scanner	A software program used to assess network devices to identify weaknesses such as unpatched operating systems, open ports, or missing/outdated virus scanning software.

is when a branch office network device connects to a corporate server, VPN concentrator, firewall, or other network device. Once connected, the branch office network device connects as if it were directly connected to the network. Figure 14.13 illustrates these concepts.

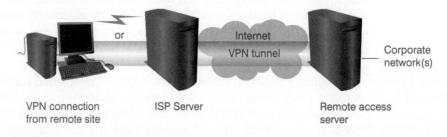

VPN connection   ISP Server   Remote access
from remote site   server

Figure 14.13   **VPN connectivity**

Tech Tip

Both sides of the VPN tunnel must match

The two devices used to create the VPN tunnel must have identical VPN settings or the VPN tunnel will not be formed.

To create a VPN connection on a Windows XP computer, open the *Network Connections* control panel. In the *Network tasks* section, select the *Create a new connection* link. The *New Connection* wizard steps you through the process. In Vista/7, use the *Network and Sharing Center* control panel to select the *Set up a connection or network* task. Select the appropriate type of IP address, the IP address of the VPN device or the domain name, a descriptive name for the connection, and security options and click *Connect*.

Security Incident Reporting

Many companies define what to do when a security incident has occurred. However, in some businesses or in an incident that occurs on a home network, people are not always sure what to do. Some tips for incident reporting and official reporting entities list in Table 14.11.

If a security incident occurs and you do not know what to do, talk to your supervisor. He or she should have the experience to guide you or know to whom he/she should go to resolve the issue. If you feel uncomfortable talking to your supervisor about this, consider the human resources department or a higher administrator. Reporting and documenting security violations is very important, especially in the business environment and it is every person's responsibility to be security-aware and responsible.

Table 14.11   Incident reporting

Type of event	Description
Virus	Disconnect the computer from the Internet and run a full scan. Once virus-free, most antivirus software companies have a process for connecting to them automatically to receive a report of the virus scan. You can also notify your Internet provider and file a complaint with the FBI Internet Crime Complaint Center.
Spyware or grayware	Use a freeware or a software application to remove the application. Many of the security suites have a method of reporting found incidents. Submit a report using the FTC Consumer Complaint Form.
Phishing	Notify the agency from which the contact was received. Report the incident to CERT (U.S. computer emergency readiness team) at phishing-report@us-cert.gov.
Child exploitation	Use parental control software, log off immediately, and notify your local police department and/or the nearest FBI field office. You can also report the event to the National Center for Exploited and Missing Children.
Software piracy	Report incidents of organized software piracy to the SIIA (Software and Information Industry Association) and the BSA (Business Software Alliance).

Wireless Network Security Overview

Security has been a big concern with wireless network installers because most people are not familiar with network or wireless security. Wireless networks by their nature are insecure. Wireless access points (APs) are normally mounted in the ceiling or on the wall where they are conspicuous. Normal networking equipment such as hubs, switches, routers, and servers are locked in a cabinet or behind a locked door in a wiring closet. Customized cabinets can be purchased to secure APs indoors and outdoors.

Data transmitted over air can be in clear text, which means that with special frame capturing software on a computer with a wireless NIC installed, the data can be captured and viewed. Negotiation between the wireless devices and the AP can be in clear text and that information can be captured. All frames include a source MAC address and someone with a computer with a wireless NIC installed can capture the frame, use the MAC address to gain access to other resources. (This is known as session hijacking or MAC spoofing.) By default, most APs transmit their SSIDs in clear text. All of these issues must be considered when installing a wireless network.

Authentication and Encryption

The original 802.11 standards define two mechanisms for wireless security: authentication and data confidentiality. Remember that authentication is the process of determining that a network device or person has permission to enter the wireless network through the access point. The two types of authentication are open and shared key. **Open authentication** allows a wireless network device to send a frame to the access point with the sender's identity (MAC address). Open authentication is used when no authentication is required. **Shared key authentication** requires the use of a shared key, which is a group of characters that the wireless network device and access point must have in common. Shared key authentication does not scale well with larger wireless networks because each device must be configured with the shared key authentication (and this is time-consuming), the users must be told of the shared key and their individual stations configured for this (which is time-consuming), or a server is used to provide the shared key automatically. Also, when manually input shared keys are used the key is not changed very often. APs that support 802.1x authentication use some form of EAP (Extensible Authentication Protocol). When any type of EAP is used, the user or client to be authenticated is called a supplicant. An authentication server holds valid usernames and passwords. The device that is in the middle that takes the client request and passes it on to the server is known as the authenticator. An AP can be an authenticator.

When shared key authentication is being used, WEP must be enabled. **WEP** (Wired Equivalent Privacy) encrypts data being transmitted. Encryption is the process of converting data into an unreadable format. WEP commonly has two versions: 64-bit and 128-bit. Some vendors may have 256-bit. 64- and 128-bit WEP may also be seen as 40- and 104-bit. This is because each of the two versions uses a 24-bit initialization vector: 40 plus 24 equals 64 and 104 plus 24 equals 128. Sometimes you might even see that in documentation or Web site wording, the author mixes the two types of numbers such as 40-bit and 128-bit, so it can be confusing.

How many characters do you type with WEP?

If 64-bit WEP is being used, five ASCII characters are entered (five times eight bits—one for each ASCII character—equals 40 bits) or 10 hexadecimal characters (10 times four bits—one for each hexadecimal character—equals 40 bits). If 128-bit WEP is being used and entering the key in ASCII, 13 characters are entered. And if hexadecimal is being used with 128-bit WEP, 26 characters are typed.

With WEP enabled, the shared "secret" key is normally entered into the wireless NIC configuration window. Vendors have a variety of ways of inputting this alphanumeric key, but normally it is input in either hexadecimal or ASCII characters.

Some wireless NIC manufacturers allow entering multiple WEP keys; however, only one key is used at a time. The multiple WEP keys are for multiple environments such as a WEP key for the business environment and a WEP key for the home wireless network using the same wireless NIC. Figure 14.14 shows the configuration dialog box for a wireless NIC and where the WEP is enabled.

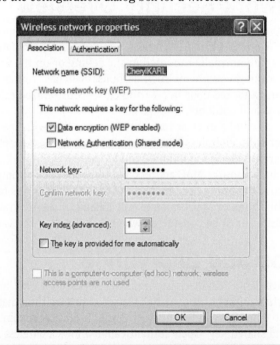

Figure 14.14   **Wireless NIC *Properties* window with WEP enabled**

Notice in Figure 14.14 that there is a checkbox for enabling WEP. The default configuration when WEP is enabled is for the *The key is provided for me automatically* checkbox to be enabled as well. The 802.11 standard does not define how the WEP key is provided to the NIC. Some bigger companies use a server that provides the key to the wireless NIC securely. However, most installations require that the WEP key be entered manually. Notice how this adapter does not allow you to specify the length of the WEP key, so it is the 64-bit version. Some vendors have configuration utilities that allow wireless NIC configuration.

How a firewall helps a wireless computer

A firewall can protect a computer connected to a wireless network; however, it cannot prevent the data being sent wirelessly from being hijacked. The firewall simply protects a hacker from accessing the computer.

WEP can be hacked. With special software on a laptop with an NIC installed, WEP can be compromised. Enabling WEP is better than no encryption whatsoever. An improvement on WEP is WPA (Wi-Fi Protected Access). WPA uses **TKIP** (Temporal Key Integrity Protocol) or **AES** (Advanced Encryption Standard) to improve security. TKIP is an improvement on WEP in that the encryption keys change. Even better than TKIP is AES, which is an encryption standard with key sizes of 128-, 192-, or 256-bits. AES has been used in wireless government networks for some time. The 802.11i wireless standard specifically deals with wireless security.

WPA2 is an improvement that includes dynamic negotiation between the AP and the client for authentication and encryption algorithms. WPA2 is a common choice for securing wireless networks. The 802.11i standard includes RSN (Robust Security Network), which includes some features of WPA2. Third-party products can be used with some vendors' wireless solutions and some vendors provide extra security of their own with their NIC cards and access points. The drawback to this is that other vendors' products are normally incompatible.

To manually configure wireless settings in Windows Vista/7, use the *Network and Internet* control panel link → *Manage Wireless Networks* → *Add* link → *Manually create a network profile* link. The *Security type* drop-down menu has the following options: No authentication (open), WEP, WPA2-Personal, WPA-Personal, WPA2-Enterprise, WPA-Enterprise, and 802.1x. If you select WPA/WPA2, then *TKIP* or *AES* are available from the *Encryption type* drop-down menu. Figure 14.15 shows this window for Windows 7.

WPS (WiFi Protected Settings) configures the SSID and WPA2 wireless security key for an AP or client devices.

Use vendor software

When a vendor provides software for controlling the wireless NIC, use it! Do not have Windows and the vendor software competing to control the wireless NIC. In XP, use the *Wireless Networks* tab to disable Windows controlling the NIC. In Vista/7, use the *Administrative Tools* control panel to select *Services*. Locate *WLAN AutoConfig* to disable.

14

Computer and
Network Security

Figure 14.15 **Windows 7 wireless security window**

It supports 802.11 a, b, g, and n devices including computers, access points, consumer electronics, and phones. The purpose of WPS is to provide a consistent wireless configuration method across various platforms and vendor products. The standard allows four ways to configure a wireless network.

- A PIN (personal identification number) is entered. This PIN is sometimes found on a sticker or display on the wireless product.
- A USB device attaches to the AP or wireless device to provide configuration information.
- A button is pushed or clicked. This method is known as PBC (push button configuration).
- The NFC (near field communication) where the wireless device is brought close to the AP (or a device known as the Registrar) and the configuration is applied. RFID tags are suited for this method.

Windows XP (SP2+), Vista, and 7 support WPS. To configure a compliant wireless router or access point, use the *Network and Sharing Center* control panel link → *Set up a New Connection or Network* → *Set Up a New Network* → *Next* and wait for the router/AP to be found → Select the device → *Next* → enter 8 digit PIN found on the router or on a sticker on the router → *Next* → type the SSID (wireless network name) in the *Type your network name* textbox → click the *Change passphrase, security level and encryption type (advanced)* down arrow → select the security method that can be used by all wireless devices on the network → enter a security key (passphrase which is used to generate a security key) → notice the "Connect automatically" checkbox is enabled → *Next*. Windows transmits the information to the router/AP. A helpful option is the *Copy the Network Profile To a USB Drive* link available at the end of the wizard. Once information is copied to a USB Flash drive, the configuration data on the drive can be used to configure other wireless computers running Windows XP, Vista, or 7.

Default Settings

All wireless networks have security features. Many access points come with a default password and SSID. Change both of these settings as soon as the access point is powered on. Default passwords are posted on the Internet and a hacker could lock out access from the access point.

Tech Tip

Never leave an access point password to the default

One of the first things to do after powering on the access point and connecting to it is change the default password.

Change the access point's default password during installation. Do not leave it to the default. The default passwords are well known by many others who could attempt to hack or penetrate the wireless network. Make the password a strong one. Use as many characters as feasible. Use uppercase and lowercase letters. Include non-alphanumeric characters such as #, %, &, or @. Common default access point SSIDs are shown in Table 14.12.

Table 14.12	**Default access point SSIDs**
Vendor	**Default SSID**
Cisco	tsunami, autoinstall, Cisco, or no SSID defined
D-link	WLAN
Linksys by Cisco	linksys
NetGear	Wireless
SMC	WLAN
SOHOware	Same as MAC address
Symbol	101
TELETRONICS	any
ZCOMAX	any, mello, or Test
ZYXEL	Wireless

As mentioned previously, the SSID (service set identifier) is used to allow wireless devices to attach to the access point or to another wireless device. Almost all access points are configured for SSID broadcasting. **SSID broadcasting** is where the access point periodically sends out a beacon frame that includes the SSID. Wireless NICs can detect this SSID automatically and attach to the access point. This can be a security issue.

WEP (wireless equivalent privacy), covered previously, is disabled by default. Even though WEP can be broken, enable it. If configuring WEP, use the largest bit size possible that will be compatible with all wireless NICs. The larger the WEP key, the stronger the encryption.

Disable SSID broadcasting

If possible and feasible, disable SSID broadcasting and manually enter the SSID into any wireless NIC's configuration. Even though this requires more effort, it protects the wireless network to some extent.

Wireless access points sometimes include other network functions such as firewall, router, and switch and sometimes include a port to add a hard drive and support network-accessible storage. Table 14.13 lists some common configuration features included in such devices.

Table 14.13	Common network device configuration settings
Option	**Description**
Wireless	Used to configure basic wireless settings such as the SSID. Also includes a link to security options such as MAC filtering, authentication, and encryption.
Security	Used to enable/disable a firewall and configure firewall features such as VPN or allow particular network ports to be opened to allow certain types of traffic through.
Storage	Allows monitoring and control of an attached storage device or even support an FTP (file transfer protocol) server.
Administration	Allows configuration of the device such as password, IP address assignment, and event logging. Could also include configuration of features such as VoIP or QoS (quality of service), which allows one type of traffic such as voice which cannot tolerate delay take priority over another type of traffic.
Maintenance	Allows viewing the current status of the various components as well as access to any logging that is enabled.

Wireless Security Conclusion

A lot of issues have been raised about wireless security. It is an important issue. The following list recaps some of the important issues and provides recommendations along with a few suggestions for a more secure wireless network.

- Change the default password and make it as long as possible. The password should include non-alphanumeric characters.
- Change the default SSID.
- Enable encryption on the access point to the highest level possible and still allow wireless NIC access. Use authentication when possible.
- Put the wireless network on its own subnetwork and place it behind a firewall if possible.
- If provided, enable MAC authentication on the access point. MAC authentication allows you to input valid MAC addresses that are allowed to associate to the access point. Even though time consuming, it is a good feature.
- If supported, authenticate using a Radius server.
- If the SSID is manually configured, periodically change the SSID.

Stop the broadcast

To protect your home wireless network, disable SSID broadcasting. As a result, all computers will have to be manually configured once, but it is worth it.

14 Computer and Network Security

- Assign a static IP address to the access point rather than using DHCP for it.
- Disable remote management of the access point.
- Place the access point in the center of the wireless network and not next to an outside window.
- Use wireless network scanning software to test the network security.
- Require that wireless clients use a VPN (virtual private network) tunnel to access the access point and wireless network.

Wireless networks have a strong presence today and in the future. The 802.11 standards are constantly being developed to tighten security for wireless networks so that it rivals a wired solution.

Wireless Network Troubleshooting

Troubleshooting wireless networks is sometimes easier than a wired network because of the mobility factor. A laptop with a wireless NIC installed can be used to troubleshoot connectivity, configuration, security, and so on. Most wireless network problems stem from inconsistent configuration. The standards deployed must be for the lowest common denominator. For example, if a wireless NIC only supports 64-bit WEP encryption, then that must be what is used even if 128-bit WEP, WPA, or WPA2 is available on some of the cards.

The list that follows are some general wireless networking tips designed to get a technician going in the right direction. Most of these tips have been discussed in previous sections, but it is nice to have the following troubleshooting list in one spot:

- Is the SSID correct?
- Is the type of wireless network (ad hoc or infrastructure) correctly configured?
- Is the wireless NIC seen by the operating system? (Use Device Manager to check.)
- Is WEP enabled? If so, is the WEP key correctly configured? Is the WEP key length correct?
- Is open or shared key authentication being used? Check the configuration.
- Is the correct security key being used? Check the configuration.
- Can any devices attach to the access point? If not, check the access point.
- Is anything causing interference or attenuation? Check antenna placement.
- Is there a channel ID overlap problem?
- If a manufacturer's utility is being used and Windows XP is installed, does the *Network Properties* window have the *Use Windows to configure my wireless network settings* checkbox unchecked? If not, uncheck this checkbox to allow the utility to configure the wireless NIC. For Vista or 7, automatic wireless network configuration is enabled by default. A program from the wireless NIC manufacturer can be installed and used instead. If the customer wants to use Windows Vista or 7 instead of the software provided, click *Start → All Programs → Accessories* locate and right-click on *Command Prompt*. At the prompt type `netsh wlan show settings`. From the output determine if the Windows automatic wireless configuration is disabled. To enable Windows Vista automatic wireless configuration type the following command: `set autoconfig enabled=yes interface="`*interface_name*`"` (where *interface_name* is the name shown from the command output).

Soft Skills—Dealing with Irate Customers

It is fitting to leave the last customer-related topic to dealing with people who are angry, upset, frustrated, and so on. This issue is faced by many technicians who have come to help or are troubleshooting a problem over the phone. Dealing with irate customers is a skill that you can fine-tune. Listening to peer technicians tell how they successfully (or unsuccessfully) dealt with a difficult customer can also help.

Some key tips for dealing with difficult customers include the following:

- Realize that not only does the customer want their computer problem fixed, but also they sometimes just need to vent, be heard, and listened to. Because a technician is the person with the knowledge for at least the start of the resolution, the technician is the front line of defense for the listening.

- Listen carefully to the customer with your full attention. Do not let your mind wander. Your body language will demonstrate that you are not listening.
- Do not argue with the customer. Show empathy. You do not have to agree with the anger, but you can empathize with it. Ask questions when appropriate. Ask questions that require more than a one-word answer so that the customer is more focused on the issue than his or her anger.
- Avoid coming across as a bureaucrat or blaming others. That just makes the customer angrier.
- Maintain your professionalism at all times no matter what the customer's reaction is.
- Do not let an angry customer ruin your day. Stay calm and do not let their increased emotional level influence your emotional level.
- Be assertive, not passive or aggressive.

The last suggestion is one that most people do not understand. Aggression is dominating a conversation or situation by threatening, bullying, being sarcastic, or showing belittling behavior and/or actions. Many technicians consistently demonstrate aggressive behavior.

Passive behavior involves letting others dominate and by commonly expressing yourself apologetically. Technicians who are passive frequently apologize while the customer is trying to explain the problem. Assertive behavior is being respectful of another person, but not allowing them to take advantage or dominate the situation. This is the middle ground you want to strive for when dealing with customers.

When dealing with an irate customer, you want to be a little bit passive or at least tone down the assertiveness a notch. Once the customer has calmed down a bit, more information about the problem can be gleaned with less anger mixed into the conversation. Dealing with angry customers is just part of a technician's job as it is with anyone who works in a service industry. Consider customers part of the job and never forget that they are the ones who must use the devices that you like to repair.

Key Terms

administrative share (p. 672)
AES (p. 681)
auditing (p. 672)
authorization (p. 670)
biometrics (p. 666)
BitLocker (p. 669)
cookie (p. 674)
EFS (p. 669)
electronic key cards (p. 665)
encryption (p. 672)
firewall (p. 673)

grayware (p. 677)
hidden share (p. 672)
local share (p. 672)
open authentication (p. 679)
phishing (p. 677)
port forwarding (p. 673)
port triggering (p. 673)
proxy server (p. 672)
security policy (p. 664)
shared key authentication
    (p. 680)

social engineering (p. 676)
spam (p. 676)
SSID broadcasting (p. 683)
TKIP (p. 681)
TPM (p. 665)
VPN (p. 677)
WEP (p. 680)
WPAD (p. 673)
WPS (p. 681)

14
Computer and
Network Security

Review Questions

1. Match the security policy component below with a definition from the list that that follows.
   _____ physical access
   _____ acceptable use
   _____ remote access
   _____ password
   a. The specific Web browser that is allowed to be installed
   b. Defines if the code used to access an account such as shared network storage is allowed to be sent using email
   c. The type of security required for a remote VPN connection
   d. The time, day, and year someone entered a network server room
2. List three common physical security resources.

3. List three advantages to electronic keys.

4. List three physical security devices used with computers and networks.

5. Describe two-factor authentication.

6. Why is biometrics more secure than a password?

7. List three biometric devices and an example of how each one might be used.

8. What type of biometric device requires you to speak into a microphone?

9. What keystrokes allow access to lock a Windows XP domain computer?

10. List two BIOS options associated with PC access.

11. List three recommendations for laptop security.

12. List five recommendations for protecting the operating system.

13. What is BitLocker?

14. What two commands could be used to format a disk volume with zeros and then overwrite the sectors with all zeros, all ones, and then a random number?

15. List three recommendations for protecting data stored on the PC.

16. List three options for executing a virus scan.

17. [T | F] A new file is created and stored in an encrypted folder. The file must be manually encrypted since it was added after the folder was encrypted.

18. Describe the security rights for a subfolder when the parent folder is shared.

19. What permissions are required to encrypt another user's file?

20. A Windows Vista computer has been bought. Detail what options are available to move the software and data from the original computer to the new one.

21. What is authorization as it relates to network security?

22. Give an analogy for authorization using nontechnical terms.

23. List three password guidelines you would recommend to one of the company's largest customers.

24. Where are domain user passwords stored?

25. Which type of network environment would be used for a company that has 300 networked computers?

26. Describe the difference between a local policy and a domain policy.

27. List two things needed before configuring a computer for a proxy server.

28. What is the purpose of a firewall?

29. What is the difference between how a software and hardware firewall are implemented?

30. [T | F] A firewalled computer still should have antispyware installed.

31. Detail how to verify if Vista has Windows Firewall enabled.

32. Which Windows Firewall security alert option allows an application access to the Internet and automatically allows the application future Internet access.

33. What Internet Explorer *General* tab section allows customization of search engine providers?

34. What is active scripting and how can it be harmful?

35. What Internet Explorer *Tools* menu option allows active scripting sites to be added?

36. What Internet Explorer *Custom security* radio button allows an option to be used?

37. [T | F] The three choices available for all Internet custom security settings are enable, disable, and prompt.

38. No one can ping a specific Windows Vista or 7 computer. What administrative tool can be used to change this default behavior?

39. What type of unsolicited Internet message records the URLs visited and keystrokes used?

40. Can grayware be transmitted through a Trojan virus?

41. What two items are designed to protect intercepted emails from being easily read? (Choose two.) [Grayware | Antivirus software | PGP | MAC | USS | S/MIME]

42. An unofficial email is sent from your bank asking you to click a link to verify your account information. What type of social engineering is this? [Phishing | Grayware | Spyware | VPN]

43. Give two instances of where a VPN might be beneficial.

44. Match the incident on the left with the action on the right.

    _____ virus   a. BSA
    _____ child exploitation b. police department
    _____ software piracy   c. CERT
    _____ phishing   d. FBI Internet crime center

45. A coworker takes the master software CDs and puts them into his laptop bag and starts to leave for the day. What should you do?

46. What are the two types of authentication used in wireless networks?

47. What is a shared key?

48. What is encryption?

49. Describe the differences among 40-bit, 64-bit, 104-bit, and 128-bit WEPs.

50. How many hexadecimal characters are typed if 64-bit WEP is being used?

51. What are two encryption alternatives to WEP?

52. Why should the default SSID and password be changed during initial configuration?

53. What is Linksys access point's default SSID?

54. [T | F] WEP is enabled by default.

55. [T | F] WEP has not been hacked and is a totally secure encryption method.

56. List three security recommendations for wireless networks.

57. List three recommendations for dealing with irate customers.

Fill-in-the-Blank

1. A/An _____ would commonly detail how to obtain permission to access and modify a shared network resource.

2. _____ are replacements for physical door keys.

3. A/An _____ can be a military personnel ID with medical history included.

4. A/An _____ tag is used inside or outside boxes stored in a warehouse to track inventory.

5. Another name for a DES card is _____, hardware token, authentication token, or authentication card.

6. _____ are found on motherboards and hold security certificates and encryption keys.

7. The term associated with authenticating someone based on a physical attribute is _____.

8. Biometrics are more expensive to implement than the traditional _____ method of authentication.

9. Another name for an eye scanner is _____.

10. The _____ BIOS security login type has full access to change BIOS options.

11. A laptop _____ allows a cable lock or alarm to be installed.

12. BitLocker is on Vista/7 Enterprise and Ultimate, and it requires _____ NTFS disk partitions.

13. `Cipher /w c:` would first write all _____, then all _____, followed by a _____ to all unused sectors; that is why the _____ command should be used first.

14. Windows XP's encryption used with NTFS partitions is called _____.

15. A non-encrypted file is moved into an encrypted folder. The file [is | is not] _____ automatically encrypted.

14
Computer and
Network Security

16. Windows XP allows only _____ users to access a shared folder simultaneously.

17. Allowing access only after someone types in their userid and password is _____.

18. The _____ network environment does not contain a network server.

19. A shared external hard drive folder is an example of a/an _____ share.

20. `C:$` is an example of a/an _____ share.

21. _____ involves logging network events such as how many times and what time of day someone logs into a computer.

22. A/An _____ server protects the address and location of another server.

23. A/An _____ firewall is an application loaded on a particular PC for protection.

24. The _____ *Internet options* tab allows configuration of the home page URL.

25. A/An _____ is data saved when using a Web browser such as the information contained in the banner advertisements.

26. A Vista computer cannot share a locally attached printer. Check and ensure _____ is enabled to remedy this situation.

27. The Internet message types used for marketing are commonly called _____.

28. Another name for badware is _____, which is designed to cause harm to the computer.

29. Unsolicited email that can fill a mail server is commonly called _____.

30. A technique used to trick someone into divulging personal or corporate knowledge is _____.

31. A secure tunnel through the Internet from one network device to a remote network device is a/an _____.

32. _____ is proving a network device has permission to join the wireless network.

33. The term given to the type of authentication used when the MAC address identifies a wireless sender is _____.

34. The _____ authentication method requires WEP.

35. The WEP secret key is normally entered in either the _____ or the _____ format.

36. When the access point periodically sends out the SSID in beacon frames, it is known as _____.

37. WPA uses _____ to improve wireless security.

Hands-On Exercises

1. Encrypting a File and Folder

Objective: To provide security for a particular file and folder, enable encryption using Windows XP, Vista, or 7

Parts: A computer with Windows XP/Vista loaded with at least one NTFS partition

Note: Two user accounts are needed and possibly created for this exercise—one that encrypts a file and the other account to test the encryption. If two user accounts are not available, most of the lab can still be performed or a second user account can be added. This lab is best demonstrated with two accounts that have local administrator rights.

Procedure: Complete the following procedure and answer the accompanying questions.

1. Power on the computer and log on using the userid and password provided by the instructor or lab assistant.

2. Access the Computer Management Console: In XP, *Start → Control Panel → Classic* view → *Administrative Tools → Computer Management*. In Vista/7, click on the *Start* button → *Control Panel → System and Maintenance* (Vista)/*System and Security* (7) → *Administrative Tools →* double-click on *Computer Management*.

3. Expand the *Storage* option and open *Disk Management*.

   How many disk partitions are available? Do any drive partitions use NTFS? If so, how many? Note that if no drive partitions use NTFS, this exercise cannot be completed.

4. Close the *Computer Management* window. Open *Windows Explorer*. Create a text file called *Security Test.txt* and save in the *My Documents* (XP) or *Documents* (Vista/7) folder.

5. Right-click the *Security text.txt* file and select *Properties*. From the *General* tab, select the *Advanced* button.

6. Enable the *Encrypt contents to secure data* and click *OK*. Click the *Apply* button and the warning message shown in Figure 14.16 appears.

7. The default would be to encrypt the Security text.txt file and to encrypt the My Documents/Documents folder. This may not be what you want to do. Select the *Encrypt the file only* radio button and the *OK* button on the screen and the one that follows.

8. In Windows Explorer, click on an empty spot in the right panel.

   Is there any indication the file is encrypted? If so, what is it? You might need to create an unencrypted file to be able to answer this question.

9. In Windows Explorer, access the *Properties* window of the Security text.txt file again and select the *Advanced* button. From the *Advanced Attributes* window, select the *Details* button.

   What user(s) can access the encrypted file?

10. Notice the certificate thumbprint number to the right of the user. EFS can request a digital certificate from a CA (certificate authority) such as a server or if one is not available, EFS can use a self-signed certificate.

    What are the first 16 hexadecimal digits used for the digital certificate? Compare these digits with a fellow classmate. Are the digital certificates the same? If so, why do you think they are the same? If they are different, why do you think they are different?

11. Notice the data recovery agent section at the bottom of the window. One or more users (such as the administrator) can be designated as a data recovery agent. A data recovery agent is issued a recovery certificate used for EFS data recovery on encrypted files. Click *Cancel* on three different windows to exit the *Properties* window.

12. From Windows Explorer, open the *Security Test.txt* file, modify and save it.

    From Windows Explorer, does the file appear to still be encrypted?

13. Log off the computer and log back on as a different user. If a different user does not exist, create one by using the *User Accounts* control panel if possible.

14. Use Windows Explorer, to locate and open the *Security Test.txt* file located under the other user name. Modify the file and save it if possible.

    Were there any problems opening, modifying, or saving the file? In one or more complete sentences, explain what happened and why you think it occurred this way.

14
Computer and
Network Security

15. Log off the computer and log back on as the original user.

16. Access the *My Documents* folder and create a new folder called *Test*. Copy the Security *Test.txt* file into the new *Test* folder.

    Is the copied file encrypted in the *Test* folder?

17. Within the *Test* folder, create a new text file called *Security Test2.txt*.

    Is the newly created file encrypted?

18. Encrypt the *Test* folder using the default encryption setting.

    Does it change anything within the folder? If so, what does it change?

19. Within the *Test* folder, create and save a new file called *Security Test3.txt*.

    Is the newly created file encrypted?

Instructor initials: _____

20. Delete the *Security Test.txt*, *Security Test2.txt*, and *Security Test3.txt* files.

    Was there any indication the files were encrypted when they were deleted?

21. Permanently delete the *Test* folder and any files created in the *My Documents/Documents* folder.

2. Making a Folder Private in XP

Objective: To provide security for a particular folder by making it private within Windows XP

Parts: A computer with Windows XP loaded with at least one NTFS partition

Note: Two user accounts are needed for this exercise—one that makes a folder private and the other account to test process. If two user accounts are not available, most of the lab can still be performed or a second user account can be added. This lab is best demonstrated with two accounts that have local administrator rights.

Procedure: Complete the following procedure and answer the accompanying questions.

1. Power on the computer and log on using the userid and password provided by the instructor or lab assistant.

2. Access the Computer Management Console: *Start → Control Panel → Classic* view → *Administrative Tools → Computer Management*.

3. Expand the *Storage* option and select *Disk Management*.

    How many disk partitions are available? Do any drive partitions use NTFS? If so, how many? Note that if no drive partitions use NTFS, this exercise cannot be completed.

4. Close the *Computer Management* window. Open Windows Explorer. Within the *My Documents* folder, create a subfolder called *Private1*. Create a text file called *Private Text1.txt* and save it to the *Private* folder. Also create a subfolder called *Private2* within *My Documents* and create a text file within the *Private2* folder called *Private Text2.txt*.

5. Using Windows Explorer, right-click the *Private1* subfolder and select *Sharing and Security*.

    What are the three tabs available?

    What is the purpose of the *Customize* tab?

6. Click the *Sharing* tab. Enable the *Make this folder private* checkbox. Click *Apply* and *OK*.

7. Return to Windows Explorer.

    Is there any visual indication that the folder is a private folder?

8. Log off and log on with another user account (preferably one with administrator rights).

9. Access *Windows Explorer* and browse to the other user account's *My Documents* area. Note that for the second account, *My Documents* is called the first user account name followed by the word documents. For example, if my login is CSchmidt, the folder would be called *CSchmidt's Documents*.

    Is the private folder (*Private1*) viewable? Is the private folder accessible? If the private folder is accessible, can you change the document stored there? If the private folder is inaccessible, what message displayed?

10. Try accessing the *Private2* folder.

    Is the *Private2* folder accessible? Can you modify and save the *Private2.txt* document located in *Private2*?

11. Log off as the second user account. Log back on with the first user account.

12. Open Windows Explorer and delete the *Private1* and *Private2* folders.

    Was there any messages that related to the *Private1* folder being private during the deletion? If so, what message(s) appeared?

3. Sharing a Folder in Windows XP

Objective: To create a folder and share its contents with another computer on the same network as well as explore security options

Parts: Two networked computers with Windows XP loaded

Procedure: Complete the following procedure and answer the accompanying questions.

1. Power on the computer and log on using the userid and password provided by the instructor or lab assistant.

2. On the first computer, use Windows Explorer to create two folders under *My Documents*. Name the folders *READ* and *WRITE*.

3. Within the *READ* folder, create a text document called *readme.txt*. Within the *WRITE* folder, create a text folder called *changeme.txt*.

4. Using Windows Explorer, right-click the *READ* folder and select *Sharing and Security*. Select the *Sharing* tab and the *Share this folder on the network* checkbox to enable it. Leave the share name as *READ*. Click *Apply* followed by *OK*.

    How can you tell this folder is shared in Windows Explorer?

5. Using Windows Explorer, right-click the *WRITE* folder and select *Sharing and Security*. Select the *Sharing* tab and the *Share this folder on the network* checkbox to enable it. Also select the *Allow network users to change my files* checkbox to enable it. Leave the share name as *WRITE*. Click *Apply* followed by *OK*.

6. Using Windows Explorer, right-click on *My Computer* and select *Properties*. Select the *Computer Name* tab.

    What is the full computer name as shown in the window?

7. Close the window. On the second computer, click the *Start* button and *Run*. In the textbox type the UNC (universal naming convention) of `\\computer_name\READ` (where `computer_name` is the name you wrote down) and press `Enter`. Note that if you get an error message, you did not type the command correctly, you mistyped the name of the computer, you did not name the share READ correctly, or you mistyped READ.

    What appears on the screen?

8. Double-click the *readme.txt* file.

    Did the file open?

9. Add a few words to the file. Click the *File* menu option and *Save*. Leave the file name the same and click the *Save* button.

    Did the file save?

10. Click *OK* and *Cancel*. Close the file and do not save. Close the *READ* window.

11. Sometimes users would like a drive letter permanently assigned in Windows Explorer to a shared folder on another computer. To do this, open Windows Explorer and select the *Tools* menu option followed by *Map Network Drive*. Accept the drive letter assigned. In the folder name, type `\\computer_name\WRITE` (where `computer_name` is the name you wrote down) and press `Enter`. Note that if you get an error message, you did not type the command correctly, you mistyped the name of the computer, you did not name the share WRITE correctly, or you mistyped WRITE.

    What appears in the address line? Does this correspond to the letter that was assigned?

14

Computer and
Network Security

12. Double-click to open the *changeme.txt* file. Add a few words to the file. Click the *File* menu option and *Save*. Leave the file name the same and click the *Save* button.

Did the file save?

13. Close the file and close the window that contains the file.

14. From Windows Explorer, scroll down until you see *WRITE on 'computer_name' (X:)* where *x:* is the drive letter assigned. You may need to use the horizontal scroll bar to see the entire name. Double-click this option. You are instantly reconnected to the network share. If you want this share to always be there, you have to enable the *Reconnect at logon* check-box when you map the network share.

Instructor initials: _____

15. Close Windows Explorer. On the original computer, use Windows Explorer to delete the *READ* folder.

Did any messages appear? If so, what did they say?

16. Use Windows Explorer to delete the *WRITE* folder.

Have a classmate print and sign their name on your answer sheet proving that they verified the deletion of the *READ* and *WRITE* folders.

4. Sharing a Folder in Windows Vista

Objective: To create a folder and share its contents with another computer on the same network as well as explore security options

Parts: Two networked computers with Windows Vista installed

Procedure: Complete the following procedure and answer the accompanying questions.

1. Power on the computer and log on using the userid and password provided by the instructor or lab assistant.

2. On the first computer, use Windows Explorer to create two folders under *Documents*. Name the folders *READ* and *WRITE*.

3. Within the *READ* folder, create a text document called *readme.txt*. Within the *WRITE* folder, create a text folder called *changeme.txt*.

4. On both computers, determine the computer name by accessing the *System* control panel. Document your findings.

Computer	Computer name
Computer 1	
Computer 2	

5. On both computers, access the *Network and Sharing Center* control panel to document the current sharing and discovery settings.

Computer 1	Computer 2
Network discovery [On | Off]	Network discovery [On | Off]
File sharing [On | Off]	File sharing [On | Off]
Public folder sharing [On (read only, password required) | On (password required) | Off]	Public folder sharing [On (read only, password required) | On (password required) | Off]
Printer sharing [On | Off]	Printer sharing [On | Off]
Password protected sharing [On | Off]	Password protected sharing [On | Off]
Media sharing [On | Off]	Media sharing [On | Off]

6. On both computers, access the *Network and Sharing Center* control panel to enable the following settings: (1) *File sharing*. If prompted, select *Yes, turn on file sharing for all public networks*. (2) *Public folder sharing* (*Turn on sharing so anyone with network access can open, change, and create files* suboption). Click *Apply*. If prompted, select *Yes, turn on network discovery and file sharing for all public networks*.

7. On both computers, ensure that the Vista Sharing Wizard is enabled, using the following process: Type **folder options** in the *Start search* textbox. Select *Folder Options* from the *Programs* list. Select the *View* tab. In the *Advanced Settings* section, locate the *Use Sharing Wizard (Recommended)* option and ensure that it is enabled. Apply changes if necessary.

8. In Windows Explorer on the first computer, right-click the *READ* folder and select *Share*. If a dialog box appears, stating that the folder is already shared, select *Change sharing permissions*. Select the name of the user with whom you want to share this document or click *Add* and add a specific username.

Notes: If you want to share with someone who is not listed, you have to use the *User Accounts* control panel to create the account.

If the local or domain policy requires a password, one should be put on the user account. Best practice is to require passwords on user accounts.

If the *Everyone* username account is selected and password protection is being used, a user account is still needed to gain access.

9. Select *Reader*. Refer to Table 14.14 for a description of the account types.

Table 14.14   **Windows Vista account types**

Account type	Permissions granted
Reader	Can view shared files and execute applications
Contributor	Only for folders to view all files and to add, delete, or modify files added by the user
Co-owner	Gives user full control of the folder

10. Click *Share*.

Document the share path that appears in the window:

_____

Describe the location of each component of the share path.

11. Click *Done*.

12. On the second computer, log on as the user given access on the first computer. If this username does not exist on this computer, log on as an administrator and create the account. Log off and log back in as the user given access on the first computer.

13. Open *Windows Explorer*. Select *Network* in left pane. In the right pane, locate and double-click on the name of the first computer.

14. Double-click through the full path until you reach the *readme.txt* document.

15. Double-click the *readme.txt* file.

Did the file open?

16. Add a few words to the file. Click the *File Save* option from the menu. Leave the filename the same and click the *Save* button.

Did the file save?

17. Close the file and close the window that contains the file.

18. Inside the *Start search* textbox, type the share path documented in Step 10 and press Enter. If an error occurs, check your typing or redo the steps to get a correct share path documented in Step 10.

What happened?

19. Close the window.

14

Computer and
Network Security

20. On the second computer, open *Windows Explorer*. Right-click *Computer* in the left pane and select *Map Network Drive*. Using the *Drive* drop-down menu, select a drive letter. In the *Folder* textbox, type the share path for the READ share documented in Step 10. Click *Finish*. The share opens with the drive letter documented in the path at the top of the window.

Instructor initials: _____

21. Re-access Windows Explorer and locate the drive letter that was just mapped to a network drive. Because Windows Vista share paths are long, a common practice is to use a mapped network drive for the share.

    How can you easily identify mapped drive letters in Windows Explorer (besides a quite high drive letter, in some cases)?

22. Close all windows on the second computer.

23. In Windows Explorer on the first computer, right-click the *WRITE* folder and select *Share*. If a dialog box appears, stating that the folder is already shared, select *Change sharing permissions*. Select the same user name as before.

24. Click the correct name in the *Name* column. Select *Contributor*. Click *Share*.

    Document the share path that appears in the window:

    _____

25. Click *Done*.

26. On the second computer, log on as the user given access on the first computer. Access the *changeme.txt* document.

27. Modify and save the *changeme.txt* file.

28. On the first computer, open the *changeme.txt* file.

    Was the file changed?

Instructor initials: _____

29. On the first computer, create a subfolder under the *READ* folder. Name the folder *SUB_READ*. Create a text file in the *SUB_READ* folder called *sub_read.txt*.

30. On the second computer in *Windows Explorer*, locate and right-click on the *SUB_READ* shared folder. Select *Properties*.

    What attributes does this folder have? [Read-only | Hidden | None]

31. On the second computer in *Windows Explorer*, locate and right-click the *sub_read.txt* file. Select *Properties*. Notice how attributes, by default, inherit the parent folder's attributes.

Instructor initials: _____

32. On the second computer, remove the mapped drive by using *Windows Explorer* to locate the mapped drive letter under *Computer* in the left pane. Right-click on the mapped drive and select *Disconnect*.

33. On the first computer, permanently delete the *READ* and *WRITE* folders and all files and subfolders contained within them.

34. On the first computer, put the sharing and discovery settings back to the original configuration. Refer to the documentation in Step 5. Show your lab partner the documented settings and the current configuration. Have your lab partner to use the table that follows to document that the computer has been put back to the original configuration.

Computer 1 (permanently deleted folders/sharing settings)
Printed name of lab partner
Signature of lab partner

35. On the second computer, put the sharing and discovery settings back to the original configuration. Refer to the documentation in Step 5. Show your lab partner the documented settings and the current configuration. Have your lab partner to use the table that follows to document that the computer has been put back to the original configuration.

Computer 2 (permanently deleted folders/sharing settings)

Printed name of lab partner

Signature of lab partner

36. On both computers, delete any user accounts that have been created. Note that you must be logged in as an administrator in order to delete accounts.

5. Sharing a Folder in Windows 7

Objective: To be able to share a folder and understand the permissions associated with a network share

Parts: Access to two Windows 7 computers with a user ID that has administrator rights

Procedure: Complete the following procedure and answer the accompanying questions.

1. Turn on both computers and verify that the operating system loads. Log in to Windows 7 using the userid and password that has full administrator rights and that is provided by your instructor or lab assistant.

2. On the first computer, use Windows Explorer to created two folders under *Documents*. Name the folders *READ* and *WRITE*.

3. Within the *READ* folder, create a text document called *readme.txt*. Within the *WRITE* folder, create a text file called *changeme.txt*.

4. On both computers, determine the computer name by accessing the *System* control panel link. Determine the IP addresses of both computers using the **ipconfig** command. Document your findings.

Computer	Computer name	IP address
Computer 1		
Computer 2		

5. On both computers, access the *Network and Sharing Center* control panel link to document the current *Advanced Sharing Settings*.

Computer 1	Computer 2
Network discovery [On | Off]	Network discovery [On | Off]
Media sharing [On | Off]	Media sharing [On | Off]
Public folder sharing [On (read only, password required) | On (password required) | Off]	Public folder sharing [On (read only, password required) | On (password required) | Off]
Printer sharing [On | Off]	Printer sharing [On | Off]
Password protected sharing [On | Off]	Password protected sharing [On | Off]
Media streaming [On | Off]	Media streaming [On | Off]

6. On both computers, enable the following settings.

   • File and printer sharing
   • Public folder sharing
   • Network discovery

7. On both computers, ensure that the Windows 7 Use Sharing Wizard is enabled by typing **folder options** in the *Search programs and files* Start button option. Select the *Folder Options* item from the resulting list → *View* tab → locate the *Advanced Settings* section → locate the *Use Sharing Wizard (Recommended)* option and ensure it is enabled. Apply changes as necessary.

   What is the current setting for the *Use Sharing Wizard* option? [Enabled | Disabled]

8. In Windows Explorer on the first computer, right-click on the *READ* folder → *Properties* → *Sharing* tab.

   Document the share network path that appears in the window.

   _____

9. Select the *Advanced sharing* button → enable the *Share this folder* checkbox → select the *Caching* button.

10. Select the *Configure Offline Availability for a Shared Folder* help link.

    What is the purpose of caching?

    [Y | N] Is offline availability enabled by default for a shared folder?

    What command can be used from a command prompt to configure caching options for a shared folder?

11. Close the help window.

12. In the Offline Settings window, leave the option to the default.

    What is the default setting for offline access?

13. Click *Ok*. In the Advanced Sharing window, select the *Permissions* button. Notice how the Everyone group lists by default.

Notes: If you want to share with someone who is not listed, use the *User Accounts* control panel to create the account, then select that account name in the Permissions window.

       If the local or domain policy requires a password, one should be put on the user account. Best practice is to require passwords on all user accounts.

       If the Everyone user account is selected and password protection is being used, a user account is still needed to gain access.

   What permissions are enabled by default for the Everyone group? [Full control | Change | Read]

14. Click *OK* on the two windows and then click the *Close* button.

15. Open the *Computer Management* console. Expand *System Tools* and *Shared Folders*. Click on *Shares* in the left panel. The READ share lists in the right panel. If the share is missing, re-do this lab from the beginning. Close the *Computer Management* window.

16. On the second computer, log on as the user given access in Step 13 or use the userid and password provided by the instructor or lab assistant.

17. On the second computer, open *Windows Explorer*. Select *Network* in the left panel. In the right panel, locate and double-click on the name of the first computer.

Notes: If the computer does not list, click on the *Start* button and in the *Search programs and files* textbox, type **\\computer_name** (where *computer_name* is the name of the first computer). Press (Enter).

18. On the second computer, locate the *READ* share and the *readme.txt* document. Double-click on the *readme.txt* file.

    [Y | N] Did the file open?

19. Add a few words to the file. Click the *File* → *Save* menu option. Leave the filename the same and click the *Save* button. When asked if you want to replace the file, click *Yes*.

    [Y | N] Did the file save?

20. Close the file and close the window that contains the file.

21. On the second computer inside the *Search programs and files* Start button option, type the share path documented in Step 8 and press (Enter). If an error occurs, check your typing or redo the steps to get a correct share path documents in Step 8.

    What happened?

22. Close the window. On the second computer, open *Windows Explorer*. Right-click *Computer* in the left panel and select *Map Network Drive*. Use the *Drive* drop-down menu to select a drive letter. In the *Folder* textbox, type the share path for the READ share documented in

Step 8. Click *Finish*. The share opens with the drive letter documented in the path at the top of the window. Note that you may have to expand the left panel to see the drive letter.

Instructor initials: _____

23. On the second computer, re-access *Windows Explorer* and locate the drive letter that was just mapped to a network drive. Because Windows share paths can be lengthy, a common practice is to use a mapped network drive for the share.

    How can you easily identify mapped drive letters in Windows Explorer (besides a quite high drive letter in some cases)?

24. Close all windows on the second computer.

25. In Windows Explorer on the first computer, right-click the *WRITE* folder → *Properties* → *Sharing* tab.

    Document the share network path that appears in the window.

    _____

26. Select the *Advanced Sharing* button → enable *Share this folder* checkbox.

27. Select the *Permissions* button.

28. Select the correct username or group and enable the *Change Allow* checkbox. Click *OK* on two windows and then click the *Close* button.

29. On the second computer, locate the *changeme.txt* document.

30. Modify and save the *changeme.txt* file.

31. On the first computer, open the *changeme.txt* file.

    [Y | N] Was the file changed?

Instructor initials: _____

32. On the second computer, try changing the name of the *changeme.txt* file.

    [Y | N] Could you change the name of the *changeme.txt* file?

33. Verify whether the filename changed on the first computer.

    [Y | N] Did the filename change on the first computer? If so, what is the new name?

34. On the second computer, right-click the *WRITE* folder and select *Always available offline*.

    What indication is given that a folder is available offline?

    [Y | N] Can a particular file be given this same attribute?

35. Disconnect the second computer from the network by removing the network cable from the network adapter.

36. From a command prompt on the second computer, ping the first computer using the IP address documented in Step 4.

    [Y | N] Did the ping succeed?

37. So with no network access, open the *WRITE* folder and access the *changeme.txt* file. Modify the file and save it.

38. Reconnect the second computer to the network.

39. From the first computer, access the *WRITE* folder.

    [Y | N] Were the document changes made when computer two was disconnected from the network saved on the first computer?

40. On the second computer, re-access the *changeme.txt* file and try to permanently delete the file.

    [Y | N] Could you permanently delete the *changeme.txt* file?

41. On the first computer, create a subfolder under the *READ* folder. Name the folder *SUB_READ*. Create a text file in the *SUB_READ* folder called *sub_file.txt*.

42. On the second computer, locate and right-click on the *SUB_READ* shared folder. Select *Properties*.

    What attributes does this folder have? [Read-only | Hidden | None]

14

Computer and
Network Security

43. On the second computer in *Windows Explorer*, locate the *sub_file.txt* file. Select *Properties*. What attributes, if any, are shown as enabled by default? [Read-only | Hidden | None]

44. Click *Cancel*. Try to modify the *sub_file.txt* file.

   [Y | N] Could you change the sub_file.txt file?

Instructor initials: _____

45. On the second computer, remove the mapped drive (and any that you created on your own) by using *Windows Explorer* to locate the mapped drive letter under *Computer* in the left panel. Right-click on the mapped drive and select *Disconnect*.

46. On the first computer, permanently delete the *READ* and *WRITE* folders and all files and subfolders contained within them.

47. On the first computer, put the *Advanced sharing settings* options back to the original configuration. Refer to the documentation in Step 5. Put the *Use Sharing Wizard* back to the original setting as documented in Step 7. Show your lab partner the documented settings and the current configuration. Have your lab partner use the table that follows to document that the computer has been put back to the original configuration.

Computer 1 (permanently deleted folders/sharing settings)
Printed name of lab partner
Signature of lab partner

48. On the second computer, put the *Advanced sharing settings* options back to the original configuration. Refer to the documentation in Step 5. Put the *Use Sharing Wizard* back to the original setting as documented in Step 7. Show your lab partner the documented settings and the current configuration. Have your lab partner use the table that follows to document that the computer has been put back to the original configuration.

Computer 2 (permanently deleted folders/sharing settings)
Printed name of lab partner
Signature of lab partner

49. On both computers, delete any user accounts that have been created. Note that you must be logged in as an administrator in order to delete user accounts.

6. Creating a Local Security Policy for Passwords

Objective: To provide additional security by requiring certain passwords parameters as a local computer security policy

Parts: A computer with Windows XP Professional/Vista/7 loaded

Procedure: Complete the following procedure and answer the accompanying questions.

Notes: Local administrator rights are required for this lab. The computer should be part of a workgroup, not a domain. However, even though domain policy requirements override local policy, the lab may still work as written.

1. Power on the computer and log on using the userid and password provided by the instructor or lab assistant.

2. Access the *Local Security Policy Console*: *Start* → *Administrative Tools* control panel → double-click *Local Security Policy*.

3. Expand the *Account Policies* option.

   What two options are available?

4. Click the *Password Policy* subcategory. Table 14.15 details each of these options.

Table 14.15 **Windows password policy option descriptions**

Option	Description
Enforce password history	The number of unique and new passwords must be used before an old password can be reused.
Maximum password age	The number of days a password has to be used before it has to be changed.
Minimum password age	The fewest number of days a user has to use the same password.
Minimum password length	The fewest number of characters required for the password. The least the password can be is zero. The more characters required, the better the security. A common setting is seven or eight. Fourteen characters is the most you can require in this setting.
Passwords must meet complexity requirements	Sets higher standards for the password such as the password cannot be the username, must be six characters or more, requires uppercase and lowercase letters, numerals, and symbols such as # or !.
Store password using reversible encryption for all users in the domain	If enabled, passwords are stored using reversible encryption. Used only if an application uses a protocol that requires knowledge of a user password for authentication purposes.

Use Table 14.16 to document the current settings.

Table 14.16 **Current password policy settings**

Option	Current setting
Enforce password history	
Maximum password age	
Minimum password age	
Minimum password length	
Passwords must meet complexity requirements	
Store password using reversible encryption for all users in the domain	

5. Change the password policy settings to the options shown in Table 14.17.

Table 14.17 **New password policy settings**

Option	New setting
Enforce password history	one password remembered
Minimum password length	seven characters
Passwords must meet complexity requirements	Enabled

6. Create a new user account by clicking the *Start* button → *User Accounts* control panel → *Manage another account* (7)/*Create a new account* (XP/Vista/7) link → type **Teststudent** for the new account name → *Next* and *Limited* radio button (XP)/*Standard user* (Vista/7) → *Create account* button. The Teststudent icon appears in the window.

What indication is given that a policy is in place?

7. Log off as the current user. Log in as *Teststudent*.

What message appeared upon logon?

8. In the *New Password* and *Confirm New Password* textboxes, type **test** followed by clicking the *OK* button (XP) or right arrow (Vista/7).

What requirements display?

14

Computer and
Network Security

9. Click *OK*. In the *New Password* and *Confirm New Password* textboxes, type `Tester9#` and click *OK*.

   What message displays?

10. Log off as *Teststudent* and log back in using the original user account.

11. Return to the *Security Policy* console. Expand *Local Policies* and select *Audit Policy*.

    What is the current setting for audit account logon events? [No auditing | Success | Failure | Success and Failure]

    List three other items that can be audited.

12. Double-click the *Audit account logon events* option. The two options are success and failure and both options can be enabled. Success logs every time someone logs into the computer. Failure logs every failed logon attempt. Enable both the *Success* and *Failure* checkboxes → *Apply* button → *OK* button.

13. Log off as the current user and log in as *Teststudent* using the password of *Tester?1*.

    What message appeared?

14. Click *OK* and this time type the correct password of *Tester9#*. Log off as Teststudent. Log back on as the original computer user.

15. To see events that have been enabled and logged, click the *Start* button → *Administrative Tools* control panel → *Event Viewer* → *Security* option in the left panel (XP). The top three events show the current successful login and the failure/successful login of *Teststudent* user.

    In Vista/7, expand the *Windows Logs* category on the left and select *Security*. Scroll down to select a line that shows as an *Audit Failure*, as shown in Figure 14.17.

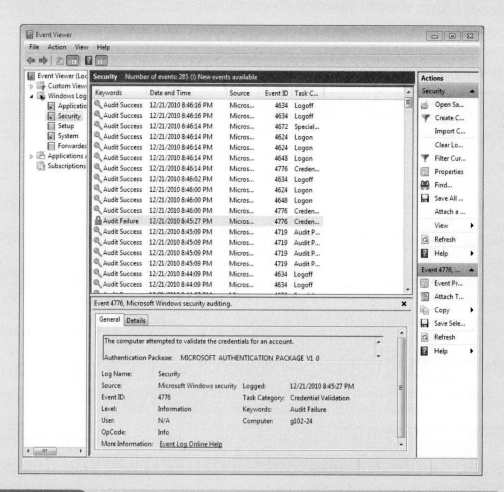

Figure 14.17   **Windows 7 *Event Viewer* Security log window**

16. Close *Event Viewer*. Return to the *Security Policy* console. Set the *Audit account logon* events setting back to the original setting. Refer to Step 11 for the original settings.

Have a classmate verify your setting and print and sign their name on your answer sheet.

17. Configure the *Password Policy* settings back to their original configuration. Refer to Step 4 for the original settings.

Have a classmate verify your setting and print and sign their name on your answer sheet.

18. Expand *Local Policies*. Select the *User Rights Assignment* option. Use Table 14.18 to document the current settings for various options.

Table 14.18   **Windows user rights assignment settings**

Option	Current setting
Access this computer from the network	
Allow log on through Remote Desktop Services	
Deny log on locally	
Force shutdown from a remote system	
Generate security audits	
Load and unload device drivers	
Restore files and directories	
Shut down the system	
Take ownership of files or other objects	

19. Select the *Security* option in the left panel. Use Table 14.19 to document the current settings for various options.

Table 14.19   **Windows security settings**

Option	Current setting
Accounts: Administrator account status	
Accounts: Guest account status	
Accounts: Rename administrator account	
Devices: Allow to format and eject removable media	
Devices: Prevent users from installing printer drivers	
Interactive logon: Message text for users attempting to log on	
Interactive logon: Prompt user to change password before expiration	
Interactive logon: Require smart card	
Network access: Let Everyone permissions apply to anonymous users	
Network access: Shares that can be accessed anonymously	
Network security: Force logoff when logon hours expire	
Shutdown: Allow system to be shut down without having to log on	

20. Close the Security Policy console. Access *User Accounts* and remove the *Teststudent* user account.

Have a classmate verify your setting and print and sign their name on your answer sheet.

21. Close the *User Accounts* window and reboot the computer.

14

Computer and Network Security

7. Configuring a Secure Wireless Network

Objective: To be able to configure a secure wireless AP (access point) or router and attach a wireless client

Parts: One wireless access point or router

A computer with an integrated wireless NIC or a wireless NIC installed as well as an Ethernet NIC

One straight-through cable

Procedure: Complete the following procedure and answer the accompanying questions.

1. Obtain the documentation for the wireless AP or router from the instructor or Internet.

2. Reset the wireless AP or router as directed by the wireless device manufacturer.

   Document the current Ethernet NIC IPv4 settings. [DHCP | Static IP address]

   If a static IP address is assigned, document the IP address, subnet mask, default gateway, and DNS configuration settings.

3. Attach a straight-through cable from the computer's Ethernet NIC to the wireless AP or router.

4. Power on the computer and log on, if necessary.

5. Configure the computer with a static IP address or DHCP, as directed by the wireless device manufacturer.

6. Open a Web browser and configure the wireless AP or router with the following parameters:
   - Change the default SSID
   - Disable SSID broadcasting enabled for this lab
   - Configure the most secure encryption and authentication supported by both the wireless NIC client and the wireless AP or router
   - Change the default password used to access the wireless AP or router

   Document the settings after you have configured them:

   SSID:

   SSID broadcasting disabled? [YES | No]

   Password for wireless device access:

   Type of security used:

7. Save the wireless AP or router configuration.

8. Disconnect the Ethernet cable.

9. Enable the wireless NIC and configure it for the appropriate SSID.

10. Configure the wireless NIC for a static IP address or DHCP, as directed by the wireless AP/router manufacturer.

11. Open a Web browser and access the wireless AP or router. If access cannot be obtained, troubleshoot as necessary or reset the wireless AP or router to default configurations and restart the lab.

    What frequency (channel) is being used by the wireless AP or router and the wireless NIC for connectivity?

12. Show the instructor the connectivity.

Instructor initials: _____

13. Open a command prompt and type **netsh wlan show settings** to see the wireless network settings.

14. If Windows XP is being used, use the **sc query w2csvc** command. (Vista does not have Wireless Zero Control service.)

15. Reset the wireless AP or router to the default configuration settings.

16. Reset the computer(s) to the original configuration settings.

Instructor initials: _____

Internet Discovery

Objective: To become familiar with researching memory chips using the Internet

Parts: A computer with Internet access

Questions: Use the Internet to answer the following questions.

1. Access the Internet Crime Complaint Center to answer the questions that follow. At the time of writing, the URL is http://www.ic3.gov/.

   What are three recommendations from the site list in regards to spam?

   What is Internet crime according to this Web site? Write the answer and the URL at which you found the answer.

2. Access the U.S. Computer Emergency Readiness Team Web site and access the technical user link to answer the questions that follow. At the time of writing, the URL is http://www.us-cert.gov/.

   What are the top three high rated vulnerabilities for the past week?

   List three recommendations made by this site for a new computer being connected to a network.

3. Access the National Institute of Standards and Technology Computer Security Resource Center Web site to answer the questions that follow.

   Access the glossary of security terms. Windows allows programming of ACLs (access control lists). What are they and how do they relate to computer security?

   Select the CSRC site map link. List one security section that you find interesting and define one term from that section that is not in the chapter.

4. Access the Business Software Alliance Web site to answer the questions that follow.

   According to the Web site, what percentage of software installed is pirated?

   Access the *Tools and Resources* link. What tool does the Business Software Alliance provide or recommend that might help a high school or college ensure that their software is legal?

Soft Skills

Objective: To enhance and fine-tune a future technician's ability to listen, communicate in both written and oral form, and support people who use computers in a professional manner

Activities:

1. Prepare a presentation on any topic related to network security. The topic can relate to wired or wireless. Share your presentation with the class.

2. In small groups, find a security policy on the Internet or use any of your school's computer policies. Critique the policy and make recommendations for how the policy can provide for stronger security.

Critical Thinking Skills

Objective: To analyze and evaluate information as well as apply learned information to new or different situations

Activities:

1. Create a wired workgroup network. Determine what security policies will be enforced before users are created. Document the security policy. Also determine what activities are logged. Share folders between the computers with security implemented. Document the shares and policies. View and capture activities logged and include with the documentation. Present your design, implementation, and monitoring to the class.

2. In teams, build a wired and wireless network with security in place. Document the security as if you were presenting it to a home network customer who hired you to build and implement it.

14

**Computer and
Network Security**

Glossary

1.44MB disk A high density 3.5-inch floppy disk having both write-protect and high density windows that cannot be used in 720KB floppy drives.

3DNow! An AMD set of instructions that allow one particular instruction to be executed by multiple items.

56Kbps modem A modem that produces higher transmission speeds and uses traditional phone lines. Actual modem speed is determined by the number of analog to digital conversions that occur through the phone system.

A

AAC (advanced audio compression) A sound file format that provides file compression.

AC (alternating current) The type of electrical power from a wall outlet.

access point A component of a wireless network that accepts associations from wireless network cards.

access time The amount of time it takes to retrieve data from memory or a device.

AC circuit tester A device used to check a wall outlet's wiring.

ACPI (advanced configuration and power interface) Allows the motherboard and operating system to control the power needs and operation modes of various devices.

ACR (advanced communications riser) Technology developed by a group of companies including AMD, VIA Technologies, Motorola, and 3Com. ACR not only supports audio, modem, and networking, but also DSL modems. It is found on motherboards and supports AMD processors.

active listening An effective communication technique used to ensure what the speaker says is accurately received.

active matrix A technology used in LCD monitors where displays have a transistor for each pixel. Contrast with passive matrix.

active terminator A type of end to a SCSI chain that allows for longer cable distance and provides correct voltage for SCSI signals.

actuator arm Holds the read/write heads over hard disk platters.

adapter Electronic circuit card that connects into an expansion slot. Also called a controller, card, controller card, circuit card, circuit board, and adapter board.

Add Printer Wizard A Windows utility used to install a local or network printer.

ad hoc mode Used in wireless networks where no access point is used. Instead, wireless devices connect to one another.

administrative share A share created by Microsoft for drive volumes and the folder that contains the majority of Windows files. An administrative share has a dollar sign at the end of its name.

ADSL (Asymmetrical DSL) Provides speeds up to 8.4Mbps, but 1.5M is the most common rate. Provides faster downloads than uploads.

Aero See *Windows Aero*.

AES (Advanced Encryption Standard) Used in wireless networks and offers encryption with 128-, 192-, and 256-bit encryption keys.

AGP (accelerated graphics port) An extension of the PCI bus (a port) that speeds up 3-D graphics in software applications. AGP is used for video adapters.

Alerts An option used to select object and counters, set when tracking is to begin, set how often the system is monitored, and set how alerts are to be handled. By default, alerts are sent to *Event Viewer's* application event log.

ALU (arithmetic logic unit) The part of the microprocessor that does mathematical manipulations.

amp A measurement of current.

amplification To increase the strength of the sound. Amplification output is measured in watts. Sound cards usually have built-in amplification to drive the speakers. Many speakers have built-in amplifiers to boost the audio signal for a fuller sound.

AMR (audio/modem riser) A motherboard connector used for a combination audio and modem adapter. Motherboard manufacturers use AMR as an option to offer a different version of the same motherboard.

antenna A component that attaches to wireless devices or is integrated into them. An antenna is used to radiate or receive radio waves.

antenna gain A measure of an antenna's output power in a particular direction compared to output power produced in any direction by an isotropic antenna.

antistatic wrist strap A strap connecting the technician to the computer that equalizes the voltage potential between the two to prevent ESD.

aperture grille An alternative to the shadow mask used by Sony in its Trinitron monitors that uses wires instead of holes to direct the color beams to the front of the monitor.

APIC (advanced programmable interrupt controller) A type of controller that supports more interrupts than the traditional 16 (24 is one example) and allows interrupt sharing between devices. There are two common types: LAPIC and I/O APIC. LAPIC is normally integrated into each CPU and has its own timer, whereas the I/O APIC is used throughout any of the peripheral buses and is integrated into the chipset.

APIPA (automatic private IP addressing) A Microsoft Windows option that allows a computer to automatically receive an IP address from the range 169.254.0.1 to 169.254.255.254.

application layer Layer seven of the OSI model that defines how applications and the computer interact with a network. Also, it is the top layer of the TCP/IP model.

application log An *Event Viewer* log that displays events associated with a specific program. Programmers who design software decide which events to display in the *Event Viewer's* application log.

Apply button Located in bottom right corner of a dialog box; clicking it saves any changes the user has applied to the window.

architecture A set of rules governing the physical structure of the computer. It regulates bit transfer rate, adapter SETUP configuration, and so on.

archive attribute A designation that can be attached to a file that marks whether the file has changed since it was last backed up by a software program. The RESTORE, XCOPY, and MSBACKUP commands use the archive attribute as well as third-party backup software applications.

aspect ratio An LCD characteristic that describes a ratio of monitor width compared to height. An LCD with an aspect ratio of 16:9 is a wide screen monitor in that it is wider than it is high.

ASR (automated system recovery) A means of creating a bootable disk with Windows XP using the Windows *Backup* tool. It replaced the ERD (emergency repair disk) used by NT and 2000 Professional.

asynchronous Transmissions that do not require a clock signal, but instead use extra bits to track the beginning and end of the data.

ATAPI (AT attachment packet interface) The hardware side of the IDE specification that supports devices like CD and tape drives.

ATA standard (AT attachment) The original IDE interface that supported two drives. Now in two types—PATA and SATA.

attenuation The amount of signal loss for a radio wave at it travels through air.

ATTRIB A command used to designate a file as hidden, archived, read-only, or as a system file.

ATX12V A specific type of ATX power supply for Intel's Pentium 4.

auditing Tracking network events such as logging onto the network domain. Auditing is sometimes called event logging or simply logging.

authentication The process of determining that a network device or person has permission to access a network.

authorization Controls what network resources such as file, folders, printers, video conferencing equipment, fax machines, scanners, and so on can be accessed and used by a legitimate network user or device.

auto-switching A type of power supply that monitors the incoming voltage from the wall outlet and automatically switches itself accordingly. Auto-switching power supplies accept voltages from 100 to 240VAC at 50 to 60Hz. They are popular in laptops and great for international travel.

average access time The time required to find and retrieve data on a disk or in memory.

average seek time The time required for a drive to move from one location to another.

B

backbone Network part that connects multiple buildings, floors, networks, and so on.

backlight A fluorescent lamp or LEDs that are always on for an LCD.

back side bus Connections between the CPU and the L2 cache.

bandwidth The communications channel width that defines its capacity for carrying data.

bank One or more memory chips that work together to transfer data to and from the CPU and a device.

baseband A networking technology where the entire cable bandwidth is used to transmit a digital signal.

baseline A snapshot of a computer's performance (memory, CPU usage, etc.) during normal operations (before a problem or slowdown is apparent).

basic disk A Windows term for a drive that has been partitioned and formatted.

basic storage A Windows term for a partition. Contrast with dynamic storage.

batch file A file that has the extension of *BAT* that executes multiple commands when a single command is entered at a prompt.

baud The number of times an analog signal changes in one second. If a signal is sent that changes 600 times in one second, the device communicates at 600 baud. Today's signaling methods (modulation techniques to be technically accurate) allow modems to send several bits in one cycle, so it is more accurate to talk in bits per second rather than baud.

Berg A type of power connector that extends from the computer's power supply to various devices.

bi-directional printing Printing that occurs from left to right and right to left to provide higher printing speeds.

biometrics A device used to authenticate someone based on one or more physical traits such as a fingerprint, eyeball (retina), or hand, or a behavioral trait such as voice or signature.

BIOS (basic input/output system) A chip that contains computer software that locates the operating system, POST, and important hardware configuration parameters. Also called ROM BIOS, Flash BIOS, or system BIOS.

bit An electrically charged 1 or 0.

BitLocker A Microsoft utility that encrypts an entire disk volume, including operating system files, user files, and swap files. The utility requires two disk partitions at a minimum.

blackout A total loss of AC power.

Bluetooth A wireless technology for personal area networks.

Blu-ray A type of optical disk technology that uses a blue laser instead of a red laser; used in CD/DVD drives to achieve higher disc capacities.

boot A term used to describe the process of a computer coming to a usable condition.

boot partition A type of partition found in Windows that contains the operating system. The boot partition can be in the same partition as the system partition, which is the part of the hard drive that holds hardware-specific files.

boot sector Previously called DBR or DOS boot record, this section of a disk contains information about the system files (the files used to boot the operating system).

boot sector virus A virus program placed in a computer's boot sector code, which can then load into memory. Once in RAM, the virus takes control of computer operations. The virus can spread to installed drives and drives located on a network.

boot volume A storage unit that contains the majority of the operating system files. Can be the same volume as the system volume, which contains the boot files.

bps (bits per second) The number of 1s and 0s transmitted per second.

broadband A networking technology where the cable bandwidth is divided into multiple channels; thus, the cable can carry simultaneous voice, video, and data.

broadcast See *broadcast address*.

broadcast address IP address used to communicate with all devices on a particular network.

brownout A loss of AC power due to electrical circuits being overloaded.

browser A program that views Web pages across the Internet. Common Web browsers are Internet Explorer, Netscape Navigator, Opera, and NeoPlanet.

BSS (basic service set) A wireless network configuration where a wireless access point is used to connect wireless devices together.

bus Electronic lines that allow 1s and 0s to move from one place to another.

bus frequency multiple A motherboard setting for the internal microprocessor speed.

busmaster DMA Another name for UDMA (ultra DMA); allows the IDE interface to control the PCI bus for faster transfers.

bus-mastering A feature that allows an adapter to take over the external data bus from the microprocessor to execute operations with another bus-mastering adapter.

bus speed The rate at which a computer pathway used for transmitting 1s and 0s operates.

bus topology Network wherein all devices connect to a single cable. If the cable fails, the network is down.

byte Eight bits grouped together as a basic unit.

C

CAB file A shortened name for a cabinet file. The file holds multiple files or drivers that are compressed into a single file. CAB files are normally located in the i386 folder on the Windows CD.

cable modem A modem that connects to the cable TV network.

cable select A setting used on IDE devices when a special cable determines which device is the master and which one is the slave.

cache memory Designed to increase microprocessor operations.

Cancel button Located in bottom right corner of the window; clicking it ignores any changes the user has made and restores parameters to their original state.

capacitive keyboard A reliable, but more expensive, keyboard.

capacitor An electronic component that can hold a charge.

CardBay A PC Card standard that allows laptop computers to be compatible with USB and IEEE 1394 serial interfaces. It is backward compatible and does not require a driver or support by the operating system.

CardBus An upgraded standard from the 16-bit local bus standard to the PCMCIA that allows 32-bit transfers at up to 33MHz speeds.

CAS (column address strobe) In a memory module, CAS indicates how long (in clock cycles) for the processor to move on to the next memory address. Therefore, the smaller the number, the better (i.e., faster). Also known as CAS latency, or CASL.

CD (compact disc) Holds large amounts of data, such as audio, video, and software applications.

CD Also known as `CHDIR` command. Used from a command prompt to change into a different directory.

CD drive A drive that holds discs (CDs) that have data, music, or software applications on them.

CD-R (compact disc-recordable) A CD drive that can create a compact disc by writing once to the disc. See also *WORM*.

CD-RW (compact disc rewritable) A CD drive that can write data multiple times to a particular disc.

Certified Wireless USB A type of USB symbol that supports high-speed, secure wireless connectivity between a USB device and a PC at speeds of 480Mbps (~10 feet) or 110Mbps (~30 feet). Wireless USB uses ultra-wideband, low-power radio over a range of 3.1 to 10.5GHz.

channel ID Used in wireless networks to define the frequency used to transmit and receive.

checkbox Provides the user the ability to enable an option or not. Clicking in the checkbox places a check mark that enables the option. Clicking again removes the check mark and disables the option.

chipset One or more motherboard chips that work in conjunction with the processor to allow certain computer features, such as motherboard memory and capacity.

CHKDSK A program that locates clusters that are disassociated from the appropriate data file.

CHS addressing (cylinders heads sectors addressing) The method the BIOS uses to talk to the hard drive based on the number of cylinders, heads, and sectors of the drive.

clamping speed The time elapsed from an overvoltage condition to when surge protection begins.

clamping voltage The voltage level at which the surge protector begins to protect the computer.

cleaning A printing process term used by Hewlett-Packard to describe the step when any residual toner is removed from the drum. The electrophotographic process equivalent term is clean.

clean install Loading an operating system on a computer that does not already have one installed.

client/server network A network environment where a computer (the server) has something (a file, a printed document, or an application, for example) that is given to another network device (the client).

clock An electronic component that provides timing signals to all motherboard components. A PC's clock is normally measured in MHz.

clock speed The rate at which timing signals are sent to the motherboard components (normally measured in MHz).

Close button Located in upper-right corner of a dialog box with an X, it is used to close the dialog box.

CL rating (CAS latency rating) The amount of time in clock cycles that passes before the CPU moves on to the next memory address.

cluster The minimum amount of space that one saved file occupies.

CMD A command issued from the Run utility in Windows to bring up a command prompt window.

CMOS (complementary metal oxide semiconductor) A special type of memory on the motherboard in which Setup configuration is saved.

CNR (communications network riser) Intel's design that allows integration of network, sound, and modem functions. It shares a PCI slot and is located right beside or between the other motherboard expansion slots.

coaxial cable Type of network cabling used in older Ethernet networks as well as mainframe and minicomputer connections. Has a copper core, surrounded by insulation and shielding from EMI.

cold boot Executes when the computer is turned on with the power switch. Executes POST.

command-based switching A technology used with SATA-PMs that limits the host adapter or port to issuing one command at a time to a single eSATA device. Contrast with FIS.

command prompt Otherwise known as a prompt. A text-based environment where commands are entered.

command switch An option used when working from a command prompt that allows a command to be controlled or operated on differently.

CompactFlash (CF) A type of removable flash memory storage that can be inserted into many devices such as disk drives, cameras, PDAs, and tablet PCs.

component/RGB video Three RCA jacks commonly found on TVs, DVD players, and projectors. The three connections are for luminescence or brightness and two jacks for color difference signals.

compression Compacting a file or folder to take up less disk space.

computer Unit that performs tasks using software applications. Also known as a microcomputer or PC.

Computer Management console A Windows tool that displays a large group of tools on one screen.

conditioning A term used by Hewlett-Packard to describe the process where the laser printer drum receives a uniform electrical charge. The equivalent electrophotographic term is charge.

conditioning roller Used in a laser printer to generate a large uniform negative voltage to be applied to the drum.

CONFIG.SYS A file that contains multiple lines used to control or configure the computer environment such as memory, CD-ROM, screen display, and so on. The file is no longer required in today's operating systems.

continuity A resistance measurement to see if a wire is good or broken.

contrast ratio An LCD characteristic that describes the difference in light intensity between the brightest white and the darkest black. A higher contrast ratio is a better characteristic.

Control Panel A Windows icon that allows computer configuration such as add or remove software, add or remove hardware, configure a screen saver, adjust the monitor, configure the mouse, install networking components, and so on.

CONVERT A command issued from a command prompt that changes an older file system into NTFS.

cookie A program written to collect information that is stored on the hard drive. This information could include your preferences when visiting a Web site, banner ads that change, or what Web sites you have visited lately.

COPY A command used from a command prompt to transfer one or more files from one place to another.

COPY CON: A command used to copy the characters entered from a keyboard (the console). An archaic way to create batch files.

counter A specific measurement for an object in Windows System Monitor tool.

counter log A Performance Tool option used to create a log file using selectable objects and counters.

cpi (characters per inch) A printing measurement that defines how many characters are printed within an inch. The larger the CPI, the smaller the font size.

cps (characters per second) The number of characters a printer prints in one second.

CPU See *processor*.

CPU bus frequency A motherboard setting for external microprocessor speed.

CPU speed The rate in which the CPU operates. It is the speed of the front side bus multiplied by the multiplier. Normally measured in MHz or GHz.

CPU throttling Reducing the clock frequency in order to reduce power consumption.

CRC (cyclic redundancy check) An advanced method of data error checking.

C-RIMM (continuity RIMM) A blank module used to fill empty memory slots on the motherboard when using RIMMs, because the memory banks must be tied together. RIMMs (a trademark of Rambus, Inc.) are packaged RDRAMs (Rambus DRAM).

crosstalk A type of EMI where signals from one wire interfere with the data on an adjacent wire.

CRT (cathode ray tube) The main part of a monitor, the picture tube.

CSMA/CA (carrier sense multiple access/collision avoidance) A common access method (set of communication rules governing networked devices) used in wireless and older Apple networks.

CSMA/CD (carrier sense multiple access/collision detect) A common access method (set of communication rules governing all network devices) used by Ethernet.

CTS (clear to send) Part of the RTS/CTS hardware handshaking communication method. Specific wires on the serial connector are used to send a signal to the other device to stop or start sending data. The CTS and RTS (request to send) signals indicate when it is okay to send data.

current A term that describes how many electrons are going through a circuit.

cylinder On a stack of hard drive platters, the same numbered concentric tracks of all platters.

D

daisy chaining Connecting multiple devices together through cabling.

data bits A serial device setting for how many bits make up a data word.

data collector set Data collected through Performance Monitor in Windows Vista and higher operating systems.

data compression A method of converting data into smaller sizes before transmission.

data link layer Layer two of the OSI model, it accurately transfers bits across the network by encapsulating (grouping) them into frames (usable sections).

dBd A measurement of antenna gain as referenced to a dipole antenna.

dBi A measurement of antenna gain as referenced to an isotropic antenna.

DBR (DOS boot record) Area of a disk that contains system files.

DC (direct current) The type of power the computer needs to operate.

DCE (data circuit terminating equipment) A term that refers to serial devices such as modems, mice, and digitizers.

DDR (double data rate) Data is transmitted on both sides of the clock signal and uses 184 pins. Sometimes called DDR SDRAM or DDR RAM.

DDR2 (double data rate 2) An upgrade to the DDR SDRAM standard and sometimes is called DDR2 RAM. It includes the following modules—DDR2-400, DDR2-533, DDR2-667, DDR2-800, and DDR2-1000. DDR2 uses 240-pin DIMMs and is not compatible with DDR; however, the higher-end (faster) DDR2 modules are backward compatible with the slower DDR2 modules.

DDR3 (double data rate 3) An upgrade from DDR2 for speeds up to 1600MHz that better supports dual and quad core processor-based systems.

DDR DIMM A type of dual in-line memory module used in AMD and Intel-based computers and higher-end servers.

DDR RAM (double data rate RAM) A memory module that can send data on both the rising and falling sides of a clock signal, unlike SDRAM that sends data only on the rising clock cycle. Therefore, DDR RAM can send twice as much data as SDRAM.

decoder In DVD drives, the MPEG-2 video must be converted, and a decoder is used to convert the data. The two types of decoders are hardware and software.

default gateway The IP address of the Layer three device, such as a router, that is directly connected to its immediate network. It tells a device on its network where to send a packet destined for a remote network.

default printer When a computer can use multiple printers, one of the printers is marked as the default. This is the printer that all applications use. A computer user must change the printer to a different one though the Print dialog window. To mark a printer as default, right-click the printer icon and click the Set as default option.

defragmentation A process of reordering and placing files in contiguous sectors.

degausser A device that demagnetizes monitors. Also called a degaussing coil.

DEL A command issued from a command prompt that is used to delete a file or folder.

density control blade A part inside the laser printer's toner cartridge that controls the amount of toner released to the drum.

DEP (data execution prevention) Software- and hardware-based security measures to prevent malicious software from executing in specific memory locations.

desktop The area of the monitor where all work is performed. It is the interface between the user and the applications, files, and hardware, and is part of the graphical user interface environment.

developing A Hewlett-Packard term used to describe the process where toner is attracted to the laser printer drum. The equivalent electrophotographic term is develop.

developing cylinder A component inside the laser printer's toner cartridge that applies a static charge to the toner so it will be attracted to the drum. Sometimes called a developing roller.

device driver Special software that allows an operating system to access a piece of hardware.

Device Manager A Windows program that is used to view and configure hardware.

DHCP (Dynamic Host Configuration Protocol) A method to automatically assign IP addresses to network devices from a pool of IP addresses.

dialog box A window used by the operating system that allows user interaction to set preferences on various software parameters.

DIB (dual independent bus) Using two buses (a back side and front side bus) to relieve the bottleneck when the CPU communicates with RAM, L2 cache, chipset, PCI bus, and so on.

digital camera A device that stores photographs that can later be transferred to a storage medium such as a CD, DVD, or hard drive. The pictures could also be directly output to a printer.

digital modem A modem that transmits directly on digital phone lines.

digital pen An input device used in the computer-aided drafting field and on touch screen monitors as well as an attachment to a monitor.

digital signature Confirms that the hardware or updated driver being installed is compatible with Windows; sometimes called driver signing.

digital tablet An input device used to illustrate or draw and frequently used in the computer-aided drafting or digital art field.

DIMM (dual in-line memory module) A style of 168-pin memory chip normally used for RAM chips on Pentium and higher motherboards.

DIN connector A round connector with small holes, normally keyed with a metal piece or notch so that the cable inserts only one way. Examples include keyboard and mouse connectors.

DIP (dual in-line package) A style of memory chip that has a row of pins down each side and is used for ROM chips.

DIP switch A physical switch located on some adapters to manually set configuration. It comes in a slide-type or a rocker-type switch.

DIR A command used from a command prompt that displays the contents of a directory.

directional antenna A type of antenna that radiates energy in a specific direction.

directory In older operating systems, an electronic container that holds files and even other directories. In today's operating systems it is known as a folder.

DirectX A Microsoft DVD technology that integrates multimedia drivers, application code, and 3D support for audio and video.

disc A term used to describe CDs and DVDs.

Disc-at-Once Sometimes called DAO, a type of drive that allows a disk to be made rather than the alternative of Track-at-Once, in which the laser stops writing normal data after a track is finished.

disk Media used to store data.

Disk Administrator A Windows program that allows testing, configuration, and preventive maintenance on hard disks.

disk cache A portion of RAM set aside for hard drive data that speeds up hard drive operations. A cache on a hard drive controller is also known as a data buffer.

Disk Cleanup A Windows utility that helps free up hard drive space by emptying the Recycle Bin, removing temporary files, removing temporary Internet files, removing offline files, and so on.

disk duplexing A technique that uses two disk controllers and allows the system to continue functioning if one hard drive fails. Data is written to both sets of hard drive systems through the two controllers. Disk duplexing is considered to be RAID level 1.

disk mirroring Protects against hard drive failure by using two or more hard drives and one disk controller. The same data is written to both drives. If one hard drive fails, the other hard drive continues to function. Disk mirroring is considered to be RAID level 1.

diskpart A command-based utility used in preparing hard disk partitions and volumes for use.

DLP (Digital Light Processing) A technology used in projectors and rear projection TVs that is an array of miniature mirrors used to create pixels on a projection surface.

DMA channel (direct memory access channel) A number assigned to an adapter that allows the adapter to bypass the microprocessor to communicate directly with the RAM chips. DMA mode allows data transfer between the hard drive and RAM without going through the CPU.

DMA mode (direct memory access mode) Allows data transfer between the hard drive and RAM without going through the CPU.

DNS server (domain name system server) Application on network server that translates Internet names into IP addresses.

docking station A part that has connections for a monitor, printer, keyboard, and mouse that allows a laptop computer to be more like a desktop system.

domain A term used in Windows server-based networks where users are required to have logins and file storage, email, and Web-based services are commonly provided.

dot matrix printer Sometimes called an impact printer because of the printer physically impacting a ribbon that places an image on the paper.

dot pitch The distance between like-colored phosphorous dots on adjacent dot triads.

dot triad A grouping of three phosphorous color dots combined to make a single image on the monitor.

double-sided memory A single memory module that contains two memory modules in one container (two banks). Data is still sent to the CPU 64 bits at a time. Some use the terms single-sided and double-sided to describe memory modules that have chips on one side (single-sided) or both sides (double-sided). Another name is double-ranked memory.

downstream A term used to describe information pulled from the Internet such as when viewing Web pages or downloading a file.

dpi (dots per inch) A printer measurement used with ink jet and laser printers that refers to how many dots are produced in an inch.

Dr. Watson A Windows utility that detects and displays troubleshooting information when a system or program error occurs.

DRAM (dynamic random access memory) One of two major RAM types that is less expensive, but slower than SRAM. DRAM requires periodic refreshing of the electrical charges holding the 1s and 0s.

driver See *device driver*.

driver roll back A new feature in Windows XP that allows an older driver to be re-installed when a new driver causes problems.

driver signing A technology that verifies whether a driver has been digitally signed and approved to work with the specific Windows operating system environment.

drive type A number that corresponds to a drive's geometry assigned during SETUP configuration.

drop-down menu Option box with down arrow; clicking the arrow reveals additional choices for the option.

D-shell connector A connector with more pins or holes on the top side than the bottom so that a cable inserts in only one direction. Examples include parallel, serial, and video ports.

DTE (data terminating equipment) A term that refers to computers and printers.

dual-boot Ability to boot from one of two installed operating systems.

dual-channel The motherboard memory controller chip handles processing of memory requests more efficiently by handling two memory paths simultaneously.

dual-core CPU Two CPUs contained in a single housing unit.

dual link A type of DVI video connector that allows higher resolutions.

dual-ported memory A type of memory used on video adapters that allows data to be read from and written to simultaneously.

dual rail power supply A term used to describe two +12 volt lines available in a power supply.

DUN (dial-up networking) A remote computer that dials into the Internet or a corporation using a modem.

DVD drive A drive that supports CDs as well as music and video DVDs.

DVD-R WORM technology used with DVD drives that is similar to CD-R drives. DVD-R discs can use one or two sides and are available in 3.95GB, 4.7GB, and 9.4GB. DVD-R discs are sometimes shown as two different types, DVD-R(A) and DVD-R(G). DVD-R(A) targets the "authoring" business for professional development of DVDs. DVD-R(G) is more for home users and lay people. Both can be read by most DVD players and drives, but DVD-R(G) drives usually cannot write to DVD-R(A) media.

DVD+R A type of read/write DVD supported by the DVD+RW Alliance that can record (one time per disc) up to 4.7GB on single-sided DVD+R discs.

DVD-RAM A type of drive that uses a laser to heat the disc and to magnetically charge it. Data can be written to the disc.

DVD-R DL (dual layer) Similar to DVD-R in that it can record one time. Uses double-layered discs to store up to 8.5GB and supported by the DVD Forum.

DVD+R DL (dual layer) Similar to DVD+R in that it can record one time. Uses double-layered discs to store up to 8.5GB and supported by the DVD+RW Alliance.

DVD-ROM A technology that produces discs with superior audio and video performance and increased storage capacity.

DVD-RW (DVD-rewritable) A type of read/write DVD format supported by the DVD Forum. Similar to DVD-R except you can erase and rewrite data. Uses 4.7GB discs and most DVD-ROM drives and DVD-Video players support this format. Sometimes known as DVD-R/W or DVD-ER.

DVD+RW (DVD read and write) A drive that can be read from, written to, and holds 3GB.

DVD±RW (DVD-rewritable) A type of read/write DVD format that is supported by both the DVD Forum and the DVD+RW Alliance. These drives reads most CD, DVD, and DVD+R DL discs and writes to CD-R, CD-RW, DVD+R, DVD-R, DVD-RW, and DVD+RW discs.

DVI A port on an AGP adapter that is used to connect ?at panel monitors to the computer.

DVI-D A type of video connector used with digital monitors.

DVI-I The most common type of DVI video connector that is used with both analog and digital monitors.

DVI port (digital video/visual interface) A port on an AGP adapter that is used to connect flat panel monitors to the computer.

dynamic disk A Windows term for volumes that can be resized and managed without rebooting.

dynamic storage A disk that has been configured for the Windows operating system. The unit can be resized and managed without rebooting and contains primary partitions, extended partitions, logical drives, and dynamic volumes.

E

ECC (error correcting code) An alternative method of checking data accuracy. ECC uses a mathematical algorithm to verify accuracy. ECC is more expensive than parity and the motherboard or memory controllers must also have additional circuitry to process ECC.

echo mode setting Sometimes called the local echo setting. The setting that displays typed commands.

ECHO OFF A command used from a command prompt that prevents characters from being displayed on the screen.

EDIT A command used to bring up a text editor. A text editor allows file creation and modification.

effective permissions The final permissions granted for a particular resource. Folder permissions are cumulative—the combination of the group and the person's permissions. The deny permission overrides any allowed permission set for a user or a group. When NTFS and shared folder permissions are both used, the most restrictive of the two becomes the effective permissions.

EFS (encrypting file system) An encryption feature of Windows 2000 and higher; only the authorized user may view or change a file encrypted with EFS.

EIDE (enhanced integrated drive electronics) A term that signifies two IDE connectors (four devices) and support of the ATAPI standard.

EISA (extended industry standard architecture) Developed by a consortium of manufacturers in response to IBM's MCA standard. EISA utilizes a 32-bit 10MHz standard.

electronic key card An alternative to a key for room or building access.

EMF (enhanced metafile) A spooled print data format that defines how data is stored on the hard drive (spooled) before being sent to the printer. EMF is the default setting and it is a 32-bit non-printer dependent format that performs faster than RAW. If you are having printing problems, and the documentation or your research directs you to change the spooling data format, this is the setting referenced. The RAW data format is printer-specific and requires extra time to convert the printing data before it is saved to the hard drive.

EMI (electromagnetic interference) Electronic noise generated by electrical devices. Also called EMR (electromagnetic radiation).

encoding The way in which binary 1s and 0s are placed on the hard drive.

encryption Method of securing data from unauthorized users. Data is converted into an unreadable format.

erase lamp A component inside a laser printer that neutralizes any charges left on the drum so that the next printed page receives no residuals from the previous page.

error correction Standard for the modem to check the data for errors rather than the microprocessor.

eSATA (external Serial ATA) A port used to connect external SATA devices to a computer.

ESCD (extended system configuration data) Data that provides the BIOS and operating system a means for communicating with plug and play devices. As the computer boots, the BIOS records legacy device configuration information. Plug and play devices use this information to configure themselves and avoid conflicts. Once an adapter has resources assigned and the resources are saved in ESCD, the resources do not have to be recalculated unless a new device is added to the computer.

ESD (electrostatic discharge) Occurs when stored up static electricity is discharged in an instantaneous surge of voltage. Cumulative effects of ESD weaken or destroy electronic components.

ESS (extended service set) A wireless network design that has multiple access points that connect to the same main wired network.

Ethernet A network system that carries computer data along with audio and video information. Ethernet adapters are the most common network cards. They may have a BNC, an RJ-45, a 15-pin female D-shell connector, or a combination of these ports. The RJ-45 connector is the most common.

Event Viewer A Windows tool used to monitor various events in the computer.

exabyte (EB) One billion times one billion bytes or 2^{60} power (1,152,921,504,606,800 bytes).

executable file A file with a *BAT*, *EXE*, or *COM* extension that starts an application, utility, or command. A file upon which the operating system can take action.

exFAT A file system type that improves upon FAT32 by having a theoretical maximum file size of 16EB, maximum volume size of 64ZB (but 512TB is current limit), smaller cluster sizes than FAT32, and an increased number of files allowed in a directory. Created for external storage media such as Flash drives and hard drives for saving images/video.

expansion slot Motherboard socket into which adapters are connected.

Explorer A Windows-based application that details certain information for all folders and files on each drive. It is used most commonly to copy or move files and folders. Sometimes called Windows Explorer.

ExpressCard A replacement for PC Card technology that supports advanced serial technologies PCI-Express or USB 2.0 connectivity through the ExpressCard slot and is used in laptop computers.

eXtended Graphics Array See *XGA*.

extended partition A hard drive division.

extension In operating systems, the adding of three or more characters following the filename and a period (.). The extension associates the file with a particular application that executes the file.

external command A command located on a disk that the operating system must locate before the command can execute.

external data bus The electronic lines that allow the microprocessor to communicate with external devices. Also known as external data path or external data lines. See also *bus*.

external data lines See *external data bus*.

F

FAT (file allocation table) A method of organizing a computer's file system.

FAT16 File system supported by DOS and all Windows versions since DOS. DOS and Windows 9x have a 2GB limit. Windows NT and higher have a 4GB limit.

FAT32 The file system used by Windows 95 Service Release 2 and higher that supports hard drives up to 2TB in size.

fault tolerance The ability to continue functioning after a hardware or software failure. An example of fault tolerance with hard drives is RAID configurations.

fax modem A device that functions as a modem and uses the printer and computer as a fax machine.

FDDI (fiber distributed data interface) High-speed fiber network that uses ring topology and token passing access method.

FDISK A command used to partition a FAT16 or FAT32 partition on a hard drive.

female port A type of connector on a motherboard or a separate adapter with recessed portions (or holes) that accept a male cable's pins.

fiber-optic cable An expensive network cabling made of plastic or glass fibers that carry data in the form of light pulses. Handles the greatest amount of data with least amount of data loss. Comes in single-mode and multi-mode.

FIFO setting A serial device setting that enables or disables the UART's buffer.

file Electronic container holding data or computer code that serves as a basic unit of storage.

filename A term used to describe the name of a file. In older operating systems, the filename was limited to eight characters plus a three-character extension. Today's operating systems allow filenames up to 255 characters long.

file system Defines how data is stored on a drive. Examples of file systems include FAT16, FAT32, and NTFS.

file virus A program that replaces or attaches to executable files (those with *.COM* or *.EXE* extensions). The virus can cause the application to not start or operate properly. It can also load into RAM and affect other executable files.

firewall Software or a hardware device that protects one or more computers from being electronically attacked.

FireWire See *IEEE 1394*.

FireWire port A serial technology developed by Apple computer. See also *IEEE 1394*.

firmware Combines hardware and software attributes. An example is a BIOS chip that has instructions (software) written into it.

FIS (Frame Information Structure) A technology that allows multiple e-SATA devices to perform simultaneous operations. It is a faster technology than command-based switching used with SATA-PMs.

Flash BIOS A type of motherboard memory that allows updates by disk or by downloading Internet files.

flash memory A type of non-volatile memory that holds data when the power is off.

flat When recording a CD, the CD has pits and flats. The pits are indentations along the track. Flats (also called lands) separate the pits.

floppy disk A flexible disk (or diskette) made of oxide-coated mylar most popular today in 3.5-inch drive sizes.

floppy drive An older storage device that accepts floppy disks.

flow control A serial device setting that determines the communication method.

flyback transformer A CRT part used to boost voltage to the high level needed by the CRT.

folder In Windows-based operating systems, an electronic container that holds files as well as other folders. Folders were previously called directories in older operating systems.

FORMAT A command used to prepare a disk for use.

formatted (disk) A disk that has been prepared to accept data.

form factor The shape and size (height, width, and depth) of motherboards, adapters, memory chips, power supplies, and so on. Before building or upgrading, make sure the device's form factor fits the computer case!

fragmentation Occurs over time as files are saved on the hard drive in clusters not adjacent to each other, which slows hard disk access time.

frame The encapsulated data found at layer 2 of the OSI model.

frequency response The number of samples taken by a sound card.

frequency response range The range of sounds a speaker can reproduce.

FSB (Front Side Bus) Part of the dual independent bus that connects the CPU to the motherboard components.

FTP (File Transfer Protocol) A standard used when transferring files from one computer to another across a network.

full-duplex A serial device setting that allows the sending and receiving device to send data simultaneously. On a cable, the ability to transmit data in both directions simultaneously.

fully buffered memory A technology used in network server memory that requires a special memory controller sometimes advertised as FBDIMMs.

fuser cleaning pad The pad located above the laser printer's fuser roller that lightly coats it with silicon to prevent the paper sticking to the roller.

fusing A Hewlett-Packard term used to describe the laser printing process where toner is melted into paper. The equivalent electrophotographic process term is fuse.

fusing roller A laser printer part responsible for heating the toner and melting it into the paper.

G

G.SHDSL A type of DSL that transmits the same both downstream and upstream.

game port An input port that connects a joystick to the computer.

GDDR4 SDRAM (graphics double data rate SDRAM) A power-efficient video memory upgrade to GDDR3 that has speeds up to 3.2GHz.

GDI (graphics device interface) The part of Windows that handles representing and transmitting graphical objects to output devices such as printers, monitors, and overhead projectors. In Windows XP, GDI+ is the improved-upon model and it handles graphical images better as well as support for file formats such as JPEG and PNG. Windows Vista further upgrades GDI with XPS (XML paper specification).

gigabyte Approximately one billion bytes of information (exactly 1,073,741,824 bytes).

gigahertz One billion cycles per second (1Ghz). Expresses the speed of a microprocessor.

GPT (GUID, or globally unique identifier, partition table) A type of partition table available in 64-bit Windows editions. GPTs can have up to 128 partitions and volumes up to 18EB.

grayware A generic term for applications or files that affect computer performance and/or cause unexpected and unsolicited events to occur. Can come from downloading shareware or freeware, infected emails, selecting an advertisement shown in a pop-up window, or through a Trojan virus. Spyware, adware, and malware are all types of grayware.

grounding Occurs when the motherboard or adapter is not installed properly and has a trace touching the computer's frame.

GUI (graphical user interface) In newer operating systems, user selects files, programs, and commands by clicking pictorial representations (icons) rather than typing commands at a command prompt.

H

HAL (hardware abstraction layer) The layer between the operating system and hardware devices that allows Windows to run different hardware configurations and components without crashing the operating system.

half-duplex A serial device setting that allows either the sending or the receiving device to send data, one device at a time. On a cable, the ability to transmit in both directions but not at the same time.

handshaking The method by which two serial devices negotiate communications.

hard drive A sealed data storage medium on which information is stored. Also called a hard disk.

hardware A tangible item, such as the keyboard or monitor.

hardware decoder Sometimes called an MPEG-2 decoder that provides the best performance (especially in older computer) when converting an MPEG DVD file into a format that can be displayed. A software decoder puts the burden on the CPU to decode and uncompress the video data from the DVD. Video card manufacturers have added MPEG-2 video decoding support to decrease the CPU's load.

HCL (hardware compatibility list) A Microsoft list of hardware that is known to work when used with a particular operating system.

HDSL (high bit-rate DSL) which provides equal speed for downloads/uploads.

hdwiz.exe The command used to open the Add Hardware wizard.

head crash Occurs when a read/write head touches a platter, causing damage to the heads or the platter.

heap Memory allocated to Windows core files that records every Windows action, such as each mouse click, each resizing of a window, and so on.

Help button Located in upper-right corner of a dialog box as a question mark button. Clicking it allows access to information on various topics.

hertz A measurement of electrical frequency equal to one cycle per second. Abbreviated Hz.

hidden attribute A designation that keeps a file from being seen in directory listings. However, with today's operating systems, this attribute does not help because the operating system makes it very easy to see hidden files.

hidden share A share that has a dollar sign ($) added to the share name so that the share is not shown to a remote networked computer.

high-level formatting Process that sets up the file system for use by the computer. It is the third and last step in preparing a hard drive for use.

HomeGroup A Windows 7 feature to make home networking easier to configure and join.

horizontal scanning frequency The rate at which a monitor's beam moves across the screen.

host Another name for a network device. It also represents one of the two parts of an IP address.

host number Portion of an IP address that represents the specific network device.

hot swapping Allows a PC Card to be inserted into a slot while the computer is powered.

HPA (Host Protected Area) A hidden part of the hard drive that is used to reinstall the operating system. It sometimes contains applications that are installed when the computer was sold. Using an HPA reduces the amount of hard drive space available to the operating system.

HPPCL (Hewlett-Packard printer control language) A popular print software that translates between the printer and the computer.

HT (Hyperthreading Technology) A technology created by Intel that is an alternative to using two processors. HT allows a single processor to handle two separate sets of instructions simultaneously.

HTML (Hypertext markup language) Programming language used to create Internet Web pages.

HTTP (hypertext transfer protocol) A standard for Internet communication.

HTTPS (HTTP over SSL) Encrypted HTTP communication through an SSL session. Web pages are encrypted and decrypted.

hub A device used with the universal serial bus or in a star network topology that allows multiple device connections. A network hub cannot look at each data frame coming through its ports like a switch does.

HVD (high voltage differential) A SCSI-2 standard that allowed longer SCSI bus lengths and required a differential terminator. HVD was removed from the SCSI-3 standards.

Hyperthreading Technology See *HT*.

HyperTransport AMD's I/O architecture in which a serial-link design allows devices to communicate in daisy chain fashion without interfering with any other communication. Thus, I/O bottleneck is mitigated.

I

I/O address (input/output address) A port address that allows an external device to communicate with the microprocessor. It is analogous to a mailbox number.

I/O APIC A type of controller that supports more interrupts than the traditional 16 that used throughout the peripheral buses and is integrated into the chipset. Compare with LAPIC which is normally integrated into each CPU and has its own timer.

ICH (I/O controller hub) A part of the chipset that controls such motherboard components as SATA ports, PCI and PCI-E slots, USB ports, audio ports, and integrated network cards. Also known as the south bridge.

icon Operating system graphic that represents a file, application, hardware, and shared network resources.

IDE (integrated drive electronics) An interface that supports internal hard drives, CD drives, DVD drives, Zip drives, and tape backup units.

IEEE 1284 A standard that defines what connections are used with printers and how data is transferred through the parallel port.

IEEE 1394 port Uses the IEEE 1394 standard for high-speed audio and video device data transfers known as FireWire. A single port supports the connectivity of up to 63 devices.

IMAP (Internet Mail Access Protocol) Used to receive email through the Internet.

infrared A technology utilizing infrared light that allows devices to communicate across a wireless network. Examples are laptop computers, printers, and hand-held computing devices.

infrared port A wireless port found on laptop computers and small portable printers used for close wireless connectivity.

infrastructure mode A type of wireless network that contains an access point for wireless devices to be connected together.

ink jet printer A type of printer that squirts ink through tiny nozzles to produce print. Ink jet printers produce high-quality, high-resolution, color output.

INT 13 interface Short for Interrupt 13, a standard that allows a system BIOS to locate data on the hard drive.

integrated motherboard A motherboard that contains ports such as the mouse, keyboard, serial, and parallel ports.

interlacing A scanning method used with monitors in which only the odd numbered pixel rows are scanned, followed by the even numbered pixel rows.

internal command A command that is part of the command interpreter that the operating system does not have to locate in order to execute. An example of an internal command is DIR.

internal data bus The electronic lines inside a microprocessor. See also *bus*.

Internet Explorer An application used to access the Internet through a network or dial-up access.

interrupt See *IRQ*.

IP address A type of network adapter address used when multiple networks are linked. Known as a Layer three address, it is a 32-bit binary number with groups of eight bits separated by a dot. This numbering scheme is also known as dotted-decimal notation. Each eight-bit group represents numbers from 0 to 255. An IP address example is 113.19.12.102.

ipconfig A command used from a command prompt in Windows to view the current IP settings.

IPv4 A type of IP address that uses 32 bits (four groups of eight bits each) shown as decimal numbers in dotted decimal format. An example of an IPv4 address is 192.168.10.1.

IPv6 A type of IP address that uses 128 bits represented by hexadecimal numbers. An example of an IPv6 IP address is fe80::13e:4586:5807:95f7. Each set of four digits represents 16 bits.

IRQ (interrupt request) A microprocessor priority system that assigns a number to each expansion adapter or port to facilitate orderly communication.

IRQ steering A PCI bus property that allows many PCI devices to share the limited and fixed number of IRQs, thus preventing competing devices from slowing or stopping CPU processing.

ISA (industry standard architecture) The oldest of the three types of computer architectures. Allows 16-bit data transfers.

ISDN (integrated services digital network) A digital phone line that has three separate channels, two B channels, and a D channel. The B channel allows 64Kbps transmission speeds. The D channel allows 16Kbps transmissions.

isotropic antenna A type of antenna used as a reference for other antennas. It is not a real antenna. An isotropic antenna theoretically transmits an equal amount of power in all directions.

ISP (Internet service provider) A vendor that provides connection to the Internet.

J

joule dissipation capacity A measure of a surge protector's ability to absorb overvoltage power surges. The higher the capacity, the better the protection.

jumper A plastic cover for two metal pins on a jumper block.

K

keyboard Allows users to communicate and input data to the computer.

keyboard port DIN connector on the motherboard into which only the keyboard cable must connect.

keyed A connector or cable that has an extra metal piece that allows correct connections.

kibibyte A binary prefix term used to describe 2^{10} or 1,024 and is abbreviated KiB. Instead of saying that it is 1 kilobyte, which people tend to think of as approximately 1,000 bytes, the term kibibyte is used.

kilobyte Approximately 1,000 bytes of information (exactly 1,024 bytes).

KMS (key management service) A service used in companies that have 25 or more Windows Vista or 7 computers to deploy. KMS is a software application installed on a computer. All newly installed Windows Vista- or 7-based computers register with the computer that has KMS installed. Every 180 days the computer is re-activated for the license. Each KMS key can be used on two computers up to 10 times. Contrast with MAK.

KVM switch (keyboard, video, mouse switch) A component that allows multiple computers to be connected to a single keyboard, monitor, and mouse.

L

L1 cache Fast memory located inside the microprocessor.

L2 cache Fast memory located inside the microprocessor on Pentium Pros and higher.

L3 cache Any cache fast memory installed on the motherboard when both L1 and L2 cache are on the processor.

LAN (local area network) A group of devices sharing resources in a single area such as a room or a building.

LAPIC (local APIC) A type of interrupt controller that supports more interrupts than the traditional 16. LAPIC is normally integrated into each CPU and has its own timer. Compare to I/O APIC which is used throughout any of the peripheral buses and is integrated into the chipset.

laptop A computer model that is portable.

laser lens A component of the CD drive that reads the data from the compact disc; susceptible to dust accumulation. Also known as the objective lens.

laser printer A type of printer that produces output using a process similar to a copier. Laser printers are the most expensive type of printer.

Last Known Good Configuration Used when the Windows configuration has been changed by adding hardware or software that is incompatible with the operating system or when an important service has been accidentally disabled.

latency In networking, the amount of delay experienced as a packet travels from source to destination.

LCD (liquid crystal display) A video technology used with laptops and flat screen monitors. The two basic types of LCD are passive matrix and active matrix.

library Windows 7 storage similar to a folder, but is automatically indexed for faster searching.

Li-ion battery A lithium battery, which is very light and can hold a charge for a long period of time; found in cell phones and portable devices such as cameras.

line conditioner Device to protect the computer from overvoltage and undervoltage conditions as well as adverse noise conditions. Also known as a power conditioner.

liquid cooling system An alternative to a fan or sink for processor cooling. Liquid is circulated through the system. Heat from the processor is transferred to the cooler liquid.

local administrator A user account that has full power over a Windows-based computer. A local administrator can install hardware and software; use all of the administrative tools; create and delete hard drive partitions; and create, delete, and manage local user accounts.

local share Something such as a printer, folder, or disc that has been made available across a network.

logical drive Dividing the extended partition into separate units, which appear as separate drive letters.

long filename Extended filenames in Windows that can be up to 255 characters in length instead of the DOS filename format of eight characters with a three-character extension.

loopback address A private IP address of 127.0.0.1 that is used to test a NIC card's basic network setup and the TCP/IP stack.

loopback plug A device used in troubleshooting that allows port testing.

lost cluster A sector on a disk that the file allocation table cannot associate with any file or directory.

M

MAC address (media access control address) One of two types of addresses assigned to network adapters, used when two devices on the same network communicate. Known as a Layer two address.

macro virus Program that attaches to a document written by a specific application such as Microsoft PowerPoint. Once the document is opened into RAM, the virus attaches to other documents.

MAK (multiple activation key) A method in which the Internet or a phone call must be made to register one or more Windows Vista or 7 computers. This method has a limited number of activations.

male port A connector on a motherboard or adapter with protruding pins that accepts a cable with a female connector.

MAN (metropolitan area network) Describes networks that span a city or town.

MAP (Microsoft Assessment and Planning Toolkit) Used for planning a Windows deployment in a corporate environment.

MAPI (Messaging Application Programming Interface) A Microsoft-proprietary protocol used with email.

marking The part of the printer that places the image on the paper. Also called the marking engine.

marking subsystem The part of the printer that places the image on the paper. Also called the marking engine.

master A jumper setting used to configure an IDE device; the controlling device on the interface.

MBR (master boot record) A program that reads the partition table to find the primary partition used to boot the system.

MCH (memory controller hub) A part of a chipset that connects directly to the processor. The MCH controls RAM and video expansion slots. It is also called the north bridge.

MD A command issued from a command prompt that is used to create a directory (folder) or subdirectory.

mebibyte A binary prefix value used to describe a value of 2^{20} or 1,048,576 and abbreviated MiB.

mechanical keyboard A keyboard that is less expensive than capacitive keyboards and more prone to failure.

mechanical mouse A mouse that uses a rubber ball to move the pointer.

megabyte Approximately one million bytes of data (exactly 1,048,576 bytes).

megahertz The speed at which microprocessors and coprocessors are measured. Equal to one million cycles per second, abbreviated MHz. See also *hertz*.

memory The part of the computer that temporarily stores applications, user documents, and system operating information.

memory address A unique address for memory chips.

memory map A graphical representation of the amount of a processor's memory addresses.

mesh topology Network where all devices connect to each other by cabling to provide link redundancy for the maximum fault tolerance.

microcomputer See *computer*.

microDIMM A type of DIMM used in portable computers such as a laptop.

microprocessor See *processor*.

Microsoft Management console Holds snap-ins or tools used to maintain the computer. Also known as the Computer Management console.

MIDI (musical instrument digital interface) An interface built into a sound card to create synthesized music.

mini PCI A 32-bit 33MHz standard used in laptops, docking stations, and printers.

MLC (multi-level cell) A cell that stores more than one bit in a memory cell that is used in a SSD (solid state drive). Contrast with SLC.

MMX Microprocessors that have 57 more multimedia instructions that speed up multimedia applications such as sound and video.

MNP (Microcom network protocol) A set of standards for error correction.

modem (modulator/demodulator) A device that connects a microcomputer to a phone line.

modem isolator See *phone line isolator*.

modulation The process of adding data to a carrier signal. Examples include frequency modulation and amplitude modulation.

Molex A type of power connector that extends from the computer's power supply to various devices.

monitor Displays information from the computer to the user.

motherboard The main circuit board of a computer. Also known as the mainboard, planar, or systemboard.

mount To make a drive available and recognizable to the operating system.

mouse A data input device that moves the cursor or selects menus and options.

mouse port A DIN connector on the motherboard that should only accept the mouse cable.

MOV (metal oxide varistor) An electronic component built into some surge protectors to absorb overvoltage spikes or surges.

MP3 (MPEG-1 audio Layer three) A sound format that compresses an audio file and has the extension of MP3.

MRW An improvement on the UDF file format used on CDs and DVDS. MRW is commonly called Mount Rainier and it is a format for CD and DVDs that saves files to read/write discs as if they were hard drives. It also supports defect management and works on different hardware platforms. MRW is natively supported in Windows Vista.

MSCDEX.EXE A DOS-based program that assigns a drive letter to the CD-ROM drive.

MSDS (material safety data sheet) A document that contains information about a product, its toxicity, storage, and disposal.

MTBF (mean time between failures) The average number of hours before a device fails.

multi-boot A situation where the computer can boot from two or more operating systems.

multi-mode A type of fiber-optic cabling that allows multiple light signals to be sent along the same cable.

multiplier A motherboard setting used to determine CPU speed (multiplier times bus speed equals CPU speed).

multisession A type of CD/DVD drive that has the ability to store data on a disc and then add to it later.

My Computer/Computer The desktop icon that allows access to files, applications, software, and hardware located in or on the computer.

My Documents/Documents The default folder (directory) location on the hard drive for files the user saves. Also, the icon that quickly accesses the default directory.

My Network Places/Network The Windows 2000 Professional and XP option used to access network resources.

N

nanosecond A billionth of a second.

NAT/PAT (Network Address Translation/Port Address Translation) Terms sometimes used interchangeably or globally to mean conserving IP addresses. A method of conserving IP addresses. NAT uses private IP addresses that become translated to public IP addresses. PAT does the same thing except uses fewer public IP addresses by "overloading" one or more public IP addresses by tracking port numbers.

native resolution The number of pixels going across and down a flat panel monitor. This resolution is the specification for which the monitor was made and is the optimum resolution.

NetBEUI A nonroutable network protocol commonly found on peer-to-peer networks. Can work only on simple networks, not on linked networks.

network Two or more devices capable of communicating and sharing resources between them.

network layer Layer three of the OSI model that coordinates data movement between two devices on separate networks.

network number Portion of an IP address that represents which network the computer is on.

network port A port used to connect a computer to other computers, including a network server.

network share A folder or network device that has been shared and is accessible from a remote computer.

network topology Maps of how the physical or logical paths of network devices connect.

NIC (network interface card) An adapter used to connect a device to a network.

NiMH battery Made of nickel-metal hydride that is being replaced by li-ion batteries.

non-parity A type of memory chip that is cheaper and does not do error checking.

nonvolatile memory Memory that remains even when the computer is powered off. ROM and flash memory are examples of nonvolatile memory.

nslookup A Windows troubleshooting tool that displays network domain names and their associated IP addresses.

NTFS File system used with Windows NT and higher.

null modem cable Connects two computers together without the use of a modem.

O

ohm A measurement of resistance.

OK button Located in bottom right-hand side of a dialog box; clicking it saves any changes applied and closes the window.

omnidirectional antenna A type of antenna that has a radiation pattern in all directions.

on-die cache L2 cache when housed in the processor packaging.

open authentication Used in wireless networks; allows a wireless device to send a frame to the access point with the sender's identity (MAC address).

operating system A piece of software used to load a computer and make it operational.

optical mouse A mouse that has optical sensors used to move the pointer.

OSI model (Open Systems Interconnect Model) A standard for information transfer across a network that was developed by the International Standards Organization. The model has seven layers—each layer uses the layer below it, and each layer provides some function to the one above it.

outline font Fonts computed from a mathematical formula, also known as vector fonts.

overclocking Manually changing the front side bus speed and/or multiplier to increase CPU and system speed, but with attendant heat increase.

overvoltage A condition when the AC voltage is over the rated amount of voltage.

ozone filter A part of the laser printer that filters out the ozone produced by the printer.

P

packet Encapsulated data found at Layer three of the OSI model.

PAE (physical address extension) A feature provided by Intel that allows up to 64GB of physical memory to be used for motherboards that support it.

pages In Windows disk caching, memory space is divided into 4KB blocks called pages. The operating system swaps or pages the application to and from the temporary swap file as needed if RAM is not large enough to handle the application.

PAN (personal area network) A network of personal devices such as PDAs, cell phones, laptop computers, and pocket video games that can communicate in close proximity through a wired network or wirelessly. Playing a game between two laptop computers wirelessly is a PAN.

paper transport The part of a printer that moves paper through the printer.

parallel port A 25-pin female D-shell connector used to connect a printer to a motherboard. Transfers eight bits of data at a time to parallel devices such as printers, tape drives, Iomega's Zip drives, and external hard drives.

parity A method of checking data accuracy.

partitioning Dividing a hard drive so that the computer system sees more than one drive.

partition table Holds the information about the types and locations of partitions created. Occupies the outermost track on the platter (Cylinder 0, Head 0, Sector 1), and is part of the Master Boot Record.

passive terminator One type of SCSI chain end that is susceptible to noise interference over long cable distances. Used with SCSI-1 devices.

pass through terminator Used with SCSI devices; has an extra connector on it and allows a device that does not have terminators to be terminated through the connector that attaches to the cable.

PATA (parallel ATA) A technology used with IDE devices that allows two devices per channel.

patch A piece of software that fixes a specific problem in an application or operating system.

path Reference that tells where a file is located among drives and folders (directories).

PC (personal computer) A common name for a computer, taken from the IBM PC brand.

PC Card A common local bus architecture used in laptops. Also known as PCMCIA.

PCI (Peripheral Component Interconnect) A common 64-bit, 66MHz local bus standard found in today's computers.

PCIe A point-to-point serial bus used for motherboard adapters. Each bit can travel over a lane and each lane allows transfers up to 250MBps with a maximum of 32 lanes (which gives a total of 8GBps transfer rate).

PCI-X A parallel PCI bus that can operate at 66, 133, 266, 533, and 1066MHz and is backward compatible with the previous versions of the bus, but allows for faster speeds.

PCL (printer command language) A type of printer PDL (page description language) such as HPPCL used on HP printers; handles the overall page look and has commands that treat the entire document as a single graphic.

PCMCIA (Personal Computer Memory Card Industry Association) See *PC Card*.

PDA (personal digital assistant) A handheld computer normally used to manage schedules, contact names, phone numbers, and addresses; write simple notes, and exchange email.

PDL (page description language) Software inside the printer that translates between the printer and the computer. Examples are HPPCL and PostScript.

PDSL (power line DSL) A type of DSL that has data speeds from 256K to 2.7Mbps using electrical lines.

Performance Logs and Alerts A Windows XP utility that allows the creation of graphs, bar charts, and text reports.

Performance Monitor Windows tool that monitors resources such as memory and CPU usage, and allows creation of graphs, bar charts, and text reports.

Performance utility Windows utility that monitors memory and other hardware parameters usage aspects.

petabyte (PB) One thousand terabytes (2^{50} power) (1,125,899,906,842,600 bytes).

phishing (pronounced fishing) A type of social engineering that attempts to get personal information through email from a company that appears legitimate. Targets obtaining ATM/debit or credit card numbers and PINs, Social Security numbers, bank account numbers, an Internet banking login ID and password, an email address, security information such as a mother's maiden name, full name, home address, or phone number.

phone line isolator A surge protector for the modem, protecting against power fluctuations in a phone line. Also known as a modem isolator.

physical layer Layer one of the OSI model; it defines how bits are sent and received across the network without regard to their structure.

physical network topology A term that describes how a network is wired.

picosecond A trillionth of a second.

picture cell The smallest image shown on the front of a monitor made up of three color phosphorous dots.

PIF (program information file) The customized property settings of a DOS application when run inside an NTVDM special environment. NTVDM simulates a DOS environment inside Windows.

pin 1 A designated pin on every cable and connector that must be mated when attaching the two. Usually designated by a stenciled or etched number, a color stripe, and so on.

pin firing The act of a printwire coming out of a dot matrix printer's printhead and impacting the paper.

ping A network troubleshooting command used to test TCP/IP communications and determine if a network path is available, whether any delays exist along the path, and if a remote network device is reachable. Use `ping` with the private IP address 127.0.0.1 to test a NIC's basic network setup.

pipeline Separate internal data buses that operate simultaneously inside the microprocessor.

pipe symbol A character (|) used at the command prompt that allows control of where or how the output of the command is processed. For example, a command can be "piped" to display only one screen at a time.

pit Area along the track of a compact disc.

pixel Short for picture element. The smallest displayable unit on a monitor.

platter A metal disk of a hard drive on which binary data is recorded.

plenum cable A type of cable that is treated with fire retardant materials so it is less of a fire risk.

plug and play (PnP) A bus specification that allows automatic configuration of an adapter.

polymorphic virus A program that changes constantly to avoid detection by antivirus scanning.

POP (Point of Presence) An Internet access point.

POP3 (Post Office Protocol) Used to retrieve email from a mail server.

port A connector located on the motherboard or on a separate adapter.

port forwarding Sending data through a firewall based on a particular port number or protocol.

port triggering Temporarily sending data through a firewall based on a pre-configured condition.

port replicator A part that is similar to a docking station. It attaches to the laptop computer and allows more devices such as a monitor, keyboard, and mouse to be connected.

POST (power on self test) Startup software contained in the BIOS chip that tests individual hardware components.

PostScript A type of printer software that translates between the printer and the computer.

power A measurement expressed in watts that represents how much work is being done.

power good signal A signal sent to the motherboard from the power supply during POST that signifies that power is acceptable.

power rating A measurement expressed in watts-per-channel that represents how loud the speaker volume can go up without distorting the sound.

power supply A device that converts AC voltage into DC voltage that the computer can use.

power supply tester A tool used to check DC voltages sourced from the power supply.

PPP (point-to-point protocol) A connection-oriented Layer two protocol that encapsulates data for transmission over remote networks.

preemptive multitasking A type of multitasking used with 32-bit applications in Windows that allows the operating system to determine which application gets the microprocessor's attention and for how long.

prefix notation A method used to describe a subnet mask. It includes a forward slash followed by a number such as /24. The number is how many consecutive bits are set in the subnet mask.

presentation layer Layer six of the OSI model that defines how data is formatted, encoded, converted, and presented from the sender to the receiver, even though a different computer language is used.

preventive maintenance Something that is done to prolong the life of a device.

primary corona A wire in the laser printer responsible for generating a large negative voltage to be applied uniformly to the laser's drum.

primary partition The first detected drive on the hard drive.

print cartridge The container that holds the ink and the nozzles for the ink jet printer. Also known as an ink cartridge.

print driver A piece of software that coordinates between the operating system and the printer.

print engine The part of a printer that translates commands from the computer and provides feedback when necessary. The print engine is the brains of the printer operation.

printhead The part of the dot matrix printer that holds the printwires and impacts the ribbon.

print server A device (computer or separate device) that connects to a printer used by multiple people through a network.

print spooler Also known as a print manager. A software program that intercepts the request to print and sends print information to the hard drive where it is sent to the printer whenever the microprocessor is not busy with other tasks. A print spooler allows multiple print jobs to be queued inside the computer so other work can be performed.

printwire A component of the dot matrix printer's printhead that is a single wire that connects to a spring and impacts a ribbon to make a single dot on the paper.

processor The central 32- or 64-bit electronic chip that determines the processing power of a computer. Also known as microprocessor or CPU (central processing unit).

Program Compatibility wizard Used to check for software application compatibility with a newer Windows version.

PROMPT A command used to change how the command prompt appears. See also *command prompt*.

proxy server A server that acts as a go-between for an application and another server.

PS/2 mouse A mouse that connects to a 6-pin DIN port.

PVC (polyvinyl chloride) Cable that has a plastic insulation or jacket that is cheaper and easier to install than plenum cable. It can have flame-retardant added.

Q

QPI (Quick Path Interconnect) An Intel technology used as an alternative to the FSB (front side bus) in which a point-to-point connection is made between the processor and a motherboard component.

quad-core CPU Four processors on a single motherboard by having either two dual-core CPUs installed on the same motherboard (Intel's solution) or two dual-core CPUs installed in a single socket (AMD's solution).

Quick Launch bar Located to the right of the *Start* button in the taskbar, clicking a quick launch icon opens the application.

R

radiation pattern Sometimes called a propagation pattern. It is the direction(s) the radio frequency is sent or received.

radio button Similar to a checkbox, it is a round space on a dialog box that allows the user to enable an option by clicking it. A solid dot in the button means the option is enabled; an absence of the dot means a disabled option.

RADSL (rate-adaptive DSL) A type of DSL developed by Westell that allows a modem to adapt to phone line condition, speeds up to 2.2Mbps

RAID (redundant array of independent disks) Allows writing to multiple hard drives for larger storage areas, better performance, and fault tolerance.

RAID 0 Also called disk striping without parity. Data is alternatively written on two or more hard drives, but are seen by the system as one logical drive. RAID level 0 does not protect data if a hard drive fails; it only increases system performance.

RAID 1 Also called disk mirroring or disk duplexing. It protects against hard drive failure. See also *disk mirroring and disk duplexing*. Requires two drives at a minimum.

RAID 5 A term that describes putting data on three or more hard drives, and one of the three drives is used for parity. See also *RAID*.

RAM (random access memory) A volatile type of memory that loses its data when power to the computer is shut off.

RAM drive A virtual hard disk created from RAM.

RAS (row address strobe) A signal that selects a specific memory row.

raster A monitor's brightness pattern.

RAW volume A part of a hard drive that has been set aside as a volume but has never been high-level formatted and does not contain a specific type of file system.

RD The Windows command used to remove a directory (folder).

RDRAM Proprietary memory developed by Rambus, Inc.

read/write head The part of a floppy or hard drive that electronically writes binary data on disks.

read-ahead caching A type of disk caching that attempts to guess what the next data requested will be and loads that data into RAM.

read-only attribute A designation that can be applied to a file so the file is not accidentally erased.

Recovery Console A Windows XP tool that allows the administrator to boot the computer to a command prompt and access the hard drive.

Recycle Bin Location in Windows-based operating systems where user-deleted files and folders are held. This data is not discarded from the computer. The user must empty the Recycle Bin to erase the data completely.

refresh (process) Rewrite the information inside memory chips.

refresh rate The maximum time a monitor's screen is scanned in one second.

REGEDIT A Windows utility used to modify and back up the registry.

REGEDT32 One of two Windows registry editors. See also *registry* and *REGEDIT*.

region code A setting on a DVD drive or disc that specifies a geographic region. The drive's region code must match the disc's region code in order to play.

registered memory Memory modules that have extra chips (registers) near the bottom of the module that delay all data transfers by one clock tick to ensure accuracy.

register size The number of bits the CPU can process at one time.

registry A central Windows database file that holds hardware and software configuration information.

Reliability Monitor A tool that provides a visual graph in Windows Vista or 7 of how stable the system is and details on events that might have affected the system reliability.

resistance A measurement in ohms of how much opposition is applied to a circuit.

resolution The number of pixels shown on a monitor or the output of a printer.

Resource Monitor A graphic tool that shows performance for the main system components.

restore point A snapshot image of the registry and some of the dynamic system files that have been saved previously by the System Restore utility. This is used when the Windows computer has a problem.

return The center (round) AC outlet plug. Other terms used are common or neutral.

RFI (radio frequency interference) A specific type of EMI noise that occurs in the radio frequency range. Often results from operation of nearby electrical appliances or devices.

RIMM A trademark of Rambus, Inc. that is a type of memory module used on video adapters and that may be used on future motherboards.

ring topology Network that is physically wired like a star network but, logically, passes control from one device to the next in a continuous fashion using a token.

riser board A board that connects to the motherboard that holds adapters.

ROM (read-only memory) A non-volatile type of memory that keeps data in chips even when the computer is shut off.

ROM BIOS (ROM basic input/output system) See *BIOS*.

root directory The starting place for all files on a disk. A floppy is limited to 127 entries and a hard drive to 512 entries. The designation for a floppy drive's root directory is A:\ and for the hard drive it is C:\.

router A network device that determines the best path to send a packet. Works at OSI model Layer three.

RS232C A serial interface standard.

RTS (request to send) Part of the RTS/CTS hardware handshaking communication method. Specific wires on the serial connector are used to send a signal to the other device to stop or start sending data. The CTS (clear to send) and RTS signals indicate when it is okay to send data.

RTS/CTS (request to send/clear to send) A method of serial device handshaking that uses signals on specific pins of the connector to signal the other device when to stop or send data.

S

S/PDIF (Sony/Phillips digital interface format) Defines how audio signals are carried between audio devices and stereo components. It can also be used to connect the output of a DVD player in a PC to a home theater or some other external device.

Safe Mode Windows option used when the computer stalls, slows down, does not work properly, has improper video settings or intermittent errors, or when a new hardware/software installation causes problems. In Safe Mode, Windows starts with minimum device drivers and services.

sag A momentary undervoltage condition that occurs when the wall outlet AC voltage drops.

SAS (serial attached SCSI) SAS devices connect in a point-to-point bus. Used in the enterprise environment where high reliability and high mean time between failures is important.

SATA (serial ATA) A point-to-point architecture for IDE devices that provides faster access for attached devices.

SATA-PM (Serial ATA port multiplier) A device used to connect multiple eSATA devices to a single eSATA port.

satellite modem A type of modem that can provide Internet access at speeds faster than an analog modem, but slower than cable or DSL access.

scalable font A font that can be created at any size. An outline font is an example of a scalable font.

SCANDISK A software program used to detect and repair lost clusters.

scanner An input device that allows documents to be brought into the computer and, from there, displayed, printed, saved, or emailed.

SCSI (small computer system interface) An interface standard that connects multiple small devices to the same adapter via a SCSI bus.

SCSI ID The priority number assigned to each device connected by a SCSI chain.

SDRAM (synchronous DRAM) Provides very fast burst memory access (approximately 100MHz) by placing new memory addresses on the address bus before prior memory address retrieval and execution completes.

SDSL (symmetrical DSL) A type of DSL that transmits at identical speeds downstream and upstream.

SE (single ended) A type of SCSI electrical signal and terminator used with most SCSI devices. Both active and passive terminators can be used with this signaling method.

sector The smallest amount of storage space on a disk or platter, holding 512 bytes of data.

Secure Sockets Layer See *SSL*.

security log A type of *Event Viewer* log that displays information such as when different users login, including both valid and invalid users.

security policy One or more documents that provide rules and guidelines related to computer and network security.

serial ATA See *SATA*

serial port Either a 9-pin male D-shell connector or a 25-pin male D-shell connector. Transmits one bit at a time and is used for input devices such as mice, modems, digitizers, trackballs, and so on.

server-based network A basic type of LAN wherein users login to a controlling computer, called a server, that knows who is authorized to connect to the LAN and what resources the user is authorized to access. Usually found in businesses comprising of 10 or more computers.

service Windows process that provides a specific function to the computer.

service pack Upgrade or patch provided by a manufacturer for an operating system.

service release Software available from a manufacturer to fix a known problem (bug) in its applications program.

Session-at-Once A type of CD drive that allows multiples sessions to be recorded on a single disc. These discs can normally be read by computer-based CD drives, but not audio CD drives such as ones found in a vehicle. Compare with Disc-at-Once and Track-at-Once.

session layer Layer five of the OSI model that manages communication and administrative functions between two network devices.

Setup Software that tells the computer about itself and the hardware it supports, such as how much RAM memory, type of hard drive installed, current date and time, and so on.

SFX12V A type of power supply used with MicroAtx and FlexATX motherboards.

SGRAM (synchronous graphics RAM) Memory chips used on video adapters and graphics accelerators to speed up graphics-intensive functions.

Shadow Copy A Windows Vista and 7 technology used with the System Restore program that uses a block-level image instead of monitoring certain files for file changes.

shadow mask A screen used in monitors that direct the electron beams to the front of the monitor.

shared key authentication A method of authentication used in wireless networks that uses a group of characters that both the wireless device and the access point have in common.

shared system memory The amount of motherboard RAM used for video because the amount of video memory on the video adapter or built into the motherboard is not enough for the application(s) being used.

shielding Cancels out and keeps magnetic interference from devices.

shortcut Icon with a bent arrow in lower left corner. It is a link to a file, a folder, or a program on a disk. If the file is a document, it opens the application used to create the document.

short filename An older filename that has a maximum of 11 characters (eight characters for the name and three characters for the extension).

Show Desktop Clicking this icon reduces all open windows on the screen and shows the desktop. Click it again and the original document reappears.

SID (security identifier) A unique number assigned to a Microsoft-based computer.

sidebar A feature in Windows Vista that is a collection of customizable desktop gadgets.

signature pad An input device that allows someone to sign and digitally store his or her name.

SIM (System Image Manager) Used in Windows Vista/7 to deploy an image of one computer to multiple computers.

simple volume A Windows term for the storage unit that contains the files needed to load the operating system. The system volume and the boot volume can be the same unit.

single An IDE setting used when only one device connects to the interface and cable.

single link A type of DVI video connection that allows resolutions up to 1920×1080.

single-mode A type of fiber-optic cabling that sends one light beam down the cable.

single-ported memory Memory that can be written to or read from, but not simultaneously.

single-sided memory A memory module that the CPU accesses at one time. The module has one "bank" of memory and 64 bits are transferred out of the memory module to the CPU. More appropriately called single-banked memory. Note that the memory module may or may not have all of its "chips" on one side.

site survey Used in wireless network design to determine the best wireless hardware placement for the optimum coverage area.

slave An IDE setting for the second device added to the cable. The device should be a slower device than the master.

SLC (single-level memory cell) A cell that stores one bit in a memory cell and is more expensive and longer lasting than an MLC.

SmartMedia A card, smaller than a credit card, used to hold audio and video files.

SMP (symmetric multiprocessing) The ability for an operating system to support two CPUs simultaneously.

SMTP (simple mail transfer protocol) A standard used for email or for transferring messages across a network from one device to another.

SNMP (simple network management protocol) A standard that supports network monitoring and management.

social engineering A technique used to trick people into divulging information including their own personal information or corporate knowledge.

SO-DIMM (small outline-DIMM) Special, smaller DIMM used in laptop computers.

software An application consisting of a set of instructions that makes the hardware work.

software decoder A type of DVD decoder that puts the burden on the CPU to decode and uncompress the MPEG-2 video data from the DVD. Video card manufacturers have added MPEG-2 video decoding support to decrease the CPU's load. Contrast with hardware decoder.

solder joint A solder connection on the back of motherboards and adapters.

SO-RIMM (small outline-RIMM) Special, smaller RIMM used in laptop computers.

sound card An adapter card (also known as an audio card) with several ports that converts digital signals to audible sound, and also the reverse. Common devices that connect to the ports include microphones, speakers, and joysticks.

spam Email that is unsolicited and comes from unknown people or businesses.

spanned volume A Windows term used to describe hard drive space created from multiple hard drives.

SPD (serial presence detect) An extra EEPROM feature that allows the system BIOS to read the EEPROM (which contains memory information such as capacity, voltage, error detection, refresh rates, data width, etc.) and adjust motherboard timings for best CPU to RAM performance.

spike An overvoltage condition of short duration and intensity.

SPS (standby power supply) A device that provides power to the computer only after it first detects an AC voltage power out condition.

SRAM (static random access memory) SRAM is faster but more expensive than DRAM. SRAM is also known as cache memory, or L2 cache.

SSD (solid state drive) A drive that uses non-volatile Flash memory and no moving parts to store data. It is faster but more expensive than a hard drive.

SSE (streaming SIMD extension) Intel's microprocessor technology that speeds up 3-D applications.

SSID (service set identifier) A set of up to 32 alphanumeric characters used in wireless networks to differentiate between different networks.

SSID broadcasting Used with wireless network access points to periodically send out a beacon frame that includes the SSID. Wireless devices can automatically detect the SSID from this beacon.

SSL (Secure Sockets Layer) A protocol used to transmit Internet messages securely.

standoff A plastic connector on the bottom side of a motherboard.

start bit A bit used in asynchronous communications that signals the beginning of each data byte.

Start button Located in the lower left hand corner of the Windows desktop, it is used to access and launch applications, files, utilities, and help, and to add/remove hardware and software.

star topology Most common Ethernet network topology where each device connects to a central hub or switch. If an individual device or cable fails, the rest of the network keeps working. But, if the hub or switch fails, the entire network goes down.

stealth virus A virus program that presents a fake image to anti-virus scanning to make itself invisible to scanning.

stop bit A bit used in asynchronous communications that signals the end of each data byte.

STP (shielded twisted pair) Network cable with extra foil to prevent outside noise from interfering with data on the cable.

straight-through cable A cable without physically crossed (twisted) wires.

straight-through serial cable A serial cable used to connect an external modem to a computer's serial port.

striped volume A Windows term describing how data is written across two to 32 hard drives. It is different from a spanned volume in that each drive is used alternately instead of filling the first hard drive before going to the second hard drive. Other names include striping or RAID 0.

subdirectory A directory contained within another directory. Today's subdirectories are called folders.

subnet A portion of a network number that has been subdivided so that multiple networks can use separate parts of a single network number. Subnets allow more efficient use of IP addresses. Also called subnetwork or subnetwork number.

subnet mask A number the computer uses to determine which part of an IP address represents the network and which portion represents the host.

surge An overvoltage condition like a spike but with a longer duration.

surge protector A device to help protect power supplies from overvoltage conditions. Also known as surge strip or surge suppressor.

SVGA (super VGA) A type of monitor that displays at least an 800×600 resolution and connects to a 15-pin D-shell connector.

swap file A temporary file in hard disk space used by Windows that varies in size depending on the amount of RAM installed, available hard drive space, and the amount of memory needed to run the application.

switch In star networks, a Layer two central controlling device. Looks at each data frame as it comes through each port.

SXGA+ (super extended graphics array) An improvement over SXGA to support resolutions up to 1400×1050.

synchronous Transmissions that require the use of a clock signal.

system attribute A file designation to mark a file as a system file. By default, files with this attribute set do not show in directory listings.

System Configuration utility A Windows utility that allows boot files and settings to be enabled/disabled for troubleshooting purposes. The command that brings this utility up is `msconfig.exe`.

system file A specific file needed to allow the computer to boot. A file type that is also known as a startup file.

System Monitor Windows utility that monitors specific computer components and allows creation of graphs, bar charts, and text reports.

system partition A type of active hard drive partition that contains the hardware-specific files needed to load the operating system.

system resources The collective set of interrupt, I/O address, and DMA configuration parameters.

System Restore A utility that makes a snapshot of the registry and backs up certain dynamic system files. When a problem occurs, this utility can be used to take your system back to a time before the error started.

System State Contains a group of interrelated files including the registry, system files, boot files, and COM+ Class Registration database. One cannot back up or restore these files individually.

system volume Windows term describing the storage space that holds Windows operating system files used to boot the computer.

T

tab Often found along the top of dialog boxes. Clicking a tab displays a group of related standard options that users may change to their personal preferences.

taskbar On a Windows program, the bar that runs across the bottom of the desktop. It holds buttons that represent files and applications currently loaded into RAM. It also holds icons representing direct access to system tools.

Task Manager Windows-based utility that displays memory and processor usage data, and displays currently loaded applications as well as currently running processes.

TCP (Transmission Control Protocol) TCP is an OSI model layer four standard that ensures reliable communication between two devices.

TCP/IP (Transmission Control Protocol/Internet Protocol) TCP/IP is the most widely used network protocol by businesses and homes to connect to the Internet. Developed by the Defense Advanced Research Projects Agency in the 1970s, it is the basis of the Internet.

Telnet An application that allows connection to a remote network device.

terabyte (TB) Approximately one trillion bytes of information (240 power) (1,099,511,627,776 bytes).

textbox An area with a dialog box where the user may type preferred parameters applied to the software in use.

TFT (thin film transistor) A type of array used in LCDs to direct the liquid crystal to block the light from the backlight.

TFX12V A type of power supply used with MicroATX and FlexATX motherboards.

thermal wax transfer A type of printer that uses wax-based inks similar to the solid ink printer, but it prints in lower resolutions.

thin client A type of computer that does not have all the ports and components (such as a hard drive) as a traditional PC.

thread A unit of programming code that receives a slice of time from Windows so it can run concurrently with other units of code or threads.

throttle management The ability to control processor speed by slowing the processor down when it is not being used heavily or is running too hot.

TKIP (Temporal Key Integrity Protocol) A method of encryption that is an improvement over WEP because the encryption keys periodically change.

token passing The common access method (set of communication rules governing network devices) used by fiber and Token Ring networks.

Token Ring A type of adapter for networks. The ports on this type of adapter have an RJ-45 or a 9-pin female D-shell connector. Some adapters have a green sticker with 4/16 on it to indicate 4Mbps/16Mbps run speeds.

toner puddling A side effect sometimes experienced on laser printers that use Resolution Enhancement Technology. The toner dial must be adjusted to reduce the amount of toner released to the paper so that it does not appear to have too much toner in one area of the paper.

touch screen An alternative way to input device into a computer. Used in kiosks.

tower A computer model that sits under a desk.

TPM (Trusted Platform Module) A motherboard chip used for hardware and software authentication. The TPM can authenticate hardware devices. Applications can use the TPM for file and folder encryption, local passwords, email, VPN/PKI authentication, and wireless authentication.

Trace log A *Performance Tool* option used to trigger data recording once a threshold has been reached.

tracert A network troubleshooting command that displays the path a data packet takes through a network, thus allowing one to see where a fault occurs in larger networks.

track A concentric circle on a formatted floppy disk or a hard drive platter.

track pad An input device commonly found on notebook computers.

track stick An input device commonly found on notebook computers.

Track-at-Once Sometimes called TAO. A technology in which the laser stops writing normal data after a track is finished. This type of drive supports the disc having both audio and data. Compare with Disc-at-Once.

trackball An input device that replaces a mouse.

transfer corona A wire inside the laser printer that applies a positive charge to the back of the paper so the toner is attracted to the paper as it moves through the printer.

transfer roller A roller inside the laser printer that replaces the transfer corona. The roller applies a positive charge to the back of the paper so the toner is attracted to the paper as it moves through the printer.

transferring A Hewlett-Packard term used to describe the laser printer process where the toner (image) moves from the drum to the paper. The equivalent electrophotographic process term is transfer.

transport layer Layer four of the OSI model, it determines details on how the data is sent, supervises the validity of the transmission, and defines protocol for structuring messages.

tri-core CPU A single unit that contains three processors.

Trojan horse virus A virus program that appears to be a normal application, but, when executed, changes something. It does not replicate, but could gather information that can later be used to hack into one's computer.

TrueType font A type of outline font that can be scaled and rotated.

TV tuner card An adapter that allows a computer to receive and display television-based video on a computer monitor.

TVS rating (transient voltage suppressor) Measure of the surge protector's ability to guard against overvoltage conditions. The lower the TVS rating, the better.

twisted cable A type of floppy or hard drive cable having crossed wires and that physically moves the drive selection jumper from the second to the first position.

twisted-pair cable Network cable of eight copper wires twisted into four pairs. Comes shielded and unshielded.

TYPE A command used to display a file's contents on the screen.

Type A-B-C fire extinguisher Used on either Type A, Type B, or Type C fires.

Type C fire extinguisher Used only on electrical fires.

U

UAC (User Access Control) A dialog box that appears in Windows Vista and higher operating systems that asks permission to do something that might be harmful or change the operating system environment. Some changes require an administrator password to continue.

UART (universal asynchronous receiver/transmitter) A chip that coordinates the serial port or device activity.

UDMA (ultra DMA) Allows the IDE interface to control the PCI bus for faster transfers.

UDP (user datagram protocol) A Layer four connectionless standard that applications use to communicate with a remote device.

UDSL (ultra high speed DSL) A type of DSL technology also known as Uni-DSL.

unbuffered memory Memory that does not delay all data transfers by one clock tick to ensure accuracy as registered memory does. Used in low- to medium-powered computers.

unbuffered SDRAM A type of memory used frequently in low- to medium-priced home computers.

UNC (universal naming convention) Used at the command prompt to obtain network shares.

undervoltage A condition that occurs when AC power drops below 100 volts, which may cause the computer's power supply to draw too much current and overheat.

upgrade Installing a newer or more powerful operating system where one already exists. An upgrade can also be installing newer hardware.

Upgrade Advisor A Microsoft tool that can be downloaded and executed to determine if a Windows XP, Vista, or 7 computer can function well with a higher version of Windows installed.

UPS (uninterruptible power supply) A device that provides power for a limited time to a computer or device during a power outage.

upstream A term used to describe information that is sent to the Internet, such as transmitting email or uploading a file to a server.

URL (uniform resource locator) A method of accessing Internet resources.

usable host numbers The number of host bits (and associated IP addresses) that can be used by network devices residing in a subnetwork.

usable subnets The number of subnetworks that can be used when an IP network number is subdivided to allow more efficient use of IP addresses.

USB (universal serial bus) A bus that allows 127 devices to be connected to a single computer port.

USB flash drive Sometimes called a flash drive or a memory stick, a USB flash drive allows storage via a USB port.

USB OTG (USB on the go) Allows two USB devices to communicate without the use of a PC or a hub that is backward compatible with the USB 2.0 standard.

USB port A port on the motherboard or on an adapter that allows the connection of up to 127 devices.

user profile All settings associated with a specific user, including desktop settings, network configurations, and applications that the user has access to. It is part of the registry.

USMT (user state migration tool) A tool used by IT staff to perform large deployments of Windows XP Professional.

UTP (unshielded twisted pair) Most common network cable. Comes in different categories for different uses. See also *twisted-pair cable*.

UVGA (ultra VGA) A type of monitor that displays at least a 1024×768 resolution or greater and connects to a 15-pin D-shell connector.

UXGA (ultra extended graphics array) Describes resolutions up to 1600×1200 and over 16 million colors. Sometimes used on powerful laptops and when using applications in which more of the screen needs to be seen (such as spreadsheets).

V

VCM (virtual channel memory) A memory chip alternative to SDRAM. Developed by NEC Electronics, Inc., it fits in DIMM slots, but the chipset must support it.

VDSL2 (very-high-bitrate DSL 2) An improvement over VDSL that supports voice, video, data, and HDTV transmissions.

vector font A font derived from a mathematical formula. Plotters frequently use vector fonts.

verifier.exe A command used to verify installed drivers.

vertical scan rate The rate at which the monitor's electron beam draws the entire screen.

VGA (video graphics array) A type of monitor that displays at least a 640×480 resolution or greater and connects to a 15-pin D-shell connector.

VGA port A type of 15-pin three-row video port that normally has a CRT monitor attached.

video capture card An adapter that allows video to be taken from a camera, DVD, recorder, or live video, edited if necessary, and saved.

video port A connector on a motherboard or separate adapter for hooking up the monitor. Two variations are the VGA and DVI. VGA connects CRT monitors. DVI is commonly used with flat panel monitors.

video processor Sometimes known as the video coprocessor or video accelerator. The processor on the video adapter that coordinates communication between the adapter and the main microprocessor.

viewable size The diagonal length of an LCD screen.

virtual machine A way for the operating system to appear as a separate computer to each application. In Windows 98 and higher, each 32-bit application runs in its own virtual machine and each 16-bit DOS application runs in its own virtual machine. Virtual machine is also a term used to describe one computer that has two or more operating systems installed that are unaware of each other due to virtualization software.

virtual memory A method of simulating extra memory by using the hard disk space as if it were RAM.

virus Program designed to change the way a computer originally operated.

VIS (viewable image size) The actual area of the monitor seen by a user.

VMM (virtual memory manager) A Windows component that uses hard disk space as if it were RAM.

VoIP (Voice over IP) A way of sending phone calls over the Internet or over networks that traditionally transmitted only data.

volatile memory Memory that does not remain when power is removed.

volt The measurement for voltage.

voltage An electronic measurement of the pressure pushing electrons through a circuit. Voltage is measured in volts.

volume A hard drive term used to describe all of a hard drive or hard drive portions that have been combined into one unit. In Windows Vista and 7, all hard drive divisions are called volumes.

VPN (virtual private network) A remote computer connecting to a remote network by "tunneling" over an intermediate network, such as the Internet or a LAN.

VRAM (video RAM) Dual-ported memory found on video adapters.

W

Wake on LAN A BIOS and adapter feature that allows a network administrator to remotely control power to a workstation, and allows a computer to come out of the sleep mode.

Wake on Ring A BIOS and adapter feature that allows a computer to come out of sleep mode when the telephone rings, so the computer can accept fax, email, and so on, when the user is absent.

WAN (wide area network) Two or more LANs communicating, often across large distances. The most famous WAN is the Internet.

warm boot Restarting the computer by pressing Ctrl+Alt+Del. Puts less strain on the computer than a cold boot.

watt Electrical measure in which computer power supplies are rated.

WDT (Windows Deployment Toolkit) A GUI shell used to deploy Windows in a corporate environment.

wear leveling The process of writing and erasing data in different memory blocks of SSDs (solid state drives) to prolong the life of the drive.

Web cam Short for Web camera and a small camera used for communicating with video across the Internet.

WEP (Wired Equivalent Privacy) A type of encryption that is sometimes used in wireless networks.

WFP (Windows file protection) Windows 2000 and XP feature that protects system files. If WFP detects a file that is altered, deleted, or overwritten, it obtains a copy of the original file and places the copied file in the proper folder. Windows Vista and 7 use WRP (Windows Resource Protection)

wide XGA See *WXGA*.

wildcard A special character used at the command prompt when typing commands. The ? character is used to designate "any" for a single character place, whereas the * character denotes any characters from that place forward.

Windows Aero A look and feel for the computing environment in Windows Vista and higher that includes transparent icons, animations, and customized desktop gadgets.

Windows Defender A Microsoft application in Windows Vista and higher that is used to detect spyware.

Windows Explorer See *Explorer*.

Windows XP mode A downloadable program for Vista/7 to provide a virtual Windows XP mode for applications that will not work in the normal operating system environment.

WinRE (Windows recovery environment) An alternative to Console Recovery found on the Windows Vista and 7 installation disc that includes multiple tools used to troubleshoot Windows when it does not work properly.

WINS server (Windows Internet Naming Service server) Keeps track of IP addresses assigned to a specific computer name.

wireless broadband A feature available from service providers that allows PC Cards, USB modems, mobile data cards, or integrated laptop connectivity to have the ability to receive, create, and communicate Internet information within a specific coverage area.

wireless network A type of network that uses air as the media to connect devices.

word size See *register size*.

workgroup A term given to a peer-to-peer Windows network. A workgroup does not use a server to authenticate users during the login process.

WORM (write once, read many) A technology that writes data once to a disk. Often used to make backups or to distribute software.

worm virus A virus program that replicates from one drive to another. The most common worm virus today is an email message that, once opened, sends the virus to every address in the user's address book.

WPAD (Web Proxy Autodiscovery) A method of discovering the proxy server IP address and port number.

WPS (WiFi Protected Settings) A method used to easily configure a wireless device for the SSID and WPA2 security.

write amplification The minimum amount of storage space affected by a request to write data on a solid state drive. For example, if the SSD has 128KB erase block with a 4KB file to be saved, 128KB of memory is erased before the 4KB file is written.

write-behind caching A type of disk caching that stores data on the RAM and later records it to the disk.

writing A Hewlett-Packard term used to describe the laser printer process where 1s and 0s are placed on the drum surface. The equivalent electrophotographic process term is expose.

WRP (Windows Resource Protection) A tool that protects system files and registry keys in Windows Vista and Windows 7. Replaces WFP, which Windows 2000 and XP use.

WUXGA (wide ultra extended graphics array) Describes resolutions of 1920×1200.

WXGA (wide XGA) Resolutions up to 1366×768 using over 16 million colors are supported. This is usually used by those who like to view a DVD on a computer monitor. Other variations include WSXGA and WUXGA.

X

x2/DSL A DSL technology provided by 3COM that allows a 56K modem to be upgraded to DSL when made available in a geographic area.

XCOPY An external command used to transfer files from one place to another in the command prompt environment.

xDSL Used to describe the various types of digital subscriber lines (DSLs) available for connecting to the Internet. Examples include ADSL, CDSL, DSL Lite, HDSL, RADSL, SDSL, VDSL, and x2/DSL.

XGA (extended graphics array) Developed by IBM to describe resolutions of 1024x768 and 64K of colors.

XON/XOFF A method of handshaking that uses special control characters to coordinate data transmissions.

XPS (XML paper specification) The Windows Vista graphics language for print drivers. XPS handles representing and transmitting graphical objects to output devices such as printers, monitors, and overhead projectors. Documents sent to printers that support XPS will not have to be converted to a printer-specific language. XPS not only affects printing, but also document viewing.

Z

ZIF socket (zero insertion force socket) A common CPU socket that has a lever that provides easy access for CPU removal.

Index

Symbols and Numbers

A

Index

Index

Index

Index

Index

Credits

A Word about Trademarks

All product names identified in this book are trademarks or registered trademarks of their respective companies. We have used the names in an editorial fashion only, and to the benefit of the trademark owner, with no intention of infringing the trademark. IBM and Lotus are trademarks of International Business Machines. Intel, Pentium, Intel386, Celeron, Intel486, OverDrive, Xeon, Camino, HyperThreading, 440ZX, 440EX, 450NX, 3GIO, MMX, MMX2, Itanium, and Itanium 2 are trademarks of Intel Corp. AMD, Athlon, AMD-760, Duron, Sempron, Tirion, Opteron, 3DNow!, DirectConnect, and HyperTransport are trademarks of Advanced Micro Devices, Inc. Alpha is a trademark of Digital Corp. Windows, Windows 95, Windows 98, NT Workstation, Windows NT, Windows 2000, Windows XP, Windows Vista, Windows 7, DirectX, MSD, Terminal, HyperTerminal, and Word are trademarks of Microsoft Corporation. Apple, PowerPC, QuickTime, and FireWire are trademarks of Apple Computer. RapidIO is a trademark of Motorola, Inc. Cyrix is a trademark of Cyrix Corp. DEC is a trademark of Digital Equipment Corporation, Inc. Northern Telecom is a trademark of Nortel Networks, Corp. CardBay and PCMCIA are registered trademarks of the Personal Computer Memory Card International Association. ALI is a trademark of Acer Labs, Inc. VIAtechnologies is a trademark of VIA Technologies, Inc. Compaq is a trademark of Compaq Corp. HP is a trademark of Hewlett-Packard Company. Zenith is a trademark of Zenith Electronics. Epson is a trademark of Seiko Epson. NEC is a trademark of NEC Corp. Wyse is a trademark of Wyse Technology. AST is a trademark of AST Research, Inc. Acer is a trademark of Acer America Corp. Tandy is a trademark of Tandy Corp. Olivetti is a trademark of Olivetti S.p.A. SiS is a trademark of Silicon Integrated Systems Corp. OPTi is a trademark of OPTi, Inc. Award is a trademark of Award Software International, Inc. PhoenixBIOS is a trademark of Phoenix Technologies Ltd. AMI BIOS is a trademark of American Megatrends, Inc. Dell is a trademark of Dell Computer Corp. Norton Utilities is a trademark of Symantec Corp. EZ-Drive is a trademark of Western Digital Corp. Seagate and Cheetah are trademarks of Seagate Technology. Sound Blaster is a trademark of Creative Labs. Hayes is a trademark of Hayes Microcomputer. x2 is a trademark of 3Com Corporation. Toshiba is a trademark of Toshiba America Information Systems. iLink and Trinitron are trademarks of Sony Electronics Inc. WordPerfect is a trademark of Corel Corp. Macromedia Flash and Macromedia Shockwave are trademarks of Macromedia, Inc. Acrobat Reader is a trademark of Adobe Systems, Inc. RealPlayer is a trademark of RealNetworks, Inc. WinZip is a trademark of WinZip Computing, Inc. Download Accelerator Plus is a trademark of Speedbit Ltd. Go!Zilla is a trademark of Radiate. NetSonic is a trademark of Redmond Ventures, Inc. Eudora Light is a trademark of QUALCOMM, Inc. Solaris is a trademark of Sun Microsystems, Inc. BenQ is a trademark of BenQ America Corp. Canon and PowerShot are trademarks of Canon, Inc.

Chapter 1

Figure 1.2: HO/AFP/Getty Images/Newscom
Figure 1.7: marekuliasz/Shutterstock
Figure 1.8: Piotr Rzeszutek/Shutterstock
Figure 1.10: Cheryl A. Schmidt
Figure 1.11: Adam Wasilewski/Shutterstock
Figure 1.13: Cheryl A. Schmidt
Figure 1.15: Fred Dimmick/iStockphoto.com
Figure 1.16: Hans-Walter Untch/iStockphoto.com
Figure 1.18: Hemera/Jupiter Images
Figure 1.19: Handout/MCT/Newscom
Figure 1.20: Jakub Krechowicz/Shutterstock
Figures 1.23, 1.24: iStockphoto.com
Figure 1.26: Cheryl A. Schmidt
Figure 1.29: Courtesy Gigabyte Technology
Figure 1.30: © Krys Bailey/Alamy

Chapter 2

Figure 2.2: Courtesy of Intel Corporation
Figure 2.3: AMD, the AMD Arrow logo, AMD Opteron, AMD Athlon and combinations thereof, are trademarks of Advanced Micro Devices, Inc.
Figure 2.11: Courtesy of Intel Corporation
Figure 2.12: Cheryl A. Schmidt
Figure 2.13: Norman Chan/Shutterstock
Figures 2.14, 2.16: Cheryl A. Schmidt
Figure 2.17: Péter Gudella/Shutterstock
Figure 2.18: Cheryl A. Schmidt
Figure 2.28: Ruslan Kudrin/Shutterstock
Figure 2.29: Cheryl A. Schmidt
Figure 2.30: ExpressCard—PCMCIA
Figure 2.33: Cheryl A. Schmidt
Figure 2.36: Wikipedia, The Free Encyclopedia

Chapter 3

Figure 3.2: Bernd Lauter/photolibray.com
Figures 3.12, 3.14 (left and right), 3.16, 3.17, 3.18: Cheryl A. Schmidt

Chapter 4

Figures 4.4, 4.6: Cheryl A. Schmidt
Figure 4.8 (left): © ICP-FR/Alamy
Figure 4.8 (middle): nart/Shutterstock
Figure 4.8 (right): © ICP-FR/Alamy
Figure 4.9: Newegg Inc.
Figure 4.11 (left): Cheryl A. Schmidt
Figure 4.11 (right): any_keen/Shutterstock
Figures 4.13, 4.14: Cheryl A. Schmidt
Figure 4.15: The Dell logo is trademark of Dell, Inc.
Figure 4.17: Cheryl A. Schmidt

Figure 4.18: Photo courtesy of Tripp Lite
Figure 4.19: Handout/KRT/Newscom
Figure 4.21: © MARKA/Alamy
Figure 4.22: Cheryl A. Schmidt

Chapter 6

Figure 6.3 (left): Crucial/Micron Technology, Inc.
Figure 6.3 (right): Oleksiy Mark/Shutterstock
Figure 6.8: Cheryl A. Schmidt
Figure 6.9: Andrew Howe/iStockphoto.com
Figure 6.14: Scott B. Rosen
Figure 6.15: Dino O./Shutterstock

Chapter 7

Figure 7.1: Cheryl A. Schmidt
Figure 7.4: © Eye-Stock/Alamy
Figure 7.9: blider/Shutterstock
Figure 7.10: Courtesy Western Digital Corporation
Figure 7.11: Cheryl A. Schmidt
Figure 7.12: any_keen/Shutterstock
Figure 7.13: Courtesy of StarTech.com
Figure 7.14 (left): Vicente Barcelo Varona/Shutterstock
Figure 7.14 (right): Wikipedia, The Free Encyclopedia
Figure 7.15: © oliver leedham/Alamy
Figure 7.16: Seagate Technology, Inc.
Figure 7.17: Cheryl A. Schmidt
Figure 7.21: Courtesy of Western Digital Corporation
Figure 7.22: Seagate Technology, Inc
Figure 7.24: Cheryl A. Schmidt
Figure 7.26: © Jeff Morgan 03/Alamy
Figure 7.29: Cheryl A. Schmidt
Figure 7.30: Thomas Staiger/Shutterstock
Figure 7.39: Cheryl A. Schmidt

Chapter 8

Figure 8.5: © imagebroker/Alamy
Figure 8.6: Handout/MCT/Newscom
Figure 8.7: Lasse Kristensen/Shutterstock
Figure 8.9: Peter Gudella/Shutterstock
Figure 8.17: Handout/KRT/Newscom
Figure 8.19: © David J. Green—Technology/Alamy
Figure 8.20: Michal Mrozek/iStockphoto.com

Chapter 9

Figure 9.5: Cheryl A. Schmidt
Figure 9.9: XFX
Figure 9.10: VisionTek Products LLC
Figure 9.11: Epson America, Inc.
Figures 9.13, 9.14, 9.16: Cheryl A. Schmidt
Figure 9.18: Hewlett-Packard Company
Figures 9.19, 9.21: Cheryl A. Schmidt
Figure 9.22: Hewlett-Packard Company

Chapter 10

Figures 10.2, 10.9, 10.10, 10.12: Cheryl A. Schmidt

Chapter 13

Figure 13.10: Senko Advanced Components, Inc.
Figure 13.12: Courtesy of SETT, LLC
     (www.get-sett.com)
Figure 13.13: Mario Aguilar/Shutterstock
Figure 13.14: chrisho/iStockphoto.com
Figure 13.20: Norman Chan/Shutterstock
Figure 13.21: Rob Bouwman/Shutterstock
Figure 13.22: Cheryl A. Schmidt
Figure 13.23: Linksys
Figures 13.25, 13.27: Cheryl A. Schmidt
Figure 13.36: tatniz/Shutterstock
Figure 13.37: © Georgios Kollidas/Alamy
Figure 13.38: © NetGear
Figure 13.39: Cheryl A. Schmidt
Figure 13.49: Courtesy of Cisco Systems, Inc. Unauthorized
     use not permitted.
Figures 13.53, 13.54, 13.55, 13.56, 13.57: Courtesy of Cheryl
     A. Schmidt

Chapter 14

Figure 14.1: © imagebroker/Alamy
Figure 14.2: Courtesy of RSA Security, Inc.
Figure 14.3: Vartanov Anatoly/Shutterstock
Figure 14.4: Long Ha/iStockphoto.com
Figure 14.5: Panasonic Corporation of North America
Figure 14.6: Peter von Felbert/photolibrary.com